SportingNews BOOKS

PRO FOOTBALL GUIDE

2006 EDITION

CONTENTS

Sporting News Contributors:
Editors: Corrie Anderson
Cover design: Chad Painter; **Page layout:** Chad Painter, David Niehaus

ON THE COVER: Tyrone Carter and James Farrior by Albert Dickson / TSN.

NFL statistics compiled by STATS, Inc., a News Corporation company; 8130 Lehigh Avenue, Morton Grove, IL 60053. STATS is a trademark of Sports Team Analysis and Tracking Systems, Inc.

Copyright © 2006 by The Sporting News, a division of Vulcan Sports Media; 14500 South Outer Forty, Suite 300, Chesterfield, MO 63017
All rights reserved. Printed in the U.S.A.

No part of the *Pro Football Guide* may be reproduced or transmitted in any form or by any means, electronic or mechanical, including photocopy, recording or any information storage and retrieval system now known or to be invented, without permission in writing from the publisher, except by a reviewer who wishes to quote brief passages in connection with a review written for inclusion in a magazine, newspaper or broadcast.

ISBN: 0-89204-850-6

10 9 8 7 6 5 4 3 2 1

2006 SEASON

NFL directory

Team information

Schedule

College draft

Playoff plan

NFL DIRECTORY

COMMISSIONER'S OFFICE

Address
280 Park Avenue
New York, NY 10017
Phone
212-450-2000
212-681-7573 (FAX)
Commissioner
Paul Tagliabue
President and COO of NFL Network, executive VP of media
Steve Bornstein
Exec. VP of community & public affairs
Joe Browne

Exec. VP, finance and strat. transactions
Eric Grubman
Exec. VP and COO of league and football development
Roger Goodell
Exec. vice president for labor relations
Harold Henderson
Executive vice president
Jeff Pash

COMMUNICATIONS
Vice president of public relations
Greg Aiello

Sr. dir. of international public affairs
Pete Abitante
Director of community affairs
Beth Colleton
Director of media services
Leslie Hammond
Director of corporate communications
Brian McCarthy
AFC Info Manager
Steve Alic
NFC Info Manager
Michael Signora

OTHER ORGANIZATIONS

NFL FILMS, INC.

Address
1 NFL Plaza
Mt. Laurel, NJ 08054
Phone
856-222-3500
President
Steve Sabol

PRO FOOTBALL HALL OF FAME

Address
2121 George Halas Drive, N.W.
Canton, OH 44708
Phone
330-456-8207
330-456-8175 (FAX)
Executive director
Stephen A. Terry
VP/communications & exhibits
Joe Horrigan
VP/operations & marketing
Dave Motts
VP/merchandising & licensing
Judy Kuntz

NFL PLAYERS ASSOCIATION

Address
2021 L Street, N.W.
Washington, DC 20036
Phone
202-463-2200
202-835-9775 (FAX)
Executive director
Gene Upshaw
Assistant executive director
Doug Allen
Assistant director of retired players
Dee Becker
General counsel
Richard Berthelsen
Director of communications
Carl Francis
Director of player development
Stacey Robinson
Director of agent administration & salary cap
Mark Levin

NFL ALUMNI INC.

Address
3696 N. Federal Highway
Suite 202
Ft. Lauderdale, FL 33308-6263
Phone
954-630-2100
954-630-2535 (FAX)
President/CEO
Frank Krauser
Chairman of the board
Lee Nystrom
COO
Remy Mackowski
Vice president
Martin Lerch
Director of player and media relations
Amy Glanzman

DIVISIONAL ALIGNMENT

AMERICAN FOOTBALL CONFERENCE

AFC EAST	AFC NORTH	AFC SOUTH	AFC WEST
Buffalo Bills	Baltimore Ravens	Houston Texans	Denver Broncos
Miami Dolphins	Cincinnati Bengals	Indianapolis Colts	Kansas City Chiefs
New England Patriots	Cleveland Browns	Jacksonville Jaguars	Oakland Raiders
New York Jets	Pittsburgh Steelers	Tennessee Titans	San Diego Chargers

NATIONAL FOOTBALL CONFERENCE

NFC EAST	NFC NORTH	NFC SOUTH	NFC WEST
Dallas Cowboys	Chicago Bears	Atlanta Falcons	Arizona Cardinals
New York Giants	Detroit Lions	Carolina Panthers	St. Louis Rams
Philadelphia Eagles	Green Bay Packers	New Orleans Saints	San Francisco 49ers
Washington Redskins	Minnesota Vikings	Tampa Bay Buccaneers	Seattle Seahawks

ARIZONA CARDINALS
NFC WEST DIVISION

2006 SEASON

CLUB DIRECTORY

President
William V. Bidwill
Vice president
William V. Bidwill Jr.
Vice president and general counsel
Michael J. Bidwill
Vice president-football operations
Rod Graves
Senior director of football operations
John Idzik
National scout
Steve Keim
Director of media relations
Mark Dalton
Media relations manager
Chris Melvin
Director of community relations
Luis Zendejas

Head coach
Dennis Green

Assistant coaches
Larry Brooks (defensive line)
Frank Bush (asst. head
  coach/linebackers)
Rick Courtright (defensive quality
  control)
Carl Hargrave (tight ends)
Bill Khayat (offensive quality
  control)
Mike Kruczek (quarterbacks)
Daryl Lawrence (asst. strength
  and conditioning)
Steve Loney (offensive line)
Clancy Pendergast (defensive
  coordinator)
Keith Rowen (offensive
  coordinator)
Richard Solomon (defensive
  backs)
Keith Vulgamott (asst. strength
  and conditioning)
Steve Wetzel (strength and
  conditioning)
Kirby Wilson (running backs)
Mike Wilson (wide receivers)
Gary Zauner (special teams
  coordinator)

OFFSEASON MOVES

Key additions
G	Milford Brown	FA/Texans
DT	Kendrick Clancy	FA/Giants
RB	Edgerrin James	FA/Colts
WR	Troy Walters	FA/Colts

Key losses
DT	Russell Davis	FA/Seahawks
QB	Josh McCown	FA/Lions

SCHEDULE

Sept.	10—SAN FRANCISCO	4:15
Sept.	17—at Seattle	4:05
Sept.	24—ST. LOUIS	4:15
Oct.	1—at Atlanta	1:00
Oct.	8—KANSAS CITY	4:05
Oct.	16—CHICAGO (Mon.)	8:30
Oct.	22—at Oakland	4:15
Oct.	29—at Green Bay	1:00
Nov.	5—Open week	
Nov.	12—DALLAS	4:15
Nov.	19—DETROIT	4:05
Nov.	26—at Minnesota	1:00
Dec.	3—at St. Louis	1:00
Dec.	10—SEATTLE	4:05
Dec.	17—DENVER	4:05
Dec.	24—at San Francisco	4:05
Dec.	31—at San Diego	4:15

All times are Eastern.
All games Sunday unless noted.

DRAFT CHOICES

Matt Leinart, QB, Southern California
(first round/10th pick overall).
Taitusi "Deuce" Lutui, G, Southern
California (2/41).
Leonard Pope, TE, Georgia (3/72).
Gabriel Watson, DT, Michigan (4/107).
Brandon Johnson, OLB, Louisville
(5/142).
Jon Lewis, DT, Virginia Tech (6/177).
Todd Watkins, WR, Brigham Young
(7/218).

MISCELLANEOUS TEAM DATA

Stadium (capacity, surface):
Cardinals Stadium (63,400, grass)
Business address:
P.O. Box 888
Phoenix, AZ 85001-0888
Business phone:
602-379-0101
Ticket information:
602-379-0102
Team colors:
Cardinal red, black and white
Flagship radio station:
KTAR, 620 AM; KMVP, 860 AM

Website:
www.azcardinals.com
Training site:
Northern Arizona University
Flagstaff, Ariz.
928-523-1818

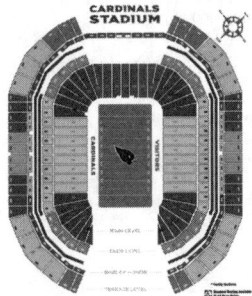

ARIZONA CARDINALS

No.	QUARTERBACKS	Ht./Wt.	Born	NFL Exp.	College	How acq.	'05 Games GP/GS
7	Matt Leinart	6-4/224	5/11/83	R	USC	D1/06	—
16	John Navarre	6-6/250	9/9/80	2	Michigan	D7/04	1/0
13	Kurt Warner	6-2/200	6/22/71	9	Northern Iowa	FA/05	10/10
	RUNNING BACKS						
22	Damien Anderson	5-11/212	7/17/79	5	Northwestern	FA/02	5/0
28	J.J. Arrington	5-9/214	1/23/83	2	California	D2/05	15/5
30	Obafemi Ayanbadejo (FB)	6-2/231	3/5/75	9	San Diego St.	FA/04	16/2
42	James Hodgins (FB)	6-1/264	4/30/77	8	San Jose St.	FA/03	1/0
32	Edgerrin James	6-0/214	8/1/78	8	Miami (Fla.)	FA/06	15/15
31	Marcel Shipp	5-11/230	8/8/78	6	Massachusetts	FA/01	15/11
	RECEIVERS						
89	Adam Bergen (TE)	6-4/263	9/3/83	2	Lehigh	FA/05	16/9
81	Anquan Boldin	6-1/218	10/3/80	4	Florida State	D2/03	14/14
83	Eric Edwards (TE)	6-5/256	8/4/80	3	LSU	FA/04	16/9
11	Larry Fitzgerald	6-3/223	8/31/83	3	Pittsburgh	D1/04	16/16
48	Nathan Hodel (TE)	6-2/256	11/12/77	5	Illinois	FA/01	16/0
80	Bryant Johnson	6-2/214	3/7/81	4	Penn State	D1a/03	14/4
19	LeRon McCoy	6-2/205	1/24/82	2	Indiana (Pa.)	D7/05	10/4
82	Leonard Pope (TE)	6-7/256	9/9/83	R	Georgia	D3/06	—
86	Troy Walters	5-7/172	12/15/76	7	Stanford	FA/06	16/1
14	Todd Watkins	6-3/199	6/22/83	R	BYU	D7/06	—
	OFFENSIVE LINEMEN						
73	Jeremy Bridges (G)	6-4/301	4/19/80	3	Southern Miss	FA/04	7/3
61	Elton Brown (G)	6-5/329	5/22/82	2	Virginia	D4/05	9/9
67	Milford Brown (G)	6-4/331	8/15/80	5	Florida State	FA/06	13/12
75	Leonard Davis (T)	6-6/381	9/5/78	6	Texas	D1/01	15/15
60	Nick Leckey (C)	6-3/286	3/12/82	3	Kansas State	D6/04	14/9
76	Taitusi Lutui (G)	6-4/330	5/5/83	R	USC	D2/06	—
65	Shawn Lynch (C)	6-4/294	7/25/79	2	Duke	W-Min/05	2/1
66	Alan Reuber (T)	6-6/323	1/26/81	2	Texas A&M	W-Min/04	0/0
79	Oliver Ross (T)	6-5/322	9/27/74	8	Iowa State	FA/05	12/12
71	Alex Stepanovich (C)	6-4/301	9/25/81	3	Ohio State	D4/04	9/9
78	Fred Wakefield (T)	6-7/312	9/17/78	6	Illinois	FA/01	16/9
74	Reggie Wells (G/C)	6-4/323	11/3/80	4	Clarion	D6a/03	9/9
	DEFENSIVE LINEMEN						
92	Bertrand Berry (E)	6-3/275	8/15/75	9	Notre Dame	FA/04	8/8
93	Tim Bulman (T)	6-4/283	10/31/82	2	Boston College	FA/05	8/1
70	Kendrick Clancy (T)	6-1/305	9/17/78	7	Mississippi	FA/06	16/15
90	Darnell Dockett (T)	6-4/301	5/27/81	3	Florida State	D3/04	16/16
95	Kenny King (E)	6-3/285	4/23/81	4	Alabama	D5/03	0/0
63	Jonathan Lewis (T)	6-0/304	7/12/84	R	Virginia Tech	D6/06	—
91	Langston Moore (T)	6-1/303	7/17/81	3	South Carolina	W-Cin/05	8/1
56	Chike Okeafor (E)	6-4/265	3/27/76	8	Purdue	FA/05	16/16
97	Calvin Pace (E)	6-4/262	10/28/80	4	Wake Forest	D1b/03	5/1
96	Anton Palepoi (E)	6-3/283	1/19/78	5	UNLV	FA/05	3/0
94	Antonio Smith (E)	6-3/274	10/21/81	2	Oklahoma State	D5/04	11/8
98	Gabe Watson (T)	6-3/335	9/24/83	R	Michigan	D4/06	—
	LINEBACKERS						
55	Darryl Blackstock	6-3/238	5/30/83	2	Virginia	D3b/05	14/1
43	Mark Brown	6-0/238	5/19/80	4	Auburn	FA/06	15/11
58	Karlos Dansby	6-4/243	11/3/81	3	Auburn	D2/04	15/15
51	James Darling	6-1/247	12/29/74	10	Washington State	FA/01	14/14
54	Gerald Hayes	6-1/242	10/10/80	4	Pittsburgh	D3/03	0/0
57	Orlando Huff	6-2/250	8/14/78	6	Fresno State	FA/05	16/12
59	Brandon Johnson	6-5/227	5/5/83	R	Louisville	D5/06	—
53	Isaac Keys	6-3/245	6/6/78	3	Morehouse	FA/04	6/0
52	Lance Mitchell	6-2/245	10/9/81	2	Oklahoma	D5/05	12/0
	DEFENSIVE BACKS						
41	Jack Brewer (S)	6-0/194	1/8/79	4	Minnesota	FA/06	6/0
33	Dyshod Carter (DB)	5-10/195	6/18/78	4	Kansas State	FA/02	3/0
47	Aaron Francisco (S)	6-2/206	7/5/83	2	Brigham Young	FA/05	11/0
25	Eric Green (CB)	5-11/198	3/16/82	2	Virginia Tech	D3a/05	12/5
34	Robert Griffith (S)	5-11/200	11/30/70	13	San Diego State	FA/05	16/16
27	David Macklin (CB)	5-10/200	7/14/78	7	Penn State	FA/04	16/15
20	Lamont Reid (CB)	6-0/193	5/4/82	2	N.C. State	FA/05	10/1
21	Antrel Rolle (CB)	6-1/197	12/16/82	2	Miami (Fla.)	D1/05	5/4
35	Ernest Shazor (S)	6-4/226	7/4/83	2	Michigan	FA/05	2/0
26	Robert Tate (CB)	5-11/193	10/19/73	9	Cincinnati	FA/02	13/5
24	Adrian Wilson (S)	6-3/222	10/12/79	6	N.C. State	D3/01	16/16
	SPECIALISTS						
3	Nick Novak (K)	6-0/186	8/21/81	2	Maryland	FA/05	10/0
10	Scott Player (P)	6-1/213	12/17/69	9	Florida State	FA/98	16/0
1	Neil Rackers (K)	6-0/206	8/16/76	7	Illinois	FA/03	15/0

Abbreviations: D1-draft pick, first round; W-claimed on waivers; T-obtained in trade; FA-free-agent acquisition.

2005 regular-season record: 5-11
Position: 3rd in NFC West

Sept.11—at N.Y. Giants	L	19-42
Sept.18—ST. LOUIS	L	12-17
Sept.25—at Seattle	L	12-37
Oct. 2—SAN FRANCISCO	W	31-14
Oct. 9—CAROLINA	L	20-24
Oct. 16—Open date		
Oct. 23—TENNESSEE	W	20-10
Oct. 30—at Dallas	L	13-34
Nov. 6—SEATTLE	L	19-33
Nov. 13—at Detroit	L	21-29
Nov. 20—at St. Louis	W	38-28
Nov. 27—JACKSONVILLE	L	17-24
Dec. 4—at San Francisco	W	17-10
Dec. 11—WASHINGTON	L	13-17
Dec. 18—at Houston	L	19-30
Dec. 24—PHILADELPHIA	W	27-21
Jan. 1—at Indianapolis	L	13-17

SCORING BY PERIODS

	Q1	Q2	Q3	Q4	OT	Pts.
Cardinals	27	111	74	99	0	311
Opponents	87	105	103	92	0	387

TEAM STATISTICS

	Ariz.	Opp.
TOTAL FIRST DOWNS	304	272
Rushing	58	83
Passing	224	158
Penalty	22	31
3rd Down: Made/Att.	91/239	67/196
3rd Down Pct.	38.1	34.2
4th Down: Made/Att.	5/16	4/11
4th Down Pct.	31.3	36.4
POSSESSION AVG.	31:20	28:40
TOTAL NET YARDS	5575	4729
Avg. per Game	348.4	295.6
Total Plays	1075	936
Avg. per Play	5.2	5.1
NET YARDS RUSHING	1138	1632
Avg. per Game	71.1	102.0
Total Rushes	360	411
NET YARDS PASSING	4437	3097
Avg. per Game	277.3	193.6
Sacked/Yards Lost	45/286	37/217
Gross Yards	4723	3314
Att./Completions	670/419	488/301
Completion Pct.	62.5	61.7
Had Intercepted	21	15
PUNTS/AVERAGE	74/43.3	85/44.1
NET PUNTING AVG.	74/37.0	85/37.8
PENALTIES/YARDS	145/1184	103/819
FUMBLES/LOST	26/16	24/11
TOUCHDOWNS	26	46
Rushing	2	22
Passing	21	17
Returns	3	7

SCORING (NONKICKERS)

	TD	RTD	PTD	MTD	2Pt.	Pts.
Fitzgerald	10	0	10	0	0	60
Boldin	7	0	7	0	1	44
Arrington	2	2	0	0	0	12
Dansby	2	0	0	2	0	12
Bergen	1	0	1	0	0	6
Edwards	1	0	1	0	0	6
B. Johnson	1	0	1	0	0	6
Macklin	1	0	0	1	0	6
McCoy	1	0	1	0	0	6
Ayanbadejo	0	0	0	0	2	4
Cardinals	26	2	21	3	3	162
Opponents	46	22	17	7	1	280

2-Pt. conversions: Cardinals 3-6; Opponents 1-1.

(KICKERS)

	XPM/XPA	FGM/FGA	Pts.
Rackers	20/20	40/42	140
Novak	0/0	3/3	9
Cardinals	20/20	43/45	149
Opponents	44/45	21/24	107

RUSHING

	Att.	Yds.	Avg.	Lg.	TD
Shipp	157	451	2.9	19	0
Arrington	112	370	3.3	32	2
McCown	29	139	4.8	12	0
Ayanbadejo	22	46	2.1	11	0
Boldin	12	45	3.8	11	0
Fitzgerald	8	41	5.1	15	0
Warner	13	28	2.2	13	0
Jackson	4	11	2.8	3	0
Anderson	2	7	3.5	6	0
B. Johnson	1	0	0.0	0	0
Cardinals	360	1138	3.2	32	2
Opponents	411	1632	4.0	t88	22

RECEIVING

	No.	Yds.	Avg.	Lg.	TD
Fitzgerald	103	1409	13.7	47	10
Boldin	102	1402	13.7	t54	7
B. Johnson	40	432	10.8	41	1
Shipp	35	255	7.3	28	0
Ayanbadejo	34	231	6.8	18	0
Bergen	28	270	9.6	32	1
Arrington	25	139	5.6	15	0
McCoy	18	191	10.6	24	1
Edwards	12	133	11.1	63	1
Lee	11	152	13.8	49	0
Newhouse	4	45	11.3	17	0
Johnson	3	29	9.7	13	0
Jackson	2	31	15.5	19	0
Baxter	1	4	4.0	4	0
Warner	1	0	0.0	0	0
Cardinals	419	4723	11.3	63	21
Opponents	301	3314	11.0	t65	17

INTERCEPTIONS

	No.	Yds.	Avg.	Lg.	TD
Dansby	3	31	10.3	t18	2
Macklin	2	79	39.5	t60	1
Tate	2	47	23.5	25	0

	No.	Yds.	Avg.	Lg.	TD
Darling	2	22	11.0	15	0
Wilson	1	36	36.0	36	0
Rolle	1	29	29.0	29	0
Dockett	1	14	14.0	14	0
Green	1	13	13.0	13	0
Griffith	1	11	11.0	11	0
Huff	1	3	3.0	3	0
Cardinals	15	285	19.0	t60	3
Opponents	21	334	15.9	71	1

SACKS: Wilson 8.0, Okeafor 7.5, Berry 6.0, Dansby 4.0, Kolodziej 3.0, A. Smith 3.0, Blackstock 1.0, Darling 1.0, Huff 1.0, Moore 1.0, Pace 1.0, Dockett 0.5. Cardinals 37.0; Opponents 45.0.

PUNTING

	No.	Yds.	Avg.	In. 20	Lg.
Player	73	3206	43.9	18	60
Cardinals	74	3206	43.3	18	60
Opponents	85	3752	44.1	26	58

PUNT RETURNS

	No.	FC	Yds.	Avg.	Lg.	TD
Swinton	42	14	334	8.0	32	0
Moses	7	0	40	5.7	12	0
B. Johnson	1	2	9	9.0	9	0
Cardinals	50	16	383	7.7	32	0
Opponents	39	14	328	8.4	t52	1

KICK RETURNS

	No.	Yds.	Avg.	Lg.	TD
Swinton	63	1456	23.1	90	0
Moses	7	177	25.3	35	0
B. Johnson	2	45	22.5	24	0
Anderson	1	7	7.0	7	0
Ayanbadejo	1	16	16.0	16	0
Green	1	4	4.0	4	0
Jackson	1	14	14.0	14	0
Cardinals	76	1719	22.6	90	0
Opponents	60	1700	28.3	t95	3

FIELD GOALS

	1-19	20-29	30-39	40-49	50+
Rackers	0/0	11/11	10/10	13/14	6/7
Novak	1/1	0/0	2/2	0/0	0/0
Cardinals	1/1	11/11	12/12	13/14	6/7
Opponents	0/0	10/10	3/4	7/7	1/3

Rackers: (24G, 42G) (29G, 26G, 48G, 35G) (54G, 39G, 50G, 39G) (40G, 45G, 48G, 23G, 43G, 24G) (39G, 49G) (33G, 24G) (52G, 47G) (23G, 31G, 50G, 44G) (51G, 28G) (32G, 33G, 51G) (43N, 42G) () (44G, 20G) (26G, 42G) (32G, 32G, 54N) (28G, 42G)
Novak: () () () () () () () () () () () (30G, 35G, 19G) () () ()
Opponents: () (29G) (33G, 23G, 47G) () (46G, 53N, 62N) (53G) (21G, 21G) (26G, 28G) (26G, 20G) (47G, 32G) (30G, 38N) (48G) (41G) (27G, 41G, 26G) () (44G)

PASSING

	Att.	Cmp.	Yds.	Pct.	Avg. Gain	TD	Pct. TD	Int.	Pct. Int.	Long	Sack/Lost	Rating
Warner	375	242	2713	64.5	7.23	11	2.9	9	2.4	63	23/158	85.8
McCown	270	163	1836	60.4	6.80	9	3.3	11	4.1	49	18/101	74.9
Navarre	24	14	174	58.3	7.25	1	4.2	1	4.2	43	4/27	77.4
Boldin	1	0	0	0.0	0.00	0	0.0	0	0.0	...	0/0	39.6
Cardinals	670	419	4723	62.5	7.05	21	3.1	21	3.1	63	45/286	81.0
Opponents	488	301	3314	61.7	6.79	17	3.5	15	3.1	t65	37/217	80.6

ATLANTA FALCONS
NFC SOUTH DIVISION

ATLANTA FALCONS

2006 SEASON

CLUB DIRECTORY

Owner and CEO
Arthur Blank
President/general manager
Rich McKay
Senior personnel executive
Billy Devaney
VP of football communications
Reggie Roberts
Senior director of media relations
Frank Kleha
Director of college scouting
Phil Emery
Director of pro personnel
Les Snead
Director of football administration
Brian Xanders

Head coach
Jim Mora

Assistant coaches
Sal Alosi (strength and
conditioning)
Clancy Barone (tight ends)
Chris Beake (linebackers)
Tom Cable (offensive line)
Chris Dalman (offensive asst.)
Joe DeCamillis (special teams
coordinator)
Ed Donatell (defensive coordinator)
Alex Gibbs (consultant/offensive
line)
Bill Johnson (defensive line)
Billy Johnson (asst. strength and
conditioning)
Greg Knapp (offensive coordinator)
Joe Lombardi (defensive asst.)
Brett Maxie (defensive backs)
Bill Musgrave (quarterbacks)
Robert Prince (asst. quarterbacks)
George Stewart (wide receivers)
Emmitt Thomas (secondary/
senior defensive asst.)
Ollie Wilson (running backs)

SCHEDULE

Sept.	10—at Carolina	1:00
Sept.	17—TAMPA BAY	1:00
Sept.	25—at New Orleans (Mon.)	8:30
Oct.	1—ARIZONA	1:00
Oct.	8—Open date	
Oct.	15—N.Y. GIANTS	1:00
Oct.	22—PITTSBURGH	1:00
Oct.	29—at Cincinnati	1:00
Nov.	5—at Detroit	1:00
Nov.	12—CLEVELAND	1:00
Nov.	19—at Baltimore	1:00
Nov.	26—NEW ORLEANS	1:00
Dec.	3—at Washington	1:00
Dec.	10—at Tampa Bay	1:00
Dec.	16—DALLAS (Sat.)	8:00
Dec.	24—CAROLINA	1:00
Dec.	31—at Philadelphia	1:00

All times are Eastern.
All games Sunday unless noted.

DRAFT CHOICES

Jimmy Williams, CB, Virginia Tech
(second round/37th pick overall).
Jerious Norwood, RB, Mississippi State
(3/79).
Quinn Ojinnaka, OT, Syracuse (5/139).
Adam Jennings, WR, Fresno State (6/184).
D.J. Shockley, QB, Georgia (7/223).

OFFSEASON MOVES

Key additions
DE	John Abraham	trade/Jets
FS	Chris Crocker	trade/Browns
LT	Wayne Gandy	trade/Saints
SS	Lawyer Milloy	FA/Bills

Key losses
FS	Keion Carpenter	FA
FS	Ronnie Heard	FA
FS	Kevin McCadam	FA/Panthers
K	Todd Peterson	FA
SS	Bryan Scott	trade/Saints
DE	Brady Smith	released
OT	Barry Stokes	FA/Lions
WR	Dez White	FA

MISCELLANEOUS TEAM DATA

Stadium (capacity, surface):
Georgia Dome
(71,228, artificial)
Business address:
4400 Falcon Parkway
Flowery Branch, GA 30542
Business phone:
770-965-3115
Ticket information:
404-223-8444
Team colors:
Black, red, silver and white
Flagship radio station:
Z-93, 92.9 FM
Website:
www.atlantafalcons.com

Training site:
4400 Falcon Parkway
Flowery Branch, GA 30542
770-965-3115

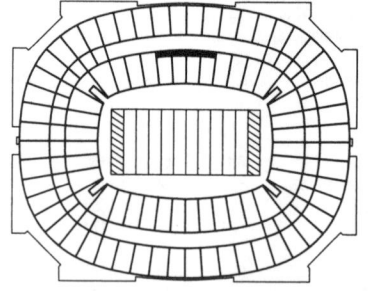

ATLANTA FALCONS

No.	QUARTERBACKS	Ht./Wt.	Born	NFL Exp.	College	How acq.	'05 Games GP/GS
3	Bryan Randall	6-0/222	8/16/83	1	Virginia Tech	FA/05	0/0
8	Matt Schaub	6-5/237	6/25/81	3	Virginia	D3/04	16/1
1	D.J. Shockley	6-0/214	3/25/83	R	Georgia	D7/06	—
7	Michael Vick	6-0/203	6/26/80	6	Virginia Tech	D1/01	15/15
	RUNNING BACKS						
34	DeAndra Cobb	5-10/196	5/18/81	2	Michigan State	D6/05	3/0
45	T.J. Duckett	6-0/254	2/17/81	5	Michigan State	D1/02	14/0
41	Kevin Dudley	6-1/237	1/2/82	2	Michigan	FA/05	1/0
28	Warrick Dunn	5-9/180	1/5/75	10	Florida State	FA/02	16/16
33	Justin Griffith (FB)	5-11/232	4/13/81	4	Mississippi State	D4/03	16/15
44	Fred McCrary (FB)	6-0/247	9/19/72	10	Mississippi State	FA/04	15/0
32	Jerious Norwood	5-11/205	7/29/83	R	Mississippi State	D3/06	—
	RECEIVERS						
80	Eric Beverly (TE)	6-3/300	3/28/74	9	Miami (Ohio)	FA/04	16/2
85	Dwayne Blakley (TE)	6-4/257	8/10/79	3	Missouri	FA/05	16/1
83	Alge Crumpler (TE)	6-2/262	12/23/77	6	North Carolina	D2/01	16/16
86	Brian Finneran	6-5/210	1/31/76	8	Villanova	FA/00	16/7
12	Michael Jenkins	6-4/217	6/18/82	3	Ohio State	D1b/04	14/12
81	Adam Jennings	5-11/175	11/17/82	R	Fresno State	D6/06	—
82	Jerome Pathon	6-0/195	12/16/75	9	Washington	FA/05	8/0
48	Derek Rackley (TE)	6-4/250	7/18/77	7	Minnesota	FA/00	16/0
84	Roddy White	6-1/204	11/2/81	2	UAB	D1/05	16/8
	OFFENSIVE LINEMEN						
69	Ben Claxton (G)	6-2/301	7/30/80	2	Mississippi	W-Pit/05	2/0
79	Shawn Draper (TE)	6-3/280	7/5/79	1	Alabama	FA/05	0/0
65	Kynan Forney (G)	6-3/307	9/8/78	6	Hawaii	D7b/01	16/16
72	Wayne Gandy (T)	6-4/315	2/10/71	13	Auburn	T-NO/06	16/16
66	Austin King (C/G)	6-5/303	4/11/81	4	Northwestern	FA/04	16/1
61	Matt Lehr (G)	6-2/293	4/25/79	6	Virginia Tech	FA/05	15/15
62	Todd McClure (C)	6-1/286	2/16/77	8	LSU	D7a/99	16/16
76	Quinn Ojinnaka (T)	6-5/292	4/23/84	R	Syracuse	D5/06	—
70	Frank Omiyale (T)	6-4/310	11/23/82	1	Tennessee Tech	D5b/05	0/0
74	Todd Weiner (T)	6-4/297	9/16/75	9	Kansas State	FA/02	15/15
	DEFENSIVE LINEMEN						
55	John Abraham (E)	6-4/256	5/6/78	7	South Carolina	T-NYJ/06	16/15
95	Jonathan Babineaux (T)	6-2/286	10/12/81	2	Iowa	D2/05	16/6
75	Rod Coleman (T)	6-2/285	8/16/76	8	East Carolina	FA/04	16/16
92	Chauncey Davis (E)	6-2/274	1/27/83	2	Florida State	D4/05	16/5
97	Patrick Kerney (E)	6-5/273	12/30/76	8	Virginia	D1/99	16/16
99	Jonathan Jackson (E)	6-3/250	10/17/82	1	Oklahoma	FA/05	0/0
96	Antwan Lake (T)	6-4/308	7/10/79	4	West Virginia	FA/04	13/2
93	Chad Lavalais (T)	6-1/293	4/15/79	3	LSU	D5/04	14/14
94	Josh Savage (E)	6-4/276	9/28/80	3	Utah	FA/05	1/0
71	Darrell Shropshire (T)	6-2/301	3/18/83	2	South Carolina	D7/05	10/0
	LINEBACKERS						
52	Jordan Beck	6-2/231	4/18/83	2	Cal Poly	D3/05	0/0
59	Michael Boley	6-3/236	8/24/82	2	Southern Miss	D5a/05	16/11
56	Keith Brooking	6-2/245	10/30/75	9	Georgia Tech	D1/98	16/16
50	Ed Hartwell	6-1/250	5/27/78	6	Western Illinois	D4/01	5/5
54	John Leake	6-0/230	8/28/81	2	Clemson	FA/06	11/0
53	Martin Patterson	6-1/243	2/18/83	1	Texas Christian	FA/05	0/0
98	Ike Reese	6-2/222	10/16/73	9	Michigan State	FA/05	16/0
51	Demorrio Williams	6-0/232	7/6/80	3	Nebraska	D4/04	16/16
	DEFENSIVE BACKS						
29	Chris Cash (CB)	5-10/185	7/13/80	5	USC	FA/05	3/0
25	Chris Crocker (S)	5-11/194	3/9/80	4	Marshall	T-Cle/06	16/16
40	Diamond Ferri (S)	5-10/214	8/6/81	1	Syracuse	FA/05	0/0
21	DeAngelo Hall (CB)	5-10/197	11/19/83	3	Virginia Tech	D1a/04	15/15
26	Omare Lowe (S)	6-1/195	4/20/78	5	Washington	W-Sea/05	16/1
23	Kevin Mathis (S)	5-9/185	4/29/74	9	Texas A&M-Comm.	FA/02	0/0
36	Lawyer Milloy (S)	6-0/190	11/14/73	11	Washington	FA/06	16/16
39	Cam Newton (DB)	6-1/203	5/19/82	2	Furman	FA/05	6/0
20	Allen Rossum (CB)	5-8/178	10/22/75	9	Notre Dame	FA/02	10/0
22	Leigh Torrence	6-0/183	1/4/82	2	Stanford	FA/05	10/0
37	Ahmad Treaudo	5-10/181	4/15/82	2	Southern	FA/05	1/0
27	Jason Webster (CB)	5-9/187	9/8/77	7	Texas A&M	FA/04	15/13
24	Jimmy Williams (CB)	6-2/213	3/8/84	R	Virginia Tech	D2/06	—
	SPECIALISTS						
9	Michael Koenen (P/K)	5-11/185	7/13/82	2	Western Washington	FA/05	16/0
11	Seth Marler (K)	6-1/200	3/27/81	3	Tulane	FA/06	0/0

Abbreviations: D1-draft pick, first round; W-claimed on waivers; T-obtained in trade; FA-free-agent acquisition.

ATLANTA FALCONS

2005 regular-season record: 8-8
Position: 3rd in NFC South

Sept.12—PHILADELPHIA	W	14-10
Sept.18—at Seattle	L	18-21
Sept.25—at Buffalo	W	24-16
Oct. 2—MINNESOTA	W	30-10
Oct. 9—NEW ENGLAND	L	28-31
Oct.16—at New Orleans	W	34-31
Oct.24—N.Y. JETS	W	27-14
Oct.30—Open date		
Nov. 6—at Miami	W	17-10
Nov.13—GREEN BAY	L	25-33
Nov.20—TAMPA BAY	L	27-30
Nov.24—at Detroit	W	27-7
Dec. 4—at Carolina	L	6-24
Dec.12—NEW ORLEANS	W	36-17
Dec.18—at Chicago	L	3-16
Dec.24—at Tampa Bay (OT)	L	24-27
Jan. 1—CAROLINA	L	11-44

SCORING BY PERIODS

	Q1	Q2	Q3	Q4	OT	Pts.
Falcons	78	132	49	92	0	351
Opponents	79	111	57	91	3	341

TEAM STATISTICS

	Atl.	Opp.
TOTAL FIRST DOWNS	313	319
Rushing	139	122
Passing	149	167
Penalty	25	30
3rd Down: Made/Att.	94/219	58/192
3rd Down Pct.	42.9	30.2
4th Down: Made/Att.	5/14	10/16
4th Down Pct.	35.7	62.5
POSSESSION AVG.	29:58	30:02
TOTAL NET YARDS	5225	5200
Avg. per Game	326.6	325.0
Total Plays	1021	1001
Avg. per Play	5.1	5.2
NET YARDS RUSHING	2546	2063
Avg. per Game	159.1	128.9
Total Rushes	531	438
NET YARDS PASSING	2679	3137
Avg. per Game	167.4	196.1
Sacked/Yards Lost	39/228	37/257
Gross Yards	2907	3394
Att./Completions	451/247	526/320
Completion Pct.	54.8	60.8
Had Intercepted	13	16
PUNTS/AVERAGE	78/42.3	79/43.1
NET PUNTING AVG.	78/36.9	79/39.0
PENALTIES/YARDS	114/1043	114/981
FUMBLES/LOST	26/16	22/13
TOUCHDOWNS	39	38
Rushing	17	18
Passing	19	18
Returns	3	2

SCORING (NONKICKERS)

	Tot. TD	RTD	PTD	MTD	2Pt.	Tot. Pts.
Duckett	8	8	0	0	0	48
Vick	6	6	0	0	0	36
Crumpler	5	0	5	0	1	32
Dunn	4	3	1	0	0	24
Finneran	2	0	2	0	3	18
Griffith	3	0	3	0	0	18
Jenkins	3	0	3	0	0	18
R. White	3	0	3	0	0	18
Blakley	1	0	1	0	0	6
Davis	1	0	0	1	0	6
D. Hall	1	0	0	1	0	6
D. White	1	0	1	0	0	6
D. Williams	1	0	0	1	0	6
Falcons	39	17	19	3	4	244
Opponents	38	18	18	2	0	228

2-Pt. conversions: Falcons 4-4; Opponents 0-0.

(KICKERS)

	XPM/XPA	FGM/FGA	Pts.
Peterson	35/35	23/25	104
Koenen	0/0	1/2	3
Falcons	35/35	24/27	107
Opponents	38/38	25/30	113

RUSHING

	Att.	Yds.	Avg.	Lg.	TD
Dunn	280	1416	5.1	65	3
Vick	102	597	5.9	32	6
Duckett	121	380	3.1	25	8
Schaub	9	76	8.4	23	0
Griffith	15	65	4.3	19	0
R. White	4	12	3.0	16	0
Falcons	531	2546	4.8	65	17
Opponents	438	2063	4.7	t70	18

RECEIVING

	No.	Yds.	Avg.	Lg.	TD
Crumpler	65	877	13.5	48	5
Finneran	50	611	12.2	53	2
Jenkins	36	508	14.1	58	3
Dunn	29	220	7.6	24	1
R. White	29	446	15.4	t54	3
Griffith	21	111	5.3	17	3
Duckett	6	63	10.5	19	0
Blakley	4	30	7.5	10	1
McCrary	3	12	4.0	11	0
D. White	2	25	12.5	t14	1
Pathon	1	18	18.0	18	0
Vick	1	-14	-14.0	-14	0
Falcons	247	2907	11.8	58	19
Opponents	320	3394	10.6	t55	18

INTERCEPTIONS

	No.	Yds.	Avg.	Lg.	TD
D. Hall	6	177	29.5	65	0

	No.	Yds.	Avg.	Lg.	TD
Brooking	4	50	12.5	22	0
D. Williams	2	6	3.0	6	0
Carpenter	2	1	0.5	1	0
Webster	1	19	19.0	19	0
Scott	1	15	15.0	15	0
Falcons	16	268	16.8	65	0
Opponents	13	163	12.5	51	0

SACKS: Coleman 10.5, Kerney 6.5, Brooking 3.5, Lake 3.5, B. Smith 3.0, D. Williams 3.0, Lavalais 2.5, Shropshire 2.0, Davis 1.0, Scott 1.0, Babineaux 0.5. Falcons 37.0; Opponents 39.0.

PUNTING

	No.	Yds.	Avg.	In. 20	Lg.
Koenen	78	3300	42.3	23	67
Falcons	78	3300	42.3	23	67
Opponents	79	3401	43.1	30	65

PUNT RETURNS

	No.	FC	Yds.	Avg.	Lg.	TD
Rossum	17	12	145	8.5	29	0
D. Hall	8	2	82	10.3	27	0
Jenkins	3	0	19	6.3	15	0
Finneran	2	8	7	3.5	5	0
Cobb	1	0	8	8.0	8	0
Falcons	31	23	261	8.4	29	0
Opponents	35	14	238	6.8	28	0

KICK RETURNS

	No.	Yds.	Avg.	Lg.	TD
Rossum	31	702	22.6	47	0
Cobb	16	359	22.4	39	0
Bryant	8	137	17.1	23	0
Griffith	8	149	18.6	23	0
Pathon	3	54	18.0	21	0
Duckett	2	36	18.0	18	0
D. Hall	2	45	22.5	23	0
Falcons	70	1482	21.2	47	0
Opponents	59	1138	19.3	45	0

FIELD GOALS

	1-19	20-29	30-39	40-49	50+
Peterson	0/0	9/10	11/11	3/4	0/0
Koenen	0/0	0/0	0/0	0/0	1/2
Falcons	0/0	9/10	11/11	3/4	1/2
Opponents	2/2	5/6	6/6	9/13	3/3

Peterson: () (30G) (27G) (38G, 26G, 39G) (33G) (37G, 36G) (22G, 41G) (21G) (37G) (31G, 20G) (21G, 23G) (36G, 43G, 49N) (43G, 20G) (30G) (31G, 28B) (29G)
Koenen: () () () () (58G) () () () (55N) () ()
() () ()
Opponents: (49N, 49N, 44G) () (36G, 41G, 30G) (43G) (29G) (19G, 47B) () (28G) (46G, 23G, 53G, 51G) (31G, 45G, 45G) () (20G) (47G) (35G, 29G, 39G, 44N) (50G, 27N, 41G) (19G, 41G, 34G)

PASSING

	Att.	Cmp.	Yds.	Pct.	Avg. Gain	TD	TD%	Int.	Pct. Int.	Long	Sack/Lost	Rating
Vick	387	214	2412	55.3	6.23	15	3.9	13	3.4	58	33/201	73.1
Schaub	64	33	495	51.6	7.73	4	6.3	0	0.0	53	6/27	98.1
Falcons	451	247	2907	54.8	6.45	19	4.2	13	2.9	58	39/228	76.6
Opponents	526	320	3394	60.8	6.45	18	3.4	16	3.0	t55	37/257	78.4

BALTIMORE RAVENS
AFC NORTH DIVISION

2006 SEASON

CLUB DIRECTORY

Owner
Steve Bisciotti
President
Dick Cass
General manager
Ozzie Newsome
Vice president of football administration
Pat Moriarty
Director of player development
O.J. Brigance
Director of college scouting
Eric DeCosta
Director of pro personnel
George Kokinis
Senior vice president/public & community relations
Kevin Byrne
Senior director of publications
Francine Lubera
Senior director of operations
Bob Eller
Director of media relations
Chad Steele

Head coach
Brian Billick

Assistant coaches
Clarence Brooks (defensive line)
Mark Carrier (secondary)
Jim Fassel (offensive coordinator)
John Fassel (special teams asst.)
Chris Foerster (offensive line/ assistant head coach)
Jedd Fisch (asst. quarterbacks/ wide receivers)
Jeff FitzGerald (linebackers)
Jeff Friday (strength and conditioning)
Frank Gansz Jr. (special teams coordinator)
Wade Harman (tight ends/asst. offensive line)
Mike Johnson (wide receivers)
Tony Nathan (running backs)
Rick Neuheisel (quarterbacks)
Mike Pettine (outside linebackers)
Paul Ricci (asst. strength and conditioning)
Greg Roman (asst. offensive line)
Rex Ryan (defensive coordinator)
Dennis Thurman (secondary)

SCHEDULE

Sept. 10—at Tampa Bay	1:00
Sept. 17—OAKLAND	1:00
Sept. 24—at Cleveland	4:05
Oct. 1—SAN DIEGO	1:00
Oct. 9—at Denver (Mon.)	8:30
Oct. 15—CAROLINA	1:00
Oct. 22—Open date	
Oct. 29—at New Orleans	1:00
Nov. 5—CINCINNATI	1:00
Nov. 12—at Tennessee	1:00
Nov. 19—ATLANTA	1:00
Nov. 26—PITTSBURGH	1:00
Nov. 30—at Cincinnati (Thurs.)	8:00
Dec. 10—at Kansas City	1:00
Dec. 17—CLEVELAND	1:00
Dec. 24—at Pittsburgh	1:00
Dec. 31—BUFFALO	1:00

All times are Eastern.
All games Sunday unless noted.

DRAFT CHOICES

Haloti Ngata, DT, Oregon (first round/12th pick overall).
Chris Chester, C, Oklahoma (2/56).
David Pittman, CB, Northwestern State (3/87).
Demetrius Williams, WR, Oregon (4/111).
P.J. Daniels, RB, Georgia Tech (4/132).
Dawan Landry, FS, Georgia Tech (5/146).
Quinn Sypniewski, TE, Colorado (5/166).
Sam Koch, P, Nebraska (6/203).
Derrick Martin, CB, Wyoming (6/208).
Ryan LaCasse, OLB, Syracuse (7/219).

OFFSEASON MOVES

Key additions
RB	Mike Anderson	FA/Broncos
P	Leo Araguz	FA/Seahawks
DT	Justin Bannan	FA/Bills
DE	Trevor Pryce	FA/Broncos

Key losses
S	Will Demps	FA/Giants
TE	Darnell Dinkins	FA/Browns
DT	Maake Kemoeatu	FA/Panthers
RB	Chester Taylor	FA/Vikings
DE	Anthony Weaver	FA/Dolphins
QB	Anthony Wright	FA/Bengals
P	Dave Zastudil	FA/Browns

MISCELLANEOUS TEAM DATA

Stadium (capacity, surface):
M&T Bank Stadium (70,701, Sportexe Momentum Turf)
Business address:
1 Winning Drive
Owings Mills, MD 21117
Business phone:
410-701-4000
Ticket information:
410-261-RAVE (7283)
Team colors:
Purple, black and metallic gold
Flagship radio stations:
WBAL, 1090 AM; 98 Rock, 97.9 FM
Website:
www.baltimoreravens.com
Training site:
McDaniel College
Westminster, Md.
410-701-4000

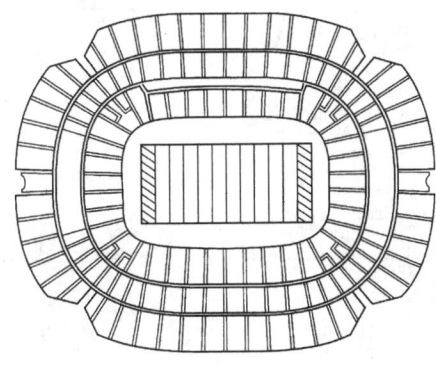

BALTIMORE RAVENS

No.	QUARTERBACKS	Ht./Wt.	Born	NFL Exp.	College	How acq.	'05 Games GP/GS
7	Kyle Boller	6-3/220	6/17/81	4	California	D1b/03	9/9
12	Brian St. Pierre	6-3/230	11/28/79	2	Boston College	FA/05	0/0
	RUNNING BACKS						
38	Mike Anderson	6-0/230	9/21/73	7	Utah	FA/06	15/15
30	P.J. Daniels	5-10/214	12/21/82	R	Georgia Tech	D4b/06	—
33	Justin Green (FB)	5-11/242	4/30/82	2	Montana	D5/05	12/4
31	Jamal Lewis	5-11/245	8/29/79	7	Tennessee	D1a/00	15/15
34	Ovie Mughelli (FB)	6-1/255	6/10/80	4	Wake Forest	D4b/03	13/5
39	Alan Ricard (FB)	5-11/237	1/17/77	6	Louisiana-Monroe	FA/00	2/2
36	B.J. Sams	5-10/185	10/29/80	3	McNeese State	FA/04	14/0
32	Musa Smith	6-0/232	5/31/82	4	Georgia	D3/03	1/0
	RECEIVERS						
44	Bobby Blizzard (TE)	6-3/273	3/22/80	1	North Carolina	FA/06	0/0
14	Romby Bryant	6-1/181	12/21/79	2	Tulsa	FA/06	3/0
89	Mark Clayton	5-10/193	7/2/82	2	Oklahoma	D1/05	14/10
81	Devard Darling	6-1/215	4/16/82	2	Washington State	D3/04	10/0
86	Todd Heap (TE)	6-5/252	3/16/80	6	Arizona State	D1/01	16/16
85	Derrick Mason	5-10/190	1/17/74	10	Michigan State	FA/05	16/16
84	Clarence Moore	6-6/211	9/24/82	3	Northern Arizona	D6b/04	4/1
88	Quinn Sypniewski (TE)	6-6/270	4/14/82	R	Colorado	D5b/06	—
83	Daniel Wilcox (TE)	6-1/245	3/23/77	3	Appalachian State	FA/04	13/3
87	Demetrius Williams	6-2/198	3/28/83	R	Oregon	D4a/06	—
	OFFENSIVE LINEMEN						
60	Jason Brown (G)	6-3/309	5/5/83	2	North Carolina	D4/05	6/1
65	Chris Chester (C)	6-3/305	1/12/83	R	Oklahoma	D2/06	—
73	Rob Droege (T)	6-6/302	2/15/81	1	Missouri	FA/05	0/0
62	Mike Flynn (C)	6-3/305	6/15/74	9	Maine	FA/97	16/16
70	Matt Katula (C)	6-6/272	8/22/82	2	Wisconsin	FA/05	16/0
64	Edwin Mulitalo (G)	6-3/345	9/1/74	8	Arizona	D4b/99	16/15
75	Jonathan Ogden (T)	6-9/345	7/31/74	11	UCLA	D1a/96	16/16
79	Tony Pashos (T)	6-6/337	8/3/80	3	Illinois	D5b/03	16/7
69	Brian Rimpf (G)	6-5/319	2/11/81	2	East Carolina	D7/04	15/7
63	Thatcher Szalay (G)	6-4/303	1/18/79	3	Montana	FA/05	4/0
78	Adam Terry (T)	6-8/330	9/1/82	2	Syracuse	D2b/05	7/0
68	Keydrick Vincent (G)	6-5/325	4/13/78	6	Mississippi	FA/05	9/9
	DEFENSIVE LINEMEN						
94	Justin Bannan (T)	6-3/305	4/18/79	5	Colorado	FA/06	16/7
93	Dwan Edwards (T)	6-3/315	5/16/81	3	Oregon State	D2/04	12/1
91	Aubrayo Franklin (T)	6-1/320	8/27/80	4	Tennessee	D5a/03	15/1
97	Kelly Gregg (T)	6-0/310	11/1/76	7	Oklahoma	FA/00	16/16
95	Jarret Johnson (E)	6-3/285	8/14/81	4	Alabama	D4a/03	16/12
92	Haloti Ngata (T)	6-4/340	1/21/84	R	Oregon	D1/06	—
90	Trevor Pryce (E)	6-5/295	8/3/75	10	Clemson	FA/06	16/16
56	Gary Stills (E)	6-2/250	7/11/74	8	West Virginia	FA/06	16/0
55	Terrell Suggs (E)	6-3/260	10/11/82	4	Arizona State	D1a/03	16/16
	LINEBACKERS						
53	Dan Cody	6-5/255	12/1/81	2	Oklahoma	D2/05	0/0
54	Roderick Green	6-2/250	4/26/82	3	Central Missouri St.	D5/04	16/0
58	Dennis Haley	6-1/247	2/18/82	2	Virginia	FA/05	4/0
98	Ryan LaCasse	6-2/257	2/6/83	R	Syracuse	D7/06	—
52	Ray Lewis	6-1/245	5/15/75	11	Miami	D1b/96	6/6
57	Bart Scott	6-2/235	8/18/80	5	Southern Illinois	FA/02	16/10
51	Mike Smith	6-1/240	9/2/81	2	Texas Tech	D7/05	6/0
96	Adalius Thomas	6-2/270	8/18/77	7	Southern Miss	D6a/00	16/16
59	Zac Woodfin	6-1/235	3/19/83	2	UAB	FA/05	1/0
	DEFENSIVE BACKS						
45	Robb Butler (S)	6-0/217	9/14/81	2	Robert Morris	FA/05	0/0
35	Corey Ivy (CB)	5-8/188	3/29/77	6	Oklahoma	FA/06	16/5
26	Dawan Landry (S)	6-0/220	12/30/82	R	Georgia Tech	D5a/06	—
29	Derrick Martin (CB)	5-10/202	5/16/85	R	Wyoming	D6b/06	—
21	Chris McAlister (CB)	6-1/206	6/14/77	8	Arizona	D1/99	14/13
42	Zach Norton (CB)	5-11/183	11/19/81	2	Cincinnati	FA/04	3/0
25	Evan Oglesby (CB)	5-10/185	12/18/81	2	North Alabama	FA/05	3/0
24	David Pittman (CB)	5-11/187	10/14/83	R	Northwestern State	D3/06	—
20	Ed Reed (S)	5-11/200	9/11/78	5	Miami	D1/02	10/10
22	Samari Rolle (CB)	6-0/175	8/10/76	9	Florida State	FA/05	16/16
46	B.J. Ward (S)	6-3/208	11/4/81	2	Florida State	FA/05	15/0
	SPECIALISTS						
2	Leo Araguz (P)	5-11/190	1/18/70	8	Stephen F. Austin	FA/06	4/0
8	Aaron Elling (K)	6-2/201	5/31/78	4	Wyoming	FA/05	9/0
4	Sam Koch (P)	6-1/230	8/13/82	R	Nebraska	D6a/06	—
3	Matt Stover (K)	5-11/178	1/27/68	17	Louisiana Tech	FA/91	16/0

Abbreviations: D1-draft pick, first round; W-claimed on waivers; T-obtained in trade; FA-free-agent acquisition.

BALTIMORE RAVENS

2005 regular-season record: 6-10
Position: 3rd in AFC North

Sept.11—INDIANAPOLIS	L	7-24	
Sept.18—at Tennessee	L	10-25	
Sept.25—Open date			
Oct. 2—N.Y. JETS	W	13-3	
Oct. 9—at Detroit	L	17-35	
Oct. 16—CLEVELAND	W	16-3	
Oct. 23—at Chicago	L	6-10	
Oct. 31—at Pittsburgh	L	19-20	
Nov. 6—CINCINNATI	L	9-21	
Nov.13—at Jacksonville	L	3-30	
Nov.20—PITTSBURGH (OT)	W	16-13	
Nov.27—at Cincinnati	L	29-42	
Dec. 4—HOUSTON	W	16-15	
Dec.11—at Denver	L	10-12	
Dec.19—GREEN BAY	W	48-3	
Dec.25—MINNESOTA	W	30-23	
Jan. 1—at Cleveland	L	16-20	

SCORING BY PERIODS

	Q1	Q2	Q3	Q4	OT	Pts.
Ravens	50	77	44	91	3	265
Opponents	54	75	90	80	0	299

TEAM STATISTICS

	Bal.	Opp.
TOTAL FIRST DOWNS ..	286	277
Rushing	97	79
Passing	163	161
Penalty	26	37
3rd Down: Made/Att. ..	95/243	79/219
3rd Down Pct.	39.1	36.1
4th Down: Made/Att. ..	11/19	4/12
4th Down Pct.	57.9	33.3
POSSESSION AVG.	30:22	29:38
TOTAL NET YARDS	4693	4549
Avg. per Game	293.3	284.3
Total Plays	1056	998
Avg. per Play	4.4	4.6
NET YARDS RUSHING ..	1605	1591
Avg. per Game	100.3	99.4
Total Rushes	452	431
NET YARDS PASSING....	3088	2958
Avg. per Game	193.0	184.9
Sacked/Yards Lost	42/293	42/270
Gross Yards	3381	3228
Att./Completions	562/335	525/296
Completion Pct.	59.6	56.4
Had Intercepted	21	11
PUNTS/AVERAGE	86/42.8	89/40.5
NET PUNTING AVG.	86/35.6	89/33.0
PENALTIES/YARDS	139/1067	110/844
FUMBLES/LOST	28/15	28/15
TOUCHDOWNS	25	30
Rushing	5	8
Passing	17	18
Returns	3	4

SCORING (NONKICKERS)

	Tot. TD	RTD	PTD	MTD	2Pt.	Tot. Pts.
Heap	7	0	7	0	0	42
J. Lewis	4	3	1	0	0	24
Clayton	3	1	2	0	0	18
Mason	3	0	3	0	0	18
A. Thomas	3	0	0	3	0	18
Hymes	2	0	2	0	0	12
Boller	1	1	0	0	0	6
C. Taylor	1	0	1	0	0	6
Wilcox	1	0	1	0	0	6
J. Green	0	0	0	0	1	2
Ravens	25	5	17	3	1	152
Opponents	30	8	18	4	1	184

2-Pt. conversions: Ravens 1-2; Opponents 1-1.

(KICKERS)

	XPM/XPA	FGM/FGA	Pts.
Stover	23/23	30/34	113
Ravens	23/23	30/35	113
Opponents	28/29	29/31	115

RUSHING

	Att.	Yds.	Avg.	Lg.	TD
J. Lewis	269	906	3.4	25	3
C. Taylor	117	487	4.2	52	0
Wright	18	68	3.8	22	0
Boller	23	66	2.9	9	1
Clayton	8	33	4.1	t11	1
Stewart	4	24	6.0	13	0
White	6	17	2.8	5	0
J. Green	5	4	0.8	4	0
Sanders	1	0	0.0	0	0
Zastudil	1	0	0.0	0	0
Ravens	452	1605	3.6	52	5
Opponents	431	1591	3.7	t77	8

RECEIVING

	No.	Yds.	Avg.	Lg.	TD
Mason	86	1073	12.5	t39	3
Heap	75	855	11.4	48	7
Clayton	44	471	10.7	t47	2
C. Taylor	41	292	7.1	20	1
J. Lewis	32	191	6.0	t15	1
Wilcox	20	154	7.7	t17	1
Hymes	11	132	12.0	21	2
J. Green	7	32	4.6	8	0
Dinkins	6	55	9.2	15	0
Moore	3	59	19.7	24	0
Mughelli	3	13	4.3	6	0
Mu. Smith	3	5	1.7	4	0
Johnson	2	31	15.5	19	0
Ricard	2	18	9.0	11	0
Ravens	335	3381	10.1	48	17
Opponents	296	3228	10.9	56	18

INTERCEPTIONS

	No.	Yds.	Avg.	Lg.	TD
Sanders	2	57	28.5	33	0
A. Thomas	2	48	24.0	28	1
Suggs	2	38	19.0	38	0
Reed	1	23	23.0	23	0
Williams	1	14	14.0	14	0
Rolle	1	11	11.0	11	0
R. Lewis	1	0	0.0	0	0
McAlister	1	0	0.0	0	0
Ravens	11	191	17.4	38	1
Opponents	21	256	12.2	37	3

SACKS: A. Thomas 9.0, Suggs 8.0, Polley 4.0, Scott 4.0, Boulware 2.5, Gregg 2.5, R. Green 2.0, Weaver 2.0, J. Johnson 1.5, Williams 1.5, Franklin 1.0, Kemoeatu 1.0, R. Lewis 1.0. Ravens 42.0; Opponents 42.0.

PUNTING

	No.	Yds.	Avg.	In. 20	Lg.
Elling	1	32	32.0	1	32
Zastudil	84	3653	43.5	11	60
Ravens	86	3685	42.8	12	60
Opponents	89	3605	40.5	30	61

PUNT RETURNS

	No.	FC	Yds.	Avg.	Lg.	TD
Sams	33	10	401	12.2	51	0
Clayton	6	2	30	5.0	10	0
Ravens	39	13	431	11.1	51	0
Opponents	55	12	481	8.7	t62	1

KICK RETURNS

	No.	Yds.	Avg.	Lg.	TD
Sams	44	998	22.7	87	0
C. Taylor	12	253	21.1	45	0
White	2	18	9.0	9	0
Dinkins	1	10	10.0	10	0
J. Green	1	10	10.0	10	0
Ravens	60	1289	21.5	87	0
Opponents	62	1352	21.8	59	0

FIELD GOALS

	1-19	20-29	30-39	40-49	50+
Stover	1/1	8/8	10/11	11/14	0/0
Elling	0/0	0/0	0/0	0/0	0/1
Ravens	1/1	8/8	10/11	11/14	0/1
Opponents	0/0	12/12	9/9	8/10	0/0

Stover: (38N, 47N, 45N) (30G) (42G, 25G) (46G) (39G, 27G, 38G) (40G, 29G) (22G, 43N, 49G, 49G, 47G) (34G, 32G, 31G) (41G) (47G, 25G, 44G) () (38G) (29G) (23G, 40G) (37G, 38G, 19G) (21G, 43G, 31G)
Elling: () () () () () () () () () () (54N) () () () () ()
Opponents: (20G) (39G, 29G, 47G) (21G) () (24G) (23G, 47N) (42G, 37G) (48N) (48G, 33G, 26G) (44G, 37G) (26G, 31G) (39G, 26G, 22G, 29G, 39G) (47G, 48G) (27G) (36G, 40G, 46G) (21G, 39G)

PASSING

	Att.	Cmp.	Yds.	Pct.	Avg. Gain	TD	Pct. TD	Int.	Pct. Int.	Long	Sack/Lost	Rating
Boller	293	171	1799	58.4	6.14	11	3.8	12	4.1	t47	23/146	71.8
Wright	266	164	1582	61.7	5.95	6	2.3	9	3.4	48	19/147	71.7
Clayton	1	0	0	0.0	0.00	0	0.0	0	0.0	...	0/0	39.6
Hymes	2	0	0	0.0	0.00	0	0.0	0	0.0	...	0/0	39.6
Ravens	562	335	3381	59.6	6.02	17	3.0	21	3.7	48	42/293	71.3
Opponents	525	296	3228	56.4	6.15	18	3.4	11	2.1	56	42/270	77.4

BUFFALO BILLS
AFC EAST DIVISION

2006 SEASON

CLUB DIRECTORY

Owner and president
Ralph C. Wilson Jr.
General manager/football operations
Marv Levy
Assistant general manager
Tom Modrak
**Executive vice president
business operations**
Scott Berchtold
Director of pro personnel
John Guy
Coordinator of college scouting
Doug Majeski
Director of community affairs
Gretchen Geitter
Media relations manager
Bill Hudock

Head coach
Dick Jauron

Assistant coaches
Bobby April (asst. head
coach/special teams)
John Allaire (strength and
conditioning)
George Catavolos (defensive
backs)
Charlie Coiner (tight ends)
DeMontie Cross (defensive/
special teams asst.)
Steve Fairchild (offensive
coordinator)
Perry Fewell (defensive
coordinator)
Bill Kollar (defensive line)
Chuck Lester (asst. to the head
coach/offensive line)
Jim McNally (offensive line)
Turk Schonert (quarterbacks)
Matt Sheldon (linebackers)
Eric Studesville (running backs)
Tyke Tolbert (wide receivers)
Alex Van Pelt (offensive quality
control)
Larry Zierlein (asst. offensive line)

OFFSEASON MOVES

Key additions
S	Matt Bowen	FA/Redskins
WR	Andre' Davis	FA/Patriots
C	Melvin Fowler	FA/Vikings
QB	Craig Nall	FA/Packers
WR	Peerless Price	FA/Cowboys
TE	Robert Royal	FA/Redskins
DT	Larry Tripplett	FA/Colts

Key losses
DT	Sam Adams	released/Bengals
DT	Justin Bannan	FA/Ravens
S	Lawyer Milloy	released/Falcons
WR	Eric Moulds	trade/Texans
TE	Mark Campbell	released/Saints

SCHEDULE

Sept.	10—at New England	1:00
Sept.	17—at Miami	1:00
Sept.	24—NEW YORK JETS	1:00
Oct.	1—MINNESOTA	1:00
Oct.	8—at Chicago	1:00
Oct.	15—at Detroit	1:00
Oct.	22—NEW ENGLAND	1:00
Oct.	29—Open date	
Nov.	5—GREEN BAY	1:00
Nov.	12—at Indianapolis	1:00
Nov.	19—at Houston	1:00
Nov.	26—JACKSONVILLE	1:00
Dec.	3—SAN DIEGO	1:00
Dec.	10—at N.Y. Jets	1:00
Dec.	17—MIAMI	1:00
Dec.	24—TENNESSEE	1:00
Dec.	31—at Baltimore	1:00

All times are Eastern.
All games Sunday unless noted.

DRAFT CHOICES

Donte Whitner, SS, Ohio State (first round/eighth pick overall).
John McCargo, DT, N.C. State (1/26).
Ashton Youboty, CB, Ohio State (3/70).
Ko Simpson, FS, South Carolina (4/105).
Kyle Williams, DT, LSU (5/134).
Brad Butler, OT, Virginia (5/143).
Keith Ellison, OLB, Oregon State (6/178).
Terrance Pennington, OT, New Mexico (7/216).
Aaron Merz, G, California (7/248).

MISCELLANEOUS TEAM DATA

Stadium (capacity, surface):
Ralph Wilson Stadium (73,967, AstroPlay)
Business address:
One Bills Drive
Orchard Park, N.Y. 14127
Business phone:
716-648-1800
Ticket information:
877-BB-TICKS
Team colors:
Dark navy, red, royal and nickel gray
Flagship radio station:
WGRF, 96.9 FM (97 ROCK)
Website:
www.buffalobills.com
Training site:
St. John Fisher College
Rochester, N.Y.
716-648-1800

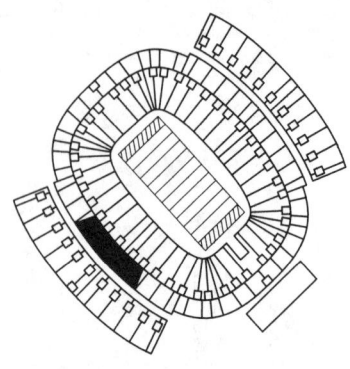

No.	QUARTERBACKS	Ht./Wt.	Born	NFL Exp.	College	How acq.	'05 Games GP/GS
10	Kelly Holcomb	6-2/212	7/9/73	10	Middle Tennessee	FA/05	10/8
7	J.P. Losman	6-2/217	3/12/81	3	Tulane	D1b/04	9/8
16	Craig Nall	6-3/228	4/21/79	3	Northwestern St.	FA/06	0/0
	RUNNING BACKS						
35	Joe Burns	5-9/215	9/15/79	5	Georgia Tech	FA/02	16/0
25	Lionel Gates	6-0/223	3/13/82	1	Louisville	D7/05	0/0
21	Willis McGahee	6-0/228	10/20/81	4	Miami	D1/03	16/15
31	Daimon Shelton (FB)	6-0/262	9/15/72	9	Sacramento State	FA/04	16/11
28	Anthony Thomas	6-2/225	11/7/77	6	Michigan	FA/06	10/2
20	Shaud Williams	5-7/193	10/2/80	3	Alabama	FA/04	16/0
	RECEIVERS						
89	Sam Aiken	6-2/204	12/14/80	4	North Carolina	D4b/03	16/2
18	Andre' Davis	6-1/195	6/12/79	5	Virginia Tech	FA/06	9/4
87	Tim Euhus (TE)	6-5/249	10/2/80	3	Oregon State	D4/04	11/3
83	Lee Evans	5-10/197	3/11/81	3	Wisconsin	D1a/04	16/15
85	Kevin Everett (TE)	6-5/241	2/5/82	1	Miami	D3/05	0/0
88	Ryan Neufeld (TE)	6-4/250	11/22/75	6	UCLA	FA/03	13/0
11	Roscoe Parrish	5-10/170	7/16/82	2	Miami	D2/05	10/1
81	Peerless Price	5-11/190	10/27/76	8	Tennessee	W-Dal/06	7/1
82	Josh Reed	5-10/208	5/1/80	5	LSU	D2a/02	16/6
84	Robert Royal (TE)	6-4/257	5/15/79	4	LSU	FA/06	15/14
19	Jonathan Smith	5-10/194	11/28/81	3	Georgia Tech	D7b/04	7/1
	OFFENSIVE LINEMEN						
66	Bennie Anderson (G)	6-5/345	2/17/77	6	Tennessee State	FA/05	16/14
60	Brad Butler (T)	6-7/309	9/18/83	R	Virginia	D5b/06	—
67	Melvin Fowler (C/G)	6-3/305	3/31/79	5	Maryland	FA/06	11/9
69	Mike Gandy (T)	6-4/310	1/3/79	6	Notre Dame	FA/05	16/16
73	Justin Geisinger (G)	6-4/320	5/24/82	1	Vanderbilt	D6/05	0/0
74	Aaron Gibson (G)	6-6/370	9/27/77	6	Wisconsin	FA/06	0/0
76	Greg Jerman (T)	6-5/310	1/24/79	5	Baylor	FA/05	10/3
62	Aaron Merz (G)	6-4/340	8/27/83	R	California	D7b/06	—
61	Terrance Pennington (T)	6-7/325	9/25/83	R	New Mexico	D7a/06	—
71	Jason Peters (T)	6-4/328	1/22/82	3	Arkansas	FA/04	16/10
75	Duke Preston (C)	6-5/311	6/12/82	2	Illinois	D4/05	15/1
70	Tutan Reyes (T)	6-3/305	10/28/77	7	Mississippi	FA/06	16/0
54	Mike Schneck (C)	6-0/237	8/4/77	8	Wisconsin	W-Pit/05	16/0
58	Chris Villarrial (G)	6-3/318	6/9/73	11	Indiana (Pa.)	FA/04	15/15
	DEFENSIVE LINEMEN						
77	Tim Anderson (T)	6-3/304	11/22/80	3	Ohio State	D3/04	16/12
92	Ryan Denney (E)	6-7/275	6/15/77	5	BYU	D2b/02	16/0
90	Chris Kelsay (E)	6-4/275	10/31/79	4	Nebraska	D2/03	16/16
97	John McCargo (T)	6-2/302	8/19/83	R	N.C. State	D1b/06	—
93	Lauvale Sape (T)	6-1/296	8/29/80	4	Utah	D6/03	9/0
94	Aaron Schobel (E)	6-4/262	9/1/77	6	TCU	D2a/01	16/16
98	Larry Tripplett (T)	6-2/295	1/18/79	5	Washington	FA/06	15/4
95	Kyle Williams (T)	6-2/297	6/10/83	R	LSU	D5a/06	—
	LINEBACKERS						
55	Angelo Crowell	6-1/235	8/16/81	4	Virginia	D3/03	15/13
64	Keith Ellison	6-1/228	2/6/84	R	Oregon State	D6/06	—
50	Liam Ezekiel	6-0/249	10/30/82	2	Northeastern	FA/05	2/0
59	London Fletcher	5-10/245	5/19/75	9	John Carroll	FA/02	16/16
53	Mario Haggan	6-3/248	3/3/80	4	Mississippi State	D7/03	16/0
96	Jeff Posey	6-4/241	8/14/75	9	Southern Miss	FA/03	16/15
51	Takeo Spikes	6-2/242	12/17/76	9	Auburn	FA/03	3/3
57	Josh Stamer	6-2/238	10/11/77	4	South Dakota	FA/03	16/0
	DEFENSIVE BACKS						
26	Rashad Baker (S)	5-10/198	2/22/82	3	Tennessee	FA/04	14/0
41	Matt Bowen (S)	6-1/207	11/12/76	7	Iowa	FA/06	13/1
22	Nate Clements (CB)	6-0/209	12/12/79	6	Ohio State	D1/01	16/16
33	Jabari Greer (CB)	5-11/169	2/2/82	3	Tennessee	FA/04	16/2
29	Eric King (CB)	5-8/184	5/10/82	2	Wake Forest	D5/05	16/1
42	Jim Leonhard (S)	5-8/190	10/27/82	2	Wisconsin	FA/05	10/0
24	Terrence McGee (CB)	5-9/195	10/14/80	4	Northwestern State	D4a/03	15/14
40	Ko Simpson (S)	6-1/209	11/9/83	R	South Carolina	D4/06	—
37	Kiwaukee Thomas (CB)	5-11/192	6/19/77	7	Georgia Southern	FA/06	10/0
23	Troy Vincent (S)	6-1/200	6/8/71	15	Wisconsin	FA/04	16/16
36	Donte Whitner (S)	5-11/205	7/24/85	R	Ohio State	D1a/06	—
27	Coy Wire (S)	6-0/205	11/7/78	5	Stanford	D3/02	13/0
38	Ashton Youboty (CB)	6-0/189	7/7/84	R	Ohio State	D3/06	—
	SPECIALISTS						
9	Rian Lindell (K)	6-3/235	1/20/77	7	Washington State	FA/03	16/0
8	Brian Moorman (P)	6-0/175	2/5/76	6	Pittsburg State	FA/01	16/0

Abbreviations: D1-draft pick, first round; W-claimed on waivers; T-obtained in trade; FA-free-agent acquisition.

BUFFALO BILLS

BUFFALO BILLS

2005 regular-season record: 5-11
Position: 3rd in AFC East

Sept.11—HOUSTON	W	22-7
Sept.18—at Tampa Bay	L	3-19
Sept.25—ATLANTA	L	16-24
Oct. 2—at New Orleans	L	7-19
Oct. 9—MIAMI	W	20-14
Oct. 16—N.Y. JETS	W	27-17
Oct. 23—at Oakland	L	17-38
Oct. 30—at New England	L	16-21
Nov. 6—Open date		
Nov.13—KANSAS CITY	W	14-3
Nov.20—at San Diego	L	10-48
Nov.27—CAROLINA	L	9-13
Dec. 4—at Miami	L	23-24
Dec.11—NEW ENGLAND	L	7-35
Dec.17—DENVER	L	17-28
Dec.24—at Cincinnati	W	37-27
Jan. 1—at N.Y. Jets	L	26-30

SCORING BY PERIODS

	Q1	Q2	Q3	Q4	OT	Pts.
Bills	80	86	46	59	0	271
Opponents	34	135	75	123	0	367

TEAM STATISTICS

	Buf.	Opp.
TOTAL FIRST DOWNS ..	259	343
Rushing	96	146
Passing	129	169
Penalty	34	28
3rd Down: Made/Att.	74/201	93/200
3rd Down Pct.	36.8	46.5
4th Down: Made/Att.	6/16	7/12
4th Down Pct.	37.5	58.3
POSSESSION AVG.	29:04	30:56
TOTAL NET YARDS	4122	5496
Avg. per Game	257.6	343.5
Total Plays	930	1030
Avg. per Play	4.4	5.3
NET YARDS RUSHING ..	1607	2205
Avg. per Game	100.4	137.8
Total Rushes	428	489
NET YARDS PASSING....	2515	3291
Avg. per Game	157.2	205.7
Sacked/Yards Lost	43/337	38/269
Gross Yards	2852	3560
Att./Completions	459/269	503/314
Completion Pct.	58.6	62.4
Had Intercepted	16	17
PUNTS/AVERAGE	71/45.7	62/40.2
NET PUNTING AVG.	71/39.1	62/34.4
PENALTIES/YARDS	120/897	124/904
FUMBLES/LOST	26/10	24/13
TOUCHDOWNS	26	44
Rushing	6	22
Passing	18	19
Returns	2	3

SCORING (NONKICKERS)

	Tot. TD	RTD	PTD	MTD	2Pt.	Tot. Pts.
Evans	7	0	7	0	0	42
McGahee	5	5	0	0	0	30
Moulds	4	0	4	0	0	24
McGee	2	0	0	2	0	12
Reed	2	0	2	0	0	12
Burns	1	0	1	0	0	6
Holcomb	1	1	0	0	0	6
Parrish	1	0	1	0	0	6
Peters	1	0	1	0	0	6
Shelton	1	0	1	0	0	6
J. Smith	1	0	1	0	0	6
Bills	26	6	18	2	0	158
Opponents	44	22	19	3	0	266

(KICKERS)

	XPM/XPA	FGM/FGA	Pts.
Lindell	26/26	29/35	113
Bills	26/26	29/35	113
Opponents	44/44	19/25	101

RUSHING

	Att.	Yds.	Avg.	Lg.	TD
McGahee	325	1247	3.8	27	5
S. Williams	45	161	3.6	28	0
Losman	31	154	5.0	30	0
Evans	4	38	9.5	39	0
Holcomb	18	11	0.6	8	1
J. Smith	1	1	1.0	1	0
Shelton	1	0	0.0	0	0
Parrish	2	-2	-1.0	4	0
Reed	1	-3	-3.0	-3	0
Bills	428	1607	3.8	39	6
Opponents	489	2205	4.5	59	22

RECEIVING

	No.	Yds.	Avg.	Lg.	TD
Moulds	81	816	10.1	t55	4
Evans	48	743	15.5	65	7
Reed	32	449	14.0	t51	2
McGahee	28	178	6.4	19	0
Campbell	19	139	7.3	27	0
S. Williams	17	118	6.9	23	0
Parrish	15	148	9.9	28	1
Shelton	13	98	7.5	21	1
J. Smith	5	56	11.2	19	1
Aiken	4	57	14.3	22	0
Euhus	3	17	5.7	9	0
Peters	2	5	2.5	4	1
Burns	1	19	19.0	t19	1
Neufeld	1	9	9.0	9	0
Bills	269	2852	10.6	65	18
Opponents	314	3560	11.3	57	19

INTERCEPTIONS

	No.	Yds.	Avg.	Lg.	TD
McGee	4	97	24.3	t46	1
Vincent	4	78	19.5	42	0
Crowell	2	3	1.5	2	0
Clements	2	0	0.0	0	0
Fletcher	1	20	20.0	20	0
Baker	1	18	18.0	18	0
Kelsay	1	17	17.0	17	0
Milloy	1	0	0.0	0	0
Schobel	1	0	0.0	0	0
Bills	17	233	13.7	t46	1
Opponents	16	209	13.1	42	2

SACKS: Schobel 12.0, Denney 4.0, Fletcher 4.0, Adams 3.0, Crowell 3.0, Posey 3.0, Kelsay 2.5, Bannan 1.5, T. Anderson 1.0, Baker 1.0, Greer 1.0, Milloy 1.0, Spikes 1.0. Bills 38.0; Opponents 43.0.

PUNTING

	No.	Yds.	Avg.	In. 20	Lg.
Moorman	71	3242	45.7	22	68
Bills	71	3242	45.7	22	68
Opponents	62	2492	40.2	22	61

PUNT RETURNS

	No.	FC	Yds.	Avg.	Lg.	TD
Parrish	14	9	186	13.3	43	0
Clements	8	3	52	6.5	13	0
J. Smith	6	5	41	6.8	17	0
Bills	28	17	279	10.0	43	0
Opponents	42	10	285	6.8	29	0

KICK RETURNS

	No.	Yds.	Avg.	Lg.	TD
McGee	46	1391	30.2	t99	1
Parrish	10	261	26.1	45	0
J. Smith	5	124	24.8	44	0
Reed	4	69	17.3	24	0
Burns	3	46	15.3	19	0
Neufeld	3	39	13.0	23	0
Shelton	2	26	13.0	16	0
Euhus	1	0	0.0	0	0
Leonhard	1	36	36.0	36	0
Bills	75	1992	26.6	t99	1
Opponents	64	1308	20.4	t95	1

FIELD GOALS

	1-19	20-29	30-39	40-49	50+
Lindell	0/0	8/9	11/13	7/10	3/3
Bills	0/0	8/9	11/13	7/10	3/3
Opponents	0/0	10/10	5/6	4/9	0/0

Lindell: (35G, 21G, 42G, 39G, 31G) (40G) (36G, 41G, 30G) (45N) (24G, 47G) (50G, 38G) (41G) (46N, 23G, 35G, 41G) (28N, 31N) (53G) (31G, 45G, 33G) () (32N) (31G) (21G, 24G, 48N, 22G) (21G, 24G, 52G, 36G) Opponents: () (40G) (27G) (23G, 40G, 32N, 20G, 37G) () (44G) (25G) (44N) (35G, 44N, 43N) (28G, 38G) (25G, 45N, 25G) (23G) () () (31G, 27G) (49G, 43N, 25G, 34G)

PASSING

	Att.	Cmp.	Yds.	Pct.	Avg. Gain	TD	Pct. TD	Int.	Pct. Int.	Long	Sack/Lost	Rating
Holcomb	230	155	1509	67.4	6.56	10	4.3	8	3.5	65	17/140	85.6
Losman	228	113	1340	49.6	5.88	8	3.5	8	3.5	58	26/197	64.9
Parrish	1	1	3	100.0	3.00	0	0.0	0	0.0	3	0/0	79.2
Bills	459	269	2852	58.6	6.21	18	3.9	16	3.5	65	43/337	75.4
Opponents	503	314	3560	62.4	7.08	19	3.8	17	3.4	57	38/269	82.1

CAROLINA PANTHERS
NFC SOUTH DIVISION

2006 SEASON

CLUB DIRECTORY

Owner & founder
Jerry Richardson
President, Panthers Football LLC
Mark Richardson
President, Panthers Stadium LLC
Jon Richardson
General manager
Marty Hurney
Director of player development
Donnie Shell
Director of communications
Charlie Dayton
Director of pro scouting
Mark Koncz
Director of college scouting
Tony Softli
Director of community relations
Riley Fields

Head coach
John Fox

Assistant coaches
Geep Chryst (quality control/
offense)
Danny Crossman (special teams)
Ken Flajole (linebackers)
Mike Gillhamer (secondary/
safeties)
Dan Henning (offensive
coordinator)
Tony Levine (special teams asst.)
David Magazu (tight ends)
Mike Maser (offensive line)
Mike McCoy (quarterbacks)
Sam Mills III (quality
control/defense)
Rod Perry (secondary)
Jerry Simmons (strength and
conditioning)
Jim Skipper (asst. head coach/
running backs)
Sal Sunseri (defensive line)
Mike Trgovac (defensive
coordinator)
Richard Williamson (wide
receivers)

OFFSEASON MOVES

Key additions
WR	Keyshawn Johnson	FA/Cowboys
DT	Damione Lewis	FA/Rams
DT	Maake Kemoeatu	FA/Ravens
LB	Keith Adams	FA/Eagles
LB	Na'il Diggs	FA/Packers
S	Shaun Williams	FA/Giants

Key losses
DT	Brentson Buckner	released
RB	Stephen Davis	released
LB	Will Witherspoon	FA/Rams
G	Tutan Reyes	FA/Bills
WR	Ricky Proehl	FA
S	Marlon McCree	FA/Chargers
LB	Brandon Short	FA/Giants

SCHEDULE

Sept.	10—ATLANTA	1:00
Sept.	17—at Minnesota	1:00
Sept.	24—at Tampa Bay	1:00
Oct.	1—NEW ORLEANS	1:00
Oct.	8—CLEVELAND	1:00
Oct.	15—at Baltimore	1:00
Oct.	22—at Cincinnati	1:00
Oct.	29—DALLAS	8:15
Nov.	5—Open date	
Nov.	13—TAMPA BAY (Mon.)	8:30
Nov.	19—ST. LOUIS	1:00
Nov.	26—at Washington	1:00
Dec.	4—at Philadelphia (Mon.)	8:30
Dec.	10—N.Y. GIANTS	1:00
Dec.	17—PITTSBURGH	1:00
Dec.	24—at Atlanta	1:00
Dec.	31—at New Orleans	1:00

All times are Eastern.
All games Sunday unless noted.

DRAFT CHOICES

DeAngelo Williams, RB, Memphis (first
round/27th pick overall).
Richard Marshall, CB, Fresno State
(2/58).
James Anderson, OLB, Virginia Tech
(3/88).
Rashad Butler, OT, Miami (3/89).
Nate Salley, FS, Ohio State (4/121).
Jeff King, TE, Virginia Tech (5/155).
Will Montgomery, G, Virginia Tech
(7/234).
Stanley McClover, DE, Auburn (7/237).

MISCELLANEOUS TEAM DATA

Stadium (capacity, surface):
Bank of America Stadium
(73,298, grass)
Business address:
800 S. Mint St.
Charlotte, NC 28202-1502
Business phone:
704-358-7000
Ticket information:
704-358-7800
Team colors:
Panther blue, black and silver
Flagship radio station:
WBT, 99.3 FM; 1110 AM
Website:
www.panthers.com
Training site:
Wofford College
Spartanburg, S.C.
704-358-7000

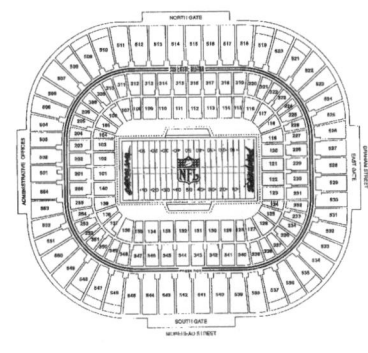

CAROLINA PANTHERS

No.	QUARTERBACKS	Ht./Wt.	Born	NFL Exp.	College	How acq.	'05 Games GP/GS
17	Jake Delhomme	6-2/215	1/10/75	8	La-Lafayette	FA/03	16/16
3	Stefan LeFors	6-0/208	6/7/81	1	Louisville	D4/04	0/0
16	Chris Weinke	6-4/232	7/31/72	6	Florida State	D4/01	3/0
	RUNNING BACKS						
49	Casey Cramer (FB)	6-2/235	1/5/82	3	Dartmouth	FA/04	1/0
26	DeShaun Foster	6-0/222	1/10/80	5	UCLA	D2/02	15/5
37	Nick Goings (FB)	6-0/225	1/26/78	6	Pittsburgh	FA/01	16/1
45	Brad Hoover (FB)	6-0/245	11/11/76	7	Western Carolina	FA/00	15/15
22	Jamal Robertson	5-10/210	1/10/77	5	Ohio Northern	FA/04	6/0
32	Eric Shelton	6-1/246	6/23/83	2	Louisville	D2/05	0/0
34	DeAngelo Williams	5-8/216	4/25/83	R	Memphis	D1/06	—
	RECEIVERS						
18	Drew Carter	6-3/200	9/5/81	2	Ohio State	D5/04	3/0
83	Keary Colbert	5-10/193	5/21/82	3	USC	D2/04	16/16
84	Michael Gaines (TE)	6-3/280	3/30/80	3	Central Florida	D7/04	11/6
88	Karl Hankton	6-2/202	7/24/70	8	Trinity (Ill.)	FA/00	16/0
19	Keyshawn Johnson	6-4/214	7/22/72	11	USC	FA/06	16/14
87	Jeff King (TE)	6-4/253	2/19/83	R	Virginia Tech	D5/06	—
86	Kris Mangum (TE)	6-4/252	8/15/73	9	Mississippi	D7/97	14/9
82	Mike Seidman (TE)	6-4/261	2/11/81	4	UCLA	D3a/03	12/1
89	Steve Smith	5-9/185	5/12/79	6	Utah	D3/01	16/16
	OFFENSIVE LINEMEN						
75	Chad Beasley (T)	6-5/300	11/13/78	2	Virginia Tech	FA/06	0/0
79	Rashad Butler (T)	6-5/294	2/10/83	R	Miami	D3b/06	—
78	Todd Fordham (T)	6-5/319	10/9/73	10	Florida State	T-Pit/04	16/0
69	Jordan Gross (T)	6-4/300	7/20/80	4	Utah	D1/03	16/16
63	Geoff Hangartner (C/G)	6-5/301	4/22/82	2	Texas A&M	D5b/05	4/0
75	Justin Hartwig (C)	6-4/312	11/21/78	5	Kansas	FA/06	16/16
61	Dave Kadela (T)	6-6/304	5/6/78	4	Virginia Tech	FA/03	0/0
71	Evan Mathis (G)	6-5/312	11/1/81	2	Alabama	D3a/05	9/0
66	Will Montgomery (G)	6-3/312	2/13/83	R	Virginia Tech	D7a/06	—
68	Mike Wahle (G)	6-6/304	3/29/77	9	Navy	FA/05	16/16
70	Travelle Wharton (T)	6-4/312	5/19/81	3	South Carolina	D3/04	16/16
	DEFENSIVE LINEMEN						
92	Tony Brown (E)	6-1/280	9/29/80	2	Memphis	FA/06	0/0
67	Jordan Carstens (T)	6-5/300	1/22/81	3	Iowa State	FA/04	16/15
98	Atiyyah Ellison (T)	6-4/305	9/29/81	1	Missouri	D3b/05	0/0
92	Jovan Haye (E)	6-2/287	6/21/82	2	Vanderbilt	D6a/05	2/0
77	Kris Jenkins (T)	6-4/335	8/3/79	6	Maryland	D2/01	1/1
99	Maake Kemoeatu (T)	6-5/340	1/10/79	5	Utah	FA/06	16/16
91	Damione Lewis (NT)	6-2/301	3/1/78	6	Miami	FA/06	16/7
75	Stanley McClover (E)	6-2/263	12/16/84	R	Auburn	D7b/06	—
94	Kindal Moorehead (T)	6-2/285	10/14/78	4	Alabama	D5/03	15/0
90	Julius Peppers (E)	6-6/283	1/18/80	5	North Carolina	D1/02	16/16
93	Mike Rucker (E)	6-5/275	2/28/75	8	Nebraska	D2b/99	15/14
96	Al Wallace (E)	6-5/275	3/25/74	7	Maryland	T-Mia/02	16/2
	LINEBACKERS						
50	Keith Adams	5-11/223	11/22/79	6	Clemson	FA/06	16/16
42	James Anderson	6-2/230	9/26/83	R	Virginia Tech	D3a/06	—
54	Vinny Ciurciu	6-0/235	5/2/80	4	Boston College	FA/03	15/1
58	Thomas Davis	6-0/231	3/22/83	2	Georgia	D1/05	16/2
53	Na'il Diggs	6-4/237	7/8/78	7	Ohio State	FA/06	9/6
52	Chris Draft	5-11/232	2/26/76	9	Stanford	FA/05	16/3
48	Corey Jenkins	6-0/222	8/25/76	3	South Carolina	FA/06	0/0
56	Jason Kyle	6-3/242	5/12/72	12	Arizona State	FA/01	16/0
55	Dan Morgan	6-2/245	12/19/78	6	Miami	D1/01	13/13
59	Adam Seward	6-2/248	6/15/82	2	UNLV	D5a/05	4/0
57	Sean Tufts	6-3/236	3/26/82	3	Colorado	D6/04	12/0
	DEFENSIVE BACKS						
28	Colin Branch (S)	5-11/205	3/2/80	4	Stanford	D4/03	0/0
20	Chris Gamble (CB)	6-1/181	3/11/83	3	Ohio State	D1/04	15/15
29	Jermaine Hardy (CB)	5-10/213	3/20/82	2	Virginia	FA/05	3/0
23	Reggie Howard (CB)	6-0/190	5/17/77	6	Memphis	FA/06	15/7
21	Ken Lucas (CB)	6-0/205	1/23/79	6	Mississippi	FA/05	15/15
31	Richard Marshall (CB)	5-11/189	12/12/84	R	Fresno State	D2/06	—
25	Kevin McCadam (S)	6-1/219	3/6/79	5	Virginia Tech	FA/06	16/0
30	Mike Minter (S)	5-10/195	1/15/74	10	Nebraska	D2/97	16/16
33	Nate Salley (S)	6-2/216	2/5/84	R	Ohio State	D4/06	—
24	Garnell Wilds (CB)	5-11/196	6/8/81	2	Virginia Tech	FA/05	3/0
36	Shaun Williams (S)	6-2/218	10/10/76	8	UCLA	FA/06	8/0
	SPECIALISTS						
7	Jason Baker (P)	6-1/201	5/17/78	6	Iowa	T-Den/05	16/0
4	John Kasay (K)	5-10/198	10/27/69	16	Georgia	FA/95	16/0

Abbreviations: D1-draft pick, first round; W-claimed on waivers; T-obtained in trade; FA-free-agent acquisition.

2005 regular-season record: 11-5
Position: 2nd in NFC South

Sept.11—NEW ORLEANS	L	20-23
Sept.18—NEW ENGLAND	W	27-17
Sept.25—at Miami	L	24-27
Oct. 3—GREEN BAY	W	32-29
Oct. 9—at Arizona	W	24-20
Oct. 16—at Detroit	W	21-20
Oct. 23—Open date		
Oct. 30—MINNESOTA	W	38-13
Nov. 6—at Tampa Bay	W	34-14
Nov.13—N.Y. JETS	W	30-3
Nov.20—at Chicago	L	3-13
Nov.27—at Buffalo	W	13-9
Dec. 4—ATLANTA	W	24-6
Dec.11—TAMPA BAY	L	10-20
Dec.18—at New Orleans	W	27-10
Dec.24—DALLAS	L	20-24
Jan. 1—at Atlanta	W	44-11

2005 postseason record: 2-1

Jan. 8—at N.Y. Giants#	W	23-0
Jan. 15—at Chicago*	W	29-21
Jan. 22—at Seattle§	L	14-34

#NFC wild-card game. *NFC divisional play-off game. §NFC championship game.

SCORING BY PERIODS

	Q1	Q2	Q3	Q4	OT	Pts.
Panthers	96	117	53	125	0	391
Opponents	72	73	42	72	0	259

TEAM STATISTICS

	Car.	Opp.
TOTAL FIRST DOWNS ..	278	262
Rushing	82	72
Passing	157	160
Penalty	39	30
3rd Down: Made/Att. ..	92/218	90/221
3rd Down Pct.	42.2	40.7
4th Down: Made/Att. ..	2/6	5/16
4th Down Pct.	33.3	31.3
POSSESSION AVG.	30:48	29:12
TOTAL NET YARDS	4950	4522
Avg. per Game	309.4	282.6
Total Plays	964	981
Avg. per Play	5.1	4.6
NET YARDS RUSHING ..	1679	1465
Avg. per Game	104.9	91.6
Total Rushes	487	408
NET YARDS PASSING....	3271	3057
Avg. per Game	204.4	191.1
Sacked/Yards Lost	28/214	45/294
Gross Yards	3485	3351
Att./Completions	449/269	528/305
Completion Pct.	59.9	57.8
Had Intercepted	16	23
PUNTS/AVERAGE	73/43.2	79/45.1
NET PUNTING AVG.	73/38.6	79/37.4
PENALTIES/YARDS	91/732	128/1045
FUMBLES/LOST	23/10	25/19

TOUCHDOWNS	45	27
Rushing	17	9
Passing	25	15
Returns	3	3

SCORING (NONKICKERS)

	TD	RTD	PTD	MTD	2Pt.	Pts.
S. Smith	13	1	12	0	0	78
S. Davis	12	12	0	0	0	72
Proehl	4	0	4	0	0	24
Foster	3	2	1	0	0	18
Colbert	2	0	2	0	0	12
Gaines	2	0	2	0	0	12
Mangum	2	0	2	0	0	12
Carter	1	0	1	0	0	6
Delhomme	1	1	0	0	0	6
Gamble	1	0	0	1	0	6
Gardner	1	0	1	0	0	6
Manning Jr.	1	0	0	1	0	6
Robertson	1	1	0	0	0	6
Witherspoon	1	0	0	1	0	6
Panthers	45	17	25	3	0	270
Opponents	27	9	15	3	3	168

2-Pt. conversions: Panthers 0-1; Opponents 3-5.

(KICKERS)

	XPM/XPA	FGM/FGA	Pts.
Kasay	43/44	26/34	121
Panthers	43/44	26/34	121
Opponents	22/22	23/27	91

RUSHING

	Att.	Yds.	Avg.	Lg.	TD
Foster	205	879	4.3	t70	2
S. Davis	180	549	3.1	39	12
Goings	37	133	3.6	17	0
Robertson	14	41	2.9	11	1
Delhomme	24	31	1.3	12	1
S. Smith	4	25	6.3	t20	1
Hoover	10	22	2.2	4	0
Colbert	1	6	6.0	6	0
Smart	3	6	2.0	6	0
Weinke	8	-5	-0.6	1	0
Proehl	1	-8	-8.0	-8	0
Panthers	487	1679	3.4	t70	17
Opponents	408	1465	3.6	58	9

RECEIVING

	No.	Yds.	Avg.	Lg.	TD
S. Smith	103	1563	15.2	t80	12
Foster	34	372	10.9	47	1
Colbert	25	282	11.3	42	2
Proehl	25	441	17.6	69	4
Mangum	23	202	8.8	24	2
Goings	14	151	10.8	30	0
Hoover	14	87	6.2	12	0
Gaines	12	155	12.9	38	2
Gardner	9	84	9.3	15	1
Carter	5	103	20.6	40	1
S. Davis	5	45	9.0	21	0
Panthers	269	3485	13.0	t80	25
Opponents	305	3351	11.0	86	15

INTERCEPTIONS

	No.	Yds.	Avg.	Lg.	TD
Gamble	7	157	22.4	t61	1
Lucas	6	70	11.7	32	0
McCree	3	73	24.3	46	0
Wallace	2	38	19.0	38	0
Witherspoon..	2	35	17.5	t35	1
Manning Jr.....	2	20	10.0	10	0
Minter	1	47	47.0	47	0
Panthers	23	440	19.1	t61	2
Opponents	25	335	20.9	t64	3

SACKS: Peppers 10.5, Rucker 7.5, Moorehead 5.0, Wallace 5.0, Carstens 4.0, Morgan 3.0, Witherspoon 2.5, Draft 2.0, T. Davis 1.5, Minter 1.5, Buckner 1.0, Short 0.5. Panthers 45.0; Opponents 28.0.

PUNTING

	No.	Yds.	Avg.	In. 20	Lg.
Baker	72	3118	43.3	23	59
Kasay	1	36	36.0	0	36
Panthers	73	3154	43.2	23	59
Opponents	79	3562	45.1	18	69

PUNT RETURNS

	No.	FC	Yds.	Avg.	Lg.	TD
S. Smith	27	6	286	10.6	44	0
Gamble	14	5	158	11.3	76	0
Panthers	41	11	444	10.8	76	0
Opponents	36	20	235	6.5	31	0

KICK RETURNS

	No.	Yds.	Avg.	Lg.	TD
Smart	29	615	21.2	60	0
Robertson	16	343	21.4	42	0
S. Smith	3	61	20.3	33	0
Gaines	2	24	12.0	13	0
Goings	1	21	21.0	21	0
Hoover	1	10	10.0	10	0
Mangum	1	9	9.0	9	0
Panthers	53	1083	20.4	60	0
Opponents	80	1702	21.3	47	0

FIELD GOALS

	1-19	20-29	30-39	40-49	50+
Kasay	1/1	8/8	8/8	6/9	3/8
Panthers	1/1	8/8	8/8	6/9	3/8
Opponents	0/0	6/6	9/11	7/9	1/1

Kasay: (39G, 46G) (51G, 52G) (52G) (32G, 38G) (46G, 53N, 62N) (52B) (56N, 44G) (30G, 20G) (23G, 42G, 28G) (46N, 38G) (25G, 45N, 25G) (20G) (42N, 39G) (32G, 50N, 29G) (24G, 47G) (19G, 41G, 34G)

Opponents: (29G, 48G, 47G) (45G) (27G, 32G) () (39G, 49G) (47B, 52G, 25G) (53N) () (22G) (33G, 39G) (31G, 45G, 33G) (36G, 43G, 49N) (34G, 36G) (44G) (24G, 32B) (29G)

PASSING

	Att.	Cmp.	Yds.	Pct.	Avg. Gain	TD	Pct. TD	Int.	Pct. Int.	Long	Sack/Lost	Rating
Delhomme	435	262	3421	60.2	7.86	24	5.5	16	3.7	t80	28/214	88.1
Weinke	13	7	64	53.8	4.92	1	7.7	0	0.0	18	0/0	93.1
Foster	1	0	0	0.0	0.00	0	0.0	0	0.0	...	0/0	39.6
Panthers	449	269	3485	59.9	7.76	25	5.6	16	3.6	t80	28/214	88.1
Opponents	528	305	3351	57.8	6.35	15	2.8	23	4.4	86	45/294	68.0

CAROLINA PANTHERS

CHICAGO BEARS
NFC NORTH DIVISION

2006 SEASON

CLUB DIRECTORY

Chairman of the board
Michael B. McCaskey
President/CEO
Ted Phillips
General manager
Jerry Angelo
Vice president
Timothy E. McCaskey
Senior director of special projects
Patrick McCaskey
**Senior director of business
development & alumni relations**
Brian McCaskey
Senior director of ticket operations
George McCaskey
Senior director of administration
John Bostrom
**Senior director of corporate
communications**
Scott Hagel
**Senior director of corporate sales &
marketing**
Dave Greeley
Senior director of finance & treasurer
Karen Murphy
Director of pro personnel
Bobby DePaul
Director of college scouting
Greg Gabriel

Head coach
Lovie Smith

Assistant coaches
Bob Babich (asst. head coach/
linebackers)
Mike Bajakian (offensive quality
control)
Rob Boras (tight ends)
Gill Byrd (defensive quality control)
Darryl Drake (wide receivers)
Harold Goodwin (asst. offensive
line)
Harry Heistand (offensive line)
Don Johnson (defensive line)
Lloyd Lee (defensive asst.)
Kevin O'Dea (asst. special teams)
Ron Rivera (defensive coordinator)
Tim Spencer (running backs)
Dave Toub (special teams
coordinator)
Ron Turner (offensive coordinator)
Steven Wilks (defensive backs)
Wade Wilson (quarterbacks)

OFFSEASON MOVES

Key additions
QB Brian Griese	FA/Bucs
CB Ricky Manning	FA/Panthers
DB Dante Wesley	FA/Panthers

Key losses
CB Jerry Azumah	retired
WR Eddie Berlin	released
QB Jeff Blake	FA
S Mike Green	trade/Seahawks

SCHEDULE

Sept.	10—at Green Bay	4:15
Sept.	17—DETROIT	1:00
Sept.	24—at Minnesota	1:00
Oct.	1—SEATTLE	8:15
Oct.	8—BUFFALO	1:00
Oct.	16—at Arizona (Mon.)	8:30
Oct.	22—Open date	
Oct.	29—SAN FRANCISCO	1:00
Nov.	5—MIAMI	1:00
Nov.	12—at N.Y. Giants	1:00
Nov.	19—at N.Y. Jets	1:00
Nov.	26—at New England	1:00
Dec.	3—MINNESOTA	1:00
Dec.	11—at St. Louis (Mon.)	8:30
Dec.	17—TAMPA BAY	1:00
Dec.	24—at Detroit	1:00
Dec.	31—GREEN BAY	1:00

All times are Eastern.
All games Sunday unless noted.

DRAFT CHOICES

Danieal Manning, SS, Abilene Christian
(second round/42nd pick overall).
Devin Hester, WR, Miami (2/57).
Dusty Dvoracek, DT, Oklahoma (3/73).
Jamar Williams, ILB, Arizona State
(4/120).
Mark Anderson, DE, Alabama (5/159).
J.D. Runnels, FB, Oklahoma (6/195).
Tyler Reed, G, Penn State (6/200).

MISCELLANEOUS TEAM DATA

Stadium (capacity, surface):
Soldier Field (61,500, grass)
Business address:
Halas Hall at Conway Park
1000 Football Drive
Lake Forest, IL 60045
Business phone:
847-295-6600
Ticket information:
847-295-6600
Team colors:
Navy blue, orange and white
Flagship radio station:
WBBM, 780 AM
Website:
www.chicagobears.com
Training site:
Olivet Nazarene University
Bourbonnais, Ill.
847-295-6600

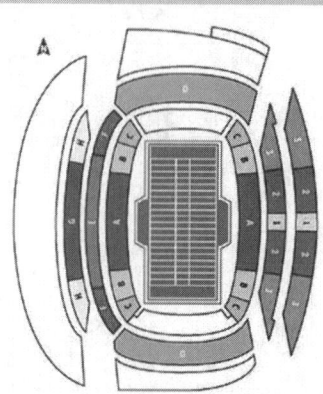

CHICAGO BEARS

No.	QUARTERBACKS	Ht./Wt.	Born	NFL Exp.	College	How acq.	'05 Games GP/GS
14	Brian Griese	6-3/214	3/18/75	9	Michigan	W-TB/06	6/6
8	Rex Grossman	6-1/218	8/23/80	4	Florida	D1b/03	2/1
18	Kyle Orton	6-4/233	11/14/82	2	Purdue	D4/05	15/15
2	B.J. Symons	6-2/215	11/19/80	1	Texas Tech	FA/06	0/0
	RUNNING BACKS						
32	Cedric Benson	5-11/222	12/28/82	2	Texas	D1/05	9/1
25	Tony Hollings	5-10/218	12/1/81	4	Georgia Tech	FA/06	2/0
47	Bryan Johnson (FB)	6-1/242	1/18/78	7	Boise State	T-Was/04	7/6
20	Thomas Jones	5-10/220	8/19/78	7	Virginia	FA/04	15/15
37	Jason McKie (FB)	5-11/240	5/22/80	4	Temple	FA/02	8/2
29	Adrian Peterson	5-10/210	7/1/79	4	Georgia Southern	D6a/02	16/0
48	J.D. Runnels (FB)	6-0/238	6/19/84	R	Oklahoma	D6a/06	—
	RECEIVERS						
80	Bernard Berrian	6-1/185	12/27/80	3	Fresno State	D3/04	11/2
16	Mark Bradley	6-1/201	1/29/82	2	Oklahoma	D2/05	7/4
88	Desmond Clark (TE)	6-3/255	4/20/77	8	Wake Forest	FA/03	16/16
17	Airese Currie	5-11/186	11/16/82	1	Clemson	D5/05	0/0
12	Justin Gage	6-4/210	1/25/81	4	Missouri	D5b/03	15/11
85	John Gilmore (TE)	6-4/262	9/21/79	5	Penn State	FA/02	16/0
87	Muhsin Muhammad	6-2/217	5/5/73	11	Michigan State	FA/05	15/15
82	Gabe Reid (TE)	6-4/260	5/28/77	2	Brigham Young	FA/03	16/3
	OFFENSIVE LINEMEN						
74	Ruben Brown (G)	6-3/300	2/13/72	12	Pittsburgh	FA/04	12/12
79	Steve Edwards (T)	6-5/330	2/20/79	4	UCF	FA/02	7/0
62	Lennie Friedman (G)	6-3/283	10/13/76	7	Duke	FA/05	11/0
63	Roberto Garza (C/G)	6-2/296	3/26/79	6	Texas A&M-Kingsville	FA/05	16/7
57	Olin Kreutz (C)	6-2/292	6/9/77	9	Washington	D3/98	16/16
65	Patrick Mannelly (LS)	6-5/265	4/18/75	9	Duke	D6b/98	16/0
60	Terrence Metcalf (G)	6-3/318	1/28/78	5	Mississippi	D3b/02	13/13
69	Fred Miller (T)	6-7/320	2/6/73	11	Baylor	FA/05	15/15
72	Qasim Mitchell (G)	6-6/355	12/3/79	4	North Carolina A&T	FA/03	3/0
64	Tyler Reed (G)	6-3/303	10/6/82	R	Penn State	D6b/06	—
78	John St. Clair (T)	6-4/320	7/31/77	5	Virginia	FA/05	13/2
76	John Tait (T)	6-6/315	1/26/75	8	Brigham Young	FA/04	15/15
	DEFENSIVE LINEMEN						
75	Mark Anderson (E)	6-4/254	5/26/83	R	Alabama	D5/06	—
70	Alfonso Boone (T)	6-4/318	1/11/76	6	Central State	FA/00	16/1
96	Alex Brown (E)	6-3/262	6/4/79	5	Florida	D4/02	16/16
98	Dusty Dvoracek (T)	6-2/301	3/3/81	R	Oklahoma	D3/06	—
67	Jamaal Green (E)	6-2/272	6/5/80	2	Miami (Fla.)	W-Phi/05	0/0
91	Tommie Harris (T)	6-3/300	4/29/83	3	Oklahoma	D1/04	16/16
97	Michael Haynes (E)	6-3/274	9/13/80	4	Penn State	D1a/03	10/0
71	Israel Idonije (E)	6-7/290	11/17/80	3	Manitoba	FA/03	11/1
99	Tank Johnson (T)	6-3/300	12/7/81	3	Washington	D2/04	16/4
93	Adewale Ogunleye (E)	6-4/260	8/9/77	6	Indiana	T-Mia/04	15/15
95	Ian Scott (T)	6-2/305	11/8/81	4	Florida	D4b/03	14/13
	LINEBACKERS						
94	Brendon Ayanbadejo	6-1/230	9/6/76	4	UCLA	T-Mia/05	16/0
55	Lance Briggs	6-1/238	11/12/80	4	Arizona	D3/03	16/16
58	Jeremy Cain	6-1/235	12/8/81	3	Massachusetts	FA/04	3/0
92	Hunter Hillenmeyer	6-4/238	10/28/80	4	Vanderbilt	FA/03	13/12
53	Leon Joe	6-1/235	10/26/81	3	Maryland	W-Ari/05	14/1
59	Joe Odom	6-1/235	12/14/79	4	Purdue	D6a/03	2/0
54	Brian Urlacher	6-4/258	5/25/78	7	New Mexico	D1/00	16/16
52	Jamar Williams	6-0/236	6/14/84	R	Arizona State	D4/06	—
	DEFENSIVE BACKS						
30	Mike Brown (S)	5-10/212	2/13/78	6	Nebraska	D2/00	12/12
81	Rashied Davis (CB)	5-10/180	7/24/79	2	San Jose State	FA/05	12/0
46	Chris Harris (S)	6-1/206	8/6/82	2	Louisiana-Monroe	D6/05	14/13
23	Devin Hester	5-10/186	11/4/82	R	Miami	D2b/06	—
26	Daven Holly (CB)	5-10/192	8/8/82	2	Cincinnati	W-SF/05	3/0
35	Todd Johnson (S)	6-1/200	12/18/78	3	Florida	D4a/03	14/2
38	Danieal Manning (S)	5-11/202	8/9/82	R	Abilene Christian	D2a/06	—
24	Ricky Manning (CB)	5-8/185	11/18/80	4	UCLA	FA/06	16/3
36	Brandon McGowan (DB)	5-11/200	9/16/83	2	Maine	FA/05	8/3
27	Chris Thompson (CB)	6-0/191	5/19/82	2	Nicholls State	W-Jac/05	12/1
33	Charles Tillman (CB)	6-1/196	2/23/81	4	La-Lafayette	D2/03	15/15
31	Nathan Vasher (CB)	5-10/180	11/17/81	3	Texas	D4a/04	16/15
21	Dante Wesley (CB)	6-0/211	4/5/79	5	Arkansas-Pine Bluff	FA/06	16/0
24	Cameron Worrell (S)	5-11/199	12/14/79	4	Fresno State	FA/03	0/0
	SPECIALISTS						
9	Robbie Gould (K)	6-1/181	12/6/82	2	Penn State	FA/05	13/0
4	Brad Maynard (P)	6-1/186	2/9/74	10	Ball State	FA/01	16/0

Abbreviations: D1-draft pick, first round; W-claimed on waivers; T-obtained in trade; FA-free-agent acquisition.

CHICAGO BEARS

2005 regular-season record: 11-5
Position: 1st in NFC North

Sept.11—at Washington	L	7-9
Sept.18—DETROIT	W	38-6
Sept.25—CINCINNATI	L	7-24
Oct. 2—Open date		
Oct. 9—at Cleveland	L	10-20
Oct. 16—MINNESOTA	W	28-3
Oct. 23—BALTIMORE	W	10-6
Oct. 30—at Detroit (OT)	W	19-13
Nov. 6—at New Orleans	W	20-17
Nov.13—SAN FRANCISCO	W	17-9
Nov.20—CAROLINA	W	13-3
Nov.27—at Tampa Bay	W	13-10
Dec. 4—GREEN BAY	W	19-7
Dec.11—at Pittsburgh	L	9-21
Dec.18—ATLANTA	W	16-3
Dec.25—at Green Bay	W	24-17
Jan. 1—at Minnesota	L	10-34

2005 postseason record: 0-1
Jan. 15—CAROLINA*	L	21-29

*NFC divisional playoff game.

SCORING BY PERIODS

	Q1	Q2	Q3	Q4	OT	Pts.
Bears	54	82	54	64	6	260
Opponents	35	69	34	64	0	202

TEAM STATISTICS

	Chi.	Opp.
TOTAL FIRST DOWNS ..	233	259
Rushing	99	83
Passing	111	153
Penalty	23	23
3rd Down: Made/Att. ..	62/215	76/238
3rd Down Pct.	28.8	31.9
4th Down: Made/Att. ..	7/16	6/20
4th Down Pct.	43.8	30.0
POSSESSION AVG.	28:41	31:19
TOTAL NET YARDS	4101	4509
Avg. per Game	256.3	281.8
Total Plays	937	1034
Avg. per Play	4.4	4.4
NET YARDS RUSHING ..	2099	1637
Avg. per Game	131.2	102.3
Total Rushes	488	443
NET YARDS PASSING....	2002	2872
Avg. per Game	125.1	179.5
Sacked/Yards Lost	31/199	41/275
Gross Yards	2201	3147
Att./Completions	418/219	550/313
Completion Pct.	52.4	56.9
Had Intercepted	15	24
PUNTS/AVERAGE	98/40.5	97/41.1
NET PUNTING AVG.	98/35.0	97/35.1
PENALTIES/YARDS	105/850	118/1016
FUMBLES/LOST	32/13	26/10
TOUCHDOWNS	28	20
Rushing	11	9
Passing	11	10
Returns	6	1

SCORING (NONKICKERS)

	Tot. TD	RTD	PTD	MTD	2Pt.	Tot. Pts.
Jones	9	9	0	0	0	54
Muhammad	4	0	4	0	0	24
Clark	2	0	2	0	0	12
Edwards	2	0	2	0	0	12
Gage	2	0	2	0	0	12
Peterson	2	2	0	0	0	12
Vasher	2	0	0	2	0	12
Briggs	1	0	0	1	0	6
M. Brown	1	0	0	1	0	6
Gilmore	1	0	1	0	0	6
Tillman	1	0	0	1	0	6
Wade	1	0	0	1	0	6
Bears	28	11	11	6	0	168
Opponents	20	9	10	1	0	120

(KICKERS)

	XPM/XPA	FGM/FGA	Pts.
Gould	19/20	21/27	82
Brien	7/7	1/4	10
Bears	26/27	22/31	92
Opponents	19/20	21/29	82

RUSHING

	Att.	Yds.	Avg.	Lg.	TD
Jones	314	1335	4.3	42	9
Peterson	76	391	5.1	36	2
Benson	67	272	4.1	36	0
Orton	24	44	1.8	15	0
Berrian	2	31	15.5	37	0
McKie	3	22	7.3	13	0
Johnson	1	5	5.0	5	0
Blake	1	-1	-1.0	-1	0
Bears	488	2099	4.3	42	11
Opponents	443	1637	3.7	t61	9

RECEIVING

	No.	Yds.	Avg.	Lg.	TD
Muhammad	64	750	11.7	33	4
Gage	31	346	11.2	25	2
Jones	26	143	5.5	41	0
Clark	24	229	9.5	31	2
Bradley	18	230	12.8	54	0
Berrian	13	246	18.9	54	0
Edwards	10	66	6.6	13	2
Wade	10	80	8.0	17	0
Peterson	7	48	6.9	18	0
Johnson	5	15	3.0	7	0
McKie	4	15	3.8	11	0
Reid	3	20	6.7	10	0
Berlin	2	9	4.5	9	0
Benson	1	3	3.0	3	0
Gilmore	1	1	1.0	t1	1
Bears	219	2201	10.1	54	11
Opponents	313	3147	10.1	56	10

INTERCEPTIONS

	No.	Yds.	Avg.	Lg.	TD
Vasher	8	145	18.1	46	1
Tillman	5	172	34.4	95	1

	No.	Yds.	Avg.	Lg.	TD
M. Brown	3	116	38.7	72	1
C. Harris	3	44	14.7	44	0
Briggs	2	30	15.0	20	1
M. Green	1	14	14.0	14	0
Scott	1	3	3.0	3	0
Hillenmeyer	1	0	0.0	0	0
Bears	24	524	21.8	95	4
Opponents	15	66	4.4	25	0

SACKS: Ogunleye 10.0, A. Brown 6.0, Urlacher 6.0, T. Johnson 5.0, T. Harris 3.0, Briggs 2.0, Boone 1.5, Haynes 1.5, Azumah 1.0, M. Brown 1.0, C. Harris 1.0, Hillenmeyer 1.0, Idonije 1.0, Tillman 1.0. Bears 41.0; Opponents 31.0.

PUNTING

	No.	Yds.	Avg.	In. 20	Lg.
Gould	1	28	28.0	0	28
Maynard	96	3937	41.0	24	63
Bears	98	3965	40.5	24	63
Opponents	97	3982	41.1	27	59

PUNT RETURNS

	No.	FC	Yds.	Avg.	Lg.	TD
Wade	33	9	317	9.6	t73	1
Berrian	8	3	69	8.6	24	0
Davis	5	1	31	6.2	21	0
Bears	46	13	417	9.1	t73	1
Opponents	39	13	312	8.0	t85	1

KICK RETURNS

	No.	Yds.	Avg.	Lg.	TD
Azumah	32	705	22.0	40	0
Davis	11	251	22.8	34	0
Bradley	4	70	17.5	23	0
McKie	3	29	9.7	17	0
Peterson	2	32	16.0	19	0
Gilmore	1	5	5.0	5	0
Idonije	1	0	0.0	0	0
Vasher	1	0	0.0	0	0
Bears	55	1092	19.9	40	0
Opponents	63	1255	19.9	45	0

FIELD GOALS

	1-19	20-29	30-39	40-49	50+
Gould	0/0	9/9	9/10	3/8	0/0
Brien	0/0	0/0	0/2	1/2	0/0
Bears	0/0	9/9	9/12	4/10	0/0
Opponents	2/2	7/8	7/10	4/6	1/3

Gould: () () () (44G, 48N) () (23G, 47N) (38G, 20G) (35G, 47N, 28G) (39N, 37G) (33G, 39G) (25G, 36G) (21G, 40G, 25G, 35G, 43N) (29G) (35G, 29G, 39G, 44N) (45G) (22G)

Brien: () (48G, 48N, 36N) (39N) () () () () () () () ()

Opponents: (40G, 43G, 19G) () (33G) (19G, 44G) (52N, 23G, 32B) (40G, 29G) (46N, 32G, 30G) (22G) (30G, 52N, 34G, 29G) (46N, 38G) (27G, 29N) () () (30G) (38N, 39N, 26G) (54G, 27G)

PASSING

	Att.	Cmp.	Yds.	Pct.	Avg. Gain	TD	Pct. TD	Int.	Pct. Int.	Long	Sack/Lost	Rating
Orton	368	190	1869	51.6	5.08	9	2.4	13	3.5	54	30/190	59.7
Grossman	39	20	259	51.3	6.64	1	2.6	2	5.1	54	1/9	59.7
Blake	9	8	55	88.9	6.11	1	11.1	0	0.0	17	0/0	129.2
Maynard	2	1	18	50.0	9.00	0	0.0	0	0.0	18	0/0	81.3
Bears	418	219	2201	52.4	5.27	11	2.6	15	3.6	54	31/199	61.5
Opponents	550	313	3147	56.9	5.72	10	1.8	24	4.4	56	41/275	61.2

CINCINNATI BENGALS
AFC NORTH DIVISION

2006 SEASON

CLUB DIRECTORY

President
Mike Brown
Sr. vice president—player personnel
Pete Brown
Executive vice president
Katie Blackburn
Vice president—player personnel
Paul Brown
Director of business development
Troy Blackburn
Director of football operations
Jim Lippincott
Director of player personnel
Duke Tobin
Public relations director
Jack Brennan
Director of player relations
Eric Ball

Head coach
Marvin Lewis

Assistant coaches
Paul Alexander (asst. head
  coach/offensive line)
Jim Anderson (running backs)
Bob Bratkowski (offensive
  coordinator)
Chuck Bresnahan (defensive
  coordinator)
Louie Cioffi (asst. defensive backs)
Kevin Coyle (defensive backs)
Paul Guenther (staff asst.)
Jay Hayes (defensive line)
Jonathan Hayes (tight ends)
Ricky Hunley (linebackers)
Chip Morton (strength and
  conditioning)
Ray Oliver (asst. strength and
  conditioning)
Darrin Simmons (special teams)
Bob Surace (asst. offensive line)
Hue Jackson (wide receivers)
Ken Zampese (quarterbacks)

OFFSEASON MOVES

Key additions
DT Sam Adams	FA/Bills
WR Antonio Chatman	FA/Packers
S Dexter Jackson	FA/Bucs
QB Anthony Wright	FA/Ravens

Key losses
DE Duane Clemons	released
QB Jon Kitna	FA/Lions
SS Ifeanyi Ohalete	FA
DE Carl Powell	FA
TE Matt Schobel	FA/Eagles
WR Kevin Walter	FA/Texans
LB Nate Webster	FA/Broncos

SCHEDULE

Sept.	10—at Kansas City	1:00
Sept.	17—CLEVELAND	1:00
Sept.	24—at Pittsburgh	1:00
Oct.	1—NEW ENGLAND	4:15
Oct.	8—Open date	
Oct.	15—at Tampa Bay	1:00
Oct.	22—CAROLINA	1:00
Oct.	29—ATLANTA	1:00
Nov.	5—at Baltimore	1:00
Nov.	12—SAN DIEGO	1:00
Nov.	19—at New Orleans	1:00
Nov.	26—at Cleveland	1:00
Nov.	30—BALTIMORE (Thurs.)	8:00
Dec.	10—OAKLAND	1:00
Dec.	18—at Indianapolis (Mon.)	8:30
Dec.	24—at Denver	4:15
Dec.	31—PITTSBURGH	1:00

All times are Eastern.
All games Sunday unless noted.

DRAFT CHOICES

Johnathan Joseph, CB, South Carolina
(first round/24th pick overall).
Andrew Whitworth, OT, LSU (2/55).
Frostee Rucker, DE, Southern California
(3/91).
Domata Peko, DT, Michigan State
(4/123).
A.J. Nicholson, ILB, Florida State (5/157).
Reggie McNeal, QB, Texas A&M (6/193).
Ethan Kilmer, WR, Penn State (7/209).
Bennie Brazell, WR, LSU (7/231).

MISCELLANEOUS TEAM DATA

Stadium (capacity, surface):
Paul Brown Stadium
(65,378, synthetic)
Business address:
One Paul Brown Stadium
Cincinnati, OH 45202-3492
Business phone:
513-621-3550
Ticket information:
513-621-TDTD (8383)
Team colors:
Black, orange and white
Flagship radio stations:
WCKY, 1360 AM (Homer); WOFX, 92.5
  FM (The Fox); WLW, 700 AM (The Big
  One)
Website:
www.bengals.com
Training site:
Georgetown College
Georgetown, Ky.
502-868-6300

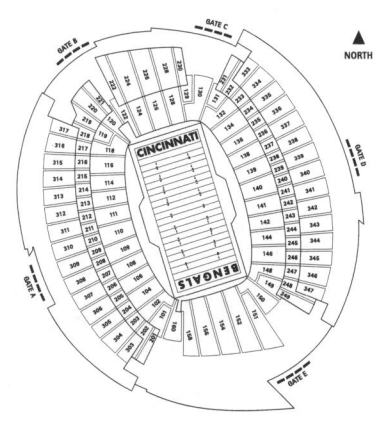

CINCINNATI BENGALS

No.	QUARTERBACKS	Ht./Wt.	Born	NFL Exp.	College	How acq.	'05 Games GP/GS
11	Doug Johnson	6-2/225	10/27/77	7	Florida	FA/06	0/0
6	Craig Krenzel	6-4/228	7/1/81	3	Ohio State	FA/05	0/0
9	Carson Palmer	6-5/230	12/27/79	4	USC	D1/03	16/16
2	Anthony Wright	6-1/211	2/14/76	8	South Carolina	FA/06	9/7
	RUNNING BACKS						
31	Jeremi Johnson (FB)	5-11/265	9/4/80	4	Western Kentucky	D4b/03	16/11
32	Rudi Johnson	5-10/220	10/1/79	5	Auburn	D4/01	16/14
23	Chris Perry	6-0/224	12/27/81	3	Michigan	D1/04	14/2
33	Kenny Watson (FB)	5-11/218	3/13/78	5	Penn State	FA/03	1/0
35	Quincy Wilson	5-9/210	4/26/81	2	West Virginia	FA/04	0/0
	RECEIVERS						
81	Bennie Brazell	6-1/176	6/2/82	R	LSU	D7b/06	—
13	Jamall Broussard	5-9/172	8/19/81	3	San Jose State	W-Car/05	0/0
83	Antonio Chatman	5-9/184	2/12/79	4	Cincinnati	FA/06	16/3
15	Chris Henry	6-4/197	5/17/83	2	West Virginia	D3/05	14/5
84	T.J. Houshmandzadeh	6-1/197	9/26/77	6	Oregon State	D7/01	14/12
85	Chad Johnson	6-1/192	1/9/78	6	Oregon State	D2/01	16/16
82	Reggie Kelly (TE)	6-4/255	2/22/77	8	Mississippi State	FA/03	15/14
43	Ethan Kilmer	6-0/205	1/31/83	R	Penn State	D7b/06	—
10	Reggie McNeal	6-2/197	9/20/83	R	Texas A&M	D6/06	—
88	Tab Perry	6-3/229	1/20/82	2	UCLA	D6/05	16/0
14	P.K. Sam	6-3/210	2/26/83	2	Florida State	FA/06	0/0
47	Darnell Sanders (TE)	6-6/270	3/16/79	5	Ohio State	FA/06	0/0
48	Brad St. Louis (TE)	6-3/247	8/19/76	7	Missouri State	D7/00	16/0
86	Tony Stewart (TE)	6-5/260	8/9/79	6	Penn State	FA/02	14/3
87	Kelley Washington	6-3/218	8/21/79	4	Tennessee	D3/03	7/0
	OFFENSIVE LINEMEN						
71	Willie Anderson (T)	6-5/340	7/11/75	11	Auburn	D1/96	16/16
79	Stacy Andrews (T)	6-5/346	6/2/81	2	Mississippi	D4/04	14/0
74	Rich Braham (C)	6-4/305	11/6/70	12	West Virginia	FA/00	15/15
53	Eric Ghiaciuc (C)	6-4/300	5/28/81	2	Central Michigan	D4/05	5/1
76	Levi Jones (T)	6-5/310	8/24/79	5	Arizona State	D1/02	15/15
75	Scott Kooistra (G)	6-6/320	10/14/80	4	N.C. State	D7/03	15/1
50	Larry Moore (C)	6-3/300	6/1/75	9	BYU	FA/02	4/0
65	Eric Steinbach (G)	6-6/297	4/4/80	4	Iowa	D2/03	16/16
77	Andrew Whitworth (T)	6-7/334	12/12/81	R	LSU	D2/06	—
64	Ben Wilkerson (G)	6-4/300	11/22/82	2	LSU	FA/05	0/0
63	Bobbie Williams (G)	6-4/330	9/25/76	5	Arkansas	FA/04	16/16
	DEFENSIVE LINEMEN						
95	Sam Adams (T)	6-4/335	6/13/73	13	Texas A&M	FA/06	14/9
96	Matthias Askew (T)	6-5/308	7/1/82	3	Michigan State	D4a/04	1/0
68	Jonathan Fanene (E)	6-3/290	3/19/82	2	Utah	D7/05	3/1
91	Robert Geathers (E)	6-2/271	8/11/83	3	Georgia	Db4/04	16/16
94	Domata Peko (T)	6-1/322	11/27/84	R	Michigan State	D4/06	—
98	Bryan Robinson (T)	6-4/296	6/22/74	10	Fresno State	FA/05	10/9
92	Frostee Rucker (E)	6-3/263	9/14/83	R	USC	D3/06	—
90	Justin Smith (E)	6-4/270	9/30/79	6	Missouri	D1/01	16/16
66	Shaun Smith (T)	6-2/320	8/19/81	3	South Carolina	FA/03	13/5
97	John Thornton (T)	6-3/297	10/2/76	8	West Virginia	FA/03	16/16
	LINEBACKERS						
59	Landon Johnson	6-1/227	3/13/81	3	Purdue	D3/04	16/10
58	Caleb Miller	6-3/225	9/3/80	3	Arkansas	D3/04	7/0
57	Hannibal Navies	6-3/249	7/19/77	8	Colorado	FA/06	15/1
52	A.J. Nicholson	6-0/235	6/25/83	R	Florida State	D5/06	—
99	David Pollack	6-2/265	6/19/82	2	Georgia	D1/05	14/5
56	Brian Simmons	6-3/244	6/21/75	8	North Carolina	D1b/98	16/16
51	Odell Thurman	6-0/233	7/9/83	2	Georgia	D2/05	16/15
55	Marcus Wilkins	6-2/235	1/2/80	5	Texas	FA/02	15/0
	DEFENSIVE BACKS						
21	Rashad Bauman (CB)	5-8/184	5/7/79	5	Oregon	D3a/02	11/1
41	Patrick Body (CB)	6-2/201	1/17/82	2	Toledo	FA/05	6/0
27	Greg Brooks (CB)	5-11/175	12/16/80	2	Southern Miss	D6/04	11/0
26	Tony Bua (S)	5-11/212	2/11/80	2	Arkansas	FA/05	0/0
28	Dexter Jackson (S)	6-0/205	7/28/77	8	Florida State	FA/06	11/10
20	Tory James (CB)	6-2/186	5/18/73	10	LSU	FA/03	16/16
22	Johnathan Joseph (CB)	5-11/193	4/16/84	R	South Carolina	D1/06	—
34	Kevin Kaesviharn (S)	6-1/194	8/29/76	6	Augustana (S.D.)	FA/01	16/16
42	Anthony Mitchell (S)	6-1/198	12/13/74	7	Tuskegee	FA/99	16/0
24	Deltha O'Neal (CB)	5-11/191	1/30/77	7	California	T-Den/04	15/14
25	Keiwan Ratliff (CB)	5-11/190	4/9/81	3	Florida	D2/04	16/3
40	Madieu Williams (S)	6-1/193	10/18/81	3	Maryland	D2/04	4/3
	SPECIALISTS						
17	Shayne Graham (K)	6-0/197	12/9/77	6	Virginia Tech	W-Car/03	16/0
19	Kyle Larson (P)	6-1/204	9/2/80	3	Nebraska	FA/04	16/0

Abbreviations: D1-draft pick, first round; W-claimed on waivers; T-obtained in trade; FA-free-agent acquisition.

2005 regular-season record: 11-5
Position: 1st in AFC North

Sept.11—at Cleveland	W	27-13
Sept.18—MINNESOTA	W	37-8
Sept.25—at Chicago	W	24-7
Oct. 2—HOUSTON	W	16-10
Oct. 9—at Jacksonville	L	20-23
Oct. 16—at Tennessee	W	31-23
Oct. 23—PITTSBURGH	L	13-27
Oct. 30—GREEN BAY	W	21-14
Nov. 6—at Baltimore	W	21-9
Nov.13—Open date		
Nov.20—INDIANAPOLIS	L	37-45
Nov.27—BALTIMORE	W	42-29
Dec. 4—at Pittsburgh	W	38-31
Dec.11—CLEVELAND	W	23-20
Dec.18—at Detroit	W	41-17
Dec.24—BUFFALO	L	27-37
Jan. 1—at Kansas City	L	3-37

2005 postseason record: 0-1

Jan. 8—PITTSBURGH#	L	17-31

#AFC wild-card game.

SCORING BY PERIODS

	Q1	Q2	Q3	Q4	OT	Pts.
Bengals	84	147	98	92	0	421
Opponents	60	102	89	99	0	350

TEAM STATISTICS

	Cin.	Opp.
TOTAL FIRST DOWNS ..	342	321
Rushing	109	109
Passing	203	185
Penalty	30	27
3rd Down: Made/Att. ..	84/196	81/190
3rd Down Pct.	42.9	42.6
4th Down: Made/Att. ..	3/10	6/14
4th Down Pct.	30.0	42.9
POSSESSION AVG.	30:51	29:08
TOTAL NET YARDS	5730	5419
Avg. per Game	358.1	338.7
Total Plays	1018	976
Avg. per Play	5.6	5.6
NET YARDS RUSHING ..	1910	1850
Avg. per Game	119.4	115.6
Total Rushes	459	429
NET YARDS PASSING ..	3820	3569
Avg. per Game	238.8	223.1
Sacked/Yards Lost	21/115	28/180
Gross Yards	3935	3749
Att./Completions	538/362	519/324
Completion Pct.	67.3	62.4
Had Intercepted	14	31
PUNTS/AVERAGE	61/42.5	50/42.1
NET PUNTING AVG.	61/35.6	50/37.4
PENALTIES/YARDS	110/920	110/985
FUMBLES/LOST	18/6	31/13
TOUCHDOWNS	48	39

	Cin.	Opp.
Rushing	15	16
Passing	32	21
Returns	1	2

SCORING (NONKICKERS)

	Tot. TD	RTD	PTD	MTD	2Pt.	Tot. Pts.
Ru. Johnson ..	12	12	0	0	0	72
C. Johnson	9	0	9	0	0	54
Houshmandzadeh	8	1	7	0	0	48
Henry	6	0	6	0	0	36
J. Johnson	3	0	3	0	0	18
C. Perry	2	0	2	0	0	12
T. Perry	2	1	1	0	0	12
Schobel	1	0	1	0	1	8
Kelly	1	0	1	0	0	6
Palmer	1	1	0	0	0	6
Thurman	1	0	0	1	0	6
Walter	1	0	1	0	0	6
Washington	1	0	1	0	0	6
Bengals	48	15	32	1	1	290
Opponents	39	16	21	2	2	238

2-Pt. conversions: Bengals 1-1; Opponents 2-2.

(KICKERS)

	XPM/XPA	FGM/FGA	Pts.
Graham	47/47	28/32	131
Bengals	47/47	28/32	131
Opponents	37/37	25/28	112

RUSHING

	Att.	Yds.	Avg.	Lg.	TD
Ru. Johnson ..	337	1458	4.3	33	12
C. Perry	61	279	4.6	30	0
Houshmandzadeh	8	62	7.8	17	1
Palmer	34	41	1.2	14	1
C. Johnson	5	33	6.6	11	0
J. Johnson	8	14	1.8	5	0
Kitna	2	14	7.0	11	0
T. Perry	3	9	3.0	7	1
Luchey	1	0	0.0	0	0
Bengals	459	1910	4.2	33	15
Opponents	429	1850	4.3	t49	16

RECEIVING

	No.	Yds.	Avg.	Lg.	TD
C. Johnson	97	1432	14.8	t70	9
Houshmandzadeh	78	956	12.3	t43	7
C. Perry	51	328	6.4	28	2
Henry	31	422	13.6	47	6
Ru. Johnson ..	23	90	3.9	15	0
Walter	19	211	11.1	33	1
Schobel	18	193	10.7	28	1
Kelly	15	90	6.0	16	1
J. Johnson	12	65	5.4	t27	3
Washington ..	10	101	10.1	t18	1
T. Perry	4	21	5.3	13	1

	No.	Yds.	Avg.	Lg.	TD
Stewart	4	26	6.5	10	0
Bengals	362	3935	10.9	t70	32
Opponents	324	3749	11.6	t68	21

INTERCEPTIONS

	No.	Yds.	Avg.	Lg.	TD
O'Neal	10	103	10.3	37	0
Thurman	5	59	11.8	t30	1
James	5	5	1.0	5	0
Ratliff	3	52	17.3	35	0
Kaesviharn	3	9	3.0	6	0
Simmons	2	15	7.5	16	0
Ohalete	1	15	15.0	15	0
M. Williams ..	1	2	2.0	2	0
Thornton	1	0	0.0	0	0
Bengals	31	260	8.4	37	1
Opponents	14	247	17.6	55	1

SACKS: J. Smith 6.0, Pollack 4.5, Simmons 4.0, Geathers 3.0, Clemons 2.0, Thornton 2.0, Thurman 1.5, Kaesviharn 1.0, Mitchell 1.0, Powell 1.0. Bengals 28.0; Opponents 21.0.

PUNTING

	No.	Yds.	Avg.	In. 20	Lg.
Larson	60	2591	43.2	13	75
Bengals	61	2591	42.5	13	75
Opponents	50	2106	42.1	18	56

PUNT RETURNS

	No.	FC	Yds.	Avg.	Lg.	TD
Ratliff	28	14	157	5.6	13	0
Bengals	28	14	157	5.6	13	0
Opponents	32	7	260	8.1	27	0

KICK RETURNS

	No.	Yds.	Avg.	Lg.	TD
T. Perry	64	1562	24.4	94	0
Schobel	2	4	2.0	4	0
O'Neal	1	14	14.0	14	0
Bengals	67	1580	23.6	94	0
Opponents	85	1787	21.0	t99	1

FIELD GOALS

	1-19	20-29	30-39	40-49	50+
Graham	0/0	11/11	10/11	7/9	0/1
Bengals	0/0	11/11	10/11	7/9	0/1
Opponents	1/1	12/12	7/8	3/4	2/3

Graham: (32G, 23G) (40G, 29G, 30G) (33G) (24G, 42N, 27G, 46G) (31G, 48G) (52N, 21G) (30N, 26G, 39G) () (48N) (43G, 41G, 44G) (26G, 31G) (30G) (21G, 27G, 37G) (28G, 33G) (31G, 27G) (49G)
Opponents: (29G, 34G) () (39N) (28G) (32G, 51G, 53G) (24G, 29G, 47G) (27G, 39G) () (34G, 32G, 31G) (19G) (54N) (23G) (41G, 29G) (45G) (21G, 24G, 48N, 22G) (39G, 24G, 23G)

PASSING

	Att.	Cmp.	Yds.	Pct.	Avg. Gain	TD	Pct. TD	Int.	Pct. Int.	Long	Sack/Lost	Rating
Palmer	509	345	3836	67.8	7.54	32	6.3	12	2.4	t70	19/105	101.1
Kitna	29	17	99	58.6	3.41	0	0.0	2	6.9	16	2/10	36.4
Bengals	538	362	3935	67.3	7.31	32	5.9	14	2.6	t70	21/115	97.6
Opponents	519	324	3749	62.4	7.22	21	4.0	31	6.0	t68	28/180	72.8

CINCINNATI BENGALS

CLEVELAND BROWNS
AFC NORTH DIVISION

2006 SEASON

CLUB DIRECTORY

Owner
Randy Lerner
Senior vice president and general manager
Phil Savage
Executive vice president and chief financial officer
Doug Jacobs
Executive vice president and chief operating officer
Lew Merletti
Vice president of communications
Bill Bonsiewicz
Vice president of new media and publishing
Vic Carucci
Vice president of event and stadium operations
Don Renzulli
Vice president of broadcasting and production
George Veras
Vice president of broadcasting and production
Mike Keenan

Head coach
Romeo Crennel

Assistant coaches
Dave Atkins (running backs)
Maurice Carthon (offensive coordinator)
Ben Coates (tight ends)
Carl Crennel II (offensive quality control)
Jeff Davidson (asst. head coach/ offensive line)
Todd Grantham (defensive coordinator)
Mike Haluchak (linebackers)
John Lott (head strength and conditioning)
Randy Melvin (defensive line)
Terry Robiskie (wide receivers)
Jerry Rosburg (special teams coordinator)
Rip Scherer (quarterbacks)
Bob Trott (defensive asst.)
Mel Tucker (defensive backs)
Jeff Uhlenhake (offensive line asst.)
Cory Undlin (defensive quality control)

OFFSEASON MOVES

Key additions
C	LeCharles Bentley	FA/Saints
QB	Ken Dorsey	trade/49ers
WR	Joe Jurevicius	FA/Seahawks
LB	Willie McGinest	FA/Patriots
OT	Kevin Shaffer	FA/Falcons
NT	Ted Washington	FA/Raiders
P	Dave Zastudil	FA/Ravens

Key losses
WR	Antonio Bryant	FA/49ers
S	Chris Crocker	trade/Falcons
QB	Trent Dilfer	trade/49ers
DE	Kenard Lang	FA/Broncos
OT	L.J. Shelton	FA/Dolphins
LB	Ben Taylor	FA/Packers

SCHEDULE

Sept. 10—NEW ORLEANS		1:00
Sept. 17—at Cincinnati		1:00
Sept. 24—BALTIMORE		4:05
Oct. 1—at Oakland		4:15
Oct. 8—at Carolina		1:00
Oct. 15—Open date		
Oct. 22—DENVER		4:05
Oct. 29—N.Y. JETS		4:15
Nov. 5—at San Diego		4:15
Nov. 12—at Atlanta		1:00
Nov. 19—PITTSBURGH		1:00
Nov. 26—CINCINNATI		1:00
Dec. 3—KANSAS CITY		1:00
Dec. 7—at Pittsburgh (Thurs.)		8:00
Dec. 17—at Baltimore		1:00
Dec. 24—TAMPA BAY		1:00
Dec. 31—at Houston		1:00

All times are Eastern.
All games Sunday unless noted.

DRAFT CHOICES

Kamerion Wimbley, DE, Florida State (first round/13th pick overall).
D'Qwell Jackson, ILB, Maryland (2/34).
Travis Wilson, WR, Oklahoma (3/78).
Leon Williams, ILB, Miami (4/110).
Isaac Sowells, G, Indiana (4/112).
Jerome Harrison, RB, Washington State (5/145).
DeMario Minter, CB, Georgia (5/152).
Lawrence Vickers, FB, Colorado (6/180).
Babatunde Oshinowo, DT, Stanford (6/181).
Justin Hamilton, SS, Virginia Tech (7/222).

MISCELLANEOUS TEAM DATA

Stadium (capacity, surface):
Cleveland Browns Stadium (73,200, grass)
Business address:
76 Lou Groza Boulevard
Berea, OH 44017
Business phone:
440-891-5000
Ticket information:
440-891-5050
Team colors:
Brown, orange and white
Flagship radio station:
WMMS, 100.7 FM
Website:
www.clevelandbrowns.com
Training site:
76 Lou Groza Boulevard
Berea, Ohio
440-891-5000

CLEVELAND BROWNS

No.	QUARTERBACKS	Ht./Wt.	Born	NFL Exp.	College	How acq.	'05 Games GP/GS
3	Derek Anderson	6-6/242	6/15/83	1	Oregon State	W-Bal/05	0/0
5	Ken Dorsey	6-4/218	4/22/81	4	Miami	T-SF/06	3/3
9	Charlie Frye	6-4/225	8/28/81	2	Akron	D3/05	7/5
	RUNNING BACKS						
34	Reuben Droughns	5-11/207	8/21/78	7	Oregon	T-Den/05	16/16
31	William Green	6-0/215	12/17/79	5	Boston College	D1/02	8/0
35	Jerome Harrison	5-9/199	2/26/83	R	Washington State	D5a/06	—
36	Corey McIntyre	6-0/246	1/25/79	2	West Virginia	FA/04	15/1
42	Terrelle Smith (FB)	6-0/255	3/12/78	7	Arizona State	FA/04	16/15
44	Lee Suggs	6-0/210	8/11/80	4	Virginia Tech	D4/03	8/0
47	Lawrence Vickers (FB)	6-0/233	5/8/83	R	Colorado	D6a/06	—
29	Jason Wright	5-10/210	7/12/82	2	Northwestern	FA/05	3/0
	RECEIVERS						
16	Josh Cribbs	6-1/192	6/9/83	2	Kent State	FA/05	14/0
87	Darnell Dinkins (TE)	6-3/255	1/20/77	4	Pitt	FA/06	16/4
17	Braylon Edwards	6-3/210	2/21/83	2	Michigan	D1/05	10/7
82	Steve Heiden (TE)	6-5/265	9/21/76	8	South Dakota St.	T-SD/02	15/13
89	Paul Irons (TE)	6-2/242	12/23/83	2	Florida State	FA/05	2/1
88	Frisman Jackson	6-3/220	6/12/79	5	Western Illinois	FA/02	12/0
84	Joe Jurevicius	6-5/230	12/23/74	9	Penn State	FA/06	16/11
86	Dennis Northcutt	5-11/175	12/22/77	7	Arizona	D2/00	16/7
85	John Owens (TE)	6-3/270	1/10/80	4	Notre Dame	FA/05	0/0
81	Travis Wilson	6-2/213	2/11/84	R	Oklahoma	D3/06	—
80	Kellen Winslow (TE)	6-4/254	7/21/83	3	Miami	D1/04	0/0
	OFFENSIVE LINEMEN						
63	Joe Andruzzi (G)	6-3/312	8/23/75	10	Southern Conn. St.	FA/05	13/13
00	LeCharles Bentley (C)	6-2/313	11/7/79	5	Ohio State	FA/06	14/14
65	Kirk Chambers (T)	6-7/313	3/19/79	3	Stanford	D6/04	15/0
60	Cosey Coleman (G)	6-4/322	10/27/78	7	Tennessee	FA/05	14/14
74	Nat Dorsey (T)	6-7/322	9/9/83	3	Georgia Tech	T-Min/05	9/0
62	Bob Hallen (C/G)	6-3/295	3/9/75	9	Kent State	FA/06	9/3
64	Ryan Pontbriand (C)	6-2/255	10/1/79	4	Rice	D5a/03	11/0
77	Kevin Shaffer (T)	6-5/290	3/2/80	5	Tulsa	FA/06	16/16
61	Isaac Sowells (G/T)	6-4/324	5/4/82	R	Indiana	D4b/06	—
72	Ryan Tucker (T)	6-6/320	6/12/75	10	TCU	FA/02	16/16
68	Dave Yovanovits (T)	6-3/294	3/6/81	4	Temple	FA/06	2/1
	DEFENSIVE LINEMEN						
98	Nick Eason (E)	6-3/301	5/29/80	4	Clemson	FA/04	16/0
75	Simon Fraser (E)	6-6/288	3/27/83	2	Ohio State	FA/05	16/0
91	Andrew Hoffman (T)	6-4/296	2/15/82	1	Virginia	D6b/05	0/0
78	Ethan Kelley (T)	6-2/310	2/12/80	3	Baylor	W-NE/05	11/2
97	Alvin McKinley (E)	6-3/310	6/9/78	7	Mississippi State	W-Car/01	16/16
96	Babatunde Oshinowo (T)	6-1/302	1/14/83	R	Stanford	D6b/06	—
69	J'Vonne Parker (E)	6-4/310	6/7/82	2	Rutgers	FA/05	4/0
99	Orpheus Roye (E)	6-4/320	1/21/73	11	Florida State	FA/00	16/16
92	Ted Washington (T)	6-5/365	4/13/68	16	Louisville	FA/06	16/16
	LINEBACKERS						
54	Andra Davis	6-1/255	12/23/78	5	Florida	D5/02	16/16
58	D'Qwell Jackson	6-0/228	9/26/83	R	Maryland	D2/06	—
56	Justin Kurpeikis	6-3/254	7/17/77	4	Penn State	FA/05	0/0
55	Willie McGinest	6-5/270	12/11/71	13	USC	FA/06	16/16
90	David McMillan	6-3/260	9/20/81	2	Kansas	D5/05	4/0
59	Nick Speegle	6-6/241	11/29/81	2	New Mexico	D6a/05	14/0
52	Matt Stewart	6-3/232	8/31/79	6	Vanderbilt	FA/05	14/12
51	Chaun Thompson	6-2/250	5/22/80	4	West Texas A&M	D2/03	16/15
53	Mason Unck	6-3/235	9/7/80	3	Arizona State	FA/03	16/0
94	Leon Williams	6-2/238	7/30/83	R	Miami	D4a/06	—
95	Kamerion Wimbley	6-3/245	10/13/83	R	Florida State	D1/06	—
	DEFENSIVE BACKS						
24	Gary Baxter (CB)	6-2/215	11/24/78	6	Baylor	FA/05	5/5
28	Leigh Bodden (CB)	6-1/200	9/24/81	4	Duquesne	FA/03	13/11
40	Justin Hamilton (S)	6-3/217	9/17/82	R	Virginia Tech	D7/06	—
20	Pete Hunter (CB)	6-2/208	5/25/80	5	Virginia Union	FA/05	4/0
26	Sean Jones (S)	6-2/212	3/2/82	3	Georgia	D2/04	16/0
37	Shawn Mayer (S)	6-0/202	3/4/79	3	Penn State	FA/06	0/0
33	Daylon McCutcheon (CB)	5-10/190	12/9/76	8	USC	D3a/99	16/16
22	DeMario Minter (CB)	5-11/190	2/20/84	R	Georgia	D5b/06	—
30	Antonio Perkins (CB)	5-11/190	1/9/82	2	Oklahoma	D4/05	1/0
21	Brodney Pool (S)	6-1/201	5/24/84	2	Oklahoma	D2/05	13/0
27	Brian Russell (S)	6-2/204	2/5/78	5	San Diego State	FA/05	16/16
	SPECIALISTS						
4	Phil Dawson (K)	5-11/200	1/23/75	8	Texas	FA/99	16/0
15	Dave Zastudil (P)	6-3/215	10/26/78	5	Ohio	FA/06	16/0

Abbreviations: D1-draft pick, first round; W-claimed on waivers; T-obtained in trade; FA-free-agent acquisition.

CLEVELAND BROWNS

2005 regular-season record: 6-10
Position: 4th in AFC North

Sept.11—CINCINNATI	L	13-27
Sept.18—at Green Bay	W	26-24
Sept.25—at Indianapolis	L	6-13
Oct. 2—Open date		
Oct. 9—CHICAGO	W	20-10
Oct. 16—at Baltimore	L	3-16
Oct. 23—DETROIT	L	10-13
Oct. 30—at Houston	L	16-19
Nov. 6—TENNESSEE	W	20-14
Nov.13—at Pittsburgh	L	21-34
Nov.20—MIAMI	W	22-0
Nov.27—at Minnesota	L	12-24
Dec. 4—JACKSONVILLE	L	14-20
Dec.11—at Cincinnati	L	20-23
Dec.18—at Oakland	W	9-7
Dec.24—PITTSBURGH	L	0-41
Jan. 1—BALTIMORE	W	20-16

SCORING BY PERIODS

	Q1	Q2	Q3	Q4	OT	Pts.
Browns	56	65	52	59	0	232
Opponents	58	102	81	60	0	301

TEAM STATISTICS

	Cle.	Opp.
TOTAL FIRST DOWNS ..	241	292
Rushing	76	116
Passing	149	161
Penalty	16	15
3rd Down: Made/Att. ..	67/203	87/215
3rd Down Pct.	33.0	40.5
4th Down: Made/Att. ..	7/18	8/18
4th Down Pct.	38.9	44.4
POSSESSION AVG.	28:00	32:00
TOTAL NET YARDS	4550	5069
Avg. per Game	284.4	316.8
Total Plays	938	1021
Avg. per Play	4.9	5.0
NET YARDS RUSHING ..	1503	2202
Avg. per Game	93.9	137.6
Total Rushes	395	527
NET YARDS PASSING....	3047	2867
Avg. per Game	190.4	179.2
Sacked/Yards Lost	46/276	23/142
Gross Yards	3323	3009
Att./Completions	497/297	471/279
Completion Pct.	59.8	59.2
Had Intercepted	17	15
PUNTS/AVERAGE	80/40.4	72/42.5
NET PUNTING AVG.	80/33.8	72/35.1
PENALTIES/YARDS	99/770	97/716
FUMBLES/LOST	27/13	21/8
TOUCHDOWNS	22	31
Rushing	4	11
Passing	15	19
Returns	3	1

SCORING (NONKICKERS)

	Tot. TD	RTD	PTD	MTD	2Pt.	Tot. Pts.
Bryant	4	0	4	0	0	24
Edwards	3	0	3	0	0	18
Heiden	3	0	3	0	0	18
Northcutt	3	0	2	1	0	18
Droughns	2	2	0	0	0	12
Bodden	1	0	0	1	0	6
Cribbs	1	0	0	1	0	6
Frye	1	1	0	0	0	6
F. Jackson	1	0	1	0	0	6
Shea	1	0	1	0	0	6
Smith	1	0	1	0	0	6
Wright	1	1	0	0	0	6
Browns	22	4	15	3	0	132
Opponents	31	11	19	1	0	186

2-Pt. conversions: Browns 0-1; Opponents 0-0.

(KICKERS)

	XPM/XPA	FGM/FGA	Pts.
Dawson	19/21	27/29	100
Browns	19/21	27/29	100
Opponents	31/31	28/35	115

RUSHING

	Att.	Yds.	Avg.	Lg.	TD
Droughns	309	1232	4.0	t75	2
Green	20	78	3.9	17	0
Frye	18	60	3.3	16	1
Dilfer	20	46	2.3	12	0
Northcutt	2	33	16.5	31	0
Wright	11	27	2.5	t6	1
Suggs	8	15	1.9	7	0
Smith	6	9	1.5	4	0
Bryant	1	3	3.0	3	0
Browns	395	1503	3.8	t75	4
Opponents	527	2202	4.2	t80	11

RECEIVING

	No.	Yds.	Avg.	Lg.	TD
Bryant	69	1009	14.6	54	4
Heiden	43	401	9.3	t62	3
Northcutt	42	441	10.5	t58	2
Droughns	39	369	9.5	51	0
Edwards	32	512	16.0	t80	3
F. Jackson	24	287	12.0	t68	1
Shea	18	153	8.5	27	1
Smith	12	58	4.8	9	1
Suggs	6	26	4.3	8	0
Green	5	30	6.0	14	0
Wright	3	15	5.0	15	0
Irons	2	16	8.0	14	0
Cribbs	1	7	7.0	7	0
Faine	1	-1	-1.0	-1	0
Browns	297	3323	11.2	t80	15
Opponents	279	3009	10.8	t51	19

INTERCEPTIONS

	No.	Yds.	Avg.	Lg.	TD
Russell	3	50	16.7	37	0
Bodden	3	6	2.0	6	0
Crocker	2	35	17.5	24	0
McCutcheon ..	2	14	7.0	14	0
Baxter	2	10	5.0	10	0
Andra. Davis ..	1	14	14.0	14	0
Pool	1	1	1.0	1	0
Stewart	1	0	0.0	0	0
Browns	15	130	8.7	37	0
Opponents	17	215	12.6	72	0

SACKS: McKinley 5.0, Thompson 5.0, Roye 3.0, Crocker 2.0, Andra. Davis 2.0, Eason 2.0, Lang 2.0, Kelley 1.0, Pool 1.0. Browns 23.0; Opponents 46.0.

PUNTING

	No.	Yds.	Avg.	In. 20	Lg.
Dawson	2	53	26.5	2	31
Richardson	78	3181	40.8	22	61
Browns	80	3234	40.4	24	61
Opponents	72	3058	42.5	19	60

PUNT RETURNS

	No.	FC	Yds.	Avg.	Lg.	TD
Northcutt	35	13	368	10.5	t62	1
Cribbs	1	0	5	5.0	5	0
Jones	1	0	0	0.0	0	0
Browns	37	13	373	10.1	t62	1
Opponents	36	9	347	9.6	51	0

KICK RETURNS

	No.	Yds.	Avg.	Lg.	TD
Cribbs	45	1094	24.3	t90	1
Droughns	5	119	23.8	35	0
Green	5	79	15.8	22	0
McIntyre	3	47	15.7	17	0
Perkins	3	82	27.3	35	0
Shea	3	29	9.7	13	0
Smith	2	24	12.0	13	0
F. Jackson	1	15	15.0	15	0
Wright	1	17	17.0	17	0
Browns	68	1506	22.1	t90	1
Opponents	56	1182	21.1	63	0

FIELD GOALS

	1-19	20-29	30-39	40-49	50+
Dawson	2/2	11/11	9/11	5/5	0/0
Browns	2/2	11/11	9/11	5/5	0/0
Opponents	0/0	10/10	11/12	6/10	1/3

Dawson: (29G, 34G) (21G, 39G) (40G, 22G) (19G, 44G) (24G) (30G) (28G, 29G, 37G) (37G, 19G, 39N) () (23G, 40G, 24G) (32G, 38G) (34N) (41G, 29G) (44G, 24G, 37G) () (21G, 39G)

Opponents: (32G, 23G) (34G) (20G, 23G) (44G, 48N) (39G, 27G, 38G) (47N, 47G, 50G) (38G, 37G, 35G, 38N, 40G) (50N) (42G, 33G, 44B) () (43G) (24G, 29G) (21G, 27G, 37G) (51N, 46B) (26G, 31G) (21G, 43G, 31G)

PASSING

	Att.	Cmp.	Yds.	Pct.	Avg. Gain	TD	Pct. TD	Int.	Pct. Int.	Long	Sack/Lost	Rating
Dilfer	333	199	2321	59.8	6.97	11	3.3	12	3.6	t80	23/139	76.9
Frye	164	98	1002	59.8	6.11	4	2.4	5	3.0	45	22/135	72.8
Browns	497	297	3323	59.8	6.69	15	3.0	17	3.4	t80	46/276	75.5
Opponents	471	279	3009	59.2	6.39	19	4.0	15	3.2	t51	23/142	78.2

DALLAS COWBOYS
NFC EAST DIVISION

2006 SEASON

CLUB DIRECTORY

Owner, president and general manager
  Jerry Jones
COO/executive vice president/director
  of player personnel
  Stephen Jones
Vice president/chief sales and
  marketing officer
  Jerry Jones Jr.
Vice president of college and pro
  scouting
  Jeff Ireland
Director of football operations
  Bruce Mays
Director of public relations
  Rich Dalrymple
Director of community relations
  Emily Robbins

Head coach
Bill Parcells

Assistant coaches
  Todd Bowles (secondary)
  Vincent Brown (inside linebackers)
  Bruce DeHaven (special teams)
  Todd Haley (wide receivers/
    passing game)
  Joe Juraszek (strength and
    conditioning)
  Freddie Kitchens (tight ends)
  David Lee (offensive quality
    control)
  Anthony Lynn (running backs)
  Mike MacIntyre (safeties)
  Chris Palmer (quarterbacks)
  Paul Pasqualoni (linebackers)
  Kacy Rodgers (defensive line)
  Tony Sparano (asst. head coach/
    offensive line/running game)
  Mike Zimmer (defensive
    coordinator)

OFFSEASON MOVES

Key additions
LB	Akin Ayodele	FA/Jaguars
LB	Rocky Boiman	FA/Titans
FS	Marcus Coleman	FA/Texans
T	Jason Fabini	FA/Jets
TE	Ryan Hannam	FA/Seahawks
G	Kyle Kosier	FA/Lions
WR	Terrell Owens	FA/Eagles
K	Mike Vanderjagt	FA/Colts

Key losses
G	Larry Allen	released/49ers
TE	Dan Campbell	FA/Lions
LB	Scott Fujita	FA/Saints
DT	La'Roi Glover	released/Rams
WR	Keyshawn Johnson	released/Panthers
OT	Torrin Tucker	FA/Bucs

SCHEDULE

Sept.	10—at Jacksonville	4:15
Sept.	17—WASHINGTON	8:15
Sept.	24—Open date	
Oct.	1—at Tennessee	1:00
Oct.	8—at Philadelphia	4:15
Oct.	15—HOUSTON	1:00
Oct.	23—N.Y. GIANTS (Mon.)	8:30
Oct.	29—at Carolina	8:15
Nov.	5—at Washington	1:00
Nov.	12—at Arizona	4:15
Nov.	19—INDIANAPOLIS	1:00
Nov.	23—TAMPA BAY (Thurs.)	4:15
Dec.	3—at N.Y. Giants	1:00
Dec.	10—NEW ORLEANS	1:00
Dec.	16—at Atlanta (Sat.)	8:00
Dec.	25—PHILADELPHIA (Mon.)	5:00
Dec.	31—DETROIT	1:00

All times are Eastern.
All games Sunday unless noted.

DRAFT CHOICES

Bobby Carpenter, OLB, Ohio State (first round/18th pick overall).
Anthony Fasano, TE, Notre Dame (2/53).
Jason Hatcher, DE, Grambling State (3/92).
Skyler Green, WR, LSU (4/125).
Pat Watkins, FS, Florida State (5/138).
Montavious Stanley, DT, Louisville (6/182).
Pat McQuistan, OT, Weber State (7/211).
E.J. Whitley, C, Texas Tech (7/224).

MISCELLANEOUS TEAM DATA

Stadium (capacity, surface):
  Texas Stadium
  (65,675, artificial)
Business address:
  One Cowboys Parkway
  Irving, TX 75063
Business phone:
  972-556-9900
Ticket information:
  972-785-5000
Team colors:
  Blue, metallic silver blue and white
Flagship radio station:
  KLUV, 98.7 FM
Website:
  www.dallascowboys.com
Training site:
  Residence Inn
  Oxnard, CA

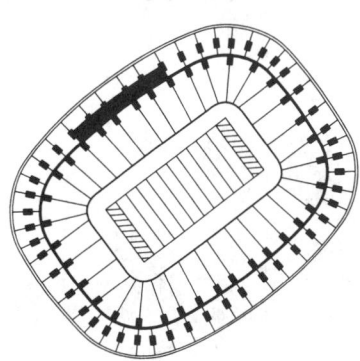

DALLAS COWBOYS

No.	QUARTERBACKS	Ht./Wt.	Born	NFL Exp.	College	How acq.	'05 Games GP/GS
11	Drew Bledsoe	6-5/238	2/14/72	14	Washington State	FA/05	16/16
7	Drew Henson	6-4/233	2/13/80	3	Michigan	T-Hou/04	0/0
9	Tony Romo	6-2/219	4/21/80	3	Eastern Illinois	FA/03	16/0
	RUNNING BACKS						
24	Marion Barber	5-11/221	6/10/83	2	Minnesota	D4a/05	13/2
21	Julius Jones	5-10/205	8/14/81	3	Notre Dame	D2/04	13/12
39	Lousaka Polite (FB)	6-0/246	9/14/81	2	Pitt	FA/04	14/3
28	Tyson Thompson	6-1/215	5/21/81	2	San Jose State	FA/05	15/0
	RECEIVERS						
18	Terrance Copper	6-0/201	3/12/82	3	East Carolina	FA/04	16/0
84	Patrick Crayton	6-0/200	4/7/79	3	N.W. Oklahoma	D7b/04	11/0
15	Tom Crowder	6-1/207	1/21/81	1	Arkansas	FA/04	0/0
47	Anthony Fasano (TE)	6-4/250	4/20/84	R	Notre Dame	D2/06	—
83	Terry Glenn	5-11/193	7/23/74	11	Ohio State	T-GB/03	16/16
10	Skyler Green	5-9/191	9/12/84	R	LSU	D4/06	—
48	Ryan Hannam (TE)	6-2/248	2/24/80	5	Northern Iowa	FA/06	16/5
86	Ahmad Merritt	5-10/195	2/5/77	4	Wisconsin	FA/05	0/0
81	Terrell Owens	6-3/226	12/7/73	11	Chattanooga	W-Phi/06	7/7
88	Brett Pierce (TE)	6-5/250	1/7/81	3	Stanford	FA/04	10/1
80	Sean Ryan (TE)	6-5/257	3/27/80	3	Boston College	D5/04	3/1
87	J.R. Tolver	6-1/202	1/13/80	1	San Diego State	FA/05	0/0
82	Jason Witten (TE)	6-5/261	5/6/82	4	Tennessee	D3/03	16/16
	OFFENSIVE LINEMEN						
76	Flozell Adams (T)	6-7/343	5/18/75	9	Michigan State	D2/98	6/6
75	Marc Colombo (T)	6-8/325	10/8/78	4	Boston College	FA/05	5/0
69	Jason Fabini (T)	6-7/304	8/25/74	9	Cincinnati	FA/06	9/9
65	Andre Gurode (C)	6-4/314	3/6/78	5	Colorado	D2a/02	16/2
52	Al Johnson (C)	6-5/296	1/27/79	3	Wisconsin	D2/03	16/16
63	Kyle Kosier (G)	6-5/309	11/27/78	5	Arizona State	FA/06	16/11
77	Pat McQuistan (T)	6-6/315	4/30/83	R	Weber State	D7a/06	—
72	Stephen Peterman (G)	6-4/300	1/11/82	2	LSU	D3/04	3/0
79	Rob Petitti (T)	6-6/347	5/21/82	2	Pitt	D6b/05	16/16
62	Marco Rivera (G)	6-4/307	4/26/72	10	Penn State	FA/05	14/14
64	Shannon Snell (G)	6-4/310	4/27/82	1	Florida	FA/05	0/0
70	E.J. Whitley (G/C)	6-5/309	2/16/82	R	Texas Tech	D7b/06	—
	DEFENSIVE LINEMEN						
99	Chris Canty (E)	6-7/279	11/10/82	2	Virginia	D4b/05	16/2
93	Kenyon Coleman (E)	6-5/284	4/10/79	4	UCLA	T-Oak/03	12/5
98	Greg Ellis (E)	6-6/271	8/14/75	9	North Carolina	D1/98	16/13
95	Jason Ferguson (T)	6-3/305	11/28/74	9	Georgia	FA/05	16/5
78	Junior Glymph (E)	6-5/270	9/2/80	3	Carson-Newman	FA/05	3/0
97	Jason Hatcher (E)	6-6/283	7/13/82	R	Grambling State	D3/06	—
92	Thomas Johnson (T)	6-2/294	6/24/81	2	Middle Tennessee	FA/05	2/0
91	L.P. Ladouceur (E)	6-4/257	3/13/81	2	California	FA/05	13/0
66	Jay Ratliff (E)	6-3/275	8/29/81	2	Auburn	D7/05	4/1
96	Marcus Spears (E)	6-4/307	3/8/83	2	LSU	D1b/05	16/10
60	Montavious Stanley (T)	6-2/314	9/10/81	R	Louisville	D6/06	—
	LINEBACKERS						
50	Akin Ayodele	6-2/251	9/17/79	5	Purdue	FA/06	16/11
59	Rocky Boiman	6-4/236	1/24/80	5	Notre Dame	FA/06	15/2
57	Kevin Burnett	6-3/230	12/24/82	2	Tennessee	D2/05	13/0
54	Bobby Carpenter	6-2/254	8/1/83	R	Ohio State	D1/06	—
55	Ryan Fowler	6-3/243	5/20/82	2	Duke	FA/04	14/3
56	Bradie James	6-2/245	1/17/81	4	LSU	D4/03	16/16
58	Scott Shanle	6-2/237	11/23/79	4	Nebraska	W-Stl/03	15/8
51	Al Singleton	6-2/236	8/7/75	10	Temple	FA/03	8/7
53	Kalen Thornton	6-3/240	5/12/82	1	Texas	FA/04	0/0
94	DeMarcus Ware	6-4/251	7/31/82	2	Troy State	D1a/05	16/16
	DEFENSIVE BACKS						
32	Marcus Coleman (S)	6-2/206	5/24/74	11	Texas Tech	FA/06	15/11
29	Keith Davis (S)	5-10/193	12/30/79	4	Sam Houston State	FA/02	16/15
26	Aaron Glenn (CB)	5-9/185	7/16/72	13	Texas A&M	FA/05	16/7
42	Anthony Henry (CB)	6-1/205	11/3/76	6	South Florida	FA/05	12/10
33	Nathan Jones (DB)	5-10/184	6/13/82	3	Rutgers	D7a/04	16/0
41	Terence Newman (CB)	5-11/190	9/4/78	4	Kansas State	D1/03	16/16
20	Willie Pile (S)	6-2/206	5/25/80	3	Virginia Tech	FA/05	16/1
35	Jacques Reeves (CB)	5-11/190	10/8/82	3	Purdue	D7b/04	16/0
25	Pat Watkins (S)	6-5/212	12/18/82	R	Florida State	D5/06	—
31	Roy Williams (S)	6-0/226	8/14/80	5	Oklahoma	D1/02	16/16
	SPECIALISTS						
1	Mat McBriar (P)	6-1/210	7/8/79	3	Hawaii	FA/04	16/0
13	Mike Vanderjagt (K)	6-5/211	3/24/70	9	West Virginia	FA/06	16/0

Abbreviations: D1-draft pick, first round; W-claimed on waivers; T-obtained in trade; FA-free-agent acquisition.

DALLAS COWBOYS

2005 regular-season record: 9-7
Position: 3rd in NFC East

Sept.11—at San Diego	W	28-24
Sept.19—WASHINGTON	L	13-14
Sept.25—at San Francisco	W	34-31
Oct. 2—at Oakland	L	13-19
Oct. 9—PHILADELPHIA	W	33-10
Oct. 16—N.Y. GIANTS (OT)	W	16-13
Oct. 23—at Seattle	L	10-13
Oct. 30—ARIZONA	W	34-13
Nov. 6—Open date		
Nov. 14—at Philadelphia	W	21-20
Nov. 20—DETROIT	W	20-7
Nov. 24—DENVER (OT)	L	21-24
Dec. 4—at N.Y. Giants	L	10-17
Dec. 11—KANSAS CITY	W	31-28
Dec. 18—at Washington	L	7-35
Dec. 24—at Carolina	W	24-20
Jan. 1—ST. LOUIS	L	10-20

SCORING BY PERIODS

	Q1	Q2	Q3	Q4	OT	Pts.
Cowboys	69	99	54	100	3	325
Opponents	68	112	61	64	3	308

TEAM STATISTICS

	Dal.	Opp.
TOTAL FIRST DOWNS ..	318	256
Rushing	97	87
Passing	177	150
Penalty	44	19
3rd Down: Made/Att.	94/232	73/211
3rd Down Pct.	40.5	34.6
4th Down: Made/Att.	7/13	7/11
4th Down Pct.	53.8	63.6
POSSESSION AVG.	32:24	27:36
TOTAL NET YARDS	5202	4814
Avg. per Game	325.1	300.9
Total Plays	1071	946
Avg. per Play	4.9	5.1
NET YARDS RUSHING ..	1861	1731
Avg. per Game	116.3	108.2
Total Rushes	521	414
NET YARDS PASSING....	3341	3083
Avg. per Game	208.8	192.7
Sacked/Yards Lost	50/298	37/236
Gross Yards	3639	3319
Att./Completions	500/300	495/271
Completion Pct.	60.0	54.7
Had Intercepted	17	15
PUNTS/AVERAGE	82/42.4	95/41.0
NET PUNTING AVG.	82/36.9	95/37.1
PENALTIES/YARDS	99/739	142/1015
FUMBLES/LOST	36/14	21/11
TOUCHDOWNS	38	35
Rushing	13	13
Passing	23	18
Returns	2	4

SCORING (NONKICKERS)

	Tot. TD	RTD	PTD	MTD	2Pt.	Tot. Pts.
T. Glenn	8	1	7	0	0	48
Johnson	6	0	6	0	1	38
Witten	6	0	6	0	0	36
Barber	5	5	0	0	0	30
J. Jones	5	5	0	0	0	30
Bledsoe	2	2	0	0	0	12
Crayton	2	0	2	0	0	12
Campbell	1	0	1	0	0	6
Henry	1	0	0	1	0	6
Polite	1	0	1	0	0	6
Ro. Williams ..	1	0	0	1	0	6
Cowboys	38	13	23	2	1	230
Opponents	35	13	18	4	0	210

2-Pt. conversions: Cowboys 1-2; Opponents 0-0.

(KICKERS)

	XPM/XPA	FGM/FGA	Pts.
Cortez	13/14	12/16	49
Cundiff	14/14	5/8	29
Suisham	8/8	3/4	17
Cowboys	35/36	20/28	95
Opponents	35/35	21/27	98

RUSHING

	Att.	Yds.	Avg.	Lg.	TD
J. Jones	257	993	3.9	51	5
Barber	138	538	3.9	t28	5
Thompson	46	182	4.0	16	0
Thomas	36	80	2.2	12	0
Bledsoe	34	50	1.5	9	2
Price	1	9	9.0	9	0
Polite	2	8	4.0	6	0
Newman	1	4	4.0	4	0
Johnson	1	3	3.0	3	0
Crayton	1	0	0.0	0	0
Romo	2	-2	-1.0	-1	0
T. Glenn	2	-4	-2.0	t6	1
Cowboys	521	1861	3.6	51	13
Opponents	414	1731	4.2	55	13

RECEIVING

	No.	Yds.	Avg.	Lg.	TD
Johnson	71	839	11.8	34	6
Witten	66	757	11.5	34	6
T. Glenn	62	1136	18.3	t71	7
J. Jones	35	218	6.2	26	0
Crayton	22	341	15.5	t63	2
Barber	18	115	6.4	21	0
Polite	9	72	8.0	15	1
Price	6	96	16.0	58	0
Campbell	3	24	8.0	18	1
Thompson	3	16	5.3	8	0
Pierce	2	15	7.5	10	0
Thomas	2	5	2.5	5	0
Copper	1	5	5.0	5	0
Cowboys	300	3639	12.1	t71	23
Opponents	271	3319	12.2	t89	18

INTERCEPTIONS

	No.	Yds.	Avg.	Lg.	TD
A. Glenn	4	10	2.5	10	0
Henry	3	102	34.0	t58	1
Ro. Williams ..	3	52	17.3	t46	1
Newman	3	16	5.3	12	0
Nguyen	1	7	7.0	7	0
Singleton	1	0	0.0	0	0
Cowboys	15	187	12.5	t58	2
Opponents	17	326	19.2	t65	2

SACKS: Ellis 8.0, Ware 8.0, Glover 3.0, Canty 2.5, B. James 2.5, Ro. Williams 2.5, Fujita 2.0, Shanle 1.5, Spears 1.5, Burnett 1.0, Ferguson 1.0, Newman 1.0, Nguyen 1.0, Ratliff 1.0, Coleman 0.5. Cowboys 37.0; Opponents 50.0.

PUNTING

	No.	Yds.	Avg.	In. 20	Lg.
Cundiff	1	35	35.0	0	35
McBriar	81	3439	42.5	28	63
Cowboys	82	3474	42.4	28	63
Opponents	95	3892	41.0	26	59

PUNT RETURNS

	No.	FC	Yds.	Avg.	Lg.	TD
Crayton	23	9	166	7.2	25	0
Price	12	6	63	5.3	11	0
Newman	10	6	55	5.5	26	0
Cowboys	45	21	284	6.3	26	0
Opponents	33	18	250	7.6	32	0

KICK RETURNS

	No.	Yds.	Avg.	Lg.	TD
Thompson	57	1399	24.5	49	0
Barber	3	58	19.3	21	0
Copper	2	32	16.0	21	0
Campbell	1	14	14.0	14	0
A. Glenn	1	20	20.0	20	0
Cowboys	64	1523	23.8	49	0
Opponents	66	1432	21.7	49	0

FIELD GOALS

	1-19	20-29	30-39	40-49	50+
Cortez	0/0	5/6	4/4	3/6	0/0
Cundiff	1/1	1/1	2/5	0/0	1/1
Suisham	0/0	3/3	0/0	0/1	0/0
Cowboys	1/1	9/10	6/9	3/7	1/1
Opponents	0/0	8/9	2/3	7/8	4/7

Cortez: () (41N, 33G, 41G) () (29G, 30G) (28G, 33G, 37G, 45G) (49B, 48N, 29G, 28G, 45G) (29N, 21G) () () () () () () Cundiff: () () () () () () () (19G, 56G) (34N) (34G) (34G) (38N) (24G, 32B) () Suisham: () () () () () () () (21G, 21G) () () () () () () () (22G, 47N)
Opponents: (33G) () (20G) (30G, 23G, 49G, 43G) (23G) (50G, 45G, 55G, 50G) (52G, 47G) (48G, 20G, 60N) (50N) (24G) (27G, 33N) (41N) () (24G, 47G) (49G, 27N, 53N, 20G)

PASSING

	Att.	Cmp.	Yds.	Pct.	Avg. Gain	TD	Pct. TD	Int.	Pct. Int.	Long	Sack/Lost	Rating
Bledsoe	499	300	3639	60.1	7.29	23	4.6	17	3.4	t71	49/295	83.7
Johnson	1	0	0	0.0	0.00	0	0.0	0	0.0	...	0/0	39.6
Cowboys	500	300	3639	60.0	7.28	23	4.6	17	3.4	t71	50/298	83.6
Opponents	495	271	3319	54.7	6.71	18	3.6	15	3.0	t89	37/236	75.1

DENVER BRONCOS
AFC WEST DIVISION

CLUB DIRECTORY

President/chief executive officer
Pat Bowlen
Executive VP of business operations
Joe Ellis
General manager
Ted Sundquist
Vice president of public relations
Jim Saccomano
Director of operations
Chip Conway
Assistant general manager
Rick Smith
Director of college scouting
Jim Goodman
Vice president of community development
Cindy Galloway-Kellogg
Director of media relations
Paul Kirk

OFFSEASON MOVES

Key additions
DE Kenard Lang   FA/Browns
WR Javon Walker   trade/Packers
Key losses
RB Mike Anderson   released/Ravens
DE Trevor Pryce   released/Ravens
TE Jeb Putzier   released/Texans

**Head coach/
executive VP
of football
operations**
Mike Shanahan

Assistant coaches
Jeremy Bates (offensive asst.)
Chip Beake (offensive asst.)
Ronnie Bradford (special teams coach)
Tim Brewster (tight ends)
Jacob Burney (defensive line)
Larry Coyer (defensive coordinator)
Rick Dennison (offensive coordinator)
Kirk Doll (linebackers)
Mike Heimerdinger (asst. head coach)
Pat McPherson (quarterbacks)
Andre Patterson (defensive lines/tackles)
Jim Ryan (defensive asst.)
Greg Saporta (asst. strength and conditioning)
Bob Slowik (defensive backs)
Ryan Slowik (defensive asst.)
Cedric Smith (asst. strength and conditioning)
Jimmy Spencer (asst. defensive backs)
Bobby Turner (running backs)
Rich Tuten (strength and conditioning)
Steve Watson (wide receivers)

SCHEDULE

Sept. 10—at St. Louis	1:00
Sept. 17—KANSAS CITY	4:15
Sept. 24—at New England	8:15
Oct. 1—Open date	
Oct. 9—BALTIMORE (Mon.)	8:30
Oct. 15—OAKLAND	8:15
Oct. 22—at Cleveland	4:05
Oct. 29—INDIANAPOLIS	4:15
Nov. 5—at Pittsburgh	4:15
Nov. 12—at Oakland	4:05
Nov. 19—SAN DIEGO	4:15
Nov. 23—at Kansas City (Thurs.)	8:00
Dec. 3—SEATTLE	4:15
Dec. 10—at San Diego	4:15
Dec. 17—at Arizona	4:05
Dec. 24—CINCINNATI	4:15
Dec. 31—SAN FRANCISCO	4:15

All times are Eastern.
All games Sunday unless noted.

DRAFT CHOICES

Jay Cutler, QB, Vanderbilt (first round/11th pick overall).
Tony Scheffler, TE, Western Michigan (2/61).
Brandon Marshall, WR, Central Florida (4/119).
Elvis Dumervil, DE, Louisville (4/126).
Domenik Hixon, WR, Akron (4/130).
Chris Kuper, G, North Dakota (5/161).
Greg Eslinger, C, Minnesota (6/198).

MISCELLANEOUS TEAM DATA

Stadium (capacity, surface):
Invesco Field at Mile High (76,125, grass)
Business address:
13655 Broncos Parkway
Englewood, CO 80112
Business phone:
303-649-9000
Ticket information:
720-258-3333
Team colors:
Orange, navy blue and white
Flagship radio station:
KOA, 850 AM
Website:
www.denverbroncos.com
Training site:
Dove Valley Headquarters
Englewood, CO
303-649-9000

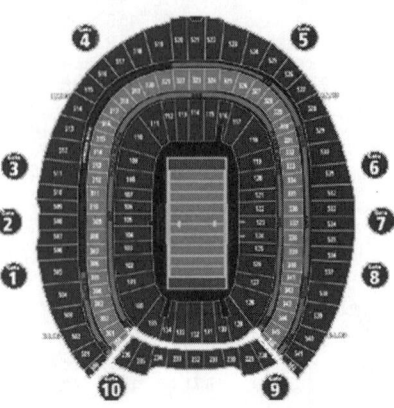

No.	QUARTERBACKS	Ht./Wt.	Born	NFL Exp.	College	How acq.	'05 Games GP/GS
6	Jay Cutler	6-3/227	4/29/83	R	Vanderbilt	D1/06	—
16	Jake Plummer	6-2/212	12/19/74	10	Arizona State	FA/03	16/16
11	Bradlee Van Pelt	6-2/231	7/3/80	2	Colorado State	D7c/04	3/0
	RUNNING BACKS						
26	Tatum Bell	5-11/213	3/2/81	3	Oklahoma State	D2/04	15/1
34	Cedric Cobbs	6-0/225	1/9/81	2	Arkansas	FA/05	0/0
33	Ron Dayne	5-10/245	3/14/78	7	Wisconsin	FA/05	10/0
39	Kyle Johnson (FB)	6-0/242	12/15/78	3	Syracuse	FA/03	16/14
37	Cecil Sapp	5-11/229	12/12/78	3	Colorado State	FA/03	16/0
	RECEIVERS						
81	Charlie Adams	6-2/190	10/23/79	4	Hofstra	FA/04	16/2
82	Stephen Alexander (TE)	6-4/250	11/7/75	9	Oklahoma	FA/05	16/15
14	Todd Devoe	6-2/198	4/5/80	2	Central Missouri St.	FA/05	14/0
	Domenik Hixon	6-2/192	10/8/84	R	Akron	D4c/06	—
89	Nate Jackson	6-3/223	6/4/79	4	Menlo	T-SF/03	2/0
87	David Kircus	6-1/185	2/19/80	3	Grand Valley State	FA/06	0/0
83	Mike Leach (TE)	6-2/245	10/18/76	7	William & Mary	FA/02	16/0
85	Ashley Lelie	6-3/200	2/16/80	5	Hawaii	D1/02	16/13
	Brandon Marshall	6-4/228	3/23/84	R	Central Florida	D4a/06	—
88	Chad Mustard (TE)	6-6/288	10/8/77	3	North Dakota	FA/06	0/0
	Tony Scheffler (TE)	6-5/261	2/15/83	R	Western Michigan	D2/06	—
80	Rod Smith	6-0/200	5/15/70	12	Missouri Southern	FA/94	16/16
13	David Terrell	6-3/212	3/13/79	6	Michigan	FA/05	1/0
	Javon Walker	6-3/215	10/14/78	5	Florida State	T-GB/06	1/1
17	Darius Watts	6-2/188	12/19/81	3	Marshall	D2/04	6/0
	OFFENSIVE LINEMEN						
69	P.J. Alexander (G)	6-4/297	12/23/78	3	Syracuse	FA/03	0/0
68	Martin Bibla (G)	6-3/306	10/4/79	4	Miami	FA/06	0/0
65	Cooper Carlisle (G)	6-5/295	8/11/77	7	Florida	D4b/00	16/16
	Greg Eslinger (C)	6-3/292	4/23/83	R	Minnesota	D6/06	—
72	George Foster (T)	6-5/338	6/9/80	4	Georgia	D1/03	16/16
74	Cornell Green (T)	6-6/315	8/25/76	7	Central Florida	FA/04	14/0
50	Ben Hamilton (G)	6-4/283	8/18/77	5	Minnesota	D4a/01	16/16
	Chris Kuper (G)	6-4/305	12/19/82	R	North Dakota	D5/06	—
78	Matt Lepsis (T)	6-4/290	1/13/74	10	Colorado	FA/97	16/16
62	Chris Myers (G)	6-5/301	9/15/81	2	Miami	D6/05	9/0
66	Tom Nalen (C)	6-3/286	5/13/71	13	Boston College	D7c/94	16/16
	DEFENSIVE LINEMEN						
98	Courtney Brown (E)	6-4/290	2/14/78	7	Penn State	FA/05	14/13
	Elvis Dumervil (E)	5-11/258	1/19/84	R	Louisville	D4b/06	—
91	Ebenezer Ekuban (E)	6-3/275	5/29/76	8	North Carolina	T-Cle/05	16/4
60	John Engelberger (E)	6-4/268	10/18/76	7	Virginia Tech	T-SF/05	14/0
94	Armon Gordon (T)	6-2/305	10/13/81	3	Stanford	W/06	0/0
90	Corey Jackson (E)	6-8/265	11/6/78	2	Nevada	FA/05	0/0
	Kenard Lang (E)	6-3/280	1/31/75	10	Miami	FA/06	16/5
96	Michael Myers (T)	6-2/300	1/20/76	9	Alabama	T-Cle/05	16/15
97	Chukie Nwokorie (E)	6-3/288	7/10/75	6	Purdue	FA/05	0/0
97	Demetrin Veal (T)	6-2/288	8/11/81	3	Tennessee	FA/04	15/0
61	Gerard Warren (T)	6-4/325	7/25/78	6	Florida	T-Cle/05	16/16
	LINEBACKERS						
51	Keith Burns	6-2/235	5/16/72	13	Oklahoma State	FA/05	15/1
54	Patrick Chukwurah	6-1/250	3/1/79	6	Wyoming	FA/04	14/0
52	Ian Gold	6-0/223	8/23/78	7	Michigan	FA/05	16/16
53	Louis Green	6-3/228	9/23/79	3	Alcorn State	FA/03	14/0
58	Nate Webster	6-0/235	11/29/77	7	Miami	FA/06	1/0
59	Ray Wells	6-1/234	8/20/80	3	Arizona	FA/06	0/0
55	D.J. Williams	6-1/242	7/20/82	3	Miami	D1/04	16/14
56	Al Wilson	6-0/240	6/21/77	8	Tennessee	D1/99	15/15
	DEFENSIVE BACKS						
45	Roc Alexander (CB)	5-10/186	9/23/81	3	Washington	FA/04	10/0
24	Champ Bailey (CB)	6-0/192	6/22/78	7	Georgia	T-Was/04	14/14
42	Sam Brandon (S)	6-2/200	7/5/79	5	UNLV	D4/02	14/0
40	Curome Cox (CB)	6-1/199	2/28/81	2	Maryland	FA/04	13/1
25	Nick Ferguson (S)	5-11/201	11/27/74	7	Georgia Tech	FA/03	16/16
22	Domonique Foxworth (CB)	6-0/183	3/27/83	2	Maryland	D3b/05	16/7
47	John Lynch (S)	6-2/220	9/25/71	14	Stanford	FA/04	16/16
41	Karl Paymah (CB)	6-0/204	11/29/82	2	Washington State	D3a/05	13/0
27	Darrent Williams (CB)	5-9/176	9/27/82	2	Oklahoma State	D2/05	12/9
32	Chris Young (S)	6-0/210	1/23/80	4	Georgia Tech	D7a/02	0/0
	SPECIALISTS						
1	Jason Elam (K)	5-11/200	3/8/70	14	Hawaii	D3b/93	16/0
3	Paul Ernster (P)	6-0/217	1/26/82	2	Northern Arizona	D7/05	1/0
10	Todd Sauerbrun (P)	5-10/215	1/4/73	12	West Virginia	T-Car/05	16/0

Abbreviations: D1-draft pick, first round; W-claimed on waivers; T-obtained in trade; FA-free-agent acquisition.

DENVER BRONCOS

DENVER BRONCOS

2005 regular-season record: 13-3
Position: 1st in AFC West

Sept.11—at Miami	L	10-34
Sept.18—SAN DIEGO	W	20-17
Sept.26—KANSAS CITY	W	30-10
Oct. 2—at Jacksonville	W	20-7
Oct. 9—WASHINGTON	W	21-19
Oct. 16—NEW ENGLAND	W	28-20
Oct. 23—at N.Y. Giants	L	23-24
Oct. 30—PHILADELPHIA	W	49-21
Nov. 6—Open date		
Nov.13—at Oakland	W	31-17
Nov.20—N.Y. JETS	W	27-0
Nov.24—at Dallas (OT)	W	24-21
Dec. 4—at Kansas City	L	27-31
Dec.11—BALTIMORE	W	12-10
Dec.17—at Buffalo	W	28-17
Dec.24—OAKLAND	W	22-3
Dec.31—at San Diego	W	23-7

2005 postseason record: 1-1

Jan. 14—NEW ENGLAND*	W	27-13
Jan. 22—PITTSBURGH§	L	17-34

*AFC divisional playoff game. §AFC championship game.

SCORING BY PERIODS

	Q1	Q2	Q3	Q4	OT	Pts.
Broncos	81	143	83	85	3	395
Opponents	44	61	37	116	0	258

TEAM STATISTICS

	Den.	Opp.
TOTAL FIRST DOWNS ..	330	295
Rushing	145	82
Passing	162	183
Penalty	23	30
3rd Down: Made/Att. ..	76/210	76/207
3rd Down Pct.	36.2	36.7
4th Down: Made/Att. ..	14/19	10/19
4th Down Pct.	73.7	52.6
POSSESSION AVG.	32:37	27:23
TOTAL NET YARDS	5766	5006
Avg. per Game	360.4	312.9
Total Plays	1030	985
Avg. per Play	5.6	5.1
NET YARDS RUSHING ..	2539	1363
Avg. per Game	158.7	85.2
Total Rushes	542	344
NET YARDS PASSING....	3227	3643
Avg. per Game	201.7	227.7
Sacked/Yards Lost	23/146	28/190
Gross Yards	3373	3833
Att./Completions	465/279	613/344
Completion Pct.	60.0	56.1
Had Intercepted	7	20
PUNTS/AVERAGE	73/43.2	81/44.9
NET PUNTING AVG.	73/38.0	81/38.2
PENALTIES/YARDS	97/756	139/989
FUMBLES/LOST	19/9	29/16
TOUCHDOWNS	46	31
Rushing	25	10

	Den.	Opp.
Passing	18	20
Returns	3	1

SCORING (NONKICKERS)

	TD	RTD	PTD	MTD	2Pt.	Tot. Pts.
Mi. Anderson..	13	12	1	0	0	78
Bell	8	8	0	0	0	48
K. Johnson	6	1	5	0	0	36
Smith	6	0	6	0	0	36
Bailey	2	0	0	2	0	12
Carswell	2	0	2	0	0	12
Plummer	2	2	0	0	0	12
S. Alexander ..	1	0	1	0	0	6
Dayne	1	1	0	0	0	6
Devoe	1	0	1	0	0	6
Duke	1	0	1	0	0	6
Lelie	1	0	1	0	0	6
Van Pelt	1	1	0	0	0	6
Da. Williams ..	1	0	0	1	0	6
Putzier	0	0	0	0	1	2
Broncos	46	25	18	3	1	280
Opponents	31	10	20	1	0	186

2-Pt. conversions: Broncos 1-2; Opponents 0-1.

(KICKERS)

	XPM/XPA	FGM/FGA	Pts.
Elam	43/44	24/32	115
Broncos	43/44	24/32	115
Opponents	30/30	14/18	72

RUSHING

	Att.	Yds.	Avg.	Lg.	TD
Mi. Anderson	239	1014	4.2	t44	12
Bell	173	921	5.3	68	8
Dayne	53	270	5.1	55	1
Plummer	46	151	3.3	22	2
Lelie	5	84	16.8	39	0
Van Pelt	11	48	4.4	11	1
Sapp	5	21	4.2	10	0
Adams	5	14	2.8	13	0
K. Johnson	4	9	2.3	4	1
Smith	1	7	7.0	7	0
Broncos	542	2539	4.7	68	25
Opponents	344	1363	4.0	61	10

RECEIVING

	No.	Yds.	Avg.	Lg.	TD
Smith	85	1105	13.0	72	6
Lelie	42	770	18.3	56	1
Putzier	37	481	13.0	32	0
Adams	21	203	9.7	21	0
S. Alexander ..	21	170	8.1	15	1
Mi. Anderson	18	212	11.8	t66	1
Bell	18	104	5.8	14	0
K. Johnson	17	160	9.4	33	5
Devoe	9	87	9.7	t44	1
Dayne	3	17	5.7	7	0
Carswell	2	3	1.5	t2	2
Duke	2	22	11.0	21	1

PASSING

	Att.	Cmp.	Yds.	Pct.	Avg. Gain	TD	Pct. TD	Int.	Pct. Int.	Long	Sack/Lost	Rating
Plummer	456	277	3366	60.7	7.38	18	3.9	7	1.5	72	22/135	90.2
Van Pelt	8	2	7	25.0	0.88	0	0.0	0	0.0	5	0/0	39.6
Smith	1	0	0	0.0	0.00	0	0.0	0	0.0	...	1/11	39.6
Broncos	465	279	3373	60.0	7.25	18	3.9	7	1.5	72	23/146	88.9
Opponents	613	344	3833	56.1	6.25	20	3.3	20	3.3	t91	28/190	72.2

	No.	Yds.	Avg.	Lg.	TD
Sapp	2	17	8.5	12	0
Watts	2	22	11.0	12	0
Broncos	279	3373	12.1	72	18
Opponents	344	3833	11.1	t91	20

INTERCEPTIONS

	No.	Yds.	Avg.	Lg.	TD
Bailey	8	139	17.4	t65	2
Ferguson	5	59	11.8	30	0
Da. Williams	2	108	54.0	t80	1
Foxworth	2	23	11.5	23	0
Lynch	2	2	1.0	1	0
Cox	1	48	48.0	48	0
Broncos	20	379	19.0	t80	3
Opponents	7	43	6.1	25	0

SACKS: Ekuban 4.0, Lynch 4.0, Pryce 4.0, Gold 3.0, Warren 3.0, Wilson 3.0, Brown 2.0, Coleman 1.0, M. Myers 1.0, Veal 1.0, Da. Williams 1.0. Broncos 28.0; Opponents 23.0.

PUNTING

	No.	Yds.	Avg.	In. 20	Lg.
Sauerbrun	72	3157	43.8	24	66
Broncos	73	3157	43.2	24	66
Opponents	81	3633	44.9	25	64

PUNT RETURNS

	No.	FC	Yds.	Avg.	Lg.	TD
Da. Williams	17	12	148	8.7	52	0
Adams	16	5	133	8.3	32	0
Broncos	33	17	281	8.5	52	0
Opponents	36	15	266	7.4	20	0

KICK RETURNS

	No.	Yds.	Avg.	Lg.	TD
Da. Williams	18	431	23.9	36	0
R. Alexander ..	12	261	21.8	31	0
Adams	10	218	21.8	32	0
Sapp	2	28	14.0	20	0
Mi. Anderson	1	18	18.0	18	0
Carswell	1	0	0.0	0	0
Engelberger ..	1	5	5.0	5	0
K. Johnson	1	8	8.0	8	0
Veal	1	6	6.0	6	0
Broncos	47	975	20.7	36	0
Opponents	67	1696	25.3	87	0

FIELD GOALS

	1-19	20-29	30-39	40-49	50+
Elam	0/0	9/10	5/5	9/13	1/4
Broncos	0/0	9/10	5/5	9/13	1/4
Opponents	0/0	3/3	6/8	4/5	1/2

Elam: (28G) (45G, 53N, 53N, 41G) (30G, 51G, 25G, 46N) (41N, 46B, 33G, 42G) () (49G, 42G, 27G, 49N) () (22G, 38G, 25G) (26G, 47G) (24G) (22G, 40G) (47G, 48G) () (29G, 33G, 34G, 52N) (28N)

Opponents: (29G, 44G) (42G) (28G) () (34G, 38B, 36G) (39G, 53N, 38G) (52G) () (45N, 40G) () (34N) (34G) (29G) (31G) (43G) ()

DETROIT LIONS
NFC NORTH DIVISION

2006 SEASON

CLUB DIRECTORY

Chairman and owner
William Clay Ford
Vice chairman
William Clay Ford Jr.
President and CEO
Matt Millen
Executive vice president and COO
Tom Lewand
Sr. VP of finance and CFO
Tom Lesnau
Sr. VP of communications
Bill Keenist
Asst. G.M. & senior VP of legal affairs
Martin Mayhew
Director of pro personnel
Sheldon White
Director of college scouting
Scott McEwen
Director of media relations
Matt Barnhart
Manager of football administration
Jeff Leinen

OFFSEASON MOVES

Key additions

WR Corey Bradford	FA/Texans
CB Jamar Fletcher	FA/Chargers
WR Mike Furrey	FA/Rams
RB Arlen Harris	FA/Rams
DT Tyoka Jackson	FA/Rams
QB Jon Kitna	FA/Bengals
QB Josh McCown	FA/Cardinals
OT Barry Stokes	FA/Falcons
G Rex Tucker	FA/Rams

Key losses

QB Jeff Garcia	FA/Eagles
CB Andre Goodman	FA/Dolphins
QB Joey Harrington	released
G Kyle Kosier	FA/Cowboys
CB R.W. McQuarters	FA/Giants
RB Paul Smith	FA

Head coach
Rod Marinelli

Assistant coaches
Jason Arapoff (strength and conditioning)
Mike Barry (asst. offensive line)
Larry Beightol (offensive line)
Malcolm Blacken (asst. strength and conditioning)
Kippy Brown (wide receivers)
Pat Carter (tight ends)
Don Clemons (defensive quality control)
Joe Cullen (defensive line)
Adam Gase (offensive quality control)
Donnie Henderson (defensive coordinator)
Shawn Jefferson (offensive asst.)
Stan Kwan (asst. special teams/offensive asst.)
Clayton Lopez (defensive backs)
Mike Martz (offensive coordinator)
Wilbert Montgomery (running backs)
Chuck Priefer (special teams coordinator)
Fred Reed (defensive asst.)
Cedric Saunders (asst. to the head coach/football operations)
Phil Snow (linebackers)

SCHEDULE

Sept.	10—SEATTLE	1:00
Sept.	17—at Chicago	1:00
Sept.	24—GREEN BAY	1:00
Oct.	1—at St. Louis	4:05
Oct.	8—at Minnesota	1:00
Oct.	15—BUFFALO	1:00
Oct.	22—at N.Y. Jets	1:00
Oct.	29—Open date	
Nov.	5—ATLANTA	1:00
Nov.	12—SAN FRANCISCO	1:00
Nov.	19—at Arizona	4:05
Nov.	23—MIAMI (Thurs.)	12:30
Dec.	3—at New England	1:00
Dec.	10—MINNESOTA	1:00
Dec.	17—at Green Bay	1:00
Dec.	24—CHICAGO	1:00
Dec	31—at Dallas	1:00

All times are Eastern.
All games Sunday unless noted.

DRAFT CHOICES

Ernie Sims, OLB, Florida State (first round/ninth pick overall).
Daniel Bullocks, SS, Nebraska (2/40).
Brian Calhoun, RB, Wisconsin (3/74).
Jonathan Scott, OT, Texas (5/141).
Alton "Dee" McCann, CB, West Virginia (6/179).
Fred Matua, G, Southern California (7/217).
Anthony Cannon, OLB, Tulane (7/247).

MISCELLANEOUS TEAM DATA

Stadium (capacity, surface):
Ford Field
(65,000, FieldTurf)
Business address:
222 Republic Drive
Allen Park, MI 48101
Business phone:
313-216-4000
Ticket information:
313-262-2000
Team colors:
Honolulu blue and silver
Flagship radio station:
WKRK, 97.1 FM
Website:
www.detroitlions.com

Training site:
222 Republic Drive
Allen Park, MI 48101
313-216-4000

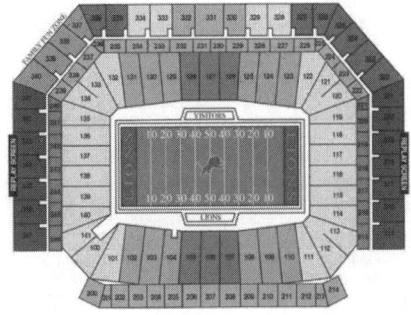

DETROIT LIONS

No.	QUARTERBACKS	Ht./Wt.	Born	NFL Exp.	College	How acq.	'05 Games GP/GS
8	Jon Kitna	6-2/220	9/21/72	10	Central Washington	FA/06	3/0
12	Josh McCown	6-4/212	7/4/79	5	Sam Houston State	FA/06	9/6
6	Dan Orlovsky	6-5/230	8/18/83	2	Connecticut	D5/05	2/0
	RUNNING BACKS						
24	Shawn Bryson (FB)	6-1/230	11/20/76	8	Tennessee	FA/03	16/2
29	Brian Calhoun	5-10/190	5/8/84	R	Wisconsin	D3/06	—
33	Arlen Harris	5-10/212	4/22/80	4	Virginia	FA/06	16/0
34	Kevin Jones	5-11/221	8/21/82	3	Virginia Tech	D1b/04	13/13
21	Artose Pinner	5-10/235	1/5/78	4	Kentucky	D4/03	16/2
30	Cory Schlesinger (FB)	6-0/247	6/23/72	12	Nebraska	D6b/95	11/8
	RECEIVERS						
17	Corey Bradford	6-1/201	12/8/75	9	Jackson State	FA/06	16/6
89	Dan Campbell (TE)	6-5/262	4/13/76	8	Texas A&M	FA/06	16/12
18	Eddie Drummond	5-9/190	4/12/80	5	Penn State	FA/02	12/0
82	Casey FitzSimmons (TE)	6-4/258	10/10/80	4	Carroll (Mont.)	FA/03	14/2
87	Mike Furrey	6-0/185	5/12/77	4	Northern Iowa	FA/06	16/11
84	Glenn Martinez	6-2/183	11/30/81	2	Saginaw Valley St.	FA/05	5/0
49	Sean McHugh (TE)	6-5/262	5/27/82	3	Penn State	W-GB/05	3/0
81	Marcus Pollard (TE)	6-3/247	2/8/72	12	Bradley	FA/05	16/16
80	Charles Rogers	6-3/202	5/23/81	4	Michigan State	D1/03	9/3
83	Scottie Vines	6-2/220	4/17/79	3	Wyoming	FA/04	13/11
88	Mike Williams	6-5/229	1/4/84	2	USC	D1/05	14/4
11	Roy Williams	6-2/212	12/20/81	3	Texas	D1/04	13/12
	OFFENSIVE LINEMEN						
76	Jeff Backus (T)	6-5/305	9/21/77	6	Michigan	D1/01	16/16
79	Kelly Butler (T)	6-7/334	7/24/82	2	Purdue	D6/04	16/16
64	Rick DeMulling (G)	6-4/304	7/21/77	6	Idaho	FA/05	13/5
63	Brock Gutierrez (C)	6-3/304	9/25/73	10	Central Michigan	FA/05	14/0
69	Tyrone Hopson (G)	6-2/294	5/28/76	5	Eastern Kentucky	FA/04	0/0
67	Fred Matua (C/G)	6-2/305	1/14/84	R	USC	D7a/06	—
48	Don Muhlbach (C)	6-4/256	8/17/81	3	Texas A&M	FA/04	13/0
51	Dominic Raiola (C)	6-1/295	12/30/78	6	Nebraska	D2a/01	16/16
73	Jonathan Scott (T/G)	6-6/310	1/10/83	R	Texas	D5/06	—
68	Barry Stokes (G)	6-4/310	12/20/73	7	Eastern Michigan	FA/06	16/1
74	Rex Tucker (T/G)	6-5/315	12/20/76	7	Texas A&M	FA/06	8/3
65	Damien Woody (G/C)	6-3/325	11/3/77	8	Boston College	FA/04	16/16
	DEFENSIVE LINEMEN						
94	Marcus Bell (T)	6-2/339	6/1/79	6	Memphis	D4b/01	15/0
75	Shaun Cody (T)	6-4/292	1/22/83	2	USC	D2/05	16/2
95	Jared DeVries (E)	6-4/275	6/11/76	8	Iowa	D3/99	16/0
98	Kalimba Edwards (E)	6-6/265	12/26/79	5	South Carolina	D2/02	16/2
96	James Hall (E)	6-2/280	2/4/77	7	Michigan	FA/00	14/14
91	Tyoka Jackson (T)	6-2/280	11/22/71	12	Penn State	FA/06	16/2
78	Cory Redding (E)	6-4/290	11/15/80	4	Texas	D3/03	16/15
92	Shaun Rogers (T)	6-4/345	3/12/79	6	Texas	D2b/01	14/14
90	Bill Swancutt (E)	6-4/270	9/4/82	2	Oregon State	D6a/05	8/1
72	Dan Wilkinson (T)	6-4/335	3/13/73	13	Ohio State	FA/04	16/16
	LINEBACKERS						
97	Boss Bailey	6-3/233	10/14/79	4	Georgia	D2/03	11/11
99	Anthony Cannon	6-0/224	12/31/84	R	Tulane	D7b/06	—
55	Donte' Curry	6-1/233	7/22/78	6	Morris Brown	W-Was/02	13/2
52	James Davis	6-2/240	4/26/79	4	West Virginia	D5b/03	16/14
54	Teddy Lehman	6-2/238	11/18/81	3	Oklahoma	D2/04	5/0
53	Paris Lenon	6-2/245	11/26/77	5	Richmond	FA/06	16/12
59	Alex Lewis	6-0/227	6/11/81	3	Wisconsin	D5/04	1/1
50	Ernie Sims	5-11/230	12/23/84	R	Florida State	D1/06	—
57	LeVar Woods	6-3/244	3/15/78	6	Iowa	FA/01	6/3
	DEFENSIVE BACKS						
28	Idrees Bashir (S)	6-2/198	12/7/78	6	Memphis	FA/06	11/0
32	Dre' Bly (CB)	5-9/185	5/22/77	8	North Carolina	FA/03	12/11
25	Fernando Bryant (CB)	5-10/175	3/26/77	8	Alabama	FA/04	2/2
27	Daniel Bullocks (S)	6-0/212	2/28/83	R	Nebraska	D2/06	—
35	Jamar Fletcher (CB)	5-10/186	8/28/79	6	Wisconsin	FA/06	14/0
36	Vernon Fox (S)	5-9/200	10/9/79	5	Fresno State	FA/04	14/0
42	Terrence Holt (S)	6-2/208	3/5/80	4	N.C. State	D5a/03	10/10
26	Kenoy Kennedy (S)	6-1/215	11/15/77	7	Arkansas	FA/05	16/16
45	Dee McCann (CB)	5-11/198	4/24/83	R	West Virginia	D6/06	—
38	Jon McGraw (S)	6-3/206	4/2/79	5	Kansas State	T-NYJ/05	8/2
23	Keith Smith (CB)	5-11/192	3/20/80	3	McNeese State	D3/04	15/2
31	Stanley Wilson (CB)	6-0/185	11/5/82	2	Stanford	D3/05	9/0
	SPECIALISTS						
4	Jason Hanson (K)	5-11/182	6/17/70	15	Washington State	D2b/92	15/0
2	Nick Harris (P)	6-2/218	7/23/78	6	California	FA/03	16/0

Abbreviations: D1-draft pick, first round; W-claimed on waivers; T-obtained in trade; FA-free-agent acquisition.

2005 regular-season record: 5-11
Position: 3rd in NFC North

Sept.11—GREEN BAY	W	17-3
Sept.18—at Chicago	L	6-38
Sept.25—Open date		
Oct. 2—at Tampa Bay	L	13-17
Oct. 9—BALTIMORE	W	35-17
Oct. 16—CAROLINA	L	20-21
Oct. 23—at Cleveland	W	13-10
Oct. 30—CHICAGO (OT)	L	13-19
Nov. 6—at Minnesota	L	14-27
Nov.13—ARIZONA	W	29-21
Nov.20—at Dallas	L	7-20
Nov.24—ATLANTA	L	7-27
Dec. 4—MINNESOTA	L	16-21
Dec.11—at Green Bay (OT)	L	13-16
Dec.18—CINCINNATI	L	17-41
Dec.24—at New Orleans	W	13-12
Jan. 1—at Pittsburgh	L	21-35

SCORING BY PERIODS

	Q1	Q2	Q3	Q4	OT	Pts.
Lions	69	72	43	70	0	254
Opponents	84	136	66	50	9	345

TEAM STATISTICS

	Det.	Opp.
TOTAL FIRST DOWNS ..	258	308
Rushing	69	109
Passing	151	166
Penalty	38	33
3rd Down: Made/Att. ..	87/224	82/208
3rd Down Pct.	38.8	39.4
4th Down: Made/Att.	7/17	6/11
4th Down Pct.	41.2	54.5
POSSESSION AVG.	29:13	30:47
TOTAL NET YARDS	4319	5158
Avg. per Game	269.9	322.4
Total Plays	955	1006
Avg. per Play	4.5	5.1
NET YARDS RUSHING ..	1471	2040
Avg. per Game	91.9	127.5
Total Rushes	404	488
NET YARDS PASSING....	2848	3118
Avg. per Game	178.0	194.9
Sacked/Yards Lost	31/173	31/187
Gross Yards	3021	3305
Att./Completions	520/297	487/295
Completion Pct.	57.1	60.6
Had Intercepted	18	19
PUNTS/AVERAGE	84/43.5	72/40.3
NET PUNTING AVG.	84/36.9	72/34.5
PENALTIES/YARDS	115/838	130/953
FUMBLES/LOST	21/12	24/12
TOUCHDOWNS	28	39
Rushing	10	15
Passing	15	19
Returns	3	5

SCORING (NONKICKERS)

	Tot. TD	RTD	PTD	MTD	2Pt.	Tot. Pts.
R. Williams	8	0	8	0	0	48
Jones	5	5	0	0	0	30
Pinner	3	3	0	0	0	18
Pollard	3	0	3	0	0	18
Bailey	1	0	0	1	0	6
Bryson	1	1	0	0	0	6
FitzSimmons ..	1	0	1	0	0	6
Garcia	1	1	0	0	0	6
Kennedy	1	0	0	1	0	6
C. Rogers	1	0	1	0	0	6
S. Rogers	1	0	1	0	0	6
Schlesinger	1	0	1	0	0	6
M. Williams	1	0	1	0	0	6
Lions	28	10	15	3	0	170
Opponents	39	15	19	5	1	236

2-Pt. conversions: Lions 0-0; Opponents 1-1.

(KICKERS)

	XPM/XPA	FGM/FGA	Pts.
Hanson	27/27	19/24	84
Lions	27/28	19/24	84
Opponents	37/37	24/30	109

RUSHING

	Att.	Yds.	Avg.	Lg.	TD
Jones	186	664	3.6	40	5
Pinner	106	349	3.3	19	3
Bryson	64	306	4.8	t77	1
Harrington	24	80	3.3	15	0
Garcia	17	51	3.0	14	1
Smith	4	16	4.0	6	0
Vines	1	7	7.0	7	0
Schlesinger....	1	1	1.0	1	0
Drummond	1	-3	-3.0	-3	0
Lions	404	1471	3.6	t77	10
Opponents	488	2040	4.2	t64	15

RECEIVING

	No.	Yds.	Avg.	Lg.	TD
Pollard	46	516	11.2	86	3
R. Williams	45	687	15.3	t51	8
Vines	40	417	10.4	40	0
Bryson	37	284	7.7	63	0
M. Williams	29	350	12.1	49	1
Pinner	21	181	8.6	24	0
Jones	20	109	5.5	28	0
Johnson	17	133	7.8	25	0
C. Rogers	14	197	14.1	t35	1
FitzSimmons..	10	45	4.5	11	1
Schlesinger	8	31	3.9	8	1
Smith	6	49	8.2	11	0
Edwards	2	15	7.5	8	0
Harrington	1	-4	-4.0	-4	0
Martinez	1	11	11.0	11	0
Lions	297	3021	10.2	86	15
Opponents	295	3305	11.2	t80	19

INTERCEPTIONS

	No.	Yds.	Avg.	Lg.	TD
Bly	6	54	9.0	28	0
Goodman	3	17	5.7	21	0
Kennedy	2	64	32.0	t64	1
Holt	2	51	25.5	51	0
McQuarters	2	25	12.5	19	0
Bailey	1	34	34.0	t34	1
Bra. Walker....	1	22	22.0	22	0
Lehman	1	21	21.0	17	0
Wayne	1	20	20.0	20	0
Lions	19	308	16.2	t64	2
Opponents	18	271	15.1	t41	2

SACKS: K. Edwards 7.0, S. Rogers 5.5, Hall 5.0, DeVries 3.0, Wilkinson 3.0, Cody 1.5, Bailey 1.0, Redding 1.0, K. Smith 1.0, Woods 1.0. Lions 31.0; Opponents 31.0.

PUNTING

	No.	Yds.	Avg.	In. 20	Lg.
N. Harris	84	3656	43.5	34	60
Lions	84	3656	43.5	34	60
Opponents	72	2899	40.3	20	61

PUNT RETURNS

	No.	FC	Yds.	Avg.	Lg.	TD
Drummond ..	26	11	157	6.0	38	0
McQuarters ..	10	2	117	11.7	49	0
Lions	36	13	274	7.6	49	0
Opponents....	50	17	520	10.4	t81	2

KICK RETURNS

	No.	Yds.	Avg.	Lg.	TD
Drummond	49	1077	22.0	48	0
McQuarters	16	381	23.8	73	0
Bryson	4	55	13.8	25	0
Martinez	2	42	21.0	24	0
DeVries	1	7	7.0	7	0
Johnson	1	14	14.0	14	0
Lions	73	1576	21.6	73	0
Opponents	55	1239	22.5	t90	1

FIELD GOALS

	1-19	20-29	30-39	40-49	50+
Hanson	1/1	9/9	3/3	4/7	2/4
Lions	1/1	9/9	3/3	4/7	2/4
Opponents	1/1	8/8	7/9	5/7	3/5

Hanson: (21G) () (44G, 23G) () (47B, 52G, 25G) (47N, 47G, 50G) (46N, 32G, 30G) (51N) (26G, 20G) (50N) () (45G, 26G, 28G) (19G, 23G) (45G) (21G, 39G) ()
Opponents: (50G) (48G, 48N, 36N) (43G, 46N) (46G) (52B) (30G) (38G, 20G) (21G, 52N, 40G) (51G, 28G) (19G, 56G) (21G, 23G) () (36G, 38B, 39G, 28G) (28G, 33G) (35G, 47G, 33G, 20G) ()

PASSING

	Att.	Cmp.	Yds.	Pct.	Avg. Gain	TD	Pct. TD	Int.	Pct. Int.	Long	Sack/Lost	Rating
Harrington	330	188	2021	57.0	6.12	12	3.6	12	3.6	86	24/136	72.0
Garcia	173	102	937	59.0	5.42	3	1.7	6	3.5	49	6/34	65.1
Orlovsky	17	7	63	41.2	3.71	0	0.0	0	0.0	20	1/3	51.8
Lions	520	297	3021	57.1	5.81	15	2.9	18	3.5	86	31/173	69.1
Opponents	487	295	3305	60.6	6.79	19	3.9	19	3.9	t80	31/187	77.6

DETROIT LIONS

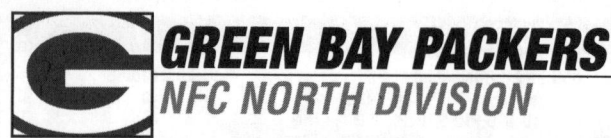

GREEN BAY PACKERS
NFC NORTH DIVISION

2006 SEASON

CLUB DIRECTORY

Chairman of the board/chief executive officer
Robert E. Harlan
President & chief operating officer
John Jones
Executive VP, general manager and director of football operations
Ted Thompson
VP of player finance/general counsel
Andrew Brandt
Director of pro personnel
Reggie McKenzie
Director of college scouting
John Dorsey
Director of public relations
Jeff Blumb
Manager of community relations
Cathy Dworak

OFFSEASON MOVES

Key additions
DT	Kenderick Allen	FA/Giants
WR	Marc Boerigter	FA/Chiefs
K	Billy Cundiff	FA/Bucs
S	Marquand Manuel	FA/Seahawks
DT	Ryan Pickett	FA/Rams
LB	Ben Taylor	FA/Browns
CB	Charles Woodson	FA/Raiders

Key losses
WR	Antonio Chatman	FA/Bengals
LB	Na'il Diggs	released/Panthers
RB	Tony Fisher	FA/Rams
C	Mike Flanagan	FA/Texans
NT	Grady Jackson	FA
LB	Paris Lenon	FA/Lions
K	Ryan Longwell	FA/Vikings
WR	Terrence Murphy	released
QB	Craig Nall	FA/Bills
OL	Grey Ruegamer	FA/Giants
LB	Robert Thomas	released/Raiders
WR	Javon Walker	trade/Broncos

Head coach
Mike McCarthy

Assistant coaches
Edgar Bennett (running backs)
James Campen (asst. offensive line)
Tom Clements (quarterbacks)
Rock Gullickson (strength and conditioning)
Carl Hairston (defensive ends)
Jeff Jagodzinski (offensive coordinator)
Ty Knott (offensive quality control)
Eric Lewis (defensive quality control)
Ben McAdoo (tight ends)
Winston Moss (linebackers)
Robert Nunn (defensive tackles)
Joe Philbin (offensive line)
Jimmy Robinson (wide receivers)
Bob Sanders (defensive coordinator)
Kurt Schottenheimer (secondary)
Shawn Slocum (asst. special teams)
Mike Stock (special teams coordinator)
Lionel Washington (defensive nickel package/cornerbacks)

SCHEDULE

Sept. 10—CHICAGO	4:15
Sept. 17—NEW ORLEANS	1:00
Sept. 24—at Detroit	1:00
Oct. 2—at Philadelphia (Mon.)	8:30
Oct. 8—ST. LOUIS	1:00
Oct. 15—Open date	
Oct. 22—at Miami	1:00
Oct. 29—ARIZONA	1:00
Nov. 5—at Buffalo	1:00
Nov. 12—at Minnesota	1:00
Nov. 19—NEW ENGLAND	1:00
Nov. 27—at Seattle (Mon.)	8:30
Dec. 3—N.Y. JETS	1:00
Dec. 10—at San Francisco	4:05
Dec. 17—DETROIT	1:00
Dec. 21—MINNESOTA (Thurs.)	8:00
Dec. 31—at Chicago	1:00

All times are Eastern.
All games Sunday unless noted.

DRAFT CHOICES

A.J. Hawk, OLB, Ohio State (first round/fifth pick overall).
Daryn Colledge, OT, Boise State (2/47).
Greg Jennings, WR, Western Michigan (2/52).
Abdul Hodge, ILB, Iowa (3/67).
Jason Spitz, C, Louisville (3/75).
Cory Rodgers, WR, Texas Christian (4/104).
Will Blackmon, WR, Boston College (4/115).
Ingle Martin, QB, Furman (5/148).
Tony Moll, OT, Nevada (5/165).
Johnny Jolly, DT, Texas A&M (6/183).
Tyrone Culver, FS, Fresno State (6/185).
Dave Tollefson, DE, Northwest Missouri State (7/253).

MISCELLANEOUS TEAM DATA

Stadium (capacity, surface):
Lambeau Field
(72,601, grass)
Business address:
P.O. Box 10628
Green Bay, WI 54307-0628
Business phone:
920-569-7500
Ticket information:
920-569-7501
Team colors:
Dark green, gold and white
Flagship radio station:
WTMJ, 620 AM
Website:
www.packers.com
Training site:
Clarke Hinkle Field
Green Bay, Wis.
920-569-7500

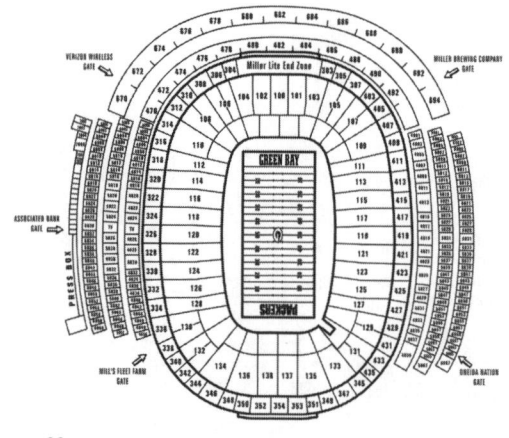

2006 TRAINING CAMP ROSTER

No.	QUARTERBACKS	Ht./Wt.	Born	NFL Exp.	College	How acq.	'05 Games GP/GS
4	Brett Favre	6-2/224	10/10/69	16	Southern Miss	T-Atl./92	16/16
7	Ingle Martin	6-2/224	8/15/82	R	Furman	D5a/06	—
12	Aaron Rodgers	6-2/223	12/2/83	2	California	D1/05	3/0
	RUNNING BACKS						
44	Najeh Davenport	6-1/250	2/8/79	5	Miami	D4/02	5/1
35	Samkon Gado	5-10/226	11/13/82	2	Liberty	FA/05	8/5
30	Ahman Green	6-0/218	2/16/77	9	Nebraska	T-Sea/00	5/5
33	William Henderson (FB)	6-1/251	2/19/171	12	North Carolina	D3b/95	16/8
23	Noah Herron	5-10/224	4/3/82	2	Northwestern	FA/05	7/0
48	Vonta Leach (FB)	6-0/246	11/6/81	3	East Carolina	FA/04	16/5
	RECEIVERS						
83	Marc Boerigter	6-3/220	5/4/78	5	Hastings	FA/06	10/0
80	Donald Driver	6-0/192	2/2/75	8	Alcorn State	D7b/99	16/16
89	Robert Ferguson	6-1/210	12/17/79	5	Texas A&M	D2/01	11/7
88	Bubba Franks (TE)	6-6/265	1/6/78	7	Miami	D1/00	10/8
82	Rod Gardner	6-2/213	10/26/77	5	Clemson	W-Car/05	12/1
85	Greg Jennings	5-10/192	9/21/83	R	Western Michigan	D2b/06	—
86	Donald Lee (TE)	6-3/255	8/31/80	3	Mississippi State	FA/05	15/5
87	David Martin (TE)	6-4/262	3/13/79	6	Tennessee	D6/01	12/8
81	Cory Rodgers	6-0/197	2/22/83	R	Texas Christian	D4a/06	—
	OFFENSIVE LINEMEN						
71	Kevin Barry (G/T)	6-4/335	7/20/79	5	Arizona	FA/02	16/1
76	Chad Clifton (T)	6-5/330	6/26/76	7	Tennessee	D2/00	16/16
73	Daryn Colledge (G)	6-4/299	2/11/82	R	Boise State	D2a/06	—
62	Junius Coston (G)	6-3/310	11/5/83	1	North Carolina A&T	D5a/05	0/0
60	Rob Davis (C)	6-3/283	12/10/68	11	Shippensburg	FA/97	16/0
70	Adrian Klemm (T)	6-3/312	5/21/77	5	Hawaii	FA/05	16/8
61	Wayne Lucier (C)	6-3/300	12/5/79	2	Colorado	FA/06	0/0
75	Tony Moll (G)	6-4/300	8/23/83	R	Nevada	D5b/06	—
72	Jason Spitz (C)	6-3/313	12/19/82	R	Louisville	D3b/06	—
65	Mark Tauscher (T)	6-4/320	6/17/77	6	Wisconsin	D7a/00	16/16
63	Scott Wells (C)	6-2/300	1/7/81	3	Tennessee	D7/04	16/10
68	Chris White (C)	6-2/285	2/28/83	2	Southern Miss	FA/05	1/0
78	Will Whitticker (G)	6-5/336	8/2/82	2	Michigan State	D7b/05	15/14
	DEFENSIVE LINEMEN						
97	Kenderick Allen (T)	6-6/315	9/14/78	4	LSU	FA/06	14/0
90	Colin Cole (T)	6-2/299	6/24/80	3	Iowa	FA/04	16/4
94	Kabeer Gbaja-Biamila (E)	6-4/252	9/24/77	7	San Diego State	D5a/00	16/16
77	Cullen Jenkins (T)	6-3/292	1/20/81	3	Central Michigan	FA/04	16/12
93	Johnny Jolly (T)	6-2/310	2/21/83	R	Texas A&M	D6a/06	—
74	Aaron Kampman (E)	6-4/284	11/30/79	5	Iowa	D5a/02	16/16
96	Michael Montgomery (E)	6-5/276	8/18/83	2	Texas A&M	D6a/05	12/0
98	Kenny Peterson (T)	6-3/295	11/21/78	4	Ohio State	D3/03	16/0
79	Ryan Pickett (T)	6-2/310	10/8/79	6	Ohio State	FA/06	16/16
91	Dave Tollefson (E)	6-4/263	5/19/81	R	NW Missouri State	D7/06	—
99	Corey Williams (T)	6-4/310	8/17/80	3	Arkansas State	D6/04	12/0
	LINEBACKERS						
56	Nick Barnett	6-2/233	5/27/81	4	Oregon State	D1/03	16/16
50	A.J. Hawk	6-1/246	1/6/84	R	Ohio State	D1/06	—
55	Abdul Hodge	5-11/233	9/9/82	R	Iowa	D3a/06	—
54	Roy Manning	6-2/245	12/4/81	2	Michigan	FA/05	15/2
51	Brady Poppinga	6-3/259	9/21/79	2	Brigham Young	D4b/05	12/1
58	Ben Taylor	6-2/245	8/31/78	5	Virginia Tech	FA/06	16/16
59	Tracy White	6-0/230	4/14/81	4	Howard	FA/06	15/0
	DEFENSIVE BACKS						
27	Will Blackmon (CB)	5-11/191	10/27/84	R	Boston College	D4b/06	—
28	Ahmad Carroll (CB)	5-10/185	8/4/83	3	Arkansas	D1/04	16/16
36	Nick Collins (S)	5-11/201	8/16/83	2	Bethune-Cookman	D2a/05	16/16
29	Tyrone Culver (S)	6-1/200	7/6/83	R	Fresno State	D6b/06	—
34	Patrick Dendy (CB)	6-0/190	3/10/82	2	Rice	FA/05	4/0
39	Therrian Fontenot (CB)	5-10/187	6/28/81	2	Fresno State	FA/05	1/0
31	Al Harris (CB)	6-1/185	12/7/74	9	Texas A&M-Kingsville	T-Phi/03	16/16
37	Mike Hawkins (CB)	6-2/178	7/15/83	2	Oklahoma	D5b/05	11/1
26	Jason Horton (CB)	6-0/193	2/16/80	3	North Carolina A&T	FA/04	9/0
22	Marquand Manuel (S)	6-0/209	7/11/79	5	Florida	FA/06	16/10
20	Mark Roman (S)	5-11/200	3/26/77	7	LSU	FA/04	16/16
25	Marviel Underwood (S)	5-10/197	2/17/82	2	San Diego State	D4a/05	16/0
21	Charles Woodson (CB)	6-1/200	10/7/76	9	Michigan	FA/06	6/6
	SPECIALISTS						
2	Billy Cundiff (K)	6-2/200	3/30/80	5	Drake	FA/06	6/0
16	Dave Rayner (K)	6-2/209	10/26/82	2	Michigan State	W-Ind/06	14/0
9	Jon Ryan (P)	6-0/202	11/26/81	1	University of Regina	FA/06	0/0
11	B.J. Sander (P)	6-4/218	7/29/80	2	Ohio State	D3c/04	14/0

Abbreviations: D1-draft pick, first round; W-claimed on waivers; T-obtained in trade; FA-free-agent acquisition.

GREEN BAY PACKERS

GREEN BAY PACKERS

2005 regular-season record: 4-12
Position: 4th in NFC North

Sept.11—at Detroit	L	3-17
Sept.18—CLEVELAND	L	24-26
Sept.25—TAMPA BAY	L	16-17
Oct. 3—at Carolina	L	29-32
Oct. 9—NEW ORLEANS	W	52-3
Oct. 16—Open date		
Oct. 23—at Minnesota	L	20-23
Oct. 30—at Cincinnati	L	14-21
Nov. 6—PITTSBURGH	L	10-20
Nov.13—at Atlanta	W	33-25
Nov.21—MINNESOTA	L	17-20
Nov.27—at Philadelphia	L	14-19
Dec. 4—at Chicago	L	7-19
Dec.11—DETROIT (OT)	W	16-13
Dec.18—at Baltimore	L	3-48
Dec.25—CHICAGO	L	17-24
Jan. 1—SEATTLE	W	23-17

SCORING BY PERIODS

	Q1	Q2	Q3	Q4	OT	Pts.
Packers	77	100	36	82	3	298
Opponents	88	100	59	97	0	344

TEAM STATISTICS

	G.B.	Opp.
TOTAL FIRST DOWNS	318	280
Rushing	76	107
Passing	206	143
Penalty	36	30
3rd Down: Made/Att.	91/221	74/206
3rd Down Pct.	41.2	35.9
4th Down: Made/Att.	9/19	3/8
4th Down Pct.	47.4	37.5
POSSESSION AVG.	30:48	29:12
TOTAL NET YARDS	5118	4690
Avg. per Game	319.9	293.1
Total Plays	1051	969
Avg. per Play	4.9	4.8
NET YARDS RUSHING	1352	2010
Avg. per Game	84.5	125.6
Total Rushes	398	504
NET YARDS PASSING	3766	2680
Avg. per Game	235.4	167.5
Sacked/Yards Lost	27/198	35/196
Gross Yards	3964	2876
Att./Completions	626/383	430/252
Completion Pct.	61.2	58.6
Had Intercepted	30	10
PUNTS/AVERAGE	70/38.9	85/42.3
NET PUNTING AVG.	70/33.5	85/36.9
PENALTIES/YARDS	119/918	98/975
FUMBLES/LOST	31/15	33/11
TOUCHDOWNS	34	37
Rushing	11	10
Passing	20	22
Returns	3	5

SCORING (NONKICKERS)

	Tot.					Tot.
	TD	RTD	PTD	MTD	2Pt.	Pts.
Gado	7	6	1	0	0	42
Chatman	5	0	4	1	0	30

	Tot.					Tot.
	TD	RTD	PTD	MTD	2Pt.	Pts.
Driver	5	0	5	0	0	30
Ferguson	3	0	3	0	1	20
D. Martin	3	0	3	0	1	20
Davenport	2	2	0	0	0	12
Fisher	2	1	1	0	0	12
Herron	2	2	0	0	0	12
D. Lee	2	0	2	0	0	12
Barnett	1	0	0	1	0	6
Franks	1	0	1	0	0	6
Harris	1	0	0	1	0	6
Packers	34	11	20	3	2	208
Opponents	37	10	22	5	1	224

2-Pt. conversions: Packers 2-3; Opponents 1-2.

(KICKERS)

	XPM/XPA	FGM/FGA	Pts.
Longwell	30/31	20/27	90
Packers	30/31	20/27	90
Opponents	33/35	29/34	120

RUSHING

	Att.	Yds.	Avg.	Lg.	TD
Gado	143	582	4.1	t64	6
Green	77	255	3.3	13	0
Fisher	60	173	2.9	17	1
Herron	45	121	2.7	17	2
Davenport	30	105	3.5	24	2
Favre	18	62	3.4	20	0
Chatman	8	34	4.3	11	0
R. Lee	11	16	1.5	4	0
Driver	2	13	6.5	9	0
Rodgers	2	7	3.5	8	0
Henderson	1	-5	-5.0	-5	0
Sander	1	-11	-11.0	-11	0
Packers	398	1352	3.4	t64	11
Opponents	504	2010	4.0	43	10

RECEIVING

	No.	Yds.	Avg.	Lg.	TD
Driver	86	1221	14.2	59	5
Chatman	49	549	11.2	25	4
Fisher	48	347	7.2	15	1
D. Lee	33	294	8.9	27	2
Henderson	30	264	8.8	32	0
Ferguson	27	366	13.6	51	3
D. Martin	27	224	8.3	t21	3
Franks	25	207	8.3	24	1
Green	19	147	7.7	20	0
Gado	10	77	7.7	30	1
Thurman	7	92	13.1	33	0
Leach	5	19	3.8	9	0
Murphy	5	36	7.2	12	0
Gardner	4	67	16.8	33	0
J. Walker	4	27	6.8	9	0
Davenport	2	3	1.5	2	0
R. Lee	1	5	5.0	5	0
W. Williams	1	19	19.0	19	0
Packers	383	3964	10.3	59	20
Opponents	252	2876	11.4	t80	22

INTERCEPTIONS

	No.	Yds.	Avg.	Lg.	TD
Harris	3	30	10.0	t22	1
Carroll	2	38	19.0	38	0
Roman	2	18	9.0	12	0
Barnett	1	95	95.0	t95	1
R. Thomas	1	24	24.0	24	0
Collins	1	0	0.0	0	0
Packers	10	205	20.5	t95	2
Opponents	30	370	12.3	95	3

SACKS: Gbaja-Biamila 8.0, Kampman 6.5, Harris 3.0, Jenkins 3.0, Peterson 3.0, Cole 2.0, Poppinga 2.0, C. Williams 2.0, Lenon 1.5, Barnett 1.0, G. Jackson 1.0, Montgomery 1.0. Packers 35.0; Opponents 27.0.

PUNTING

	No.	Yds.	Avg.	In. 20	Lg.
Flinn	6	218	36.3	0	42
Sander	64	2508	39.2	11	53
Packers	70	2726	38.9	11	53
Opponents	85	3597	42.3	29	63

PUNT RETURNS

	No.	FC	Yds.	Avg.	Lg.	TD
Chatman	45	18	381	8.5	t85	1
Packers	45	18	381	8.5	t85	1
Opponents	49	12	339	6.9	49	0

KICK RETURNS

	No.	Yds.	Avg.	Lg.	TD
Carroll	19	390	20.5	57	0
R. Lee	15	319	21.3	35	0
Davenport	10	189	18.9	27	0
Thurman	8	136	17.0	23	0
Chatman	5	91	18.2	33	0
Murphy	5	91	18.2	29	0
Jones	4	80	20.0	25	0
Leach	3	39	13.0	20	0
Ferguson	2	44	22.0	22	0
Henderson	2	20	10.0	10	0
Peterson	1	5	5.0	5	0
C. Williams	1	14	14.0	14	0
Packers	75	1418	18.9	57	0
Opponents	65	1404	21.6	73	0

FIELD GOALS

	1-19	20-29	30-39	40-49	50+
Longwell	0/0	7/7	6/10	3/5	4/5
Packers	0/0	7/7	6/10	3/5	4/5
Opponents	1/1	11/11	10/10	6/10	1/2

Longwell: (50G) (34G) (42N, 32G) () (26G) (53N, 53G, 42N, 39G) () (40G, 31N) (46G, 23G, 53G, 51G) (46G) () () (36G, 38B, 39G, 28G) (27G) (38N, 39N, 26G) (26G, 32G, 28G)
Opponents: (21G) (21G, 39G) (42G) (32G, 38G) (33G, 43N, 43N) (27G, 22G, 56G) () (32G, 24G, 51B) (37G) (49N, 24G, 27G) (44G, 38G, 37G, 33G) (21G, 40G, 25G, 35G, 43N) (19G, 23G) (23G, 40G) (45G) (44G)

PASSING

	Att.	Cmp.	Yds.	Pct.	Avg. Gain	TD	Pct. TD	Int.	Pct. Int.	Long	Sack/Lost	Rating
Favre	607	372	3881	61.3	6.39	20	3.3	29	4.8	59	24/170	70.9
Rodgers	16	9	65	56.3	4.06	0	0.0	1	6.3	16	3/28	39.8
Fisher	1	1	14	100.0	14.00	0	0.0	0	0.0	14	0/0	118.8
Sander	1	1	4	100.0	4.00	0	0.0	0	0.0	4	0/0	83.3
Gado	1	0	0	0.0	0.00	0	0.0	0	0.0	...	0/0	39.6
Packers	626	383	3964	61.2	6.33	20	3.2	30	4.8	59	27/198	70.1
Opponents	430	252	2876	58.6	6.69	22	5.1	10	2.3	t80	35/196	86.2

HOUSTON TEXANS
AFC SOUTH DIVISION

2006 SEASON

CLUB DIRECTORY

Chairman and chief executive officer
Bob McNair
Vice chairman
Phillip Burguieres
Senior vice president and general manager of football operations
Charley Casserly
VP/communications
Tony Wyllie
Director of pro scouting
Chuck Banker
Coordinator of college scouting
Mike Maccagnan
Vice president/operations
Barry Asimos
Director of media relations
Kevin Cooper
Director of community relations
Regina Woolfolk

Head coach
Gary Kubiak

Assistant coaches
Martin Bayless (asst. defensive backs)
John Benton (offensive line)
Troy Calhoun (offensive coordinator/quarterbacks)
Chick Harris (running backs)
Jon Hoke (defensive backs)
Johnny Holland (linebackers)
Bob Karmelowicz (defensive line)
Joe Marciano (special teams coordinator)
Mike McDaniel (offensive quality control)
Brian Pariani (tight ends)
Robert Saleh (defensive quality control)
Kyle Shanahan (wide receivers)
Mike Sherman (asst. head coach/offense)
Richard Smith (defensive coordinator)
Tracy Simien (asst. defensive line)

OFFSEASON MOVES

Key additions

LB	Sam Cowart	FA/Vikings
FB	Jameel Cook	FA/Bucs
C	Mike Flanagan	FA/Packers
WR	Eric Moulds	trade/Bills
TE	Jeb Putzier	FA/Broncos
QB	Sage Rosenfels	FA/Dolphins
WR	Kevin Walter	FA/Bengals
DE	Anthony Weaver	FA/Ravens

Key losses

WR	Corey Bradford	FA/Lions
G	Milford Brown	FA/Cardinals
S	Marcus Coleman	released/Cowboys
LB	Jerry DeLoach	released
WR	Jabar Gaffney	FA/Eagles
RB	Moran Norris	released
DT	Gary Walker	released
C	Todd Washington	released

SCHEDULE

Sept.	10—PHILADELPHIA	1:00
Sept.	17—at Indianapolis	1:00
Sept.	24—WASHINGTON	1:00
Oct.	1—MIAMI	1:00
Oct.	8—Open date	
Oct.	15—at Dallas	1:00
Oct.	22—JACKSONVILLE	1:00
Oct.	29—at Tennessee	1:00
Nov.	5—at N.Y. Giants	1:00
Nov.	12—at Jacksonville	1:00
Nov.	19—BUFFALO	1:00
Nov.	26—at N.Y. Jets	1:00
Dec.	3—at Oakland	4:05
Dec.	10—TENNESSEE	1:00
Dec.	17—at New England	1:00
Dec.	24—INDIANAPOLIS	1:00
Dec.	31—CLEVELAND	1:00

All times are Eastern.
All games Sunday unless noted.

DRAFT CHOICES

Mario Williams, DE, N.C. State (first round/first pick overall).
DeMeco Ryans, OLB, Alabama (2/33).
Charles Spencer, OT, Pittsburgh (3/65).
Eric Winston, OT, Miami (3/66).
Owen Daniels, TE, Wisconsin (4/98).
Wali Lundy, RB, Virginia (6/170).
David Anderson, WR, Colorado State (7/251).

MISCELLANEOUS TEAM DATA

Stadium (capacity, surface):
Reliant Stadium (71,054, grass)
Business address:
Two Reliant Park
Houston, TX 77054
Business phone:
832-667-2000
Ticket information:
832-667-2002
Team colors:
Deep steel blue, battle red, liberty white
Flagship radio station:
KILT, 610 AM
Website:
www.houstontexans.com
Training site:
Reliant Park practice facility
Houston, TX
832-667-2000

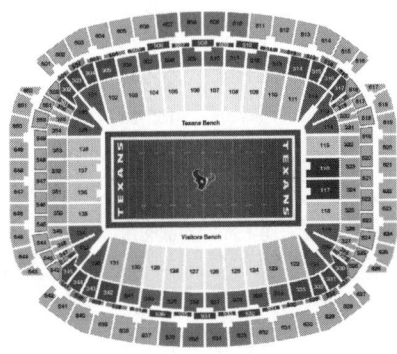

2006 TRAINING CAMP ROSTER

HOUSTON TEXANS

No.	QUARTERBACKS	Ht./Wt.	Born	NFL Exp.	College	How acq.	'05 Games GP/GS
8	David Carr	6-3/220	7/21/79	5	Fresno State	D1/02	16/16
15	Dave Ragone	6-3/245	10/3/79	4	Louisville	D3c/03	0/0
18	Sage Rosenfels	6-4/222	3/6/78	6	Iowa State	FA/06	4/1
	RUNNING BACKS						
43	Jameel Cook (FB)	5-10/237	2/8/79	6	Illinois	FA/06	16/0
37	Domanick Davis	5-9/221	10/1/80	4	LSU	D4/03	11/11
33	Wali Lundy	5-10/214	9/8/83	R	Virginia	D6/06	—
34	Vernand Morency	5-10/212	2/4/80	2	Oklahoma State	D3/05	13/1
32	Antowain Smith	6-2/232	3/14/72	10	Houston	FA/06	16/7
	RECEIVERS						
14	David Anderson	5-11/192	7/28/83	R	Colorado State	D7/06	—
88	Derick Armstrong	6-2/206	4/2/79	4	Arkansas-Monticello	FA/03	13/3
87	Mark Bruener (TE)	6-4/258	9/16/72	12	Washington	FA/04	16/15
81	Owen Daniels (TE)	6-4/253	11/9/82	R	Wisconsin	D4/06	—
86	Chris Doering	6-4/201	5/19/73	6	Florida	FA/06	0/0
80	Andre Johnson	6-3/219	7/11/81	4	Miami	D1/03	13/13
83	Bennie Joppru	6-4/260	1/5/80	4	Michigan	D2/03	0/0
13	Jerome Mathis	5-11/181	7/26/83	2	Hampton	D4/05	12/0
11	Donovan Morgan	6-2/187	7/29/82	2	Louisiana-Lafayette	FA/05	3/0
84	Eric Moulds	6-2/210	7/17/73	11	Mississippi State	T-Buf/06	15/15
79	Matt Murphy (TE)	6-5/260	2/23/80	4	Maryland	FA/03	9/2
89	Jeb Putzier (TE)	6-4/256	1/20/79	5	Boise State	FA/06	16/4
17	Kendrick Starling	6-0/193	12/27/79	3	Auburn	FA/04	0/0
82	Ben Steele (TE)	6-5/250	5/27/78	2	Mesa State	FA/06	2/0
85	Kevin Walter	6-3/218	8/4/81	4	Eastern Michigan	FA/06	16/2
	OFFENSIVE LINEMEN						
58	Mike Flanagan (C)	6-5/301	11/10/73	9	UCLA	FA/06	14/14
63	Drew Hodgdon (C)	6-3/296	11/15/81	2	Arizona State	D5/05	4/3
62	David Loverne (G)	6-3/299	5/22/76	5	San Jose State	FA/06	0/0
76	Steve McKinney (G)	6-4/302	10/15/75	9	Texas A&M	FA/02	16/16
48	Bryan Pittman (C)	6-3/275	1/20/77	4	Washington	FA/03	16/0
69	Chester Pitts (G)	6-4/329	6/26/79	5	San Diego State	D2b/02	16/16
76	Ephraim Salaam (T)	6-7/295	6/19/76	9	San Diego State	FA/06	5/2
77	Charles Spencer (T)	6-5/352	3/17/82	R	Pitt	D3a/06	—
71	Todd Wade (T)	6-8/317	10/30/76	7	Mississippi	FA/04	9/9
78	Seth Wand (T)	6-7/330	8/6/79	4	NW Missouri State	D3b/03	13/0
70	Fred Weary (G)	6-4/308	9/30/77	5	Tennessee	D3a/02	4/4
72	Zach Wiegert (T)	6-5/305	8/16/72	12	Nebraska	FA/03	12/12
73	Eric Winston (T)	6-7/310	11/17/83	R	Miami	D3b/06	—
	DEFENSIVE LINEMEN						
93	Jason Babin (E)	6-2/259	5/24/80	3	Western Michigan	D1b/04	12/3
75	Travis Johnson (E)	6-4/296	4/26/82	2	Florida State	D1/05	15/3
94	N.D. Kalu (E)	6-3/265	8/3/75	9	Rice	FA/06	15/8
97	Alfred Malone (T)	6-5/308	2/21/82	2	Troy	FA/05	2/0
91	Seth Payne (T)	6-4/315	2/12/75	10	Cornell	ED/02	16/14
98	Antwan Peek (E)	6-3/238	10/29/79	4	Cincinnati	D3a/03	16/16
99	Robaire Smith (T)	6-4/328	11/15/77	7	Michigan State	FA/04	16/16
92	Anthony Weaver (E)	6-3/290	7/28/80	5	Notre Dame	FA/06	10/8
90	Mario Williams (E)	6-7/295	1/31/85	R	N.C. State	D1/06	—
	LINEBACKERS						
50	Charlie Anderson	6-4/243	12/8/81	3	Mississippi	D6/04	16/0
57	Sam Cowart	6-2/245	2/26/75	8	Florida State	FA/06	15/14
54	Troy Evans	6-1/237	12/3/77	5	Cincinnati	FA/02	16/0
56	Morlon Greenwood	6-0/238	7/17/78	6	Syracuse	FA/05	16/16
53	Shantee Orr	6-0/250	5/28/81	4	Michigan	FA/03	16/12
51	DaShon Polk	6-2/240	3/13/77	7	Arizona	FA/04	16/11
96	Wali Rainer	6-2/240	4/19/77	8	Virginia	FA/06	16/5
59	DeMeco Ryans	6-2/236	7/28/84	R	Alabama	D2/06	—
52	Kailee Wong	6-2/246	5/23/76	9	Stanford	FA/02	5/5
	DEFENSIVE BACKS						
24	C.C. Brown (S)	6-0/208	1/27/83	2	La-Lafayette	D6/05	16/13
31	Phillip Buchanon (CB)	5-10/185	9/19/80	5	Miami (Fla.)	T-Oak/05	10/6
26	Glenn Earl (S)	6-1/215	6/10/81	3	Notre Dame	D4/04	10/7
38	Demarcus Faggins (CB)	5-10/180	6/13/79	5	Kansas State	D6a/02	13/10
28	Chris McKenzie (CB)	5-8/182	3/17/82	2	Arizona State	FA/05	3/0
23	Dunta Robinson (CB)	5-10/174	4/11/82	3	South Carolina	D1/04	16/16
21	Lewis Sanders (CB)	6-1/210	6/22/78	7	Maryland	FA/05	12/3
30	Jason Simmons (S)	5-9/199	3/30/76	9	Arizona State	FA/02	14/1
42	Michael Stone (S)	6-0/201	2/13/78	5	Memphis	FA/06	13/3
22	Ramon Walker (S)	6-0/212	11/8/79	4	Pittsburgh	D5b/02	16/0
	SPECIALISTS						
3	Kris Brown (K)	5-11/205	12/23/76	8	Nebraska	FA/02	16/0
7	Chad Stanley (P)	6-3/216	1/29/76	7	Stephen F. Austin	FA/02	16/0

Abbreviations: D1-draft pick, first round; W-claimed on waivers; T-obtained in trade; FA-free-agent acquisition.

2005 regular-season record: 2-14
Position: 4th in AFC South

Sept.11—at Buffalo	L	7-22	
Sept.18—PITTSBURGH	L	7-27	
Sept.25—Open date			
Oct. 2—at Cincinnati	L	10-16	
Oct. 9—TENNESSEE	L	20-34	
Oct. 16—at Seattle	L	10-42	
Oct. 23—INDIANAPOLIS	L	20-38	
Oct. 30—CLEVELAND	W	19-16	
Nov. 6—at Jacksonville	L	14-21	
Nov.13—at Indianapolis	L	17-31	
Nov.20—KANSAS CITY	L	17-45	
Nov.27—ST. LOUIS (OT)	L	27-33	
Dec. 4—at Baltimore	L	15-16	
Dec.11—at Tennessee	L	10-13	
Dec.18—ARIZONA	W	30-19	
Dec.24—JACKSONVILLE	L	20-38	
Jan. 1—at San Francisco (OT)	L	17-20	

SCORING BY PERIODS

	Q1	Q2	Q3	Q4	OT	Pts.
Texans	40	111	64	45	0	260
Opponents	84	115	83	140	9	431

TEAM STATISTICS

	Hou.	Opp.
TOTAL FIRST DOWNS ..	243	348
Rushing	89	123
Passing	142	188
Penalty	12	37
3rd Down: Made/Att. ..	75/219	75/196
3rd Down Pct.	34.2	38.3
4th Down: Made/Att.	8/17	13/20
4th Down Pct.	47.1	65.0
POSSESSION AVG.	28:10	31:50
TOTAL NET YARDS	4053	5824
Avg. per Game	253.3	364.0
Total Plays	954	1012
Avg. per Play	4.2	5.8
NET YARDS RUSHING ..	1816	2303
Avg. per Game	113.5	143.9
Total Rushes	437	506
NET YARDS PASSING ..	2237	3521
Avg. per Game	139.8	220.1
Sacked/Yards Lost	68/424	37/206
Gross Yards	2661	3727
Att./Completions	449/270	469/304
Completion Pct.	60.1	64.8
Had Intercepted	13	7
PUNTS/AVERAGE	77/38.8	63/40.1
NET PUNTING AVG.	77/35.7	63/34.4
PENALTIES/YARDS	106/854	105/846
FUMBLES/LOST	30/11	24/9
TOUCHDOWNS	26	50
Rushing	9	21

	Hou.	Opp.
Passing	15	24
Returns	2	5

SCORING (NONKICKERS)

	Tot. TD	RTD	PTD	MTD	2Pt.	Tot. Pts.
D. Davis	6	2	4	0	0	36
Bradford	5	0	5	0	1	32
Wells	4	4	0	0	0	24
Mathis	3	0	1	2	0	18
Gaffney	2	0	2	0	0	12
An. Johnson	2	0	2	0	0	12
Morency	2	2	0	0	0	12
Carr	1	1	0	0	0	6
Norris	1	0	1	0	0	6
Texans	26	9	15	2	1	158
Opponents	50	21	24	5	0	300

2-Pt. conversions: Texans 1-2; Opponents 0-2.

(KICKERS)

	XPM/XPA	FGM/FGA	Pts.
K. Brown	24/24	26/34	102
Texans	24/24	26/34	102
Opponents	47/47	28/32	131

RUSHING

	Att.	Yds.	Avg.	Lg.	TD
D. Davis	230	976	4.2	44	2
Wells	90	325	3.6	t14	4
Carr	56	308	5.5	20	1
Morency	46	184	4.0	t25	2
Gaffney	4	13	3.3	10	0
An. Johnson	6	10	1.7	5	0
K. Brown	1	4	4.0	4	0
Stanley	1	0	0.0	0	0
Banks	2	-2	-1.0	-1	0
Bradford	1	-2	-2.0	-2	0
Texans	437	1816	4.2	44	9
Opponents	506	2303	4.6	49	21

RECEIVING

	No.	Yds.	Avg.	Lg.	TD
An. Johnson	63	688	10.9	t53	2
Gaffney	55	492	8.9	29	2
D. Davis	39	337	8.6	33	4
Bradford	34	436	12.8	t50	5
Rivers	24	168	7.0	20	0
Wells	22	179	8.1	20	0
Morency	10	87	8.7	16	0
Armstrong	9	115	12.8	28	0
Mathis	5	65	13.0	t34	1
Morgan	4	42	10.5	14	0
Bruener	2	22	11.0	19	0
Murphy	2	26	13.0	14	0
Norris	1	4	4.0	t4	1
Texans	270	2661	9.9	t53	15
Opponents	304	3727	12.3	t56	24

HOUSTON TEXANS

INTERCEPTIONS

	No.	Yds.	Avg.	Lg.	TD
Earl	2	2	1.0	2	0
Sanders	1	29	29.0	29	0
Coleman	1	6	6.0	6	0
C. Brown	1	5	5.0	5	0
Evans	1	3	3.0	3	0
Robinson	1	1	1.0	1	0
Texans	7	46	6.6	29	0
Opponents	13	225	17.3	t57	3

SACKS: Orr 7.0, Peek 6.0, Babin 4.0, Payne 4.0, Polk 3.5, Greenwood 2.0, Smith 1.5, C. Anderson 1.0, DeLoach 1.0, T. Johnson 1.0, Malone 1.0, McKenzie 1.0, Robinson 1.0, Simmons 1.0, G. Walker 1.0, Wong 1.0. Texans 37.0; Opponents 68.0.

PUNTING

	No.	Yds.	Avg.	In. 20	Lg.
Stanley	77	2990	38.8	29	61
Texans	77	2990	38.8	29	61
Opponents	63	2528	40.1	17	59

PUNT RETURNS

	No.	FC	Yds.	Avg.	Lg.	TD
Buchanon	12	6	101	8.4	37	0
Mathis	12	6	68	5.7	19	0
D. Davis	3	1	24	8.0	21	0
Morgan	3	0	30	10.0	23	0
Texans	30	7	223	7.4	37	0
Opponents	33	27	219	6.6	t52	1

KICK RETURNS

	No.	Yds.	Avg.	Lg.	TD
Mathis	54	1542	28.6	t99	2
Morency	20	437	21.9	31	0
Wells	5	106	21.2	40	0
Hollings	2	46	23.0	28	0
Bruener	1	11	11.0	11	0
D. Davis	1	29	29.0	29	0
Norris	1	2	2.0	2	0
Texans	84	2173	25.9	t99	2
Opponents	55	1194	21.7	71	0

FIELD GOALS

	1-19	20-29	30-39	40-49	50+
K. Brown	0/0	9/9	12/17	4/6	1/2
Texans	0/0	9/9	12/17	4/6	1/2
Opponents	0/0	9/9	11/11	7/10	1/2

K. Brown: () () (28G) (32G, 38G, 43G, 47G) (39G, 56N) () (38G, 37G, 35G, 38N, 40G) () (24G) (22G) (39G, 46N, 35G) (39G, 26G, 22G, 29G, 39G) (30G, 37B, 31N) (27G, 41G, 26G) (37G, 53G, 38N, 48N) (21G, 31N)
Opponents: (35G, 21G, 42G, 39G, 31G) (37G, 35G) (24G, 42N, 27G, 46G) (52G, 58N, 49G) () (36G) (28G, 29G, 37G) () (45G) (35G) (37G, 47G) (38G) (46N, 23G, 21G) (26G, 42G) (40N, 26G) (42G, 33G)

PASSING

	Att.	Cmp.	Yds.	Pct.	Avg. Gain	TD	Pct. TD	Int.	Pct. Int.	Long	Sack/Lost	Rating
Carr	423	256	2488	60.5	5.88	14	3.3	11	2.6	t53	68/424	77.2
Banks	25	14	173	56.0	6.92	1	4.0	2	8.0	31	0/0	57.6
D. Davis	1	0	0	0.0	0.00	0	0.0	0	0.0	...	0/0	39.6
Texans	449	270	2661	60.1	5.93	15	3.3	13	2.9	t53	68/424	76.0
Opponents	469	304	3727	64.8	7.95	24	5.1	7	1.5	t56	37/206	100.0

INDIANAPOLIS COLTS
AFC SOUTH DIVISION

INDIANAPOLIS COLTS

2006 SEASON

CLUB DIRECTORY

Owner and CEO
James Irsay
President
Bill Polian
Senior executive vice president
Pete Ward
Vice president of football operations
Chris Polian
Assistant general manager/scouting
Dom Anile
Executive vice president
Bob Terpening
Executive director of administration
Bill Brooks
Vice president of public relations
Craig Kelley
Director of pro personnel
Clyde Powers
Director of college scouting
Mike Butler
Director of player development
Steve Champlin
**Director of community relations/
marketing communications**
Nicole Duncan

Head coach
Tony Dungy

Assistant coaches
Jim Caldwell (asst. coach/
quarterbacks)
Clyde Christensen (wide receivers)
Leslie Frazier (special asst. to the
head coach/defensive backs)
Richard Howell (asst. strength
and conditioning)
Gene Huey (running backs)
Ron Meeks (defensive
coordinator)
Pete Metzelaars (offensive quality
control)
Tom Moore (offensive
coordinator)
Howard Mudd (offensive line)
Mike Murphy (linebackers)
Russ Purnell (special teams)
Diron Reynolds (defensive quality
control)
John Teerlinck (defensive line)
Ricky Thomas (tight ends)
Jon Torine (strength and
conditioning)
Alan Williams (defensive backs)

OFFSEASON MOVES

Key additions
K   Adam Vinatieri   FA/Patriots
Key losses
RB Edgerrin James   FA/Cardinals
LB David Thornton   FA/Titans
DT Larry Tripplett   FA/Bills
K   Mike Vanderjagt   FA/Cowboys

SCHEDULE

Sept.	10—at N.Y. Giants	8:15
Sept.	17—HOUSTON	1:00
Sept.	24—JACKSONVILLE	1:00
Oct.	1—at N.Y. Jets	1:00
Oct.	8—TENNESSEE	1:00
Oct.	15—Open date	
Oct.	22—WASHINGTON	4:15
Oct.	29—at Denver	4:15
Nov.	5—at New England	8:15
Nov.	12—BUFFALO	1:00
Nov.	19—at Dallas	1:00
Nov.	26—PHILADELPHIA	1:00
Dec.	3—at Tennessee	1:00
Dec.	10—at Jacksonville	1:00
Dec.	18—CINCINNATI (Mon.)	8:30
Dec.	24—at Houston	1:00
Dec.	31—MIAMI	1:00

All times are Eastern.
All games Sunday unless noted.

DRAFT CHOICES

Joseph Addai, RB, LSU, (first round/30th
pick overall).
Tim Jennings, CB, Georgia (2/62).
Freddie Keiaho, ILB, San Diego State
(3/94).
Michael Toudouze, G, Texas Christian
(5/162).
Charlie Johnson, OT, Oklahoma State
(6/199).
Antoine Bethea, FS, Howard (6/207).
T.J. Rushing, CB, Stanford (7/238).

MISCELLANEOUS TEAM DATA

Stadium (capacity, surface):
RCA Dome (55,506, FieldTurf)
Business address:
P.O. Box 535000
Indianapolis, IN 46253
Business phone:
317-297-2658
Ticket information:
317-297-7000
Team colors:
Royal blue and white
Flagship radio stations:
WNDE, 1260 AM
WFBQ, 94.7 FM
Website:
www.colts.com
Training site:
Rose Hulman Technical Institute
Terre Haute, Ind.
812-872-6885

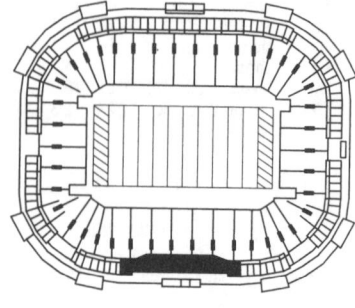

No.	QUARTERBACKS	Ht./Wt.	Born	NFL Exp.	College	How acq.	'05 Games GP/GS
18	Peyton Manning	6-5/230	3/24/76	9	Tennessee	D1/98	16/16
12	Jim Sorgi	6-5/196	12/3/80	3	Wisconsin	D6b/04	5/0
	RUNNING BACKS						
29	Joseph Addai	5-11/214	5/3/83	R	LSU	D1/06	—
31	Kory Chapman	6-1/202	7/13/80	2	Jacksonville St.	FA/05	3/0
23	James Mungro	5-9/214	2/13/78	5	Syracuse	W-Det/02	12/0
34	Vashon Pearson	5-10/205	1/23/83	1	Mississippi	FA/05	0/0
33	Dominic Rhodes	5-9/203	1/17/79	5	Midwestern State	FA/01	13/1
	RECEIVERS						
10	Roscoe Crosby	6-2/210	2/6/83	1	Clemson	FA/05	0/0
14	Montiese Culton	6-2/180	1/18/82	1	Tulsa	FA/05	0/0
44	Dallas Clark (TE)	6-3/252	6/12/79	4	Iowa	D1/03	15/14
81	Bryan Fletcher (TE)	6-5/230	3/23/79	2	UCLA	FA/04	16/12
88	Marvin Harrison	6-0/175	8/25/72	11	Syracuse	D1/96	15/15
80	Ben Hartsock (TE)	6-4/262	7/5/80	3	Ohio State	D3/04	7/0
85	Aaron Moorehead	6-3/200	11/5/80	4	Illinois	FA/03	2/0
48	Justin Snow (TE)	6-3/240	12/21/76	7	Baylor	FA/00	16/0
84	John Standeford	6-4/206	4/15/82	1	Purdue	FA/05	0/0
83	Brandon Stokley	5-11/197	6/23/76	8	La-Lafayette	FA/03	15/4
86	Ben Utecht (TE)	6-6/249	6-30-81	2	Minnesota	FA/04	12/2
87	Reggie Wayne	6-0/198	11/17/78	6	Miami	D1/01	16/16
	OFFENSIVE LINEMEN						
71	Ryan Diem (T)	6-6/331	7/1/79	6	Northern Illinois	D4/01	14/14
76	Makoa Freitas (T)	6-4/307	11/23/79	4	Arizona	D6b/03	0/0
57	Dylan Gandy (G)	6-3/300	3/8/82	2	Texas Tech	D4a/05	16/2
78	Tarik Glenn (T)	6-5/332	5/25/76	10	California	D1/97	16/16
74	Charlie Johnson (T)	6-4/298	5/2/84	R	Oklahoma State	D6a/06	—
62	Mike Johnson (C)	6-4/290	3/26/82	1	Kansas State	FA/05	0/0
67	Bo Lacy (T)	6-4/303	11/22/80	1	Arkansas	FA/05	0/0
65	Ryan Lilja (G)	6-2/285	10/15/81	3	Kansas State	FA/04	16/16
63	Jeff Saturday (C)	6-2/295	6/8/75	8	North Carolina	FA/99	16/16
73	Jake Scott (G)	6-5/280	4/16/81	3	Idaho	D5/04	16/16
75	Michael Toudouze (T)	6-7/310	4/27/83	R	Texas Christian	D5/06	—
69	Matt Ulrich (G)	6-2/309	12/30/81	2	Northwestern	FA/05	5/0
	DEFENSIVE LINEMEN						
79	Raheem Brock (E)	6-4/274	6/10/78	5	Temple	D7/02	16/16
72	Vincent Burns (T)	6-2/260	6/21/81	1	Kentucky	D3/05	0/0
93	Dwight Freeney (E)	6-1/268	2/19/80	5	Syracuse	D1/02	16/13
98	Robert Mathis (E)	6-2/235	2/26/81	4	Alabama A&M	D5a/03	13/0
90	Montae Reagor (T)	6-3/285	6/29/77	8	Texas Tech	FA/03	13/12
95	Darrell Reid (T)	6-2/288	6/20/82	2	Minnesota	FA/05	8/1
97	Corey Simon (T)	6-2/293	3/2/77	7	Florida State	W-Phi./05	13/13
91	Josh Thomas (E)	6-5/271	6/26/81	3	Syracuse	FA/04	12/2
99	Jonathan Welsh (E)	6-3/244	6/9/82	2	Wisconsin	D5a/05	6/0
	LINEBACKERS						
58	Gary Brackett	5-11/235	5/23/80	4	Rutgers	FA/03	16/16
51	Gilbert Gardner	6-1/228	5/9/82	3	Purdue	D3/04	11/3
55	Jonathan Goddard	6-0/248	5/11/81	2	Marshall	FA/05	1/0
56	Tyjuan Hagler	6-0/236	12/3/81	1	Cincinnati	D5c/05	0/0
59	Cato June	6-0/227	11/18/79	4	Michigan	D6a/03	13/13
54	Freddie Keiaho	5-11/232	12/18/82	R	San Diego State	D3/06	—
40	Chris Laskowski	5-9/210	9/12/81	1	Florida Atlantic	FA/05	0/0
94	Rob Morris	6-2/243	1/18/75	7	Brigham Young	D1/00	14/0
53	Keith O'Neil	6-0/235	8/26/80	4	Northern Arizona	W-Dal/05	11/0
52	Keyon Whiteside	6-0/229	1/31/80	4	Tennessee	D5b/03	0/0
	DEFENSIVE BACKS						
41	Antoine Bethea (S)	5-11/203	7/27/84	R	Howard	D6b/06	—
42	Jason David (CB)	5-8/172	6/12/82	3	Washington State	D4b/04	16/16
20	Mike Doss (S)	5-10/207	3/24/81	4	Ohio State	D2/03	15/14
43	Matt Giordano (S)	5-10/196	10/16/82	2	California	D4b/05	15/0
25	Nick Harper (CB)	5-10/182	9/10/74	6	Fort Valley State	FA/01	15/15
26	Kelvin Hayden (CB)	5-10/190	7/23/83	2	Illinois	D2/05	16/0
27	Von Hutchins (CB)	5-9/181	2/14/81	3	Mississippi	D6/04	3/0
28	Marlin Jackson (CB/S)	6-1/198	6/30/83	2	Michigan	D1/05	15/1
35	Tim Jennings (CB)	5-8/185	12/24/83	R	Georgia	D2/06	—
36	Dexter Reid (S)	5-11/203	3/18/81	3	North Carolina	W-NE/05	16/0
45	T.J. Rushing (CB)	5-10/180	6/8/83	R	Stanford	D7/06	—
21	Bob Sanders (S)	5-8/206	2/24/81	3	Iowa	D2/04	14/14
38	Gerome Sapp (S)	6-1/216	2/8/81	4	Notre Dame	FA/04	16/2
	SPECIALISTS						
17	Hunter Smith (P)	6-2/209	8/9/77	8	Notre Dame	D7a/99	16/0
4	Adam Vinatieri (K)	6-0/202	12/28/72	11	South Dakota St.	FA/06	16/0

Abbreviations: D1-draft pick, first round; W-claimed on waivers; T-obtained in trade; FA-free-agent acquisition.

INDIANAPOLIS COLTS

INDIANAPOLIS COLTS

2005 regular-season record: 14-2
Position: 1st in AFC South

Sept.11—at Baltimore	W	24-7
Sept.18—JACKSONVILLE	W	10-3
Sept.25—CLEVELAND	W	13-6
Oct. 2—at Tennessee	W	31-10
Oct. 9—at San Francisco	W	28-3
Oct. 17—ST. LOUIS	W	45-28
Oct. 23—at Houston	W	38-20
Oct. 30—Open date		
Nov. 7—at New England	W	40-21
Nov.13—HOUSTON	W	31-17
Nov.20—at Cincinnati	W	45-37
Nov.28—PITTSBURGH	W	26-7
Dec. 4—TENNESSEE	W	35-3
Dec.11—at Jacksonville	W	26-18
Dec.18—SAN DIEGO	L	17-26
Dec.24—at Seattle	L	13-28
Jan. 1—ARIZONA	W	17-13

2005 postseason record: 0-1

Jan. 15—PITTSBURGH*	L	18-21

*AFC divisional playoff game.

SCORING BY PERIODS

	Q1	Q2	Q3	Q4	OT	Pts.
Colts	90	122	119	108	0	439
Opponents	61	63	47	76	0	247

TEAM STATISTICS

	Ind.	Opp.
TOTAL FIRST DOWNS ..	363	269
Rushing	116	91
Passing	217	163
Penalty	30	15
3rd Down: Made/Att. ..	91/187	76/207
3rd Down Pct.	48.7	36.7
4th Down: Made/Att. ..	8/13	14/24
4th Down Pct.	61.5	58.3
POSSESSION AVG.	30:22	29:38
TOTAL NET YARDS	5799	4913
Avg. per Game	362.4	307.1
Total Plays	1000	953
Avg. per Play	5.8	5.2
NET YARDS RUSHING ..	1703	1762
Avg. per Game	106.4	110.1
Total Rushes	465	398
NET YARDS PASSING....	4096	3151
Avg. per Game	256.0	196.9
Sacked/Yards Lost	20/95	46/318
Gross Yards	4191	3469
Att./Completions	515/347	509/343
Completion Pct.	67.4	67.4
Had Intercepted	11	18
PUNTS/AVERAGE	52/44.3	67/41.7
NET PUNTING AVG.	52/37.1	67/36.9
PENALTIES/YARDS	94/690	119/857
FUMBLES/LOST	14/8	32/13
TOUCHDOWNS	53	27

	Ind.	Opp.
Rushing	18	9
Passing	31	17
Returns	4	1

SCORING (NONKICKERS)

	Tot. TD	RTD	PTD	MTD	2Pt.	Tot. Pts.
James	14	13	1	0	0	84
Harrison	12	0	12	0	0	72
Wayne	5	0	5	0	0	30
Clark	4	0	4	0	0	24
Rhodes	4	4	0	0	0	24
Fletcher	3	0	3	0	0	18
Walters	3	0	3	0	0	18
June	2	0	0	2	0	12
Utecht	2	0	2	0	0	12
Carthon	1	1	0	0	0	6
Reagor	1	0	0	1	0	6
Stokley	1	0	1	0	0	6
Tripplett	1	0	0	1	0	6
Colts	53	18	31	4	0	318
Opponents	27	9	17	1	2	166

2-Pt. conversions: Colts 0-1; Opponents 2-3.

(KICKERS)

	XPM/XPA	FGM/FGA	Pts.
Vanderjagt	52/52	23/25	121
Colts	52/52	23/26	121
Opponents	24/24	19/27	81

RUSHING

	Att.	Yds.	Avg.	Lg.	TD
James	360	1506	4.2	33	13
Rhodes	40	118	3.0	24	4
Manning	33	45	1.4	12	0
Carthon	13	18	1.4	7	1
Mungro	7	15	2.1	7	0
Sorgi	12	1	0.1	6	0
Colts	465	1703	3.7	33	18
Opponents	398	1762	4.4	t83	9

RECEIVING

	No.	Yds.	Avg.	Lg.	TD
Wayne	83	1055	12.7	t66	5
Harrison	82	1146	14.0	t80	12
James	44	337	7.7	20	1
Stokley	41	543	13.2	45	1
Clark	37	488	13.2	56	4
Fletcher	18	202	11.2	23	3
Walters	14	152	10.9	39	3
Rhodes	12	88	7.3	15	0
Moorehead	7	75	10.7	24	0
Mungro	3	28	9.3	17	0
Utecht	3	59	19.7	t26	2
Hartsock	2	8	4.0	7	0
Carthon	1	10	10.0	10	0
Colts	347	4191	12.1	t80	31
Opponents	343	3469	10.1	t68	17

INTERCEPTIONS

	No.	Yds.	Avg.	Lg.	TD
June	5	115	23.0	36	2
Brackett	3	50	16.7	31	0
Harper	3	41	13.7	21	0
David	2	13	6.5	13	0
Doss	2	8	4.0	8	0
Gardner	1	16	16.0	16	0
Jackson	1	16	16.0	16	0
Sanders	1	0	0.0	0	0
Colts	18	259	14.4	36	2
Opponents	11	136	12.4	36	0

SACKS: Mathis 11.5, Freeney 11.0, Brock 6.5, Reagor 5.5, Tripplett 4.0, Thomas 3.0, Thornton 2.0, Brackett 1.0, Gardner 1.0, Labinjo 0.5. Colts 46.0; Opponents 20.0.

PUNTING

	No.	Yds.	Avg.	In. 20	Lg.
H. Smith	52	2301	44.3	23	58
Colts	52	2301	44.3	23	58
Opponents	67	2791	41.7	17	62

PUNT RETURNS

	No.	FC	Yds.	Avg.	Lg.	TD
Walters	21	25	172	8.2	29	0
David	1	0	0	0.0	0	0
Harrison	1	0	10	10.0	10	0
Jackson	1	0	0	0.0	0	0
Colts	24	25	182	7.6	29	0
Opponents	25	15	272	10.9	29	0

KICK RETURNS

	No.	Yds.	Avg.	Lg.	TD
Rhodes	41	855	20.9	39	0
Carthon	5	92	18.4	25	0
Mungro	2	39	19.5	22	0
Jefferson	1	11	11.0	11	0
Utecht	1	7	7.0	7	0
Walters	1	13	13.0	13	0
Colts	51	1017	19.9	39	0
Opponents	89	1978	22.2	t89	1

FIELD GOALS

	1-19	20-29	30-39	40-49	50+
Vanderjagt	1/1	9/9	6/7	7/8	0/0
Rayner	0/0	0/0	0/0	0/0	0/1
Colts	1/1	9/9	6/7	7/8	0/1
Opponents	0/0	8/8	3/5	8/12	0/2

Vanderjagt: (20G) (41G) (20G, 23G) (20G) () (48N, 22G) (36G) (35G, 20G) (45G) (19G) (29G, 48G, 44G, 28G) () (40G, 34G, 38G, 46G) (32G) (24G, 31B, 32G) (44G)

Rayner: () () () () () () () () () () () () () (59N) () ()

Opponents: (38N, 47N, 45N) (42N, 28G) (40G, 22G) (34G, 38N) (30G) (29G, 49G) () () (24G) (43G, 41G, 44G) (41N) (51N, 24G) (27G) (36G, 20G, 48G, 49G) (57N) (28G, 42G)

PASSING

	Att.	Cmp.	Yds.	Pct.	Avg. Gain	TD	Pct. TD	Int.	Pct. Int.	Long	Sack/Lost	Rating
Manning	453	305	3747	67.3	8.27	28	6.2	10	2.2	t80	17/81	104.1
Sorgi	61	42	444	68.9	7.28	3	4.9	1	1.6	45	3/14	99.4
H. Smith	1	0	0	0.0	0.00	0	0.0	0	0.0	...	0/0	39.6
Colts	515	347	4191	67.4	8.14	31	6.0	11	2.1	t80	20/95	103.3
Opponents	509	343	3469	67.4	6.82	17	3.3	18	3.5	t68	46/318	83.0

JACKSONVILLE JAGUARS
AFC SOUTH DIVISION

2006 SEASON

CLUB DIRECTORY

Chairman & CEO
Wayne Weaver
Senior vice president/football operations
Paul Vance
Vice president of communications & media
Dan Edwards
Vice president of player personnel
James Harris
Director of pro personnel
Charles Bailey
Director of college scouting
Gene Smith
Director of football operations
Skip Richardson

OFFSEASON MOVES

Key additions
LB	Nick Greisen	FA/Giants
OL	Stockar McDougle	FA/Dolphins
CB	Brian Williams	FA/Vikings
OL	Mike Williams	FA/Bills

Key losses
LB	Akin Ayodele	FA/Cowboys
S	Deke Cooper	FA/Dolphins
OT	Mike Pearson	FA/Dolphins
WR	Jimmy Smith	retired
LB	Tracy White	FA/Packers
LB	Jamie Winborn	FA/Bucs
CB	Kenny Wright	FA/Redskins

Head coach
Jack Del Rio

Assistant coaches
Ken Anderson (quarterbacks)
Mark Asanovich (strength and conditioning)
Dave Campo (asst. head coach/secondary)
Mark Duffner (linebackers)
Les Ebert (asst. strength and conditioning)
Ray Hamilton (defensive line)
Andy Heck (offensive line)
Mark Michaels (asst. special teams)
Ted Monachino (asst. defensive line)
Kennedy Pola (running backs)
Alvin Reynolds (defensive backs)
Alfredo Roberts (tight ends)
Pete Rodriguez (special teams coordinator)
Carl Smith (offensive coordinator)
Mike Smith (defensive coordinator)
Mike Tice (asst. head coach/offense)
Steve Walters (wide receivers)

SCHEDULE

Sept.	10—DALLAS	4:15
Sept.	18—PITTSBURGH (Mon.)	8:30
Sept.	24—at Indianapolis	1:00
Oct.	1—at Washington	4:15
Oct.	8—N.Y. JETS	4:05
Oct.	15—Open date	
Oct.	22—at Houston	1:00
Oct.	29—at Philadelphia	1:00
Nov.	5—TENNESSEE	1:00
Nov.	12—HOUSTON	1:00
Nov.	20—N.Y. GIANTS (Mon.)	8:30
Nov.	26—at Buffalo	1:00
Dec.	3—at Miami	1:00
Dec.	10—INDIANAPOLIS	1:00
Dec.	17—at Tennessee	1:00
Dec.	24—NEW ENGLAND	1:00
Dec.	31—at Kansas City	1:00

All times are Eastern.
All games Sunday unless noted.

DRAFT CHOICES

Marcedes Lewis, TE, UCLA (first round/28th pick overall).
Maurice Drew, RB, UCLA (2/60).
Clint Ingram, OLB, Oklahoma (3/80).
Brent Hawkins, DE, Illinois State (5/160).
James Wyche, DE, Syracuse (7/213).
Demetrice Webb, CB, Florida (7/236).

MISCELLANEOUS TEAM DATA

Stadium (capacity, surface):
ALLTEL Stadium (67,164, grass)
Business address:
One ALLTEL Stadium Place
Jacksonville, FL 32202
Business phone:
904-633-6000
Ticket information:
904-633-2000
Team colors:
Teal, black and gold
Flagship radio station:
WOKV, 690 AM
Website:
www.jaguars.com
Training site:
ALLTEL Stadium
Jacksonville, Fla.
904-633-6000

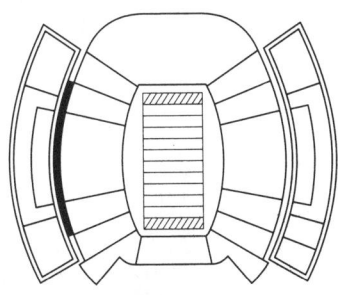

JACKSONVILLE JAGUARS

No.	QUARTERBACKS	Ht./Wt.	Born	NFL Exp.	College	How acq.	'05 Games GP/GS
9	David Garrard	6-2/244	2/14/78	5	East Carolina	D4a/02	7/5
5	Quinn Gray	6-3/246	5/21/79	2	Florida A&M	FA/03	1/0
7	Byron Leftwich	6-5/245	1/14/80	4	Marshall	D1/03	11/11
	RUNNING BACKS						
40	Rich Alexis	6-0/213	5/6/81	1	Washington	FA/05	2/0
32	Maurice Drew	5-7/206	3/23/85	R	UCLA	D2/06	—
33	Greg Jones (FB)	6-1/250	4/4/81	3	Florida State	D2/04	14/13
34	Alvin Pearman	5-9/205	8/10/82	2	Virginia	D4/05	16/0
28	Fred Taylor	6-1/234	1/27/76	8	Florida	D1a/98	11/11
22	LaBrandon Toefield	5-11/232	9/24/80	4	LSU	D4b/03	9/2
36	Derrick Wimbush (FB)	6-1/211	8/26/80	2	Fort Valley State	FA/05	14/1
	RECEIVERS						
80	Kyle Brady (TE)	6-6/278	1/14/72	12	Penn State	FA/99	16/14
85	Cortez Hankton	6-0/200	1/20/81	4	Texas Southern	FA/03	5/0
89	Kahlil Hill	6-2/200	3/18/79	1	Iowa	FA/06	0/0
86	Brian Jones (TE)	6-3/235	8/23/81	3	Arkansas-Pine Bluff	FA/04	13/1
18	Matt Jones	6-6/242	2/22/83	2	Arkansas	D1/05	16/1
89	Marcedes Lewis (TE)	6-6/252	5/19/84	R	UCLA	D1/06	—
84	Chad Owens	5-7/181	4/3/82	2	Hawaii	D6a/05	1/0
19	Ernest Wilford	6-4/223	1/14/79	3	Virginia Tech	D4/04	16/8
11	Reggie Williams	6-4/223	5/17/83	3	Washington	D1/04	16/7
87	George Wrighster (TE)	6-2/260	4/1/81	4	Oregon	D4a/03	16/6
83	Todd Yoder (TE)	6-4/250	3/18/78	7	Vanderbilt	FA/04	0/0
88	Joe Zelenka (TE)	6-3/270	3/9/76	8	Wake Forest	FA/01	16/0
	OFFENSIVE LINEMEN						
69	Khalif Barnes (T)	6-6/305	4/21/82	2	Washington	D2/05	13/12
61	Dan Connolly (G)	6-4/318	9/2/82	2	SE Missouri State	FA/05	4/0
79	Carlos Joseph (T)	6-6/334	7/14/80	1	Miami	FA/06	0/0
67	Vince Manuwai (G)	6-2/312	7/12/80	4	Hawaii	D3/03	16/16
73	Stockar McDougle (T/G)	6-6/335	1/11/77	7	Oklahoma	FA/06	8/2
63	Brad Meester (C)	6-3/300	3/23/77	7	Northern Iowa	D2/00	12/12
65	Chris Naeole (G)	6-3/320	12/25/74	10	Colorado	FA/02	15/15
62	Dennis Norman	6-5/312	1/26/80	5	Princeton	FA/05	16/4
74	Maurice Williams (T)	6-5/310	1/26/79	6	Michigan	FA/05	16/16
77	Mike Williams (T/G)	6-6/360	1/11/80	5	Texas	FA/06	9/6
	DEFENSIVE LINEMEN						
90	Omari Hand (E)	6-4/265	7/3/80	1	Tennessee	FA/05	0/0
97	Reggie Hayward (E)	6-5/270	3/14/79	6	Iowa State	FA/05	15/15
98	John Henderson (T)	6-7/328	1/9/79	5	Tennessee	D1/02	16/15
91	Anthony Maddox (T)	6-1/295	11/22/78	2	Delta State	D4a/04	5/0
93	Bobby McCray (E)	6-5/251	11/1/81	2	Florida	D7/04	16/1
92	Rob Meier (T)	6-5/293	8/29/77	7	Washington State	D7b/00	16/2
78	Elton Patterson (E)	6-2/271	6/13/81	2	Central Florida	FA/06	0/0
95	Paul Spicer (E)	6-4/287	8/18/75	6	Saginaw Valley	FA/00	15/14
99	Marcus Stroud (T)	6-6/312	6/25/78	6	Georgia	D1/01	16/16
75	Marcellus Wiley (E)	6-4/278	11/30/74	10	Columbia	FA/05	11/1
90	James Wyche (E)	6-5/262	4/19/82	R	Syracuse	D7a/06	—
	LINEBACKERS						
58	Jorge Cordova	6-2/250	9/25/81	1	Nevada	D3/04	0/0
54	Greg Favors	6-1/244	9/30/74	9	Mississippi State	FA/04	1/0
50	Tony Gilbert	6-1/244	10/16/79	4	Georgia	FA/03	16/0
54	Nick Greisen	6-1/245	8/10/79	5	Wisconsin	FA/06	16/12
57	Brent Hawkins	6-2/240	9/1/83	R	Illinois State	D5/06	—
51	Clint Ingram	6-1/244	3/21/83	R	Oklahoma	D3/06	—
59	James Kinney	6-1/240	6/5/82	1	Missouri	FA/05	0/0
54	Mike Peterson	6-1/230	6/17/76	8	Florida	FA/03	16/16
52	Daryl Smith	6-2/234	4/14/82	3	Georgia Tech	D2/04	16/16
53	Pat Thomas	6-1/237	1/26/83	2	N.C. State	D6b/05	9/0
	DEFENSIVE BACKS						
21	Terry Cousin (CB)	5-9/185	4/11/75	10	South Carolina	FA/05	16/5
20	Donovin Darius (S)	6-1/225	8/12/75	9	Syracuse	D1b/98	2/2
37	Deon Grant (S)	6-2/210	3/14/79	6	Tennessee	FA/04	16/16
27	Rashean Mathis (CB)	6-1/200	8/27/80	4	Bethune-Cookman	D2/03	16/16
26	David Richardson (CB)	6-0/202	9/9/81	3	Cal Poly	FA/04	7/0
38	Chris Roberson (CB)	5-11/185	6/3/83	2	Eastern Michigan	D7/05	6/0
43	Gerald Sensabaugh (S)	6-1/211	6/13/83	2	North Carolina	D5/05	16/2
41	Nick Sorensen (S)	6-3/210	7/31/78	6	Virginia Tech	FA/03	10/0
31	Scott Starks (CB)	5-9/172	6/27/83	2	Wisconsin	D3/05	16/0
25	Demetrice Webb (CB)	5-10/183	12/8/84	R	Florida	D7b/06	—
29	Brian Williams (CB)	5-11/198	7/2/179	5	N.C. State	FA/06	14/9
	SPECIALISTS						
2	Chris Hanson (P)	6-1/223	10/25/76	6	Marshall	FA/01	16/0
10	Josh Scobee (K)	6-1/190	6/23/82	2	Louisiana Tech	D5a/04	16/0

Abbreviations: D1-draft pick, first round; W-claimed on waivers; T-obtained in trade; FA-free-agent acquisition.

2005 REVIEW

2005 regular-season record: 12-4
Position: 2nd in AFC South

Sept.11—SEATTLE	W	26-14
Sept.18—at Indianapolis	L	3-10
Sept.25—at N.Y. Jets (OT)	W	26-20
Oct. 2—DENVER	L	7-20
Oct. 9—CINCINNATI	W	23-20
Oct. 16—at Pittsburgh (OT)	W	23-17
Oct. 23—Open date		
Oct. 30—at St. Louis	L	21-24
Nov. 6—HOUSTON	W	21-14
Nov. 13—BALTIMORE	W	30-3
Nov. 20—at Tennessee	W	31-28
Nov. 27—at Arizona	W	24-17
Dec. 4—at Cleveland	W	20-14
Dec. 11—INDIANAPOLIS	L	18-26
Dec. 18—SAN FRANCISCO	W	10-9
Dec. 24—at Houston	W	38-20
Jan. 1—TENNESSEE	W	40-13

2005 postseason record: 0-1
Jan. 7—at New England#	L	3-28

#AFC wild-card game.

SCORING BY PERIODS

	Q1	Q2	Q3	Q4	OT	Pts.
Jaguars	67	70	113	99	12	361
Opponents	30	117	36	86	0	269

TEAM STATISTICS

	Jac.	Opp.
TOTAL FIRST DOWNS ..	301	273
Rushing	97	79
Passing	170	158
Penalty	34	36
3rd Down: Made/Att. ..	93/225	67/205
3rd Down Pct.	41.3	32.7
4th Down: Made/Att. ..	4/10	4/14
4th Down Pct.	40.0	28.6
POSSESSION AVG.	31:33	28:27
TOTAL NET YARDS	5149	4655
Avg. per Game	321.8	290.9
Total Plays	1021	963
Avg. per Play	5.0	4.8
NET YARDS RUSHING ..	1959	1709
Avg. per Game	122.4	106.8
Total Rushes	502	434
NET YARDS PASSING	3190	2946
Avg. per Game	199.4	184.1
Sacked/Yards Lost	32/162	47/277
Gross Yards	3352	3223
Att./Completions	487/283	482/285
Completion Pct.	58.1	59.1
Had Intercepted	6	19
PUNTS/AVERAGE	83/42.4	88/42.8
NET PUNTING AVG.	83/36.9	88/36.7
PENALTIES/YARDS	121/1006	130/1055
FUMBLES/LOST	27/11	21/9
TOUCHDOWNS	42	30
Rushing	18	4
Passing	21	22
Returns	3	4

SCORING (NONKICKERS)

	Tot.TD	RTD	PTD	MTD	2Pt.	Tot.Pts.
Wilford	7	0	7	0	0	42
J. Smith	6	0	6	0	0	36
M. Jones	5	0	5	0	0	30
G. Jones	4	4	0	0	0	24
Toefield	4	4	0	0	0	24
Garrard	3	3	0	0	1	20
F. Taylor	3	3	0	0	0	18
Leftwich	2	2	0	0	0	12
Wimbush	2	1	0	1	0	12
Wrighster	2	0	2	0	0	12
Brady	1	0	1	0	0	6
Mathis	1	0	1	0	0	6
Pearman	1	1	0	0	0	6
Peterson	1	0	0	1	0	6
Jaguars	42	18	21	3	1	254
Opponents	30	4	22	4	0	180

2-Pt. conversions: Jaguars 1-1; Opponents 0-0.

(KICKERS)

	XPM/XPA	FGM/FGA	Pts.
Scobee	38/39	23/30	107
Jaguars	38/39	23/30	107
Opponents	29/30	20/27	89

RUSHING

	Att.	Yds.	Avg.	Lg.	TD
F. Taylor	194	787	4.1	t71	3
G. Jones	151	575	3.8	27	4
Garrard	31	172	5.5	28	3
Pearman	39	149	3.8	45	1
Toefield	36	142	3.9	t32	4
Leftwich	31	67	2.2	9	2
M. Jones	12	51	4.3	25	0
Wimbush	3	12	4.0	7	1
R. Williams	2	3	1.5	10	0
Gray	3	1	0.3	3	0
Jaguars	502	1959	3.9	t71	18
Opponents	434	1709	3.9	51	4

RECEIVING

	No.	Yds.	Avg.	Lg.	TD
J. Smith	70	1023	14.6	t45	6
Wilford	41	681	16.6	39	7
M. Jones	36	432	12.0	42	5
R. Williams	35	445	12.7	41	0
Pearman	32	240	7.5	19	0
Brady	18	157	8.7	33	1
F. Taylor	13	83	6.4	13	0
Wrighster	13	120	9.2	27	2
G. Jones	10	65	6.5	10	0
Wimbush	5	26	5.2	6	0
Hankton	3	15	5.0	8	0
B. Jones	3	49	16.3	41	0
Toefield	3	17	5.7	11	0

	No.	Yds.	Avg.	Lg.	TD
Manuwai	1	-1	-1.0	-1	0
Jaguars	283	3352	11.8	t45	21
Opponents	285	3223	11.3	t83	22

INTERCEPTIONS

	No.	Yds.	Avg.	Lg.	TD
Mathis	5	79	15.8	t41	1
Cousin	4	18	4.5	14	0
Peterson	3	54	18.0	t26	1
Grant	3	29	9.7	29	0
Wright	2	4	2.0	4	0
Cooper	1	0	0.0	0	0
D. Smith	1	0	0.0	0	0
Jaguars	19	184	9.7	t41	2
Opponents	6	90	15.0	37	0

SACKS: Hayward 8.5, Spicer 7.5, Meier 6.0, Peterson 6.0, McCray 5.5, D. Smith 4.0, Henderson 3.0, Ayodele 2.5, Grant 1.5, Maddox 1.0, Stroud 1.0, Cousin 0.5. Jaguars 47.0; Opponents 32.0.

PUNTING

	No.	Yds.	Avg.	In.20	Lg.
Hanson	82	3517	42.9	33	74
Jaguars	83	3517	42.4	33	74
Opponents	88	3763	42.8	22	75

PUNT RETURNS

	No.	FC	Yds.	Avg.	Lg.	TD
Pearman	49	15	410	8.4	24	0
Owens	3	0	6	2.0	6	0
Mathis	1	0	-1	-1.0	-1	0
Jaguars	53	15	415	7.8	24	0
Opponents	29	15	236	8.1	t72	1

KICK RETURNS

	No.	Yds.	Avg.	Lg.	TD
Wimbush	39	955	24.5	t91	1
Pearman	8	187	23.4	34	0
Alexis	1	31	31.0	31	0
Brady	1	24	24.0	24	0
G. Jones	1	0	0.0	0	0
Jaguars	50	1197	23.9	t91	1
Opponents	56	1327	23.7	85	0

FIELD GOALS

	1-19	20-29	30-39	40-49	50+
Scobee	0/0	9/9	7/8	5/10	2/3
Jaguars	0/0	9/9	7/8	5/10	2/3
Opponents	0/0	2/2	8/10	9/14	1/1

Scobee: (23G, 41G, 43N, 29G, 41G) (42N, 28G) (32G, 40G) () (32G, 51G, 53G) (23G) (49N, 44N) () (48G, 33G, 26G) (31G) (30G, 38N) (24G, 29G) (27G) (52N, 32G) (40N, 26G) (46G, 38G)
Opponents: () (41G) (35G, 25G) (41N, 46B, 33G, 42G) (31G, 48G) (29G, 46N) (41G) () (41G) () (43N, 42G) (34N) (40G, 34G, 38G, 46G) (35G, 47G, 33G) (37G, 53G, 38N, 48N) ()

PASSING

	Att.	Cmp.	Yds.	Pct.	Avg.Gain	TD	Pct.TD	Int.	Pct.Int.	Long	Sack/Lost	Rating
Leftwich	302	175	2123	57.9	7.03	15	5.0	5	1.7	t45	23/110	89.3
Garrard	168	98	1117	58.3	6.65	4	2.4	1	0.6	37	8/45	83.9
Gray	14	8	100	57.1	7.14	2	14.3	0	0.0	26	1/7	119.0
M. Jones	3	2	12	66.7	4.00	0	0.0	0	0.0	6	0/0	74.3
Jaguars	487	283	3352	58.1	6.88	21	4.3	6	1.2	t45	32/162	88.4
Opponents	482	285	3223	59.1	6.69	22	4.6	19	3.9	t83	47/277	78.0

KANSAS CITY CHIEFS
AFC WEST DIVISION

2006 SEASON

CLUB DIRECTORY

Founder
Lamar Hunt
Chairman of the board
Clark Hunt
Vice chairman of the board
Jack Steadman
President/G.M./chief executive officer
Carl Peterson
Executive vice president/assistant G.M.
Dennis Thum
VP of player personnel
Bill Kuharich
Senior vice president of administration
Bill Newman
VP of football operations
Lynn Stiles
Director of college scouting
Chuck Cook
Director of public relations
Bob Moore
Director of community relations
Brenda Sniezek

Head coach
Herm Edwards

Assistant coaches
Don Blackmon (linebackers)
Gunther Cunningham (defensive coordinator)
Dick Curl (asst. to the head coach/offense)
Jon Embree (tight ends)
David Gibbs (defensive backs)
Jeff Hurd (strength and conditioning)
Charlie Joiner (wide receivers)
Mike Ketchum (offensive asst./quality control)
Tim Krumrie (defensive line)
Billy Long (asst. strength and conditioning)
John Matsko (offensive line)
Mike Priefer (special teams)
James Saxon (running backs)
Terry Shea (quarterbacks)
Mike Solari (offensive coordinator)
Darvin Wallis (defensive asst./quality control)

OFFSEASON MOVES

Key additions
DT Ron Edwards	FA/Bills
RB Quentin Griffin	FA/Broncos
CB Lenny Walls	FA/Broncos

Key losses
LB Shawn Barber	released/Eagles
WR Marc Boerigter	FA/Packers
QB Todd Collins	FA/Redskins
WR Chris Horn	FA/Saints
CB Dexter McCleon	released
FB Tony Richardson	FA/Vikings
DE Gary Stills	FA/Ravens
CB Eric Warfield	released/Patriots

SCHEDULE

Sept. 10—CINCINNATI	1:00
Sept. 17—at Denver	4:15
Sept. 24—Open date	
Oct. 1—SAN FRANCISCO	1:00
Oct. 8—at Arizona	4:05
Oct. 15—at Pittsburgh	4:15
Oct. 22—SAN DIEGO	1:00
Oct. 29—SEATTLE	1:00
Nov. 5—at St. Louis	1:00
Nov. 12—at Miami	1:00
Nov. 19—OAKLAND	1:00
Nov. 23—DENVER (Thurs.)	8:00
Dec. 3—at Cleveland	1:00
Dec. 10—BALTIMORE	1:00
Dec. 17—at San Diego	4:05
Dec. 23—at Oakland (Sat.)	8:00
Dec. 31—JACKSONVILLE	1:00

All times are Eastern.
All games Sunday unless noted.

DRAFT CHOICES

Tamba Hali, DE, Penn State (first round/20th pick overall).
Bernard Pollard, SS, Purdue (2/54).
Brodie Croyle, QB, Alabama (3/85).
Marcus Maxey, CB, Miami (5/154).
Tre' Stallings, G, Mississippi (6/186).
Jeff Webb, WR, San Diego State (6/190).
Jarrad Page, SS, UCLA (7/228).

MISCELLANEOUS TEAM DATA

Stadium (capacity, surface):
Arrowhead Stadium
(79,451, grass)
Business address:
One Arrowhead Drive
Kansas City, MO 64129
Business phone:
816-920-9300
Ticket information:
816-920-9400
Team colors:
Red, gold and white
Flagship radio station:
KCFX, 101 FM
Website:
www.kcchiefs.com
Training site:
U. of Wisconsin-River Falls
River Falls, Wis.
715-425-4580

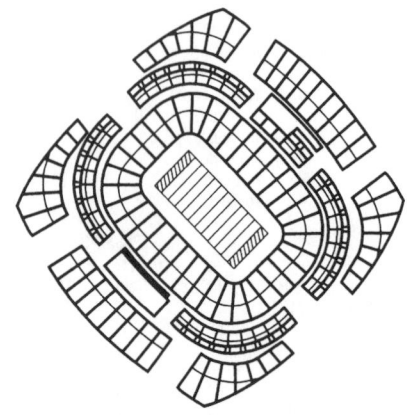

No.	QUARTERBACKS	Ht./Wt.	Born	NFL Exp.	College	How acq.	'05 Games GP/GS
4	Brodie Croyle	6-2/206	2/6/83	R	Alabama	D3/06	—
10	Trent Green	6-3/217	7/9/70	13	Indiana	T-StL/01	16/16
11	Damon Huard	6-3/215	7/9/73	9	Washington	FA/04	0/0
	Casey Printers	6-2/216	5/16/81	R	Florida A&M	FA/06	0/0
	RUNNING BACKS						
22	Dee Brown	5-10/215	5/12/78	5	Syracuse	FA/05	8/0
42	Ronnie Cruz (FB)	6-0/237	6/11/81	2	Northern State	FA/04	14/0
34	Quentin Griffin	5-7/195	1/12/81	4	Oklahoma	W-Den/06	0/0
31	Priest Holmes	5-9/213	10/7/73	10	Texas	FA/01	7/7
27	Larry Johnson	6-1/230	11/19/79	4	Penn State	D1/03	16/9
	RECEIVERS						
89	Jason Dunn (TE)	6-6/276	11/15/73	10	Eastern Kentucky	FA/00	16/1
83	Kendall Gammon (TE)	6-4/255	10/23/68	15	Pittsburg State	FA/00	10/0
88	Tony Gonzalez (TE)	6-5/251	2/27/76	10	California	D1/97	16/16
82	Dante Hall	5-8/187	9/20/78	7	Texas A&M	D5a/00	16/2
87	Eddie Kennison	6-1/201	1/20/73	11	LSU	FA/01	16/16
14	Jeris McIntyre	6-0/207	7/4/81	2	Auburn	D6/04	0/018
18	Samie Parker	5-11/190	3/25/81	3	Oregon	D4a/04	12/9
12	Craphonso Thorpe	6-1/187	6/27/83	1	Florida State	D4/05	0/0
80	Jeff Webb	6-2/211	1/31/82	R	San Diego State	D6b/06	—
84	Kris Wilson (TE/FB)	6-2/251	8/22/81	2	Pittsburgh	D2b/04	14/1
	OFFENSIVE LINEMEN						
65	Jordan Black (T)	6-5/304	1/28/80	3	Notre Dame	D5/03	16/10
67	Chris Bober (C/G)	6-5/310	12/24/76	6	Nebraska-Omaha	FA/04	16/2
66	Johnathan Ingram (C)	6-2/300	9/20/80	2	San Diego State	FA/04	2/0
77	Willie Roaf (T)	6-5/320	4/18/70	14	Louisiana Tech	T-N.O./02	10/10
79	Kevin Sampson (T)	6-4/312	6/19/81	3	Syracuse	D7/04	4/1
68	Will Shields (G)	6-3/320	9/15/71	14	Nebraska	D3/93	16/16
61	Tre Stallings (G)	6-3/315	1/8/83	R	Mississippi	D6a/06	—
71	Will Svitek (T)	6-6/300	1/8/82	2	Stanford	D6a/05	1/0
54	Brian Waters (G)	6-3/318	2/18/77	7	North Texas	FA/00	16/16
76	John Welbourn (G)	6-5/310	3/30/76	8	California	T-Phi/04	12/9
62	Casey Wiegmann (C)	6-2/285	7/20/73	11	Iowa	FA/01	16/16
	DEFENSIVE LINEMEN						
69	Jared Allen (E)	6-6/265	4/3/82	3	Idaho State	D4b/04	16/15
93	John Browning (T)	6-5/297	9/30/73	11	West Virginia	D3/96	16/12
94	Lional Dalton (T)	6-1/315	2/21/75	9	Eastern Michigan	FA/04	16/14
95	Ron Edwards (T)	6-3/320	7/12/79	6	Texas A&M	FA/06	4/4
71	Eddie Freeman (E)	6-5/307	1/4/78	3	UAB	FA/06	0/0
91	Tamba Hali (E)	6-3/275	11/3/83	R	Penn State	D1/06	—
92	Carlos Hall (E)	6-4/261	1/16/79	5	Arkansas	T-Ten/05	14/2
98	Eric Hicks (E)	6-6/280	6/17/76	9	Maryland	FA/98	16/14
94	Junior Siavii (T)	6-5/336	11/14/78	3	Oregon	D2a/04	14/0
90	Ryan Sims (T)	6-4/315	5/4/80	5	North Carolina	D1/02	6/5
64	Zach Ville (E)	6-2/275	4/24/82	1	Missouri	FA/06	0/0
96	Jimmy Wilkerson (E)	6-2/280	1/4/81	4	Oklahoma	D6/03	16/2
	LINEBACKERS						
99	Kendrell Bell	6-1/257	7/2/78	6	Georgia	FA/05	16/14
97	Keyaron Fox	6-3/235	1/24/82	3	Georgia Tech	D3/04	2/0
53	Kris Griffin	6-3/232	5/27/81	2	Indiana (Pa.)	FA/05	8/0
51	Boomer Grigsby	6-0/249	11/15/81	2	Illinois State	D5a/05	16/0
56	Derrick Johnson	6-3/242	11/22/82	2	Texas	D1/05	16/16
50	Kawika Mitchell	6-1/253	10/10/79	4	South Florida	D2/03	16/16
55	Rich Scanlon	6-2/249	12/23/80	3	Syracuse	FA/04	16/0
	DEFENSIVE BACKS						
24	William Bartee (CB/S)	6-1/200	6/25/77	7	Oklahoma	D2/00	16/0
26	Julian Battle (CB)	6-2/205	7/11/81	4	Tennessee	D3/03	0/0
41	Scott Connot (S)	6-3/216	6/24/81	1	South Dakota State	FA/04	0/0
46	Kevin Garrett (CB)	5-10/194	7/29/80	3	Southern Methodist	FA/06	0/0
47	Alphonso Hodge (CB)	5-11/203	5/30/82	1	Miami (Ohio)	D5b/05	0/0
39	Chris Johnson (CB)	6-11/184	9/25/79	2	Louisville	FA/06	14/1
29	Sammy Knight (S)	6-0/215	9/10/75	10	USC	FA/05	16/16
45	Marcus Maxey (CB)	6-0/192	2/2/83	R	Miami	D5/06	—
44	Jarrad Page (S)	6-0/219	10/19/84	R	UCLA	D7/06	—
49	Bernard Pollard (S)	6-1/224	12/23/84	R	Purdue	D2/06	—
20	Benny Sapp (CB)	5-9/190	1/20/81	3	Northern Iowa	FA/04	16/3
23	Patrick Surtain (CB)	5-11/192	6/19/76	9	Southern Miss	T-Mia/05	15/15
43	Lenny Walls (CB)	6-4/192	9/26/79	5	Boston College	FA/06	7/3
25	Greg Wesley (S)	6-2/206	3/19/78	7	Arkansas-Pine Bluff	D3/00	16/16
21	Jerome Woods (S)	6-3/205	3/17/73	11	Memphis	D1/96	7/0
	SPECIALISTS						
2	Dustin Colquitt (P)	6-2/207	5/6/82	2	Tennessee	D3/05	16/0
1	Lawrence Tynes (K)	6-1/202	5/3/78	3	Troy	FA/04	16/0

Abbreviations: D1-draft pick, first round; W-claimed on waivers; T-obtained in trade; FA-free-agent acquisition.

KANSAS CITY CHIEFS

KANSAS CITY CHIEFS

2005 regular-season record: 10-6
Position: 2nd in AFC West

Sept.11—N.Y. JETS	W	27-7
Sept.18—at Oakland	W	23-17
Sept.26—at Denver	L	10-30
Oct. 2—PHILADELPHIA	L	31-37
Oct. 9—Open date		
Oct. 16—WASHINGTON	W	28-21
Oct. 21—at Miami	W	30-20
Oct. 30—at San Diego	L	20-28
Nov. 6—OAKLAND	W	27-23
Nov.13—at Buffalo	L	3-14
Nov.20—at Houston	W	45-17
Nov.27—NEW ENGLAND	W	26-16
Dec. 4—DENVER	W	31-27
Dec.11—at Dallas	L	28-31
Dec.17—at N.Y. Giants	L	17-27
Dec.24—SAN DIEGO	W	20-7
Jan. 1—CINCINNATI	W	37-3

SCORING BY PERIODS

	Q1	Q2	Q3	Q4	OT	Pts.
Chiefs	85	136	79	103	0	403
Opponents	51	110	76	88	0	325

TEAM STATISTICS

	K.C.	Opp.
TOTAL FIRST DOWNS	347	292
Rushing	138	84
Passing	182	189
Penalty	27	19
3rd Down: Made/Att.	91/213	78/206
3rd Down Pct.	42.7	37.9
4th Down: Made/Att.	10/16	7/19
4th Down Pct.	62.5	36.8
POSSESSION AVG.	32:09	27:51
TOTAL NET YARDS	6192	5249
Avg. per Game	387.0	328.1
Total Plays	1059	971
Avg. per Play	5.8	5.4
NET YARDS RUSHING	2382	1570
Avg. per Game	148.9	98.1
Total Rushes	520	383
NET YARDS PASSING	3810	3679
Avg. per Game	238.1	229.9
Sacked/Yards Lost	32/204	29/183
Gross Yards	4014	3862
Att./Completions	507/317	559/325
Completion Pct.	62.5	58.1
Had Intercepted	10	16
PUNTS/AVERAGE	65/39.4	69/45.7
NET PUNTING AVG.	65/35.2	69/40.0
PENALTIES/YARDS	115/890	90/805
FUMBLES/LOST	23/13	33/15

	K.C.	Opp.
TOUCHDOWNS	46	38
Rushing	26	11
Passing	17	25
Returns	3	2

SCORING (NONKICKERS)

	Tot. TD	RTD	PTD	MTD	2Pt.	Tot. Pts.
L. Johnson	21	20	1	0	0	126
Holmes	7	6	1	0	0	42
Kennison	5	0	5	0	0	30
D. Hall	4	0	3	1	0	24
Parker	3	0	3	0	0	18
Gonzalez	2	0	2	0	0	12
Brown	1	0	1	0	0	6
Knight	1	0	0	1	0	6
Richardson	1	0	1	0	0	6
Warfield	1	0	0	1	0	6
Boerigter	0	0	0	0	1	2
Chiefs	46	26	17	3	1	278
Opponents	38	11	25	2	2	232

2-Pt. conversions: Chiefs 1-1; Opponents 2-5.

(KICKERS)

	XPM/XPA	FGM/FGA	Pts.
Tynes	44/45	27/33	125
Chiefs	44/45	27/33	125
Opponents	33/33	20/26	93

RUSHING

	Att.	Yds.	Avg.	Lg.	TD
L. Johnson	336	1750	5.2	t49	20
Holmes	119	451	3.8	t35	6
Green	35	82	2.3	13	0
Kennison	7	43	6.1	23	0
Brown	7	21	3.0	7	0
Richardson	6	20	3.3	8	0
D. Hall	7	11	1.6	7	0
Wilson	1	6	6.0	6	0
Collins	2	-2	-1.0	-1	0
Chiefs	520	2382	4.6	t49	26
Opponents	383	1570	4.1	t65	11

RECEIVING

	No.	Yds.	Avg.	Lg.	TD
Gonzalez	78	905	11.6	39	2
Kennison	68	1102	16.2	55	5
Parker	36	533	14.8	49	3
D. Hall	34	436	12.8	t52	3
L. Johnson	33	343	10.4	36	1
Holmes	21	197	9.4	t60	1
Horn	18	187	10.4	50	0
Richardson	9	68	7.6	22	1
Boerigter	8	119	14.9	38	0

	No.	Yds.	Avg.	Lg.	TD
Dunn	5	53	10.6	24	0
Brown	3	23	7.7	9	1
Wilson	3	33	11.0	16	0
Cruz	1	15	15.0	15	0
Chiefs	317	4014	12.7	t60	17
Opponents	325	3862	11.9	t78	25

INTERCEPTIONS

	No.	Yds.	Avg.	Lg.	TD
Wesley	6	106	17.7	51	0
Surtain	4	57	14.3	53	0
Knight	2	12	6.0	12	0
McCleon	2	0	0.0	0	0
Warfield	1	57	57.0	t57	1
K. Mitchell	1	0	0.0	0	0
Chiefs	16	232	14.5	t57	1
Opponents	10	196	19.6	t40	1

SACKS: Allen 11.0, Hicks 4.0, Sapp 2.5, Browning 2.0, D. Johnson 2.0, Knight 2.0, K. Mitchell 2.0, Bell 1.5, Dalton 1.0, C. Hall 1.0. Chiefs 29.0; Opponents 32.0.

PUNTING

	No.	Yds.	Avg.	In. 20	Lg.
Colquitt	65	2564	39.4	27	62
Chiefs	65	2564	39.4	27	62
Opponents	69	3155	45.7	19	61

PUNT RETURNS

	No.	FC	Yds.	Avg.	Lg.	TD
D. Hall	42	6	276	6.6	52	0
Kennison	1	1	17	17.0	17	0
Chiefs	43	7	293	6.8	52	0
Opponents	23	21	179	7.8	47	0

KICK RETURNS

	No.	Yds.	Avg.	Lg.	TD
D. Hall	65	1560	24.0	t96	1
Horn	3	31	10.3	11	0
Chiefs	68	1591	23.4	t96	1
Opponents	83	2053	24.7	t99	1

FIELD GOALS

	1-19	20-29	30-39	40-49	50+
Tynes	1/1	8/8	12/13	4/8	2/3
Chiefs	1/1	8/8	12/13	4/8	2/3
Opponents	0/0	7/9	6/7	6/8	1/2

Tynes: (41G, 38G, 32N) (31G, 46B, 39G, 42G) (28G) (38G) (20G, 38G) (30G, 51G, 52G) (34G, 20G) (27G, 47G) (35G, 44N, 43N) (35G) (25G, 20G, 33G, 47G) (34G) (41N) (19G) (52N) (39G, 24G, 23G)
Opponents: (28B) (29G, 50N) (30G, 51G, 25G, 46N) (40B, 44G, 37G, 26G) () (33G, 23G) () (32G, 49G, 48G) (28N, 31N) (22G) (29G) (22G, 40G) (34G) (41G, 35G) () (49G)

PASSING

	Att.	Cmp.	Yds.	Pct.	Avg. Gain	TD	Pct. TD	Int.	Pct. Int.	Long	Sack/Lost	Rating
Green	507	317	4014	62.5	7.92	17	3.4	10	2.0	t60	32/204	90.1
Chiefs	507	317	4014	62.5	7.92	17	3.4	10	2.0	t60	32/204	90.1
Opponents	559	325	3862	58.1	6.91	25	4.5	16	2.9	t78	29/183	82.3

MIAMI DOLPHINS
AFC EAST DIVISION

CLUB DIRECTORY

Owner/chairman of the board
H. Wayne Huizenga
CEO, Dolphin Enterprises
Joe Bailey
President/COO
Bryan Wiedmeier
General manager
Randy Mueller
Sr. vice president/operations
Bill Galante
Director of pro personnel
George Paton
Director of college scouting
Ron Labadie
Assistant director of player personnel
Mike Baugh
Sr. vice president/media relations
Harvey Greene
Director of media relations
Neal Gulkis

Head coach
Nick Saban

Assistant coaches
Keith Armstrong (special teams)
Charlie Baggett (asst. head coach/offense/wide receivers)
Dom Capers (special asst. to the head coach)
James Coley (offensive quality control)
Bo Davis (asst. strength and conditioning/asst. defensive line)
Tim Davis (asst. offensive line)
Derek Dooley (tight ends)
George Edwards (linebackers)
Jason Garrett (quarterbacks)
Bert Hill (associate strength and conditioning)
Hudson Houck (offensive line)
Travis Jones (asst. defensive line)
Mike Mularkey (offensive coordinator)
Mel Phillips (secondary)
Glenn Pires (defensive quality control)
Dan Quinn (defensive line)
Kirby Smart (safeties)
Patrick Suddes (defensive asst.)
Bobby Williams (running backs)

OFFSEASON MOVES

Key additions
CB	Will Allen	FA/Giants
FB	Fred Beasley	FA/49ers
WR	Kelly Campbell	FA/Vikings
S	Deke Cooper	FA/Jaguars
QB	Daunte Culpepper	trade/Vikings
CB	Andre Goodman	FA/Lions
QB	Joey Harrington	trade/Lions
CB	Renaldo Hill	FA/Raiders
LB	Sedrick Hodge	FA/Saints
OT	Mike Pearson	FA/Jaguars
TE	Justin Peelle	FA/Chargers
OT	L.J. Shelton	FA/Browns

Key losses
WR	David Boston	FA
QB	Gus Frerotte	released/Rams
WR	Bryan Gilmore	FA/49ers
S	Tebucky Jones	released/Patriots
CB	Sam Madison	released/Giants
QB	Sage Rosenfels	FA/Texans

SCHEDULE

Sept.	7—at Pittsburgh (Thurs.)	8:30
Sept.	17—BUFFALO	1:00
Sept.	24—TENNESSEE	1:00
Oct.	1—at Houston	1:00
Oct.	8—at New England	1:00
Oct.	15—at N.Y. Jets	4:15
Oct.	22—GREEN BAY	1:00
Oct.	29—Open date	
Nov.	5—at Chicago	1:00
Nov.	12—KANSAS CITY	1:00
Nov.	19—MINNESOTA	1:00
Nov.	23—at Detroit (Thurs.)	12:30
Dec.	3—JACKSONVILLE	1:00
Dec.	10—NEW ENGLAND	1:00
Dec.	17—at Buffalo	1:00
Dec.	25—N.Y. JETS (Mon.)	8:30
Dec.	31—at Indianapolis	1:00

All times are Eastern.
All games Sunday unless noted.

DRAFT CHOICES

Jason Allen, CB, Tennessee (first round/16th pick overall).
Derek Hagan, WR, Arizona State (3/82).
Joe Toledo, OT, Washington (4/114).
Fred Evans, DT, Texas State (7/212).
Rodrique Wright, DT, Texas (7/226).
Devin Aromashodu, WR, Auburn (7/233).

MISCELLANEOUS TEAM DATA

Stadium (capacity, surface):
Dolphin Stadium
(75,540, grass)
Business address:
7500 S.W. 30th St.
Davie, FL 33314
Business phone:
954-452-7000
Ticket information:
888-346-7849
Team colors:
Aqua, coral, blue and white
Flagship radio station:
790 AM The Ticket
Website:
www.miamidolphins.com

Training site:
Nova Southeastern University
Davie, Fla.
954-452-7000

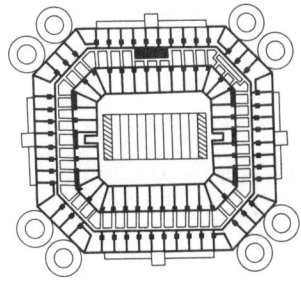

MIAMI DOLPHINS

No.	QUARTERBACKS	Ht./Wt.	Born	NFL Exp.	College	How acq.	'05 Games GP/GS
8	Daunte Culpepper	6-4/264	1/28/177	7	Central Florida	T-Min/06	7/7
3	Joey Harrington	6-4/220	10/21/78	5	Oregon	T-Mia/06	12/11
17	Cleo Lemon	6-2/215	8/16/79	3	Arkansas State	T-SD/05	1/0
	Marcus Vick	6-0/213	3/20/84	1	Virginia Tech	FA/06	—
	RUNNING BACKS						
36	Darian Barnes (FB)	6-2/241	2/28/80	5	Hampton	FA/05	9/5
40	Fred Beasley (FB)	6-0/246	9/18/74	9	Auburn	FA/06	9/7
23	Ronnie Brown	6-0/233	12/12/81	2	Auburn	D1/05	15/14
28	Travis Minor	5-10/205	6/30/79	6	Florida State	D3a/01	16/0
31	Sammy Morris	6-0/220	3/23/77	7	Texas Tech	D5/00	16/2
	RECEIVERS						
19	Devin Aromashodu	6-2/201	5/23/84	R	Auburn	D7c/06	—
86	Marty Booker	6-0/212	7/31/76	8	Louisiana-Monroe	T-Chi/04	15/11
80	Kelly Campbell	5-10/173	7/23/80	5	Georgia Tech	FA/06	0/0
84	Chris Chambers	5-11/210	8/12/78	6	Wisconsin	D2/01	16/16
18	Fred Gibson	6-4/196	10/26/81	2	Georgia	FA/05	0/0
82	Derek Hagan	6-1/208	9/21/84	R	Arizona State	D3/06	—
47	Teyo Johnson (TE)	6-6/260	11/29/81	4	Stanford	FA/06	7/3
81	Randy McMichael (TE)	6-3/250	6/28/79	5	Georgia	D4/02	16/16
87	Justin Peelle (TE)	6-4/255	3/15/79	5	Oregon	FA/06	16/4
88	Cliff Russell	5-11/193	2/8/79	4	Utah	FA/05	2/0
83	Wes Welker	5-9/190	5/1/81	3	Texas Tech	FA/04	16/1
15	Jason Willis	6-1/196	7/26/80	2	Oregon	FA/06	0/0
	OFFENSIVE LINEMEN						
79	Anthony Alabi (T)	6-5/313	2/16/81	2	TCU	D5/05	0/0
65	Joe Berger (T)	6-5/303	5/25/82	2	Michigan Tech	D6b/05	3/0
69	C.J. Brooks (G)	6-5/310	8/21/82	2	Maryland	FA/05	0/0
72	Vernon Carey (T)	6-5/325	7/31/81	3	Miami	D1/04	16/14
66	Rex Hadnot (G)	6-2/323	1/28/82	3	Houston	D6/04	16/16
78	Jeno James (G)	6-3/315	1/12/77	7	Auburn	FA/04	16/16
77	Damion McIntosh (T)	6-4/325	3/25/77	7	Kansas State	FA/04	16/16
68	Seth McKinney (C)	6-3/305	6/12/79	5	Texas A&M	D3/02	13/13
71	Mike Pearson (T)	6-7/297	8/22/80	5	Florida	FA/06	4/2
70	L.J. Shelton (T)	6-6/335	3/21/76	8	Eastern Michigan	FA/06	16/16
74	Wade Smith (C)	6-4/315	4/26/81	3	Memphis	D3a/03	0/0
67	Joe Toledo (G)	6-5/335	10/20/82	R	Washington	D4/06	—
	DEFENSIVE LINEMEN						
96	David Bowens (E)	6-3/260	7/3/77	7	Western Illinois	FA/01	16/0
93	Kevin Carter (E)	6-5/290	9/21/73	12	Florida	FA/05	16/16
97	John Denney (E/LS)	6-5/270	12/13/78	2	BYU	FA/05	16/0
	Fred Evans (T)	6-3/320	11/6/83	R	Texas State	D7a/06	—
90	Vonnie Holliday (T)	6-5/290	12/11/75	9	North Carolina	FA/05	16/16
98	Matt Roth (E)	6-4/278	10/14/82	2	Iowa	D2/05	16/0
93	Josh Shaw (T)	6-2/290	9/7/79	3	Michigan State	FA/04	1/0
99	Jason Taylor (E)	6-6/255	9/1/74	10	Akron	D3a/97	16/16
94	Keith Traylor (T)	6-2/340	9/3/69	15	Central Oklahoma	FA/05	13/13
92	Kevin Vickerson (T)	6-5/305	1/8/83	2	Michigan State	D7/05	0/0
75	Manny Wright (T)	6-6/329	4/13/84	2	USC	D5/05	3/0
	Rodrique Wright (T)	6-5/300	7/31/84	R	Texas	D7b/06	—
90	Jeff Zgonina (T)	6-2/285	5/24/70	14	Purdue	FA/03	16/3
	LINEBACKERS						
52	Channing Crowder	6-2/242	12/2/83	2	Florida	D3/05	16/13
50	Sedrick Hodge	6-4/246	9/13/78	6	North Carolina	FA/06	13/12
53	Mike Labinjo	6-0/241	7/8/80	3	Michigan State	FA/06	7/1
58	Eddie Moore	6-0/230	7/5/80	4	Tennessee	D2/03	5/0
56	Derrick Pope	5-11/233	5/4/82	3	Alabama	D7/04	12/2
59	Donnie Spragan	6-3/239	7/12/76	6	Stanford	FA/05	16/9
54	Zach Thomas	5-11/230	9/1/73	11	Texas Tech	D5c/96	14/14
	DEFENSIVE BACKS						
32	Jason Allen (S)	6-2/200	7/5/83	R	Tennessee	D1/06	—
25	Will Allen (CB)	5-10/196	8/5/78	6	Syracuse	FA/06	16/16
37	Yeremiah Bell (S)	6-1/200	3/3/78	3	Eastern Kentucky	D6c/03	16/0
35	Deke Cooper (S)	6-2/210	10/18/77	5	Notre Dame	FA/06	16/12
21	Travis Daniels (CB)	6-1/192	9/8/82	2	LSU	D4/05	16/14
29	Andre' Goodman (CB)	5-10/185	8/11/78	5	South Carolina	FA/06	15/8
24	Renaldo Hill (S)	5-11/189	11/12/78	6	Michigan State	FA/06	16/13
20	Eddie Jackson (CB)	6-0/190	12/19/80	3	Arkansas	W-Car/05	15/1
42	Norman LeJeune (S)	6-0/200	5/10/80	2	LSU	D7/03	5/0
27	Will Poole (CB)	5-10/192	7/24/81	2	USC	D4/04	0/0
44	Siddeeq Shabazz (S)	5-11/200	2/5/81	4	New Mexico State	FA/06	2/0
26	Travares Tillman (S)	6-1/190	10/8/77	6	Georgia Tech	FA/05	16/10
	SPECIALISTS						
5	Donnie Jones (P)	6-2/222	7/5/80	3	LSU	W-Sea/05	16/0
10	Olindo Mare (K)	5-10/195	6/6/73	10	Syracuse	FA/97	16/0

Abbreviations: D1-draft pick, first round; W-claimed on waivers; T-obtained in trade; FA-free-agent acquisition.

2005 regular-season record: 9-7
Position: 2nd in AFC East

Sept.11—DENVER	W	34-10
Sept.18—at N.Y. Jets	L	7-17
Sept.25—CAROLINA	W	27-24
Oct. 2—Open date		
Oct. 9—at Buffalo	L	14-20
Oct. 16—at Tampa Bay	L	13-27
Oct. 21—KANSAS CITY	L	20-30
Oct. 30—at New Orleans	W	21-6
Nov. 6—ATLANTA	L	10-17
Nov.13—NEW ENGLAND	L	16-23
Nov.20—at Cleveland	L	0-22
Nov.27—at Oakland	W	33-21
Dec. 4—BUFFALO	W	24-23
Dec.11—at San Diego	W	23-21
Dec.18—N.Y. JETS	W	24-20
Dec.24—TENNESSEE	W	24-10
Jan. 1—at New England	W	28-26

SCORING BY PERIODS

	Q1	Q2	Q3	Q4	OT	Pts.
Dolphins	44	78	57	139	0	318
Opponents	94	67	71	85	0	317

TEAM STATISTICS

	Mia.	Opp.
TOTAL FIRST DOWNS ..	274	319
Rushing	93	94
Passing	159	183
Penalty	22	42
3rd Down: Made/Att. ..	79/225	95/236
3rd Down Pct.	35.1	40.3
4th Down: Made/Att.	6/15	8/19
4th Down Pct.	40.0	42.1
POSSESSION AVG.	27:25	32:35
TOTAL NET YARDS	5198	5078
Avg. per Game	324.9	317.4
Total Plays	1026	1078
Avg. per Play	5.1	4.7
NET YARDS RUSHING ..	1898	1771
Avg. per Game	118.6	110.7
Total Rushes	444	480
NET YARDS PASSING....	3300	3307
Avg. per Game	206.3	206.7
Sacked/Yards Lost	26/158	49/375
Gross Yards	3458	3682
Att./Completions	556/291	549/323
Completion Pct.	52.3	58.8
Had Intercepted	16	14
PUNTS/AVERAGE	89/43.1	92/43.0
NET PUNTING AVG.	89/39.0	92/37.0
PENALTIES/YARDS	132/1055	105/827
FUMBLES/LOST	31/14	35/17
TOUCHDOWNS	34	35
Rushing	11	11
Passing	22	23
Returns	1	1

SCORING (NONKICKERS)

	Tot. TD	RTD	PTD	MTD	2Pt.	Tot. Pts.
Chambers	11	0	11	0	0	66
R. Williams	6	6	0	0	0	36
Brown	5	4	1	0	0	30
McMichael	5	0	5	0	0	30
Booker	3	0	3	0	0	18
Gilmore	1	0	1	0	0	6
Heller	1	0	1	0	0	6
Morris	1	1	0	0	0	6
Taylor	1	0	0	1	0	8
Dolphins	34	11	22	1	0	210
Opponents	35	11	23	1	1	214

2-Pt. conversions: Dolphins 0-1; Opponents 1-3.

(KICKERS)

	XPM/XPA	FGM/FGA	Pts.
Mare	33/33	25/30	108
Dolphins	33/33	25/30	108
Opponents	31/32	24/24	103

RUSHING

	Att.	Yds.	Avg.	Lg.	TD
Brown	207	907	4.4	t65	4
R. Williams	168	743	4.4	35	6
Chambers	12	92	7.7	61	0
Frerotte	27	61	2.3	14	0
Morris	16	58	3.6	t9	1
Minor	5	17	3.4	9	0
Rosenfels	6	15	2.5	12	0
Welker	1	5	5.0	5	0
Evans	1	0	0.0	0	0
Jones	1	0	0.0	0	0
Dolphins	444	1898	4.3	t65	11
Opponents	480	1771	3.7	t75	11

RECEIVING

	No.	Yds.	Avg.	Lg.	TD
Chambers	82	1118	13.6	t77	11
McMichael	60	582	9.7	43	5
Booker	39	686	17.6	t60	3
Brown	32	232	7.3	38	1
Welker	29	434	15.0	47	0
R. Williams	17	93	5.5	19	0
Diamond	8	54	6.8	18	0
Morris	8	54	6.8	18	0
Gilmore	5	105	21.0	t44	1
Boston	4	80	20.0	54	0
Evans	4	17	4.3	5	0
Heller	1	1	1.0	t1	1
Holmes	1	2	2.0	2	0
Minor	1	0	0.0	0	0
Dolphins	291	3458	11.9	t77	22
Opponents	323	3682	11.4	t60	23

INTERCEPTIONS

	No.	Yds.	Avg.	Lg.	TD
Schulters	4	78	19.5	37	0
Tillman	3	38	12.7	22	0
Madison	2	11	5.5	11	0
Howard	1	5	5.0	5	0
Daniels	1	4	4.0	4	0
Bell	1	0	0.0	0	0
Spragan	1	0	0.0	0	0
Z. Thomas	1	0	0.0	0	0
Dolphins	14	136	9.7	37	0
Opponents	16	127	7.9	33	0

SACKS: Taylor 12.0, D. Bowens 6.0, Carter 6.0, Holliday 5.0, Bell 3.0, Howard 2.0, Jones 2.0, Schulters 2.0, Z. Thomas 2.0, Traylor 2.0, Zgonina 2.0, Roth 1.0, Seau 1.0, Spragan 1.0, Wright 1.0. Dolphins 49.0; Opponents 26.0.

PUNTING

	No.	Yds.	Avg.	In. 20	Lg.
Jones	88	3827	43.5	31	63
Mare	1	8	8.0	0	8
Dolphins	89	3835	43.1	31	63
Opponents	92	3957	43.0	31	63

PUNT RETURNS

	No.	FC	Yds.	Avg.	Lg.	TD
Welker	43	23	390	9.1	47	0
Dolphins	43	23	390	9.1	47	0
Opponents	46	14	227	4.9	37	0

KICK RETURNS

	No.	Yds.	Avg.	Lg.	TD
Welker	61	1379	22.6	46	0
Gilmore	3	84	28.0	29	0
Minor	2	22	11.0	19	0
D. Bowens	1	5	5.0	5	0
Heller	1	11	11.0	11	0
Dolphins	68	1501	22.1	46	0
Opponents	56	1425	25.4	65	0

FIELD GOALS

	1-19	20-29	30-39	40-49	50+
Mare	0/0	9/10	9/12	6/6	1/2
Dolphins	0/0	9/10	9/12	6/6	1/2
Opponents	0/0	7/7	7/7	7/7	3/3

Mare: (29G, 44G) (21N) (27G, 32G) () (47G, 53G) (33G, 23G) (37G, 36G, 41G, 46G, 36N) (28G) (31N, 36G) () (38N, 27G) (23G) (29G, 39G, 20G) (53N, 32G) (25G) (36G, 38G, 41G, 42G)
Opponents: (28G) (41G) (52G) (24G, 47G) (36G, 32G) (30G, 51G, 52G) (26G, 49G) (21G) (35G, 32G, 33G) (23G, 40G, 24G) () () () (42G, 42G) (24G) (49G, 33G)

PASSING

	Att.	Cmp.	Yds.	Pct.	Avg. Gain	TD	Pct. TD	Int.	Pct. Int.	Long	Sack/Lost	Rating
Frerotte	494	257	2996	52.0	6.06	18	3.6	13	2.6	t60	26/158	71.9
Rosenfels	61	34	462	55.7	7.57	4	6.6	3	4.9	t77	0/0	81.5
Booker	1	0	0	0.0	0.00	0	0.0	0	0.0	...	0/0	39.6
Dolphins	556	291	3458	52.3	6.22	22	4.0	16	2.9	t77	26/158	72.8
Opponents	549	323	3682	58.8	6.71	23	4.2	14	2.6	t60	49/375	82.4

MIAMI DOLPHINS

MINNESOTA VIKINGS
NFC NORTH DIVISION

2006 SEASON

CLUB DIRECTORY

Owner/chairman
Zygi Wilf
Owner/president
Mark Wilf
Owner/vice chairman
Leonard Wilf
Ownership partners
Reggie Fowler, Alan Landis,
David Mandelbaum
VP of public affairs/stadium development
Lester Bagley
Vice president of football operations
Rob Brzezinski
Vice president of player personnel
Fran Foley
Vice president of sales and marketing
Steve LaCroix
Vice president of finance
Steve Poppen
VP of operations and legal counsel
Kevin Warren
Director of college scouting
Scott Studwell
Director of football administration
Dave Blando
Director of public relations
Bob Hagan
Director of community relations
Brad Madson

Head coach
Brad Childress

Assistant coaches
Darrell Bevell (offensive coordinator)
Mike Tomlin (defensive coordinator)
Paul Ferraro (special teams
coordinator)
Juney Barnett (asst. strength and
conditioning)
Eric Bieniemy (running backs)
Brendan Daly (defensive quality
control)
Karl Dunbar (defensive line)
Jim Hueber (asst. offensive line)
Jeff Imamura (defensive asst.)
Jimmie Johnson (tight ends)
Tom Kanavy (strength and
conditioning)
Clay Matchett (offensive asst.)
Pat Morris (offensive line)
Brian Murphy (asst. special
teams)
Chad O'Shea (offensive quality
control)
Fred Pagac (linebackers)
Kevin Rogers (quarterbacks)
Kevin Stefanski (asst. to the head
coach)
Martin Streight (asst. strength
and conditioning)
Joe Woods (defensive backs)
Darrell Wyatt (wide receivers)

SCHEDULE

Sept.	11—at Washington (Mon.)	7:00
Sept.	17—CAROLINA	1:00
Sept.	24—CHICAGO	1:00
Oct.	1—at Buffalo	1:00
Oct.	8—DETROIT	1:00
Oct.	15—Open date	
Oct.	22—at Seattle	4:15
Oct.	30—NEW ENGLAND (Mon.)	8:30
Nov.	5—at San Francisco	4:05
Nov.	12—GREEN BAY	1:00
Nov.	19—at Miami	1:00
Nov.	26—ARIZONA	1:00
Dec.	3—at Chicago	1:00
Dec.	10—at Detroit	1:00
Dec.	17—N.Y. JETS	1:00
Dec.	21—at Green Bay (Thurs.)	8:00
Dec.	31—ST. LOUIS	1:00

All times are Eastern.
All games Sunday unless noted.

DRAFT CHOICES

Chad Greenway, OLB, Iowa (first round,
17th overall pick).
Cedric Griffin, CB, Texas (2/48).
Ryan Cook, C, New Mexico (2/51).
Tarvaris Jackson, QB, Alabama State
(2/64).
Ray Edwards, DE, Purdue (4/127).
Greg Blue, FS, Georgia (5/149).

OFFSEASON MOVES

Key additions
G Steve Hutchinson	FA/Seahawks
LB Ben Leber	FA/Chargers
K Ryan Longwell	FA/Packers
QB Mike McMahon	FA/Eagles
FB Tony Richardson	FA/Chiefs
DL DeQuincy Scott	FA/Chargers
OL Jason Whittle	FA/Giants
S Tank Williams	FA/Titans

Key losses
RB Michael Bennett	FA/Saints
SS Corey Chavous	FA/Rams
LB Sam Cowart	FA/Texans
QB Daunte Culpepper	trade/Dolphins
LB Keith Newman	FA
CB Brian Williams	FA/Jaguars

MISCELLANEOUS TEAM DATA

Stadium (capacity, surface):
Metrodome (64,121, FieldTurf)
Business address:
9520 Viking Drive
Eden Prairie, MN 55344
Business phone:
952-828-6500
Ticket information:
612-338-4537
Team colors:
Purple, gold and white
Flagship radio station:
KFAN, 1130 AM
Website:
www.vikings.com

Training site:
Minnesota State University-
Mankato
Mankato, Minn.
952-828-6500

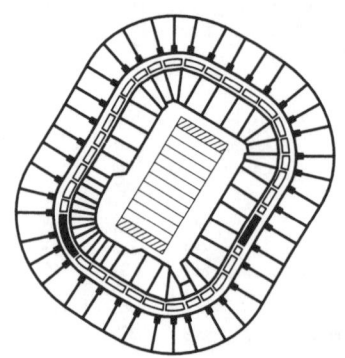

No.	QUARTERBACKS	Ht./Wt.	Born	NFL Exp.	College	How acq.	'05 Games GP/GS
2	Tarvaris Jackson	6-1/232	4/21/83	R	Alabama State	D2c/06	—
14	Brad Johnson	6-5/226	9/13/68	13	Florida State	FA/05	15/9
4	Mike McMahon	6-2/215	2/8/79	6	Rutgers	FA/06	9/7
7	J.T. O'Sullivan	6-2/220	8/25/79	2	California-Davis	FA/05	0/0
	RUNNING BACKS						
22	Adimchinobe Echemandu	5-10/226	11/21/80	3	California	FA/05	2/0
35	Ciatrick Fason	6-1/209	10/29/82	2	Florida	D4/05	13/0
44	Joey Goodspeed (FB)	6-1/247	2/22/78	5	Notre Dame	FA/06	0/0
30	Mewelde Moore	5-11/209	7/24/82	3	Tulane	D4/04	16/8
49	Tony Richardson (FB)	6-1/238	12/17/71	12	Auburn	FA/06	16/16
29	Chester Taylor	5-11/213	9/22/79	5	Toledo	FA/06	15/1
	RECEIVERS						
83	Jeff Dugan (TE)	6-4/258	4/8/81	3	Maryland	D7/04	1/0
19	Ryan Hoag	6-2/200	11/23/79	1	Gustavus Adolphus	FA/04	0/0
12	Kelvin Kight	6-0/209	7/2/82	1	Florida	FA/06	0/0
40	Jim Kleinsasser (TE)	6-3/272	1/31/77	7	North Dakota	D2/99	16/16
	Billy McMullen	6-4/215	3/8/1980	4	Virginia	T-Phi/06	16/0
33	Richard Owens (TE)	6-4/273	11/4/80	3	Louisville	FA/04	16/2
17	Jimmy Redmond	6-0/190	8/18/77	3	McNeese State	FA/06	0/0
18	Koren Robinson	6-1/205	3/19/80	6	N.C. State	FA/05	14/5
87	Marcus Robinson	6-3/215	2/27/75	9	South Carolina	FA/04	15/9
89	Travis Taylor	6-1/210	3/30/78	7	Florida	FA/05	16/13
85	Jermaine Wiggins (TE)	6-2/260	1/18/75	7	Georgia	FA/04	16/8
82	Troy Williamson	6-1/203	4/30/83	2	South Carolina	D1a/05	14/3
	OFFENSIVE LINEMEN						
78	Matt Birk (C)	6-4/309	7/23/76	9	Harvard	D6/98	0/0
62	Ryan Cook (G/C)	6-6/328	5/8/83	R	New Mexico	D2b/06	—
73	Adam Goldberg (T)	6-7/310	8/12/80	3	Wyoming	FA/04	16/12
64	Anthony Herrera (G/C)	6-2/315	6/14/80	3	Tennessee	FA/04	10/6
79	Artis Hicks (G)	6-4/320	11/28/78	4	Memphis	T-Phi/06	14/14
76	Steve Hutchinson (G)	6-5/313	11/1/77	6	Michigan	FA/06	16/16
72	Marcus Johnson (T)	6-6/310	12/1/81	2	Mississippi	D2/05	14/8
67	Chris Liwienski (G)	6-5/325	8/2/75	7	Indiana	FA/99	15/9
46	Cullen Loeffler (C)	6-5/241	1/27/81	3	Texas	FA/03	16/0
74	Bryant McKinnie (T)	6-8/335	9/23/79	5	Miami	D1/02	16/16
75	Mike Rosenthal (T)	6-7/318	6/10/77	7	Notre Dame	FA/03	16/12
65	Jason Whittle (C/G)	6-4/305	3/7/75	8	Missouri State	FA/06	14/0
	DEFENSIVE LINEMEN						
	Ray Edwards (E)	6-4/268	1/1/85	R	Purdue	D4/06	—
99	Erasmus James (E)	6-4/266	11/4/82	2	Wisconsin	D1b/05	15/9
97	Spencer Johnson (T)	6-3/286	12/12/81	3	Auburn	FA/04	10/2
90	Steve Martin (T)	6-4/320	5/31/74	11	Missouri	FA/04	0/0
96	C.J. Mosley (T)	6-2/312	8/6/83	2	Missouri	D6/05	12/2
98	Darrion Scott (E)	6-3/289	10/25/81	3	Ohio State	D3/04	16/15
92	DeQuincy Scott (E)	6-1/260	3/5/78	5	Southern Miss	FA/06	16/0
95	Kenechi Udeze (E)	6-3/281	3/5/83	3	USC	D1/04	3/2
93	Kevin Williams (T)	6-5/311	8/16/80	4	Oklahoma State	D1/03	14/14
94	Pat Williams (T)	6-3/317	10/24/72	9	Texas A&M	FA/05	16/16
	LINEBACKERS						
50	Rod Davis	6-2/239	4/2/81	3	Southern Miss	D5/04	16/1
59	Heath Farwell	6-0/235	12/31/81	2	San Diego State	FA/05	7/0
52	Chad Greenway	6-2/242	1/13/83	R	Iowa	D1/06	—
58	Napoleon Harris	6-2/255	2/25/79	5	Northwestern	T-Oak/05	15/3
56	E.J. Henderson	6-1/245	8/3/80	4	Maryland	D2/03	15/14
51	Ben Leber	6-3/244	12/7/78	5	Kansas State	FA/06	9/6
54	Dontarrious Thomas	6-2/241	9/2/80	3	Auburn	D2/04	14/2
	DEFENSIVE BACKS						
20	Greg Blue (S)	6-2/216	3/12/82	R	Georgia	D5/06	—
36	Dovonte Edwards (CB)	6-0/182	10/17/82	2	N.C. State	FA/05	12/0
37	Dustin Fox (S)	5-10/190	10/8/82	2	Ohio State	D3/05	0/0
23	Cedric Griffin (CB)	6-0/199	11/11/82	R	Texas	D2a/06	—
25	Will Hunter (CB)	5-10/190	3/24/79	2	Syracuse	FA/05	13/0
24	Willie Offord (S)	6-1/216	12/22/78	5	South Carolina	D3/02	3/1
42	Darren Sharper (S)	6-2/210	11/3/75	10	William & Mary	FA/05	14/14
21	Fred Smoot (CB)	5-11/174	4/17/79	6	Mississippi State	FA/05	11/8
31	Marvin Ward (CB)	5-11/205	8/7/82	1	Northwestern	FA/05	0/0
25	Tank Williams (S)	6-3/223	6/30/80	5	Stanford	FA/06	16/16
26	Antoine Winfield (CB)	5-9/180	6/24/77	8	Ohio State	FA/04	16/16
	SPECIALISTS						
5	Chris Kluwe (P)	6-4/215	12/24/81	2	UCLA	W-Sea/05	15/0
8	Ryan Longwell (K)	6-0/202	8/16/74	10	California	FA/06	16/0

Abbreviations: D1-draft pick, first round; W-claimed on waivers; T-obtained in trade; FA-free-agent acquisition.

MINNESOTA VIKINGS

2005 regular-season record: 9-7
Position: 2nd in NFC North

Sept.11—TAMPA BAY	L	13-24
Sept.18—at Cincinnati	L	8-37
Sept.25—NEW ORLEANS	W	33-16
Oct. 2—at Atlanta	L	10-30
Oct. 9—Open date		
Oct. 16—at Chicago	L	3-28
Oct. 23—GREEN BAY	W	23-20
Oct. 30—at Carolina	L	13-38
Nov. 6—DETROIT	W	27-14
Nov. 13—at N.Y. Giants	W	24-21
Nov. 21—at Green Bay	W	20-17
Nov. 27—CLEVELAND	W	24-12
Dec. 4—at Detroit	W	21-16
Dec. 11—ST. LOUIS	W	27-13
Dec. 18—PITTSBURGH	L	3-18
Dec. 25—at Baltimore	L	23-30
Jan. 1—CHICAGO	W	34-10

SCORING BY PERIODS

	Q1	Q2	Q3	Q4	OT	Pts.
Vikings	54	89	82	81	0	306
Opponents	51	136	60	97	0	344

TEAM STATISTICS

	Min.	Opp.
TOTAL FIRST DOWNS	285	304
Rushing	83	96
Passing	169	177
Penalty	33	31
3rd Down: Made/Att.	64/196	95/221
3rd Down Pct.	32.7	43.0
4th Down: Made/Att.	4/9	5/13
4th Down Pct.	44.4	38.5
POSSESSION AVG.	28:46	31:14
TOTAL NET YARDS	4613	5173
Avg. per Game	288.3	323.3
Total Plays	945	1029
Avg. per Play	4.9	5.0
NET YARDS RUSHING	1467	1841
Avg. per Game	91.7	115.1
Total Rushes	381	462
NET YARDS PASSING	3146	3332
Avg. per Game	196.6	208.3
Sacked/Yards Lost	54/303	34/207
Gross Yards	3449	3539
Att./Completions	510/323	533/319
Completion Pct.	63.3	59.8
Had Intercepted	16	24
PUNTS/AVERAGE	81/43.3	72/41.8
NET PUNTING AVG.	81/35.7	72/36.8
PENALTIES/YARDS	128/1013	137/990
FUMBLES/LOST	25/14	22/11
TOUCHDOWNS	33	37
Rushing	10	14
Passing	18	23
Returns	5	0

SCORING (NONKICKERS)

	TD	RTD	PTD	MTD2Pt.	Tot. Pts.
Robinson	5	0	5	0 1	32
M. Bennett	5	3	2	0 0	30
Fason	4	4	0	0 0	24
Moore	4	1	2	1 0	24
Taylor	4	0	4	0 0	24
Robinson	3	1	1	1 0	18
Sharper	2	0	0	2 0	12
Williamson	2	0	2	0 0	12
Burleson	1	0	1	0 0	6
Culpepper	1	1	0	0 0	6
Edwards	1	0	0	1 0	6
Wiggins	1	0	1	0 0	6
Vikings	33	10	18	5 1	200
Opponents	37	14	23	0 1	226

2-Pt. conversions: Vikings 1-2; Opponents 1-3.

(KICKERS)

	XPM/XPA	FGM/FGA	Pts.
Edinger	31/31	25/34	106
Vikings	31/31	25/34	106
Opponents	34/34	28/33	118

RUSHING

	Att.	Yds.	Avg.	Lg.	TD
Moore	155	662	4.3	33	1
M. Bennett	126	473	3.8	t61	3
Culpepper	24	147	6.1	18	1
Fason	32	62	1.9	15	4
Johnson	18	53	2.9	16	0
Williamson	3	28	9.3	11	0
Robinson	4	27	6.8	t13	1
M. Williams	13	20	1.5	9	0
Taylor	2	3	1.5	5	0
Hill	2	-2	-1.0	-1	0
Burleson	2	-6	-3.0	-2	0
Vikings	381	1467	3.9	t61	10
Opponents	462	1841	4.0	t71	14

RECEIVING

	No.	Yds.	Avg.	Lg.	TD
Wiggins	69	568	8.2	24	1
Taylor	50	604	12.1	31	4
Moore	37	339	9.2	29	2
Robinson	31	515	16.6	68	5
Burleson	30	328	10.9	20	1
M. Bennett	27	124	4.6	20	2
Williamson	24	372	15.5	56	2
Kleinsasser	22	171	7.8	15	0
Robinson	22	347	15.8	t80	1
M. Williams	8	52	6.5	25	0
Owens	2	18	9.0	12	0
Angulo	1	11	11.0	11	0
Vikings	323	3449	10.7	t80	18
Opponents	319	3539	11.1	t70	23

INTERCEPTIONS

	No.	Yds.	Avg.	Lg.	TD
Sharper	9	276	30.7	t92	2

B. Williams	4	59	14.8	31	0
Winfield	4	5	1.3	4	0
Chavous	2	0	0.0	0	0
Smoot	2	0	0.0	0	0
Edwards	1	51	51.0	t51	1
Newman	1	1	1.0	1	0
Offord	1	0	0.0	0	0
Vikings	24	392	16.3	t92	3
Opponents	16	220	13.8	55	0

SACKS: Johnstone 7.5, James 4.0, Scott 4.0, K. Williams 4.0, Mosley 3.0, Newman 3.0, Cowart 2.0, Williams 1.5, Harris 1.0, Henderson 1.0, R. Smith 1.0, Udeze 1.0, B. Williams 1.0. Vikings 34.0; Opponents 54.0.

PUNTING

	No.	Yds.	Avg.	In. 20	Lg.
D. Bennett	8	300	37.5	1	53
Edinger	2	75	37.5	1	40
Kluwe	71	3130	44.1	17	62
Vikings	81	3505	43.3	19	62
Opponents	72	3013	41.8	25	60

PUNT RETURNS

	No.	FC	Yds.	Avg.	Lg.	TD
Moore	21	9	245	11.7	t71	1
Howry	12	5	78	6.5	19	0
Burleson	5	0	21	4.2	10	0
Robinson	2	0	0	0.0	0	0
Taylor	1	0	0	0.0	0	0
Vikings	41	14	344	8.4	t71	1
Opponents	45	17	495	11.0	72	0

KICK RETURNS

	No.	Yds.	Avg.	Lg.	TD
Robinson	47	1221	26.0	t86	1
Williamson	12	192	16.0	28	0
Moore	4	72	18.0	27	0
Owens	3	25	8.3	16	0
Fason	2	4	2.0	4	0
Henderson	1	13	13.0	13	0
Herrera	1	6	6.0	6	0
M. Williams	1	16	16.0	16	0
Vikings	71	1549	21.8	t86	1
Opponents	67	1416	21.1	48	0

FIELD GOALS

	1-19	20-29	30-39	40-49	50+
Edinger	0/0	11/11	3/8	8/10	3/5
Vikings	0/0	11/11	3/8	8/10	3/5
Opponents	1/1	9/10	9/9	7/8	2/5

Edinger: (53G, 22G) () (24G, 33N, 28G, 48G, 34G) (43G) (52N, 23G, 32B) (27G, 22G, 56G) (33N) (21G, 52N, 40G) (40N, 32B, 48G) (49N, 24G, 27G) (43G) () (37G, 44G) (20G, 32B) (36G, 40G, 46G) (54G, 27G)
Opponents: (41G) (40G, 29G, 30G) (22G) (38G, 26G, 39G) () (53N, 53G, 42N, 39G) (56N, 44G) (51N) (35G, 48G, 28N) (46G) (32G, 38G) (45G, 26G, 28G) (51G, 23G) (21G, 41G, 26G) (37G, 38G, 19G) (22G)

PASSING

	Att.	Cmp.	Yds.	Pct.	Avg. Gain	TD	Pct. TD	Int.	Pct. Int.	Long	Sack/Lost	Rating
Johnson	294	184	1885	62.6	6.41	12	4.1	4	1.4	t80	23/134	88.9
Culpepper	216	139	1564	64.4	7.24	6	2.8	12	5.6	68	31/169	72.0
Vikings	510	323	3449	63.3	6.76	18	3.5	16	3.1	t80	54/303	81.7
Opponents	533	319	3539	59.8	6.64	23	4.3	24	4.5	t70	34/207	75.2

MINNESOTA VIKINGS

NEW ENGLAND PATRIOTS
AFC EAST DIVISION

2006 SEASON

CLUB DIRECTORY

Chairman and owner
Robert K. Kraft
Vice chairman and president
Jonathan A. Kraft
Vice president of player personnel
Scott Pioli
VP and chief marketing officer
Lou Imbriano
VP of community affairs & corporate philanthropy
Rena Clark
Vice president of finance
Jim Hausmann
Vice president of marketing operations
Jen Ferron
Chief administrative counsel
Jack Mula
Executive director of media relations
Stacey James
Director of football/head coach administration
Berj Najarian
Director of college scouting
Thomas Dimitroff
Director of pro personnel
Nick Caserio
Director of operations
Matt Caracciolo

Head coach
Bill Belichick

Assistant coaches
Joel Collier (asst. secondary)
Brian Daboll (wide receivers)
Ivan Fears (running backs)
Pepper Johnson (defensive line)
Pete Mangurian (tight ends)
Josh McDaniels (offensive coordinator)
Harold Nash (asst. strength and conditioning)
Matt Patricia (asst. offensive line)
Dean Pees (defensive coordinator)
Dante Scarnecchia (asst. head coach/offensive line)
Brad Seely (special teams)
Mike Woicik (strength and conditioning)

OFFSEASON MOVES

Key additions
WR Reche Caldwell	FA/Chargers
S Tebucky Jones	FA/Dolphins
S Mel Mitchell	FA/Saints
CB Eric Warfield	FA/Chiefs

Key losses
OT Tom Ashworth	FA/Seahawks
LB Matt Chatham	FA/Jets
WR Tim Dwight	FA/Jets
TE Christian Fauria	FA/Redskins
WR David Givens	FA/Titans
LB Willie McGinest	FA/Browns
K Adam Vinatieri	FA/Colts

SCHEDULE

Sept.	10—BUFFALO	1:00
Sept.	17—at N.Y. Jets	4:15
Sept.	24—DENVER	8:15
Oct.	1—at Cincinnati	4:15
Oct.	8—MIAMI	1:00
Oct.	15—Open date	
Oct.	22—at Buffalo	1:00
Oct.	30—at Minnesota (Mon.)	8:30
Nov.	5—INDIANAPOLIS	8:15
Nov.	12—N.Y. JETS	1:00
Nov.	19—at Green Bay	1:00
Nov.	26—CHICAGO	1:00
Dec.	3—DETROIT	1:00
Dec.	10—at Miami	1:00
Dec.	17—HOUSTON	1:00
Dec.	24—at Jacksonville	1:00
Dec.	31—at Tennessee	1:00

All times are Eastern.
All games Sunday unless noted.

DRAFT CHOICES

Laurence Maroney, RB, Minnesota (first round/21st pick overall).
Chad Jackson, WR, Florida (2/36).
Dave Thomas, TE, Texas (3/86).
Garrett Mills, TE, Tulsa (4/106).
Stephen Gostkowski, K, Memphis (4/118).
Ryan O'Callaghan, G, California (5/136).
Jeremy Mincey, DE, Florida (6/191).
Dan Stevenson, G, Notre Dame (6/205).
Le Kevin Smith, DT, Nebraska (6/206).
Willie Andrews, CB, Baylor (7/229).

MISCELLANEOUS TEAM DATA

Stadium (capacity, surface):
Gillette Stadium
(68,756, grass)
Business address:
One Patriot Place
Foxborough, MA 02035
Business phone:
508-543-8200
Ticket information:
508-543-1776
Team colors:
Red, white, blue and silver
Flagship radio station:
WBCN, 104.1 FM
Website:
www.patriots.com

Training site:
Gillette Stadium
Foxborough, MA
508-543-8200

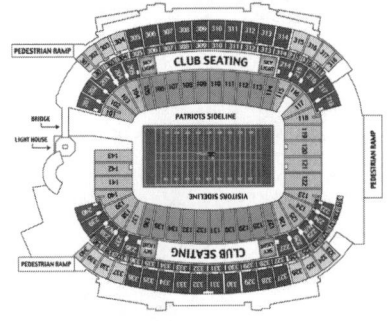

NEW ENGLAND PATRIOTS

No.	QUARTERBACKS	Ht./Wt.	Born	NFL Exp.	College	How acq.	'05 Games GP/GS
12	Tom Brady	6-4/225	8/3/77	7	Michigan	D6b/00	16/16
16	Matt Cassel	6-5/230	5/17/82	2	USC	D7a/05	2/0
	RUNNING BACKS						
28	Corey Dillon	6-1/225	10/24/74	10	Washington	T-Cin/04	12/10
44	Heath Evans (FB)	6-0/245	12/30/78	6	Auburn	FA/05	12/3
33	Kevin Faulk	5-8/202	6/5/76	8	LSU	D2/99	8/2
39	Laurence Maroney	6-0/215	2/5/85	R	Minnesota	D1/06	—
45	Garrett Mills (FB)	6-1/248	10/12/83	R	Tulsa	D4a/06	—
35	Patrick Pass (FB)	5-10/217	12/31/77	7	Georgia	D7b/00	12/4
	RECEIVERS						
83	Deion Branch	5-9/193	7/18/79	5	Louisville	D2/02	16/15
80	Troy Brown	5-10/196	7/2/71	14	Marshall	D8/93	13/3
87	Reche Caldwell	6-0/215	3/28/79	5	Florida	FA/06	16/2
82	Daniel Graham (TE)	6-3/257	11/16/78	5	Colorado	D1/02	11/9
17	Chad Jackson	6-1/213	3/6/85	R	Florida	D2/06	—
81	Bethel Johnson	5-11/200	2/11/79	4	Texas A&M	D2b/03	11/1
	Zuriel Smith	5-11/166	1/15/80	2	Hampton	FA/06	0/0
86	David Thomas (TE)	6-3/252	7/5/83	R	Texas	D3/06	—
84	Ben Watson (TE)	6-3/253	12/18/80	3	Georgia	D1b/04	15/9
	OFFENSIVE LINEMEN						
76	Brandon Gorin (T)	6-6/308	7/17/78	5	Purdue	FA/02	12/8
71	Russ Hochstein (G/C)	6-4/305	10/7/77	6	Nebraska	FA/02	16/7
77	Nick Kaczur (T)	6-4/319	7/28/79	2	Toledo	D3b/05	14/11
67	Dan Koppen (C)	6-2/296	9/12/79	4	Boston College	D5/03	9/9
72	Matt Light (T)	6-4/305	6/23/78	6	Purdue	D2/01	3/3
70	Logan Mankins (G)	6-4/307	3/10/82	2	Fresno State	D1/05	16/16
64	Gene Mruczkowski (G/C)	6-2/305	6/6/80	4	Purdue	FA/03	7/0
61	Stephen Neal (G)	6-4/305	10/9/76	5	CS Bakersfield	FA/01	16/16
68	Ryan O'Callaghan (G)	6-7/344	7/19/83	R	California	D5/06	—
66	Lonie Paxton (C)	6-2/260	3/13/78	7	Sacramento State	FA/00	16/0
63	Dan Stevenson (G)	6-5/300	10/4/82	R	Notre Dame	D6a/06	—
69	Ross Tucker (G)	6-4/316	3/2/79	6	Princeton	FA/05	1/0
	DEFENSIVE LINEMEN						
97	Jarvis Green (E)	6-3/290	1/12/79	5	LSU	D4b/02	15/5
91	Marquise Hill (E)	6-6/300	8/7/82	3	LSU	D2/04	8/0
90	Dan Klecko (E)	5-11/275	1/12/81	4	Temple	D4a/03	10/0
58	Jeremy Mincey (E)	6-4/259	12/14/83	R	Florida	D6a/06	—
93	Richard Seymour (E)	6-6/310	10/6/79	6	Georgia	D1/01	12/12
65	Le Kevin Smith (T)	6-3/316	7/21/82	R	Nebraska	D6c/06	—
94	Ty Warren (E)	6-5/300	2/6/81	4	Texas A&M	D1/03	16/16
75	Vince Wilfork (T)	6-2/325	11/4/81	3	Miami	D1a/04	16/16
99	Mike Wright (T)	6-4/295	3/1/82	2	Cincinnati	FA/05	13/0
	LINEBACKERS						
49	Eric Alexander	6-2/240	2/8/82	3	LSU	FA/04	1/0
95	Tully Banta-Cain	6-2/250	8/28/80	4	California	D7b/03	13/0
52	Monty Beisel	6-3/238	8/20/78	6	Kansas State	FA/05	15/6
54	Tedy Bruschi	6-1/247	6/9/73	11	Arizona	D3/96	9/9
47	Ryan Claridge	6-2/259	4/12/81	2	UNLV	D5/05	0/0
59	Rosevelt Colvin	6-3/250	9/5/77	8	Purdue	FA/03	16/11
51	Don Davis	6-1/235	12/17/72	11	Kansas	FA/03	16/0
53	Larry Izzo	5-10/228	9/26/74	11	Rice	FA/01	16/0
50	Mike Vrabel	6-4/261	8/14/75	10	Ohio State	FA/01	16/16
	DEFENSIVE BACKS						
	Willie Andrews (S)	5-10/189	11/2/83	R	Baylor	D7/06	—
21	Randall Gay (CB)	5-11/186	5/5/82	3	LSU	FA/04	5/2
37	Rodney Harrison (S)	6-1/220	12/15/72	13	Western Illinois	FA/03	3/3
25	Artrell Hawkins (CB)	5-10/190	11/24/76	9	Cincinnati	FA/05	5/4
27	Ellis Hobbs (CB)	5-8/188	5/16/83	2	Iowa State	D3a/05	16/8
34	Tebucky Jones (S)	6-2/220	10/6/74	9	Syracuse	FA/06	6/6
24	Mel Mitchell (S)	6-1/222	2/10/79	5	Western Kentucky	FA/06	13/0
32	Hank Poteat (S)	5-9/192	8/30/77	6	Pittsburgh	FA/05	10/1
22	Asante Samuel (CB)	5-10/185	1/6/81	4	Central Florida	D4b/03	15/15
36	James Sanders (S)	5-11/214	11/11/83	2	Fresno State	D4/05	10/2
30	Chad Scott (CB)	6-1/202	9/6/74	10	Maryland	FA/05	3/0
29	Guss Scott (S)	5-10/205	5/21/82	2	Florida	D3/04	5/2
23	Eric Warfield (CB)	6-0/200	3/3/76	9	Nebraska	FA/06	11/10
26	Eugene Wilson (S)	5-10/195	8/17/80	4	Illinois	D2a/03	16/16
	SPECIALISTS						
3	Steve Gostkowski (K)	6-1/212	1/28/84	R	Memphis	D4b/06	—
7	Martin Gramatica (K)	5-8/170	11/27/75	7	Kansas State	FA/06	0/0
8	Josh Miller (P)	6-4/225	7/14/70	11	Arizona	FA/04	16/0

Abbreviations: D1-draft pick, first round; W-claimed on waivers; T-obtained in trade; FA-free-agent acquisition.

2005 regular-season record: 10-6
Position: 1st in AFC East

Sept. 8—OAKLAND	W	30-20
Sept.18—at Carolina	L	17-27
Sept.25—at Pittsburgh	W	23-20
Oct. 2—SAN DIEGO	L	17-41
Oct. 9—at Atlanta	W	31-28
Oct. 16—at Denver	L	20-28
Oct. 23—Open date		
Oct. 30—BUFFALO	W	21-16
Nov. 7—INDIANAPOLIS	L	21-40
Nov.13—at Miami	W	23-16
Nov.20—NEW ORLEANS	W	24-17
Nov.27—at Kansas City	L	16-26
Dec. 4—N.Y. JETS	W	16-3
Dec.11—at Buffalo	W	35-7
Dec.17—TAMPA BAY	W	28-0
Dec.26—at N.Y. Jets	W	31-21
Jan. 1—MIAMI	L	26-28

2005 postseason record: 1-1

Jan. 7—JACKSONVILLE#	W	28-3
Jan. 14—at Denver*	L	13-27

#AFC wild-card game. *AFC divisional play-off game.

SCORING BY PERIODS

	Q1	Q2	Q3	Q4	OT	Pts.
Patriots	90	74	97	118	0	379
Opponents	55	117	56	110	0	338

TEAM STATISTICS

	N.E.	Opp.
TOTAL FIRST DOWNS	334	306
Rushing	101	94
Passing	204	179
Penalty	29	33
3rd Down: Made/Att.	93/221	92/219
3rd Down Pct.	42.1	42.0
4th Down: Made/Att.	13/17	3/9
4th Down Pct.	76.5	33.3
POSSESSION AVG.	30:19	29:41
TOTAL NET YARDS	5632	5283
Avg. per Game	352.0	330.2
Total Plays	1031	997
Avg. per Play	5.5	5.3
NET YARDS RUSHING	1512	1580
Avg. per Game	94.5	98.8
Total Rushes	439	437
NET YARDS PASSING	4120	3703
Avg. per Game	257.5	231.4
Sacked/Yards Lost	28/202	33/223
Gross Yards	4322	3926
Att./Completions	564/352	527/296
Completion Pct.	62.4	56.2
Had Intercepted	15	10
PUNTS/AVERAGE	77/44.6	81/43.7
NET PUNTING AVG.	77/38.3	81/37.8
PENALTIES/YARDS	110/921	132/1068
FUMBLES/LOST	19/9	13/8
TOUCHDOWNS	46	38
Rushing	16	11
Passing	28	25
Returns	2	2

SCORING (NONKICKERS)

	TD	RTD	PTD	MTD	2Pt.	Pts.
Dillon	13	12	1	0	0	78
Branch	5	0	5	0	0	30
Vrabel	4	0	3	1	0	24
Watson	4	0	4	0	0	24
Dwight	3	0	3	0	0	18
Graham	3	0	3	0	0	18
Pass	3	3	0	0	0	18
T. Brown	2	0	2	0	0	12
Fauria	2	0	2	0	0	12
Givens	2	0	2	0	0	12
Ashworth	1	0	1	0	0	6
Brady	1	1	0	0	0	6
Davis	1	0	1	0	0	6
B. Johnson	1	0	1	0	0	6
Sanders	1	0	1	0	0	6
Evans	0	0	0	0	1	2
Patriots	46	16	28	2	1	278
Opponents	38	11	25	2	1	232

2-Pt. conversions: Patriots 1-4; Opponents 1-4.

(KICKERS)

	XPM/XPA	FGM/FGA	Pts.
Vinatieri	40/41	20/25	100
Flutie	1/1	0/0	1
Patriots	41/42	20/25	101
Opponents	34/34	24/30	106

RUSHING

	Att.	Yds.	Avg.	Lg.	TD
Dillon	209	733	3.5	29	12
Pass	54	245	4.5	31	3
Evans	51	192	3.8	21	0
Faulk	51	145	2.8	13	0
Brady	27	89	3.3	15	1
Cloud	23	59	2.6	15	0
Zereoue	7	14	2.0	12	0
Givens	2	13	6.5	9	0
Cassel	6	12	2.0	9	0
Dwight	4	11	2.8	12	0
Flutie	5	-1	-0.2	2	0
Patriots	439	1512	3.4	31	16
Opponents	437	1580	3.6	68	11

RECEIVING

	No.	Yds.	Avg.	Lg.	TD
Branch	78	998	12.8	51	5
Givens	59	738	12.5	40	2
T. Brown	39	466	11.9	71	2
Faulk	29	260	9.0	23	0
Watson	29	441	15.2	35	4
Dillon	22	181	8.2	25	1
Pass	22	227	10.3	39	0
Dwight	19	332	17.5	59	3
Graham	16	235	14.7	145	3
Evans	10	88	8.8	19	0
Davis	9	190	21.1	t60	1
Fauria	8	57	7.1	18	2
B. Johnson	4	67	16.8	t55	1
Childress	3	32	10.7	21	0
Vrabel	3	4	1.3	t2	3

	No.	Yds.	Avg.	Lg.	TD
Ashworth	1	1	1.0	t1	1
Zereoue	1	5	5.0	5	0
Patriots	352	4322	12.3	71	28
Opponents	296	3926	13.3	t85	25

INTERCEPTIONS

	No.	Yds.	Avg.	Lg.	TD
Samuel	3	15	5.0	15	0
Hobbs	3	8	2.7	8	0
Vrabel	2	23	11.5	t24	1
Sanders	1	39	39.0	t39	1
Wilson	1	0	0.0	0	0
Patriots	10	85	8.5	t39	2
Opponents	15	188	12.5	t74	2

SACKS: Colvin 7.0, McGinest 6.0, Vrabel 4.5, Seymour 4.0, J. Green 2.5, Bruschi 2.0, Warren 1.5, Beisel 1.0, Chatham 1.0, Hawkins 1.0, Poteat 1.0, Banta-Cain 0.5, Klecko 0.5, Wilfork 0.5. Patriots 33.0; Opponents 28.0.

PUNTING

	No.	Yds.	Avg.	In. 20	Lg.
Jo. Miller	76	3431	45.1	22	59
Patriots	77	3431	44.6	22	59
Opponents	81	3537	43.7	27	68

PUNT RETURNS

	No.	FC	Yds.	Avg.	Lg.	TD
Dwight	32	13	273	8.5	29	0
T. Brown	7	5	30	4.3	7	0
B. Johnson	1	0	11	11.0	11	0
Patriots	40	18	314	7.9	29	0
Opponents	42	14	405	9.6	76	0

KICK RETURNS

	No.	Yds.	Avg.	Lg.	TD
B. Johnson	31	694	22.4	54	0
Hobbs	15	361	24.1	37	0
Dwight	10	250	25.0	38	0
Faulk	4	81	20.3	26	0
Davis	3	108	36.0	65	0
Pass	2	31	15.5	21	0
Banta-Cain	1	14	14.0	14	0
Cloud	1	15	15.0	15	0
Izzo	1	0	0.0	0	0
M. Stone	1	0	0.0	0	0
Watson	1	1	1.0	1	0
Patriots	70	1555	22.2	65	0
Opponents	68	1487	21.9	46	0

FIELD GOALS

	1-19	20-29	30-39	40-49	50+
Vinatieri	0/0	7/7	9/10	4/6	0/2
Patriots	0/0	7/7	9/10	4/6	0/2
Opponents	0/0	6/6	9/12	6/8	3/4

Vinatieri: (26G) (45G) (53N, 48G, 35G, 43G) (37N, 24G) (29G) (39G, 53N, 38G) (44N) () (35G, 32G, 33G) (37G) (29G) (45N, 21G, 34G, 22G) () () (26G) (49G, 33G) Opponents: (43N) (51G, 52G) (33G, 52N, 24G) (42G, 21G) (33G, 58G) () (46N, 23G, 35G, 41G) (35G, 20G) (31N, 36G) (30N, 46G) (25G, 20G, 33G, 47G) (38G) (32N) () () (36G, 38G, 41G, 42G)

PASSING

	Att.	Cmp.	Yds.	Pct.	Avg. Gain	TD	Pct. TD	Int.	Pct. Int.	Long	Sack/Lost	Rating
Brady	530	334	4110	63.0	7.75	26	4.9	14	2.6	71	26/188	92.3
Cassel	24	13	183	54.2	7.63	2	8.3	1	4.2	36	1/1	89.4
Flutie	10	5	29	50.0	2.90	0	0.0	0	0.0	13	1/13	56.3
Patriots	564	352	4322	62.4	7.66	28	5.0	15	2.7	71	28/202	91.5
Opponents	527	296	3926	56.2	7.45	25	4.7	10	1.9	t85	33/223	87.8

NEW ENGLAND PATRIOTS

NEW ORLEANS SAINTS
NFC SOUTH DIVISION

2006 SEASON

CLUB DIRECTORY

Owner
Tom Benson
Owner/executive vice president of administration
Rita LeBlanc
Executive vice president/general manager of football operations
Mickey Loomis
Director of player personnel
Rick Mueller
Senior football administrator
Russ Ball
Director of college scouting
Rick Reiprish
College scouting coordinator
Rick Thompson
Director of media & public relations
Greg Bensel

Head coach
Sean Payton

Assistant coaches
Dennis Allen (asst. defensive line)
Adam Bailey (asst. strength and conditioning)
John Bomamego (special teams)
Pete Carmichael Jr. (quarterbacks)
Dan Dalrymple (strength and conditioning)
Gary Gibbs (defensive coordinator)
Tom Hayes (secondary/cornerbacks)
George Henshaw (senior asst./running backs)
Marion Hobby (defensive line)
Curtis Johnson (wide receivers)
Terry Malone (tight ends)
Doug Marrone (offensive coordinator/offensive line)
Greg McMahon (asst. special teams)
John Morton (offensive asst./passing game)
Tony Oden (defensive asst./secondary)
Joe Vitt (asst. head coach/linebackers)

OFFSEASON MOVES

Key additions
RB	Michael Bennett	FA/Vikings
QB	Drew Brees	FA/Chargers
C	Jeff Faine	trade/Browns
LB	Scott Fujita	FA/Cowboys
WR	Chris Horn	FA/Chiefs
QB	Jamie Martin	FA/Rams
FS	Bryan Scott	trade/Falcons
LB	Anthony Simmons	FA/Seahawks
S	Omar Stoutmire	FA/Redskins
DT	Hollis Thomas	trade/Eagles

Key losses
C	LeCharles Bentley	FA/Browns
QB	Aaron Brooks	released/Raiders
CB	Fakhir Brown	FA/Rams
LT	Wayne Gandy	trade/Falcons
LB	Sedrick Hodge	FA/Dolphins
DE	Darren Howard	FA/Eagles
S	Mel Mitchell	FA/Patriots
LB	T.J. Slaughter	FA/49ers

SCHEDULE

Sept.	10—at Cleveland	1:00
Sept.	17—at Green Bay	1:00
Sept.	25—ATLANTA (Mon.)	8:30
Oct.	1—at Carolina	1:00
Oct.	8—TAMPA BAY	1:00
Oct.	15—PHILADELPHIA	1:00
Oct.	22—Open date	
Oct.	29—BALTIMORE	1:00
Nov.	5—at Tampa Bay	1:00
Nov.	12—at Pittsburgh	1:00
Nov.	19—CINCINNATI	1:00
Nov.	26—at Atlanta	1:00
Dec.	3—SAN FRANCISCO	1:00
Dec.	10—at Dallas	1:00
Dec.	17—WASHINGTON	1:00
Dec.	24—at N.Y. Giants	1:00
Dec.	31—CAROLINA	1:00

All times are Eastern.
All games Sunday unless noted.

DRAFT CHOICES

Reggie Bush, RB, Southern California (first round/second pick overall).
Roman Harper, FS, Alabama (2/43).
Jahri Evans, OT, Bloomsburg (4/108).
Rob Ninkovich, DE, Purdue (5/135).
Mike Hass, WR, Oregon State (6/171).
Josh "Bernard" Lay, CB, Pittsburgh (6/174).
Zach Strief, G, Northwestern (7/210).
Marques Colston, TE, Hofstra (7/252).

MISCELLANEOUS TEAM DATA

Stadium (capacity, surface):
Louisiana Superdome
(64,900, Sportexe Momentum)
Business address:
5800 Airline Drive
Metairie, LA 70003
Business phone:
504-733-0255
Ticket information:
504-731-1700
Team colors:
Old gold, black and white
Flagship radio station:
WWL, 870 AM
Website:
www.neworleanssaints.com
Training site:
TBD

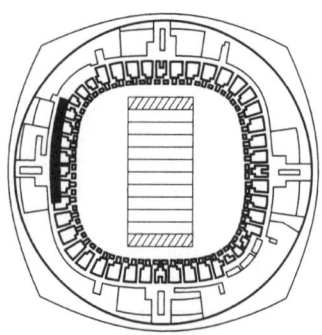

No.	QUARTERBACKS	Ht./Wt.	Born	NFL Exp.	College	How acq.	'05 Games GP/GS
	Todd Bouman	6-2/226	8/1/72	9	St. Cloud State	T-Min/03	16/3
	Drew Brees	6-0/209	1/15/79	6	Purdue	FA/06	16/16
0	Jamie Martin	6-2/205	2/8/70	12	Weber State	FA/06	8/5
	Adrian McPherson	6-3/218	5/8/83	1	Florida State	D5/05	0/0
	RUNNING BACKS						
8	Michael Bennett	5-9/209	8/13/78	6	Wisconsin	FA/06	16/6
	Reggie Bush	6-0/203	3/2/85	R	USC	D1/06	—
4	Mike Karney (FB)	5-11/258	7/6/81	3	Arizona State	D5/04	16/14
5	Fred McAfee	5-10/197	6/20/68	15	Mississippi College	FA/00	16/0
6	Deuce McAllister	6-1/232	12/27/78	6	Mississippi	D1/01	5/5
6	Nate Schurman (FB)	6-2/247	11/8/81	1	Missouri State	FA/06	0/0
7	Aaron Stecker	5-10/213	11/13/75	7	Western Illinois	FA/04	15/4
	RECEIVERS						
9	Mark Campbell (TE)	6-6/260	12/6/75	7	Michigan	FA/06	14/10
2	Marques Colston	6-4/231	6/5/83	R	Hofstra	D7b/06	—
5	Ernie Conwell (TE)	6-2/255	8/17/72	11	Washington	FA/03	9/9
8	Mike Hass (TE)	6-1/209	1/2/83	R	Oregon State	D6a/06	—
9	Devery Henderson	5-11/200	3/26/82	3	LSU	D2/04	14/3
6	Zach Hilton (TE)	6-8/268	7/2/80	4	North Carolina	FA/03	15/6
1	Chris Horn	5-11/195	7/13/77	3	Rocky Mountain	FA/06	14/3
7	Joe Horn	6-1/213	1/16/72	11	Itwamba JC	FA/00	13/13
2	Nate Lawrie (TE)	6-7/256	10/781	2	Yale	W-TB/05	6/0
4	Michael Lewis	5-8/173	11/14/71	6	None	FA/01	2/0
5	Chase Lyman	6-4/210	9/4/82	2	California	D4/05	—
8	Nate Poole	6-2/204	2/1/77	5	Marshall	FA/05	7/0
6	Lance Moore	5-9/177	8/31/83	1	Toledo	FA/06	—
3	Donte' Stallworth	6-0/196	11/10/80	5	Tennessee	D1a/02	16/13
4	Levon Thomas	6-1/201	7/7/83	1	Georgia Tech	FA/06	—
	OFFENSIVE LINEMEN						
0	Ben Archibald (T)	6-3/320	8/26/78	2	Brigham Young	FA/03	6/0
0	Jammal Brown (T)	6-6/313	3/30/81	2	Oklahoma	D1/05	13/13
3	Jahri Evans (G)	6-4/318	8/22/83	R	Bloomsburg	D4/06	—
9	Jeff Faine (C)	6-3/291	4/6/81	4	Notre Dame	T-Cle/06	14/14
6	Jonathan Goodwin (G/C)	6-3/318	12/2/78	5	Michigan	FA/06	16/10
4	Augie Hoffmann (G)	6-2/315	2/23/81	2	Boston College	FA/06	—
1	Montrae Holland (G)	6-2/322	5/21/80	4	Florida State	D4/03	15/10
5	Jermane Mayberry (G)	6-4/325	8/29/73	11	Texas A&M-Kingsville	FA/05	11/8
7	Jamar Nesbit (G/T)	6-4/328	12/17/76	8	South Carolina	FA/04	16/4
3	Chad Setterstrom (T)	6-3/310	6/13/80	2	Northern Iowa	FA/05	—
8	Jon Stinchcomb (T)	6-5/315	8/27/79	4	Georgia	D2/03	0/0
4	Zach Strief (T)	6-7/349	9/22/83	R	Northwestern	D7a/06	—
	DEFENSIVE LINEMEN						
2	Tony Bryant (E)	6-6/282	9/3/76	7	Florida State	FA/04	16/1
4	Charles Grant (E)	6-3/290	9/3/78	5	Georgia	D1b/02	16/14
7	Rodney Leisle (T)	6-3/315	2/5/81	2	UCLA	D5/04	1/0
3	Rob Ninkovich (E)	6-2/252	2/1/84	R	Purdue	D5/06	—
1	Will Smith (E)	6-3/282	7/4/81	3	Ohio State	D1/04	16/9
7	Johnathan Sullivan (T)	6-3/315	1/21/81	4	Georgia	D1/03	15/0
9	Hollis Thomas (T)	6-0/306	1/10/74	11	Northern Illinois	T-Phi/06	16/12
9	Jimmy Verdon (T)	6-3/280	11/4/81	2	Arizona State	D7/05	4/0
8	Willie Whitehead (T)	6-3/300	1/26/73	8	Auburn	FA/99	16/15
6	Brian Young (T)	6-2/298	7/8/77	7	UTEP	FA/04	16/16
	LINEBACKERS						
0	James Allen	6-2/245	11/11/79	5	Oregon State	D3/02	3/0
7	Colby Bockwoldt	6-1/237	4/14/81	3	Brigham Young	D7/04	16/16
6	Alfred Fincher	6-1/238	8/15/83	2	Connecticut	D3/05	11/0
2	Scott Fujita	6-5/250	4/28/79	5	California	FA/06	16/8
1	Terrence Melton	6-1/235	1/1/77	3	Rice	FA/04	15/2
1	Anthony Simmons	6-0/240	6/20/76	8	Clemson	FA/06	0/0
5	Courtney Watson	6-1/246	9/18/80	3	Notre Dame	D2/04	9/6
	DEFENSIVE BACKS						
0	Jay Bellamy (S)	5-11/200	7/8/72	13	Rutgers	FA/01	3/3
9	Josh Bullocks (S)	6-0/207	2/28/83	2	Nebraska	D2/05	16/13
1	Jason Craft (CB)	5-10/187	2/13/76	8	Colorado State	T-Jax/04	16/4
7	Steve Gleason (S)	5-11/212	3/19/77	6	Washington State	FA/00	13/1
1	Roman Harper (S)	6-1/200	12/11/82	R	Alabama	D2/06	—
2	Josh Lay (CB)	6-0/197	9/8/82	R	Pitt	D6b/06	—
4	Mike McKenzie (CB)	6-0/194	4/26/76	8	Memphis	T-GB/04	15/15
8	Bryan Scott (S)	6-1/219	4/13/81	4	Penn State	T-Atl/06	16/13
4	Dwight Smith (S)	5-10/201	8/13/78	6	Akron	FA/05	15/15
3	Omar Stoutmire (S)	5-11/205	7/9/74	10	Fresno State	FA/06	10/0
2	Fred Thomas (CB)	5-9/185	9/11/73	11	Tennessee-Martin	FA/00	16/11
1	Joey Thomas (CB)	6-1/190	8/29/80	3	Montana State	W-GB/05	11/1
	SPECIALISTS						
7	Mitch Berger (P)	6-4/228	6/24/72	12	Colorado	FA/03	16/0
	John Carney (K)	5-11/185	4/20/64	17	Notre Dame	FA/01	16/0
7	Kevin Houser (LS)	6-2/252	8/23/77	7	Ohio State	FA/02	16/0

Abbreviations: D1-draft pick, first round; W-claimed on waivers; T-obtained in trade; FA-free-agent acquisition.

NEW ORLEANS SAINTS

2005 REVIEW

NEW ORLEANS SAINTS

2005 regular-season record: 3-13
Position: 4th in NFC South

Sept.11—at Carolina	W	23-20
Sept.19—N.Y. GIANTS	L	10-27
Sept.25—at Minnesota	L	16-33
Oct. 2—BUFFALO	W	19-7
Oct. 9—at Green Bay	L	3-52
Oct. 16—ATLANTA	L	31-34
Oct. 23—at St. Louis	L	17-28
Oct. 30—MIAMI	L	6-21
Nov. 6—CHICAGO	L	17-20
Nov. 13—Open date		
Nov. 20—at New England	L	17-24
Nov. 27—at N.Y. Jets	W	21-19
Dec. 4—TAMPA BAY	L	3-10
Dec. 12—at Atlanta	L	17-36
Dec. 18—CAROLINA	L	10-27
Dec. 24—DETROIT	L	12-13
Jan. 1—at Tampa Bay	L	13-27

SCORING BY PERIODS

	Q1	Q2	Q3	Q4	OT	Pts.
Saints	47	97	22	69	0	235
Opponents	103	126	59	110	0	398

TEAM STATISTICS

	N.O.	Opp.
TOTAL FIRST DOWNS ..	312	281
Rushing	89	103
Passing	182	145
Penalty	41	33
3rd Down: Made/Att. ..	82/211	89/220
3rd Down Pct.	38.9	40.5
4th Down: Made/Att. ..	2/12	3/4
4th Down Pct.	16.7	75.0
POSSESSION AVG.	30:32	29:28
TOTAL NET YARDS	5031	4994
Avg. per Game	314.4	312.1
Total Plays	1017	946
Avg. per Play	4.9	5.3
NET YARDS RUSHING ..	1688	2145
Avg. per Game	105.5	134.1
Total Rushes	423	503
NET YARDS PASSING....	3343	2849
Avg. per Game	208.9	178.1
Sacked/Yards Lost	41/261	25/165
Gross Yards	3604	3014
Att./Completions	553/308	418/241
Completion Pct.	55.7	57.7
Had Intercepted	24	10
PUNTS/AVERAGE	71/43.2	76/45.6
NET PUNTING AVG.	71/38.7	76/39.0
PENALTIES/YARDS	135/1130	127/985
FUMBLES/LOST	23/19	19/9
TOUCHDOWNS	23	43
Rushing	8	16
Passing	15	20
Returns	0	7

SCORING (NONKICKERS)

	TD	RTD	PTD	MTD	2Pt.	Tot. Pts.
Stallworth	7	0	7	0	0	42
Henderson	3	0	3	0	0	18
McAllister	3	3	0	0	0	18
Smith	3	3	0	0	0	18
Brooks	2	2	0	0	0	12
Hakim	2	0	2	0	0	12
Conwell	1	0	1	0	0	6
Hilton	1	0	1	0	0	6
Horn	1	0	1	0	0	6
Saints	23	8	15	0	0	138
Opponents	43	16	20	7	0	262

2-Pt. conversions: Saints 0-1; Opponents 0-0.

(KICKERS)

	XPM/XPA	FGM/FGA	Pts.
Carney	22/22	25/32	97
Saints	22/22	25/32	97
Opponents	43/43	31/39	136

RUSHING

	Att.	Yds.	Avg.	Lg.	TD
Smith	166	659	4.0	42	3
Stecker	95	363	3.8	32	0
McAllister	93	335	3.6	26	3
Brooks	45	281	6.2	22	2
Bouman	8	15	1.9	6	0
Karney	6	12	2.0	3	0
A. Thomas	7	12	1.7	4	0
Henderson	1	9	9.0	9	0
Stallworth	2	2	1.0	3	0
Saints	423	1688	4.0	42	8
Opponents	503	2145	4.3	64	16

RECEIVING

	No.	Yds.	Avg.	Lg.	TD
Stallworth	70	945	13.5	43	7
Horn	49	654	13.3	30	1
Hilton	35	396	11.3	29	1
Stecker	35	281	8.0	41	0
Hakim	34	489	14.4	42	2
Henderson	22	343	15.6	66	3
McAllister	17	117	6.9	22	0
Conwell	13	165	12.7	31	1
Smith	12	46	3.8	8	0
Karney	10	61	6.1	10	0
L. Hall	6	36	6.0	8	0
Poole	3	63	21.0	42	0
A. Thomas	2	8	4.0	6	0
Saints	308	3604	11.7	66	15
Opponents	241	3014	12.5	68	20

INTERCEPTIONS

	No.	Yds.	Avg.	Lg.	TD
Craft	3	63	21.0	39	0
Smith	2	53	26.5	28	0
F. Thomas	2	4	2.0	4	0
Bullocks	1	51	51.0	51	0
McKenzie	1	11	11.0	11	0
Slaughter	1	0	0.0	0	0
Saints	10	182	18.2	51	0
Opponents	24	456	19.0	t95	3

SACKS: W. Smith 8.5, Bryant 4.0, Howard 3.5, F. Thomas 3.0, Ch. Grant 2.5, Craft 1.0, Smith 1.0, Watson 1.0, Whitehead 0.5. Saints 25.0; Opponents 41.0.

PUNTING

	No.	Yds.	Avg.	In. 20	Lg.
Berger	71	3066	43.2	28	69
Saints	71	3066	43.2	28	69
Opponents	76	3462	45.6	23	59

PUNT RETURNS

	No.	FC	Yds.	Avg.	Lg.	TD
Hakim	34	4	260	7.6	42	0
Stallworth	7	1	52	7.4	27	0
M. Lewis	4	0	8	2.0	5	0
F. Thomas	1	0	0	0.0	0	0
Saints	46	5	320	7.0	42	0
Opponents	33	26	260	7.9	23	0

KICK RETURNS

	No.	Yds.	Avg.	Lg.	TD
Stecker	31	672	21.7	46	0
McAfee	22	485	22.0	34	0
Hakim	9	171	19.0	29	0
M. Lewis	8	137	17.1	20	0
L. Hall	2	9	4.5	5	0
Whitehead	2	12	6.0	12	0
Smith	1	30	30.0	30	0
Saints	75	1516	20.2	46	0
Opponents	61	1404	23.0	82	0

FIELD GOALS

	1-19	20-29	30-39	40-49	50+
Carney	1/1	12/13	4/6	8/12	0/0
Saints	1/1	12/13	4/6	8/12	0/0
Opponents	0/0	10/10	13/15	8/12	0/2

Carney: (29G, 48G, 47G) (21G, 29N) (22G) (23G, 40G, 32N, 20G, 37G) (33G, 43N, 43N) (19G, 47B) (45B, 22G) (26G, 49G) (22G) (30N, 46G) () (26G) (47G) (44G) (35G, 47G, 33G, 20G) (25G, 24G)
Opponents: (39G, 46G) (39G, 30G) (24G, 33N, 28G, 48G, 34G) (45N) (26G) (37G, 36G) (48N) (37G, 36G, 41G, 46G, 36N) (35G, 47N, 28G) (37G) (29G, 45G, 41G, 38G, 53N) (43B, 28G) (43G, 20G) (32G, 50N, 29G) (21G, 39G) (46G, 26G)

PASSING

	Att.	Cmp.	Yds.	Pct.	Avg. Gain	TD	Pct. TD	Int.	Pct. Int.	Long	Sack/Lost	Rating
Brooks	431	240	2882	55.7	6.69	13	3.0	17	3.9	66	33/202	70.0
Bouman	122	68	722	55.7	5.92	2	1.6	7	5.7	43	8/59	54.7
Saints	553	308	3604	55.7	6.52	15	2.7	24	4.3	66	41/261	66.6
Opponents	418	241	3014	57.7	7.21	20	4.8	10	2.4	68	25/165	86.2

NEW YORK GIANTS
NFC EAST DIVISION

NEW YORK GIANTS

2006 SEASON

CLUB DIRECTORY

President
John K. Mara
Chairman
Steven Tisch
Senior vice president and general manager
Ernie Accorsi
Assistant general manager
Kevin Abrams
Director/player personnel
Jerry Reese
Director/pro personnel
Dave Gettleman
Director/research and development
Raymond J. Walsh Jr.
Vice president for player evaluation
Chris Mara
Director/college scouting
Jerry Shay
Vice president of communications
Pat Hanlon
Director of community relations
Allison Stangeby

Head coach
Tom Coughlin

Assistant coaches
Andy Barnett (asst. strength and conditioning)
Andre Curtis (defensive quality control)
John DeFilippo (offensive quality control)
Dave DeGuglielmo (asst. offensive line)
Pat Flaherty (offensive line)
Peter Giunta (defensive backs)
Kevin Gilbride (quarterbacks)
John Hufnagel (offensive coordinator)
Jerald Ingram (running backs)
Tim Lewis (defensive coordinator)
Dave Merritt (asst. secondary)
Jerry Palmieri (strength and conditioning)
Michael Pope (tight ends)
Tom Quinn (asst. special teams)
Bill Sheridan (linebackers)
Mike Sullivan (wide receivers)
Mike Sweatman (special teams)
Mike Waufle (defensive line)

OFFSEASON MOVES

Key additions
LB LaVar Arrington — released/Redskins
S Will Demps — FA/Ravens
CB Sam Madison — released/Dolphins
CB R.W. McQuarters — FA/Lions
CB Jason Bell — FA/Texans
S Quentin Harris — FA/Cardinals
C Grey Ruegamer — FA/Packers
LB Brandon Short — FA/Panthers
Key losses
DT Kendrick Clancy — FA/Cardinals
CB Will Allen — FA/Dolphins
LB Nick Greisen — FA/Jaguars
LB Barrett Green — released
S Brent Alexander — retired

SCHEDULE

Sept. 10—INDIANAPOLIS 8:15
Sept. 17—at Philadelphia 1:00
Sept. 24—at Seattle 4:15
Oct. 1—Open date
Oct. 8—WASHINGTON 1:00
Oct. 15—at Atlanta 1:00
Oct. 23—at Dallas (Mon.) 8:30
Oct. 29—TAMPA BAY 1:00
Nov. 5—HOUSTON 1:00
Nov. 12—CHICAGO 1:00
Nov. 20—at Jacksonville (Mon.) 8:30
Nov. 26—at Tennessee 1:00
Dec. 3—DALLAS 1:00
Dec. 10—at Carolina 1:00
Dec. 17—PHILADELPHIA 1:00
Dec. 24—NEW ORLEANS 1:00
Dec. 30—at Washington (Sat.) 8:00
All times are Eastern.
All games Sunday unless noted.

DRAFT CHOICES

Mathias Kiwanuka, DE, Boston College (first round/32nd pick overall).
Sinorice Moss, WR, Miami (2/44).
Gerris Wilkinson, ILB, Georgia Tech (3/96).
Barry Cofield, DT, Northwestern (4/124).
Guy Whimper, OT, East Carolina (4/129).
Charlie Peprah, SS, Alabama (5/158).
Gerrick McPhearson, CB, Maryland (7/232).

MISCELLANEOUS TEAM DATA

Stadium (capacity, surface):
Giants Stadium (80,242, artificial)
Business address:
Giants Stadium
East Rutherford, N.J. 07073
Business phone:
201-935-8111
Ticket information:
201-935-8222
Team colors:
Blue, white and red
Flagship radio station:
WFAN, 660 AM
Website:
www.giants.com
Training site:
University at Albany
Albany, N.Y.
201-935-8111

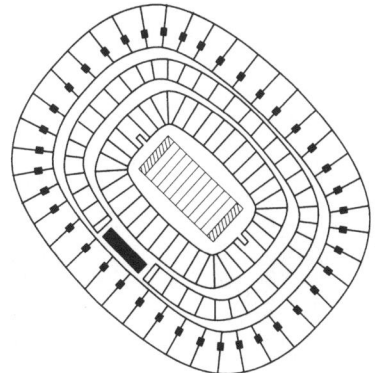

– 65 –

NEW YORK GIANTS

No.	QUARTERBACKS	Ht./Wt.	Born	NFL Exp.	College	How acq.	'05 Games GP/GS
8	Tim Hasselbeck	6-1/211	4/6/78	4	Boston College	W-Was/05	5/0
12	Jared Lorenzen	6-4/275	2/14/81	1	Kentucky	FA/04	0/0
10	Eli Manning	6-4/218	1/3/81	3	Mississippi	T-SD/04	16/16
	RUNNING BACKS						
21	Tiki Barber	5-10/200	4/7/75	10	Virginia	D2/97	16/16
20	Jim Finn (FB)	6-0/245	12/2/76	7	Pennsylvania	FA/03	16/13
44	Tony Jackson (FB)	6-3/265	7/5/82	1	Iowa	FA/06	0/0
27	Brandon Jacobs	6-4/264	7/6/82	2	Southern Illinois	D4/05	16/0
29	Chad Morton	5-8/203	4/4/77	7	USC	FA/05	16/0
34	Derrick Ward	5-11/233	8/30/80	3	Ottawa	D7c/04	14/0
	RECEIVERS						
88	Sean Berton (TE)	6-4/272	10/31/79	4	N.C. State	W-Min/05	14/0
17	Plaxico Burress	6-5/226	8/12/77	7	Michigan State	FA/05	16/15
84	Tim Carter	6-0/200	9/21/79	5	Auburn	D2/02	15/1
15	Michael Jennings	5-11/175	9/7/79	1	Florida State	FA/04	0/0
83	Matt Kranchick (TE)	6-7/260	12/13/79	3	Penn State	FA/05	6/1
89	Sinorice Moss	5-8/185	12/28/83	R	Miami	D2/06	—
87	Willie Ponder	6-0/205	2/14/80	4	SE Missouri St.	D6a/03	11/0
82	Visanthe Shiancoe (TE)	6-4/250	6/18/80	4	Morgan State	D3/03	16/4
80	Jeremy Shockey (TE)	6-5/253	8/18/80	5	Miami	D1/02	15/15
86	Jamaar Taylor	6-0/197	2/25/81	3	Texas A&M	D6/04	5/0
81	Amani Toomer	6-3/208	9/8/74	11	Michigan	D2/96	16/16
85	David Tyree	6-0/205	1/3/80	4	Syracuse	D6c/03	13/0
	OFFENSIVE LINEMEN						
66	David Diehl (G)	6-5/315	9/15/80	4	Illinois	D5/03	16/16
61	Lewis Kelly (G)	6-4/306	4/21/77	4	S.C. State	FA/05	1/0
67	Kareem McKenzie (T)	6-6/327	5/24/79	6	Penn State	FA/05	14/14
60	Shaun O'Hara (C)	6-3/306	6/23/77	7	Rutgers	FA/00	16/16
77	Luke Petitgout (T)	6-6/310	6/16/76	8	Notre Dame	D1/99	16/15
65	Grey Ruegamer (G)	6-4/305	6/11/76	7	Arizona State	FA/06	13/2
69	Rich Seubert (G)	6-3/305	3/30/79	5	Western Illinois	FA/01	4/1
76	Chris Snee (G)	6-2/314	1/8/82	2	Boston College	D2/04	16/16
79	Guy Whimper (T)	6-4/300	5/21/83	R	East Carolina	D4b/06	—
71	Bob Whitfield (T)	6-5/310	10/18/71	15	Stanford	FA/06	16/2
	DEFENSIVE LINEMEN						
95	Adrian Awasom (E)	6-5/275	10/25/83	2	North Texas	FA/05	5/0
96	Barry Cofield (T)	6-4/304	3/19/84	R	Northwestern	D4a/06	—
99	Damane Duckett (T)	6-6/300	1/21/81	3	East Carolina	FA/04	8/0
94	William Joseph (T)	6-5/315	9/3/79	4	Miami	D1/03	10/10
97	Mathias Kiwanuka (E)	6-5/265	3/8/83	R	Boston College	D1/06	—
90	Ryan Kuehl (T)	6-5/280	1/18/72	9	Virginia	FA/03	16/0
93	Eric Moore (E)	6-4/261	2/28/81	2	Florida State	D6/05	8/0
98	Fred Robbins (T)	6-4/325	3/25/77	7	Wake Forest	FA/04	16/6
75	Jonas Seawright (T)	6-6/312	4/12/82	1	North Carolina	FA/05	0/0
92	Michael Strahan (E)	6-5/275	11/21/71	14	Texas Southern	D2/93	16/16
91	Justin Tuck (E)	6-5/275	3/29/83	2	Notre Dame	D3/05	14/1
72	Osi Umenyiora (E)	6-3/280	11/16/80	4	Troy	D2/03	16/16
	LINEBACKERS						
55	LaVar Arrington	6-3/253	6/20/78	7	Penn State	FA/06	12/8
57	Chase Blackburn	6-3/247	6/10/83	2	Akron	FA/05	15/2
51	Carlos Emmons	6-5/250	9/3/73	11	Arkansas State	FA/04	9/8
58	Antonio Pierce	6-1/240	10/26/78	6	Arizona	FA/05	13/13
54	Brandon Short	6-3/253	7/11/77	7	Penn State	FA/06	16/15
53	Reggie Torbor	6-2/254	1/25/81	3	Auburn	D4/04	14/9
59	Gerris Wilkinson	6-3/233	4/5/83	R	Georgia Tech	D3/06	—
	DEFENSIVE BACKS						
33	Jason Bell (CB)	6-0/186	4/1/78	6	UCLA	FA/06	16/0
37	James Butler (S)	6-3/210	9/7/82	2	Georgia Tech	FA/05	16/1
39	Curtis DeLoatch (CB)	6-2/217	10/4/81	3	North Carolina A&T	FA/04	16/13
47	Will Demps (S)	6-0/205	11/7/79	5	San Diego State	FA/06	11/11
26	Quentin Harris (S)	6-1/214	1/26/77	5	Syracuse	FA/06	16/1
22	Sam Madison (CB)	5-11/185	4/23/74	10	Louisville	FA/06	15/15
43	Adrian Mayes (SS)	6-1/211	11/17/80	3	LSU	FA/06	3/0
38	Gerrick McPhearson (CB)	5-10/196	12/29/83	R	Maryland	D7/06	—
25	R.W. McQuarters (CB)	5-10/195	12/21/76	9	Oklahoma State	FA/06	16/11
36	Charlie Peprah (S)	5-10/206	2/24/83	R	Alabama	D5/06	—
24	Will Peterson (CB)	6-0/200	6/15/79	6	Western Illinois	D3/01	2/2
41	Frank Walker (CB)	5-10/198	8/6/80	4	Tuskegee	D6b/03	7/0
23	Corey Webster (CB)	6-0/199	3/2/82	2	LSU	D2/05	15/2
28	Gibril Wilson (DB)	6-0/197	11/12/81	3	Tennessee	D5/04	16/16
	SPECIALISTS						
18	Jeff Feagles (P)	6-1/215	3/7/66	19	Miami	FA/03	16/0
2	Jay Feely (K)	5-10/206	5/23/76	6	Michigan	FA/05	16/0

Abbreviations: D1-draft pick, first round; W-claimed on waivers; T-obtained in trade; FA-free-agent acquisition.

2005 regular-season record: 11-5
Position: 1st in NFC East

Sept.11—ARIZONA	W	42-19
Sept.19—at New Orleans	W	27-10
Sept.25—at San Diego	L	23-45
Oct. 2—ST. LOUIS	W	44-24
Oct. 9—Open date		
Oct. 16—at Dallas (OT)	L	13-16
Oct. 23—DENVER	W	24-23
Oct. 30—WASHINGTON	W	36-0
Nov. 6—at San Francisco	W	24-6
Nov.13—MINNESOTA	L	21-24
Nov.20—PHILADELPHIA	W	27-17
Nov.27—at Seattle (OT)	L	21-24
Dec. 4—DALLAS	W	17-10
Dec.11—at Philadelphia (OT)	W	26-23
Dec.17—KANSAS CITY	W	27-17
Dec.24—at Washington	L	20-35
Dec.31—at Oakland	W	30-21

2005 postseason record: 0-1
Jan. 8—CAROLINA#	L	0-23

#NFC wild-card game.

SCORING BY PERIODS

	Q1	Q2	Q3	Q4	OT	Pts.
Giants	84	136	84	115	3	422
Opponents	55	95	95	63	6	314

TEAM STATISTICS

	NYG	Opp.
TOTAL FIRST DOWNS	312	302
Rushing	106	83
Passing	172	189
Penalty	34	30
3rd Down: Made/Att.	90/227	94/236
3rd Down Pct.	39.6	39.8
4th Down: Made/Att.	6/13	6/12
4th Down Pct.	46.2	50.0
POSSESSION AVG.	30:26	29:34
TOTAL NET YARDS	5787	5240
Avg. per Game	361.7	327.5
Total Plays	1055	1049
Avg. per Play	5.5	5.0
NET YARDS RUSHING	2209	1656
Avg. per Game	138.1	103.5
Total Rushes	469	428
NET YARDS PASSING	3578	3584
Avg. per Game	223.6	224.0
Sacked/Yards Lost	28/184	41/268
Gross Yards	3762	3852
Att./Completions	558/294	580/329
Completion Pct.	52.7	56.7
Had Intercepted	17	17
PUNTS/AVERAGE	73/42.1	88/41.5
NET PUNTING AVG.	73/37.0	88/35.7
PENALTIES/YARDS	143/1115	136/1180
FUMBLES/LOST	17/8	29/20
TOUCHDOWNS	45	36
Rushing	17	12

	NYG	Opp.
Passing	24	20
Returns	4	4

SCORING (NONKICKERS)

	Tot. TD	RTD	PTD	MTD	2Pt.	Tot. Pts.
Barber	11	9	2	0	1	68
Shockey	7	0	7	0	1	44
Burress	7	0	7	0	0	42
Jacobs	7	7	0	0	0	42
Toomer	7	0	7	0	0	42
Blackburn	1	0	0	1	0	6
Manning	1	1	0	0	0	6
Morton	1	0	0	1	0	6
Pierce	1	0	0	1	0	6
Ponder	1	0	0	1	0	6
Tyree	1	0	1	0	0	6
Giants	45	17	24	4	2	274
Opponents	36	12	20	4	0	216

2-Pt. conversions: Giants 2-2; Opponents 0-1.

(KICKERS)

	XPM/XPA	FGM/FGA	Pts.
Feely	43/43	35/42	148
Giants	43/43	35/42	148
Opponents	35/35	21/30	98

RUSHING

	Att.	Yds.	Avg.	Lg.	TD
Barber	357	1860	5.2	t95	9
Ward	35	123	3.5	12	0
Jacobs	38	99	2.6	21	7
Manning	29	80	2.8	14	1
T. Carter	6	46	7.7	22	0
Ponder	1	4	4.0	4	0
Cloud	1	0	0.0	0	0
Hasselbeck	2	-3	-1.5	-1	0
Giants	469	2209	4.7	t95	17
Opponents	428	1656	3.9	62	12

RECEIVING

	No.	Yds.	Avg.	Lg.	TD
Burress	76	1214	16.0	t78	7
Shockey	65	891	13.7	59	7
Toomer	60	684	11.4	37	7
Barber	54	530	9.8	48	2
Finn	13	98	7.5	15	0
T. Carter	10	186	18.6	44	0
Shiancoe	8	91	11.4	17	0
Tyree	5	52	10.4	18	1
Ward	2	13	6.5	8	0
Berton	1	3	3.0	3	0
Giants	294	3762	12.8	t78	24
Opponents	329	3852	11.7	t72	20

INTERCEPTIONS

	No.	Yds.	Avg.	Lg.	TD
Alexander	4	45	11.3	24	0
Pierce	2	41	20.5	24	0
Wilson	2	36	18.0	19	0
Williams	2	34	17.0	34	0
Butler	2	16	8.0	16	0
F. Walker	1	71	71.0	71	0
Torbor	1	37	37.0	37	0
Blackburn	1	31	31.0	t31	1
DeLoatch	1	20	20.0	20	0
Emmons	1	6	6.0	6	0
W. Allen	0	17	-	17	0
Giants	17	354	20.8	71	1
Opponents	17	302	17.8	t92	2

SACKS: Umenyiora 14.5, Strahan 11.5, Wilson 3.0, Pierce 2.5, Allen 2.0, Clancy 2.0, Joseph 2.0, Robbins 1.5, Greisen 1.0, Tuck 1.0. Giants 41.0; Opponents 28.0.

PUNTING

	No.	Yds.	Avg.	In. 20	Lg.
Feagles	73	3070	42.1	26	56
Giants	73	3070	42.1	26	56
Opponents	88	3651	41.5	30	61

PUNT RETURNS

	No.	FC	Yds.	Avg.	Lg.	TD
Morton	47	16	453	9.6	58	1
Blackburn	1	0	0	0.0	0	0
Butler	1	0	0	0.0	0	0
Giants	49	16	453	9.2	58	1
Opponents	36	15	309	8.6	t71	1

KICK RETURNS

	No.	Yds.	Avg.	Lg.	TD
Ponder	35	905	25.9	t95	1
Morton	24	559	23.3	41	0
Jacobs	2	58	29.0	33	0
Allen	1	2	2.0	2	0
Shiancoe	1	5	5.0	5	0
Giants	63	1529	24.3	t95	1
Opponents	85	1867	22.0	t86	1

FIELD GOALS

	1-19	20-29	30-39	40-49	50+
Feely	0/0	11/13	13/14	8/10	3/5
Giants	0/0	11/13	13/14	8/10	3/5
Opponents	1/1	6/7	4/6	8/14	2/2

Feely: () (39G, 30G) (22G, 40G, 28G) (38G, 32G, 23G) (50G, 45G) (52G) (39G, 50G, 51N, 33G, 39G, 44G) (22G) (35G, 48G, 28N) (26G, 27G) (39G, 43G, 40N, 54N, 45N) (27G, 33N) (24G, 21G, 27G, 36G) (41G, 35G) (47G, 29B, 38G) (25G, 38G, 46G) Opponents: (24G, 42G) (21G, 29N) (44G) (37G, 48N) (49B, 48N, 29G, 28G, 45G) (49G, 42G, 27G, 49N) () (48G, 52G) (40N, 32B, 48G) (20G, 38N) (36G) (34G) (42G, 49N, 36G, 50G) (19G) () ()

PASSING

	Att.	Cmp.	Yds.	Pct.	Avg. Gain	TD	Pct. TD	Int.	Pct. Int.	Long	Sack/Lost	Rating
Manning	557	294	3762	52.8	6.75	24	4.3	17	3.1	t78	28/184	75.9
Barber	1	0	0	0.0	0.00	0	0.0	0	0.0	...	0/0	39.6
Giants	558	294	3762	52.7	6.74	24	4.3	17	3.0	t78	28/184	75.7
Opponents	580	329	3852	56.7	6.64	20	3.4	17	2.9	t72	41/268	76.3

NEW YORK GIANTS

NEW YORK JETS
AFC EAST DIVISION

NEW YORK JETS

2006 SEASON

CLUB DIRECTORY

Chairman and CEO
Woody Johnson
President
Jay Cross
General manager
Mike Tannenbaum
Director, pro personnel
JoJo Wooden
VP, public relations
Ron Colangelo
Senior director, football administration
David Socie
Senior director, operations
Clay Hampton
Senior director, college scouting
Jesse Kaye
Assistant director, college scouting
Joey Clinkscales
National scouts
Jim Cochran, Mike Davis

Head coach
Eric Mangini

Assistant coaches
Richie Anderson (tight ends/
asst. wide receivers)
Brett Bech (asst. strength and
conditioning)
Corwin Brown (defensive backs)
Bryan Cox (asst. defensive line)
Mike Devlin (tight ends/asst.
offensive line)
Andy Dickerson (coaches' asst.)
Sam Gash (asst. running
backs/special teams)
Jim Herrmann (linebackers)
Rick Lyle (asst. strength and
conditioning)
Denny Marcin (defensive line)
Jason Mandolesi (defensive
quality control)
Noel Mazzone (wide receivers)
Jason Michael (offensive quality
control)
Markus Paul (head strength and
conditioning)
Jimmy Raye (running backs)
Brian Schottenheimer (offensive
coordinator)
Bob Sutton (defensive
coordinator)
Mike Westhoff (special teams
coordinator)
Tony Wise (offensive line)

SCHEDULE

Sept.	10—at Tennessee	1:00
Sept.	17—NEW ENGLAND	4:15
Sept.	24—at Buffalo	1:00
Oct.	1—INDIANAPOLIS	1:00
Oct.	8—at Jacksonville	4:05
Oct.	15—MIAMI	4:15
Oct.	22—DETROIT	1:00
Oct.	29—at Cleveland	4:15
Nov.	5—Open date	
Nov.	12—at New England	1:00
Nov.	19—CHICAGO	1:00
Nov.	26—HOUSTON	1:00
Dec.	3—at Green Bay	1:00
Dec.	10—BUFFALO	1:00
Dec.	17—at Minnesota	1:00
Dec.	25—at Miami (Mon.)	8:30
Dec.	31—OAKLAND	1:00

All times are Eastern.
All games Sunday unless noted.

DRAFT CHOICES

D'Brickashaw Ferguson, OT, Virginia
(first round/fourth pick overall).
Nick Mangold, C, Ohio State (1/29).
Kellen Clemens, QB, Oregon (2/49).
Anthony Schlegel, ILB, Ohio State
(3/76).
Eric Smith, SS, Michigan State (3/97).
Brad Smith, WR, Missouri (4/103).
Leon Washington, RB, Florida State
(4/117).
Jason Pociask, TE, Wisconsin (5/150).
Drew Coleman, CB, Texas Christian
(6/189).
Titus Adams, DT, Nebraska (7/220).

OFFSEASON MOVES

Key additions
LB	Matt Chatham	FA/Patriots
WR	Tim Dwight	FA/Patriots
CB	Andre Dyson	FA/Seahawks
WR	Brad Kassell	FA/Titans
QB	Patrick Ramsey	trade/Redskins
C	Trey Teague	FA/Bills
DT	Kimo von Oelhoffen	FA/Steelers

Key losses
DE	John Abraham	trade/Falcons
RT	Jason Fabini	released/Cowboys
QB	Jay Fiedler	released
CB	Ty Law	released
C	Kevin Mawae	released/Titans
NT	James Reed	FA
FB	Jerald Sowell	released/Bucs

MISCELLANEOUS TEAM DATA

Stadium (capacity, surface):
The Meadowlands
(80,062, FieldTurf)
Business address:
Training facilities
1000 Fulton Avenue
Hempstead, NY 11550
City office
50 W. 57th,
New York, NY 10019
Business phone:
516-560-8100, 212-969-1800
Ticket information:
516-560-8200
Team colors:
Green and white

Flagship radio station:
ESPN Radio, 1050 AM
Website:
www.newyorkjets.com
Training site:
Hofstra University
Hempstead, N.Y.
516-560-8288

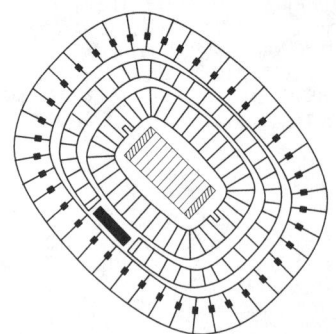

NEW YORK JETS

No.	QUARTERBACKS	Ht./Wt.	Born	NFL Exp.	College	How acq.	'05 Games GP/GS
5	Brooks Bollinger	6-1/205	11/15/79	4	Wisconsin	D6/03	11/9
6	Kellen Clemens	6-2/223	6/6/83	R	Oregon	D2/06	
3	Kliff Kingsbury	6-4/231	8/9/79	2	Texas Tech	FA/05	1/0
10	Chad Pennington	6-3/225	6/26/76	7	Marshall	D1c/00	3/3
11	Patrick Ramsey	6-2/223	2/14/79	5	Tulane	T-Was/06	4/1
	RUNNING BACKS						
35	B.J. Askew (FB)	6-3/233	8/19/80	4	Michigan	D3/03	10/1
23	Derrick Blaylock	5-9/210	8/23/79	6	Stephen F. Austin	FA/05	7/1
27	Terry Butler	6-1/200	8/2/82	2	Villanova	FA/05	1/0
34	Cedric Houston (FB)	5-11/223	6/28/82	2	Tennessee	D6a/05	12/4
44	Luke Lawton	5-11/237	8/26/80	2	McNeese State	FA/05	4/0
28	Curtis Martin	5-11/210	5/1/73	12	Pittsburgh	FA/98	12/12
29	Leon Washington	5-8/202	8/29/82	R	Florida State	D4b/06	—
	RECEIVERS						
81	Chris Baker (TE)	6-3/258	11/18/79	5	Michigan State	D3/02	8/8
87	Laveranues Coles	5-11/193	12/29/77	7	Florida State	T-Was/05	16/16
89	Jerricho Cotchery	6-0/207	6/16/82	3	N.C. State	D4a/04	16/1
85	James Dearth (TE/LS)	6-4/270	1/22/76	6	Tarleton State	FA/00	16/0
83	Joel Dreessen (TE)	6-4/260	7/26/82	2	Colorado State	D6b/05	14/0
17	Tim Dwight	5-8/180	7/13/75	9	Iowa	FA/06	16/1
88	Doug Jolley (TE)	6-4/250	1/2/79	5	Brigham Young	T-Oak/05	16/7
86	Justin McCareins	6-2/215	12/11/78	6	Northern Illinois	T-Ten/04	16/16
82	Jason Pociask (TE)	6-2/259	2/9/83	R	Wisconsin	D5/06	—
84	Dante Ridgeway	5-11/206	4/18/84	2	Ball State	D6a/05	7/0
16	Brad Smith	6-2/210	12/12/83	R	Missouri	D4a/06	—
	OFFENSIVE LINEMEN						
65	Anthony Clement (T)	6-8/337	4/10/76	9	Louisiana-Lafayette	FA/06	14/6
60	D'Brickashaw Ferguson (T)	6-6/305	12/10/83	R	Virginia	D1a/06	1/0
79	Adrian Jones (T)	6-4/296	6/10/81	3	Kansas	D4b/04	16/16
64	Norm Katnik (C)	6-4/280	7/2/81	2	Southern California	FA/05	0/0
66	Pete Kendall (G)	6-5/280	7/9/73	11	Boston College	FA/00	16/16
74	Nick Mangold (C)	6-4/300	1/13/84	R	Ohio State	D1b/06	—
65	Brandon Moore (G)	6-3/295	6/3/80	4	Illinois	FA/02	16/16
76	Steve Morley (G)	6-7/330	8/18/81	2	St. Mary's (Canada)	T-GB/05	7/0
67	Doug Nienhuis (T)	6-6/307	2/16/82	2	Oregon State	D7b/05	7/0
72	Isaac Snell (T)	6-6/288	11/4/81	3	N. Dakota State	FA/05	0/0
70	Trey Teague (C)	6-5/300	12/27/74	9	Tennessee	FA/06	16/16
	DEFENSIVE LINEMEN						
94	Titus Adams (T)	6-4/305	1/28/83	R	Nebraska	D7/06	—
96	Dave Ball (E)	6-5/277	1/4/81	3	UCLA	D5/04	5/0
92	Shaun Ellis (E)	6-5/285	6/24/77	7	Tennessee	D1a/00	13/13
97	Trevor Johnson (E)	6-4/260	2/26/81	3	Nebraska	D7b/04	9/0
95	Matt McChesney (T)	6-4/290	11/6/81	2	Colorado	W-StL/05	3/0
75	Monsanto Pope (T/E)	6-3/300	1/27/78	5	Virginia	FA/06	2/0
91	Sione Pouha (T)	6-4/318	2/3/79	2	Utah	D3/05	14/0
63	Dewayne Robertson (T)	6-1/317	10/16/81	4	Kentucky	D1/03	13/12
67	Kimo von Oelhoffen (E)	6-4/299	1/30/71	13	Boise State	FA/06	16/16
	LINEBACKERS						
50	Eric Barton	6-2/245	9/29/77	8	Maryland	FA/04	4/3
58	Matt Chatham	6-4/250	6/28/77	7	South Dakota	FA/06	15/0
98	Jamar Enzor	6-1/238	12/28/81	2	Cincinnati	W-Jac/05	1/0
54	Victor Hobson	6-0/252	2/3/80	4	Michigan	D2/03	16/16
55	Brad Kassell	6-3/242	1/7/80	5	North Texas	FA/06	16/14
57	Darrell McClover	6-2/226	8/25/81	3	Miami	D7a/04	0/0
58	Ryan Myers	6-2/245	2/27/80	2	Akron	FA/04	15/0
56	Anthony Schlegel	6-1/250	3/1/81	R	Ohio State	D3a/06	—
99	Bryan Thomas	6-4/266	6/7/79	5	UAB	D1/02	16/4
51	Jonathan Vilma	6-1/230	4/16/82	3	Miami	D1/04	16/16
	DEFENSIVE BACKS						
36	David Barrett (CB)	5-10/195	12/22/77	7	Arkansas	FA/04	13/8
	Drew Coleman (CB)	5-8/183	4/22/83	R	TCU	D6/05	0/0
26	Erik Coleman (S)	5-10/200	5/6/82	3	Washington State	D5/04	16/16
22	Andre Dyson (CB)	5-10/183	5/25/79	6	Utah	FA/06	10/6
32	D.J. Johnson (CB)	5-11/215	5/3/80	2	Iowa	FA/05	8/0
41	Andre Maddox (S)	6-1/205	10/8/82	2	N.C. State	D5/05	0/1
10	Justin Miller (CB)	5-10/201	2/14/84	2	Clemson	D2b/05	16/8
	Kerry Rhodes (S)	6-3/208	8/2/82	2	Louisville	D4/05	16/16
33	Eric Smith (S)	6-1/209	3/17/83	R	Michigan State	D3b/06	—
21	Derrick Strait (CB)	5-11/189	8/27/80	3	Oklahoma	D3/04	16/2
42	Rashad Washington (S)	6-1/217	3/15/80	3	Kansas State	D7d/04	16/0
	SPECIALISTS						
7	Ben Graham (P)	6-5/230	11/2/73	2	Deakin (Australia)	FA/05	16/0
1	Mike Nugent (K)	6-0/182	3/2/82	2	Ohio State	D2a/05	16/0

Abbreviations: D1-draft pick, first round; W-claimed on waivers; T-obtained in trade; FA-free-agent acquisition.

NEW YORK JETS

2005 regular-season record: 4-12
Position: 4th in AFC East

Sept.11—at Kansas City	L	7-27
Sept.18—MIAMI	W	17-7
Sept.25—JACKSONVILLE (OT)	L	20-26
Oct. 2—at Baltimore	L	3-13
Oct. 9—TAMPA BAY	W	14-12
Oct. 16—at Buffalo	L	17-27
Oct. 24—at Atlanta	L	14-27
Oct. 30—Open date		
Nov. 6—SAN DIEGO	L	26-31
Nov. 13—at Carolina	L	3-30
Nov. 20—at Denver	L	0-27
Nov. 27—NEW ORLEANS	L	19-21
Dec. 4—at New England	L	3-16
Dec. 11—OAKLAND	W	26-10
Dec. 18—at Miami	L	20-24
Dec. 26—NEW ENGLAND	L	21-31
Jan. 1—BUFFALO	W	30-26

SCORING BY PERIODS

	Q1	Q2	Q3	Q4	OT	Pts.
Jets	23	83	50	84	0	240
Opponents	85	109	58	97	6	355

TEAM STATISTICS

	NYJ	Opp.
TOTAL FIRST DOWNS ..	251	321
Rushing	74	136
Passing	146	151
Penalty	31	34
3rd Down: Made/Att.	72/204	88/212
3rd Down Pct.	35.3	41.5
4th Down: Made/Att.	8/19	14/17
4th Down Pct.	42.1	82.4
POSSESSION AVG.	26:37	33:23
TOTAL NET YARDS	3970	4940
Avg. per Game	248.1	308.8
Total Plays	907	1047
Avg. per Play	4.4	4.7
NET YARDS RUSHING ..	1328	2185
Avg. per Game	83.0	136.6
Total Rushes	384	554
NET YARDS PASSING....	2642	2755
Avg. per Game	165.1	172.2
Sacked/Yards Lost	53/347	30/193
Gross Yards	2989	2948
Att./Completions	470/268	463/284
Completion Pct.	57.0	61.3
Had Intercepted	15	21
PUNTS/AVERAGE	75/43.3	62/45.0
NET PUNTING AVG.	75/37.7	62/39.5
PENALTIES/YARDS	98/801	115/981
FUMBLES/LOST	36/19	24/7
TOUCHDOWNS	25	38
Rushing	10	19
Passing	11	17
Returns	4	2

SCORING (NONKICKERS)

	Tot. TD	RTD	PTD	MTD	2Pt.	Tot. Pts.
Coles	5	0	5	0	0	30
C. Martin	5	5	0	0	0	30
Sowell	3	1	2	0	0	18
Houston	2	2	0	0	0	12
McCareins	2	0	2	0	0	12
Testaverde	2	2	0	0	0	12
Baker	1	0	1	0	0	6
Brown	1	0	0	1	0	6
Jolley	1	0	1	0	0	6
Law	1	0	0	1	0	6
Miller	1	0	0	1	0	6
Reed	1	0	0	1	0	6
Jets	25	10	11	4	0	150
Opponents	38	19	17	2	0	228

2-Pt. conversions: Jets 0-1; Opponents 0-0.

(KICKERS)

	XPM/XPA	FGM/FGA	Pts.
Nugent	24/24	22/28	90
Jets	24/24	22/28	90
Opponents	37/37	30/35	127

RUSHING

	Att.	Yds.	Avg.	Lg.	TD
C. Martin	220	735	3.3	49	5
Houston	81	302	3.7	17	2
Bollinger	35	135	3.9	15	0
Askew	13	59	4.5	14	0
Blaylock	17	53	3.1	11	0
Pennington	6	27	4.5	14	0
McCareins	1	8	8.0	8	0
Cotchery	1	4	4.0	4	0
Testaverde	7	4	0.6	2	2
Sowell	1	1	1.0	t1	1
Fiedler	1	0	0.0	0	0
Graham	1	0	0.0	0	0
Jets	384	1328	3.5	49	10
Opponents	554	2185	3.9	65	19

RECEIVING

	No.	Yds.	Avg.	Lg.	TD
Coles	73	845	11.6	43	5
McCareins	43	713	16.6	45	2
Jolley	29	324	11.2	t60	1
Sowell	28	155	5.5	28	2
C. Martin	24	118	4.9	14	0
Cotchery	19	251	13.2	45	0
Baker	18	269	14.9	47	1
Chrebet	15	153	10.2	20	0
Houston	8	66	8.3	16	0
Dreessen	5	41	8.2	17	0
Blaylock	3	17	5.7	10	0
Ridgeway	2	26	13.0	17	0
Askew	1	11	11.0	11	0
Jets	268	2989	11.2	t60	11
Opponents	284	2948	10.4	t50	17

INTERCEPTIONS

	No.	Yds.	Avg.	Lg.	TD
Law	10	195	19.5	t74	1
Barrett	5	28	5.6	13	0
Brown	2	51	25.5	t33	1
Coleman	2	4	2.0	4	0
Vilma	1	1	1.0	1	0
Rhodes	1	0	0.0	0	0
Jets	21	279	13.3	t74	2
Opponents	15	147	9.8	53	1

SACKS: J. Abraham 10.5, Robertson 3.5, B. Thomas 3.5, Legree 3.0, Ellis 2.5, Reed 2.0, Brown 1.5, Hobson 1.0, Rhodes 1.0, Washington 1.0, Vilma 0.5. Jets 30.0; Opponents 53.0.

PUNTING

	No.	Yds.	Avg.	In. 20	Lg
Graham	74	3233	43.7	18	59
Nugent	1	18	18.0	1	18
Jets	75	3251	43.3	19	59
Opponents	62	2787	45.0	17	60

PUNT RETURNS

	No.	FC	Yds.	Avg.	Lg.	TD
Cotchery	23	7	182	7.9	18	0
Miller	6	1	9	1.5	12	0
McCareins	5	4	28	5.6	12	0
Jets	34	12	219	6.4	18	0
Opponents	36	15	305	8.5	23	0

KICK RETURNS

	No.	Yds.	Avg.	Lg.	TD
Miller	60	1577	26.3	t95	1
Cotchery	4	105	26.3	30	0
Baker	2	11	5.5	11	0
Houston	2	18	9.0	18	0
Barrett	1	0	0.0	0	0
Blaylock	1	17	17.0	17	0
Lawton	1	0	0.0	0	0
Jets	71	1728	24.3	t95	1
Opponents	60	1250	20.8	50	0

FIELD GOALS

	1-19	20-29	30-39	40-49	50+
Nugent	0/0	8/9	7/7	7/10	0/2
Jets	0/0	8/9	7/7	7/10	0/2
Opponents	1/1	10/12	9/10	8/9	2/3

Nugent: (28B) (41G) (35G, 25G) (21G) (40N, 48N) (44G) () (51N, 35G, 22G) (22G) () (29G, 45G, 41G, 38G, 53N) (38G) (33G, 20G, 35G, 21G) (42G, 42G) () (49G, 43N, 25G, 34G)
Opponents: (41G, 38G, 32N) (21N) (32G, 40G) (42G, 25G) (35G, 36G, 43G, 30G) (50G, 38G) (22G, 41G) (18G) (23G, 42G, 28G) (26G, 47G) () (45N, 21G, 34G, 22G) (42G, 29N) (53N, 32G) (26G) (21G, 24G, 52G, 36G)

PASSING

	Att.	Cmp.	Yds.	Pct.	Avg. Gain	TD	Pct. TD	Int.	Pct. Int.	Long	Sack/Lost	Rating
Bollinger	266	150	1558	56.4	5.86	7	2.6	6	2.3	t60	32/193	72.9
Testaverde	106	60	777	56.6	7.33	1	0.9	6	5.7	47	12/102	59.4
Pennington	83	49	530	59.0	6.39	2	2.4	3	3.6	37	9/52	70.9
Fiedler	13	8	107	61.5	8.23	1	7.7	0	0.0	t23	0/0	113.3
Kingsbury	2	1	17	50.0	8.50	0	0.0	0	0.0	17	0/0	79.2
Jets	470	268	2989	57.0	6.36	11	2.3	15	3.2	t60	53/347	70.6
Opponents	463	284	2948	61.3	6.37	17	3.7	21	4.5	t50	30/193	73.1

OAKLAND RAIDERS
AFC WEST DIVISION

2006 SEASON

CLUB DIRECTORY

Owner
Al Davis
Chief executive
Amy Trask
Personnel executive
Mike Lombardi
Senior administrator
Morris Bradshaw
Finance
Marc Badain, Tom Blanda
Public relations director
Mike Taylor

Head coach
Art Shell

Assistant coaches
Fred Biletnikoff (wide receivers)
Willie Brown (defensive backs/
squad development)
Ted Daisher (special teams)
Irv Eatman (co-offensive line)
Jeff Fish (strength and
conditioning)
Robert Ford (offensive quality
control)
Don Martindale (linebackers)
George Martinez (defensive
quality control)
Jim McElwain (quarterbacks)
Keith Millard (defensive line)
Chuck Pagano (defensive backs)
Skip Peete (running backs)
Rob Ryan (defensive coordinator)
John Shoop (tight ends)
Darryl Sims (asst. defensive line)
Jackie Slater (co-offensive line)
Tom Walsh (offensive coordinator)
Lorenzo Ward (asst. defensive
backs/asst. special teams)

OFFSEASON MOVES

Key additions
QB	Aaron Brooks	FA/Saints
G	Kelvin Garmon	FA/Browns
DE	Lance Johnstone	FA/Vikings
CB	Tyrone Poole	FA/Patriots
CB	Duane Starks	FA/Patriots

Key losses
QB	Kerry Collins	released
TE	Zeron Flemister	FA
DB	Renaldo Hill	FA/Dolphins
DT	Ed Jasper	FA/Eagles
G	Ron Stone	released
DT	Ted Washington	released/Browns
CB	Charles Woodson	FA/Packers

SCHEDULE

Sept.	11—SAN DIEGO (Mon.)	10:15
Sept.	17—at Baltimore	1:00
Sept.	24—Open date	
Oct.	1—CLEVELAND	4:15
Oct.	8—at San Francisco	4:05
Oct.	15—at Denver	8:15
Oct.	22—ARIZONA	4:15
Oct.	29—PITTSBURGH	4:15
Nov.	6—at Seattle (Mon.)	8:30
Nov.	12—DENVER	4:05
Nov.	19—at Kansas City	1:00
Nov.	26—at San Diego	4:05
Dec.	3—HOUSTON	4:05
Dec.	10—at Cincinnati	1:00
Dec.	17—ST. LOUIS	4:15
Dec.	23—KANSAS CITY (Sat.)	8:00
Dec.	31—at N.Y. Jets	1:00

All times are Eastern.
All games Sunday unless noted.

DRAFT CHOICES

Michael Huff, SS, Texas (first round/
seventh pick overall).
Thomas Howard, OLB, Texas-El Paso
(2/38).
Paul McQuistan, G, Weber State (3/69).
Darnell Bing, SS, Southern California
(4/101).
Kevin Boothe, OT, Cornell (6/176).
Chris Morris, C, Michigan State (7/214).
Kevin McMahan, WR, Maine (7/255).

MISCELLANEOUS TEAM DATA

Stadium (capacity, surface):
Network Associates Coliseum
(63,142, grass)
Business address:
1220 Harbor Bay Parkway
Alameda, CA 94502
Business phone:
510-864-5000
Ticket information:
800-949-2626
Team colors:
Silver and black
Flagship radio station:
KSFO, 560 AM
Website:
www.raiders.com
Training site:
Napa, Calif.
707-256-1000

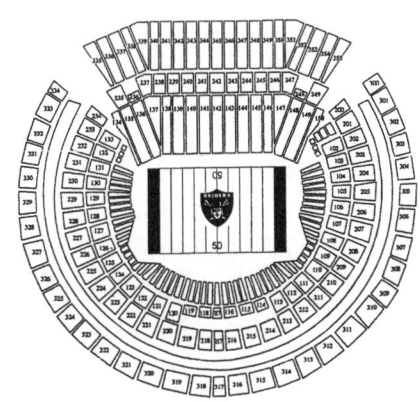

OAKLAND RAIDERS

No.	QUARTERBACKS	Ht./Wt.	Born	NFL Exp.	College	How acq.	'05 Games GP/GS
2	Aaron Brooks	6-4/220	3/24/76	8	Virginia	FA/06	13/13
8	Marques Tuiasosopo	6-1/220	3/22/79	6	Washington	D2/01	1/1
16	Andrew Walter	6-6/233	5/11/82	1	Arizona State	D3a/05	0/0
	RUNNING BACKS						
32	Zack Crockett (FB)	6-2/240	12/2/72	12	Florida State	FA/99	16/10
25	Justin Fargas	6-1/220	1/25/80	4	Southern California	D3b/03	14/0
49	John Paul Foschi	6-4/270	5/19/82	2	Georgia Tech	FA/04	10/5
28	DeJuan Green	5-11/205	5/13/80	1	South Florida	FA/04	0/0
34	LaMont Jordan	5-10/230	11/11/78	6	Maryland	FA/05	14/14
45	Zach Tuiasosopo	6-2/249	12/19/81	1	Washington	FA/05	0/0
	RECEIVERS						
83	Courtney Anderson (TE)	6-7/270	11/19/80	3	San Jose State	D7a/04	14/13
89	Ronald Curry	6-2/220	5/28/79	4	North Carolina	D7/02	2/0
82	Carlos Francis	5-9/190	1/3/81	3	Texas Tech	D4/04	0/0
85	Doug Gabriel	6-2/215	8/27/80	4	Central Florida	D5/03	14/2
5	Kevin McMahan	6-2/199	3/2/83	R	Maine	D7b/06	—
19	Johnnie Morant	6-4/220	12/7/81	3	Syracuse	D5/04	1/0
18	Randy Moss	6-4/210	2/13/77	9	Marshall	T-Min/05	16/15
84	Jerry Porter	6-2/220	7/14/78	7	West Virginia	D2/00	16/14
87	Alvis Whitted	6-0/185	9/4/74	9	N.C. State	FA/02	15/0
86	Randal Williams (TE)	6-3/211	5/21/78	6	New Hampshire	FA/05	16/4
	OFFENSIVE LINEMEN						
70	Brad Badger (G)	6-4/320	1/11/75	10	Stanford	FA/02	16/8
67	Kevin Boothe (T)	6-5/312	7/5/83	R	Cornell	D6/06	—
76	Robert Gallery (T)	6-7/325	7/26/80	3	Iowa	D1/04	16/16
69	Kelvin Garmon (G)	6-2/350	10/26/76	8	Baylor	FA/06	0/0
60	Roderick Green (T)	6-6/276	6/23/82	3	Ark. Pine-Bluff	FA/06	16/0
64	Jake Grove (C)	6-4/300	1/22/80	3	Virginia Tech	D2/04	10/8
71	Corey Hulsey (G)	6-4/325	7/26/77	5	Clemson	FA/03	11/0
75	Brad Lekkerkerker (T)	6-7/330	5/8/78	2	California-Davis	FA/04	1/0
79	Paul McQuistan (G)	6-6/313	4/3/83	R	Weber State	D3/06	—
61	Chris Morris (C)	6-4/298	2/22/83	R	Michigan State	D7a/06	—
68	William Obeng (T)	6-6/307	4/14/83	1	San Jose State	FA/05	0/0
65	Barry Sims (G)	6-5/300	12/1/74	8	Utah	FA/99	16/16
78	Chad Slaughter (G/T)	6-8/340	6/4/78	6	Alcorn State	FA/03	11/0
73	Cameron Spikes (G)	6-4/313	11/6/76	8	Texas A&M	FA/06	0/0
67	Ron Stone (G)	6-5/325	7/20/71	14	Boston College	FA/04	16/16
62	Adam Treu (C/G)	6-5/300	6/24/74	10	Nebraska	D3/97	16/10
66	Langston Walker (T)	6-8/345	9/3/79	5	California	D2a/02	6/6
	DEFENSIVE LINEMEN						
56	Derrick Burgess (E)	6-2/266	8/12/78	5	Mississippi	FA/05	16/12
98	Bobby Hamilton (E)	6-5/285	7/1/71	12	Southern Miss	FA/04	14/13
77	Anttaj Hawthorne (T)	6-3/321	11/15/81	2	Wisconsin	D6a/05	2/0
96	Grant Irons (E)	6-6/285	7/7/79	5	Notre Dame	FA/02	15/1
51	Lance Johnstone (E)	6-4/250	6/11/73	11	Temple	FA/06	15/1
93	Tommy Kelly (T)	6-6/300	12/27/80	3	Mississippi State	FA/04	16/12
90	Terdell Sands (T)	6-7/335	10/31/79	4	Chattanooga	FA/03	9/0
99	Warren Sapp (T)	6-2/300	12/19/72	12	Miami	FA/04	10/10
	LINEBACKERS						
59	Darnell Bing	6-2/225	9/10/84	R	USC	D4/06	—
91	Tyler Brayton	6-6/280	11/20/79	4	Colorado	D1b/03	16/3
55	Danny Clark	6-2/245	5/9/77	7	Illinois	FA/05	16/15
53	Thomas Howard	6-3/237	7/14/83	R	UTEP	D2/06	—
52	Kirk Morrison	6-1/234	2/19/82	2	San Diego State	D3b/05	16/15
57	Ryan Riddle	6-2/260	7/5/81	2	California	D6b/05	12/0
54	Sam Williams	6-5/265	7/28/80	4	Fresno State	D3a/03	0/0
	DEFENSIVE BACKS						
21	Nnamdi Asomugha (CB)	6-2/210	7/6/81	4	California	D1a/03	16/16
23	Chris Carr (CB)	5-10/180	4/30/83	2	Boise State	FA/05	16/0
40	Jarrod Cooper (S)	6-0/215	3/31/78	6	Kansas State	W-Car/04	16/10
36	Derrick Gibson (S)	6-2/215	3/22/79	6	Florida State	D1/01	6/6
24	Michael Huff (S)	6-0/205	3/6/83	R	Texas	D1/06	—
38	Tyrone Poole (CB)	5-8/188	2/3/72	11	Fort Valley State	FA/06	1/1
26	Stanford Routt (CB)	6-1/190	7/23/83	2	Houston	D2/05	14/2
30	Stuart Schweigert (S)	6-1/210	6/21/81	3	Purdue	D3/04	16/13
22	Duane Starks (CB)	5-10/174	5/23/74	9	Miami	FA/06	7/6
25	Denard Walker (CB)	6-1/190	8/9/73	10	LSU	FA/04	9/0
27	Fabian Washington (CB)	5-11/188	6/9/83	2	Nebraska	D1/05	16/11
	SPECIALISTS						
6	Tim Duncan (K)	6-2/210	6/12/79	2	Oklahoma	FA/06	0/0
11	Sebastian Janikowski (K)	6-2/250	3/2/78	7	Florida State	D1/00	16/0
9	Shane Lechler (P)	6-2/225	8/7/76	7	Texas A&M	D5/00	16/0

Abbreviations: D1-draft pick, first round; W-claimed on waivers; T-obtained in trade; FA-free-agent acquisition.

2005 regular-season record: 4-12
Position: 4th in AFC West

Sept. 8—at New England	L	20-30
Sept.18—KANSAS CITY	L	17-23
Sept.25—at Philadelphia	L	20-23
Oct. 2—DALLAS	W	19-13
Oct. 9—Open date		
Oct. 16—SAN DIEGO	L	14-27
Oct. 23—BUFFALO	W	38-17
Oct. 30—at Tennessee	W	34-25
Nov. 6—at Kansas City	L	23-27
Nov. 13—DENVER	L	17-31
Nov. 20—at Washington	W	16-13
Nov. 27—MIAMI	L	21-33
Dec. 4—at San Diego	L	10-34
Dec. 11—at N.Y. Jets	L	10-26
Dec. 18—CLEVELAND	L	7-9
Dec. 24—at Denver	L	3-22
Dec. 31—N.Y. GIANTS	L	21-30

SCORING BY PERIODS

	Q1	Q2	Q3	Q4	OT	Pts.
Raiders	64	81	48	97	0	290
Opponents	75	132	84	92	0	383

TEAM STATISTICS

	Oak.	Opp.
TOTAL FIRST DOWNS ..	294	299
Rushing	80	100
Passing	189	165
Penalty	25	34
3rd Down: Made/Att. ..	85/214	92/226
3rd Down Pct.	39.7	40.7
4th Down: Made/Att. ..	7/14	9/27
4th Down Pct.	50.0	33.3
POSSESSION AVG.	28:07	31:53
TOTAL NET YARDS	4951	5292
Avg. per Game	309.4	330.8
Total Plays	997	1029
Avg. per Play	5.0	5.1
NET YARDS RUSHING ..	1369	2049
Avg. per Game	85.6	128.1
Total Rushes	361	507
NET YARDS PASSING....	3582	3243
Avg. per Game	223.9	202.7
Sacked/Yards Lost	45/301	36/238
Gross Yards	3883	3481
Att./Completions	591/316	486/296
Completion Pct.	53.5	60.9
Had Intercepted	14	5
PUNTS/AVERAGE	82/45.7	76/41.5
NET PUNTING AVG.	82/37.9	76/37.8
PENALTIES/YARDS	147/1132	101/825
FUMBLES/LOST	26/9	22/14

	Oak.	Opp.
TOUCHDOWNS	33	40
Rushing	11	18
Passing	21	18
Returns	1	4

SCORING (NONKICKERS)

	TD	RTD	PTD	MTD	2Pt.	Tot. Pts.
Jordan	11	9	2	0	1	68
Moss	8	0	8	0	0	48
Porter	5	0	5	0	0	30
C. Anderson ..	3	0	3	0	0	18
Gabriel	3	0	3	0	0	18
Collins	1	1	0	0	0	6
Cooper	1	0	0	1	0	6
Crockett	1	1	0	0	0	6
Raiders	33	11	21	1	1	200
Opponents	40	18	18	4	1	244

2-Pt. conversions: Raiders 1-3; Opponents 1-3.

(KICKERS)

	XPM/XPA	FGM/FGA	Pts.
Janikowski	30/30	20/30	90
Raiders	30/30	20/30	90
Opponents	34/37	35/38	139

RUSHING

	Att.	Yds.	Avg.	Lg.	TD
Jordan	272	1025	3.8	26	9
Crockett	60	208	3.5	24	1
Whitted	2	51	25.5	27	0
Collins	17	39	2.3	t18	1
Fargas	5	28	5.6	15	0
M. Tuiasosopo	2	19	9.5	10	0
Gabriel	1	5	5.0	5	0
Lechler	1	2	2.0	2	0
Porter	1	-8	-8.0	-8	0
Raiders	361	1369	3.8	27	11
Opponents	507	2049	4.0	t95	18

RECEIVING

	No.	Yds.	Avg.	Lg.	TD
Porter	76	942	12.4	t49	5
Jordan	70	563	8.0	28	2
Moss	60	1005	16.8	79	8
Gabriel	37	554	15.0	38	3
C. Anderson ..	24	303	12.6	36	3
Whitted	14	183	13.1	26	0
Crockett	13	111	8.5	23	0
Williams	13	164	12.6	34	0
Foschi	6	37	6.2	11	0
Curry	2	12	6.0	8	0
Fargas	1	9	9.0	9	0
Raiders	316	3883	12.3	79	21
Opponents	296	3481	11.8	t78	18

INTERCEPTIONS

	No.	Yds.	Avg.	Lg.	TD
Schweigert	2	35	17.5	33	0
Sapp	1	3	3.0	3	0
Hill	1	0	0.0	0	0
C. Woodson ..	1	0	0.0	0	0
Raiders	5	38	7.6	33	0
Opponents	14	336	24.0	t80	4

SACKS: Burgess 16.0, Sapp 5.0, Kelly 4.5, Hamilton 2.0, Jasper 2.0, Brayton 1.0, Clark 1.0, Gibson 1.0, Grant 1.0, Routt 1.0, Sands 1.0, Cooper 0.5. Raiders 36.0; Opponents 45.0.

PUNTING

	No.	Yds.	Avg.	In. 20	Lg.
Lechler	82	3744	45.7	26	64
Raiders	82	3744	45.7	26	64
Opponents	76	3156	41.5	32	71

PUNT RETURNS

	No.	FC	Yds.	Avg.	Lg.	TD
Carr	34	7	186	5.5	34	0
C. Woodson	3	0	20	6.7	15	0
Raiders	37	7	206	5.6	34	0
Opponents	39	16	460	11.8	58	0

KICK RETURNS

	No.	Yds.	Avg.	Lg.	TD
Carr	73	1752	24.0	62	0
Gabriel	4	64	16.0	21	0
Flemister	2	16	8.0	8	0
Hulsey	1	0	0.0	0	0
Raiders	80	1832	22.9	62	0
Opponents	56	1369	24.4	60	0

FIELD GOALS

	1-19	20-29	30-39	40-49	50+
Janikowski	1/1	7/8	5/6	7/12	0/3
Raiders	1/1	7/8	5/6	7/12	0/3
Opponents	0/0	14/14	14/15	7/8	0/1

Janikowski: (43N) (29G, 50N) (49N, 28G, 26G, 37N) (30G, 23G, 49G, 43G) () (25G) (22G, 32G) (32G, 49G, 48G) (45N, 40G) (30G, 45N, 25G, 19G) () (37G, 61N) (42G, 29N) (51N, 46B) (43G) ()

Opponents: (26G) (31G, 46B, 39G, 42G) (23G) (29G, 30G) (32G, 33G) (41G) (39G, 24G) (27G, 47G) (22G, 38G, 25G) (24G, 45G) (38N, 27G) (41G, 32G) (33G, 20G, 35G, 21G) (44G, 24G, 37G) (29G, 33G, 34G, 52N) (25G, 38G, 46G)

PASSING

	Att.	Cmp.	Yds.	Pct.	Avg. Gain	TD	Pct. TD	Int.	Pct. Int.	Long	Sack/Lost	Rating
Collins	565	302	3759	53.5	6.65	20	3.5	12	2.1	79	39/261	77.3
M. Tuiasosopo	26	14	124	53.8	4.77	1	3.8	2	7.7	t20	6/40	47.6
Raiders	591	316	3883	53.5	6.57	21	3.6	14	2.4	79	45/301	76.0
Opponents	486	296	3481	60.9	7.16	18	3.7	5	1.0	t78	36/238	90.7

OAKLAND RAIDERS

PHILADELPHIA EAGLES
NFC EAST DIVISION

2006 SEASON

CLUB DIRECTORY

Chairman/chief executive officer
Jeffrey Lurie
President
Joe Banner
Sr. VP/business operations
Mark Donovan
General manager
Tom Heckert
Director of pro personnel
Scott Cohen
Vice president of player personnel
Jason Licht
Director of football media relations
Derek Boyko
Manager of community relations
Julie Dubin

Head coach & executive VP for football operations
Andy Reid

Assistant coaches
Juan Castillo (offensive line)
Dave Culley (wide receivers)
John Harbaugh (special teams coordinator)
Pete Jenkins (defensive line)
Jim Johnson (defensive coordinator)
Sean McDermott (secondary/safeties)
Tom Melvin (tight ends)
Marty Mornhinweg (asst. head coach/offensive coordinator)
Mike Reed (defensive asst./quality control)
Robert Rogucki (strength and conditioning asst.)
Bill Shuey (offensive asst./quality control)
Pat Shurmur (quarterbacks)
Steve Spagnuolo (linebackers)
Trent Walters (secondary)
Ted Williams (running backs)
Mike Wolf (strength and conditioning)

OFFSEASON MOVES

Key additions
LB	Shawn Barber	FA/Chiefs
WR	Jabar Gaffney	FA/Texans
QB	Jeff Garcia	FA/Lions
DE	Darren Howard	FA/Saints
DT	Ed Jasper	FA/Raiders
TE	Matt Schobel	FA/Bengals

Key losses
LB	Keith Adams	FA/Panthers
OL	Artis Hicks	trade/Vikings
DE	N.D. Kalu	FA/Texans
DT	Hollis Thomas	trade/Saints

SCHEDULE

Sept.	10—at Houston	1:00
Sept.	17—N.Y. GIANTS	1:00
Sept.	24—at San Francisco	4:15
Oct.	2—GREEN BAY (Mon.)	8:30
Oct.	8—DALLAS	4:15
Oct.	15—at New Orleans	1:00
Oct.	22—at Tampa Bay	1:00
Oct.	29—JACKSONVILLE	1:00
Nov.	5—Open date	
Nov.	12—WASHINGTON	1:00
Nov.	19—TENNESSEE	1:00
Nov.	26—at Indianapolis	1:00
Dec.	4—CAROLINA (Mon.)	8:30
Dec.	10—at Washington	1:00
Dec.	17—at N.Y. Giants	1:00
Dec.	25—at Dallas (Mon.)	5:00
Dec.	31—ATLANTA	1:00

All times are Eastern.
All games Sunday unless noted.

DRAFT CHOICES

Brodrick Bunkley, DT, Florida State (first round/14th pick overall).
Winston Justice, OT, Southern California (2/39).
Chris Gocong, DE, Cal Poly (3/71).
Max Jean-Gilles, G, Georgia (4/99).
Jason Avant, WR, Michigan (4/109).
Jeremy Bloom, WR, Colorado (5/147).
Omar Gaither, OLB, Tennessee (5/168).
LaJuan Ramsey, DT, Southern California (6/204).

MISCELLANEOUS TEAM DATA

Stadium (capacity, surface):
Lincoln Financial Field
(68,400, grass)
Business address:
NovaCare Complex
One NovaCare Way
Philadelphia, PA 19145
Business phone:
215-463-2500
Ticket information:
215-463-5500
Team colors:
Midnight green, silver and white
Flagship radio station:
WYSP, 94.1 FM
Website:
www.philadelphiaeagles.com
Training site:
Lehigh University
Bethlehem, Pa.
215-463-2500

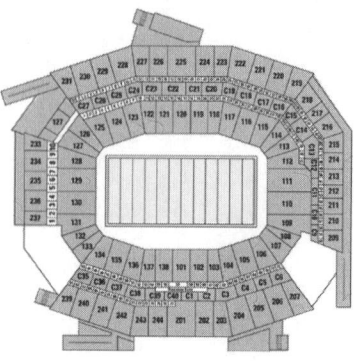

No.	QUARTERBACKS	Ht./Wt.	Born	NFL Exp.	College	How acq.	'05 Games GP/GS
10	Koy Detmer	6-1/195	7/5/73	9	Colorado	D7a/97	16/0
7	Jeff Garcia	6-1/200	2/24/70	8	San Jose State	FA/06	6/5
5	Donovan McNabb	6-2/240	11/25/76	8	Syracuse	D1/99	9/9
	RUNNING BACKS						
28	Correll Buckhalter	6-0/222	10/6/78	4	Nebraska	D4/01	0/0
34	Reno Mahe	5-10/212	6/3/80	4	BYU	FA/03	15/0
23	Ryan Moats	5-8/210	12/17/82	2	Louisiana Tech	D3/05	7/1
49	Josh Parry (FB)	6-2/250	4/5/78	3	San Jose State	FA/04	16/11
35	Bruce Perry	5-10/200	3/22/81	2	Maryland	D7b/04	2/1
38	Thomas Tapeh	6-1/243	3/28/80	3	Minnesota	D5/04	0/0
36	Brian Westbrook	5-10/205	9/2/79	5	Villanova	D3/02	12/12
	RECEIVERS						
81	Jason Avant	6-0/209	4/20/83	R	Michigan	D4b/06	—
88	Mike Bartrum (TE)	6-4/245	6/23/70	13	Marshall	FA/00	16/0
	Hank Baskett	6-4/220	9/4/82	1	New Mexico	FA/06	—
11	Jeremy Bloom	5-9/173	4/2/82	R	Colorado	D5a/06	—
86	Reggie Brown	6-2/195	1/13/81	2	Georgia	D2a/05	16/11
19	Carl Ford	6-0/174	10/8/80	2	Toledo	W-Chi/05	10/0
84	Jabar Gaffney	6-1/205	12/1/80	5	Florida	FA/06	16/13
83	Greg Lewis	6-0/180	2/12/80	4	Illinois	FA/03	16/16
85	Darnerien McCants	6-3/214	8/1/77	5	Delaware State	FA/05	12/0
87	Todd Pinkston	6-3/180	4/23/77	7	Southern Miss	D2a/00	0/0
89	Matt Schobel (TE)	6-5/257	11/4/78	5	TCU	FA/06	16/1
82	L.J. Smith (TE)	6-3/258	5/13/80	4	Rutgers	D2/03	16/16
41	Stephen Spach (TE)	6-4/250	7/18/82	2	Fresno State	FA/05	13/1
	OFFENSIVE LINEMEN						
73	Shawn Andrews (T)	6-4/340	12/25/82	2	Arkansas	D1/04	16/16
76	Calvin Armstrong (T)	6-7/325	3/31/82	1	Washington State	D6/05	0/0
61	Adrien Clarke (G)	6-5/330	3/26/81	2	Ohio State	D7/04	14/4
66	Trey Darilek (G)	6-5/310	4/23/81	3	UTEP	D4/04	15/0
63	Hank Fraley (C)	6-2/300	9/21/77	6	Robert Morris	W-Pit/00	8/8
79	Todd Herremans (T)	6-6/321	10/13/82	2	Saginaw Valley St.	D4b/05	4/4
67	Jamaal Jackson (G)	6-4/330	5/8/80	2	Delaware State	FA/03	8/8
62	Max Jean-Gilles (G)	6-4/356	11/19/83	R	Georgia	D4a/06	—
74	Winston Justice (T)	6-6/300	9/14/84	R	USC	D2/06	—
69	Jon Runyan (T)	6-7/330	11/27/73	11	Michigan	FA/00	16/16
72	Tra Thomas (T)	6-7/349	11/20/74	9	Florida State	D1/98	10/10
	DEFENSIVE LINEMEN						
78	Brodrick Bunkley (T)	6-2/300	11/23/83	R	Florida State	D1/06	—
58	Trent Cole	6-2/236	10/5/82	2	Cincinnati	D5a/05	15/7
57	Chris Gocong (E)	6-2/254	11/16/83	R	Cal Poly	D3/06	—
96	Paul Grasmanis (T)	6-3/298	8/2/74	11	Notre Dame	FA/00	2/0
90	Darren Howard (E)	6-3/275	11/19/76	7	Kansas State	FA/06	12/9
94	Ed Jasper (T)	6-2/293	1/18/73	10	Texas A&M	FA/06	15/1
93	Jevon Kearse (E)	6-4/265	9/3/76	8	Florida	FA/04	15/15
95	Jerome McDougle (E)	6-2/264	12/15/78	4	Miami	D1/03	0/0
98	Mike Patterson (T)	5-11/291	9/1/83	2	USC	D1/05	16/7
77	LaJuan Ramsey (T)	6-2/294	3/19/84	R	USC	D6/06	—
91	Sam Rayburn (T)	6-3/303	10/20/80	4	Tulsa	FA/03	16/2
75	Juqua Thomas (E)	6-2/250	5/15/78	6	Oklahoma State	FA/05	16/1
97	Darwin Walker (T)	6-3/294	6/15/77	6	Tennessee	W-Ari/00	13/12
	LINEBACKERS						
56	Shawn Barber	6-2/240	1/14/75	9	Richmond	FA/06	3/0
96	Omar Gaither	6-1/233	3/18/84	R	Tennessee	D5b/06	—
55	Dhani Jones	6-1/240	2/22/78	6	Michigan	FA/04	16/16
51	Matt McCoy	6-0/234	10/14/82	2	San Diego State	D2b/05	4/0
50	Greg Richmond	6-1/235	7/15/81	1	Oklahoma State	FA/04	0/0
53	Mark Simoneau	6-0/245	1/16/77	7	Kansas State	FA/04	16/0
54	Jeremiah Trotter	6-1/262	1/20/77	9	Stephen F. Austin	FA/02	15/15
	DEFENSIVE BACKS						
24	Sheldon Brown (CB)	5-10/200	3/19/79	5	South Carolina	D2b/02	16/16
37	Sean Considine (S)	6-0/212	10/28/81	2	Iowa	D4a/05	6/0
20	Brian Dawkins (S)	6-0/210	10/13/73	11	Clemson	D2b/96	16/16
29	Roderick Hood (CB)	5-11/196	10/3/81	4	Auburn	FA/03	16/6
32	Michael Lewis (S)	6-1/211	4/29/80	5	Colorado	D2a/02	16/16
27	Quintin Mikell (S)	5-10/206	9/16/80	4	Boise State	FA/03	16/0
26	Lito Sheppard (CB)	5-10/194	4/8/81	5	Florida	D1/02	10/10
33	Donald Strickland (CB)	5-10/187	11/24/80	4	Colorado	FA/05	4/0
21	Matt Ware (CB)	6-2/210	12/2/82	3	UCLA	D3/04	16/0
31	Dexter Wynn (CB)	5-9/177	2/25/81	3	Colorado State	D6/04	10/0
	SPECIALISTS						
2	David Akers (K)	5-10/200	12/9/74	8	Louisville	FA/99	12/0
8	Dirk Johnson (P)	6-0/205	6/1/75	4	Northern Colorado	FA/03	7/0

Abbreviations: D1-draft pick, first round; W-claimed on waivers; T-obtained in trade; FA-free-agent acquisition.

PHILADELPHIA EAGLES

PHILADELPHIA EAGLES

2005 regular-season record: 6-10
Position: 4th in NFC East

Sept.12—at Atlanta	L	10-14	
Sept.18—SAN FRANCISCO	W	42-3	
Sept.25—OAKLAND	W	23-20	
Oct. 2—at Kansas City	W	37-31	
Oct. 9—at Dallas	L	10-33	
Oct. 16—Open date			
Oct. 23—SAN DIEGO	W	20-17	
Oct. 30—at Denver	L	21-49	
Nov. 6—at Washington	L	10-17	
Nov.14—DALLAS	L	20-21	
Nov. 20—at N.Y. Giants	L	17-27	
Nov.27—GREEN BAY	W	19-14	
Dec. 5—SEATTLE	L	0-42	
Dec.11—N.Y. GIANTS (OT)	L	23-26	
Dec.18—at St. Louis	W	17-16	
Dec.24—at Arizona	L	21-27	
Jan. 1—WASHINGTON	L	20-31	

SCORING BY PERIODS

	Q1	Q2	Q3	Q4	OT	Pts.
Eagles	62	88	81	79	0	310
Opponents	113	119	50	103	3	388

TEAM STATISTICS

	Phi.	Opp.
TOTAL FIRST DOWNS ..	282	290
Rushing	73	91
Passing	182	171
Penalty	27	28
3rd Down: Made/Att.	72/220	80/233
3rd Down Pct.	32.7	34.3
4th Down: Made/Att. ..	3/12	7/11
4th Down Pct.	25.0	63.6
POSSESSION AVG.	28:22	31:38
TOTAL NET YARDS	5109	5206
Avg. per Game	319.3	325.4
Total Plays	1027	1038
Avg. per Play	5.0	5.0
NET YARDS RUSHING ..	1432	1883
Avg. per Game	89.5	117.7
Total Rushes	365	506
NET YARDS PASSING....	3677	3323
Avg. per Game	229.8	207.7
Sacked/Yards Lost	42/226	29/184
Gross Yards	3903	3507
Att./Completions	620/337	503/297
Completion Pct.	54.4	59.0
Had Intercepted	20	17
PUNTS/AVERAGE	100/40.7	104/41.9
NET PUNTING AVG.	100/37.0	104/35.7
PENALTIES/YARDS	134/1130	112/910
FUMBLES/LOST	34/14	25/10
TOUCHDOWNS	35	46
Rushing	11	15
Passing	21	24
Returns	3	7

SCORING (NONKICKERS)

	Tot. TD	RTD	PTD	MTD	2Pt.	Tot. Pts.
Westbrook	7	3	4	0	1	44
Owens	6	0	6	0	0	36
R. Brown	4	0	4	0	0	24
McMahon	3	3	0	0	0	18
Moats	3	3	0	0	0	18
Smith	3	0	3	0	0	18
Bartrum	2	0	2	0	0	12
S. Brown	2	0	0	2	0	12
Gordon	1	1	0	0	0	6
G. Lewis	1	0	1	0	0	6
McMullen	1	0	1	0	0	6
McNabb	1	1	0	0	0	6
Ware	1	0	1	0	0	6
Eagles	35	11	21	3	1	212
Opponents	46	15	24	7	0	276

2-Pt. conversions: Eagles 1-2; Opponents 0-0.

(KICKERS)

	XPM/XPA	FGM/FGA	Pts.
Akers	23/23	16/22	71
France	5/5	6/7	23
Cortez	3/3	0/0	3
Simoneau	1/2	0/0	1
Eagles	32/33	22/29	98
Opponents	46/46	22/27	112

RUSHING

	Att.	Yds.	Avg.	Lg.	TD
Westbrook	156	617	4.0	31	3
Moats	55	278	5.1	t59	3
Gordon	54	182	3.4	11	1
McMahon	34	118	3.5	19	3
Mahe	20	87	4.4	13	0
Perry	16	74	4.6	11	0
McNabb	25	55	2.2	11	1
G. Lewis	2	13	6.5	8	0
R. Brown	1	5	5.0	5	0
Owens	1	2	2.0	2	0
Detmer	1	1	1.0	1	0
Eagles	365	1432	3.9	t59	11
Opponents	506	1883	3.7	t67	15

RECEIVING

	No.	Yds.	Avg.	Lg.	TD
Smith	61	682	11.2	48	3
Westbrook	61	616	10.1	62	4
G. Lewis	48	561	11.7	34	1
Owens	47	763	16.2	t91	6
R. Brown	43	571	13.3	t56	4
McMullen	18	268	14.9	38	1
Parry	13	89	6.8	13	0
Mahe	12	68	5.7	12	0
Gordon	11	79	7.2	18	0
Spach	7	42	6.0	8	0
C. Lewis	5	64	12.8	17	0
McCants	5	87	17.4	22	0
Moats	4	7	1.8	9	0
Bartrum	2	6	3.0	t3	2

SCORING (right column top)

	No.	Yds.	Avg.	Lg.	TD
Eagles	337	3903	11.6	t91	21
Opponents	297	3507	11.8	t61	24

INTERCEPTIONS

	No.	Yds.	Avg.	Lg.	TD
S. Brown	4	67	16.8	t40	1
Sheppard	3	72	24.0	34	0
Dawkins	3	24	8.0	24	0
Hood	3	17	5.7	17	0
M. Lewis	2	13	6.5	13	0
Trotter	1	2	2.0	2	0
Jones	1	0	0.0	0	0
Eagles	17	195	11.5	t40	1
Opponents	20	339	17.0	t72	4

SACKS: Kearse 7.5, Cole 5.0, Dawkins 3.5, Patterson 3.5, Walker 2.5, Kalu 2.0, S. Brown 1.0, M. Lewis 1.0, Rayburn 1.0, Sheppard 1.0, Trotter 1.0. Eagles 29.0; Opponents 42.0.

PUNTING

	No.	Yds.	Avg.	In. 20	Lg.
Hodges	19	699	36.8	6	51
D. Johnson	39	1615	41.4	11	59
Landeta	34	1483	43.6	7	56
Murphy	7	275	39.3	1	44
Eagles	100	4072	40.7	25	59
Opponents	104	4361	41.9	27	62

PUNT RETURNS

	No.	FC	Yds.	Avg.	Lg.	TD
Wynn	22	10	110	5.0	27	0
Mahe	21	9	269	12.8	44	0
Westbrook	8	2	60	7.5	23	0
Sheppard	2	3	9	4.5	8	0
Eagles	53	24	448	8.5	44	0
Opponents	57	18	310	5.4	25	0

KICK RETURNS

	No.	Yds.	Avg.	Lg.	TD
Hood	38	900	23.7	53	0
Wynn	16	284	17.8	27	0
Perry	10	273	27.3	49	0
Gordon	3	64	21.3	25	0
Moats	2	26	13.0	15	0
Mahe	1	19	19.0	19	0
Patterson	1	12	12.0	12	0
Eagles	71	1578	22.2	53	0
Opponents	67	1416	21.1	t96	1

FIELD GOALS

	1-19	20-29	30-39	40-49	50+
Akers	0/0	3/3	7/8	5/9	1/2
France	0/0	3/3	1/1	2/3	0/0
Eagles	0/0	6/6	8/9	7/12	1/2
Opponents	0/0	12/12	8/9	1/4	1/2

Akers: (49N, 49N, 44G) (43N) (23G) () () () (34G) (48G, 20G, 60N) (20G, 38N) (44G, 38G, 37G, 33G) () (42G, 49N, 36G, 50G) (31G) () (49G, 35G)
France: () () () () (40B, 44G, 37G, 26G) (23G) (23G, 40G)
Opponents: () (32G) (49N, 28G, 26G, 37N) (38G) (28G, 33G, 37G, 45G) (34G, 40B) () (24G) () (26G, 27G) () (40N) (24G, 21G, 27G, 36G) (26G, 53G, 28G) (32G, 32G, 54N) (25G)

PASSING

	Att.	Cmp.	Yds.	Pct.	Avg. Gain	TD	Pct. TD	Int.	Pct. Int.	Long	Sack/Lost	Rating
McNabb	357	211	2507	59.1	7.02	16	4.5	9	2.5	t91	19/112	85.0
McMahon	207	94	1158	45.4	5.59	5	2.4	8	3.9	48	19/96	55.2
Detmer	56	32	238	57.1	4.25	0	0.0	3	5.4	24	3/15	45.1
Eagles	620	337	3903	54.4	6.30	21	3.4	20	3.2	t91	42/226	71.5
Opponents	503	297	3507	59.0	6.97	24	4.8	17	3.4	t61	29/184	82.2

PITTSBURGH STEELERS
AFC NORTH DIVISION

2006 SEASON

CLUB DIRECTORY

Chairman
Daniel M. Rooney
President
Arthur J. Rooney II
Vice president
John R. McGinley
Vice president
Arthur J. Rooney Jr.
Administration advisor
Charles H. Noll
Director of football operations
Kevin Colbert
Communications coordinator
Dave Lockett
Public relations/media manager
Burt Lauten
Pro personnel coordinator
Doug Whaley
College scouting coordinator
Ron Hughes

Head coach
Bill Cowher

Assistant coaches
Bruce Arians (wide receivers)
Keith Butler (linebackers)
James Daniel (tight ends)
Chet Fuhrman (conditioning)
Russ Grimm (asst. head
coach/offensive line)
Dick Hoak (running backs)
Ray Horton (asst. defensive
backs)
Dick LeBeau (defensive
coordinator)
John Mitchell (defensive line)
Darren Perry (defensive backs)
Matt Raich (offensive quality
control)
Lou Spanos (defensive quality
control)
Kevin Spencer (special teams)
Mark Whipple (quarterbacks)
Ken Whisenhunt (offensive
coordinator)

OFFSEASON MOVES

Key additions
FS Ryan Clark   FA/Redskins
Key losses
RB Jerome Bettis   retired
FS Chris Hope   FA/Titans
QB Tommy Maddox   released
WR Antwaan Randle El   FA/Redskins
DT Kimo von Oelhoffen FA/Jets

SCHEDULE

Sept.	7—MIAMI (Thurs.)	8:30
Sept.	18—at Jacksonville (Mon.)	8:30
Sept.	24—CINCINNATI	1:00
Oct.	1—Open date	
Oct.	8—at San Diego	8:15
Oct.	15—KANSAS CITY	4:15
Oct.	22—at Atlanta	1:00
Oct.	29—at Oakland	4:15
Nov.	5—DENVER	4:15
Nov.	12—NEW ORLEANS	1:00
Nov.	19—at Cleveland	1:00
Nov.	26—at Baltimore	1:00
Dec.	3—TAMPA BAY	1:00
Dec.	7—CLEVELAND (Thurs.)	8:00
Dec.	17—at Carolina	1:00
Dec.	24—BALTIMORE	1:00
Dec.	31—at Cincinnati	1:00

All times are Eastern.
All games Sunday unless noted.

DRAFT CHOICES

Santonio Holmes, WR, Ohio State (first round/25th pick overall).
Anthony Smith, FS, Syracuse (3/83).
Willie Reid, WR, Florida State (3/95).
Willie Colon, G, Hofstra (4/131).
Orien Harris, DT, Miami (4/133).
Omar Jacobs, QB, Bowling Green (5/164).
Charles Davis, TE, Purdue (5/167).
Marvin Philip, C, California (6/201).
Cedric Humes, RB, Virginia Tech (7/240).

MISCELLANEOUS TEAM DATA

Stadium (capacity, surface):
Heinz Field
(65,050, grass/DDGrassmaster)
Business address:
3400 South Water St.
Pittsburgh, PA 15203-2349
Business phone:
412-432-7800
Ticket information:
412-323-1200
Team colors:
Black and gold
Flagship radio station:
WDVE, 102.5 FM
Website:
www.steelers.com
Training site:
St. Vincent College
Latrobe, Pa.
412-539-8515

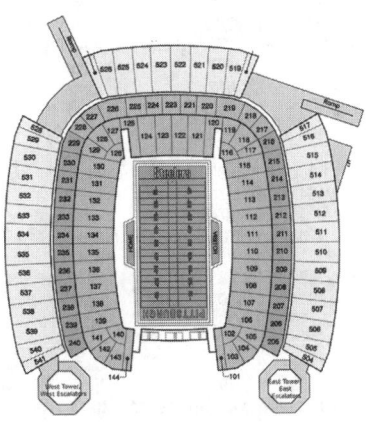

PITTSBURGH STEELERS

No.	QUARTERBACKS	Ht./Wt.	Born	NFL Exp.	College	How acq.	'05 Games GP/GS
16	Charlie Batch	6-2/220	12/5/74	9	Eastern Michigan	FA/02	4/2
4	Omar Jacobs	6-4/232	5/3/84	R	Bowling Green	D5a/06	—
7	Ben Roethlisberger	6-5/241	3/2/82	3	Miami (Ohio)	D1/04	12/12
	RUNNING BACKS						
34	Verron Haynes	5-9/222	2/17/79	5	Georgia	D5/02	14/0
30	Cedric Humes	6-1/227	8/7/83	R	Virginia Tech	D7/06	—
35	Dan Kreider (FB)	5-11/255	3/11/77	7	New Hampshire	FA/00	16/9
39	Willie Parker	5-10/209	11/11/80	3	North Carolina	FA/04	15/15
22	Duce Staley	5-11/242	2/27/75	10	South Carolina	FA/04	5/1
	RECEIVERS						
82	Eugene Baker	6-2/183	3/18/76	8	Kent State	FA/06	0/0
87	Charles Davis (TE)	6-6/263	3/13/83	R	Purdue	D5b/06	—
10	Santonio Holmes	5-11/189	3/3/84	R	Ohio State	D1/06	—
89	Lee Mays	6-2/193	9/18/78	5	UTEP	D6/02	0/0
83	Heath Miller (TE)	6-5/255	10/22/82	2	Virginia	D1/05	16/14
81	Sean Morey	5-11/200	2/26/76	5	Brown	FA/04	15/0
11	Quincy Morgan	6-1/215	9/23/77	6	Kansas State	FA/05	16/0
15	Willie Reid	5-11/189	9/19/82	R	Florida State	D3b/06	—
84	Jerame Tuman (TE)	6-4/253	3/24/76	8	Michigan	FA/03	15/9
86	Hines Ward	6-0/215	3/8/76	9	Georgia	D3b/98	15/15
85	Nate Washington	6-1/185	8/28/83	2	Tiffin	FA/05	1/0
80	Cedrick Wilson	5-10/183	12/17/78	6	Tennessee	FA/05	16/1
	OFFENSIVE LINEMEN						
72	Barrett Brooks (T)	6-4/325	5/5/72	11	Kansas State	FA/03	16/0
74	Willie Colon (G/T)	6-3/315	4/9/83	R	Hofstra	D4a/06	—
79	Trai Essex (T)	6-4/316	12/5/82	2	Northwestern	D3/05	6/4
66	Alan Faneca (G)	6-5/307	12/7/76	9	LSU	D1/98	16/16
64	Jeff Hartings (C)	6-3/299	9/7/72	11	Penn State	FA/01	16/16
68	Chris Kemoeatu (G)	6-3/344	1/4/83	1	Utah	D6/05	0/0
56	Chukky Okobi (C)	6-1/318	10/18/78	6	Purdue	D5/01	16/0
62	Marvin Philip (C)	6-1/307	2/3/82	R	California	D6/06	—
73	Kendall Simmons (G)	6-3/313	3/11/79	5	Auburn	D1/02	16/16
77	Marvel Smith (T)	6-5/321	8/6/78	7	Arizona State	D2/00	13/12
78	Max Starks (T)	6-7/337	1/10/82	3	Florida	D3/04	16/16
60	Greg Warren (C)	6-3/252	10/18/81	2	North Carolina	FA/05	16/0
	DEFENSIVE LINEMEN						
93	Rodney Bailey (E)	6-3/306	10/7/79	6	Ohio State	FA/06	8/0
98	Casey Hampton (T)	6-1/325	9/3/77	6	Texas	D1/01	16/15
71	Orien Harris (T)	6-3/302	6/3/83	R	Miami	D4b/06	—
76	Chris Hoke (T)	6-3/296	4/6/76	6	Brigham Young	FA/02	15/0
99	Brett Keisel (E)	6-5/285	9/19/78	5	Brigham Young	D7b/02	16/0
90	Travis Kirschke (T)	6-3/298	9/6/74	10	UCLA	FA/04	16/0
96	Shaun Nua (E)	6-5/270	5/22/81	2	Brigham Young	D7a/05	0/0
91	Aaron Smith (E)	6-5/298	4/9/76	8	Northern Colorado	D4/99	16/16
	LINEBACKERS						
51	James Farrior	6-2/243	1/6/75	10	Virginia	FA/02	14/14
50	Larry Foote	6-0/239	6/12/80	5	Michigan	D4/02	16/16
94	Andre Frazier	6-5/234	6/29/82	2	Cincinnati	FA/05	11/0
53	Clark Haggans	6-4/243	1/10/77	7	Colorado State	D5a/00	13/13
97	Arnold Harrison	6-3/225	9/20/82	1	Georgia	FA/05	0/0
92	James Harrison	6-0/242	5/4/78	3	Kent State	FA/04	16/3
57	Clint Kriewaldt	6-1/248	3/16/76	8	Wis.-Stevens Point	FA/03	16/2
55	Joey Porter	6-3/250	3/22/77	8	Colorado State	D3a/99	16/16
54	Rian Wallace	6-2/241	5/24/82	2	Temple	D5/05	4/0
	DEFENSIVE BACKS						
23	Tyrone Carter (S)	5-8/190	3/31/76	7	Minnesota	FA/04	16/0
25	Ryan Clark (S)	5-11/200	10/12/79	5	LSU	FA/06	13/13
21	Ricardo Colclough (CB)	5-11/186	4/18/82	3	Tusculum	D2/04	14/0
29	Chidi Iwuoma (CB)	5-8/184	2/19/78	6	California	FA/02	16/0
31	Mike Logan (S)	6-1/211	9/15/74	10	West Virginia	FA/01	12/1
20	Bryant McFadden (CB)	5-11/188	11/21/81	2	Florida State	D2/05	12/1
43	Troy Polamalu (S)	5-10/212	4/19/81	4	USC	D1/03	16/16
27	Anthony Smith (S)	6-0/192	9/20/83	R	Syracuse	D3a/06	—
24	Ike Taylor (CB)	6-1/191	5/5/80	4	La.-Lafayette	D4/03	16/15
26	Deshea Townsend (CB)	5-10/190	9/8/75	9	Alabama	D4a/98	16/15
	SPECIALISTS						
17	Chris Gardocki (P)	6-1/192	2/7/70	16	Clemson	FA/04	16/0
3	Jeff Reed (K)	5-11/232	4/9/79	5	North Carolina	FA/02	16/0

Abbreviations: D1-draft pick, first round; W-claimed on waivers; T-obtained in trade; FA-free-agent acquisition.

2005 regular-season record: 11-5
Position: 2nd in AFC North

Sept.11—TENNESSEE	W	34-7
Sept.18—at Houston	W	27-7
Sept.25—NEW ENGLAND	L	20-23
Oct. 2—Open date		
Oct. 10—at San Diego	W	24-22
Oct. 16—JACKSONVILLE (OT)	L	17-23
Oct. 23—at Cincinnati	W	27-13
Oct. 31—BALTIMORE	W	20-19
Nov. 6—at Green Bay	W	20-10
Nov.13—CLEVELAND	W	34-21
Nov.20—at Baltimore (OT)	L	13-16
Nov.26—at Indianapolis	L	7-26
Dec. 4—CINCINNATI	L	31-38
Dec.11—CHICAGO	W	21-9
Dec.18—at Minnesota	W	18-3
Dec.24—at Cleveland	W	41-0
Jan. 1—DETROIT	W	35-21

2005 postseason record: 4-0

Jan. 8—at Cincinnati#	W	31-17
Jan. 15—at Indianapolis*	W	21-18
Jan. 22—at Denver§	W	34-17
Feb. 5—SEATTLE+	W	21-10

#AFC wild-card game. *AFC divisional playoff game. §AFC championship game. +Super Bowl 40.

SCORING BY PERIODS

	Q1	Q2	Q3	Q4	OT	Pts.
Steelers	99	121	103	66	0	389
Opponents	78	49	54	68	9	258

TEAM STATISTICS

	Pit.	Opp.
TOTAL FIRST DOWNS ..	297	275
Rushing	120	75
Passing	144	179
Penalty	33	21
3rd Down: Made/Att. ..	68/192	92/232
3rd Down Pct.	35.4	39.7
4th Down: Made/Att.	5/12	6/17
4th Down Pct.	41.7	35.3
POSSESSION AVG.	31:16	28:44
TOTAL NET YARDS	5149	4544
Avg. per Game	321.8	284.0
Total Plays	960	998
Avg. per Play	5.4	4.6
NET YARDS RUSHING ..	2223	1376
Avg. per Game	138.9	86.0
Total Rushes	549	402
NET YARDS PASSING....	2926	3168
Avg. per Game	182.9	198.0
Sacked/Yards Lost	32/178	47/312
Gross Yards	3104	3480
Att./Completions	379/228	549/315
Completion Pct.	60.2	57.4
Had Intercepted	14	15
PUNTS/AVERAGE	69/41.7	80/43.3
NET PUNTING AVG.	69/34.5	80/34.7
PENALTIES/YARDS	99/876	120/1031
FUMBLES/LOST	22/9	30/15

PASSING

	Att.	Cmp.	Yds.	Pct.	Avg. Gain	TD	Pct. TD	Int.	Pct. Int.	Long	Sack/Lost	Rating
Roethlisberger	268	168	2385	62.7	8.90	17	6.3	9	3.4	t85	23/129	98.6
Maddox	71	34	406	47.9	5.72	2	2.8	4	5.6	32	8/43	51.7
Batch	36	23	246	63.9	6.83	1	2.8	1	2.8	43	1/6	81.5
Randle El	3	3	67	100.0	22.33	1	33.3	0	0.0	t51	0/0	158.3
Gardocki	1	0	0	0.0	0.0	0	0.0	0	0.0		0/0	39.6
Steelers	379	228	3104	60.2	8.19	21	5.5	14	3.7	t85	32/178	89.4
Opponents	549	315	3480	57.4	6.34	15	2.7	15	2.7	t80	47/312	74.0

TOUCHDOWNS

	Pit.	Opp.
TOUCHDOWNS	45	27
Rushing	21	10
Passing	21	15
Returns	3	2

SCORING (NONKICKERS)

	Tot. TD	RTD	PTD	MTD	2Pt.	Tot. Pts.
Ward	11	0	11	0	0	66
Bettis	9	9	0	0	0	54
Miller	6	0	6	0	0	36
Parker	5	4	1	0	0	30
Haynes	3	3	0	0	0	18
Randle El	3	0	1	2	0	18
Roethlisberger	3	3	0	0	0	18
Morgan	2	0	2	0	0	12
Batch	1	1	0	0	0	6
Polamalu	1	0	0	1	0	6
Staley	1	1	0	0	0	6
Steelers	45	21	21	3	0	272
Opponents	27	10	15	2	0	162

2-Pt. conversions: Steelers 0-0; Opponents 0-1.

(KICKERS)

	XPM/XPA	FGM/FGA	Pts.
Reed	45/45	24/29	117
Steelers	45/45	24/29	117
Opponents	24/25	24/30	96

RUSHING

	Att.	Yds.	Avg.	Lg.	TD
Parker	255	1202	4.7	t80	4
Bettis	110	368	3.3	39	9
Haynes	74	274	3.7	20	3
Staley	38	148	3.9	17	1
Randle El	12	73	6.1	43	0
Roethlisberger	31	69	2.2	13	3
Batch	11	30	2.7	15	1
Maddox	8	26	3.3	16	0
Kreider	3	21	7.0	12	0
Ward	3	10	3.3	7	0
Herron	3	2	0.7	1	0
Wilson	1	0	0.0	0	0
Steelers	549	2223	4.0	t80	21
Opponents	402	1376	3.4	36	10

RECEIVING

	No.	Yds.	Avg.	Lg.	TD
Ward	69	975	14.1	t85	11
Miller	39	459	11.8	50	6
Randle El	35	558	15.9	t63	1
Wilson	26	451	17.3	46	0
Parker	18	218	12.1	48	1
Haynes	11	113	10.3	18	0
Morgan	9	150	16.7	t31	2
Kreider	7	43	6.1	9	0
Staley	6	34	5.7	9	0
Bettis	4	40	10.0	16	0
Tuman	3	57	19.0	27	0
Kranchick	1	6	6.0	6	0
Steelers	228	3104	13.6	t85	21
Opponents	315	3480	11.0	t80	15

INTERCEPTIONS

	No.	Yds.	Avg.	Lg.	TD
Hope	3	60	20.0	55	0
Polamalu	2	42	21.0	36	0
Townsend	2	26	13.0	26	0
Porter	2	9	4.5	9	0
J. Harrison	1	25	25.0	25	0
Colclough	1	14	14.0	14	0
Carter	1	3	3.0	3	0
McFadden	1	0	0.0	0	0
A. Smith	1	0	0.0	0	0
I. Taylor	1	0	0.0	0	0
Steelers	15	179	11.9	55	0
Opponents	14	194	13.9	t41	1

SACKS: Porter 10.5, Haggans 9.0, von Oelhoffen 3.5, Foote 3.0, J. Harrison 3.0, Keisel 3.0, Polamalu 3.0, Townsend 3.0, Farrior 2.0, A. Smith 2.0, Carter 1.0, Colclough 1.0, Frazier 1.0, Kirschke 1.0, McFadden 1.0. Steelers 47.0; Opponents 32.0.

PUNTING

	No.	Yds.	Avg.	In. 20	Lg.
Gardocki	67	2803	41.8	22	65
Roethlisberger	2	72	36.0	1	39
Steelers	69	2875	41.7	23	65
Opponents	80	3463	43.3	19	58

PUNT RETURNS

	No.	FC	Yds.	Avg.	Lg.	TD
Randle El	44	12	448	10.2	t81	2
Iwuoma	1	0	3	3.0	3	0
I. Taylor	1	0	19	19.0	19	0
Steelers	46	13	470	10.2	t81	2
Opponents	37	12	336	9.1	36	0

KICK RETURNS

	No.	Yds.	Avg.	Lg.	TD
Morgan	23	583	25.3	74	0
Colclough	22	473	21.5	63	0
I. Taylor	3	59	19.7	24	0
Wilson	3	53	17.7	29	0
Keisel	2	23	11.5	12	0
J. Harrison	1	-2	-2.0	-2	0
Kreider	1	3	3.0	3	0
Randle El	1	16	16.0	16	0
Steelers	56	1208	21.6	74	0
Opponents	77	1685	21.9	94	0

FIELD GOALS

	1-19	20-29	30-39	40-49	50+
Reed	0/0	9/9	9/9	6/9	0/2
Steelers	0/0	9/9	9/9	6/9	0/2
Opponents	0/0	8/8	5/8	11/13	0/1

Reed: (44G, 27G) (37G, 35G) (33G, 52N, 24G) (29G, 46N) (27G, 39G) (42G, 37G) (32G, 24G, 51B) (42G, 33G, 44B) (44G, 37G) (41N) (23G) () (21G, 41G, 26G) (26G, 31G) ()
Opponents: (47N) () (53N, 48G, 35G, 43G) (34G, 32G, 41G) (23G) (30N, 26G, 39G) (22G, 43N, 40G, 49G, 47G) (40G, 31N) () (47G, 25G, 44G) (29G, 48G, 44G, 28G) (30G) (29G) (20G, 32B) () ()

ST. LOUIS RAMS
NFC WEST DIVISION

ST. LOUIS RAMS

2006 SEASON

CLUB DIRECTORY

Chairman/owner
Georgia Frontiere
Vice chairman/owner
Stan Kroenke
President
John Shaw
President/football operations
Jay Zygmunt
General manager
Charley Armey
Executive vice president
Bob Wallace
Director of player personnel
Lawrence McCutcheon
Vice president/operations
John Oswald
Director of football media
Duane Lewis

Head coach
Scott Linehan

Assistant coaches
Brian Baker (defensive line)
Joe Baker (defensive quality control)
Paul Boudreau (offensive line)
Jim Chaney (asst. offensive line)
Dana LeDuc (strength and conditioning)
Todd Downing (coaching asst.)
Henry Ellard (wide receivers)
Judd Garrett (tight ends)
Randy Hanson (offensive quality control)
Jim Haslett (defensive coordinator)
Jeff Horton (special asst./offense)
Bob Ligashesky (special teams)
Ron Milus (asst. secondary)
Wayne Moses (running backs)
Doug Nussmeier (quarterbacks)
Greg Olson (offensive coordinator)
Willy Robinson (secondary)
Brad Roll (asst. strength and conditioning)
Rick Venturi (asst. head coach/linebackers)

OFFSEASON MOVES

Key additions
CB	Fakhir Brown	FA/Saints
SS	Corey Chavous	FA/Vikings
RB	Tony Fisher	FA/Packers
QB	Gus Frerotte	FA/Dolphins
DT	La'Roi Glover	FA/Cowboys
WR	Brad Pyatt	FA/Colts
LB	Raonall Smith	FA/Vikings
OT	Todd Steussie	FA/Bucs
P	Matt Turk	FA/Dolphins
LB	Will Witherspoon	FA/Panthers

Key losses
S	Adam Archuleta	FA/Redskins
WR	Mike Furrey	FA/Lions
RB	Arlen Harris	FA/Lions
CB	Corey Ivy	FA/Ravens
DT	Tyoka Jackson	FA/Lions
CB	Chris Johnson	FA/Chiefs
DT	Damione Lewis	FA/Panthers
TE	B. Manumaleuna	trade/Chargers
QB	Jamie Martin	FA/Saints
DT	Ryan Pickett	FA/Packers

SCHEDULE

Sept.	10—DENVER	1:00
Sept.	17—at San Francisco	4:05
Sept.	24—at Arizona	4:15
Oct.	1—DETROIT	4:05
Oct.	8—at Green Bay	1:00
Oct.	15—SEATTLE	1:00
Oct.	22—Open date	
Oct.	29—at San Diego	4:05
Nov.	5—KANSAS CITY	1:00
Nov.	12—at Seattle	4:15
Nov.	19—at Carolina	1:00
Nov.	26—SAN FRANCISCO	1:00
Dec.	3—ARIZONA	1:00
Dec.	11—CHICAGO (Mon.)	8:30
Dec.	17—at Oakland	4:15
Dec.	24—WASHINGTON	1:00
Dec.	31—at Minnesota	1:00

All times are Eastern.
All games Sunday unless noted.

DRAFT CHOICES

Tye Hill, CB, Clemson (first round/15th pick overall).
Joe Klopfenstein, TE, Colorado (2/46).
Claude Wroten, DT, LSU (3/68).
Jon Alston, OLB, Stanford (3/77).
Dominique Byrd, TE, Southern California (3/93).
Victor Adeyanju, DE, Indiana (4/113).
Marques Hagans, WR, Virginia (5/144).
Tim McGarigle, ILB, Northwestern (7/221).
Mark Setterstrom, G, Minnesota (7/242).
Tony Palmer, G, Missouri (7/243).

MISCELLANEOUS TEAM DATA

Stadium (capacity, surface):
Edward Jones Dome (66,000, artificial)
Business address:
1 Rams Way
St. Louis, MO 63045
Business phone:
314-982-7267
Ticket information:
314-425-8830
Team colors:
Rams millennium blue, Rams century gold
Flagship radio station:
KLOU, 103.3 FM; KATZ, 1600 AM; KTRS, 550 AM
Training site:
Rams Park
St. Louis, MO 63045
Website:
www.stlouisrams.com

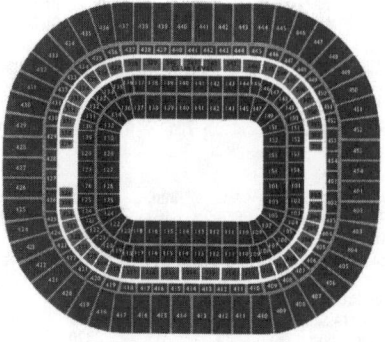

ST. LOUIS RAMS

No. QUARTERBACKS	Ht./Wt.	Born	NFL Exp.	College	How acq.	'05 Games GP/GS
10 Marc Bulger	6-3/215	4/5/77	6	West Virginia	FA/01	8/8
12 Ryan Fitzpatrick	6-2/221	11/24/82	2	Harvard	D7a/05	4/3
11 Gus Frerotte	6-3/237	7/31/71	13	Tulsa	FA/06	16/15
9 Jeff Smoker	6-3/223	6/13/81	1	Michigan State	FA/05	0/0
RUNNING BACKS						
28 Marshall Faulk	5-10/211	2/26/73	13	San Diego State	T-Ind./99	16/1
30 Tony Fisher	6-1/222	10/12979	5	Notre Dame	FA/06	14/4
44 Madison Hedgecock (FB)	6-3/259	8/27/81	2	North Carolina	D7b/05	16/7
39 Steven Jackson	6-2/233	7/22/83	3	Oregon State	D1/04	15/15
45 Chris Massey (FB)	6-0/245	8/21/79	5	Marshall	D7/02	16/0
27 Paul Smith (FB)	5-11/234	1/31/78	7	UTEP	FA/06	12/5
RECEIVERS						
80 Isaac Bruce	6-0/188	11/10/72	13	Memphis	D2/94	11/10
86 Dominique Byrd (TE)	6-2/260	2/7/84	R	USC	D3c/06	—
48 Jerome Collins (TE)	6-4/267	8/18/82	2	Notre Dame	D5/05	3/0
83 Kevin Curtis	5-11/186	7/17/78	4	Utah State	D3/03	16/9
15 Marques Hagans	5-10/209	12/29/82	R	Virginia	D5/06	—
81 Torry Holt	6-0/190	6/5/76	8	N.C. State	D1/99	14/14
Joe Klopfenstein (TE)	6-5/255	11/9/83	R	Colorado	D2/06	—
89 Dane Looker	6-0/194	4/5/76	5	Washington	FA/02	16/0
84 Shaun McDonald	5-10/183	6/13/81	4	Arizona State	D4a/03	16/2
88 Brad Pyatt	5-11/195	4/16/80	4	Northern Colorado	FA/06	0/0
17 Dominique Thompson	6-1/190	12/28/82	2	William & Mary	FA/05	2/0
87 Aaron Walker (TE)	6-6/252	3/14/80	3	Florida	FA/05	0/0
OFFENSIVE LINEMEN						
70 Alex Barron (T)	6-8/320	9/28/82	2	Florida State	D1/05	12/11
68 Richie Incognito (G)	6-3/305	7/5/83	1	Nebraska	D3b/05	0/0
67 Andy McCollum (C)	6-4/300	6/2/70	13	Toledo	FA/99	16/16
76 Orlando Pace (T)	6-7/325	11/4/75	10	Ohio State	D1/97	16/16
65 Tony Palmer (G)	6-2/330	2/23/83	R	Missouri	D7c/06	—
60 Blaine Saipaia (G/T)	6-3/310	8/25/78	3	Colorado State	FA/04	9/3
66 Mark Setterstrom (G)	6-4/314	3/3/84	R	Minnesota	D7b/06	—
79 Todd Steussie (T)	6-6/320	12/1/70	13	California	FA/06	15/0
75 Claude Terrell (G)	6-2/343	4/20/82	2	New Mexico	D4b/05	14/10
62 Adam Timmerman (G)	6-4/310	8/14/71	12	South Dakota St.	FA/99	16/16
63 Larry Turner (C)	6-2/290	3/8/82	3	Eastern Kentucky	D7b/04	7/0
DEFENSIVE LINEMEN						
94 Victor Adeyanju (E)	6-4/268	2/11/83	R	Indiana	D4/06	—
90 Jeremy Calahan (T)	6-3/295	7/7/83	2	Rice	FA/05	1/0
97 La'Roi Glover (T)	6-2/282	7/4/74	11	San Diego State	FA/06	16/13
93 Brandon Green (E)	6-2/264	9/5/80	3	Rice	FA/05	16/1
95 Anthony Hargrove (E)	6-3/269	7/20/83	3	Georgia Tech	D3/04	16/15
98 Brian Howard (T)	6-4/278	9/9/81	3	Idaho	FA/04	5/0
73 Jimmy Kennedy (T)	6-4/320	11/15/79	4	Penn State	D1/03	15/9
91 Leonard Little (E)	6-3/261	10/19/74	9	Tennessee	D3/98	14/14
99 Claude Wroten (T)	6-1/292	9/16/83	R	LSU	D3a/06	—
LINEBACKERS						
Jon Alston	6-0/218	6/4/83	R	Stanford	D3b/06	—
54 Brandon Chillar	6-2/253	10/21/82	3	UCLA	D4/04	16/7
52 Dexter Coakley	5-10/231	10/20/72	10	Appalachian State	FA/05	12/9
57 Trev Faulk	6-3/254	8/6/81	3	LSU	FA/03	16/5
Tim McGarigle	6-0/240	10/25/83	R	Northwestern	D7a/06	—
56 Raonall Smith	6-2/241	10/22/78	4	Washington State	FA/06	16/6
50 Pisa Tinoisamoa	6-1/235	7/15/81	4	Hawaii	D2/03	16/16
58 Drew Wahlroos	6-3/230	6/7/80	3	Colorado	FA/04	15/0
51 Will Witherspoon	6-1/231	8/19/80	4	Georgia	FA/06	15/15
DEFENSIVE BACKS						
20 Dwight Anderson (CB)	5-10/172	7/5/81	3	South Dakota	FA/04	3/0
21 O.J. Atogwe (S)	5-11/219	6/23/81	2	Stanford	D3a/05	12/0
32 Ronald Bartell (CB)	6-1/211	2/22/82	2	Howard	D2/05	10/7
26 Fakhir Brown (CB)	5-11/192	9/21/77	7	Grambling State	FA/06	12/4
23 Jerametrius Butler (CB)	5-10/181	11/28/78	5	Kansas State	D5/01	0/0
27 Dwaine Carpenter (S)	6-1/203	11/4/76	4	North Carolina A&T	FA/05	3/0
42 Jerome Carter (S)	6-0/217	10/25/82	2	Florida State	D4a/05	14/2
25 Corey Chavous (S)	6-1/205	1/15/76	9	Vanderbilt	FA/06	16/16
22 Travis Fisher (CB)	5-10/189	9/12/79	5	Central Florida	D2/02	8/8
24 DeJuan Groce (CB)	5-10/192	2/17/80	4	Nebraska	D4b/03	15/15
31 Tye Hill (CB)	5-10/185	6/3/82	R	Clemson	D1/06	—
SPECIALISTS						
1 Matt Turk (P)	6-5/235	6/16/68	12	Wis-Whitewater	FA/06	0/0
14 Jeff Wilkins (K)	6-2/205	4/19/72	13	Youngstown State	FA/97	16/0

Abbreviations: D1-draft pick, first round; W-claimed on waivers; T-obtained in trade; FA-free-agent acquisition.

ST. LOUIS RAMS

2005 regular-season record: 6-10
Position: 2nd in NFC West

Sept.11—at San Francisco	L	25-28	
Sept.18—at Arizona	W	17-12	
Sept.25—TENNESSEE	W	31-27	
Oct. 2—at N.Y. Giants	L	24-44	
Oct. 9—SEATTLE	L	31-37	
Oct. 17—at Indianapolis	L	28-45	
Oct. 23—NEW ORLEANS	W	28-17	
Oct. 30—JACKSONVILLE	W	24-21	
Nov. 6—Open date			
Nov. 13—at Seattle	L	16-31	
Nov.20—ARIZONA	L	28-38	
Nov.27—at Houston (OT)	W	33-27	
Dec. 4—WASHINGTON	L	9-24	
Dec. 11—at Minnesota	L	13-27	
Dec.18—PHILADELPHIA	L	16-17	
Dec.24—SAN FRANCISCO	L	20-24	
Jan. 1—at Dallas	W	20-10	

SCORING BY PERIODS

	Q1	Q2	Q3	Q4	OT	Pts.
Rams	67	123	54	113	6	363
Opponents	110	124	92	103	0	429

TEAM STATISTICS

	St.L.	Opp.
TOTAL FIRST DOWNS ..	314	321
Rushing	82	116
Passing	209	178
Penalty	23	27
3rd Down: Made/Att. ..	77/211	80/199
3rd Down Pct.	36.5	40.2
4th Down: Made/Att. ..	14/21	2/9
4th Down Pct.	66.7	22.2
POSSESSION AVG.	30:14	29:46
TOTAL NET YARDS	5571	5602
Avg. per Game	348.2	350.1
Total Plays	1025	1007
Avg. per Play	5.4	5.6
NET YARDS RUSHING ..	1535	2178
Avg. per Game	95.9	136.1
Total Rushes	380	459
NET YARDS PASSING....	4036	3424
Avg. per Game	252.3	214.0
Sacked/Yards Lost	46/315	41/195
Gross Yards	4351	3619
Att./Completions	599/392	507/314
Completion Pct.	65.4	61.9
Had Intercepted	24	13
PUNTS/AVERAGE	73/41.2	68/40.0
NET PUNTING AVG.	73/33.9	68/36.0
PENALTIES/YARDS	131/941	117/1066
FUMBLES/LOST	24/13	27/14
TOUCHDOWNS	40	50
Rushing	13	22
Passing	23	26
Returns	4	2

SCORING (NONKICKERS)

	TD	RTD	PTD	MTD	2Pt.	Tot. Pts.
S. Jackson	10	8	2	0	0	60
Holt	9	0	9	0	0	54
Curtis	7	1	6	0	0	42
Bruce	3	0	3	0	0	18
Fitzpatrick	2	2	0	0	0	12
M. Faulk	1	0	1	0	1	8
Harris	1	1	0	0	1	8
Archuleta	1	0	0	1	0	6
Cason	1	1	0	0	0	6
Chillar	1	0	0	1	0	6
Cleeland	1	0	1	0	0	6
Furrey	1	0	0	1	0	6
Johnson	1	0	0	1	0	6
Manumaleuna	1	0	1	0	0	6
Rams	40	13	23	4	2	246
Opponents	50	22	26	2	1	302

2-Pt. conversions: Rams 2-3; Opponents 1-1.

(KICKERS)

	XPM/XPA	FGM/FGA	Pts.
J. Wilkins	36/36	27/31	117
Rams	36/36	27/31	117
Opponents	49/49	26/33	127

RUSHING

	Att.	Yds.	Avg.	Lg.	TD
S. Jackson	254	1046	4.1	51	8
M. Faulk	65	292	4.5	20	0
Cason	10	65	6.5	14	1
Fitzpatrick	14	64	4.6	t14	2
Bulger	9	29	3.2	9	0
Harris	13	21	1.6	10	1
McDonald	1	7	7.0	7	0
Martin	9	6	0.7	9	0
Curtis	1	5	5.0	t5	1
Holt	1	2	2.0	2	0
Manumaleuna	1	2	2.0	2	0
Hedgecock	1	0	0.0	0	0
J. Wilkins	1	-4	-4.0	-4	0
Rams	380	1535	4.0	51	13
Opponents	459	2178	4.7	t73	22

RECEIVING

	No.	Yds.	Avg.	Lg.	TD
Holt	102	1331	13.0	44	9
Curtis	60	801	13.4	t83	6
McDonald	46	523	11.4	31	0
M. Faulk	44	291	6.6	18	1
S. Jackson	43	320	7.4	27	2
Bruce	36	525	14.6	t46	3
Looker	23	237	10.3	23	0
Manumaleuna	13	129	9.9	33	1
Hedgecock	9	69	7.7	15	0
Cleeland	5	17	3.4	t9	1
Harris	4	34	8.5	17	0
Williams	3	21	7.0	12	0
Bulger	1	1	1.0	1	0
Cason	1	11	11.0	11	0
Robinson	1	28	28.0	28	0
Thompson	1	13	13.0	13	0
Rams	392	4351	11.1	t83	23
Opponents	314	3619	11.5	52	26

INTERCEPTIONS

	No.	Yds.	Avg.	Lg.	TD
Furrey	4	143	35.8	t67	1
Tinoisamoa	2	35	17.5	20	0
Groce	2	0	0.0	0	0
Archuleta	1	85	85.0	t85	0
Atogwe	1	42	42.0	42	0
Hawthorne	1	24	24.0	24	0
Ivy	1	19	19.0	19	0
Coakley	1	16	16.0	16	0
Rams	13	364	28.0	t85	2
Opponents	24	268	11.2	37	0

SACKS: Little 9.5, Hargrove 6.5, Archuleta 3.5, Green 3.0, Kennedy 3.0, T. Jackson 2.5, Coakley 2.0, Ivy 2.0, Pickett 2.0, Tinoisamoa 1.5, Atogwe 1.0, Lewis 1.0, Claiborne 0.5. Rams 41.0; Opponents 46.0.

PUNTING

	No.	Yds.	Avg.	In. 20	Lg.
Barker	50	2137	42.7	13	63
Hodges	22	836	38.0	3	55
J. Wilkins	1	35	35.0	0	35
Rams	73	3008	41.2	16	63
Opponents	68	2722	40.0	18	55

PUNT RETURNS

	No.	FC	Yds.	Avg.	Lg.	TD
Looker	8	2	69	8.6	17	0
McDonald	8	6	33	4.1	14	0
Allen	7	6	38	5.4	12	0
Furrey	4	2	28	7.0	13	0
Fair	3	6	7	2.3	8	0
Rams	30	23	175	5.8	17	0
Opponents	39	14	410	10.5	t75	1

KICK RETURNS

	No.	Yds.	Avg.	Lg.	TD
Johnson	38	857	22.6	t99	1
Allen	23	472	20.5	32	0
Fair	10	182	18.2	35	0
Cason	2	48	24.0	29	0
Harris	1	21	21.0	21	0
Rams	74	1580	21.4	t99	1
Opponents	70	1781	25.4	90	0

FIELD GOALS

	1-19	20-29	30-39	40-49	50+
J. Wilkins	0/0	6/7	8/8	9/11	4/5
Rams	0/0	6/7	8/8	9/11	4/5
Opponents	0/0	7/7	13/13	4/11	2/2

J. Wilkins: (30G, 41G, 33G, 41G) (29G) (46G) (37G, 48N) (40G) (29G, 49G) (48N) (41G) (31G, 36G, 39G) (47G, 32G) (37G, 47N) () (51G, 23G) (26G, 53G, 28G) (50G, 51G) (49G, 27N, 53N, 20G)
Opponents: () (29G, 26G, 48G, 35G) (41G, 39G) (38G, 32G, 23G) (34G, 44G, 28G) (48N, 22G) (45B, 22G) (49N, 44N) (31G) (32G, 33G, 51G) (39G, 46N, 35G) (45N, 38G) (37G, 44G) (31G) (56G) (22G, 47N)

PASSING

	Att.	Cmp.	Yds.	Pct.	Avg. Gain	TD	Pct. TD	Int.	Pct. Int.	Long	Sack/Lost	Rating
Bulger	287	192	2297	66.9	8.00	14	4.9	9	3.1	t57	26/188	94.4
Martin	177	124	1277	70.1	7.21	5	2.8	7	4.0	t83	11/78	83.5
Fitzpatrick	135	76	777	56.3	5.76	4	3.0	8	5.9	t56	9/49	58.2
Rams	599	392	4351	65.4	7.26	23	3.8	24	4.0	t83	46/315	83.0
Opponents	507	314	3619	61.9	7.14	26	5.1	13	2.6	52	41/195	89.8

SAN DIEGO CHARGERS
AFC WEST DIVISION

2006 SEASON

CLUB DIRECTORY

Owner
Alex G. Spanos
President/CEO
Dean A. Spanos
Executive vice president
Michael A. Spanos
Executive vice president-general manager
A.J. Smith
Executive vice president-chief operating officer
Jim Steeg
Executive vice president of football operations
Ed McGuire
Executive vice president-chief financial officer
Jeanne Bonk
Vice president-chief marketing officer
Ken Derrett
Director of marketing programs and business development
A.G. Spanos
Assistant general manager-director of player personnel
Buddy Nix
Director of college scouting
Jimmy Raye
Assistant director of college scouting
John Spanos
Director of pro scouting
Dennis Abraham
Director of public relations
Bill Johnston
Director of public affairs & corporate/community relations
Kimberley Layton

Head coach
Marty Schottenheimer

Assistant coaches
Cam Cameron (offensive coordinator)
Wade Phillips (defensive coordinator)
Rob Chudzinski (tight ends)
Steve Crosby (special teams)
John "Jack" Henry (offensive line)
James Lofton (wide receivers)
Greg Manusky (linebackers)
Wayne Nunnely (defensive line)
John Ramsdell (quarterbacks)
Clarence Shelmon (running backs)
Brian Stewart (secondary)
Hal Hunter (asst. offensive line)
John Pagano (asst. linebackers/quality control)
Dave Redding (strength and conditioning)
Matt Schiotz (asst. strength and conditioning)
John Wuehrmann (coaching administrator)

SCHEDULE

Sept.	11—at Oakland (Mon.)	10:15
Sept.	17—TENNESSEE	4:15
Sept.	24—Open date	
Oct.	1—at Baltimore	1:00
Oct.	8—PITTSBURGH	8:15
Oct.	15—at San Francisco	4:15
Oct.	22—at Kansas City	1:00
Oct.	29—ST. LOUIS	4:05
Nov.	5—CLEVELAND	4:15
Nov.	12—at Cincinnati	1:00
Nov.	19—at Denver	4:15
Nov.	26—OAKLAND	4:05
Dec.	3—at Buffalo	1:00
Dec.	10—DENVER	4:15
Dec.	17—KANSAS CITY	4:05
Dec.	24—at Seattle	4:15
Dec.	31—ARIZONA	4:15

All times are Eastern.
All games Sunday unless noted.

DRAFT CHOICES

Antonio Cromartie, CB, Florida State (first round/19th pick overall).
Marcus McNeill, OT, Auburn (2/50).
Charlie Whitehurst, QB, Clemson (3/81).
Tim Dobbins, ILB, Iowa State (5/151).
Jeromey Clary, OT, Kansas State (6/187).
Kurt Smith, K, Virginia (6/188).
Chase Page, DT, North Carolina (7/225).
Jimmy Martin, C, Virginia Tech (7/227).

OFFSEASON MOVES

Key additions
FS Marlon McCree	FA/Panthers
TE Brandon Manumaleuna	trade/Rams
TE Aaron Shea	FA/Browns
WR Rashaun Woods	trade/49ers

Key losses
QB Drew Brees	FA/Saints
WR Reche Caldwell	FA/Patriots
CB Jamar Fletcher	FA/Lions
LB Ben Leber	FA/Vikings
DE DeQuincy Scott	FA/Vikings

MISCELLANEOUS TEAM DATA

Stadium (capacity, surface):
Qualcomm Stadium
(70,000, grass)
Business address:
P.O. Box 609609
San Diego, CA 92160-9609
Business phone:
858-874-4500
Ticket information:
877-CHARGERS
Team colors:
Navy blue, white and gold
Flagship radio station:
KIOZ, Rock 105.3 FM
Website:
www.chargers.com
Training site:
Chargers Park
San Diego, CA
858-874-4500

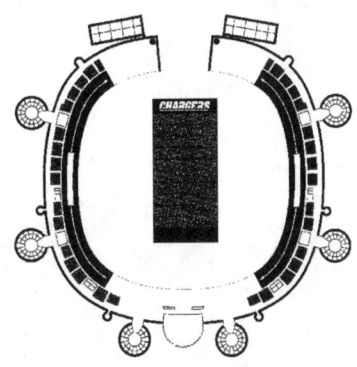

SAN DIEGO CHARGERS

No.	QUARTERBACKS	Ht./Wt.	Born	NFL Exp.	College	How acq.	'05 Games GP/GS
7	A.J. Feeley	6-3/225	5/16/77	6	Oregon	T-Mia/05	0/0
17	Philip Rivers	6-5/228	12/8/81	3	N.C. State	D1/04	2/0
6	Charlie Whitehurst	6-4/223	8/6/82	R	Clemson	D3/06	—
	RUNNING BACKS						
41	Lorenzo Neal (FB)	5-11/255	12/27/70	14	Fresno State	FA/03	16/15
34	Andrew Pinnock (FB)	5-10/260	3/12/80	4	South Carolina	D7/03	11/0
43	Darren Sproles	5-6/187	6/20/83	2	Kansas State	D4/05	15/0
21	LaDainian Tomlinson	5-10/221	6/23/79	6	TCU	D1/01	16/16
33	Michael Turner	5-10/237	2/13/82	3	Northern Illinois	D5b/04	16/0
	RECEIVERS						
85	Antonio Gates (TE)	6-4/260	6/18/80	4	Kent State	FA/03	15/15
83	Vincent Jackson	6-5/238	1/14/83	2	Northern Colorado	D2/05	7/0
89	Ryan Krause (TE)	6-3/256	6/16/81	2	Nebraska-Omaha	D6/04	3/0
49	Brandon Manumaleuna (TE)	6-2/288	1/4/80	6	Arizona	T-StL/06	14/14
87	Keenan McCardell	6-1/191	1/6/70	15	UNLV	T-TB/04	16/16
81	Kassim Osgood	6-5/209	5/20/80	4	San Diego State	FA/03	12/3
88	Eric Parker	6-0/180	4/14/79	5	Tennessee	FA/02	16/9
84	Aaron Shea (TE)	6-3/255	12/5/76	7	Michigan	FA/06	12/4
86	Rashaun Woods	6-2/202	10/17/80	2	Oklahoma State	T-SF/06	14/0
	OFFENSIVE LINEMEN						
50	David Binn (C)	6-3/223	2/6/72	13	California	FA/94	16/0
66	Jeromey Clary (T)	6-6/309	11/5/83	R	Kansas State	D6a/06	—
68	Kris Dielman (G)	6-4/310	2/3/81	4	Indiana	FA/03	16/14
79	Mike Goff (G)	6-5/311	1/6/76	9	Iowa	FA/04	16/16
61	Nick Hardwick (C)	6-4/295	9/12/81	3	Purdue	D3/04	13/13
69	Ben Johnson (T)	6-6/329	4/7/80	1	Wisconsin	FA/06	0/0
75	Leander Jordan (T)	6-4/316	9/15/77	7	Indiana (Pa.)	FA/04	13/9
71	Cory Lekkerkerker (T)	6-7/324	7/25/81	2	Cal-Davis	FA/05	1/0
67	Jimmy Martin (T)	6-4/303	10/19/82	R	Virginia Tech	D7b/06	—
73	Marcus McNeill (T)	6-7/336	11/16/83	R	Auburn	D2/06	—
63	Scott Mruczkowski (C)	6-4/321	4/5/82	2	Bowling Green	D7/05	6/0
72	Roman Oben (T)	6-4/305	10/9/72	11	Louisville	T-TB/04	8/8
70	Shane Olivea (T)	6-3/312	10/7/81	3	Ohio State	D7b/04	15/15
60	Wes Sims (G)	6-3/317	4/8/81	2	Oklahoma	D6/05	2/0
	DEFENSIVE LINEMEN						
97	Ryon Bingham (T)	6-3/303	6/6/81	2	Nebraska	D7a/04	1/0
93	Luis Castillo (T)	6-3/305	8/4/83	2	Northwestern	D1b/05	16/15
74	Jacques Cesaire (T)	6-2/295	8/30/80	4	Southern Conn. St.	FA/03	16/5
99	Igor Olshansky (T)	6-6/309	5/3/82	3	Oregon	D2/04	14/12
96	Chase Page (T)	6-4/285	5/20/83	R	North Carolina	D7a/06	—
98	Derreck Robinson (T)	6-5/287	3/3/82	2	Iowa	FA/06	3/0
76	Jamal Williams (T)	6-3/348	4/28/76	9	Oklahoma State	SD-2/98	16/16
	LINEBACKERS						
54	Stephen Cooper	6-1/235	6/19/79	4	Maine	FA/03	16/2
51	Tim Dobbins	6-1/246	12/10/82	R	Iowa State	D5/06	—
59	Donnie Edwards	6-2/227	4/6/73	11	UCLA	FA/02	16/16
53	Steve Foley	6-4/265	9/11/75	8	Louisiana-Monroe	FA/04	13/13
94	Akbar Gbaja-Biamila	6-5/270	5/6/79	3	San Diego State	FA/06	0/0
58	Randall Godfrey	6-2/245	4/6/73	11	Georgia	FA/04	14/14
92	Marques Harris	6-1/231	9/20/81	2	Southern Utah St.	FA/06	11/0
56	Shawne Merriman	6-4/245	5/25/84	2	Maryland	D1a/05	15/10
95	Shaun Phillips	6-3/262	5/13/81	3	Purdue	D4/04	15/3
52	Carlos Polk	6-2/250	2/22/77	6	Nebraska	D4/01	0/0
57	Matt Wilhelm	6-2/254	2/2/81	4	Ohio State	D4/03	16/0
	DEFENSIVE BACKS						
25	Antonio Cromartie (CB)	6-2/208	4/15/84	R	Florida State	D1/06	—
36	Markus Curry (CB)	5-11/181	4/7/81	1	Michigan	FA/05	0/0
29	Drayton Florence (CB)	6-0/195	12/19/80	4	Tuskegee	D2a/03	13/12
42	Clinton Hart (S)	6-0/205	7/20/77	4	Central Florida CC	W-Phi/04	16/5
23	Quentin Jammer (CB)	6-0/204	6/19/79	5	Texas	D1/02	16/16
27	Bhawoh Jue (S)	6-0/199	5/24/79	6	Penn State	FA/05	14/14
48	Terrence Kiel (S)	5-11/207	11/24/80	4	Texas A&M	D2b/03	12/12
24	Andre Lott (CB)	5-10/196	5/31/79	4	Tennessee	FA/06	0/0
20	Marlon McCree (S)	5-11/202	3/17/77	6	Kentucky	FA/06	16/15
31	Hanik Milligan (S)	6-3/200	11/3/79	3	Houston	D6/03	16/0
28	Jerrell Pippens (S)	6-2/195	6/30/80	3	Nebraska	FA/04	2/0
22	Raymond Walls (CB)	5-10/188	7/24/79	6	Southern Miss	FA/06	7/2
	SPECIALISTS						
10	Nate Kaeding (K)	6-0/187	3/26/82	3	Iowa	D3a/04	16/0
5	Mike Scifres (P)	6-2/236	10/8/80	4	Western Illinois	D5/03	16/0
8	Kurt Smith (K)	6-0/184	1/9/83	R	Virginia	D6b/06	—

Abbreviations: D1-draft pick, first round; W-claimed on waivers; T-obtained in trade; FA-free-agent acquisition.

2005 regular-season record: 9-7
Position: 3rd in AFC West

Sept.11—DALLAS	L	24-28
Sept.18—at Denver	L	17-20
Sept.25—N.Y. GIANTS	W	45-23
Oct. 2—at New England	W	41-17
Oct. 10—PITTSBURGH	L	22-24
Oct. 16—at Oakland	W	27-14
Oct. 23—at Philadelphia	L	17-20
Oct. 30—KANSAS CITY	W	28-20
Nov. 6—at N.Y. Jets	W	31-26
Nov. 13—Open date		
Nov. 20—BUFFALO	W	48-10
Nov. 27—at Washington (OT)	W	23-17
Dec. 4—OAKLAND	W	34-10
Dec. 11—MIAMI	L	21-23
Dec. 18—at Indianapolis	W	26-17
Dec. 24—at Kansas City	L	7-20
Dec. 31—DENVER	L	7-23

SCORING BY PERIODS

	Q1	Q2	Q3	Q4	OT	Pts.
Chargers	93	139	74	106	6	418
Opponents	36	126	77	73	0	312

TEAM STATISTICS

	S.D.	Opp.
TOTAL FIRST DOWNS ..	337	306
Rushing	116	90
Passing	191	189
Penalty	30	27
3rd Down: Made/Att. ..	88/208	79/212
3rd Down Pct.	42.3	37.3
4th Down: Made/Att. ..	11/17	10/20
4th Down Pct.	64.7	50.0
POSSESSION AVG.	31:34	28:26
TOTAL NET YARDS	5567	4948
Avg. per Game	347.9	309.3
Total Plays	1022	999
Avg. per Play	5.4	5.0
NET YARDS RUSHING ..	2072	1349
Avg. per Game	129.5	84.3
Total Rushes	465	386
NET YARDS PASSING....	3495	3599
Avg. per Game	218.4	224.9
Sacked/Yards Lost	31/243	46/289
Gross Yards	3738	3888
Att./Completions	526/338	567/338
Completion Pct.	64.3	59.6
Had Intercepted	16	10
PUNTS/AVERAGE	71/43.7	78/42.0
NET PUNTING AVG.	71/38.0	78/37.6
PENALTIES/YARDS	110/890	110/831
FUMBLES/LOST	22/12	23/10
TOUCHDOWNS	51	36

	S.D.	Opp.
Rushing	22	14
Passing	27	20
Returns	2	2

SCORING (NONKICKERS)

	TD	RTD	PTD	MTD	2Pt.	Tot. Pts.
Tomlinson	20	18	2	0	0	120
Gates	10	0	10	0	0	60
McCardell	9	0	9	0	0	54
E. Parker	3	0	3	0	0	18
Turner	3	3	0	0	0	18
Hart	2	0	0	0	2	12
Brees	1	1	0	0	0	6
Caldwell	1	0	1	0	0	6
Neal	1	0	1	0	0	6
Peelle	1	0	1	0	0	6
Chargers	51	22	27	2	0	306
Opponents	36	14	20	2	0	218

2-Pt. conversions: Chargers 0-1; Opponents 0-1.

(KICKERS)

	XPM/XPA	FGM/FGA	Pts.
Kaeding	49/49	21/24	112
Chargers	49/49	21/24	112
Opponents	34/35	20/29	94

RUSHING

	Att.	Yds.	Avg.	Lg.	TD
Tomlinson	339	1462	4.3	62	18
Turner	57	335	5.9	t83	3
Neal	29	98	3.4	9	0
E. Parker	4	55	13.8	30	0
Sproles	8	50	6.3	21	0
Brees	21	49	2.3	9	1
Caldwell	2	10	5.0	7	0
McCardell	2	6	3.0	3	0
Osgood	1	4	4.0	4	0
Pinnock	1	4	4.0	4	0
Rivers	1	-1	-1.0	-1	0
Chargers	465	2072	4.5	t83	22
Opponents	386	1349	3.5	46	14

RECEIVING

	No.	Yds.	Avg.	Lg.	TD
Gates	89	1101	12.4	38	10
McCardell	70	917	13.1	54	9
E. Parker	57	725	12.7	49	3
Tomlinson	51	370	7.3	41	2
Caldwell	28	352	12.6	43	1
Neal	24	145	6.0	21	1
Peelle	11	38	3.5	11	1
Jackson	3	59	19.7	21	0
Sproles	3	10	3.3	6	0
Osgood	2	21	10.5	15	0
Chargers	338	3738	11.1	54	27
Opponents	338	3888	11.5	56	20

INTERCEPTIONS

	No.	Yds.	Avg.	Lg.	TD
Jue	3	28	9.3	20	0
Edwards	2	15	7.5	14	0
Hart	1	110	110.0	t70	2
Fletcher	1	19	19.0	19	0
Jammer	1	14	14.0	14	0
Wilhelm	1	10	10.0	10	0
Florence	1	9	9.0	9	0
Chargers	10	205	20.5	t70	2
Opponents	16	230	14.4	51	1

SACKS: Merriman 10.0, Phillips 7.0, Foley 4.5, Scott 4.5, Castillo 3.5, Edwards 3.0, Olshansky 3.0, Leber 2.0, Cooper 1.5, Cesaire 1.0, Davis 1.0, Fletcher 1.0, Godfrey 1.0, Harris 1.0, Kiel 1.0, Wilhelm 1.0. Chargers 46.0; Opponents 31.0.

PUNTING

	No.	Yds.	Avg.	In.20	Lg.
Scifres	71	3104	43.7	25	71
Chargers	71	3104	43.7	25	71
Opponents	78	3274	42.0	19	65

PUNT RETURNS

	No.	FC	Yds.	Avg.	Lg.	TD
E. Parker	18	9	106	5.9	15	0
Sproles	18	5	108	6.0	23	0
McCardell	3	3	31	10.3	14	0
Chargers	39	17	245	6.3	23	0
Opponents	26	19	244	9.4	52	0

KICK RETURNS

	No.	Yds.	Avg.	Lg.	TD
Sproles	63	1528	24.3	58	0
Caldwell	3	99	33.0	60	0
E. Parker	1	16	16.0	16	0
Pinnock	1	24	24.0	24	0
Turner	1	0	0.0	0	0
Chargers	69	1667	24.2	60	0
Opponents	83	1856	22.4	54	0

FIELD GOALS

	1-19	20-29	30-39	40-49	50+
Kaeding	1/1	3/3	9/9	8/11	0/0
Chargers	1/1	3/3	9/9	8/11	0/0
Opponents	0/0	8/9	6/7	5/5	1/8

Kaeding: (33G) (42G) (44G) (42G, 21G) (34G, 32G, 41G) (32G, 33G) (34G, 40B) () (18G) (28G, 38G) (42N, 46N, 48G) (41G, 32G) () (36G, 20G, 48G, 49G) ()
Opponents: () (45G, 53N, 53N, 41G) (22G, 40G, 28G) (37N, 24G) (40G) () (23G, 40G) (34G, 20G) (51N, 35G, 22G) (53G) (38G, 53N) (37G, 61N) (29G, 39G, 20G) (59N, 32G) (52N) (28N)

PASSING

	Att.	Cmp.	Yds.	Pct.	Avg. Gain	TD	Pct. TD	Int.	Pct. Int.	Long	Sack/Lost	Rating
Brees	500	323	3576	64.6	7.15	24	4.8	15	3.0	54	27/223	89.2
Rivers	22	12	115	54.5	5.23	0	0.0	1	4.5	22	3/16	50.4
Tomlinson	4	3	47	75.0	11.75	3	75.0	0	0.0	t26	0/0	153.1
Chargers	526	338	3738	64.3	7.11	27	5.1	16	3.0	54	31/243	89.7
Opponents	567	338	3888	59.6	6.86	20	3.5	10	1.8	56	46/289	84.7

SAN DIEGO CHARGERS

SAN FRANCISCO 49ERS
NFC WEST DIVISION

2006 SEASON

CLUB DIRECTORY

Owner
Denise DeBartolo-York
Owner
John York
Owner
The DeBartolo Corporation
Vice president/CFO
Larry MacNeil
Vice president business affairs/general counsel
Ed Goines
Vice president/operations
Murlan Fowell
Vice president player personnel
Scot McCloughan
Vice president/sales and marketing
David Peart
Director of football operations
Paraag Marathe
Director of football administration
Terry Tumey
Ticket manager
Lynn Carrozzi
Director of security
Fred Formosa
Director of stadium operations
Jim Mercurio
Equipment manager
Steve Urbianak
Video operations director
Keith Yanagi

Head coach
Mike Nolan

Assistant coaches
Duane Carlisle (asst. strength and conditioning)
Billy Davis (defensive coordinator)
Gary Emanuel (defensive line)
Pep Hamilton (offensive asst./quarterbacks)
Bishop Harris (running backs)
Pete Hoener (tight ends)
Jim Hostler (quarterbacks)
Vance Joseph (asst. defensive backs)
Johnnie Lynn (defensive backs)
Larry Mac Duff (special teams coordinator)
Johnny Parker (strength/conditioning)
Jeff Rodgers (asst. special teams)
Mike Singletary (asst. head coach/linebackers)
Jerry Sullivan (wide receivers)
Jason Tarver (defensive asst./defensive quality control)
Norv Turner (offensive coordinator)
George Warhop (offensive line)

OFFSEASON MOVES

Key additions
G	Larry Allen	FA/Cowboys
WR	Antonio Bryant	FA/Browns
WR	Bryan Gilmore	FA/Dolphins
CB	Walt Harris	FA/Redskins
LB	T.J. Slaughter	FA/Saints
CB	Sammy Davis	trade/Chargers
S	Chad Williams	FA/Ravens

Key losses
FB	Fred Beasley	FA/Dolphins
DE	Andre Carter	FA/Redskins
WR	Brandon Lloyd	trade/Redskins
LB	Julian Peterson	FA/Seahawks
CB	Ahmed Plummer	released
WR	Rashaun Woods	trade/Chargers

SCHEDULE

Sept.	10—at Arizona	4:15
Sept.	17—ST. LOUIS	4:05
Sept.	24—PHILADELPHIA	4:15
Oct.	1—at Kansas City	1:00
Oct.	8—OAKLAND	4:05
Oct.	15—SAN DIEGO	4:15
Oct.	22—Open date	
Oct.	29—at Chicago	1:00
Nov.	5—MINNESOTA	4:05
Nov.	12—at Detroit	1:00
Nov.	19—SEATTLE	4:05
Nov.	26—at St. Louis	1:00
Dec.	3—at New Orleans	1:00
Dec.	10—GREEN BAY	4:05
Dec.	14—at Seattle (Thurs.)	8:00
Dec.	24—ARIZONA	4:05
Dec.	31—at Denver	4:15

All times are Eastern.
All games Sunday unless noted.

DRAFT CHOICES

Vernon Davis, TE, Maryland (first round/sixth pick overall).
Manny Lawson, OLB, N.C. State (1/22).
Brandon Williams, WR, Wisconsin (3/84).
Michael Robinson, WR, Penn State (4/100).
Parys Haralson, DE, Tennessee (5/140).
Delanie Walker, WR, Central Missouri State (6/175).
Marcus Hudson, FS, N.C. State (6/192).
Melvin Oliver, DE, LSU (6/197).
Vickiel Vaughn, FS, Arkansas (7/254).

MISCELLANEOUS TEAM DATA

Stadium (capacity, surface):
Monster Park at Candlestick Point (69,734, grass)
Business address:
4949 Centennial Blvd.
Santa Clara, CA 95054
Business phone:
408-562-4949
Ticket information:
415-656-4900
Team colors:
Forty Niners gold and cardinal
Flagship radio station:
KNBR, 680 AM
Website:
www.sf49ers.com
Training site:
4949 Centennial Blvd.
Santa Clara, CA 95054-1229
408-562-4949

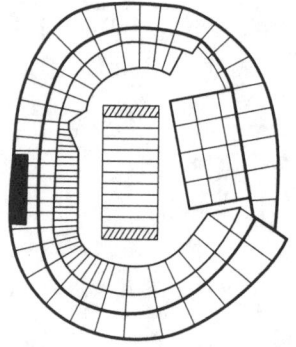

SAN FRANCISCO 49ERS

No.	QUARTERBACKS	Ht./Wt.	Born	NFL Exp.	College	How acq.	'05 Games GP/GS
8	Trent Dilfer	6-4/225	3/13/72	13	Fresno State	T-Cle/06	11/11
2	Jesse Palmer	6-2/225	10/5/78	4	Florida	W-NYG/05	0/0
3	Cody Pickett	6-3/227	6/30/80	2	Washington	D7a/04	5/2
11	Alex Smith	6-4/217	5/7/84	2	Utah	D1/05	9/7
	RUNNING BACKS						
32	Kevan Barlow	6-1/238	1/7/79	6	Pittsburgh	D3/01	12/12
21	Frank Gore	5-10/208	5/14/83	2	Miami (Fla.)	D3a/05	14/1
44	Chris Hetherington (FB)	6-3/245	11/27/72	11	Yale	FA/05	16/6
43	Maurice Hicks	5-11/200	7/22/78	3	North Carolina A&T	FA/04	14/3
22	Terry Jackson (FB)	6-0/232	1/10/76	8	Florida	D5/99	16/0
35	Michael Robinson	6-1/218	2/6/83	R	Penn State	D4/06	—
14	Delanie Walker (FB)	6-1/241	8/12/84	R	Central Missouri St.	D6a/06	—
	RECEIVERS						
18	Otis Amey	5-10/197	12/4/81	2	Sacramento State	FA/05	11/0
47	Billy Bajema (TE)	6-5/259	10/31/82	2	Oklahoma State	D7d/05	15/7
83	Arnaz Battle	6-1/217	2/22/80	4	Notre Dame	D6/03	10/8
81	Antonio Bryant	6-1/196	3/9/81	5	Pittsburgh	FA/06	16/15
85	Vernon Davis (TE)	6-3/253	1/31/84	R	Maryland	D1a/06	—
84	Bryan Gilmore	6-0/195	1/21/78	7	Midwestern State	FA/06	15/1
86	Brian Jennings (TE)	6-5/245	10/14/76	7	Arizona State	D7b/00	16/0
82	Eric Johnson (TE)	6-3/256	9/15/79	6	Yale	D7b/01	0/0
49	Terry Jones (TE)	6-3/260	12/3/79	5	Alabama	W-Bal/05	8/5
89	Rasheed Marshall	5-11/185	7/11/81	2	West Virginia	D5b/05	12/0
19	Marcus Maxwell	6-4/205	7/8/83	2	Oregon	D7b/05	4/0
15	Jason McAddley	6-2/200	7/28/79	5	Alabama	FA/05	12/2
48	Trent Smith (TE)	6-5/243	9/15/79	4	Oklahoma	W-Bal/05	5/2
17	Brandon Williams	5-10/179	2/24/84	R	Wisconsin	D3/06	—
	OFFENSIVE LINEMEN						
71	Larry Allen (G)	6-3/325	11/27/71	13	Sonoma State	FA/06	16/16
64	David Baas (C/G)	6-4/319	9/28/81	2	Michigan	D2/05	13/5
78	Patrick Estes (T)	6-6/268	2/4/83	2	Virginia	D7c/05	7/0
77	Kwame Harris (T)	6-7/310	3/15/82	4	Stanford	D1/03	16/16
66	Eric Heitmann (G)	6-3/305	2/24/80	5	Stanford	D7a/02	16/16
75	Jonas Jennings (T)	6-3/325	11/21/77	6	Georgia	FA/05	3/3
62	Jeremy Newberry (C)	6-5/310	3/23/76	9	California	D2/98	10/10
65	Justin Smiley (G)	6-3/301	11/11/81	3	Alabama	D2a/04	16/16
68	Adam Snyder (T)	6-5/316	1/30/82	2	Oregon	D3b/05	16/8
	DEFENSIVE LINEMEN						
91	Anthony Adams (T)	6-0/300	6/18/80	4	Penn State	D2/03	16/16
94	Marques Douglas (E)	6-2/290	3/5/77	7	Howard	FA/05	16/15
95	Ronald Fields (E)	6-2/298	9/13/81	2	Mississippi State	D5a/05	4/0
96	Melvin Oliver (E)	6-3/276	7/25/83	R	Louisiana State	D6c/06	—
90	Isaac Sopoaga (T)	6-2/321	9/4/81	2	Hawaii	D4a/04	16/1
97	Bryant Young (E)	6-3/291	1/27/72	13	Notre Dame	D1//94	13/13
	LINEBACKERS						
98	Parys Haralson	6-1/253	1/24/84	R	Tennessee	D5/06	—
99	Manny Lawson	6-5/240	7/3/84	R	N.C. State	D1b/06	—
57	James Maxwell	6-4/242	8/8/81	3	Gardner-Webb	FA/05	11/1
56	Brandon Moore	6-1/242	1/16/79	5	Oklahoma	FA/02	16/10
52	T.J. Slaughter	6-0/233	2/20/77	7	Southern Miss	FA/06	10/1
58	Corey Smith	6-2/250	11/2/79	4	N.C. State	FA/04	14/0
50	Derek Smith	6-2/245	1/18/75	10	Arizona State	FA/01	16/16
53	Jeff Ulbrich	6-0/249	2/17/77	7	Hawaii	D3b/00	5/5
59	Renauld Williams	6-0/211	2/23/81	3	Hofstra	FA/05	2/0
	DEFENSIVE BACKS						
20	Mike Adams (S)	5-11/193	3/24/81	3	Delaware	FA/04	14/10
31	Sammy Davis (CB)	6-0/195	4/8/80	4	Texas A&M	T-SD/06	16/4
38	Bert Emanuel (S)	6-2/213	6/18/82	2	UCLA	FA/05	11/8
27	Walt Harris (CB)	5-11/192	8/10/74	11	Mississippi State	FA/06	13/12
41	Marcus Hudson (S)	6-1/194	11/15/82	R	N.C. State	D6b/06	—
23	Derrick Johnson (CB)	5-11/188	2/9/82	2	Washington	D6/05	14/5
28	Keith Lewis (S)	6-0/202	10/20/81	3	Oregon	D6b/04	16/4
33	Tony Parrish (S)	6-0/210	11/23/75	9	Washington	FA/02	9/9
29	Kris Richard (CB)	5-11/190	10/28/78	5	USC	D1/02	1/0
24	Mike Rumph (CB)	6-2/205	11/8/79	5	Miami (Fla.)	D1/02	3/3
36	Shawntae Spencer (CB)	6-1/181	2/22/82	3	Pittsburgh	D2b/04	15/14
26	Bruce Thornton (CB)	5-10/198	1/31/80	3	Georgia	W-Dal/05	12/11
35	B.J. Tucker (CB)	5-10/188	10/12/80	4	Wisconsin	W-Sea/05	6/0
40	Vickiel Vaughn (S)	6-0/204	10/24/83	R	Arkansas	D7/06	—
25	Chad Williams (S)	5-9/207	1/22/79	5	Southern Miss	FA/06	16/3
	SPECIALISTS						
4	Andy Lee (P)	6-0/206	8/11/82	3	Pittsburgh	D6/04	16/0
6	Joe Nedney (K)	6-5/225	3/22/73	10	San Jose State	FA/05	15/0

Abbreviations: D1-draft pick, first round; W-claimed on waivers; T-obtained in trade; FA-free-agent acquisition.

SAN FRANCISCO 49ERS

2005 regular-season record: 4-12
Position: 4th in NFC West

Sept.11—ST. LOUIS	W	28-25
Sept.18—at Philadelphia	L	3-42
Sept.25—DALLAS	L	31-34
Oct. 2—at Arizona	L	14-31
Oct. 9—INDIANAPOLIS	L	3-28
Oct. 16—Open date		
Oct. 23—at Washington	L	17-52
Oct. 30—TAMPA BAY	W	15-10
Nov. 6—N.Y. GIANTS	L	6-24
Nov.13—at Chicago	L	9-17
Nov.20—SEATTLE	L	25-27
Nov.27—at Tennessee	L	22-33
Dec. 4—ARIZONA	L	10-17
Dec.11—at Seattle	L	3-41
Dec.18—at Jacksonville	L	9-10
Dec.24—at St. Louis	W	24-20
Jan. 1—HOUSTON (OT)	W	20-17

SCORING BY PERIODS

	Q1	Q2	Q3	Q4	OT	Pts.
49ers	44	94	51	47	3	239
Opponents	70	150	91	117	0	428

TEAM STATISTICS

	S.F.	Opp.
TOTAL FIRST DOWNS ..	191	335
Rushing	70	115
Passing	96	205
Penalty	25	15
3rd Down: Made/Att. ..	49/204	87/226
3rd Down Pct.	24.0	38.5
4th Down: Made/Att. ..	5/8	11/19
4th Down Pct.	62.5	57.9
POSSESSION AVG.	27:18	32:42
TOTAL NET YARDS	3587	6259
Avg. per Game	224.2	391.2
Total Plays	865	1090
Avg. per Play	4.1	5.7
NET YARDS RUSHING ..	1689	1832
Avg. per Game	105.6	114.5
Total Rushes	428	486
NET YARDS PASSING	1898	4427
Avg. per Game	118.6	276.7
Sacked/Yards Lost	48/292	28/193
Gross Yards	2190	4620
Att./Completions	389/204	576/374
Completion Pct.	52.4	64.9
Had Intercepted	21	16
PUNTS/AVERAGE	108/41.2	71/40.1
NET PUNTING AVG.	108/36.3	71/33.7
PENALTIES/YARDS	106/780	120/961
FUMBLES/LOST	31/14	18/10
TOUCHDOWNS	23	49
Rushing	9	19
Passing	8	28
Returns	6	2

SCORING (NONKICKERS)

	Tot. TD	RTD	PTD	MTD	2Pt.	Tot. Pts.
Lloyd	5	0	5	0	0	30
Barlow	3	3	0	0	0	18
Battle	3	0	3	0	0	18
Gore	3	3	0	0	0	18
Hicks	3	3	0	0	0	18
M. Adams	1	0	0	1	0	6
Amey	1	0	0	1	0	6
D. Johnson	1	0	0	1	0	6
Parrish	1	0	0	1	0	6
D. Smith	1	0	0	1	0	6
Spencer	1	0	0	1	0	6
Jackson	0	0	0	0	1	2
49ers	23	9	8	6	1	140
Opponents	49	19	28	2	2	298

2-Pt. conversions: 49ers 1-2; Opponents 2-5.

(KICKERS)

	XPM/XPA	FGM/FGA	Pts.
Nedney	19/19	26/28	97
Cortez	2/2	0/1	2
49ers	21/21	26/29	99
Opponents	43/44	29/36	130

RUSHING

	Att.	Yds.	Avg.	Lg.	TD
Gore	127	608	4.8	t72	3
Barlow	176	581	3.3	29	3
Hicks	59	308	5.2	t73	3
A. Smith	30	103	3.4	19	0
Pickett	13	42	3.2	12	0
Rattay	7	18	2.6	13	0
Battle	8	11	1.4	9	0
Dorsey	4	11	2.8	6	0
Jackson	2	11	5.5	11	0
Hetherington	1	3	3.0	3	0
Marshall	1	-7	-7.0	-7	0
49ers	428	1689	3.9	t73	9
Opponents	486	1832	3.8	40	19

RECEIVING

	No.	Yds.	Avg.	Lg.	TD
Lloyd	48	733	15.3	t89	5
Battle	32	363	11.3	39	3
Barlow	31	241	7.8	24	0
Morton	21	288	13.7	30	0
Gore	15	131	8.7	47	0
Hicks	12	47	3.9	11	0
Jackson	10	67	6.7	12	0
Jones	9	76	8.4	21	0
McAddley	7	125	17.9	38	0
Bajema	5	54	10.8	24	0
Hetherington	5	26	5.2	11	0
Bush	3	21	7.0	10	0
T. Smith	3	7	2.3	6	0
Beasley	2	12	6.0	6	0
Marshall	1	-1	-1.0	-1	0
49ers	204	2190	10.7	t89	8
Opponents	374	4620	12.4	t78	28

INTERCEPTIONS

	No.	Yds.	Avg.	Lg.	TD
Spencer	4	85	21.3	t61	1
M. Adams	4	36	9.0	t40	1
Parrish	2	34	17.0	t34	1
Thornton	2	0	0.0	0	0
Emanuel	1	38	38.0	35	0
D. Smith	1	13	13.0	13	0
B. Moore	1	12	12.0	12	0
Lewis	1	2	2.0	2	0
49ers	16	220	13.8	t61	3
Opponents	21	265	12.6	34	1

SACKS: Young 8.0, B. Moore 5.0, Carter 4.5, J. Peterson 3.0, A. Adams 2.5, M. Adams 1.0, Douglas 1.0, D. Johnson 1.0, Emanuel 0.5, Hall 0.5. 49ers 28.0; Opponents 48.0.

PUNTING

	No.	Yds.	Avg.	In. 20	Lg.
Lee	107	4447	41.6	15	58
49ers	108	4447	41.2	15	58
Opponents	71	2846	40.1	22	56

PUNT RETURNS

	No.	FC	Yds.	Avg.	Lg.	TD
Marshall	17	10	87	5.1	13	0
Amey	11	2	125	11.4	t75	1
49ers	28	12	212	7.6	t75	1
Opponents	62	20	471	7.6	25	0

KICK RETURNS

	No.	Yds.	Avg.	Lg.	TD
Hicks	34	689	20.3	40	0
Marshall	26	488	18.8	29	0
Amey	14	241	17.2	25	0
McAddley	7	122	17.4	22	0
49ers	81	1540	19.0	40	0
Opponents	48	960	20.0	35	0

FIELD GOALS

	1-19	20-29	30-39	40-49	50+
Nedney	0/0	4/4	10/11	10/10	2/3
Cortez	0/0	0/0	0/1	0/0	0/0
49ers	0/0	4/4	10/12	10/10	2/3
Opponents	1/1	8/8	7/9	9/10	4/8

Nedney: () (32G) (20G) () (30G) (47G) (45G, 47G, 41G, 46G, 28G, 39N) (48G, 52G) (30G, 52N, 34G, 29G) (33G, 31G, 40G, 22G) () (48G) (39G) (35G, 47G, 33G) (56G) (42G, 33G)

Cortez: () () () () () () () () () (34N) () () () () ()

Opponents: (30G, 41G, 33G, 41G) (43N) () (40G, 45G, 48G, 23G, 43G, 24G) () (27G) (47G, 52N) (22G) (39N, 37G) (21G, 51N, 47G) (35G, 41G, 21G, 22G) (30G, 35G, 19G) (52G, 50N, 52G) (52N, 32G) (50G, 51G) (21G, 31N)

PASSING

	Att.	Cmp.	Yds.	Pct.	Avg. Gain	TD	Pct. TD	Int.	Pct. Int.	Long	Sack/Lost	Rating
A. Smith	165	84	875	50.9	5.30	1	0.6	11	6.7	47	29/185	40.8
Rattay	97	56	667	57.7	6.88	5	5.2	6	6.2	t89	10/63	70.3
Dorsey	90	48	481	53.3	5.34	2	2.2	2	2.2	44	6/28	66.9
Pickett	35	14	140	40.0	4.00	0	0.0	2	5.7	28	3/16	28.3
Battle	2	2	27	100.0	13.50	0	0.0	0	0.0	24	0/0	118.8
49ers	389	204	2190	52.4	5.63	8	2.1	21	5.4	t89	48/292	53.6
Opponents	576	374	4620	64.9	8.02	28	4.9	16	2.8	t78	28/193	94.2

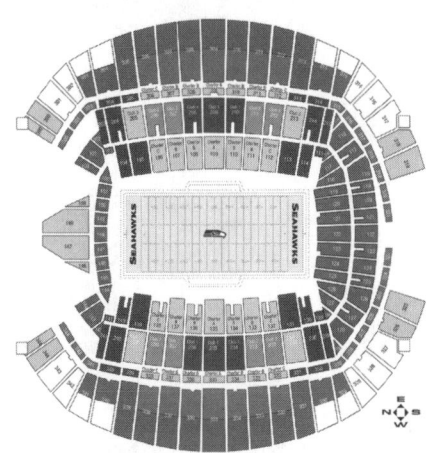

SEATTLE SEAHAWKS
NFC WEST DIVISION

2006 SEASON

CLUB DIRECTORY

Owner
Paul Allen
President of football operations
Tim Ruskell
CEO
Tod Leiweke
Vice president of football administration
Mike Reinfeldt
Vice president/administration
Gary Wright
Director of communication & broadcasting
Dave Pearson
Community outreach director
Sandy Gregory
Director of pro personnel
Will Lewis

Executive VP of football operations/ head coach
Mike Holmgren

Assistant coaches
Teryl Austin (defensive backs)
Dwaine Board (defensive line)
Bob Casullo (special teams)
Mike Clark (strength and conditioning)
Nolan Cromwell (wide receivers)
Keith Gilbertson (asst. offensive line)
Gil Haskell (offensive coordinator)
Tom Headlee (quality control/ defense)
John Jamison (special teams asst.)
Darren Krein (asst. strength and conditioning)
Bill Laveroni (offensive line)
Jim Lind (tight ends)
Larry Marmie (defensive asst./ secondary)
John Marshall (defensive coordinator)
Stump Mitchell (running backs)
Gary Reynolds (quality control/ offense)
Ray Rhodes (defensive coordinator)
Zerick Rollins (linebackers)
Jim Zorn (quarterbacks)

OFFSEASON MOVES

Key additions
OL	Tom Ashworth	FA/Patriots
WR	Nate Burleson	FA/Vikings
DT	Russell Davis	FA/Cardinals
FS	Mike Green	trade/Bears
OLB	Julian Peterson	FA/49ers

Key losses
CB	Andre Dyson	released/Jets
TE	Ryan Hannam	FA/Cowboys
G	Steve Hutchinson	FA/Vikings
WR	Joe Jurevicius	FA/Browns
FS	Marquand Manuel	FA/Packers
LB	Jamie Sharper	released

SCHEDULE

Sept.	10—at Detroit	1:00
Sept.	17—ARIZONA	4:05
Sept.	24—N.Y. GIANTS	4:15
Oct.	1—at Chicago	8:15
Oct.	8—Open date	
Oct.	15—at St. Louis	1:00
Oct.	22—MINNESOTA	4:15
Oct.	29—at Kansas City	1:00
Nov.	6—OAKLAND (Mon.)	8:30
Nov.	12—ST. LOUIS	4:15
Nov.	19—at San Francisco	4:05
Nov.	27—GREEN BAY (Mon.)	8:30
Dec.	3—at Denver	4:15
Dec.	10—at Arizona	4:05
Dec.	14—SAN FRANCISCO (Thurs.)	8:00
Dec.	24—SAN DIEGO	4:15
Dec.	31—at Tampa Bay	1:00

All times are Eastern.
All games Sunday unless noted.

DRAFT CHOICES

Kelly Jennings, CB, Miami (first round/31st pick overall).
Darryl Tapp, DE, Virginia Tech (2/63).
Rob Sims, G, Ohio State (4/128).
David Kirtman, FB, Southern California (5/163).
Ryan Plackemeier, P, Wake Forest (7/239).
Ben Obomanu, WR, Auburn (7/249).

MISCELLANEOUS TEAM DATA

Stadium (capacity, surface):
Qwest Field (67,000, FieldTurf)
Business address:
11220 N.E. 53rd Street
Kirkland, WA 98033
Business phone:
425-827-9777
Ticket information:
800-635-4295
Team colors:
Seahawks blue, Seahawks navy and Seahawks bright green
Flagship radio station:
KIRO, 710 AM
Website:
www.seahawks.com
Training site:
Eastern Washington University
Cheney, Wash.
425-827-9777

SEATTLE SEAHAWKS

No.	QUARTERBACKS	Ht./Wt.	Born	NFL Exp.	College	How acq.	'05 Games GP/GS
11	David Greene	6-3/226	6/22/82	1	Georgia	D3a/05	0/0
5	Gibran Hamdan	6-6/240	2/8/81	2	Indiana	FA/05	0/0
8	Matt Hasselbeck	6-4/223	9/25/75	8	Boston College	T-GB/01	16/16
15	Seneca Wallace	5-11/196	8/6/80	4	Iowa State	D4a/03	7/0
	RUNNING BACKS						
37	Shaun Alexander	5-11/225	8/30/77	7	Alabama	D1a/00	16/16
34	David Kirtman (FB)	5-11/232	2/12/83	R	USC	D5/06	—
20	Maurice Morris	5-11/202	12/1/79	5	Oregon	D2a/02	16/1
39	Josh Scobey	6-0/216	12/11/79	4	Kansas State	W-Ari/05	16/0
38	Mack Strong (FB)	6-0/245	9/11/71	14	Georgia	FA/93	16/7
43	Leonard Weaver (FB)	6-0/251	9/23/82	2	Carson-Newman	FA/05	16/0
	RECEIVERS						
85	Alex Bannister	6-5/207	4/23/79	6	Eastern Kentucky	D5/01	2/0
83	Nate Burleson	6-0/192	8/19/81	4	Nevada	FA/06	12/9
84	Bobby Engram	5-10/188	1/7/73	11	Penn State	FA/01	13/13
18	D.J. Hackett	6-2/199	7/31/81	2	Colorado	FA/05	13/3
19	Keenan Howry	5-10/172	6/17/81	4	Oregon	FA/06	4/0
82	Darrell Jackson	6-0/201	12/6/78	7	Florida	D3/00	6/6
13	Kevin Kasper	6-1/197	12/23/77	4	Iowa	FA/06	0/0
88	Itula Mili (TE)	6-4/260	4/20/73	10	Brigham Young	D6/97	2/0
87	Ben Obomanu	6-1/205	10/30/83	R	Auburn	D7b/06	—
86	Jerramy Stevens (TE)	6-7/260	11/13/79	5	Washington	D1/02	16/12
10	Taco Wallace	6-1/190	4/14/81	3	Kansas State	D7/03	1/0
81	Peter Warrick	5-11/192	6/19/77	7	Florida State	FA/05	13/5
	OFFENSIVE LINEMEN						
68	Tom Ashworth (T)	6-6/305	10/10/77	5	Colorado	FA/06	14/11
62	Chris Gray (G)	6-4/308	6/19/70	14	Auburn	FA/98	16/16
73	Wayne Hunter (T)	6-5/303	7/2/81	4	Hawaii	D3/03	1/0
71	Walter Jones (T)	6-5/315	1/19/74	10	Florida State	D1b/97	15/15
75	Sean Locklear (T)	6-4/301	5/29/81	3	N.C. State	D3/04	16/16
67	Rob Sims (G)	6-2/307	12/6/83	R	Ohio State	D4/06	—
65	Chris Spencer (C)	6-3/308	3/28/82	2	Mississippi	D1/05	8/0
61	Robbie Tobeck (C)	6-4/297	3/6/70	13	Washington State	FA/00	16/16
74	Ray Willis (T)	6-5/325	8/13/82	2	Florida State	D4/05	6/0
77	Floyd Womack (T)	6-4/333	11/15/78	6	Mississippi State	D4c/01	11/1
	DEFENSIVE LINEMEN						
99	Rocky Bernard (T)	6-3/293	4/19/79	5	Texas A&M	D5a/02	16/6
91	Chuck Darby (T)	6-0/298	10/22/75	6	South Carolina St.	FA/05	14/14
95	Russell Davis (T)	6-4/310	3/28/75	8	North Carolina	FA/06	3/3
94	Bryce Fisher (E)	6-3/272	5/12/77	6	Air Force	FA/05	16/15
97	Jeb Huckeba (E)	6-4/252	5/20/82	2	Arkansas	D5/05	5/5
92	Alain Kashama (E)	6-4/270	12/8/79	3	Michigan	T-Chi/05	1/0
72	Kemp Rasmussen (E)	6-3/265	5/25/79	5	Indiana	FA/06	15/0
69	Joe Tafoya (E)	6-4/265	9/6/78	6	Arizona	W-Atl/05	15/1
55	Darryl Tapp (E)	6-1/252	9/13/84	R	Virginia Tech	D2/06	—
93	Craig Terrill (T)	6-2/290	6/27/80	3	Purdue	D6/04	16/0
90	Marcus Tubbs (T)	6-4/320	5/16/81	3	Texas	D1/04	13/12
98	Grant Wistrom (E)	6-4/272	7/3/76	9	Nebraska	FA/04	16/16
	LINEBACKERS						
57	Kevin Bentley	6-1/240	12.29/79	5	Northwestern	FA/05	15/3
56	Leroy Hill	6-1/229	9/14/82	2	Clemson	D3b/05	15/9
58	Isaiah Kacyvenski	6-1/252	10/3/77	7	Harvard	D4b/00	16/0
53	Niko Koutouvides	6-2/238	3/25/81	3	Purdue	D4/04	12/0
54	D.D. Lewis	6-1/241	1/8/79	5	Texas	FA/02	12/12
92	Julian Peterson	6-3/235	7/28/78	7	Michigan State	FA/06	15/14
51	Lofa Tatupu	6-0/240	11/15/82	2	USC	D2/05	16/16
50	Cornelius Wortham	6-1/231	1/25/82	2	Alabama	D7a/05	8/0
	DEFENSIVE BACKS						
27	Jordan Babineaux (S)	6-0/200	8/31/82	3	Southern Arkansas	FA/04	16/4
28	Michael Boulware (S)	6-3/223	9/17/81	3	Florida State	D2/04	16/16
40	Oliver Celestin (CB)	6-0/207	2/25/81	3	Texas Southern	FA/06	12/0
25	Lance Frazier (CB)	5-10/183	5/23/81	3	West Virginia	FA/06	0/0
32	Mike Green (S)	6-0/195	12/6/76	7	Northwestern St.	T-Chi/06	16/3
26	Ken Hamlin (S)	6-2/209	1/20/81	4	Arkansas	D2/03	6/6
31	Kelly Herndon (CB)	5-10/180	11/3/76	5	Toledo	FA/05	12/6
21	Kelly Jennings (CB)	5-11/178	11/30/82	R	Miami	D1/06	—
35	Etric Pruitt (DB)	6-0/196	8/16/81	3	Southern Miss	FA/05	6/0
23	Marcus Trufant (CB)	5-11/199	12/25/80	4	Washington State	D1/03	15/15
22	Jimmy Williams (CB)	5-11/190	3/10/79	6	Vanderbilt	FA/05	14/1
	SPECIALISTS						
3	Josh Brown (K)	6-0/202	4/29/79	4	Nebraska	D7/03	16/0
1	Ryan Plackemeier (P)	6-3/253	3/5/84	R	Wake Forest	D7a/06	—
16	Tom Rouen (P)	6-3/225	6/9/68	14	Colorado	FA/05	12/0

Abbreviations: D1-draft pick, first round; W-claimed on waivers; T-obtained in trade; FA-free-agent acquisition.

2005 regular-season record: 13-3
Position: 1st in NFC West

Sept.11—at Jacksonville	L	14-26
Sept.18—ATLANTA	W	21-18
Sept.25—ARIZONA	W	37-12
Oct. 2—at Washington (OT)	L	17-20
Oct. 9—at St. Louis	W	37-31
Oct. 16—HOUSTON	W	42-10
Oct. 23—DALLAS	W	13-10
Oct. 30—Open date		
Nov. 6—at Arizona	W	33-19
Nov. 13—ST. LOUIS	W	31-16
Nov. 20—at San Francisco	W	27-25
Nov. 27—N.Y. GIANTS (OT)	W	24-21
Dec. 5—at Philadelphia	W	42-0
Dec. 11—SAN FRANCISCO	W	41-3
Dec. 18—at Tennessee	W	28-24
Dec. 24—INDIANAPOLIS	W	28-13
Jan. 1—at Green Bay	L	17-23

2005 postseason record: 2-1

Jan. 14—WASHINGTON*	W	20-10
Jan. 22—CAROLINA§	W	34-14
Feb. 5—at Pittsburgh+	L	10-21

*NFC divisional playoff game. §NFC championship game. +Super Bowl 40.

SCORING BY PERIODS

	Q1	Q2	Q3	Q4	OT	Pts.
Seahawks	93	148	121	87	3	452
Opponents	44	80	83	61	3	271

TEAM STATISTICS

	Sea.	Opp.
TOTAL FIRST DOWNS	361	295
Rushing	142	78
Passing	192	194
Penalty	27	23
3rd Down: Made/Att.	76/192	89/234
3rd Down Pct.	39.6	38.0
4th Down: Made/Att.	7/8	12/19
4th Down Pct.	87.5	63.2
POSSESSION AVG.	29:17	30:43
TOTAL NET YARDS	5915	5069
Avg. per Game	369.7	316.8
Total Plays	1020	1041
Avg. per Play	5.8	4.9
NET YARDS RUSHING	2457	1510
Avg. per Game	153.6	94.4
Total Rushes	519	420
NET YARDS PASSING	3458	3559
Avg. per Game	216.1	222.4
Sacked/Yards Lost	27/174	50/302
Gross Yards	3632	3861
Att./Completions	474/307	571/331
Completion Pct.	64.8	58.0
Had Intercepted	10	16
PUNTS/AVERAGE	80/41.0	77/40.1
NET PUNTING AVG.	80/34.7	77/36.0
PENALTIES/YARDS	94/846	123/909
FUMBLES/LOST	18/7	25/11

	Sea.	Opp.
TOUCHDOWNS	57	24
Rushing	29	5
Passing	25	18
Returns	3	1

SCORING (NONKICKERS)

	Tot. TD	RTD	PTD	MTD	2Pt.	Tot. Pts.
Alexander	28	27	1	0	0	168
Jurevicius	10	0	10	0	0	60
Stevens	5	0	5	0	0	30
Engram	3	0	3	0	0	18
Jackson	3	0	3	0	0	18
Dyson	2	0	0	2	0	12
Hackett	2	0	2	0	0	12
Hannam	1	0	1	0	0	6
Hasselbeck	1	1	0	0	0	6
Morris	1	1	0	0	0	6
Tatupu	1	0	0	1	0	6
Seahawks	57	29	25	3	0	342
Opponents	24	5	18	1	2	148

2-Pt. conversions: Seahawks 0-0; Opponents 2-3.

(KICKERS)

	XPM/XPA	FGM/FGA	Pts.
J. Brown	56/57	18/25	110
Seahawks	56/57	18/25	110
Opponents	21/21	34/42	123

RUSHING

	Att.	Yds.	Avg.	Lg.	TD
Alexander	370	1880	5.1	t88	27
Morris	71	288	4.1	49	1
Hasselbeck	36	124	3.4	23	1
Weaver	17	80	4.7	24	0
Strong	17	78	4.6	16	0
Jackson	1	7	7.0	7	0
Warrick	1	5	5.0	5	0
S. Wallace	6	-5	-0.8	0	0
Seahawks	519	2457	4.7	t88	29
Opponents	420	1510	3.6	50	5

RECEIVING

	No.	Yds.	Avg.	Lg.	TD
Engram	67	778	11.6	56	3
Jurevicius	55	694	12.6	52	10
Stevens	45	554	12.3	t35	5
Jackson	38	482	12.7	48	3
Hackett	28	400	14.3	47	2
Strong	22	166	7.5	27	0
Alexander	15	78	5.2	9	1
Hannam	13	89	6.8	20	1
Warrick	11	180	16.4	42	0
Urban	7	151	21.6	46	0
Morris	5	48	9.6	20	0
Weaver	1	12	12.0	12	0
Seahawks	307	3632	11.8	56	25
Opponents	331	3861	11.7	63	18

INTERCEPTIONS

	No.	Yds.	Avg.	Lg.	TD
Boulware	4	107	26.8	40	0
Babineaux	3	56	18.7	25	0
Tatupu	3	55	18.3	t38	1
Herndon	2	12	6.0	10	0
Williams	2	6	3.0	6	0
Dyson	1	72	72.0	t72	1
Trufant	1	7	7.0	7	0
Seahawks	16	315	19.7	t72	2
Opponents	10	93	9.3	33	0

SACKS: Fisher 9.0, R. Bernard 8.5, Hill 7.5, Tubbs 5.5, Tatupu 4.0, Wistrom 4.0, Darby 2.5, Boulware 2.0, Terrill 2.0, Tafoya 1.0, Trufant 1.0. Seahawks 50.0; Opponents 27.0.

PUNTING

	No.	Yds.	Avg.	In. 20	Lg.
Araguz	18	723	40.2	4	53
J. Brown	1	20	20.0	1	20
Rouen	61	2539	41.6	20	62
Seahawks	80	3282	41.0	25	62
Opponents	77	3091	40.1	23	67

PUNT RETURNS

	No.	FC	Yds.	Avg.	Lg.	TD
Williams	24	22	139	5.8	24	0
Warrick	6	0	29	4.8	10	0
Engram	1	1	9	9.0	9	0
Seahawks	31	23	177	5.7	24	0
Opponents	41	16	343	8.4	44	0

KICK RETURNS

	No.	Yds.	Avg.	Lg.	TD
Scobey	59	1326	22.5	53	0
Morris	1	21	21.0	21	0
Tafoya	1	0	0.0	0	0
Seahawks	61	1347	22.1	53	0
Opponents	82	1802	22.0	t99	1

FIELD GOALS

	1-19	20-29	30-39	40-49	50+
J. Brown	0/0	5/5	4/5	4/7	5/8
Seahawks	0/0	5/5	4/5	4/7	5/8
Opponents	0/0	8/9	16/18	7/10	3/5

J. Brown: () () (33G, 23G, 47G) (53G, 47N, 47N) (34G, 44G, 28G) () (55G, 50G) (26G, 28G) (31G) (21G, 51N, 47G) (36G) (40N) (52G, 50N, 52G) (36B) (57N) (44G)
Opponents: (23G, 41G, 43N, 29G, 41G) (30G) (54G, 39G, 50G, 39G) (39B, 40G, 39G) (40G) (39G, 56N) (29N, 21G) (23G, 31G, 50G, 44G) (31G, 36G, 39G) (33G, 31G, 40G, 22G) (39G, 43G, 40N, 54N, 45N) () (39G) (38G) (24G, 31B, 32G) (26G, 32G, 28G)

PASSING

	Att.	Cmp.	Yds.	Pct.	Avg. Gain	TD	Pct. TD	Int.	Pct. Int.	Long	Sack/Lost	Rating
Hasselbeck	449	294	3459	65.5	7.70	24	5.3	9	2.0	56	24/154	98.2
S. Wallace	25	13	173	52.0	6.92	1	4.0	1	4.0	42	3/20	70.9
Seahawks	474	307	3632	64.8	7.66	25	5.3	10	2.1	56	27/174	96.8
Opponents	571	331	3861	58.0	6.76	18	3.2	16	2.8	63	50/302	77.4

SEATTLE SEAHAWKS

TAMPA BAY BUCCANEERS
NFC SOUTH DIVISION

2006 SEASON

CLUB DIRECTORY

Owner
Malcolm Glazer
Executive vice president
Bryan Glazer
Executive vice president
Joel Glazer
Executive vice president
Edward Glazer
General manager
Bruce Allen
Director of football operations
Mark Arteaga
Chief operating officer
Eric Land
Director of player personnel
Ruston Webster
Director of pro personnel
Mark Dominik
Director of college scouting
Dennis Hickey
Personnel executive
Doug Williams
Director of player development
TBA
Director of public relations
Jeff Kamis

Head coach
Jon Gruden

Assistant coaches
Joe Barry (linebackers)
Tim Berbenich (offensive quality
  control)
Richard Bisaccia (special teams)
Casey Bradley (defensive quality
  control)
Greg Burns (defensive backs)
Jethro Franklin (defensive line)
Jay Gruden (offensive asst.)
Nathaniel Hackett (offensive
  quality control)
Paul Hackett (quarterbacks)
Paul Kelly (asst. to the head
  coach/football operations)
Monte Kiffin (defensive coordinator)
Aaron Kromer (senior asst./
  offensive line)
Jimmy Lake (asst. defensive backs)
Richard Mann (wide receivers)
Ron Middleton (tight ends/asst.
  special teams)
Mike Morris (head strength and
  conditioning)
Kurt Schultz (asst. strength and
  conditioning)
Art Valero (running backs)

OFFSEASON MOVES

Key additions
G	Toniu Fonoti	FA/Vikings
OT	Torrin Tucker	FA/Cowboys
LB	Jamie Winborn	FA/Jaguars

Key losses
QB	Brian Griese	released/Bears
FS	Dexter Jackson	FA/Bengals

SCHEDULE

Sept.	10—BALTIMORE	1:00
Sept.	17—at Atlanta	1:00
Sept.	24—CAROLINA	1:00
Oct.	1—Open date	
Oct.	8—at New Orleans	1:00
Oct.	15—CINCINNATI	1:00
Oct.	22—PHILADELPHIA	1:00
Oct.	29—at N.Y. Giants	1:00
Nov.	5—NEW ORLEANS	1:00
Nov.	13—at Carolina (Mon.)	8:30
Nov.	19—WASHINGTON	1:00
Nov.	23—at Dallas (Thurs.)	4:15
Dec.	3—at Pittsburgh	1:00
Dec.	10—ATLANTA	1:00
Dec.	17—at Chicago	1:00
Dec.	24—at Cleveland	1:00
Dec.	31—SEATTLE	1:00

All times are Eastern.
All games Sunday unless noted.

DRAFT CHOICES

Davin Joseph, G, Oklahoma (first
round/23rd pick overall).
Jeremy Trueblood, OT, Boston College
(2/59).
Maurice Stovall, WR, Notre Dame
(3/90).
Alan Zemaitis, CB, Penn State (4/122).
Julian Jenkins, DE, Stanford (5/156).
Bruce Gradkowski, QB, Toledo (6/194).
T.J. Williams, TE, N.C. State (6/202).
Justin Phinisee, CB, Oregon (7/235).
Charles Bennett, OLB, Clemson (7/241).
Tim Massaquoi, TE, Michigan (7/244).

MISCELLANEOUS TEAM DATA

Stadium (capacity, surface):
Raymond James Stadium
  (65,657, grass)
Business address:
One Buccaneer Place
Tampa, FL 33607
Business phone:
813-870-2700
Ticket information:
813-879-2827
Team colors:
Buccaneer red, pewter, black and
  orange
Flagship radio station:
WFUS, 103.5 FM
Website:
www.buccaneers.com
Training site:
Disney Wide World of Sports
Orlando, Fla.

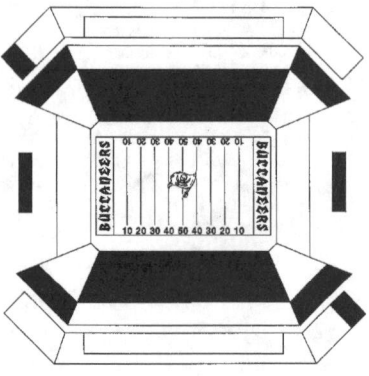

No.	QUARTERBACKS	Ht./Wt.	Born	NFL Exp.	College	How acq.	'05 Games GP/GS
7	Bruce Gradkowski	6-1/217	1/27/83	R	Toledo	D6a/06	—
12	Luke McCown	6-3/212	7/12/81	1	Louisiana Tech	T-Cle/05	0/0
13	Tim Rattay	6-0/200	3/15/77	7	Louisiana Tech	T-SF/05	4/4
2	Chris Simms	6-4/220	8/29/80	4	Texas	D3/03	11/10
	RUNNING BACKS						
40	Mike Alstott (FB)	6-1/248	12/21/73	11	Purdue	D2/96	16/7
34	Earnest Graham	5-9/215	1/15/80	3	Florida	FA/04	16/0
32	Michael Pittman	6-0/218	8/14/75	9	Fresno State	FA/02	16/4
33	Jerald Sowell (FB)	6-0/237	1/21/74	10	Tulane	FA/06	16/14
24	Cadillac Williams	5-11/217	4/21/82	2	Auburn	D1/05	14/14
	RECEIVERS						
88	Anthony Becht (TE)	6-5/272	8/8/77	7	West Virginia	FA/05	16/16
16	Larry Brackins	6-4/205	11/5/82	1	Pearl River C.C.	D5b/05	0/0
80	Michael Clayton	6-4/197	10/13/82	3	LSU	D1/04	14/10
84	Joey Galloway	5-11/197	11/20/71	12	Ohio State	T-Dal./04	16/16
19	Ike Hilliard	5-11/210	4/5/76	10	Florida	FA/05	16/2
89	Mark Jones	5-9/185	11/3/80	3	Tennessee	W-NYG/05	16/0
48	Tim Massaquoi (TE)	6-2/255	7/8/82	R	Michigan	D7c/06	—
83	Dave Moore (TE)	6-2/250	11/11/69	15	Pittsburgh	FA/04	16/1
86	Edell Shepherd	6-1/175	5/18/80	4	San Jose State	FA/03	16/0
81	Alex Smith (TE)	6-4/258	5/22/82	2	Stanford	D3a/05	16/10
85	Maurice Stovall	6-4/216	2/21/85	R	Notre Dame	D3/06	—
82	Paris Warren	6-3/213	9/6/82	1	Utah	D7b/05	0/0
45	T.J. Williams (TE)	6-2/269	9/24/82	R	N.C. State	D6b/06	—
	OFFENSIVE LINEMEN						
72	Dan Buenning (G)	6-4/320	10/26/81	2	Wisconsin	D4/05	16/16
61	Chris Colmer (T)	6-5/306	11/21/80	1	N.C. State	D3b/05	0/0
69	Anthony Davis (T)	6-4/322	3/27/80	3	Virginia Tech	FA/04	16/16
78	Toniu Fonoti (G)	6-4/350	11/26/81	4	Nebraska	FA/06	3/3
75	Davin Joseph (G)	6-2/304	11/22/83	R	Oklahoma	D1/06	—
79	Sean Mahan (G/C)	6-3/301	5/28/80	4	Notre Dame	D5/03	16/16
77	Jeb Terry (G)	6-5/311	4/10/81	2	North Carolina	D5/04	16/0
65	Jeremy Trueblood (T)	6-8/319	5/10/83	R	Boston College	D2/06	—
68	Torrin Tucker (T)	6-6/315	12/25/79	4	Southern Miss	FA/06	16/10
76	John Wade (C)	6-5/299	1/25/75	9	Marshall	FA/03	16/16
67	Kenyatta Walker (T)	6-5/302	2/1/79	6	Florida	D1/01	16/16
	DEFENSIVE LINEMEN						
91	Jon Bradley (T)	6-0/301	1/13/81	3	Arkansas State	FA/04	13/0
64	Anthony Bryant (T)	6-3/332	11/6/81	2	Alabama	D6/05	4/0
95	Chris Hovan (T)	6-2/296	5/12/78	7	Boston College	FA/05	16/16
73	Julian Jenkins (E)	6-4/277	10/25/83	R	Stanford	D5/06	—
92	Anthony McFarland (T)	6-0/300	12/18/77	8	LSU	D1/99	15/15
97	Simeon Rice (E)	6-5/268	2/24/74	11	Illinois	FA/01	15/15
94	Greg Spires (E)	6-1/265	8/12/74	9	Florida State	FA/02	16/16
90	Dewayne White (E/T)	6-2/273	10/19/79	4	Louisville	D2/03	16/1
98	Andrew Williams (E)	6-2/263	4/18/79	3	Miami	W-SF/05	0/0
96	Ellis Wyms (T/E)	6-3/279	4/12/79	6	Mississippi State	D6b/01	16/1
	LINEBACKERS						
93	Charles Bennett	6-3/258	4/4/83	R	Clemson	D7b/06	—
55	Derrick Brooks	6-0/235	4/18/73	12	Florida State	D1b/95	16/16
52	Antoine Cash	6-1/223	3/5/82	2	Southern Miss	W-Atl/05	3/0
58	Marquis Cooper	6-3/213	3/11/82	3	Washington	D3/04	12/0
54	Wesly Mallard	6-1/230	11/21/78	5	Oregon	W-NE/05	9/0
56	Ryan Nece	6-3/224	2/24/79	5	UCLA	FA/02	16/14
53	Shelton Quarles	6-1/225	9/11/71	10	Vanderbilt	FA/97	16/16
51	Barrett Ruud	6-3/241	5/20/83	2	Nebraska	D2/05	16/0
50	Jamie Winborn	5-11/242	5/14/79	6	Vanderbilt	FA/06	8/2
	DEFENSIVE BACKS						
46	Blue Adams (CB)	5-9/182	10/15/79	3	Cincinnati	FA/05	13/0
26	Will Allen (S)	6-1/193	6/17/82	3	Ohio State	D4/04	13/8
20	Ronde Barber (CB)	5-10/184	4/7/75	10	Virginia	D3b/97	16/16
21	Juran Bolden (CB)	6-2/207	6/27/74	9	Mississippi Delta J.C.	FA/05	16/2
27	Torrie Cox (CB)	5-10/181	10/29/80	4	Pittsburgh	D6/03	15/0
25	Brian Kelly (CB)	5-11/193	1/14/76	9	USC	D2b/98	16/16
28	Donte Nicholson (S)	6-1/209	12/18/81	2	Oklahoma	D5a/05	9/0
39	Kalvin Pearson (S)	5-10/190	10/22/78	4	Grambling State	FA/04	14/1
23	Jermaine Phillips (S)	6-1/214	3/27/79	5	Georgia	D5/02	13/13
35	Justin Phinisee (CB)	5-10/195	1/1/83	R	Oregon	D7a/06	—
29	Alan Zemaitis (CB)	6-2/194	8/24/82	R	Penn State	D4/06	—
	SPECIALISTS						
9	Josh Bidwell (P)	6-3/220	3/13/76	7	Oregon	FA/04	16/0
3	Matt Bryant (K)	5-9/200	5/29/75	4	Baylor	FA/05	15/0

Abbreviations: D1-draft pick, first round; W-claimed on waivers; T-obtained in trade; FA-free-agent acquisition.

TAMPA BAY BUCCANEERS

TAMPA BAY BUCCANEERS

2005 regular-season record: 11-5
Position: 1st in NFC South

Sept.11—at Minnesota	W	24-13
Sept.18—BUFFALO	W	19-3
Sept.25—at Green Bay	W	17-16
Oct. 2—DETROIT	W	17-13
Oct. 9—at N.Y. Jets	L	12-14
Oct. 16—MIAMI	W	27-13
Oct. 23—Open date		
Oct. 30—at San Francisco	L	10-15
Nov. 6—CAROLINA	L	14-34
Nov.13—WASHINGTON	W	36-35
Nov.20—at Atlanta	W	30-27
Nov.27—CHICAGO	L	10-13
Dec. 4—at New Orleans	W	10-3
Dec.11—at Carolina	W	20-10
Dec.17—at New England	L	0-28
Dec.24—ATLANTA (OT)	W	27-24
Jan. 1—NEW ORLEANS	W	27-13

2005 postseason record: 0-1
Jan. 7—WASHINGTON# L 10-17
#NFC wild-card game.

SCORING BY PERIODS

	Q1	Q2	Q3	Q4	OT	Pts.
Buccaneers	64	103	48	82	3	300
Opponents......	50	100	57	67	0	274

TEAM STATISTICS

	T.B.	Opp.
TOTAL FIRST DOWNS ..	268	254
Rushing	83	75
Passing	161	148
Penalty	24	31
3rd Down: Made/Att. ..	87/221	75/214
3rd Down Pct.	39.4	35.0
4th Down: Made/Att. ..	4/7	7/18
4th Down Pct.	57.1	38.9
POSSESSION AVG.	30:45	29:15
TOTAL NET YARDS	4716	4444
Avg. per Game	294.8	277.8
Total Plays	985	950
Avg. per Play	4.8	4.7
NET YARDS RUSHING ..	1826	1515
Avg. per Game	114.1	94.7
Total Rushes	457	438
NET YARDS PASSING	2890	2929
Avg. per Game	180.6	183.1
Sacked/Yards Lost	41/281	36/229
Gross Yards	3171	3158
Att./Completions	487/303	476/275
Completion Pct.	62.2	57.8
Had Intercepted	14	17
PUNTS/AVERAGE	90/45.6	80/43.9
NET PUNTING AVG.	90/37.5	80/36.7
PENALTIES/YARDS	131/1085	108/830
FUMBLES/LOST	16/9	25/13
TOUCHDOWNS	33	28
Rushing	13	10
Passing	17	15
Returns	3	3

SCORING (NONKICKERS)

	Tot. TD	RTD	PTD	MTD	2Pt.	Tot. Pts.
Galloway	10	0	10	0	0	60
Alstott	7	6	1	0	1	44
C. Williams	6	6	0	0	0	36
Pittman	2	1	1	0	0	12
Smith............	2	0	2	0	0	12
Allen	1	0	0	1	0	6
Cook	1	0	1	0	0	6
Hilliard	1	0	1	0	0	6
McFarland	1	0	0	1	0	6
Shepherd........	1	0	1	0	0	6
D. White	1	0	0	1	0	6
Buccaneers	33	13	17	3	1	202
Opponents	28	10	15	3	1	170

2-Pt. conversions: Buccaneers 1-1;
Opponents 1-1.

(KICKERS)

	XPM/XPA	FGM/FGA	Pts.
M. Bryant	31/31	21/25	94
France................	1/1	1/2	4
Buccaneers	32/32	22/27	98
Opponents	26/27	26/33	104

RUSHING

	Att.	Yds.	Avg.	Lg.	TD
C. Williams	290	1178	4.1	t71	6
Pittman	70	436	6.2	64	1
Graham...........	28	83	3.0	16	0
Alstott	34	80	2.4	9	6
Simms	19	31	1.6	10	0
Griese	13	12	0.9	7	0
Galloway	2	4	2.0	4	0
Clayton	1	2	2.0	2	0
Buccaneers	457	1826	4.0	t71	13
Opponents	438	1515	3.5	31	10

RECEIVING

	No.	Yds.	Avg.	Lg.	TD
Galloway	83	1287	15.5	t80	10
Smith	41	367	9.0	24	2
Pittman	36	300	8.3	t41	1
Hilliard	35	282	8.1	22	1
Clayton	32	372	11.6	41	0
Alstott	25	222	8.9	24	1
C. Williams	20	81	4.1	15	0
Becht	16	112	7.0	17	0
Cook	7	43	6.1	11	1
Shepherd........	6	103	17.2	46	1
Moore	1	5	5.0	5	0
Simms	1	-3	-3.0	-3	0
Buccaneers	303	3171	10.5	t80	17
Opponents	275	3158	11.5	62	15

INTERCEPTIONS

	No.	Yds.	Avg.	Lg.	TD
Barber...........	5	105	21.0	42	0
Kelly	4	19	4.8	14	0
Allen	3	26	8.7	26	0
Bolden	2	46	23.0	28	0

	No.	Yds.	Avg.	Lg.	TD
D. Jackson	1	21	21.0	21	0
Rice	1	6	6.0	6	0
Brooks	1	0	0.0	0	0
Buccaneers	17	223	13.1	42	0
Opponents	14	480	34.3	t88	2

SACKS: Rice 14.0, Spires 4.0, Brooks 3.0,
D. White 3.0, Barber 2.0, McFarland 2.0,
Nece 2.0, Wyms 2.0, D. Jackson 1.0, Kelly
1.0, Quarles 1.0. Buccaneers 36.0;
Opponents 41.0.

PUNTING

	No.	Yds.	Avg.	In. 20	Lg.
Bidwell	90	4101	45.6	24	61
Buccaneers	90	4101	45.6	24	61
Opponents	80	3509	43.9	18	62

PUNT RETURNS

	No.	FC	Yds.	Avg.	Lg.	TD
Jones	51	18	492	9.6	31	0
Buccaneers ..	51	18	492	9.6	31	0
Opponents....	49	16	466	9.5	44	0

KICK RETURNS

	No.	Yds.	Avg.	Lg.	TD
Cox	24	464	19.3	30	0
Shepherd	20	414	20.7	30	0
Jones	5	95	19.0	24	0
Graham..........	4	74	18.5	22	0
Pittman	3	85	28.3	37	0
Alstott	1	2	2.0	2	0
Bradley	1	2	2.0	2	0
Smith	1	12	12.0	12	0
Buccaneers	59	1148	19.5	37	0
Opponents	63	1368	21.7	t94	1

FIELD GOALS

	1-19	20-29	30-39	40-49	50+
M. Bryant	0/0	2/4	8/8	10/11	1/2
France...........	0/0	1/1	0/0	0/1	0/0
Buccaneers	0/0	3/5	8/8	10/12	1/2
Opponents	0/0	9/10	7/8	8/12	2/3

M. Bryant: (41G) (40G) (42G) (43G, 46N)
(35G, 36G, 43G, 30G) (36G, 32G) (47G,
52N) ( ) ( ) (31G, 45G, 45G) (27G, 29N) ( )
(34G, 36G) ( ) (50G, 27N, 41G) (46G, 26G)
France: ( ) ( ) ( ) ( ) ( ) ( ) ( ) ( ) ( ) ( ) (43B,
28G) ( ) ( ) ( )
Opponents: (53G, 22G) (40G) (42N, 32G)
(44G, 23G) (40N, 48N) (47G, 53G) (45G,
47G, 41G, 46G, 28G, 39N) (30G, 20G) (35G,
40G) (31G, 20G, 55N) (25G, 36G) (26G)
(42N, 39G) ( ) (31G, 28B) (25G, 24G)

PASSING

	Att.	Cmp.	Yds.	Pct.	Avg. Gain	TD	Pct. TD	Int.	Pct. Int.	Long	Sack/Lost	Rating
Simms	313	191	2035	61.0	6.50	10	3.2	7	2.2	t78	29/205	81.4
Griese	174	112	1136	64.4	6.53	7	4.0	7	4.0	t80	12/76	79.6
Buccaneers	487	303	3171	62.2	6.51	17	3.5	14	2.9	t80	41/281	80.7
Opponents	476	275	3158	57.8	6.63	15	3.2	17	3.6	62	36/229	73.5

TENNESSEE TITANS
AFC SOUTH DIVISION

2006 SEASON

CLUB DIRECTORY

Owner
K.S. "Bud" Adams Jr.

Executive vice president/general manager
Floyd Reese

Vice president of administration
Don MacLachlan

Director of player personnel
Rich Snead

Director of media relations and services
Robbie Bohren

Vice president for community affairs
Bob Hyde

Head coach/ executive vice president
Jeff Fisher

Assistant coaches
Matt Burke (defensive asst./ quality control)
Chuck Cecil (defensive asst./ quality control)
Norm Chow (offensive coordinator)
Dave McGinnis (linebackers)
Craig Johnson (quarterbacks)
Alan Lowry (special teams)
Mike Munchak (offensive line)
Jim Schwartz (defensive coordinator)
Ray Sherman (wide receivers)
Sherman Smith (running backs)
Jim Washburn (defensive line)
Steve Watterson (strength and conditioning)
Everett Withers (defensive backs)
John Zernhelt (tight ends)

OFFSEASON MOVES

Key additions
WR	David Givens	FA/Patriots
S	Chris Hope	FA/Steelers
C	Kevin Mawae	FA/Jets
LB	David Thornton	FA/Colts

Key losses
C	Justin Hartwig	FA/Panthers
OT	Brad Hopkins	retired
LB	Brad Kassell	FA/Jets
S	Tank Williams	FA/Vikings

SCHEDULE

Sept. 10—N.Y. JETS	1:00
Sept. 17—at San Diego	4:15
Sept. 24—at Miami	1:00
Oct. 1—DALLAS	1:00
Oct. 8—at Indianapolis	1:00
Oct. 15—at Washington	1:00
Oct. 22—Open date	
Oct. 29—HOUSTON	1:00
Nov. 5—at Jacksonville	1:00
Nov. 12—BALTIMORE	1:00
Nov. 19—at Philadelphia	1:00
Nov. 26—N.Y. GIANTS	1:00
Dec. 3—INDIANAPOLIS	1:00
Dec. 10—at Houston	1:00
Dec. 17—JACKSONVILLE	1:00
Dec. 24—at Buffalo	1:00
Dec. 31—NEW ENGLAND	1:00

All times are Eastern.
All games Sunday unless noted.

DRAFT CHOICES

Vince Young, QB, Texas (first round/third pick overall).
LenDale White, RB, Southern California (2/45).
Calvin Lowry, SS, Penn State (4/102).
Stephen Tulloch, ILB, N.C. State (4/116).
Terna Nande, OLB, Miami (Ohio) (5/137).
Jesse Mahelona, DT, Tennessee (5/169).
Jonathan Orr, WR, Wisconsin (6/172).
Cortland Finnegan, FS, Samford (7/215).
Spencer Toone, OLB, Utah (7/245).
Quinton Ganther, RB, Utah (7/246).

MISCELLANEOUS TEAM DATA

Stadium (capacity, surface):
Coliseum
(68,804, grass)

Business address:
460 Great Circle Road
Nashville, TN 37228

Business phone:
615-565-4000

Ticket information:
615-565-4200

Team colors:
Navy, red, Titan blue and white

Flagship radio station:
WKDF, 103.3 FM

Website:
www.titansonline.com

Training site:
460 Great Circle Road
Nashville, TN 37228
615-565-4000

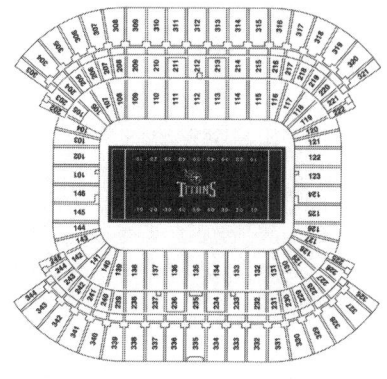

TENNESSEE TITANS

No.	QUARTERBACKS	Ht./Wt.	Born	NFL Exp.	College	How acq.	'05 Games GP/GS
8	Matt Mauck	6-1/213	2/12/79	2	LSU	FA/05	2/1
9	Steve McNair	6-2/235	2/14/73	12	Alcorn State	D1/95	14/14
7	Billy Volek	6-2/214	4/28/76	7	Fresno State	FA/00	6/1
10	Vince Young	6-5/229	5/18/83	R	Texas	D1/06	—
	RUNNING BACKS						
29	Chris Brown	6-3/219	4/17/81	4	Colorado	D3/03	15/14
44	Troy Fleming (FB)	6-0/230	10/1/80	3	Tennessee	D6/04	13/2
35	Quinton Ganther	5-9/214	7/15/84	R	Utah	D7c/06	—
20	Travis Henry	5-9/215	10/29/78	6	Tennessee	T-Buf/05	9/1
42	Damien Nash	5-10/210	4/14/82	2	Missouri	D5a/05	3/0
25	LenDale White	6-0/238	12/20/84	R	USC	D2/06	—
	RECEIVERS						
83	Drew Bennett	6-5/206	8/26/78	6	UCLA	FA/01	13/10
87	Tyrone Calico	6-4/222	11/9/80	4	Middle Tennessee	D2/03	12/6
89	David Givens	6-0/215	8/16/80	5	Notre Dame	FA/06	13/10
81	Brandon Jones	6-2/208	10/6/82	2	Oklahoma	D3b/05	10/8
88	Erron Kinney (TE)	6-5/275	7/28/77	7	Florida	D3a/00	14/14
14	Jonathan Orr	6-1/193	3/20/83	R	Wisconsin	D6/06	—
82	Courtney Roby	6-0/189	1/10/83	2	Indiana	D3a/05	13/6
80	Bo Scaife (TE)	6-3/249	1/6/81	2	Texas	D6/05	16/5
84	Ben Troupe (TE)	6-4/262	9/1/82	3	Florida	D2a/04	15/11
19	Bobby Wade	5-10/192	2/25/81	4	Arizona	W/Chi/05	14/1
86	Roydell Williams	6-1/187	3/14/81	2	Tulane	D4c/05	10/2
	OFFENSIVE LINEMEN						
54	Eugene Amano (G/C)	6-3/295	8/1/82	3	Southeast Missouri	D7b/04	16/0
58	Ken Amato (LS)	6-2/245	5/18/77	4	Montana State	FA/03	7/0
60	Jacob Bell (G/T)	6-4/306	3/2/81	3	Miami (Ohio)	D5a/04	9/1
57	Jon Dorenbos (C)	6-0/250	7/21/80	4	UTEP	FA/05	9/0
70	Daniel Loper (T)	6-6/306	1/15/82	2	Texas Tech	D5b/05	0/0
68	Kevin Mawae (C)	6-4/289	1/23/71	13	LSU	FA/06	6/6
75	Benji Olson (G)	6-4/320	6/5/75	9	Washington	D5/98	16/16
69	Zach Piller (G)	6-5/321	5/2/76	8	Florida	D3/99	16/16
71	Michael Roos (T)	6-7/320	10/5/82	2	Eastern Washington	D2/05	16/16
76	David Stewart (T)	6-6/317	8/28/82	2	Mississippi State	D4b/05	0/0
	DEFENSIVE LINEMEN						
96	Jared Clauss (T)	6-4/294	4/7/81	3	Iowa	D7/04	15/1
92	Albert Haynesworth (T)	6-6/320	6/17/81	5	Tennessee	D1/02	14/14
91	Travis LaBoy (E)	6-3/253	8/10/81	3	Hawaii	D2b/04	15/7
99	Rien Long (T)	6-6/300	8/7/81	4	Washington State	D4/03	16/1
94	Jesse Mahelona (T)	6-0/311	4/7/83	R	Tennessee	D5b/06	—
98	Antwan Odom (E)	6-4/277	9/24/81	3	Alabama	D2c/04	16/
95	Bo Schobel (E)	6-5/264	3/24/81	3	TCU	D4a/04	8/0
90	Randy Starks (T)	6-3/307	12/14/83	3	Maryland	D3a/04	16/16
93	Kyle Vanden Bosch (E)	6-4/278	11/17/78	6	Nebraska	FA/05	16/16
	LINEBACKERS						
53	Keith Bulluck	6-3/235	4/4/77	7	Syracuse	D1/00	16/16
57	Terna Nande	6-0/230	6/17/83	R	Miami (Ohio)	D5a/06	—
51	Robert Reynolds	6-3/242	5/20/81	3	Ohio State	D5b/04	15/1
59	Peter Sirmon	6-2/237	2/18/77	7	Oregon	D4b/00	14/13
56	Cody Spencer	6-2/242	6/1/81	3	North Texas	W-Oak/04	16/0
50	David Thornton	6-2/230	11/1/78	5	North Carolina	FA/06	16/16
49	Spencer Toone	6-2/240	8/25/80	R	Utah	D7b/06	—
55	Stephen Tulloch	5-11/235	1/1/85	R	N.C. State	D4b/06	—
	DEFENSIVE BACKS						
24	Tony Beckham (CB)	6-1/187	10/1/78	5	Wisconsin-Stout	D4b/02	15/2
39	Cortland Finnegan (CB)	5-10/188	2/2/84	R	Samford	D7a/06	—
22	Vincent Fuller (S)	6-1/187	8/3/82	2	Virginia Tech	D4a/05	2/0
30	Rich Gardner (CB)	5-10/199	2/1/81	3	Penn State	D3b/04	13/0
21	Reynaldo Hill (CB)	5-11/187	8/28/82	2	Florida	D7/05	15/10
24	Chris Hope (S)	5-11/206	9/29/80	5	Florida State	FA/06	16/16
32	Pacman Jones (CB)	5-10/183	9/30/83	2	West Virginia	D1/05	15/13
37	Calvin Lowry (S)	5-11/200	2/13/83	R	Penn State	D4a/06	—
23	Donnie Nickey (S)	6-3/215	4/25/80	4	Ohio State	D5/03	16/0
31	Marcus Randall (S)	6-2/219	3/14/82	2	LSU	FA/05	3/0
40	Justin Sandy (S)	6-0/214	2/22/82	3	Northern Iowa	FA/04	2/1
28	Lamont Thompson (S)	6-1/220	7/30/78	5	Washington State	FA/03	16/16
36	Michael Waddell (CB)	5-10/187	1/9/81	3	North Carolina	D4/04	16/1
26	Andre Woolfolk (CB)	6-2/197	1/26/80	4	Oklahoma	D1/03	13/
	SPECIALISTS						
2	Rob Bironas (K)	6-0/205	1/29/78	2	Georgia Southern	FA/05	16/0
15	Craig Hentrich (P)	6-3/213	5/18/71	13	Notre Dame	FA/98	16/0

Abbreviations: D1-draft pick, first round; W-claimed on waivers; T-obtained in trade; FA-free-agent acquisition.

2005 regular-season record: 4-12
Position: 3rd in AFC South

Sept.11—at Pittsburgh	L	7-34
Sept.18—BALTIMORE	W	25-10
Sept.25—at St. Louis	L	27-31
Oct. 2—INDIANAPOLIS	L	10-31
Oct. 9—at Houston	W	34-20
Oct. 16—CINCINNATI	L	23-31
Oct. 23—at Arizona	L	10-20
Oct. 30—OAKLAND	L	25-34
Nov. 6—at Cleveland	L	14-20
Nov. 13—Open date		
Nov.20—JACKSONVILLE	L	28-31
Nov.27—SAN FRANCISCO	W	33-22
Dec. 4—at Indianapolis	L	3-35
Dec.11—HOUSTON	W	13-10
Dec.18—SEATTLE	L	24-28
Dec.24—at Miami	L	10-24
Jan. 1—at Jacksonville	L	13-40

SCORING BY PERIODS

	Q1	Q2	Q3	Q4	OT	Pts.
Titans	50	88	83	78	0	299
Opponents	79	132	108	102	0	421

TEAM STATISTICS

	Ten.	Opp.
TOTAL FIRST DOWNS ..	279	294
Rushing	72	89
Passing	191	180
Penalty	16	25
3rd Down: Made/Att. ..	75/218	71/200
3rd Down Pct.	34.4	35.5
4th Down: Made/Att. ..	9/31	7/11
4th Down Pct.	29.0	63.6
POSSESSION AVG.	31:13	28:47
TOTAL NET YARDS	5122	5110
Avg. per Game	320.1	319.4
Total Plays	1022	960
Avg. per Play	5.0	5.3
NET YARDS RUSHING ..	1525	1894
Avg. per Game	95.3	118.4
Total Rushes	397	449
NET YARDS PASSING....	3597	3216
Avg. per Game	224.8	201.0
Sacked/Yards Lost	31/200	41/246
Gross Yards	3797	3462
Att./Completions	594/358	470/296
Completion Pct.	60.3	63.0
Had Intercepted	14	9
PUNTS/AVERAGE	78/43.2	85/44.1
NET PUNTING AVG.	78/37.8	85/37.5
PENALTIES/YARDS	125/1002	95/779
FUMBLES/LOST	27/12	20/11
TOUCHDOWNS	33	51
Rushing	8	12
Passing	20	33
Returns	5	6

SCORING (NONKICKERS)

	Tot.					Tot.
	TD	RTD	PTD	MTD	2Pt.	Pts.
Brown	7	5	2	0	0	42
Bennett	4	0	4	0	0	24
Troupe	4	0	4	0	0	24
B. Jones	2	0	2	0	0	12
Kinney	2	0	2	0	0	12
Odom	2	0	0	2	0	12
Payton	2	2	0	0	0	12
Scaife	2	0	2	0	0	12
R. Williams	2	0	2	0	0	12
Fleming	1	0	1	0	0	6
Hill	1	0	0	1	0	6
P. Jones	1	0	0	1	0	6
Kassell	1	0	0	1	0	6
McNair	1	1	0	0	0	6
Roby	1	0	1	0	0	6
Titans	33	8	20	5	0	200
Opponents	51	12	33	6	2	310

2-Pt. conversions: Titans 0-1; Opponents 2-2.

(KICKERS)

	XPM/XPA	FGM/FGA	Pts.
Bironas	30/32	23/29	99
Titans	30/32	23/29	99
Opponents	48/49	21/27	111

RUSHING

	Att.	Yds.	Avg.	Lg.	TD
Brown	224	851	3.8	t38	5
Henry	88	335	3.8	29	0
McNair	32	139	4.3	19	1
Payton	33	105	3.2	15	2
Mauck	7	39	5.6	12	0
Nash	6	32	5.3	8	0
Roby	2	16	8.0	11	0
Bennett	1	3	3.0	3	0
Volek	1	3	3.0	3	0
B. Jones	1	1	1.0	1	0
Wade	1	1	1.0	1	0
Hentrich	1	0	0.0	0	0
Titans	397	1525	3.8	t38	8
Opponents	449	1894	4.2	52	12

RECEIVING

	No.	Yds.	Avg.	Lg.	TD
Bennett	58	738	12.7	t55	4
Kinney	55	543	9.9	27	2
Troupe	55	530	9.6	35	4
Scaife	37	273	7.4	19	2
Brown	25	327	13.1	57	2
B. Jones	23	299	13.0	t38	2
Calico	22	191	8.7	18	0
Roby	21	289	13.8	32	1
R. Williams	21	299	14.2	t50	2
Henry	13	117	9.0	42	0
Fleming	10	69	6.9	18	1
Payton	6	30	5.0	9	0
Wade	4	40	10.0	15	0

	No.	Yds.	Avg.	Lg.	TD
Nash	3	14	4.7	7	0
Guenther	2	13	6.5	8	0
Nickey	1	26	26.0	26	0
Roos	1	-7	-7.0	-7	0
Small	1	6	6.0	6	0
Titans	358	3797	10.6	57	20
Opponents	296	3462	11.7	t63	33

INTERCEPTIONS

	No.	Yds.	Avg.	Lg.	TD
Hill	3	88	29.3	t52	1
Bulluck	2	16	8.0	16	0
Kassell	1	21	21.0	t21	1
Woolfolk	1	3	3.0	3	0
Ta. Williams	1	1	1.0	1	0
Thompson	1	0	0.0	0	0
Titans	9	129	14.3	t52	2
Opponents	14	293	20.9	t85	4

SACKS: Vanden Bosch 12.5, LaBoy 6.5, Bulluck 5.0, Long 3.5, Haynesworth 3.0, Starks 3.0, Sirmon 2.5, Odom 2.0, Schobel 1.0, Thompson 1.0, Clauss 0.5, Waddell 0.5. Titans 41.0; Opponents 31.0.

PUNTING

	No.	Yds.	Avg.	In. 20	Lg.
Hentrich	78	3371	43.2	21	59
Titans	78	3371	43.2	21	59
Opponents	85	3746	44.1	16	74

PUNT RETURNS

	No.	FC	Yds.	Avg.	Lg.	TD
P. Jones	29	8	272	9.4	t52	1
Thurman	9	5	31	3.4	11	0
B. Jones	5	0	75	15.0	32	0
Thompson	1	0	31	31.0	31	0
Ta. Williams..	1	0	9	9.0	9	0
Titans	45	13	418	9.3	t52	1
Opponents	32	20	144	4.5	15	0

KICK RETURNS

	No.	Yds.	Avg.	Lg.	TD
P. Jones	43	1127	26.2	85	0
Roby	22	495	22.5	59	0
Payton	2	24	12.0	24	0
Thurman	2	42	21.0	25	0
Fleming	1	9	9.0	9	0
Titans	70	1697	24.2	85	0
Opponents	57	1290	22.6	50	0

FIELD GOALS

	1-19	20-29	30-39	40-49	50+
Bironas	0/0	10/10	6/7	5/7	2/5
Titans	0/0	10/10	6/7	5/7	2/5
Opponents	1/1	6/6	9/14	5/5	0/1

Bironas: (47N) (39G, 29G, 47G) (41G, 39G) (34G, 38N) (52G, 58N, 49G) (24G, 29G, 47G) (53G) (39G, 24G) (50N) () (35G, 41G, 21G, 22G) (51N, 24G) (46N, 23G, 21G) (38G) (24G) ()
Opponents: (44G, 27G) (30G) (46G) (20G) (32G, 38G, 43G, 47G) (52N, 21G) (33G, 24G) (22G, 32G) (37G, 19G, 39N) (31G) (34N) () (30G, 37B, 31N) (36B) (25G) (46G, 38G)

PASSING

	Att.	Cmp.	Yds.	Pct.	Avg. Gain	TD	Pct. TD	Int.	Pct. Int.	Long	Sack/Lost	Rating
McNair	476	292	3161	61.3	6.64	16	3.4	11	2.3	57	20/134	82.4
Volek	88	50	474	56.8	5.39	4	4.5	2	2.3	t55	9/45	77.6
Mauck	27	15	136	55.6	5.04	0	0.0	1	3.7	17	1/8	53.9
Hentrich	2	1	26	50.0	13.00	0	0.0	0	0.0	26	0/0	95.8
Bennett	1	0	0	0.0	0.00	0	0.0	0	0.0	...	0/0	39.6
Titans	594	358	3797	60.3	6.39	20	3.4	14	2.4	57	31/200	80.3
Opponents	470	296	3462	63.0	7.37	33	7.0	9	1.9	t63	41/246	100.7

TENNESSEE TITANS

WASHINGTON REDSKINS
NFC EAST DIVISION

2006 SEASON

CLUB DIRECTORY

Owner, chairman and CEO
Daniel M. Snyder
Chief operating officer
Mitch Gershman
Senior vice president of stadium operations
Michael Dillow
Vice president of football operations
Vinny Cerrato
Director of pro personnel
Louis Riddick
Director of public relations
Patrick Wixted

Head coach
Joe Gibbs

Assistant coaches
Greg Blache (defensive coordinator/ defensive line)
Don Breaux (offensive coordinator)
Joe Bugel (asst. head coach/ offense)
Jack Burns (offensive asst.)
Earnest Byner (running backs)
Bobby Crumpler (strength and conditioning)
Coy Gibbs (quality control/offense)
Jerry Gray (secondary/cornerbacks)
John Hastings (head strength and conditioning)
Stan Hixon (wide receivers)
Steve Jackson (passing game/ safeties)
Bill Lazor (quarterbacks)
Dale Lindsey (linebackers)
Kirk Olivadotti (defensive line/ special teams)
Al Saunders (associate head coach/offense)
Bob Saunders (asst. head coach/special projects)
Rennie Simmons (tight ends)
Danny Smith (special teams)
Tony Spinosa (asst. strength and conditioning)
Gregg Williams (asst. head coach/defense)

OFFSEASON MOVES

Key additions
SS	Adam Archuleta	FA/Rams
DE	Andre Carter	FA/49ers
QB	Todd Collins	FA/Chiefs
TE	Christian Fauria	FA/Patriots
WR	Brandon Lloyd	trade/49ers
WR	Antwaan Randle El	FA/Steelers
CB	Kenny Wright	FA/Jaguars

Key losses
LB	LaVar Arrington	FA/Giants
OL	Ray Brown	retired
SS	Ryan Clark	FA/Steelers
CB	Walt Harris	FA
C	Cory Raymer	FA
TE	Robert Royal	FA/Bills

SCHEDULE

Sept.	11—MINNESOTA (Mon.)	7:00
Sept.	17—at Dallas	8:15
Sept.	24—at Houston	1:00
Oct.	1—JACKSONVILLE	4:15
Oct.	8—at N.Y. Giants	1:00
Oct.	15—TENNESSEE	1:00
Oct.	22—at Indianapolis	4:15
Oct.	29—Open date	
Nov.	5—DALLAS	1:00
Nov.	12—at Philadelphia	1:00
Nov.	19—at Tampa Bay	1:00
Nov.	26—CAROLINA	1:00
Dec.	3—ATLANTA	1:00
Dec.	10—Philadelphia	1:00
Dec.	17—at New Orleans	1:00
Dec.	24—at St. Louis	1:00
Dec.	30—N.Y. GIANTS (Sat.)	8:00

All times are Eastern.
All games Sunday unless noted.

DRAFT CHOICES

Roger "Rocky" McIntosh, OLB, Miami (second round/35th overall pick).
Anthony Montgomery, DT, Minnesota (5/153).
Reed Doughty, SS, Northern Colorado (6/173).
Kedric Golston, DT, Georgia (6/196).
Kili Lefotu, G, Arizona (7/230).
Kevin Simon, ILB, Tennessee (7/250).

MISCELLANEOUS TEAM DATA

Stadium (capacity, surface):
FedEx Field (91,665, grass)
Business address:
21300 Redskin Park Drive
Ashburn, VA 20147
Business phone:
703-726-7000
Ticket information:
301-276-6050
Team colors:
Burgundy and gold
Flagship radio station:
WJFK, 106.7 FM
Website:
www.redskins.com
Training site:
Redskins Park
Ashburn, VA
703-726-7000

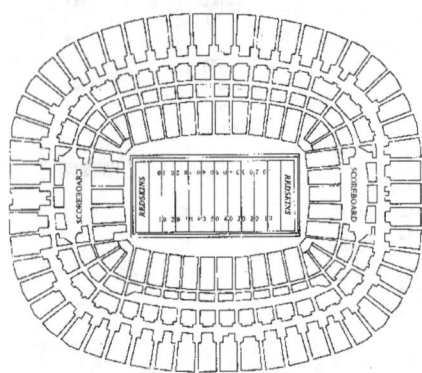

No.	QUARTERBACKS	Ht./Wt.	Born	NFL Exp.	College	How acq.	'05 Games GP/GS
9	Casey Bramlet	6-4/209	4/2/81	3	Wyoming	FA/06	0/0
8	Mark Brunell	6-1/217	9/17/70	13	Washington	T-Jax/04	16/15
17	Jason Campbell	6-5/227	12/31/81	1	Auburn	D1b/05	0/0
15	Todd Collins	6-4/228	11/5/71	12	Michigan	FA/06	1/0
	RUNNING BACKS						
46	Ladell Betts	5-10/222	8/27/79	5	Iowa	D2/02	12/0
40	Nehemiah Broughton	5-11/245	11/4/82	2	The Citadel	D7/05	4/0
49	Kerry Carter	6-1/238	12/19/80	4	Stanford	FA/06	0/0
41	Rock Cartwright (FB)	5-7/223	12/3/79	5	Kansas State	D7c/02	16/0
26	Clinton Portis	5-11/205	9/1/81	5	Miami (Fla.)	T-Den/04	16/16
	RECEIVERS						
47	Chris Cooley (TE)	6-3/265	7/11/82	3	Utah State	D3/04	16/16
13	Ataveus Cash	6-1/205	5/2/79	2	Hampton	FA/06	0/0
36	Jimmy Farris	6-0/200	4/13/78	4	Montana	FA/05	4/0
48	Christian Fauria (TE)	6-4/250	9/22/71	12	Colorado	FA/06	16/0
34	Taylor Jacobs	6-0/198	5/30/81	4	Florida	D2/03	15/3
87	Robert Johnson (TE)	6-6/278	6/20/80	3	Auburn	FA/05	2/0
18	Ron Johnson	6-3/220	5/23/80	3	Minnesota	FA/06	0/0
85	Brandon Lloyd	6-0/192	7/5/81	4	Illinois	T-SF/06	16/15
89	Santana Moss	5-10/185	6/1/79	6	Miami (Fla.)	T-NYJ/05	16/16
30	David Patten	5-10/190	8/19/74	10	Western Carolina	FA/05	9/7
82	Antwaan Randle El	5-10/192	8/17/79	5	Indiana	FA/06	16/15
45	Mike Sellers (TE)	6-3/260	7/21/75	7	None	FA/01	15/6
16	Richard Smith	5-10/191	7/16/80	2	Arkansas	FA/05	0/0
83	James Thrash	6-0/200	4/28/75	10	Missouri Southern	T-Phi/04	12/2
	OFFENSIVE LINEMEN						
71	Ethan Albright (C)	6-5/265	5/1/71	12	North Carolina	FA/01	16/0
66	Derrick Dockery (G)	6-6/345	9/7/80	4	Texas	D3/03	16/16
76	Jon Jansen (T)	6-6/305	1/28/76	7	Michigan	D2/99	16/16
67	Kili Lefotu (G)	6-5/315	11/22/83	R	Arizona	D7a/06	—
69	Jim Molinaro (T)	6-6/309	4/27/81	3	Notre Dame	D6/04	3/0
68	Ikechuku Ndukwe (G)	6-5/325	7/17/82	1	Northwestern	FA/05	0/0
62	Mike Pucillo (G)	6-4/311	7/14/79	4	Auburn	FA/06	10/6
61	Casey Rabach (C/G)	6-4/301	9/24/77	5	Wisconsin	FA/05	16/16
60	Chris Samuels (T)	6-5/310	7/28/77	7	Alabama	D1b/00	16/16
77	Randy Thomas (G)	6-5/306	1/19/76	8	Mississippi State	FA/03	14/14
72	Tyson Walter (G)	6-4/303	3/17/78	5	Ohio State	FA/06	0/0
	DEFENSIVE LINEMEN						
73	Ryan Boschetti (T)	6-4/300	10/7/81	3	UCLA	FA/04	13/1
99	Andre Carter (E)	6-4/265	5/12/79	6	California	FA/06	16/14
90	Nic Clemons (E)	6-6/298	2/3/80	2	Georgia	FA/03	8/0
93	Phillip Daniels (E)	6-3/288	3/4/73	11	Georgia	FA/04	16/16
92	Demetric Evans (E)	6-3/300	9/3/79	5	Georgia	FA/01	16/3
64	Kedric Golston (T)	6-4/300	5/30/83	R	Georgia	D6b/06	—
96	Cornelius Griffin (T)	6-3/300	12/3/76	7	Alabama	FA/04	13/12
74	Aki Jones (T)	6-4/295	5/21/82	1	Fordham	FA/05	4/0
91	Cedric Killings (T)	6-2/310	12/14/77	4	Carson-Newman	FA/04	10/1
94	Anthony Montgomery (T)	6-5/305	3/8/84	R	Minnesota	D5/06	—
75	Karon Riley (E)	6-2/268	8/23/78	5	Minnesota	FA/06	0/0
95	Joe Salave'a (T)	6-3/295	3/23/75	8	Arizona	FA/04	14/13
97	Renaldo Wynn (E)	6-3/292	9/3/74	10	Notre Dame	FA/02	16/15
	LINEBACKERS						
50	Khary Campbell	6-3/250	4/4/79	5	Bowling Green	FA/02	15/0
58	Chris Clemons	6-3/234	10/30/81	3	Georgia	FA/04	14/1
57	Warrick Holdman	6-1/235	11/22/75	8	Texas A&M	FA/05	14/7
98	Lemar Marshall	6-2/227	12/17/76	5	Michigan State	FA/01	16/16
59	Robert McCune	6-0/244	3/9/79	2	Louisville	D5/05	5/0
52	Rocky McIntosh	6-2/231	11/15/82	R	Miami	D2/06	—
54	Kevin Simon	5-10/235	6/12/83	R	Tennessee	D7b/06	—
53	Marcus Washington	6-3/247	10/17/77	7	Auburn	FA/04	16/16
	DEFENSIVE BACKS						
30	Adam Archuleta (S)	6-0/223	11/27/77	6	Arizona State	FA/06	14/14
29	Curry Burns (S)	6-0/216	2/12/81	3	Louisville	FA/05	0/0
23	Reed Doughty (S)	6-1/210	11/4/82	R	Northern Colorado	D6a/06	—
32	Ade Jimoh (CB)	6-1/190	4/18/80	4	Utah State	FA/03	16/0
35	Christian Morton (CB)	6-0/180	4/28/81	3	Illinois	FA/05	5/1
34	Dimitri Patterson (CB)	5-11/196	6/18/83	2	Tuskegee	FA/05	3/0
20	Pierson Prioleau (S)	5-11/188	8/6/77	8	Virginia Tech	FA/05	15/6
22	Carlos Rogers (CB)	6-0/196	7/2/81	2	Auburn	D1a/05	12/5
24	Shawn Springs (CB)	6-0/204	3/11/75	10	Ohio State	FA/04	15/15
21	Sean Taylor (S)	6-2/231	4/1/83	3	Miami (Fla.)	D1/04	15/15
25	Kenny Wright (CB)	6-1/207	9/14/77	8	Northwestern St.	FA/06	16/16
	SPECIALISTS						
4	Derrick Frost (P)	6-4/200	11/25/80	3	Northern Iowa	FA/05	14/0
10	John Hall (K)	6-3/240	3/17/74	10	Wisconsin	FA/03	10/0

Abbreviations: D1-draft pick, first round; W-claimed on waivers; T-obtained in trade; FA-free-agent acquisition.

WASHINGTON REDSKINS

WASHINGTON REDSKINS

2005 regular-season record: 10-6
Position: 2nd in NFC East

Sept.11—CHICAGO	W	9-7
Sept.19—at Dallas	W	14-13
Sept.25—Open date		
Oct. 2—SEATTLE (OT)	W	20-17
Oct. 9—at Denver	L	19-21
Oct. 16—at Kansas City	L	21-28
Oct. 23—SAN FRANCISCO	W	52-17
Oct. 30—at N.Y. Giants	L	0-36
Nov. 6—PHILADELPHIA	W	17-10
Nov.13—at Tampa Bay	L	35-36
Nov.20—OAKLAND	L	13-16
Nov.27—SAN DIEGO (OT)	L	17-23
Dec. 4—at St. Louis	W	24-9
Dec.11—at Arizona	W	17-13
Dec.18—DALLAS	W	35-7
Dec.24—N.Y. GIANTS	W	35-20
Jan. 1—at Philadelphia	W	31-20

2005 postseason record: 1-1

Jan. 7—at Tampa Bay#	W	17-10
Jan. 14—at Seattle*	L	10-20

#NFC wild-card game. *NFC divisional play-off game.

SCORING BY PERIODS

	Q1	Q2	Q3	Q4	OT	Pts.
Redskins	69	114	101	72	3	359
Opponents	63	78	86	60	6	293

TEAM STATISTICS

	Was.	Opp.
TOTAL FIRST DOWNS	301	258
Rushing	114	74
Passing	166	158
Penalty	21	26
3rd Down: Made/Att.	97/230	81/222
3rd Down Pct.	42.2	36.5
4th Down: Made/Att.	6/11	5/13
4th Down Pct.	54.5	38.5
POSSESSION AVG.	31:33	28:27
TOTAL NET YARDS	5289	4767
Avg. per Game	330.6	297.9
Total Plays	1037	981
Avg. per Play	5.1	4.9
NET YARDS RUSHING	2183	1686
Avg. per Game	136.4	105.4
Total Rushes	525	411
NET YARDS PASSING	3106	3081
Avg. per Game	194.1	192.6
Sacked/Yards Lost	31/240	35/237
Gross Yards	3346	3318
Att./Completions	481/278	535/291
Completion Pct.	57.8	54.4
Had Intercepted	11	16
PUNTS/AVERAGE	87/40.3	88/41.3
NET PUNTING AVG.	87/36.5	88/37.7
PENALTIES/YARDS	108/925	105/879
FUMBLES/LOST	29/16	32/12
TOUCHDOWNS	44	32
Rushing	15	15
Passing	25	15
Returns	4	2

SCORING (NONKICKERS)

	Tot. TD	RTD	PTD	MTD	2Pt.	Tot. Pts.
Portis	11	11	0	0	1	68
Moss	9	0	9	0	0	54
Sellers	8	1	7	0	0	48
Cooley	7	0	7	0	0	42
Betts	3	1	1	1	0	18
Cartwright	2	2	0	0	0	12
Brown	1	0	0	1	0	6
Marshall	1	0	0	1	0	6
Royal	1	0	1	0	0	6
Taylor	1	0	0	1	0	6
Redskins	44	15	25	4	1	266
Opponents	32	15	15	2	2	198

2-Pt. conversions: Redskins 1-2; Opponents 2-2.

(KICKERS)

	XPM/XPA	FGM/FGA	Pts.
Hall	27/27	12/14	63
Novak	15/15	5/7	30
Redskins	42/42	17/21	93
Opponents	29/29	22/31	95

RUSHING

	Att.	Yds.	Avg.	Lg.	TD
Portis	352	1516	4.3	t47	11
Betts	89	338	3.8	22	1
Cartwright	27	199	7.4	52	2
Brunell	42	111	2.6	25	0
Thrash	1	8	8.0	8	0
Brown	2	7	3.5	4	0
Broughton	1	3	3.0	3	0
Ramsey	7	3	0.4	5	0
Sellers	1	1	1.0	t1	1
Moss	3	-3	-1.0	3	0
Redskins	525	2183	4.2	52	15
Opponents	411	1686	4.1	t72	15

RECEIVING

	No.	Yds.	Avg.	Lg.	TD
Moss	84	1483	17.7	t78	9
Cooley	71	774	10.9	32	7
Portis	30	216	7.2	23	0
Patten	22	217	9.9	32	0
Royal	18	131	7.3	29	1
Thrash	14	194	13.9	41	0
Sellers	12	72	6.0	t19	7
Jacobs	11	100	9.1	24	0
Betts	10	78	7.8	26	1
Cartwright	2	23	11.5	17	0
Kozlowski	2	26	13.0	18	0
Farris	1	18	18.0	18	0
Johnson	1	14	14.0	14	0
Redskins	278	3346	12.0	t78	25
Opponents	291	3318	11.4	t70	15

INTERCEPTIONS

	No.	Yds.	Avg.	Lg.	TD
Marshall	4	55	13.8	27	1
Clark	3	10	3.3	6	0
Taylor	2	34	17.0	32	0
Rogers	2	14	7.0	14	0
Washington	1	41	41.0	41	0
Patterson	1	20	20.0	20	0
Springs	1	2	2.0	2	0
Griffin	1	0	0.0	0	0
W. Harris	1	0	0.0	0	0
Redskins	16	176	11.0	41	1
Opponents	11	183	16.6	36	1

SACKS: Daniels 8.0, Washington 7.5, Griffin 4.0, Evans 3.0, Prioleau 3.0, C. Clemons 2.0, Marshall 2.0, Taylor 1.0, Clark 0.5, Salave'a 0.5, Wynn 0.5. Redskins 35.0; Opponents 31.0.

PUNTING

	No.	Yds.	Avg.	In. 20	Lg.
Frost	76	3074	40.4	23	55
Groom	11	429	39.0	2	57
Redskins	87	3503	40.3	25	57
Opponents	88	3636	41.3	26	65

PUNT RETURNS

	No.	FC	Yds.	Avg.	Lg.	TD
Brown	13	12	63	4.8	16	0
Thrash	10	15	77	7.7	18	0
Moss	7	1	40	5.7	14	0
Redskins	30	28	180	6.0	18	0
Opponents	40	18	189	4.7	19	0

KICK RETURNS

	No.	Yds.	Avg.	Lg.	TD
Betts	24	621	25.9	t94	1
Brown	19	439	23.1	t91	1
Thrash	7	170	24.3	31	0
Cartwright	4	82	20.5	25	0
Parson	3	71	23.7	35	0
Sellers	3	50	16.7	20	0
Broughton	1	5	5.0	5	0
Evans	1	0	0.0	0	0
Redskins	62	1438	23.2	t94	2
Opponents	72	1503	20.9	49	0

FIELD GOALS

	1-19	20-29	30-39	40-49	50+
Hall	1/1	3/3	3/3	5/6	0/1
Novak	0/0	1/1	3/5	1/1	0/0
Redskins	1/1	4/4	6/8	6/7	0/1
Opponents	1/1	3/4	9/10	7/13	2/3

Hall: (40G, 43G, 19G) () () () () (24G) (33G, 40G) (24G, 45G) (38G, 53N) (45N, 38G) (41G) () () (25G)
Novak: () () (39B, 40G, 39G) (34G, 38B, 36G) () (27G) () () () () () () () ()
Opponents: () (41N, 33G, 41G) (53G, 47N, 47N) () (20G, 38G) (47G) (39G, 50G, 51N, 33G, 39G, 44G) (34G) () (30G, 45N, 25G, 19G) (42N, 46N, 48G) () (44G, 20G) (38N) (47G, 29B, 38G) (49G, 35G)

PASSING

	Att.	Cmp.	Yds.	Pct.	Avg. Gain	TD	Pct. TD	Int.	Pct. Int.	Long	Sack/Lost	Rating
Brunell	454	262	3050	57.7	6.72	23	5.1	10	2.2	t78	27/213	85.9
Ramsey	25	15	279	60.0	11.16	1	4.0	1	4.0	t72	4/27	95.3
Portis	2	1	17	50.0	8.50	1	50.0	0	0.0	t17	0/0	118.8
Redskins	481	278	3346	57.8	6.96	25	5.2	11	2.3	t78	31/240	87.0
Opponents	535	291	3318	54.4	6.20	15	2.8	16	3.0	t70	35/237	70.1

SCHEDULE

PRESEASON

(All times Eastern)

HALL OF FAME WEEKEND

SUNDAY, AUGUST 6

Oakland vs. Philidelphia at Canton, Ohio 8:00

WEEK 1

THURSDAY, AUGUST 10

Cleveland at Philadelphia 7:30
Indianapolis at St. Louis 8:00

FRIDAY, AUGUST 11

Indianapolis at St. Louis 8:00
Denver at Detroit 7:30
N.Y. Jets at Tampa Bay 7:30
N.Y. Giants at Baltimore 8:00
New England at Atlanta 8:00
Chicago at San Francisco 10:00

SATURDAY, AUGUST 12

Pittsburgh at Arizona 4:05
Buffalo at Carolina 7:30
Jacksonville at Miami 7:30
New Orleans at Tennessee 8:00
Kansas City at Houston 8:00
Dallas at Seattle 10:00

SUNDAY, AUGUST 13

Washington at Cincinnati 8:00

MONDAY, AUGUST 14

Oakland at Minnesota 8:00

WEEK 2

THURSDAY, AUGUST 17

Kansas City at N.Y. Giants 8:00
Philadelphia at Baltimore 8:00

FRIDAY, AUGUST 18

Cincinnati at Buffalo 7:00
Detroit at Cleveland 7:30
San Diego at Chicago 8:00

SATURDAY, AUGUST 19

Miami at Tampa Bay 7:30
Carolina at Jacksonville 7:30
N.Y. Jets at Washington 8:00
Minnesota at Pittsburgh 8:00
Arizona at New England 8:00
Houston at St. Louis 8:00
Tennessee at Denver 9:00

SUNDAY, AUGUST 20

Seattle at Indianapolis 8:00

MONDAY, AUGUST 21

Dallas at New Orleans 8:00

WEEK 3

THURSDAY, AUGUST 24

Miami at Carolina 8:00

FRIDAY, AUGUST 25

Pittsburgh at Philadelphia 8:00
Baltimore at Minnesota 8:00
Arizona at Chicago 8:00

SATURDAY, AUGUST 26

Cleveland at Buffalo 6:00
Indianapolis at New Orleans 7:00
Washington at New England 8:00
San Francisco at Dallas 8:00
Atlanta at Tennessee 8:00
Tampa Bay at Jacksonville 8:00
St. Louis at Kansas City 8:30
Seattle at San Diego 10:00

SUNDAY, AUGUST 27

Houston at Denver 8:00

MOMDAY, AUGUST 28

Green Bay at Cincinnati 8:00

WEEK 4

THURSDAY, AUGUST 31

Jacksonville at Atlanta 7:30
Buffalo at Detroit 7:30
St. Louis at Miami 7:30
New England at N.Y. Giants 7:30
Carolina at Pittsburgh 7:30
Baltimore at Washington 8:00
Tampa Bay at Houston 8:00
Minnesota at Dallas 8:00
Chicago at Cleveland 8:00
New Orleans at Kansas City 8:30
Oakland at Seattle 10:00
Denver at Arizona 10:05

FRIDAY, SEPTEMBER 1

Cincinnati at Indianapolis 7:00

REGULAR SEASON

(All times Eastern)

WEEK 1

THURSDAY, SEPTEMBER 7

Miami at Pittsburgh 8:30

SUNDAY, SEPTEMBER 10

Atlanta at Carolina 1:00
Baltimore at Tampa Bay 1:00
Buffalo at New England 1:00
Cincinnati at Kansas City 1:00
Denver at St. Louis 1:00
New Orleans at Cleveland 1:00
N.Y. Jets at Tennessee 1:00
Philadelphia at Houston 1:00
Seattle at Detroit 1:00

Chicago at Green Bay 4:15
Dallas at Jacksonville 4:15
San Francisco at Arizona 4:15
Indianapolis at N.Y. Giants 8:15

MONDAY, SEPTEMBER 11

Minnesota at Washington 7:00
San Diego at Oakland 10:15

WEEK 2

SUNDAY, SEPTEMBER 17

Buffalo at Miami 1:00
Carolina at Minnesota 1:00
Cleveland at Cincinnati 1:00
Detroit at Chicago 1:00

Houston at Indianapolis....................................... 1:00
New Orleans at Green Bay.................................... 1:00
N.Y. Giants at Philadelphia.................................. 1:00
Oakland at Baltimore 1:00
Tampa Bay at Atlanta 1:00
Arizona at Seattle... 4:05
St. Louis at San Francisco................................... 4:05
Kansas City at Denver... 4:15
New England at N.Y. Jets..................................... 4:15
Tennessee at San Diego....................................... 4:15
Washington at Dallas... 8:15

MONDAY, SEPTEMBER 18

Pittsburgh at Jacksonville.................................... 8:30

WEEK 3

SUNDAY, SEPTEMBER 24

Carolina at Tampa Bay 1:00
Chicago at Minnesota.. 1:00
Cincinnati at Pittsburgh 1:00
Green Bay at Detroit 1:00
Jacksonville at Indianapolis.................................. 1:00
N.Y. Jets at Buffalo... 1:00
Tennessee at Miami.. 1:00
Washington at Houston 1:00
Baltimore at Cleveland 4:05
N.Y. Giants at Seattle 4:15
Philadelphia at San Francisco............................... 4:15
St. Louis at Arizona 4:15
Denver at New England 8:15

MONDAY, SEPTEMBER 25

Atlanta at New Orleans 8:30
Open date: Dallas, Kansas City, Oakland, San Diego

WEEK 4

SUNDAY, OCTOBER 1

Arizona at Atlanta... 1:00
Dallas at Tennessee 1:00
Indianapolis at N.Y. Jets 1:00
Miami at Houston 1:00
Minnesota at Buffalo... 1:00
New Orleans at Carolina 1:00
San Diego at Baltimore.. 1:00
San Francisco at Kansas City................................ 1:00
Detroit at St. Louis 4:05
Cleveland at Oakland 4:15
Jacksonville at Washington 4:15
New England at Cincinnati 4:15
Seattle at Chicago.. 8:15

MONDAY, OCTOBER 2

Green Bay at Philadelphia..................................... 8:30
Open date: Denver, N.Y. Giants, Pittsburgh, Tampa Bay

WEEK 5

SUNDAY, OCTOBER 8

Buffalo at Chicago 1:00
Cleveland at Carolina 1:00
Detroit at Minnesota 1:00
Miami at New England 1:00
St. Louis at Green Bay... 1:00
Tampa Bay at New Orleans................................... 1:00
Tennessee at Indianapolis.................................... 1:00
Washington at N.Y. Giants 1:00
Kansas City at Arizona 4:05
N.Y. Jets at Jacksonville 4:05
Oakland at San Francisco 4:05
Dallas at Philadelphia.. 4:15
Pittsburgh at San Diego....................................... 8:15

MONDAY, OCTOBER 9

Baltimore at Denver.. 8:30
Open date: Atlanta, Cincinnati, Houston, Seattle

WEEK 6

SUNDAY, OCTOBER 15

Buffalo at Detroit 1:00
Carolina at Baltimore 1:00
Cincinnati at Tampa Bay 1:00
Houston at Dallas 1:00
N.Y. Giants at Atlanta 1:00
Philadelphia at New Orleans 1:00
Seattle at St. Louis... 1:00
Tennessee at Washington 1:00
Kansas City at Pittsburgh 4:15
Miami at N.Y. Jets.. 4:15
San Diego at San Francisco.................................. 4:15
Oakland at Denver.. 8:15

MONDAY, OCTOBER 16

Chicago at Arizona.. 8:30
Open date: Cleveland, Green Bay, Indianapolis, Jacksonville,
Minnesota, New England

WEEK 7

SUNDAY, OCTOBER 22

Carolina at Cincinnati.. 1:00
Detroit at N.Y. Jets... 1:00
Green Bay at Miami 1:00
Jacksonville at Houston....................................... 1:00
New England at Buffalo.. 1:00
Philadelphia at Tampa Bay 1:00
Pittsburgh at Atlanta... 1:00
San Diego at Kansas City..................................... 1:00
Denver at Cleveland.. 4:05
Arizona at Oakland 4:15
Minnesota at Seattle... 4:15
Washington at Indianapolis 4:15

MONDAY, OCTOBER 23

N.Y. Giants at Dallas 8:30
Open date: Baltimore, Chicago, New Orleans, San Francisco, St.
Louis, Tennessee

WEEK 8

SUNDAY, OCTOBER 29

Arizona at Green Bay 1:00
Atlanta at Cincinnati 1:00
Baltimore at New Orleans 1:00
Houston at Tennessee... 1:00
Jacksonville at Philadelphia.................................. 1:00
Seattle at Kansas City 1:00
San Francisco at Chicago 1:00
Tampa Bay at N.Y. Giants.................................... 1:00
St. Louis at San Diego... 4:05
Indianapolis at Denver... 4:15
N.Y. Jets at Cleveland 4:15
Pittsburgh at Oakland 4:15
Dallas at Carolina... 8:15

MONDAY, OCTOBER 30

New England at Minnesota.................................... 8:30
Open date: Buffalo, Detroit, Miami, Washington

WEEK 9

SUNDAY, NOVEMBER 5

Atlanta at Detroit.. 1:00
Cincinnati at Baltimore... 1:00
Dallas at Washington... 1:00
Green Bay at Buffalo... 1:00
Houston at N.Y. Giants.. 1:00
Kansas City at St. Louis....................................... 1:00
Miami at Chicago.. 1:00
New Orleans at Tampa Bay................................... 1:00
Tennessee at Jacksonville.................................... 1:00
Minnesota at San Francisco.................................. 4:05
Cleveland at San Diego.. 4:15
Denver at Pittsburgh... 4:15
Indianapolis at New England 8:15

MONDAY, NOVEMBER 6

Oakland at Seattle... 8:30
Open date: Arizona, Carolina, N.Y. Jets, Philadelphia

WEEK 10

SUNDAY, NOVEMBER 12

Baltimore at Tennessee 1:00
Buffalo at Indianapolis 1:00
Chicago at N.Y. Giants 1:00
Cleveland at Atlanta 1:00
Green Bay at Minnesota 1:00
Houston at Jacksonville 1:00
Kansas City at Miami 1:00
New Orleans at Pittsburgh 1:00
N.Y. Jets at New England 1:00
San Diego at Cincinnati 1:00
San Francisco at Detroit 1:00
Washington at Philadelphia 1:00
Denver at Oakland 4:05
Dallas at Arizona 4:15
St. Louis at Seattle 4:15
*Note: One of the Sunday games will move to 8:15 Sunday night.

MONDAY, NOVEMBER 13

Tampa Bay at Carolina 8:30

WEEK 11

SUNDAY, NOVEMBER 19

Atlanta at Baltimore 1:00
Buffalo at Houston 1:00
Chicago at N.Y. Jets 1:00
Cincinnati at New Orleans 1:00
Indianapolis at Dallas 1:00
Minnesota at Miami 1:00
New England at Green Bay 1:00
Oakland at Kansas City 1:00
Pittsburgh at Cleveland 1:00
St. Louis at Carolina 1:00
Tennessee at Philadelphia 1:00
Washington at Tampa Bay 1:00
Detroit at Arizona 4:05
Seattle at San Francisco 4:05
San Diego at Denver 4:15
*Note: One of the Sunday games will move to 8:15 Sunday night.

MONDAY, NOVEMBER 20

N.Y. Giants at Jacksonville 8:30

WEEK 12

THURSDAY, NOVEMBER 23

Miami at Detroit.. 12:30
Tampa Bay at Dallas 4:15
Denver at Kansas City 8:00

SUNDAY, NOVEMBER 26

Arizona at Minnesota 1:00
Carolina at Washington 1:00
Chicago at New England 1:00
Cincinnati at Cleveland 1:00
Houston at N.Y. Jets 1:00
Jacksonville at Buffalo 1:00
New Orleans at Atlanta 1:00
N.Y. Giants at Tennessee 1:00
Philadelphia at Indianapolis 1:00
Pittsburgh at Baltimore 1:00
San Francisco at St. Louis 1:00
Oakland at San Diego 4:05
*Note: One of the Sunday games will move to 8:15 Sunday night.

MONDAY, NOVEMBER 27

Green Bay at Seattle 8:30

WEEK 13

THURSDAY, NOVEMBER 30

Baltimore at Cincinnati.. 8:00

SUNDAY, DECEMBER 3

Arizona at St. Louis 1:00
Atlanta at Washington 1:00
Dallas at N.Y. Giants 1:00
Detroit at New England 1:00
Indianapolis at Tennessee 1:00
Jacksonville at Miami 1:00
Kansas City at Cleveland 1:00
Minnesota at Chicago 1:00
N.Y. Jets at Green Bay 1:00
San Diego at Buffalo 1:00
San Francisco at New Orleans 1:00
Tampa Bay at Pittsburgh.. 1:00
Houston at Oakland 4:05
Seattle at Denver 4:15
*Note: One of the Sunday games will move to 8:15 Sunday night.

MONDAY, DECEMBER 4

Carolina at Philadelphia 8:30

WEEK 14

THURSDAY, DECEMBER 7

Cleveland at Pittsburgh.. 8:00

SUNDAY, DECEMBER 10

Atlanta at Tampa Bay 1:00
Baltimore at Kansas City 1:00
Buffalo at N.Y. Jets 1:00
Indianapolis at Jacksonville 1:00
Minnesota at Detroit 1:00
New England at Miami 1:00
New Orleans at Dallas 1:00
N.Y. Giants at Carolina 1:00
Oakland at Cincinnati 1:00
Philadelphia at Washington 1:00
Tennessee at Houston 1:00
Green Bay at San Francisco.. 4:05
Seattle at Arizona 4:05
Denver at San Diego 4:15
*Note: One of the Sunday games will move to 8:15 Sunday night.

MONDAY, DECEMBER 11

Chicago at St. Louis 8:30

WEEK 15

THURSDAY, DECEMBER 14

San Francisco at Seattle 8:00

SATURDAY, DECEMBER 16

Dallas at Atlanta.. 8:00

SUNDAY, DECEMBER 17

Cleveland at Baltimore 1:00
Detroit at Green Bay 1:00
Houston at New England 1:00
Jacksonville at Tennessee.. 1:00
Miami at Buffalo 1:00
N.Y. Jets at Minnesota 1:00
Philadelphia at N.Y. Giants 1:00
Pittsburgh at Carolina 1:00
Tampa Bay at Chicago 1:00
Washington at New Orleans 1:00
Denver at Arizona 4:05
Kansas City at San Diego... 4:05
St. Louis at Oakland 4:15
*Note: One of the Sunday games will move to 8:15 Sunday night.

MONDAY, DECEMBER 18

Cincinnati at Indianapolis... 8:30

WEEK 16

THURSDAY, DECEMBER 21
Minnesota at Green Bay.. 8:00

SATURDAY, DECEMBER 23
Kansas City at Oakland 8:00

SUNDAY, DECEMBER 24
Baltimore at Pittsburgh... 1:00
Carolina at Atlanta... 1:00
Chicago at Detroit.. 1:00
Indianapolis at Houston... 1:00
New England at Jacksonville 1:00
New Orleans at N.Y. Giants 1:00
Tampa Bay at Cleveland... 1:00
Tennessee at Buffalo.. 1:00
Washington at St. Louis 1:00
Arizona at San Francisco... 4:05
Cincinnati at Denver... 4:15
San Diego at Seattle 4:15

MONDAY, DECEMBER 25
Philadelphia at Dallas... 5:00
N.Y. Jets at Miami... 8:30

WEEK 17

SATURDAY, DECEMBER 30
N.Y. Giants at Washington 8:00

SUNDAY, DECEMBER 31
Atlanta at Philadelphia 1:00
Buffalo at Baltimore... 1:00
Carolina at New Orleans 1:00
Cleveland at Houston... 1:00
Detroit at Dallas... 1:00
Green Bay at Chicago.. 1:00
Jacksonville at Kansas City 1:00
Miami at Indianapolis... 1:00
New England at Tennessee 1:00
Oakland at N.Y. Jets.. 1:00
Pittsburgh at Cincinnati 1:00
Seattle at Tampa Bay... 1:00
St. Louis at Minnesota.. 1:00
Arizona at San Diego 4:15
San Francisco at Denver.. 4:15
*Note: One of the Sunday games will move to 8:15 Sunday night.

NATIONALLY TELEVISED GAMES

(All times Eastern)

PRESEASON

Sun.,	Aug.	6	Oakland vs. Philadelphia	(8:00, NBC)
Thurs.	Aug.	10	Indianapolis at St. Louis	(8:00, FOX)
Fri.	Aug.	11	New England at Atlanta	(8:00, CBS)
Sun.	Aug.	13	Washington at Cincinnati	(8:00, NBC)
Mon.	Aug.	14	Oakland at Minnesota	(8:00, ESPN)
Thurs.	Aug.	17	Kansas City at N.Y. Giants	(8:00, FOX)
Fri.	Aug.	18	San Diego at Chicago	(8:00, CBS)
Sat.	Aug.	19	Arizona at New England	(8:00, NFL Network)
Sun.	Aug.	20	Seattle at Indianapolis	(8:00, NBC)
Mon.	Aug.	21	Dal. at N. Orleans (Shreveport)	(8:00, ESPN)
Thurs.	Aug.	24	Miami at Carolina	(8:00, FOX)
Fri.	Aug.	25	Pittsburgh at Philadelphia	(8:00, ESPN)
Sat.	Aug.	26	Tampa Bay at Jacksonville	(8:00, CBS)
Sun.	Aug.	27	Houston at Denver	(8:00, NFL Network)
Mon.	Aug.	28	Green Bay at Cincinnati	(8:00, ESPN)

REGULAR SEASON

Thurs.	Sept.	7	Miami at Pittsburgh	(8:30, NBC)
Sun.	Sept.	10	Dallas at Jacksonville	(4:15, FOX)
			Indianapolis at N.Y. Giants	(8:15, NBC)
Mon.	Sept.	11	Minnesota at Washington	(7:00, ESPN)
			San Diego at Oakland	(10:15, ESPN)
Sun.	Sept.	17	Kansas City at Denver	(4:15, CBS)
			Washington at Dallas	(8:15, NBC)
Mon.	Sept.	18	Pittsburgh at Jacksonville	(8:30, ESPN)
Sun.	Sept.	24	N.Y. Giants at Seattle	(4:15, FOX)
			Denver at New England	(8:15, NBC)
Mon.	Sept.	25	Atlanta at New Orleans	(8:30, ESPN)
Sun.	Oct.	1	New England at Cincinnati	(4:15, CBS)
			Seattle at Chicago	(8:15, NBC)
Mon.	Oct.	2	Green Bay at Philadelphia	(8:30, ESPN)
Sun.	Oct.	8	Dallas at Philadelphia	(4:15, FOX)
			Pittsburgh at San Diego	(8:15, NBC)
Mon.	Oct.	9	Baltimore at Denver	(8:30, ESPN)
Sun.	Oct.	15	San Diego at San Francisco	(4:15, CBS)
			Oakland at Denver	(8:15, NBC)
Mon.	Oct.	16	Chicago at Arizona	(8:30, ESPN)
Sun.	Oct.	22	Washington at Indianapolis	(4:15, FOX)
Mon.	Oct.	23	N.Y. Giants at Dallas	(8:30, ESPN)
Sun.	Oct.	29	Indianapolis at Denver	(4:15, CBS)
			Dallas at Carolina	(8:15, NBC)
Mon.	Oct.	30	New England at Minnesota	(8:30, ESPN)
Sun.	Nov.	5	Denver at Pittsburgh	(4:15, CBS)
			Indianapolis at New England	(8:15, NBC)
Mon.	Nov.	6	Oakland at Seattle	(8:30, ESPN)
Sun.	Nov.	12	Dallas at Arizona	(4:15, FOX)

			To be determined	(8:15, NBC)
Mon.	Nov.	13	Tampa Bay at Carolina	(8:30, ESPN)
Sun.	Nov.	19	San Diego at Denver	(4:15, CBS)
			To be determined	(8:15, NBC)
Mon.	Nov.	20	N.Y. Giants at Jacksonville	(8:30, ESPN)
Thurs.	Nov.	23	Miami at Detroit	(12:30, CBS)
			Tampa Bay at Dallas	(4:15, FOX)
			Denver at Kansas City	(8:00, NFL Network)
Sun.	Nov.	26	To be determined	(4:15, FOX)
			To be determined	(8:15, NBC)
Mon.	Nov.	27	Green Bay at Seattle	(8:30, ESPN)
Thurs.	Nov.	30	Baltimore at Cincinnati	(8:00, NFL Network)
Sun.	Dec	3	Seattle at Denver	(4:15, FOX)
			To be determined	(8:15, NBC)
Mon.	Dec.	4	Carolina at Philadelphia	(8:30, ESPN)
Thurs.	Dec.	7	Cleveland at Pittsburgh	(8:00, NFL Network)
Sun.	Dec.	10	Denver at San Diego	(4:15, CBS)
			To be determined	(8:15, NBC)
Mon.	Dec.	11	Chicago at St. Louis	(8:30, ESPN)
Thurs.	Dec.	14	San Francisco at Seattle	(8:00, NFL Network)
Sat.	Dec.	16	Dallas at Atlanta	(8:00, NFL Network)
Sun.	Dec.	17	St. Louis at Oakland	(4:15, FOX)
			To be determined	(8:15, NBC)
Mon.	Dec.	18	Cincinnati at Indianapolis	(8:30, ESPN)
Thurs.	Dec.	21	Minnesota at Green Bay	(8:00, NFL Network)
Sat.	Dec.	23	Kansas City at Oakland	(8:00, NFL Network)
Sun.	Dec.	24	Cincinnati at Denver	(4:15, CBS)
Mon.	Dec.	25	Philadelphia at Dallas	(5:00, TBD)
			N.Y. Jets at Miami	(8:30, TBD)
Sat.,	Dec.	30	N.Y. Giants at Washington	(8:00, NFL Network)
Sun.	Dec.	31	To be determined	(4:15, CBS)
			Arizona at San Diego	(4:15, FOX)
			To be determined	(8:15, NBC)

POSTSEASON

Sat.	Jan. 6	AFC, NFC wild-card playoffs (NBC)	
Sun.	Jan. 7	AFC, NFC wild-card playoffs (CBS and FOX)	
Sun.	Jan. 7	AFC, NFC divisional playoffs (CBS and FOX)	
Sat.	Jan. 13	AFC, NFC divisional playoffs (CBS and FOX)	
Sun.	Jan. 14	AFC, NFC divisional playoffs (CBS and FOX)	
Sun.	Jan. 21	AFC, NFC championship games (CBS and FOX)	
Sun.	Feb. 4	Super Bowl XLI, Dolphin Stadium, Miami (CBS)	
Sat.	Feb. 10	Pro Bowl, Aloha Stadium, Honolulu (CBS)	

INTERCONFERENCE GAMES

(All times Eastern)

Sun.	Sept. 10—Baltimore at Tampa Bay	1:00
	New Orleans at Cleveland	1:00
	Philadelphia at Houston	1:00
	Denver at St. Louis	1:00
	Dallas at Jacksonville	4:15
	Indianapolis at N.Y. Giants	8:15
Sun.	Sept. 24—Washington at Houston	1:00
Sun.	Oct. 1—Dallas at Tennessee	1:00
	San Francisco at Kansas City	1:00
	Minnesota at Buffalo	1:00
	Jacksonville at Washington	4:15
Sun.	Oct. 8—Cleveland at Carolina	1:00
	Buffalo at Chicago	1:00
	Oakland at San Francisco	4:05
	Kansas City at Arizona	4:05
Sun.	Oct. 15—Carolina at Baltimore	1:00
	Buffalo at Detroit	1:00
	Cincinnati at Tampa Bay	1:00
	Houston at Dallas	1:00
	Tennessee at Washington	1:00
	San Diego at San Francisco	4:15
Sun.	Oct. 22—Carolina at Cincinnati	1:00
	Detroit at N.Y. Jets	1:00
	Pittsburgh at Atlanta	1:00
	Green Bay at Miami	1:00
	Washington at Indianapolis	4:15
	Arizona at Oakland	4:15
Sun.	Oct. 29—Baltimore at New Orleans	1:00
	Atlanta at Cincinnati	1:00
	Jacksonville at Philadelphia	1:00
	Seattle at Kansas City	1:00
	St. Louis at San Diego	4:05

Mon.	Oct. 30—New England at Minnesota	8:30
Sun.	Nov. 5—Green Bay at Buffalo	1:00
	Miami at Chicago	1:00
	Houston at N.Y. Giants	1:00
	Kansas City at St. Louis	1:00
Mon.	Nov. 6—Oakland at Seattle	8:30
Sun.	Nov. 12—Cleveland at Atlanta	1:00
	New Orleans at Pittsburgh	1:00
Sun.	Nov. 19—Minnesota at Miami	1:00
	New England at Green Bay	1:00
	Chicago at N.Y. Jets	1:00
	Atlanta at Baltimore	1:00
	Cincinnati at New Orleans	1:00
	Indianapolis at Dallas	1:00
	Tennessee at Philadelphia	1:00
Mon.	Nov. 20—N.Y. Giants at Jacksonville	8:30
Thurs.	Nov. 23—Miami at Detroit	1:00
Sun.	Nov. 26—Chicago at New England	1:00
	Philadelphia at Indianapolis	1:00
	N.Y. Giants at Tennessee	1:00
Sun.	Dec. 3—Detroit at New England	1:00
	N.Y. Jets at Green Bay	1:00
	Tampa Bay at Pittsburgh	1:00
	Seattle at Denver	4:15
Sun.	Dec. 17—N.Y. Jets at Minnesota	1:00
	Pittsburgh at Carolina	1:00
	Denver at Arizona	4:05
	St. Louis at Oakland	4:15
Sun.	Dec. 24—Tampa Bay at Cleveland	1:00
	San Diego at Seattle	4:15
Sun.	Dec. 31—San Francisco at Denver	4:15
	Arizona at Seattle	4:15

2006 STRENGTH OF SCHEDULE

(Teams are ranked from most difficult to easiest schedules, based on 2006 opponents' combined 2005 records. Ties based on percentage were broken using number of opponents who made the playoffs.)

	Team	Opp. Wins	Opp. Losses	Opp. Ties	Opp. Pct.
1.	N.Y. Giants (22)	139	117	0	.543
2.	Cincinnati (T10)	139	117	0	.543
3.	New Orleans (18)	138	118	0	.539
	Tampa Bay (T20)	138	118	0	.539
5.	Pittsburgh (12)	136	120	0	.531
6.	Tennessee (T20)	135	121	0	.527
7.	Kansas City (4)	135	121	0	.527
8.	Baltimore (T6)	134	122	0	.523
	Houston (T14)	134	122	0	.523
10.	Philadelphia (30)	133	123	0	.520
11.	Washington (28)	132	124	0	.516
12.	Denver (T10)	132	124	0	.516
	Oakland (8)	132	124	0	.516
14.	Cleveland (9)	131	125	0	.512
15.	Atlanta (16)	130	126	0	.508
16.	St. Louis (32)	130	126	0	.508
17.	Dallas (26)	129	127	0	.504
18.	Carolina (19)	129	127	0	.504
19.	Arizona (31)	128	128	0	.500
20.	Jacksonville (13)	125	131	0	.488
21.	San Diego (2)	125	131	0	.488
22.	Indianapolis (T14)	124	132	0	.484
23.	Buffalo (T6)	122	134	0	.477
24.	San Francisco (27)	122	134	0	.477
25.	New England (3)	121	135	0	.473
26.	Detroit (23)	121	135	0	.473
27.	Miami (1)	120	136	0	.469
28.	N.Y. Jets (5)	119	137	0	.465
29.	Minnesota (25)	117	139	0	.457
30.	Seattle (29)	117	139	0	.457
31.	Green Bay (17)	115	141	0	.449
32.	Chicago (24)	114	142	0	.445

NOTE: Number in parentheses is 2005 preseason rank.

COLLEGE DRAFT

ROUND-BY-ROUND SELECTIONS, APRIL 29-30, 2006

FIRST ROUND

Team	Player selected	Pos.	College	Draft pick origination
1. Houston	Mario Williams	DE	N.C. State	
2. New Orleans	Reggie Bush	RB	Southern California	
3. Tennessee	Vince Young	QB	Texas	
4. N.Y. Jets	D'Brickashaw Ferguson	OT	Virginia	
5. Green Bay	A.J. Hawk	OLB	Ohio State	
6. San Francisco	Vernon Davis	TE	Maryland	
7. Oakland	Michael Huff	SS	Texas	
8. Buffalo	Donte Whitner	SS	Ohio State	
9. Detroit	Ernie Sims	OLB	Florida State	
10. Arizona	Matt Leinart	QB	Southern California	
11. Denver	Jay Cutler	QB	Vanderbilt	From St. Louis
12. Baltimore	Haloti Ngata	DT	Oregon	From Cleveland
13. Cleveland	Kamerion Wimbley	DE	Florida State	From Baltimore
14. Philadelphia	Brodrick Bunkley	DT	Florida State	
15. St. Louis	Tye Hill	CB	Clemson	From Atlanta through Denver
16. Miami	Jason Allen	CB	Tennessee	
17. Minnesota	Chad Greenway	OLB	Iowa	
18. Dallas	Bobby Carpenter	OLB	Ohio State	
19. San Diego	Antonio Cromartie	CB	Florida State	
20. Kansas City	Tamba Hali	DE	Penn State	
21. New England	Laurence Maroney	RB	Minnesota	
22. San Francisco	Manny Lawson	OLB	N.C. State	From Washington through Denver
23. Tampa Bay	Davin Joseph	G	Oklahoma	
24. Cincinnati	Johnathan Joseph	CB	South Carolina	
25. Pittsburgh	Santonio Holmes	WR	Ohio State	From N.Y. Giants
26. Buffalo	John McCargo	DT	N.C. State	From Chicago
27. Carolina	DeAngelo Williams	RB	Memphis	
28. Jacksonville	Marcedes Lewis	TE	UCLA	
29. N.Y. Jets	Nick Mangold	C	Ohio State	From Denver
30. Indianapolis	Joseph Addai	RB	LSU	
31. Seattle	Kelly Jennings	CB	Miami	
32. N.Y. Giants	Mathias Kiwanuka	DE	Boston College	From Pittsburgh

SECOND ROUND

Team	Player selected	Pos.	College	Draft pick origination
33. Houston	DeMeco Ryans	OLB	Alabama	
34. Cleveland	D'Qwell Jackson	ILB	Maryland	From New Orleans
35. Washington	Roger "Rocky" McIntosh	OLB	Miami	From N.Y. Jets
36. New England	Chad Jackson	WR	Florida	From Green Bay
37. Atlanta	Jimmy Williams	CB	Virginia Tech	From San Fran. through Denver and Green Bay
38. Oakland	Thomas Howard	OLB	Texas-El Paso	
39. Philadelphia	Winston Justice	OT	Southern California	From Tennessee
40. Detroit	Daniel Bullocks	SS	Nebraska	
41. Arizona	Taitusi "Deuce" Lutui	G	Southern California	
42. Chicago	Danieal Manning	SS	Abilene Christian	From Buffalo
43. New Orleans	Roman Harper	FS	Alabama	From Cleveland
44. N.Y. Giants	Sinorice Moss	WR	Miami	From Baltimore
45. Tennessee	LenDale White	RB	Southern California	From Philadelphia
46. St. Louis	Joe Klopfenstein	TE	Colorado	
47. Green Bay	Daryn Colledge	OT	Boise State	From Atlanta
48. Minnesota	Cedric Griffin	CB	Texas	
49. N.Y. Jets	Kellen Clemens	QB	Oregon	From Dallas
50. San Diego	Marcus McNeill	OT	Auburn	
51. Minnesota	Ryan Cook	C	New Mexico	From Miami
52. Green Bay	Greg Jennings	WR	Western Michigan	From New England
53. Dallas	Anthony Fasano	TE	Notre Dame	From Washington through N.Y. Jets
54. Kansas City	Bernard Pollard	SS	Purdue	
55. Cincinnati	Andrew Whitworth	OT	Louisiana State	
56. Baltimore	Chris Chester	C	Oklahoma	From N.Y. Giants
57. Chicago	Devin Hester	WR	Miami	
58. Carolina	Richard Marshall	CB	Fresno State	
59. Tampa Bay	Jeremy Trueblood	OT	Boston College	
60. Jacksonville	Maurice Drew	RB	UCLA	
61. Denver	Tony Scheffler	TE	Western Michigan	
62. Indianapolis	Tim Jennings	CB	Georgia	
63. Seattle	Darryl Tapp	DE	Virginia Tech	
64. Minnesota	Tarvaris Jackson	QB	Alabama State	From Pittsburgh

THIRD ROUND

Team	Player selected	Pos.	College	Draft pick origination
65. Houston	Charles Spencer	OT	Pittsburgh	
66. Houston	Eric Winston	OT	Miami	From New Orleans
67. Green Bay	Abdul Hodge	ILB	Iowa	
68. St. Louis	Claude Wroten	DT	LSU	From San Francisco through Denver
69. Oakland	Paul McQuistan	G	Weber State	
70. Buffalo	Ashton Youboty	CB	Ohio State	From Tennessee
71. Philadelphia	Chris Gocong	DE	Cal Poly	From N.Y. Jets
72. Arizona	Leonard Pope	TE	Georgia	
73. Chicago	Dusty Dvoracek	DT	Oklahoma	From Buffalo
74. Detroit	Brian Calhoun	RB	Wisconsin	
75. Green Bay	Jason Spitz	C	Louisville	From Baltimore through New England
76. N.Y. Jets	Anthony Schlegel	ILB	Ohio State	From Philadelphia
77. St. Louis	Jon Alston	OLB	Stanford	
78. Cleveland	Travis Wilson	WR	Oklahoma	
79. Atlanta	Jerious Norwood	RB	Mississippi State	
80. Jacksonville	Clint Ingram	OLB	Oklahoma	From Dallas
81. San Diego	Charlie Whitehurst	QB	Clemson	
82. Miami	Derek Hagan	WR	Arizona State	
83. Pittsburgh	Anthony Smith	FS	Syracuse	From Minnesota
84. San Francisco	Brandon Williams	WR	Wisconsin	From Washington
85. Kansas City	Brodie Croyle	QB	Alabama	
86. New England	Dave Thomas	TE	Texas	
87. Baltimore	David Pittman	CB	Northwestern State	From N.Y. Giants
88. Carolina	James Anderson	OLB	Virginia Tech	From Chicago
89. Carolina	Rashad Butler	OT	Miami	
90. Tampa Bay	Maurice Stovall	WR	Notre Dame	
91. Cincinnati	Frostee Rucker	DE	Southern California	
92. Dallas	Jason Hatcher	DE	Grambling State	From Jacksonville
93. St. Louis	Dominique Byrd	TE	Southern California	From Denver through Atlanta and Green Bay
94. Indianapolis	Freddie Keiaho	ILB	San Diego State	
95. Pittsburgh	Willie Reid	WR	Florida State	From Seattle through Minnesota
96. N.Y. Giants	Gerris Wilkinson	ILB	Georgia Tech	From Pittsburgh
97. N.Y. Jets*	Eric Smith	SS	Michigan State	

FOURTH ROUND

Team	Player selected	Pos.	College	Draft pick origination
98. Houston	Owen Daniels	TE	Wisconsin	
99. Philadelphia	Max Jean-Gilles	G	Georgia	From New Orleans
100. San Francisco	Michael Robinson	WR	Penn State	
101. Oakland	Darnell Bing	SS	Southern California	
102. Tennessee	Calvin Lowry	SS	Penn State	
103. N.Y. Jets	Brad Smith	WR	Missouri	
104. Green Bay	Cory Rodgers	WR	Texas Christian	
105. Buffalo	Ko Simpson	FS	South Carolina	
106. New England	Garrett Mills	TE	Tulsa	From Detroit
107. Arizona	Gabriel Watson	DT	Michigan	
108. New Orleans	Jahri Evans	OT	Bloomsburg	From Philadelphia
109. Philadelphia	Jason Avant	WR	Michigan	From St. Louis through Green Bay
110. Cleveland	Leon Williams	ILB	Miami	
111. Baltimore	Demetrius Williams	WR	Oregon	
112. Cleveland	Isaac Sowells	G	Indiana	From Atlanta
113. St. Louis	Victor Adeyanju	DE	Indiana	From San Diego
114. Miami	Joe Toledo	OT	Washington	
115. Green Bay	Will Blackmon	WR	Boston College	From Minnesota through Philadelphia
116. Tennessee	Stephen Tulloch	ILB	N.C. State	From Dallas through Philadelphia
117. N.Y. Jets	Leon Washington	RB	Florida State	From Kansas City
118. New England	Stephen Gostkowski	K	Memphis	
119. Denver	Brandon Marshall	WR	Central Florida	From Washington
120. Chicago	Jamar Williams	ILB	Arizona State	
121. Carolina	Nate Salley	FS	Ohio State	
122. Tampa Bay	Alan Zemaitis	CB	Penn State	
123. Cincinnati	Domata Peko	DT	Michigan State	
124. N.Y. Giants	Barry Cofield	DT	Northwestern	
125. Dallas	Skyler Green	WR	LSU	From Jacksonville
126. Denver	Elvis Dumervil	DE	Louisville	
127. Minnesota	Ray Edwards	DE	Purdue	From Indianapolis through Philadelphia
128. Seattle	Rob Sims	G	Ohio State	
129. N.Y. Giants	Guy Whimper	OT	East Carolina	From Pittsburgh
130. Denver*	Domenik Hixon	WR	Akron	
131. Pittsburgh*	Willie Colon	G	Hofstra	
132. Baltimore*	P.J. Daniels	RB	Georgia Tech	
133. Pittsburgh*	Orien Harris	DT	Miami (Fla.)	

FIFTH ROUND

	Team	Player selected	Pos.	College	Draft pick origination
134.	Buffalo	Kyle Williams	DT	LSU	From Houston
135.	New Orleans	Rob Ninkovich	DE	Purdue	
136.	New England	Ryan O'Callaghan	G	California	From Oakland
137.	Tennessee	Terna Nande	OLB	Miami (Ohio)	
138.	Dallas	Pat Watkins	FS	Florida State	From N.Y. Jets
139.	Atlanta	Quinn Ojinnaka	OT	Syracuse	From Green Bay
140.	San Francisco	Parys Haralson	DE	Tennessee	
141.	Detroit	Jonathan Scott	OT	Texas	
142.	Arizona	Brandon Johnson	OLB	Louisville	
143.	Buffalo	Brad Butler	OT	Virginia	
144.	St. Louis	Marques Hagans	WR	Virginia	
145.	Cleveland	Jerome Harrison	RB	Washington State	
146.	Baltimore	Dawan Landry	FS	Georgia Tech	
147.	Philadelphia	Jeremy Bloom	WR	Colorado	
148.	Green Bay	Ingle Martin	QB	Furman	From Atlanta
149.	Minnesota	Greg Blue	FS	Georgia	
150.	N.Y. Jets	Jason Pociask	TE	Wisconsin	From Dallas
151.	San Diego	Tim Dobbins	ILB	Iowa State	
152.	Cleveland	DeMario Minter	CB	Georgia	From New England
153.	Washington	Anthony Montgomery	DT	Minnesota	
154.	Kansas City	Marcus Maxey	CB	Miami (Fla.)	
155.	Carolina	Jeff King	TE	Virginia Tech	
156.	Tampa Bay	Julian Jenkins	DE	Stanford	
157.	Cincinnati	A.J. Nicholson	ILB	Florida State	
158.	N.Y. Giants	Charlie Peprah	SS	Alabama	
159.	Chicago	Mark Anderson	DE	Alabama	
160.	Jacksonville	Brent Hawkins	DE	Illinois State	
161.	Denver	Chris Kuper	G	North Dakota	
162.	Indianapolis	Michael Toudouze	G	Texas Christian	
163.	Seattle	David Kirtman	FB	Southern California	
164.	Pittsburgh	Omar Jacobs	QB	Bowling Green	
165.	Green Bay*	Tony Moll	OT	Nevada	
166.	Baltimore*	Quinn Sypniewski	TE	Colorado	
167.	Pittsburgh*	Charles Davis	TE	Purdue	
168.	Philadelphia*	Omar Gaither	OLB	Tennessee	
169.	Tennessee*	Jesse Mahelona	DT	Tennessee	

SIXTH ROUND

	Team	Player selected	Pos.	College	Draft pick origination
170.	Houston	Wali Lundy	RB	Virginia	
171.	New Orleans	Mike Hass	WR	Oregon State	
172.	Tennessee	Jonathan Orr	WR	Wisconsin	
173.	Washington	Reed Doughty	SS	Northern Colorado	From N.Y. Jets
174.	New Orleans	Josh "Bernard" Lay	CB	Pittsburgh	From Green Bay
175.	San Francisco	Delanie Walker	WR	Central Missouri State	
176.	Oakland	Kevin Boothe	OT	Cornell	
177.	Arizona	Jon Lewis	DT	Virginia Tech	
178.	Buffalo	Keith Ellison	OLB	Oregon State	
179.	Detroit	Alton "Dee" McCann	CB	West Virginia	
180.	Cleveland	Lawrence Vickers	FB	Colorado	
181.	Cleveland	Babatunde Oshinowo	DT	Stanford	From Baltimore
182.	Dallas	Montavious Stanley	DT	Louisville	From Philadelphia
183.	Green Bay	Johnny Jolly	DT	Texas A&M	From St. Louis
184.	Atlanta	Adam Jennings	WR	Fresno State	
185.	Green Bay	Tyrone Culver	FS	Fresno State	From Minnesota through Philadelphia
186.	Kansas City	Tre' Stallings	G	Mississippi	From Dallas
187.	San Diego	Jeromey Clary	OT	Kansas State	
188.	San Diego	Kurt Smith	K	Virginia	From Miami
189.	N.Y. Jets	Drew Coleman	CB	Texas Christian	From Wash. through N.Y. Jets and Dallas
190.	Kansas City	Jeff Webb	WR	San Diego State	
191.	New England	Jeremy Mincey	DE	Florida	
192.	San Francisco	Marcus Hudson	FS	N.C. State	From Tampa Bay
193.	Cincinnati	Reggie McNeal	QB	Texas A&M	
194.	Tampa Bay	Bruce Gradkowski	QB	Toledo	From New York Giants
195.	Chicago	J.D. Runnels	FB	Oklahoma	
196.	Washington	Kedric Golston	DT	Georgia	From Carolina
197.	San Francisco	Melvin Oliver	DE	LSU	From Jacksonville
198.	Denver	Greg Eslinger	C	Minnesota	
199.	Indianapolis	Charlie Johnson	OT	Oklahoma State	
200.	Chicago	Tyler Reed	G	Penn State	From Seattle

Team	Player selected	Pos.	College	Draft pick origination
201. Pittsburgh	Marvin Philip	C	California	
202. Tampa Bay*	T.J. Williams	TE	North Carolina State	
203. Baltimore*	Sam Koch	P	Nebraska	
204. Philadelphia*	LaJuan Ramsey	DT	Southern California	
205. New England*	Dan Stevenson	G	Notre Dame	
206. New England*	Le Kevin Smith	DT	Nebraska	
207. Indianapolis*	Antoine Bethea	FS	Howard	
208. Baltimore*	Derrick Martin	CB	Wyoming	

SEVENTH ROUND

Team	Player selected	Pos.	College	Draft pick origination
209. Cincinnati	Ethan Kilmer	WR	Penn State	From Houston
210. New Orleans	Zach Strief	G	Northwestern	
211. Dallas	Pat McQuistan	G	Weber State	From N.Y. Jets
212. Miami	Fred Evans	DT	Texas State	From Green Bay
213. Jacksonville	James Wyche	DE	Syracuse	From San Francisco
214. Oakland	Chris Morris	C	Michigan State	
215. Tennessee	Cortland Finnegan	FS	Samford	
216. Buffalo	Terrance Pennington	OT	New Mexico	
217. Detroit	Fred Matua	G	Southern California	
218. Arizona	Todd Watkins	WR	Brigham Young	
219. Baltimore	Ryan LaCasse	OLB	Syracuse	
220. N.Y. Jets	Titus Adams	DT	Nebraska	From Philadelphia
221. St. Louis	Tim McGarigle	ILB	Northwestern	
222. Cleveland	Justin Hamilton	SS	Virginia Tech	
223. Atlanta	D.J. Shockley	QB	Georgia	
224. Dallas	E.J. Whitley	C	Texas Tech	
225. San Diego	Chase Page	DT	North Carolina	
226. Miami	Rodrique Wright	DT	Texas	
227. San Diego	Jimmy Martin	C	Virginia Tech	From Minnesota
228. Kansas City	Jarrad Page	SS	UCLA	
229. New England	Willie Andrews	CB	Baylor	
230. Washington	Kili Lefotu	G	Arizona	
231. Cincinnati	Bennie Brazell	WR	LSU	
232. N.Y. Giants	Gerrick McPhearson	CB	Maryland	
233. Miami	Devin Aromashodu	WR	Auburn	From Chicago
234. Carolina	Will Montgomery	G	Virginia Tech	
235. Tampa Bay	Justin Phinisee	CB	Oregon	
236. Jacksonville	Demetrice Webb	CB	Florida	From Jacksonville through San Francisco
237. Carolina	Stanley McClover	DE	Auburn	From Denver
238. Indianapolis	T.J. Rushing	CB	Stanford	From Indianapolis through Tennessee
239. Seattle	Ryan Plackemeier	P	Wake Forest	
240. Pittsburgh	Cedric Humes	RB	Virginia Tech	
241. Tampa Bay*	Charles Bennett	OLB	Clemson	
242. St. Louis*	Mark Setterstrom	G	Minnesota	
243. St. Louis*	Tony Palmer	G	Missouri	
244. Tampa Bay*	Tim Massaquoi	TE	Michigan	
245. Tennessee*	Spencer Toone	OLB	Utah	
246. Tennessee*	Quinton Ganther	RB	Utah	
247. Detroit*	Anthony Cannon	OLB	Tulane	
248. Buffalo*	Aaron Merz	G	California	
249. Seattle*	Ben Obomanu	WR	Auburn	
250. Washington*	Kevin Simon	ILB	Tennessee	
251. Houston*	David Anderson	WR	Colorado State	
252. New Orleans*	Marques Colston	TE	Hofstra	
253. Green Bay*	Dave Tollefson	DE	Northwest Missouri State	
254. San Francisco*	Vickiel Vaughn	FS	Arkansas	
255. Oakland*	Kevin McMahan	WR	Maine	

*Compensatory selection

2006 DRAFT DISTRIBUTIONS
SELECTIONS PER ROUND BY TEAM

Club	1	2	3	4	5	6	7	Total Picks	Club	1	2	3	4	5	6	7	Total Picks
Green Bay	1	2	2	2	2	2	1	12	N.Y. Giants	1	1	1	2	1	0	1	7
N.Y. Jets	2	1	2	2	1	1	1	10	Arizona	1	1	1	1	1	1	1	7
St. Louis	1	1	3	1	1	0	3	10	Oakland	1	1	1	1	0	1	2	7
Baltimore	1	1	1	2	2	2	1	10	Indianapolis	1	1	1	0	1	1	2	7
Cleveland	1	1	1	2	2	2	1	10	Detroit	1	1	0	1	1	2	1	7
New England	1	1	1	2	1	3	1	10	Kansas City	1	1	1	0	1	2	1	7
Tennessee	1	1	0	2	2	1	3	10	Denver	1	1	0	3	1	1	0	7
Tampa Bay	1	1	1	1	1	2	3	10	Chicago	0	2	1	1	1	2	0	7
Buffalo	2	0	1	1	2	1	2	9	Minnesota	1	3	0	1	1	0	0	6
San Francisco	2	0	1	1	1	3	1	9	Jacksonville	1	1	1	0	1	0	2	6
Pittsburgh	1	0	2	2	2	1	1	9	Seattle	1	1	0	1	1	0	2	6
Carolina	1	1	2	1	1	0	2	8	Miami	1	0	1	1	0	0	3	6
Philadelphia	1	1	1	2	2	1	0	8	Washington	0	1	0	0	1	2	2	6
Cincinnati	1	1	1	1	1	1	2	8	Atlanta	0	1	1	0	1	1	1	5
Dallas	1	1	1	1	1	1	2	8	Total Picks	32	32	33	36	37	39	47	255
San Diego	1	1	1	0	1	2	2	8									
New Orleans	1	1	0	1	1	2	2	8									
Houston	1	1	2	1	0	1	1	7									

SELECTIONS BY COLLEGE

College		College		College		College	
Southern California	11	Fresno State	3	Arkansas	1	Oklahoma State	1
Miami (Fla.)	9	Georgia Tech	3	Baylor	1	Samford	1
Ohio State	9	Maryland	3	Bloomsburg	1	Texas State	1
Virginia Tech	9	Michigan	3	Boise State	1	Texas Tech	1
Florida State	8	Michigan State	3	Bowling Green	1	Texas-El Paso	1
Georgia	7	Northwestern	3	Brigham Young	1	Toledo	1
LSU	7	Notre Dame	3	Cal Poly	1	Tulane	1
N.C. State	6	Texas Christian	3	Central Florida	1	Tulsa	1
Oklahoma	6	UCLA	3	Central Missouri State	1	Vanderbilt	1
Penn State	6	Arizona State	2	Colorado State	1	Wake Forest	1
Texas	6	Hofstra	2	Cornell	1	Washington	1
Alabama	5	Indiana	2	East Carolina	1	Washington State	1
Tennessee	5	Iowa	2	Furman	1	West Virginia	1
Virginia	5	Memphis	2	Grambling State	1	Wyoming	1
Wisconsin	5	Missouri	2	Howard	1		
Auburn	4	New Mexico	2	Illinois State	1		
Colorado	4	Oregon State	2	Iowa State	1		
Louisville	4	Pittsburgh	2	Kansas State	1		
Minnesota	4	San Diego State	2	Maine	1		
Nebraska	4	South Carolina	2	Miami (Ohio)	1		
Oregon	4	Texas A&M	2	Mississippi	1		
Purdue	4	Utah	2	Mississippi State	1		
Stanford	4	Weber State	2	Nevada	1		
Syracuse	4	Western Michigan	2	North Carolina	1		
Boston College	3	Abilene Christian	1	North Dakota	1		
California	3	Akron	1	Northern Colorado	1		
Clemson	3	Alabama State	1	Northwest Missouri State	1		
Florida	3	Arizona	1	Northwestern State	1		

SELECTIONS BY POSITION

Position		Position	
Wide receivers	33	Free safeties	12
Cornerbacks	23	Inside linebackers	12
Defensive tackles	23	Quarterbacks	12
Defensive ends	21	Strong safeties	12
Guards	21	Centers	9
Offensive tackles	20	Fullbacks	3
Outside linebackers	19	Kickers	2
Tight ends	17	Punters	2
Running backs	14		

PLAYOFF PLAN

TIEBREAKING PROCEDURES

(Note: Tie games count as one-half win and one-half loss for both clubs.)

DIVISION TIES

TWO CLUBS

1. Head-to-head (best won-lost-tied percentage in games between the clubs).
2. Best won-lost-tied percentage in games played within the division.
3. Best won-lost-tied percentage in common games.
4. Best won-lost-tied percentage in games played within the conference.
5. Strength of victory.
6. Strength of schedule.
7. Best combined ranking among conference teams in points scored and points allowed.
8. Best combined ranking among all teams in points scored and points allowed.
9. Best net points in common games.
10. Best net points in all games.
11. Best net touchdowns in all games.
12. Coin toss.

THREE OR MORE CLUBS

(Note: If two clubs remain tied after other clubs are eliminated during any step, tiebreaker reverts to Step 1 of two-club format.)

1. Head-to-head (best won-lost-tied percentage in games between the clubs).
2. Best won-lost-tied percentage in games played within the division.
3. Best won-lost-tied percentage in common games.
4. Best won-lost-tied percentage in games played within the conference.
5. Strength of victory.
6. Strength of schedule.
7. Best combined ranking among conference teams in points scored and points allowed.
8. Best combined ranking among all teams in points scored and points allowed.
9. Best net points in common games.
10. Best net points in all games.
11. Best net touchdowns in all games.
12. Coin toss.

WILD-CARD TIES

If necessary to break ties to determine the three wild-card clubs from each conference, the following steps will be taken:

1. If all the tied clubs are from the same division, apply division tiebreaker.
2. If the tied clubs are from different divisions, apply the steps listed in the right-hand column.
3. When the first wild-card team has been identified, the procedure is repeated to name the second wild-card club (i.e. eliminate all but the highest-ranked club in each division prior to proceeding to Step 2), and repeated a third time, if necessary, to identify the third wild-card team. In situations where three teams from the same division are involved in the procedure, the original seeding of the teams remains the same for subsequent applications of the tiebreaker if the top-ranked team in that division qualifies for a wild-card berth.

TWO CLUBS

1. Head-to-head, if applicable.
2. Best won-lost-tied percentage in the games played within the conference.
3. Best won-lost-tied percentage in common games, minimum of four.

4. Strength of victory.
5. Strength of schedule.
6. Best combined ranking among conference teams in points scored and points allowed.
7. Best combined ranking among all teams in points scored and points allowed.
8. Best net points in conference games.
9. Best net points in all games.
10. Best net touchdowns in all games.
11. Coin toss.

THREE OR MORE CLUBS

(Note: If two clubs remain tied after other clubs are eliminated, tiebreaker reverts to Step 1 of two-club format.)

1. Apply division tiebreaker to eliminate all but highest-ranked club in each division prior to proceeding to Step 2. The original seeding within a division upon application of the division tiebreaker remains the same for all subsequent applications of the procedure that are necessary to identify the wild-card participants.
2. Head-to-head sweep (apply only if one club has defeated each of the others or one club has lost to each of the others).
3. Best won-lost-tied percentage in the games played within the conference.
4. Best won-lost-tied percentage in common games, minimum of four.
5. Strength of victory.
6. Strength of schedule.
7. Best combined ranking among conference teams in points scored and points allowed.
8. Best combined ranking among all teams in points scored and points allowed.
9. Best net points in conference games.
10. Best net points in all games.
11. Best net touchdowns in all games.
12. Coin toss.

OTHER TIEBREAKING PROCEDURES

1. In comparing records against common opponents among tied teams, the best won-lost-tied percentage is the deciding factor since teams may have played an unequal number of games.
2. To determine home-field priority among division winners, apply wild-card tiebreakers.
3. To determine home-field priority for wild-card qualifiers, apply division tiebreakers (if teams are from the same division) or wild-card tiebreakers (if teams are from different divisions).

2005 REVIEW

Final Standings

Weeks 1 through 17

Wild-card games

Divisional playoffs

Conference championships

Super Bowl 39

Pro Bowl

Player participation

Attendance

Trades

FINAL STANDINGS

AMERICAN FOOTBALL CONFERENCE

EAST DIVISION

	W	L	T	Pct.	Pts.	Opp.	Home	Away	vs. AFC	vs. NFC	vs. AFC East
New England*	10	6	0	.625	379	338	5-3	5-3	7-5	3-1	5-1
Miami	9	7	0	.563	318	317	5-3	4-4	7-5	2-2	3-3
Buffalo	5	11	0	.313	271	367	4-4	1-7	5-7	0-4	2-4
N.Y. Jets	4	12	0	.250	240	355	4-4	0-8	3-9	1-3	2-4

NORTH DIVISION

	W	L	T	Pct.	Pts.	Opp.	Home	Away	vs. AFC	vs. NFC	vs. AFC East
Cincinnati*	11	5	0	.688	421	350	5-3	6-2	7-5	4-0	5-1
Pittsburgh†	11	5	0	.688	389	258	5-3	6-2	7-5	4-0	4-2
Baltimore	6	10	0	.375	265	299	6-2	0-8	4-8	2-2	2-4
Cleveland	6	10	0	.375	232	301	4-4	2-6	4-8	2-2	1-5

SOUTH DIVISION

	W	L	T	Pct.	Pts.	Opp.	Home	Away	vs. AFC	vs. NFC	vs. AFC East
Indianapolis*	14	2	0	.875	439	247	7-1	7-1	11-1	3-1	6-0
Jacksonville†	12	4	0	.750	361	269	6-2	6-2	9-3	3-1	4-2
Tennessee	4	12	0	.250	299	421	3-5	1-7	3-9	1-3	2-4
Houston	2	14	0	.125	260	431	2-6	0-8	1-11	1-3	0-6

WEST DIVISION

	W	L	T	Pct.	Pts.	Opp.	Home	Away	vs. AFC	vs. NFC	vs. AFC East
Denver*	13	3	0	.813	395	258	8-0	5-3	10-2	3-1	5-1
Kansas City	10	6	0	.625	403	325	7-1	3-5	9-3	1-3	4-2
San Diego	9	7	0	.563	418	312	4-4	5-3	7-5	2-2	3-3
Oakland	4	12	0	.250	290	383	2-6	2-6	2-10	2-2	0-6

*Division champion. †Wild-card team.

NATIONAL FOOTBALL CONFERENCE

EAST DIVISION

	W	L	T	Pct.	Pts.	Opp.	Home	Away	vs. AFC	vs. NFC	vs. AFC East
N.Y. Giants*	11	5	0	.688	422	314	7-1	4-4	3-1	8-4	4-2
Washington†	10	6	0	.625	359	293	6-2	4-4	0-4	10-2	5-1
Dallas	9	7	0	.563	325	308	5-3	4-4	2-2	7-5	3-3
Philadelphia	6	10	0	.375	310	388	4-4	2-6	3-1	3-9	0-6

NORTH DIVISION

	W	L	T	Pct.	Pts.	Opp.	Home	Away	vs. AFC	vs. NFC	vs. AFC East
Chicago*	11	5	0	.688	260	202	7-1	4-4	1-3	10-2	5-1
Minnesota	9	7	0	.563	306	344	6-2	3-5	1-3	8-4	5-1
Detroit	5	11	0	.313	254	345	3-5	2-6	2-2	3-9	1-5
Green Bay	4	12	0	.250	298	344	3-5	1-7	0-4	4-8	1-5

SOUTH DIVISION

	W	L	T	Pct.	Pts.	Opp.	Home	Away	vs. AFC	vs. NFC	vs. AFC East
Tampa Bay*	11	5	0	.688	300	274	6-2	5-3	2-2	9-3	5-1
Carolina†	11	5	0	.688	391	259	5-3	6-2	3-1	8-4	4-2
Atlanta	8	8	0	.500	351	341	4-4	4-4	3-1	5-7	2-4
New Orleans	3	13	0	.188	235	398	1-7	2-6	2-2	1-11	1-5

WEST DIVISION

	W	L	T	Pct.	Pts.	Opp.	Home	Away	vs. AFC	vs. NFC	vs. AFC East
Seattle*	13	3	0	.813	452	271	8-0	5-3	3-1	10-2	6-0
St. Louis	6	10	0	.375	363	429	3-5	3-5	3-1	3-9	1-5
Arizona	5	11	0	.313	311	387	3-5	2-6	1-3	4-8	3-3
San Francisco	4	12	0	.250	239	428	3-5	1-7	1-3	3-9	2-4

*Division champion. †Wild-card team.

AFC PLAYOFFS
AFC wild card: NEW ENGLAND 28, Jacksonville 3
Pittsburgh 31, CINCINNATI 17
AFC semifinals: DENVER 27, New England 13
Pittsburgh 21, INDIANAPOLIS 18
AFC championship: Pittsburgh 34, DENVER 17

NFC PLAYOFFS
NFC wild card: Washington 17, TAMPA BAY 10
Carolina 23, N.Y. GIANTS 0
NFC semifinals: SEATTLE 20, Washington 10
Carolina 29, CHICAGO 21
NFC championship: SEATTLE 34, Carolina 14

SUPER BOWL XL
PITTSBURGH 21, Seattle 10

WEEK 1

STANDINGS

AMERICAN FOOTBALL CONFERENCE

EAST DIVISION

	W	L	T	Pct.	PF	PA
Buffalo	1	0	0	1.000	22	7
Miami	1	0	0	1.000	34	10
New England	1	0	0	1.000	30	20
N.Y. Jets	0	1	0	.000	7	27

NORTH DIVISION

	W	L	T	Pct.	PF	PA
Cincinnati	1	0	0	1.000	27	13
Pittsburgh	1	0	0	1.000	34	7
Baltimore	0	1	0	.000	7	24
Cleveland	0	1	0	.000	13	27

SOUTH DIVISION

	W	L	T	Pct.	PF	PA
Indianapolis	1	0	0	1.000	24	7
Jacksonville	1	0	0	1.000	26	14
Houston	0	1	0	.000	7	22
Tennessee	0	1	0	.000	7	34

WEST DIVISION

	W	L	T	Pct.	PF	PA
Kansas City	1	0	0	1.000	27	7
Denver	0	1	0	.000	10	34
Oakland	0	1	0	.000	20	30
San Diego	0	1	0	.000	24	28

NATIONAL FOOTBALL CONFERENCE

EAST DIVISION

	W	L	T	Pct.	PF	PA
Dallas	1	0	0	1.000	28	24
N.Y. Giants	1	0	0	1.000	42	19
Washington	1	0	0	1.000	9	7
Philadelphia	0	1	0	.000	10	14

NORTH DIVISION

	W	L	T	Pct.	PF	PA
Detroit	1	0	0	1.000	17	3
Chicago	0	1	0	.000	7	9
Green Bay	0	1	0	.000	3	17
Minnesota	0	1	0	.000	13	24

SOUTH DIVISION

	W	L	T	Pct.	PF	PA
Atlanta	1	0	0	1.000	14	10
New Orleans	1	0	0	1.000	23	20
Tampa Bay	1	0	0	1.000	24	13
Carolina	0	1	0	.000	20	23

WEST DIVISION

	W	L	T	Pct.	PF	PA
San Francisco	1	0	0	1.000	28	25
Arizona	0	1	0	.000	19	42
Seattle	0	1	0	.000	14	26
St. Louis	0	1	0	.000	25	28

TOP PERFORMANCES

100-YARD RUSHING GAMES

Player, team & opponent	Att.	Yds.	TD
Willie Parker, Pit. vs. Ten.	22	161	1
Carnell Williams, T.B. at Min.	27	148	1
Rudi Johnson, Cin. at Cle.	26	126	1
Clinton Portis, Was. vs. Chi.	21	121	0
Warrick Dunn, Atl. vs. Phi.	21	117	0
Willis McGahee, Buf. vs. Hou.	22	117	0
Larry Johnson, K.C. vs. NYJ	9	110	2

300-YARD PASSING GAMES

Player, team & opponent	Att.	Cmp.	Yds.	TD	Int.
Marc Bulger, St.L. at S.F.	56	34	362	2	1
Tom Brady, N.E. vs. Oak.	38	24	306	2	0

100-YARD RECEIVING GAMES

Player, team & opponent	Rec.	Yds.	TD
Larry Fitzgerald, Ariz. at NYG	13	155	1
Steve Smith, Car. vs. N.O.	8	138	1
Randy Moss, Oak. at N.E.	5	130	1
Jimmy Smith, Jac. vs. Sea.	7	130	2
Frisman Jackson, Cle. vs. Cin.	8	128	1
Torry Holt, St.L. at S.F.	10	125	0
Chris Baker, NYJ at K.C.	7	124	1
Keenan McCardell, S.D. vs. Dal.	9	123	2
Terrell Owens, Phi. at Atl.	7	112	0
Marty Booker, Mia. vs. Den.	5	104	1

RESULTS

THURSDAY, SEPTEMBER 8
NEW ENGLAND 30, Oakland 20

SUNDAY, SEPTEMBER 11
PITTSBURGH 34, Tennessee 7
WASHINGTON 9, Chicago 7
Cincinnati 27, CLEVELAND 13
JACKSONVILLE 26, Seattle 14
Tampa Bay 24, MINNESOTA 13
KANSAS CITY 27, N.Y. Jets 7
MIAMI 34, Denver 10
BUFFALO 22, Houston 7
New Orleans 23, CAROLINA 20
DETROIT 17, Green Bay 3
Dallas 28, SAN DIEGO 24
N.Y. GIANTS 42, Arizona 19
SAN FRANCISCO 28, St. Louis 25
Indianapolis 24, BALTIMORE 7

MONDAY, SEPTEMBER 12
ATLANTA 14, Philadelphia 10

PATRIOTS 30, RAIDERS 20
Thursday, September 8

Oakland	7	7	0	6—20
New England	10	7	6	7—30

First Quarter
Oak.—C. Anderson 2 pass from Collins (Janikowski kick); 3:09.
N.E.—FG, Vinatieri 26, 7:56.
N.E.—Branch 18 pass from Brady (Vinatieri kick), 12:55.

Second Quarter
Oak.—Moss 73 pass from Collins (Janikowski kick); 6:08.
N.E.—Dwight 5 pass from Brady (Vinatieri kick), 10:11.

Third Quarter
N.E.—Dillon 8 run (kick blocked), 9:55.

Fourth Quarter
N.E.—Dillon 2 run (Vinatieri kick), 5:31.
Oak.—C. Anderson 5 pass from Collins (pass failed), 11:56.
Attendance—68,756.

	Oakland	New England
First downs	19	22
Rushes-yards	22-92	31-73
Passing	246	306
Punt returns	3-15	4-44
Kickoff returns	6-151	3-79
Interception returns	0-0	0-0
Comp.-att.-int.	18-39-0	24-38-0
Sacked-yards lost	2-19	0-0
Punts	8-45	7-38
Fumbles-lost	2-1	0-0
Penalties-yards	16-149	7-46
Time of possession	27:40	32:20

INDIVIDUAL STATISTICS
RUSHING—Oakland, Jordan 18-70, Crockett 3-20, Collins 1-2. New England, Dillon 23-63, Faulk 5-11, Brady 3-(minus 1).
PASSING—Oakland, Collins 18-39-0-265. New England, Brady 24-38-0-306.
RECEIVING—Oakland, Moss 5-130, Jordan 5-40, Porter 3-48, C. Anderson 3-18, Whitted 2-29. New England, Branch 7-99, T. Brown 6-51, Faulk 3-18, Watson 2-55, Givens 2-31, Dillon 2-30, Graham 1-17, Dwight 1-5.
MISSED FIELD GOAL ATTEMPTS—Oakland, Janikowski 43.
INTERCEPTIONS—None.
KICKOFF RETURNS—Oakland, Carr 6-151. New England, Faulk 2-42, Hobbs 1-37.
PUNT RETURNS—Oakland, Carr 3-15. New England, Dwight 4-44.
SACKS—New England, Vrabel 1, J. Green 1.

STEELERS 34, TITANS 7
Sunday, September 11

Tennessee	7	0	0	0— 7
Pittsburgh	7	13	14	0—34

First Quarter
Ten.—Troupe 1 pass from McNair (Bironas kick), 6:37.
Pit.—Miller 3 pass from Roethlisberger (Reed kick), 12:18.

Second Quarter
Pit.—FG, Reed 44, 4:10.
Pit.—Randle El 63 pass from Roethlisberger (Reed kick), 6:11.
Pit.—FG, Reed 27, 14:39.

Third Quarter
Pit.—Parker 11 run (Reed kick), 3:23.
Pit.—Haynes 5 run (Reed kick), 12:57.
....Attendance—62,931.

	Tennessee	Pittsburgh
First downs	16	18
Rushes-yards	23-97	41-206
Passing	206	218
Punt returns	1-10	1-0
Kickoff returns	6-132	2-40
Interception returns	0-0	2-20
Comp.-att.-int.	18-27-2	9-11-0
Sacked-yards lost	3-13	0-0
Punts	2-46	3-46
Fumbles-lost	4-2	0-0
Penalties-yards	7-49	3-27
Time of possession	29:10	30:50

INDIVIDUAL STATISTICS
RUSHING—Tennessee, Brown 11-63, Henry 10-35, McNair 2-(minus 1). Pittsburgh, Parker 22-161, Haynes 11-33, Roethlisberger 3-5, Herron 3-2, Randle El 1-6, Ward 1-(minus 1).
PASSING—Tennessee, McNair 18-26-1-219, Volek 0-1-1-0. Pittsburgh, Roethlisberger 9-11-0-218.
RECEIVING—Tennessee, Kinney 5-58, Troupe 4-28, Bennett 3-79, B. Jones 2-30, Scaife 2-22, Calico 2-2. Pittsburgh, Randle El 2-89, Wilson 2-26, Ward 2-25, Parker 1-48, Tuman 1-27, Miller 1-3.
MISSED FIELD GOAL ATTEMPTS—Tennessee, Bironas 47.
INTERCEPTIONS—Pittsburgh, Colclough 1-14, Polamalu 1-6.
KICKOFF RETURNS—Tennessee, Roby 6-132. Pittsburgh, I. Taylor 2-40.
PUNT RETURNS—Tennessee, Thurman 1-10. Pittsburgh, Randle El 1-0.
SACKS—Pittsburgh, Porter 1, Haggans 1, Frazier 1.

REDSKINS 9, BEARS 7
Sunday, September 11

Chicago	0	0	7	0—7
Washington	0	6	3	0—9

Second Quarter
Was.—FG, Hall 40, 7:26.
Was.—FG, Hall 43, 14:00.

Third Quarter
Chi.—T. Jones 1 run (Brien kick), 3:32.
Was.—FG, Hall 19, 12:06.
Attendance—90,138.

	Chicago	Washington
First downs	11	18
Rushes-yards	18-41	40-164
Passing	125	159
Punt returns	2-(-3)	2-5
Kickoff returns	4-70	2-41
Interception returns	1-3	1-7
Comp.-att.-int.	15-28-1	14-25-1
Sacked-yards lost	3-16	3-16
Punts	7-42	3-38
Fumbles-lost	3-1	4-2
Penalties-yards	8-86	5-45
Time of possession	25:45	34:15

INDIVIDUAL STATISTICS
RUSHING—Chicago, T. Jones 15-31, Benson 3-10. Washington, Portis 21-121, Betts 12-41, Brunell 5-(minus 2), A. Brown 1-3, Ramsey 1-1.
PASSING—Chicago, Orton 15-28-1-141. Washington, Brunell 8-14-0-70, Ramsey 6-11-1-105.
RECEIVING—Chicago, Muhammad 6-59, Clark 3-26, T. Jones 2-14, Bradley 1-22, Gage 1-10, Berrian 1-9, M. Edwards 1-1. Washington, Moss 4-96, Cooley 3-34, Patten 3-19, Thrash 3-15, Royal 1-11.
MISSED FIELD GOAL ATTEMPTS—None.
INTERCEPTIONS—Chicago, Vasher 1-3. Washington, Marshall 1-7.
KICKOFF RETURNS—Chicago, Bradley 4-70. Washington, Betts 1-25, A. Brown 1-16.
PUNT RETURNS—Chicago, Berrian 2-(minus 3). Washington, A. Brown 2-5.
SACKS—Chicago, Urlacher 1, Ogunleye 1, Briggs 1. Washington, Griffin 1, Evans 1, Team 1.

BENGALS 27, BROWNS 13
Sunday, September 11

Cincinnati	0	17	10	0—27
Cleveland	3	7	0	3—13

First Quarter
Cle.—FG, Dawson 29, 10:23.

Second Quarter
Cin.—Ru. Johnson 1 run (Graham kick), 1:16.
Cin.—FG, Graham 32, 6:14.
Cle.—F. Jackson 68 pass from Dilfer (Dawson kick), 9:57.
Cin.—Walter 20 pass from Palmer (Graham kick), 14:15.

Third Quarter
Cin.—J. Johnson 18 pass from Palmer (Graham kick), 5:12.
Cin.—FG, Graham 23, 6:36.

Fourth Quarter
Cle.—FG, Dawson 34, 5:12.
Attendance—73,013.

	Cincinnati	Cleveland
First downs	26	16
Rushes-yards	32-148	18-95
Passing	272	278
Punt returns	2-18	2-20
Kickoff returns	4-108	6-133
Interception returns	2-30	1-0
Comp.-att.-int.	26-34-1	26-43-2
Sacked-yards lost	2-8	0-0
Punts	3-47	2-46
Fumbles-lost	2-1	3-1
Penalties-yards	5-40	7-56
Time of possession	34:13	25:47

INDIVIDUAL STATISTICS

RUSHING—Cincinnati, Ru. Johnson 26-126, C. Perry 5-11, C. Johnson 1-11. Cleveland, Droughns 12-78, Green 4-12, Dilfer 2-5.

PASSING—Cincinnati, Palmer 26-34-1-280. Cleveland, Dilfer 26-43-2-278.

RECEIVING—Cincinnati, C. Johnson 9-91, Houshmandzadeh 5-75, C. Perry 5-37, Walter 4-47, Ru. Johnson 2-12, J. Johnson 1-18. Cleveland, F. Jackson 8-128, Bryant 5-65, Northcutt 4-16, Heiden 3-32, Droughns 3-22, Edwards 2-16, Faine 1-(minus 1).

MISSED FIELD GOAL ATTEMPTS—None.

INTERCEPTIONS—Cincinnati, Ratliff 1-16, Thurman 1-14. Cleveland, Bodden 1-0.

KICKOFF RETURNS—Cincinnati, T. Perry 4-108. Cleveland, Droughns 5-119, Cribbs 1-14.

PUNT RETURNS—Cincinnati, Ratliff 2-18. Cleveland, Northcutt 2-20.

SACKS—Cleveland, Thompson 1, Crocker 1.

JAGUARS 26, SEAHAWKS 14
Sunday, September 11

Seattle	0	14	0	0—14
Jacksonville	6	7	7	6—26

First Quarter
Jac.—FG, Scobee 23, 3:57.
Jac.—FG, Scobee 41, 11:11.

Second Quarter
Sea.—Jurevicius 33 pass from Hasselbeck (J. Brown kick), :08.
Jac.—J. Smith 30 pass from Leftwich (Scobee kick), 10:43.
Sea.—Jackson 9 pass from Hasselbeck (J. Brown kick), 14:13.

Third Quarter
Jac.—J. Smith 7 pass from Leftwich (Scobee kick), 6:21.

Fourth Quarter
Jac.—FG, Scobee 29, 10:28.
Jac.—FG, Scobee 41, 13:05.
Attendance—65,204.

	Seattle	Jacksonville
First downs	20	18
Rushes-yards	19-97	31-119
Passing	225	243
Punt returns	1-5	3-24
Kickoff returns	3-81	3-63
Interception returns	0-0	2-29
Comp.-att.-int.	21-36-2	18-32-0
Sacked-yards lost	3-21	3-15
Punts	5-46	4-44
Fumbles-lost	3-3	1-0
Penalties-yards	5-29	6-31
Time of possession	25:49	34:11

INDIVIDUAL STATISTICS

RUSHING—Seattle, Alexander 14-73, Hasselbeck 2-16, Morris 2-6, Strong 1-2. Jacksonville, F. Taylor 20-76, Leftwich 4-9, Toefield 4-4, M. Jones 2-28, Pearman 1-2.

PASSING—Seattle, Hasselbeck 21-36-2-246. Jacksonville, Leftwich 17-31-0-252, M. Jones 1-1-0-6.

RECEIVING—Seattle, Engram 8-79, Jackson 6-65, Jurevicius 3-64, Stevens 3-41, Strong 1-(minus 3). Jacksonville, J. Smith 7-130, R. Williams 4-41, M. Jones 2-22, F. Taylor 2-14, Wrighster 1-27, Wilford 1-14, G. Jones 1-10.

MISSED FIELD GOAL ATTEMPTS—Jacksonville, Scobee 43.

INTERCEPTIONS—Jacksonville, Grant 1-29, D. Smith 1-0.

KICKOFF RETURNS—Seattle, Scobey 3-81. Jacksonville, Wimbush 2-46, Pearman 1-17.

PUNT RETURNS—Seattle, Warrick 1-5. Jacksonville, Pearman 3-24.

SACKS—Seattle, Trufant 1, B. Fisher 1, R. Bernard 1. Jacksonville, Ayodele 1, Hayward 1, Grant 0.5, McCray 0.5.

BUCCANEERS 24, VIKINGS 13
Sunday, September 11

Tampa Bay	0	17	0	7—24
Minnesota	7	0	3	3—13

First Quarter
Min.—Sharper 88 interception return (Edinger kick), 12:16.

Second Quarter
T.B.—Smith 23 pass from Griese (M. Bryant kick), :05.
T.B.—Smith 2 pass from Griese (M. Bryant kick), 10:22.
T.B.—FG, M. Bryant 41, 14:43.

Third Quarter
Min.—FG, Edinger 53, 11:08.

Fourth Quarter
Min.—FG, Edinger 22, 8:47.
T.B.—C. Williams 71 run (M. Bryant kick), 13:37.
Attendance—63,939.

	Tampa Bay	Minnesota
First downs	12	15
Rushes-yards	31-146	15-33
Passing	199	215
Punt returns	3-27	5-54
Kickoff returns	4-83	5-89
Interception returns	3-16	2-88
Comp.-att.-int.	18-29-2	22-33-3
Sacked-yards lost	2-14	3-18
Punts	6-47	4-54
Fumbles-lost	1-0	4-2
Penalties-yards	13-99	9-70
Time of possession	30:34	29:26

INDIVIDUAL STATISTICS

RUSHING—Tampa Bay, C. Williams 27-148, Griese 2-(minus 2), Galloway 1-0, Alstott 1-0. Minnesota, M. Williams 6-15, M. Bennett 6-(minus 1), Culpepper 3-19.

PASSING—Tampa Bay, Griese 18-29-2-213. Minnesota, Culpepper 22-33-3-233.

RECEIVING—Tampa Bay, Galloway 5-97, Clayton 4-57, Smith 4-34, Cook 2-7, Alstott 1-7, Becht 1-7, I. Hilliard 1-4. Minnesota, Kleinsasser 4-42, Wiggins 4-33, Burleson 3-45, T. Taylor 3-38, M. Robinson 3-22, M. Bennett 3-21, M. Williams 2-32.

MISSED FIELD GOAL ATTEMPTS—None.

INTERCEPTIONS—Tampa Bay, Kelly 2-16, Brooks 1-0. Minnesota, Sharper 1-88, Smoot 1-0.

KICKOFF RETURNS—Tampa Bay, Cox 4-83. Minnesota, Moore 3-66, Williamson 2-23.

PUNT RETURNS—Tampa Bay, Jones 3-27. Minnesota, Howry 5-54.

SACKS—Tampa Bay, Rice 1, McFarland 1, Team 1. Minnesota, P. Williams 1, Johnstone 1.

CHIEFS 27, JETS 7
Sunday, September 11

N.Y. Jets	0	0	0	7— 7
Kansas City	14	3	3	7—27

First Quarter
K.C.—L. Johnson 35 run (Tynes kick), 1:21.
K.C.—Holmes 3 run (Tynes kick), 11:56.

Second Quarter
K.C.—FG, Tynes 41, 2:58.

Third Quarter
K.C.—FG, Tynes 38, 10:47.

Fourth Quarter
K.C.—L. Johnson 4 run (Tynes kick), :04.
NYJ—Baker 23 pass from Fiedler (Nugent kick), 14:31.
Attendance—78,014.

	N.Y. Jets	Kansas City
First downs	19	23
Rushes-yards	23-57	34-198
Passing	333	191
Punt returns	2-8	0-0
Kickoff returns	6-182	2-39
Interception returns	1-0	1-53
Comp.-att.-int.	27-44-1	15-26-1
Sacked-yards lost	3-19	1-9
Punts	3-44	2-49
Fumbles-lost	7-2	1-0
Penalties-yards	8-80	4-26
Time of possession	31:29	28:31

INDIVIDUAL STATISTICS

RUSHING—New York, C. Martin 20-57, Pennington 2-0, Fiedler 1-0. Kansas City, Holmes 22-85, L. Johnson 9-110, Richardson 1-4, D. Hall 1-0, Green 1-(minus 1).

PASSING—New York, Pennington 21-34-1-264, Fiedler 6-10-0-88. Kansas City, Green 15-26-1-200.

RECEIVING—New York, Baker 7-124, Coles 6-66, Sowell 3-52, McCareins 3-39, Chrebet 3-33, C. Martin 3-20, Jolley 2-18. Kansas City, Kennison 4-76, Gonzalez 4-51, Parker 2-23, Cruz 1-15, L. Johnson 1-11, Horn 1-11, D. Hall 1-8, Holmes 1-5.

MISSED FIELD GOAL ATTEMPTS—New York, Nugent 28. Kansas City, Tynes 32.

INTERCEPTIONS—New York, Law 1-0. Kansas City, Surtain 1-53.

KICKOFF RETURNS—New York, Miller 6-182. Kansas City, D. Hall 2-39.

PUNT RETURNS—New York, Cotchery 1-8, Miller 1-0.

SACKS—New York, J. Abraham 1. Kansas City, D. Johnson 1, S. Knight 1, Allen 1.

DOLPHINS 34, BRONCOS 10
Sunday, September 11

Denver	0	3	0	7—10
Miami	3	3	7	21—34

First Quarter
Mia.—FG, Mare 29, 9:10.

Second Quarter
Mia.—FG, Mare 44, 2:24.
Den.—FG, Elam 28, 13:09.

Third Quarter
Mia.—McMichael 2 pass from Frerotte (Mare kick), 10:13.

Fourth Quarter
Mia.—Morris 9 run (Mare kick), 1:49.
Den.—K. Johnson 2 pass from Plummer (Elam kick), 5:41.
Mia.—Booker 60 pass from Frerotte (Mare kick), 5:51.
Mia.—Taylor 85 fumble return (Mare kick), 15:00.
Attendance—72,324.

	Denver	Miami
First downs	19	21
Rushes-yards	20-70	33-151
Passing	242	275
Punt returns	1-13	4-64
Kickoff returns	5-118	2-51
Interception returns	1-11	2-29
Comp.-att.-int.	22-48-2	24-36-1
Sacked-yards lost	1-9	0-0
Punts	7-45	3-47
Fumbles-lost	2-1	3-2
Penalties-yards	7-73	11-69
Time of possession	27:42	32:18

BILLS 22, TEXANS 7
Sunday, September 11

Houston	0	7	0	0— 7
Buffalo	6	13	0	3—22

First Quarter
Buf.—FG, Lindell 35, 5:36.
Buf.—FG, Lindell 21, 13:17.

Second Quarter
Buf.—FG, Lindell 42, 1:03.
Buf.—FG, Lindell 39, 3:53.
Hou.—Carr 1 run (K. Brown kick), 8:23.
Buf.—Peters 1 pass from Losman (Lindell kick), 14:31.

Fourth Quarter
Buf.—FG, Lindell 31, 7:49.
Attendance—71,781.

	Houston	Buffalo
First downs	12	20
Rushes-yards	23-95	36-152
Passing	25	164
Punt returns	1-6	2-19
Kickoff returns	7-141	2-32
Interception returns	0-0	3-22
Comp.-att.-int.	9-21-3	17-28-0
Sacked-yards lost	5-45	1-6
Punts	5-43	5-41

	Houston	Buffalo
Fumbles-lost	2-2	0-0
Penalties-yards	6-38	10-71
Time of possession	21:45	38:15

INDIVIDUAL STATISTICS

RUSHING—Houston, D. Davis 14-48, Carr 7-40, An. Johnson 2-7. Buffalo, McGahee 22-117, S. Williams 7-14, Losman 6-31, Evans 1-(minus 10).

PASSING—Houston, Carr 9-21-3-70. Buffalo, Losman 17-28-0-170.

RECEIVING—Houston, An. Johnson 3-18, Wells 2-10, D. Davis 2-9, Bruener 1-19, Murphy 1-14. Buffalo, Moulds 4-40, Evans 3-68, McGahee 3-15, Campbell 2-18, S. Williams 2-11, Shelton 1-11, Reed 1-6, Peters 1-1.

MISSED FIELD GOAL ATTEMPTS—None.

INTERCEPTIONS—Buffalo, Vincent 2-22, Milloy 1-0.

KICKOFF RETURNS—Houston, Morency 5-101, D. Davis 1-29, Bruener 1-11. Buffalo, Shelton 1-16, McGee 1-16.

PUNT RETURNS—Houston, Buchanon 1-6. Buffalo, Clements 2-19.

SACKS—Houston, Simmons 1. Buffalo, Schobel 2, Spikes 1, Kelsay 1, Greer 1.

SAINTS 23, PANTHERS 20
Sunday, September 11

New Orleans	7	7	3	6—23
Carolina	7	0	7	6—20

First Quarter
N.O.—McAllister 4 run (Carney kick), 9:37.
Car.—S. Smith 33 pass from Delhomme (Kasay kick), 14:23.

Second Quarter
N.O.—McAllister 2 run (Carney kick), 10:23.

Third Quarter
N.O.—FG, Carney 29, 10:29.
Car.—S. Davis 1 run (Kasay kick), 14:39.

Fourth Quarter
N.O.—FG, Carney 48, 3:04.
Car.—FG, Kasay 39, 8:43.
Car.—FG, Kasay 46, 13:56.
N.O.—FG, Carney 47, 14:57.
Attendance—72,920.

	New Orleans	Carolina
First downs	21	20
Rushes-yards	33-101	25-141
Passing	190	209
Punt returns	1-0	0-0
Kickoff returns	4-75	5-76
Interception returns	2-16	0-0
Comp.-att.-int.	18-24-0	19-31-2
Sacked-yards lost	1-2	1-3
Punts	2-44	1-35
Fumbles-lost	3-2	3-2
Penalties-yards	9-74	11-84
Time of possession	32:36	27:24

INDIVIDUAL STATISTICS

RUSHING—New Orleans, McAllister 26-64, Brooks 3-32, A. Smith 3-2, Stecker 1-3. Carolina, S. Davis 13-81, Foster 9-41, Delhomme 2-17, Goings 1-2.

PASSING—New Orleans, Brooks 18-24-0-192. Carolina, Delhomme 19-31-2-212.

RECEIVING—New Orleans, Conwell 6-71, Horn 5-66, Stallworth 4-47, McAllister 2-5, Hilton 1-3. Carolina, S. Smith 8-138, Foster 3-15, Mangum 2-22, Goings 2-15, Hoover 2-11, Colbert 2-11.

MISSED FIELD GOAL ATTEMPTS—None.

INTERCEPTIONS—New Orleans, M. McKenzie 1-11, Craft 1-5.

KICKOFF RETURNS—New Orleans, M. Lewis 4-75. Carolina, Smart 3-46, Goings 1-21, Mangum 1-9.

PUNT RETURNS—New Orleans, M. Lewis 1-0.

SACKS—New Orleans, W. Smith 1. Carolina.

LIONS 17, PACKERS 3
Sunday, September 11

Green Bay	0	3	0	0— 3
Detroit	7	0	3	7—17

First Quarter
Det.—Pollard 9 pass from Harrington (Hanson kick), 10:04.

Second Quarter
G.B.—FG, Longwell 50, 12:01.

Third Quarter
Det.—FG, Hanson 21, 6:26.

Fourth Quarter
Det.—M. Williams 3 pass from Harrington (Hanson kick), 10:47.
  Attendance—61,877.

	Green Bay	Detroit
First downs	13	18
Rushes-yards	17-46	31-102
Passing	170	152
Punt returns	3-19	6-12
Kickoff returns	4-83	2-29
Interception returns	0-0	2-0
Comp.-att.-int.	27-44-2	15-28-0
Sacked-yards lost	4-31	2-15
Punts	6-41	7-42
Fumbles-lost	4-1	2-0
Penalties-yards	14-100	4-38
Time of possession	31:04	28:56

INDIVIDUAL STATISTICS
RUSHING—Green Bay, Green 12-58, Davenport 3-0, Favre 1-(minus 1), Sander 1-(minus 11). Detroit, Jones 25-87, Harrington 3-14, Bryson 3-1.
PASSING—Green Bay, Favre 27-44-2-201. Detroit, Harrington 15-28-0-167.
RECEIVING—Green Bay, Green 5-34, Driver 4-48, Franks 4-27, J. Walker 4-27, Fisher 4-24, Henderson 3-20, Chatman 1-11, D. Martin 1-6, Ferguson 1-4. Detroit, Pollard 5-58, K. Johnson 2-38, R. Williams 2-13, Jones 2-9, C. Rogers 1-31, P. Smith 1-8, Bryson 1-7, M. Williams 1-3.
MISSED FIELD GOAL ATTEMPTS—None.
INTERCEPTIONS—Detroit, Kennedy 1-0, Holt 1-0.
KICKOFF RETURNS—Green Bay, Ferguson 2-44, Chatman 1-22, Davenport 1-17. Detroit, Drummond 2-29.
PUNT RETURNS—Green Bay, Chatman 3-19. Detroit, Drummond 6-12.
SACKS—Green Bay, Kampman 1, Gbaja-Biamila 0.5, Jenkins 0.5. Detroit, S. Rogers 1, Hall 1, K. Edwards 1, Team 1.

COWBOYS 28, CHARGERS 24
Sunday, September 11

Dallas 0   14   7   7—28
San Diego 7   7   10   0—24

First Quarter
S.D.—Tomlinson 2 run (Kaeding kick), 8:07.
Second Quarter
Dal.—Crayton 20 pass from Bledsoe (Cortez kick), 1:26.
Dal.—K. Johnson 13 pass from Bledsoe (Cortez kick), 5:14.
S.D.—McCardell 20 pass from Brees (Kaeding kick), 12:53.
Third Quarter
S.D.—McCardell 17 pass from Brees (Kaeding kick), 4:29.
Dal.—J. Jones 5 run (Cortez kick), 9:19.
S.D.—FG, Kaeding 33, 14:48.
Fourth Quarter
Dal.—K. Johnson 2 pass from Bledsoe (Cortez kick), 11:54.
  Attendance—67,679.

...	Dallas	San Diego
First downs	23	19
Rushes-yards	33-109	26-103
Passing	192	188
Punt returns	1-2	2-25
Kickoff returns	4-78	5-162
Interception returns	2-1	0-0
Comp.-att.-int.	18-24-0	18-35-2
Sacked-yards lost	4-34	2-21
Punts	3-41	2-32
Fumbles-lost	3-1	0-0
Penalties-yards	8-46	8-62
Time of possession	31:09	28:51

INDIVIDUAL STATISTICS
RUSHING—Dallas, J. Jones 26-93, Bledsoe 4-7, A. Thomas 3-9. San Diego, Tomlinson 19-72, Neal 3-15, Turner 2-7, Caldwell 1-7, Brees 1-2.
PASSING—Dallas, Bledsoe 18-24-0-226. San Diego, Brees 18-35-2-209.
RECEIVING—Dallas, Crayton 6-89, K. Johnson 5-65, T. Glenn 3-42, J. Jones 3-18, Witten 1-12. San Diego, McCardell 9-123, E. Parker 5-75, Peelle 2-(minus 4), Caldwell 1-9, Neal 1-6.
MISSED FIELD GOAL ATTEMPTS—None.
INTERCEPTIONS—Dallas, Henry 1-1, A. Glenn 1-0.
KICKOFF RETURNS—Dallas, Barber 3-58, A. Glenn 1-20. San Diego, Sproles 4-146, E. Parker 1-16.
PUNT RETURNS—Dallas, Crayton 1-2. San Diego, Sproles 2-25.
SACKS—Dallas, Glover 1, Ro. Williams 0.5, Ellis 0.5. San Diego, Foley 1, Leber 1, Phillips 1, Davis 1.

GIANTS 42, CARDINALS 19
Sunday, September 11

Arizona 0   13   6   0—19
N.Y. Giants 7   0   21   14—42

First Quarter
NYG—Shockey 20 pass from Manning (Feely kick), 7:03.
Second Quarter
Ariz.—FG, Rackers 24, 3:24.
Ariz.—Dansby 18 interception return (Rackers kick), 3:46.
Ariz.—FG, Rackers 42, 11:41.
Third Quarter
NYG—Jacobs 5 run (Feely kick), 2:47.
NYG—Barber 21 run (Feely kick), 3:12.
Ariz.—Fitzgerald 1 pass from Warner (pass failed), 7:56.
NYG—Ponder 95 kickoff return (Feely kick), 8:15.
Fourth Quarter
NYG—Burress 13 pass from Manning (Feely kick), 3:34.
NYG—Morton 52 punt return (Feely kick), 6:35.
  Attendance—78,387.

	Arizona	N.Y. Giants
First downs	20	14
Rushes-yards	21-31	25-121
Passing	287	154
Punt returns	1-(-5)	6-88
Kickoff returns	7-180	5-224
Interception returns	2-20	2-88
Comp.-att.-int.	32-56-2	10-23-2
Sacked-yards lost	3-29	3-18
Punts	7-45	6-42
Fumbles-lost	0-0	0-0
Penalties-yards	10-53	7-52
Time of possession	35:45	24:15

INDIVIDUAL STATISTICS
RUSHING—Arizona, Arrington 8-5, Shipp 7-10, Warner 3-11, O. Ayanbadejo 2-2, J. Jackson 1-3. New York, Barber 13-62, Jacobs 6-39, Ward 4-23, Hasselbeck 2-(minus 3).
PASSING—Arizona, Warner 27-46-1-264, McCown 5-10-1-52. New York, Manning 10-23-2-172.
RECEIVING—Arizona, Fitzgerald 13-155, O. Ayanbadejo 5-29, Boldin 4-62, Arrington 4-22, B. Johnson 2-27, Shipp 2-5, Bergen 1-10, Lee 1-6. New York, Burress 5-76, Barber 2-60, Shockey 2-29, T. Carter 1-7.
MISSED FIELD GOAL ATTEMPTS—None.
INTERCEPTIONS—Arizona, Dansby 2-20. New York, F. Walker 1-71, Wilson 1-17.
KICKOFF RETURNS—Arizona, Swinton 6-164, O. Ayanbadejo 1-16. New York, Ponder 4-191, Jacobs 1-33.
PUNT RETURNS—Arizona, Swinton 1-(minus 5). New York, Morton 6-88.
SACKS—Arizona, Berry 1, Huff 1, Dansby 1. New York, Strahan 1.5, Joseph 1, Pierce 0.5.

49ERS 28, RAMS 25
Sunday, September 11

St. Louis 3   6   3   13—25
San Francisco 0   21   7   0—28

First Quarter
St.L.—FG, J. Wilkins 30, 10:32.
Second Quarter
St.L.—FG, J. Wilkins 41, 1:53.
S.F.—Lloyd 35 pass from Rattay (Nedney kick), 5:15.
S.F.—Amey 75 punt return (Nedney kick), 8:12.
S.F.—Battle 6 pass from Rattay (Nedney kick), 13:44.
St.L.—FG, J. Wilkins 33, 15:00.
Third Quarter
S.F.—Barlow 9 run (Nedney kick), 3:28.
St.L.—FG, J. Wilkins 41, 13:08.
Fourth Quarter
St.L.—Bruce 29 pass from Bulger (run failed), 1:38.
St.L.—Manumaleuna 6 pass from Bulger (J. Wilkins kick), 12:47.
  Attendance—67,918.

	St. Louis	San Francisco
First downs	26	12
Rushes-yards	26-89	21-34
Passing	316	183
Punt returns	2-14	1-75
Kickoff returns	4-55	5-123
Interception returns	0-0	1-0

	St. Louis	San Francisco
Comp.-att.-int.	34-56-1	13-18-0
Sacked-yards lost	7-46	2-9
Punts	4-33	5-41
Fumbles-lost	0-0	2-2
Penalties-yards	7-48	5-30
Time of possession	39:23	20:37

INDIVIDUAL STATISTICS

RUSHING—St. Louis, S. Jackson 19-60, M. Faulk 3-12, Bulger 2-8, McDonald 1-7, Manumaleuna 1-2. San Francisco, Barlow 14-22, Gore 4-17, Rattay 2-(minus 2), Battle 1-(minus 3).

PASSING—St. Louis, Bulger 34-56-1-362. San Francisco, Rattay 11-16-0-165, Battle 2-2-0-27.

RECEIVING—St. Louis, Holt 10-125, McDonald 7-73, Curtis 7-63, Bruce 3-61, S. Jackson 3-13, R. Williams 1-12, Manumaleuna 1-6, Looker 1-5, M. Faulk 1-4. San Francisco, Battle 5-59, Lloyd 3-65, Gore 2-21, Barlow 2-17, Morton 1-30.

MISSED FIELD GOAL ATTEMPTS—None.

INTERCEPTIONS—San Francisco, M. Adams 1-0.

KICKOFF RETURNS—St. Louis, C. Johnson 4-55. San Francisco, Hicks 4-106, Amey 1-17.

PUNT RETURNS—St. Louis, McDonald 2-14. San Francisco, Amey 1-75.

SACKS—St. Louis, Little 2. San Francisco, Young 3, J. Peterson 2.5, M. Adams 1, Carter 0.5.

COLTS 24, RAVENS 7
Sunday, September 11

Indianapolis	0	3	14	7—24
Baltimore	0	0	0	7— 7

Second Quarter
Ind.—FG, Vanderjagt 20, 14:45.
Third Quarter
Ind.—Harrison 28 pass from Manning (Vanderjagt kick), 6:17.
Ind.—Utecht 26 pass from Manning (Vanderjagt kick), 9:52.
Fourth Quarter
Ind.—June 30 interception return (Vanderjagt kick), 12:21.
Bal.—Wilcox 17 pass from Wright (Stover kick), 14:47.
Attendance—70,501.

	Indianapolis	Baltimore
First downs	19	22
Rushes-yards	26-86	21-77
Passing	254	324
Punt returns	1-0	3-51
Kickoff returns	1-14	4-78
Interception returns	3-61	0-0
Comp.-att.-int.	21-36-0	34-54-3
Sacked-yards lost	0-0	3-31
Punts	7-39	4-40
Fumbles-lost	0-0	2-1
Penalties-yards	7-45	8-45
Time of possession	27:09	32:51

INDIVIDUAL STATISTICS

RUSHING—Indianapolis, James 23-88, Manning 3-(minus 2). Baltimore, J. Lewis 16-48, C. Taylor 4-27, Boller 1-2.

PASSING—Indianapolis, Manning 21-36-0-254. Baltimore, Wright 19-31-2-214, Boller 15-23-1-141.

RECEIVING—Indianapolis, Stokley 7-83, Harrison 6-69, Wayne 4-50, James 3-26, Utecht 1-26. Baltimore, Mason 8-99, Wilcox 8-78, Clayton 5-44, Heap 4-38, Dinkins 3-30, Moore 2-36, C. Taylor 2-22, J. Lewis 1-4, Hymes 1-4.

MISSED FIELD GOAL ATTEMPTS—Baltimore, Stover 38, 47, 45.

INTERCEPTIONS—Indianapolis, Brackett 2-31, June 1-30.

KICKOFF RETURNS—Indianapolis, Carthon 1-14. Baltimore, Sams 3-68, J. Green 1-10.

PUNT RETURNS—Indianapolis, Walters 1-0. Baltimore, Sams 3-51.

SACKS—Indianapolis, Tripplett 2, Mathis 1.

FALCONS 14, EAGLES 10
Monday, September 12

Philadelphia	0	7	0	3—10
Atlanta	14	0	0	0—14

First Quarter
Atl.—Vick 7 run (T. Peterson kick), 11:54.
Atl.—Duckett 1 run (T. Peterson kick), 14:51.
Second Quarter
Phi.—Westbrook 9 pass from McNabb (Akers kick), 3:39.
Fourth Quarter
Phi.—FG, Akers 44, 5:40.
Attendance—70,806.

	Philadelphia	Atlanta
First downs	18	18
Rushes-yards	14-51	40-200
Passing	250	119
Punt returns	3-28	2-0
Kickoff returns	3-48	2-53
Interception returns	1-0	1-38
Comp.-att.-int.	24-45-1	12-23-1
Sacked-yards lost	2-7	4-37
Punts	5-43	7-40
Fumbles-lost	3-2	3-2
Penalties-yards	8-55	7-88
Time of possession	26:09	33:51

INDIVIDUAL STATISTICS

RUSHING—Philadelphia, Westbrook 12-47, Gordon 1-4, McNabb 1-0. Atlanta, Dunn 21-117, Vick 11-68, Duckett 8-15.

PASSING—Philadelphia, McNabb 24-45-1-257. Atlanta, Vick 12-23-1-156.

RECEIVING—Philadelphia, Owens 7-112, Westbrook 7-64, G. Lewis 5-44, Smith 3-29, R. Brown 1-7, Parry 1-1. Atlanta, Crumpler 4-54, Jenkins 3-80, Finneran 2-12, Blakley 1-9, Griffith 1-1, Dunn 1-0.

MISSED FIELD GOAL ATTEMPTS—Philadelphia, Akers 49, 49.

INTERCEPTIONS—Philadelphia, Dawkins 1-0. Atlanta, D. Hall 1-38.

KICKOFF RETURNS—Philadelphia, Hood 3-48. Atlanta, Rossum 2-53.

PUNT RETURNS—Philadelphia, Wynn 3-28. Atlanta, Rossum 2-0.

SACKS—Philadelphia, Dawkins 1.5, Walker 1.5, M. Lewis 1. Atlanta, Kerney 1, R. Coleman 1.

WEEK 2

AMERICAN FOOTBALL CONFERENCE

EAST DIVISION

	W	L	T	Pct.	PF	PA
Buffalo	1	1	0	.500	25	26
Miami	1	1	0	.500	41	27
New England	1	1	0	.500	47	47
N.Y. Jets	1	1	0	.500	24	34

NORTH DIVISION

	W	L	T	Pct.	PF	PA
Cincinnati	2	0	0	1.000	64	21
Pittsburgh	2	0	0	1.000	61	14
Cleveland	1	1	0	.500	39	51
Baltimore	0	2	0	.000	17	49

SOUTH DIVISION

	W	L	T	Pct.	PF	PA
Indianapolis	2	0	0	1.000	34	10
Jacksonville	1	1	0	.500	29	24
Tennessee	1	1	0	.500	32	44
Houston	0	2	0	.000	14	49

WEST DIVISION

	W	L	T	Pct.	PF	PA
Kansas City	2	0	0	1.000	50	24
Denver	1	1	0	.500	30	51
Oakland	0	2	0	.000	37	53
San Diego	0	2	0	.000	41	48

NATIONAL FOOTBALL CONFERENCE

EAST DIVISION

	W	L	T	Pct.	PF	PA
N.Y. Giants	2	0	0	1.000	69	29
Washington	2	0	0	1.000	23	20
Dallas	1	1	0	.500	41	38
Philadelphia	1	1	0	.500	52	17

NORTH DIVISION

	W	L	T	Pct.	PF	PA
Chicago	1	1	0	.500	45	15
Detroit	1	1	0	.500	23	41
Green Bay	0	2	0	.000	27	43
Minnesota	0	2	0	.000	21	61

SOUTH DIVISION

	W	L	T	Pct.	PF	PA
Tampa Bay	2	0	0	1.000	43	16
Atlanta	1	1	0	.500	32	31
Carolina	1	1	0	.500	47	40
New Orleans	1	1	0	.500	33	47

WEST DIVISION

	W	L	T	Pct.	PF	PA
San Francisco	1	1	0	.500	31	67
Seattle	1	1	0	.500	35	44
St. Louis	1	1	0	.500	42	40
Arizona	0	2	0	.000	31	59

TOP PERFORMANCES

100-YARD RUSHING GAMES

Player, team & opponent	Att.	Yds.	TD
Shaun Alexander, Sea. vs. Atl.	28	144	1
Thomas Jones, Chi. vs. Det.	20	139	2
Edgerrin James, Ind. vs. Jac.	27	128	0
Carnell Williams, T.B. vs. Buf.	24	128	1
Willie Parker, Pit. at Hou.	25	111	1

300-YARD PASSING GAMES

Player, team & opponent	Att.	Cmp.	Yds.	TD	Int.
Aaron Brooks, N.O. vs. NYG	45	27	375	1	3
Brett Favre, G.B. vs. Cle.	44	32	342	3	2
Donovan McNabb, Phi. vs. S.F.	29	23	342	5	0
Carson Palmer, Cin. vs. Min.	40	27	337	3	1
Trent Dilfer, Cle. at G.B.	32	21	336	3	0
Kurt Warner, Ariz. vs. St.L.	42	29	327	0	1

100-YARD RECEIVING GAMES

Player, team & opponent	Rec.	Yds.	TD
Santana Moss, Was. at Dal.	5	159	2
Terry Glenn, Dal. vs. Was.	6	157	1
Joe Horn, N.O. vs. NYG	9	143	1
Terrell Owens, Phi. vs. S.F.	5	143	2
Donte' Stallworth, N.O. vs. NYG	8	141	0
Chad Johnson, Cin. vs. Min.	7	139	1
Darrell Jackson, Sea. vs. Atl.	8	131	0
Randy Moss, Oak. vs. K.C.	5	127	1
Anquan Boldin, Ariz. vs. St.L.	8	119	0
L.J. Smith, Phi. vs. S.F.	9	119	1
Braylon Edwards, Cle. at G.B.	3	107	1
Donald Driver, G.B. vs. Cle.	6	105	1
Steve Heiden, Cle. at G.B.	6	104	2

RESULTS

SUNDAY, SEPTEMBER 18
Pittsburgh 27, HOUSTON 7
TAMPA BAY 19, Buffalo 3
INDIANAPOLIS 10, Jacksonville 3
PHILADELPHIA 42, San Francisco 3
CHICAGO 38, Detroit 6
CINCINNATI 37, Minnesota 8
CAROLINA 27, New England 17
TENNESSEE 25, Baltimore 10
SEATTLE 21, Atlanta 18
DENVER 20, San Diego 17
St. Louis 17, ARIZONA 12
N.Y. JETS 17, Miami 7
Cleveland 26, GREEN BAY 24
Kansas City 23, OAKLAND 17

MONDAY, SEPTEMBER 19
N.Y. Giants 27, NEW ORLEANS 10
Washington 14, DALLAS 13

2005 REVIEW Week 2

STEELERS 27, TEXANS 7

Sunday, September 18

Pittsburgh	10	10	7	0—27
Houston	0	0	7	0— 7

First Quarter

Pit.—FG, Reed 37, 4:53.
Pit.—Ward 16 pass from Roethlisberger (Reed kick), 6:56.

Second Quarter

Pit.—Ward 14 pass from Roethlisberger (Reed kick), :05.
Pit.—FG, Reed 35, 11:02.

Third Quarter

Hou.—D. Davis 3 pass from Carr (K. Brown kick), 7:55.
Pit.—Parker 10 run (Reed kick), 11:09.
Attendance—70,742.

	Pittsburgh	Houston
First downs	18	16
Rushes-yards	32-135	25-113
Passing	253	108
Punt returns	2-10	1-6
Kickoff returns	1-19	5-101
Interception returns	0-0	0-0
Comp.-att.-int.	14-21-0	16-26-0
Sacked-yards lost	1-1	8-59
Punts	1-39	4-40
Fumbles-lost	0-0	1-1
Penalties-yards	5-40	7-58
Time of possession	29:06	30:54

INDIVIDUAL STATISTICS

RUSHING—Pittsburgh, Parker 25-111, Haynes 7-24. Houston, D. Davis 15-59, Carr 7-46, Wells 3-8.

PASSING—Pittsburgh, Roethlisberger 14-21-0-254. Houston, Carr 16-26-0-167.

RECEIVING—Pittsburgh, Ward 6-84, Randle El 3-75, Wilson 2-76, Haynes 1-8, Kreider 1-7, Tuman 1-4. Houston, D. Davis 4-33, An. Johnson 4-20, Bradford 2-49, Armstrong 2-42, Gaffney 2-7, Murphy 1-12, Wells 1-4.

MISSED FIELD GOAL ATTEMPTS—None.

INTERCEPTIONS—None.

KICKOFF RETURNS—Pittsburgh, I. Taylor 1-19. Houston, Morency 5-101.

PUNT RETURNS—Pittsburgh, Randle El 2-10. Houston, Buchanon 1-6.

SACKS—Pittsburgh, Polamalu 3, Haggans 1, Townsend 1, Porter 1, Colclough 1, J. Harrison 1. Houston, Peek 1.

BUCCANEERS 19, BILLS 3

Sunday, September 18

Buffalo	0	3	0	0— 3
Tampa Bay	0	9	7	3—19

Second Quarter

T.B.—Safety, 5:31.
T.B.—Alstott 1 run (M. Bryant kick), 12:24.
Buf.—FG, Lindell 40, 13:59.

Third Quarter

T.B.—C. Williams 3 run (M. Bryant kick), 9:51.

Fourth Quarter

T.B.—FG, M. Bryant 40, 5:38.
Attendance—64,777.

	Buffalo	Tampa Bay
First downs	8	18
Rushes-yards	17-47	40-191
Passing	100	127
Punt returns	3-20	3-50
Kickoff returns	3-105	3-49
Interception returns	0-0	0-0
Comp.-att.-int.	13-31-0	16-22-0
Sacked-yards lost	2-12	1-9
Punts	7-44	6-46
Fumbles-lost	0-0	0-0
Penalties-yards	3-20	13-99
Time of possession	21:10	38:50

INDIVIDUAL STATISTICS

RUSHING—Buffalo, McGahee 13-34, Losman 4-13. Tampa Bay, C. Williams 24-128, Pittman 7-46, Alstott 6-19, Griese 3-(minus 2).

PASSING—Buffalo, Losman 11-28-0-113, Holcomb 2-3-0-(minus 1).

Tampa Bay, Griese 16-22-0-136.

RECEIVING—Buffalo, Reed 6-71, S. Williams 3-22, Evans 1-12, Moulds 1-8, Campbell 1-0, McGahee 1-(minus 1). Tampa Bay, Clayton 6-84, Pittman 3-20, I. Hilliard 2-15, Alstott 2-9, Becht 2-6, Smith 1-2.

MISSED FIELD GOAL ATTEMPTS—None.

INTERCEPTIONS—None.

KICKOFF RETURNS—Buffalo, McGee 3-105. Tampa Bay, Jones 3-49.

PUNT RETURNS—Buffalo, Clements 3-20. Tampa Bay, Jones 3-50.

SACKS—Buffalo, Milloy 1. Tampa Bay, Quarles 1, Rice 1.

COLTS 10, JAGUARS 3

Sunday, September 18

Jacksonville	0	0	3	0— 3
Indianapolis	0	0	0	10—10

Third Quarter

Jac.—FG, Scobee 28, 8:01.

Fourth Quarter

Ind.—Carthon 6 run (Vanderjagt kick), 6:33.
Ind.—FG, Vanderjagt 41, 13:10.
Attendance—56,460.

	Jacksonville	Indianapolis
First downs	12	18
Rushes-yards	24-128	38-146
Passing	175	122
Punt returns	5-46	2-12
Kickoff returns	3-62	2-51
Interception returns	1-14	0-0
Comp.-att.-int.	16-29-0	13-28-1
Sacked-yards lost	6-23	0-0
Punts	7-46	7-46
Fumbles-lost	6-0	0-0
Penalties-yards	7-60	6-45
Time of possession	31:20	28:40

INDIVIDUAL STATISTICS

RUSHING—Jacksonville, F. Taylor 16-81, G. Jones 3-29, Leftwich 3-11, M. Jones 2-7. Indianapolis, James 27-128, Carthon 6-5, Rhodes 4-10, Mungro 1-3.

PASSING—Jacksonville, Leftwich 16-29-1-198. Indianapolis, Manning 13-28-1-122.

RECEIVING—Jacksonville, R. Williams 4-38, J. Smith 3-49, F. Taylor 3-18, Toefield 2-6, B. Jones 1-41, Wilford 1-25, Brady 1-12, M. Jones 1-9. Indianapolis, James 4-39, Harrison 3-36, Wayne 3-19, Stokley 2-24, Clark 1-4.

MISSED FIELD GOAL ATTEMPTS—Jacksonville, Scobee 42.

INTERCEPTIONS—Jacksonville, Peterson 1-14.

KICKOFF RETURNS—Jacksonville, Pearman 3-62. Indianapolis, Rhodes 2-51.

PUNT RETURNS—Jacksonville, Owens 3-6, Pearman 2-40. Indianapolis, Walters 2-12.

SACKS—Indianapolis, Reagor 3, Freeney 1, Brock 1, Mathis 1.

EAGLES 42, 49ERS 3

Sunday, September 18

San Francisco	0	0	3	0— 3
Philadelphia	14	14	7	7—42

First Quarter

Phi.—Owens 68 pass from McNabb (Akers kick), :57.
Phi.—Smith 6 pass from McNabb (Akers kick), 7:45.

Second Quarter

Phi.—Owens 42 pass from McNabb (Akers kick), 3:18.
Phi.—Westbrook 2 pass from McNabb (Simoneau kick), 3:38.

Third Quarter

S.F.—FG, Nedney 32, 10:52.
Phi.—G. Lewis 6 pass from McNabb (Akers kick), 14:02.

Fourth Quarter

Phi.—Gordon 6 run (Akers kick), 11:17.
Attendance—67,727.

	San Francisco	Philadelphia
First downs	8	30
Rushes-yards	17-58	30-140
Passing	84	443
Punt returns	1-0	4-13
Kickoff returns	7-131	1-22

	San Francisco	Philadelphia
Interception returns	0-0	3-51
Comp.-att.-int.	13-27-3	33-39-0
Sacked-yards lost	3-23	2-15
Punts	7-43	2-33
Fumbles-lost	0-0	2-1
Penalties-yards	2-15	6-50
Time of possession	22:03	37:57

INDIVIDUAL STATISTICS

RUSHING—San Francisco, Barlow 10-34, Gore 4-15, Battle 2-6, A. Smith 1-3. Philadelphia, Westbrook 15-89, Gordon 12-40, Mahe 2-12, McMahon 1-(minus 1).

PASSING—San Francisco, Rattay 13-26-3-107, A. Smith 0-1-0-0. Philadelphia, McNabb 23-29-0-342, Detmer 9-9-0-94, McMahon 1-1-0-22.

RECEIVING—San Francisco, Battle 4-44, Barlow 3-31, Lloyd 3-17, Jackson 1-8, Morton 1-4, Bush 1-3. Philadelphia, Smith 9-119, Owens 5-143, G. Lewis 4-39, R. Brown 3-37, Westbrook 3-31, Parry 3-20, Spach 2-14, McMullen 1-24, McCants 1-22, Mahe 1-6, Gordon 1-3.

MISSED FIELD GOAL ATTEMPTS—Philadelphia, Akers 43.

INTERCEPTIONS—Philadelphia, Sheppard 1-34, Hood 1-17, Dh. Jones 1-0.

KICKOFF RETURNS—San Francisco, Amey 4-71, Hicks 3-60. Philadelphia, Hood 1-22.

PUNT RETURNS—San Francisco, Amey 1-0. Philadelphia, Wynn 4-13.

SACKS—San Francisco, Douglas 1, A. Adams 1. Philadelphia, Sheppard 1, Kalu 1, Walker 1.

BEARS 38, LIONS 6
Sunday, September 18

Detroit	6	0	0	0— 6
Chicago	10	21	0	7—38

First Quarter
Chi.—T. Jones 3 run (Brien kick), 4:50.
Det.—R. Williams 51 pass from Harrington (kick blocked), 5:06.
Chi.—FG, Brien 48, 8:56.

Second Quarter
Chi.—Wade 73 punt return (Brien kick), 3:26.
Chi.—Muhammad 28 pass from Orton (Brien kick), 13:46.
Chi.—M. Brown 41 interception return (Brien kick), 14:03.

Fourth Quarter
Chi.—T. Jones 16 run (Brien kick), 2:47.
Attendance—62,019.

	Detroit	Chicago
First downs	14	18
Rushes-yards	17-29	37-187
Passing	205	149
Punt returns	2-20	3-87
Kickoff returns	6-159	2-67
Interception returns	0-0	5-88
Comp.-att.-int.	21-43-5	15-22-0
Sacked-yards lost	3-11	2-12
Punts	4-43	4-42
Fumbles-lost	0-0	0-0
Penalties-yards	3-30	6-40
Time of possession	26:48	33:12

INDIVIDUAL STATISTICS

RUSHING—Detroit, Jones 8-22, Bryson 4-5, P. Smith 2-11, Harrington 2-(minus 6), Drummond 1-(minus 3). Chicago, T. Jones 20-139, Benson 16-49, Blake 1-(minus 1).

PASSING—Detroit, Harrington 19-37-5-196, Orlovsky 2-6-0-20. Chicago, Orton 14-21-0-150, Blake 1-1-0-0.

RECEIVING—Detroit, K. Johnson 6-32, R. Williams 5-96, C. Rogers 3-31, Pollard 2-31, FitzSimmons 2-10, P. Smith 1-10, Jones 1-5, Bryson 1-1. Chicago, Muhammad 6-81, Clark 2-19, T. Jones 2-19, M. Edwards 2-10, Gage 1-21, Bradley 1-9, Wade 1-2.

MISSED FIELD GOAL ATTEMPTS—Chicago, Brien 48, 36.

INTERCEPTIONS—Chicago, Vasher 2-24, M. Brown 1-41, Briggs 1-20, Scott 1-3.

KICKOFF RETURNS—Detroit, Drummond 6-159. Chicago, Azumah 2-67.

PUNT RETURNS—Detroit, Drummond 2-20. Chicago, Wade 3-87.

SACKS—Detroit, Bailey 1, S. Rogers 1. Chicago, Urlacher 2, Azumah 1.

BENGALS 37, VIKINGS 8
Sunday, September 18

Minnesota	0	0	0	8— 8
Cincinnati	14	13	7	3—37

First Quarter
Cin.—C. Johnson 70 pass from Palmer (Graham kick), :52.
Cin.—Houshmandzadeh 12 pass from Palmer (Graham kick), 7:41.

Second Quarter
Cin.—FG, Graham 40, 9:58.
Cin.—FG, Graham 29, 11:41.
Cin.—Schobel 8 pass from Palmer (Graham kick), 14:48.

Third Quarter
Cin.—Houshmandzadeh 16 run (Graham kick), 12:54.

Fourth Quarter
Cin.—FG, Graham 30, 9:19.
Min.—Culpepper 5 run (M. Robinson pass from Culpepper), 11:43.
Attendance—65,763.

	Minnesota	Cincinnati
First downs	21	26
Rushes-yards	14-77	39-167
Passing	227	337
Punt returns	1-5	2-15
Kickoff returns	8-101	1-18
Interception returns	1-0	5-38
Comp.-att.-int.	21-37-5	27-40-1
Sacked-yards lost	2-9	0-0
Punts	3-47	3-42
Fumbles-lost	2-2	1-0
Penalties-yards	7-49	17-115
Time of possession	21:20	38:40

INDIVIDUAL STATISTICS

RUSHING—Minnesota, Moore 8-29, M. Bennett 3-36, Culpepper 2-10, M. Williams 1-2. Cincinnati, Ru. Johnson 22-90, C. Perry 9-47, Palmer 4-3, Houshmandzadeh 2-24, J. Johnson 2-3.

PASSING—Minnesota, Culpepper 21-37-5-236. Cincinnati, Palmer 27-40-1-337.

RECEIVING—Minnesota, T. Taylor 7-75, Burleson 3-48, Wiggins 3-17, Williamson 2-44, M. Robinson 2-40, Moore 2-7, Kleinsasser 1-6, M. Bennett 1-(minus 1). Cincinnati, C. Johnson 7-139, Houshmandzadeh 5-55, Henry 4-45, C. Perry 4-33, Schobel 2-36, R. Kelly 2-7, T. Perry 1-13, Walter 1-6, Ru. Johnson 1-3.

MISSED FIELD GOAL ATTEMPTS—None.

INTERCEPTIONS—Minnesota, Offord 1-0. Cincinnati, O'Neal 3-27, Kaesviharn 1-6, James 1-5.

KICKOFF RETURNS—Minnesota, Williamson 5-66, M. Williams 1-16, Henderson 1-13, Moore 1-6. Cincinnati, T. Perry 1-18.

PUNT RETURNS—Minnesota, Howry 1-5. Cincinnati, Ratliff 2-15.

SACKS—Cincinnati, J. Smith 1, Powell 1.

PANTHERS 27, PATRIOTS 17
Sunday, September 18

New England	7	0	10	0—17
Carolina	7	10	3	7—27

First Quarter
N.E.—Graham 1 pass from Brady (Vinatieri kick), 11:20.
Car.—S. Davis 1 run (Kasay kick), 13:47.

Second Quarter
Car.—FG, Kasay 51, 11:22.
Car.—S. Davis 1 run (Kasay kick), 13:15.

Third Quarter
Car.—FG, Kasay 52, 3:25.
N.E.—FG, Vinatieri 45, 8:35.
N.E.—Vrabel 24 interception return (Vinatieri kick), 8:52.

Fourth Quarter
Car.—S. Davis 1 run (Kasay kick), :14.
Attendance—73,528.

	New England	Carolina
First downs	14	17
Rushes-yards	16-39	36-104
Passing	249	146
Punt returns	1-0	6-128
Kickoff returns	6-146	4-105
Interception returns	1-24	1-0
Comp.-att.-int.	23-44-1	11-26-1
Sacked-yards lost	2-21	1-8
Punts	7-48	7-42
Fumbles-lost	2-2	0-0
Penalties-yards	12-86	6-45
Time of possession	28:01	31:59

INDIVIDUAL STATISTICS

RUSHING—New England, Dillon 14-36, Faulk 2-3. Carolina, S. Davis 25-77, Foster 7-37, Delhomme 3-(minus 2), Proehl 1-(minus 8).

PASSING—New England, Brady 23-44-1-270. Carolina, Delhomme 11-26-1-154.

RECEIVING—New England, Branch 8-60, Givens 5-56, T. Brown 3-87, Faulk 3-27, Dwight 2-32, Watson 1-7, Graham 1-1. Carolina, S. Smith 4-34, Proehl 3-63, Mangum 2-18, Foster 1-23, Goings 1-16.

MISSED FIELD GOAL ATTEMPTS—None.

INTERCEPTIONS—New England, Vrabel 1-24. Carolina, Witherspoon 1-0.

KICKOFF RETURNS—New England, Hobbs 5-123, Faulk 1-23. Carolina, Smart 4-105.

PUNT RETURNS—New England, Dwight 1-0. Carolina, S. Smith 5-52, Gamble 1-76.

SACKS—New England, Wilfork 0.5, Colvin 0.5. Carolina, Rucker 1, T. Davis 1.

TITANS 25, RAVENS 10
Sunday, September 18

Baltimore	0	0	3	7—10
Tennessee	7	6	3	9—25

First Quarter
Ten.—Fleming 2 pass from McNair (Bironas kick), 7:10.
Second Quarter
Ten.—FG, Bironas 39, 1:52.
Ten.—FG, Bironas 29, 14:59.
Third Quarter
Bal.—FG, Stover 30, 6:06.
Ten.—FG, Bironas 47, 7:50.
Fourth Quarter
Ten.—Kassell 21 interception return (Bironas kick), 3:07.
Bal.—Mason 12 pass from Wright (Stover kick), 8:36.
Ten.—Safety, 12:17.
Attendance—69,149.

	Baltimore	Tennessee
First downs	12	16
Rushes-yards	13-14	29-97
Passing	168	193
Punt returns	3-5	5-21
Kickoff returns	4-76	3-104
Interception returns	0-0	1-21
Comp.-att.-int.	25-41-1	19-37-0
Sacked-yards lost	6-44	1-2
Punts	10-38	8-45
Fumbles-lost	1-1	1-1
Penalties-yards	10-73	5-47
Time of possession	26:54	33:06

INDIVIDUAL STATISTICS

RUSHING—Baltimore, J. Lewis 10-9, C. Taylor 3-5. Tennessee, Henry 18-62, Brown 8-33, McNair 3-2.

PASSING—Baltimore, Wright 25-40-1-212, Hymes 0-1-0-0. Tennessee, McNair 19-36-0-195, Bennett 0-1-0-0.

RECEIVING—Baltimore, Mason 8-60, Heap 5-56, J. Lewis 4-32, C. Taylor 3-21, Clayton 2-17, Dinkins 2-14, Hymes 1-12. Tennessee, Bennett 3-52, Brown 3-25, Fleming 3-21, B. Jones 2-29, Calico 2-22, Kinney 2-13, Henry 2-4, Roby 1-24, Troupe 1-5.

MISSED FIELD GOAL ATTEMPTS—None.

INTERCEPTIONS—Tennessee, Kassell 1-21.

KICKOFF RETURNS—Baltimore, Sams 3-66, Dinkins 1-10. Tennessee, Roby 2-81, P. Jones 1-23.

PUNT RETURNS—Baltimore, Sams 3-5. Tennessee, Thurman 5-21.

SACKS—Baltimore, R. Green 1. Tennessee, Vanden Bosch 3, Bulluck 1, Sirmon 1, Starks 0.5, LaBoy 0.5.

SEAHAWKS 21, FALCONS 18
Sunday, September 18

Atlanta	0	0	10	8—18
Seattle	0	21	0	0—21

Second Quarter
Sea.—Jurevicius 6 pass from Hasselbeck (J. Brown kick), 6:36.
Sea.—Alexander 14 run (J. Brown kick), 11:04.
Sea.—Stevens 35 pass from Hasselbeck (J. Brown kick), 14:32.
Third Quarter
Atl.—Finneran 5 pass from Vick (T. Peterson kick), 4:46.
Atl.—FG, T. Peterson 30, 8:00.

Fourth Quarter
Atl.—Duckett 1 run (Crumpler pass from Schaub), 11:02.
Attendance—66,030.

	Atlanta	Seattle
First downs	14	24
Rushes-yards	28-115	34-163
Passing	108	265
Punt returns	2-29	3-19
Kickoff returns	4-81	3-58
Interception returns	0-0	0-0
Comp.-att.-int.	11-20-0	20-31-0
Sacked-yards lost	3-15	2-16
Punts	7-50	7-38
Fumbles-lost	1-0	1-1
Penalties-yards	3-24	10-79
Time of possession	23:25	36:35

INDIVIDUAL STATISTICS

RUSHING—Atlanta, Dunn 16-54, Vick 8-43, Duckett 4-18. Seattle, Alexander 28-144, Hasselbeck 4-9, Morris 2-10.

PASSING—Atlanta, Vick 11-19-0-123, Schaub 0-1-0-0. Seattle, Hasselbeck 20-31-0-281.

RECEIVING—Atlanta, Finneran 5-35, Crumpler 3-53, Jenkins 1-22, D. White 1-11, Griffith 1-2. Seattle, Jackson 8-131, Engram 5-77, Stevens 3-49, Alexander 2-11, Strong 1-7, Jurevicius 1-6.

MISSED FIELD GOAL ATTEMPTS—None.

INTERCEPTIONS—None.

KICKOFF RETURNS—Atlanta, Bryant 4-81. Seattle, Scobey 3-58.

PUNT RETURNS—Atlanta, D. Hall 1-27, Finneran 1-2. Seattle, Warrick 2-10, Engram 1-9.

SACKS—Atlanta, Brooking 1, Lavalais 1. Seattle, Tatupu 1, R. Bernard 1, B. Fisher 1.

BRONCOS 20, CHARGERS 17
Sunday, September 18

San Diego	0	14	0	3—17
Denver	3	0	7	10—20

First Quarter
Den.—FG, Elam 45, 12:02.
Second Quarter
S.D.—Tomlinson 16 run (Kaeding kick), 2:47.
S.D.—Tomlinson 4 run (Kaeding kick), 10:05.
Third Quarter
Den.—Bailey 25 interception return (Elam kick), :11.
Fourth Quarter
Den.—K. Johnson 3 run (Elam kick), 6:14.
S.D.—FG, Kaeding 42, 9:39.
Den.—FG, Elam 41, 14:55.
Attendance—75,310.

	San Diego	Denver
First downs	15	21
Rushes-yards	24-79	26-98
Passing	134	233
Punt returns	1-0	4-66
Kickoff returns	3-71	3-64
Interception returns	1-8	1-25
Comp.-att.-int.	15-23-1	23-37-1
Sacked-yards lost	4-41	3-15
Punts	6-46	3-44
Fumbles-lost	1-1	3-1
Penalties-yards	7-42	5-45
Time of possession	26:55	33:05

INDIVIDUAL STATISTICS

RUSHING—San Diego, Tomlinson 19-52, Neal 3-9, Sproles 1-12, Turner 1-6. Denver, Mi. Anderson 15-49, Dayne 8-44, Plummer 2-2, K. Johnson 1-3.

PASSING—San Diego, Brees 15-23-1-175. Denver, Plummer 23-37-1-248.

RECEIVING—San Diego, Gates 6-80, McCardell 4-54, E. Parker 3-30, Neal 1-6, Sproles 1-5. Denver, Smith 8-83, Lelie 6-62, Mi. Anderson 3-41, Adams 3-31, Putzier 1-16, Watts 1-10, S. Alexander 1-5.

MISSED FIELD GOAL ATTEMPTS—Denver, Elam 53, 53.

INTERCEPTIONS—San Diego, Jue 1-8. Denver, Bailey 1-25.

KICKOFF RETURNS—San Diego, Sproles 3-71. Denver, Da. Williams 3-64.

PUNT RETURNS—San Diego, Sproles 1-0. Denver, Da. Williams 4-66.

SACKS—San Diego, Kiel 1, Foley 1, Scott 1. Denver, Lynch 1, Gold 1, C. Brown 1, Veal 1.

RAMS 17, CARDINALS 12
Sunday, September 18

St. Louis	7	3	7	0—17
Arizona	3	3	3	3—12

First Quarter
St.L.—Holt 19 pass from Bulger (J. Wilkins kick), 3:18.
Ariz.—FG, Rackers 29, 9:22.

Second Quarter
Ariz.—FG, Rackers 26, 6:16.
St.L.—FG, J. Wilkins 29, 11:18.

Third Quarter
Ariz.—FG, Rackers 48, 4:37.
St.L.—S. Jackson 7 run (J. Wilkins kick), 9:15.

Fourth Quarter
Ariz.—FG, Rackers 35, 8:01.
Attendance—45,160.

	St. Louis	Arizona
First downs	16	18
Rushes-yards	22-108	16-82
Passing	189	297
Punt returns	3-14	3-19
Kickoff returns	1-25	4-83
Interception returns	1-0	1-14
Comp.-att.-int.	18-29-1	29-42-1
Sacked-yards lost	4-27	5-30
Punts	7-43	5-47
Fumbles-lost	1-0	3-1
Penalties-yards	4-30	8-72
Time of possession	28:51	31:09

INDIVIDUAL STATISTICS
RUSHING—St. Louis, S. Jackson 18-93, M. Faulk 3-15, Bulger 1-0. Arizona, Shipp 12-54, Fitzgerald 2-25, J. Jackson 1-3, Warner 1-0.
PASSING—St. Louis, Bulger 18-29-1-216. Arizona, Warner 29-42-1-327.
RECEIVING—St. Louis, Bruce 5-64, Holt 4-70, Curtis 2-29, S. Jackson 2-16, M. Faulk 2-8, Manumaleuna 1-13, McDonald 1-9, R. Williams 1-7. Arizona, Boldin 8-119, Shipp 5-39, Fitzgerald 4-76, Lee 4-40, O. Ayanbadejo 3-16, Bergen 2-15, B. Johnson 2-15, T. Johnson 1-13.
MISSED FIELD GOAL ATTEMPTS—None.
INTERCEPTIONS—St. Louis, Groce 1-0. Arizona, Dockett 1-14.
KICKOFF RETURNS—St. Louis, C. Johnson 1-25. Arizona, Swinton 4-83.
PUNT RETURNS—St. Louis, McDonald 3-14. Arizona, Swinton 3-19.
SACKS—St. Louis, Kennedy 2, Archuleta 1, Little 0.5, Pickett 0.5, Team 1. Arizona, Berry 2, Dansby 1, Okeafor 1.

JETS 17, DOLPHINS 7
Sunday, September 18

Miami	0	0	0	7— 7
N.Y. Jets	7	3	0	7—17

First Quarter
NYJ—Coles 7 pass from Pennington (Nugent kick), 5:28.

Second Quarter
NYJ—FG, Nugent 41, 13:58.

Fourth Quarter
Mia.—McMichael 4 pass from Frerotte (Mare kick), :47.
NYJ—Sowell 1 pass from Pennington (Nugent kick), 6:41.
Attendance—77,918.

	Miami	N.Y. Jets
First downs	15	20
Rushes-yards	18-66	34-98
Passing	169	173
Punt returns	5-26	3-12
Kickoff returns	4-73	0-0
Interception returns	0-0	1-1
Comp.-att.-int.	20-43-1	19-30-0
Sacked-yards lost	2-8	2-17
Punts	7-41	7-44
Fumbles-lost	3-0	3-0
Penalties-yards	10-88	5-40
Time of possession	26:01	33:59

INDIVIDUAL STATISTICS
RUSHING—Miami, Brown 12-35, Morris 4-23, Chambers 1-8, H. Evans 1-0. New York, C. Martin 31-72, Blaylock 2-14, Pennington 1-12.
PASSING—Miami, Frerotte 20-43-1-177. New York, Pennington 19-30-0-190.
RECEIVING—Miami, McMichael 8-77, Chambers 3-21, Diamond 3-14, Welker 2-21, Boston 2-18, Booker 1-21, Brown 1-5. New York, McCareins 5-87, Coles 5-68, Chrebet 3-22, Sowell 3-4, C. Martin 2-6, Baker 1-3.
MISSED FIELD GOAL ATTEMPTS—Miami, Mare 21.
INTERCEPTIONS—New York, Barrett 1-1.
KICKOFF RETURNS—Miami, Welker 4-73.
PUNT RETURNS—Miami, Welker 5-26. New York, Miller 2-12, McCareins 1-0.
SACKS—Miami, Seau 1, Carter 1. New York, J. Abraham 1, Ellis 1.

BROWNS 26, PACKERS 24
Sunday, September 18

Cleveland	7	6	6	7—26
Green Bay	7	0	0	17—24

First Quarter
G.B.—Driver 42 pass from Favre (Longwell kick), 5:12.
Cle.—Heiden 1 pass from Dilfer (Dawson kick), 11:12.

Second Quarter
Cle.—FG, Dawson 21, 1:13.
Cle.—FG, Dawson 39, 14:47.

Third Quarter
Cle.—Edwards 80 pass from Dilfer (kick blocked), 12:34.

Fourth Quarter
G.B.—FG, Longwell 34, 3:20.
G.B.—Ferguson 19 pass from Favre (Longwell kick), 11:20.
Cle.—Heiden 62 pass from Dilfer (Dawson kick), 13:10.
G.B.—Fisher 4 pass from Favre (Longwell kick), 14:56.
Attendance—70,400.

	Cleveland	Green Bay
First downs	19	27
Rushes-yards	23-55	30-116
Passing	336	336
Punt returns	1-(-11)	1-9
Kickoff returns	4-100	5-88
Interception returns	2-14	0-0
Comp.-att.-int.	21-32-0	32-44-2
Sacked-yards lost	0-0	1-6
Punts	4-45	3-34
Fumbles-lost	2-0	2-0
Penalties-yards	6-40	6-41
Time of possession	24:49	35:11

INDIVIDUAL STATISTICS
RUSHING—Cleveland, Droughns 20-50, Dilfer 3-5. Green Bay, Green 16-54, Davenport 8-36, Favre 3-19, Fisher 2-(minus 1), Chatman 1-8.
PASSING—Cleveland, Dilfer 21-32-0-336. Green Bay, Favre 32-44-2-342.
RECEIVING—Cleveland, Heiden 6-104, Droughns 4-29, Edwards 3-107, Northcutt 3-39, Bryant 3-32, Green 1-14, F. Jackson 1-11. Green Bay, Driver 6-105, Green 5-45, Henderson 5-27, Chatman 4-71, Ferguson 4-47, Murphy 3-23, Franks 3-15, Leach 1-5, Fisher 1-4.
MISSED FIELD GOAL ATTEMPTS—None.
INTERCEPTIONS—Cleveland, McCutcheon 1-14, Baxter 1-0.
KICKOFF RETURNS—Cleveland, Perkins 3-82, Green 1-18. Green Bay, Davenport 3-54, Carroll 2-34.
PUNT RETURNS—Cleveland, Northcutt 1-(minus 11). Green Bay, Chatman 1-9.
SACKS—Cleveland, Roye 1.

CHIEFS 23, RAIDERS 17
Sunday, September 18

Kansas City	7	10	3	3—23
Oakland	0	10	7	0—17

First Quarter
K.C.—Holmes 1 run (Tynes kick), 5:30.

Second Quarter
Oak.—Jordan 1 run (Janikowski kick), :03.
K.C.—L. Johnson 6 run (Tynes kick), 1:45.
Oak.—FG, Janikowski 29, 6:30.
K.C.—FG, Tynes 31, 12:34.

Third Quarter
Oak.—Moss 64 pass from Collins (Janikowski kick), 5:42.
K.C.—FG, Tynes 39, 15:00.

Fourth Quarter
K.C.—FG, Tynes 42, 6:14.
Attendance—62,273.

	Kansas City	Oakland
First downs	17	16
Rushes-yards	36-125	18-72
Passing	229	255
Punt returns	4-32	2-34
Kickoff returns	4-136	6-130
Interception returns	0-0	0-0
Comp.-att.-int.	18-28-0	21-35-0
Sacked-yards lost	1-8	2-8
Punts	3-40	4-51
Fumbles-lost	1-1	3-2
Penalties-yards	9-78	7-84
Time of possession	34:34	25:26

INDIVIDUAL STATISTICS

RUSHING—Kansas City, Holmes 19-75, L. Johnson 9-41, Green 4-2, D. Hall 2-(minus 7), Kennison 1-8, Wilson 1-6. Oakland, Jordan 15-59, Collins 2-11, Crockett 1-2.

PASSING—Kansas City, Green 18-28-0-237. Oakland, Collins 21-35-0-263.

RECEIVING—Kansas City, Gonzalez 5-44, Kennison 4-52, Parker 3-86, Holmes 3-15, Horn 2-25, D. Hall 1-15. Oakland, Jordan 6-32, Moss 5-127, Porter 5-68, Crockett 3-24, Curry 2-12.

MISSED FIELD GOAL ATTEMPTS—Kansas City, Tynes 46. Oakland, Janikowski 50.

INTERCEPTIONS—None.

KICKOFF RETURNS—Kansas City, D. Hall 4-136. Oakland, Carr 6-130.

PUNT RETURNS—Kansas City, D. Hall 4-32. Oakland, Carr 2-34.

SACKS—Kansas City, K. Mitchell 1, Sapp 1. Oakland, Burgess 1.

GIANTS 27, SAINTS 10
Monday, September 19

N.Y. Giants	14	7	3	3—27
New Orleans	0	10	0	0—10

First Quarter
NYG—Jacobs 1 run (Feely kick), 1:35.
NYG—Barber 6 pass from Manning (Feely kick), 10:47.

Second Quarter
N.O.—Horn 21 pass from Brooks (Carney kick), :49.
NYG—Barber 12 run (Feely kick), 13:06.
N.O.—FG, Carney 21, 14:55.

Third Quarter
NYG—FG, Feely 39, 7:12.

Fourth Quarter
NYG—FG, Feely 30, 8:23.
Attendance—68,031.

	N.Y. Giants	New Orleans
First downs	15	23
Rushes-yards	29-92	22-72
Passing	165	350
Punt returns	2-7	4-35
Kickoff returns	3-37	5-76
Interception returns	3-30	0-0
Comp.-att.-int.	13-24-0	27-45-3
Sacked-yards lost	0-0	4-25
Punts	5-46	3-40
Fumbles-lost	2-1	3-3
Penalties-yards	9-86	13-92
Time of possession	28:08	31:52

INDIVIDUAL STATISTICS

RUSHING—New York, Barber 22-83, Jacobs 3-5, Manning 3-0, Ponder 1-4. New Orleans, McAllister 15-47, A. Smith 4-15, Brooks 3-10.

PASSING—New York, Manning 13-24-0-165. New Orleans, Brooks 27-45-3-375.

RECEIVING—New York, Burress 5-64, Shockey 5-64, Toomer 2-31, Barber 1-6. New Orleans, Horn 9-143, Stallworth 8-141, McAllister 6-44, Henderson 3-42, Karney 1-5.

MISSED FIELD GOAL ATTEMPTS—New Orleans, Carney 29.

INTERCEPTIONS—New York, Alexander 1-24, Emmons 1-6, Williams 1-0.

KICKOFF RETURNS—New York, Jacobs 1-25, Ponder 1-10, K. Allen 1-2. New Orleans, M. Lewis 4-62, Whitehead 1-12.

PUNT RETURNS—New York, Morton 1-7, Butler 1-0. New Orleans, M. Lewis 3-8, Stallworth 1-27.

SACKS—New York, Umenyiora 2, Strahan 1, Clancy 1.

REDSKINS 14, COWBOYS 13
Monday, September 19

Washington	0	0	0	14—14
Dallas	0	3	7	3—13

Second Quarter
Dal.—FG, Cortez 33, 3:40.

Third Quarter
Dal.—T. Glenn 70 pass from Bledsoe (Cortez kick), 2:09.

Fourth Quarter
Dal.—FG, Cortez 41, 9:02.
Was.—Moss 39 pass from Brunell (Novak kick), 11:14.
Was.—Moss 70 pass from Brunell (Novak kick), 12:25.
Attendance—65,207.

	Washington	Dallas
First downs	14	14
Rushes-yards	25-104	29-90
Passing	242	261
Punt returns	1-9	4-29
Kickoff returns	4-82	3-94
Interception returns	0-0	1-12
Comp.-att.-int.	20-34-1	21-36-0
Sacked-yards lost	5-49	0-0
Punts	8-40	6-48
Fumbles-lost	1-1	3-0
Penalties-yards	12-80	7-60
Time of possession	27:53	32:07

INDIVIDUAL STATISTICS

RUSHING—Washington, Portis 17-52, Brunell 4-35, Betts 4-17. Dallas, J. Jones 22-81, Thompson 3-4, Bledsoe 2-5, A. Thomas 2-0.

PASSING—Washington, Brunell 20-34-1-291. Dallas, Bledsoe 21-36-0-261.

RECEIVING—Washington, Moss 5-159, Portis 4-25, Thrash 3-42, Royal 3-19, Cooley 2-20, Patten 1-12, Jacobs 1-9, Betts 1-5. Dallas, T. Glenn 6-157, Witten 4-35, J. Jones 4-24, K. Johnson 2-26, A. Thomas 2-5, Pierce 1-10, Crayton 1-5, P. Price 1-(minus 1).

MISSED FIELD GOAL ATTEMPTS—Dallas, Cortez 41.

INTERCEPTIONS—Dallas, Newman 1-12.

KICKOFF RETURNS—Washington, Betts 4-82. Dallas, Thompson 3-94.

PUNT RETURNS—Washington, Thrash 1-9. Dallas, Crayton 4-29.

SACKS—Dallas, Nguyen 1, Shanle 1, Ro. Williams 1, Canty 1, Ellis 0.5, Spears 0.5.

WEEK 3

STANDINGS

AMERICAN FOOTBALL CONFERENCE

EAST DIVISION

	W	L	T	Pct.	PF	PA
Miami	2	1	0	.667	68	51
New England	2	1	0	.667	70	67
Buffalo	1	2	0	.333	41	50
N.Y. Jets	1	2	0	.333	44	60

NORTH DIVISION

	W	L	T	Pct.	PF	PA
Cincinnati	3	0	0	1.000	88	28
Pittsburgh	2	1	0	.667	81	37
Cleveland	1	2	0	.333	45	64
Baltimore	0	2	0	.000	17	49

SOUTH DIVISION

	W	L	T	Pct.	PF	PA
Indianapolis	3	0	0	1.000	47	16
Jacksonville	2	1	0	.667	55	44
Tennessee	1	2	0	.333	59	75
Houston	0	2	0	.000	14	49

WEST DIVISION

	W	L	T	Pct.	PF	PA
Denver	2	1	0	.667	60	61
Kansas City	2	1	0	.667	60	54
San Diego	1	2	0	.333	86	71
Oakland	0	3	0	.000	57	76

NATIONAL FOOTBALL CONFERENCE

EAST DIVISION

	W	L	T	Pct.	PF	PA
Washington	2	0	0	1.000	23	20
Dallas	2	1	0	.667	75	69
N.Y. Giants	2	1	0	.667	92	74
Philadelphia	2	1	0	.667	75	37

NORTH DIVISION

	W	L	T	Pct.	PF	PA
Detroit	1	1	0	.500	23	41
Chicago	1	2	0	.333	52	39
Minnesota	1	2	0	.333	54	77
Green Bay	0	3	0	.000	43	60

SOUTH DIVISION

	W	L	T	Pct.	PF	PA
Tampa Bay	3	0	0	1.000	60	32
Atlanta	2	1	0	.667	56	47
Carolina	1	2	0	.333	71	67
New Orleans	1	2	0	.333	49	80

WEST DIVISION

	W	L	T	Pct.	PF	PA
Seattle	2	1	0	.667	72	56
St. Louis	2	1	0	.667	73	67
San Francisco	1	2	0	.333	62	101
Arizona	0	3	0	.000	43	96

TOP PERFORMANCES

100-YARD RUSHING GAMES

Player, team & opponent	Att.	Yds.	TD
LaDainian Tomlinson, S.D. vs. NYG	21	192	3
Carnell Williams, T.B. at G.B.	37	158	0
Shaun Alexander, Sea. vs. Ariz.	22	140	4
Willis McGahee, Buf. vs. Atl.	27	140	1
Ronnie Brown, Mia. vs. Car.	23	132	1
Edgerrin James, Ind. vs. Cle.	27	108	1
Thomas Jones, Chi. vs. Cin.	27	106	1
Mewelde Moore, Min. vs. N.O.	23	101	0

300-YARD PASSING GAMES

Player, team & opponent	Att.	Cmp.	Yds.	TD	Int.
Tom Brady, N.E. at Pit.	41	31	372	0	1
Donovan McNabb, Phi. vs. Oak.	52	30	365	2	1
Drew Bledsoe, Dal. at S.F.	38	24	363	2	2
Eli Manning, NYG at S.D.	41	24	352	2	0
Kerry Collins, Oak. at Phi.	42	24	345	2	0
Daunte Culpepper, Min. vs. N.O.	29	21	300	3	0

100-YARD RECEIVING GAMES

Player, team & opponent	Rec.	Yds.	TD
Steve Smith, Car. at Mia.	11	170	3
Torry Holt, St.L. vs. Ten.	9	163	1
Brandon Lloyd, S.F. vs. Dal.	4	142	2
Brian Westbrook, Phi. vs. Oak.	6	140	1
Terry Glenn, Dal. at S.F.	5	137	0
David Givens, N.E. at Pit.	9	130	0
Darrell Jackson, Sea. vs. Ariz.	8	125	0
Eddie Kennison, K.C. at Den.	8	112	0
Hines Ward, Pit. vs. N.E.	4	110	2
Jeremy Shockey, NYG at S.D.	6	101	0
Courtney Anderson, Oak. at Phi.	5	100	0

RESULTS

SUNDAY, SEPTEMBER 25
INDIANAPOLIS 13, Cleveland 6
Atlanta 24, BUFFALO 16
MIAMI 27, Carolina 24
Cincinnati 24, CHICAGO 7
Tampa Bay 17, GREEN BAY 16
MINNESOTA 33, New Orleans 16
ST. LOUIS 31, Tennessee 27
Jacksonville 26, N.Y. JETS 20 (OT)
PHILADELPHIA 23, Oakland 20
SEATTLE 37, Arizona 12
New England 23, PITTSBURGH 20
Dallas 34, SAN FRANCISCO 31
SAN DIEGO 45, N.Y. Giants 23

MONDAY, SEPTEMBER 26
DENVER 30, Kansas City 10
Open Date: Baltimore, Detroit, Houston, Washington

COLTS 13, BROWNS 6

Sunday, September 25

Cleveland	0	3	0	3— 6
Indianapolis	7	3	3	0—13

First Quarter
Ind.—James 2 run (Vanderjagt kick), 10:49.
Second Quarter
Cle.—FG, Dawson 40, 1:47.
Ind.—FG, Vanderjagt 20, 11:46.
Third Quarter
Ind.—FG, Vanderjagt 23, 7:53.
Fourth Quarter
Cle.—FG, Dawson 22, :51.
Attendance—57,127.

	Cleveland	Indianapolis
First downs	14	20
Rushes-yards	23-75	33-111
Passing	188	228
Punt returns	1-12	2-10
Kickoff returns	4-61	3-61
Interception returns	1-0	0-0
Comp.-att.-int.	22-29-0	19-23-1
Sacked-yards lost	4-20	0-0
Punts	5-42	3-40
Fumbles-lost	1-0	1-0
Penalties-yards	7-62	3-15
Time of possession	28:22	31:38

INDIVIDUAL STATISTICS
RUSHING—Cleveland, Droughns 22-76, Green 1-(minus 1). Indianapolis, James 27-108, Carthon 3-6, Manning 3-(minus 3).
PASSING—Cleveland, Dilfer 22-29-0-208. Indianapolis, Manning 19-23-1-228.
RECEIVING—Cleveland, Bryant 7-75, Edwards 4-43, Droughns 3-32, F. Jackson 2-29, Heiden 2-12, Suggs 2-7, Northcutt 1-7, Green 1-3. Indianapolis, Wayne 6-97, Harrison 6-53, James 2-29, Fletcher 2-26, Clark 2-14, Stokley 1-9.
MISSED FIELD GOAL ATTEMPTS—None.
INTERCEPTIONS—Cleveland, McCutcheon 1-0.
KICKOFF RETURNS—Cleveland, Green 4-61. Indianapolis, Carthon 3-61.
PUNT RETURNS—Cleveland, Northcutt 1-12. Indianapolis, Walters 2-10.
SACKS—Indianapolis, Freeney 3, Mathis 1.

FALCONS 24, BILLS 16

Sunday, September 25

Atlanta	7	10	0	7—24
Buffalo	3	10	3	0—16

First Quarter
Buf.—FG, Lindell 36, 5:28.
Atl.—Blakley 9 pass from Vick (T. Peterson kick), 11:16.
Second Quarter
Buf.—FG, Lindell 41, :15.
Atl.—Jenkins 15 pass from Vick (T. Peterson kick), 4:53.
Buf.—McGahee 8 run (Lindell kick), 11:05.
Atl.—FG, T. Peterson 27, 15:00.
Third Quarter
Buf.—FG, Lindell 30, 4:50.
Fourth Quarter
Atl.—Duckett 12 run (T. Peterson kick), 2:53.
Attendance—72,032.

	Atlanta	Buffalo
First downs	24	18
Rushes-yards	36-236	35-172
Passing	167	36
Punt returns	2-14	2-24
Kickoff returns	4-56	2-55
Interception returns	1-3	1-17
Comp.-att.-int.	15-27-1	10-23-1
Sacked-yards lost	0-0	4-39
Punts	4-36	3-47
Fumbles-lost	1-1	1-1
Penalties-yards	7-75	3-35
Time of possession	29:11	30:49

INDIVIDUAL STATISTICS
RUSHING—Atlanta, Dunn 15-97, Duckett 12-75, Vick 9-64. Buffalo, McGahee 27-140, Losman 5-20, S. Williams 2-11, J. Smith 1-1.
PASSING—Atlanta, Vick 15-27-1-167. Buffalo, Losman 10-23-1-75.
RECEIVING—Atlanta, Finneran 4-57, Jenkins 4-48, Crumpler 3-35, Blakley 2-11, Griffith 1-11, Dunn 1-5. Buffalo, Moulds 3-18, Reed 2-24, Evans 2-7, Aiken 1-12, Shelton 1-8, J. Smith 1-6.
MISSED FIELD GOAL ATTEMPTS—None.
INTERCEPTIONS—Atlanta, D. Hall 1-3. Buffalo, Kelsay 1-17.
KICKOFF RETURNS—Atlanta, Bryant 4-56. Buffalo, McGee 2-55.
PUNT RETURNS—Atlanta, D. Hall 1-10, Jenkins 1-4. Buffalo, J. Smith 2-24.
SACKS—Atlanta, R. Coleman 2, Davis 1, Kerney 0.5, Lavalais 0.5.

DOLPHINS 27, PANTHERS 24

Sunday, September 25

Carolina	3	14	0	7—24
Miami	14	7	0	6—27

First Quarter
Mia.—Brown 1 run (Mare kick), 4:51.
Car.—FG, Kasay 52, 7:49.
Mia.—McMichael 18 pass from Frerotte (Mare kick), 14:50.
Second Quarter
Car.—S. Smith 1 pass from Delhomme (Kasay kick), 9:16.
Mia.—Chambers 42 pass from Frerotte (Mare kick), 11:21.
Car.—S. Smith 3 pass from Delhomme (Kasay kick), 14:06.
Fourth Quarter
Mia.—FG, Mare 27, 7:28.
Car.—S. Smith 53 pass from Delhomme (Kasay kick), 7:48.
Mia.—FG, Mare 32, 14:56.
Attendance—72,288.

	Carolina	Miami
First downs	23	16
Rushes-yards	26-61	30-144
Passing	238	171
Punt returns	3-17	1-4
Kickoff returns	4-85	4-80
Interception returns	1-0	1-37
Comp.-att.-int.	19-35-1	14-33-1
Sacked-yards lost	4-47	0-0
Punts	5-45	6-45
Fumbles-lost	3-2	0-0
Penalties-yards	4-39	13-138
Time of possession	32:13	27:47

INDIVIDUAL STATISTICS
RUSHING—Carolina, S. Davis 16-36, Foster 8-27, S. Smith 2-(minus 2). Miami, Brown 23-132, Morris 5-10, Welker 1-5, Frerotte 1-(minus 3).
PASSING—Carolina, Delhomme 19-35-1-285. Miami, Frerotte 14-33-1-171.
RECEIVING—Carolina, S. Smith 11-170, Foster 3-48, Mangum 2-32, S. Davis 2-16, Proehl 1-19. Miami, Chambers 6-93, Booker 2-15, Morris 1-18, McMichael 1-18, Gilmore 1-12.
MISSED FIELD GOAL ATTEMPTS—None.
INTERCEPTIONS—Carolina, Gamble 1-0. Miami, Schulters 1-37.
KICKOFF RETURNS—Carolina, Smart 3-73, S. Smith 1-12. Miami, Welker 4-80.
PUNT RETURNS—Carolina, Gamble 2-17, S. Smith 1-0. Miami, Welker 1-4.
SACKS—Miami, Z. Thomas 1, Carter 1, Schulters 1, T. Jones 1.

BENGALS 24, BEARS 7

Sunday, September 25

Cincinnati	10	0	7	7—24
Chicago	0	0	0	7— 7

First Quarter
Cin.—C. Johnson 18 pass from Palmer (Graham kick), 1:14.
Cin.—FG, Graham 33, 9:29.
Third Quarter
Cin.—Henry 36 pass from Palmer (Graham kick), 7:57.
Fourth Quarter
Chi.—T. Jones 2 run (Brien kick), 1:30.
Cin.—C. Johnson 40 pass from Palmer (Graham kick), 3:04.
Attendance—62,045.

	Cincinnati	Chicago
First downs	11	16
Rushes-yards	34-83	28-106
Passing	161	149
Punt returns	3-17	4-12
Kickoff returns	2-56	5-88
Interception returns	5-2	0-0
Comp.-att.-int.	16-23-0	17-39-5
Sacked-yards lost	1-8	0-0
Punts	9-40	6-42
Fumbles-lost	2-1	4-1
Penalties-yards	9-77	7-88
Time of possession	31:08	28:52

INDIVIDUAL STATISTICS

RUSHING—Cincinnati, Ru. Johnson 25-84, Palmer 6-(minus 3), C. Perry 1-2, J. Johnson 1-1, C. Johnson 1-(minus 1). Chicago, T. Jones 27-106, Orton 1-0.

PASSING—Cincinnati, Palmer 16-23-0-169. Chicago, Orton 17-39-5-149.

RECEIVING—Cincinnati, Henry 4-51, C. Johnson 3-77, C. Perry 3-20, Houshmandzadeh 2-13, Ru. Johnson 2-(minus 2), Stewart 1-6, Schobel 1-4. Chicago, T. Jones 5-8, Muhammad 4-58, Wade 4-47, Bradley 2-26, Peterson 1-7, M. Edwards 1-3.

MISSED FIELD GOAL ATTEMPTS—Chicago, Brien 39.

INTERCEPTIONS—Cincinnati, M. Williams 1-2, Ratliff 1-1, James 1-0, O'Neal 1-0, Simmons 1-(minus 1).

KICKOFF RETURNS—Cincinnati, T. Perry 2-56. Chicago, Azumah 5-88.

PUNT RETURNS—Cincinnati, Ratliff 3-17. Chicago, Wade 4-12.

SACKS—Chicago, Ogunleye 1.

BUCCANEERS 17, PACKERS 16
Sunday, September 25

Tampa Bay	7	10	0	0—17
Green Bay	6	7	0	3—16

First Quarter
T.B.—Galloway 5 pass from Griese (M. Bryant kick), 9:52.
G.B.—Ferguson 37 pass from Favre (kick failed), 12:54.

Second Quarter
T.B.—Galloway 10 pass from Griese (M. Bryant kick), 4:25.
T.B.—FG, M. Bryant 42, 8:12.
G.B.—Chatman 20 pass from Favre (Longwell kick), 10:33.

Fourth Quarter
G.B.—FG, Longwell 32, 7:42.
Attendance—70,518.

	Tampa Bay	Green Bay
First downs	19	15
Rushes-yards	41-161	25-75
Passing	132	185
Punt returns	2-23	3-23
Kickoff returns	4-68	4-86
Interception returns	3-29	1-38
Comp.-att.-int.	17-26-1	14-24-3
Sacked-yards lost	2-7	2-10
Punts	6-47	2-49
Fumbles-lost	1-0	1-1
Penalties-yards	8-103	8-65
Time of possession	34:22	25:38

INDIVIDUAL STATISTICS

RUSHING—Tampa Bay, C. Williams 37-158, Griese 3-0, Pittman 1-3. Green Bay, Green 19-58, Davenport 3-5, Chatman 1-10, Favre 1-7, Henderson 1-(minus 5).

PASSING—Tampa Bay, Griese 17-26-1-139. Green Bay, Favre 14-24-3-195.

RECEIVING—Tampa Bay, Galloway 5-53, Clayton 5-44, I. Hilliard 2-14, Cook 1-11, Becht 1-9, Alstott 1-4, Smith 1-4, C. Williams 1-0. Green Bay, Ferguson 4-68, Green 3-27, Driver 2-49, Chatman 2-37, Henderson 2-4, D. Martin 1-10.

MISSED FIELD GOAL ATTEMPTS—Green Bay, Longwell 42.

INTERCEPTIONS—Tampa Bay, Allen 2-26, Kelly 1-3. Green Bay, Carroll 1-38.

KICKOFF RETURNS—Tampa Bay, Cox 4-68. Green Bay, Murphy 2-54, Davenport 2-32.

PUNT RETURNS—Tampa Bay, Jones 2-23. Green Bay, Chatman 3-23.

SACKS—Tampa Bay, Nece 1, Spires 1. Green Bay, Kampman 1, Team 1.

VIKINGS 33, SAINTS 16
Sunday, September 25

New Orleans	0	6	3	7—16
Minnesota	17	7	0	9—33

First Quarter
Min.—T. Taylor 24 pass from Culpepper (Edinger kick), :13.
Min.—FG, Edinger 24, 7:42.
Min.—T. Taylor 13 pass from Culpepper (Edinger kick), 14:27.

Second Quarter
Min.—Williamson 53 pass from Culpepper (Edinger kick), 9:23.
N.O.—Conwell 13 pass from Brooks (pass failed), 13:06.

Third Quarter
N.O.—FG, Carney 22, 9:22.

Fourth Quarter
N.O.—McAllister 1 run (Carney kick), 3:20.
Min.—FG, Edinger 28, 8:43.
Min.—FG, Edinger 48, 10:31.
Min.—FG, Edinger 34, 13:52.
Attendance—63,952.

	New Orleans	Minnesota
First downs	15	21
Rushes-yards	20-114	39-146
Passing	182	274
Punt returns	3-9	3-8
Kickoff returns	8-193	4-91
Interception returns	0-0	2-2
Comp.-att.-int.	12-32-2	21-29-0
Sacked-yards lost	3-17	6-26
Punts	6-42	5-48
Fumbles-lost	2-2	0-0
Penalties-yards	14-84	8-60
Time of possession	21:47	38:13

INDIVIDUAL STATISTICS

RUSHING—New Orleans, McAllister 14-63, Brooks 3-29, A. Smith 3-22. Minnesota, Moore 23-101, Culpepper 9-35, M. Williams 4-2, M. Bennett 2-4, K. Robinson 1-4.

PASSING—New Orleans, Brooks 12-32-2-199. Minnesota, Culpepper 21-29-0-300.

RECEIVING—New Orleans, McAllister 4-19, Henderson 3-95, Conwell 3-65, Horn 1-11, Poole 1-9. Minnesota, Wiggins 6-60, Williamson 3-83, T. Taylor 3-40, M. Williams 3-4, M. Robinson 2-80, Owens 2-18, Kleinsasser 1-12, Moore 1-3.

MISSED FIELD GOAL ATTEMPTS—Minnesota, Edinger 33.

INTERCEPTIONS—Minnesota, Winfield 1-1, Newman 1-1.

KICKOFF RETURNS—New Orleans, McAfee 7-184, Stecker 1-9. Minnesota, K. Robinson 4-91.

PUNT RETURNS—New Orleans, Stallworth 3-9. Minnesota, Howry 3-8.

SACKS—New Orleans, Bryant 2.5, F. Thomas 2, Watson 1, Howard 0.5. Minnesota, Johnstone 1, Udeze 1, Newman 0.5, Scott 0.5.

RAMS 31, TITANS 27
Sunday, September 25

Tennessee	10	0	14	3—27
St. Louis	0	17	7	7—31

First Quarter
Ten.—Troupe 16 pass from McNair (Bironas kick), 8:39.
Ten.—FG, Bironas 41, 10:59.

Second Quarter
St.L.—Archuleta 85 interception return (J. Wilkins kick), 2:32.
St.L.—FG, J. Wilkins 46, 7:05.
St.L.—M. Faulk 13 pass from Bulger (J. Wilkins kick), 12:52.

Third Quarter
St.L.—Holt 32 pass from Bulger (J. Wilkins kick), 5:30.
Ten.—B. Jones 4 pass from McNair (Bironas kick), 11:38.
Ten.—Odom 25 fumble return (Bironas kick), 12:23.

Fourth Quarter
St.L.—Curtis 10 pass from Bulger (J. Wilkins kick), :06.
Ten.—FG, Bironas 39, 8:58.
Attendance—65,835.

	Tennessee	St. Louis
First downs	18	22
Rushes-yards	24-87	21-101
Passing	248	259
Punt returns	1-0	1-1
Kickoff returns	4-109	4-94
Interception returns	1-1	2-109
Comp.-att.-int.	24-39-2	21-28-1
Sacked-yards lost	2-13	4-33
Punts	5-43	4-43
Fumbles-lost	1-1	4-3
Penalties-yards	11-80	11-75
Time of possession	32:50	27:10

INDIVIDUAL STATISTICS

RUSHING—Tennessee, Brown 20-83, Henry 3-0, McNair 1-4. St. Louis, S. Jackson 12-48, M. Faulk 6-50, Bulger 3-3.

PASSING—Tennessee, McNair 24-39-2-261. St. Louis, Bulger 21-28-1-292.

RECEIVING—Tennessee, Kinney 7-64, Bennett 6-96, B. Jones 5-40, Troupe 2-22, Brown 2-5, Calico 1-18, Henry 1-16. St. Louis, Holt 9-163, Curtis 5-56, M. Faulk 3-31, Looker 2-25, Bruce 1-11, S. Jackson 1-6.

MISSED FIELD GOAL ATTEMPTS—None.

INTERCEPTIONS—Tennessee, Ta. Williams 1-1. St. Louis, Archuleta 1-85, Hawthorne 1-24.

KICKOFF RETURNS—Tennessee, P. Jones 4-109. St. Louis, C. Johnson 4-94.

PUNT RETURNS—Tennessee, Thurman 1-0. St. Louis, McDonald 1-1.

SACKS—Tennessee, Vanden Bosch 2, LaBoy 1, Starks 1. St. Louis, Little 1, Green 1.

JAGUARS 26, JETS 20

Sunday, September 25

Jacksonville	3	7	3	7	6—26
N.Y. Jets	0	7	7	6	0—20

First Quarter
Jac.—FG, Scobee 32, 10:23.

Second Quarter
Jac.—Wilford 21 pass from Leftwich (Scobee kick), 9:10.
NYJ—Sowell 1 run (Nugent kick), 13:09.

Third Quarter
NYJ—Reed 33 fumble return (Nugent kick), 2:43.
Jac.—FG, Scobee 40, 9:55.

Fourth Quarter
Jac.—F. Taylor 3 run (Scobee kick), :03.
NYJ—FG, Nugent 35, 5:17.
NYJ—FG, Nugent 25, 13:46.

Overtime
Jac.—J. Smith 36 pass from Leftwich, 6:05.
Attendance—77,422.

	Jacksonville	N.Y. Jets
First downs	16	12
Rushes-yards	47-139	25-89
Passing	169	79
Punt returns	5-31	3-(-3)
Kickoff returns	4-93	3-75
Interception returns	2-9	1-0
Comp.-att.-int.	16-24-1	11-22-2
Sacked-yards lost	2-8	4-16
Punts	6-50	7-49
Fumbles-lost	3-2	3-1
Penalties-yards	9-85	6-44
Time of possession	40:31	25:34

INDIVIDUAL STATISTICS

RUSHING—Jacksonville, F. Taylor 37-98, Pearman 4-22, G. Jones 4-7, Leftwich 2-12. New York, C. Martin 18-67, Pennington 3-15, Blaylock 3-6, Sowell 1-1.

PASSING—Jacksonville, Leftwich 16-23-1-177, M. Jones 0-1-0-0. New York, Pennington 9-19-2-76, Fiedler 2-3-0-19.

RECEIVING—Jacksonville, R. Williams 5-54, M. Jones 4-31, J. Smith 2-41, Wilford 2-35, B. Jones 2-8, Pearman 1-8. New York, Coles 4-17, Baker 3-45, C. Martin 2-4, McCareins 1-16, Chrebet 1-13.

MISSED FIELD GOAL ATTEMPTS—None.

INTERCEPTIONS—Jacksonville, Mathis 1-9, D. Cooper 1-0. New York, Rhodes 1-0.

KICKOFF RETURNS—Jacksonville, Wimbush 4-93. New York, Miller 3-75.

PUNT RETURNS—Jacksonville, Pearman 4-32, Mathis 1-(minus 1). New York, Miller 3-(minus 3).

SACKS—Jacksonville, Spicer 3, Hayward 1. New York, J. Abraham 1, B. Thomas 1.

EAGLES 23, RAIDERS 20

Sunday, September 25

Oakland	7	3	0	10—20
Philadelphia	0	6	14	3—23

First Quarter
Oak.—Jordan 8 pass from Collins (Janikowski kick), 2:38.

Second Quarter
Phi.—Westbrook 18 run (kick blocked), 10:27.
Oak.—FG, Janikowski 28, 14:11.

Third Quarter
Phi.—Owens 4 pass from McNabb (Akers kick), 4:40.
Phi.—Westbrook 5 pass from McNabb (Akers kick), 14:15.

Fourth Quarter
Oak.—FG, Janikowski 26, 2:06.
Oak.—Gabriel 27 pass from Collins (Janikowski kick), 12:43.
Phi.—FG, Akers 23, 14:51.
Attendance—67,735.

	Oakland	Philadelphia
First downs	18	26
Rushes-yards	22-21	18-83
Passing	344	365
Punt returns	5-17	3-17
Kickoff returns	4-44	4-98
Interception returns	1-3	0-0
Comp.-att.-int.	24-42-0	30-52-1
Sacked-yards lost	1-1	1-0
Punts	6-45	7-37
Fumbles-lost	2-0	1-1
Penalties-yards	13-94	9-70
Time of possession	29:57	30:03

INDIVIDUAL STATISTICS

RUSHING—Oakland, Jordan 16-19, Crockett 3-9, Fargas 1-2, Collins 1-(minus 1), Porter 1-(minus 8). Philadelphia, Westbrook 13-68, McNabb 3-8, G. Lewis 1-8, Gordon 1-(minus 1).

PASSING—Oakland, Collins 24-42-0-345. Philadelphia, McNabb 30-52-1-365.

RECEIVING—Oakland, C. Anderson 5-100, Moss 5-86, Jordan 5-53, Porter 5-40, Gabriel 2-35, Whitted 2-31. Philadelphia, Owens 9-80, Westbrook 6-140, G. Lewis 6-70, Smith 5-50, Gordon 3-19, R. Brown 1-6.

MISSED FIELD GOAL ATTEMPTS—Oakland, Janikowski 49, 37.

INTERCEPTIONS—Oakland, Sapp 1-3.

KICKOFF RETURNS—Oakland, Carr 3-35, Gabriel 1-9. Philadelphia, Wynn 3-72, Hood 1-26.

PUNT RETURNS—Oakland, Carr 4-17, C. Woodson 1-0. Philadelphia, Wynn 3-17.

SACKS—Oakland, Grant 1. Philadelphia, Patterson 1.

SEAHAWKS 37, CARDINALS 12

Sunday, September 25

Arizona	3	6	3	0—12
Seattle	7	3	14	13—37

First Quarter
Ariz.—FG, Rackers 54, 5:14.
Sea.—Alexander 25 run (J. Brown kick), 10:40.

Second Quarter
Ariz.—FG, Rackers 39, :53.
Sea.—FG, J. Brown 33, 8:17.
Ariz.—FG, Rackers 50, 11:19.

Third Quarter
Sea.—Alexander 1 run (J. Brown kick), 3:09.
Sea.—Alexander 1 run (J. Brown kick), 3:39.
Ariz.—FG, Rackers 39, 9:54.

Fourth Quarter
Sea.—Alexander 1 run (J. Brown kick), :04.
Sea.—FG, J. Brown 23, 6:10.
Sea.—FG, J. Brown 47, 13:32.
Attendance—64,843.

	Arizona	Seattle
First downs	15	29
Rushes-yards	21-90	37-163
Passing	176	284
Punt returns	2-16	4-14
Kickoff returns	8-142	2-57
Interception returns	0-0	1-17
Comp.-att.-int.	18-36-1	21-32-0
Sacked-yards lost	3-26	0-0
Punts	5-49	4-36
Fumbles-lost	2-1	0-0
Penalties-yards	12-71	3-25
Time of possession	26:31	33:29

INDIVIDUAL STATISTICS

RUSHING—Arizona, Shipp 10-41, Arrington 5-9, Boldin 2-18, Fitzgerald 2-(minus 1), Warner 1-13, McCown 1-10. Seattle, Alexander 22-140, Morris 11-4, Strong 2-11, Weaver 2-8.

PASSING—Arizona, McCown 10-23-1-97, Warner 8-13-0-105. Seattle, Hasselbeck 20-31-0-242, S. Wallace 1-1-0-42.

RECEIVING—Arizona, Boldin 6-88, Fitzgerald 3-41, Lee 3-29, Shipp 2-16, Johnson 1-10, Bergen 1-9, O. Ayanbadejo 1-5, Arrington 1-4. Seattle, ackson 8-125, Engram 5-54, Stevens 3-34, Jurevicius 2-16, Warrick 1-42, trong 1-8, Hannam 1-5.

MISSED FIELD GOAL ATTEMPTS—None.

INTERCEPTIONS—Seattle, Babineaux 1-17.

KICKOFF RETURNS—Arizona, Swinton 5-83, B. Johnson 2-45, J. Jackson -14. Seattle, Scobey 2-57.

PUNT RETURNS—Arizona, Swinton 2-16. Seattle, Warrick 3-14, J. illiams 1-0.

SACKS—Seattle, Hill 1, Boulware 1, B. Fisher 1.

PATRIOTS 23, STEELERS 20
Sunday, September 25

ew England	7	0	3	13—23
ittsburgh	10	0	3	7—20

First Quarter
.E.—Dillon 4 run (Vinatieri kick), 5:13.
it.—Ward 85 pass from Roethlisberger (Reed kick), 5:28.
it.—FG, Reed 33, 10:18.

Third Quarter
it.—FG, Reed 24, 8:52.
.E.—FG, Vinatieri 48, 14:46.

Fourth Quarter
.E.—Dillon 7 run (Vinatieri kick), 4:23.
.E.—FG, Vinatieri 35, 11:41.
it.—Ward 4 pass from Roethlisberger (Reed kick), 13:39.
.E.—FG, Vinatieri 43, 14:59.
Attendance—64,868.

	New England	Pittsburgh
irst downs	24	14
ushes-yards	30-80	23-79
assing	346	190
unt returns	4-55	3-20
ickoff returns	5-128	4-79
iterception returns	0-0	1-5
omp.-att.-int.	31-41-1	12-28-0
acked-yards lost	3-26	4-26
unts	4-45	6-44
umbles-lost	3-2	1-1
enalties-yards	10-118	5-35
ime of possession	35:23	24:37

INDIVIDUAL STATISTICS

RUSHING—New England, Dillon 22-61, Faulk 7-14, Pass 1-5. Pittsburgh, arker 17-55, Roethlisberger 3-17, Haynes 2-7, Wilson 1-0.

PASSING—New England, Brady 31-41-1-372. Pittsburgh, Roethlisberger 2-28-0-216.

RECEIVING—New England, Givens 9-130, Faulk 7-71, Branch 6-78, T. rown 4-43, Dillon 2-23, Pass 1-14, Watson 1-10, B. Johnson 1-3. ittsburgh, Ward 4-110, Randle El 2-56, Wilson 2-16, Haynes 1-18, Miller 1-3, Morgan 1-9, Parker 1-(minus 6).

MISSED FIELD GOAL ATTEMPTS—New England, Vinatieri 53. Pittsburgh, eed 52.

INTERCEPTIONS—Pittsburgh, Hope 1-5.

KICKOFF RETURNS—New England, B. Johnson 3-69, Hobbs 2-59. ittsburgh, Colclough 3-81, J. Harrison 1-(minus 2).

PUNT RETURNS—New England, Dwight 4-55. Pittsburgh, Randle El 3-0.

SACKS—New England, McGinest 2, Seymour 2. Pittsburgh, Farrior 1, aggans 1, J. Harrison 1.

COWBOYS 34, 49ERS 31
Sunday, September 25

allas	0	12	7	15—34
an Francisco	7	17	7	0—31

First Quarter
.F.—Battle 15 pass from Rattay (Nedney kick), 11:31.

Second Quarter
al.—Bledsoe 6 run (kick failed), 6:14.
.F.—Lloyd 89 pass from Rattay (Nedney kick), 7:17.
.F.—Parrish 34 interception return (Nedney kick), 8:18.
al.—Witten 6 pass from Bledsoe (pass failed), 11:27.
.F.—FG, Nedney 20, 14:45.

Third Quarter
al.—J. Jones 1 run (Cortez kick), 5:36.
.F.—Lloyd 13 pass from Rattay (Nedney kick), 14:20.

Fourth Quarter
Dal.—J. Jones 1 run (Cortez kick), :09.
Dal.—K. Johnson 14 pass from Bledsoe (K. Johnson pass from Bledsoe), 13:09.
Attendance—68,247.

	Dallas	San Francisco
First downs	26	19
Rushes-yards	32-95	25-124
Passing	348	266
Punt returns	2-8	1-10
Kickoff returns	6-114	5-94
Interception returns	2-7	2-34
Comp.-att.-int.	24-38-2	21-34-2
Sacked-yards lost	2-15	2-3
Punts	3-42	5-40
Fumbles-lost	2-1	2-1
Penalties-yards	6-45	8-67
Time of possession	32:05	27:55

INDIVIDUAL STATISTICS

RUSHING—Dallas, J. Jones 26-85, Bledsoe 3-5, Thompson 1-3, Polite 1-2, Crayton 1-0. San Francisco, Barlow 12-65, Gore 7-42, Rattay 4-21, Battle 2-(minus 4).

PASSING—Dallas, Bledsoe 24-38-2-363. San Francisco, Rattay 21-34-2-269.

RECEIVING—Dallas, Witten 6-85, T. Glenn 5-137, K. Johnson 5-74, Crayton 4-39, J. Jones 4-28. San Francisco, Battle 6-68, Lloyd 4-142, Barlow 4-28, Morton 4-19, Hetherington 1-7, Gore 1-5, T. Smith 1-0.

MISSED FIELD GOAL ATTEMPTS—None.

INTERCEPTIONS—Dallas, Nguyen 1-7, Singleton 1-0. San Francisco, Parrish 2-34.

KICKOFF RETURNS—Dallas, Thompson 5-103, Copper 1-11. San Francisco, Hicks 3-66, Amey 2-28.

PUNT RETURNS—Dallas, Crayton 2-8. San Francisco, Amey 1-10.

SACKS—Dallas, Ellis 1, Ware 1. San Francisco, Young 1, B. Moore 1.

CHARGERS 45, GIANTS 23
Sunday, September 25

N.Y. Giants	3	17	0	3—23
San Diego	7	14	14	10—45

First Quarter
NYG—FG, Feely 22, 6:32.
S.D.—Tomlinson 1 run (Kaeding kick), 10:37.

Second Quarter
S.D.—McCardell 15 pass from Brees (Kaeding kick), 1:55.
S.D.—Tomlinson 3 run (Kaeding kick), 5:25.
NYG—Burress 5 pass from Manning (Feely kick), 11:26.
NYG—Tyree 4 pass from Manning (Feely kick), 13:05.
NYG—FG, Feely 40, 14:49.

Third Quarter
S.D.—McCardell 26 pass from Tomlinson (Kaeding kick), 1:52.
S.D.—Gates 14 pass from Brees (Kaeding kick), 12:01.

Fourth Quarter
NYG—FG, Feely 28, 2:46.
S.D.—Tomlinson 5 run (Kaeding kick), 6:30.
S.D.—FG, Kaeding 44, 11:05.
Attendance—65,373.

	N.Y. Giants	San Diego
First downs	23	25
Rushes-yards	23-86	33-268
Passing	338	217
Punt returns	1-(-2)	2-10
Kickoff returns	7-161	5-134
Interception returns	0-0	0-0
Comp.-att.-int.	24-41-0	20-23-0
Sacked-yards lost	2-14	0-0
Punts	4-44	2-43
Fumbles-lost	2-1	1-1
Penalties-yards	12-83	7-50
Time of possession	29:55	30:05

INDIVIDUAL STATISTICS

RUSHING—New York, Barber 15-60, Ward 4-13, Manning 3-13, Jacobs 1-0. San Diego, Tomlinson 21-192, Turner 7-12, Neal 2-14, E. Parker 1-30, Sproles 1-21, Brees 1-(minus 1).

PASSING—New York, Manning 24-41-0-352. San Diego, Brees 19-22-0-191, Tomlinson 1-1-0-26.

RECEIVING—New York, Shockey 6-101, Tyree 5-52, Burress 5-52, Toomer 4-84, T. Carter 2-53, Shiancoe 1-5, Barber 1-5. San Diego, Gates 6-

92, Tomlinson 6-28, McCardell 4-80, E. Parker 2-12, Neal 1-4, Peelle 1-1.
MISSED FIELD GOAL ATTEMPTS—None.
INTERCEPTIONS—None.
KICKOFF RETURNS—New York, Ponder 6-156, Shiancoe 1-5. San Diego, Sproles 4-134, Turner 1-0.
PUNT RETURNS—New York, Morton 1-(minus 2). San Diego, Sproles 2-10.
SACKS—San Diego, Edwards 1, Harris 1.

BRONCOS 30, CHIEFS 10
Monday, September 26

Kansas City	0	3	0	7—10
Denver	17	3	7	3—30

First Quarter
Den.—FG, Elam 30, 7:10.
Den.—Mi. Anderson 44 run (Elam kick), 11:31.
Den.—Smith 12 pass from Plummer (Elam kick), 12:24.
Second Quarter
Den.—FG, Elam 51, 9:01.
K.C.—FG, Tynes 28, 14:36.
Third Quarter
Den.—Plummer 1 run (Elam kick), 6:26.
Fourth Quarter
Den.—FG, Elam 25, 2:30.
K.C.—Parker 21 pass from Green (Tynes kick), 13:00.
Attendance—76,381.

	Kansas City	Denver
First downs	18	24
Rushes-yards	22-74	37-221
Passing	211	137
Punt returns	1-10	2-1
Kickoff returns	5-125	1-32
Interception returns	0-0	0-0
Comp.-att.-int.	23-44-0	13-18-0
Sacked-yards lost	2-10	1-15
Punts	6-38	1-55
Fumbles-lost	1-1	2-0
Penalties-yards	13-118	4-30
Time of possession	29:52	30:08

INDIVIDUAL STATISTICS
RUSHING—Kansas City, Holmes 14-61, L. Johnson 8-13. Denver, Mi Anderson 20-98, Bell 5-47, Plummer 5-9, Dayne 3-6, Lelie 2-56, K. Johnson 2-5.
PASSING—Kansas City, Green 23-44-0-221. Denver, Plummer 13-18-0 152.
RECEIVING—Kansas City, Kennison 8-112, Gonzalez 5-29, Holmes 3-33 D. Hall 3-18, Parker 2-21, Wilson 1-6, Richardson 1-3. Denver, Smith 7-88 Adams 2-23, Lelie 1-16, Sapp 1-12, Watts 1-12, S. Alexander 1-9.
MISSED FIELD GOAL ATTEMPTS—Denver, Elam 46.
INTERCEPTIONS—None.
KICKOFF RETURNS—Kansas City, D. Hall 5-125. Denver, Da. Williams 1 32.
PUNT RETURNS—Kansas City, D. Hall 1-10. Denver, Da. Williams 1-1 Adams 1-0.
SACKS—Kansas City, Hicks 1. Denver, Ekuban 1, Warren 1.

STANDINGS

AMERICAN FOOTBALL CONFERENCE

EAST DIVISION
	W	L	T	Pct.	PF	PA
Miami	2	1	0	.667	68	51
New England	2	2	0	.500	87	108
Buffalo	1	3	0	.250	48	69
N.Y. Jets	1	3	0	.250	47	73

NORTH DIVISION
	W	L	T	Pct.	PF	PA
Cincinnati	4	0	0	1.000	104	38
Pittsburgh	2	1	0	.667	81	37
Baltimore	1	2	0	.333	30	52
Cleveland	1	2	0	.333	45	64

SOUTH DIVISION
	W	L	T	Pct.	PF	PA
Indianapolis	4	0	0	1.000	78	26
Jacksonville	2	2	0	.500	62	64
Tennessee	1	3	0	.250	69	106
Houston	0	3	0	.000	24	65

WEST DIVISION
	W	L	T	Pct.	PF	PA
Denver	3	1	0	.750	80	68
Kansas City	2	2	0	.500	91	91
San Diego	2	2	0	.500	127	88
Oakland	1	3	0	.250	76	89

NATIONAL FOOTBALL CONFERENCE

EAST DIVISION
	W	L	T	Pct.	PF	PA
Washington	3	0	0	1.000	43	37
N.Y. Giants	3	1	0	.750	136	98
Philadelphia	3	1	0	.750	112	68
Dallas	2	2	0	.500	88	88

NORTH DIVISION
	W	L	T	Pct.	PF	PA
Chicago	1	2	0	.333	52	39
Detroit	1	2	0	.333	36	58
Minnesota	1	3	0	.250	64	107
Green Bay	0	4	0	.000	72	92

SOUTH DIVISION
	W	L	T	Pct.	PF	PA
Tampa Bay	4	0	0	1.000	77	45
Atlanta	3	1	0	.750	86	57
Carolina	2	2	0	.500	103	96
New Orleans	2	2	0	.500	68	87

WEST DIVISION
	W	L	T	Pct.	PF	PA
Seattle	2	2	0	.500	89	76
St. Louis	2	2	0	.500	97	111
Arizona	1	3	0	.250	74	110
San Francisco	1	3	0	.250	76	132

TOP PERFORMANCES

100-YARD RUSHING GAMES
Player, team & opponent	Att.	Yds.	TD
LaDainian Tomlinson, S.D. at N.E.	25	134	2
Deuce McAllister, N.O. vs. Buf.	27	130	0
Tiki Barber, NYG vs. St.L.	24	128	1
Warrick Dunn, Atl. vs. Min.	18	126	1
LaMont Jordan, Oak. vs. Dal.	26	126	1
Mike Anderson, Den. at Jac.	23	115	0

300-YARD PASSING GAMES
Player, team & opponent	Att.	Cmp.	Yds.	TD	Int.
Marc Bulger, St.L. at NYG	62	40	442	2	3
Josh McCown, Ariz. vs. S.F.	46	32	385	2	0
Donovan McNabb, Phi. at K.C.	48	33	369	3	1
Brett Favre, G.B. at Car.	47	28	303	4	1
Brian Griese, T.B. vs. Det.	39	22	302	2	3

100-YARD RECEIVING GAMES
Player, team & opponent	Rec.	Yds.	TD
Plaxico Burress, NYG vs. St.L.	10	204	2
Terrell Owens, Phi. at K.C.	11	171	1
Joey Galloway, T.B. vs. Det.	7	166	1
Donte' Stallworth, N.O. vs. Buf.	8	129	0
Randy Moss, Oak. vs. Dal.	4	123	0
Shaun McDonald, St.L. at NYG	9	121	0
Anquan Boldin, Ariz. vs. S.F.	8	116	1
Marvin Harrison, Ind. at Ten.	9	109	2
Eddie Kennison, K.C. vs. Phi.	7	109	1
Jimmy Smith, Jac. vs. Den.	5	109	1
Antonio Gates, S.D. at N.E.	6	108	0
Bobby Engram, Sea. at Was.*	9	106	0
T.J. Houshmandzadeh, Cin. vs. Hou.	8	105	0
Larry Fitzgerald, Ariz. vs. S.F.	7	102	1
Brandon Lloyd, S.F. at Ariz.	7	102	0

*Overtime game.

RESULTS

SUNDAY, OCTOBER 2
Indianapolis 31, TENNESSEE 10
CINCINNATI 16, Houston 10
San Diego 41, NEW ENGLAND 17
NEW ORLEANS 19, Buffalo 7
TAMPA BAY 17, Detroit 13
WASHINGTON 20, Seattle 17 (OT)
Denver 20, JACKSONVILLE 7
N.Y. GIANTS 44, St. Louis 24
BALTIMORE 13, N.Y. Jets 3
OAKLAND 19, Dallas 13
ATLANTA 30, Minnesota 10
Philadelphia 37, KANSAS CITY 31
ARIZONA 31, San Francisco 14

MONDAY, OCTOBER 3
CAROLINA 32, Green Bay 29
Open Date: Chicago, Cleveland, Miami, Pittsburgh

COLTS 31, TITANS 10
Sunday, October 2

Indianapolis	7	10	7	7—31
Tennessee	3	0	0	7—10

First Quarter
Ind.—Wayne 25 pass from Manning (Vanderjagt kick), 3:29.
Ten.—FG, Bironas 34, 10:02.

Second Quarter
Ind.—FG, Vanderjagt 20, 7:43.
Ind.—Harrison 11 pass from Manning (Vanderjagt kick), 13:43.

Third Quarter
Ind.—James 8 pass from Manning (Vanderjagt kick), 7:05.

Fourth Quarter
Ind.—Harrison 24 pass from Manning (Vanderjagt kick), 1:51.
Ten.—Scaife 6 pass from McNair (Bironas kick), 10:29.
Attendance—69,149.

	Indianapolis	Tennessee
First downs	22	18
Rushes-yards	26-100	19-109
Passing	264	204
Punt returns	0-0	1-1
Kickoff returns	1-17	6-137
Interception returns	1-0	0-0
Comp.-att.-int.	20-27-0	28-37-1
Sacked-yards lost	0-0	2-16
Punts	2-56	3-38
Fumbles-lost	1-0	1-0
Penalties-yards	1-10	9-76
Time of possession	25:48	34:12

INDIVIDUAL STATISTICS
RUSHING—Indianapolis, James 21-90, Carthon 4-7, Manning 1-3. Tennessee, Brown 10-31, McNair 4-40, Payton 4-37, B. Jones 1-1.
PASSING—Indianapolis, Manning 20-27-0-264. Tennessee, McNair 28-37-1-220.
RECEIVING—Indianapolis, Harrison 9-109, Clark 4-47, Wayne 2-48, Fletcher 2-38, James 2-12, Carthon 1-10. Tennessee, Kinney 7-42, Scaife 7-39, Troupe 4-34, R. Williams 2-33, B. Jones 2-22, Bennett 2-20, Brown 2-17, Calico 1-9, Fleming 1-4.
MISSED FIELD GOAL ATTEMPTS—Tennessee, Bironas 38.
INTERCEPTIONS—Indianapolis, Sanders 1-0.
KICKOFF RETURNS—Indianapolis, Carthon 1-17. Tennessee, P. Jones 4-95, Thurman 2-42.
PUNT RETURNS—Tennessee, Thurman 1-1.
SACKS—Indianapolis, Mathis 1, Thomas 1.

BENGALS 16, TEXANS 10
Sunday, October 2

Houston	0	3	7	0—10
Cincinnati	3	7	0	6—16

First Quarter
Cin.—FG, Graham 24, 10:25.

Second Quarter
Hou.—FG, K. Brown 28, 1:29.
Cin.—J. Johnson 1 pass from Palmer (Graham kick), 13:51.

Third Quarter
Hou.—Norris 4 pass from Carr (K. Brown kick), 7:20.

Fourth Quarter
Cin.—FG, Graham 27, 9:56.
Cin.—FG, Graham 46, 13:50.
Attendance—65,714.

	Houston	Cincinnati
First downs	18	22
Rushes-yards	23-126	25-98
Passing	128	273
Punt returns	1-4	2-7
Kickoff returns	5-130	2-55
Interception returns	0-0	0-0
Comp.-att.-int.	17-26-0	25-34-0
Sacked-yards lost	7-46	2-3
Punts	4-36	2-48
Fumbles-lost	1-1	1-0
Penalties-yards	9-90	14-117
Time of possession	25:26	34:34

INDIVIDUAL STATISTICS
RUSHING—Houston, D. Davis 19-81, Carr 3-35, Wells 1-10. Cincinnati, Ru. Johnson 19-88, C. Perry 4-6, Houshmandzadeh 1-5, Palmer 1-(minus 1).
PASSING—Houston, Carr 17-26-0-174. Cincinnati, Palmer 25-34-0-276.
RECEIVING—Houston, Gaffney 6-88, D. Davis 4-31, An. Johnson 3-38, Wells 2-5, Bradford 1-8, Norris 1-4. Cincinnati, Houshmandzadeh 8-105, C. Johnson 7-67, C. Perry 4-29, Henry 2-34, R. Kelly 2-20, Schobel 1-20, J. Johnson 1-1.
MISSED FIELD GOAL ATTEMPTS—Cincinnati, Graham 42.
INTERCEPTIONS—None.
KICKOFF RETURNS—Houston, Mathis 5-130. Cincinnati, T. Perry 2-55.
PUNT RETURNS—Houston, Buchanon 1-4. Cincinnati, Ratliff 2-7.
SACKS—Houston, Wong 1, Robinson 1. Cincinnati, Kaesviharn 1, Simmons 1, J. Smith 1, Thurman 1, A. Mitchell 1, Pollack 1, Geathers 1.

CHARGERS 41, PATRIOTS 17
Sunday, October 2

San Diego	3	14	14	10—41
New England	7	10	0	0—17

First Quarter
S.D.—FG, Kaeding 42, 8:38.
N.E.—Dillon 1 run (Vinatieri kick), 13:26.

Second Quarter
S.D.—McCardell 11 pass from Brees (Kaeding kick), 8:39.
N.E.—Dwight 30 pass from Brady (Vinatieri kick), 9:31.
S.D.—Tomlinson 8 run (Kaeding kick), 12:13.
N.E.—FG, Vinatieri 24, 14:39.

Third Quarter
S.D.—Tomlinson 1 run (Kaeding kick), 8:44.
S.D.—Caldwell 28 pass from Brees (Kaeding kick), 14:41.

Fourth Quarter
S.D.—FG, Kaeding 21, 10:16.
S.D.—Hart 40 interception return (Kaeding kick), 14:26.
Attendance—68,756.

	San Diego	New England
First downs	26	18
Rushes-yards	40-183	18-72
Passing	248	231
Punt returns	3-24	1-8
Kickoff returns	4-80	8-203
Interception returns	2-41	0-0
Comp.-att.-int.	19-24-0	21-36-2
Sacked-yards lost	0-0	1-8
Punts	3-50	4-46
Fumbles-lost	0-0	1-0
Penalties-yards	7-50	4-62
Time of possession	36:38	23:22

INDIVIDUAL STATISTICS
RUSHING—San Diego, Tomlinson 25-134, Turner 11-44, Sproles 2-8, Brees 1-(minus 1), E. Parker 1-(minus 2). New England, Dillon 14-63, Brady 2-4, Pass 1-6, Cassel 1-(minus 1).
PASSING—San Diego, Brees 19-24-0-248. New England, Brady 19-32-1-224, Cassel 2-4-1-15.
RECEIVING—San Diego, Gates 6-108, E. Parker 4-51, Tomlinson 3-34, Caldwell 2-36, McCardell 1-11, Peelle 1-5, Neal 1-4, Sproles 1-(minus 1). New England, Pass 8-55, Givens 6-66, Dwight 2-41, T. Brown 2-25, Dillon 1-23, Watson 1-23, Branch 1-6.
MISSED FIELD GOAL ATTEMPTS—New England, Vinatieri 37.
INTERCEPTIONS—San Diego, Edwards 1-1, Jue 1-0.
KICKOFF RETURNS—San Diego, Sproles 4-80. New England, B. Johnson 5-143, Hobbs 3-60.
PUNT RETURNS—San Diego, Sproles 3-24. New England, Dwight 1-8.
SACKS—San Diego, Leber 1.

SAINTS 19, BILLS 7
Sunday, October 2

Buffalo	7	0	0	0— 7
New Orleans	0	13	0	6—19

First Quarter
Buf.—McGahee 1 run (Lindell kick), 5:20.

Second Quarter
N.O.—FG, Carney 23, 5:55.
N.O.—Brooks 4 run (Carney kick), 9:22.

J.O.—FG, Carney 40, 14:50.

Fourth Quarter
J.O.—FG, Carney 20, 10:01.
J.O.—FG, Carney 37, 13:51.
Attendance—58,688.

	Buffalo	New Orleans
First downs	13	23
Rushes-yards	23-141	41-167
Passing	67	166
Punt returns	1-8	4-25
Kickoff returns	6-216	2-45
Interception returns	0-0	1-39
Comp.-att.-int.	10-21-1	15-26-0
Sacked-yards lost	4-36	1-6
Punts	5-53	4-40
Fumbles-lost	3-1	0-0
Penalties-yards	12-79	4-26
Time of possession	23:40	36:20

INDIVIDUAL STATISTICS
RUSHING—Buffalo, McGahee 16-84, Losman 4-38, S. Williams 2-19, Holcomb 1-0. New Orleans, McAllister 27-130, Brooks 7-33, A. Smith 4-(minus 2), Karney 3-6.

PASSING—Buffalo, Losman 7-15-1-75, Holcomb 3-6-0-28. New Orleans, Brooks 15-26-0-172.

RECEIVING—Buffalo, J. Smith 2-30, Evans 2-27, McGahee 2-17, Moulds 2-14, Reed 1-14, S. Williams 1-1. New Orleans, Stallworth 8-129, McAllister 2-16, L. Hall 1-8, Henderson 1-7, Conwell 1-5, Karney 1-4, A. Smith 1-3.

MISSED FIELD GOAL ATTEMPTS—Buffalo, Lindell 45. New Orleans, Carney 32.

INTERCEPTIONS—New Orleans, Craft 1-39.

KICKOFF RETURNS—Buffalo, McGee 4-159, J. Smith 1-44, Burns 1-13. New Orleans, McAfee 2-45.

PUNT RETURNS—Buffalo, J. Smith 1-8. New Orleans, Hakim 2-13, Stallworth 2-12.

SACKS—Buffalo, Fletcher 1. New Orleans, Howard 2, Ch. Grant 1, W. Smith 1.

BUCCANEERS 17, LIONS 13
Sunday, October 2

Detroit	0	10	0	3—13
Tampa Bay	3	7	7	0—17

First Quarter
T.B.—FG, M. Bryant 43, 7:01.

Second Quarter
Det.—FG, Hanson 44, 3:30.
Det.—Jones 8 run (Hanson kick), 10:02.
T.B.—Pittman 41 pass from Griese (M. Bryant kick), 13:48.

Third Quarter
T.B.—Galloway 80 pass from Griese (M. Bryant kick), :55.

Fourth Quarter
Det.—FG, Hanson 23, 7:31.
Attendance—64,994.

	Detroit	Tampa Bay
First downs	11	17
Rushes-yards	25-91	22-69
Passing	135	284
Punt returns	3-25	3-15
Kickoff returns	3-33	2-29
Interception returns	3-87	0-0
Comp.-att.-int.	15-27-0	22-39-3
Sacked-yards lost	2-2	3-18
Punts	6-43	3-47
Fumbles-lost	1-1	1-1
Penalties-yards	8-55	7-55
Time of possession	28:25	31:35

INDIVIDUAL STATISTICS
RUSHING—Detroit, Jones 12-38, Pinner 6-28, Harrington 4-12, Bryson 3-13. Tampa Bay, C. Williams 11-13, Pittman 5-30, Graham 4-15, Griese 1-7, Galloway 1-4.

PASSING—Detroit, Harrington 15-27-0-137. Tampa Bay, Griese 22-39-3-302.

RECEIVING—Detroit, R. Williams 3-54, M. Williams 3-22, K. Johnson 2-15, Pinner 2-11, Pollard 2-5, C. Rogers 1-15, FitzSimmons 1-11, Bryson 1-4. Tampa Bay, Galloway 7-166, Pittman 6-96, Clayton 2-11, Becht 2-9, Alstott 2-7, C. Williams 2-6, Smith 1-7.

MISSED FIELD GOAL ATTEMPTS—Tampa Bay, M. Bryant 46.

INTERCEPTIONS—Detroit, Holt 1-51, McQuarters 1-19, Lehman 1-17.

KICKOFF RETURNS—Detroit, Drummond 2-26, DeVries 1-7. Tampa Bay, Cox 1-17, Smith 1-12.

PUNT RETURNS—Detroit, Drummond 3-17. Tampa Bay, Jones 3-15.

SACKS—Detroit, K. Edwards 2, DeVries 1. Tampa Bay, Barber 1, Rice 1.

REDSKINS 20, SEAHAWKS 17
Sunday, October 2

Seattle	3	0	7	7	0—17
Washington	0	7	10	0	3—20

First Quarter
Sea.—FG, J. Brown 53, 9:02.

Second Quarter
Was.—Royal 1 pass from Brunell (Novak kick), 12:21.

Third Quarter
Was.—Sellers 4 pass from Brunell (Novak kick), 7:41.
Sea.—Alexander 3 run (J. Brown kick), 10:50.
Was.—FG, Novak 40, 14:57.

Fourth Quarter
Sea.—Jackson 6 pass from Hasselbeck (J. Brown kick), 13:37.
Overtime
Was.—FG, Novak 39, 5:31.
Attendance—90,215.

	Seattle	Washington
First downs	21	26
Rushes-yards	23-119	39-141
Passing	235	211
Punt returns	1-(-3)	1-9
Kickoff returns	3-44	4-95
Interception returns	1-2	0-0
Comp.-att.-int.	26-38-0	20-36-1
Sacked-yards lost	1-7	2-15
Punts	3-33	2-41
Fumbles-lost	1-0	0-0
Penalties-yards	8-84	2-10
Time of possession	26:09	39:22

INDIVIDUAL STATISTICS
RUSHING—Seattle, Alexander 20-98, Hasselbeck 2-16, Strong 1-5. Washington, Portis 25-90, Betts 12-35, Brunell 2-16.

PASSING—Seattle, Hasselbeck 26-38-0-242. Washington, Brunell 20-36-1-226.

RECEIVING—Seattle, Engram 9-106, Jackson 7-55, Stevens 3-31, Hannam 3-23, Strong 2-6, Jurevicius 1-17, Alexander 1-4. Washington, Moss 6-87, Cooley 4-61, Patten 3-15, Thrash 2-30, Portis 2-18, Royal 2-11, Sellers 1-4.

MISSED FIELD GOAL ATTEMPTS—Seattle, J. Brown 47, 47. Washington, Novak 39.

INTERCEPTIONS—Seattle, K. Herndon 1-2.

KICKOFF RETURNS—Seattle, Scobey 2-44, Morris 1-0. Washington, Betts 4-95.

PUNT RETURNS—Seattle, J. Williams 1-(minus 3). Washington, Moss 1-9.

SACKS—Seattle, Tatupu 1, Boulware 1. Washington, Marshall 1.

BRONCOS 20, JAGUARS 7
Sunday, October 2

Denver	0	14	0	6—20
Jacksonville	0	0	7	0— 7

Second Quarter
Den.—Carswell 2 pass from Plummer (Elam kick), 8:12.
Den.—Carswell 1 pass from Plummer (Elam kick), 14:17.

Third Quarter
Jac.—J. Smith 45 pass from Leftwich (Scobee kick), 6:08.

Fourth Quarter
Den.—FG, Elam 33, 6:12.
Den.—FG, Elam 42, 12:18.
Attendance—66,045.

	Denver	Jacksonville
First downs	24	13
Rushes-yards	44-188	11-12
Passing	118	229
Punt returns	2-31	3-24
Kickoff returns	1-22	3-87
Interception returns	2-53	0-0
Comp.-att.-int.	19-26-0	20-34-2
Sacked-yards lost	3-18	2-11
Punts	4-49	6-42

	Denver	Jacksonville
Fumbles-lost	0-0	4-2
Penalties-yards	5-30	15-119
Time of possession	38:05	21:55

INDIVIDUAL STATISTICS

RUSHING—Denver, Mi. Anderson 23-115, Bell 15-60, Plummer 3-(minus 3), Dayne 2-3, Adams 1-13. Jacksonville, F. Taylor 8-14, Leftwich 1-3, G. Jones 1-2, M. Jones 1-(minus 7).

PASSING—Denver, Plummer 19-26-0-136. Jacksonville, Leftwich 20-34-2-240.

RECEIVING—Denver, Smith 4-33, S. Alexander 3-27, Mi. Anderson 3-27, Putzier 2-15, Carswell 2-3, Lelie 1-13, Adams 1-9, Bell 1-6, Sapp 1-5, K. Johnson 1-(minus 2). Jacksonville, J. Smith 5-109, Pearman 4-42, M. Jones 3-27, R. Williams 3-22, Wilford 2-17, F. Taylor 1-13, Wrighster 1-6, G. Jones 1-4.

MISSED FIELD GOAL ATTEMPTS—Denver, Elam 41, 46.

INTERCEPTIONS—Denver, N. Ferguson 1-30, Foxworth 1-23.

KICKOFF RETURNS—Denver, Adams 1-22. Jacksonville, Pearman 3-87.

PUNT RETURNS—Denver, Adams 2-31. Jacksonville, Pearman 3-24.

SACKS—Denver, Wilson 1, Warren 1. Jacksonville, Hayward 1.5, Meier 1, Spicer 0.5.

GIANTS 44, RAMS 24
Sunday, October 2

St. Louis	7	10	0	7—24
N.Y. Giants	17	10	7	10—44

First Quarter
NYG—Burress 31 pass from Manning (Feely kick), 2:09.
NYG—FG, Feely 38, 6:21.
St.L.—S. Jackson 13 pass from Bulger (J. Wilkins kick), 9:57.
NYG—Toomer 1 pass from Manning (Feely kick), 12:10.
Second Quarter
NYG—Burress 17 pass from Manning (Feely kick), 2:48.
NYG—FG, Feely 32, 5:35.
St.L.—S. Jackson 1 run (J. Wilkins kick), 10:55.
St.L.—FG, J. Wilkins 37, 13:13.
Third Quarter
NYG—Shockey 31 pass from Manning (Feely kick), 9:41.
Fourth Quarter
NYG—FG, Feely 23, 6:33.
St.L.—Holt 22 pass from Bulger (J. Wilkins kick), 9:32.
NYG—Barber 16 run (Feely kick), 13:08.
Attendance—78,453.

	St. Louis	N.Y. Giants
First downs	27	24
Rushes-yards	15-42	29-164
Passing	434	292
Punt returns	1-5	1-11
Kickoff returns	7-65	3-65
Interception returns	0-0	3-95
Comp.-att.-int.	40-62-3	19-35-0
Sacked-yards lost	1-8	1-4
Punts	2-34	2-45
Fumbles-lost	3-2	0-0
Penalties-yards	11-103	11-90
Time of possession	32:04	27:56

INDIVIDUAL STATISTICS

RUSHING—St. Louis, S. Jackson 10-17, M. Faulk 3-16, Bulger 1-9, Hedgecock 1-0. New York, Barber 24-128, Jacobs 2-16, Manning 2-(minus 2), T. Carter 1-22.

PASSING—St. Louis, Bulger 40-62-3-442. New York, Manning 19-35-0-296.

RECEIVING—St. Louis, McDonald 9-121, Looker 8-90, Holt 7-84, Curtis 6-78, S. Jackson 5-42, M. Faulk 3-24, R. Williams 1-2, Bulger 1-1. New York, Burress 10-204, Shockey 4-57, Toomer 3-20, Barber 2-15.

MISSED FIELD GOAL ATTEMPTS—St. Louis, J. Wilkins 48.

INTERCEPTIONS—New York, Torbor 1-37, Williams 1-34, Pierce 1-24.

KICKOFF RETURNS—St. Louis, C. Johnson 6-146, Harris 1-21. New York, Ponder 3-65.

PUNT RETURNS—St. Louis, McDonald 1-5. New York, Morton 1-11.

SACKS—St. Louis, Hargrove 1. New York, Strahan 1.

RAVENS 13, JETS 3
Sunday, October 2

N.Y. Jets	0	0	3	0— 3
Baltimore	3	3	7	0—13

First Quarter
Bal.—FG, Stover 42, 8:29.
Second Quarter
Bal.—FG, Stover 25, 11:13.
Third Quarter
NYJ—FG, Nugent 21, 3:43.
Bal.—J. Lewis 1 run (Stover kick), 11:48.
Attendance—70,479.

	N.Y. Jets	Baltimore
First downs	8	17
Rushes-yards	15-28	45-115
Passing	124	144
Punt returns	4-32	4-56
Kickoff returns	4-89	2-52
Interception returns	1-0	0-0
Comp.-att.-int.	14-28-0	15-21-1
Sacked-yards lost	5-25	0-0
Punts	9-42	5-46
Fumbles-lost	0-0	1-1
Penalties-yards	5-39	3-19
Time of possession	21:59	38:01

INDIVIDUAL STATISTICS

RUSHING—New York, C. Martin 13-30, Blaylock 2-(minus 2). Baltimore, J. Lewis 29-81, C. Taylor 11-32, Wright 5-2.

PASSING—New York, Bollinger 14-28-0-149. Baltimore, Wright 15-21-1-144.

RECEIVING—New York, McCareins 3-59, Baker 3-29, C. Martin 3-15, Jolley 2-15, Coles 1-16, Blaylock 1-10, Sowell 1-5. Baltimore, Mason 5-54, Heap 4-39, C. Taylor 2-24, Ricard 1-11, Wilcox 1-10, Clayton 1-4, Mughelli 1-2.

MISSED FIELD GOAL ATTEMPTS—None.

INTERCEPTIONS—New York, Coleman 1-0.

KICKOFF RETURNS—New York, Miller 3-78, Baker 1-11. Baltimore, Sams 2-52.

PUNT RETURNS—New York, Cotchery 4-32. Baltimore, Sams 4-56.

SACKS—Baltimore, R. Lewis 1, Boulware 1, A. Thomas 1, R. Green 1, Polley 0.5, Suggs 0.5.

RAIDERS 19, COWBOYS 13
Sunday, October 2

Dallas	0	3	3	7—13
Oakland	10	0	3	6—19

First Quarter
Oak.—FG, Janikowski 30, 7:38.
Oak.—Jordan 2 run (Janikowski kick), 11:53.
Second Quarter
Dal.—FG, Cortez 29, 9:01.
Third Quarter
Oak.—FG, Janikowski 23, 6:45.
Dal.—FG, Cortez 30, 13:55.
Fourth Quarter
Oak.—FG, Janikowski 49, 4:35.
Dal.—Crayton 63 pass from Bledsoe (Cortez kick), 6:09.
Oak.—FG, Janikowski 43, 10:31.
Attendance—62,400.

	Dallas	Oakland
First downs	16	16
Rushes-yards	32-116	30-129
Passing	187	204
Punt returns	0-0	5-35
Kickoff returns	1-22	2-59
Interception returns	0-0	1-0
Comp.-att.-int.	11-27-1	13-23-0
Sacked-yards lost	4-25	3-14
Punts	5-45	4-45
Fumbles-lost	0-0	1-0
Penalties-yards	6-35	13-85
Time of possession	30:46	29:14

INDIVIDUAL STATISTICS

RUSHING—Dallas, J. Jones 22-76, Thompson 7-32, Barber 2-1, Bledsoe 1-7. Oakland, Jordan 26-126, Collins 2-(minus 1), Crockett 1-2, Fargas 1-1.

PASSING—Dallas, Bledsoe 11-26-1-212, K. Johnson 0-1-0-0. Oakland, Collins 13-23-0-218.

RECEIVING—Dallas, Witten 5-49, T. Glenn 2-64, Crayton 1-63, K. Johnson 1-16, J. Jones 1-12, Thompson 1-8. Oakland, Moss 4-123, Jordan 4-22, Porter 3-41, C. Anderson 2-32.

MISSED FIELD GOAL ATTEMPTS—None.

INTERCEPTIONS—Oakland, C. Woodson 1-0.

KICKOFF RETURNS—Dallas, Thompson 1-22. Oakland, Carr 2-59.

PUNT RETURNS—Oakland, Carr 4-30, C. Woodson 1-5.

SACKS—Dallas, Ware 1, Canty 0.5, K. Coleman 0.5, Shanle 0.5, Ratliff 0.5. Oakland, Burgess 2, Gibson 1, Sapp 1.

FALCONS 30, VIKINGS 10
Sunday, October 2

Minnesota	0	0	0	10—10
Atlanta	7	17	3	3—30

First Quarter
Atl.—Crumpler 5 pass from Vick (T. Peterson kick), 7:16.

Second Quarter
Atl.—Duckett 1 run (T. Peterson kick), 2:05.
Atl.—Dunn 37 run (T. Peterson kick), 11:20.
Atl.—FG, T. Peterson 38, 14:59.

Third Quarter
Atl.—FG, T. Peterson 26, 14:56.

Fourth Quarter
Min.—FG, Edinger 43, 6:47.
Atl.—FG, T. Peterson 39, 9:36.
Min.—Williamson 16 pass from Culpepper (Edinger kick), 12:27.
Attendance—69,552.

	Minnesota	Atlanta
First downs	17	22
Rushes-yards	16-63	41-285
Passing	198	83
Punt returns	2-0	3-14
Kickoff returns	5-101	1-36
Interception returns	0-0	2-43
Comp.-att.-int.	23-34-2	11-22-0
Sacked-yards lost	9-52	1-5
Punts	5-46	3-35
Fumbles-lost	3-1	1-0
Penalties-yards	11-84	8-65
Time of possession	27:23	32:37

INDIVIDUAL STATISTICS

RUSHING—Minnesota, Moore 14-57, Culpepper 1-10, M. Bennett 1-(minus 4). Atlanta, Dunn 18-126, Duckett 14-40, Vick 4-58, Schaub 4-56, Griffith 1-5.

PASSING—Minnesota, Culpepper 23-34-2-250. Atlanta, Schaub 5-14-0-39, Vick 6-8-0-49.

RECEIVING—Minnesota, Moore 6-63, T. Taylor 5-62, Williamson 4-39, Wiggins 3-25, M. Bennett 2-31, Kleinsasser 2-13, M. Robinson 1-17. Atlanta, Finneran 3-31, Crumpler 3-16, R. White 2-12, Jenkins 1-12, Blakley 1-10, Dunn 1-7.

MISSED FIELD GOAL ATTEMPTS—None.

INTERCEPTIONS—Atlanta, D. Hall 1-37, Brooking 1-6.

KICKOFF RETURNS—Minnesota, K. Robinson 4-95, Herrera 1-6. Atlanta, Rossum 1-36.

PUNT RETURNS—Minnesota, K. Robinson 2-0. Atlanta, Rossum 3-14.

SACKS—Minnesota, Cowart 1. Atlanta, D. Williams 2, R. Coleman 2, B. Smith 2, Brooking 1, Scott 1, Kerney 1.

EAGLES 37, CHIEFS 31
Sunday, October 2

Philadelphia	0	13	11	13—37
Kansas City	10	14	0	7—31

First Quarter
K.C.—Holmes 3 run (Tynes kick), 5:01.
K.C.—FG, Tynes 38, 13:00.

Second Quarter
K.C.—Kennison 8 pass from Green (Tynes kick), 1:17.
Phi.—S. Brown 40 interception return (conversion failed), 10:19.
K.C.—D. Hall 96 kickoff return (Tynes kick), 10:33.
Phi.—Owens 7 pass from McNabb (France kick), 13:46.

Third Quarter
Phi.—FG, France 44, 2:46.
Phi.—Bartrum 3 pass from McNabb (Westbrook pass from McNabb), 13:06.

Fourth Quarter
Phi.—FG, France 37, 3:22.
Phi.—Smith 1 pass from McNabb (France kick), 6:03.
Phi.—FG, France 26, 11:38.
K.C.—D. Hall 15 pass from Green (Tynes kick), 13:36.
Attendance—78,742.

	Philadelphia	Kansas City
First downs	25	19
Rushes-yards	17-28	27-144
Passing	368	209
Punt returns	2-2	1-0
Kickoff returns	4-108	8-234
Interception returns	2-60	1-0
Comp.-att.-int.	33-48-1	19-30-2
Sacked-yards lost	1-1	3-12
Punts	3-38	4-48
Fumbles-lost	3-1	2-2
Penalties-yards	3-25	6-40
Time of possession	30:57	29:03

INDIVIDUAL STATISTICS

RUSHING—Philadelphia, Westbrook 9-15, Gordon 4-14, McNabb 4-(minus 1). Kansas City, Holmes 18-84, L. Johnson 7-34, Kennison 1-23, Green 1-3.

PASSING—Philadelphia, McNabb 33-48-1-369. Kansas City, Green 19-30-2-221.

RECEIVING—Philadelphia, Owens 11-171, Smith 9-67, Westbrook 6-33, G. Lewis 3-50, Gordon 2-33, Parry 1-12, Bartrum 1-3. Kansas City, Kennison 7-109, Holmes 5-24, D. Hall 4-45, Gonzalez 2-5, Boerigter 1-38.

MISSED FIELD GOAL ATTEMPTS—Philadelphia, France 40.

INTERCEPTIONS—Philadelphia, S. Brown 2-60. Kansas City, McCleon 1-0.

KICKOFF RETURNS—Philadelphia, Hood 4-108. Kansas City, D. Hall 8-234.

PUNT RETURNS—Philadelphia, Wynn 2-2. Kansas City, D. Hall 1-0.

SACKS—Philadelphia, Dawkins 1, Patterson 1, Kearse 1. Kansas City, Allen 1.

CARDINALS 31, 49ERS 14
Sunday, October 2

San Francisco	14	0	0	0—14
Arizona	0	12	6	13—31

First Quarter
S.F.—D. Smith 0 fumble return (Nedney kick), :09.
S.F.—D. Johnson 78 fumble return (Nedney kick), 7:03.

Second Quarter
Ariz.—FG, Rackers 40, 6:14.
Ariz.—FG, Rackers 45, 12:16.
Ariz.—Fitzgerald 17 pass from McCown (pass failed), 14:55.

Third Quarter
Ariz.—FG, Rackers 48, 6:03.
Ariz.—FG, Rackers 23, 12:19.

Fourth Quarter
Ariz.—FG, Rackers 43, 1:46.
Ariz.—Boldin 27 pass from McCown (Rackers kick), 6:31.
Ariz.—Rackers 24, 9:00.
Attendance—103,467.

	San Francisco	Arizona
First downs	8	24
Rushes-yards	14-51	34-97
Passing	117	366
Punt returns	2-7	5-71
Kickoff returns	2-38	1-19
Interception returns	0-0	1-22
Comp.-att.-int.	17-31-1	32-46-0
Sacked-yards lost	5-43	3-19
Punts	7-47	3-45
Fumbles-lost	5-3	3-3
Penalties-yards	8-52	4-37
Time of possession	22:12	37:48

INDIVIDUAL STATISTICS

RUSHING—San Francisco, Barlow 10-45, Gore 2-4, Hetherington 1-3, Rattay 1-(minus 1). Arizona, Shipp 16-42, Arrington 7-13, McCown 6-32, O. Ayanbadejo 4-9, Boldin 1-1.

PASSING—San Francisco, Rattay 11-21-1-126, A. Smith 6-10-0-34. Arizona, McCown 32-46-0-385.

RECEIVING—San Francisco, Lloyd 7-102, Morton 3-46, Barlow 3-10, Gore 2-(minus 12), Bush 1-8, Beasley 1-6. Arizona, Boldin 8-116, Fitzgerald 7-102, Shipp 5-52, B. Johnson 4-50, O. Ayanbadejo 3-18, Lee 2-28, T. Johnson 2-16, Edwards 1-3.

MISSED FIELD GOAL ATTEMPTS—None.

INTERCEPTIONS—Arizona, Tate 1-22.

KICKOFF RETURNS—San Francisco, Hicks 2-38. Arizona, Swinton 1-19.

PUNT RETURNS—San Francisco, Amey 2-7. Arizona, Swinton 5-71.

SACKS—San Francisco, Young 2, Team 1. Arizona, Berry 2, Wilson 1, Pace 1, Kolodziej 1.

PANTHERS 32, PACKERS 29
Monday, October 3

Green Bay	7	0	6	16—29
Carolina	7	16	3	6—32

First Quarter
Car.—Mangum 2 pass from Delhomme (Kasay kick), 2:30.
G.B.—D. Martin 21 pass from Favre (Longwell kick), 7:30.

Second Quarter
Car.—FG, Kasay 32, 2:07.
Car.—Gaines 19 pass from Delhomme (kick blocked), 6:30.
Car.—S. Davis 11 run (Kasay kick), 11:41.

Third Quarter
Car.—FG, Kasay 38, 7:10.
G.B.—Driver 26 pass from Favre (pass failed), 11:54.

Fourth Quarter
Car.—S. Davis 1 run (pass failed), :16.
G.B.—D. Lee 16 pass from Favre (D. Martin pass from Favre), 3:11.
G.B.—Chatman 4 pass from Favre (Ferguson pass from Favre), 11:53.
Attendance—73,657.

	Green Bay	Carolina
First downs	22	17
Rushes-yards	19-58	33-90
Passing	294	196
Punt returns	4-29	4-17
Kickoff returns	7-123	3-112
Interception returns	0-0	1-32
Comp.-att.-int.	28-47-1	17-24-0
Sacked-yards lost	1-9	2-10
Punts	5-45	5-43
Fumbles-lost	1-1	1-1
Penalties-yards	8-86	8-75
Time of possession	28:51	31:09

INDIVIDUAL STATISTICS

RUSHING—Green Bay, Green 14-36, Davenport 4-10, Favre 1-12. Carolina, S. Davis 19-51, Foster 9-38, Hoover 2-4, Delhomme 2-(minus 3), Goings 1-0.

PASSING—Green Bay, Favre 28-47-1-303. Carolina, Delhomme 17-24-0-206.

RECEIVING—Green Bay, Driver 6-92, D. Martin 5-53, Green 4-23, Chatman 3-36, Ferguson 3-24, Henderson 2-42, Murphy 2-13, D. Lee 1-16, Leach 1-3, Davenport 1-1. Carolina, Colbert 4-52, Foster 3-55, Hoover 3-20, Gaines 2-42, S. Smith 2-12, Mangum 2-4, S. Davis 1-21.

MISSED FIELD GOAL ATTEMPTS—None.

INTERCEPTIONS—Carolina, Lucas 1-32.

KICKOFF RETURNS—Green Bay, Davenport 4-86, Murphy 3-37. Carolina, Smart 2-79, S. Smith 1-33.

PUNT RETURNS—Green Bay, Chatman 4-29. Carolina, Gamble 2-12, S. Smith 2-5.

SACKS—Green Bay, Gbaja-Biamila 2. Carolina, Rucker 1.

WEEK 5

STANDINGS

AMERICAN FOOTBALL CONFERENCE

EAST DIVISION

	W	L	T	Pct.	PF	PA
New England	3	2	0	.600	118	136
Miami	2	2	0	.500	82	71
Buffalo	2	3	0	.400	68	83
N.Y. Jets	2	3	0	.400	61	85

NORTH DIVISION

	W	L	T	Pct.	PF	PA
Cincinnati	4	1	0	.800	124	61
Pittsburgh	3	1	0	.750	105	59
Cleveland	2	2	0	.500	65	74
Baltimore	1	3	0	.250	47	87

SOUTH DIVISION

	W	L	T	Pct.	PF	PA
Indianapolis	5	0	0	1.000	106	29
Jacksonville	3	2	0	.600	85	84
Tennessee	2	3	0	.400	103	126
Houston	0	4	0	.000	44	99

WEST DIVISION

	W	L	T	Pct.	PF	PA
Denver	4	1	0	.800	101	87
Kansas City	2	2	0	.500	91	91
San Diego	2	3	0	.400	149	112
Oakland	1	3	0	.250	76	89

NATIONAL FOOTBALL CONFERENCE

EAST DIVISION

	W	L	T	Pct.	PF	PA
N.Y. Giants	3	1	0	.750	136	98
Washington	3	1	0	.750	62	58
Dallas	3	2	0	.600	121	98
Philadelphia	3	2	0	.600	122	101

NORTH DIVISION

	W	L	T	Pct.	PF	PA
Detroit	2	2	0	.500	71	75
Chicago	1	3	0	.250	62	59
Minnesota	1	3	0	.250	64	107
Green Bay	1	4	0	.200	124	95

SOUTH DIVISION

	W	L	T	Pct.	PF	PA
Tampa Bay	4	1	0	.800	89	59
Atlanta	3	2	0	.600	114	88
Carolina	3	2	0	.600	127	116
New Orleans	2	3	0	.400	71	139

WEST DIVISION

	W	L	T	Pct.	PF	PA
Seattle	3	2	0	.600	126	107
St. Louis	2	3	0	.400	128	148
Arizona	1	4	0	.200	94	134
San Francisco	1	4	0	.200	79	160

TOP PERFORMANCES

100-YARD RUSHING GAMES

Player, team & opponent	Att.	Yds.	TD
Thomas Jones, Chi. at Cle.	24	137	0
Fred Taylor, Jac. vs. Cin.	24	132	0
Domanick Davis, Hou. vs. Ten.	19	130	0
Tatum Bell, Den. vs. Was.	12	127	2
Shaun Alexander, Sea. at St.L.	25	119	2
Corey Dillon, N.E. at Atl.	23	106	0
Edgerrin James, Ind. at S.F.	21	105	1
Clinton Portis, Was. at Den.	20	103	0

300-YARD PASSING GAMES

Player, team & opponent	Att.	Cmp.	Yds.	TD	Int.
Josh McCown, Ariz. vs. Car.	46	29	398	2	3
Tom Brady, N.E. at Atl.	27	22	350	3	1
Marc Bulger, St.L. vs. Sea.	40	26	336	2	1
Mark Brunell, Was. at Den.	53	30	322	2	0
Matt Hasselbeck, Sea. at St.L.	38	27	316	2	0

100-YARD RECEIVING GAMES

Player, team & opponent	Rec.	Yds.	TD
Anquan Boldin, Ariz. vs. Car.	10	162	1
Joe Jurevicius, Sea. at St.L.	9	137	1
Larry Fitzgerald, Ariz. vs. Car.	9	136	1
Torry Holt, St.L. vs. Sea.	8	126	1
Daniel Graham, N.E. at Atl.	5	119	1
Steve Smith, Car. at Ariz.	8	119	2
Terry Glenn, Dal. vs. Phi.	7	118	2
Santana Moss, Was. at Den.	8	116	0
Az-Zahir Hakim, N.O. at G.B.	5	108	0
Deion Branch, N.E. at Atl.	8	107	0
Brian Finneran, Atl. vs. N.E.	5	103	0

RESULTS

SUNDAY, OCTOBER 9
N.Y. JETS 14, Tampa Bay 12
CLEVELAND 20, Chicago 10
Tennessee 34, HOUSTON 20
GREEN BAY 52, New Orleans 3
Seattle 37, ST. LOUIS 31
BUFFALO 20, Miami 14
DETROIT 35, Baltimore 17
New England 31, ATLANTA 28
Indianapolis 28, SAN FRANCISCO 3
Carolina 24, ARIZONA 20
DALLAS 33, Philadelphia 10
DENVER 21, Washington 19
JACKSONVILLE 23, Cincinnati 20
MONDAY, OCTOBER 10
Pittsburgh 24, SAN DIEGO 22
Open Date: Kansas City, Minnesota, N.Y. Giants, Oakland

JETS 14, BUCCANEERS 12
Sunday, October 9

Tampa Bay	3	6	0	3—12
N.Y. Jets	0	7	7	0—14

First Quarter
T.B.—FG, M. Bryant 35, 6:51.

Second Quarter
T.B.—FG, M. Bryant 36, 3:39.
NYJ—C. Martin 2 run (Nugent kick), 7:28.
T.B.—FG, M. Bryant 43, 14:55.

Third Quarter
NYJ—C. Martin 1 run (Nugent kick), 5:55.

Fourth Quarter
T.B.—FG, M. Bryant 30, 11:00.
　Attendance—77,852.

	Tampa Bay	N.Y. Jets
First downs	20	15
Rushes-yards	26-84	27-62
Passing	201	150
Punt returns	4-18	4-29
Kickoff returns	2-21	5-109
Interception returns	1-0	1-43
Comp.-att.-int.	27-42-1	13-19-1
Sacked-yards lost	3-25	2-13
Punts	5-52	4-43
Fumbles-lost	2-0	3-2
Penalties-yards	12-87	6-46
Time of possession	33:11	26:49

INDIVIDUAL STATISTICS
RUSHING—Tampa Bay, Pittman 13-46, Graham 7-18, Alstott 3-12, Griese 3-8. New York, C. Martin 23-59, Blaylock 3-1, Testaverde 1-9.

PASSING—Tampa Bay, Griese 27-42-1-226. New York, Testaverde 13-19-1-163.

RECEIVING—Tampa Bay, Pittman 7-41, Galloway 5-87, Smith 5-46, I. Hilliard 5-27, Becht 2-6, Alstott 1-9, Shepherd 1-9, Cook 1-1. New York, Coles 6-89, Jolley 3-46, Cotchery 2-14, Baker 1-11, Blaylock 1-3.

MISSED FIELD GOAL ATTEMPTS—New York, Nugent 40, 48.

INTERCEPTIONS—Tampa Bay, Barber 1-0. New York, Law 1-43.

KICKOFF RETURNS—Tampa Bay, Graham 1-22, Cox 1-(minus 1). New York, Miller 4-109, Baker 1-0.

PUNT RETURNS—Tampa Bay, Jones 4-18. New York, Cotchery 4-29.

SACKS—Tampa Bay, Rice 1, Nece 1. New York, Robertson 2, Ellis 0.5, Brown 0.5.

BROWNS 20, BEARS 10
Sunday, October 9

Chicago	0	3	7	0—10
Cleveland	3	3	0	14—20

First Quarter
Cle.—FG, Dawson 19, 10:43.

Second Quarter
Chi.—FG, Gould 44, 5:59.
Cle.—FG, Dawson 44, 14:23.

Third Quarter
Chi.—M. Edwards 8 pass from Orton (Gould kick), 9:31.

Fourth Quarter
Cle.—Bryant 33 pass from Dilfer (Dawson kick), 11:58.
Cle.—Bryant 28 pass from Dilfer (Dawson kick), 12:36.
　Attendance—73,079.

	Chicago	Cleveland
First downs	16	15
Rushes-yards	34-176	22-76
Passing	90	202
Punt returns	1-0	1-15
Kickoff returns	5-114	3-61
Interception returns	2-72	0-0
Comp.-att.-int.	16-26-0	23-34-2
Sacked-yards lost	4-27	3-16
Punts	4-45	6-41
Fumbles-lost	4-3	0-0
Penalties-yards	7-57	5-55
Time of possession	31:14	28:46

INDIVIDUAL STATISTICS
RUSHING—Chicago, T. Jones 24-137, Benson 5-6, Orton 3-14, Peterson 2-19. Cleveland, Droughns 17-72, Green 2-1, Dilfer 2-(minus 1), T. Smith 1-4.

PASSING—Chicago, Orton 16-26-0-117. Cleveland, Dilfer 23-34-2-218.

RECEIVING—Chicago, Muhammad 6-52, Bradley 4-33, Clark 2-9, T. Jones 2-5, Reid 1-10, M. Edwards 1-8. Cleveland, Bryant 6-83, Shea 6-65, Droughns 4-21, Northcutt 3-23, Heiden 2-11, T. Smith 1-8, Green 1-7.

MISSED FIELD GOAL ATTEMPTS—Chicago, Gould 48.

INTERCEPTIONS—Chicago, M. Brown 1-72, Tillman 1-0.

KICKOFF RETURNS—Chicago, Azumah 3-82, Peterson 2-32. Cleveland, Cribbs 3-61.

PUNT RETURNS—Chicago, Wade 1-0. Cleveland, Northcutt 1-15.

SACKS—Chicago, Urlacher 1, Briggs 1, T. Harris 1. Cleveland, McKinley 1, Thompson 1, Crocker 1, Pool 1.

TITANS 34, TEXANS 20
Sunday, October 9

Tennessee	7	3	14	10—34
Houston	0	6	3	11—20

First Quarter
Ten.—Troupe 10 pass from McNair (Bironas kick), 9:06.

Second Quarter
Hou.—FG, K. Brown 32, :22.
Hou.—FG, K. Brown 38, 7:51.
Ten.—FG, Bironas 52, 12:40.

Third Quarter
Hou.—FG, K. Brown 43, 2:34.
Ten.—Payton 5 run (Bironas kick), 8:54.
Ten.—Bennett 16 pass from McNair (Bironas kick), 12:44.

Fourth Quarter
Ten.—FG, Bironas 49, :54.
Hou.—FG, K. Brown 47, 3:28.
Ten.—McNair 1 run (Bironas kick), 7:15.
Hou.—Bradford 3 pass from Carr (Bradford pass from Carr), 13:05.
　Attendance—70,430.

	Tennessee	Houston
First downs	22	14
Rushes-yards	31-90	28-161
Passing	220	96
Punt returns	2-8	3-20
Kickoff returns	4-145	7-171
Interception returns	1-3	0-0
Comp.-att.-int.	22-31-0	18-27-1
Sacked-yards lost	0-0	7-35
Punts	4-47	5-45
Fumbles-lost	1-0	2-0
Penalties-yards	7-65	6-39
Time of possession	31:09	28:51

INDIVIDUAL STATISTICS
RUSHING—Tennessee, Brown 22-78, Payton 8-11, McNair 1-1. Houston, D. Davis 19-130, Carr 5-24, Wells 3-7, Gaffney 1-0.

PASSING—Tennessee, McNair 22-31-0-220. Houston, Carr 18-27-1-131.

RECEIVING—Tennessee, Troupe 8-67, Bennett 5-99, Kinney 4-27, B. Jones 3-21, Brown 1-13, Roos 1-(minus 7). Houston, D. Davis 8-43, Bradford 4-35, Gaffney 2-24, Mathis 2-15, Rivers 1-7, Wells 1-7.

MISSED FIELD GOAL ATTEMPTS—Tennessee, Bironas 58.

INTERCEPTIONS—Tennessee, Woolfolk 1-3.

KICKOFF RETURNS—Tennessee, P. Jones 4-145. Houston, Mathis 6-141, Morency 1-30.

PUNT RETURNS—Tennessee, Ta. Williams 1-9, Thurman 1-(minus 1). Houston, Buchanon 2-19, Mathis 1-1.

SACKS—Tennessee, Odom 2, Vanden Bosch 1.5, Long 1.5, Bulluck 1, LaBoy 1.

PACKERS 52, SAINTS 3
Sunday, October 9

New Orleans	3	0	0	0— 3
Green Bay	14	21	10	7—52

First Quarter
N.O.—FG, Carney 33, 6:09.
G.B.—Davenport 1 run (Longwell kick), 12:36.
G.B.—Harris 22 interception return (Longwell kick), 14:03.

Second Quarter

G.B.—Davenport 4 run (Longwell kick), 6:10.

G.B.—Ferguson 25 pass from Favre (Longwell kick), 8:18.

G.B.—D. Martin 1 pass from Favre (Longwell kick), 14:36.

Third Quarter

G.B.—D. Lee 26 pass from Favre (Longwell kick), 3:36.

G.B.—FG, Longwell 26, 11:23.

Fourth Quarter

G.B.—Barnett 95 interception return (Longwell kick), 6:41.

Attendance—70,580.

	New Orleans	Green Bay
First downs	14	21
Rushes-yards	26-95	28-94
Passing	159	215
Punt returns	4-20	4-22
Kickoff returns	8-183	1-25
Interception returns	0-0	3-117
Comp.-att.-int.	14-35-3	20-28-0
Sacked-yards lost	4-18	0-0
Punts	6-48	6-38
Fumbles-lost	2-2	1-0
Penalties-yards	11-107	6-36
Time of possession	31:03	28:57

INDIVIDUAL STATISTICS

RUSHING—New Orleans, A. Smith 12-36, McAllister 11-31, Brooks 2-32, Stecker 1-(minus 4). Green Bay, Davenport 12-54, Fisher 7-19, R. Lee 7-7, Favre 1-9, Chatman 1-5.

PASSING—New Orleans, Brooks 9-22-2-146, Bouman 5-13-1-31. Green Bay, Favre 19-27-0-215, Rodgers 1-1-0-0.

RECEIVING—New Orleans, Hakim 5-108, McAllister 3-33, Conwell 3-24, Stallworth 1-6, A. Smith 1-4, Hilton 1-2. Green Bay, Fisher 6-40, Driver 5-48, Ferguson 3-84, D. Martin 2-7, D. Lee 1-26, Henderson 1-8, Davenport 1-2, Leach 1-0.

MISSED FIELD GOAL ATTEMPTS—New Orleans, Carney 43, 43.

INTERCEPTIONS—Green Bay, Harris 2-22, Barnett 1-95.

KICKOFF RETURNS—New Orleans, McAfee 6-129, A. Smith 1-30, Stecker 1-24. Green Bay, Jones 1-25.

PUNT RETURNS—New Orleans, Hakim 4-20. Green Bay, Chatman 4-22.

SACKS—Green Bay, C. Williams 2, Harris 1, Peterson 1.

SEAHAWKS 37, RAMS 31

Sunday, October 9

Seattle	14	10	10	3—37
St. Louis	7	14	7	3—31

First Quarter

St.L.—C. Johnson 99 kickoff return (J. Wilkins kick), :14.

Sea.—Alexander 1 run (J. Brown kick), 5:26.

Sea.—Stevens 29 pass from Hasselbeck (J. Brown kick), 13:23.

Second Quarter

St.L.—Curtis 25 pass from Bulger (J. Wilkins kick), 1:11.

Sea.—Jurevicius 24 pass from Hasselbeck (J. Brown kick), 5:55.

St.L.—Holt 26 pass from Bulger (J. Wilkins kick), 12:58.

Sea.—FG, J. Brown 34, 15:00.

Third Quarter

Sea.—FG, J. Brown 44, 5:37.

Sea.—Alexander 18 run (J. Brown kick), 8:45.

St.L.—S. Jackson 4 run (J. Wilkins kick), 14:34.

Fourth Quarter

Sea.—FG, J. Brown 28, 7:28.

St.L.—FG, J. Wilkins 40, 11:06.

Attendance—65,707.

	Seattle	St. Louis
First downs	26	20
Rushes-yards	30-134	17-77
Passing	299	309
Punt returns	2-28	4-6
Kickoff returns	5-117	6-202
Interception returns	1-3	0-0
Comp.-att.-int.	27-38-0	26-40-1
Sacked-yards lost	4-17	4-27
Punts	6-40	6-34
Fumbles-lost	0-0	2-1
Penalties-yards	7-50	7-74
Time of possession	30:54	29:06

INDIVIDUAL STATISTICS

RUSHING—Seattle, Alexander 25-119, Hasselbeck 4-4, Strong 1-11. St. Louis, S. Jackson 17-77.

PASSING—Seattle, Hasselbeck 27-38-0-316. St. Louis, Bulger 26-40-1-336.

RECEIVING—Seattle, Jurevicius 9-137, Hackett 5-43, Stevens 3-65, Strong 3-25, Alexander 3-16, Hannam 2-12, Urban 1-11, Warrick 1-7. St. Louis, Holt 8-126, S. Jackson 6-62, Curtis 5-63, McDonald 5-55, Robinson 1-28, Cleeland 1-2.

MISSED FIELD GOAL ATTEMPTS—None.

INTERCEPTIONS—Seattle, Tatupu 1-3.

KICKOFF RETURNS—Seattle, Scobey 5-117. St. Louis, C. Johnson 6-202.

PUNT RETURNS—Seattle, J. Williams 2-28. St. Louis, Fair 3-7, McDonald 1-(minus 1).

SACKS—Seattle, R. Bernard 1.5, Darby 1, Hill 1, Terrill 0.5. St. Louis, T. Jackson 2, Ivy 1, Little 0.5, Archuleta 0.5.

BILLS 20, DOLPHINS 14

Sunday, October 9

Miami	0	0	7	7—14
Buffalo	10	7	0	3—20

First Quarter

Buf.—McGahee 1 run (Lindell kick), 3:37.

Buf.—FG, Lindell 24, 10:45.

Second Quarter

Buf.—Moulds 2 pass from Holcomb (Lindell kick), 6:52.

Third Quarter

Mia.—Heller 1 pass from Frerotte (Mare kick), 9:10.

Fourth Quarter

Mia.—McMichael 30 pass from Frerotte (Mare kick), 6:42.

Buf.—FG, Lindell 47, 10:25.

Attendance—72,160.

	Miami	Buffalo
First downs	16	21
Rushes-yards	20-113	36-99
Passing	210	137
Punt returns	5-33	2-1
Kickoff returns	5-104	3-105
Interception returns	0-0	3-6
Comp.-att.-int.	21-33-3	20-26-0
Sacked-yards lost	2-16	3-32
Punts	3-41	6-50
Fumbles-lost	4-2	5-1
Penalties-yards	18-102	7-63
Time of possession	24:48	35:12

INDIVIDUAL STATISTICS

RUSHING—Miami, Brown 17-97, Frerotte 2-16, D. Jones 1-0. Buffalo, McGahee 31-86, Holcomb 4-11, S. Williams 1-2.

PASSING—Miami, Frerotte 21-33-3-226. Buffalo, Holcomb 20-26-0-169.

RECEIVING—Miami, Brown 6-19, Chambers 4-60, Booker 3-72, Welker 2-24, H. Evans 2-10, McMichael 1-30, Morris 1-8, Diamond 1-2, Heller 1-1. Buffalo, Moulds 7-59, Evans 3-65, Campbell 3-15, Reed 2-13, Shelton 2-10, McGahee 2-5, S. Williams 1-2.

MISSED FIELD GOAL ATTEMPTS—None.

INTERCEPTIONS—Buffalo, Vincent 1-6, Clements 1-0, McGee 1-0.

KICKOFF RETURNS—Miami, Welker 4-93, Heller 1-11. Buffalo, McGee 2-80, J. Smith 1-25.

PUNT RETURNS—Miami, Welker 5-33. Buffalo, J. Smith 2-1.

SACKS—Miami, Taylor 2, Howard 1. Buffalo, Denney 1, Kelsay 1.

LIONS 35, RAVENS 17

Sunday, October 9

Baltimore	0	10	0	7—17
Detroit	14	0	7	14—35

First Quarter

Det.—Jones 14 run (Hanson kick), 5:20.

Det.—Jones 1 run (Hanson kick), 10:20.

Second Quarter

Bal.—J. Lewis 15 pass from Wright (Stover kick), 6:46.

Bal.—FG, Stover 46, 15:00.

Third Quarter

Det.—Pinner 1 run (Hanson kick), 13:25.

Fourth Quarter

Det.—FitzSimmons 2 pass from Harrington (Hanson kick), :05.

Bal.—Heap 6 pass from Wright (Stover kick), 6:01.

Det.—Bryson 77 run (Hanson kick), 7:55.

Attendance—61,201.

	Baltimore	Detroit
First downs	26	22
Rushes-yards	30-159	37-169
Passing	228	97
Punt returns	3-24	4-75
Kickoff returns	5-96	3-48
Interception returns	2-38	2-21
Comp.-att.-int.	20-37-2	10-23-2
Sacked-yards lost	1-2	1-0
Punts	4-41	4-46
Fumbles-lost	2-2	1-0
Penalties-yards	21-147	7-46
Time of possession	29:46	30:14

INDIVIDUAL STATISTICS

RUSHING—Baltimore, J. Lewis 19-95, C. Taylor 9-46, Wright 2-18. Detroit, Jones 26-58, Pinner 9-32, Bryson 1-77, Harrington 1-2.

PASSING—Baltimore, Wright 20-37-2-230. Detroit, Harrington 10-23-2-97.

RECEIVING—Baltimore, Mason 6-65, C. Taylor 4-24, Clayton 3-21, Heap 2-54, J. Lewis 2-17, Moore 1-23, Hymes 1-21, Mughelli 1-5. Detroit, K. Johnson 3-25, R. Williams 2-24, Bryson 1-18, P. Smith 1-11, Vines 1-10, M. Williams 1-7, FitzSimmons 1-2.

MISSED FIELD GOAL ATTEMPTS—None.

INTERCEPTIONS—Baltimore, Suggs 1-38, McAlister 1-0. Detroit, Bly 2-17.

KICKOFF RETURNS—Baltimore, Sams 5-96. Detroit, McQuarters 1-19, Drummond 1-15, K. Johnson 1-14.

PUNT RETURNS—Baltimore, Sams 3-24. Detroit, McQuarters 4-75.

SACKS—Baltimore. Detroit, K. Edwards 1.

PATRIOTS 31, FALCONS 28
Sunday, October 9

New England	14	0	14	3—31
Atlanta	0	13	0	15—28

First Quarter
N.E.—Pass 6 run (Vinatieri kick), 9:55.
N.E.—Graham 45 pass from Brady (Vinatieri kick), 13:57.

Second Quarter
Atl.—Griffith 2 pass from Schaub (T. Peterson kick), 1:36.
Atl.—FG, T. Peterson 33, 13:35.
Atl.—FG, Koenen 58, 14:59.

Third Quarter
N.E.—Watson 33 pass from Brady (Vinatieri kick), 1:01.
N.E.—B. Johnson 55 pass from Brady (Vinatieri kick), 9:10.

Fourth Quarter
Atl.—Crumpler 25 pass from Schaub (T. Peterson kick), :37.
Atl.—D. White 14 pass from Schaub (Finneran pass from Schaub), 11:08.
N.E.—FG, Vinatieri 29, 14:43.
Attendance—71,079.

	New England	Atlanta
First downs	20	22
Rushes-yards	30-141	26-116
Passing	342	284
Punt returns	2-5	1-8
Kickoff returns	5-86	6-119
Interception returns	0-0	1-0
Comp.-att.-int.	22-27-1	18-34-0
Sacked-yards lost	1-8	3-14
Punts	6-44	7-46
Fumbles-lost	0-0	0-0
Penalties-yards	11-83	8-84
Time of possession	32:25	27:35

INDIVIDUAL STATISTICS

RUSHING—New England, Dillon 23-106, Pass 6-34, Brady 1-1. Atlanta, Dunn 19-83, Duckett 5-30, Schaub 2-3.

PASSING—New England, Brady 22-27-1-350. Atlanta, Schaub 18-34-0-298.

RECEIVING—New England, Branch 8-107, Graham 5-119, Givens 2-14, Dillon 2-13, B. Johnson 1-55, Watson 1-33, Pass 1-6, T. Brown 1-2, Dwight 1-1. Atlanta, Crumpler 6-99, Finneran 5-103, Jenkins 3-55, Dunn 2-23, D. White 1-14, Griffith 1-2, R. White 0-2.

MISSED FIELD GOAL ATTEMPTS—None.

INTERCEPTIONS—Atlanta, D. Williams 1-0.

KICKOFF RETURNS—New England, B. Johnson 4-86, M. Stone 1-0. Atlanta, Rossum 6-119.

PUNT RETURNS—New England, Dwight 2-5. Atlanta, Rossum 1-8.

SACKS—New England, Beisel 1, Colvin 1, J. Green 0.5, Vrabel 0.5. Atlanta, B. Smith 1.

COLTS 28, 49ERS 3
Sunday, October 9

Indianapolis	7	7	0	14—28
San Francisco	0	0	3	0— 3

First Quarter
Ind.—Rhodes 6 run (Vanderjagt kick), 7:19.

Second Quarter
Ind.—June 24 interception return (Vanderjagt kick), 8:31.

Third Quarter
S.F.—FG, Nedney 30, 5:19.

Fourth Quarter
Ind.—James 4 run (Vanderjagt kick), :05.
Ind.—Walters 18 pass from Manning (Vanderjagt kick), 9:02.
Attendance—68,084.

	Indianapolis	San Francisco
First downs	22	12
Rushes-yards	28-120	28-133
Passing	245	44
Punt returns	3-16	1-7
Kickoff returns	0-0	5-101
Interception returns	4-52	2-13
Comp.-att.-int.	23-31-2	9-23-4
Sacked-yards lost	1-10	5-30
Punts	2-42	5-42
Fumbles-lost	1-1	2-1
Penalties-yards	10-80	7-40
Time of possession	30:52	29:08

INDIVIDUAL STATISTICS

RUSHING—Indianapolis, James 21-105, Rhodes 5-18, Sorgi 2-(minus 3). San Francisco, Barlow 18-99, Gore 8-31, A. Smith 2-3.

PASSING—Indianapolis, Manning 23-31-2-255. San Francisco, A. Smith 9-23-4-74.

RECEIVING—Indianapolis, Wayne 6-75, Stokley 6-59, James 4-42, Clark 3-36, Harrison 2-17, Walters 1-18, Rhodes 1-8. San Francisco, Barlow 3-29, Gore 1-14, Morton 1-13, Bush 1-10, Beasley 1-6, Hetherington 1-2, Bajema 1-0.

MISSED FIELD GOAL ATTEMPTS—None.

INTERCEPTIONS—Indianapolis, June 2-39, David 1-13, Doss 1-0. San Francisco, D. Smith 1-13, B. Thornton 1-0.

KICKOFF RETURNS—San Francisco, Hicks 3-62, Amey 2-39.

PUNT RETURNS—Indianapolis, Walters 3-16. San Francisco, Amey 1-7.

SACKS—Indianapolis, Mathis 2, Thornton 1, Freeney 1, Brock 1. San Francisco, Carter 1.

PANTHERS 24, CARDINALS 20
Sunday, October 9

Carolina	3	7	0	14—24
Arizona	0	17	3	0—20

First Quarter
Car.—FG, Kasay 46, 9:19.

Second Quarter
Ariz.—Fitzgerald 26 pass from McCown (Rackers kick), :05.
Car.—S. Smith 65 pass from Delhomme (Kasay kick), 2:31.
Ariz.—FG, Rackers 39, 4:34.
Ariz.—Boldin 20 pass from McCown (Rackers kick), 9:52.

Third Quarter
Ariz.—FG, Rackers 49, 9:49.

Fourth Quarter
Car.—S. Davis 1 run (Kasay kick), :03.
Car.—S. Smith 4 pass from Delhomme (Kasay kick), 8:06.
Attendance—38,809.

	Carolina	Arizona
First downs	15	19
Rushes-yards	27-87	27-72
Passing	243	396
Punt returns	0-0	3-33
Kickoff returns	3-95	4-109
Interception returns	3-84	1-25
Comp.-att.-int.	18-29-1	29-46-3
Sacked-yards lost	0-0	1-2
Punts	5-43	3-42
Fumbles-lost	1-1	1-1
Penalties-yards	4-30	8-55
Time of possession	25:48	34:12

INDIVIDUAL STATISTICS

RUSHING—Carolina, S. Davis 18-46, Foster 8-42, Delhomme 1-(minus 1). Arizona, Shipp 13-22, McCown 5-29, Arrington 4-14, Boldin 3-7, O. Ayanbadejo 1-0, B. Johnson 1-0.

PASSING—Carolina, Delhomme 18-29-1-243. Arizona, McCown 29-46-3-398.

RECEIVING—Carolina, S. Smith 8-119, Gardner 3-33, Mangum 3-31, Foster 2-47, Proehl 1-11, Gaines 1-2. Arizona, Boldin 10-162, Fitzgerald 9-136, O. Ayanbadejo 4-24, B. Johnson 2-9, Shipp 2-6, Lee 1-49, Arrington 1-12.

MISSED FIELD GOAL ATTEMPTS—Carolina, Kasay 53, 62.

INTERCEPTIONS—Carolina, McCree 2-46, Wallace 1-38. Arizona, Tate 1-25.

KICKOFF RETURNS—Carolina, Robertson 3-95. Arizona, Swinton 4-109.

PUNT RETURNS—Arizona, Swinton 3-33.

SACKS—Carolina, Morgan 1.

COWBOYS 33, EAGLES 10
Sunday, October 9

Philadelphia	0	3	7	0—10
Dallas	17	10	3	3—33

First Quarter

Dal.—T. Glenn 15 pass from Bledsoe (Cortez kick), 1:59.
Dal.—T. Glenn 38 pass from Bledsoe (Cortez kick), 7:19.
Dal.—FG, Cortez 28, 14:41.

Second Quarter

Phi.—FG, France 23, 4:37.
Dal.—Polite 12 pass from Bledsoe (Cortez kick), 9:38.
Dal.—FG, Cortez 33, 14:51.

Third Quarter

Dal.—FG, Cortez 37, 3:21.
Phi.—S. Brown 80 fumble return (France kick), 13:48.

Fourth Quarter

Dal.—FG, Cortez 45, 10:21.
Attendance—63,199.

	Philadelphia	Dallas
First downs	6	28
Rushes-yards	9-19	46-167
Passing	110	289
Punt returns	1-0	7-84
Kickoff returns	6-96	3-87
Interception returns	0-0	0-0
Comp.-att.-int.	16-30-0	24-35-0
Sacked-yards lost	4-35	0-0
Punts	8-47	2-41
Fumbles-lost	0-0	2-1
Penalties-yards	8-54	5-48
Time of possession	19:17	40:43

INDIVIDUAL STATISTICS

RUSHING—Philadelphia, Westbrook 6-12, McNabb 2-2, Gordon 1-5. Dallas, Thompson 20-75, J. Jones 16-72, A. Thomas 4-5, Bledsoe 3-14, Romo 2-(minus 2), K. Johnson 1-3.

PASSING—Philadelphia, McNabb 13-26-0-131, Detmer 3-4-0-14. Dallas, Bledsoe 24-35-0-289.

RECEIVING—Philadelphia, Owens 5-50, G. Lewis 3-36, Westbrook 3-24, Smith 2-22, Spach 2-10, R. Brown 1-3. Dallas, T. Glenn 7-118, Witten 7-80, K. Johnson 6-47, Crayton 2-30, Polite 1-12, Thompson 1-2.

MISSED FIELD GOAL ATTEMPTS—None.

INTERCEPTIONS—None.

KICKOFF RETURNS—Philadelphia, Wynn 5-78, Hood 1-18. Dallas, Thompson 3-87.

PUNT RETURNS—Philadelphia, Wynn 1-0. Dallas, Crayton 7-84.

SACKS—Dallas, Ro. Williams 1, Newman 1, Ware 1, Ratliff 0.5, Ellis 0.5.

BRONCOS 21, REDSKINS 19
Sunday, October 9

Washington	7	3	0	9—19
Denver	7	7	7	0—21

First Quarter

Den.—Bell 34 run (Elam kick), 3:20.
Was.—Sellers 2 pass from Brunell (Novak kick), 11:13.

Second Quarter

Den.—Lelie 5 pass from Plummer (Elam kick), 2:53.
Was.—FG, Novak 34, 13:18.

Third Quarter

Den.—Bell 55 run (Elam kick), 8:33.

Fourth Quarter

Was.—FG, Novak 36, 8:35.
Was.—Cooley 11 pass from Brunell (pass failed), 13:51.
Attendance—75,880.

	Washington	Denver
First downs	28	11
Rushes-yards	26-125	28-165
Passing	322	92
Punt returns	3-24	0-0
Kickoff returns	3-85	4-74
Interception returns	0-0	0-0
Comp.-att.-int.	30-53-0	10-26-0
Sacked-yards lost	0-0	0-0
Punts	5-37	8-41
Fumbles-lost	1-1	0-0
Penalties-yards	10-67	6-43
Time of possession	33:49	26:11

INDIVIDUAL STATISTICS

RUSHING—Washington, Portis 20-103, Brunell 4-17, Betts 2-5. Denver, Bell 12-127, Mi. Anderson 11-34, Plummer 5-4.

PASSING—Washington, Brunell 30-53-0-322. Denver, Plummer 10-25-0-92, Smith 0-1-0-0.

RECEIVING—Washington, Moss 8-116, Cooley 8-82, Patten 7-63, Portis 2-27, Betts 2-21, Thrash 1-7, Royal 1-4, Sellers 1-2. Denver, Smith 2-23, Mi. Anderson 2-16, Adams 2-11, Putzier 1-31, Lelie 1-5, Bell 1-5, K. Johnson 1-1.

MISSED FIELD GOAL ATTEMPTS—Washington, Novak 38.

INTERCEPTIONS—None.

KICKOFF RETURNS—Washington, Thrash 2-57, Betts 1-28. Denver, Adams 2-56, Da. Williams 1-18, Carswell 1-0.

PUNT RETURNS—Washington, Moss 2-17, Thrash 1-7.

SACKS—None.

JAGUARS 23, BENGALS 20
Sunday, October 9

Cincinnati	0	7	6	7—20
Jacksonville	10	3	7	3—23

First Quarter

Jac.—Wrighster 26 pass from Leftwich (Scobee kick), 4:29.
Jac.—FG, Scobee 32, 14:10.

Second Quarter

Jac.—FG, Scobee 51, 4:53.
Cin.—C. Johnson 14 pass from Palmer (Graham kick), 9:24.

Third Quarter

Jac.—Wilford 11 pass from Leftwich (Scobee kick), 2:44.
Cin.—FG, Graham 31, 7:55.
Cin.—FG, Graham 48, 10:31.

Fourth Quarter

Jac.—FG, Scobee 53, 5:15.
Cin.—Henry 25 pass from Palmer (Graham kick), 9:44.
Attendance—66,137.

	Cincinnati	Jacksonville
First downs	20	19
Rushes-yards	26-132	37-181
Passing	232	161
Punt returns	2-8	1-8
Kickoff returns	3-82	4-73
Interception returns	0-0	0-0
Comp.-att.-int.	22-33-0	10-24-0
Sacked-yards lost	2-7	0-0
Punts	6-36	5-40
Fumbles-lost	2-1	1-1
Penalties-yards	12-94	10-98
Time of possession	30:35	29:25

INDIVIDUAL STATISTICS

RUSHING—Cincinnati, Ru. Johnson 18-76, C. Perry 7-55, Palmer 1-1. Jacksonville, F. Taylor 24-132, Leftwich 5-0, G. Jones 4-24, Pearman 3-15, R. Williams 1-10.

PASSING—Cincinnati, Palmer 22-33-0-239. Jacksonville, Leftwich 10-24-0-161.

RECEIVING—Cincinnati, C. Johnson 5-52, Henry 3-85, Schobel 3-23, Walter 3-17, Washington 2-30, C. Perry 2-21, Ru. Johnson 2-7, R. Kelly 1-5, J. Johnson 1-(minus 1). Jacksonville, J. Smith 3-43, R. Williams 2-41, Wrighster 2-40, Pearman 1-19, Wilford 1-11, Brady 1-7.

MISSED FIELD GOAL ATTEMPTS—None.

INTERCEPTIONS—None.

KICKOFF RETURNS—Cincinnati, T. Perry 3-82. Jacksonville, Wimbush 4-73.

PUNT RETURNS—Cincinnati, Ratliff 2-8. Jacksonville, Pearman 1-8.
SACKS—Jacksonville, D. Smith 1, Stroud 1.

STEELERS 24, CHARGERS 22

Monday, October 10

Pittsburgh	0	14	0	10—24
San Diego	0	7	6	9—22

Second Quarter
Pit.—Roethlisberger 7 run (Reed kick), 5:46.
Pit.—Bettis 1 run (Reed kick), 13:23.
S.D.—Gates 11 pass from Brees (Kaeding kick), 14:26.
Third Quarter
S.D.—FG, Kaeding 34, 5:18.
S.D.—FG, Kaeding 32, 11:06.
Fourth Quarter
S.D.—FG, Kaeding 41, 3:19.
Pit.—Miller 16 pass from Roethlisberger (Reed kick), 4:30.
S.D.—Tomlinson 2 run (run failed), 10:18.
Pit.—FG, Reed 40, 14:54.
    Attendance—68,537.

	Pittsburgh	San Diego
First downs	25	20
Rushes-yards	32-104	21-66
Passing	207	213
Punt returns	1-0	2-11
Kickoff returns	6-138	5-157
Interception returns	1-25	0-0
Comp.-att.-int.	17-26-0	20-35-1
Sacked-yards lost	3-18	1-6
Punts	6-43	4-48
Fumbles-lost	1-1	1-1
Penalties-yards	11-104	9-100
Time of possession	33:23	26:37

INDIVIDUAL STATISTICS

RUSHING—Pittsburgh, Bettis 17-54, Parker 10-26, Roethlisberger 2-15, Randle El 2-7, Kreider 1-2. San Diego, Tomlinson 18-62, Brees 2-3, Neal 1-1.

PASSING—Pittsburgh, Roethlisberger 17-26-0-225. San Diego, Brees 20-35-1-219.

RECEIVING—Pittsburgh, Ward 6-83, Miller 4-36, Randle El 3-50, Wilson 1-22, Bettis 1-16, Parker 1-14, Haynes 1-4. San Diego, Tomlinson 7-68, E. Parker 5-72, Gates 5-61, Caldwell 1-7, Osgood 1-6, McCardell 1-5.

MISSED FIELD GOAL ATTEMPTS—None.

INTERCEPTIONS—Pittsburgh, J. Harrison 1-25.

KICKOFF RETURNS—Pittsburgh, Colclough 3-56, Wilson 2-45, Morgan 1-37. San Diego, Sproles 5-157.

PUNT RETURNS—Pittsburgh, Randle El 1-0. San Diego, Sproles 2-11.

SACKS—Pittsburgh, Porter 1. San Diego, Merriman 1, Phillips 1, Foley 0.5, Scott 0.5.

WEEK 6

STANDINGS

AMERICAN FOOTBALL CONFERENCE

EAST DIVISION

	W	L	T	Pct.	PF	PA
Buffalo	3	3	0	.500	95	100
New England	3	3	0	.500	138	164
Miami	2	3	0	.400	95	98
N.Y. Jets	2	4	0	.333	78	112

NORTH DIVISION

	W	L	T	Pct.	PF	PA
Cincinnati	5	1	0	.833	155	84
Pittsburgh	3	2	0	.600	122	82
Baltimore	2	3	0	.400	63	90
Cleveland	2	3	0	.400	68	90

SOUTH DIVISION

	W	L	T	Pct.	PF	PA
Indianapolis	6	0	0	1.000	151	57
Jacksonville	4	2	0	.667	108	101
Tennessee	2	4	0	.333	126	157
Houston	0	5	0	.000	54	141

WEST DIVISION

	W	L	T	Pct.	PF	PA
Denver	5	1	0	.833	129	107
Kansas City	3	2	0	.600	119	112
San Diego	3	3	0	.500	176	126
Oakland	1	4	0	.200	90	116

NATIONAL FOOTBALL CONFERENCE

EAST DIVISION

	W	L	T	Pct.	PF	PA
Dallas	4	2	0	.667	137	111
N.Y. Giants	3	2	0	.600	149	114
Philadelphia	3	2	0	.600	122	101
Washington	3	2	0	.600	83	86

NORTH DIVISION

	W	L	T	Pct.	PF	PA
Chicago	2	3	0	.400	90	62
Detroit	2	3	0	.400	91	96
Green Bay	1	4	0	.200	124	95
Minnesota	1	4	0	.200	67	135

SOUTH DIVISION

	W	L	T	Pct.	PF	PA
Tampa Bay	5	1	0	.833	116	72
Atlanta	4	2	0	.667	148	119
Carolina	4	2	0	.667	148	136
New Orleans	2	4	0	.333	102	173

WEST DIVISION

	W	L	T	Pct.	PF	PA
Seattle	4	2	0	.667	168	117
St. Louis	2	4	0	.333	156	193
Arizona	1	4	0	.200	94	134
San Francisco	1	4	0	.200	79	160

TOP PERFORMANCES

100-YARD RUSHING GAMES

Player, team & opponent	Att.	Yds.	TD
Curtis Martin, NYJ at Buf.	18	148	1
Edgerrin James, Ind. vs. St.L.	23	143	3
Willis McGahee, Buf. vs. NYJ	29	143	1
Shaun Alexander, Sea. vs. Hou.	22	141	4
LaDainian Tomlinson, S.D. at Oak.	31	140	1
Michael Pittman, T.B. vs. Mia.	15	127	1
Tatum Bell, Den. vs. N.E.	13	114	1
Maurice Morris, Sea. vs. Hou.	8	104	1
Warrick Dunn, Atl. at N.O.	22	100	1

300-YARD PASSING GAMES

Player, team & opponent	Att.	Cmp.	Yds.	TD	Int.
Mark Brunell, Was. at K.C.	41	25	331	3	0
Drew Bledsoe, Dal. vs. NYG*	37	26	312	1	1

100-YARD RECEIVING GAMES

Player, team & opponent	Rec.	Yds.	TD
Santana Moss, Was. at K.C.	10	173	2
Chad Johnson, Cin. at Ten.	8	135	1
Jeremy Shockey, NYG at Dal.*	5	129	1
Rod Smith, Den. vs. N.E.	6	123	1
Steve Smith, Car. at Det.	6	123	1
Keyshawn Johnson, Dal. vs. NYG*	8	120	0
Justin McCareins, NYJ at Buf.	5	116	0
Marcus Pollard, Det. vs. Car.	3	105	0
Priest Holmes, K.C. vs. Was.	5	100	1

*Overtime game.

RESULTS

SUNDAY, OCTOBER 16
BALTIMORE 16, Cleveland 3
Jacksonville 23, PITTSBURGH 17 (OT)
Cincinnati 31, TENNESSEE 23
Carolina 21, DETROIT 20
DALLAS 16, N.Y. Giants 13 (OT)
CHICAGO 28, Minnesota 13
Atlanta 34, NEW ORLEANS 31
TAMPA BAY 27, Miami 13
KANSAS CITY 28, Washington 21
BUFFALO 27, N.Y. Jets 17
San Diego 27, OAKLAND 14
DENVER 28, New England 20
SEATTLE 42, Houston 10

MONDAY, OCTOBER 17
INDIANAPOLIS 45, St. Louis 28

Open Date: Arizona, Green Bay, Philadelphia, San Francisco

RAVENS 16, BROWNS 3
Sunday, October 16

Cleveland........................	0	0	3	0— 3
Baltimore........................	10	6	0	0—16

First Quarter
Bal.—Heap 3 pass from Wright (Stover kick), 6:11.
Bal.—FG, Stover 39, 11:52.

Second Quarter
Bal.—FG, Stover 27, 2:22.
Bal.—FG, Stover 38, 15:00.

Third Quarter
Cle.—FG, Dawson 24, 7:23.
   Attendance—70,196.

	Cleveland	Baltimore
First downs	12	16
Rushes-yards....................................	18-70	33-150
Passing..	116	201
Punt returns.....................................	5-38	3-74
Kickoff returns.................................	4-75	1-7
Interception returns	1-10	1-0
Comp.-att.-int.	16-30-1	23-31-1
Sacked-yards lost	4-31	1-12
Punts...	6-50	5-48
Fumbles-lost....................................	3-2	1-0
Penalties-yards	8-53	11-97
Time of possession	22:55	37:05

INDIVIDUAL STATISTICS
RUSHING—Cleveland, Droughns 15-55, Green 2-15, Dilfer 1-0. Baltimore, J. Lewis 24-59, C. Taylor 8-92, Wright 1-(minus 1).

PASSING—Cleveland, Dilfer 16-30-1-147. Baltimore, Wright 23-31-1-213.

RECEIVING—Cleveland, Northcutt 4-60, Heiden 4-38, Bryant 4-34, Shea 3-17, Droughns 1-(minus 2). Baltimore, Mason 8-85, Heap 6-79, C. Taylor 4-8, J. Lewis 2-11, Hymes 1-19, Clayton 1-9, Wilcox 1-2.

MISSED FIELD GOAL ATTEMPTS—None.

INTERCEPTIONS—Cleveland, Baxter 1-10. Baltimore, R. Lewis 1-0.

KICKOFF RETURNS—Cleveland, Cribbs 3-61, McIntyre 1-14. Baltimore, Sams 1-7.

PUNT RETURNS—Cleveland, Northcutt 5-38. Baltimore, Sams 3-74.

SACKS—Cleveland, McKinley 1. Baltimore, Polley 1.5, A. Thomas 1, Suggs 1, Gregg 0.5.

JAGUARS 23, STEELERS 17
Sunday, October 16

Jacksonville	7	3	7	0	6—23
Pittsburgh.............................	0	14	0	3	0—17

First Quarter
Jac.—G. Jones 7 run (Scobee kick), 13:48.

Second Quarter
Pit.—Miller 15 pass from Maddox (Reed kick), :08.
Pit.—Randle El 72 punt return (Reed kick), 1:10.
Jac.—FG, Scobee 23, 15:00.

Third Quarter
Jac.—M. Jones 10 pass from Leftwich (Scobee kick), 3:14.

Fourth Quarter
Pit.—FG, Reed 29, 5:22.

Overtime
Jac.—Mathis 41 interception return, 3:36.
   Attendance—63,891.

	Jacksonville	Pittsburgh
First downs	17	16
Rushes-yards....................................	35-93	30-73
Passing..	153	145
Punt returns.....................................	3-15	5-94
Kickoff returns.................................	2-40	2-77
Interception returns	3-54	1-0
Comp.-att.-int.	19-35-1	11-28-3
Sacked-yards lost	3-24	2-9
Punts...	9-47	6-32
Fumbles-lost....................................	1-0	2-1
Penalties-yards	10-106	7-80
Time of possession	36:09	27:27

INDIVIDUAL STATISTICS
RUSHING—Jacksonville, G. Jones 18-77, Pearman 15-22, Leftwich 1-1, M. Jones 1-(minus 7). Pittsburgh, Parker 21-55, Bettis 4-4, Maddox 3-15, Haynes 2-(minus 1).

PASSING—Jacksonville, Leftwich 19-35-1-177. Pittsburgh, Maddox 11-28-3-154.

RECEIVING—Jacksonville, Pearman 5-35, R. Williams 3-50, J. Smith 3-32, Brady 3-15, M. Jones 2-20, Wilford 2-15, G. Jones 1-10. Pittsburgh, Miller 4-72, Randle El 3-27, Morgan 2-33, Haynes 1-11, Wilson 1-11.

MISSED FIELD GOAL ATTEMPTS—Pittsburgh, Reed 46.

INTERCEPTIONS—Jacksonville, Mathis 1-41, Peterson 1-14, Cousin 1-(minus 1). Pittsburgh, McFadden 1-0.

KICKOFF RETURNS—Jacksonville, Wimbush 2-40. Pittsburgh, Morgan 1-74, Kreider 1-3.

PUNT RETURNS—Jacksonville, Pearman 3-15. Pittsburgh, Randle El 5-94.

SACKS—Jacksonville, Hayward 2. Pittsburgh, Porter 1, A. Smith 1, J. Harrison 1.

BENGALS 31, TITANS 23
Sunday, October 16

Cincinnati	0	7	10	14—31
Tennessee	0	10	7	6—23

Second Quarter
Ten.—Brown 4 run (Bironas kick), 2:10.
Ten.—FG, Bironas 24, 12:50.
Cin.—C. Perry 1 pass from Palmer (Graham kick), 14:27.

Third Quarter
Cin.—FG, Graham 21, 7:32.
Ten.—Brown 9 run (Bironas kick), 10:28.
Cin.—Thurman 30 interception return (Graham kick), 13:59.

Fourth Quarter
Ten.—FG, Bironas 29, 10:06.
Cin.—C. Johnson 15 pass from Palmer (Graham kick), 10:41.
Cin.—Ru. Johnson 1 run (Graham kick), 12:34.
Ten.—FG, Bironas 47, 14:28.
   Attendance—69,149.

	Cincinnati	Tennessee
First downs	24	21
Rushes-yards....................................	28-119	24-118
Passing..	268	259
Punt returns.....................................	1-7	2-34
Kickoff returns.................................	3-70	6-117
Interception returns	2-33	0-0
Comp.-att.-int.	27-33-0	26-41-2
Sacked-yards lost	1-4	0-0
Punts...	4-48	3-42
Fumbles-lost....................................	0-0	3-1
Penalties-yards	4-32	5-69
Time of possession	29:04	30:56

INDIVIDUAL STATISTICS
RUSHING—Cincinnati, Ru. Johnson 18-80, C. Perry 6-28, Palmer 3-4, T. Perry 1-7. Tennessee, Brown 18-84, Roby 2-16, Payton 2-11, McNair 2-7.

PASSING—Cincinnati, Palmer 27-33-0-272. Tennessee, McNair 26-41-2-259.

RECEIVING—Cincinnati, C. Perry 9-45, C. Johnson 8-135, Walter 4-65, Washington 2-13, Schobel 1-5, Henry 1-5, Ru. Johnson 1-3, J. Johnson 1-1. Tennessee, Bennett 7-61, B. Jones 5-82, Kinney 4-52, Troupe 4-22, Brown 3-28, Scaife 1-9, Calico 1-3, Roby 1-2.

MISSED FIELD GOAL ATTEMPTS—Cincinnati, Graham 52.

INTERCEPTIONS—Cincinnati, Thurman 1-30, Kaesviharn 1-3.

KICKOFF RETURNS—Cincinnati, T. Perry 3-70. Tennessee, Roby 6-117.

PUNT RETURNS—Cincinnati, Ratliff 1-7. Tennessee, B. Jones 2-34.

SACKS—Tennessee, Haynesworth 1.

PANTHERS 21, LIONS 20
Sunday, October 16

Carolina...........................	7	7	0	7—21
Detroit.............................	0	14	3	3—20

First Quarter
Car.—Gardner 4 pass from Delhomme (Kasay kick), 14:06.

Second Quarter
Det.—Bailey 34 interception return (Hanson kick), :43.
Car.—S. Smith 80 pass from Delhomme (Kasay kick), 1:00.

Det.—Kennedy 64 interception return (Hanson kick), 6:32.

Third Quarter
Det.—FG, Hanson 52, 14:20.

Fourth Quarter
Det.—FG, Hanson 25, 9:52.
Car.—Proehl 3 pass from Weinke (Kasay kick), 14:28.
    Attendance—61,083.

	Carolina	Detroit
First downs	14	11
Rushes-yards	25-54	24-52
Passing	263	157
Punt returns	4-14	2-3
Kickoff returns	5-72	4-112
Interception returns	1-27	3-98
Comp.-att.-int.	20-32-3	17-28-1
Sacked-yards lost	2-20	6-44
Punts	5-38	5-43
Fumbles-lost	3-1	4-3
Penalties-yards	10-73	10-75
Time of possession	27:57	32:03

INDIVIDUAL STATISTICS
RUSHING—Carolina, S. Davis 13-27, Goings 4-15, Robertson 4-7, Delhomme 2-5, Weinke 2-0. Detroit, Jones 12-21, Bryson 5-12, Pinner 4-7, Harrington 3-12.

PASSING—Carolina, Delhomme 15-25-3-236, Weinke 5-7-0-47. Detroit, Harrington 17-28-1-201.

RECEIVING—Carolina, S. Smith 6-123, Proehl 5-50, Gardner 4-32, Colbert 3-53, Goings 2-25. Detroit, K. Johnson 4-23, Pollard 3-105, M. Williams 2-27, Bryson 2-9, Jones 2-3, Pinner 1-13, Vines 1-13, P. Smith 1-4, FitzSimmons 1-4.

MISSED FIELD GOAL ATTEMPTS—Carolina, Kasay 52. Detroit, Hanson 47.

INTERCEPTIONS—Carolina, Lucas 1-27. Detroit, Kennedy 1-64, Bailey 1-34, Bly 1-0.

KICKOFF RETURNS—Carolina, Robertson 5-72. Detroit, McQuarters 3-87, Bryson 1-25.

PUNT RETURNS—Carolina, S. Smith 4-14. Detroit, McQuarters 2-3.

SACKS—Carolina, Rucker 2, Morgan 1, Wallace 1, Carstens 1, Peppers 1. Detroit, Cody 1.5, S. Rogers 0.5.

COWBOYS 16, GIANTS 13
Sunday, October 16

N.Y. Giants	3	3	0	7	0—13
Dallas	0	7	0	6	3—16

First Quarter
NYG—FG, Feely 50, 4:24.

Second Quarter
NYG—FG, Feely 45, 6:18.
Dal.—Witten 2 pass from Bledsoe (Cortez kick), 14:20.

Fourth Quarter
Dal.—FG, Cortez 29, 2:16.
Dal.—FG, Cortez 28, 10:20.
NYG—Shockey 24 pass from Manning (Feely kick), 14:41.

Overtime
Dal.—FG, Cortez 45, 3:47.
    Attendance—62,278.

	N.Y. Giants	Dallas
First downs	11	25
Rushes-yards	19-91	38-92
Passing	179	293
Punt returns	0-0	3-10
Kickoff returns	4-78	5-100
Interception returns	1-20	1-43
Comp.-att.-int.	14-29-1	26-37-1
Sacked-yards lost	4-36	3-19
Punts	5-42	3-40
Fumbles-lost	3-3	3-3
Penalties-yards	6-32	6-44
Time of possession	23:01	40:46

INDIVIDUAL STATISTICS
RUSHING—New York, Barber 14-64, Ward 3-15, Manning 1-10, Jacobs 1-2. Dallas, A. Thomas 21-47, Barber 11-30, Thompson 3-13, Bledsoe 3-2.

PASSING—New York, Manning 14-29-1-215. Dallas, Bledsoe 26-37-1-312.

RECEIVING—New York, Shockey 5-129, Burress 5-55, Toomer 2-11, T. Carter 1-15, Barber 1-5. Dallas, K. Johnson 8-120, T. Glenn 6-64, Witten 5-56, Crayton 4-46, Barber 2-21, Campbell 1-5.

MISSED FIELD GOAL ATTEMPTS—Dallas, Cortez 49, 48.

INTERCEPTIONS—New York, DeLoatch 1-20. Dallas, Henry 1-43.

KICKOFF RETURNS—New York, Ponder 4-78. Dallas, Thompson 5-100.

PUNT RETURNS—Dallas, Crayton 3-10.

SACKS—New York, Strahan 2, Umenyiora 1. Dallas, Glover 2, Ware 1, Ellis 1.

BEARS 28, VIKINGS 3
Sunday, October 16

Minnesota	0	3	0	0—	3
Chicago	0	7	7	14—	28

Second Quarter
Min.—FG, Edinger 23, 8:05.
Chi.—Clark 3 pass from Orton (Gould kick), 14:23.

Third Quarter
Chi.—Clark 2 pass from Orton (Gould kick), 7:32.

Fourth Quarter
Chi.—T. Jones 24 run (Gould kick), 1:57.
Chi.—T. Jones 1 run (Gould kick), 10:49.
    Attendance—62,143.

	Minnesota	Chicago
First downs	16	16
Rushes-yards	19-80	30-95
Passing	203	97
Punt returns	3-11	3-63
Kickoff returns	5-91	2-54
Interception returns	1-0	2-99
Comp.-att.-int.	26-49-2	16-25-1
Sacked-yards lost	4-34	3-20
Punts	6-44	5-39
Fumbles-lost	0-0	2-2
Penalties-yards	14-91	8-58
Time of possession	32:22	27:38

INDIVIDUAL STATISTICS
RUSHING—Minnesota, Moore 14-57, M. Bennett 3-8, Culpepper 1-14, M. Williams 1-1. Chicago, T. Jones 23-89, Orton 4-4, Benson 3-2.

PASSING—Minnesota, Culpepper 26-48-2-237, B. Johnson 0-1-0-0. Chicago, Orton 16-25-1-117.

RECEIVING—Minnesota, Wiggins 10-68, Moore 5-52, M. Robinson 4-41, Williamson 4-35, T. Taylor 2-37, K. Robinson 1-4. Chicago, Muhammad 5-48, Clark 4-19, M. Edwards 2-13, Bradley 1-15, Peterson 1-7, T. Jones 1-6, Reid 1-5, Wade 1-4.

MISSED FIELD GOAL ATTEMPTS—Minnesota, Edinger 52, 32.

INTERCEPTIONS—Minnesota, Chavous 1-0. Chicago, Tillman 1-55, C. Harris 1-44.

KICKOFF RETURNS—Minnesota, K. Robinson 5-91. Chicago, Azumah 2-54.

PUNT RETURNS—Minnesota, Howry 3-11. Chicago, Wade 3-63.

SACKS—Minnesota, K. Williams 1, Harris 1, Scott 0.5, Johnstone 0.5. Chicago, Urlacher 2, Idonije 1, T. Harris 1.

FALCONS 34, SAINTS 31
Sunday, October 16

Atlanta	3	14	0	17—	34
New Orleans	7	3	7	14—	31

First Quarter
Atl.—FG, T. Peterson 37, 5:21.
N.O.—A. Smith 24 run (Carney kick), 11:23.

Second Quarter
N.O.—FG, Carney 19, 5:05.
Atl.—D. Hall 66 fumble return (T. Peterson kick), 10:56.
Atl.—D. Williams 59 blocked FG return (T. Peterson kick), 15:00.

Third Quarter
N.O.—A. Smith 1 run (Carney kick), 7:21.

Fourth Quarter
Atl.—Griffith 12 pass from Vick (T. Peterson kick), 2:43.
N.O.—Stallworth 27 pass from Brooks (Carney kick), 8:04.
Atl.—Dunn 21 run (T. Peterson kick), 10:23.
N.O.—Henderson 15 pass from Brooks (Carney kick), 14:14.
Atl.—FG, T. Peterson 36, 15:00.
    Attendance—65,562.

	Atlanta	New Orleans
First downs	21	32
Rushes-yards	33-160	32-211
Passing	106	245
Punt returns	0-0	4-7

	Atlanta	New Orleans
Kickoff returns	6-143	4-71
Interception returns	1-22	1-51
Comp.-att.-int.	11-23-1	22-33-1
Sacked-yards lost	1-6	2-14
Punts	4-47	2-37
Fumbles-lost	0-0	1-1
Penalties-yards	10-79	8-55
Time of possession	26:34	33:26

INDIVIDUAL STATISTICS

RUSHING—Atlanta, Dunn 22-100, Vick 8-51, Duckett 2-5, Griffith 1-4. New Orleans, Stecker 16-86, A. Smith 12-88, Brooks 3-28, Henderson 1-9.

PASSING—Atlanta, Vick 11-23-1-112. New Orleans, Brooks 22-33-1-259.

RECEIVING—Atlanta, Crumpler 4-52, Jenkins 2-24, Dunn 2-15, Griffith 2-11, R. White 1-10. New Orleans, Stallworth 7-83, Hakim 6-85, Henderson 4-53, Stecker 2-0, Hilton 1-18, Poole 1-12, Karney 1-8.

MISSED FIELD GOAL ATTEMPTS—New Orleans, Carney 47.

INTERCEPTIONS—Atlanta, Brooking 1-22. New Orleans, Bullocks 1-51.

KICKOFF RETURNS—Atlanta, Rossum 6-143. New Orleans, Hakim 4-71.

PUNT RETURNS—New Orleans, Hakim 4-7.

SACKS—Atlanta, Kerney 1, R. Coleman 1. New Orleans, W. Smith 1.

BUCCANEERS 27, DOLPHINS 13
Sunday, October 16

Miami	3	0	3	7—13
Tampa Bay	10	0	17	0—27

First Quarter

T.B.—Galloway 7 pass from Griese (M. Bryant kick), 5:55.
Mia.—FG, Mare 47, 9:44.
T.B.—FG, M. Bryant 36, 13:50.

Third Quarter

Mia.—FG, Mare 53, 3:14.
T.B.—FG, M. Bryant 32, 10:28.
T.B.—Pittman 57 run (M. Bryant kick), 13:28.
T.B.—Allen 33 fumble return (M. Bryant kick), 14:54.

Fourth Quarter

Mia.—Brown 8 run (Mare kick), 5:04.
Attendance—65,168.

	Miami	Tampa Bay
First downs	13	15
Rushes-yards	18-64	34-180
Passing	243	162
Punt returns	4-70	3-20
Kickoff returns	6-130	1-23
Interception returns	0-0	0-0
Comp.-att.-int.	21-43-0	18-26-0
Sacked-yards lost	4-24	3-27
Punts	6-39	7-49
Fumbles-lost	3-2	1-1
Penalties-yards	9-60	9-65
Time of possession	24:21	35:39

INDIVIDUAL STATISTICS

RUSHING—Miami, Brown 9-22, R. Williams 5-8, Chambers 3-25, Frerotte 1-9. Tampa Bay, Graham 17-50, Pittman 15-127, Clayton 1-2, Griese 1-1.

PASSING—Miami, Frerotte 21-43-0-267. Tampa Bay, Griese 12-16-0-120, Simms 6-10-0-69.

RECEIVING—Miami, R. Williams 6-22, Welker 3-97, Chambers 3-50, McMichael 3-20, Brown 2-44, Morris 2-18, Booker 1-12, Gilmore 1-4. Tampa Bay, Galloway 9-96, Clayton 2-27, I. Hilliard 2-19, Smith 2-0, Alstott 1-23, Becht 1-13, Pittman 1-11.

MISSED FIELD GOAL ATTEMPTS—None.

INTERCEPTIONS—None.

KICKOFF RETURNS—Miami, Welker 6-130. Tampa Bay, Cox 1-23.

PUNT RETURNS—Miami, Welker 4-70. Tampa Bay, Jones 3-20.

SACKS—Miami, Carter 1, Z. Thomas 1, Bell 1. Tampa Bay, Brooks 1, Rice 1, Spires 1, D. White 1.

CHIEFS 28, REDSKINS 21
Sunday, October 16

Washington	0	7	14	0—21
Kansas City	3	3	15	7—28

First Quarter

K.C.—FG, Tynes 20, 12:15.

Second Quarter

Was.—Moss 4 pass from Brunell (Novak kick), 1:29.
K.C.—FG, Tynes 38, 9:06.

Third Quarter

K.C.—Holmes 6 run (Boerigter pass from Green), 3:22.
Was.—Moss 78 pass from Brunell (Novak kick), 4:12.
K.C.—S. Knight 80 fumble return (Tynes kick), 9:20.
Was.—Cooley 11 pass from Brunell (Novak kick), 14:30.

Fourth Quarter

K.C.—Holmes 60 pass from Green (Tynes kick), 1:39.
Attendance—78,083.

	Washington	Kansas City
First downs	26	18
Rushes-yards	28-101	32-96
Passing	297	178
Punt returns	0-0	2-2
Kickoff returns	6-118	4-72
Interception returns	0-0	0-0
Comp.-att.-int.	25-41-0	15-25-0
Sacked-yards lost	4-34	1-3
Punts	4-47	5-34
Fumbles-lost	3-3	2-0
Penalties-yards	5-54	4-24
Time of possession	32:20	27:40

INDIVIDUAL STATISTICS

RUSHING—Washington, Portis 21-77, Cartwright 4-14, Brunell 2-2, Thrash 1-8. Kansas City, Holmes 14-18, L. Johnson 13-53, Green 5-25.

PASSING—Washington, Brunell 25-41-0-331. Kansas City, Green 15-25-0-181.

RECEIVING—Washington, Moss 10-173, Cooley 6-54, Portis 4-51, Thrash 2-29, Patten 2-22, Sellers 1-2. Kansas City, Holmes 5-100, Parker 2-25, Boerigter 2-20, D. Hall 2-15, Gonzalez 2-13, Dunn 1-6, L. Johnson 1-2.

MISSED FIELD GOAL ATTEMPTS—None.

INTERCEPTIONS—None.

KICKOFF RETURNS—Washington, Thrash 5-113, Broughton 1-5. Kansas City, D. Hall 4-72.

PUNT RETURNS—Kansas City, D. Hall 2-2.

SACKS—Washington, Griffin 1. Kansas City, Allen 3, Browning 1.

BILLS 27, JETS 17
Sunday, October 16

N.Y. Jets	0	10	7	0—17
Buffalo	7	10	7	3—27

First Quarter

Buf.—J. Smith 8 pass from Holcomb (Lindell kick), 6:15.

Second Quarter

Buf.—Moulds 15 pass from Holcomb (Lindell kick), 4:55.
NYJ—FG, Nugent 44, 9:07.
NYJ—C. Martin 1 run (Nugent kick), 14:30.
Buf.—FG, Lindell 50, 15:00.

Third Quarter

Buf.—McGahee 1 run (Lindell kick), 8:28.
NYJ—Testaverde 1 run (Nugent kick), 13:19.

Fourth Quarter

Buf.—FG, Lindell 38, 9:06.
Attendance—72,045.

	N.Y. Jets	Buffalo
First downs	17	24
Rushes-yards	21-149	39-177
Passing	126	164
Punt returns	2-21	1-8
Kickoff returns	3-68	4-109
Interception returns	2-18	2-27
Comp.-att.-int.	12-26-2	18-26-2
Sacked-yards lost	5-35	1-8
Punts	5-39	4-43
Fumbles-lost	2-1	1-0
Penalties-yards	7-50	13-99
Time of possession	21:25	38:35

INDIVIDUAL STATISTICS

RUSHING—New York, C. Martin 18-148, Testaverde 3-1. Buffalo, McGahee 29-143, S. Williams 6-34, Holcomb 3-(minus 2), Evans 1-2.

PASSING—New York, Testaverde 12-26-2-161. Buffalo, Holcomb 18-26-2-172.

RECEIVING—New York, McCareins 5-116, Coles 4-33, C. Martin 2-3, Chrebet 1-9. Buffalo, Moulds 7-63, McGahee 3-24, Evans 3-22, Campbell 2-34, Reed 1-17, J. Smith 1-8, Peters 1-4.

MISSED FIELD GOAL ATTEMPTS—None.

INTERCEPTIONS—New York, Brown 1-18, Law 1-0. Buffalo, McGee 1-18, Crowell 1-1.

KICKOFF RETURNS—New York, Miller 3-68. Buffalo, McGee 3-104, Neufeld 1-5.

PUNT RETURNS—New York, McCareins 1-12, Cotchery 1-9. Buffalo, J. Smith 1-8.

SACKS—New York, Ellis 1. Buffalo, Denney 2, Adams 1, Crowell 1, T. Anderson 1.

CHARGERS 27, RAIDERS 14
Sunday, October 16

San Diego	14	10	3	0—27
Oakland	7	0	7	0—14

First Quarter
S.D.—Tomlinson 35 pass from Brees (Kaeding kick), 6:18.
S.D.—Tomlinson 7 run (Kaeding kick), 10:58.
Oak.—Jordan 4 run (Janikowski kick), 14:03.

Second Quarter
S.D.—FG, Kaeding 32, 4:35.
S.D.—Peelle 4 pass from Tomlinson (Kaeding kick), 12:21.

Third Quarter
S.D.—FG, Kaeding 33, 8:58.
Oak.—Jordan 1 run (Janikowski kick), 14:26.
Attendance—52,666.

	San Diego	Oakland
First downs	22	19
Rushes-yards	41-190	13-39
Passing	156	271
Punt returns	3-12	3-15
Kickoff returns	3-99	6-137
Interception returns	1-20	0-0
Comp.-att.-int.	15-21-0	24-48-1
Sacked-yards lost	2-12	4-21
Punts	7-43	6-47
Fumbles-lost	2-0	0-0
Penalties-yards	5-35	8-51
Time of possession	35:18	24:42

INDIVIDUAL STATISTICS
RUSHING—San Diego, Tomlinson 31-140, Turner 7-50, Caldwell 1-3, Neal 1-2, Brees 1-(minus 5). Oakland, Jordan 12-36, Crockett 1-3.

PASSING—San Diego, Brees 14-20-0-164, Tomlinson 1-1-0-4. Oakland, Collins 24-48-1-292.

RECEIVING—San Diego, Neal 4-27, Peelle 3-20, Tomlinson 2-39, McCardell 2-20, Gates 2-17, Caldwell 1-32, E. Parker 1-13. Oakland, Jordan 6-58, Gabriel 5-84, Porter 5-63, Whitted 4-34, Ra. Williams 2-39, C. Anderson 2-14.

MISSED FIELD GOAL ATTEMPTS—None.

INTERCEPTIONS—San Diego, Jue 1-20.

KICKOFF RETURNS—San Diego, Caldwell 3-99. Oakland, Carr 6-137.

PUNT RETURNS—San Diego, E. Parker 2-(minus 2), McCardell 1-14. Oakland, Carr 2-0, C. Woodson 1-15.

SACKS—San Diego, Olshansky 2, Scott 1, Cesaire 1. Oakland, Burgess 2.

BRONCOS 28, PATRIOTS 20
Sunday, October 16

New England	3	0	3	14—20
Denver	0	21	7	0—28

First Quarter
N.E.—FG, Vinatieri 39, 9:23.

Second Quarter
Den.—Bell 3 run (Elam kick), 2:24.
Den.—Smith 6 pass from Plummer (Elam kick), 7:08.
Den.—K. Johnson 1 pass from Plummer (Elam kick), 14:12.

Third Quarter
Den.—Mi. Anderson 2 run (Elam kick), 4:24.
N.E.—FG, Vinatieri 38, 9:07.

Fourth Quarter
N.E.—Pass 8 run (Vinatieri kick), :04.
N.E.—Givens 8 pass from Brady (Vinatieri kick), 6:59.
Attendance—76,571.

	New England	Denver
First downs	22	20
Rushes-yards	19-89	34-178
Passing	299	254
Punt returns	6-38	3-8
Kickoff returns	2-32	1-30
Interception returns	0-0	0-0
Comp.-att.-int.	24-46-0	17-24-0
Sacked-yards lost	0-0	1-8
Punts	7-52	7-52
Fumbles-lost	1-0	1-0
Penalties-yards	8-55	11-82
Time of possession	27:43	32:17

INDIVIDUAL STATISTICS
RUSHING—New England, Pass 10-64, Zereoue 7-14, Brady 1-12, Dwight 1-(minus 1). Denver, Mi. Anderson 15-57, Bell 13-114, Plummer 5-6, K. Johnson 1-1.

PASSING—New England, Brady 24-46-0-299. Denver, Plummer 17-24-0-262.

RECEIVING—New England, Branch 7-87, Givens 7-58, Pass 6-89, Dwight 1-49, Watson 1-6, Zereoue 1-5, Graham 1-5. Denver, Smith 6-123, Lelie 3-81, Putzier 3-32, Bell 3-20, S. Alexander 1-5, K. Johnson 1-1.

MISSED FIELD GOAL ATTEMPTS—New England, Vinatieri 53.

INTERCEPTIONS—None.

KICKOFF RETURNS—New England, B. Johnson 1-20, Hobbs 1-12. Denver, Da. Williams 1-30.

PUNT RETURNS—New England, Dwight 6-38. Denver, Da. Williams 2-2, Adams 1-6.

SACKS—New England, McGinest 0.5, Klecko 0.5.

SEAHAWKS 42, TEXANS 10
Sunday, October 16

Houston	0	3	7	0—10
Seattle	14	7	7	14—42

First Quarter
Sea.—Alexander 4 run (J. Brown kick), 6:48.
Sea.—Alexander 5 run (J. Brown kick), 13:52.

Second Quarter
Hou.—FG, K. Brown 39, 7:10.
Sea.—Jurevicius 3 pass from Hasselbeck (J. Brown kick), 13:15.

Third Quarter
Sea.—Alexander 1 run (J. Brown kick), 6:37.
Hou.—D. Davis 27 pass from Carr (K. Brown kick), 11:25.

Fourth Quarter
Sea.—Alexander 23 run (J. Brown kick), 1:43.
Sea.—Morris 11 run (J. Brown kick), 9:46.
Attendance—66,196.

	Houston	Seattle
First downs	14	31
Rushes-yards	22-67	42-320
Passing	160	139
Punt returns	0-0	4-18
Kickoff returns	4-90	3-81
Interception returns	1-3	0-0
Comp.-att.-int.	19-33-0	14-20-1
Sacked-yards lost	3-19	3-29
Punts	6-38	1-41
Fumbles-lost	1-0	2-0
Penalties-yards	13-95	6-45
Time of possession	28:27	31:33

INDIVIDUAL STATISTICS
RUSHING—Houston, D. Davis 18-40, Morency 2-15, Carr 2-12. Seattle, Alexander 22-141, Morris 8-104, Weaver 5-21, Hasselbeck 4-40, S. Wallace 2-(minus 2), Strong 1-16.

PASSING—Houston, Carr 19-33-0-179. Seattle, Hasselbeck 14-20-1-168.

RECEIVING—Houston, Gaffney 10-87, Bradford 4-38, D. Davis 2-28, Wells 1-16, Rivers 1-6, Armstrong 1-4. Seattle, Warrick 3-53, Jurevicius 3-29, Strong 3-20, Urban 2-37, Stevens 2-28, Alexander 1-1.

MISSED FIELD GOAL ATTEMPTS—Houston, K. Brown 56.

INTERCEPTIONS—Houston, Evans 1-3.

KICKOFF RETURNS—Houston, Morency 2-45, Mathis 2-45. Seattle, Scobey 3-81.

PUNT RETURNS—Seattle, J. Williams 4-18.

SACKS—Houston, Payne 1, Peek 1, C. Anderson 1. Seattle, Wistrom 1, R. Bernard 1, Terrill 1.

COLTS 45, RAMS 28
Monday, October 17

St. Louis	17	3	0	8—28
Indianapolis	0	14	10	21—45

First Quarter
St.L.—S. Jackson 21 run (J. Wilkins kick), 2:56.
St.L.—FG, J. Wilkins 29, 6:43.
St.L.—Curtis 57 pass from Bulger (J. Wilkins kick), 11:29.

Second Quarter
Ind.—James 1 run (Vanderjagt kick), 5:16.
Ind.—Wayne 3 pass from Manning (Vanderjagt kick), 13:03.
St.L.—FG, J. Wilkins 49, 14:30.

Third Quarter
Ind.—FG, Vanderjagt 22, 4:58.
Ind.—James 8 run (Vanderjagt kick), 11:44.

Fourth Quarter
Ind.—Rhodes 1 run (Vanderjagt kick), :02.
Ind.—Harrison 6 pass from Manning (Vanderjagt kick), 5:35.
Ind.—James 1 run (Vanderjagt kick), 6:48.
St.L.—Cleeland 9 pass from J. Martin (M. Faulk run), 11:32.
    Attendance—57,307.

	St. Louis	Indianapolis
First downs	20	31
Rushes-yards	21-105	38-176
Passing	244	187
Punt returns	0-0	1-19
Kickoff returns	8-151	5-94
Interception returns	0-0	3-67
Comp.-att.-int.	23-29-3	22-32-0
Sacked-yards lost	1-11	2-4
Punts	2-43	1-36
Fumbles-lost	2-1	2-1
Penalties-yards	9-50	3-15
Time of possession	27:06	32:54

INDIVIDUAL STATISTICS
RUSHING—St. Louis, S. Jackson 17-88, M. Faulk 4-17. Indianapolis, James 23-143, Rhodes 11-29, Manning 2-6, Sorgi 2-(minus 2).

PASSING—St. Louis, J. Martin 17-21-2-134, Bulger 6-8-1-121. Indianapolis, Manning 22-32-0-191.

RECEIVING—St. Louis, Holt 6-70, S. Jackson 5-39, M. Faulk 4-21, Curtis 3-73, Looker 2-25, Cleeland 2-18, Manumaleuna 1-9. Indianapolis, Wayne 7-59, Harrison 4-39, Stokley 4-38, Clark 3-31, James 3-16, Rhodes 1-8.

MISSED FIELD GOAL ATTEMPTS—Indianapolis, Vanderjagt 48.

INTERCEPTIONS—Indianapolis, June 2-46, Harper 1-21.

KICKOFF RETURNS—St. Louis, C. Johnson 8-151. Indianapolis, Rhodes 5-94.

PUNT RETURNS—Indianapolis, Walters 1-19.

SACKS—St. Louis, Tinoisamoa 1, Hargrove 1. Indianapolis, Mathis 1.

WEEK 7

STANDINGS

AMERICAN FOOTBALL CONFERENCE

EAST DIVISION

	W	L	T	Pct.	PF	PA
New England	3	3	0	.500	138	164
Buffalo	3	4	0	.429	112	138
Miami	2	4	0	.333	115	128
N.Y. Jets	2	5	0	.286	92	139

NORTH DIVISION

	W	L	T	Pct.	PF	PA
Cincinnati	5	2	0	.714	168	111
Pittsburgh	4	2	0	.667	149	95
Baltimore	2	4	0	.333	69	100
Cleveland	2	4	0	.333	78	103

SOUTH DIVISION

	W	L	T	Pct.	PF	PA
Indianapolis	7	0	0	1.000	189	77
Jacksonville	4	2	0	.667	108	101
Tennessee	2	5	0	.286	136	177
Houston	0	6	0	.000	74	179

WEST DIVISION

	W	L	T	Pct.	PF	PA
Denver	5	2	0	.714	152	131
Kansas City	4	2	0	.667	149	132
San Diego	3	4	0	.429	193	146
Oakland	2	4	0	.333	128	133

NATIONAL FOOTBALL CONFERENCE

EAST DIVISION

	W	L	T	Pct.	PF	PA
N.Y. Giants	4	2	0	.667	173	137
Philadelphia	4	2	0	.667	142	118
Washington	4	2	0	.667	135	103
Dallas	4	3	0	.571	147	124

NORTH DIVISION

	W	L	T	Pct.	PF	PA
Chicago	3	3	0	.500	100	68
Detroit	3	3	0	.500	104	106
Minnesota	2	4	0	.333	90	155
Green Bay	1	5	0	.167	144	118

SOUTH DIVISION

	W	L	T	Pct.	PF	PA
Tampa Bay	5	1	0	.833	116	72
Atlanta	5	2	0	.714	175	133
Carolina	4	2	0	.667	148	136
New Orleans	2	5	0	.286	119	201

WEST DIVISION

	W	L	T	Pct.	PF	PA
Seattle	5	2	0	.714	181	127
St. Louis	3	4	0	.429	184	210
Arizona	2	4	0	.333	114	144
San Francisco	1	5	0	.167	96	212

TOP PERFORMANCES

100-YARD RUSHING GAMES

Player, team & opponent	Att.	Yds.	TD
Warrick Dunn, Atl. vs. NYJ	24	155	0
Edgerrin James, Ind. at Hou.	21	139	2
Thomas Jones, Chi. vs. Bal.	25	139	0
Willie Parker, Pit. at Cin.	18	131	1
LaMont Jordan, Oak. vs. Buf.	28	122	3
Mike Anderson, Den. at NYG	24	120	1
Clinton Portis, Was. vs. S.F.	19	101	3
Reuben Droughns, Cle. vs. Det.	19	100	0

300-YARD PASSING GAMES

Player, team & opponent	Att.	Cmp.	Yds.	TD	Int.
Brett Favre, G.B. at Min.	36	28	315	2	0

100-YARD RECEIVING GAMES

Player, team & opponent	Rec.	Yds.	TD
Donald Driver, G.B. at Min.	8	114	1
Santana Moss, Was. vs. S.F.	5	112	1
Doug Gabriel, Oak. vs. Buf.	5	101	0
Az-Zahir Hakim, N.O. at St.L.	6	100	1

RESULTS

FRIDAY, OCTOBER 21
Kansas City 30, MIAMI 20

SUNDAY, OCTOBER 23
Indianapolis 38, HOUSTON 20
WASHINGTON 52, San Francisco 17
Detroit 13, CLEVELAND 10
Pittsburgh 27, CINCINNATI 13
MINNESOTA 23, Green Bay 20
ST. LOUIS 28, New Orleans 17
PHILADELPHIA 20, San Diego 17
SEATTLE 13, Dallas 10
CHICAGO 10, Baltimore 6
OAKLAND 38, Buffalo 17
N.Y. GIANTS 24, Denver 23
ARIZONA 20, Tennessee 10

MONDAY, OCTOBER 24
ATLANTA 27, N.Y. Jets 14

Open Date: Carolina, Jacksonville, New England, Tampa Bay

CHIEFS 30, DOLPHINS 20

Friday, October 21

Kansas City	7	7	10	6—30
Miami	0	6	7	7—20

First Quarter
K.C.—Holmes 5 run (Tynes kick), 4:32.

Second Quarter
Mia.—FG, Mare 33, 7:38.
K.C.—L. Johnson 2 run (Tynes kick), 13:04.
Mia.—FG, Mare 23, 14:55.

Third Quarter
Mia.—Brown 65 run (Mare kick), :20.
K.C.—Holmes 35 run (Tynes kick), 1:01.
K.C.—FG, Tynes 30, 11:23.

Fourth Quarter
K.C.—FG, Tynes 51, 1:35.
K.C.—FG, Tynes 52, 4:19.
Mia.—Chambers 77 pass from Rosenfels (Mare kick), 12:25.
  Attendance—68,350.

	Kansas City	Miami
First downs	24	9
Rushes-yards	45-185	14-94
Passing	277	192
Punt returns	5-19	2-55
Kickoff returns	3-65	7-162
Interception returns	1-15	0-0
Comp.-att.-int.	20-34-0	12-31-1
Sacked-yards lost	2-12	2-10
Punts	5-45	8-46
Fumbles-lost	0-0	1-0
Penalties-yards	7-63	4-30
Time of possession	41:40	18:20

INDIVIDUAL STATISTICS

RUSHING—Kansas City, L. Johnson 23-93, Holmes 18-90, Kennison 2-4, Green 2-(minus 2). Miami, Brown 8-95, R. Williams 6-(minus 1).

PASSING—Kansas City, Green 20-34-0-289. Miami, Frerotte 11-29-1-125, Booker 0-1-0-0, Rosenfels 1-1-0-77.

RECEIVING—Kansas City, Gonzalez 7-67, D. Hall 3-39, Dunn 2-42, Boerigter 2-34, Kennison 2-24, Horn 1-50, L. Johnson 1-26, Holmes 1-6, Richardson 1-1. Miami, McMichael 3-29, Chambers 2-88, Welker 2-41, Booker 2-26, Brown 2-15, H. Evans 1-3.

MISSED FIELD GOAL ATTEMPTS—None.

INTERCEPTIONS—Kansas City, Wesley 1-15.

KICKOFF RETURNS—Kansas City, D. Hall 3-65. Miami, Welker 7-162.

PUNT RETURNS—Kansas City, D. Hall 5-19. Miami, Welker 2-55.

SACKS—Kansas City, Hicks 1, Bell 0.5, Sapp 0.5. Miami, T. Jones 1, Schulters 1.

COLTS 38, TEXANS 20

Sunday, October 23

Indianapolis	7	7	10	14—38
Houston	0	14	0	6—20

First Quarter
Ind.—James 1 run (Vanderjagt kick), 11:18.

Second Quarter
Ind.—Clark 31 pass from Manning (Vanderjagt kick), 3:38.
Hou.—D. Davis 8 run (K. Brown kick), 11:45.
Hou.—Gaffney 8 pass from Carr (K. Brown kick), 14:30.

Third Quarter
Ind.—James 9 run (Vanderjagt kick), 3:42.
Ind.—FG, Vanderjagt 36, 14:43.

Fourth Quarter
Ind.—Harrison 7 pass from Manning (Vanderjagt kick), 3:22.
Ind.—Reagor 37 fumble return (Vanderjagt kick), 6:53.
Hou.—Mathis 89 kickoff return (pass failed), 7:04.
  Attendance—70,621.

	Indianapolis	Houston
First downs	30	13
Rushes-yards	34-205	33-133
Passing	232	6
Punt returns	1-9	0-0

	Indianapolis	Houston
Kickoff returns	3-60	7-266
Interception returns	1-20	1-1
Comp.-att.-int.	21-27-1	6-9-1
Sacked-yards lost	2-5	5-42
Punts	0-0	4-37
Fumbles-lost	1-1	3-1
Penalties-yards	6-35	3-15
Time of possession	33:19	26:41

INDIVIDUAL STATISTICS

RUSHING—Indianapolis, James 21-139, Rhodes 6-50, Manning 6-12, Mungro 1-4. Houston, D. Davis 28-98, Carr 5-35.

PASSING—Indianapolis, Manning 21-27-1-237. Houston, Carr 6-9-1-48.

RECEIVING—Indianapolis, Wayne 9-89, Harrison 7-65, Clark 3-51, Stokley 1-24, James 1-8. Houston, Gaffney 4-25, Rivers 1-16, D. Davis 1-7.

MISSED FIELD GOAL ATTEMPTS—None.

INTERCEPTIONS—Indianapolis, Harper 1-20. Houston, Robinson 1-1.

KICKOFF RETURNS—Indianapolis, Rhodes 3-60. Houston, Mathis 7-266.

PUNT RETURNS—Indianapolis, Walters 1-9.

SACKS—Indianapolis, Brock 1, Thornton 1, Freeney 1, Mathis 1, Reagor 0.5, Thomas 0.5. Houston, Payne 1, Orr 1.

REDSKINS 52, 49ERS 17

Sunday, October 23

San Francisco	7	0	0	10—17
Washington	14	21	10	7—52

First Quarter
Was.—Sellers 2 pass from Brunell (Novak kick), 4:15.
Was.—Portis 5 run (Novak kick), 10:12.
S.F.—Barlow 17 run (Nedney kick), 13:51.

Second Quarter
Was.—Portis 1 run (Novak kick), 9:21.
Was.—Moss 32 pass from Brunell (Novak kick), 13:07.
Was.—Sellers 19 pass from Brunell (Novak kick), 14:03.

Third Quarter
Was.—Portis 1 run (Novak kick), 3:56.
Was.—FG, Novak 27, 11:33.

Fourth Quarter
Was.—Cartwright 4 run (Novak kick), 5:34.
S.F.—FG, Nedney 47, 10:25.
S.F.—Gore 72 run (Nedney kick), 13:00.
  Attendance—90,224.

	San Francisco	Washington
First downs	9	24
Rushes-yards	26-140	39-204
Passing	54	253
Punt returns	2-12	5-56
Kickoff returns	9-153	4-82
Interception returns	0-0	1-32
Comp.-att.-int.	8-16-1	14-21-0
Sacked-yards lost	5-38	1-7
Punts	7-42	4-40
Fumbles-lost	3-1	0-0
Penalties-yards	5-29	8-60
Time of possession	26:42	33:18

INDIVIDUAL STATISTICS

RUSHING—San Francisco, Barlow 14-54, Gore 9-89, A. Smith 2-4, Marshall 1-(minus 7). Washington, Portis 19-101, Betts 12-92, Cartwright 5-14, Ramsey 3-(minus 3).

PASSING—San Francisco, A. Smith 8-16-1-92. Washington, Brunell 13-20-0-252, Ramsey 1-1-0-8.

RECEIVING—San Francisco, Lloyd 2-43, Morton 2-19, T. Smith 2-7, Bajema 1-24, Marshall 1-(minus 1). Washington, Moss 5-112, Patten 2-56, Cooley 2-48, Sellers 2-21, Portis 1-12, Kozlowski 1-8, Betts 1-3.

MISSED FIELD GOAL ATTEMPTS—None.

INTERCEPTIONS—Washington, Taylor 1-32.

KICKOFF RETURNS—San Francisco, Hicks 8-133, Marshall 1-20. Washington, Cartwright 4-82.

PUNT RETURNS—San Francisco, Marshall 2-12. Washington, Thrash 4-50, Moss 1-6.

SACKS—San Francisco, B. Moore 1. Washington, Washington 1, Marshall 1, Griffin 1, Team 2.

LIONS 13, BROWNS 10

Sunday, October 23

Detroit	0	7	3	3—13
Cleveland	3	7	0	0—10

First Quarter
Cle.—FG, Dawson 30, 6:30.

Second Quarter
Det.—Garcia 1 run (Hanson kick), 9:34.
Cle.—Cribbs 90 kickoff return (Dawson kick), 9:46.

Third Quarter
Det.—FG, Hanson 47, 5:31.

Fourth Quarter
Det.—FG, Hanson 50, :53.
Attendance—72,923.

	Detroit	Cleveland
First downs	19	11
Rushes-yards	37-119	22-118
Passing	210	56
Punt returns	1-18	3-27
Kickoff returns	3-50	4-152
Interception returns	3-7	0-0
Comp.-att.-int.	22-34-0	10-19-3
Sacked-yards lost	0-0	4-17
Punts	5-39	6-37
Fumbles-lost	1-1	1-0
Penalties-yards	11-72	8-50
Time of possession	37:17	22:43

INDIVIDUAL STATISTICS
RUSHING—Detroit, Jones 21-74, Pinner 7-24, Bryson 5-20, Garcia 4-1. Cleveland, Droughns 19-100, Dilfer 1-12, Green 1-3, Bryant 1-3.

PASSING—Detroit, Garcia 22-34-0-210. Cleveland, Dilfer 10-19-3-73.

RECEIVING—Detroit, M. Williams 5-95, Vines 5-34, Bryson 4-24, Schlesinger 2-10, FitzSimmons 2-10, Jones 2-10, Pinner 1-22, Pollard 1-5. Cleveland, Edwards 3-30, Droughns 2-9, Heiden 2-8, Bryant 1-15, Shea 1-9, Green 1-2.

MISSED FIELD GOAL ATTEMPTS—Detroit, Hanson 47.

INTERCEPTIONS—Detroit, McQuarters 1-6, Bly 1-5, Goodman 1-(minus 4).

KICKOFF RETURNS—Detroit, McQuarters 3-50. Cleveland, Cribbs 4-152.

PUNT RETURNS—Detroit, McQuarters 1-18. Cleveland, Northcutt 3-27.

SACKS—Detroit, Wilkinson 2, DeVries 2.

STEELERS 27, BENGALS 13

Sunday, October 23

Pittsburgh	0	7	17	3—27
Cincinnati	3	3	0	7—13

First Quarter
Cin.—FG, Graham 26, 12:23.

Second Quarter
Pit.—Miller 2 pass from Roethlisberger (Reed kick), 2:45.
Cin.—FG, Graham 39, 14:32.

Third Quarter
Pit.—FG, Reed 27, 4:51.
Pit.—Parker 37 run (Reed kick), 7:12.
Pit.—Ward 4 pass from Roethlisberger (Reed kick), 15:00.

Fourth Quarter
Pit.—FG, Reed 39, 8:04.
Cin.—Palmer 4 run (Graham kick), 13:03.
Attendance—66,104.

	Pittsburgh	Cincinnati
First downs	20	20
Rushes-yards	47-221	19-91
Passing	83	211
Punt returns	3-20	1-(-6)
Kickoff returns	2-31	6-115
Interception returns	2-55	1-0
Comp.-att.-int.	9-14-1	21-36-2
Sacked-yards lost	1-10	2-16
Punts	2-39	4-38
Fumbles-lost	1-1	0-0
Penalties-yards	5-65	4-35
Time of possession	35:29	24:31

INDIVIDUAL STATISTICS
RUSHING—Pittsburgh, Parker 18-131, Bettis 13-56, Haynes 11-35, Roethlisberger 4-(minus 5), Ward 1-4. Cincinnati, Ru. Johnson 12-65, Palmer 3-8, C. Perry 3-1, Houshmandzadeh 1-17.

PASSING—Pittsburgh, Roethlisberger 9-14-1-93. Cincinnati, Palmer 21-36-2-227.

RECEIVING—Pittsburgh, Miller 6-58, Ward 3-35. Cincinnati, Houshmandzadeh 7-75, C. Perry 5-43, C. Johnson 4-94, R. Kelly 2-8, Ru. Johnson 2-1, Washington 1-6.

MISSED FIELD GOAL ATTEMPTS—Cincinnati, Graham 30.

INTERCEPTIONS—Pittsburgh, Hope 1-55, A. Smith 1-0. Cincinnati, James 1-0.

KICKOFF RETURNS—Pittsburgh, Morgan 2-31. Cincinnati, T. Perry 6-115.

PUNT RETURNS—Pittsburgh, Randle El 3-20. Cincinnati, Ratliff 1-(minus 6).

SACKS—Pittsburgh, von Oelhoffen 1, Kirschke 1. Cincinnati, Clemons 1.

VIKINGS 23, PACKERS 20

Sunday, October 23

Green Bay	0	17	0	3—20
Minnesota	0	0	10	13—23

Second Quarter
G.B.—Driver 22 pass from Favre (Longwell kick), 2:49.
G.B.—Chatman 4 pass from Favre (Longwell kick), 10:27.
G.B.—FG, Longwell 53, 14:38.

Third Quarter
Min.—FG, Edinger 27, 4:58.
Min.—M. Robinson 27 pass from Culpepper (Edinger kick), 10:12.

Fourth Quarter
Min.—FG, Edinger 22, 5:59.
Min.—Moore 14 pass from Culpepper (Edinger kick), 11:50.
G.B.—FG, Longwell 39, 14:36.
Min.—FG, Edinger 56, 15:00.
Attendance—64,278.

	Green Bay	Minnesota
First downs	19	24
Rushes-yards	23-45	26-108
Passing	329	255
Punt returns	0-0	3-9
Kickoff returns	5-90	5-147
Interception returns	0-0	0-0
Comp.-att.-int.	29-37-0	23-31-0
Sacked-yards lost	0-0	5-25
Punts	3-45	2-39
Fumbles-lost	2-0	3-1
Penalties-yards	6-50	4-21
Time of possession	29:57	30:03

INDIVIDUAL STATISTICS
RUSHING—Green Bay, Green 16-49, Fisher 5-2, Favre 1-0, Chatman 1-(minus 6). Minnesota, Moore 13-45, Culpepper 7-41, M. Bennett 6-22.

PASSING—Green Bay, Favre 28-36-0-315, Fisher 1-1-0-14. Minnesota, Culpepper 23-31-0-280.

RECEIVING—Green Bay, Driver 8-114, Chatman 5-31, Franks 3-38, D. Lee 3-21, Ferguson 2-52, D. Martin 2-30, Green 2-18, Fisher 2-17, Henderson 2-8. Minnesota, Wiggins 6-56, Moore 4-60, M. Robinson 3-60, Burleson 3-37, T. Taylor 3-36, K. Robinson 2-9, Williamson 1-13, Kleinsasser 1-9.

MISSED FIELD GOAL ATTEMPTS—Green Bay, Longwell 53, 42.

INTERCEPTIONS—None.

KICKOFF RETURNS—Green Bay, Jones 3-55, R. Lee 2-35. Minnesota, K. Robinson 5-147.

PUNT RETURNS—Minnesota, Moore 3-9.

SACKS—Green Bay, G. Jackson 1, Peterson 1, Poppinga 1, Cole 1, Kampman 0.5, Lenon 0.5.

RAMS 28, SAINTS 17

Sunday, October 23

New Orleans	14	0	0	3—17
St. Louis	0	7	0	21—28

First Quarter
N.O.—Stallworth 11 pass from Brooks (Carney kick), 3:24.
N.O.—Hakim 17 pass from Brooks (Carney kick), 10:00.

Second Quarter
St.L.—S. Jackson 6 run (J. Wilkins kick), 10:35.

Fourth Quarter
N.O.—FG, Carney 22, 1:29.

St.L.—S. Jackson 1 run (J. Wilkins kick), 5:27.
St.L.—Curtis 5 run (J. Wilkins kick), 9:02.
St.L.—Furrey 67 interception return (J. Wilkins kick), 13:05.
  Attendance—64,586.

	New Orleans	St. Louis
First downs	24	16
Rushes-yards	32-119	27-109
Passing	213	189
Punt returns	5-45	0-0
Kickoff returns	5-100	4-92
Interception returns	0-0	1-67
Comp.-att.-int.	18-39-1	18-29-0
Sacked-yards lost	4-17	1-9
Punts	4-38	5-44
Fumbles-lost	1-1	1-1
Penalties-yards	9-102	8-65
Time of possession	33:57	26:03

INDIVIDUAL STATISTICS

RUSHING—New Orleans, A. Smith 14-56, Stecker 12-33, Brooks 3-28, Karney 1-3, Bouman 1-0, Stallworth 1-(minus 1). St. Louis, S. Jackson 20-97, J. Martin 4-(minus 2), M. Faulk 2-9, Curtis 1-5.

PASSING—New Orleans, Brooks 18-39-1-230. St. Louis, J. Martin 18-29-0-198.

RECEIVING—New Orleans, Hakim 6-100, Stallworth 4-53, Stecker 3-32, Henderson 2-21, A. Smith 2-14, Karney 1-10. St. Louis, M. Faulk 5-28, Looker 4-43, Curtis 3-69, McDonald 2-20, S. Jackson 2-19, Thompson 1-13, Manumaleuna 1-6.

MISSED FIELD GOAL ATTEMPTS—New Orleans, Carney 45. St. Louis, J. Wilkins 48.

INTERCEPTIONS—St. Louis, Furrey 1-67.

KICKOFF RETURNS—New Orleans, Hakim 5-100. St. Louis, Fair 2-48, C. Johnson 2-44.

PUNT RETURNS—New Orleans, Hakim 5-45.

SACKS—New Orleans, Whitehead 0.5, Ch. Grant 0.5. St. Louis, Archuleta 2, Coakley 1, Kennedy 1.

EAGLES 20, CHARGERS 17
Sunday, October 23

San Diego	0	0	7	10	17
Philadelphia	0	7	3	10	20

Second Quarter
Phi.—Owens 4 pass from McNabb (France kick), 10:13.
Third Quarter
Phi.—FG, France 23, 5:18.
S.D.—McCardell 19 pass from Brees (Kaeding kick), 11:39.
Fourth Quarter
S.D.—Gates 8 pass from Brees (Kaeding kick), 1:12.
S.D.—FG, Kaeding 34, 5:39.
Phi.—FG, France 40, 8:36.
Phi.—Ware 65 blocked FG return (France kick), 12:35.
  Attendance—67,747.

	San Diego	Philadelphia
First downs	15	22
Rushes-yards	20-21	14-24
Passing	270	262
Punt returns	3-14	1-1
Kickoff returns	5-81	4-65
Interception returns	2-33	2-35
Comp.-att.-int.	23-40-2	35-54-2
Sacked-yards lost	3-29	3-25
Punts	7-45	6-41
Fumbles-lost	2-1	0-0
Penalties-yards	9-72	10-72
Time of possession	28:47	31:13

INDIVIDUAL STATISTICS

RUSHING—San Diego, Tomlinson 17-7, Neal 2-5, Brees 1-9. Philadelphia, Westbrook 10-25, McNabb 4-(minus 1).

PASSING—San Diego, Brees 23-40-2-299. Philadelphia, McNabb 35-54-2-287.

RECEIVING—San Diego, Gates 8-72, McCardell 5-78, Caldwell 4-97, Tomlinson 4-26, Neal 1-21, Peelle 1-5. Philadelphia, Westbrook 10-75, Owens 7-53, Smith 6-63, G. Lewis 4-30, Gordon 3-6, Parry 2-9, McMullen 1-36, R. Brown 1-11, Spach 1-4.

MISSED FIELD GOAL ATTEMPTS—San Diego, Kaeding 40.

INTERCEPTIONS—San Diego, Fletcher 1-19, Edwards 1-14. Philadelphia, Sheppard 1-33, Trotter 1-2.

KICKOFF RETURNS—San Diego, Sproles 5-81. Philadelphia, Moats 2-26, Hood 1-20, Mahe 1-19.

PUNT RETURNS—San Diego, E. Parker 2-6, Sproles 1-8. Philadelphia, Sheppard 1-1.

SACKS—San Diego, Merriman 1, Fletcher 1, Godfrey 1. Philadelphia, Trotter 1, S. Brown 1, Kearse 1.

SEAHAWKS 13, COWBOYS 10
Sunday, October 23

Dallas	7	0	0	3	10
Seattle	0	3	0	10	13

First Quarter
Dal.—K. Johnson 5 pass from Bledsoe (Cortez kick), 13:57.
Second Quarter
Sea.—FG, J. Brown 55, 14:27.
Fourth Quarter
Dal.—FG, Cortez 21, 12:54.
Sea.—Hannam 1 pass from Hasselbeck (J. Brown kick), 14:20.
Sea.—FG, J. Brown 50, 15:00.
  Attendance—67,046.

	Dallas	Seattle
First downs	16	20
Rushes-yards	39-164	22-72
Passing	111	217
Punt returns	5-17	2-7
Kickoff returns	3-94	2-36
Interception returns	2-0	2-56
Comp.-att.-int.	13-24-2	23-42-2
Sacked-yards lost	5-25	1-7
Punts	9-40	9-37
Fumbles-lost	4-0	2-1
Penalties-yards	9-81	9-83
Time of possession	34:08	25:52

INDIVIDUAL STATISTICS

RUSHING—Dallas, Barber 22-95, Thompson 6-34, A. Thomas 6-19, Bledsoe 3-1, P. Price 1-9, Polite 1-6. Seattle, Alexander 21-61, Hasselbeck 1-11.

PASSING—Dallas, Bledsoe 13-24-2-136. Seattle, Hasselbeck 23-42-2-224.

RECEIVING—Dallas, T. Glenn 4-35, K. Johnson 4-28, Witten 2-47, P. Price 1-19, Thompson 1-6, Barber 1-1. Seattle, Jurevicius 6-54, Stevens 5-60, Hackett 4-36, Urban 3-57, Strong 2-8, Hannam 2-6, Warrick 1-3.

MISSED FIELD GOAL ATTEMPTS—Dallas, Cortez 29.

INTERCEPTIONS—Dallas, Newman 1-0, Ro. Williams 1-0. Seattle, Boulware 1-31, Babineaux 1-25.

KICKOFF RETURNS—Dallas, Thompson 3-94. Seattle, Scobey 2-36.

PUNT RETURNS—Dallas, P. Price 5-17. Seattle, J. Williams 2-7.

SACKS—Dallas, B. James 1. Seattle, B. Fisher 2, Wistrom 1, Darby 1, Tubbs 1.

BEARS 10, RAVENS 6
Sunday, October 23

Baltimore	0	6	0	0	6
Chicago	7	0	3	0	10

First Quarter
Chi.—M. Edwards 9 pass from Orton (Gould kick), 14:41.
Second Quarter
Bal.—FG, Stover 40, 6:14.
Bal.—FG, Stover 29, 14:34.
Third Quarter
Chi.—FG, Gould 23, 12:08.
  Attendance—62,102.

	Baltimore	Chicago
First downs	12	17
Rushes-yards	22-66	29-143
Passing	133	133
Punt returns	3-11	3-34
Kickoff returns	3-64	2-36
Interception returns	0-0	0-0
Comp.-att.-int.	18-32-0	15-29-0
Sacked-yards lost	4-31	2-12
Punts	9-44	7-37
Fumbles-lost	2-0	1-0
Penalties-yards	11-100	9-60
Time of possession	28:22	31:38

INDIVIDUAL STATISTICS

RUSHING—Baltimore, J. Lewis 15-34, Wright 5-11, C. Taylor 2-21. Chicago, T. Jones 25-139, Benson 2-6, Orton 2-(minus 2).

PASSING—Baltimore, Wright 18-32-0-164. Chicago, Orton 15-29-0-145.

RECEIVING—Baltimore, Heap 7-71, Mason 2-38, Hymes 2-25, Wilcox 2-8, J. Lewis 2-6, J. Green 1-8, Ricard 1-7, C. Taylor 1-1. Chicago, Clark 4-50, Bradley 4-37, Muhammad 3-39, Berrian 2-15, M. Edwards 1-9, T. Jones 1- (minus 5).

MISSED FIELD GOAL ATTEMPTS—Chicago, Gould 47.

INTERCEPTIONS—None.

KICKOFF RETURNS—Baltimore, Sams 3-64. Chicago, Azumah 2-36.

PUNT RETURNS—Baltimore, Sams 3-11. Chicago, Wade 3-34.

SACKS—Baltimore, A. Thomas 1, Team 1. Chicago, T. Johnson 2, Ogunleye 1, Boone 0.5, Haynes 0.5.

RAIDERS 38, BILLS 17
Sunday, October 23

Buffalo	7	3	0	7—17
Oakland	0	17	7	14—38

First Quarter
Buf.—Evans 5 pass from Holcomb (Lindell kick), 8:23.

Second Quarter
Oak.—FG, Janikowski 25, :13.
Oak.—Moss 22 pass from Collins (Janikowski kick), 3:17.
Buf.—FG, Lindell 41, 10:56.
Oak.—Jordan 1 run (Janikowski kick), 14:20.

Third Quarter
Oak.—Jordan 17 run (Janikowski kick), 4:50.

Fourth Quarter
Buf.—Reed 9 pass from Holcomb (Lindell kick), :07.
Oak.—Jordan 7 run (Janikowski kick), 6:11.
Oak.—Crockett 2 run (Janikowski kick), 14:46.
Attendance—42,779.

	Buffalo	Oakland
First downs	15	26
Rushes-yards	23-84	37-162
Passing	126	254
Punt returns	3-22	4-31
Kickoff returns	7-162	4-80
Interception returns	0-0	0-0
Comp.-att.-int.	19-27-0	19-27-0
Sacked-yards lost	3-33	2-7
Punts	4-45	3-46
Fumbles-lost	1-1	3-1
Penalties-yards	7-51	8-53
Time of possession	27:09	32:51

INDIVIDUAL STATISTICS
RUSHING—Buffalo, McGahee 16-50, S. Williams 4-27, Evans 1-7, Shelton 1-0, Holcomb 1-0. Oakland, Jordan 28-122, Crockett 7-33, Collins 2-7.

PASSING—Buffalo, Holcomb 19-27-0-159. Oakland, Collins 19-27-0-261.

RECEIVING—Buffalo, Moulds 4-36, Reed 4-31, McGahee 3-36, Evans 3-19, Campbell 2-7, J. Smith 1-12, S. Williams 1-10, Shelton 1-8. Oakland, Gabriel 5-101, Porter 4-43, Jordan 4-40, Moss 3-43, Foschi 2-11, Crockett 1-23.

MISSED FIELD GOAL ATTEMPTS—None.

INTERCEPTIONS—None.

KICKOFF RETURNS—Buffalo, McGee 3-98, J. Smith 3-55, Reed 1-9. Oakland, Carr 4-80.

PUNT RETURNS—Buffalo, Clements 2-12, Parrish 1-10. Oakland, Carr 4-31.

SACKS—Buffalo, Crowell 1, Schobel 1. Oakland, Burgess 2, Sapp 1.

GIANTS 24, BRONCOS 23
Sunday, October 23

Denver	6	7	7	3—23
N.Y. Giants	7	3	0	14—24

First Quarter
Den.—FG, Elam 49, 5:03.
NYG—Burress 18 pass from Manning (Feely kick), 7:58.
Den.—FG, Elam 42, 13:19.

Second Quarter
Den.—Mi. Anderson 2 run (Elam kick), 9:15.
NYG—FG, Feely 52, 13:57.

Third Quarter
Den.—K. Johnson 4 pass from Plummer (Elam kick), 1:34.

Fourth Quarter
Den.—FG, Elam 27, 1:42.
NYG—Barber 4 run (Feely kick), 5:53.
NYG—Toomer 2 pass from Manning (Feely kick), 14:55.
Attendance—78,516.

	Denver	N.Y. Giants
First downs	20	22
Rushes-yards	33-191	20-97
Passing	194	214
Punt returns	3-18	1-0
Kickoff returns	4-74	4-124
Interception returns	1-0	0-0
Comp.-att.-int.	18-29-0	23-42-1
Sacked-yards lost	0-0	0-0
Punts	3-34	4-46
Fumbles-lost	1-1	1-1
Penalties-yards	6-53	7-52
Time of possession	34:01	25:59

INDIVIDUAL STATISTICS
RUSHING—Denver, Mi. Anderson 24-120, Bell 8-60, Plummer 1-11. New York, Barber 19-86, T. Carter 1-11.

PASSING—Denver, Plummer 18-29-0-194. New York, Manning 23-42-1-214.

RECEIVING—Denver, Lelie 5-64, Smith 3-51, S. Alexander 3-22, Putzier 3-19, K. Johnson 2-37, Bell 2-1. New York, Toomer 8-62, Burress 6-84, Barber 6-24, Shockey 3-44.

MISSED FIELD GOAL ATTEMPTS—Denver, Elam 49.

INTERCEPTIONS—Denver, Bailey 1-0.

KICKOFF RETURNS—Denver, Da. Williams 2-49, Adams 1-17, K. Johnson 1-8. New York, Ponder 4-124.

PUNT RETURNS—Denver, Da. Williams 2-2, Adams 1-16. New York, Morton 1-0.

SACKS—None.

CARDINALS 20, TITANS 10
Sunday, October 23

Tennessee	10	0	0	0—10
Arizona	0	10	3	7—20

First Quarter
Ten.—B. Jones 38 pass from Volek (Bironas kick), 3:21.
Ten.—FG, Bironas 53, 12:18.

Second Quarter
Ariz.—FG, Rackers 33, 5:37.
Ariz.—Macklin 60 interception return (Rackers kick), 10:16.

Third Quarter
Ariz.—FG, Rackers 24, 14:31.

Fourth Quarter
Ariz.—Fitzgerald 34 pass from McCown (Rackers kick), 9:40.
Attendance—39,482.

	Tennessee	Arizona
First downs	16	9
Rushes-yards	28-90	22-55
Passing	258	118
Punt returns	9-79	4-10
Kickoff returns	2-57	3-88
Interception returns	1-22	1-60
Comp.-att.-int.	26-45-1	12-28-1
Sacked-yards lost	3-11	4-22
Punts	7-42	10-50
Fumbles-lost	4-2	0-0
Penalties-yards	11-90	9-71
Time of possession	33:30	26:30

INDIVIDUAL STATISTICS
RUSHING—Tennessee, Payton 12-30, Brown 10-37, Mauck 4-20, Volek 1-3, Hentrich 1-0. Arizona, Shipp 14-8, Arrington 5-30, Boldin 2-15, McCown 1-2.

PASSING—Tennessee, Volek 18-32-1-198, Mauck 8-13-0-71. Arizona, McCown 12-28-1-140.

RECEIVING—Tennessee, Calico 6-51, Kinney 5-60, R. Williams 5-43, Troupe 3-15, B. Jones 2-50, Scaife 2-14, Payton 2-5, Roby 1-31. Arizona, Fitzgerald 4-71, Shipp 3-34, B. Johnson 2-21, Arrington 2-7, Bergen 1-7.

MISSED FIELD GOAL ATTEMPTS—None.

INTERCEPTIONS—Tennessee, Hill 1-22. Arizona, Macklin 1-60.

KICKOFF RETURNS—Tennessee, Roby 2-57. Arizona, Swinton 3-88.

PUNT RETURNS—Tennessee, P. Jones 6-38, B. Jones 3-41. Arizona, Swinton 4-10.

SACKS—Tennessee, Thompson 1, Vanden Bosch 1, Long 1, LaBoy 1. Arizona, Okeafor 1.5, Dansby 1, Dockett 0.5.

FALCONS 27, JETS 14

Monday, October 24

N.Y. Jets	0	7	0	7—14
Atlanta	10	10	7	0—27

First Quarter
Atl.—Vick 1 run (T. Peterson kick), 9:25.
Atl.—FG, T. Peterson 22, 14:18.

Second Quarter
Atl.—Davis 24 fumble return (T. Peterson kick), 2:37.
Atl.—FG, T. Peterson 41, 8:02.
NYJ—Testaverde 1 run (Nugent kick), 12:11.

Third Quarter
Atl.—Vick 1 run (T. Peterson kick), 8:25.

Fourth Quarter
NYJ—C. Martin 1 run (Nugent kick), 3:08.
Attendance—70,995.

	N.Y. Jets	Atlanta
First downs	16	19
Rushes-yards	18-37	38-205
Passing	194	105
Punt returns	1-18	2-17
Kickoff returns	4-118	3-74
Interception returns	3-5	1-0
Comp.-att.-int.	23-38-1	11-26-3
Sacked-yards lost	4-40	3-11
Punts	5-47	4-40
Fumbles-lost	4-3	2-0
Penalties-yards	5-44	4-30
Time of possession	26:38	33:22

INDIVIDUAL STATISTICS

RUSHING—New York, C. Martin 14-28, Bollinger 2-8, Testaverde 2-1 Atlanta, Dunn 24-155, Vick 9-18, Griffith 5-32.

PASSING—New York, Bollinger 12-20-0-94, Testaverde 11-18-1-140 Atlanta, Vick 11-26-3-116.

RECEIVING—New York, Coles 9-96, Chrebet 4-37, C. Martin 3-26, Sowel 3-14, McCareins 2-46, Baker 1-8, Cotchery 1-7. Atlanta, Crumpler 4-66, R White 2-20, Dunn 2-6, McCrary 1-11, Jenkins 1-8, Griffith 1-5.

MISSED FIELD GOAL ATTEMPTS—None.

INTERCEPTIONS—New York, Barrett 1-4, Vilma 1-1, Law 1-0. Atlanta, D Hall 1-0.

KICKOFF RETURNS—New York, Miller 3-100, Houston 1-18. Atlanta Cobb 3-74.

PUNT RETURNS—New York, Cotchery 1-18. Atlanta, Rossum 2-17.

SACKS—New York, J. Abraham 1.5, Robertson 1, B. Thomas 0.5. Atlanta D. Williams 1, Lake 1, Shropshire 1, R. Coleman 1.

WEEK 8

AMERICAN FOOTBALL CONFERENCE

EAST DIVISION

	W	L	T	Pct.	PF	PA
New England	4	3	0	.571	159	180
Miami	3	4	0	.429	136	134
Buffalo	3	5	0	.375	128	159
N.Y. Jets	2	5	0	.286	92	139

NORTH DIVISION

	W	L	T	Pct.	PF	PA
Cincinnati	6	2	0	.750	189	125
Pittsburgh	5	2	0	.714	169	114
Baltimore	2	5	0	.286	88	120
Cleveland	2	5	0	.286	94	122

SOUTH DIVISION

	W	L	T	Pct.	PF	PA
Indianapolis	7	0	0	1.000	189	77
Jacksonville	4	3	0	.571	129	125
Tennessee	2	6	0	.250	161	211
Houston	1	6	0	.143	93	195

WEST DIVISION

	W	L	T	Pct.	PF	PA
Denver	6	2	0	.750	201	152
Kansas City	4	3	0	.571	169	160
San Diego	4	4	0	.500	221	166
Oakland	3	4	0	.429	162	158

NATIONAL FOOTBALL CONFERENCE

EAST DIVISION

	W	L	T	Pct.	PF	PA
N.Y. Giants	5	2	0	.714	209	137
Dallas	5	3	0	.625	181	137
Philadelphia	4	3	0	.571	163	167
Washington	4	3	0	.571	135	139

NORTH DIVISION

	W	L	T	Pct.	PF	PA
Chicago	4	3	0	.571	119	81
Detroit	3	4	0	.429	117	125
Minnesota	2	5	0	.286	103	193
Green Bay	1	6	0	.143	158	139

SOUTH DIVISION

	W	L	T	Pct.	PF	PA
Atlanta	5	2	0	.714	175	133
Carolina	5	2	0	.714	186	149
Tampa Bay	5	2	0	.714	126	87
New Orleans	2	6	0	.250	125	222

WEST DIVISION

	W	L	T	Pct.	PF	PA
Seattle	5	2	0	.714	181	127
St. Louis	4	4	0	.500	208	231
Arizona	2	5	0	.286	127	178
San Francisco	2	5	0	.286	111	222

100-YARD RUSHING GAMES

Player, team & opponent	Att.	Yds.	TD
Tiki Barber, NYG vs. Was.	24	206	1
Steven Jackson, St.L. vs. Jac.	25	179	0
Fred Taylor, Jac. at St.L.	22	165	1
Willis McGahee, Buf. at N.E.	31	136	0
Marion Barber, Dal. vs. Ariz.	27	127	2
Mike Anderson, Den. vs. Phi.	21	126	1
Tatum Bell, Den. vs. Phi.	14	107	2
Ronnie Brown, Mia. at N.O.	23	106	0
Kevan Barlow, S.F. vs. T.B.	26	101	0

300-YARD PASSING GAMES

Player, team & opponent	Att.	Cmp.	Yds.	TD	Int.
Trent Green, K.C. at S.D.	43	31	347	2	0
Jake Delhomme, Car. vs. Min.	30	21	341	3	0
Drew Brees, S.D. vs. K.C.	43	25	324	3	1
Jake Plummer, Den. vs. Phi.	35	22	309	4	0

100-YARD RECEIVING GAMES

Player, team & opponent	Rec.	Yds.	TD
Steve Smith, Car. vs. Min.	11	201	1
Terrell Owens, Phi. at Den.	3	154	1
Joey Galloway, T.B. at S.F.	8	149	1
Antonio Gates, S.D. vs. K.C.	10	145	3
Ernest Wilford, Jac. at St.L.	6	145	1
Eric Moulds, Buf. at N.E.	9	125	1
Jerry Porter, Oak. at Ten.	6	123	2
Eddie Kennison, K.C. at S.D.	7	115	1
Kevin Curtis, St.L. vs. Jac.	3	105	1

SUNDAY, OCTOBER 30
HOUSTON 19, Cleveland 16
ST. LOUIS 24, Jacksonville 21
CAROLINA 38, Minnesota 13
Oakland 34, TENNESSEE 25
CINCINNATI 21, Green Bay 14
DALLAS 34, Arizona 13
N.Y. GIANTS 36, Washington 0
Chicago 19, DETROIT 13 (OT)
Miami 21, NEW ORLEANS 6
SAN DIEGO 28, Kansas City 20
SAN FRANCISCO 15, Tampa Bay 10
DENVER 49, Philadelphia 21
NEW ENGLAND 21, Buffalo 16

MONDAY, OCTOBER 31
PITTSBURGH 20, Baltimore 19

Open Date: Atlanta, Indianapolis, N.Y. Jets, Seattle

2005 REVIEW *Week 8*

– 157 –

TEXANS 19, BROWNS 16

Sunday, October 30

Cleveland	10	3	0	3—16
Houston	7	3	3	6—19

First Quarter
Hou.—Mathis 34 pass from Carr (K. Brown kick), 4:05.
Cle.—Shea 8 pass from Dilfer (Dawson kick), 9:55.
Cle.—FG, Dawson 28, 14:55.

Second Quarter
Cle.—FG, Dawson 29, 10:46.
Hou.—FG, K. Brown 38, 14:50.

Third Quarter
Hou.—FG, K. Brown 37, 11:12.

Fourth Quarter
Hou.—FG, K. Brown 35, :52.
Cle.—FG, Dawson 37, 9:54.
Hou.—FG, K. Brown 40, 12:15.
Attendance—70,064.

	Cleveland	Houston
First downs	16	11
Rushes-yards	33-156	37-117
Passing	169	120
Punt returns	2-21	1-20
Kickoff returns	5-118	5-177
Interception returns	1-0	0-0
Comp.-att.-int.	12-25-0	10-20-1
Sacked-yards lost	2-16	2-18
Punts	4-33	4-39
Fumbles-lost	2-2	1-0
Penalties-yards	1-5	5-35
Time of possession	29:04	30:56

INDIVIDUAL STATISTICS
RUSHING—Cleveland, Droughns 20-99, Green 10-48, Dilfer 3-9. Houston, D. Davis 28-91, Carr 8-16, Gaffney 1-10.
PASSING—Cleveland, Dilfer 12-25-0-185. Houston, Carr 10-20-1-138.
RECEIVING—Cleveland, Bryant 4-98, Heiden 4-43, Edwards 2-32, Shea 1-8, Green 1-4. Houston, Gaffney 5-64, D. Davis 2-25, Mathis 1-34, Bradford 1-8, Armstrong 1-7.
MISSED FIELD GOAL ATTEMPTS—Houston, K. Brown 38.
INTERCEPTIONS—Cleveland, Bodden 1-0.
KICKOFF RETURNS—Cleveland, Cribbs 4-102, McIntyre 1-16. Houston, Mathis 5-177.
PUNT RETURNS—Cleveland, Northcutt 2-21. Houston, Buchanon 1-20.
SACKS—Cleveland, Andra. Davis 1, Lang 1. Houston, Polk 1, G. Walker 1

RAMS 24, JAGUARS 21

Sunday, October 30

Jacksonville	7	7	7	0—21
St. Louis	14	3	0	7—24

First Quarter
St.L.—Chillar 29 blocked punt return (J. Wilkins kick), 2:13.
Jac.—F. Taylor 71 run (Scobee kick), 2:36.
St.L.—Curtis 83 pass from J. Martin (J. Wilkins kick), 4:06.

Second Quarter
Jac.—Wilford 20 pass from Leftwich (Scobee kick), 12:44.
St.L.—FG, J. Wilkins 41, 15:00.

Third Quarter
Jac.—M. Jones 15 pass from Leftwich (Scobee kick), 9:53.

Fourth Quarter
St.L.—S. Jackson 19 pass from J. Martin (J. Wilkins kick), 2:15.
Attendance—65,251.

	Jacksonville	St. Louis
First downs	16	15
Rushes-yards	28-221	33-200
Passing	206	186
Punt returns	3-26	0-0
Kickoff returns	4-106	4-66
Interception returns	3-20	1-37
Comp.-att.-int.	18-31-1	13-21-3
Sacked-yards lost	2-7	2-14
Punts	3-26	5-41
Fumbles-lost	1-1	0-0
Penalties-yards	4-25	9-59
Time of possession	31:22	28:38

INDIVIDUAL STATISTICS
RUSHING—Jacksonville, F. Taylor 22-165, G. Jones 4-2, Pearman 1-45, Leftwich 1-9. St. Louis, S. Jackson 25-179, M. Faulk 6-23, J. Martin 2-(minus 2).
PASSING—Jacksonville, Leftwich 18-31-1-213. St. Louis, J. Martin 13-21-3-200.
RECEIVING—Jacksonville, Wilford 6-145, M. Jones 4-38, J. Smith 2-27, F. Taylor 2-(minus 1), Pearman 2-(minus 5), Wimbush 1-5, Brady 1-4. St. Louis, Curtis 3-105, Looker 3-23, McDonald 2-41, S. Jackson 2-21, Manumaleuna 2-7, M. Faulk 1-3.
MISSED FIELD GOAL ATTEMPTS—Jacksonville, Scobee 49, 44.
INTERCEPTIONS—Jacksonville, Mathis 2-20, Grant 1-0. St. Louis, Furrey 1-37.
KICKOFF RETURNS—Jacksonville, Wimbush 4-106. St. Louis, Fair 4-66.
PUNT RETURNS—Jacksonville, Pearman 3-26.
SACKS—Jacksonville, Peterson 1, Spicer 1. St. Louis, Green 1, Claiborne 0.5, Pickett 0.5.

PANTHERS 38, VIKINGS 13

Sunday, October 30

Minnesota	0	0	7	6—13
Carolina	7	17	7	7—38

First Quarter
Car.—S. Davis 7 run (Kasay kick), 4:41.

Second Quarter
Car.—FG, Kasay 44, 5:15.
Car.—S. Davis 1 run (Kasay kick), 11:03.
Car.—S. Smith 13 pass from Delhomme (Kasay kick), 14:22.

Third Quarter
Min.—Moore 4 run (Edinger kick), 3:15.
Car.—Mangum 1 pass from Delhomme (Kasay kick), 7:35.

Fourth Quarter
Car.—Colbert 25 pass from Delhomme (Kasay kick), 7:22.
Min.—M. Robinson 5 run from B. Johnson (run failed), 13:05.
Attendance—73,502.

	Minnesota	Carolina
First downs	14	27
Rushes-yards	18-82	39-111
Passing	171	338
Punt returns	1-13	3-24
Kickoff returns	7-136	2-33
Interception returns	0-0	0-0
Comp.-att.-int.	16-32-0	21-31-0
Sacked-yards lost	4-19	1-3
Punts	5-49	2-42
Fumbles-lost	0-0	0-0
Penalties-yards	10-60	6-53
Time of possession	24:09	35:51

INDIVIDUAL STATISTICS
RUSHING—Minnesota, Moore 9-30, B. Johnson 4-30, M. Bennett 2-6, Culpepper 1-18, M. Williams 1-0, Burleson 1-(minus 2). Carolina, S. Davis 17-40, Foster 12-51, Goings 5-20, Weinke 3-(minus 4), Delhomme 1-2, Hoover 1-2.
PASSING—Minnesota, B. Johnson 13-28-0-162, Culpepper 3-4-0-28. Carolina, Delhomme 21-30-0-341, Weinke 0-1-0-0.
RECEIVING—Minnesota, M. Robinson 4-77, Wiggins 3-36, M. Williams 3-16, T. Taylor 2-17, Williamson 1-36, Burleson 1-6, Kleinsasser 1-1, Moore 1-1. Carolina, S. Smith 11-201, Gaines 2-67, Colbert 2-32, Proehl 2-18, Foster 1-8, S. Davis 1-7, Gardner 1-7, Mangum 1-1.
MISSED FIELD GOAL ATTEMPTS—Minnesota, Edinger 33. Carolina, Kasay 56.
INTERCEPTIONS—None.
KICKOFF RETURNS—Minnesota, K. Robinson 4-80, Williamson 3-56. Carolina, Smart 1-20, Gaines 1-13.
PUNT RETURNS—Minnesota, Moore 1-13. Carolina, S. Smith 2-20, Gamble 1-4.
SACKS—Minnesota, James 1. Carolina, Morgan 1, Witherspoon 1, Moorehead 1, Carstens 1.

RAIDERS 34, TITANS 25

Sunday, October 30

Oakland	17	7	3	7—34
Tennessee	0	22	0	3—25

First Quarter
Oak.—Porter 26 pass from Collins (Janikowski kick), 2:56.
Oak.—FG, Janikowski 22, 8:36.
Oak.—Jordan 18 pass from Collins (Janikowski kick), 14:25.
Second Quarter
Ten.—Roby 19 pass from McNair (kick failed), 4:47.
Ten.—Brown 38 run (pass failed), 7:02.
Oak.—J. Cooper 0 fumble return (Janikowski kick), 9:13.
Ten.—FG, Bironas 39, 14:09.
Ten.—Hill 52 interception return (Bironas kick), 14:48.
Third Quarter
Oak.—FG, Janikowski 32, 13:31.
Fourth Quarter
Ten.—FG, Bironas 24, 7:12.
Oak.—Porter 44 pass from Collins (Janikowski kick), 10:23.
Attendance—69,149.

	Oakland	Tennessee
First downs	17	19
Rushes-yards	23-92	25-140
Passing	232	186
Punt returns	0-0	2-39
Kickoff returns	6-140	3-69
Interception returns	0-0	1-52
Comp.-att.-int.	17-29-1	26-40-0
Sacked-yards lost	2-6	6-43
Punts	3-52	3-42
Fumbles-lost	1-0	3-2
Penalties-yards	7-55	9-79
Time of possession	24:23	35:37

INDIVIDUAL STATISTICS
RUSHING—Oakland, Jordan 20-67, Whitted 1-24, Crockett 1-2, Collins 1-(minus 1). Tennessee, Brown 19-97, McNair 5-41, Henry 1-2.
PASSING—Oakland, Collins 17-29-1-238. Tennessee, McNair 26-40-0-229.
RECEIVING—Oakland, Porter 6-123, Jordan 5-69, Moss 3-26, Foschi 2-14, Ra. Williams 1-6. Tennessee, Roby 7-83, Kinney 5-69, Scaife 5-19, R. Williams 3-25, Brown 2-13, Troupe 2-9, Calico 1-6, Guenther 1-5.
MISSED FIELD GOAL ATTEMPTS—None.
INTERCEPTIONS—Tennessee, Hill 1-52.
KICKOFF RETURNS—Oakland, Carr 4-119, Gabriel 1-21, Hulsey 1-0. Tennessee, Roby 2-45, Payton 1-24.
PUNT RETURNS—Tennessee, P. Jones 2-39.
SACKS—Oakland, Sapp 3, Clark 1, Jasper 1, Brayton 1. Tennessee, Long 1, LaBoy 0.5, Waddell 0.5.

BENGALS 21, PACKERS 14
Sunday, October 30

Green Bay	0	7	0	7—14
Cincinnati	7	7	0	7—21

First Quarter
Cin.—C. Perry 4 pass from Palmer (Graham kick), 6:15.
Second Quarter
G.B.—Fisher 1 run (Longwell kick), 5:25.
Cin.—Houshmandzadeh 8 pass from Palmer (Graham kick), 11:53.
Fourth Quarter
Cin.—J. Johnson 27 pass from Palmer (Graham kick), 1:43.
G.B.—Franks 1 pass from Favre (Longwell kick), 11:49.
Attendance—65,940.

	Green Bay	Cincinnati
First downs	23	21
Rushes-yards	22-76	27-95
Passing	277	222
Punt returns	4-39	1-3
Kickoff returns	4-103	3-69
Interception returns	1-0	5-31
Comp.-att.-int.	26-39-5	22-34-1
Sacked-yards lost	1-2	2-15
Punts	3-42	6-42
Fumbles-lost	1-0	1-0
Penalties-yards	7-29	3-58
Time of possession	29:49	30:11

INDIVIDUAL STATISTICS
RUSHING—Green Bay, Fisher 17-51, Favre 2-4, Driver 1-9, Gado 1-8, R. Lee 1-4. Cincinnati, Ru. Johnson 22-72, C. Perry 3-18, C. Johnson 1-8, Houshmandzadeh 1-(minus 3).
PASSING—Green Bay, Favre 26-39-5-279. Cincinnati, Palmer 22-34-1-237.

RECEIVING—Green Bay, Chatman 8-97, Franks 7-62, Driver 5-76, D. Lee 3-28, Fisher 2-7, Henderson 1-9. Cincinnati, C. Perry 6-25, Houshmandzadeh 5-77, C. Johnson 5-62, Henry 2-22, J. Johnson 1-27, Schobel 1-12, Walter 1-12, Ru. Johnson 1-0.
MISSED FIELD GOAL ATTEMPTS—None.
INTERCEPTIONS—Green Bay, Carroll 1-0. Cincinnati, O'Neal 2-21, Thurman 2-10, James 1-0.
KICKOFF RETURNS—Green Bay, R. Lee 4-103. Cincinnati, T. Perry 2-55, O'Neal 1-14.
PUNT RETURNS—Green Bay, Chatman 4-39. Cincinnati, Ratliff 1-3.
SACKS—Green Bay, Harris 1, Lenon 1. Cincinnati, Clemons 1.

COWBOYS 34, CARDINALS 13
Sunday, October 30

Arizona	3	7	3	0—13
Dallas	10	14	3	7—34

First Quarter
Ariz.—FG, Rackers 52, 5:17.
Dal.—Barber 28 run (Suisham kick), 6:24.
Dal.—FG, Suisham 21, 12:03.
Second Quarter
Ariz.—Boldin 44 pass from McCown (Rackers kick), 2:07.
Dal.—K. Johnson 5 pass from Bledsoe (Suisham kick), 11:49.
Dal.—Barber 10 run (Suisham kick), 14:00.
Third Quarter
Ariz.—FG, Rackers 47, 3:47.
Dal.—FG, Suisham 21, 11:57.
Fourth Quarter
Dal.—Henry 58 interception return (Suisham kick), 3:06.
Attendance—62,068.

	Arizona	Dallas
First downs	12	21
Rushes-yards	24-71	32-146
Passing	142	202
Punt returns	3-59	3-25
Kickoff returns	7-127	3-83
Interception returns	0-0	2-58
Comp.-att.-int.	16-34-2	19-24-0
Sacked-yards lost	3-19	3-18
Punts	5-43	3-53
Fumbles-lost	1-0	2-1
Penalties-yards	8-56	0-0
Time of possession	27:11	32:49

INDIVIDUAL STATISTICS
RUSHING—Arizona, Shipp 12-44, McCown 4-16, Arrington 4-5, O. Ayanbadejo 2-1, Fitzgerald 1-5, Boldin 1-0. Dallas, Barber 27-127, Thompson 4-19, Bledsoe 1-0.
PASSING—Arizona, McCown 16-33-2-161, Boldin 0-1-0-0. Dallas, Bledsoe 19-24-0-220.
RECEIVING—Arizona, Fitzgerald 4-36, Shipp 4-25, Boldin 3-69, B. Johnson 2-14, Arrington 1-8, Bergen 1-7, O. Ayanbadejo 1-2. Dallas, K. Johnson 6-54, Witten 5-71, T. Glenn 3-65, Barber 2-15, P. Price 1-5, Polite 1-5, Pierce 1-5.
MISSED FIELD GOAL ATTEMPTS—None.
INTERCEPTIONS—Dallas, Henry 1-58, A. Glenn 1-0.
KICKOFF RETURNS—Arizona, Swinton 7-127. Dallas, Thompson 3-83.
PUNT RETURNS—Arizona, Swinton 3-59. Dallas, P. Price 3-25.
SACKS—Arizona, Berry 1, Wilson 1, Lan. Moore 1. Dallas, Ellis 1.5, Fujita 1, B. James 0.5.

GIANTS 36, REDSKINS 0
Sunday, October 30

Washington	0	0	0	0— 0
N.Y. Giants	6	13	17	0—36

First Quarter
NYG.—FG, Feely 39, 3:31.
NYG.—FG, Feely 50, 14:43.
Second Quarter
NYG.—Jacobs 3 run (Feely kick), 2:29.
NYG.—FG, Feely 33, 12:46.
NYG.—FG, Feely 39, 14:58.
Third Quarter
NYG.—Shockey 10 pass from Manning (Feely kick), 1:43.
NYG.—FG, Feely 44, 10:56.
NYG.—Barber 4 run (Feely kick), 13:53.
Attendance—78,630.

	Washington	N.Y. Giants
First downs	7	19
Rushes-yards	13-38	45-262
Passing	87	124
Punt returns	2-13	6-42
Kickoff returns	6-105	1-24
Interception returns	1-0	1-17
Comp.-att.-int.	14-34-1	12-31-1
Sacked-yards lost	5-40	2-22
Punts	8-43	4-43
Fumbles-lost	3-3	2-0
Penalties-yards	10-88	9-73
Time of possession	20:39	39:21

INDIVIDUAL STATISTICS

RUSHING—Washington, Portis 4-9, Ramsey 3-5, Betts 3-2, Cartwright 2-21, Brunell 1-1. New York, Barber 24-206, Ward 13-42, Jacobs 8-14.

PASSING—Washington, Brunell 11-28-1-65, Ramsey 3-6-0-62. New York, Manning 12-31-1-146.

RECEIVING—Washington, Moss 4-34, Cooley 3-19, Portis 3-13, Thrash 1-28, Jacobs 1-24, Patten 1-6, Sellers 1-3. New York, Burress 4-42, Shockey 3-29, Toomer 2-43, T. Carter 1-19, Ward 1-8, Barber 1-5.

MISSED FIELD GOAL ATTEMPTS—New York, Feely 51.

INTERCEPTIONS—Washington, Clark 1-0. New York, Pierce 1-17.

KICKOFF RETURNS—Washington, Betts 5-105, Evans 1-0. New York, Ponder 1-24.

PUNT RETURNS—Washington, Thrash 1-8, Moss 1-5. New York, Morton 6-42.

SACKS—Washington, Evans 1, C. Clemons 1. New York, Umenyiora 2, Strahan 1, Joseph 1, K. Allen 1.

BEARS 19, LIONS 13
Sunday, October 30

Chicago	0	13	0	0	6—19
Detroit	3	0	7	3	0—13

First Quarter
Det.—FG, Hanson 32, 10:49.

Second Quarter
Chi.—Muhammad 23 pass from Orton (Gould kick), 5:31.
Chi.—FG, Gould 38, 13:09.
Chi.—FG, Gould 20, 14:43.

Third Quarter
Det.—Jones 6 run (Hanson kick), 11:45.

Fourth Quarter
Det.—FG, Hanson 30, 1:40.

Overtime
Chi.—Tillman 22 interception return, 6:17.
Attendance—61,814.

	Chicago	Detroit
First downs	14	17
Rushes-yards	29-115	29-93
Passing	218	185
Punt returns	2-0	3-6
Kickoff returns	4-122	5-96
Interception returns	1-22	0-0
Comp.-att.-int.	17-31-0	23-35-1
Sacked-yards lost	2-12	2-12
Punts	8-36	7-43
Fumbles-lost	2-1	0-0
Penalties-yards	10-75	5-40
Time of possession	30:22	35:55

INDIVIDUAL STATISTICS

RUSHING—Chicago, T. Jones 22-72, Peterson 4-8, Benson 3-35. Detroit, Jones 18-66, Bryson 4-6, Garcia 4-6, Pinner 2-8, Vines 1-7.

PASSING—Chicago, Orton 17-31-0-230. Detroit, Garcia 23-35-1-197.

RECEIVING—Chicago, Bradley 5-88, Muhammad 4-49, T. Jones 3-25, Gage 2-47, M. Edwards 1-13, Clark 1-7, Peterson 1-1. Detroit, Vines 5-61, Bryson 5-40, Jones 5-13, Pollard 3-35, M. Williams 3-27, Martinez 1-11, Pinner 1-10.

MISSED FIELD GOAL ATTEMPTS—Detroit, Hanson 46.

INTERCEPTIONS—Chicago, Tillman 1-22.

KICKOFF RETURNS—Chicago, Azumah 4-122. Detroit, Drummond 5-96.

PUNT RETURNS—Chicago, Wade 2-0. Detroit, Drummond 3-6.

SACKS—Chicago, T. Johnson 1, A. Brown 1. Detroit, Hall 1, Redding 1.

DOLPHINS 21, SAINTS 6
Sunday, October 30

Miami	3	6	2	10—21
New Orleans	3	0	3	0— 6

First Quarter
N.O.—FG, Carney 26, 8:12.
Mia.—FG, Mare 37, 14:27.

Second Quarter
Mia.—FG, Mare 36, 7:42.
Mia.—FG, Mare 41, 15:00.

Third Quarter
N.O.—FG, Carney 49, 11:23.
Mia.—Safety, 13:08.

Fourth Quarter
Mia.—Chambers 12 pass from Frerotte (Mare kick), :51.
Mia.—FG, Mare 46, 5:32.
Attendance—61,643.

	Miami	New Orleans
First downs	20	14
Rushes-yards	47-188	17-90
Passing	154	113
Punt returns	1-11	0-0
Kickoff returns	4-73	3-75
Interception returns	1-5	1-28
Comp.-att.-int.	16-28-1	14-31-1
Sacked-yards lost	2-14	6-68
Punts	4-46	5-47
Fumbles-lost	2-1	3-1
Penalties-yards	5-34	8-77
Time of possession	36:23	23:37

INDIVIDUAL STATISTICS

RUSHING—Miami, Brown 23-106, R. Williams 17-82, Frerotte 6-(minus 1), Chambers 1-1. New Orleans, Brooks 6-34, A. Smith 6-33, Stecker 4-23, Karney 1-0.

PASSING—Miami, Frerotte 16-28-1-168. New Orleans, Brooks 14-31-1-181.

RECEIVING—Miami, Chambers 4-25, Booker 3-40, McMichael 3-20, Welker 3-17, Brown 2-12, Boston 1-54. New Orleans, Horn 7-99, Stallworth 3-52, Stecker 3-16, Henderson 1-14.

MISSED FIELD GOAL ATTEMPTS—Miami, Mare 36.

INTERCEPTIONS—Miami, Howard 1-5. New Orleans, D. Smith 1-28.

KICKOFF RETURNS—Miami, Welker 4-67. New Orleans, Stecker 3-75.

PUNT RETURNS—Miami, Welker 1-11.

SACKS—Miami, Traylor 1, Zgonina 1, Carter 1, Holliday 1, Bell 1, Team 1. New Orleans, Howard 1, W. Smith 1.

CHARGERS 28, CHIEFS 20
Sunday, October 30

Kansas City	0	3	7	10—20
San Diego	7	14	0	7—28

First Quarter
S.D.—Gates 19 pass from Brees (Kaeding kick), 10:30.

Second Quarter
S.D.—E. Parker 17 pass from Tomlinson (Kaeding kick), :04.
K.C.—FG, Tynes 34, 13:04.
S.D.—Gates 20 pass from Brees (Kaeding kick), 14:33.

Third Quarter
K.C.—Gonzalez 16 pass from Green (Tynes kick), 8:15.

Fourth Quarter
K.C.—FG, Tynes 20, 3:00.
S.D.—Gates 35 pass from Brees (Kaeding kick), 5:50.
K.C.—Kennison 7 pass from Green (Tynes kick), 12:48.
Attendance—65,750.

...	Kansas City	San Diego
First downs	21	22
Rushes-yards	21-95	22-83
Passing	323	341
Punt returns	3-54	3-29
Kickoff returns	4-101	4-84
Interception returns	1-51	0-0
Comp.-att.-int.	31-43-0	26-44-1
Sacked-yards lost	4-24	0-0
Punts	6-40	6-49
Fumbles-lost	1-1	2-1
Penalties-yards	9-59	4-38
Time of possession	31:19	28:41

INDIVIDUAL STATISTICS

RUSHING—Kansas City, Holmes 14-38, L. Johnson 6-55, Green 1-2. San Diego, Tomlinson 17-69, Neal 3-10, Sproles 1-3, Brees 1-1.

PASSING—Kansas City, Green 31-43-0-347. San Diego, Brees 25-43-1-324, Tomlinson 1-1-0-17.

RECEIVING—Kansas City, Kennison 7-115, Gonzalez 7-97, Horn 7-58, L. Johnson 3-28, Holmes 3-15, D. Hall 2-16, Richardson 1-9, Boerigter 1-9. San Diego, Gates 10-145, McCardell 5-73, E. Parker 4-63, Tomlinson 3-23, Neal 2-21, Caldwell 1-16, Peelle 1-0.

MISSED FIELD GOAL ATTEMPTS—None.

INTERCEPTIONS—Kansas City, Wesley 1-51.

KICKOFF RETURNS—Kansas City, D. Hall 4-101. San Diego, Sproles 4-84.

PUNT RETURNS—Kansas City, D. Hall 3-54. San Diego, Sproles 3-29.

SACKS—San Diego, Merriman 2, Castillo 1.5, Cooper 0.5.

49ERS 15, BUCCANEERS 10

Sunday, October 30

Tampa Bay	0	3	0	7—10
San Francisco	0	6	6	3—15

Second Quarter

S.F.—FG, Nedney 45, 9:00.
T.B.—FG, M. Bryant 47, 14:42.
S.F.—FG, Nedney 47, 15:00.

Third Quarter

S.F.—FG, Nedney 41, 8:44.
S.F.—FG, Nedney 46, 12:15.

Fourth Quarter

T.B.—Galloway 78 pass from Simms (M. Bryant kick), 4:27.
S.F.—FG, Nedney 28, 13:04.
Attendance—63,358.

	Tampa Bay	San Francisco
First downs	13	9
Rushes-yards	20-43	39-158
Passing	232	50
Punt returns	5-29	4-18
Kickoff returns	4-84	3-63
Interception returns	0-0	2-36
Comp.-att.-int.	21-34-2	8-19-0
Sacked-yards lost	5-32	0-0
Punts	8-44	9-41
Fumbles-lost	1-1	1-0
Penalties-yards	8-65	7-65
Time of possession	29:41	30:19

INDIVIDUAL STATISTICS

RUSHING—Tampa Bay, C. Williams 13-20, Pittman 4-5, Simms 3-18. San Francisco, Barlow 26-101, Gore 10-40, Pickett 2-12, Dorsey 1-5.

PASSING—Tampa Bay, Simms 21-34-2-264. San Francisco, Dorsey 7-18-0-40, Pickett 1-1-0-10.

RECEIVING—Tampa Bay, Galloway 8-149, Clayton 4-30, Alstott 3-24, Smith 2-43, I. Hilliard 1-7, C. Williams 1-5, Pittman 1-3, Shepherd 1-3. San Francisco, Barlow 2-21, Lloyd 2-18, Morton 1-7, Jackson 1-6, Bajema 1-5, Gore 1-(minus 7).

MISSED FIELD GOAL ATTEMPTS—Tampa Bay, M. Bryant 52. San Francisco, Nedney 39.

INTERCEPTIONS—San Francisco, Spencer 1-24, B. Moore 1-12.

KICKOFF RETURNS—Tampa Bay, Jones 2-46, Cox 2-38. San Francisco, Hicks 3-63.

PUNT RETURNS—Tampa Bay, Jones 5-29. San Francisco, Marshall 4-18.

SACKS—San Francisco, Young 2, D. Johnson 1, A. Adams 1, Carter 1.

BRONCOS 49, EAGLES 21

Sunday, October 30

Philadelphia	0	7	14	0—21
Denver	14	14	0	21—49

First Quarter

Den.—Mi. Anderson 2 run (Elam kick), 4:43.
Den.—K. Johnson 6 pass from Plummer (Elam kick), 10:30.

Second Quarter

Den.—Smith 2 pass from Plummer (Elam kick), 2:44.
Den.—S. Alexander 3 pass from Plummer (Elam kick), 7:13.
Phi.—Smith 1 pass from McNabb (Cortez kick), 13:47.

Third Quarter

Phi.—Owens 91 pass from McNabb (Cortez kick), 5:14.
Phi.—Westbrook 14 pass from McNabb (Cortez kick), 13:27.

Fourth Quarter

Den.—Devoe 44 pass from Plummer (Elam kick), 5:07.
Den.—Bell 67 run (Elam kick), 8:29.
Den.—Bell 6 run (Elam kick), 14:34.
Attendance—76,530.

	Philadelphia	Denver
First downs	12	28
Rushes-yards	19-79	36-255
Passing	272	309
Punt returns	2-10	6-4
Kickoff returns	7-166	3-71
Interception returns	0-0	2-1
Comp.-att.-int.	12-34-2	22-35-0
Sacked-yards lost	2-11	1-0
Punts	8-43	7-39
Fumbles-lost	1-0	1-0
Penalties-yards	10-70	6-50
Time of possession	23:00	37:00

INDIVIDUAL STATISTICS

RUSHING—Philadelphia, Westbrook 13-48, McNabb 3-13, Gordon 2-16, Owens 1-2. Denver, Mi. Anderson 21-126, Bell 14-107, Plummer 1-22.

PASSING—Philadelphia, McNabb 12-34-2-283. Denver, Plummer 22-35-0-309.

RECEIVING—Philadelphia, Westbrook 4-56, Owens 3-154, R. Brown 2-44, G. Lewis 1-15, Gordon 1-13, Smith 1-1. Denver, Smith 5-76, Devoe 5-59, Lelie 3-81, Adams 3-25, Putzier 2-39, S. Alexander 2-7, Mi. Anderson 1-16, K. Johnson 1-6.

MISSED FIELD GOAL ATTEMPTS—None.

INTERCEPTIONS—Denver, Lynch 1-1, Foxworth 1-0.

KICKOFF RETURNS—Philadelphia, Hood 6-149, Wynn 1-17. Denver, R. Alexander 1-26, Da. Williams 1-26, Adams 1-19.

PUNT RETURNS—Philadelphia, Wynn 2-10. Denver, Adams 3-5, Da. Williams 3-(minus 1).

SACKS—Philadelphia, Kearse 1. Denver, Pryce 1, Da. Williams 1.

PATRIOTS 21, BILLS 16

Sunday, October 30

Buffalo	0	3	7	6—16
New England	0	0	7	14—21

Second Quarter

Buf.—FG, Lindell 23, 6:19.

Third Quarter

N.E.—Branch 33 pass from Brady (Vinatieri kick), 2:28.
Buf.—Moulds 55 pass from Holcomb (Lindell kick), 3:51.

Fourth Quarter

Buf.—FG, Lindell 35, 1:58.
Buf.—FG, Lindell 41, 4:53.
N.E.—Dillon 1 run (Vinatieri kick), 7:54.
N.E.—Dillon 1 run (Vinatieri kick), 9:28.
Attendance—68,756.

	Buffalo	New England
First downs	24	18
Rushes-yards	39-147	22-93
Passing	247	180
Punt returns	3-33	1-11
Kickoff returns	4-64	5-106
Interception returns	0-0	1-0
Comp.-att.-int.	20-33-1	14-21-0
Sacked-yards lost	2-16	3-19
Punts	2-39	5-46
Fumbles-lost	1-1	2-2
Penalties-yards	12-74	7-57
Time of possession	39:20	20:40

INDIVIDUAL STATISTICS

RUSHING—Buffalo, McGahee 31-136, S. Williams 5-14, Parrish 2-(minus 2), Holcomb 1-(minus 1). New England, Dillon 18-72, Pass 3-17, Brady 1-4.

PASSING—Buffalo, Holcomb 20-33-1-263. New England, Brady 14-21-0-199.

RECEIVING—Buffalo, Moulds 9-125, S. Williams 3-37, McGahee 2-21, Reed 2-19, Shelton 1-21, Parrish 1-17, Evans 1-14, Campbell 1-9. New England, Givens 7-58, Branch 3-92, Pass 1-23, Graham 1-15, Andre. Davis 1-6, Dwight 1-5.

MISSED FIELD GOAL ATTEMPTS—Buffalo, Lindell 46. New England, Vinatieri 44.

INTERCEPTIONS—New England, Samuel 1-0.

KICKOFF RETURNS—Buffalo, Reed 2-42, McGee 2-22. New England, B. Johnson 3-69, Hobbs 1-23, Banta-Cain 1-14.

PUNT RETURNS—Buffalo, Parrish 3-33. New England, B. Johnson 1-11.

SACKS—Buffalo, Schobel 2, Kelsay 0.5, Bannan 0.5. New England, Vrabel 1, Colvin 1.

STEELERS 20, RAVENS 19

Monday, October 31

Baltimore	7	3	0	9—19
Pittsburgh	7	3	7	3—20

First Quarter
Pit.—Miller 4 pass from Roethlisberger (Reed kick), 8:57.
Bal.—C. Taylor 13 pass from Wright (Stover kick), 13:06.

Second Quarter
Pit.—FG, Reed 42, 1:39.
Bal.—FG, Stover 22, 9:57.

Third Quarter
Pit.—Miller 8 pass from Roethlisberger (Reed kick), 7:13.

Fourth Quarter
Bal.—FG, Stover 40, 1:04.
Bal.—FG, Stover 49, 6:20.
Bal.—FG, Stover 47, 11:39.
Pit.—FG, Reed 37, 13:24.
Attendance—64,178.

	Baltimore	Pittsburgh
First downs	20	19
Rushes-yards	27-72	28-101
Passing	246	160
Punt returns	1-10	0-0
Kickoff returns	4-75	5-127
Interception returns	1-28	2-0
Comp.-att.-int.	25-44-2	18-31-1
Sacked-yards lost	2-6	2-17
Punts	1-41	3-41
Fumbles-lost	1-1	2-1
Penalties-yards	6-38	4-19
Time of possession	31:04	28:56

INDIVIDUAL STATISTICS

RUSHING—Baltimore, J. Lewis 17-61, C. Taylor 8-9, Wright 2-2. Pittsburgh, Parker 14-63, Bettis 8-22, Roethlisberger 4-4, Haynes 1-7, Randle El 1-5.

PASSING—Baltimore, Wright 25-44-2-252. Pittsburgh, Roethlisberger 18-30-1-177, Gardocki 0-1-0-0.

RECEIVING—Baltimore, Mason 7-91, C. Taylor 5-55, Heap 5-38, Wilcox 3-17, Hymes 1-21, P. Johnson 1-12, Dinkins 1-11, J. Green 1-7, J. Lewis 1-0. Pittsburgh, Ward 8-75, Randle El 3-31, Miller 3-18, Morgan 2-35, Parker 2-18.

MISSED FIELD GOAL ATTEMPTS—Baltimore, Stover 43.

INTERCEPTIONS—Baltimore, A. Thomas 1-28. Pittsburgh, I. Taylor 1-0, Hope 1-0.

KICKOFF RETURNS—Baltimore, Sams 4-75. Pittsburgh, Colclough 4-68, Morgan 1-59.

PUNT RETURNS—Baltimore, Sams 1-10.

SACKS—Baltimore, Gregg 1, Suggs 0.5, Boulware 0.5. Pittsburgh, Haggans 1, Keisel 1.

WEEK 9

AMERICAN FOOTBALL CONFERENCE

EAST DIVISION

	W	L	T	Pct.	PF	PA
New England	4	4	0	.500	180	220
Buffalo	3	5	0	.375	128	159
Miami	3	5	0	.375	146	151
N.Y. Jets	2	6	0	.250	118	170

NORTH DIVISION

	W	L	T	Pct.	PF	PA
Cincinnati	7	2	0	.778	210	134
Pittsburgh	6	2	0	.750	189	124
Cleveland	3	5	0	.375	114	136
Baltimore	2	6	0	.250	97	141

SOUTH DIVISION

	W	L	T	Pct.	PF	PA
Indianapolis	8	0	0	1.000	229	98
Jacksonville	5	3	0	.625	150	139
Tennessee	2	7	0	.222	175	231
Houston	1	7	0	.125	107	216

WEST DIVISION

	W	L	T	Pct.	PF	PA
Denver	6	2	0	.750	201	152
Kansas City	5	3	0	.625	196	183
San Diego	5	4	0	.556	252	192
Oakland	3	5	0	.375	185	185

NATIONAL FOOTBALL CONFERENCE

EAST DIVISION

	W	L	T	Pct.	PF	PA
N.Y. Giants	6	2	0	.750	233	143
Dallas	5	3	0	.625	181	137
Washington	5	3	0	.625	152	149
Philadelphia	4	4	0	.500	173	184

NORTH DIVISION

	W	L	T	Pct.	PF	PA
Chicago	5	3	0	.625	139	98
Detroit	3	5	0	.375	131	152
Minnesota	3	5	0	.375	130	207
Green Bay	1	7	0	.125	168	159

SOUTH DIVISION

	W	L	T	Pct.	PF	PA
Atlanta	6	2	0	.750	192	143
Carolina	6	2	0	.750	220	163
Tampa Bay	5	3	0	.625	140	121
New Orleans	2	7	0	.222	142	242

WEST DIVISION

	W	L	T	Pct.	PF	PA
Seattle	6	2	0	.750	214	146
St. Louis	4	4	0	.500	208	231
Arizona	2	6	0	.250	146	211
San Francisco	2	6	0	.250	117	246

TOP PERFORMANCES

100-YARD RUSHING GAMES

Player, team & opponent	Att.	Yds.	TD
Shaun Alexander, Sea. at Ariz.	23	173	2
Reuben Droughns, Cle. vs. Ten.	20	116	0
Antowain Smith, N.O. vs. Chi.	17	110	0
Larry Johnson, K.C. vs. Oak.	22	107	2
LaDainian Tomlinson, S.D. at NYJ	25	107	3
Michael Bennett, Min. vs. Det.	18	106	0
Edgerrin James, Ind. at N.E.	34	104	1

300-YARD PASSING GAMES

Player, team & opponent	Att.	Cmp.	Yds.	TD	Int.
Kurt Warner, Ariz. vs. Sea.	48	29	334	1	3
Peyton Manning, Ind. at N.E.	37	28	321	3	1
Donovan McNabb, Phi. at Was.	35	22	304	1	1

100-YARD RECEIVING GAMES

Player, team & opponent	Rec.	Yds.	TD
Antonio Gates, S.D. at NYJ	8	132	0
Marvin Harrison, Ind. at N.E.	9	128	2
Reggie Wayne, Ind. at N.E.	9	124	1
Scottie Vines, Det. at Min.	9	109	0
Steve Smith, Car. at T.B.	5	106	1
Larry Fitzgerald, Ariz. vs. Sea.	8	102	0

RESULTS

SUNDAY, NOVEMBER 6
Atlanta 17, MIAMI 10
JACKSONVILLE 21, Houston 14
Carolina 34, TAMPA BAY 14
Cincinnati 21, BALTIMORE 9
CLEVELAND 20, Tennessee 14
MINNESOTA 27, Detroit 14
San Diego 31, N.Y. JETS 26
KANSAS CITY 27, Oakland 23
Chicago 20, NEW ORLEANS 17
N.Y. Giants 24, SAN FRANCISCO 6
Seattle 33, ARIZONA 19
Pittsburgh 20, GREEN BAY 10
WASHINGTON 17, Philadelphia 10

MONDAY, NOVEMBER 7
Indianapolis 40, NEW ENGLAND 21

Open Date: Buffalo, Dallas, Denver, St. Louis

2005 REVIEW *Week 9*

FALCONS 17, DOLPHINS 10

Sunday, November 6

Atlanta	7	7	3	0—17
Miami	0	10	0	0—10

First Quarter
Atl.—Dunn 1 run (T. Peterson kick), 4:36.

Second Quarter
Mia.—R. Williams 23 run (Mare kick), 4:10.
Atl.—Finneran 11 pass from Vick (T. Peterson kick), 10:20.
Mia.—FG, Mare 28, 13:04.

Third Quarter
Atl.—FG, T. Peterson 21, 10:44.
Attendance—72,187.

	Atlanta	Miami
First downs	27	11
Rushes-yards	41-162	25-105
Passing	220	103
Punt returns	2-1	1-0
Kickoff returns	3-72	3-56
Interception returns	1-1	0-0
Comp.-att.-int.	22-31-0	13-22-1
Sacked-yards lost	3-8	0-0
Punts	3-38	6-44
Fumbles-lost	3-2	1-0
Penalties-yards	4-28	7-60
Time of possession	36:15	23:45

INDIVIDUAL STATISTICS
RUSHING—Atlanta, Dunn 25-88, Vick 8-38, Griffith 7-20, R. White 1-16. Miami, Brown 12-67, R. Williams 10-52, Chambers 2-(minus 13), Frerotte 1-(minus 1).
PASSING—Atlanta, Vick 22-31-0-228. Miami, Frerotte 13-22-1-103.
RECEIVING—Atlanta, Finneran 8-92, Crumpler 6-65, Dunn 4-23, R. White 3-50, Griffith 1-(minus 2). Miami, Chambers 3-40, McMichael 3-21, Booker 2-15, Brown 2-11, Morris 2-10, Welker 1-6.
MISSED FIELD GOAL ATTEMPTS—None.
INTERCEPTIONS—Atlanta, Carpenter 1-1.
KICKOFF RETURNS—Atlanta, Rossum 3-72. Miami, Welker 3-56.
PUNT RETURNS—Atlanta, Rossum 2-1. Miami, Welker 1-0.
SACKS—Miami, Taylor 1, Traylor 1, D. Bowens 1.

JAGUARS 21, TEXANS 14

Sunday, November 6

Houston	0	7	7	0—14
Jacksonville	0	0	7	14—21

Second Quarter
Hou.—Bradford 31 pass from Carr (K. Brown kick), 4:42.

Third Quarter
Jac.—Wilford 12 pass from Leftwich (Scobee kick), 6:14.
Hou.—Wells 7 run (K. Brown kick), 13:41.

Fourth Quarter
Jac.—Leftwich 8 run (Scobee kick), 4:12.
Jac.—G. Jones 12 run (Scobee kick), 12:07.
Attendance—64,613.

	Houston	Jacksonville
First downs	17	18
Rushes-yards	23-88	27-98
Passing	191	214
Punt returns	2-0	3-8
Kickoff returns	4-80	2-46
Interception returns	0-0	0-0
Comp.-att.-int.	22-30-0	19-25-0
Sacked-yards lost	6-28	2-4
Punts	5-44	6-38
Fumbles-lost	5-1	1-0
Penalties-yards	4-30	6-45
Time of possession	30:56	29:04

INDIVIDUAL STATISTICS
RUSHING—Houston, Wells 13-56, Morency 8-24, Carr 2-8. Jacksonville, F. Taylor 12-48, G. Jones 7-27, Leftwich 4-10, Pearman 2-7, Wimbush 2-6.
PASSING—Houston, Carr 22-30-0-219. Jacksonville, Leftwich 19-25-0-218.
RECEIVING—Houston, An. Johnson 9-91, Bradford 5-71, Wells 5-45, Gaffney 1-7, Armstrong 1-6, Morency 1-(minus 1). Jacksonville, Pearman 5-34, Wilford 4-89, J. Smith 4-52, M. Jones 3-21, F. Taylor 2-15, Wrighster 1-7.

MISSED FIELD GOAL ATTEMPTS—None.
INTERCEPTIONS—None.
KICKOFF RETURNS—Houston, Hollings 2-46, Wells 1-17, Morency 1-17. Jacksonville, Wimbush 2-46.
PUNT RETURNS—Houston, Buchanon 2-0. Jacksonville, Pearman 3-8.
SACKS—Houston, Payne 1, T. Johnson 1. Jacksonville, Peterson 1, Grant 1, D. Smith 1, Spicer 1, Meier 1, McCray 1.

PANTHERS 34, BUCCANEERS 14

Sunday, November 6

Carolina	10	7	10	7—34
Tampa Bay	0	7	0	7—14

First Quarter
Car.—FG, Kasay 30, 5:15.
Car.—S. Davis 4 run (Kasay kick), 11:55.

Second Quarter
T.B.—Galloway 50 pass from Simms (M. Bryant kick), :09.
Car.—S. Davis 1 run (Kasay kick), 9:01.

Third Quarter
Car.—Gamble 61 interception return (Kasay kick), 2:34.
Car.—FG, Kasay 20, 10:53.

Fourth Quarter
Car.—S. Smith 35 pass from Delhomme (Kasay kick), :53.
T.B.—Alstott 1 run (M. Bryant kick), 7:19.
Attendance—65,014.

	Carolina	Tampa Bay
First downs	15	18
Rushes-yards	32-77	17-44
Passing	210	226
Punt returns	3-46	3-45
Kickoff returns	2-53	7-155
Interception returns	2-101	0-0
Comp.-att.-int.	11-18-0	25-42-2
Sacked-yards lost	1-6	6-33
Punts	6-50	6-44
Fumbles-lost	1-0	2-2
Penalties-yards	5-24	8-42
Time of possession	28:37	31:23

INDIVIDUAL STATISTICS
RUSHING—Carolina, Foster 16-23, S. Davis 12-48, Goings 3-6, Delhomme 1-0. Tampa Bay, C. Williams 11-29, Pittman 5-14, Alstott 1-1.
PASSING—Carolina, Delhomme 11-18-0-216. Tampa Bay, Simms 25-42-2-259.
RECEIVING—Carolina, S. Smith 5-106, Foster 2-16, Proehl 1-62, Colbert 1-18, Mangum 1-13, S. Davis 1-1. Tampa Bay, Galloway 5-83, Pittman 4-29, I. Hilliard 4-28, Smith 3-41, C. Williams 3-25, Clayton 2-22, Alstott 2-21, Becht 2-10.
MISSED FIELD GOAL ATTEMPTS—None.
INTERCEPTIONS—Carolina, Gamble 2-101.
KICKOFF RETURNS—Carolina, Smart 2-53. Tampa Bay, Cox 7-155.
PUNT RETURNS—Carolina, S. Smith 2-41, Gamble 1-5. Tampa Bay, Jones 3-45.
SACKS—Carolina, Peppers 3, Rucker 2, Wallace 1. Tampa Bay, D. White 1.

BENGALS 21, RAVENS 9

Sunday, November 6

Cincinnati	0	14	0	7—21
Baltimore	3	3	0	3— 9

First Quarter
Bal.—FG, Stover 34, 11:27.

Second Quarter
Cin.—Ru. Johnson 1 run (Graham kick), 9:04.
Cin.—T. Perry 8 pass from Palmer (Graham kick), 13:10.
Bal.—FG, Stover 32, 14:49.

Fourth Quarter
Bal.—FG, Stover 31, 2:14.
Cin.—Henry 3 pass from Palmer (Graham kick), 8:55.
Attendance—70,540.

	Cincinnati	Baltimore
First downs	25	17
Rushes-yards	35-95	25-118
Passing	234	122
Punt returns	2-13	1-(-1)
Kickoff returns	3-61	4-105
Interception returns	0-0	0-0
Comp.-att.-int.	19-26-0	19-31-0
Sacked-yards lost	2-14	3-31
Punts	2-47	3-48
Fumbles-lost	4-1	2-1
Penalties-yards	5-54	7-40
Time of possession	33:26	26:34

INDIVIDUAL STATISTICS

RUSHING—Cincinnati, Ru. Johnson 29-97, Palmer 5-(minus 6), C. Perry 1-4. Baltimore, J. Lewis 15-49, Stewart 4-24, Wright 3-36, C. Taylor 3-9.

PASSING—Cincinnati, Palmer 19-26-0-248. Baltimore, Wright 19-30-0-153, Hymes 0-1-0-0.

RECEIVING—Cincinnati, C. Johnson 5-91, Houshmandzadeh 5-61, Henry 3-17, C. Perry 2-11, Walter 1-33, Ru. Johnson 1-15, Schobel 1-12, T. Perry 1-8. Baltimore, Mason 5-60, C. Taylor 5-26, Heap 4-28, Wilcox 2-16, P. Johnson 1-19, J. Green 1-2, Hymes 1-2.

MISSED FIELD GOAL ATTEMPTS—Cincinnati, Graham 48.

INTERCEPTIONS—None.

KICKOFF RETURNS—Cincinnati, T. Perry 3-61. Baltimore, Sams 4-105.

PUNT RETURNS—Cincinnati, Ratliff 2-13. Baltimore, Sams 1-(minus 1).

SACKS—Cincinnati, Simmons 1, Geathers 1, Thornton 1. Baltimore, A. Thomas 1, Scott 0.5, Gregg 0.5.

BROWNS 20, TITANS 14
Sunday, November 6

Tennessee	0	7	0	7—14
Cleveland	7	0	10	3—20

First Quarter
Cle.—Northcutt 58 pass from Dilfer (Dawson kick), 10:59.
Second Quarter
Ten.—Kinney 24 pass from McNair (Bironas kick), 13:36.
Third Quarter
Cle.—FG, Dawson 37, 2:51.
Cle.—Wright 6 run (Dawson kick), 8:48.
Fourth Quarter
Cle.—FG, Dawson 19, 1:25.
Ten.—Brown 15 run (Bironas kick), 7:47.
Attendance—72,594.

	Tennessee	Cleveland
First downs	19	16
Rushes-yards	24-98	32-169
Passing	225	272
Punt returns	1-31	3-11
Kickoff returns	5-76	1-4
Interception returns	1-0	1-1
Comp.-att.-int.	18-42-1	18-34-1
Sacked-yards lost	1-10	0-0
Punts	7-35	5-41
Fumbles-lost	1-0	1-1
Penalties-yards	2-15	9-63
Time of possession	27:36	32:24

INDIVIDUAL STATISTICS

RUSHING—Tennessee, Brown 22-95, McNair 1-2, Payton 1-1. Cleveland, Droughns 20-116, Wright 8-19, Dilfer 2-3, Northcutt 1-31, T. Smith 1-0.

PASSING—Tennessee, McNair 18-41-1-235, Hentrich 0-1-0-0. Cleveland, Dilfer 18-34-1-272.

RECEIVING—Tennessee, Kinney 5-74, R. Williams 5-61, Scaife 5-59, Roby 1-29, Brown 1-8, Fleming 1-4. Cleveland, Droughns 4-73, Northcutt 3-80, Bryant 3-79, Wright 3-15, Heiden 2-15, T. Smith 2-8, Edwards 1-2.

MISSED FIELD GOAL ATTEMPTS—Tennessee, Bironas 50. Cleveland, Dawson 39.

INTERCEPTIONS—Tennessee, Bulluck 1-0. Cleveland, Pool 1-1.

KICKOFF RETURNS—Tennessee, P. Jones 5-76. Cleveland, Cribbs 1-4.

PUNT RETURNS—Tennessee, Thompson 1-31. Cleveland, Northcutt 2-6, Cribbs 1-5.

SACKS—Cleveland, Andra. Davis 1.

VIKINGS 27, LIONS 14
Sunday, November 6

Detroit	0	7	0	7—14
Minnesota	3	21	0	3—27

First Quarter
Min.—FG, Edinger 21, 9:05.
Second Quarter
Min.—M. Bennett 5 pass from B. Johnson (Edinger kick), 7:34.
Min.—Fason 3 run (Edinger kick), 9:15.
Min.—Burleson 15 pass from B. Johnson (Edinger kick), 10:58.
Det.—Pinner 1 run (Hanson kick), 14:12.
Fourth Quarter
Det.—Pollard 23 pass from Harrington (Hanson kick), :05.
Min.—FG, Edinger 40, 7:30.
Attendance—63,813.

	Detroit	Minnesota
First downs	20	19
Rushes-yards	20-58	35-164
Passing	231	121
Punt returns	2-12	3-34
Kickoff returns	6-122	3-101
Interception returns	0-0	2-34
Comp.-att.-int.	28-48-2	15-22-0
Sacked-yards lost	4-32	3-15
Punts	5-53	5-47
Fumbles-lost	1-1	1-1
Penalties-yards	6-31	3-18
Time of possession	30:21	29:39

INDIVIDUAL STATISTICS

RUSHING—Detroit, Jones 7-15, Pinner 6-11, Harrington 4-17, Bryson 3-15. Minnesota, M. Bennett 18-106, Moore 11-49, Fason 5-10, B. Johnson 1-(minus 1).

PASSING—Detroit, Harrington 28-48-2-263. Minnesota, B. Johnson 15-22-0-136.

RECEIVING—Detroit, Vines 9-109, Bryson 6-30, M. Williams 4-43, Pollard 4-42, Pinner 2-26, Schlesinger 2-5, Jones 1-8. Minnesota, T. Taylor 4-27, Williamson 3-26, Burleson 2-16, Moore 1-26, M. Robinson 1-12, Wiggins 1-11, Kleinsasser 1-8, M. Bennett 1-5, K. Robinson 1-5.

MISSED FIELD GOAL ATTEMPTS—Detroit, Hanson 51. Minnesota, Edinger 52.

INTERCEPTIONS—Minnesota, Sharper 1-30, Winfield 1-4.

KICKOFF RETURNS—Detroit, Drummond 6-122. Minnesota, K. Robinson 3-101.

PUNT RETURNS—Detroit, Drummond 2-12. Minnesota, Moore 2-30, Burleson 1-4.

SACKS—Detroit, K. Edwards 2, K. Smith 1. Minnesota, Johnstone 2, Newman 1, B. Williams 1.

CHARGERS 31, JETS 26
Sunday, November 6

San Diego	14	7	7	3—31
N.Y. Jets	0	10	3	13—26

First Quarter
S.D.—Tomlinson 4 run (Kaeding kick), 7:16.
S.D.—Tomlinson 25 pass from Brees (Kaeding kick), 12:39.
Second Quarter
NYJ—C. Martin 1 run (Nugent kick), :03.
S.D.—Tomlinson 1 run (Kaeding kick), 7:06.
NYJ—FG, Nugent 35, 11:23.
Third Quarter
NYJ—FG, Nugent 22, 3:50.
S.D.—Tomlinson 1 run (Kaeding kick), 11:09.
Fourth Quarter
NYJ—Sowell 5 pass from Bollinger (Nugent kick), 2:33.
S.D.—FG, Kaeding 18, 6:25.
NYJ—Coles 8 pass from Bollinger (pass failed), 8:46.
Attendance—77,662.

	San Diego	N.Y. Jets
First downs	27	19
Rushes-yards	35-133	25-89
Passing	262	180
Punt returns	0-0	1-15
Kickoff returns	6-145	6-169
Interception returns	0-0	1-10
Comp.-att.-int.	20-27-1	17-31-0
Sacked-yards lost	1-8	3-24
Punts	2-58	2-44
Fumbles-lost	1-1	0-0
Penalties-yards	12-124	5-35
Time of possession	33:04	26:56

INDIVIDUAL STATISTICS

RUSHING—San Diego, Tomlinson 25-107, Turner 4-18, Neal 3-6, Brees 2-(minus 2), Sproles 1-4. New York, C. Martin 21-72, Houston 2-10, Bollinger 2-7.

PASSING—San Diego, Brees 20-27-1-270. New York, Bollinger 11-20-0-106, Testaverde 6-11-0-98.

RECEIVING—San Diego, Gates 8-132, Caldwell 5-43, Tomlinson 3-46, McCardell 2-25, Jackson 1-18, Neal 1-6. New York, Coles 6-64, Sowell 4-23, Chrebet 3-39, Baker 2-49, McCareins 1-17, Jolley 1-12.

MISSED FIELD GOAL ATTEMPTS—New York, Nugent 51.

INTERCEPTIONS—New York, Barrett 1-10.

KICKOFF RETURNS—San Diego, Sproles 6-145. New York, Miller 6-169.

PUNT RETURNS—New York, Cotchery 1-15.

SACKS—San Diego, Phillips 2, Merriman 1. New York, J. Abraham 1.

CHIEFS 27, RAIDERS 23
Sunday, November 6

Oakland	3	6	0	14—23
Kansas City	0	6	7	14—27

First Quarter
Oak.—FG, Janikowski 32, 6:10.

Second Quarter
Oak.—FG, Janikowski 49, :13.
K.C.—FG, Tynes 27, 10:01.
K.C.—FG, Tynes 47, 14:31.
Oak.—FG, Janikowski 48, 14:55.

Third Quarter
K.C.—Richardson 6 pass from Green (Tynes kick), 14:05.

Fourth Quarter
K.C.—L. Johnson 15 run (Tynes kick), 2:04.
Oak.—Porter 4 pass from Collins (pass failed), 4:29.
Oak.—Moss 7 pass from Collins (Jordan run), 13:15.
K.C.—L. Johnson 1 run (Tynes kick), 15:00.
Attendance—79,033.

	Oakland	Kansas City
First downs	21	18
Rushes-yards	26-101	24-114
Passing	162	207
Punt returns	2-(-6)	5-32
Kickoff returns	5-191	6-83
Interception returns	0-0	1-14
Comp.-att.-int.	21-40-1	22-35-0
Sacked-yards lost	1-13	3-28
Punts	5-47	5-42
Fumbles-lost	2-0	3-1
Penalties-yards	9-84	11-87
Time of possession	31:54	28:06

INDIVIDUAL STATISTICS

RUSHING—Oakland, Jordan 19-93, Crockett 5-3, Gabriel 1-5, Collins 1-0. Kansas City, L. Johnson 22-107, D. Hall 1-7, Green 1-0.

PASSING—Oakland, Collins 21-40-1-175. Kansas City, Green 22-35-0-235.

RECEIVING—Oakland, Porter 7-68, Jordan 5-25, Gabriel 3-37, C. Anderson 2-26, Ra. Williams 2-11, Moss 1-7, Foschi 1-1. Kansas City, Gonzalez 5-70, Kennison 5-60, Horn 4-25, L. Johnson 3-48, D. Hall 3-24, Richardson 2-8.

MISSED FIELD GOAL ATTEMPTS—None.

INTERCEPTIONS—Kansas City, Wesley 1-14.

KICKOFF RETURNS—Oakland, Carr 5-191. Kansas City, D. Hall 4-63, Horn 2-20.

PUNT RETURNS—Oakland, Carr 2-(minus 6). Kansas City, D. Hall 5-32.

SACKS—Oakland, Kelly 3. Kansas City, K. Mitchell 1.

BEARS 20, SAINTS 17
Sunday, November 6

Chicago	7	3	7	3—20
New Orleans	3	7	0	7—17

First Quarter
N.O.—FG, Carney 22, 2:42.
Chi.—Gage 4 pass from Orton (Gould kick), 8:34.

Second Quarter
N.O.—Stallworth 15 pass from Brooks (Carney kick), 5:03.
Chi.—FG, Gould 35, 14:38.

Third Quarter
Chi.—Peterson 6 run (Gould kick), 7:31.

Fourth Quarter
N.O.—Brooks 1 run (Carney kick), 7:16.
Chi.—FG, Gould 28, 14:54.
Attendance—32,637.

	Chicago	New Orleans
First downs	15	15
Rushes-yards	32-183	33-133
Passing	131	150
Punt returns	4-35	1-7
Kickoff returns	3-60	5-110
Interception returns	2-5	2-29
Comp.-att.-int.	12-26-2	16-26-2
Sacked-yards lost	2-6	3-20
Punts	6-49	7-44
Fumbles-lost	1-1	2-2
Penalties-yards	8-60	6-70
Time of possession	26:18	33:42

INDIVIDUAL STATISTICS

RUSHING—Chicago, Benson 14-79, T. Jones 11-40, Peterson 6-58, Orton 1-6. New Orleans, A. Smith 17-110, Stecker 13-29, Brooks 3-(minus 6).

PASSING—Chicago, Orton 12-26-2-137. New Orleans, Brooks 16-26-2-170.

RECEIVING—Chicago, Gage 4-28, Muhammad 3-85, Clark 1-10, M. Edwards 1-9, Wade 1-8, Peterson 1-3, T. Jones 1-(minus 6). New Orleans, Stallworth 3-37, Horn 2-27, Stecker 2-17, Hilton 2-13, Karney 2-11, A. Smith 2-7, Poole 1-42, Hakim 1-10, L. Hall 1-6.

MISSED FIELD GOAL ATTEMPTS—Chicago, Gould 47.

INTERCEPTIONS—Chicago, Vasher 1-5, Hillenmeyer 1-0. New Orleans, D. Smith 1-25, F. Thomas 1-4.

KICKOFF RETURNS—Chicago, Azumah 3-60. New Orleans, Stecker 4-110, Whitehead 1-0.

PUNT RETURNS—Chicago, Wade 4-35. New Orleans, Hakim 1-7.

SACKS—Chicago, C. Harris 1, Hillenmeyer 1, Ogunleye 1. New Orleans, Bryant 1, D. Smith 1.

GIANTS 24, 49ERS 6
Sunday, November 6

N.Y. Giants	3	7	0	14—24
San Francisco	0	0	6	0— 6

First Quarter
NYG—FG, Feely 22, 5:36.

Second Quarter
NYG—Shockey 32 pass from Manning (Feely kick), 14:47.

Third Quarter
S.F.—FG, Nedney 48, 4:36.
S.F.—FG, Nedney 52, 10:18.

Fourth Quarter
NYG—Jacobs 1 run (Feely kick), 1:41.
NYG—Jacobs 1 run (Feely kick), 8:42.
Attendance—63,820.

	N.Y. Giants	San Francisco
First downs	19	9
Rushes-yards	32-93	22-52
Passing	251	86
Punt returns	6-35	3-30
Kickoff returns	3-81	5-103
Interception returns	1-19	0-0
Comp.-att.-int.	18-33-0	12-21-1
Sacked-yards lost	0-0	3-16
Punts	5-46	7-45
Fumbles-lost	1-0	1-0
Penalties-yards	10-81	12-80
Time of possession	33:05	26:55

INDIVIDUAL STATISTICS

RUSHING—New York, Barber 21-71, Jacobs 5-3, Ward 3-22, Manning 3-(minus 3). San Francisco, Barlow 10-4, Gore 7-33, Pickett 5-15.

PASSING—New York, Manning 18-33-0-251. San Francisco, Pickett 12-21-1-102.

RECEIVING—New York, Burress 5-79, Shockey 4-77, Toomer 3-45, Barber 2-32, Finn 2-10, T. Carter 1-12, Berton 1-3. San Francisco, Barlow 6-41, Battle 2-17, Morton 1-24, Lloyd 1-13, Hetherington 1-4, Gore 1-3.

MISSED FIELD GOAL ATTEMPTS—None.

INTERCEPTIONS—New York, Alexander 1-2.

KICKOFF RETURNS—New York, Ponder 3-81. San Francisco, Marshall 4-81, McAddley 1-22.

PUNT RETURNS—New York, Morton 6-35. San Francisco, Marshall 3-30.

SACKS—New York, Pierce 1, Wilson 1, Umeniyiora 1.

SEAHAWKS 33, CARDINALS 19
Sunday, November 6

Seattle	3	14	10	6—33
Arizona	3	3	10	3—19

First Quarter
Ariz.—FG, Rackers 23, 7:04.
Sea.—FG, J. Brown 26, 14:00.

Second Quarter
Sea.—Jurevicius 4 pass from Hasselbeck (J. Brown kick), 2:00.
Ariz.—FG, Rackers 31, 8:44.
Sea.—Hasselbeck 1 run (J. Brown kick), 14:21.

Third Quarter
Sea.—Alexander 88 run (J. Brown kick), :20.
Ariz.—FG, Rackers 50, 4:31.
Sea.—FG, J. Brown 28, 8:12.
Ariz.—B. Johnson 6 pass from Warner (Rackers kick), 14:25.

Fourth Quarter
Ariz.—FG, Rackers 44, 2:51.
Sea.—Alexander 14 run (kick blocked), 9:41.
Attendance—43,542.

	Seattle	Arizona
First downs	22	23
Rushes-yards	33-208	20-71
Passing	162	307
Punt returns	0-0	2-11
Kickoff returns	6-165	7-177
Interception returns	3-31	0-0
Comp.-att.-int.	13-20-0	29-48-3
Sacked-yards lost	1-0	4-27
Punts	4-46	1-36
Fumbles-lost	1-0	1-1
Penalties-yards	6-52	9-78
Time of possession	28:03	31:57

INDIVIDUAL STATISTICS
RUSHING—Seattle, Alexander 23-173, Morris 5-30, Hasselbeck 4-2, Strong 1-3. Arizona, Shipp 13-20, Arrington 5-40, Fitzgerald 1-9, O. Ayanbadejo 1-2.
PASSING—Seattle, Hasselbeck 13-20-0-162. Arizona, Warner 29-48-3-334.
RECEIVING—Seattle, Jurevicius 4-31, Engram 3-28, Stevens 2-28, Urban 1-46, Morris 1-12, Strong 1-9, Hannam 1-8. Arizona, Fitzgerald 8-102, B. Johnson 6-66, Arrington 4-22, McCoy 3-25, O. Ayanbadejo 2-25, Newhouse 2-22, Bergen 2-5, Edwards 1-63, Shipp 1-4.
MISSED FIELD GOAL ATTEMPTS—None.
INTERCEPTIONS—Seattle, Babineaux 1-14, K. Herndon 1-10, Trufant 1-7.
KICKOFF RETURNS—Seattle, Scobey 6-165. Arizona, Moses 7-177.
PUNT RETURNS—Arizona, Moses 2-11.
SACKS—Seattle, Hill 1.5, B. Fisher 1.5, Tubbs 0.5, Darby 0.5. Arizona, Okeafor 1.

STEELERS 20, PACKERS 10
Sunday, November 6

Pittsburgh	6	7	0	7—20
Green Bay	3	0	7	0—10

First Quarter
Pit.—FG, Reed 32, 3:20.
Pit.—FG, Reed 24, 8:15.
G.B.—FG, Longwell 40, 14:00.

Second Quarter
Pit.—Polamalu 77 fumble return (Reed kick), 1:16.

Third Quarter
G.B.—Gado 1 run (Longwell kick), 7:34.

Fourth Quarter
Pit.—Staley 3 run (Reed kick), 8:44.
Attendance—70,607.

	Pittsburgh	Green Bay
First downs	13	16
Rushes-yards	33-154	29-65
Passing	59	203
Punt returns	3-13	4-66
Kickoff returns	3-59	5-81
Interception returns	1-3	1-24
Comp.-att.-int.	9-16-1	20-35-1
Sacked-yards lost	1-6	1-11
Punts	4-46	3-49
Fumbles-lost	3-0	3-2
Penalties-yards	4-53	8-74
Time of possession	26:52	33:08

INDIVIDUAL STATISTICS
RUSHING—Pittsburgh, Staley 15-76, Batch 8-14, Parker 5-13, Haynes 3-10, Randle El 2-41. Green Bay, Gado 26-62, R. Lee 2-3, Favre 1-0.
PASSING—Pittsburgh, Batch 9-16-1-65. Green Bay, Favre 20-35-1-214.
RECEIVING—Pittsburgh, Kreider 2-13, Miller 2-11, Staley 2-9, Ward 1-12, Wilson 1-10, Parker 1-10. Green Bay, Driver 5-64, Chatman 4-43, Henderson 3-36, Franks 3-22, D. Lee 3-21, W. Williams 1-19, Gado 1-9.
MISSED FIELD GOAL ATTEMPTS—Pittsburgh, Reed 51. Green Bay, Longwell 31.
INTERCEPTIONS—Pittsburgh, T. Carter 1-3. Green Bay, R. Thomas 1-24.
KICKOFF RETURNS—Pittsburgh, Morgan 3-59. Green Bay, R. Lee 3-49, Thurman 1-18, C. Williams 1-14.
PUNT RETURNS—Pittsburgh, Randle El 3-13. Green Bay, Chatman 4-66.
SACKS—Pittsburgh, McFadden 1. Green Bay, Gbaja-Biamila 1.

REDSKINS 17, EAGLES 10
Sunday, November 6

Philadelphia	7	0	3	0—10
Washington	0	10	7	0—17

First Quarter
Phi.—R. Brown 56 pass from McNabb (Akers kick), 12:05.

Second Quarter
Was.—FG, Hall 24, 2:23.
Was.—Sellers 1 run (Hall kick), 10:43.

Third Quarter
Phi.—FG, Akers 34, 8:34.
Was.—Portis 6 run (Hall kick), 12:13.
Attendance—90,298.

	Philadelphia	Washington
First downs	17	17
Rushes-yards	23-45	29-78
Passing	291	215
Punt returns	1-8	2-0
Kickoff returns	3-74	3-86
Interception returns	0-0	1-6
Comp.-att.-int.	22-35-1	21-29-0
Sacked-yards lost	2-13	2-9
Punts	7-37	6-43
Fumbles-lost	2-0	3-1
Penalties-yards	5-64	4-35
Time of possession	28:03	31:57

INDIVIDUAL STATISTICS
RUSHING—Philadelphia, Westbrook 17-24, McNabb 3-12, Gordon 3-9. Washington, Portis 21-67, Brunell 4-4, Betts 2-4, Moss 1-2, Sellers 1-1.
PASSING—Philadelphia, McNabb 22-35-1-304. Washington, Brunell 21-29-0-224.
RECEIVING—Philadelphia, R. Brown 5-94, G. Lewis 5-57, Westbrook 4-55, McMullen 3-60, Spach 2-14, Parry 2-14, Smith 1-10. Washington, Cooley 7-85, Moss 7-79, Sellers 3-26, Portis 3-8, Betts 1-26.
MISSED FIELD GOAL ATTEMPTS—None.
INTERCEPTIONS—Washington, Clark 1-6.
KICKOFF RETURNS—Philadelphia, Hood 3-74. Washington, Betts 3-86.
PUNT RETURNS—Philadelphia, Sheppard 1-8. Washington, Thrash 2-0.
SACKS—Philadelphia, Kearse 1, Cole 1. Washington, Daniels 1, Washington 1.

COLTS 40, PATRIOTS 21
Monday, November 7

Indianapolis	7	14	10	9—40
New England	7	0	7	7—21

First Quarter
Ind.—Harrison 1 pass from Manning (Vanderjagt kick), 2:30.
N.E.—Branch 16 pass from Brady (Vinatieri kick), 9:08.

Second Quarter
Ind.—James 2 run (Vanderjagt kick), 3:10.
Ind.—Wayne 10 pass from Manning (Vanderjagt kick), 14:51.

Third Quarter
Ind.—Rhodes 4 run (Vanderjagt kick), 6:24.
N.E.—Graham 31 pass from Brady (Vinatieri kick), 9:14.
Ind.—FG, Vanderjagt 35, 10:15.

Fourth Quarter
Ind.—FG, Vanderjagt 20, 1:02.
N.E.—T. Brown 19 pass from Brady (Vinatieri kick), 4:45.
Ind.—Harrison 30 pass from Manning (pass failed), 9:07.
  Attendance—68,756.

	Indianapolis	New England
First downs	28	17
Rushes-yards	38-132	14-34
Passing	321	254
Punt returns	1-0	1-29
Kickoff returns	4-98	8-142
Interception returns	0-0	1-(-1)
Comp.-att.-int.	28-37-1	25-40-0
Sacked-yards lost	0-0	2-31
Punts	1-49	3-48
Fumbles-lost	0-0	3-2
Penalties-yards	7-32	4-24
Time of possession	36:41	23:19

INDIVIDUAL STATISTICS
RUSHING—Indianapolis, James 34-104, Manning 3-24, Rhodes 1-4. New England, Dillon 12-40, Brady 1-(minus 1), Cloud 1-(minus 5).

PASSING—Indianapolis, Manning 28-37-1-321. New England, Brady 22-33-0-265, Flutie 3-7-0-20.

RECEIVING—Indianapolis, Harrison 9-128, Wayne 9-124, Stokley 4-34, James 3-9, Fletcher 2-22, Clark 1-4. New England, Branch 5-58, T. Brown 5-57, Graham 5-41, Givens 4-64, Watson 3-36, Dillon 3-29.

MISSED FIELD GOAL ATTEMPTS—None.

INTERCEPTIONS—New England, Vrabel 1-(minus 1).

KICKOFF RETURNS—Indianapolis, Rhodes 3-87, Jefferson 1-11. New England, B. Johnson 7-118, Hobbs 1-24.

PUNT RETURNS—Indianapolis, Walters 1-0. New England, Dwight 1-29.

SACKS—Indianapolis, Brock 1, Mathis 1.

STANDINGS

AMERICAN FOOTBALL CONFERENCE

EAST DIVISION

	W	L	T	Pct.	PF	PA
New England	5	4	0	.556	203	236
Buffalo	4	5	0	.444	142	162
Miami	3	6	0	.333	162	174
N.Y. Jets	2	7	0	.222	121	200

NORTH DIVISION

	W	L	T	Pct.	PF	PA
Cincinnati	7	2	0	.778	210	134
Pittsburgh	7	2	0	.778	223	145
Cleveland	3	6	0	.333	135	170
Baltimore	2	7	0	.222	100	171

SOUTH DIVISION

	W	L	T	Pct.	PF	PA
Indianapolis	9	0	0	1.000	260	115
Jacksonville	6	3	0	.667	180	142
Tennessee	2	7	0	.222	175	231
Houston	1	8	0	.111	124	247

WEST DIVISION

	W	L	T	Pct.	PF	PA
Denver	7	2	0	.778	232	169
Kansas City	5	4	0	.556	199	197
San Diego	5	4	0	.556	252	192
Oakland	3	6	0	.333	202	216

NATIONAL FOOTBALL CONFERENCE

EAST DIVISION

	W	L	T	Pct.	PF	PA
Dallas	6	3	0	.667	202	157
N.Y. Giants	6	3	0	.667	254	167
Washington	5	4	0	.556	187	185
Philadelphia	4	5	0	.444	193	205

NORTH DIVISION

	W	L	T	Pct.	PF	PA
Chicago	6	3	0	.667	156	107
Detroit	4	5	0	.444	160	173
Minnesota	4	5	0	.444	154	228
Green Bay	2	7	0	.222	201	184

SOUTH DIVISION

	W	L	T	Pct.	PF	PA
Carolina	7	2	0	.778	250	166
Atlanta	6	3	0	.667	217	176
Tampa Bay	6	3	0	.667	176	156
New Orleans	2	7	0	.222	142	242

WEST DIVISION

	W	L	T	Pct.	PF	PA
Seattle	7	2	0	.778	245	162
St. Louis	4	5	0	.444	224	262
Arizona	2	7	0	.222	167	240
San Francisco	2	7	0	.222	126	263

TOP PERFORMANCES

100-YARD RUSHING GAMES

Player, team & opponent	Att.	Yds.	TD
Shaun Alexander, Sea. vs. St.L.	33	165	3
Clinton Portis, Was. at T.B.	23	144	1
Larry Johnson, K.C. at Buf.	27	132	0
Edgerrin James, Ind. vs. Hou.	26	122	1
Adrian Peterson, Chi. vs. S.F.	24	120	1
Greg Jones, Jac. vs. Bal.	25	106	1
Samkon Gado, G.B. at Atl.	25	103	2

300-YARD PASSING GAMES

Player, team & opponent	Att.	Cmp.	Yds.	TD	Int.
Gus Frerotte, Mia. vs. N.E.	47	25	360	2	1
Kurt Warner, Ariz. at Det.	45	29	359	1	0
Kerry Collins, Oak. vs. Den.	50	26	310	2	3
Marc Bulger, St.L. at Sea.	40	28	304	1	1

100-YARD RECEIVING GAMES

Player, team & opponent	Rec.	Yds.	TD
Larry Fitzgerald, Ariz. at Det.	9	141	1
Joey Galloway, T.B. vs. Was.	7	131	1
Hines Ward, Pit. vs. Cle.	8	124	1
Matt Jones, Jac. vs. Bal.	5	117	1
Roy Williams, Det. vs. Ariz.	7	117	3
Donald Driver, G.B. at Atl.	10	114	0
Tiki Barber, NYG vs. Min.	8	111	0
Marvin Harrison, Ind. vs. Hou.	7	108	1
Marty Booker, Mia. vs. N.E.	5	102	0

RESULTS

SUNDAY, NOVEMBER 13
CHICAGO 17, San Francisco 9
DETROIT 29, Arizona 21
INDIANAPOLIS 31, Houston 17
JACKSONVILLE 30, Baltimore 3
New England 23, MIAMI 16
Minnesota 24, N.Y. GIANTS 21
BUFFALO 14, Kansas City 3
CAROLINA 30, N.Y. Jets 3
Denver 31, OAKLAND 17
SEATTLE 31, St. Louis 16
Green Bay 33, ATLANTA 25
TAMPA BAY 36, Washington 35
PITTSBURGH 34, Cleveland 21

MONDAY, NOVEMBER 14
Dallas 21, PHILADELPHIA 20

Open Date: Cincinnati, New Orleans, San Diego, Tennessee

BEARS 17, 49ERS 9

Sunday, November 13

San Francisco	0	3	3	3— 9
Chicago	0	7	0	10—17

Second Quarter
S.F.—FG, Nedney 30, 6:03.
Chi.—Vasher 108 missed FG return (Gould kick), 15:00.
Third Quarter
S.F.—FG, Nedney 34, 5:22.
Fourth Quarter
Chi.—Peterson 7 run (Gould kick), :27.
S.F.—FG, Nedney 29, 4:06.
Chi.—FG, Gould 37, 7:20.
Attendance—62,153.

	San Francisco	Chicago
First downs	9	12
Rushes-yards	46-133	40-172
Passing	28	67
Punt returns	2-0	4-31
Kickoff returns	3-46	4-83
Interception returns	1-0	1-3
Comp.-att.-int.	1-13-1	8-14-1
Sacked-yards lost	0-0	0-0
Punts	7-40	5-38
Fumbles-lost	3-1	5-3
Penalties-yards	10-80	5-34
Time of possession	31:06	28:54

INDIVIDUAL STATISTICS

RUSHING—San Francisco, Barlow 25-63, Gore 14-55, Pickett 6-15, Jackson 1-0. Chicago, Peterson 24-120, Benson 12-50, Orton 3-(minus 3), B. Johnson 1-5.

PASSING—San Francisco, Pickett 1-13-1-28. Chicago, Orton 8-13-1-67, Maynard 0-1-0-0.

RECEIVING—San Francisco, Lloyd 1-28. Chicago, Clark 2-43, B. Johnson 2-2, Wade 1-11, Gage 1-6, Muhammad 1-3, McKie 1-2.

MISSED FIELD GOAL ATTEMPTS—San Francisco, Nedney 52. Chicago, Gould 39.

INTERCEPTIONS—San Francisco, Spencer 1-0. Chicago, M. Brown 1-3.

KICKOFF RETURNS—San Francisco, McAddley 2-30, Marshall 1-16. Chicago, Azumah 4-83.

PUNT RETURNS—San Francisco, Marshall 2-0. Chicago, Wade 4-31.

SACKS—None.

LIONS 29, CARDINALS 21

Sunday, November 13

Arizona	0	3	8	10—21
Detroit	9	10	7	3—29

First Quarter
Det.—R. Williams 7 pass from Harrington (Hanson kick), 3:43.
Det.—Safety, 12:14.
Second Quarter
Det.—R. Williams 21 pass from Harrington (Hanson kick), 3:47.
Ariz.—FG, Rackers 51, 9:27.
Det.—FG, Hanson 26, 15:00.
Third Quarter
Ariz.—Arrington 1 run (O. Ayanbadejo run), 5:07.
Det.—R. Williams 29 pass from Harrington (Hanson kick), 8:57.
Fourth Quarter
Ariz.—FG, Rackers 28, :51.
Det.—FG, Hanson 20, 6:25.
Ariz.—Fitzgerald 8 pass from Warner (Rackers kick), 12:36.
Attendance—61,091.

	Arizona	Detroit
First downs	21	22
Rushes-yards	16-38	32-157
Passing	359	226
Punt returns	5-29	1-13
Kickoff returns	5-97	4-106
Interception returns	0-0	0-0
Comp.-att.-int.	29-45-0	21-31-0
Sacked-yards lost	0-0	1-5
Punts	4-38	6-44
Fumbles-lost	2-1	0-0
Penalties-yards	9-80	7-50
Time of possession	25:32	34:28

INDIVIDUAL STATISTICS

RUSHING—Arizona, Arrington 8-24, Shipp 4-3, O. Ayanbadejo 3-11, Warner 1-0. Detroit, Jones 14-81, Bryson 7-44, Pinner 7-19, Harrington 4-13.

PASSING—Arizona, Warner 29-45-0-359. Detroit, Harrington 21-31-0-231.

RECEIVING—Arizona, Fitzgerald 9-141, McCoy 6-70, O. Ayanbadejo 6-51, J. Jackson 2-31, Newhouse 2-23, Bergen 1-32, Shipp 1-7, Arrington 1-4, Warner 1-0. Detroit, R. Williams 7-117, Pollard 4-47, Vines 2-17, Bryson 2-17, T. Edwards 2-15, Jones 2-12, C. Rogers 1-4, Schlesinger 1-2.

MISSED FIELD GOAL ATTEMPTS—None.

INTERCEPTIONS—None.

KICKOFF RETURNS—Arizona, Swinton 5-97. Detroit, Drummond 4-106.

PUNT RETURNS—Arizona, Moses 5-29. Detroit, Drummond 1-13.

SACKS—Arizona, Darling 1.

COLTS 31, TEXANS 17

Sunday, November 13

Houston	0	7	10	0—17
Indianapolis	7	14	7	3—31

First Quarter
Ind.—Clark 14 pass from Manning (Vanderjagt kick), 10:31.
Second Quarter
Ind.—James 5 run (Vanderjagt kick), 3:46.
Ind.—Stokley 21 pass from Manning (Vanderjagt kick), 9:24.
Hou.—Wells 14 run (K. Brown kick), 13:07.
Third Quarter
Hou.—Gaffney 13 pass from Carr (K. Brown kick), 6:34.
Ind.—Harrison 30 pass from Manning (Vanderjagt kick), 9:06.
Hou.—FG, K. Brown 24, 14:01.
Fourth Quarter
Ind.—FG, Vanderjagt 45, 3:30.
Attendance—57,209.

	Houston	Indianapolis
First downs	11	26
Rushes-yards	24-83	29-126
Passing	126	293
Punt returns	3-9	3-7
Kickoff returns	6-143	4-82
Interception returns	0-0	0-0
Comp.-att.-int.	16-25-0	26-35-0
Sacked-yards lost	3-12	1-4
Punts	6-37	3-46
Fumbles-lost	2-0	3-2
Penalties-yards	4-35	6-50
Time of possession	27:25	32:35

INDIVIDUAL STATISTICS

RUSHING—Houston, Wells 15-58, Morency 6-18, Carr 2-9, An. Johnson 1-(minus 2). Indianapolis, James 26-122, Manning 3-4.

PASSING—Houston, Carr 16-25-0-138. Indianapolis, Manning 26-35-0-297.

RECEIVING—Houston, An. Johnson 4-42, Morency 3-19, Wells 3-19, Gaffney 2-29, Armstrong 2-25, Rivers 2-6. Indianapolis, Wayne 8-72, Harrison 7-108, Stokley 6-73, James 3-26, Clark 2-18.

MISSED FIELD GOAL ATTEMPTS—None.

INTERCEPTIONS—None.

KICKOFF RETURNS—Houston, Morency 6-143. Indianapolis, Rhodes 3-60, Mungro 1-22.

PUNT RETURNS—Houston, Buchanon 3-9. Indianapolis, Walters 1-7, Jackson 1-0, David 1-0.

SACKS—Houston, Peek 1. Indianapolis, Reagor 1, Freeney 1, Tripplett 1.

JAGUARS 30, RAVENS 3

Sunday, November 13

Baltimore	3	0	0	0— 3
Jacksonville	0	10	7	13—30

First Quarter
Bal.—FG, Stover 41, 9:17.
Second Quarter
Jac.—M. Jones 32 pass from Leftwich (Scobee kick), 8:14.
Jac.—FG, Scobee 48, 15:00.
Third Quarter
Jac.—G. Jones 1 run (Scobee kick), 12:40.

Fourth Quarter

Jac.—FG, Scobee 33, 3:33.
Jac.—FG, Scobee 26, 12:20.
Jac.—Peterson 26 interception return (Scobee kick), 12:59.
Attendance—66,107.

	Baltimore	Jacksonville
First downs	8	20
Rushes-yards	17-53	35-133
Passing	110	205
Punt returns	2-46	7-59
Kickoff returns	4-85	2-63
Interception returns	0-0	3-31
Comp.-att.-int.	19-33-3	16-30-0
Sacked-yards lost	4-32	1-6
Punts	7-45	5-41
Fumbles-lost	0-0	0-0
Penalties-yards	9-86	5-42
Time of possession	25:31	34:29

INDIVIDUAL STATISTICS

RUSHING—Baltimore, J. Lewis 14-44, Boller 2-9, Clayton 1-0. Jacksonville, G. Jones 25-106, Leftwich 4-3, Pearman 3-9, M. Jones 2-12, Toefield 1-3.

PASSING—Baltimore, Boller 19-33-3-142. Jacksonville, Leftwich 16-30-0-211.

RECEIVING—Baltimore, Heap 5-58, J. Lewis 5-13, Mason 4-63, Mu. Smith 3-5, Clayton 2-3. Jacksonville, M. Jones 5-117, J. Smith 3-43, Wrighster 2-10, Wimbush 2-9, Toefield 1-11, Wilford 1-10, G. Jones 1-7, Pearman 1-4.

MISSED FIELD GOAL ATTEMPTS—None.

INTERCEPTIONS—Jacksonville, Cousin 2-5, Peterson 1-26.

KICKOFF RETURNS—Baltimore, Sams 4-85. Jacksonville, Wimbush 2-63.

PUNT RETURNS—Baltimore, Sams 2-46. Jacksonville, Pearman 7-59.

SACKS—Baltimore, J. Johnson 0.5, Scott 0.5. Jacksonville, McCray 2, Peterson 1, Meier 1.

PATRIOTS 23, DOLPHINS 16

Sunday, November 13

New England	0	3	9	11—23
Miami	0	7	0	9—16

Second Quarter

Mia.—Chambers 3 pass from Frerotte (Mare kick), 10:38.
N.E.—FG, Vinatieri 35, 14:57.

Third Quarter

N.E.—FG, Vinatieri 32, 9:33.
N.E.—Watson 16 pass from Brady (pass failed), 15:00.

Fourth Quarter

N.E.—FG, Vinatieri 33, 2:36.
Mia.—FG, Mare 36, 6:46.
Mia.—Chambers 15 pass from Frerotte (pass failed), 12:01.
N.E.—Watson 17 pass from Brady (H. Evans run), 12:44.
Attendance—73,405.

	New England	Miami
First downs	19	22
Rushes-yards	25-91	25-77
Passing	274	360
Punt returns	3-0	3-13
Kickoff returns	4-100	4-112
Interception returns	1-8	2-22
Comp.-att.-int.	21-36-2	25-47-1
Sacked-yards lost	2-1	0-0
Punts	6-44	6-45
Fumbles-lost	1-0	3-1
Penalties-yards	6-38	4-69
Time of possession	30:27	29:33

INDIVIDUAL STATISTICS

RUSHING—New England, H. Evans 17-84, Cloud 7-8, Brady 1-(minus 1). Miami, Brown 14-64, R. Williams 11-13.

PASSING—New England, Brady 21-36-2-275. Miami, Frerotte 25-47-1-360.

RECEIVING—New England, Branch 5-82, Dwight 3-70, Watson 3-37, T. Brown 3-36, H. Evans 3-18, Fauria 2-23, B. Johnson 2-9. Miami, McMichael 7-81, Chambers 6-69, Booker 5-102, Brown 4-28, Welker 2-61, R. Williams 1-19.

MISSED FIELD GOAL ATTEMPTS—Miami, Mare 31.

INTERCEPTIONS—New England, Hobbs 1-8. Miami, Tillman 1-22, Bell 1-0.

KICKOFF RETURNS—New England, B. Johnson 4-100. Miami, Welker 4-112.

PUNT RETURNS—New England, Dwight 2-(minus 2), T. Brown 1-2. Miami, Welker 3-13.

SACKS—Miami, Carter 1, Taylor 1.

VIKINGS 24, GIANTS 21

Sunday, November 13

Minnesota	0	7	14	3—24
N.Y. Giants	0	6	7	8—21

Second Quarter

Min.—Sharper 92 interception return (Edinger kick), :17.
NYG—FG, Feely 35, 3:11.
NYG—FG, Feely 48, 11:21.

Third Quarter

Min.—K. Robinson 86 kickoff return (Edinger kick), :11.
NYG—Toomer 23 pass from Manning (Feely kick), 3:14.
Min.—Moore 71 punt return (Edinger kick), 9:33.

Fourth Quarter

NYG—Barber 3 run (Barber run), 13:39.
Min.—FG, Edinger 48, 14:50.
Attendance—78,637.

	Minnesota	N.Y. Giants
First downs	11	25
Rushes-yards	21-12	29-124
Passing	125	281
Punt returns	3-87	5-93
Kickoff returns	4-158	4-81
Interception returns	4-149	0-0
Comp.-att.-int.	18-31-0	23-48-4
Sacked-yards lost	4-19	2-10
Punts	8-43	5-43
Fumbles-lost	1-1	1-1
Penalties-yards	7-90	9-75
Time of possession	24:25	35:35

INDIVIDUAL STATISTICS

RUSHING—Minnesota, M. Bennett 19-16, Fason 1-0, Burleson 1-(minus 4). New York, Barber 23-95, Manning 2-24, Ward 2-(minus 2), T. Carter 1-5, Jacobs 1-2.

PASSING—Minnesota, B. Johnson 18-31-0-144. New York, Manning 23-48-4-291.

RECEIVING—Minnesota, Wiggins 6-42, M. Bennett 6-11, Burleson 2-14, K. Robinson 1-44, T. Taylor 1-11, M. Robinson 1-11, Williamson 1-11. New York, Barber 8-111, Toomer 6-61, Shockey 5-55, Burress 3-50, Finn 1-12, T. Carter 0-2.

MISSED FIELD GOAL ATTEMPTS—Minnesota, Edinger 40, 32. New York, Feely 28.

INTERCEPTIONS—Minnesota, Sharper 3-123, B. Williams 1-26.

KICKOFF RETURNS—Minnesota, K. Robinson 4-158. New York, Ponder 4-81.

PUNT RETURNS—Minnesota, Moore 3-87. New York, Morton 5-93.

SACKS—Minnesota, Scott 1, Newman 0.5, P. Williams 0.5. New York, Umenyiora 2, Strahan 1, Wilson 1.

BILLS 14, CHIEFS 3

Sunday, November 13

Kansas City	3	0	0	0— 3
Buffalo	0	7	7	0—14

First Quarter

K.C.—FG, Tynes 35, 13:43.

Second Quarter

Buf.—Evans 33 pass from Losman (Lindell kick), 13:07.

Third Quarter

Buf.—Evans 29 pass from Losman (Lindell kick), 6:44.
Attendance—72,093.

	Kansas City	Buffalo
First downs	22	9
Rushes-yards	32-150	28-61
Passing	166	148
Punt returns	4-14	0-0
Kickoff returns	3-56	2-32
Interception returns	0-0	3-53
Comp.-att.-int.	23-40-3	13-22-0
Sacked-yards lost	6-54	2-14
Punts	3-35	5-48
Fumbles-lost	2-1	2-2

	Kansas City	Buffalo
Penalties-yards	8-65	5-37
Time of possession	34:43	25:17

INDIVIDUAL STATISTICS

RUSHING—Kansas City, L. Johnson 27-132, Richardson 2-8, De. Brown 1-7, Green 1-4, D. Hall 1-(minus 1). Buffalo, McGahee 20-66, Losman 4-3, S. Williams 3-(minus 1), Holcomb 1-(minus 7).

PASSING—Kansas City, Green 23-40-3-220. Buffalo, Losman 9-16-0-137, Holcomb 4-6-0-25.

RECEIVING—Kansas City, Gonzalez 8-81, L. Johnson 5-46, Kennison 4-41, D. Hall 2-19, Boerigter 2-18, Horn 2-15. Buffalo, Moulds 5-26, Campbell 4-42, Evans 3-66, Reed 1-28.

MISSED FIELD GOAL ATTEMPTS—Kansas City, Tynes 44, 43. Buffalo, Lindell 28, 31.

INTERCEPTIONS—Buffalo, McGee 1-33, Baker 1-18, Crowell 1-2.

KICKOFF RETURNS—Kansas City, D. Hall 3-56. Buffalo, Reed 1-18, McGee 1-14.

PUNT RETURNS—Kansas City, D. Hall 4-14.

SACKS—Kansas City, Allen 2. Buffalo, Schobel 2, Fletcher 1, Crowell 1, Denney 1, Bannan 1.

PANTHERS 30, JETS 3
Sunday, November 13

N.Y. Jets	0	3	0	0— 3
Carolina	7	3	0	20—30

First Quarter
Car.—Colbert 19 pass from Delhomme (Kasay kick), 7:48.

Second Quarter
NYJ—FG, Nugent 22, 5:49.
Car.—FG, Kasay 23, 14:13.

Fourth Quarter
Car.—S. Davis 1 run (Kasay kick), 1:35.
Car.—FG, Kasay 42, 3:51.
Car.—FG, Kasay 28, 7:25.
Car.—Witherspoon 35 interception return (Kasay kick), 9:30.
Attendance—73,529.

	N.Y. Jets	Carolina
First downs	15	15
Rushes-yards	32-137	36-101
Passing	77	119
Punt returns	1-4	2-25
Kickoff returns	7-133	2-35
Interception returns	2-11	4-42
Comp.-att.-int.	11-21-4	10-20-2
Sacked-yards lost	3-21	0-0
Punts	3-42	3-43
Fumbles-lost	3-2	0-0
Penalties-yards	5-50	3-25
Time of possession	28:47	31:13

INDIVIDUAL STATISTICS

RUSHING—New York, C. Martin 19-75, Houston 10-53, Bollinger 2-5, Cotchery 1-4. Carolina, S. Davis 27-81, Foster 6-20, Delhomme 2-(minus 2), Hoover 1-2.

PASSING—New York, Bollinger 11-21-4-98. Carolina, Delhomme 10-20-2-119.

RECEIVING—New York, Coles 3-30, Jolley 2-25, McCareins 2-21, Sowell 2-8, Cotchery 1-8, C. Martin 1-6. Carolina, Foster 3-43, S. Smith 3-34, Colbert 2-29, Gaines 1-11, Hoover 1-2.

MISSED FIELD GOAL ATTEMPTS—None.

INTERCEPTIONS—New York, Law 1-7, Coleman 1-4. Carolina, Lucas 2-3, Witherspoon 1-35, Gamble 1-4.

KICKOFF RETURNS—New York, Miller 7-133. Carolina, Smart 1-24, Gaines 1-11.

PUNT RETURNS—New York, Cotchery 1-4. Carolina, S. Smith 1-18, Gamble 1-7.

SACKS—Carolina, Peppers 1.5, Moorehead 1, Rucker 0.5.

BRONCOS 31, RAIDERS 17
Sunday, November 13

Denver	0	13	10	8—31
Oakland	0	0	0	17—17

Second Quarter
Den.—Smith 27 pass from Plummer (Elam kick), :06.
Den.—FG, Elam 22, 6:48.
Den.—FG, Elam 38, 15:00.

Third Quarter
Den.—Mi. Anderson 1 run (Elam kick), 7:39.
Den.—FG, Elam 25, 14:01.

Fourth Quarter
Oak.—Moss 29 pass from Collins (Janikowski kick), :44.
Oak.—FG, Janikowski 40, 2:57.
Den.—Da. Williams 80 interception return (Putzier pass from Plummer), 7:58.
Oak.—Gabriel 14 pass from Collins (Janikowski kick), 13:01.
Attendance—62,779.

	Denver	Oakland
First downs	18	20
Rushes-yards	38-121	17-60
Passing	205	275
Punt returns	1-52	2-9
Kickoff returns	2-49	6-139
Interception returns	3-126	0-0
Comp.-att.-int.	16-22-0	26-50-3
Sacked-yards lost	0-0	4-35
Punts	4-44	5-47
Fumbles-lost	2-2	1-0
Penalties-yards	4-30	9-58
Time of possession	30:47	29:13

INDIVIDUAL STATISTICS

RUSHING—Denver, Mi. Anderson 17-65, Bell 16-44, Plummer 3-7, Adams 2-5. Oakland, Jordan 14-48, Crockett 3-12.

PASSING—Denver, Plummer 16-22-0-205. Oakland, Collins 26-50-3-310.

RECEIVING—Denver, Smith 5-50, Lelie 3-76, Putzier 3-33, Bell 3-15, K. Johnson 1-17, S. Alexander 1-14. Oakland, Jordan 7-60, Moss 6-87, Gabriel 5-58, Whitted 3-53, Porter 3-27, C. Anderson 1-18, Crockett 1-7.

MISSED FIELD GOAL ATTEMPTS—Oakland, Janikowski 45.

INTERCEPTIONS—Denver, Da. Williams 1-80, N. Ferguson 1-28, Bailey 1-18.

KICKOFF RETURNS—Denver, R. Alexander 2-49. Oakland, Carr 6-139.

PUNT RETURNS—Denver, Da. Williams 1-52. Oakland, Carr 2-9.

SACKS—Denver, Pryce 1, M. Myers 1, Ekuban 1, C. Brown 1.

SEAHAWKS 31, RAMS 16
Sunday, November 13

St. Louis	3	0	6	7—16
Seattle	0	10	14	7—31

First Quarter
St.L.—FG, J. Wilkins 31, 5:10.

Second Quarter
Sea.—Alexander 6 run (J. Brown kick), 6:15.
Sea.—FG, J. Brown 31, 14:45.

Third Quarter
St.L.—FG, J. Wilkins 36, 2:38.
Sea.—Alexander 4 run (J. Brown kick), 5:40.
Sea.—Hackett 31 pass from Hasselbeck (J. Brown kick), 10:01.
St.L.—FG, J. Wilkins 39, 14:20.

Fourth Quarter
St.L.—Holt 14 pass from Bulger (J. Wilkins kick), 8:00.
Sea.—Alexander 17 run (J. Brown kick), 13:48.
Attendance—67,192.

	St. Louis	Seattle
First downs	22	21
Rushes-yards	21-75	36-174
Passing	278	243
Punt returns	2-16	1-19
Kickoff returns	6-112	5-114
Interception returns	2-49	1-4
Comp.-att.-int.	28-40-1	17-29-2
Sacked-yards lost	3-26	0-0
Punts	2-42	3-40
Fumbles-lost	2-1	0-0
Penalties-yards	8-49	3-69
Time of possession	30:47	29:13

INDIVIDUAL STATISTICS

RUSHING—St. Louis, S. Jackson 17-70, Bulger 2-9, M. Faulk 1-0, J. Wilkins 1-(minus 4). Seattle, Alexander 33-165, Strong 2-7, Hasselbeck 1-2.

PASSING—St. Louis, Bulger 28-40-1-304. Seattle, Hasselbeck 17-29-2-243.

RECEIVING—St. Louis, Curtis 6-51, M. Faulk 5-54, S. Jackson 5-45, Holt 4-45, Manumaleuna 3-51, McDonald 2-26, Bruce 1-16, Looker 1-12, Cleeland 1-4. Seattle, Engram 6-70, Stevens 4-49, Jurevicius 3-27, Hackett 2-78, Hannam 1-10, Alexander 1-9.

MISSED FIELD GOAL ATTEMPTS—None.

INTERCEPTIONS—St. Louis, Furrey 1-33, Coakley 1-16. Seattle, Boulware 1-4.

KICKOFF RETURNS—St. Louis, Allen 6-112. Seattle, Scobey 5-114.

PUNT RETURNS—St. Louis, Allen 2-16. Seattle, J. Williams 1-19.

SACKS—Seattle, Tatupu 1, R. Bernard 1, Hill 1.

PACKERS 33, FALCONS 25
Sunday, November 13

Green Bay	14	3	6	10—33
Atlanta	0	14	0	11—25

First Quarter
G.B.—Gado 9 run (Longwell kick), 4:51.
G.B.—Gado 1 pass from Favre (Longwell kick), 7:10.

Second Quarter
Atl.—Dunn 21 pass from Vick (T. Peterson kick), 2:42.
Atl.—Vick 1 run (T. Peterson kick), 5:32.
G.B.—FG, Longwell 46, 14:20.

Third Quarter
G.B.—FG, Longwell 23, 5:08.
G.B.—FG, Longwell 53, 13:09.

Fourth Quarter
Atl.—FG, T. Peterson 37, 4:52.
G.B.—FG, Longwell 51, 10:59.
G.B.—Gado 2 run (Longwell kick), 11:26.
Atl.—R. White 19 pass from Vick (Finneran pass from Vick), 13:17.
Attendance—71,001.

	Green Bay	Atlanta
First downs	25	19
Rushes-yards	29-107	29-129
Passing	244	192
Punt returns	2-14	3-34
Kickoff returns	2-57	8-156
Interception returns	0-0	1-6
Comp.-att.-int.	27-40-1	20-30-0
Sacked-yards lost	1-12	3-17
Punts	3-42	5-39
Fumbles-lost	2-0	6-3
Penalties-yards	4-58	8-58
Time of possession	32:56	27:04

INDIVIDUAL STATISTICS
RUSHING—Green Bay, Gado 25-103, Favre 3-2, R. Lee 1-2. Atlanta, Dunn 17-76, Vick 7-20, Duckett 4-31, R. White 1-2.

PASSING—Green Bay, Favre 26-39-1-252, Sander 1-1-0-4. Atlanta, Vick 20-30-0-209.

RECEIVING—Green Bay, Driver 10-114, Franks 4-34, Gado 4-5, D. Lee 3-31, Chatman 2-27, Henderson 2-24, Thurman 1-16, R. Lee 1-5. Atlanta, Dunn 6-52, Crumpler 5-40, Finneran 4-50, Duckett 2-27, R. White 2-22, Pathon 1-18.

MISSED FIELD GOAL ATTEMPTS—None.

INTERCEPTIONS—Atlanta, D. Williams 1-6.

KICKOFF RETURNS—Green Bay, R. Lee 2-57. Atlanta, Rossum 8-156.

PUNT RETURNS—Green Bay, Chatman 2-14. Atlanta, Rossum 3-34.

SACKS—Green Bay, Barnett 1, Kampman 1, Harris 1. Atlanta, Babineaux 0.5, Kerney 0.5.

BUCCANEERS 36, REDSKINS 35
Sunday, November 13

Washington	3	10	15	7—35
Tampa Bay	7	14	7	8—36

First Quarter
T.B.—Alstott 2 run (M. Bryant kick), 7:44.
Was.—FG, Hall 33, 11:27.

Second Quarter
T.B.—Alstott 1 run (M. Bryant kick), 7:08.
Was.—Betts 94 kickoff return (Hall kick), 7:24.
T.B.—Galloway 24 pass from Simms (M. Bryant kick), 9:52.
Was.—FG, Hall 40, 13:24.

Third Quarter
Was.—Sellers 7 pass from Brunell (Portis pass from Brunell), 1:46.
Was.—Betts 17 pass from Brunell (Hall kick), 9:41.
T.B.—I. Hilliard 4 pass from Simms (M. Bryant kick), 13:07.

Fourth Quarter
Was.—Portis 8 run (Hall kick), 6:41.
T.B.—Shepherd 30 pass from Simms (Alstott run), 14:02.
Attendance—65,421.

	Washington	Tampa Bay
First downs	23	19
Rushes-yards	33-185	27-61
Passing	204	279
Punt returns	2-3	1-4
Kickoff returns	5-170	6-121
Interception returns	0-0	2-34
Comp.-att.-int.	23-35-2	15-29-0
Sacked-yards lost	2-22	0-0
Punts	2-42	4-45
Fumbles-lost	3-1	1-1
Penalties-yards	6-41	2-15
Time of possession	34:25	25:35

INDIVIDUAL STATISTICS
RUSHING—Washington, Portis 23-144, Betts 7-26, Brunell 3-15. Tampa Bay, C. Williams 10-20, Alstott 9-21, Pittman 5-15, Simms 3-5.

PASSING—Washington, Brunell 23-35-2-226. Tampa Bay, Simms 15-29-0-279.

RECEIVING—Washington, Cooley 6-66, Moss 4-79, Patten 3-24, Betts 3-19, Portis 2-9, Royal 2-2, Kozlowski 1-18, Sellers 1-7, Thrash 1-2. Tampa Bay, Galloway 7-131, Shepherd 3-87, I. Hilliard 3-37, Alstott 1-18, Cook 1-6.

MISSED FIELD GOAL ATTEMPTS—None.

INTERCEPTIONS—Tampa Bay, Bolden 1-28, Rice 1-6.

KICKOFF RETURNS—Washington, Betts 5-170. Tampa Bay, Cox 4-81, Shepherd 2-40.

PUNT RETURNS—Washington, Thrash 1-3, Moss 1-0. Tampa Bay, Jones 1-4.

SACKS—Tampa Bay, Rice 2.

STEELERS 34, BROWNS 21
Sunday, November 13

Cleveland	7	0	0	14—21
Pittsburgh	0	17	7	10—34

First Quarter
Cle.—Droughns 5 run (Dawson kick), 5:07.

Second Quarter
Pit.—Bettis 1 run (Reed kick), 6:40.
Pit.—FG, Reed 42, 12:49.
Pit.—Batch 1 run (Reed kick), 14:54.

Third Quarter
Pit.—Ward 51 pass from Randle El (Reed kick), 1:41.

Fourth Quarter
Pit.—FG, Reed 33, :12.
Cle.—Bodden 59 blocked FG return (Dawson kick), 10:37.
Pit.—Haynes 10 run (Reed kick), 13:07.
Cle.—Bryant 9 pass from Dilfer (Dawson kick), 14:39.
Attendance—63,491.

	Cleveland	Pittsburgh
First downs	16	25
Rushes-yards	19-61	41-159
Passing	242	223
Punt returns	0-0	3-16
Kickoff returns	7-119	3-52
Interception returns	0-0	1-9
Comp.-att.-int.	17-34-1	18-27-0
Sacked-yards lost	2-11	0-0
Punts	4-37	2-44
Fumbles-lost	1-1	0-0
Penalties-yards	9-75	4-30
Time of possession	23:37	36:23

INDIVIDUAL STATISTICS
RUSHING—Cleveland, Droughns 17-56, Dilfer 1-5, T. Smith 1-0. Pittsburgh, Staley 17-64, Haynes 9-41, Bettis 9-28, Batch 3-16, Randle El 2-10, Maddox 1-0.

PASSING—Cleveland, Dilfer 17-34-1-253. Pittsburgh, Batch 13-19-0-150, Maddox 4-7-0-22, Randle El 1-1-0-51.

RECEIVING—Cleveland, Bryant 5-82, Droughns 4-67, Northcutt 4-31, Edwards 2-64, T. Smith 1-9, Heiden 1-0. Pittsburgh, Ward 8-124, Wilson 3-48, Randle El 2-19, Staley 2-16, Haynes 2-10, Kranchick 1-6.

MISSED FIELD GOAL ATTEMPTS—Pittsburgh, Reed 44.

INTERCEPTIONS—Pittsburgh, Porter 1-9.

KICKOFF RETURNS—Cleveland, Cribbs 3-65, T. Smith 2-24, Wright 1-17, Shea 1-13. Pittsburgh, Colclough 1-29, Morgan 1-15, Wilson 1-8.

PUNT RETURNS—Pittsburgh, Randle El 3-16.

SACKS—Pittsburgh, Porter 1, Haggans 1.

COWBOYS 21, EAGLES 20

Monday, November 14

Dallas	7	0	0	14—21
Philadelphia	7	7	3	3—20

First Quarter
Phi.—Westbrook 15 run (Akers kick), 6:06.
Dal.—Barber 1 run (Suisham kick), 14:05.

Second Quarter
Phi.—McNabb 2 run (Akers kick), 13:13.

Third Quarter
Phi.—FG, Akers 48, 6:54.

Fourth Quarter
Phi.—FG, Akers 20, 5:48.
Dal.—T. Glenn 20 pass from Bledsoe (Suisham kick), 11:56.
Dal.—Ro. Williams 46 interception return (Suisham kick), 12:17.
  Attendance—67,739.

	Dallas	Philadelphia
First downs	13	21
Rushes-yards	24-58	36-181
Passing	183	178
Punt returns	1-1	6-65
Kickoff returns	5-107	4-89
Interception returns	1-46	1-5
Comp.-att.-int.	17-24-1	21-39-1
Sacked-yards lost	2-13	2-5
Punts	9-43	7-38
Fumbles-lost	1-0	3-0
Penalties-yards	4-31	14-95
Time of possession	24:15	35:45

INDIVIDUAL STATISTICS

RUSHING—Dallas, Barber 13-46, J. Jones 8-16, Bledsoe 2-6, T. Glenn 1-(minus 10). Philadelphia, Westbrook 16-86, Gordon 13-57, McNabb 5-22, McMahon 1-9, Mahe 1-7.

PASSING—Dallas, Bledsoe 17-24-1-196. Philadelphia, McNabb 19-34-1-169, McMahon 2-5-0-14.

RECEIVING—Dallas, K. Johnson 5-56, Witten 3-27, Barber 3-0, T. Glenn 2-31, P. Price 1-58, Campbell 1-18, J. Jones 1-3, Polite 1-3. Philadelphia, Smith 6-56, Westbrook 5-32, G. Lewis 3-42, R. Brown 3-15, Parry 2-16, C. Lewis 1-17, McMullen 1-5.

MISSED FIELD GOAL ATTEMPTS—Philadelphia, Akers 60.

INTERCEPTIONS—Dallas, Ro. Williams 1-46. Philadelphia, Sheppard 1-5.

KICKOFF RETURNS—Dallas, Thompson 5-107. Philadelphia, Hood 4-89.

PUNT RETURNS—Dallas, P. Price 1-1. Philadelphia, Westbrook 4-32, Mahe 2-33.

SACKS—Dallas, B. James 1, Ellis 1. Philadelphia, Cole 2.

STANDINGS

AMERICAN FOOTBALL CONFERENCE

EAST DIVISION

	W	L	T	Pct.	PF	PA
New England	6	4	0	.600	227	253
Buffalo	4	6	0	.400	152	210
Miami	3	7	0	.300	162	196
N.Y. Jets	2	8	0	.200	121	227

NORTH DIVISION

	W	L	T	Pct.	PF	PA
Cincinnati	7	3	0	.700	247	179
Pittsburgh	7	3	0	.700	236	161
Cleveland	4	6	0	.400	157	170
Baltimore	3	7	0	.300	116	184

SOUTH DIVISION

	W	L	T	Pct.	PF	PA
Indianapolis	10	0	0	1.000	305	152
Jacksonville	7	3	0	.700	211	170
Tennessee	2	8	0	.200	203	262
Houston	1	9	0	.100	141	292

WEST DIVISION

	W	L	T	Pct.	PF	PA
Denver	8	2	0	.800	259	169
Kansas City	6	4	0	.600	244	214
San Diego	6	4	0	.600	300	202
Oakland	4	6	0	.400	218	229

NATIONAL FOOTBALL CONFERENCE

EAST DIVISION

	W	L	T	Pct.	PF	PA
Dallas	7	3	0	.700	222	164
N.Y. Giants	7	3	0	.700	281	184
Washington	5	5	0	.500	200	201
Philadelphia	4	6	0	.400	210	232

NORTH DIVISION

	W	L	T	Pct.	PF	PA
Chicago	7	3	0	.700	169	110
Minnesota	5	5	0	.500	174	245
Detroit	4	6	0	.400	167	193
Green Bay	2	8	0	.200	218	204

SOUTH DIVISION

	W	L	T	Pct.	PF	PA
Carolina	7	3	0	.700	253	179
Tampa Bay	7	3	0	.700	206	183
Atlanta	6	4	0	.600	244	206
New Orleans	2	8	0	.200	159	266

WEST DIVISION

	W	L	T	Pct.	PF	PA
Seattle	8	2	0	.800	272	187
St. Louis	4	6	0	.400	252	300
Arizona	3	7	0	.300	205	268
San Francisco	2	8	0	.200	151	290

TOP PERFORMANCES

100-YARD RUSHING GAMES

Player, team & opponent	Att.	Yds.	TD
Larry Johnson, K.C. at Hou.	36	211	2
Reuben Droughns, Cle. vs. Mia.	30	166	1
Mewelde Moore, Min. at G.B.	22	122	0
Carnell Williams, T.B. at Atl.	19	116	1
Shaun Alexander, Sea. at S.F.	24	115	2
Mike Anderson, Den. vs. NYJ	26	113	3
Tiki Barber, NYG vs. Phi.	21	112	0

300-YARD PASSING GAMES

Player, team & opponent	Att.	Cmp.	Yds.	TD	Int.
Peyton Manning, Ind. at Cin.	40	24	365	3	1
Aaron Brooks, N.O. at N.E.	50	27	343	2	1
Drew Brees, S.D. vs. Buf.	33	28	339	4	0
Carson Palmer, Cin. vs. Ind.	38	25	335	2	1
Michael Vick, Atl. vs. T.B.	38	21	306	2	0

100-YARD RECEIVING GAMES

Player, team & opponent	Rec.	Yds.	TD
Chad Johnson, Cin. vs. Ind.	8	189	1
Steve Smith, Car. at Chi.	14	169	0
Jerry Porter, Oak. at Was.	6	142	1
Torry Holt, St.L. vs. Ariz.	11	129	1
Dallas Clark, Ind. at Cin.	6	125	1
Brandon Lloyd, S.F. vs. Sea.	7	119	1
Reggie Wayne, Ind. at Cin.	5	117	1
Plaxico Burress, NYG vs. Phi.	6	113	1
Roddy White, Atl. vs. T.B.	4	108	0
Anquan Boldin, Ariz. at St.L.	8	105	1
Larry Fitzgerald, Ariz. at St.L.	9	104	1

RESULTS

SUNDAY, NOVEMBER 20
CLEVELAND 22, Miami 0
CHICAGO 13, Carolina 3
NEW ENGLAND 24, New Orleans 17
N.Y. GIANTS 27, Philadelphia 17
DALLAS 20, Detroit 7
Arizona 38, ST. LOUIS 28
Jacksonville 31, TENNESSEE 28
Tampa Bay 30, ATLANTA 27
Oakland 16, WASHINGTON 13
BALTIMORE 16, Pittsburgh 13 (OT)
DENVER 27, N.Y. Jets 0
SAN DIEGO 48, Buffalo 10
Seattle 27, SAN FRANCISCO 25
Indianapolis 45, CINCINNATI 37
Kansas City 45, HOUSTON 17

MONDAY, NOVEMBER 21
Minnesota 20, GREEN BAY 17

BROWNS 22, DOLPHINS 0
Sunday, November 20

Miami	0	0	0	0— 0
Cleveland	9	3	10	0—22

First Quarter
Cle.—Droughns 75 run (kick failed), 1:51.
Cle.—FG, Dawson 23, 7:57.

Second Quarter
Cle.—FG, Dawson 40, 15:00.

Third Quarter
Cle.—T. Smith 6 pass from Dilfer (Dawson kick), 9:36.
Cle.—FG, Dawson 24, 13:25.
Attendance—72,773.

	Miami	Cleveland
First downs	12	19
Rushes-yards	25-139	39-181
Passing	55	195
Punt returns	2-23	2-47
Kickoff returns	5-98	1-16
Interception returns	1-16	2-11
Comp.-att.-int.	9-28-2	17-29-1
Sacked-yards lost	2-12	0-0
Punts	6-44	4-36
Fumbles-lost	1-0	0-0
Penalties-yards	7-43	5-35
Time of possession	24:32	35:28

INDIVIDUAL STATISTICS
...RUSHING—Miami, R. Williams 13-83, Brown 12-56. Cleveland, Droughns 30-166, Dilfer 4-3, Wright 3-8, Northcutt 1-2, T. Smith 1-2.
....PASSING—Miami, Frerotte 4-18-0-53, Rosenfels 5-10-2-14. Cleveland, Dilfer 11-18-0-137, Frye 6-11-1-58.
...RECEIVING—Miami, Chambers 3-12, Welker 2-12, Gilmore 1-39, Diamond 1-7, Brown 1-2, Morris 1-(minus 5). Cleveland, Edwards 6-90, Bryant 4-60, Heiden 4-31, T. Smith 1-6, Northcutt 1-5, Droughns 1-3.
...MISSED FIELD GOAL ATTEMPTS—None.
....INTERCEPTIONS—Miami, Tillman 1-16. Cleveland, Crocker 1-11, Stewart 1-0.
...KICKOFF RETURNS—Miami, Welker 4-79, Minor 1-19. Cleveland, Cribbs 1-16.
....PUNT RETURNS—Miami, Welker 2-23. Cleveland, Northcutt 2-47.
....SACKS—Cleveland, Thompson 1, McKinley 1.

BEARS 13, PANTHERS 3
Sunday, November 20

Carolina	0	0	0	3— 3
Chicago	10	3	0	0—13

First Quarter
Chi.—Muhammad 3 pass from Orton (Gould kick), 3:10.
Chi.—FG, Gould 33, 9:19.

Second Quarter
Chi.—FG, Gould 39, 7:08.

Fourth Quarter
Car.—FG, Kasay 38, 6:29.
Attendance—62,156.

	Carolina	Chicago
First downs	13	15
Rushes-yards	16-55	31-122
Passing	183	136
Punt returns	2-18	3-3
Kickoff returns	4-51	2-26
Interception returns	1-10	2-68
Comp.-att.-int.	22-39-2	15-26-1
Sacked-yards lost	8-52	0-0
Punts	7-42	7-44
Fumbles-lost	3-0	0-0
Penalties-yards	7-62	9-75
Time of possession	29:18	30:42

INDIVIDUAL STATISTICS
RUSHING—Carolina, Foster 9-41, S. Davis 4-6, Delhomme 2-8, Goings 1-0. Chicago, T. Jones 25-87, Peterson 4-37, Orton 2-(minus 2).
PASSING—Carolina, Delhomme 22-38-2-235, Foster 0-1-0-0. Chicago, Orton 15-26-1-136.

RECEIVING—Carolina, S. Smith 14-169, Foster 3-20, Proehl 2-19, Gaines 2-15, Gardner 1-12. Chicago, Gage 7-81, Muhammad 6-49, B. Johnson 2-6.
MISSED FIELD GOAL ATTEMPTS—Carolina, Kasay 46.
INTERCEPTIONS—Carolina, Manning Jr. 1-10. Chicago, Vasher 2-68.
KICKOFF RETURNS—Carolina, Smart 4-51. Chicago, Azumah 2-26.
PUNT RETURNS—Carolina, S. Smith 2-18. Chicago, Wade 3-3.
SACKS—Chicago, Ogunleye 3, A. Brown 2, T. Harris 1, Haynes 1, Boone 1.

PATRIOTS 24, SAINTS 17
Sunday, November 20

New Orleans	0	7	0	10—17
New England	7	7	7	3—24

First Quarter
N.E.—Branch 2 pass from Brady (Vinatieri kick), 12:30.

Second Quarter
N.E.—Vrabel 1 pass from Brady (Vinatieri kick), 1:30.
N.O.—Stallworth 7 pass from Brooks (Carney kick), 13:48.

Third Quarter
N.E.—Andre. Davis 60 pass from Brady (Vinatieri kick), 10:41.

Fourth Quarter
N.E.—FG, Vinatieri 37, 7:08.
N.O.—Stallworth 12 pass from Brooks (Carney kick), 10:00.
N.O.—FG, Carney 46, 12:40.
Attendance—68,756.

	New Orleans	New England
First downs	23	20
Rushes-yards	21-87	30-132
Passing	338	194
Punt returns	4-28	1-23
Kickoff returns	4-114	3-59
Interception returns	0-0	1-0
Comp.-att.-int.	27-50-1	15-29-0
Sacked-yards lost	1-5	3-28
Punts	4-32	5-47
Fumbles-lost	0-0	1-1
Penalties-yards	11-99	5-50
Time of possession	32:57	27:03

INDIVIDUAL STATISTICS
RUSHING—New Orleans, A. Smith 11-32, Stecker 7-25, Brooks 3-30. New England, H. Evans 16-74, Pass 13-53, Brady 1-5.
PASSING—New Orleans, Brooks 27-50-1-343. New England, Brady 15-29-0-222.
RECEIVING—New Orleans, Horn 6-80, Stallworth 6-76, Stecker 6-72, Hilton 6-72, Hakim 2-41, Karney 1-2. New England, Branch 5-38, Watson 4-66, Pass 2-36, H. Evans 2-21, Andre. Davis 1-60, Vrabel 1-1.
MISSED FIELD GOAL ATTEMPTS—New Orleans, Carney 30.
INTERCEPTIONS—New England, Wilson 1-0.
KICKOFF RETURNS—New Orleans, Stecker 4-114. New England, Dwight 2-36, Hobbs 1-23.
PUNT RETURNS—New Orleans, Hakim 4-28. New England, Dwight 1-23.
SACKS—New Orleans, W. Smith 1.5, Ch. Grant 1, Bryant 0.5. New England, McGinest 1.

GIANTS 27, EAGLES 17
Sunday, November 20

Philadelphia	0	0	10	7—17
N.Y. Giants	0	10	3	14—27

Second Quarter
NYG—FG, Feely 26, :45.
NYG—Toomer 1 pass from Manning (Feely kick), 12:05.

Third Quarter
Phi.—R. Brown 22 pass from McMahon (Akers kick), 5:55.
NYG—FG, Feely 27, 9:02.
Phi.—FG, Akers 20, 13:27.

Fourth Quarter
NYG—Shockey 1 pass from Manning (Feely kick), 2:46.
Phi.—McMahon 1 run (Akers kick), 7:27.
NYG—Burress 61 pass from Manning (Feely kick), 9:36.
Attendance—78,626.

	Philadelphia	N.Y. Giants
First downs	20	17
Rushes-yards	30-106	29-115

	Philadelphia	N.Y. Giants
Passing	298	200
Punt returns	4-27	2-8
Kickoff returns	4-86	3-66
Interception returns	0-0	1-19
Comp.-att.-int.	18-39-1	17-26-0
Sacked-yards lost	0-0	5-18
Punts	6-29	6-39
Fumbles-lost	3-0	2-0
Penalties-yards	7-105	6-58
Time of possession	29:31	30:29

INDIVIDUAL STATISTICS

RUSHING—Philadelphia, Westbrook 16-66, McMahon 9-31, Gordon 4-4, G. Lewis 1-5. New York, Barber 21-112, Manning 3-7, Jacobs 3-0, Ward 2-(minus 4).

PASSING—Philadelphia, McMahon 18-39-1-298. New York, Manning 17-26-0-218.

RECEIVING—Philadelphia, Smith 7-84, Westbrook 4-57, R. Brown 3-88, G. Lewis 3-64, McMullen 1-5. New York, Burress 6-113, Toomer 6-56, Barber 2-22, Shiancoe 1-15, Finn 1-11, Shockey 1-1.

MISSED FIELD GOAL ATTEMPTS—Philadelphia, Akers 38.

INTERCEPTIONS—New York, Wilson 1-19.

KICKOFF RETURNS—Philadelphia, Hood 4-86. New York, Morton 3-66.

PUNT RETURNS—Philadelphia, Mahe 2-19, Westbrook 2-8. New York, Morton 1-8, Blackburn 1-0.

SACKS—Philadelphia, Kearse 2.5, Cole 2, Patterson 0.5.

COWBOYS 20, LIONS 7
Sunday, November 20

Detroit	0	7	0	0— 7
Dallas	7	6	7	0—20

First Quarter
Dal.—Barber 6 run (Cundiff kick), 8:02.

Second Quarter
Dal.—FG, Cundiff 19, 8:21.
Det.—Jones 2 run (Hanson kick), 12:11.
Dal.—FG, Cundiff 56, 14:57.

Third Quarter
Dal.—Barber 4 run (Cundiff kick), 12:39.
Attendance—62,670.

	Detroit	Dallas
First downs	11	26
Rushes-yards	19-57	42-149
Passing	169	104
Punt returns	1-(-6)	3-24
Kickoff returns	5-95	2-42
Interception returns	0-0	0-0
Comp.-att.-int.	17-25-0	12-23-0
Sacked-yards lost	1-0	1-6
Punts	5-40	3-32
Fumbles-lost	1-1	2-1
Penalties-yards	17-129	5-40
Time of possession	23:58	36:02

INDIVIDUAL STATISTICS

RUSHING—Detroit, Jones 12-29, Bryson 4-15, Pinner 1-7, Harrington 1-5, Schlesinger 1-1. Dallas, J. Jones 21-92, Barber 15-53, Bledsoe 4-2, Thompson 2-2.

PASSING—Detroit, Harrington 17-25-0-169. Dallas, Bledsoe 12-23-0-110.

RECEIVING—Detroit, R. Williams 5-72, C. Rogers 4-41, Jones 3-38, Bryson 2-13, Pollard 2-5, FitzSimmons 1-0. Dallas, K. Johnson 5-37, T. Glenn 3-35, Witten 2-15, J. Jones 1-13, Polite 1-10.

MISSED FIELD GOAL ATTEMPTS—Detroit, Hanson 50.

INTERCEPTIONS—None.

KICKOFF RETURNS—Detroit, Drummond 4-79, McQuarters 1-16. Dallas, Thompson 1-21, Copper 1-21.

PUNT RETURNS—Detroit, Drummond 1-(minus 6). Dallas, Newman 2-14, P. Price 1-10.

SACKS—Detroit, K. Edwards 1. Dallas, Ellis 1.

CARDINALS 38, RAMS 28
Sunday, November 20

Arizona	3	10	3	22—38
St. Louis	3	7	7	11—28

First Quarter
St.L.—FG, J. Wilkins 47, 7:25.
Ariz.—FG, Rackers 32, 13:38.

Second Quarter
St.L.—Holt 22 pass from Bulger (J. Wilkins kick), :53.
Ariz.—Boldin 13 pass from Warner (Rackers kick), 6:07.
Ariz.—FG, Rackers 33, 14:34.

Third Quarter
Ariz.—FG, Rackers 51, 3:51.
St.L.—Bruce 46 pass from Bulger (J. Wilkins kick), 7:22.

Fourth Quarter
Ariz.—Bergen 9 pass from Warner (Boldin pass from Warner), 6:49.
St.L.—FG, J. Wilkins 32, 11:25.
Ariz.—Fitzgerald 7 pass from Warner (Rackers kick), 11:49.
Ariz.—Arrington 7 run (Rackers kick), 13:06.
St.L.—Curtis 26 pass from J. Martin (Harris pass from J. Martin), 14:25.
Attendance—65,750.

	Arizona	St. Louis
First downs	27	19
Rushes-yards	26-94	12-6
Passing	278	351
Punt returns	2-17	0-0
Kickoff returns	5-199	6-159
Interception returns	0-0	0-0
Comp.-att.-int.	27-39-0	33-43-0
Sacked-yards lost	1-7	5-34
Punts	2-31	3-45
Fumbles-lost	2-1	2-2
Penalties-yards	10-111	9-54
Time of possession	31:45	28:15

INDIVIDUAL STATISTICS

RUSHING—Arizona, Arrington 11-45, Shipp 8-30, O. Ayanbadejo 3-6, Warner 2-1, Fitzgerald 1-9, J. Jackson 1-3. St. Louis, S. Jackson 12-6.

PASSING—Arizona, Warner 27-39-0-285. St. Louis, Bulger 19-24-0-224, J. Martin 14-19-0-161.

RECEIVING—Arizona, Fitzgerald 9-104, Boldin 8-105, Bergen 4-35, Arrington 2-23, McCoy 2-10, Edwards 1-7, Shipp 1-1. St. Louis, Holt 11-129, Curtis 9-98, Bruce 4-83, McDonald 3-37, S. Jackson 3-16, Looker 1-10, Hedgecock 1-9, M. Faulk 1-3.

MISSED FIELD GOAL ATTEMPTS—None.

INTERCEPTIONS—None.

KICKOFF RETURNS—Arizona, Swinton 5-199. St. Louis, Allen 6-159.

PUNT RETURNS—Arizona, Swinton 2-17.

SACKS—Arizona, Wilson 3, Blackstock 1, Okeafor 1. St. Louis, Green 1.

JAGUARS 31, TITANS 28
Sunday, November 20

Jacksonville	0	7	14	10—31
Tennessee	0	14	7	7—28

Second Quarter
Ten.—Brown 15 pass from McNair (Bironas kick), 7:52.
Jac.—Brady 1 pass from Leftwich (Scobee kick), 13:50.
Ten.—Brown 1 run (Bironas kick), 14:45.

Third Quarter
Jac.—Leftwich 2 run (Scobee kick), 6:03.
Ten.—Odom 27 fumble return (Bironas kick), 7:52.
Jac.—Wilford 18 pass from Leftwich (Scobee kick), 10:58.

Fourth Quarter
Jac.—M. Jones 7 pass from Leftwich (Scobee kick), 5:39.
Jac.—FG, Scobee 31, 13:08.
Ten.—R. Williams 8 pass from McNair (Bironas kick), 14:50.
Attendance—69,149.

	Jacksonville	Tennessee
First downs	22	16
Rushes-yards	30-49	21-63
Passing	246	191
Punt returns	2-23	3-30
Kickoff returns	3-69	6-196
Interception returns	1-0	0-0
Comp.-att.-int.	22-38-0	20-30-1
Sacked-yards lost	2-12	3-17
Punts	6-50	8-47
Fumbles-lost	1-1	0-0
Penalties-yards	3-15	11-73
Time of possession	31:54	28:06

INDIVIDUAL STATISTICS

RUSHING—Jacksonville, G. Jones 16-33, Leftwich 6-9, F. Taylor 6-(minus 8), Garrard 1-12, Pearman 1-3. Tennessee, Brown 20-61, McNair 1-2.

PASSING—Jacksonville, Leftwich 22-38-0-258. Tennessee, McNair 20-30-1-208.

RECEIVING—Jacksonville, J. Smith 5-89, Wilford 5-47, M. Jones 3-46, Brady 3-43, Pearman 2-18, G. Jones 2-7, R. Williams 1-9, Manuwai 1-(minus 1). Tennessee, Bennett 6-55, Kinney 5-37, Brown 4-58, Roby 2-24, B. Jones 1-21, R. Williams 1-8, Fleming 1-5.

MISSED FIELD GOAL ATTEMPTS—None.

INTERCEPTIONS—Jacksonville, Wright 1-0.

KICKOFF RETURNS—Jacksonville, Wimbush 2-48, Pearman 1-21. Tennessee, P. Jones 6-196.

PUNT RETURNS—Jacksonville, Pearman 2-23. Tennessee, P. Jones 3-30.

SACKS—Jacksonville, D. Smith 1, Meier 1, Spicer 1. Tennessee, Vanden Bosch 1, LaBoy 0.5, Clauss 0.5.

BUCCANEERS 30, FALCONS 27
Sunday, November 20

Tampa Bay	10	3	7	10	30
Atlanta	0	10	7	10	27

First Quarter
T.B.—FG, M. Bryant 31, 4:16.
T.B.—McFarland 0 fumble return (M. Bryant kick), 7:57.
Second Quarter
T.B.—FG, M. Bryant 45, 6:22.
Atl.—FG, T. Peterson 31, 10:29.
Atl.—Duckett 1 run (T. Peterson kick), 14:44.
Third Quarter
Atl.—Crumpler 4 pass from Vick (T. Peterson kick), 5:38.
T.B.—Alstott 1 run (M. Bryant kick), 9:28.
Fourth Quarter
Atl.—FG, T. Peterson 20, 2:03.
Atl.—Jenkins 10 pass from Vick (T. Peterson kick), 7:24.
T.B.—C. Williams 9 run (M. Bryant kick), 13:05.
T.B.—FG, M. Bryant 45, 14:18.
Attendance—70,794.

	Tampa Bay	Atlanta
First downs	15	26
Rushes-yards	27-140	36-150
Passing	118	293
Punt returns	1-2	1-19
Kickoff returns	4-66	6-112
Interception returns	0-0	1-5
Comp.-att.-int.	11-19-1	21-38-0
Sacked-yards lost	0-0	3-13
Punts	3-50	2-39
Fumbles-lost	0-0	2-2
Penalties-yards	8-55	11-87
Time of possession	23:58	36:02

INDIVIDUAL STATISTICS
RUSHING—Tampa Bay, C. Williams 19-116, Alstott 4-8, Simms 3-10, Pittman 1-6. Atlanta, Dunn 18-82, Duckett 14-51, Vick 4-17.

PASSING—Tampa Bay, Simms 11-19-1-118. Atlanta, Vick 21-38-0-306.

RECEIVING—Tampa Bay, Clayton 3-48, Smith 3-43, C. Williams 3-13, Becht 1-12, Alstott 1-2. Atlanta, Jenkins 5-69, Crumpler 5-49, R. White 4-108, Finneran 3-40, Dunn 2-20, Duckett 1-19, McCrary 1-1.

MISSED FIELD GOAL ATTEMPTS—Atlanta, Koenen 55.

INTERCEPTIONS—Atlanta, Brooking 1-5.

KICKOFF RETURNS—Tampa Bay, Shepherd 3-47, Graham 1-19. Atlanta, Rossum 4-76, Duckett 2-36.

PUNT RETURNS—Tampa Bay, Jones 1-2. Atlanta, Rossum 1-19.

SACKS—Tampa Bay, Brooks 1, McFarland 1, Rice 1.

RAIDERS 16, REDSKINS 13
Sunday, November 20

Oakland	3	0	7	6	16
Washington	7	6	0	0	13

First Quarter
Was.—Marshall 17 interception return (Hall kick), 4:26.
Oak.—FG, Janikowski 30, 14:29.
Second Quarter
Was.—FG, Hall 24, 7:03.
Was.—FG, Hall 45, 14:44.
Third Quarter
Oak.—Porter 49 pass from Collins (Janikowski kick), 1:58.

Fourth Quarter
Oak.—FG, Janikowski 25, 7:04.
Oak.—FG, Janikowski 19, 13:52.
Attendance—90,129.

	Oakland	Washington
First downs	16	13
Rushes-yards	29-50	27-108
Passing	286	138
Punt returns	2-13	1-3
Kickoff returns	4-67	4-88
Interception returns	0-0	1-17
Comp.-att.-int.	19-36-1	14-32-0
Sacked-yards lost	1-3	2-17
Punts	5-42	6-36
Fumbles-lost	1-0	3-3
Penalties-yards	10-101	6-50
Time of possession	31:35	28:25

INDIVIDUAL STATISTICS
RUSHING—Oakland, Jordan 27-52, Collins 2-(minus 2). Washington, Portis 22-92, Cartwright 3-6, Brunell 2-10.

PASSING—Oakland, Collins 19-36-1-289. Washington, Brunell 14-32-0-155.

RECEIVING—Oakland, Porter 6-142, Jordan 5-37, Moss 3-40, Crockett 2-18, C. Anderson 2-15, Gabriel 1-37. Washington, Cooley 5-74, Moss 4-53, Jacobs 3-17, Cartwright 1-17, Portis 1-(minus 6).

MISSED FIELD GOAL ATTEMPTS—Oakland, Janikowski 45.

INTERCEPTIONS—Washington, Marshall 1-17.

KICKOFF RETURNS—Oakland, Carr 4-67. Washington, Parson 3-71, Sellers 1-17.

PUNT RETURNS—Oakland, Carr 2-13. Washington, Moss 1-3.

SACKS—Oakland, Burgess 2. Washington, C. Clemons 1.

RAVENS 16, STEELERS 13
Sunday, November 20

Pittsburgh	0	6	0	7	0—13
Baltimore	0	13	0	0	3—16

Second Quarter
Bal.—FG, Stover 47, :43.
Pit.—FG, Reed 44, 5:07.
Bal.—Hymes 3 pass from Boller (Stover kick), 8:51.
Pit.—FG, Reed 37, 10:31.
Bal.—FG, Stover 25, 14:46.
Fourth Quarter
Pit.—Parker 11 pass from Maddox (Reed kick), 9:45.
Overtime
Bal.—FG, Stover 44, 10:51.
Attendance—70,601.

	Pittsburgh	Baltimore
First downs	17	18
Rushes-yards	25-70	38-104
Passing	212	137
Punt returns	4-12	5-54
Kickoff returns	5-71	4-130
Interception returns	1-26	1-0
Comp.-att.-int.	21-38-1	21-36-1
Sacked-yards lost	6-34	5-26
Punts	8-42	8-44
Fumbles-lost	1-1	1-1
Penalties-yards	10-62	11-70
Time of possession	34:00	36:51

INDIVIDUAL STATISTICS
RUSHING—Pittsburgh, Parker 18-59, Maddox 4-11, Bettis 2-0, Haynes 1-0. Baltimore, C. Taylor 19-59, J. Lewis 13-28, Boller 6-17.

PASSING—Pittsburgh, Maddox 19-36-1-230, Randle El 2-2-0-16. Baltimore, Boller 21-36-1-163.

RECEIVING—Pittsburgh, Ward 6-81, Miller 5-37, Randle El 4-50, Parker 2-22, Kreider 2-14, Wilson 1-25, Haynes 1-17. Baltimore, Clayton 4-43, Mason 4-42, Heap 4-29, C. Taylor 4-26, J. Green 3-8, Hymes 2-15.

MISSED FIELD GOAL ATTEMPTS—None.

INTERCEPTIONS—Pittsburgh, Townsend 1-26. Baltimore, Suggs 1-0.

KICKOFF RETURNS—Pittsburgh, Colclough 4-55, Morgan 1-16. Baltimore, C. Taylor 3-101, Sams 1-29.

PUNT RETURNS—Pittsburgh, Randle El 4-12. Baltimore, Sams 5-54.

SACKS—Pittsburgh, A. Smith 1, Foote 1, von Oelhoffen 1, Haggans 1, T. Carter 1. Baltimore, Scott 2, Weaver 2, Polley 1, J. Johnson 1.

BRONCOS 27, JETS 0
Sunday, November 20

N.Y. Jets	0	0	0	0— 0
Denver	7	10	0	10—27

First Quarter
Den.—Mi. Anderson 1 run (Elam kick), 12:26.
Second Quarter
Den.—FG, Elam 26, 9:40.
Den.—Mi. Anderson 1 run (Elam kick), 10:34.
Fourth Quarter
Den.—FG, Elam 47, 1:57.
Den.—Mi. Anderson 3 run (Elam kick), 13:04.
Attendance—76,255.

	N.Y. Jets	Denver
First downs	10	28
Rushes-yards	8-19	48-191
Passing	176	213
Punt returns	1-13	1-4
Kickoff returns	5-116	1-23
Interception returns	0-0	2-1
Comp.-att.-int.	20-32-2	18-26-0
Sacked-yards lost	3-19	2-12
Punts	3-51	2-47
Fumbles-lost	4-3	1-1
Penalties-yards	7-41	3-30
Time of possession	17:32	42:28

INDIVIDUAL STATISTICS

RUSHING—New York, C. Martin 4-7, Bollinger 2-4, McCareins 1-8, Testaverde 1-0. Denver, Mi. Anderson 26-113, Bell 10-34, Plummer 6-20, Sapp 5-21, Adams 1-3.

PASSING—New York, Testaverde 15-25-2-152, Bollinger 4-5-0-26, Kingsbury 1-2-0-17. Denver, Plummer 18-26-0-225.

RECEIVING—New York, Coles 6-62, McCareins 5-73, Ridgeway 2-26, Sowell 2-8, Houston 1-7, Dreessen 1-7, Jolley 1-4, Cotchery 1-4, C. Martin 1-4. Denver, Smith 5-57, Lelie 4-81, Mi. Anderson 3-16, Adams 2-21, Putzier 1-26, S. Alexander 1-9, Devoe 1-8, Bell 1-6.

MISSED FIELD GOAL ATTEMPTS—None.

INTERCEPTIONS—Denver, Lynch 1-1, Bailey 1-0.

KICKOFF RETURNS—New York, Miller 5-116. Denver, R. Alexander 1-23.

PUNT RETURNS—New York, Cotchery 1-13. Denver, Da. Williams 1-4.

SACKS—New York, Rhodes 1, Hobson 1. Denver, Gold 1, Wilson 1, Coleman 1.

CHARGERS 48, BILLS 10
Sunday, November 20

Buffalo	3	7	0	0—10
San Diego	14	21	3	10—48

First Quarter
S.D.—Tomlinson 1 run (Kaeding kick), 5:29.
Buf.—FG, Lindell 53, 8:20.
S.D.—Gates 27 pass from Brees (Kaeding kick), 14:28.
Second Quarter
S.D.—E. Parker 23 pass from Brees (Kaeding kick), 7:38.
S.D.—Neal 2 pass from Brees (Kaeding kick), 11:48.
Buf.—Shelton 3 pass from Losman (Lindell kick), 13:37.
S.D.—McCardell 29 pass from Brees (Kaeding kick), 14:23.
Third Quarter
S.D.—FG, Kaeding 28, 10:59.
Fourth Quarter
S.D.—FG, Kaeding 38, :46.
S.D.—Turner 8 run (Kaeding kick), 10:54.
Attendance—65,602.

	Buffalo	San Diego
First downs	12	28
Rushes-yards	13-65	34-141
Passing	137	337
Punt returns	0-0	2-0
Kickoff returns	9-239	3-51
Interception returns	0-0	1-10
Comp.-att.-int.	20-36-1	28-33-0
Sacked-yards lost	6-31	1-2
Punts	4-49	1-53

	Buffalo	San Diego
Fumbles-lost	3-1	2-0
Penalties-yards	9-65	2-10
Time of possession	22:30	37:30

INDIVIDUAL STATISTICS

RUSHING—Buffalo, McGahee 10-39, Losman 2-30, S. Williams 1-(minus 4). San Diego, Tomlinson 19-67, Turner 8-48, McCardell 2-6, E. Parker 1-14, Pinnock 1-4, Osgood 1-4, Brees 1-(minus 1), Rivers 1-(minus 1).

PASSING—Buffalo, Losman 20-36-1-168. San Diego, Brees 28-33-0-339.

RECEIVING—Buffalo, Moulds 5-38, Evans 4-69, Parrish 2-14, Euhus 2-12, Shelton 2-7, S. Williams 2-2, Aiken 1-15, Reed 1-9, McGahee 1-2. San Diego, McCardell 6-88, Gates 5-77, Neal 5-22, E. Parker 4-69, Caldwell 3-40, Tomlinson 3-22, Osgood 1-15, Sproles 1-6.

MISSED FIELD GOAL ATTEMPTS—None.

INTERCEPTIONS—San Diego, Wilhelm 1-10.

KICKOFF RETURNS—Buffalo, Parrish 6-176, McGee 1-42, Neufeld 1-11, Shelton 1-10. San Diego, Sproles 3-51.

PUNT RETURNS—San Diego, Sproles 2-0.

SACKS—Buffalo, Posey 1. San Diego, Merriman 2, Edwards 1, Castillo 1, Phillips 1, Cooper 1.

SEAHAWKS 27, 49ERS 25
Sunday, November 20

Seattle	3	14	10	0—27
San Francisco	3	6	3	13—25

First Quarter
Sea.—FG, J. Brown 21, 4:57.
S.F.—FG, Nedney 33, 10:57.
Second Quarter
Sea.—Alexander 8 run (J. Brown kick), 1:51.
S.F.—FG, Nedney 31, 4:53.
Sea.—Hackett 12 pass from Hasselbeck (J. Brown kick), 8:32.
S.F.—FG, Nedney 40, 13:00.
Third Quarter
S.F.—FG, Nedney 22, 8:36.
Sea.—Alexander 1 run (J. Brown kick), 11:09.
Sea.—FG, J. Brown 47, 12:37.
Fourth Quarter
S.F.—Lloyd 22 pass from Dorsey (Nedney kick), :42.
S.F.—Hicks 1 run (pass failed), 14:32.
Attendance—63,590.

	Seattle	San Francisco
First downs	21	17
Rushes-yards	34-145	26-110
Passing	228	226
Punt returns	2-15	2-12
Kickoff returns	5-116	6-125
Interception returns	0-0	0-0
Comp.-att.-int.	19-31-0	18-29-0
Sacked-yards lost	1-5	4-23
Punts	5-43	4-44
Fumbles-lost	0-0	2-1
Penalties-yards	5-75	6-34
Time of possession	28:20	31:40

INDIVIDUAL STATISTICS

RUSHING—Seattle, Alexander 24-115, Hasselbeck 6-7, Morris 2-17, Warrick 1-5, Strong 1-1. San Francisco, Barlow 12-21, Hicks 11-83, Dorsey 3-6.

PASSING—Seattle, Hasselbeck 19-31-0-233. San Francisco, Dorsey 18-29-0-249.

RECEIVING—Seattle, Engram 6-93, Hackett 6-67, Jurevicius 4-40, Stevens 1-27, Alexander 1-7, Strong 1-(minus 1). San Francisco, Lloyd 7-119, Jackson 2-23, Morton 2-22, Barlow 2-17, McAddley 1-29, T. Jones 1-19, Battle 1-11, Bajema 1-5, Hicks 1-4.

MISSED FIELD GOAL ATTEMPTS—Seattle, J. Brown 51.

INTERCEPTIONS—None.

KICKOFF RETURNS—Seattle, Scobey 5-116. San Francisco, Marshall 6-125.

PUNT RETURNS—Seattle, J. Williams 2-15. San Francisco, Marshall 2-12.

SACKS—Seattle, R. Bernard 2, Hill 1, B. Fisher 1. San Francisco, Carter 1.

COLTS 45, BENGALS 37
Sunday, November 20

Indianapolis	14	21	7	3—45
Cincinnati	10	17	7	3—37

First Quarter

Ind.—Rhodes 4 run (Vanderjagt kick), 6:04.
Cin.—FG, Graham 43, 10:13.
Ind.—Wayne 66 pass from Manning (Vanderjagt kick), 10:30.
Cin.—C. Johnson 68 pass from Palmer (Graham kick), 11:37.

Second Quarter

Ind.—Fletcher 9 pass from Manning (Vanderjagt kick), :48.
Cin.—Ru. Johnson 1 run (Graham kick), 5:47.
Ind.—James 1 run (Vanderjagt kick), 7:49.
Ind.—Clark 21 pass from Manning (Vanderjagt kick), 11:19.
Cin.—FG, Graham 41, 13:31.
Cin.—Ru. Johnson 1 run (Graham kick), 14:48.

Third Quarter

Cin.—Henry 15 pass from Palmer (Graham kick), 2:08.
Ind.—James 2 run (Vanderjagt kick), 10:31.

Fourth Quarter

Ind.—FG, Vanderjagt 19, 8:44.
Cin.—FG, Graham 44, 13:37.
Attendance—65,995.

	Indianapolis	Cincinnati
First downs	28	23
Rushes-yards	30-92	26-164
Passing	359	328
Punt returns	0-0	1-0
Kickoff returns	7-107	8-181
Interception returns	1-16	1-35
Comp.-att.-int.	24-40-1	25-38-1
Sacked-yards lost	1-6	1-7
Punts	2-39	1-18
Fumbles-lost	0-0	0-0
Penalties-yards	4-30	9-85
Time of possession	32:02	27:58

INDIVIDUAL STATISTICS

RUSHING—Indianapolis, James 24-89, Manning 4-(minus 3), Rhodes 2-6. Cincinnati, Ru. Johnson 16-76, C. Perry 8-82, Houshmandzadeh 1-5, Palmer 1-1.

PASSING—Indianapolis, Manning 24-40-1-365. Cincinnati, Palmer 25-38-1-335.

RECEIVING—Indianapolis, Clark 6-125, Wayne 5-117, Harrison 5-42, James 3-18, Stokley 2-40, Fletcher 2-16, Mungro 1-7. Cincinnati, C. Johnson 8-189, Houshmandzadeh 5-47, C. Perry 4-41, Henry 3-31, Ru. Johnson 2-9, Schobel 1-9, R. Kelly 1-8, J. Johnson 1-1.

MISSED FIELD GOAL ATTEMPTS—None.

INTERCEPTIONS—Indianapolis, Jackson 1-16. Cincinnati, Ratliff 1-35.

KICKOFF RETURNS—Indianapolis, Rhodes 5-83, Mungro 1-17, Utecht 1-7. Cincinnati, T. Perry 8-181.

PUNT RETURNS—Cincinnati, Ratliff 1-0.

SACKS—Indianapolis, Mathis 1. Cincinnati, J. Smith 0.5, Pollack 0.5.

CHIEFS 45, TEXANS 17

Sunday, November 20

Kansas City	10	21	0	14—45
Houston	7	0	10	0—17

First Quarter

K.C.—FG, Tynes 35, 5:28.
K.C.—L. Johnson 23 run (Tynes kick), 10:40.
Hou.—Mathis 99 kickoff return (K. Brown kick), 10:55.

Second Quarter

K.C.—Kennison 26 pass from Green (Tynes kick), 4:46.
K.C.—L. Johnson 1 run (Tynes kick), 8:37.
K.C.—Warfield 57 interception return (Tynes kick), 14:57.

Third Quarter

Hou.—D. Davis 3 run (K. Brown kick), 6:06.
Hou.—FG, K. Brown 22, 14:18.

Fourth Quarter

K.C.—Kennison 7 pass from Green (Tynes kick), 6:22.
K.C.—Parker 6 pass from Green (Tynes kick), 10:25.
Attendance—70,481.

	Kansas City	Houston
First downs	28	14
Rushes-yards	42-226	19-78
Passing	220	181
Punt returns	3-5	1-37
Kickoff returns	4-94	8-278
Interception returns	1-57	1-29
Comp.-att.-int.	19-29-1	19-36-1

	Kansas City	Houston
Sacked-yards lost	0-0	1-1
Punts	4-40	4-40
Fumbles-lost	1-0	4-2
Penalties-yards	5-30	6-43
Time of possession	36:58	23:02

INDIVIDUAL STATISTICS

RUSHING—Kansas City, L. Johnson 36-211, De. Brown 2-8, Collins 2-(minus 2), Green 1-11, Kennison 1-(minus 2). Houston, D. Davis 13-57, Carr 3-18, An. Johnson 1-5, Stanley 1-0, Wells 1-(minus 2).

PASSING—Kansas City, Green 19-29-1-220. Houston, Carr 19-36-1-182.

RECEIVING—Kansas City, Gonzalez 9-98, Kennison 4-57, Parker 2-23, Wilson 1-16, D. Hall 1-11, De. Brown 1-9, L. Johnson 1-6. Houston, An. Johnson 6-50, Gaffney 5-35, D. Davis 3-53, Bradford 3-20, Armstrong 1-14, Rivers 1-10.

MISSED FIELD GOAL ATTEMPTS—None.

INTERCEPTIONS—Kansas City, Warfield 1-57. Houston, L. Sanders 1-29.

KICKOFF RETURNS—Kansas City, D. Hall 4-94. Houston, Mathis 7-266, Wells 1-12.

PUNT RETURNS—Kansas City, D. Hall 3-5. Houston, Buchanon 1-37.

SACKS—Kansas City, C. Hall 1.

VIKINGS 20, PACKERS 17

Monday, November 21

Minnesota	0	7	7	6—20
Green Bay	7	7	0	3—17

First Quarter

G.B.—Driver 15 pass from Favre (Longwell kick), 12:44.

Second Quarter

Min.—Edwards 51 interception return (Edinger kick), 13:56.
G.B.—Driver 53 pass from Favre (Longwell kick), 14:34.

Third Quarter

Min.—Fason 1 run (Edinger kick), 14:14.

Fourth Quarter

Min.—FG, Edinger 24, 4:47.
G.B.—FG, Longwell 46, 11:57.
Min.—FG, Edinger 27, 15:00.
Attendance—70,610.

	Minnesota	Green Bay
First downs	22	13
Rushes-yards	37-160	14-21
Passing	171	215
Punt returns	5-40	4-21
Kickoff returns	4-72	4-72
Interception returns	2-53	1-0
Comp.-att.-int.	18-30-1	20-33-2
Sacked-yards lost	5-25	2-12
Punts	5-39	7-36
Fumbles-lost	2-1	1-0
Penalties-yards	6-77	5-31
Time of possession	37:33	22:27

INDIVIDUAL STATISTICS

RUSHING—Minnesota, Moore 22-122, M. Bennett 5-10, Fason 5-7, B. Johnson 4-13, Williamson 1-8. Green Bay, Gado 10-7, Fisher 4-14.

PASSING—Minnesota, B. Johnson 18-30-1-196. Green Bay, Favre 20-33-2-227.

RECEIVING—Minnesota, Wiggins 7-67, K. Robinson 3-51, T. Taylor 2-33, Moore 2-16, M. Bennett 2-13, Kleinsasser 1-11, Williamson 1-5. Green Bay, Driver 5-84, D. Lee 4-37, Fisher 4-25, Thurman 2-15, Gado 1-30, Chatman 1-14, Franks 1-9, Henderson 1-8, Ferguson 1-5.

MISSED FIELD GOAL ATTEMPTS—Minnesota, Edinger 49.

INTERCEPTIONS—Minnesota, Edwards 1-51, B. Williams 1-2. Green Bay, Collins 1-0.

KICKOFF RETURNS—Minnesota, K. Robinson 3-63, Owens 1-9. Green Bay, R. Lee 2-38, Thurman 2-34.

PUNT RETURNS—Minnesota, Moore 5-40. Green Bay, Chatman 4-21.

SACKS—Minnesota, James 1, Johnstone 1. Green Bay, Kampman 3, Cole 1, Jenkins 0.5, Gbaja-Biamila 0.5.

WEEK 12

STANDINGS

AMERICAN FOOTBALL CONFERENCE

EAST DIVISION

	W	L	T	Pct.	PF	PA
New England	6	5	0	.545	243	279
Buffalo	4	7	0	.364	161	223
Miami	4	7	0	.364	195	217
N.Y. Jets	2	9	0	.182	140	248

NORTH DIVISION

	W	L	T	Pct.	PF	PA
Cincinnati	8	3	0	.727	289	208
Pittsburgh	7	4	0	.636	243	187
Cleveland	4	7	0	.364	169	194
Baltimore	3	8	0	.273	145	226

SOUTH DIVISION

	W	L	T	Pct.	PF	PA
Indianapolis	11	0	0	1.000	331	159
Jacksonville	8	3	0	.727	235	187
Tennessee	3	8	0	.273	236	284
Houston	1	10	0	.091	168	325

WEST DIVISION

	W	L	T	Pct.	PF	PA
Denver	9	2	0	.818	283	190
Kansas City	7	4	0	.636	270	230
San Diego	7	4	0	.636	323	219
Oakland	4	7	0	.364	239	262

NATIONAL FOOTBALL CONFERENCE

EAST DIVISION

	W	L	T	Pct.	PF	PA
Dallas	7	4	0	.636	243	188
N.Y. Giants	7	4	0	.636	302	208
Philadelphia	5	6	0	.455	229	246
Washington	5	6	0	.455	217	224

NORTH DIVISION

	W	L	T	Pct.	PF	PA
Chicago	8	3	0	.727	182	120
Minnesota	6	5	0	.545	198	257
Detroit	4	7	0	.364	174	220
Green Bay	2	9	0	.182	232	223

SOUTH DIVISION

	W	L	T	Pct.	PF	PA
Carolina	8	3	0	.727	266	188
Atlanta	7	4	0	.636	271	213
Tampa Bay	7	4	0	.636	216	196
New Orleans	3	8	0	.273	180	285

WEST DIVISION

	W	L	T	Pct.	PF	PA
Seattle	9	2	0	.818	296	208
St. Louis	5	6	0	.455	285	327
Arizona	3	8	0	.273	222	292
San Francisco	2	9	0	.182	173	323

TOP PERFORMANCES

100-YARD RUSHING GAMES

Player, team & opponent	Att.	Yds.	TD
LaDainian Tomlinson, S.D. at Was.*	25	184	3
Tiki Barber, NYG at Sea.*	26	151	0
Edgerrin James, Ind. vs. Pit.	29	124	0
Brian Westbrook, Phi. vs. G.B.	20	120	1
Larry Johnson, K.C. vs. N.E.	31	119	1
Warrick Dunn, Atl. at Det.	17	116	0
Rudi Johnson, Cin. vs. Bal.	27	114	2
Jamal Lewis, Bal. at Cin.	23	113	1
Samkon Gado, G.B. at Phi.	26	111	1
Shaun Alexander, Sea. vs. NYG*	31	110	1
Steven Jackson, St.L. at Hou.*	25	110	1

300-YARD PASSING GAMES

Player, team & opponent	Att.	Cmp.	Yds.	TD	Int.
Eli Manning, NYG at Sea.*	53	29	344	2	1
Steve McNair, Ten. vs. S.F.	41	23	343	3	1
Trent Green, K.C. vs. N.E.	26	19	323	1	0
Kurt Warner, Ariz. vs. Jac.	46	29	315	2	1
Ryan Fitzpatrick, St.L. at Hou.*	30	19	310	3	1
Carson Palmer, Cin. vs. Bal.	30	22	302	3	1

100-YARD RECEIVING GAMES

Player, team & opponent	Rec.	Yds.	TD
Andre Johnson, Hou. vs. St.L.*	12	159	1
T.J. Houshmandzadeh, Cin. vs. Bal.	9	147	1
Joey Galloway, T.B. vs. Chi.	7	138	0
Joe Jurevicius, Sea. vs. NYG*	8	137	2
Torry Holt, St.L. at Hou.*	10	130	1
Marvin Harrison, Ind. vs. Pit.	4	128	1
Jeremy Shockey, NYG at Sea.*	10	127	1
Anquan Boldin, Ariz. vs. Jac.	10	115	0
Plaxico Burress, NYG at Sea.*	6	109	1
Chris Brown, Ten. vs. S.F.	3	105	1
Alge Crumpler, Atl. at Det.	7	104	2
Chris Chambers, Mia. at Oak.	6	101	0

*Overtime game.

RESULTS

THURSDAY, NOVEMBER 24
Atlanta 27, DETROIT 7
Denver 24, DALLAS 21 (OT)

SUNDAY, NOVEMBER 27
Carolina 13, BUFFALO 9
KANSAS CITY 26, New England 16
MINNESOTA 24, Cleveland 12
Chicago 13, TAMPA BAY 10
CINCINNATI 42, Baltimore 29
TENNESSEE 33, San Francisco 22
San Diego 23, WASHINGTON 17 (OT)
St. Louis 33, HOUSTON 27 (OT)
Jacksonville 24, ARIZONA 17
PHILADELPHIA 19, Green Bay 14
Miami 33, OAKLAND 21
SEATTLE 24, N.Y. Giants 21 (OT)
New Orleans 21, N.Y. JETS 19

MONDAY, NOVEMBER 28
INDIANAPOLIS 26, Pittsburgh 7

FALCONS 27, LIONS 7

Thursday, November 24

Atlanta	10	7	10	0—27
Detroit	0	0	0	7— 7

First Quarter
Atl.—FG, T. Peterson 21, 4:47.
Atl.—Duckett 1 run (T. Peterson kick), 14:08.
Second Quarter
Atl.—Crumpler 6 pass from Vick (T. Peterson kick), 4:16.
Third Quarter
Atl.—Crumpler 32 pass from Vick (T. Peterson kick), 3:14.
Atl.—FG, T. Peterson 23, 9:49.
Fourth Quarter
Det.—R. Williams 31 pass from Garcia (Hanson kick), 5:42.
Attendance—62,390.

	Atlanta	Detroit
First downs	22	20
Rushes-yards	45-256	13-75
Passing	146	229
Punt returns	2-54	2-13
Kickoff returns	0-0	5-101
Interception returns	2-53	1-20
Comp.-att.-int.	12-22-1	25-48-2
Sacked-yards lost	0-0	5-29
Punts	4-49	4-48
Fumbles-lost	1-1	3-2
Penalties-yards	11-84	9-50
Time of possession	34:19	25:41

INDIVIDUAL STATISTICS
RUSHING—Atlanta, Duckett 19-72, Dunn 17-116, Vick 6-57, Schaub 2-7, Griffith 1-4. Detroit, Bryson 6-26, Jones 4-32, Pinner 2-12, Garcia 1-5.
PASSING—Atlanta, Vick 12-22-1-146. Detroit, Garcia 14-24-1-154, Harrington 6-13-1-61, Orlovsky 5-11-0-43.
RECEIVING—Atlanta, Crumpler 7-104, R. White 2-25, Griffith 2-17, Dunn 1-0. Detroit, M. Williams 6-84, Vines 6-70, Bryson 5-18, R. Williams 3-55, Pollard 3-24, C. Rogers 1-4, Pinner 1-3.
MISSED FIELD GOAL ATTEMPTS—None.
INTERCEPTIONS—Atlanta, D. Hall 1-34, Webster 1-19. Detroit, Wayne 1-20.
KICKOFF RETURNS—Detroit, Drummond 5-101.
PUNT RETURNS—Atlanta, Rossum 2-54. Detroit, Drummond 2-13.
SACKS—Atlanta, Kerney 1.5, R. Coleman 1.5, Lake 1.5, Brooking 0.5.

BRONCOS 24, COWBOYS 21

Thursday, November 24

Denver	7	7	7	0	3—24
Dallas	7	7	0	7	0—21

First Quarter
Den.—Bailey 65 interception return (Elam kick), 6:50.
Dal.—K. Johnson 14 pass from Bledsoe (Cundiff kick), 11:14.
Second Quarter
Den.—Smith 20 pass from Plummer (Elam kick), :43.
Dal.—Bledsoe 1 run (Cundiff kick), 12:07.
Third Quarter
Den.—Dayne 16 run (Elam kick), 9:13.
Fourth Quarter
Dal.—Witten 4 pass from Bledsoe (Cundiff kick), 1:24.
Overtime
Den.—FG, Elam 24, 1:21.
Attendance—63,273.

	Denver	Dallas
First downs	13	23
Rushes-yards	20-144	32-85
Passing	149	229
Punt returns	1-8	4-10
Kickoff returns	5-100	4-95
Interception returns	2-66	1-4
Comp.-att.-int.	15-24-1	29-44-2
Sacked-yards lost	2-13	1-3
Punts	7-44	5-48
Fumbles-lost	1-1	1-0
Penalties-yards	10-67	7-40
Time of possession	24:51	36:30

INDIVIDUAL STATISTICS
RUSHING—Denver, Mi. Anderson 11-31, Dayne 7-98, Plummer 2-15. Dallas, J. Jones 20-55, Barber 9-28, Bledsoe 3-2.
PASSING—Denver, Plummer 15-24-1-162. Dallas, Bledsoe 29-44-2-232.
RECEIVING—Denver, Smith 5-57, Putzier 4-69, Dayne 2-10, Mi. Anderson 2-6, K. Johnson 1-13, Adams 1-7. Dallas, Witten 9-82, K. Johnson 6-59, J. Jones 5-9, T. Glenn 4-56, P. Price 2-15, Polite 1-8, Copper 1-5, Barber 1-(minus 2).
MISSED FIELD GOAL ATTEMPTS—Dallas, Cundiff 34.
INTERCEPTIONS—Denver, Bailey 1-65, N. Ferguson 1-1. Dallas, Newman 1-4.
KICKOFF RETURNS—Denver, R. Alexander 4-73, Da. Williams 1-27. Dallas, Thompson 3-81, Campbell 1-14.
PUNT RETURNS—Denver, Da. Williams 1-8. Dallas, P. Price 2-10, Newman 2-0.
SACKS—Denver, Pryce 1. Dallas, Canty 1, Ellis 1.

PANTHERS 13, BILLS 9

Sunday, November 27

Carolina	0	3	3	7—13
Buffalo	0	6	0	3— 9

Second Quarter
Car.—FG, Kasay 25, :04.
Buf.—FG, Lindell 31, 12:57.
Buf.—FG, Lindell 45, 15:00.
Third Quarter
Car.—FG, Kasay 25, 15:00.
Fourth Quarter
Buf.—FG, Lindell 33, 4:56.
Car.—Gaines 3 pass from Delhomme (Kasay kick), 12:44.
Attendance—71,440.

	Carolina	Buffalo
First downs	19	14
Rushes-yards	33-113	23-55
Passing	182	161
Punt returns	4-45	0-0
Kickoff returns	3-40	4-86
Interception returns	1-0	0-0
Comp.-att.-int.	20-27-0	16-29-1
Sacked-yards lost	1-9	5-36
Punts	2-41	4-48
Fumbles-lost	2-1	1-0
Penalties-yards	4-20	4-31
Time of possession	35:44	24:16

INDIVIDUAL STATISTICS
RUSHING—Carolina, Foster 22-74, S. Davis 7-25, Goings 2-9, Colbert 1-6, Delhomme 1-(minus 1). Buffalo, McGahee 21-53, Losman 2-2.
PASSING—Carolina, Delhomme 20-27-0-191. Buffalo, Losman 16-29-1-197.
RECEIVING—Carolina, Colbert 4-32, Foster 4-24, S. Smith 3-55, Hoover 3-20, Gaines 3-18, Mangum 2-18, Proehl 1-24. Buffalo, Moulds 7-84, Evans 5-45, Parrish 2-30, Reed 1-29, Neufeld 1-9.
MISSED FIELD GOAL ATTEMPTS—Carolina, Kasay 45.
INTERCEPTIONS—Carolina, Gamble 1-0.
KICKOFF RETURNS—Carolina, Smart 3-40. Buffalo, Parrish 3-72, Burns 1-14.
PUNT RETURNS—Carolina, S. Smith 4-45.
SACKS—Carolina, Rucker 1, Minter 1, Peppers 1, Carstens 1, Wallace 1. Buffalo, Schobel 1.

CHIEFS 26, PATRIOTS 16

Sunday, November 27

New England	0	3	7	6—16
Kansas City	7	12	7	0—26

First Quarter
K.C.—L. Johnson 1 run (Tynes kick), 5:57.
Second Quarter
K.C.—FG, Tynes 25, 1:06.
K.C.—FG, Tynes 20, 4:22.
N.E.—FG, Vinatieri 29, 8:08.
K.C.—FG, Tynes 33, 13:09.
K.C.—FG, Tynes 47, 14:58.

Third Quarter

K.C.—D. Hall 52 pass from Green (Tynes kick), 4:32.

N.E.—Pass 1 run (Vinatieri kick), 10:39.

Fourth Quarter

N.E.—Fauria 1 pass from Brady (pass failed), 4:57.

Attendance—78,025.

	New England	Kansas City
First downs	20	24
Rushes-yards	18-74	37-112
Passing	232	308
Punt returns	2-9	2-20
Kickoff returns	7-147	4-100
Interception returns	0-0	4-26
Comp.-att.-int.	22-40-4	19-26-0
Sacked-yards lost	3-16	2-15
Punts	3-48	3-36
Fumbles-lost	1-0	1-1
Penalties-yards	2-22	5-35
Time of possession	25:35	34:25

INDIVIDUAL STATISTICS

RUSHING—New England, Pass 8-26, H. Evans 6-11, Dwight 2-17, Brady 1-15, Cloud 1-5. Kansas City, L. Johnson 31-119, Green 4-(minus 2), Richardson 1-0, Kennison 1-(minus 5).

PASSING—New England, Brady 22-40-4-248. Kansas City, Green 19-26-0-323.

RECEIVING—New England, Dwight 5-76, Branch 5-49, H. Evans 3-25, Watson 3-14, Graham 2-37, T. Brown 1-25, Andre. Davis 1-23, Fauria 1-1, Pass 1-(minus 2). Kansas City, Parker 5-76, L. Johnson 5-53, Gonzalez 4-63, Kennison 3-65, D. Hall 2-66.

MISSED FIELD GOAL ATTEMPTS—None.

INTERCEPTIONS—Kansas City, Wesley 3-26, S. Knight 1-0.

KICKOFF RETURNS—New England, Dwight 6-147, Izzo 1-0. Kansas City, D. Hall 4-100.

PUNT RETURNS—New England, T. Brown 2-9. Kansas City, D. Hall 2-20.

SACKS—New England, Warren 1, Colvin 1. Kansas City, S. Knight 1, Allen 1, Bell 1.

VIKINGS 24, BROWNS 12

Sunday, November 27

Cleveland	0	3	3	6—12
Minnesota	3	7	7	7—24

First Quarter

Min.—FG, Edinger 43, 7:02.

Second Quarter

Min.—M. Robinson 15 pass from B. Johnson (Edinger kick), 10:38.

Cle.—FG, Dawson 32, 14:56.

Third Quarter

Min.—M. Robinson 15 pass from B. Johnson (Edinger kick), 7:36.

Cle.—FG, Dawson 38, 11:33.

Fourth Quarter

Min.—M. Robinson 2 pass from B. Johnson (Edinger kick), 6:13.

Cle.—Northcutt 9 pass from Dilfer (run failed), 13:54.

Attendance—63,814.

	Cleveland	Minnesota
First downs	20	18
Rushes-yards	20-78	31-81
Passing	184	200
Punt returns	4-26	1-2
Kickoff returns	5-155	2-63
Interception returns	1-24	3-24
Comp.-att.-int.	23-36-3	19-28-1
Sacked-yards lost	5-30	2-7
Punts	4-33	6-44
Fumbles-lost	2-2	2-1
Penalties-yards	6-30	7-49
Time of possession	27:44	32:16

INDIVIDUAL STATISTICS

RUSHING—Cleveland, Droughns 19-73, Dilfer 1-5. Minnesota, Moore 21-67, Fason 3-14, B. Johnson 3-(minus 2), M. Bennett 3-(minus 3), T. Taylor 1-5.

PASSING—Cleveland, Dilfer 23-35-2-214, Frye 0-1-1-0. Minnesota, B. Johnson 19-28-1-207.

RECEIVING—Cleveland, Heiden 5-55, Droughns 5-46, F. Jackson 5-38, Edwards 4-42, Northcutt 2-17, Bryant 2-16. Minnesota, T. Taylor 5-70, Wiggins 5-67, K. Robinson 4-29, M. Robinson 3-32, Moore 2-9.

MISSED FIELD GOAL ATTEMPTS—None.

INTERCEPTIONS—Cleveland, Crocker 1-24. Minnesota, Sharper 2-24, Winfield 1-0.

KICKOFF RETURNS—Cleveland, Cribbs 5-155. Minnesota, K. Robinson 2-63.

PUNT RETURNS—Cleveland, Northcutt 4-26. Minnesota, Moore 1-2.

SACKS—Cleveland, Kelley 1, Roye 1. Minnesota, Mosley 2, Newman 1, Scott 1, Johnstone 1.

BEARS 13, BUCCANEERS 10

Sunday, November 27

Chicago	7	3	3	0—13
Tampa Bay	3	0	0	7—10

First Quarter

Chi.—Gilmore 1 pass from Orton (Gould kick), 3:10.

T.B.—FG, M. Bryant 27, 12:48.

Second Quarter

Chi.—FG, Gould 25, 14:43.

Third Quarter

Chi.—FG, Gould 36, 11:13.

Fourth Quarter

T.B.—Alstott 2 run (M. Bryant kick), 8:00.

Attendance—65,506.

	Chicago	Tampa Bay
First downs	15	15
Rushes-yards	33-118	25-107
Passing	121	168
Punt returns	3-21	6-67
Kickoff returns	3-69	4-94
Interception returns	0-0	1-0
Comp.-att.-int.	14-28-1	19-30-0
Sacked-yards lost	2-13	4-34
Punts	8-44	7-42
Fumbles-lost	3-0	1-1
Penalties-yards	4-35	5-52
Time of possession	30:03	29:57

INDIVIDUAL STATISTICS

RUSHING—Chicago, T. Jones 25-72, Peterson 5-27, Orton 3-19. Tampa Bay, C. Williams 20-84, Alstott 3-8, Pittman 1-16, Simms 1-(minus 1).

PASSING—Chicago, Orton 14-28-1-134. Tampa Bay, Simms 19-30-0-202.

RECEIVING—Chicago, Muhammad 4-38, Gage 4-32, T. Jones 3-50, Clark 2-13, Gilmore 1-1. Tampa Bay, Galloway 7-138, Smith 2-14, Alstott 2-14, Becht 2-12, C. Williams 2-7, Cook 1-9, Pittman 1-6, Moore 1-5, Simms 1-(minus 3).

MISSED FIELD GOAL ATTEMPTS—Tampa Bay, M. Bryant 29.

INTERCEPTIONS—Tampa Bay, Kelly 1-0.

KICKOFF RETURNS—Chicago, Davis 3-69. Tampa Bay, Shepherd 4-94.

PUNT RETURNS—Chicago, Davis 2-10, Wade 1-11. Tampa Bay, Jones 6-67.

SACKS—Chicago, Ogunleye 2, A. Brown 2. Tampa Bay, Rice 1, Wyms 1.

BENGALS 42, RAVENS 29

Sunday, November 27

Baltimore	0	0	14	15—29
Cincinnati	3	14	17	8—42

First Quarter

Cin.—FG, Graham 26, 14:10.

Second Quarter

Cin.—Ru. Johnson 6 run (Graham kick), 7:36.

Cin.—C. Johnson 54 pass from Palmer (Graham kick), 11:18.

Third Quarter

Cin.—Houshmandzadeh 30 pass from Palmer (Graham kick), 1:10.

Cin.—Henry 27 pass from Palmer (Graham kick), 3:50.

Cin.—FG, Graham 31, 8:42.

Bal.—Mason 28 pass from Boller (Stover kick), 13:13.

Bal.—Heap 34 pass from Boller (Stover kick), 14:45.

Fourth Quarter

Bal.—J. Lewis 5 run (Stover kick), 3:02.

Cin.—Ru. Johnson 3 run (Schobel pass from Palmer), 8:57.

Bal.—Heap 17 pass from Boller (J. Green run), 13:03.

Attendance—65,680.

	Baltimore	Cincinnati
First downs	23	23
Rushes-yards	33-133	32-135
Passing	189	302
Punt returns	2-18	3-21

	Baltimore	Cincinnati
Kickoff returns	8-145	4-114
Interception returns	1-33	2-15
Comp.-att.-int.	18-32-2	22-30-1
Sacked-yards lost	3-22	0-0
Punts	5-44	3-37
Fumbles-lost	4-1	2-2
Penalties-yards	9-91	5-45
Time of possession	29:47	30:13

INDIVIDUAL STATISTICS

RUSHING—Baltimore, J. Lewis 23-113, J. Green 5-4, Boller 4-10, Clayton 1-6. Cincinnati, Ru. Johnson 27-114, C. Perry 3-0, Palmer 1-14, Houshmandzadeh 1-7.

PASSING—Baltimore, Boller 18-32-2-211. Cincinnati, Palmer 22-30-1-302.

RECEIVING—Baltimore, Heap 6-87, J. Lewis 5-36, Mason 3-58, Clayton 2-14, Wilcox 1-9, J. Green 1-7. Cincinnati, Houshmandzadeh 9-147, C. Johnson 5-88, Henry 3-53, C. Perry 2-2, J. Johnson 1-9, Ru. Johnson 1-5, Walter 1-(minus 2).

MISSED FIELD GOAL ATTEMPTS—Baltimore, Elling 54.

INTERCEPTIONS—Baltimore, Sanders 1-33. Cincinnati, Ohalete 1-15, O'Neal 1-0.

KICKOFF RETURNS—Baltimore, Sams 8-145. Cincinnati, T. Perry 4-114.

PUNT RETURNS—Baltimore, Sams 2-18. Cincinnati, Ratliff 3-21.

SACKS—Cincinnati, J. Smith 1, Team 2.

TITANS 33, 49ERS 22
Sunday, November 27

San Francisco	0	14	0	8	22
Tennessee	3	6	21	3	33

First Quarter
Ten.—FG, Bironas 35, 14:56.

Second Quarter
S.F.—Barlow 1 run (Cortez kick), 5:40.
Ten.—FG, Bironas 41, 10:57.
Ten.—FG, Bironas 21, 13:00.
S.F.—Spencer 61 interception return (Cortez kick), 14:33.

Third Quarter
Ten.—Brown 41 pass from McNair (Bironas kick), 1:42.
Ten.—R. Williams 50 pass from McNair (Bironas kick), 3:01.
Ten.—Kinney 4 pass from McNair (Bironas kick), 10:06.

Fourth Quarter
Ten.—FG, Bironas 22, 11:25.
S.F.—Battle 17 pass from Dorsey (Jackson pass from Dorsey), 13:45.
Attendance—69,149.

	San Francisco	Tennessee
First downs	15	15
Rushes-yards	22-74	27-118
Passing	187	343
Punt returns	3-5	4-42
Kickoff returns	7-125	1-16
Interception returns	1-61	2-30
Comp.-att.-int.	23-43-2	23-41-1
Sacked-yards lost	2-5	0-0
Punts	8-45	5-46
Fumbles-lost	2-2	1-0
Penalties-yards	4-35	10-70
Time of possession	28:16	31:44

INDIVIDUAL STATISTICS

RUSHING—San Francisco, Barlow 14-40, Hicks 6-30, Battle 2-4. Tennessee, Henry 13-86, Brown 10-30, McNair 3-0, Payton 1-2.

PASSING—San Francisco, Dorsey 23-43-2-192. Tennessee, McNair 23-41-1-343.

RECEIVING—San Francisco, Battle 7-75, Barlow 4-17, Lloyd 3-30, Hicks 3-17, T. Jones 3-15, Bajema 1-20, Morton 1-10, Jackson 1-8. Tennessee, Bennett 5-52, Kinney 4-37, Troupe 4-28, Brown 3-105, R. Williams 3-95, Henry 1-14, Payton 1-4, Roby 1-4, B. Jones 1-4.

MISSED FIELD GOAL ATTEMPTS—San Francisco, Cortez 34.

INTERCEPTIONS—San Francisco, Spencer 1-61. Tennessee, Bulluck 1-16, Hill 1-14.

KICKOFF RETURNS—San Francisco, Marshall 6-106, McAddley 1-19. Tennessee, P. Jones 1-16.

PUNT RETURNS—San Francisco, Amey 3-5. Tennessee, P. Jones 4-42.

SACKS—Tennessee, Vanden Bosch 2.

CHARGERS 23, REDSKINS 17
Sunday, November 27

San Diego	0	7	0	10	6—23
Washington	3	7	7	0	0—17

First Quarter
Was.—FG, Hall 38, 9:38.

Second Quarter
S.D.—Tomlinson 1 run (Kaeding kick), 4:29.
Was.—Moss 22 pass from Brunell (Hall kick), 7:37.

Third Quarter
Was.—Cartwright 13 run (Hall kick), 11:46.

Fourth Quarter
S.D.—FG, Kaeding 48, :52.
S.D.—Tomlinson 32 run (Kaeding kick), 11:31.

Overtime
S.D.—Tomlinson 41 run, :34.
Attendance—84,930.

	San Diego	Washington
First downs	24	15
Rushes-yards	28-202	33-91
Passing	195	191
Punt returns	5-32	1-3
Kickoff returns	5-128	4-59
Interception returns	0-0	3-16
Comp.-att.-int.	22-45-3	17-27-0
Sacked-yards lost	3-20	2-3
Punts	6-38	9-38
Fumbles-lost	1-0	2-0
Penalties-yards	6-40	7-60
Time of possession	30:47	29:47

INDIVIDUAL STATISTICS

RUSHING—San Diego, Tomlinson 25-184, E. Parker 1-13, Neal 1-3, Brees 1-2. Washington, Portis 29-87, Brunell 2-(minus 1), Cartwright 1-13, Moss 1-(minus 8).

PASSING—San Diego, Brees 22-44-3-215, Tomlinson 0-1-0-0. Washington, Brunell 17-27-0-194.

RECEIVING—San Diego, E. Parker 7-98, Tomlinson 6-29, McCardell 5-45, Gates 3-39, Neal 1-4. Washington, Moss 6-65, Jacobs 4-44, Cooley 3-28, Portis 1-23, J. Farris 1-18, R. Johnson 1-14, Royal 1-2.

MISSED FIELD GOAL ATTEMPTS—San Diego, Kaeding 42, 46. Washington, Hall 53.

INTERCEPTIONS—Washington, Rogers 1-14, Springs 1-2, W. Harris 1-0.

KICKOFF RETURNS—San Diego, Sproles 5-128. Washington, A. Brown 4-59.

PUNT RETURNS—San Diego, E. Parker 5-32. Washington, A. Brown 1-3.

SACKS—San Diego, Foley 1, Phillips 1. Washington, Washington 1.5, Daniels 1, Clark 0.5.

RAMS 33, TEXANS 27
Sunday, November 27

St. Louis	0	3	7	17	6—33
Houston	7	17	0	3	0—27

First Quarter
Hou.—An. Johnson 5 pass from Carr (K. Brown kick), 8:25.

Second Quarter
Hou.—D. Davis 30 pass from Carr (K. Brown kick), 3:27.
Hou.—FG, K. Brown 39, 10:35.
St.L.—FG, J. Wilkins 37, 14:02.
Hou.—Bradford 10 pass from Carr (K. Brown kick), 14:40.

Third Quarter
St.L.—Holt 19 pass from Fitzpatrick (J. Wilkins kick), 4:27.

Fourth Quarter
St.L.—S. Jackson 1 run (J. Wilkins kick), 8:23.
Hou.—FG, K. Brown 35, 12:11.
St.L.—Bruce 43 pass from Fitzpatrick (J. Wilkins kick), 14:34.
St.L.—FG, J. Wilkins 47, 14:56.

Overtime
St.L.—Curtis 56 pass from Fitzpatrick, 6:14.
Attendance—70,010.

	St. Louis	Houston
First downs	22	26
Rushes-yards	29-138	31-124
Passing	291	288

	St. Louis	Houston
Punt returns	0-0	3-30
Kickoff returns	4-68	5-146
Interception returns	1-15	1-6
Comp.-att.-int.	21-33-1	25-35-1
Sacked-yards lost	7-33	3-5
Punts	4-42	2-39
Fumbles-lost	2-0	1-1
Penalties-yards	9-65	4-54
Time of possession	31:20	34:54

INDIVIDUAL STATISTICS

RUSHING—St. Louis, S. Jackson 25-110, Fitzpatrick 3-23, M. Faulk 1-5. Houston, D. Davis 25-78, Carr 4-39, Wells 1-10, Gaffney 1-(minus 3).

PASSING—St. Louis, Fitzpatrick 19-30-1-310, J. Martin 2-3-0-14. Houston, Carr 25-34-1-293, D. Davis 0-1-0-0.

RECEIVING—St. Louis, Holt 10-130, Bruce 4-94, McDonald 2-18, S. Jackson 2-2, Curtis 1-56, Hedgecock 1-15, M. Faulk 1-9. Houston, An. Johnson 12-159, Gaffney 5-38, D. Davis 3-42, Bradford 2-19, Wells 1-19, Rivers 1-13, Bruener 1-3.

MISSED FIELD GOAL ATTEMPTS—Houston, K. Brown 46.

INTERCEPTIONS—St. Louis, Tinoisamoa 1-15. Houston, Coleman 1-6.

KICKOFF RETURNS—St. Louis, Fair 4-68. Houston, Mathis 4-106, Wells 1-40.

PUNT RETURNS—Houston, Mathis 2-27, D. Davis 1-3.

SACKS—St. Louis, Pickett 1, Coakley 1, Atogwe 1. Houston, Polk 2.5, Greenwood 2, Orr 1, McKenzie 1, Smith 0.5.

JAGUARS 24, CARDINALS 17
Sunday, November 27

Jacksonville	7	3	7	7—24
Arizona	0	0	3	14—17

First Quarter
Jac.—Garrard 16 run (Scobee kick), 12:15.
Second Quarter
Jac.—FG, Scobee 30, 12:01.
Third Quarter
Ariz.—FG, Rackers 42, 11:00.
Jac.—Wimbush 91 kickoff return (Scobee kick), 11:17.
Fourth Quarter
Ariz.—Edwards 1 pass from Warner (Rackers kick), 1:26.
Jac.—G. Jones 25 run (Scobee kick), 10:40.
Ariz.—Fitzgerald 5 pass from Warner (Rackers kick), 12:04.
Attendance—39,198.

	Jacksonville	Arizona
First downs	19	23
Rushes-yards	33-162	16-67
Passing	133	301
Punt returns	2-9	0-0
Kickoff returns	3-138	3-57
Interception returns	1-0	0-0
Comp.-att.-int.	14-28-0	29-46-1
Sacked-yards lost	0-0	3-14
Punts	4-39	4-40
Fumbles-lost	0-0	1-1
Penalties-yards	11-81	11-105
Time of possession	31:41	28:19

INDIVIDUAL STATISTICS

RUSHING—Jacksonville, G. Jones 23-78, Garrard 6-61, Toefield 2-9, M. Jones 1-8, Pearman 1-6. Arizona, Arrington 6-39, Shipp 6-23, Warner 1-5, Boldin 1-4, J. Jackson 1-2, Fitzgerald 1-(minus 6).

PASSING—Jacksonville, Garrard 12-26-0-115, Leftwich 2-2-0-18. Arizona, Warner 29-46-1-315.

RECEIVING—Jacksonville, J. Smith 7-70, Wilford 2-28, Pearman 2-21, M. Jones 1-7, Wimbush 1-6, Brady 1-1. Arizona, Boldin 10-115, B. Johnson 5-77, Fitzgerald 4-41, Shipp 3-31, McCoy 2-40, Edwards 2-1, Baxter 1-4, Arrington 1-4, Bergen 1-2.

MISSED FIELD GOAL ATTEMPTS—Jacksonville, Scobee 38. Arizona, Rackers 43.

INTERCEPTIONS—Jacksonville, Grant 1-0.

KICKOFF RETURNS—Jacksonville, Wimbush 3-138. Arizona, Swinton 3-57.

PUNT RETURNS—Jacksonville, Pearman 2-9.

SACKS—Jacksonville, Ayodele 1.5, Meier 1, Cousin 0.5.

EAGLES 19, PACKERS 14
Sunday, November 27

Green Bay	7	7	0	0—14
Philadelphia	10	0	3	6—19

First Quarter
Phi.—FG, Akers 44, 7:44.
Phi.—Westbrook 27 run (Akers kick), 8:06.
G.B.—Gado 33 run (Longwell kick), 9:15.
Second Quarter
G.B.—D. Martin 13 pass from Favre (Longwell kick), 14:25.
Third Quarter
Phi.—FG, Akers 38, 8:20.
Fourth Quarter
Phi.—FG, Akers 37, 10:29.
Phi.—FG, Akers 33, 13:11.
Attendance—67,665.

	Green Bay	Philadelphia
First downs	18	15
Rushes-yards	30-128	35-176
Passing	164	88
Punt returns	5-39	4-35
Kickoff returns	6-98	3-64
Interception returns	0-0	2-0
Comp.-att.-int.	15-33-2	12-28-0
Sacked-yards lost	1-7	1-3
Punts	7-36	7-39
Fumbles-lost	4-3	2-1
Penalties-yards	7-40	7-50
Time of possession	28:55	31:05

INDIVIDUAL STATISTICS

RUSHING—Green Bay, Gado 26-111, Fisher 2-9, Driver 1-4, Favre 1-4. Philadelphia, Westbrook 20-120, Moats 6-24, McMahon 6-22, Gordon 3-10.

PASSING—Green Bay, Favre 15-33-2-171. Philadelphia, McMahon 12-28-0-91.

RECEIVING—Green Bay, D. Martin 4-41, Driver 3-50, Fisher 3-33, D. Lee 2-21, Ferguson 2-15, Gado 1-11. Philadelphia, Westbrook 4-11, Smith 2-28, C. Lewis 2-22, McMullen 2-10, Parry 1-11, G. Lewis 1-9.

MISSED FIELD GOAL ATTEMPTS—None.

INTERCEPTIONS—Philadelphia, M. Lewis 1-0, Hood 1-0.

KICKOFF RETURNS—Green Bay, Thurman 4-61, R. Lee 2-37. Philadelphia, Gordon 3-64.

PUNT RETURNS—Green Bay, Chatman 5-39. Philadelphia, Westbrook 2-20, Mahe 2-15.

SACKS—Green Bay, Poppinga 1. Philadelphia, Patterson 1.

DOLPHINS 33, RAIDERS 21
Sunday, November 27

Miami	7	7	9	10—33
Oakland	0	7	7	7—21

First Quarter
Mia.—Gilmore 44 pass from Frerotte (Mare kick), 3:02.
Second Quarter
Oak.—Jordan 1 run (Janikowski kick), 5:26.
Mia.—Brown 1 run (Mare kick), 14:28.
Third Quarter
Mia.—Safety, 1:27.
Oak.—Jordan 8 run (Janikowski kick), 9:11.
Mia.—McMichael 25 pass from Frerotte (Mare kick), 13:12.
Fourth Quarter
Oak.—Collins 18 run (Janikowski kick), :59.
Mia.—R. Williams 34 run (Mare kick), 11:10.
Mia.—FG, Mare 27, 13:50.
Attendance—49,097.

	Miami	Oakland
First downs	21	24
Rushes-yards	32-145	25-120
Passing	249	185
Punt returns	0-0	2-17
Kickoff returns	5-141	4-135
Interception returns	2-16	1-33
Comp.-att.-int.	18-31-1	21-37-2
Sacked-yards lost	3-12	7-41
Punts	4-51	6-34
Fumbles-lost	2-2	2-1
Penalties-yards	7-70	13-90
Time of possession	30:08	29:52

RUSHING—Miami, R. Williams 16-82, Brown 15-58, Chambers 1-5. Oakland, Jordan 23-97, Collins 2-23.

PASSING—Miami, Frerotte 18-31-1-261. Oakland, Collins 21-37-2-226.

RECEIVING—Miami, Chambers 6-101, McMichael 4-59, Brown 2-23, R. Williams 2-13, Gilmore 1-44, Welker 1-16, Diamond 1-3, Holmes 1-2. Oakland, Jordan 7-47, C. Anderson 5-50, Porter 3-57, Moss 3-28, Gabriel 1-23, Whitted 1-18, Crockett 1-3.

MISSED FIELD GOAL ATTEMPTS—Miami, Mare 38.

INTERCEPTIONS—Miami, Schulters 1-16, Tillman 1-0. Oakland, Schweigert 1-33.

KICKOFF RETURNS—Miami, Welker 5-141. Oakland, Carr 4-135.

PUNT RETURNS—Oakland, Carr 2-17.

SACKS—Miami, Taylor 3, Holliday 2, D. Bowens 2. Oakland, Burgess 2, J. Cooper 0.5, Kelly 0.5.

SEAHAWKS 24, GIANTS 21
Sunday, November 27

N.Y. Giants	0	10	3	8	0—21
Seattle	7	0	7	7	3—24

First Quarter
Sea.—Jurevicius 35 pass from Hasselbeck (J. Brown kick), 14:17.
Second Quarter
NYG—FG, Feely 39, 10:37.
NYG—Shockey 7 pass from Manning (Feely kick), 13:53.
Third Quarter
NYG—FG, Feely 43, 4:40.
Sea.—Jurevicius 16 pass from Hasselbeck (J. Brown kick), 10:24.
Fourth Quarter
Sea.—Alexander 4 run (J. Brown kick), 10:27.
NYG—Toomer 18 pass from Manning (Shockey pass from Manning), 13:01.
Overtime
Sea.—FG, J. Brown 36, 12:15.
Attendance—67,102.

	N.Y. Giants	Seattle
First downs	25	17
Rushes-yards	28-166	34-127
Passing	324	228
Punt returns	6-50	1-0
Kickoff returns	4-101	6-118
Interception returns	1-4	1-40
Comp.-att.-int.	29-53-1	21-37-1
Sacked-yards lost	3-20	3-21
Punts	7-37	9-46
Fumbles-lost	1-0	4-1
Penalties-yards	16-114	8-65
Time of possession	39:21	32:54

RUSHING—New York, Barber 26-151, Manning 2-15. Seattle, Alexander 31-110, Hasselbeck 2-7, Strong 1-10.

PASSING—New York, Manning 29-53-1-344. Seattle, Hasselbeck 21-37-1-249.

RECEIVING—New York, Shockey 10-127, Burress 6-109, Toomer 6-62, Barber 5-27, Finn 2-19. Seattle, Jurevicius 8-137, Engram 6-34, Strong 3-18, Hackett 2-47, Warrick 1-9, Alexander 1-4.

MISSED FIELD GOAL ATTEMPTS—New York, Feely 40, 54, 45.

INTERCEPTIONS—New York, Alexander 1-4. Seattle, Boulware 1-40.

KICKOFF RETURNS—New York, Morton 4-101. Seattle, Scobey 6-118.

PUNT RETURNS—New York, Morton 6-50. Seattle, J. Williams 1-0.

SACKS—New York, Umenyiora 2, Pierce 1. Seattle, Wistrom 1, R. Bernard 1, Team 1.

SAINTS 21, JETS 19
Sunday, November 27

New Orleans	0	14	0	7—21
N.Y. Jets	3	6	7	3—19

First Quarter
NYJ—FG, Nugent 29, 13:04.
Second Quarter
N.O.—Stallworth 21 pass from Brooks (Carney kick), 2:01.
NYJ—FG, Nugent 45, 7:58.
N.O.—Hilton 15 pass from Brooks (Carney kick), 12:19.
NYJ—FG, Nugent 41, 14:46.
Third Quarter
NYJ—McCareins 27 pass from Bollinger (Nugent kick), 9:25.

Fourth Quarter
NYJ—FG, Nugent 38, :04.
N.O.—Henderson 30 pass from Brooks (Carney kick), 6:28.
Attendance—77,152.

	New Orleans	N.Y. Jets
First downs	18	19
Rushes-yards	25-97	35-118
Passing	172	242
Punt returns	1-22	4-33
Kickoff returns	6-107	4-83
Interception returns	0-0	0-0
Comp.-att.-int.	17-23-0	19-28-0
Sacked-yards lost	1-9	1-9
Punts	5-43	3-44
Fumbles-lost	0-0	1-0
Penalties-yards	7-60	7-55
Time of possession	26:41	33:19

RUSHING—New Orleans, A. Smith 12-45, Stecker 11-54, Brooks 2-(minus 2). New York, C. Martin 24-91, Bollinger 6-15, Houston 5-12.

PASSING—New Orleans, Brooks 17-23-0-181. New York, Bollinger 19-28-0-251.

RECEIVING—New Orleans, Stallworth 5-48, Horn 4-47, Hilton 3-33, Karney 2-13, Henderson 1-30, Stecker 1-6, L. Hall 1-4. New York, Cotchery 4-72, Jolley 4-62, McCareins 3-71, Coles 3-58, C. Martin 3-8, Sowell 2-2.

MISSED FIELD GOAL ATTEMPTS—New York, Nugent 53.

INTERCEPTIONS—None.

KICKOFF RETURNS—New Orleans, Stecker 6-107. New York, Miller 4-83.

PUNT RETURNS—New Orleans, Hakim 1-22. New York, Cotchery 3-24, McCareins 1-9.

SACKS—New Orleans, W. Smith 1. New York, Washington 1.

COLTS 26, STEELERS 7
Monday, November 28

Pittsburgh	7	0	0	0—7
Indianapolis	10	6	7	3—26

First Quarter
Ind.—Harrison 80 pass from Manning (Vanderjagt kick), 1:44.
Ind.—FG, Vanderjagt 29, 8:53.
Pit.—Ward 12 pass from Roethlisberger (Reed kick), 13:46.
Second Quarter
Ind.—FG, Vanderjagt 48, 9:38.
Ind.—FG, Vanderjagt 44, 15:00.
Third Quarter
Ind.—Fletcher 12 pass from Manning (Vanderjagt kick), 3:13.
Fourth Quarter
Ind.—FG, Vanderjagt 28, 13:22.
Attendance—57,442.

...	Pittsburgh	Indianapolis
First downs	10	17
Rushes-yards	25-86	32-127
Passing	111	239
Punt returns	1-19	3-36
Kickoff returns	6-119	1-14
Interception returns	1-36	2-8
Comp.-att.-int.	17-26-2	15-25-1
Sacked-yards lost	3-22	2-6
Punts	6-46	5-46
Fumbles-lost	0-0	1-0
Penalties-yards	10-62	12-106
Time of possession	29:13	30:47

RUSHING—Pittsburgh, Parker 12-43, Bettis 6-9, Roethlisberger 3-21, Staley 3-6, Kreider 1-7. Indianapolis, James 29-124, Mungro 2-2, Rhodes 1-1.

PASSING—Pittsburgh, Roethlisberger 17-26-2-133. Indianapolis, Manning 15-25-1-245.

RECEIVING—Pittsburgh, Miller 4-26, Parker 4-23, Wilson 3-44, Ward 3-28, Randle El 2-5, Morgan 1-7. Indianapolis, Wayne 5-62, Harrison 4-128, Fletcher 3-28, Clark 2-19, Stokley 1-8.

MISSED FIELD GOAL ATTEMPTS—Pittsburgh, Reed 41.

INTERCEPTIONS—Pittsburgh, Polamalu 1-36. Indianapolis, Doss 1-8, David 1-0.

KICKOFF RETURNS—Pittsburgh, Colclough 3-59, Morgan 2-48, Keisel 1-12. Indianapolis, Rhodes 1-14.

PUNT RETURNS—Pittsburgh, Randle El 1-19. Indianapolis, Walters 2-26, Harrison 1-10.

SACKS—Pittsburgh, Townsend 1, Porter 1. Indianapolis, Reagor 1, Thomas 1, Freeney 0.5, Mathis 0.5.

WEEK 13

AMERICAN FOOTBALL CONFERENCE

EAST DIVISION

	W	L	T	Pct.	PF	PA
New England	7	5	0	.583	259	282
Miami	5	7	0	.417	219	240
Buffalo	4	8	0	.333	184	247
N.Y. Jets	2	10	0	.167	143	264

NORTH DIVISION

	W	L	T	Pct.	PF	PA
Cincinnati	9	3	0	.750	327	239
Pittsburgh	7	5	0	.583	274	225
Baltimore	4	8	0	.333	161	241
Cleveland	4	8	0	.333	183	214

SOUTH DIVISION

	W	L	T	Pct.	PF	PA
Indianapolis	12	0	0	1.000	366	162
Jacksonville	9	3	0	.750	255	201
Tennessee	3	9	0	.250	239	319
Houston	1	11	0	.083	183	341

WEST DIVISION

	W	L	T	Pct.	PF	PA
Denver	9	3	0	.750	310	221
Kansas City	8	4	0	.667	301	257
San Diego	8	4	0	.667	357	229
Oakland	4	8	0	.333	249	296

NATIONAL FOOTBALL CONFERENCE

EAST DIVISION

	W	L	T	Pct.	PF	PA
N.Y. Giants	8	4	0	.667	319	218
Dallas	7	5	0	.583	253	205
Washington	6	6	0	.500	241	233
Philadelphia	5	7	0	.417	229	288

NORTH DIVISION

	W	L	T	Pct.	PF	PA
Chicago	9	3	0	.750	201	127
Minnesota	7	5	0	.583	219	273
Detroit	4	8	0	.333	190	241
Green Bay	2	10	0	.167	239	242

SOUTH DIVISION

	W	L	T	Pct.	PF	PA
Carolina	9	3	0	.750	290	194
Tampa Bay	8	4	0	.667	226	199
Atlanta	7	5	0	.583	277	237
New Orleans	3	9	0	.250	183	295

WEST DIVISION

	W	L	T	Pct.	PF	PA
Seattle	10	2	0	.833	338	208
St. Louis	5	7	0	.417	294	351
Arizona	4	8	0	.333	239	302
San Francisco	2	10	0	.167	183	340

TOP PERFORMANCES

100-YARD RUSHING GAMES

Player, team & opponent	Att.	Yds.	TD
Domanick Davis, Hou. at Bal.	29	155	0
Larry Johnson, K.C. vs. Den.	30	140	2
Clinton Portis, Was. at St.L.	27	136	2
DeShaun Foster, Car. vs. Atl.	24	131	1
Rock Cartwright, Was. at St.L.	9	118	0
Tiki Barber, NYG vs. Dal.	30	115	0
Edgerrin James, Ind. vs. Ten.	28	107	1
Greg Jones, Jac. at Cle.	27	103	0

300-YARD PASSING GAMES

Player, team & opponent	Att.	Cmp.	Yds.	TD	Int.
Ben Roethlisberger, Pit. vs. Cin.	41	29	386	3	3
Kurt Warner, Ariz. at S.F.	45	29	354	1	2

100-YARD RECEIVING GAMES

Player, team & opponent	Rec.	Yds.	TD
Chris Chambers, Mia. vs. Buf.	15	238	1
Anquan Boldin, Ariz. at S.F.	11	156	1
Koren Robinson, Min. at Det.	4	148	1
Hines Ward, Pit. vs. Cin.	9	135	2
Larry Fitzgerald, Ariz. at S.F.	8	129	0
Lee Evans, Buf. at Mia.	5	117	3
Eddie Kennison, K.C. vs. Den.	4	108	0

RESULTS

SUNDAY, DECEMBER 4
INDIANAPOLIS 35, Tennessee 3
CAROLINA 24, Atlanta 6
Tampa Bay 10, NEW ORLEANS 3
Minnesota 21, DETROIT 16
Jacksonville 20, CLEVELAND 14
N.Y. GIANTS 17, Dallas 10
Cincinnati 38, PITTSBURGH 31
CHICAGO 19, Green Bay 7
BALTIMORE 16, Houston 15
MIAMI 24, Buffalo 23
Washington 24, ST. LOUIS 9
NEW ENGLAND 16, N.Y. Jets 3
Arizona 17, SAN FRANCISCO 10
KANSAS CITY 31, Denver 27
SAN DIEGO 34, Oakland 10

MONDAY, DECEMBER 5
Seattle 42, PHILADELPHIA 0

2005 REVIEW *Week 13*

COLTS 35, TITANS 3
Sunday, December 4

Tennessee	0	3	0	0— 3
Indianapolis	7	7	14	7—35

First Quarter
Ind.—Harrison 10 pass from Manning (Vanderjagt kick), 6:52.

Second Quarter
Ind.—Fletcher 13 pass from Manning (Vanderjagt kick), 10:49.
Ten.—FG, Bironas 24, 14:31.

Third Quarter
Ind.—Wayne 27 pass from Manning (Vanderjagt kick), 5:20.
Ind.—James 2 run (Vanderjagt kick), 13:32.

Fourth Quarter
Ind.—Tripplett 60 fumble return (Vanderjagt kick), 3:16.
Attendance—57,228.

	Tennessee	Indianapolis
First downs	17	21
Rushes-yards	19-53	31-105
Passing	207	187
Punt returns	1-16	0-0
Kickoff returns	6-171	2-48
Interception returns	0-0	0-0
Comp.-att.-int.	26-39-0	13-17-0
Sacked-yards lost	5-43	0-0
Punts	2-43	2-52
Fumbles-lost	2-1	1-1
Penalties-yards	7-35	5-33
Time of possession	32:57	27:03

INDIVIDUAL STATISTICS
RUSHING—Tennessee, Brown 11-32, Henry 6-18, McNair 2-3. Indianapolis, James 28-107, Manning 2-(minus 1), Sorgi 1-(minus 1).
PASSING—Tennessee, McNair 22-33-0-220, Volek 4-6-0-30. Indianapolis, Manning 13-17-0-187.
RECEIVING—Tennessee, Scaife 6-53, Bennett 6-37, Troupe 5-67, R. Williams 2-34, Calico 2-26, Henry 2-18, Brown 1-6, Fleming 1-5, Kinney 1-4. Indianapolis, Harrison 4-61, Wayne 3-50, Clark 2-37, Fletcher 2-22, James 2-17.
MISSED FIELD GOAL ATTEMPTS—Tennessee, Bironas 51.
INTERCEPTIONS—None.
KICKOFF RETURNS—Tennessee, P. Jones 6-171. Indianapolis, Rhodes 2-48.
PUNT RETURNS—Tennessee, P. Jones 1-16.
SACKS—Indianapolis, Freeney 2, Mathis 1, Brock 1, Tripplett 1.

PANTHERS 24, FALCONS 6
Sunday, December 4

Atlanta	3	3	0	0— 6
Carolina	7	7	0	10—24

First Quarter
Atl.—FG, T. Peterson 36, 10:58.
Car.—Foster 18 pass from Delhomme (Kasay kick), 14:29.

Second Quarter
Atl.—FG, T. Peterson 43, 3:19.
Car.—S. Smith 18 pass from Delhomme (Kasay kick), 11:09.

Fourth Quarter
Car.—FG, Kasay 20, 8:27.
Car.—Foster 6 run (Kasay kick), 12:41.
Attendance—73,661.

	Atlanta	Carolina
First downs	14	14
Rushes-yards	24-111	34-142
Passing	148	164
Punt returns	3-20	0-0
Kickoff returns	4-113	3-56
Interception returns	1-15	2-37
Comp.-att.-int.	17-35-2	17-27-1
Sacked-yards lost	4-23	0-0
Punts	6-36	7-45
Fumbles-lost	0-0	1-0
Penalties-yards	4-37	3-38
Time of possession	27:40	32:20

INDIVIDUAL STATISTICS
RUSHING—Atlanta, Dunn 16-80, Vick 4-27, Duckett 4-4. Carolina, Foster 24-131, S. Davis 5-8, Delhomme 4-1, Hoover 1-2.
PASSING—Atlanta, Vick 17-35-2-171. Carolina, Delhomme 17-27-1-164.
RECEIVING—Atlanta, Finneran 4-31, Crumpler 3-52, R. White 3-35, Jenkins 3-32, Griffith 2-13, Dunn 1-6, Duckett 1-2. Carolina, S. Smith 7-65, Foster 3-49, Colbert 3-24, Hoover 3-20, Proehl 1-6.
MISSED FIELD GOAL ATTEMPTS—Atlanta, T. Peterson 49.
INTERCEPTIONS—Atlanta, Scott 1-15. Carolina, McCree 1-27, Manning Jr. 1-10.
KICKOFF RETURNS—Atlanta, Rossum 1-47, D. Hall 1-23, Griffith 1-22, Pathon 1-21. Carolina, Smart 2-46, Hoover 1-10.
PUNT RETURNS—Atlanta, D. Hall 1-17, Finneran 1-5, Rossum 1-(minus 2).
SACKS—Carolina, Draft 1, Peppers 1, Witherspoon 0.5, Minter 0.5, T. Davis 0.5, Short 0.5.

BUCCANEERS 10, SAINTS 3
Sunday, December 4

Tampa Bay	0	7	0	3—10
New Orleans	0	3	0	0— 3

Second Quarter
T.B.—Galloway 30 pass from Simms (France kick), 10:16.
N.O.—FG, Carney 26, 14:14.

Fourth Quarter
T.B.—FG, France 28, 5:23.
Attendance—34,411.

	Tampa Bay	New Orleans
First downs	14	16
Rushes-yards	30-133	27-65
Passing	115	214
Punt returns	3-36	1-4
Kickoff returns	2-53	3-67
Interception returns	4-91	0-0
Comp.-att.-int.	12-21-0	18-34-4
Sacked-yards lost	1-8	2-1
Punts	5-40	4-44
Fumbles-lost	0-0	0-0
Penalties-yards	5-26	5-35
Time of possession	28:47	31:13

INDIVIDUAL STATISTICS
RUSHING—Tampa Bay, C. Williams 22-96, Pittman 4-40, Simms 4-(minus 3). New Orleans, A. Smith 18-49, Stecker 5-5, Brooks 3-9, A. Thomas 1-2.
PASSING—Tampa Bay, Simms 12-21-0-123. New Orleans, Brooks 18-34-4-215.
RECEIVING—Tampa Bay, Galloway 5-75, I. Hilliard 2-23, Pittman 2-19, C. Williams 2-7, Smith 1-(minus 1). New Orleans, Stecker 4-55, Hilton 4-50, Henderson 3-42, Stallworth 3-20, Horn 2-40, L. Hall 1-7, A. Smith 1-1.
MISSED FIELD GOAL ATTEMPTS—Tampa Bay, France 43.
INTERCEPTIONS—Tampa Bay, Barber 3-70, D. Jackson 1-21.
KICKOFF RETURNS—Tampa Bay, Shepherd 2-53. New Orleans, Stecker 3-67.
PUNT RETURNS—Tampa Bay, Jones 3-36. New Orleans, Stallworth 1-4.
SACKS—Tampa Bay, Kelly 1, Spires 1. New Orleans, W. Smith 1.

VIKINGS 21, LIONS 16
Sunday, December 4

Minnesota	7	7	7	0—21
Detroit	3	3	3	7—16

First Quarter
Det.—FG, Hanson 45, 6:54.
Min.—K. Robinson 80 pass from B. Johnson (Edinger kick), 7:04.

Second Quarter
Min.—M. Bennett 7 run (Edinger kick), 1:07.
Det.—FG, Hanson 26, 14:52.

Third Quarter
Min.—M. Bennett 5 pass from B. Johnson (Edinger kick), 4:15.
Det.—FG, Hanson 28, 13:09.

Fourth Quarter
Det.—Pinner 6 run (Hanson kick), 7:22.
Attendance—61,375.

	Minnesota	Detroit
First downs	20	19
Rushes-yards	32-103	23-105
Passing	242	118
Punt returns	5-24	3-69
Kickoff returns	4-71	4-80
Interception returns	1-0	0-0
Comp.-att.-int.	17-23-0	17-35-1
Sacked-yards lost	2-14	1-8
Punts	6-43	5-47
Fumbles-lost	0-0	1-0
Penalties-yards	11-94	3-30
Time of possession	30:41	29:19

INDIVIDUAL STATISTICS

RUSHING—Minnesota, M. Bennett 22-79, Fason 4-13, B. Johnson 4-8, K. Robinson 1-9, Moore 1-(minus 6). Detroit, Pinner 14-64, Bryson 6-29, Garcia 3-12.

PASSING—Minnesota, B. Johnson 17-23-0-256. Detroit, Garcia 17-35-1-126.

RECEIVING—Minnesota, K. Robinson 4-148, Kleinsasser 4-26, M. Robinson 3-32, M. Bennett 3-10, Burleson 2-26, T. Taylor 1-14. Detroit, R. Williams 4-34, Bryson 4-26, Pinner 3-39, Vines 2-10, Pollard 2-10, M. Williams 1-6, FitzSimmons 1-1.

MISSED FIELD GOAL ATTEMPTS—None.

INTERCEPTIONS—Minnesota, Chavous 1-0.

KICKOFF RETURNS—Minnesota, K. Robinson 3-71, Owens 1-0. Detroit, Drummond 3-68, Bryson 1-12.

PUNT RETURNS—Minnesota, Burleson 4-17, Moore 1-7. Detroit, Drummond 3-69.

SACKS—Minnesota, Mosley 1. Detroit, S. Rogers 1, Wilkinson 1.

JAGUARS 20, BROWNS 14
Sunday, December 4

Jacksonville	3	0	17	0—20
Cleveland	0	14	0	0—14

First Quarter
Jac.—FG, Scobee 24, 10:46.

Second Quarter
Cle.—Edwards 34 pass from Frye (Dawson kick), 4:19.
Cle.—Edwards 17 pass from Frye (Dawson kick), 14:16.

Third Quarter
Jac.—FG, Scobee 29, 4:47.
Jac.—Wrighster 9 pass from Garrard (Scobee kick), 9:56.
Jac.—J. Smith 12 pass from Garrard (Scobee kick), 13:49.
Attendance—70,941.

	Jacksonville	Cleveland
First downs	17	15
Rushes-yards	38-122	32-98
Passing	115	205
Punt returns	3-21	0-0
Kickoff returns	3-80	5-84
Interception returns	0-0	1-0
Comp.-att.-int.	11-20-1	13-20-0
Sacked-yards lost	1-1	5-21
Punts	4-41	6-37
Fumbles-lost	0-0	1-0
Penalties-yards	5-50	7-97
Time of possession	29:43	30:17

INDIVIDUAL STATISTICS

RUSHING—Jacksonville, Jones 27-103, Garrard 9-13, Pearman 1-3, M. Jones 1-3. Cleveland, Droughns 30-88, Frye 2-10.

PASSING—Jacksonville, Garrard 11-20-1-116. Cleveland, Frye 13-20-0-226.

RECEIVING—Jacksonville, J. Smith 3-49, Wilford 3-36, Wrighster 2-9, Brady 1-17, G. Jones 1-9, Pearman 1-(minus 4). Cleveland, Edwards 5-86, Bryant 3-63, F. Jackson 2-15, Northcutt 1-45, Shea 1-13, Heiden 1-4.

MISSED FIELD GOAL ATTEMPTS—Cleveland, Dawson 34.

INTERCEPTIONS—Cleveland, Russell 1-0.

KICKOFF RETURNS—Jacksonville, Wimbush 2-56, Brady 1-24. Cleveland, Cribbs 4-75, Shea 1-9.

PUNT RETURNS—Jacksonville, Pearman 3-21.

SACKS—Jacksonville, Peterson 1, Spicer 1, Henderson 1, D. Smith 1, McCray 1. Cleveland, Lang 1.

GIANTS 17, COWBOYS 10
Sunday, December 4

Dallas	0	0	10	0—10
N.Y. Giants	0	10	7	0—17

Second Quarter
NYG—Jacobs 1 run (Feely kick), 5:00.
NYG—FG, Feely 27, 13:02.

Third Quarter
NYG—Pierce 12 fumble return (Feely kick), :12.
Dal.—FG, Cundiff 34, 4:57.
Dal.—T. Glenn 7 pass from Bledsoe (Cundiff kick), 11:08.
Attendance—78,645.

	Dallas	N.Y. Giants
First downs	16	17
Rushes-yards	27-81	34-127
Passing	125	150
Punt returns	2-30	2-6
Kickoff returns	4-66	3-61
Interception returns	2-10	2-15
Comp.-att.-int.	15-39-2	12-31-2
Sacked-yards lost	4-21	1-2
Punts	7-40	6-45
Fumbles-lost	2-2	0-0
Penalties-yards	7-46	6-44
Time of possession	28:29	31:31

INDIVIDUAL STATISTICS

RUSHING—Dallas, J. Jones 23-74, Barber 2-8, Bledsoe 2-(minus 1). New York, Barber 30-115, Jacobs 2-2, T. Carter 1-6, Ward 1-4.

PASSING—Dallas, Bledsoe 15-39-2-146. New York, Manning 12-31-2-152.

RECEIVING—Dallas, J. Jones 9-88, T. Glenn 3-37, K. Johnson 2-16, Witten 1-5. New York, Burress 4-47, T. Carter 2-48, Finn 2-20, Shockey 2-20, Barber 1-9, Toomer 1-8.

MISSED FIELD GOAL ATTEMPTS—New York, Feely 33.

INTERCEPTIONS—Dallas, A. Glenn 2-10. New York, Alexander 1-15, Butler 1-0.

KICKOFF RETURNS—Dallas, Thompson 4-66. New York, Morton 3-61.

PUNT RETURNS—Dallas, Newman 1-26, Crayton 1-4. New York, Morton 2-6.

SACKS—Dallas, J. Ferguson 1. New York, Strahan 2, Umenyiora 1, Tuck 1.

BENGALS 38, STEELERS 31
Sunday, December 4

Cincinnati	7	14	10	7—38
Pittsburgh	14	3	7	7—31

First Quarter
Pit.—Bettis 1 run (Reed kick), 10:15.
Cin.—Houshmandzadeh 43 pass from Palmer (Graham kick), 11:38.
Pit.—Morgan 25 pass from Roethlisberger (Reed kick), 14:47.

Second Quarter
Cin.—R. Kelly 1 pass from Palmer (Graham kick), 4:52.
Cin.—Houshmandzadeh 6 pass from Palmer (Graham kick), 8:03.
Pit.—FG, Reed 23, 15:00.

Third Quarter
Cin.—FG, Graham 30, 3:59.
Pit.—Ward 20 pass from Roethlisberger (Reed kick), 5:55.
Cin.—Ru. Johnson 1 run (Graham kick), 7:03.

Fourth Quarter
Cin.—Ru. Johnson 14 run (Graham kick), 8:51.
Pit.—Ward 6 pass from Roethlisberger (Reed kick), 12:01.
Attendance—63,044.

	Cincinnati	Pittsburgh
First downs	21	28
Rushes-yards	25-102	28-95
Passing	222	379
Punt returns	1-3	2-8
Kickoff returns	5-197	6-136
Interception returns	3-58	0-0
Comp.-att.-int.	22-38-0	29-41-3
Sacked-yards lost	1-5	2-7
Punts	5-47	3-32
Fumbles-lost	0-0	4-1
Penalties-yards	4-30	7-70
Time of possession	26:42	33:18

INDIVIDUAL STATISTICS

RUSHING—Cincinnati, Ru. Johnson 21-98, Palmer 3-(minus 3), Houshmandzadeh 1-7. Pittsburgh, Parker 15-71, Bettis 8-13, Staley 3-2, Ward 1-7, Roethlisberger 1-2.

PASSING—Cincinnati, Palmer 22-38-0-227. Pittsburgh, Roethlisberger 29-41-3-386.

RECEIVING—Cincinnati, Houshmandzadeh 5-88, C. Johnson 5-54, Henry 5-52, R. Kelly 3-12, C. Perry 2-12, Ru. Johnson 1-5, Stewart 1-4. Pittsburgh, Ward 9-135, Randle El 5-47, Wilson 4-65, Miller 3-44, Bettis 3-24, Staley 2-9, Tuman 1-26, Morgan 1-25, Parker 1-11.

MISSED FIELD GOAL ATTEMPTS—None.

INTERCEPTIONS—Cincinnati, O'Neal 1-37, Simmons 1-16, Thurman 1-5.

KICKOFF RETURNS—Cincinnati, T. Perry 5-197. Pittsburgh, Morgan 3-84, Colclough 2-41, Keisel 1-11.

PUNT RETURNS—Cincinnati, Ratliff 1-3. Pittsburgh, Randle El 2-8.

SACKS—Cincinnati, J. Smith 1, Pollack 1. Pittsburgh, Haggans 1.

BEARS 19, PACKERS 7
Sunday, December 4

Green Bay	0	7	0	0— 7
Chicago	0	9	0	10—19

Second Quarter
Chi.—FG, Gould 21, 1:26.
G.B.—Gado 2 run (Longwell kick), 7:57.
Chi.—FG, Gould 40, 10:27.
Chi.—FG, Gould 25, 14:58.

Fourth Quarter
Chi.—FG, Gould 35, 6:38.
Chi.—Vasher 45 interception return (Gould kick), 11:54.
    Attendance—62,177.

	Green Bay	Chicago
First downs	26	10
Rushes-yards	24-100	31-141
Passing	258	49
Punt returns	1-3	4-36
Kickoff returns	6-102	2-29
Interception returns	1-6	2-140
Comp.-att.-int.	31-58-2	6-17-1
Sacked-yards lost	2-19	3-19
Punts	7-36	6-49
Fumbles-lost	4-2	3-1
Penalties-yards	9-70	4-61
Time of possession	34:47	25:13

INDIVIDUAL STATISTICS

RUSHING—Green Bay, Gado 20-75, Fisher 2-14, Chatman 1-11, Favre 1-0. Chicago, T. Jones 19-93, Peterson 11-48, Orton 1-0.

PASSING—Green Bay, Favre 31-58-2-277. Chicago, Orton 6-17-1-68.

RECEIVING—Green Bay, Driver 8-64, Fisher 7-69, Chatman 4-41, Ferguson 4-37, D. Martin 4-17, D. Lee 3-37, Gado 1-12. Chicago, Berrian 3-59, Clark 2-6, Wade 1-3.

MISSED FIELD GOAL ATTEMPTS—Chicago, Gould 43.

INTERCEPTIONS—Green Bay, Roman 1-6. Chicago, Tillman 1-95, Vasher 1-45.

KICKOFF RETURNS—Green Bay, Chatman 3-36, Carroll 2-43, Thurman 1-23. Chicago, Azumah 2-29.

PUNT RETURNS—Green Bay, Chatman 1-3. Chicago, Davis 3-21, Wade 1-15.

SACKS—Green Bay, Montgomery 1, Jenkins 1, Gbaja-Biamila 1. Chicago, Tillman 1, M. Brown 1.

RAVENS 16, TEXANS 15
Sunday, December 4

Houston	3	3	0	9—15
Baltimore	0	7	0	9—16

First Quarter
Hou.—FG, K. Brown 39, 11:17.

Second Quarter
Bal.—Boller 6 run (Stover kick), 1:59.
Hou.—FG, K. Brown 26, 14:56.

Fourth Quarter
Hou.—FG, K. Brown 22, :30.
Bal.—A. Thomas 20 interception return (pass failed), 7:44.
Hou.—FG, K. Brown 29, 11:29.
Hou.—FG, K. Brown 39, 13:52.
Bal.—FG, Stover 38, 14:54.
    Attendance—69,909.

	Houston	Baltimore
First downs	16	15
Rushes-yards	34-165	23-73
Passing	133	165
Punt returns	7-50	1-0
Kickoff returns	4-99	3-67
Interception returns	0-0	1-20
Comp.-att.-int.	17-37-1	17-33-0
Sacked-yards lost	5-32	4-33
Punts	6-35	8-40
Fumbles-lost	5-1	4-2
Penalties-yards	11-93	8-71
Time of possession	33:49	26:11

INDIVIDUAL STATISTICS

RUSHING—Houston, D. Davis 29-155, Carr 3-8, Wells 2-2. Baltimore, C. Taylor 11-40, J. Lewis 8-17, Boller 3-11, Clayton 1-5.

PASSING—Houston, Carr 17-37-1-165. Baltimore, Boller 17-33-0-198.

RECEIVING—Houston, Gaffney 6-40, An. Johnson 4-70, D. Davis 3-16, Wells 2-12, Armstrong 1-17, Rivers 1-10. Baltimore, Clayton 7-86, Heap 3-51, Mason 3-32, J. Lewis 3-23, C. Taylor 1-6.

MISSED FIELD GOAL ATTEMPTS—None.

INTERCEPTIONS—Baltimore, A. Thomas 1-20.

KICKOFF RETURNS—Houston, Mathis 4-99. Baltimore, Sams 2-46, C. Taylor 1-21.

PUNT RETURNS—Houston, Mathis 5-29, D. Davis 2-21. Baltimore, Sams 1-0.

SACKS—Houston, Orr 3, Peek 1. Baltimore, Suggs 3, A. Thomas 1, Scott 1.

DOLPHINS 24, BILLS 23
Sunday, December 4

Buffalo	21	0	2	0—23
Miami	0	3	0	21—24

First Quarter
Buf.—Evans 46 pass from Losman (Lindell kick), 2:13.
Buf.—Evans 56 pass from Losman (Lindell kick), 3:53.
Buf.—Evans 4 pass from Losman (Lindell kick), 12:46.

Second Quarter
Mia.—FG, Mare 23, 14:17.

Third Quarter
Buf.—Safety, 4:48.

Fourth Quarter
Mia.—R. Williams 5 run (Mare kick), 3:25.
Mia.—Brown 23 pass from Rosenfels (Mare kick), 7:25.
Mia.—Chambers 4 pass from Rosenfels (Mare kick), 14:54.
    Attendance—72,051.

	Buffalo	Miami
First downs	16	26
Rushes-yards	33-92	22-73
Passing	202	361
Punt returns	5-35	5-14
Kickoff returns	5-111	4-74
Interception returns	1-0	1-11
Comp.-att.-int.	14-27-1	34-65-1
Sacked-yards lost	2-25	3-26
Punts	8-44	7-36
Fumbles-lost	2-2	1-1
Penalties-yards	7-55	13-81
Time of possession	31:17	28:43

INDIVIDUAL STATISTICS

RUSHING—Buffalo, McGahee 27-81, Losman 3-10, S. Williams 3-1. Miami, R. Williams 11-46, Brown 9-22, Rosenfels 2-5.

PASSING—Buffalo, Losman 13-26-1-224, Parrish 1-1-0-3. Miami, Rosenfels 22-37-1-272, Frerotte 12-28-0-115.

RECEIVING—Buffalo, Evans 5-117, Reed 2-35, McGahee 2-18, Parrish 2-17, Aiken 1-22, S. Williams 1-13, Euhus 1-5. Miami, Chambers 15-238, McMichael 6-41, R. Williams 6-32, Welker 4-40, Brown 2-30, Gilmore 1-6.

MISSED FIELD GOAL ATTEMPTS—None.

INTERCEPTIONS—Buffalo, Schobel 1-0. Miami, Madison 1-11.

KICKOFF RETURNS—Buffalo, McGee 3-79, Burns 1-19, Parrish 1-13. Miami, Welker 4-74.

PUNT RETURNS—Buffalo, Parrish 4-34, Clements 1-1. Miami, Welker 5-14.

SACKS—Buffalo, Fletcher 2, Schobel 1. Miami, Spragan 1, Wright 1.

REDSKINS 24, RAMS 9

Sunday, December 4

Washington	7	3	0	14—24
St. Louis	0	7	0	2— 9

First Quarter
Was.—Portis 47 run (Hall kick), 4:31.
Second Quarter
St.L.—Fitzpatrick 7 run (J. Wilkins kick), 7:55.
Was.—FG, Hall 38, 11:49.
Fourth Quarter
Was.—Portis 1 run (Hall kick), 1:14.
St.L.—Safety, 3:05.
Was.—Cooley 4 pass from Brunell (Hall kick), 9:10.
Attendance—65,701.

	Washington	St. Louis
First downs	19	13
Rushes-yards	40-257	17-49
Passing	150	142
Punt returns	5-38	2-2
Kickoff returns	2-42	5-90
Interception returns	1-0	0-0
Comp.-att.-int.	14-22-0	21-36-1
Sacked-yards lost	1-6	3-21
Punts	4-43	8-47
Fumbles-lost	1-0	2-1
Penalties-yards	8-76	4-30
Time of possession	33:58	26:02

INDIVIDUAL STATISTICS
RUSHING—Washington, Portis 27-136, Cartwright 9-118, Brunell 3-0, Broughton 1-3. St. Louis, S. Jackson 11-24, Fitzpatrick 5-22, M. Faulk 1-3.
PASSING—Washington, Brunell 14-21-0-156, Portis 0-1-0-0. St. Louis, Fitzpatrick 21-36-1-163.
RECEIVING—Washington, Cooley 5-58, Royal 4-40, Moss 3-58, Portis 1-, Jacobs 1-(minus 1). St. Louis, Holt 6-75, Bruce 4-33, S. Jackson 4-18, McDonald 2-27, Curtis 2-6, Manumaleuna 1-6, Hedgecock 1-5, Cleeland 1-(minus 7).
MISSED FIELD GOAL ATTEMPTS—Washington, Hall 45.
INTERCEPTIONS—Washington, Rogers 1-0.
KICKOFF RETURNS—Washington, A. Brown 2-42. St. Louis, Allen 5-90.
PUNT RETURNS—Washington, A. Brown 5-38. St. Louis, Allen 2-2.
SACKS—Washington, Washington 1, Taylor 1, Prioleau 1. St. Louis.

PATRIOTS 16, JETS 3

Sunday, December 4

N.Y. Jets	0	3	0	0— 3
New England	0	6	7	3—16

Second Quarter
N.E.—FG, Vinatieri 21, 9:24.
NYJ—FG, Nugent 38, 13:58.
N.E.—FG, Vinatieri 34, 14:58.
Third Quarter
N.E.—Dillon 1 run (Vinatieri kick), 10:48.
Fourth Quarter
N.E.—FG, Vinatieri 22, :58.
Attendance—68,756.

	N.Y. Jets	New England
First downs	12	24
Rushes-yards	16-41	35-146
Passing	123	251
Punt returns	2-14	3-17
Kickoff returns	5-70	2-32
Interception returns	0-0	1-0
Comp.-att.-int.	15-37-1	27-37-0
Sacked-yards lost	2-12	2-20
Punts	6-42	4-48
Fumbles-lost	0-0	1-0
Penalties-yards	7-60	7-68
Time of possession	21:50	38:10

INDIVIDUAL STATISTICS
RUSHING—New York, C. Martin 15-29, Bollinger 1-12. New England, Dillon 16-65, Faulk 10-35, Cloud 5-27, Brady 4-19.
PASSING—New York, Bollinger 15-37-1-135. New England, Brady 27-37-0-271.
RECEIVING—New York, Coles 4-35, C. Martin 4-26, Jolley 2-26, Cotchery 2-16, Dreessen 1-17, Houston 1-11, McCareins 1-4. New England, T. Brown 7-64, Branch 5-44, Givens 5-27, Faulk 4-46, Dillon 4-19, Watson 2-43, Andre. Davis 2-28.

MISSED FIELD GOAL ATTEMPTS—New England, Vinatieri 45.
INTERCEPTIONS—New England, Hobbs 1-0.
KICKOFF RETURNS—New York, Miller 3-51, Cotchery 1-19, Lawton 1-0. New England, B. Johnson 1-17, Cloud 1-15.
PUNT RETURNS—New York, Cotchery 2-14. New England, Dwight 3-17.
SACKS—New York, J. Abraham 1, Robertson 0.5, B. Thomas 0.5. New England, Colvin 1, J. Green 1.

CARDINALS 17, 49ERS 10

Sunday, December 4

Arizona	3	0	6	8—17
San Francisco	0	7	3	0—10

First Quarter
Ariz.—FG, Novak 30, 13:58.
Second Quarter
S.F.—Hicks 1 run (Nedney kick), 13:02.
Third Quarter
Ariz.—FG, Novak 35, 3:00.
Ariz.—FG, Novak 19, 7:39.
S.F.—FG, Nedney 48, 14:54.
Fourth Quarter
Ariz.—Boldin 54 pass from Warner (O. Ayanbadejo run), 4:15.
Attendance—60,439.

	Arizona	San Francisco
First downs	18	11
Rushes-yards	23-65	20-51
Passing	339	169
Punt returns	3-17	1-1
Kickoff returns	3-57	5-76
Interception returns	3-31	2-2
Comp.-att.-int.	29-45-2	16-24-3
Sacked-yards lost	2-15	3-16
Punts	5-26	5-43
Fumbles-lost	0-0	2-1
Penalties-yards	11-80	6-44
Time of possession	34:45	25:15

INDIVIDUAL STATISTICS
RUSHING—Arizona, Arrington 18-59, Warner 3-(minus 5), O. Ayanbadejo 2-11. San Francisco, Hicks 10-17, Gore 6-22, A. Smith 4-12.
PASSING—Arizona, Warner 29-45-2-354. San Francisco, A. Smith 16-24-3-185.
RECEIVING—Arizona, Boldin 11-156, Fitzgerald 8-129, B. Johnson 3-28, Arrington 3-16, O. Ayanbadejo 2-8, McCoy 1-10, Edwards 1-7. San Francisco, Lloyd 5-47, Morton 3-66, Hicks 3-8, McAddley 2-16, Gore 1-31, Jackson 1-10, T. Jones 1-7.
MISSED FIELD GOAL ATTEMPTS—None.
INTERCEPTIONS—Arizona, Green 1-13, Griffith 1-11, Darling 1-7. San Francisco, Lewis 1-2, M. Adams 1-0.
KICKOFF RETURNS—Arizona, Swinton 2-50, Anderson 1-7. San Francisco, Marshall 5-76.
PUNT RETURNS—Arizona, Swinton 3-17. San Francisco, Marshall 1-1.
SACKS—Arizona, Wilson 1, Kolodziej 1, Dansby 1. San Francisco, B. Moore 2.

CHIEFS 31, BRONCOS 27

Sunday, December 4

Denver	7	14	3	3—27
Kansas City	7	14	3	7—31

First Quarter
Den.—Mi. Anderson 66 pass from Plummer (Elam kick), 5:46.
K.C.—D. Hall 41 pass from Green (Tynes kick), 9:11.
Second Quarter
K.C.—L. Johnson 1 run (Tynes kick), 4:55.
Den.—Mi. Anderson 1 run (Elam kick), 11:33.
K.C.—Gonzalez 25 pass from Green (Tynes kick), 13:21.
Den.—Van Pelt 7 run (Elam kick), 14:38.
Third Quarter
K.C.—FG, Tynes 34, 4:56.
Den.—FG, Elam 22, 11:51.
Fourth Quarter
Den.—FG, Elam 40, 1:29.
K.C.—L. Johnson 4 run (Tynes kick), 5:02.
Attendance—78,261.

	Denver	Kansas City
First downs	19	24
Rushes-yards	29-131	37-168
Passing	257	253

	Denver	Kansas City
Punt returns	1-1	2-10
Kickoff returns	6-113	6-143
Interception returns	2-38	2-0
Comp.-att.-int.	18-29-2	16-23-2
Sacked-yards lost	2-19	0-0
Punts	2-49	2-38
Fumbles-lost	0-0	1-1
Penalties-yards	8-55	6-45
Time of possession	27:33	32:27

INDIVIDUAL STATISTICS

RUSHING—Denver, Mi. Anderson 13-37, Dayne 8-26, Bell 5-46, Plummer 1-8, Smith 1-7, Van Pelt 1-7. Kansas City, L. Johnson 30-140, Green 3-13, De. Brown 2-1, Richardson 1-8, D. Hall 1-6.

PASSING—Denver, Plummer 18-29-2-276. Kansas City, Green 16-23-2-253.

RECEIVING—Denver, Smith 6-79, Putzier 4-50, Lelie 2-63, K. Johnson 2-(minus 1), Mi. Anderson 1-66, S. Alexander 1-9, Devoe 1-9, Bell 1-1. Kansas City, Kennison 4-108, Parker 4-39, D. Hall 2-55, L. Johnson 2-9, Gonzalez 1-25, Wilson 1-11, Dunn 1-3, Horn 1-3.

MISSED FIELD GOAL ATTEMPTS—None.

INTERCEPTIONS—Denver, Da. Williams 1-28, Bailey 1-10. Kansas City, K. Mitchell 1-0, Surtain 1-0.

KICKOFF RETURNS—Denver, Da. Williams 4-87, Sapp 1-20, Veal 1-6. Kansas City, D. Hall 6-143.

PUNT RETURNS—Denver, Da. Williams 1-1. Kansas City, D. Hall 2-10.

SACKS—Kansas City, D. Johnson 1, Hicks 1.

CHARGERS 34, RAIDERS 10
Sunday, December 4

Oakland	3	7	0	0—10
San Diego	3	14	7	10—34

First Quarter
Oak.—FG, Janikowski 37, 3:27.
S.D.—FG, Kaeding 41, 6:11.

Second Quarter
S.D.—Gates 6 pass from Brees (Kaeding kick), 3:46.
Oak.—C. Anderson 16 pass from Collins (Janikowski kick), 8:01.
S.D.—Turner 2 run (Kaeding kick), 14:42.

Third Quarter
S.D.—E. Parker 1 pass from Brees (Kaeding kick), 10:05.

Fourth Quarter
S.D.—FG, Kaeding 32, 1:27.
S.D.—Hart 70 interception return (Kaeding kick), 8:31.
Attendance—66,436.

	Oakland	San Diego
First downs	16	19
Rushes-yards	17-81	37-130
Passing	210	144
Punt returns	1-0	1-14
Kickoff returns	7-126	3-87
Interception returns	0-0	1-70
Comp.-att.-int.	22-40-1	17-22-0
Sacked-yards lost	3-26	3-16
Punts	4-38	4-43
Fumbles-lost	1-1	1-0
Penalties-yards	0-0	1-15
Time of possession	25:22	34:38

INDIVIDUAL STATISTICS

RUSHING—Oakland, Jordan 15-55, Crockett 1-24, Lechler 1-2. San Diego, Tomlinson 25-86, Turner 7-34, Neal 3-8, Sproles 2-2.

PASSING—Oakland, Collins 22-40-1-236. San Diego, Brees 17-22-0-160.

RECEIVING—Oakland, Moss 7-74, Porter 6-50, Gabriel 2-28, Crockett 2-13, Jordan 2-10, Ra. Williams 1-34, C. Anderson 1-16, Whitted 1-11. San Diego, Tomlinson 5-24, McCardell 4-60, Gates 4-51, E. Parker 3-22, Neal 1-3.

MISSED FIELD GOAL ATTEMPTS—Oakland, Janikowski 61.

INTERCEPTIONS—San Diego, Hart 1-70.

KICKOFF RETURNS—Oakland, Carr 5-103, Gabriel 1-15, Flemister 1-8. San Diego, Sproles 2-63, Pinnock 1-24.

PUNT RETURNS—Oakland, Carr 1-0. San Diego, E. Parker 1-14.

SACKS—Oakland, Hamilton 2, Sands 1. San Diego, Scott 2, Wilhelm 1.

SEAHAWKS 42, EAGLES 0
Monday, December 5

Seattle	14	21	7	0—42
Philadelphia	0	0	0	0— 0

First Quarter
Sea.—Engram 11 pass from Hasselbeck (J. Brown kick), 8:10.
Sea.—A. Dyson 72 interception return (J. Brown kick), 11:36.

Second Quarter
Sea.—Tatupu 38 interception return (J. Brown kick), 3:29.
Sea.—Alexander 2 run (J. Brown kick), 10:26.
Sea.—Alexander 1 run (J. Brown kick), 14:31.

Third Quarter
Sea.—A. Dyson 25 fumble return (J. Brown kick), :15.
Attendance—67,637.

	Seattle	Philadelphia
First downs	14	11
Rushes-yards	42-96	25-61
Passing	98	129
Punt returns	5-29	7-108
Kickoff returns	1-22	7-117
Interception returns	4-148	0-0
Comp.-att.-int.	8-17-0	17-39-4
Sacked-yards lost	0-0	4-16
Punts	9-41	8-37
Fumbles-lost	1-0	2-2
Penalties-yards	2-10	10-56
Time of possession	30:40	29:20

INDIVIDUAL STATISTICS

RUSHING—Seattle, Alexander 19-49, Morris 15-33, Weaver 5-10, Strong 2-4, S. Wallace 1-0. Philadelphia, Moats 10-26, Westbrook 9-17, McMahon 3-14, Mahe 2-3, Detmer 1-1.

PASSING—Seattle, Hasselbeck 8-15-0-98, S. Wallace 0-2-0-0. Philadelphia, Detmer 13-29-2-84, McMahon 4-10-2-61.

RECEIVING—Seattle, Stevens 4-22, Engram 3-34, Hackett 1-42. Philadelphia, Westbrook 5-38, Mahe 4-16, R. Brown 3-27, Smith 2-46, G. Lewis 1-9, McCants 1-6, Moats 1-3.

MISSED FIELD GOAL ATTEMPTS—Seattle, J. Brown 40.

INTERCEPTIONS—Seattle, A. Dyson 1-72, Tatupu 1-38, Boulware 1-32, J. Williams 1-6.

KICKOFF RETURNS—Seattle, Scobey 1-22. Philadelphia, Wynn 7-117.

PUNT RETURNS—Seattle, J. Williams 5-29. Philadelphia, Mahe 7-108.

SACKS—Seattle, Hill 1.5, Tafoya 1, Tubbs 0.5, B. Fisher 0.5, Terrill 0.5.

STANDINGS

AMERICAN FOOTBALL CONFERENCE

EAST DIVISION
	W	L	T	Pct.	PF	PA
New England	8	5	0	.615	294	289
Miami	6	7	0	.462	242	261
Buffalo	4	9	0	.308	191	282
N.Y. Jets	3	10	0	.231	169	274

NORTH DIVISION
	W	L	T	Pct.	PF	PA
Cincinnati	10	3	0	.769	350	259
Pittsburgh	8	5	0	.615	295	234
Baltimore	4	9	0	.308	171	253
Cleveland	4	9	0	.308	203	237

SOUTH DIVISION
	W	L	T	Pct.	PF	PA
Indianapolis	13	0	0	1.000	392	180
Jacksonville	9	4	0	.692	273	227
Tennessee	4	9	0	.308	252	329
Houston	1	12	0	.077	193	354

WEST DIVISION
	W	L	T	Pct.	PF	PA
Denver	10	3	0	.769	322	231
Kansas City	8	5	0	.615	329	288
San Diego	8	5	0	.615	378	252
Oakland	4	9	0	.308	259	322

NATIONAL FOOTBALL CONFERENCE

EAST DIVISION
	W	L	T	Pct.	PF	PA
N.Y. Giants	9	4	0	.692	345	241
Dallas	8	5	0	.615	284	233
Washington	7	6	0	.538	258	246
Philadelphia	5	8	0	.385	252	314

NORTH DIVISION
	W	L	T	Pct.	PF	PA
Chicago	9	4	0	.692	210	148
Minnesota	8	5	0	.615	246	286
Detroit	4	9	0	.308	203	257
Green Bay	3	10	0	.231	255	255

SOUTH DIVISION
	W	L	T	Pct.	PF	PA
Carolina	9	4	0	.692	300	214
Tampa Bay	9	4	0	.692	246	209
Atlanta	8	5	0	.615	313	254
New Orleans	3	10	0	.231	200	331

WEST DIVISION
	W	L	T	Pct.	PF	PA
Seattle	11	2	0	.846	379	211
St. Louis	5	8	0	.385	307	378
Arizona	4	9	0	.308	252	319
San Francisco	2	11	0	.154	186	381

TOP PERFORMANCES

100-YARD RUSHING GAMES
Player, team & opponent	Att.	Yds.	TD
Samkon Gado, G.B. vs. Det.*	29	171	1
Rudi Johnson, Cin. vs. Cle.	30	169	1
Larry Johnson, K.C. at Dal.	26	143	3
Domanick Davis, Hou. at Ten.	22	139	0
Tiki Barber, NYG at Phi.*	32	124	0
Ryan Moats, Phi. vs. NYG*	11	114	2
Carnell Williams, T.B. at Car.	29	112	2
Shaun Alexander, Sea. vs. S.F.	21	108	1
Clinton Portis, Was. at Ariz.	26	105	1
Corey Dillon, N.E. at Buf.	22	102	1
Jerome Bettis, Pit. vs. Chi.	17	101	2

300-YARD PASSING GAMES
Player, team & opponent	Att.	Cmp.	Yds.	TD	Int.
Trent Green, K.C. at Dal.	32	20	340	1	0
Drew Bledsoe, Dal. vs. K.C.	34	22	332	3	0
Tom Brady, N.E. at Buf.	38	29	329	2	2
Peyton Manning, Ind. at Jac.	36	24	324	2	0
Eli Manning, NYG at Phi.*	44	28	312	1	3

100-YARD RECEIVING GAMES
Player, team & opponent	Rec.	Yds.	TD
Terry Glenn, Dal. vs. K.C.	6	138	1
Marvin Harrison, Ind. at Jac.	6	137	2
Antonio Gates, S.D. vs. Mia.	13	123	1
Chris Chambers, Mia. at S.D.	8	121	2
Anquan Boldin, Ariz. vs. Was.	9	114	0
Jeremy Shockey, NYG at Phi.*	10	107	0
Mark Clayton, Bal. at Den.	7	105	1
Steve Smith, Car. vs. T.B.	5	103	0
Jimmy Smith, Jac. vs. Ind.	8	102	1

*Overtime game.

RESULTS

SUNDAY, DECEMBER 11
CINCINNATI 23, Cleveland 20
Tampa Bay 20, CAROLINA 10
N.Y. JETS 26, Oakland 10
PITTSBURGH 21, Chicago 9
TENNESSEE 13, Houston 10
Indianapolis 26, JACKSONVILLE 18
MINNESOTA 27, St. Louis 13
New England 35, BUFFALO 7
Miami 23, SAN DIEGO 21
SEATTLE 41, San Francisco 3
Washington 17, ARIZONA 13
DENVER 12, Baltimore 10
DALLAS 31, Kansas City 28
N.Y. Giants 26, PHILADELPHIA 23 (OT)
GREEN BAY 16, Detroit 13 (OT)

MONDAY, DECEMBER 12
ATLANTA 36, New Orleans 17

BENGALS 23, BROWNS 20
Sunday, December 11

Cleveland	7	7	3	3—20
Cincinnati	7	6	7	3—23

First Quarter
Cle.—Frye 3 run (Dawson kick), 6:37.
Cin.—Ru. Johnson 8 run (Graham kick), 10:42.

Second Quarter
Cle.—Heiden 2 pass from Frye (Dawson kick), 2:42.
Cin.—FG, Graham 21, 7:22.
Cin.—FG, Graham 27, 14:54.

Third Quarter
Cle.—FG, Dawson 41, 8:49.
Cin.—Houshmandzadeh 4 pass from Palmer (Graham kick), 14:58.

Fourth Quarter
Cle.—FG, Dawson 29, 10:41.
Cin.—FG, Graham 37, 15:00.
Attendance—65,788.

	Cleveland	Cincinnati
First downs	15	18
Rushes-yards	26-84	34-185
Passing	124	93
Punt returns	3-21	3-22
Kickoff returns	5-104	5-114
Interception returns	1-14	1-9
Comp.-att.-int.	16-24-1	13-27-1
Sacked-yards lost	2-14	0-0
Punts	3-42	3-40
Fumbles-lost	0-0	1-0
Penalties-yards	7-45	6-33
Time of possession	30:48	29:12

INDIVIDUAL STATISTICS
RUSHING—Cleveland, Droughns 21-74, Frye 4-14, Suggs 1-(minus 4). Cincinnati, Ru. Johnson 30-169, C. Perry 3-15, Palmer 1-1.
PASSING—Cleveland, Frye 16-24-1-138. Cincinnati, Palmer 13-27-1-93.
RECEIVING—Cleveland, Bryant 4-48, Northcutt 3-29, Heiden 3-27, Suggs 2-13, T. Smith 2-3, Shea 1-14, Droughns 1-7. Cincinnati, Houshmandzadeh 6-53, Ru. Johnson 3-11, C. Johnson 2-22, R. Kelly 2-7.
MISSED FIELD GOAL ATTEMPTS—None.
INTERCEPTIONS—Cleveland, Andra. Davis 1-14. Cincinnati, O'Neal 1-9.
KICKOFF RETURNS—Cleveland, Cribbs 4-87, McIntyre 1-17. Cincinnati, T. Perry 5-114.
PUNT RETURNS—Cleveland, Northcutt 3-21. Cincinnati, Ratliff 3-22.
SACKS—Cincinnati, Geathers 1, Thurman 0.5, J. Smith 0.5.

BUCCANEERS 20, PANTHERS 10
Sunday, December 11

Tampa Bay	7	3	3	7—20
Carolina	0	0	3	7—10

First Quarter
T.B.—C. Williams 14 run (M. Bryant kick), 10:56.

Second Quarter
T.B.—FG, M. Bryant 34, 15:00.

Third Quarter
T.B.—FG, M. Bryant 36, 10:31.
Car.—FG, Kasay 39, 13:40.

Fourth Quarter
T.B.—C. Williams 10 run (M. Bryant kick), 9:21.
Car.—Proehl 10 pass from Delhomme (Kasay kick), 14:37.
Attendance—73,467.

	Tampa Bay	Carolina
First downs	17	14
Rushes-yards	36-114	20-82
Passing	133	194
Punt returns	3-49	4-63
Kickoff returns	3-32	4-78
Interception returns	1-35	0-0
Comp.-att.-int.	20-27-0	21-33-1
Sacked-yards lost	1-5	2-26
Punts	6-43	4-45
Fumbles-lost	0-0	1-0
Penalties-yards	7-50	5-35
Time of possession	32:04	27:56

INDIVIDUAL STATISTICS
RUSHING—Tampa Bay, C. Williams 29-112, Alstott 4-2, Pittman 2-1, Simms 1-(minus 1). Carolina, Foster 14-46, S. Davis 4-23, Goings 1-7, Delhomme 1-6.
PASSING—Tampa Bay, Simms 20-27-0-138. Carolina, Delhomme 21-33-1-220.
RECEIVING—Tampa Bay, I. Hilliard 5-32, Galloway 4-39, Pittman 3-20, Smith 3-11, Alstott 2-20, C. Williams 2-4, Clayton 1-12. Carolina, S. Smith 5-103, Mangum 4-30, Goings 4-26, Proehl 3-36, Colbert 2-20, Foster 2-2, Hoover 1-3.
MISSED FIELD GOAL ATTEMPTS—Carolina, Kasay 42.
INTERCEPTIONS—Tampa Bay, Barber 1-35.
KICKOFF RETURNS—Tampa Bay, Shepherd 2-30, Alstott 1-2. Carolina, Smart 4-78.
PUNT RETURNS—Tampa Bay, Jones 3-49. Carolina, S. Smith 2-55, Gamble 2-8.
SACKS—Tampa Bay, Barber 1, Wyms 1. Carolina, Moorehead 1.

JETS 26, RAIDERS 10
Sunday, December 11

Oakland	0	3	0	7—10
N.Y. Jets	3	3	6	14—26

First Quarter
NYJ—FG, Nugent 33, 6:05.

Second Quarter
NYJ—FG, Nugent 20, 9:47.
Oak.—FG, Janikowski 42, 14:12.

Third Quarter
NYJ—FG, Nugent 35, 8:35.
NYJ—FG, Nugent 21, 12:05.

Fourth Quarter
NYJ—McCareins 4 pass from Bollinger (Nugent kick), :06.
Oak.—Porter 20 pass from M. Tuiasosopo (Janikowski kick), 5:45.
NYJ—Houston 2 run (Nugent kick), 13:04.
Attendance—77,561.

	Oakland	N.Y. Jets
First downs	14	23
Rushes-yards	17-95	43-184
Passing	84	110
Punt returns	1-4	1-7
Kickoff returns	6-136	3-62
Interception returns	0-0	2-15
Comp.-att.-int.	14-26-2	14-26-0
Sacked-yards lost	6-40	2-9
Punts	3-39	4-41
Fumbles-lost	3-2	1-0
Penalties-yards	13-88	5-69
Time of possession	24:22	35:38

INDIVIDUAL STATISTICS
RUSHING—Oakland, Jordan 14-49, M. Tuiasosopo 2-19, Whitted 1-27. New York, Houston 28-74, Askew 9-54, Bollinger 6-56.
PASSING—Oakland, M. Tuiasosopo 14-26-2-124. New York, Bollinger 14-26-0-119.
RECEIVING—Oakland, Porter 4-36, Jordan 4-30, Gabriel 2-24, Moss 2-18, C. Anderson 1-14, Ra. Williams 1-2. New York, McCareins 4-45, Sowell 4-20, Coles 3-30, Jolley 2-15, Cotchery 1-9.
MISSED FIELD GOAL ATTEMPTS—Oakland, Janikowski 29.
INTERCEPTIONS—New York, Law 1-15, Barrett 1-0.
KICKOFF RETURNS—Oakland, Carr 6-136. New York, Miller 2-62, Houston 1-0.
PUNT RETURNS—Oakland, Carr 1-4. New York, McCareins 1-7.
SACKS—Oakland, Burgess 2. New York, J. Abraham 2, Legree 1.5, Reed 1, Brown 1, B. Thomas 0.5.

STEELERS 21, BEARS 9
Sunday, December 11

Chicago	3	0	0	6—9
Pittsburgh	7	7	7	0—21

First Quarter
Pit.—Ward 14 pass from Roethlisberger (Reed kick), 5:44.
Chi.—FG, Gould 29, 12:30.

Second Quarter
Pit.—Bettis 1 run (Reed kick), 7:35.

Third Quarter

it.—Bettis 5 run (Reed kick), 9:37.

Fourth Quarter

hi.—T. Jones 1 run (kick failed), 1:22.

Attendance—61,237.

	Chicago	Pittsburgh
irst downs	15	20
ushes-yards	18-83	46-190
assing	185	173
unt returns	4-26	6-42
ickoff returns	4-54	3-59
nterception returns	0-0	0-0
omp.-att.-int.	17-35-0	13-20-0
acked-yards lost	3-22	0-0
unts	7-40	6-40
umbles-lost	2-0	4-0
enalties-yards	1-5	7-55
ime of possession	22:41	37:19

INDIVIDUAL STATISTICS

RUSHING—Chicago, T. Jones 14-72, Orton 3-8, Peterson 1-3. Pittsburgh, arker 21-68, Bettis 17-101, Haynes 4-8, Roethlisberger 2-(minus 2), reider 1-12, Randle El 1-3.

PASSING—Chicago, Orton 17-35-0-207. Pittsburgh, Roethlisberger 13-0-0-173.

RECEIVING—Chicago, Muhammad 8-91, T. Jones 4-23, Berrian 1-43, lark 1-27, Gage 1-11, B. Johnson 1-7, Wade 1-5. Pittsburgh, Ward 3-27, arker 2-45, Haynes 2-29, Wilson 2-29, Randle El 2-28, Morgan 1-10, reider 1-5.

MISSED FIELD GOAL ATTEMPTS—None.

INTERCEPTIONS—None.

KICKOFF RETURNS—Chicago, Azumah 2-37, McKie 1-17, Idonije 1-0. ittsburgh, Morgan 2-38, Colclough 1-21.

PUNT RETURNS—Chicago, Wade 4-26. Pittsburgh, Randle El 5-23, I. aylor 1-19.

SACKS—Pittsburgh, Haggans 1, Porter 1, von Oelhoffen 1.

TITANS 13, TEXANS 10

Sunday, December 11

Houston	3	7	0	0—10
Tennessee	0	3	7	3—13

First Quarter

lou.—FG, K. Brown 30, 14:57.

Second Quarter

en.—FG, Bironas 23, 10:32.

lou.—D. Davis 3 pass from Carr (K. Brown kick), 14:41.

Third Quarter

en.—P. Jones 52 punt return (Bironas kick), 11:53.

Fourth Quarter

en.—FG, Bironas 21, 14:50.

Attendance—69,149.

	Houston	Tennessee
First downs	12	15
Rushes-yards	26-152	30-93
Passing	82	208
Punt returns	2-(-2)	3-80
Kickoff returns	4-123	3-25
nterception returns	0-0	0-0
Comp.-att.-int.	17-26-0	18-30-0
Sacked-yards lost	6-34	0-0
Punts	9-36	5-43
Fumbles-lost	0-0	0-0
Penalties-yards	8-72	4-56
Time of possession	28:38	31:22

INDIVIDUAL STATISTICS

RUSHING—Houston, D. Davis 22-139, Wells 2-3, Gaffney 1-6, K. Brown 1-4. Tennessee, Brown 16-53, Henry 8-19, McNair 4-17, Payton 2-4.

PASSING—Houston, Carr 17-26-0-116. Tennessee, McNair 18-30-0-208.

RECEIVING—Houston, D. Davis 7-50, An. Johnson 3-27, Bradford 3-20, Rivers 3-18, Gaffney 1-1. Tennessee, Henry 3-54, Brown 3-49, Troupe 3-28, Calico 2-20, Bennett 2-15, Scaife 2-12, Fleming 1-15, Guenther 1-8, Payton 1-7.

MISSED FIELD GOAL ATTEMPTS—Houston, K. Brown 37, 31. Tennessee, Bironas 46.

INTERCEPTIONS—None.

KICKOFF RETURNS—Houston, Mathis 4-123. Tennessee, P. Jones 1-16, Fleming 1-9, Payton 1-0.

PUNT RETURNS—Houston, Mathis 2-(minus 2). Tennessee, P. Jones 3-80.

SACKS—Tennessee, Bulluck 2, Vanden Bosch 2, Haynesworth 1, LaBoy 0.5, Sirmon 0.5.

COLTS 26, JAGUARS 18

Sunday, December 11

Indianapolis	7	10	6	3—26
Jacksonville	0	3	0	15—18

First Quarter

Ind.—Harrison 9 pass from Manning (Vanderjagt kick), 10:20.

Second Quarter

Jac.—FG, Scobee 27, :49.

Ind.—Harrison 65 pass from Manning (Vanderjagt kick), 5:39.

Ind.—FG, Vanderjagt 40, 15:00.

Third Quarter

Ind.—FG, Vanderjagt 34, 6:46.

Ind.—FG, Vanderjagt 38, 14:15.

Fourth Quarter

Ind.—FG, Vanderjagt 46, 2:47.

Jac.—Garrard 5 run (Scobee kick), 10:52.

Jac.—J. Smith 1 pass from Garrard (Garrard run), 13:06.

Attendance—67,164.

	Indianapolis	Jacksonville
First downs	25	18
Rushes-yards	34-99	23-74
Passing	300	250
Punt returns	2-2	3-45
Kickoff returns	2-70	6-123
Interception returns	0-0	0-0
Comp.-att.-int.	24-37-0	26-35-0
Sacked-yards lost	3-24	0-0
Punts	3-46	5-39
Fumbles-lost	0-0	4-3
Penalties-yards	5-47	7-65
Time of possession	33:58	26:02

INDIVIDUAL STATISTICS

RUSHING—Indianapolis, James 30-93, Manning 4-6. Jacksonville, F. Taylor 10-19, G. Jones 7-43, Garrard 5-19, R. Williams 1-(minus 7).

PASSING—Indianapolis, Manning 24-36-0-324, H. Smith 0-1-0-0. Jacksonville, Garrard 26-35-0-250.

RECEIVING—Indianapolis, James 9-61, Harrison 6-137, Wayne 4-81, Fletcher 3-31, Clark 2-14. Jacksonville, J. Smith 8-102, Brady 5-43, Wrighster 4-21, M. Jones 3-28, Wilford 3-23, R. Williams 2-25, G. Jones 1-8.

MISSED FIELD GOAL ATTEMPTS—None.

INTERCEPTIONS—None.

KICKOFF RETURNS—Indianapolis, Rhodes 2-70. Jacksonville, Wimbush 5-92, Alexis 1-31.

PUNT RETURNS—Indianapolis, Walters 2-2. Jacksonville, Pearman 3-45.

SACKS—Jacksonville, Hayward 2, Maddox 1.

VIKINGS 27, RAMS 13

Sunday, December 11

St. Louis	0	6	7	0—13
Minnesota	7	6	14	0—27

First Quarter

Min.—K. Robinson 13 run (Edinger kick), 9:24.

Second Quarter

St.L.—FG, J. Wilkins 51, 8:06.

Min.—FG, Edinger 37, 10:08.

Min.—FG, Edinger 44, 14:01.

St.L.—FG, J. Wilkins 23, 15:00.

Third Quarter

St.L.—Fitzpatrick 14 run (J. Wilkins kick), 4:18.

Min.—M. Bennett 7 run (Edinger kick), 6:55.

Min.—Fason 1 run (Edinger kick), 11:49.

Attendance—64,005.

	St. Louis	Minnesota
First downs	20	16
Rushes-yards	29-108	29-113
Passing	229	146
Punt returns	4-25	1-0
Kickoff returns	6-111	3-104
Interception returns	0-0	5-31
Comp.-att.-int.	26-45-5	16-25-0
Sacked-yards lost	1-6	0-0

	St. Louis	Minnesota
Punts	5-42	8-38
Fumbles-lost	2-1	3-2
Penalties-yards	9-60	5-60
Time of possession	33:49	26:11

INDIVIDUAL STATISTICS

RUSHING—St. Louis, S. Jackson 19-67, M. Faulk 5-25, Fitzpatrick 5-16. Minnesota, M. Bennett 18-70, Fason 6-19, K. Robinson 2-14, Williamson 1-11, Moore 1-0, B. Johnson 1-(minus 1).

PASSING—St. Louis, Fitzpatrick 26-45-5-235. Minnesota, B. Johnson 16-25-0-146.

RECEIVING—St. Louis, Holt 10-95, Bruce 5-66, M. Faulk 4-32, McDonald 2-18, Curtis 2-13, Hedgecock 2-5, Manumaleuna 1-6. Minnesota, M. Bennett 4-6, Wiggins 3-18, Burleson 2-20, Kleinsasser 2-11, M. Robinson 1-49, K. Robinson 1-15, Williamson 1-12, T. Taylor 1-8, Moore 1-7.

MISSED FIELD GOAL ATTEMPTS—None.

INTERCEPTIONS—Minnesota, B. Williams 2-31, Winfield 1-0, Smoot 1-0, Sharper 1-0.

KICKOFF RETURNS—St. Louis, Allen 6-111. Minnesota, K. Robinson 3-104.

PUNT RETURNS—St. Louis, Allen 3-20, Furrey 1-5. Minnesota, Moore 1-0.

SACKS—Minnesota, Scott 1.

PATRIOTS 35, BILLS 7
Sunday, December 11

New England	7	7	7	14—35
Buffalo	0	0	0	7— 7

First Quarter
N.E.—Brady 3 run (Vinatieri kick), 9:27.
Second Quarter
N.E.—Dillon 12 run (Vinatieri kick), 6:47.
Third Quarter
N.E.—T. Brown 5 pass from Brady (Vinatieri kick), 9:33.
Fourth Quarter
N.E.—Fauria 2 pass from Brady (Vinatieri kick), 6:42.
N.E.—Sanders 39 interception return (Vinatieri kick), 12:17.
Buf.—Reed 51 pass from Losman (Lindell kick), 12:46.
Attendance—71,810.

	New England	Buffalo
First downs	32	8
Rushes-yards	41-159	12-14
Passing	335	169
Punt returns	3-18	2-45
Kickoff returns	1-29	6-149
Interception returns	3-39	2-20
Comp.-att.-int.	30-40-2	10-27-3
Sacked-yards lost	1-1	2-12
Punts	4-36	6-44
Fumbles-lost	0-0	0-0
Penalties-yards	9-83	7-50
Time of possession	41:59	18:01

INDIVIDUAL STATISTICS

RUSHING—New England, Dillon 22-102, Cloud 9-24, Faulk 5-14, Brady 4-17, Flutie 1-2. Buffalo, McGahee 8-3, S. Williams 3-4, Losman 1-7.

PASSING—New England, Brady 29-38-2-329, Flutie 1-2-0-7. Buffalo, Losman 10-27-3-181.

RECEIVING—New England, Faulk 6-71, T. Brown 6-45, Branch 5-83, Dillon 4-29, Givens 3-58, Watson 3-35, Fauria 2-8, Andre. Davis 1-7. Buffalo, Evans 4-83, Reed 2-76, Aiken 1-8, Parrish 1-5, McGahee 1-5, Campbell 1-4.

MISSED FIELD GOAL ATTEMPTS—Buffalo, Lindell 32.

INTERCEPTIONS—New England, Sanders 1-39, Hobbs 1-0, Samuel 1-0. Buffalo, Fletcher 1-20, Clements 1-0.

KICKOFF RETURNS—New England, B. Johnson 1-29. Buffalo, McGee 5-126, Neufeld 1-23.

PUNT RETURNS—New England, Dwight 2-15, T. Brown 1-3. Buffalo, Parrish 2-45.

SACKS—New England, Colvin 1, Seymour 1. Buffalo, Schobel 1.

DOLPHINS 23, CHARGERS 21
Sunday, December 11

Miami	0	3	17	3—23
San Diego	7	0	0	14—21

First Quarter
S.D.—McCardell 8 pass from Brees (Kaeding kick), 12:20.
Second Quarter
Mia.—FG, Mare 29, 11:21.

Third Quarter
Mia.—FG, Mare 39, 3:17.
Mia.—Chambers 8 pass from Frerotte (Mare kick), 4:25.
Mia.—Chambers 35 pass from Frerotte (Mare kick), 11:34.
Fourth Quarter
S.D.—Brees 4 run (Kaeding kick), 4:26.
Mia.—FG, Mare 20, 13:49.
S.D.—Gates 8 pass from Brees (Kaeding kick), 14:45.
Attendance—65,026.

	Miami	San Diego
First downs	14	27
Rushes-yards	26-71	27-96
Passing	229	245
Punt returns	0-0	2-1
Kickoff returns	3-90	6-145
Interception returns	1-0	0-0
Comp.-att.-int.	14-22-0	35-52-1
Sacked-yards lost	0-0	3-34
Punts	3-42	4-35
Fumbles-lost	2-2	2-2
Penalties-yards	3-12	7-49
Time of possession	19:43	40:17

INDIVIDUAL STATISTICS

RUSHING—Miami, Brown 11-30, R. Williams 11-28, Frerotte 4-13. San Diego, Tomlinson 21-75, Brees 3-11, Neal 2-6, Turner 1-4.

PASSING—Miami, Frerotte 14-22-0-229. San Diego, Brees 35-52-1-279.

RECEIVING—Miami, Chambers 8-121, Booker 3-78, McMichael 2-12 Diamond 1-18. San Diego, Gates 13-123, McCardell 7-58, Neal 5-21, E. Parker 4-37, Caldwell 4-29, Peelle 1-11, Tomlinson 1-0.

MISSED FIELD GOAL ATTEMPTS—None.

INTERCEPTIONS—Miami, Z. Thomas 1-0.

KICKOFF RETURNS—Miami, Welker 3-90. San Diego, Sproles 6-145.

PUNT RETURNS—San Diego, Sproles 2-1.

SACKS—Miami, Holliday 1, D. Bowens 1, Bell 1.

SEAHAWKS 41, 49ERS 3
Sunday, December 11

San Francisco	3	0	0	0— 3
Seattle	7	17	14	3—41

First Quarter
Sea.—Engram 28 pass from Hasselbeck (J. Brown kick), 4:20.
S.F.—FG, Nedney 39, 10:25.
Second Quarter
Sea.—Stevens 8 pass from Hasselbeck (J. Brown kick), :04.
Sea.—Jurevicius 21 pass from Hasselbeck (J. Brown kick), :22.
Sea.—FG, J. Brown 52, 7:32.
Third Quarter
Sea.—Engram 7 pass from Hasselbeck (J. Brown kick), 7:47.
Sea.—Alexander 3 run (J. Brown kick), 13:31.
Fourth Quarter
Sea.—FG, J. Brown 52, 9:45.
Attendance—66,690.

	San Francisco	Seattle
First downs	8	31
Rushes-yards	21-62	40-185
Passing	51	253
Punt returns	0-0	3-9
Kickoff returns	7-134	2-48
Interception returns	1-0	1-14
Comp.-att.-int.	9-22-1	24-30-1
Sacked-yards lost	4-26	1-6
Punts	8-37	2-39
Fumbles-lost	3-1	1-0
Penalties-yards	7-82	8-54
Time of possession	23:47	36:13

INDIVIDUAL STATISTICS

RUSHING—San Francisco, Barlow 11-33, A. Smith 6-20, Gore 2-5, Hicks 2-4. Seattle, Alexander 21-108, Morris 7-22, Weaver 5-41, Strong 4-8, S. Wallace 2-(minus 3), Hasselbeck 1-9.

PASSING—San Francisco, A. Smith 9-22-1-77. Seattle, Hasselbeck 21-25-1-226, S. Wallace 3-5-0-33.

RECEIVING—San Francisco, Lloyd 3-37, Barlow 2-30, Gore 1-6, McAddley 1-4, Hetherington 1-2, Hicks 1-(minus 2). Seattle, Engram 6-65, Jurevicius 4-63, Alexander 4-20, Hackett 3-43, Stevens 3-28, Warrick 2-22, Hannam 1-12, Strong 1-6.

MISSED FIELD GOAL ATTEMPTS—Seattle, J. Brown 50.

INTERCEPTIONS—San Francisco, B. Thornton 1-0. Seattle, Tatupu 1-14.
KICKOFF RETURNS—San Francisco, Hicks 6-114, Amey 1-20. Seattle, Scobey 2-27.
PUNT RETURNS—Seattle, J. Williams 3-9.
SACKS—San Francisco, J. Peterson 0.5, T. Hall 0.5. Seattle, Tubbs 2, Tatupu 1, Team 1.

REDSKINS 17, CARDINALS 13
Sunday, December 11

Washington	0	3	14	0—17
Arizona	0	10	3	0—13

Second Quarter
Was.—FG, Hall 41, :10.
Ariz.—McCoy 2 pass from Warner (Rackers kick), 6:33.
Ariz.—FG, Rackers 44, 13:54.
Third Quarter
Was.—Portis 15 run (Hall kick), 7:40.
Ariz.—FG, Rackers 20, 11:20.
Was.—A. Brown 91 kickoff return (Hall kick), 11:31.
Attendance—46,654.

	Washington	Arizona
First downs	16	17
Rushes-yards	34-109	18-62
Passing	122	240
Punt returns	0-0	4-34
Kickoff returns	3-136	4-99
Interception returns	1-2	3-84
Comp.-att.-int.	18-28-3	25-41-1
Sacked-yards lost	0-0	2-15
Punts	5-43	3-43
Fumbles-lost	3-0	3-3
Penalties-yards	5-63	8-65
Time of possession	33:19	26:41

INDIVIDUAL STATISTICS
RUSHING—Washington, Portis 26-105, Betts 5-6, Brunell 3-(minus 2). Arizona, Arrington 9-26, Shipp 7-27, Boldin 1-6, Warner 1-3.
PASSING—Washington, Brunell 18-28-3-122. Arizona, Warner 25-41-1-255.
RECEIVING—Washington, Moss 7-56, Cooley 4-25, Portis 3-16, Royal 2-23, Jacobs 1-7, Betts 1-(minus 5). Arizona, Boldin 9-114, B. Johnson 5-61, Fitzgerald 4-23, Bergen 3-41, McCoy 2-8, Arrington 1-6, Shipp 1-2.
MISSED FIELD GOAL ATTEMPTS—None.
INTERCEPTIONS—Washington, Taylor 1-2. Arizona, Wilson 1-36, Rolle 1-29, Macklin 1-19.
KICKOFF RETURNS—Washington, A. Brown 3-136. Arizona, Swinton 4-99.
PUNT RETURNS—Arizona, Swinton 4-34.
SACKS—Washington, Prioleau 1, Evans 1.

BRONCOS 12, RAVENS 10
Sunday, December 11

Baltimore	3	0	0	7—10
Denver	3	3	6	0—12

First Quarter
Bal.—FG, Stover 29, 2:01.
Den.—FG, Elam 47, 6:16.
Second Quarter
Den.—FG, Elam 48, 15:00.
Third Quarter
Den.—K. Johnson 7 pass from Plummer (kick failed), 8:52.
Fourth Quarter
Bal.—Clayton 39 pass from Boller (Stover kick), 13:08.
Attendance—75,651.

	Baltimore	Denver
First downs	20	17
Rushes-yards	23-72	32-96
Passing	251	222
Punt returns	0-0	1-14
Kickoff returns	3-140	3-62
Interception returns	0-0	2-10
Comp.-att.-int.	23-40-2	19-33-0
Sacked-yards lost	2-0	2-14
Punts	3-36	5-36
Fumbles-lost	3-2	1-1
Penalties-yards	3-20	4-31
Time of possession	28:06	31:54

INDIVIDUAL STATISTICS
RUSHING—Baltimore, C. Taylor 20-59, Boller 2-3, Clayton 1-10. Denver, Bell 16-63, Mi. Anderson 8-21, Dayne 4-7, Plummer 3-(minus 3), Lelie 1-8.
PASSING—Baltimore, Boller 23-39-2-251, Clayton 0-1-0-0. Denver, Plummer 19-33-0-236.
RECEIVING—Baltimore, Clayton 7-105, Mason 6-53, Heap 5-65, C. Taylor 3-14, Wilcox 2-14. Denver, Smith 5-64, K. Johnson 3-40, Adams 3-35, Lelie 2-42, Bell 2-16, S. Alexander 1-15, Devoe 1-9, Putzier 1-8, Dayne 1-7.
MISSED FIELD GOAL ATTEMPTS—None.
INTERCEPTIONS—Denver, Bailey 1-10, N. Ferguson 1-0.
KICKOFF RETURNS—Baltimore, Sams 3-140. Denver, Adams 1-25, Da. Williams 1-19, Mi. Anderson 1-18.
PUNT RETURNS—Denver, Adams 1-14.
SACKS—Baltimore, A. Thomas 1, Franklin 1. Denver, Ekuban 1, Team 1.

COWBOYS 31, CHIEFS 28
Sunday, December 11

Kansas City	7	7	7	7—28
Dallas	0	17	0	14—31

First Quarter
K.C.—L. Johnson 11 run (Tynes kick), 5:28.
Second Quarter
Dal.—FG, Cundiff 34, 7:00.
K.C.—L. Johnson 1 run (Tynes kick), 9:41.
Dal.—T. Glenn 71 pass from Bledsoe (Cundiff kick), 11:05.
Dal.—Witten 26 pass from Bledsoe (Cundiff kick), 14:20.
Third Quarter
K.C.—L. Johnson 21 run (Tynes kick), 6:21.
Fourth Quarter
Dal.—T. Glenn 6 run (Cundiff kick), 1:53.
K.C.—Kennison 47 pass from Green (Tynes kick), 11:05.
Dal.—Campbell 1 pass from Bledsoe (Cundiff kick), 14:38.
Attendance—63,432.

	Kansas City	Dallas
First downs	25	21
Rushes-yards	28-161	28-129
Passing	332	316
Punt returns	1-(-5)	0-0
Kickoff returns	6-161	5-130
Interception returns	0-0	0-0
Comp.-att.-int.	20-32-0	22-34-0
Sacked-yards lost	2-8	4-16
Punts	5-39	5-42
Fumbles-lost	1-1	1-0
Penalties-yards	3-17	5-45
Time of possession	28:12	31:48

INDIVIDUAL STATISTICS
RUSHING—Kansas City, L. Johnson 26-143, Kennison 1-15, De. Brown 1-3. Dallas, Barber 15-82, J. Jones 12-41, T. Glenn 1-6.
PASSING—Kansas City, Green 20-32-0-340. Dallas, Bledsoe 22-34-0-332.
RECEIVING—Kansas City, Gonzalez 5-94, Parker 5-79, Kennison 4-92, L. Johnson 3-28, D. Hall 2-42, Richardson 1-5. Dallas, Witten 7-93, T. Glenn 6-138, K. Johnson 3-35, Polite 3-33, Barber 2-32, Campbell 1-1.
MISSED FIELD GOAL ATTEMPTS—Kansas City, Tynes 41.
INTERCEPTIONS—None.
KICKOFF RETURNS—Kansas City, D. Hall 6-161. Dallas, Thompson 5-130.
PUNT RETURNS—Kansas City, D. Hall 1-(minus 5).
SACKS—Kansas City, Allen 2, Dalton 1, Browning 1. Dallas, Fujita 1, Burnett 1.

GIANTS 26, EAGLES 23
Sunday, December 11

N.Y. Giants	7	10	3	3	3—26
Philadelphia	7	10	0	6	0—23

First Quarter
NYG—Barber 4 pass from Manning (Feely kick), 5:38.
Phi.—Moats 40 run (Akers kick), 7:08.
Second Quarter
NYG—Manning 1 run (Feely kick), 2:29.
NYG—FG, Feely 24, 10:01.
Phi.—Moats 18 run (Akers kick), 13:07.
Phi.—FG, Akers 42, 14:39.
Third Quarter
NYG—FG, Feely 21, 11:43.

2005 REVIEW Week 14

Fourth Quarter
NYG—FG, Feely 27, 4:21.
Phi.—FG, Akers 36, 8:32.
Phi.—FG, Akers 50, 13:08.

Overtime
NYG—FG, Feely 36, 11:05.
Attendance—67,443.

	N.Y. Giants	Philadelphia
First downs	28	17
Rushes-yards	40-138	25-175
Passing	299	162
Punt returns	2-19	1-28
Kickoff returns	5-95	5-122
Interception returns	0-0	3-13
Comp.-att.-int.	28-44-3	14-32-0
Sacked-yards lost	1-13	6-28
Punts	2-35	4-37
Fumbles-lost	0-0	1-1
Penalties-yards	10-71	9-101
Time of possession	43:30	27:35

INDIVIDUAL STATISTICS
RUSHING—New York, Barber 32-124, Manning 4-8, Jacobs 2-0, T. Carter 1-4, Ward 1-2. Philadelphia, Moats 11-114, Mahe 7-42, Gordon 6-17, McMahon 1-2.

PASSING—New York, Manning 28-44-3-312. Philadelphia, McMahon 14-32-0-190.

RECEIVING—New York, Shockey 10-107, Toomer 6-54, Barber 5-71, Burress 2-37, Shiancoe 2-15, Finn 2-14, T. Carter 1-14. Philadelphia, R. Brown 5-72, Mahe 3-19, McMullen 2-46, Smith 2-25, McCants 1-20, G. Lewis 1-8.

MISSED FIELD GOAL ATTEMPTS—Philadelphia, Akers 49.

INTERCEPTIONS—Philadelphia, M. Lewis 1-13, S. Brown 1-0, Dawkins 1-0.

KICKOFF RETURNS—New York, Ponder 5-95. Philadelphia, Hood 5-122.

PUNT RETURNS—New York, Morton 2-19. Philadelphia, Mahe 1-28.

SACKS—New York, Strahan 2, Umenyiora 1.5, Robbins 1.5, Wilson 1. Philadelphia, Dawkins 1.

PACKERS 16, LIONS 13
Sunday, December 11

Detroit	13	0	0	0	—13
Green Bay	3	7	0	3	—16

First Quarter
Det.—FG, Hanson 19, 3:57.
Det.—FG, Hanson 23, 7:49.
G.B.—FG, Longwell 36, 12:34.
Det.—R. Williams 4 pass from Garcia (Hanson kick), 14:17.

Second Quarter
G.B.—Gado 64 run (Longwell kick), 10:04.

Fourth Quarter
G.B.—FG, Longwell 39, :38.

Overtime
G.B.—FG, Longwell 28, 5:17.
Attendance—70,019.

	Detroit	Green Bay
First downs	11	19
Rushes-yards	31-129	35-181
Passing	112	149
Punt returns	3-13	2-7
Kickoff returns	4-133	5-83
Interception returns	1-28	0-0
Comp.-att.-int.	13-24-0	21-32-1
Sacked-yards lost	0-0	3-21
Punts	6-41	5-34
Fumbles-lost	2-0	1-1
Penalties-yards	5-50	5-25
Time of possession	28:08	37:09

INDIVIDUAL STATISTICS
RUSHING—Detroit, Pinner 13-25, Jones 9-63, Bryson 5-16, Garcia 4-25. Green Bay, Gado 29-171, Fisher 4-0, Favre 1-7, Chatman 1-3.

PASSING—Detroit, Garcia 13-24-0-112. Green Bay, Favre 21-31-1-170, Gado 0-1-0-0.

RECEIVING—Detroit, R. Williams 4-53, Pinner 3-8, Pollard 2-13, Vines 1-22, Jones 1-9, M. Williams 1-6, Bryson 1-1. Green Bay, D. Martin 5-38, Henderson 4-38, Driver 4-32, D. Lee 3-20, Ferguson 2-28, Gado 1-9, Thurman 1-9, Fisher 1-(minus 4).

MISSED FIELD GOAL ATTEMPTS—Green Bay, Longwell 38.

INTERCEPTIONS—Detroit, Bly 1-28.

KICKOFF RETURNS—Detroit, McQuarters 3-115, Bryson 1-18. Green Bay, Carroll 3-45, Chatman 1-33, Peterson 1-5.

PUNT RETURNS—Detroit, McQuarters 3-13. Green Bay, Chatman 2-7.

SACKS—Detroit, Hall 1, S. Rogers 1, Team 1.

FALCONS 36, SAINTS 17
Monday, December 12

New Orleans	3	14	0	0	—17
Atlanta	7	14	9	6	—36

First Quarter
Atl.—Duckett 1 run (T. Peterson kick), 4:38.
N.O.—FG, Carney 47, 11:55.

Second Quarter
N.O.—A. Smith 6 run (Carney kick), 3:47.
Atl.—Vick 2 run (T. Peterson kick), 8:54.
Atl.—R. White 54 pass from Vick (T. Peterson kick), 13:11.
N.O.—Hakim 9 pass from Brooks (Carney kick), 14:49.

Third Quarter
Atl.—Vick 17 run (T. Peterson kick), 7:10.
Atl.—Safety, 14:20.

Fourth Quarter
Atl.—FG, T. Peterson 43, 6:27.
Atl.—FG, T. Peterson 20, 11:59.
Attendance—70,083.

	New Orleans	Atlanta
First downs	22	19
Rushes-yards	24-125	32-127
Passing	207	279
Punt returns	3-15	4-28
Kickoff returns	6-104	5-101
Interception returns	1-19	0-0
Comp.-att.-int.	27-46-0	13-25-1
Sacked-yards lost	3-12	0-0
Punts	8-48	6-46
Fumbles-lost	1-1	1-0
Penalties-yards	10-107	9-74
Time of possession	30:42	29:18

INDIVIDUAL STATISTICS
RUSHING—New Orleans, A. Smith 11-60, Stecker 7-35, Brooks 4-24, A. Thomas 1-3, Karney 1-3. Atlanta, Dunn 14-73, Duckett 10-13, Vick 6-38, Schaub 1-10, R. White 1-(minus 7).

PASSING—New Orleans, Brooks 27-46-0-219. Atlanta, Vick 12-23-1-231, Schaub 1-2-0-48.

RECEIVING—New Orleans, Horn 5-54, Stallworth 5-43, Hilton 4-41, Hakim 4-32, A. Smith 3-12, Stecker 2-12, L. Hall 2-11, Henderson 1-8, A. Thomas 1-6. Atlanta, Crumpler 3-94, Jenkins 3-33, R. White 2-65, Dunn 2-39, Griffith 2-12, Finneran 1-36.

MISSED FIELD GOAL ATTEMPTS—None.

INTERCEPTIONS—New Orleans, Craft 1-19.

KICKOFF RETURNS—New Orleans, Stecker 6-104. Atlanta, Griffith 3-62, D. Hall 1-22, Pathon 1-17.

PUNT RETURNS—New Orleans, Hakim 3-15. Atlanta, D. Hall 4-28.

SACKS—Atlanta, Lake 1, Lavalais 1, Shropshire 1.

WEEK 15

STANDINGS

AMERICAN FOOTBALL CONFERENCE

EAST DIVISION

	W	L	T	Pct.	PF	PA
New England	9	5	0	.643	322	289
Miami	7	7	0	.500	266	281
Buffalo	4	10	0	.286	208	310
N.Y. Jets	3	11	0	.214	189	298

NORTH DIVISION

	W	L	T	Pct.	PF	PA
Cincinnati	11	3	0	.786	391	276
Pittsburgh	9	5	0	.643	313	237
Baltimore	5	9	0	.357	219	256
Cleveland	5	9	0	.357	212	244

SOUTH DIVISION

	W	L	T	Pct.	PF	PA
Indianapolis	13	1	0	.929	409	206
Jacksonville	10	4	0	.714	283	236
Tennessee	4	10	0	.286	276	357
Houston	2	12	0	.143	223	373

WEST DIVISION

	W	L	T	Pct.	PF	PA
Denver	11	3	0	.786	350	248
San Diego	9	5	0	.643	404	269
Kansas City	8	6	0	.571	346	315
Oakland	4	10	0	.286	266	331

NATIONAL FOOTBALL CONFERENCE

EAST DIVISION

	W	L	T	Pct.	PF	PA
N.Y. Giants	10	4	0	.714	372	258
Dallas	8	6	0	.571	291	268
Washington	8	6	0	.571	293	253
Philadelphia	6	8	0	.429	269	330

NORTH DIVISION

	W	L	T	Pct.	PF	PA
Chicago	10	4	0	.714	226	151
Minnesota	8	6	0	.571	249	304
Detroit	4	10	0	.286	220	298
Green Bay	3	11	0	.214	258	303

SOUTH DIVISION

	W	L	T	Pct.	PF	PA
Carolina	10	4	0	.714	327	224
Tampa Bay	9	5	0	.643	246	237
Atlanta	8	6	0	.571	316	270
New Orleans	3	11	0	.214	210	358

WEST DIVISION

	W	L	T	Pct.	PF	PA
Seattle	12	2	0	.857	407	235
St. Louis	5	9	0	.357	323	395
Arizona	4	10	0	.286	271	349
San Francisco	2	12	0	.143	195	391

TOP PERFORMANCES

100-YARD RUSHING GAMES

Player, team & opponent	Att.	Yds.	TD
Tiki Barber, NYG vs. K.C.	29	220	2
Shaun Alexander, Sea. at Ten.	26	172	1
Larry Johnson, K.C. at NYG	31	167	2
LaMont Jordan, Oak. vs. Cle.	25	132	0
Rudi Johnson, Cin. at Det.	24	117	2
Michael Turner, S.D. at Ind.	8	113	1
Clinton Portis, Was. vs. Dal.	23	112	0
Jamal Lewis, Bal. vs. G.B.	22	105	1

300-YARD PASSING GAMES

Player, team & opponent	Att.	Cmp.	Yds.	TD	Int.
Peyton Manning, Ind. vs. S.D.	45	26	336	1	2
Brooks Bollinger, NYJ at Mia.	42	28	327	2	0
Steve McNair, Ten. vs. Sea.	38	23	310	2	0

100-YARD RECEIVING GAMES

Player, team & opponent	Rec.	Yds.	TD
David Givens, N.E. vs. T.B.	6	137	1
Rod Smith, Den. at Buf.	11	137	1
Marvin Harrison, Ind. vs. S.D.	8	135	0
Anquan Boldin, Ariz. at Hou.	8	134	1
Ben Troupe, Ten. vs. Sea.	6	116	0
Todd Heap, Bal. vs. G.B.	9	110	2
Eric Moulds, Buf. vs. Den.	9	110	0
Doug Jolley, NYJ at Mia.	9	102	1
Donte' Stallworth, N.O. vs. Car.	5	102	1

RESULTS

SATURDAY, DECEMBER 17
NEW ENGLAND 28, Tampa Bay 0
N.Y. GIANTS 27, Kansas City 17
Denver 28, BUFFALO 17

SUNDAY, DECEMBER 18
Seattle 28, TENNESSEE 24
Carolina 27, NEW ORLEANS 10
Philadelphia 17, ST. LOUIS 16
HOUSTON 30, Arizona 19
San Diego 26, INDIANAPOLIS 17
JACKSONVILLE 10, San Francisco 9
Pittsburgh 18, MINNESOTA 3
MIAMI 24, N.Y. Jets 20
Cincinnati 41, DETROIT 17
WASHINGTON 35, Dallas 7
Cleveland 9, OAKLAND 7
CHICAGO 16, Atlanta 3

MONDAY, DECEMBER 19
BALTIMORE 48, Green Bay 3

2005 REVIEW *Week 15*

– 199 –

PATRIOTS 28, BUCCANEERS 0
Saturday, December 17

Tampa Bay	0	0	0	0— 0
New England	7	14	0	7—28

First Quarter
N.E.—Ashworth 1 pass from Brady (Vinatieri kick), 6:08.

Second Quarter
N.E.—Dillon 3 run (Vinatieri kick), 12:52.
N.E.—Givens 16 pass from Brady (Vinatieri kick), 14:33.

Fourth Quarter
N.E.—Dillon 2 pass from Brady (Vinatieri kick), 3:28.
Attendance—68,756.

	Tampa Bay	New England
First downs	12	22
Rushes-yards	18-30	32-83
Passing	108	253
Punt returns	3-28	5-31
Kickoff returns	4-64	1-20
Interception returns	0-0	0-0
Comp.-att.-int.	21-34-0	20-31-0
Sacked-yards lost	7-47	1-5
Punts	7-44	6-40
Fumbles-lost	2-1	0-0
Penalties-yards	8-58	8-54
Time of possession	26:32	33:28

INDIVIDUAL STATISTICS
RUSHING—Tampa Bay, C. Williams 14-23, Pittman 2-6, Alstott 1-2, Simms 1-(minus 1). New England, Dillon 19-48, Faulk 6-18, Brady 3-6, Givens 2-13, Flutie 2-(minus 2).
PASSING—Tampa Bay, Simms 21-34-0-155. New England, Brady 20-31-0-258.
RECEIVING—Tampa Bay, I. Hilliard 5-50, Galloway 4-38, Smith 4-26, C. Williams 3-4, Clayton 2-26, Alstott 2-8, Pittman 1-3. New England, Givens 6-137, Branch 2-27, Fauria 2-20, Faulk 2-8, Dwight 1-27, Andre. Davis 1-19, Pass 1-4, Ashworth 1-1.
MISSED FIELD GOAL ATTEMPTS—None.
INTERCEPTIONS—None.
KICKOFF RETURNS—Tampa Bay, Shepherd 2-40, Graham 1-22, Bradley 1-2. New England, B. Johnson 1-20.
PUNT RETURNS—Tampa Bay, Jones 3-28. New England, Dwight 3-22, T. Brown 2-9.
SACKS—Tampa Bay, Rice 1. New England, McGinest 2, Bruschi 2, Vrabel 1, Hawkins 1, Colvin 1.

GIANTS 27, CHIEFS 17
Saturday, December 17

Kansas City	0	3	7	7—17
N.Y. Giants	0	10	3	14—27

Second Quarter
K.C.—FG, Tynes 19, 8:24.
NYG—Barber 41 run (Feely kick), 12:13.
NYG—FG, Feely 41, 14:32.

Third Quarter
K.C.—L. Johnson 14 run (Tynes kick), 2:59.
NYG—FG, Feely 35, 14:12.

Fourth Quarter
NYG—Toomer 31 pass from Manning (Feely kick), 2:08.
K.C.—L. Johnson 1 run (Tynes kick), 6:31.
NYG—Barber 20 run (Feely kick), 12:12.
Attendance—78,625.

	Kansas City	N.Y. Giants
First downs	22	22
Rushes-yards	34-188	34-223
Passing	174	183
Punt returns	2-7	1-(-4)
Kickoff returns	6-118	4-94
Interception returns	1-0	1-16
Comp.-att.-int.	15-28-1	17-32-1
Sacked-yards lost	1-2	1-3
Punts	5-38	3-39
Fumbles-lost	2-2	1-1
Penalties-yards	9-75	7-70
Time of possession	30:04	29:56

INDIVIDUAL STATISTICS
RUSHING—Kansas City, L. Johnson 31-167, Green 2-21, Richardson 1-0. New York, Barber 29-220, Ward 2-8, Manning 2-(minus 3), T. Carter 1-(minus 2).
PASSING—Kansas City, Green 15-28-1-176. New York, Manning 17-32-1-186.
RECEIVING—Kansas City, Parker 6-87, Gonzalez 4-51, Kennison 3-21, L. Johnson 2-17. New York, Toomer 5-69, Barber 5-29, Shockey 3-33, Burress 2-34, T. Carter 1-16, Ward 1-5.
MISSED FIELD GOAL ATTEMPTS—None.
INTERCEPTIONS—Kansas City, McCleon 1-0. New York, Butler 1-16.
KICKOFF RETURNS—Kansas City, D. Hall 5-107, Horn 1-11. New York, Morton 4-94.
PUNT RETURNS—Kansas City, D. Hall 2-7. New York, Morton 1-(minus 4).
SACKS—Kansas City, Hicks 1. New York, K. Allen 1.

BRONCOS 28, BILLS 17
Saturday, December 17

Denver	0	7	14	7—28
Buffalo	7	0	3	7—17

First Quarter
Buf.—McGahee 1 run (Lindell kick), 4:50.

Second Quarter
Den.—Smith 3 pass from Plummer (Elam kick), 14:17.

Third Quarter
Den.—Duke 1 pass from Plummer (Elam kick), 4:07.
Buf.—FG, Lindell 31, 9:49.
Den.—Mi. Anderson 11 run (Elam kick), 14:41.

Fourth Quarter
Den.—Mi. Anderson 6 run (Elam kick), 9:11.
Buf.—Burns 19 pass from Holcomb (Lindell kick), 11:11.
Attendance—71,887.

	Denver	Buffalo
First downs	27	17
Rushes-yards	37-178	16-75
Passing	259	197
Punt returns	2-3	0-0
Kickoff returns	3-34	5-120
Interception returns	0-0	0-0
Comp.-att.-int.	20-37-0	22-35-0
Sacked-yards lost	1-0	1-5
Punts	4-31	6-42
Fumbles-lost	3-1	1-0
Penalties-yards	9-90	12-82
Time of possession	34:43	25:17

INDIVIDUAL STATISTICS
RUSHING—Denver, Mi. Anderson 21-97, Bell 12-49, Plummer 3-19, Lelie 1-13. Buffalo, McGahee 9-36, S. Williams 5-40, Holcomb 1-2, Reed 1-(minus 3).
PASSING—Denver, Plummer 20-37-0-259. Buffalo, Holcomb 22-35-0-202.
RECEIVING—Denver, Smith 11-137, Putzier 3-56, S. Alexander 2-12, Lelie 1-40, Bell 1-9, Mi. Anderson 1-4, Duke 1-1. Buffalo, Moulds 9-110, McGahee 3-14, Shelton 2-16, S. Williams 2-15, Reed 2-12, Evans 2-5, Burns 1-19, Parrish 1-11.
MISSED FIELD GOAL ATTEMPTS—None.
INTERCEPTIONS—None.
KICKOFF RETURNS—Denver, R. Alexander 1-21, Sapp 1-8, Engelberger 1-5. Buffalo, McGee 5-120.
PUNT RETURNS—Denver, Wilson 1. Buffalo, Posey 1.
SACKS—Denver, Adams 2-3.

SEAHAWKS 28, TITANS 24
Sunday, December 18

Seattle	14	0	7	7—28
Tennessee	0	14	10	0—24

First Quarter
Sea.—Stevens 22 pass from Hasselbeck (J. Brown kick), 3:25.
Sea.—Alexander 1 run (J. Brown kick), 9:06.

Second Quarter
Ten.—Payton 3 run (Bironas kick), 8:55.
Ten.—Bennett 4 pass from McNair (Bironas kick), 14:56.

Third Quarter
Ten.—Bennett 14 pass from McNair (Bironas kick), 4:05.
Ten.—FG, Bironas 38, 8:46.
Sea.—Jurevicius 4 pass from Hasselbeck (J. Brown kick), 10:09.

Fourth Quarter
Sea.—Jackson 2 pass from Hasselbeck (J. Brown kick), 6:01.
Attendance—69,149.

	Seattle	Tennessee
First downs	26	25
Rushes-yards	33-183	26-81
Passing	276	336
Punt returns	1-5	0-0
Kickoff returns	5-94	5-101
Interception returns	0-0	0-0
Comp.-att.-int.	21-27-0	24-39-0
Sacked-yards lost	1-9	0-0
Punts	2-39	2-45
Fumbles-lost	0-0	0-0
Penalties-yards	4-38	4-30
Time of possession	30:24	29:36

INDIVIDUAL STATISTICS
RUSHING—Seattle, Alexander 26-172, Hasselbeck 5-1, Jackson 1-7, Morris 1-3. Tennessee, Brown 20-56, Payton 3-9, McNair 2-13, Bennett 1-3.

PASSING—Seattle, Hasselbeck 21-27-0-285. Tennessee, McNair 23-38-0-310, Hentrich 1-1-0-26.

RECEIVING—Seattle, Engram 6-95, Jackson 6-72, Stevens 4-53, Jurevicius 3-31, Strong 1-20, Morris 1-14. Tennessee, Bennett 8-93, Troupe 6-116, Roby 3-54, Calico 3-25, Scaife 2-13, Nickey 1-26, Payton 1-9.

MISSED FIELD GOAL ATTEMPTS—Seattle, J. Brown 36.
INTERCEPTIONS—None.
KICKOFF RETURNS—Seattle, Scobey 4-94, Tafoya 1-0. Tennessee, P. Jones 5-101.
PUNT RETURNS—Seattle, J. Williams 1-5.
SACKS—Tennessee, LaBoy 1.

PANTHERS 27, SAINTS 10
Sunday, December 18

Carolina	7	10	7	3—27
New Orleans	7	0	0	3—10

First Quarter
Car.—S. Smith 20 run (Kasay kick), 4:27.
N.O.—Stallworth 23 pass from Bouman (Carney kick), 10:18.

Second Quarter
Car.—FG, Kasay 32, 9:38.
Car.—Delhomme 2 run (Kasay kick), 14:19.

Third Quarter
Car.—S. Smith 15 pass from Delhomme (Kasay kick), 14:33.

Fourth Quarter
N.O.—FG, Carney 44, 9:13.
Car.—FG, Kasay 29, 13:58.
Attendance—32,551.

	Carolina	New Orleans
First downs	19	15
Rushes-yards	43-161	22-94
Passing	165	183
Punt returns	3-25	4-7
Kickoff returns	3-60	4-63
Interception returns	4-99	1-0
Comp.-att.-int.	13-21-1	17-34-4
Sacked-yards lost	1-11	1-10
Punts	4-44	4-50
Fumbles-lost	1-1	2-2
Penalties-yards	3-25	9-72
Time of possession	34:54	25:06

INDIVIDUAL STATISTICS
RUSHING—Carolina, Foster 21-75, Goings 16-52, Hoover 4-12, S. Smith 1-20, Delhomme 1-2. New Orleans, A. Smith 10-25, Stecker 9-59, Bouman 3-10.

PASSING—Carolina, Delhomme 13-21-1-176. New Orleans, Bouman 17-34-4-193.

RECEIVING—Carolina, S. Smith 6-85, Carter 2-48, Goings 2-36, Foster 2-9, Mangum 1-(minus 2). New Orleans, Stecker 6-42, Stallworth 5-102, Hakim 3-35, Hilton 1-7, Horn 1-6, Henderson 1-1.

MISSED FIELD GOAL ATTEMPTS—Carolina, Kasay 50.

INTERCEPTIONS—Carolina, Gamble 1-52, Minter 1-47, Lucas 1-0, Wallace 1-0. New Orleans, Slaughter 1-0.

KICKOFF RETURNS—Carolina, Robertson 2-44, S. Smith 1-16. New Orleans, McAfee 3-59, L. Hall 1-4.

PUNT RETURNS—Carolina, S. Smith 2-18, Gamble 1-7. New Orleans, Hakim 3-7, F. Thomas 1-0.

SACKS—Carolina, Carstens 1. New Orleans, Craft 1.

EAGLES 17, RAMS 16
Sunday, December 18

Philadelphia	7	0	3	7—17
St. Louis	3	10	3	0—16

First Quarter
St.L.—FG, J. Wilkins 26, 6:05.
Phi.—Moats 59 run (Akers kick), 7:26.

Second Quarter
St.L.—Holt 5 pass from Fitzpatrick (J. Wilkins kick), 4:00.
St.L.—FG, J. Wilkins 53, 8:47.

Third Quarter
St.L.—FG, J. Wilkins 28, 6:30.
Phi.—FG, Akers 31, 11:50.

Fourth Quarter
Phi.—Bartrum 3 pass from McMahon (Akers kick), :08.
Attendance—65,382.

	Philadelphia	St. Louis
First downs	13	16
Rushes-yards	28-125	36-178
Passing	76	127
Punt returns	4-42	4-26
Kickoff returns	5-138	3-62
Interception returns	1-24	3-26
Comp.-att.-int.	15-28-3	18-35-1
Sacked-yards lost	4-21	0-0
Punts	6-46	7-41
Fumbles-lost	4-1	0-0
Penalties-yards	13-115	15-115
Time of possession	27:52	32:08

INDIVIDUAL STATISTICS
RUSHING—Philadelphia, Moats 12-78, McMahon 7-17, Mahe 4-18, Gordon 4-7, R. Brown 1-5. St. Louis, M. Faulk 16-87, S. Jackson 16-82, Harris 3-6, Fitzpatrick 1-3.

PASSING—Philadelphia, McMahon 15-28-3-97. St. Louis, Fitzpatrick 10-24-1-69, J. Martin 8-11-0-58.

RECEIVING—Philadelphia, G. Lewis 4-26, McMullen 2-25, R. Brown 2-21, Mahe 2-11, Smith 2-0, Parry 1-6, Gordon 1-5, Bartrum 1-3. St. Louis, McDonald 6-51, M. Faulk 3-21, Holt 3-16, Bruce 2-16, Harris 2-12, Curtis 1-7, Looker 1-4.

MISSED FIELD GOAL ATTEMPTS—None.

INTERCEPTIONS—Philadelphia, Dawkins 1-24. St. Louis, Tinoisamoa 1-20, Furrey 1-6, Groce 1-0.

KICKOFF RETURNS—Philadelphia, Hood 5-138. St. Louis, C. Johnson 3-62.

PUNT RETURNS—Philadelphia, Mahe 4-42. St. Louis, Looker 4-26.

SACKS—St. Louis, Little 2, Ivy 1, Hargrove 1.

TEXANS 30, CARDINALS 19
Sunday, December 18

Arizona	3	7	0	9—19
Houston	0	24	3	3—30

First Quarter
Ariz.—FG, Rackers 26, 11:17.

Second Quarter
Hou.—Wells 7 run (K. Brown kick), :37.
Ariz.—Boldin 20 pass from Warner (Rackers kick), 4:44.
Hou.—Morency 25 run (K. Brown kick), 10:03.
Hou.—Wells 3 run (K. Brown kick), 13:10.
Hou.—FG, K. Brown 27, 14:52.

Third Quarter
Hou.—FG, K. Brown 41, 2:47.

Fourth Quarter
Ariz.—FG, Rackers 42, :14.
Ariz.—Fitzgerald 12 pass from Navarre (run failed), 9:28.
Hou.—FG, K. Brown 26, 14:33.
Attendance—70,024.

	Arizona	Houston
First downs	16	18
Rushes-yards	13-39	35-119
Passing	262	134
Punt returns	3-6	1-8
Kickoff returns	7-151	5-86
Interception returns	1-3	2-7
Comp.-att.-int.	25-38-2	22-33-1
Sacked-yards lost	6-39	3-16
Punts	4-49	4-40
Fumbles-lost	3-2	1-1
Penalties-yards	7-69	5-43
Time of possession	27:36	32:24

INDIVIDUAL STATISTICS

RUSHING—Arizona, Arrington 7-11, Shipp 6-28. Houston, Wells 28-87, Morency 5-32, Carr 1-2, An. Johnson 1-(minus 2).

PASSING—Arizona, Navarre 14-24-1-174, Warner 10-10-0-115, McCown 1-4-1-12. Houston, Carr 22-33-1-150.

RECEIVING—Arizona, Boldin 8-134, Fitzgerald 6-85, Bergen 3-18, McCoy 2-28, Shipp 2-14, Arrington 2-4, B. Johnson 1-12, O. Ayanbadejo 1-6. Houston, An. Johnson 7-51, Gaffney 5-39, Rivers 4-20, Bradford 3-11, Wells 1-11, Morency 1-9, Morgan 1-9.

MISSED FIELD GOAL ATTEMPTS—None.

INTERCEPTIONS—Arizona, Huff 1-3. Houston, C. Brown 1-5, Earl 1-2.

KICKOFF RETURNS—Arizona, Swinton 7-151. Houston, Mathis 3-49, Wells 2-37.

PUNT RETURNS—Arizona, Swinton 3-6. Houston, Mathis 1-8.

SACKS—Arizona, A. Smith 2, Kolodziej 1. Houston, Babin 2, Payne 1, Smith 1, DeLoach 1, Peek 1.

CHARGERS 26, COLTS 17
Sunday, December 18

San Diego	10	3	3	10—26
Indianapolis	0	0	17	0—17

First Quarter
S.D.—McCardell 29 pass from Brees (Kaeding kick), 5:47.
S.D.—FG, Kaeding 36, 13:04.

Second Quarter
S.D.—FG, Kaeding 20, 14:45.

Third Quarter
S.D.—FG, Kaeding 48, 5:30.
Ind.—FG, Vanderjagt 32, 8:19.
Ind.—James 1 run (Vanderjagt kick), 11:18.
Ind.—Clark 1 pass from Manning (Vanderjagt kick), 14:20.

Fourth Quarter
S.D.—FG, Kaeding 49, 8:19.
S.D.—Turner 83 run (Kaeding kick), 12:51.
Attendance—57,389.

	San Diego	Indianapolis
First downs	18	21
Rushes-yards	37-206	15-24
Passing	247	314
Punt returns	3-28	1-6
Kickoff returns	4-71	7-131
Interception returns	2-23	2-19
Comp.-att.-int.	22-33-2	26-45-2
Sacked-yards lost	1-8	4-22
Punts	4-42	6-45
Fumbles-lost	2-2	1-1
Penalties-yards	11-75	8-67
Time of possession	34:32	25:28

INDIVIDUAL STATISTICS

RUSHING—San Diego, Tomlinson 24-76, Turner 8-113, Neal 4-17, Brees 1-0. Indianapolis, James 13-25, Manning 2-(minus 1).

PASSING—San Diego, Brees 22-33-2-255. Indianapolis, Manning 26-45-2-336.

RECEIVING—San Diego, Gates 6-29, Caldwell 4-25, Tomlinson 4-9, McCardell 3-88, E. Parker 3-63, Jackson 2-41. Indianapolis, Wayne 10-91, Harrison 8-135, Clark 3-45, Stokley 2-29, James 2-20, Rhodes 1-16.

MISSED FIELD GOAL ATTEMPTS—Indianapolis, Rayner 59.

INTERCEPTIONS—San Diego, Jammer 1-14, Florence 1-9. Indianapolis, Brackett 1-19, Harper 1-0.

KICKOFF RETURNS—San Diego, Sproles 4-71. Indianapolis, Rhodes 7-131.

PUNT RETURNS—San Diego, McCardell 2-17, E. Parker 1-11. Indianapolis, Walters 1-6.

SACKS—San Diego, Merriman 2, Castillo 1, Olshansky 1. Indianapolis, Freeney 1.

JAGUARS 10, 49ERS 9
Sunday, December 18

San Francisco	3	3	0	3— 9
Jacksonville	0	7	0	3—10

First Quarter
S.F.—FG, Nedney 35, 4:27.

Second Quarter
Jac.—Garrard 13 run (Scobee kick), 8:34.
S.F.—FG, Nedney 47, 14:59.

Fourth Quarter
S.F.—FG, Nedney 33, :04.
Jac.—FG, Scobee 32, 5:19.
Attendance—64,764.

	San Francisco	Jacksonville
First downs	11	21
Rushes-yards	25-110	35-134
Passing	107	202
Punt returns	2-1	7-45
Kickoff returns	3-64	2-16
Interception returns	0-0	1-4
Comp.-att.-int.	8-24-1	21-40-0
Sacked-yards lost	2-16	2-14
Punts	8-42	8-39
Fumbles-lost	1-0	0-0
Penalties-yards	8-56	10-84
Time of possession	24:20	35:40

INDIVIDUAL STATISTICS

RUSHING—San Francisco, Gore 19-79, A. Smith 4-30, Hicks 2-1. Jacksonville, F. Taylor 17-61, G. Jones 12-44, Garrard 5-27, M. Jones 1-2.

PASSING—San Francisco, A. Smith 8-24-1-123. Jacksonville, Garrard 21-40-0-216.

RECEIVING—San Francisco, Gore 3-57, McAddley 1-38, Morton 1-28, Lloyd 1-6, T. Jones 1-(minus 1), Jackson 1-(minus 5). Jacksonville, J. Smith 6-70, R. Williams 4-65, Wilford 2-28, F. Taylor 2-13, M. Jones 2-11, G. Jones 2-10, Pearman 1-8, Wimbush 1-6, Brady 1-5.

MISSED FIELD GOAL ATTEMPTS—Jacksonville, Scobee 52.

INTERCEPTIONS—Jacksonville, Wright 1-4.

KICKOFF RETURNS—San Francisco, Hicks 2-47, McAddley 1-17. Jacksonville, Wimbush 1-16, G. Jones 1-0.

PUNT RETURNS—San Francisco, Marshall 2-1. Jacksonville, Pearman 7-45.

SACKS—San Francisco, B. Moore 1, Emanuel 0.5, A. Adams 0.5. Jacksonville, Peterson 1, Meier 1.

STEELERS 18, VIKINGS 3
Sunday, December 18

Pittsburgh	3	7	6	2—18
Minnesota	3	0	0	0— 3

First Quarter
Pit.—FG, Reed 21, 3:53.
Min.—FG, Edinger 20, 13:01.

Second Quarter
Pit.—Roethlisberger 3 run (Reed kick), 11:30.

Third Quarter
Pit.—FG, Reed 41, 11:11.
Pit.—FG, Reed 26, 14:24.

Fourth Quarter
Pit.—Safety, 3:15.
Attendance—64,136.

	Pittsburgh	Minnesota
First downs	14	11
Rushes-yards	39-142	17-54
Passing	133	131
Punt returns	5-85	4-41
Kickoff returns	3-56	5-83
Interception returns	2-0	0-0
Comp.-att.-int.	10-15-0	16-30-2
Sacked-yards lost	4-16	2-12
Punts	6-47	6-45
Fumbles-lost	2-1	3-1
Penalties-yards	12-129	13-95
Time of possession	36:48	23:12

INDIVIDUAL STATISTICS

RUSHING—Pittsburgh, Parker 14-81, Haynes 9-36, Bettis 9-16, Roethlisberger 6-7, Randle El 1-2. Minnesota, M. Bennett 11-43, Fason 3-0, Moore 2-5, B. Johnson 1-6.

PASSING—Pittsburgh, Roethlisberger 10-15-0-149. Minnesota, B. Johnson 16-30-2-143.

RECEIVING—Pittsburgh, Miller 2-58, Randle El 2-48, Wilson 2-16, Parker 2-16, Ward 2-11. Minnesota, K. Robinson 3-34, T. Taylor 3-28, M. Robinson 2-38, Burleson 2-24, Wiggins 2-9, Moore 2-9, Kleinsasser 1-6, M. Bennett 1-(minus 5).

MISSED FIELD GOAL ATTEMPTS—Minnesota, Edinger 32.

INTERCEPTIONS—Pittsburgh, Porter 1-0, Townsend 1-0.

KICKOFF RETURNS—Pittsburgh, Morgan 2-40, Randle El 1-16. Minnesota, K. Robinson 3-79, Fason 2-4.

PUNT RETURNS—Pittsburgh, Randle El 5-85. Minnesota, Moore 3-41, T. Taylor 1-0.

SACKS—Pittsburgh, Foote 1, Porter 0.5, von Oelhoffen 0.5. Minnesota, James 2, K. Williams 1, Johnstone 1.

DOLPHINS 24, JETS 20

Sunday, December 18

N.Y. Jets	0	10	7	3—20
Miami	7	3	0	14—24

First Quarter
Mia.—Chambers 8 pass from Frerotte (Mare kick), 10:52.

Second Quarter
Mia.—FG, Mare 32, 11:03.
NYJ—Coles 4 pass from Bollinger (Nugent kick), 13:42.
NYJ—FG, Nugent 42, 14:57.

Third Quarter
NYJ—Jolley 60 pass from Bollinger (Nugent kick), 6:11.

Fourth Quarter
Mia.—R. Williams 23 run (Mare kick), 1:15.
Mia.—Booker 50 pass from Rosenfels (Mare kick), 4:05.
NYJ—FG, Nugent 42, 10:28.
Attendance—72,650.

	N.Y. Jets	Miami
First downs	24	14
Rushes-yards	25-99	31-128
Passing	298	169
Punt returns	4-13	3-31
Kickoff returns	5-121	5-110
Interception returns	1-13	0-0
Comp.-att.-int.	28-42-0	14-29-1
Sacked-yards lost	6-29	1-6
Punts	6-39	7-42
Fumbles-lost	3-3	1-0
Penalties-yards	5-39	8-92
Time of possession	34:02	25:58

INDIVIDUAL STATISTICS

RUSHING—New York, Houston 15-84, Bollinger 5-10, Askew 4-5, Graham 1-0. Miami, R. Williams 14-70, Brown 12-45, Rosenfels 4-10, Frerotte 1-3.

PASSING—New York, Bollinger 28-42-0-327. Miami, Frerotte 8-16-1-76, Rosenfels 6-13-0-99.

RECEIVING—New York, Jolley 9-102, Coles 4-53, Cotchery 4-44, Houston 4-40, McCareins 2-57, Dreessen 2-11, Sowell 2-9, Askew 1-11. Miami, McMichael 4-42, Chambers 4-34, Booker 2-65, Brown 2-11, Welker 1-19, R. Williams 1-4.

MISSED FIELD GOAL ATTEMPTS—Miami, Mare 53.

INTERCEPTIONS—New York, Barrett 1-13.

KICKOFF RETURNS—New York, Miller 4-91, Cotchery 1-30. Miami, Welker 4-105, D. Bowens 1-5.

PUNT RETURNS—New York, Cotchery 3-13, McCareins 1-0. Miami, Welker 3-31.

SACKS—New York, Legree 1. Miami, Taylor 3, Zgonina 1, Roth 1, D. Bowens 1.

BENGALS 41, LIONS 17

Sunday, December 18

Cincinnati	17	7	7	10—41
Detroit	0	7	3	7—17

First Quarter
Cin.—FG, Graham 28, 3:19.
Cin.—Washington 18 pass from Palmer (Graham kick), 7:08.
Cin.—C. Johnson 1 pass from Palmer (Graham kick), 12:01.

Second Quarter
Det.—R. Williams 5 run from Garcia (Hanson kick), 2:18.
Cin.—Houshmandzadeh 7 pass from Palmer (Graham kick), 5:40.

Third Quarter
Cin.—Ru. Johnson 4 run (Graham kick), 5:28.
Det.—FG, Hanson 45, 9:38.

Fourth Quarter
Cin.—Ru. Johnson 16 run (Graham kick), 3:59.
Det.—C. Rogers 35 pass from Harrington (Hanson kick), 8:16.
Cin.—FG, Graham 33, 13:05.
Attendance—61,749.

	Cincinnati	Detroit
First downs	29	13
Rushes-yards	32-155	17-59
Passing	271	211
Punt returns	3-19	0-0
Kickoff returns	3-48	8-136
Interception returns	3-9	2-25
Comp.-att.-int.	30-42-2	19-28-3
Sacked-yards lost	2-9	1-4
Punts	1-51	3-46
Fumbles-lost	2-0	1-1
Penalties-yards	4-40	4-30
Time of possession	36:11	23:49

INDIVIDUAL STATISTICS

RUSHING—Cincinnati, Ru. Johnson 24-117, J. Johnson 5-10, Kitna 1-11, C. Johnson 1-9, Palmer 1-8. Detroit, Pinner 15-55, Garcia 1-2, Bryson 1-2.

PASSING—Cincinnati, Palmer 28-39-2-274, Kitna 2-3-0-6. Detroit, Garcia 13-21-3-138, Harrington 6-7-0-77.

RECEIVING—Cincinnati, C. Johnson 11-99, Houshmandzadeh 6-61, Washington 4-48, J. Johnson 3-3, R. Kelly 2-23, Schobel 2-20, Ru. Johnson 1-14, Walter 1-12. Detroit, Vines 4-27, C. Rogers 3-71, Pollard 3-42, R. Williams 3-27, Pinner 3-18, Bryson 1-13, M. Williams 1-9, Schlesinger 1-8.

MISSED FIELD GOAL ATTEMPTS—None.

INTERCEPTIONS—Cincinnati, O'Neal 1-9, James 1-0, Thornton 1-0. Detroit, Goodman 1-21, Bly 1-4.

KICKOFF RETURNS—Cincinnati, T. Perry 2-44, Schobel 1-4. Detroit, McQuarters 5-94, Martinez 2-42, Bryson 1-0.

PUNT RETURNS—Cincinnati, Ratliff 3-19.

SACKS—Cincinnati, Simmons 1. Detroit, Woods 1, S. Rogers 1.

REDSKINS 35, COWBOYS 7

Sunday, December 18

Dallas	0	0	0	7— 7
Washington	7	21	7	0—35

First Quarter
Was.—Cooley 8 pass from Brunell (Hall kick), 6:16.

Second Quarter
Was.—Cooley 2 pass from Brunell (Hall kick), 5:20.
Was.—Sellers 3 pass from Brunell (Hall kick), 13:35.
Was.—Cooley 30 pass from Brunell (Hall kick), 14:48.

Third Quarter
Was.—Betts 1 run (Hall kick), 4:45.

Fourth Quarter
Dal.—Witten 2 pass from Bledsoe (Cundiff kick), 2:50.
Attendance—90,588.

	Dallas	Washington
First downs	13	19
Rushes-yards	24-109	40-171
Passing	107	163
Punt returns	1-6	2-0
Kickoff returns	6-136	2-40
Interception returns	0-0	3-61
Comp.-att.-int.	16-29-3	12-20-0
Sacked-yards lost	7-46	0-0
Punts	6-35	6-34
Fumbles-lost	2-1	2-1
Penalties-yards	9-56	7-55
Time of possession	28:36	31:24

INDIVIDUAL STATISTICS

RUSHING—Dallas, J. Jones 12-79, Barber 10-30, Bledsoe 2-0. Washington, Portis 23-112, Betts 12-44, Cartwright 3-13, Moss 1-3, Brunell 1-(minus 1).

PASSING—Dallas, Bledsoe 16-29-3-153. Washington, Brunell 12-20-0-163.

RECEIVING—Dallas, Witten 4-41, Barber 4-26, J. Jones 3-17, T. Glenn 2-25, K. Johnson 2-20, Crayton 1-24. Washington, Cooley 6-71, Moss 2-73, Royal 1-6, Cartwright 1-6, Portis 1-4, Sellers 1-3.

MISSED FIELD GOAL ATTEMPTS—Dallas, Cundiff 38.

INTERCEPTIONS—Washington, Washington 1-41, Patterson 1-20, Griffin 1-0.

KICKOFF RETURNS—Dallas, Thompson 6-136. Washington, A. Brown 1-27, Sellers 1-13.

PUNT RETURNS—Dallas, Crayton 1-6. Washington, A. Brown 2-0.

SACKS—Washington, Daniels 4, Washington 2, Wynn 0.5, Salave'a 0.5.

BROWNS 9, RAIDERS 7
Sunday, December 18

Cleveland	0	3	3	3—9
Oakland	0	7	0	0—7

Second Quarter
Oak.—Moss 28 pass from Collins (Janikowski kick), 13:44.
Cle.—FG, Dawson 44, 15:00.

Third Quarter
Cle.—FG, Dawson 24, 13:12.

Fourth Quarter
Cle.—FG, Dawson 37, 15:00.
Attendance—41,862.

	Cleveland	Oakland
First downs	13	16
Rushes-yards	26-70	31-143
Passing	185	113
Punt returns	3-47	1-1
Kickoff returns	2-63	2-28
Interception returns	1-6	1-0
Comp.-att.-int.	21-32-1	14-30-1
Sacked-yards lost	2-13	3-19
Punts	5-43	6-49
Fumbles-lost	1-1	1-0
Penalties-yards	1-15	7-45
Time of possession	26:22	33:38

INDIVIDUAL STATISTICS

RUSHING—Cleveland, Droughns 18-53, Frye 7-11, Suggs 1-6. Oakland, Jordan 25-132, Crockett 4-10, Collins 2-1.

PASSING—Cleveland, Frye 21-32-1-198. Oakland, Collins 14-30-1-132.

RECEIVING—Cleveland, Bryant 5-86, Droughns 5-31, T. Smith 3-16, Northcutt 2-25, F. Jackson 2-21, Heiden 2-8, Cribbs 1-7, Suggs 1-4. Oakland, Porter 6-31, Jordan 5-40, Moss 1-28, Ra. Williams 1-24, Gabriel 1-9.

MISSED FIELD GOAL ATTEMPTS—Oakland, Janikowski 51, 46.

INTERCEPTIONS—Cleveland, Bodden 1-6. Oakland, Hill 1-0.

KICKOFF RETURNS—Cleveland, Cribbs 1-48, F. Jackson 1-15. Oakland, Gabriel 1-19, Carr 1-9.

PUNT RETURNS—Cleveland, Northcutt 2-47, Jones 1-0. Oakland, Carr 1-1.

SACKS—Cleveland, Thompson 1, McKinley 1, Eason 1. Oakland, Burgess 1, Routt 1.

BEARS 16, FALCONS 3
Sunday, December 18

Atlanta	0	3	0	0— 3
Chicago	0	6	10	0—16

Second Quarter
Atl.—FG, T. Peterson 30, 4:44.
Chi.—FG, Gould 35, 8:27.
Chi.—FG, Gould 29, 11:40.

Third Quarter
Chi.—T. Jones 1 run (Gould kick), 6:43.
Chi.—FG, Gould 39, 14:07.
Attendance—62,170.

	Atlanta	Chicago
First downs	12	14
Rushes-yards	31-114	32-128
Passing	117	98
Punt returns	1-0	2-30
Kickoff returns	5-81	2-12
Interception returns	1-0	2-14
Comp.-att.-int.	13-32-2	11-26-1
Sacked-yards lost	2-5	1-7
Punts	6-39	7-33
Fumbles-lost	1-1	0-0
Penalties-yards	6-75	3-16
Time of possession	30:58	29:02

INDIVIDUAL STATISTICS

RUSHING—Atlanta, Dunn 17-81, Duckett 8-(minus 2), Vick 6-35. Chicago, T. Jones 27-91, Peterson 3-6, Berrian 2-31.

PASSING—Atlanta, Vick 13-32-2-122. Chicago, Grossman 9-16-1-93, Orton 2-10-0-12.

RECEIVING—Atlanta, Finneran 6-75, Crumpler 2-14, R. White 1-19, Jenkins 1-11, Dunn 1-9, Griffith 1-8, Vick 1-(minus 14). Chicago, Muhammad 3-40, McKie 3-13, Gage 2-29, Berrian 2-20, T. Jones 1-3.

MISSED FIELD GOAL ATTEMPTS—Chicago, Gould 44.

INTERCEPTIONS—Atlanta, Carpenter 1-0. Chicago, M. Green 1-14, Vasher 1-0.

KICKOFF RETURNS—Atlanta, Griffith 4-65, Pathon 1-16. Chicago, McKie 2-12.

PUNT RETURNS—Atlanta, D. Hall 1-0. Chicago, Berrian 2-30.

SACKS—Atlanta, R. Coleman 1. Chicago, T. Johnson 1, Ogunleye 1.

RAVENS 48, PACKERS 3
Monday, December 19

Green Bay	3	0	0	0— 3
Baltimore	14	10	10	14—48

First Quarter
Bal.—Heap 2 pass from Boller (Stover kick), 3:56.
Bal.—Clayton 11 run (Stover kick), 8:08.
G.B.—FG, Longwell 27, 9:37.

Second Quarter
Bal.—Hymes 13 pass from Boller (Stover kick), 10:51.
Bal.—FG, Stover 23, 14:37.

Third Quarter
Bal.—Heap 27 pass from Boller (Stover kick), 5:17.
Bal.—FG, Stover 40, 14:43.

Fourth Quarter
Bal.—J. Lewis 3 run (Stover kick), 1:35.
Bal.—A. Thomas 35 fumble return (Stover kick), 14:43.
Attendance—70,604.

	Green Bay	Baltimore
First downs	16	25
Rushes-yards	19-107	38-182
Passing	181	253
Punt returns	2-5	2-53
Kickoff returns	9-167	2-41
Interception returns	0-0	3-24
Comp.-att.-int.	22-44-3	19-27-0
Sacked-yards lost	3-28	0-0
Punts	4-36	4-40
Fumbles-lost	2-2	1-0
Penalties-yards	10-94	7-71
Time of possession	28:28	31:32

INDIVIDUAL STATISTICS

RUSHING—Green Bay, Herron 8-27, Gado 6-45, Fisher 4-27, Rodgers 1-8. Baltimore, J. Lewis 22-105, C. Taylor 6-37, J. White 6-17, Clayton 3-14, Boller 1-9.

PASSING—Green Bay, Favre 14-29-2-144, Rodgers 8-15-1-65. Baltimore, Boller 19-27-0-253.

RECEIVING—Green Bay, Chatman 6-63, Fisher 4-27, Driver 3-56, Henderson 3-30, D. Lee 2-16, D. Martin 2-14, Ferguson 1-2, Gado 1-1. Baltimore, Heap 9-110, Mason 5-97, Clayton 2-24, J. Lewis 2-9, Hymes 1-13.

MISSED FIELD GOAL ATTEMPTS—None.

INTERCEPTIONS—Baltimore, Sanders 1-24, Williams 1-0, Rolle 1-0.

KICKOFF RETURNS—Green Bay, Carroll 5-118, Leach 3-39, Henderson 1-10. Baltimore, C. Taylor 1-21, Sams 1-20.

PUNT RETURNS—Green Bay, Chatman 2-5. Baltimore, Sams 2-53.

SACKS—Baltimore, Suggs 1, A. Thomas 1, Williams 1.

WEEK 16

STANDINGS

AMERICAN FOOTBALL CONFERENCE

EAST DIVISION

	W	L	T	Pct.	PF	PA
New England	10	5	0	.667	353	310
Miami	8	7	0	.533	290	291
Buffalo	5	10	0	.333	245	337
N.Y. Jets	3	12	0	.200	210	329

NORTH DIVISION

	W	L	T	Pct.	PF	PA
Cincinnati	11	4	0	.733	418	313
Pittsburgh	10	5	0	.667	354	237
Baltimore	6	9	0	.400	249	279
Cleveland	5	10	0	.333	212	285

SOUTH DIVISION

	W	L	T	Pct.	PF	PA
Indianapolis	13	2	0	.867	422	234
Jacksonville	11	4	0	.733	321	256
Tennessee	4	11	0	.267	286	381
Houston	2	13	0	.133	243	411

WEST DIVISION

	W	L	T	Pct.	PF	PA
Denver	12	3	0	.800	372	251
Kansas City	9	6	0	.600	366	322
San Diego	9	6	0	.600	411	289
Oakland	4	11	0	.267	269	353

NATIONAL FOOTBALL CONFERENCE

EAST DIVISION

	W	L	T	Pct.	PF	PA
N.Y. Giants	10	5	0	.667	392	293
Dallas	9	6	0	.600	315	288
Washington	9	6	0	.600	328	273
Philadelphia	6	9	0	.400	290	357

NORTH DIVISION

	W	L	T	Pct.	PF	PA
Chicago	11	4	0	.733	250	168
Minnesota	8	7	0	.533	272	334
Detroit	5	10	0	.333	233	310
Green Bay	3	12	0	.200	275	327

SOUTH DIVISION

	W	L	T	Pct.	PF	PA
Carolina	10	5	0	.667	347	248
Tampa Bay	10	5	0	.667	273	261
Atlanta	8	7	0	.533	340	297
New Orleans	3	12	0	.200	222	371

WEST DIVISION

	W	L	T	Pct.	PF	PA
Seattle	13	2	0	.867	435	248
Arizona	5	10	0	.333	298	370
St. Louis	5	10	0	.333	343	419
San Francisco	3	12	0	.200	219	411

TOP PERFORMANCES

100-YARD RUSHING GAMES

Player, team & opponent	Att.	Yds.	TD
Julius Jones, Dal. at Car.	34	194	2
Ricky Williams, Mia. vs. Ten.	26	172	1
Carnell Williams, T.B. vs. Atl.*	31	150	1
Shaun Alexander, Sea. vs. Ind.	21	139	2
Larry Johnson, K.C. vs. S.D.	32	131	1
Willie Parker, Pit. at Cle.	17	130	1
Maurice Hicks, S.F. at St.L.	10	109	1
Clinton Portis, Was. vs. NYG	27	108	1
Thomas Jones, Chi. at G.B.	25	105	1
Fred Taylor, Jac. at Hou.	22	101	1

300-YARD PASSING GAMES

Player, team & opponent	Att.	Cmp.	Yds.	TD	Int.
Jamie Martin, St.L. vs. S.F.	41	33	354	1	2
Brett Favre, G.B. vs. Chi.	51	30	317	0	4
Kelly Holcomb, Buf. at Cin.	31	24	308	1	1

100-YARD RECEIVING GAMES

Player, team & opponent	Rec.	Yds.	TD
Torry Holt, St.L. vs. S.F.	10	163	1
Santana Moss, Was. vs. NYG	5	160	3
Brandon Stokley, Ind. at Sea.	5	122	0
Andre Johnson, Hou. vs. Jac.	7	119	1
Ernest Wilford, Jac. at Hou.	4	118	1
Chad Johnson, Cin. vs. Buf.	9	117	1
Roy Williams, Det. at N.O.	4	111	0
Ashley Lelie, Den. vs. Oak.	6	110	1
Donald Driver, G.B. vs. Chi.	6	107	0
Lee Evans, Buf. at Cin.	5	107	1
Hines Ward, Pit. at Cle.	7	105	1
Ricky Proehl, Car. vs. Dal.	2	104	1
Derrick Mason, Bal. vs. Min.	9	103	1
Corey Bradford, Hou. vs. Jac.	4	101	1

*Overtime game.

RESULTS

SATURDAY, DECEMBER 24
San Francisco 24, ST. LOUIS 20
Detroit 13, NEW ORLEANS 12
Pittsburgh 41, CLEVELAND 0
Dallas 24, CAROLINA 20
Jacksonville 38, HOUSTON 20
Buffalo 37, CINCINNATI 27
WASHINGTON 35, N.Y. Giants 20
KANSAS CITY 20, San Diego 7
TAMPA BAY 27, Atlanta 24 (OT)
MIAMI 24, Tennessee 10
SEATTLE 28, Indianapolis 13
ARIZONA 27, Philadelphia 21
DENVER 22, Oakland 3

SUNDAY, DECEMBER 25
Chicago 24, GREEN BAY 17
BALTIMORE 30, Minnesota 23

MONDAY, DECEMBER 26
New England 31, N.Y. JETS 21

49ERS 24, RAMS 20

Saturday, December 24

San Francisco	7	10	0	7—24
St. Louis	3	17	0	0—20

First Quarter
S.F.—Hicks 73 run (Nedney kick), :16.
St.L.—FG, J. Wilkins 50, 7:05.

Second Quarter
St.L.—S. Jackson 3 run (J. Wilkins kick), :04.
St.L.—Holt 40 pass from J. Martin (J. Wilkins kick), 6:28.
St.L.—FG, J. Wilkins 51, 11:27.
S.F.—Gore 10 run (Nedney kick), 13:41.
S.F.—FG, Nedney 56, 15:00.

Fourth Quarter
S.F.—Gore 30 run (Nedney kick), 10:55.
Attendance—65,473.

	San Francisco	St. Louis
First downs	15	20
Rushes-yards	29-217	21-44
Passing	104	345
Punt returns	1-13	4-43
Kickoff returns	5-98	4-78
Interception returns	2-3	0-0
Comp.-att.-int.	12-16-0	33-41-2
Sacked-yards lost	5-27	1-9
Punts	6-41	3-44
Fumbles-lost	1-0	1-0
Penalties-yards	6-39	4-24
Time of possession	27:37	32:23

INDIVIDUAL STATISTICS

RUSHING—San Francisco, Hicks 10-109, Gore 10-68, A. Smith 7-21, Jackson 1-11, Battle 1-8. St. Louis, S. Jackson 16-28, M. Faulk 3-5, J. Martin 2-11.

PASSING—San Francisco, A. Smith 12-16-0-131. St. Louis, J. Martin 33-41-2-354.

RECEIVING—San Francisco, Battle 4-37, McAddley 2-38, T. Jones 2-26, Lloyd 2-18, Jackson 1-9, Hicks 1-3. St. Louis, Holt 10-163, M. Faulk 9-44, Bruce 6-73, S. Jackson 3-21, Hedgecock 2-25, Curtis 2-15, McDonald 1-13.

MISSED FIELD GOAL ATTEMPTS—None.

INTERCEPTIONS—San Francisco, Emanuel 1-3, Spencer 1-0.

KICKOFF RETURNS—San Francisco, Marshall 3-64, McAddley 2-34. St. Louis, C. Johnson 4-78.

PUNT RETURNS—San Francisco, Marshall 1-13. St. Louis, Looker 4-43.

SACKS—San Francisco, Carter 1. St. Louis, Hargrove 1.5, Lewis 1, Little 1, T. Jackson 0.5, Team 1.

LIONS 13, SAINTS 12

Saturday, December 24

Detroit	0	7	0	6—13
New Orleans	0	3	6	3—12

Second Quarter
Det.—S. Rogers 21 fumble return (Hanson kick), 9:15.
N.O.—FG, Carney 35, 13:56.

Third Quarter
N.O.—FG, Carney 47, 5:44.
N.O.—FG, Carney 33, 9:11.

Fourth Quarter
Det.—FG, Hanson 21, 7:46.
N.O.—FG, Carney 20, 13:08.
Det.—FG, Hanson 39, 15:00.
Attendance—63,747.

	Detroit	New Orleans
First downs	14	19
Rushes-yards	24-71	25-47
Passing	208	226
Punt returns	1-0	4-64
Kickoff returns	5-150	3-53
Interception returns	0-0	1-0
Comp.-att.-int.	17-30-1	21-38-0
Sacked-yards lost	1-2	1-7
Punts	6-47	4-40
Fumbles-lost	0-0	2-1
Penalties-yards	11-65	4-17
Time of possession	30:09	29:51

INDIVIDUAL STATISTICS

RUSHING—Detroit, Pinner 20-57, Bryson 4-14. New Orleans, A. Smith 13-33, Stecker 7-5, Bouman 3-6, Stallworth 1-3, A. Thomas 1-0.

PASSING—Detroit, Harrington 17-30-1-210. New Orleans, Bouman 21-38-0-233.

RECEIVING—Detroit, Pollard 6-44, R. Williams 4-111, Pinner 4-31, M. Williams 1-21, FitzSimmons 1-7, Harrington 1-(minus 4). New Orleans, Hilton 7-83, Horn 6-70, Stallworth 2-47, Stecker 2-13, A. Smith 2-5, Karney 1-8, Hakim 1-7.

MISSED FIELD GOAL ATTEMPTS—None.

INTERCEPTIONS—New Orleans, F. Thomas 1-0.

KICKOFF RETURNS—Detroit, Drummond 5-150. New Orleans, McAfee 3-53.

PUNT RETURNS—Detroit, Drummond 1-0. New Orleans, Hakim 4-64.

SACKS—Detroit, Hall 1. New Orleans, W. Smith 1.

STEELERS 41, BROWNS 0

Saturday, December 24

Pittsburgh	14	6	14	7—41
Cleveland	0	0	0	0— 0

First Quarter
Pit.—Bettis 2 run (Reed kick), 7:12.
Pit.—Ward 7 pass from Roethlisberger (Reed kick), 11:30.

Second Quarter
Pit.—FG, Reed 26, 1:39.
Pit.—FG, Reed 31, 12:43.

Third Quarter
Pit.—Parker 80 run (Reed kick), 5:58.
Pit.—Haynes 15 run (Reed kick), 13:55.

Fourth Quarter
Pit.—Morgan 31 pass from Batch (Reed kick), 8:44.
Attendance—73,136.

	Pittsburgh	Cleveland
First downs	20	12
Rushes-yards	35-209	19-63
Passing	248	123
Punt returns	5-52	1-8
Kickoff returns	1-22	7-133
Interception returns	0-0	0-0
Comp.-att.-int.	14-21-0	20-39-0
Sacked-yards lost	2-9	8-60
Punts	3-42	8-42
Fumbles-lost	1-1	5-1
Penalties-yards	3-30	4-25
Time of possession	31:39	28:21

INDIVIDUAL STATISTICS

RUSHING—Pittsburgh, Parker 17-130, Haynes 10-57, Bettis 7-24, Randle El 1-(minus 2). Cleveland, Droughns 10-36, Suggs 4-7, Frye 3-17, T. Smith 2-3.

PASSING—Pittsburgh, Roethlisberger 13-20-0-226, Batch 1-1-0-31. Cleveland, Frye 20-39-0-183.

RECEIVING—Pittsburgh, Ward 7-105, Wilson 2-63, Morgan 1-31, Miller 1-21, Randle El 1-20, Haynes 1-13, Kreider 1-4. Cleveland, Shea 5-27, Northcutt 5-23, Bryant 4-50, F. Jackson 3-41, Heiden 2-13, Droughns 1-29.

MISSED FIELD GOAL ATTEMPTS—None.

INTERCEPTIONS—None.

KICKOFF RETURNS—Pittsburgh, Morgan 1-22. Cleveland, Cribbs 6-126, Shea 1-7.

PUNT RETURNS—Pittsburgh, Randle El 4-49, Iwuoma 1-3. Cleveland, Northcutt 1-8.

SACKS—Pittsburgh, Porter 3, Keisel 2, Foote 1, Haggans 1, Townsend 1. Cleveland, McKinley 1, Eason 1.

COWBOYS 24, PANTHERS 20

Saturday, December 24

Dallas	7	3	7	7—24
Carolina	10	3	0	7—20

First Quarter
Car.—FG, Kasay 24, 4:55.
Car.—Carter 32 pass from Delhomme (Kasay kick), 5:11.
Dal.—J. Jones 8 run (Cundiff kick), 8:00.

Second Quarter
Dal.—FG, Cundiff 24, 4:00.
Car.—FG, Kasay 47, 8:10.

Third Quarter
Dal.—J. Jones 43 run (Cundiff kick), 10:10.

Fourth Quarter
Car.—Proehl 35 pass from Delhomme (Kasay kick), 12:28.
Dal.—T. Glenn 2 pass from Bledsoe (Cundiff kick), 14:36.
Attendance—73,436.

	Dallas	Carolina
First downs	22	13
Rushes-yards	41-214	24-71
Passing	180	247
Punt returns	4-10	2-14
Kickoff returns	5-132	4-104
Interception returns	1-6	1-8
Comp.-att.-int.	15-23-1	14-31-1
Sacked-yards lost	5-29	3-13
Punts	7-49	7-45
Fumbles-lost	3-1	3-1
Penalties-yards	5-44	6-49
Time of possession	34:40	25:20

INDIVIDUAL STATISTICS
RUSHING—Dallas, J. Jones 34-194, Barber 6-20, Bledsoe 1-0. Carolina, Foster 22-68, Goings 1-4, Delhomme 1-(minus 1).

PASSING—Dallas, Bledsoe 15-23-1-209. Carolina, Delhomme 14-31-1-260.

RECEIVING—Dallas, K. Johnson 6-89, T. Glenn 4-88, J. Jones 2-17, Witten 1-9, Barber 1-5, Polite 1-1. Carolina, Carter 3-55, Mangum 3-35, Proehl 2-104, Goings 2-24, Foster 2-13, S. Smith 1-18, Hoover 1-11.

MISSED FIELD GOAL ATTEMPTS—Dallas, Cundiff 32.

INTERCEPTIONS—Dallas, Ro. Williams 1-6. Carolina, Lucas 1-8.

KICKOFF RETURNS—Dallas, Thompson 5-132. Carolina, Robertson 4-104.

PUNT RETURNS—Dallas, Crayton 2-8, Newman 2-2. Carolina, Gamble 2-14.

SACKS—Dallas, Ware 3. Carolina, Peppers 3, Draft 1, Witherspoon 1.

JAGUARS 38, TEXANS 20
Saturday, December 24

Jacksonville	7	3	7	21—38
Houston	3	10	0	7—20

First Quarter
Jac.—Toefield 1 run (Scobee kick), 8:58.
Hou.—FG, K. Brown 37, 12:39.

Second Quarter
Hou.—Bradford 50 pass from Carr (K. Brown kick), 3:17.
Jac.—FG, Scobee 26, 10:25.
Hou.—FG, K. Brown 53, 13:57.

Third Quarter
Jac.—Toefield 2 run (Scobee kick), 10:57.

Fourth Quarter
Hou.—An. Johnson 53 pass from Carr (K. Brown kick), 2:45.
Jac.—F. Taylor 15 run (Scobee kick), 5:44.
Jac.—Wilford 36 pass from Garrard (Scobee kick), 12:23.
Jac.—Toefield 17 run (Scobee kick), 13:09.
Attendance—70,025.

	Jacksonville	Houston
First downs	30	18
Rushes-yards	33-172	29-107
Passing	276	263
Punt returns	0-0	1-8
Kickoff returns	4-85	4-53
Interception returns	1-14	0-0
Comp.-att.-int.	18-31-0	19-29-1
Sacked-yards lost	3-16	4-32
Punts	2-49	2-32
Fumbles-lost	2-0	1-0
Penalties-yards	6-50	7-40
Time of possession	32:18	27:42

INDIVIDUAL STATISTICS
RUSHING—Jacksonville, F. Taylor 22-101, Garrard 5-40, Toefield 4-24, M. Jones 1-5, Pearman 1-2. Houston, Wells 21-86, Morency 4-12, Carr 3-7, An. Johnson 1-2.

PASSING—Jacksonville, Garrard 18-31-0-292. Houston, Carr 19-29-1-295.

RECEIVING—Jacksonville, J. Smith 5-71, Pearman 5-44, Wilford 4-118, R. Williams 3-48, F. Taylor 1-11. Houston, An. Johnson 7-119, Bradford 4-101, Rivers 4-28, Wells 3-33, Morency 1-14.

MISSED FIELD GOAL ATTEMPTS—Jacksonville, Scobee 40. Houston, K. Brown 38, 48.

INTERCEPTIONS—Jacksonville, Cousin 1-14.

KICKOFF RETURNS—Jacksonville, Wimbush 4-85. Houston, Mathis 3-51, Norris 1-2.

PUNT RETURNS—Houston, Morgan 1-8.

SACKS—Jacksonville, Henderson 2, Peterson 1, Hayward 1. Houston, Orr 2, Malone 1.

BILLS 37, BENGALS 27
Saturday, December 24

Buffalo	6	7	7	17—37
Cincinnati	0	14	10	3—27

First Quarter
Buf.—FG, Lindell 21, 3:16.
Buf.—FG, Lindell 24, 9:23.

Second Quarter
Cin.—T. Perry 2 run (Graham kick), :31.
Buf.—Evans 3 pass from Holcomb (Lindell kick), 5:23.
Cin.—C. Johnson 41 pass from Palmer (Graham kick), 13:43.

Third Quarter
Cin.—FG, Graham 31, 10:51.
Buf.—McGee 99 kickoff return (Lindell kick), 11:03.
Cin.—Henry 27 pass from Palmer (Graham kick), 13:24.

Fourth Quarter
Buf.—Holcomb 1 run (Lindell kick), 3:31.
Cin.—FG, Graham 27, 7:33.
Buf.—FG, Lindell 22, 14:02.
Buf.—McGee 46 interception return (Lindell kick), 14:25.
Attendance—65,485.

	Buffalo	Cincinnati
First downs	19	23
Rushes-yards	25-67	23-104
Passing	288	270
Punt returns	2-38	0-0
Kickoff returns	6-256	7-125
Interception returns	2-88	1-0
Comp.-att.-int.	24-31-1	27-38-2
Sacked-yards lost	3-20	2-13
Punts	1-52	2-44
Fumbles-lost	2-0	0-0
Penalties-yards	6-55	3-15
Time of possession	30:12	29:48

INDIVIDUAL STATISTICS
RUSHING—Buffalo, McGahee 23-66, Holcomb 2-1. Cincinnati, Ru. Johnson 18-88, Palmer 4-14, T. Perry 1-2.

PASSING—Buffalo, Holcomb 24-31-1-308. Cincinnati, Palmer 25-36-2-266, Kitna 2-2-0-17.

RECEIVING—Buffalo, Moulds 10-99, Evans 5-107, Reed 3-60, McGahee 3-0, Parrish 2-31, Shelton 1-11. Cincinnati, C. Johnson 9-117, Houshmandzadeh 7-70, Walter 3-21, Schobel 2-30, Ru. Johnson 2-8, J. Johnson 2-6, Henry 1-27, Washington 1-4.

MISSED FIELD GOAL ATTEMPTS—Buffalo, Lindell 48.

INTERCEPTIONS—Buffalo, McGee 1-46, Vincent 1-42. Cincinnati, Kaesviharn 1-0.

KICKOFF RETURNS—Buffalo, McGee 5-220, Leonhard 1-36. Cincinnati, T. Perry 7-125.

PUNT RETURNS—Buffalo, Parrish 2-38.

SACKS—Buffalo, Schobel 2. Cincinnati, Simmons 1, J. Smith 1, Thornton 1.

REDSKINS 35, GIANTS 20
Saturday, December 24

N.Y. Giants	10	7	3	0—20
Washington	14	7	7	7—35

First Quarter
Was.—Moss 17 pass from Brunell (Hall kick), 8:58.
NYG—FG, Feely 47, 11:50.
NYG—Blackburn 31 interception return (Feely kick), 12:40.
Was.—Moss 59 pass from Brunell (Hall kick), 14:47.

Second Quarter
Was.—Cooley 17 pass from Portis (Hall kick), 11:45.
NYG—Toomer 25 pass from Manning (Feely kick), 14:50.

Third Quarter
Was.—Moss 72 pass from Ramsey (Hall kick), 9:15.
NYG—FG, Feely 38, 12:05.

Fourth Quarter
Was.—Portis 19 run (Hall kick), 2:17.
Attendance—90,477.

	N.Y. Giants	Washington
First downs	18	22
Rushes-yards	19-99	43-156
Passing	233	224
Punt returns	2-2	1-5
Kickoff returns	6-162	5-106
Interception returns	1-31	1-27
Comp.-att.-int.	23-42-1	13-19-1
Sacked-yards lost	1-11	1-9
Punts	3-43	5-44
Fumbles-lost	0-0	0-0
Penalties-yards	9-64	6-81
Time of possession	26:47	33:13

INDIVIDUAL STATISTICS

RUSHING—New York, Barber 16-80, Manning 2-13, Jacobs 1-6. Washington, Portis 27-108, Betts 13-36, Brunell 2-8, A. Brown 1-4.

PASSING—New York, Manning 23-41-1-244, Barber 0-1-0-0. Washington, Brunell 7-11-1-112, Ramsey 5-7-0-104, Portis 1-1-0-17.

RECEIVING—New York, Toomer 6-85, Barber 6-49, Shiancoe 3-40, Burress 3-40, Finn 3-12, Shockey 2-18. Washington, Moss 5-160, Cooley 5-41, Royal 1-13, Portis 1-10, Betts 1-9.

MISSED FIELD GOAL ATTEMPTS—New York, Feely 29.

INTERCEPTIONS—New York, Blackburn 1-31. Washington, Marshall 1-27.

KICKOFF RETURNS—New York, Morton 6-162. Washington, A. Brown 4-86, Sellers 1-20.

PUNT RETURNS—New York, Morton 2-2. Washington, A. Brown 1-5.

SACKS—New York, Greisen 1. Washington, Daniels 1.

CHIEFS 20, CHARGERS 7
Saturday, December 24

San Diego	7	0	0	0— 7
Kansas City	7	13	0	0—20

First Quarter
K.C.—L. Johnson 4 run (Tynes kick), 5:32.
S.D.—Gates 18 pass from Brees (Kaeding kick), 10:54.

Second Quarter
K.C.—Parker 42 pass from Green (Tynes kick), :07.
K.C.—L. Johnson 28 pass from Green (kick failed), 13:15.
    Attendance—75,956.

	San Diego	Kansas City
First downs	15	20
Rushes-yards	20-80	37-144
Passing	153	197
Punt returns	2-3	4-59
Kickoff returns	4-85	2-42
Interception returns	0-0	1-0
Comp.-att.-int.	18-33-1	19-35-0
Sacked-yards lost	1-8	2-10
Punts	6-41	5-31
Fumbles-lost	1-1	2-0
Penalties-yards	7-58	7-48
Time of possession	25:58	34:02

INDIVIDUAL STATISTICS

RUSHING—San Diego, Tomlinson 14-47, Brees 5-31, Neal 1-2. Kansas City, L. Johnson 32-131, Green 4-7, D. Hall 1-6.

PASSING—San Diego, Brees 18-33-1-161. Kansas City, Green 19-35-0-207.

RECEIVING—San Diego, McCardell 6-58, Gates 4-52, E. Parker 4-33, Tomlinson 3-18, Peelle 1-0. Kansas City, Gonzalez 5-58, Parker 4-58, L. Johnson 4-48, Richardson 2-20, Kennison 2-19, D. Hall 1-2, Dunn 1-2.

MISSED FIELD GOAL ATTEMPTS—Kansas City, Tynes 52.

INTERCEPTIONS—Kansas City, Surtain 1-0.

KICKOFF RETURNS—San Diego, Sproles 4-85. Kansas City, D. Hall 2-42.

PUNT RETURNS—San Diego, E. Parker 2-3. Kansas City, D. Hall 4-59.

SACKS—San Diego, Edwards 1, Foley 1. Kansas City, Allen 1.

BUCCANEERS 27, FALCONS 24
Saturday, December 24

Atlanta	7	10	0	7	0—24
Tampa Bay	7	7	0	10	3—27

First Quarter
Atl.—Griffith 4 pass from Vick (T. Peterson kick), 11:33.
T.B.—Cook 9 pass from Simms (M. Bryant kick), 14:40.

Second Quarter
T.B.—Alstott 13 pass from Simms (M. Bryant kick), 2:10.
Atl.—Jenkins 8 pass from Vick (T. Peterson kick), 11:41.
Atl.—FG, T. Peterson 31, 14:51.

Fourth Quarter
T.B.—FG, M. Bryant 50, 5:59.
Atl.—Duckett 2 run (T. Peterson kick), 10:42.
T.B.—C. Williams 6 run (M. Bryant kick), 14:35.

Overtime
T.B.—FG, M. Bryant 41, 14:45.
    Attendance—65,482.

	Atlanta	Tampa Bay
First downs	19	30
Rushes-yards	36-154	37-174
Passing	127	270
Punt returns	1-8	6-55
Kickoff returns	5-104	6-121
Interception returns	2-82	0-0
Comp.-att.-int.	16-26-0	29-42-0
Sacked-yards lost	4-34	2-15
Punts	7-45	5-43
Fumbles-lost	1-1	1-1
Penalties-yards	7-85	8-107
Time of possession	33:39	41:06

INDIVIDUAL STATISTICS

RUSHING—Atlanta, Dunn 14-59, Vick 11-63, Duckett 11-32. Tampa Bay, C. Williams 31-150, Pittman 4-17, Alstott 1-5, Simms 1-2.

PASSING—Atlanta, Vick 16-26-0-161. Tampa Bay, Simms 29-42-2-285.

RECEIVING—Atlanta, Crumpler 4-63, Jenkins 4-54, R. White 3-31, Griffith 2-4, Dunn 1-5, Finneran 1-4, McCrary 1-0. Tampa Bay, Galloway 8-97, Smith 8-75, Pittman 4-17, Alstott 3-32, Becht 3-32, Clayton 1-11, C. Williams 1-10, Cook 1-9, I. Hilliard 1-6.

MISSED FIELD GOAL ATTEMPTS—Atlanta, T. Peterson 28. Tampa Bay, M. Bryant 27.

INTERCEPTIONS—Atlanta, D. Hall 1-65, Brooking 1-17.

KICKOFF RETURNS—Atlanta, Cobb 5-104. Tampa Bay, Shepherd 5-110, Graham 1-11.

PUNT RETURNS—Atlanta, Cobb 1-8. Tampa Bay, Jones 6-55.

SACKS—Atlanta, Kerney 1, R. Coleman 1. Tampa Bay, Rice 2, Brooks 1, D. Jackson 1.

DOLPHINS 24, TITANS 10
Saturday, December 24

Tennessee	3	0	0	7—10
Miami	0	17	0	7—24

First Quarter
Ten.—FG, Bironas 24, 13:11.

Second Quarter
Mia.—FG, Mare 25, 7:29.
Mia.—Chambers 11 pass from Frerotte (Mare kick), 12:12.
Mia.—Chambers 7 pass from Frerotte (Mare kick), 14:33.

Fourth Quarter
Ten.—Bennett 55 pass from Volek (Bironas kick), 2:40.
Mia.—R. Williams 19 run (Mare kick), 13:12.
    Attendance—72,001.

	Tennessee	Miami
First downs	11	19
Rushes-yards	25-92	38-192
Passing	142	130
Punt returns	8-25	5-28
Kickoff returns	3-58	3-78
Interception returns	1-0	2-0
Comp.-att.-int.	19-37-2	14-30-1
Sacked-yards lost	4-24	3-21
Punts	9-42	9-44
Fumbles-lost	3-1	4-1
Penalties-yards	5-28	4-30
Time of possession	31:48	28:12

INDIVIDUAL STATISTICS

RUSHING—Tennessee, Henry 16-65, Brown 7-18, McNair 1-8, Wade 1-1. Miami, R. Williams 26-172, Morris 5-11, Frerotte 4-4, Chambers 3-5.

PASSING—Tennessee, Volek 14-24-0-132, McNair 5-13-2-34. Miami, Frerotte 14-30-1-151.

RECEIVING—Tennessee, Bennett 4-70, Roby 3-30, Scaife 3-18, Henry 3-10, Wade 2-14, Calico 1-9, Kinney 1-6, Payton 1-5, Fleming 1-4. Miami, Chambers 5-51, McMichael 4-42, Booker 3-50, Morris 1-5, R. Williams 1-3.

MISSED FIELD GOAL ATTEMPTS—None.

INTERCEPTIONS—Tennessee, Thompson 1-0. Miami, Spragan 1-0, Madison 1-0.

KICKOFF RETURNS—Tennessee, P. Jones 2-45, Roby 1-13. Miami, Gilmore 3-78.

PUNT RETURNS—Tennessee, P. Jones 8-25. Miami, Welker 5-28.

SACKS—Tennessee, Starks 1.5, Bulluck 1, LaBoy 0.5. Miami, Holliday 1, Carter 1, Taylor 1, D. Bowens 1.

SEAHAWKS 28, COLTS 13

Saturday, December 24

Indianapolis	3	3	0	7—13
Seattle	7	7	7	7—28

First Quarter
Ind.—FG, Vanderjagt 24, 7:09.
Sea.—Alexander 2 run (J. Brown kick), 9:18.

Second Quarter
Sea.—Stevens 15 pass from Hasselbeck (J. Brown kick), 3:14.
Ind.—FG, Vanderjagt 32, 14:23.

Third Quarter
Sea.—Alexander 6 pass from Hasselbeck (J. Brown kick), 4:03.

Fourth Quarter
Sea.—Alexander 1 run (J. Brown kick), 11:02.
Ind.—Walters 6 pass from Sorgi (Vanderjagt kick), 13:01.
Attendance—67,855.

	Indianapolis	Seattle
First downs	20	21
Rushes-yards	23-43	30-173
Passing	344	159
Punt returns	2-50	0-0
Kickoff returns	5-105	4-114
Interception returns	0-0	0-0
Comp.-att.-int.	31-43-0	17-21-0
Sacked-yards lost	2-9	2-9
Punts	3-38	5-50
Fumbles-lost	1-1	0-0
Penalties-yards	4-30	5-30
Time of possession	33:37	26:23

INDIVIDUAL STATISTICS

RUSHING—Indianapolis, James 13-41, Rhodes 5-(minus 4), Sorgi 3-7, Mungro 2-(minus 1). Seattle, Alexander 21-139, Morris 9-34.

PASSING—Indianapolis, Sorgi 22-31-0-237, Manning 9-12-0-116. Seattle, Hasselbeck 17-21-0-168.

RECEIVING—Indianapolis, Walters 8-91, Rhodes 6-27, Stokley 5-122, Clark 3-43, James 3-14, Wayne 2-21, Fletcher 2-19, Moorehead 2-16. Seattle, Stevens 5-39, Jackson 3-34, Jurevicius 2-31, Strong 1-16, Engram 1-13, Weaver 1-12, Hannam 1-9, Alexander 1-6, Hackett 1-5, Morris 1-3.

MISSED FIELD GOAL ATTEMPTS—Indianapolis, Vanderjagt 31. Seattle, J. Brown 57.

INTERCEPTIONS—None.

KICKOFF RETURNS—Indianapolis, Rhodes 5-105. Seattle, Scobey 4-114.

PUNT RETURNS—Indianapolis, Walters 2-50.

SACKS—Indianapolis, Gardner 1, Thomas 0.5, Labinjo 0.5. Seattle, Tubbs 1, Wistrom 1.

CARDINALS 27, EAGLES 21

Saturday, December 24

Philadelphia	0	7	0	14—21
Arizona	6	7	7	7—27

First Quarter
Ariz.—FG, Rackers 32, 7:36.
Ariz.—FG, Rackers 32, 11:26.

Second Quarter
Ariz.—Dansby 11 interception return (Rackers kick), 4:32.
Phi.—McMahon 1 run (Akers kick), 8:22.

Third Quarter
Ariz.—Fitzgerald 25 pass from McCown (Rackers kick), 4:24.

Fourth Quarter
Ariz.—Boldin 20 pass from McCown (Rackers kick), 3:35.
Phi.—McMullen 21 pass from McMahon (Akers kick), 4:39.
Phi.—McMahon 1 run (Akers kick), 14:34.
Attendance—44,723.

	Philadelphia	Arizona
First downs	11	19
Rushes-yards	17-43	32-75
Passing	146	285
Punt returns	5-55	9-57

	Philadelphia	Arizona
Kickoff returns	6-190	4-76
Interception returns	1-7	1-11
Comp.-att.-int.	14-36-1	27-38-1
Sacked-yards lost	4-24	2-9
Punts	10-50	8-48
Fumbles-lost	1-0	2-0
Penalties-yards	10-103	9-83
Time of possession	21:06	38:54

INDIVIDUAL STATISTICS

RUSHING—Philadelphia, Moats 9-13, Mahe 4-5, McMahon 3-21, Perry 1-4. Arizona, Shipp 13-42, Arrington 10-23, McCown 4-8, Anderson 2-7, O. Ayanbadejo 2-1, Boldin 1-(minus 6).

PASSING—Philadelphia, McMahon 12-33-1-151, Detmer 2-3-0-19. Arizona, McCown 27-38-1-294.

RECEIVING—Philadelphia, R. Brown 6-69, McCants 2-39, McMullen 2-25, Mahe 2-16, C. Lewis 1-12, Smith 1-9. Arizona, Boldin 9-81, Fitzgerald 5-93, Bergen 4-54, Edwards 4-21, B. Johnson 3-26, O. Ayanbadejo 2-19.

MISSED FIELD GOAL ATTEMPTS—Arizona, Rackers 54.

INTERCEPTIONS—Philadelphia, S. Brown 1-7. Arizona, Dansby 1-11.

KICKOFF RETURNS—Philadelphia, Perry 6-190. Arizona, Swinton 3-72, Green 1-4.

PUNT RETURNS—Philadelphia, Mahe 3-24, Wynn 2-31. Arizona, Swinton 9-57.

SACKS—Philadelphia, Kalu 1, Kearse 1. Arizona, Wilson 2, Okeafor 2.

BRONCOS 22, RAIDERS 3

Saturday, December 24

Oakland	0	0	0	3— 3
Denver	10	6	6	0—22

First Quarter
Den.—FG, Elam 29, 4:18.
Den.—Plummer 1 run (Elam kick), 14:27.

Second Quarter
Den.—Mi. Anderson 2 run (run failed), 12:43.

Third Quarter
Den.—FG, Elam 33, 1:47.
Den.—FG, Elam 34, 5:41.

Fourth Quarter
Oak.—FG, Janikowski 43, :50.
Attendance—76,212.

	Oakland	Denver
First downs	15	24
Rushes-yards	17-87	40-155
Passing	161	259
Punt returns	1-12	2-41
Kickoff returns	5-115	2-56
Interception returns	1-2	1-0
Comp.-att.-int.	17-41-1	19-29-1
Sacked-yards lost	1-17	2-9
Punts	5-59	2-43
Fumbles-lost	2-1	0-0
Penalties-yards	6-41	5-25
Time of possession	21:28	38:32

INDIVIDUAL STATISTICS

RUSHING—Oakland, Crockett 15-61, Fargas 2-26. Denver, Bell 17-71, Mi. Anderson 10-46, Dayne 8-22, Plummer 3-16, Lelie 1-7, Adams 1-(minus 7).

PASSING—Oakland, Collins 17-41-1-178. Denver, Plummer 19-29-1-268.

RECEIVING—Oakland, Moss 5-72, Porter 4-29, Ra. Williams 2-22, Gabriel 2-18, Crockett 2-17, Foschi 1-11, Fargas 1-9. Denver, Lelie 6-110, Smith 5-91, Mi. Anderson 2-20, S. Alexander 2-17, Bell 2-12, Putzier 1-17, Devoe 1-1.

MISSED FIELD GOAL ATTEMPTS—Denver, Elam 52.

INTERCEPTIONS—Oakland, Schweigert 1-2. Denver, N. Ferguson 1-0.

KICKOFF RETURNS—Oakland, Carr 4-107, Flemister 1-8. Denver, R. Alexander 1-31, Adams 1-25.

PUNT RETURNS—Oakland, Carr 1-12. Denver, Adams 2-41.

SACKS—Oakland, Burgess 1, Jasper 1. Denver, Lynch 1.

BEARS 24, PACKERS 17

Sunday, December 25

Chicago	7	7	10	0—24
Green Bay	0	7	0	10—17

First Quarter

Chi.—Muhammad 12 pass from Grossman (Gould kick), 10:00.

Second Quarter

G.B.—Herron 1 run (Longwell kick), 2:55.
Chi.—T. Jones 2 run (Gould kick), 9:55.

Third Quarter

Chi.—FG, Gould 45, 5:21.
Chi.—Briggs 10 interception return (Gould kick), 10:59.

Fourth Quarter

G.B.—Chatman 85 punt return (Longwell kick), 7:06.
G.B.—FG, Longwell 26, 13:06.
  Attendance—69,757.

	Chicago	Green Bay
First downs	16	24
Rushes-yards	33-135	21-65
Passing	157	300
Punt returns	3-30	3-90
Kickoff returns	4-60	5-97
Interception returns	4-10	1-12
Comp.-att.-int.	11-23-1	30-51-4
Sacked-yards lost	1-9	2-17
Punts	6-41	3-40
Fumbles-lost	0-0	0-0
Penalties-yards	8-55	9-69
Time of possession	26:57	33:03

INDIVIDUAL STATISTICS

RUSHING—Chicago, T. Jones 25-105, Peterson 8-30. Green Bay, Herron 14-33, Fisher 6-22, Chatman 1-10.

PASSING—Chicago, Grossman 11-23-1-166. Green Bay, Favre 30-51-4-317.

RECEIVING—Chicago, Muhammad 5-58, Berrian 3-93, Gage 2-14, T. Jones 1-1. Green Bay, Fisher 8-61, Driver 6-107, Chatman 5-45, Thurman 3-52, D. Lee 3-10, Gardner 2-23, Leach 2-11, D. Martin 1-8.

MISSED FIELD GOAL ATTEMPTS—Green Bay, Longwell 38, 39.

INTERCEPTIONS—Chicago, C. Harris 2-0, Briggs 1-10, Tillman 1-0. Green Bay, Roman 1-12.

KICKOFF RETURNS—Chicago, Davis 2-39, Azumah 1-21, Vasher 1-0. Green Bay, Carroll 5-97.

PUNT RETURNS—Chicago, Berrian 3-30. Green Bay, Chatman 3-90.

SACKS—Chicago, A. Brown 1, T. Johnson 1. Green Bay, Gbaja-Biamila 1.

RAVENS 30, VIKINGS 23

Sunday, December 25

Minnesota		7	7	6	3—23
Baltimore		7	3	7	13—30

First Quarter

Min.—T. Taylor 13 pass from B. Johnson (Edinger kick), 3:59.
Bal.—Heap 6 pass from Boller (Stover kick), 13:25.

Second Quarter

Min.—Wiggins 5 pass from B. Johnson (Edinger kick), 13:54.
Bal.—FG, Stover 37, 15:00.

Third Quarter

Min.—FG, Edinger 36, 1:31.
Bal.—Clayton 47 pass from Boller (Stover kick), 5:11.
Min.—FG, Edinger 40, 10:46.

Fourth Quarter

Bal.—Mason 39 pass from Boller (Stover kick), :13.
Bal.—FG, Stover 38, 13:05.
Bal.—FG, Stover 19, 13:57.
Min.—FG, Edinger 46, 14:45.
  Attendance—70,246.

	Minnesota	Baltimore
First downs	18	23
Rushes-yards	14-42	32-88
Passing	220	279
Punt returns	1-16	0-0
Kickoff returns	5-94	5-84
Interception returns	1-11	0-0
Comp.-att.-int.	25-36-0	24-34-1
Sacked-yards lost	3-28	2-10
Punts	4-31	2-52
Fumbles-lost	1-1	1-1
Penalties-yards	6-50	7-35
Time of possession	26:54	33:06

INDIVIDUAL STATISTICS

RUSHING—Minnesota, Moore 10-49, Fason 2-(minus 4), M. Bennett 1-(minus 1), T. Taylor 1-(minus 2). Baltimore, J. Lewis 24-74, C. Taylor 5-15, Boller 2-1, Clayton 1-(minus 2).

PASSING—Minnesota, B. Johnson 25-36-0-248. Baltimore, Boller 24-34-1-289.

RECEIVING—Minnesota, Wiggins 7-43, Moore 4-42, Burleson 4-26, T. Taylor 3-40, Kleinsasser 2-11, Williamson 1-56, Angulo 1-11, M. Bennett 1-10, K. Robinson 1-5, M. Robinson 1-4. Baltimore, Mason 9-103, Clayton 5-90, Heap 4-30, C. Taylor 3-49, J. Lewis 2-11, Mughelli 1-6.

MISSED FIELD GOAL ATTEMPTS—None.

INTERCEPTIONS—Minnesota, Sharper 1-11.

KICKOFF RETURNS—Minnesota, K. Robinson 4-78, Owens 1-16. Baltimore, C. Taylor 5-84.

PUNT RETURNS—Minnesota, Moore 1-16.

SACKS—Minnesota, R. Smith 1, Cowart 1. Baltimore, Polley 1, A. Thomas 1, Suggs 0.5, Gregg 0.5.

PATRIOTS 31, JETS 21

Monday, December 26

New England		7	14	7	3—31
N.Y. Jets		7	0	0	14—21

First Quarter

N.E.—Vrabel 1 pass from Brady (Vinatieri kick), 9:33.
NYJ—Law 74 interception return (Nugent kick), 10:42.

Second Quarter

N.E.—Vrabel 2 pass from Brady (Vinatieri kick), 8:55.
N.E.—Dillon 1 run (Vinatieri kick), 14:23.

Third Quarter

N.E.—Dillon 1 run (Vinatieri kick), 9:24.

Fourth Quarter

NYJ—Coles 11 pass from Bollinger (Nugent kick), 1:08.
N.E.—FG, Vinatieri 26, 7:45.
NYJ—Coles 27 pass from Testaverde (Nugent kick), 12:50.
  Attendance—77,569.

	New England	N.Y. Jets
First downs	26	10
Rushes-yards	50-151	10-40
Passing	170	131
Punt returns	2-20	1-3
Kickoff returns	4-50	4-83
Interception returns	1-15	1-74
Comp.-att.-int.	19-30-1	14-26-1
Sacked-yards lost	3-17	4-32
Punts	2-41	4-44
Fumbles-lost	1-0	2-2
Penalties-yards	4-30	9-69
Time of possession	43:21	16:39

INDIVIDUAL STATISTICS

RUSHING—New England, Dillon 26-77, Faulk 10-38, H. Evans 6-16, Brady 3-7, Flutie 2-(minus 1). New York, Houston 5-14, Blaylock 3-20, Bollinger 2-6.

PASSING—New England, Brady 18-29-1-185, Flutie 1-1-0-2. New York, Bollinger 11-19-1-100, Testaverde 3-7-0-63.

RECEIVING—New England, Branch 4-69, Faulk 4-19, T. Brown 3-31, Watson 2-37, Givens 2-21, Vrabel 2-3, Fauria 1-5, Pass 1-2. New York, Coles 5-71, McCareins 4-51, Cotchery 2-32, Blaylock 1-4, Sowell 1-3, Houston 1-2.

MISSED FIELD GOAL ATTEMPTS—None.

INTERCEPTIONS—New England, Samuel 1-15. New York, Law 1-74.

KICKOFF RETURNS—New England, B. Johnson 1-23, Faulk 1-16, Pass 1-10, Watson 1-1. New York, Miller 1-39, Cotchery 1-27, Blaylock 1-17, Barrett 1-0.

PUNT RETURNS—New England, Dwight 1-13, T. Brown 1-7. New York, Cotchery 1-3.

SACKS—New England, Vrabel 1, Seymour 1, Poteat 1, Colvin 0.5, McGinest 0.5. New York, Reed 1, J. Abraham 1, Vilma 0.5, Legree 0.5.

WEEK 17

STANDINGS

AMERICAN FOOTBALL CONFERENCE

EAST DIVISION

	W	L	T	Pct.	PF	PA
New England	10	6	0	.625	379	338
Miami	9	7	0	.563	318	317
Buffalo	5	11	0	.313	271	367
N.Y. Jets	4	12	0	.250	240	355

NORTH DIVISION

	W	L	T	Pct.	PF	PA
Cincinnati	11	5	0	.688	421	350
Pittsburgh	11	5	0	.688	389	258
Baltimore	6	10	0	.375	265	299
Cleveland	6	10	0	.375	232	301

SOUTH DIVISION

	W	L	T	Pct.	PF	PA
Indianapolis	14	2	0	.875	439	247
Jacksonville	12	4	0	.750	361	269
Tennessee	4	12	0	.250	299	421
Houston	2	14	0	.125	260	431

WEST DIVISION

	W	L	T	Pct.	PF	PA
Denver	13	3	0	.813	395	258
Kansas City	10	6	0	.625	403	325
San Diego	9	7	0	.563	418	312
Oakland	4	12	0	.250	290	383

NATIONAL FOOTBALL CONFERENCE

EAST DIVISION

	W	L	T	Pct.	PF	PA
N.Y. Giants	11	5	0	.688	422	314
Washington	10	6	0	.625	359	293
Dallas	9	7	0	.563	325	308
Philadelphia	6	10	0	.375	310	388

NORTH DIVISION

	W	L	T	Pct.	PF	PA
Chicago	11	5	0	.688	260	202
Minnesota	9	7	0	.563	306	344
Detroit	5	11	0	.313	254	345
Green Bay	4	12	0	.250	298	344

SOUTH DIVISION

	W	L	T	Pct.	PF	PA
Carolina	11	5	0	.688	391	259
Tampa Bay	11	5	0	.688	300	274
Atlanta	8	8	0	.500	351	341
New Orleans	3	13	0	.188	235	398

WEST DIVISION

	W	L	T	Pct.	PF	PA
Seattle	13	3	0	.813	452	271
St. Louis	6	10	0	.375	363	429
Arizona	5	11	0	.313	311	387
San Francisco	4	12	0	.250	239	428

TOP PERFORMANCES

100-YARD RUSHING GAMES

Player, team & opponent	Att.	Yds.	TD
Tiki Barber, NYG at Oak.	28	203	1
Larry Johnson, K.C. vs. Cin.	26	201	3
DeShaun Foster, Car. at Atl.	18	165	1
Willie Parker, Pit. vs. Det.	26	135	0
Willis McGahee, Buf. at NYJ	22	113	0
Clinton Portis, Was. at Phi.	27	112	2
Frank Gore, S.F. vs. Hou.*	25	108	0
Ricky Williams, Mia. at N.E.	28	108	1
LaBrandon Toefield, Jac. vs. Ten.	25	102	1

300-YARD PASSING GAMES

Player, team & opponent	Att.	Cmp.	Yds.	TD	Int.
Trent Green, K.C. vs. Cin.	29	23	344	1	0
Kerry Collins, Oak. vs. NYG	48	26	331	3	0

100-YARD RECEIVING GAMES

Player, team & opponent	Rec.	Yds.	TD
Eddie Kennison, K.C. vs. Cin.	7	151	0
Steve Smith, Car. at Atl.	9	131	1
Plaxico Burress, NYG at Oak.	5	128	1
Antonio Bryant, Cle. vs. Bal.	9	123	1
Donald Driver, G.B. vs. Sea.	6	118	0
Randy Moss, Oak. vs. NYG	7	116	2
Doug Gabriel, Oak. vs. NYG	8	100	1

*Overtime game.

RESULTS

SATURDAY, DECEMBER 31
Denver 23, SAN DIEGO 7
N.Y. Giants 30, OAKLAND 21

SUNDAY, JANUARY 1
PITTSBURGH 35, Detroit 21
GREEN BAY 23, Seattle 17
INDIANAPOLIS 17, Arizona 13
KANSAS CITY 37, Cincinnati 3
N.Y. JETS 30, Buffalo 26
Carolina 44, ATLANTA 11
Miami 28, NEW ENGLAND 26
CLEVELAND 20, Baltimore 16
TAMPA BAY 27, New Orleans 13
JACKSONVILLE 40, Tennessee 13
Washington 31, PHILADELPHIA 20
SAN FRANCISCO 20, Houston 17 (OT)
MINNESOTA 34, Chicago 10
St. Louis 20, DALLAS 10

BRONCOS 23, CHARGERS 7
Saturday, December 31

Denver	0	14	2	7—23
San Diego	0	7	0	0— 7

Second Quarter
Den.—Bell 6 run (Elam kick), 3:12.
Den.—Bell 1 run (Elam kick), 11:36.
S.D.—Tomlinson 6 run (Kaeding kick), 14:22.
Third Quarter
Den.—Safety, 9:30.
Fourth Quarter
Den.—Bell 19 run (Elam kick), 10:28.
Attendance—65,513.

	Denver	San Diego
First downs	17	15
Rushes-yards	40-157	20-91
Passing	84	145
Punt returns	3-17	5-42
Kickoff returns	3-53	4-87
Interception returns	1-48	0-0
Comp.-att.-int.	10-22-0	20-36-1
Sacked-yards lost	2-14	6-38
Punts	7-46	7-44
Fumbles-lost	1-0	3-1
Penalties-yards	4-22	8-70
Time of possession	33:22	26:38

INDIVIDUAL STATISTICS
RUSHING—Denver, Bell 17-52, Dayne 13-64, Van Pelt 10-41. San Diego, Tomlinson 19-92, Turner 1-(minus 1).
PASSING—Denver, Plummer 8-14-0-91, Van Pelt 2-8-0-7. San Diego, Rivers 12-22-1-115, Brees 8-14-0-68.
RECEIVING—Denver, K. Johnson 2-27, Lelie 2-19, Adams 2-6, Duke 1-21, Smith 1-11, S. Alexander 1-11, Putzier 1-3. San Diego, E. Parker 8-87, McCardell 6-51, Gates 3-23, Caldwell 2-18, Tomlinson 1-4.
MISSED FIELD GOAL ATTEMPTS—Denver, Elam 28.
INTERCEPTIONS—Denver, Cox 1-48.
KICKOFF RETURNS—Denver, R. Alexander 2-38, Adams 1-15. San Diego, Sproles 4-87.
PUNT RETURNS—Denver, Adams 3-17. San Diego, E. Parker 5-42.
SACKS—Denver, Lynch 2, Gold 1, Pryce 1, Ekuban 1, Warren 1. San Diego, Merriman 1, Phillips 1.

GIANTS 30, RAIDERS 21
Saturday, December 31

N.Y. Giants	7	13	7	3—30
Oakland	7	7	7	0—21

First Quarter
NYG—Barber 95 run (Feely kick), 7:01.
Oak.—Moss 15 pass from Collins (Janikowski kick), 11:27.
Second Quarter
NYG—FG, Feely 25, 2:23.
NYG—Burress 78 pass from Manning (Feely kick), 5:19.
NYG—FG, Feely 38, 13:04.
Oak.—Gabriel 8 pass from Collins (Janikowski kick), 14:41.
Third Quarter
NYG—Jacobs 1 run (Feely kick), 11:32.
Oak.—Moss 44 pass from Collins (Janikowski kick), 12:32.
Fourth Quarter
NYG—FG, Feely 46, :12.
Attendance—44,594.

	N.Y. Giants	Oakland
First downs	13	21
Rushes-yards	34-211	17-25
Passing	191	300
Punt returns	6-98	3-9
Kickoff returns	4-75	7-154
Interception returns	0-0	0-0
Comp.-att.-int.	12-24-0	26-48-0
Sacked-yards lost	2-13	3-31
Punts	6-39	9-47
Fumbles-lost	1-0	1-0
Penalties-yards	9-70	8-54
Time of possession	31:52	28:08

INDIVIDUAL STATISTICS
RUSHING—New York, Barber 28-203, Jacobs 3-10, Manning 2-(minus 2), Cloud 1-0. Oakland, Crockett 15-27, Collins 1-0, Fargas 1-(minus 2).
PASSING—New York, Manning 12-24-0-204. Oakland, Collins 26-48-0-331.
RECEIVING—New York, Barber 6-60, Burress 5-128, Shiancoe 1-16. Oakland, Gabriel 8-100, Moss 7-116, Porter 6-76, Ra. Williams 3-26, Whitted 1-7, Crockett 1-6.
MISSED FIELD GOAL ATTEMPTS—None.
INTERCEPTIONS—None.
KICKOFF RETURNS—New York, Morton 4-75. Oakland, Carr 7-154.
PUNT RETURNS—New York, Morton 6-98. Oakland, Carr 3-9.
SACKS—New York, Umenyiora 2, Clancy 1. Oakland, Burgess 1, Kelly 1.

STEELERS 35, LIONS 21
Sunday, January 1

Detroit	14	0	7	0—21
Pittsburgh	14	7	14	0—35

First Quarter
Pit.—Randle El 81 punt return (Reed kick), 1:17.
Det.—Pollard 11 pass from Harrington (Hanson kick), 5:17.
Det.—Schlesinger 1 pass from Harrington (Hanson kick), 11:27.
Pit.—Bettis 1 run (Reed kick), 14:39.
Second Quarter
Pit.—Bettis 5 run (Reed kick), 13:49.
Third Quarter
Pit.—Bettis 4 run (Reed kick), 4:00.
Det.—R. Williams 15 pass from Harrington (Hanson kick), 9:28.
Pit.—Roethlisberger 7 run (Reed kick), 14:18.
Attendance—63,794.

	Detroit	Pittsburgh
First downs	16	20
Rushes-yards	25-105	44-199
Passing	203	132
Punt returns	2-1	2-79
Kickoff returns	6-126	4-123
Interception returns	2-22	0-0
Comp.-att.-int.	17-33-0	7-16-2
Sacked-yards lost	1-9	1-3
Punts	6-39	4-41
Fumbles-lost	3-2	0-0
Penalties-yards	5-47	2-15
Time of possession	27:29	32:31

INDIVIDUAL STATISTICS
RUSHING—Detroit, Jones 18-78, Bryson 3-11, Harrington 2-11, P. Smith 2-5. Pittsburgh, Parker 26-135, Bettis 10-41, Haynes 4-17, Roethlisberger 3-5, Randle El 1-1.
PASSING—Detroit, Harrington 17-33-0-212. Pittsburgh, Roethlisberger 7-16-2-135.
RECEIVING—Detroit, Pollard 4-50, Vines 4-44, R. Williams 3-31, P. Smith 2-16, Schlesinger 2-6, Bryson 1-63, Jones 1-2. Pittsburgh, Miller 3-62, Ward 1-40, Parker 1-17, Randle El 1-13, Haynes 1-3.
MISSED FIELD GOAL ATTEMPTS—None.
INTERCEPTIONS—Detroit, Bra. Walker 1-22, Goodman 1-0.
KICKOFF RETURNS—Detroit, Drummond 6-126. Pittsburgh, Morgan 3-60, Colclough 1-63.
PUNT RETURNS—Detroit, Drummond 2-1. Pittsburgh, Randle El 2-79.
SACKS—Detroit, Hall 1. Pittsburgh, Farrior 1.

PACKERS 23, SEAHAWKS 17
Sunday, January 1

Seattle	0	7	7	3—17
Green Bay	6	7	7	3—23

First Quarter
G.B.—FG, Longwell 26, 6:16.
G.B.—FG, Longwell 32, 11:55.
Second Quarter
Sea.—Alexander 1 run (J. Brown kick), 2:00.
G.B.—Herron 11 run (Longwell kick), 6:38.
Third Quarter
Sea.—Jurevicius 5 pass from S. Wallace (J. Brown kick), 4:28.
G.B.—Chatman 9 pass from Favre (Longwell kick), 11:19.
Fourth Quarter
G.B.—FG, Longwell 28, 4:04.
Sea.—FG, J. Brown 44, 13:22.
Attendance—69,928.

– 212 –

	Seattle	Green Bay
First downs	17	21
Rushes-yards	30-98	33-68
Passing	147	246
Punt returns	1-12	3-(-5)
Kickoff returns	6-82	3-63
Interception returns	1-0	1-8
Comp.-att.-int.	15-25-1	21-37-1
Sacked-yards lost	4-27	3-13
Punts	6-37	3-33
Fumbles-lost	2-1	2-2
Penalties-yards	5-58	7-50
Time of possession	24:47	35:13

INDIVIDUAL STATISTICS

RUSHING—Seattle, Alexander 20-73, Morris 9-25, S. Wallace 1-0. Green Bay, Herron 23-61, Fisher 7-16, Rodgers 1-(minus 1), Favre 1-(minus 1), Chatman 1-(minus 7).

PASSING—Seattle, S. Wallace 9-17-1-98, Hasselbeck 6-8-0-76. Green Bay, Favre 21-37-1-259.

RECEIVING—Seattle, Hackett 4-39, Engram 3-30, Warrick 2-44, Morris 2-19, Jurevicius 2-11, Strong 1-27, Hannam 1-4. Green Bay, Driver 6-118, Fisher 6-44, Chatman 4-33, Gardner 2-44, D. Lee 2-10, Henderson 1-10.

MISSED FIELD GOAL ATTEMPTS—None.

INTERCEPTIONS—Seattle, J. Williams 1-0. Green Bay, Harris 1-8.

KICKOFF RETURNS—Seattle, Scobey 6-82. Green Bay, Carroll 2-53, Henderson 1-10.

PUNT RETURNS—Seattle, J. Williams 1-12. Green Bay, Chatman 3-(minus 5).

SACKS—Seattle, B. Fisher 1, Hill 0.5, Tubbs 0.5, Team 1. Green Bay, Gbaja-Biamila 2, Peterson 1, Jenkins 1.

COLTS 17, CARDINALS 13
Sunday, January 1

Arizona	0	3	7	3—13
Indianapolis	7	3	7	0—17

First Quarter
Ind.—Utecht 14 pass from Sorgi (Vanderjagt kick), 10:16.

Second Quarter
Ariz.—FG, Rackers 28, 1:56.
Ind.—FG, Vanderjagt 44, 12:19.

Third Quarter
Ind.—Walters 18 pass from Sorgi (Vanderjagt kick), 3:34.
Ariz.—Fitzgerald 25 pass from McCown (Rackers kick), 6:31.

Fourth Quarter
Ariz.—FG, Rackers 42, 4:01.
Attendance—57,211.

	Arizona	Indianapolis
First downs	23	15
Rushes-yards	31-129	10-11
Passing	284	207
Punt returns	1-9	2-15
Kickoff returns	4-58	4-65
Interception returns	1-15	1-16
Comp.-att.-int.	31-42-1	21-32-1
Sacked-yards lost	3-13	2-5
Punts	5-39	5-46
Fumbles-lost	2-1	1-0
Penalties-yards	12-98	7-50
Time of possession	36:41	23:19

INDIVIDUAL STATISTICS

RUSHING—Arizona, Shipp 16-57, McCown 8-42, Arrington 5-27, O. Ayanbadejo 2-3. Indianapolis, Rhodes 5-4, Sorgi 4-0, Mungro 1-7.

PASSING—Arizona, McCown 31-42-1-297. Indianapolis, Sorgi 20-30-1-207, Manning 1-2-0-5.

RECEIVING—Arizona, Boldin 8-81, Fitzgerald 6-80, Bergen 4-35, O. Ayanbadejo 4-28, Shipp 3-19, Edwards 2-31, B. Johnson 2-16, Arrington 2-7. Indianapolis, Moorehead 5-59, Walters 5-43, Rhodes 3-29, Utecht 2-33, Mungro 2-21, Harrison 2-19, Hartsock 2-8.

MISSED FIELD GOAL ATTEMPTS—None.

INTERCEPTIONS—Arizona, Darling 1-15. Indianapolis, Gardner 1-16.

KICKOFF RETURNS—Arizona, Swinton 4-58. Indianapolis, Rhodes 3-52, Walters 1-13.

PUNT RETURNS—Arizona, B. Johnson 1-9. Indianapolis, Walters 2-15.

SACKS—Arizona, A. Smith 1, Okeafor 1. Indianapolis, Brock 1.5, Brackett 1, Freeney 0.5.

CHIEFS 37, BENGALS 3
Sunday, January 1

Cincinnati	3	0	0	0— 3
Kansas City	3	17	10	7—37

First Quarter
K.C.—FG, Tynes 39, 10:17.
Cin.—FG, Graham 49, 13:48.

Second Quarter
K.C.—FG, Tynes 24, 4:33.
K.C.—L. Johnson 49 run (Tynes kick), 13:06.
K.C.—L. Johnson 14 run (Tynes kick), 13:46.

Third Quarter
K.C.—L. Johnson 20 run (Tynes kick), 2:19.
K.C.—FG, Tynes 23, 10:49.

Fourth Quarter
K.C.—De. Brown 8 pass from Green (Tynes kick), 12:13.
Attendance—77,211.

	Cincinnati	Kansas City
First downs	10	24
Rushes-yards	22-37	32-202
Passing	124	335
Punt returns	1-10	4-34
Kickoff returns	8-167	1-22
Interception returns	0-0	2-16
Comp.-att.-int.	18-32-2	23-29-0
Sacked-yards lost	1-6	2-9
Punts	7-49	2-50
Fumbles-lost	0-0	2-1
Penalties-yards	6-50	9-80
Time of possession	27:18	32:42

INDIVIDUAL STATISTICS

RUSHING—Cincinnati, Ru. Johnson 10-18, C. Perry 8-10, C. Johnson 1-6, Kitna 1-3, T. Perry 1-0, Luchey 1-0. Kansas City, L. Johnson 26-201, Green 5-(minus 1), De. Brown 1-2.

PASSING—Cincinnati, Kitna 13-24-2-76, Palmer 5-8-0-54. Kansas City, Green 23-29-0-344.

RECEIVING—Cincinnati, C. Johnson 4-55, Houshmandzadeh 3-29, Schobel 3-22, C. Perry 3-9, Stewart 2-16, T. Perry 2-0, Ru. Johnson 1-(minus 1). Kansas City, Kennison 7-151, D. Hall 5-61, Gonzalez 5-59, L. Johnson 2-21, De. Brown 2-14, Richardson 1-22, Parker 1-16.

MISSED FIELD GOAL ATTEMPTS—None.

INTERCEPTIONS—Kansas City, S. Knight 1-12, Surtain 1-4.

KICKOFF RETURNS—Cincinnati, T. Perry 7-167, Schobel 1-0. Kansas City, D. Hall 1-22.

PUNT RETURNS—Cincinnati, Ratliff 1-10. Kansas City, D. Hall 3-17, Kennison 1-17.

SACKS—Cincinnati, Pollack 2. Kansas City, Sapp 1.

JETS 30, BILLS 26
Sunday, January 1

Buffalo	3	10	10	3—26
N.Y. Jets	3	14	3	10—30

First Quarter
Buf.—FG, Lindell 21, 5:31.
NYJ—FG, Nugent 49, 10:02.

Second Quarter
Buf.—FG, Lindell 24, :48.
NYJ—Houston 3 run (Nugent kick), 1:29.
NYJ—Brown 33 interception return (Nugent kick), 1:45.
Buf.—Moulds 22 pass from Holcomb (Lindell kick), 11:03.

Third Quarter
Buf.—FG, Lindell 52, 3:08.
NYJ—FG, Nugent 25, 9:34.
Buf.—Parrish 3 pass from Holcomb (Lindell kick), 14:24.

Fourth Quarter
NYJ—FG, Nugent 34, 4:25.
Buf.—FG, Lindell 36, 8:47.
NYJ—Miller 95 kickoff return (Nugent kick), 9:02.
Attendance—76,822.

	Buffalo	N.Y. Jets
First downs	21	12
Rushes-yards	30-159	27-81
Passing	172	126
Punt returns	2-26	0-0
Kickoff returns	7-151	7-250
Interception returns	0-0	4-89

	Buffalo	N.Y. Jets
Comp.-att.-int.	23-37-4	11-20-0
Sacked-yards lost	2-12	4-27
Punts	1-48	4-40
Fumbles-lost	3-0	0-0
Penalties-yards	3-30	6-40
Time of possession	33:58	26:02

INDIVIDUAL STATISTICS

RUSHING—Buffalo, McGahee 22-113, Holcomb 4-7, S. Williams 3-0, Evans 1-39. New York, Houston 16-55, Bollinger 7-12, Blaylock 4-14.

PASSING—Buffalo, Holcomb 23-37-4-184. New York, Bollinger 11-20-0-153.

RECEIVING—Buffalo, Moulds 8-96, Parrish 4-23, Campbell 3-10, McGahee 2-22, Evans 2-17, Shelton 2-6, S. Williams 1-5, Reed 1-5. New York, Coles 4-79, McCareins 2-11, Cotchery 1-45, Sowell 1-7, Houston 1-6, Dreessen 1-6, Jolley 1-(minus 1).

MISSED FIELD GOAL ATTEMPTS—New York, Nugent 43.

INTERCEPTIONS—New York, Law 3-56, Brown 1-33.

KICKOFF RETURNS—Buffalo, McGee 6-151, Euhus 1-0. New York, Miller 6-221, Cotchery 1-29.

PUNT RETURNS—Buffalo, Parrish 2-26.

SACKS—Buffalo, Adams 2, Posey 1, Baker 1. New York, B. Thomas 1, J. Abraham 1.

PANTHERS 44, FALCONS 11
Sunday, January 1

Carolina	14	13	10	7	—44
Atlanta	3	0	0	8	—11

First Quarter
Car.—Proehl 12 pass from Delhomme (Kasay kick), 4:09.
Atl.—FG, T. Peterson 29, 12:28.
Car.—Foster 70 run (Kasay kick), 13:32.

Second Quarter
Car.—FG, Kasay 19, 11:16.
Car.—S. Smith 42 pass from Delhomme (Kasay kick), 13:06.
Car.—FG, Kasay 41, 15:00.

Third Quarter
Car.—Robertson 1 run (Kasay kick), 7:44.
Car.—FG, Kasay 34, 14:14.

Fourth Quarter
Car.—Manning Jr. 8 fumble return (Kasay kick), 10:41.
Atl.—R. White 14 pass from Schaub (Finneran pass from Schaub), 13:42.
Attendance—70,796.

	Carolina	Atlanta
First downs	23	15
Rushes-yards	38-229	15-26
Passing	174	185
Punt returns	1-8	2-15
Kickoff returns	2-28	8-181
Interception returns	1-0	0-0
Comp.-att.-int.	16-25-0	24-37-1
Sacked-yards lost	1-6	5-40
Punts	3-37	3-45
Fumbles-lost	0-0	3-3
Penalties-yards	6-55	7-70
Time of possession	35:08	24:52

INDIVIDUAL STATISTICS

RUSHING—Carolina, Foster 18-165, Robertson 10-34, Smart 3-6, Weinke 3-(minus 1), Goings 2-18, S. Smith 1-7, Hoover 1-0. Atlanta, Dunn 7-29, Duckett 6-(minus 4), R. White 1-1, Vick 1-0.

PASSING—Carolina, Delhomme 14-20-0-163, Weinke 2-5-0-17. Atlanta, Vick 15-24-1-115, Schaub 9-13-0-110.

RECEIVING—Carolina, S. Smith 9-131, Proehl 3-29, Colbert 2-11, Goings 1-9, Gaines 1-0. Atlanta, Jenkins 5-60, R. White 4-47, Finneran 4-45, Griffith 4-27, Crumpler 3-21, Duckett 2-15, Dunn 2-10.

MISSED FIELD GOAL ATTEMPTS—None.

INTERCEPTIONS—Carolina, Gamble 1-0.

KICKOFF RETURNS—Carolina, Robertson 2-28. Atlanta, Cobb 8-181.

PUNT RETURNS—Carolina, Gamble 1-8. Atlanta, Jenkins 2-15.

SACKS—Carolina, Wallace 2, Moorehead 2, Buckner 1. Atlanta, Brooking 1.

DOLPHINS 28, PATRIOTS 26
Sunday, January 1

Miami	7	6	5	10	—28
New England	7	3	3	13	—26

First Quarter
Mia.—R. Williams 2 run (Mare kick), 11:01.
N.E.—Branch 11 pass from Brady (Vinatieri kick), 14:02.

Second Quarter
Mia.—FG, Mare 36, 9:09.
Mia.—FG, Mare 38, 14:22.
N.E.—FG, Vinatieri 49, 15:00.

Third Quarter
Mia.—FG, Mare 41, 6:03.
N.E.—FG, Vinatieri 33, 10:19.
Mia.—Safety, 13:36.

Fourth Quarter
Mia.—Booker 15 pass from Frerotte (Mare kick), 5:53.
N.E.—Dwight 9 pass from Cassel (Flutie kick), 8:50.
Mia.—FG, Mare 42, 13:05.
N.E.—Watson 9 pass from Cassel (pass failed), 15:00.
Attendance—68,756.

	Miami	New England
First downs	25	16
Rushes-yards	40-148	28-55
Passing	230	204
Punt returns	2-18	1-6
Kickoff returns	4-69	6-196
Interception returns	1-0	0-0
Comp.-att.-int.	22-35-0	14-28-1
Sacked-yards lost	2-9	1-1
Punts	4-39	4-42
Fumbles-lost	0-0	2-0
Penalties-yards	9-77	6-45
Time of possession	38:06	21:54

INDIVIDUAL STATISTICS

RUSHING—Miami, R. Williams 28-108, Brown 8-21, Frerotte 4-19. New England, Pass 9-26, Faulk 6-12, H. Evans 6-7, Cassel 5-13, Brady 1-2, Dwight 1-(minus 1).

PASSING—Miami, Frerotte 22-35-0-239. New England, Cassel 11-20-0-168, Brady 3-8-1-37.

RECEIVING—Miami, Booker 7-86, Chambers 5-75, McMichael 5-35, Welker 2-20, Brown 2-13, Diamond 1-10. New England, Childress 3-32, Andre. Davis 2-47, Watson 2-39, Dwight 2-26, H. Evans 2-24, Branch 2-19, Givens 1-18.

MISSED FIELD GOAL ATTEMPTS—None.

INTERCEPTIONS—Miami, Schulters 1-0.

KICKOFF RETURNS—Miami, Welker 3-66, Minor 1-3. New England, Andre. Davis 3-108, Dwight 2-67, Pass 1-21.

PUNT RETURNS—Miami, Welker 2-18. New England, Dwight 1-6.

SACKS—Miami, Howard 1. New England, Chatham 1, Banta-Cain 0.5, Warren 0.5.

BROWNS 20, RAVENS 16
Sunday, January 1

Baltimore	0	13	3	0	—16
Cleveland	0	6	14	0	—20

Second Quarter
Bal.—FG, Stover 21, :39.
Bal.—FG, Stover 43, 6:44.
Bal.—A. Thomas 9 fumble return (Stover kick), 7:55.
Cle.—FG, Dawson 21, 12:17.
Cle.—FG, Dawson 39, 15:00.

Third Quarter
Bal.—FG, Stover 31, 6:15.
Cle.—Bryant 6 pass from Frye (Dawson kick), 7:33.
Cle.—Northcutt 62 punt return (Dawson kick), 8:55.
Attendance—69,871.

	Baltimore	Cleveland
First downs	12	12
Rushes-yards	32-129	23-54
Passing	138	172
Punt returns	6-30	6-91
Kickoff returns	4-44	5-128
Interception returns	1-48	2-50
Comp.-att.-int.	15-36-2	22-37-1
Sacked-yards lost	2-13	5-27
Punts	8-45	8-41
Fumbles-lost	2-1	4-2
Penalties-yards	8-64	9-64
Time of possession	29:34	30:26

INDIVIDUAL STATISTICS

RUSHING—Baltimore, J. Lewis 20-89, C. Taylor 8-36, Boller 2-4, Sanders -0, Zastudil 1-0. Cleveland, Droughns 19-40, Frye 2-8, Suggs 2-6.

PASSING—Baltimore, Boller 15-36-2-151. Cleveland, Frye 22-37-1-199.

RECEIVING—Baltimore, C. Taylor 4-16, Mason 3-73, J. Lewis 3-29, ayton 3-11, Heap 2-22. Cleveland, Bryant 9-123, Northcutt 6-41, Irons 2-6, T. Smith 2-8, Droughns 1-5, F. Jackson 1-4, Suggs 1-2.

MISSED FIELD GOAL ATTEMPTS—None.

INTERCEPTIONS—Baltimore, Reed 1-23. Cleveland, Russell 2-50.

KICKOFF RETURNS—Baltimore, C. Taylor 2-26, J. White 2-18. Cleveland, ribbs 5-128.

PUNT RETURNS—Baltimore, Clayton 6-30. Cleveland, Northcutt 6-91.

SACKS—Baltimore, Suggs 1.5, A. Thomas 1, Kemoeatu 1, Boulware 1, Villiams 0.5. Cleveland, Thompson 1, Roye 1.

BUCCANEERS 27, SAINTS 13

Sunday, January 1

lew Orleans	0	10	0	3—13
ampa Bay	7	10	0	10—27

First Quarter

.B.—Galloway 7 pass from Simms (M. Bryant kick), 12:08.

Second Quarter

.O.—FG, Carney 25, 1:38.

.B.—Galloway 4 pass from Simms (M. Bryant kick), 3:35.

I.O.—Henderson 24 pass from Bouman (Carney kick), 11:24.

.B.—FG, M. Bryant 46, 14:15.

Fourth Quarter

.O.—FG, Carney 24, 2:54.

.B.—FG, M. Bryant 26, 7:44.

'.B.—D. White 34 fumble return (M. Bryant kick), 13:17.

Attendance—65,379.

	New Orleans	Tampa Bay
irst downs	18	14
Rushes-yards	23-71	26-149
Passing	235	136
Punt returns	3-32	2-24
Kickoff returns	5-80	3-85
nterception returns	0-0	2-18
Comp.-att.-int.	25-37-2	12-25-0
Sacked-yards lost	4-30	1-7
Punts	3-47	6-46
Fumbles-lost	1-1	2-0
Penalties-yards	7-53	10-107
Time of possession	33:45	26:15

INDIVIDUAL STATISTICS

RUSHING—New Orleans, A. Smith 16-55, A. Thomas 4-7, Stecker 2-10, Bouman 1-(minus 1). Tampa Bay, C. Williams 22-81, Simms 2-2, Pittman 1-54, Alstott 1-2.

PASSING—New Orleans, Bouman 25-37-2-265. Tampa Bay, Simms 12-25-0-143.

RECEIVING—New Orleans, Hakim 6-71, Stallworth 6-61, Hilton 5-74, Stecker 4-16, Henderson 2-30, Horn 1-11, A. Thomas 1-2. Tampa Bay, Galloway 4-38, Pittman 3-35, I. Hilliard 2-20, Alstott 1-24, Smith 1-22, Shepherd 1-4.

MISSED FIELD GOAL ATTEMPTS—None.

INTERCEPTIONS—Tampa Bay, Bolden 1-18, Allen 1-0.

KICKOFF RETURNS—New Orleans, Stecker 3-62, McAfee 1-13, L. Hall 1-5. Tampa Bay, Pittman 3-85.

PUNT RETURNS—New Orleans, Hakim 3-32. Tampa Bay, Jones 2-24.

SACKS—New Orleans, F. Thomas 1. Tampa Bay, Rice 2, D. White 1, Spires 1.

JAGUARS 40, TITANS 13

Sunday, January 1

Tennessee	0	0	0	13—13
Jacksonville	17	10	13	0—40

First Quarter

Jac.—Pearman 6 run (Scobee kick), 3:51.

Jac.—Toefield 32 run (Scobee kick), 7:45.

Jac.—FG, Scobee 46, 13:25.

Second Quarter

Jac.—FG, Scobee 38, 4:47.

Jac.—Wimbush 6 run (Scobee kick), 10:49.

Third Quarter

Jac.—M. Jones 10 pass from Gray (Scobee kick), 10:36.

Jac.—Wilford 14 pass from Gray (kick failed), 14:26.

Fourth Quarter

Ten.—Troupe 4 pass from Volek (Bironas kick), 5:59.

Ten.—Scaife 10 pass from Volek (kick failed), 14:05.

Attendance—65,485.

	Tennessee	Jacksonville
First downs	15	25
Rushes-yards	22-99	35-122
Passing	171	213
Punt returns	2-2	3-31
Kickoff returns	7-184	2-53
Interception returns	0-0	1-9
Comp.-att.-int.	21-39-1	19-31-0
Sacked-yards lost	1-8	3-21
Punts	5-48	3-39
Fumbles-lost	2-1	2-1
Penalties-yards	18-140	7-50
Time of possession	25:49	34:11

INDIVIDUAL STATISTICS

RUSHING—Tennessee, Henry 13-48, Nash 6-32, Mauck 3-19. Jacksonville, Toefield 25-102, Pearman 6-13, Gray 3-1, Wimbush 1-6.

PASSING—Tennessee, Volek 14-25-0-114, Mauck 7-14-1-65. Jacksonville, Garrard 10-16-0-128, Gray 8-14-0-100, M. Jones 1-1-0-6.

RECEIVING—Tennessee, Troupe 9-89, Nash 3-14, Wade 2-26, Scaife 2-15, Fleming 1-11, Bennett 1-9, Roby 1-8, Small 1-6, Henry 1-1. Jacksonville, R. Williams 4-52, J. Smith 4-46, M. Jones 3-55, Hankton 3-15, Wilford 2-40, Pearman 2-16, Brady 1-10.

MISSED FIELD GOAL ATTEMPTS—None.

INTERCEPTIONS—Jacksonville, Mathis 1-9.

KICKOFF RETURNS—Tennessee, P. Jones 4-134, Roby 3-50. Jacksonville, Wimbush 2-53.

PUNT RETURNS—Tennessee, P. Jones 2-2. Jacksonville, Pearman 3-31.

SACKS—Tennessee, Haynesworth 1, Schobel 1, Sirmon 1. Jacksonville, McCray 1.

REDSKINS 31, EAGLES 20

Sunday, January 1

Washington	7	3	7	14—31
Philadelphia	10	7	3	0—20

First Quarter

Phi.—FG, Akers 49, 4:44.

Was.—Sellers 4 pass from Brunell (Hall kick), 8:19.

Phi.—R. Brown 33 pass from McMahon (Akers kick), 14:27.

Second Quarter

Phi.—R. Brown 8 pass from McMahon (Akers kick), 8:55.

Was.—FG, Hall 25, 13:59.

Third Quarter

Was.—Portis 2 run (Hall kick), 3:14.

Phi.—FG, Akers 35, 6:08.

Fourth Quarter

Was.—Portis 22 run (Hall kick), 2:41.

Was.—Taylor 39 fumble return (Hall kick), 12:44.

Attendance—67,700.

	Washington	Philadelphia
First downs	14	18
Rushes-yards	36-151	25-96
Passing	128	239
Punt returns	2-12	5-9
Kickoff returns	5-103	5-95
Interception returns	2-8	1-0
Comp.-att.-int.	9-25-1	21-42-2
Sacked-yards lost	1-13	4-22
Punts	10-41	6-44
Fumbles-lost	0-0	6-4
Penalties-yards	7-60	5-45
Time of possession	29:50	30:10

INDIVIDUAL STATISTICS

RUSHING—Washington, Portis 27-112, Betts 5-30, Brunell 4-9. Philadelphia, Perry 15-70, Moats 7-23, McMahon 3-3.

PASSING—Washington, Brunell 9-25-1-141. Philadelphia, McMahon 16-31-1-234, Detmer 5-11-1-27.

RECEIVING—Washington, Moss 4-83, Cooley 2-8, Thrash 1-41, Portis 1-5, Sellers 1-4. Philadelphia, R. Brown 7-77, G. Lewis 4-62, Smith 3-73, McMullen 3-32, Moats 3-4, C. Lewis 1-13.

MISSED FIELD GOAL ATTEMPTS—None.

INTERCEPTIONS—Washington, Marshall 1-4, Clark 1-4. Philadelphia, Hood 1-0.

KICKOFF RETURNS—Washington, A. Brown 4-73, Betts 1-30. Philadelphia, Perry 4-83, Patterson 1-12.

PUNT RETURNS—Washington, A. Brown 2-12. Philadelphia, Wynn 5-9.

SACKS—Washington, Washington 1, Prioleau 1, Griffin 1, Daniels 1. Philadelphia, Rayburn 1.

49ERS 20, TEXANS 17
Sunday, January 1

Houston	10	0	7	0	0—17
San Francisco	0	7	10	0	3—20

First Quarter
Hou.—FG, K. Brown 21, 5:46.
Hou.—Morency 3 run (K. Brown kick), 10:17.
Second Quarter
S.F.—Lloyd 14 pass from A. Smith (Nedney kick), 14:42.
Third Quarter
S.F.—FG, Nedney 42, 7:27.
Hou.—Bradford 25 pass from Banks (K. Brown kick), 9:10.
S.F.—M. Adams 40 interception return (Nedney kick), 14:50.
Overtime
S.F.—FG, Nedney 33, 11:08.
Attendance—67,970.

	Houston	San Francisco
First downs	13	19
Rushes-yards	25-88	47-182
Passing	196	142
Punt returns	3-27	2-21
Kickoff returns	4-89	4-66
Interception returns	1-0	2-71
Comp.-att.-int.	18-36-2	16-29-1
Sacked-yards lost	0-0	3-17
Punts	7-40	10-31
Fumbles-lost	0-0	1-0
Penalties-yards	8-74	5-32
Time of possession	27:05	44:03

INDIVIDUAL STATISTICS
RUSHING—Houston, Morency 21-83, Banks 2-(minus 2), Carr 1-9, Bradford 1-(minus 2). San Francisco, Gore 25-108, Hicks 18-64, A. Smith 4-10.

PASSING—Houston, Banks 14-25-2-173, Carr 4-11-0-23. San Francisco, A. Smith 16-29-1-159.

RECEIVING—Houston, Rivers 5-34, Morency 4-46, Morgan 3-33, Bradford 2-56, Mathis 2-16, Gaffney 1-8, An. Johnson 1-3. San Francisco, Lloyd 4-48, Battle 3-52, Hicks 3-17, Gore 2-13, Jackson 2-8, Hetherington 1-11, T. Jones 1-9.

MISSED FIELD GOAL ATTEMPTS—Houston, K. Brown 31.

INTERCEPTIONS—Houston, Earl 1-0. San Francisco, M. Adams 2-36.

KICKOFF RETURNS—Houston, Mathis 4-89. San Francisco, Amey 4-66.

PUNT RETURNS—Houston, Morgan 2-22, Mathis 1-5. San Francisco, Amey 2-21.

SACKS—Houston, Babin 2, Peek 1.

VIKINGS 34, BEARS 10
Sunday, January 1

Chicago	3	0	0	7—10	
Minnesota	0	17	7	10—34	

First Quarter
Chi.—FG, Gould 22, 9:46.
Second Quarter
Min.—FG, Edinger 54, :07.
Min.—Fason 2 run (Edinger kick), 7:23.
Min.—T. Taylor 17 pass from B. Johnson (Edinger kick), 14:57.
Third Quarter
Min.—Moore 7 pass from B. Johnson (Edinger kick), 11:02.
Fourth Quarter
Min.—FG, Edinger 27, :08.
Chi.—Gage 4 pass from Blake (Gould kick), 7:52.
Min.—M. Bennett 61 run (Edinger kick), 9:50.
Attendance—64,023.

	Chicago	Minnesota
First downs	13	22
Rushes-yards	33-154	18-149
Passing	97	247
Punt returns	1-12	0-0
Kickoff returns	7-148	2-47
Interception returns	0-0	0-0

	Chicago	Minnesota
Comp.-att.-int.	14-23-0	27-40-0
Sacked-yards lost	3-24	0-0
Punts	5-29	3-37
Fumbles-lost	2-0	0-0
Penalties-yards	8-45	7-45
Time of possession	33:28	26:32

INDIVIDUAL STATISTICS
RUSHING—Chicago, T. Jones 12-62, Benson 9-35, Peterson 8-35, McK 3-22, Orton 1-0. Minnesota, M. Bennett 6-82, Moore 6-57, Fason 3-3, Hill 2 (minus 2), Williamson 1-9.

PASSING—Chicago, Orton 6-14-0-59, Blake 7-8-0-44, Maynard 1-1-0 18. Minnesota, B. Johnson 27-40-0-247.

RECEIVING—Chicago, Gage 6-67, Peterson 3-30, Berlin 2-9, Berrian 1-7 Reid 1-5, Benson 1-3. Minnesota, Burleson 6-66, Moore 6-44, T. Taylor 5 68, M. Bennett 3-23, Wiggins 3-16, Williamson 2-12, Kleinsasser 1-15, K Robinson 1-3.

MISSED FIELD GOAL ATTEMPTS—None.

INTERCEPTIONS—None.

KICKOFF RETURNS—Chicago, Davis 6-143, Gilmore 1-5. Minnesota Williamson 2-47.

PUNT RETURNS—Chicago, Berrian 1-12.

SACKS—Minnesota, K. Williams 2, Henderson 1.

RAMS 20, COWBOYS 10
Sunday, January 1

St. Louis	0	10	0	10—20	
Dallas	7	3	0	0—10	

First Quarter
Dal.—Witten 19 pass from Bledsoe (Suisham kick), 12:24.
Second Quarter
St.L.—FG, J. Wilkins 49, :45.
St.L.—Cason 8 run (J. Wilkins kick), 13:08.
Dal.—FG, Suisham 22, 14:57.
Fourth Quarter
St.L.—Harris 1 run (J. Wilkins kick), 3:03.
St.L.—FG, J. Wilkins 20, 13:55.
Attendance—63,131.

	St. Louis	Dallas
First downs	20	15
Rushes-yards	33-106	22-57
Passing	147	214
Punt returns	3-23	5-28
Kickoff returns	2-48	5-143
Interception returns	2-61	0-0
Comp.-att.-int.	19-32-0	18-39-2
Sacked-yards lost	2-11	5-28
Punts	6-40	6-37
Fumbles-lost	0-0	5-2
Penalties-yards	7-40	10-78
Time of possession	33:43	26:17

INDIVIDUAL STATISTICS
RUSHING—St. Louis, M. Faulk 11-25, Cason 10-65, Harris 10-15, Holt 1-2, J. Martin 1-(minus 1). Dallas, J. Jones 15-35, Barber 6-18, Newman 1-4.

PASSING—St. Louis, J. Martin 19-32-0-158. Dallas, Bledsoe 18-39-2-242.

RECEIVING—St. Louis, Holt 4-40, Curtis 3-19, Manumaleuna 2-25, Harris 2-22, McDonald 2-14, Hedgecock 2-10, M. Faulk 2-9, Cason 1-11, Bruce 1-8. Dallas, K. Johnson 5-97, Witten 4-50, Crayton 3-45, T. Glenn 2-44, Barber 2-17, J. Jones 2-(minus 11).

MISSED FIELD GOAL ATTEMPTS—St. Louis, J. Wilkins 27, 53. Dallas, Suisham 47.

INTERCEPTIONS—St. Louis, Atogwe 1-42, Ivy 1-19.

KICKOFF RETURNS—St. Louis, Cason 2-48. Dallas, Thompson 5-143.

PUNT RETURNS—St. Louis, Furrey 3-23. Dallas, Newman 3-13, Crayton 2-15.

SACKS—St. Louis, Little 2.5, Hargrove 2, Tinoisamoa 0.5. Dallas, Ware 1, Spears 1.

WILD-CARD GAMES

REDSKINS 17, BUCCANEERS 10

Saturday, January 7

Washington	14	3	0	0—17
Tampa Bay	0	3	7	0—10

First Quarter
Was.—Portis 6 run (Hall kick), 6:20.
Was.—Taylor 51 fumble return (Hall kick), 10:45.
Second Quarter
T.B.—FG, M. Bryant 43, 4:58.
Was.—FG, Hall 47, 9:26.
Third Quarter
T.B.—Simms 2 run (M. Bryant kick), 5:20.
Attendance—65,514.

	Washington	Tampa Bay
First downs	9	17
Rushes-yards	31-95	25-75
Passing	25	168
Punt returns	3-19	4-37
Kickoff returns	3-55	4-96
Interception returns	2-34	1-3
Comp.-att.-int.	7-16-1	25-38-2
Sacked-yards lost	2-16	3-30
Punts	7-38	5-39
Fumbles-lost	3-0	3-1
Penalties-yards	4-30	3-30
Time of possession	25:31	34:29

INDIVIDUAL STATISTICS

RUSHING—Washington, Portis 16-53, Betts 10-25, Brunell 4-6, Moss 1-11. Tampa Bay, C. Williams 18-49, Alstott 4-15, Simms 3-11.

PASSING—Washington, Brunell 7-15-1-41, Portis 0-1-0-0. Tampa Bay, Simms 25-38-2-198.

RECEIVING—Washington, Moss 2-18, Cooley 2-12, Betts 1-11, Thrash 1-5, Portis 1-(minus 5). Tampa Bay, Galloway 7-69, I. Hilliard 4-38, Pittman 3-30, Becht 3-26, Smith 3-14, C. Williams 3-10, Alstott 1-7, Shepherd 1-4.

MISSED FIELD GOAL ATTEMPTS—None.

INTERCEPTIONS—Washington, Arrington 1-21, Washington 1-13. Tampa Bay, Kelly 1-3.

KICKOFF RETURNS—Washington, Betts 2-43, Sellers 1-12. Tampa Bay, Pittman 4-96.

PUNT RETURNS—Washington, A. Brown 3-19. Tampa Bay, Jones 4-37.

SACKS—Washington, Stoutmire 1, Daniels 1, Evans 1. Tampa Bay, Rice 1, Wyms 1.

PATRIOTS 28, JAGUARS 3

Saturday, January 7

Jacksonville	0	3	0	0— 3
New England	0	7	14	7—28

Second Quarter
N.E.—T. Brown 11 pass from Brady (Vinatieri kick), 2:52.
Jac.—FG, Scobee 36, 13:55.
Third Quarter
N.E.—Givens 3 pass from Brady (Vinatieri kick), 7:47.
N.E.—Watson 63 pass from Brady (Vinatieri kick), 11:57.
Fourth Quarter
N.E.—Samuel 73 interception return (Vinatieri kick), :14.
Attendance—68,756.

	Jacksonville	New England
First downs	15	17
Rushes-yards	17-87	28-118
Passing	205	189
Punt returns	3-12	4-31
Kickoff returns	5-108	2-36
Interception returns	0-0	1-73
Comp.-att.-int.	21-39-1	15-27-0
Sacked-yards lost	6-42	4-12
Punts	5-42	5-39
Fumbles-lost	2-1	4-0
Penalties-yards	8-40	4-32
Time of possession	29:34	30:26

INDIVIDUAL STATISTICS

RUSHING—Jacksonville, F. Taylor 8-24, Leftwich 3-26, G. Jones 2-15, Garrard 2-14, Pearman 2-8. New England, Dillon 17-40, Faulk 6-51, Brady 2-9, Andre. Davis 1-13, Pass 1-6, Cassel 1-(minus 1).

PASSING—Jacksonville, Leftwich 18-31-1-179, Garrard 3-8-0-68. New England, Brady 15-27-0-201.

RECEIVING—Jacksonville, M. Jones 6-94, R. Williams 4-56, Wilford 4-53, J. Smith 3-30, F. Taylor 3-13, Brady 1-1. New England, Watson 5-91, Faulk 4-45, Branch 2-36, Dillon 1-12, T. Brown 1-11, Andre. Davis 1-3, Givens 1-3.

MISSED FIELD GOAL ATTEMPTS—Jacksonville, Scobee 41.

INTERCEPTIONS—New England, Samuel 1-73.

KICKOFF RETURNS—Jacksonville, Wimbush 4-97, Alexis 1-11. New England, Hobbs 2-36.

PUNT RETURNS—Jacksonville, Pearman 3-12. New England, Dwight 4-31.

SACKS—Jacksonville, D. Smith 1, Peterson 1, Hayward 1, Meier 1. New England, McGinest 4.5, Colvin 1, Seymour 0.5.

2005 REVIEW *Wild-card games*

PANTHERS 23, GIANTS 0

Sunday, January 8

Carolina	0	10	7	6—23
N.Y. Giants	0	0	0	0— 0

Second Quarter

Car.—S. Smith 22 pass from Delhomme (Kasay kick), 5:19.
Car.—FG, Kasay 31, 14:30.

Third Quarter

Car.—S. Smith 12 run (Kasay kick), 8:03.

Fourth Quarter

Car.—FG, Kasay 45, 1:27.
Car.—FG, Kasay 18, 12:20.
Attendance—79,378.

	Carolina	N.Y. Giants
First downs	23	9
Rushes-yards	45-223	13-41
Passing	112	91
Punt returns	0-0	2-5
Kickoff returns	1-17	6-122
Interception returns	3-5	0-0
Comp.-att.-int.	15-22-0	10-18-3
Sacked-yards lost	4-28	4-22
Punts	4-38	4-39
Fumbles-lost	1-0	2-2
Penalties-yards	7-52	2-15
Time of possession	42:45	17:15

INDIVIDUAL STATISTICS

RUSHING—Carolina, Foster 27-151, Goings 12-63, Weinke 3-(minus 3), Hoover 2-0, S. Smith 1-12. New York, Barber 13-41.

PASSING—Carolina, Delhomme 15-22-0-140. New York, Manning 10-18-3-113.

RECEIVING—Carolina, S. Smith 10-84, Colbert 2-31, Mangum 1-11, Goings 1-10, Foster 1-4. New York, Shockey 3-50, Toomer 3-31, Barber 3-28, Shiancoe 1-4.

MISSED FIELD GOAL ATTEMPTS—None.

INTERCEPTIONS—Carolina, McCree 2-(minus 9), Lucas 1-14.

KICKOFF RETURNS—Carolina, Robertson 1-17. New York, Morton 6-122.

PUNT RETURNS—New York, Morton 1-5, Wilson 1-0.

SACKS—Carolina, Witherspoon 1, Peppers 1, Carstens 1, T. Davis 1. New York, Strahan 2, Jackson 1, Umenyiora 1.

STEELERS 31, BENGALS 17

Sunday, January 8

Pittsburgh	0	14	14	3—31
Cincinnati	10	7	0	0—17

First Quarter

Cin.—FG, Graham 23, 8:06.
Cin.—Ru. Johnson 20 run (Graham kick), 13:51.

Second Quarter

Pit.—Parker 19 pass from Roethlisberger (Reed kick), 1:49.
Cin.—Houshmandzadeh 7 pass from Kitna (Graham kick), 8:47.
Pit.—Ward 5 pass from Roethlisberger (Reed kick), 11:12.

Third Quarter

Pit.—Bettis 5 run (Reed kick), 9:48.
Pit.—Wilson 43 pass from Roethlisberger (Reed kick), 13:47.

Fourth Quarter

Pit.—FG, Reed 21, 4:31.
Attendance—65,870.

	Pittsburgh	Cincinnati
First downs	19	19
Rushes-yards	34-144	20-84
Passing	202	243
Punt returns	2-21	2-15
Kickoff returns	4-94	6-127
Interception returns	2-31	0-0
Comp.-att.-int.	14-21-0	25-41-2
Sacked-yards lost	1-6	4-20
Punts	3-47	3-44
Fumbles-lost	0-0	2-0
Penalties-yards	6-39	7-90
Time of possession	28:57	31:03

INDIVIDUAL STATISTICS

RUSHING—Pittsburgh, Parker 16-38, Bettis 10-52, Roethlisberger 4-3, Haynes 3-46, Randle El 1-5. Cincinnati, Ru. Johnson 13-56, Kitna 4-25, C. Perry 2-3, Larson 1-0.

PASSING—Pittsburgh, Roethlisberger 14-19-0-208, Randle El 0-1-0-0, Bettis 0-1-0-0. Cincinnati, Kitna 24-40-2-197, Palmer 1-1-0-66.

RECEIVING—Pittsburgh, Wilson 3-104, Parker 3-41, Randle El 2-15, Miller 2-15, Ward 2-10, Haynes 1-14, Tuman 1-9. Cincinnati, C. Perry 6-11, Walter 5-73, C. Johnson 4-59, Houshmandzadeh 4-25, Ru. Johnson 2-14, Schobel 2-11, Henry 1-66, R. Kelly 1-4.

MISSED FIELD GOAL ATTEMPTS—None.

INTERCEPTIONS—Pittsburgh, Farrior 1-22, Polamalu 1-4.

KICKOFF RETURNS—Pittsburgh, Morgan 2-40, I. Taylor 1-36, Colclough 1-18. Cincinnati, T. Perry 5-119, Walter 1-8.

PUNT RETURNS—Pittsburgh, Randle El 2-21. Cincinnati, Ratliff 2-15.

SACKS—Pittsburgh, Hoke 1, Foote 0.5, Polamalu 0.5, Haggans 0.5 Porter 0.5, Team 1. Cincinnati, Pollack 1.

DIVISIONAL PLAYOFFS

SEAHAWKS 20, REDSKINS 10

Saturday, January 14

Washington	0	3	0	7—10
Seattle	0	7	7	6—20

Second Quarter
Was.—FG, Hall 26, 6:01.
Sea.—Jackson 29 pass from Hasselbeck (J. Brown kick), 11:38.

Third Quarter
Sea.—Hasselbeck 6 run (J. Brown kick), 5:25.

Fourth Quarter
Sea.—FG, J. Brown 33, :44.
Was.—Moss 20 pass from Brunell (Hall kick), 3:01.
Sea.—FG, J. Brown 31, 12:06.
Attendance—67,551.

	Washington	Seattle
First downs	11	15
Rushes-yards	25-59	33-119
Passing	230	215
Punt returns	1-3	4-(-1)
Kickoff returns	5-95	3-49
Interception returns	0-0	0-0
Comp.-att.-int.	22-38-0	16-26-0
Sacked-yards lost	2-12	0-0
Punts	7-43	5-42
Fumbles-lost	1-1	5-3
Penalties-yards	7-50	2-10
Time of possession	32:15	27:45

INDIVIDUAL STATISTICS

RUSHING—Washington, Portis 17-41, Brunell 4-12, Betts 3-5, Moss 1-1. Seattle, Morris 18-49, Hasselbeck 6-21, Alexander 6-9, Strong 3-40.

PASSING—Washington, Brunell 22-37-0-242, Portis 0-1-0-0. Seattle, Hasselbeck 16-26-0-215.

RECEIVING—Washington, Moss 7-103, Cooley 4-85, Betts 3-21, Jacobs 3-19, Royal 3-3, Portis 2-11. Seattle, Jackson 9-143, Stevens 2-13, Engram 2-11, Jurevicius 1-31, Morris 1-16, Hannam 1-1.

MISSED FIELD GOAL ATTEMPTS—Washington, Hall 36.

INTERCEPTIONS—None.

KICKOFF RETURNS—Washington, Betts 4-75, J. Farris 1-20. Seattle, Scobey 3-49.

PUNT RETURNS—Washington, A. Brown 1-3. Seattle, J. Williams 4-(minus 1).

SACKS—Seattle, B. Fisher 1, Darby 1.

The Denver defense ended the Patriots' season—and talk of a New England dynasty.

BRONCOS 27, PATRIOTS 13

Saturday, January 14

New England	0	3	3	7—13
Denver	0	10	7	10—27

Second Quarter
N.E.—FG, Vinatieri 40, 11:12.
Den.—Mi. Anderson 1 run (Elam kick), 13:18.
Den.—FG, Elam 50, 14:17.

Third Quarter
N.E.—FG, Vinatieri 32, 7:11.
Den.—Mi. Anderson 1 run (Elam kick), 14:17.

Fourth Quarter
Den.—Smith 4 pass from Plummer (Elam kick), 6:22.
N.E.—Givens 4 pass from Brady (Vinatieri kick), 6:55.
Den.—FG, Elam 34, 11:40.
Attendance—76,238.

	New England	Denver
First downs	15	16
Rushes-yards	21-79	32-96
Passing	341	190
Punt returns	4-37	1-10
Kickoff returns	6-150	4-73
Interception returns	1-0	2-105
Comp.-att.-int.	20-36-2	15-26-1
Sacked-yards lost	0-0	2-7
Punts	3-49	6-46
Fumbles-lost	3-3	1-0
Penalties-yards	8-82	4-24
Time of possession	28:12	31:48

INDIVIDUAL STATISTICS

RUSHING—New England, Dillon 13-57, Faulk 7-23, Brady 1-(minus 1). Denver, Mi. Anderson 19-69, Plummer 7-8, Bell 6-19.

PASSING—New England, Brady 20-36-2-341. Denver, Plummer 15-26-1-197.

RECEIVING—New England, Branch 8-153, Givens 5-54, Faulk 2-20, Andre. Davis 1-51, T. Brown 1-33, Graham 1-18, Dillon 1-9, H. Evans 1-3. Denver, Smith 6-96, Lelie 5-50, Putzier 3-37, Mi. Anderson 1-14.

MISSED FIELD GOAL ATTEMPTS—New England, Vinatieri 43.

INTERCEPTIONS—New England, Samuel 1-0. Denver, Bailey 1-100, Lynch 1-5.

KICKOFF RETURNS—New England, Hobbs 3-89, Andre. Davis 3-61. Denver, Adams 3-54, Da. Williams 1-19.

PUNT RETURNS—New England, Dwight 3-37, T. Brown 1-0. Denver, Adams 1-10.

SACKS—New England, Vrabel 1, Seymour 1.

ALBERT DICKSON / TSN

STEELERS 21, COLTS 18
Sunday, January 15

Pittsburgh	14	0	7	0—21
Indianapolis	0	3	0	15—18

First Quarter
Pit.—Randle El 6 pass from Roethlisberger (Reed kick), 5:35.
Pit.—Miller 7 pass from Roethlisberger (Reed kick), 11:48.
Second Quarter
Ind.—FG, Vanderjagt 20, 13:40.
Third Quarter
Pit.—Bettis 1 run (Reed kick), 13:34.
Fourth Quarter
Ind.—Clark 50 pass from Manning (Vanderjagt kick), :51.
Ind.—James 3 run (Wayne pass from Manning), 10:36.
Attendance—57,449.

	Pittsburgh	Indianapolis
First downs	21	15
Rushes-yards	42-112	14-58
Passing	183	247
Punt returns	5-50	2-(-2)
Kickoff returns	3-55	3-52
Interception returns	0-0	1-5
Comp.-att.-int.	14-24-1	22-38-0
Sacked-yards lost	2-14	5-43
Punts	5-42	6-45
Fumbles-lost	1-1	1-0
Penalties-yards	2-8	9-67
Time of possession	34:52	25:08

INDIVIDUAL STATISTICS
RUSHING—Pittsburgh, Parker 17-59, Bettis 17-46, Roethlisberger 5-(minus 3), Haynes 2-8, Kreider 1-2. Indianapolis, James 13-56, Rhodes 1-2.

PASSING—Pittsburgh, Roethlisberger 14-24-1-197. Indianapolis, Manning 22-38-0-290.

RECEIVING—Pittsburgh, Ward 3-68, Miller 3-61, Randle El 3-30, Parker 3-19, Tuman 1-19, Haynes 1-0. Indianapolis, Wayne 7-97, James 5-26, Clark 4-84, Harrison 3-52, Fletcher 2-18, Stokley 1-13.

MISSED FIELD GOAL ATTEMPTS—Indianapolis, Vanderjagt 46.

INTERCEPTIONS—Indianapolis, June 1-5.

KICKOFF RETURNS—Pittsburgh, I. Taylor 2-33, Colclough 1-22. Indianapolis, Rhodes 3-52.

PUNT RETURNS—Pittsburgh, Randle El 5-50. Indianapolis, Walters 2-(minus 2).

SACKS—Pittsburgh, Farrior 2.5, Porter 1.5, von Oelhoffen 1. Indianapolis, Freeney 1, Tripplett 1.

PANTHERS 29, BEARS 21
Sunday, January 15

Carolina	7	9	7	6—29
Chicago	0	7	7	7—21

First Quarter
Car.—S. Smith 58 pass from Delhomme (Kasay kick), :55.
Second Quarter
Car.—FG, Kasay 20, :03.
Car.—FG, Kasay 38, 8:34.
Chi.—Peterson 1 run (Gould kick), 13:03.
Car.—FG, Kasay 37, 15:00.
Third Quarter
Chi.—Clark 1 pass from Grossman (Gould kick), 3:39.
Car.—S. Smith 39 pass from Delhomme (Kasay kick), 12:53.
Fourth Quarter
Chi.—McKie 3 run (Gould kick), 2:37.
Car.—Mangum 1 pass from Delhomme (kick failed), 6:56.
Attendance—62,209.

	Carolina	Chicago
First downs	21	23
Rushes-yards	31-123	27-97
Passing	311	185
Punt returns	2-(-1)	2-1
Kickoff returns	4-100	6-132
Interception returns	1-1	1-20
Comp.-att.-int.	24-33-1	17-41-1
Sacked-yards lost	1-8	1-7
Punts	5-41	7-35
Fumbles-lost	3-0	0-0
Penalties-yards	9-50	4-19
Time of possession	33:25	26:35

INDIVIDUAL STATISTICS
RUSHING—Carolina, Foster 16-54, Goings 10-34, S. Smith 3-26, Delhomme 2-9. Chicago, T. Jones 20-80, Peterson 5-9, Grossman 1-5, McKie 1-3.

PASSING—Carolina, Delhomme 24-33-1-319. Chicago, Grossman 17-41-1-192.

RECEIVING—Carolina, S. Smith 12-218, Proehl 3-28, Carter 2-43, Hoover 2-13, Goings 1-14, Colbert 1-9, Foster 1-3, Mangum 1-1, Robertson 1-(minus 10). Chicago, Berrian 5-68, Muhammad 3-58, T. Jones 3-30, Gage 3-28, Clark 2-5, Peterson 1-3.

MISSED FIELD GOAL ATTEMPTS—None.

INTERCEPTIONS—Carolina, Lucas 1-1. Chicago, Urlacher 1-20.

KICKOFF RETURNS—Carolina, Robertson 4-100. Chicago, Davis 5-115, Peterson 1-17.

PUNT RETURNS—Carolina, S. Smith 2-(minus 1). Chicago, Vasher 2-1.

SACKS—Carolina, Carstens 1. Chicago, Ogunleye 1.

Chicago's defense made headlines all season, but it was no match for Carolina's offense.

CONFERENCE CHAMPIONSHIPS

STEELERS 34, BRONCOS 17
Sunday, January 22

Pittsburgh	3	21	0	10—34
Denver	0	3	7	7—17

First Quarter
Pit.—FG, Reed 47, 10:49.

Second Quarter
Pit.—Wilson 12 pass from Roethlisberger (Reed kick), :06.
Den.—FG, Elam 23, 5:37.
Pit.—Bettis 3 run (Reed kick), 13:05.
Pit.—Ward 17 pass from Roethlisberger (Reed kick), 14:53.

Third Quarter
Den.—Lelie 30 pass from Plummer (Elam kick), 11:24.

Fourth Quarter
Pit.—FG, Reed 42, 1:22.
Den.—Mi. Anderson 3 run (Elam kick), 7:08.
Pit.—Roethlisberger 4 run (Reed kick), 12:01.
Attendance—76,775.

	Pittsburgh	Denver
First downs	20	16
Rushes-yards	33-90	21-97
Passing	268	211
Punt returns	1-13	0-0
Kickoff returns	2-42	5-121
Interception returns	2-15	0-0
Comp.-att.-int.	21-29-0	18-30-2
Sacked-yards lost	2-7	3-12
Punts	4-37	2-44
Fumbles-lost	1-0	2-2
Penalties-yards	8-61	4-20
Time of possession	36:07	23:53

INDIVIDUAL STATISTICS
RUSHING—Pittsburgh, Bettis 15-39, Parker 14-35, Roethlisberger 3-12, Ward 1-4. Denver, Mi. Anderson 9-36, Plummer 7-30, Bell 5-31.

PASSING—Pittsburgh, Roethlisberger 21-29-0-275. Denver, Plummer 18-30-2-223.

RECEIVING—Pittsburgh, Wilson 5-92, Ward 5-59, Randle El 4-52, Parker 3-20, Miller 2-31, Washington 1-13, Haynes 1-8. Denver, Bell 5-28, Smith 4-61, Putzier 4-55, Mi. Anderson 3-11, Lelie 2-68.

MISSED FIELD GOAL ATTEMPTS—None.

INTERCEPTIONS—Pittsburgh, Foote 1-14, I. Taylor 1-1.

KICKOFF RETURNS—Pittsburgh, I. Taylor 2-42. Denver, Adams 4-110, Sapp 1-11.

PUNT RETURNS—Pittsburgh, Randle El 1-13.

SACKS—Pittsburgh, Keisel 2, Porter 1. Denver, M. Myers 1, D.. Williams 1.

SEAHAWKS 34, PANTHERS 14
Sunday, January 22

Carolina	0	7	0	7—14
Seattle	10	10	7	7—34

First Quarter
Sea.—Stevens 17 pass from Hasselbeck (J. Brown kick), 9:29.
Sea.—FG, J. Brown 24, 12:37.

Second Quarter
Sea.—Alexander 1 run (J. Brown kick), :07.
Car.—S. Smith 59 punt return (Kasay kick), 5:55.
Sea.—FG, J. Brown 39, 10:57.

Third Quarter
Sea.—Jackson 20 pass from Hasselbeck (J. Brown kick), 3:51.

Fourth Quarter
Sea.—Alexander 1 run (J. Brown kick), 9:00.
Car.—Carter 47 pass from Delhomme (Kasay kick), 9:51.
Attendance—67,837.

	Carolina	Seattle
First downs	11	27
Rushes-yards	12-36	51-190
Passing	176	203
Punt returns	1-59	2-7
Kickoff returns	7-143	2-51
Interception returns	0-0	3-67
Comp.-att.-int.	15-35-3	20-28-0
Sacked-yards lost	2-20	2-16
Punts	7-35	5-39
Fumbles-lost	1-1	0-0
Penalties-yards	5-57	7-63
Time of possession	18:09	41:51

INDIVIDUAL STATISTICS
RUSHING—Carolina, Goings 5-2, Robertson 4-19, Delhomme 3-15. Seattle, Alexander 34-132, Morris 7-24, Hasselbeck 6-27, Strong 4-7.

PASSING—Carolina, Delhomme 15-35-3-196. Seattle, Hasselbeck 20-28-0-219.

RECEIVING—Carolina, Robertson 5-37, S. Smith 5-33, Carter 2-88, Proehl 1-19, Mangum 1-10, Hoover 1-9. Seattle, Jackson 6-75, Stevens 6-66, Engram 3-34, S. Wallace 1-28, Hannam 1-7, Jurevicius 1-6, Strong 1-3, Alexander 1-0.

MISSED FIELD GOAL ATTEMPTS—Seattle, J. Brown 49.

INTERCEPTIONS—Seattle, Manuel 1-32, Tatupu 1-21, Boulware 1-14.

KICKOFF RETURNS—Carolina, Smart 4-74, Robertson 3-69. Seattle, Scobey 2-51.

PUNT RETURNS—Carolina, S. Smith 1-59. Seattle, Warrick 2-7.

SACKS—Carolina, Morgan 1, Rucker 1. Seattle, R. Bernard 2.

The Steelers ran past the Broncos for their third consecutive road win and a trip to Super Bowl XL.

BOB LEVERONE / TSN

By PAUL ATTNER

Reprinted from the February 17, 2006 issue of the *Sporting News*.

THAT '70S SHOW

With an inspiring victory that conjures memories of their heyday, the Steelers finally get their thumb ring—and strike a blow for stability

This is about tears. Tears from the coach. Tears from the star running back. And maybe, if you look close enough, a tear from the team owner. This is what can make some victories so special; they aren't about the quality of how they are achieved, but rather about the joy resulting from the triumph. And when the final seconds of Super Bowl 40 tick off, the pure, wonderful emotion of it all overwhelms these three men who mean so much to what is the Pittsburgh Steelers.

For Bill Cowher, they are tears of relief, 14 years coming, tears that validate a career that lasted this long in one city only because he is blessed with the most patient of NFL owners.

For Jerome Bettis, they are tears of a dream, to come to his home city of Detroit and end a career holding the Lombardi Trophy in his arms, kissing it, knowing he had returned for one final season hoping to accomplish all of this. And to do it, oh my, the joy.

For Dan Rooney, they are tears of accomplishment, a fifth ring, rewarding a city of fans so faithful they somehow corralled enough tickets to dominate the noise inside Ford Field. "Ninety percent Steeler fans," Seahawks quarterback Matt Hasselbeck says in disgust.

These tears come after the most improbable of journeys, one that starts nine weeks ago, the Steelers standing at 7-5, wondering whether the playoffs already are out of touch—a journey that begins when their coach pulls out the corniest of phrases, telling his players to "wipe the slate clean" and start this season again. They listen, and they do just that, amassing a winning streak that reaches eight and includes four wins in a row away from home and triumphs over Indianapolis and Denver—the AFC's top two seeds—and the Seahawks, the NFC's No. 1 seed.

These tears also are tears for history, the first sixth seed to win a Super Bowl, the third franchise to win five rings, joining the Cowboys and 49ers. This is the least artistic of the eight victories, a rough, uneven, scrambling kind of game in which both teams never are in sync or firm control. Pittsburgh really doesn't do much—a handful of huge plays clustered around misfires and six punts. But Seattle uncharacteristically implodes, the league's No. 1 scoring offense stalled by awful penalties, two missed field-goal attempts and one killer interception. Still, those are the criticisms of purists;

Ward caught a touchdown pass from Randle El off a reverse—a play that all but deep-sixed the Seahawks' hopes of a comeback.

ALBERT DICKSON / TSN

for the Steelers it is a 21-10 masterpiece of pure heaven, confirmation of why they, the lowest seed, could be favorites before kickoff.

"You can't ever replace how you feel at this moment," says wide receiver Hines Ward, the game's MVP for his 123 receiving yards and one touchdown. "You win these games for so many people—for Mr. Rooney, for Bill Cowher, for Jerome. I am so happy for them. They deserve this so much. We've heard so much about the Steelers of the '70s. For us to be able to stand with them, we had to win this game."

In the days leading up to the game, Detroit becomes a Steeler town, a brawny, chilly and, finally, snowy place. After all, this is Bettis' city, and he

Randle El—a quarterback in college—completed the first-ever Super Bowl touchdown pass by a receiver.

soaks up every second. He even has some teammates over to his mom's house for a home-cooked dinner, and he stages his own fundraiser one night, a celebrity bowling tournament.

"This is amazing," he says. "To have this opportunity at home in Detroit, to win a championship in front of your friends and family and everyone who has seen me play since I was a kid, is a dream come true. It's been an incredible ride. I decided to come back to win a championship, and my mission is accomplished. So with that, I have to bid farewell." And just like that, he retires.

Cowher isn't going anywhere. He has been to this championship once before, losing Super Bowl 30 to the Cowboys; four other times he fell in the conference title game. He likes to say he didn't need this ring to confirm an already wonderful career, but he lies. And it shows on his face on the awards podium, a huge smile erasing the frustrations, overwhelming the granite jaw.

"I am not in this for my validation," he says. "I can't control that. I'm just happy for the players and the coaches and for Mr. Rooney. I'm happy for the support, and you talk about a class guy. He's inspired me."

You might have thought the NFL itself would be inspired by Super Bowl 40, given the significance of four decades of this once-modest, now-extraordinary occasion. But the league has no time for lengthy reflection, not when it continues to set all-time regular-season attendance records and has revenues approaching $5.8 billion and has convinced its television partners to pay $24 billion for a new broadcast package and can boast, albeit with shaky evidence, that up to 1 billion folks watched at least a bit of Sunday's championship.

The Steelers wrote a happy ending to Bettis' fairy-tale final season.

We are talking a lot of billions of dollars here, and there is power and influence and a swagger attached to these almost unfathomable numbers that infuse the NFL with a role in our lives far exceeding anything we could have anticipated when Green Bay and Kansas City kicked off the first Super Bowl, which, we all know, was viewed as so ho-hum it wasn't even called *super* back in 1967.

Now, the Super Bowl is no longer anything close to just a game. This could have been Hollywood or Vegas, not Detroit—well, unless you looked outside, of course—what with the stars who deem it important enough to be seen in Motown. Is that Diddy? Usher? LL Cool J? Jessica Alba? Magic? Paris Hilton? The Stones? And the penetration is worldwide: There are 234 countries that watch the game, with 54 international broadcasters using 32 different languages; 130 international

Second-year quarterback Roethlisberger didn't save his best game for the Super Bowl, but the rest of the Steelers' stars were at their brightest, so ultimately, it didn't matter.

international broadcasters using 32 different languages; 130 international media organizations from 18 nations receive credentials. Last season, 133.7 million Americans saw at least a little of the contest; only 122.3 million voted in the 2004 presidential election. And, of course, Super Bowl 40 again will be the highest-rated television event of the year.

Still, amid all the hugeness of this 40th renewal—does the NFL always answer yes at the drive-through when asked, "Do you want to super-size?"—it is just as important to see this game in another context: how it represents what the league once was, what it has become and what it might be in the future.

Three days before kickoff, Gene Upshaw, executive director of the players association, makes not-so-subtle hints about the intent of the union if a new collective bargaining agreement can't be negotiated. He uses such words as *lockout* and *decertification*—ridiculous words given the economic fortunes of the NFL and its players. No one seriously thinks it will develop into a situation in which no new CBA will exist when the current one expires after the 2007 season. No one seriously thinks that the labor messes that have sullied both the NBA and NHL recently will afflict the NFL, either.

Yet, the mere fact both Tagliabue and Upshaw want a new agreement but still don't have one says volumes about the discord that exists within Tagliabue's constituency. If you want to see how much the league has changed, just consider the owners of Pittsburgh and Seattle. Rooney's family has owned the Steelers since 1932. He sits daily in his office at the team complex; his sons are integral parts of the organization; he knows all of his players by name. Paul Allen has owned the Seahawks for eight-plus years; it is just another business interest for one of the world's richest men, a co-founder of Microsoft. For recreation, Rooney flies his own small plane; Allen finances private spaceships that fly into other worlds.

With the death of Giants owner Wellington Mara last fall, Rooney is the lone owner with links to the core foundation of the NFL. Allen is the new NFL ownership, the driven deep pockets who want to grow wealth as much as cultivate championships. And it is those owners—Dan Snyder, Jerry Jones, Bob McNair, Robert Kraft—who have stalled the new CBA. They have developed new streams of revenue through parking, signage, sponsorships and local media rights that have generated extra income above what other clubs can equal. In a league of *share and share alike* that has flourished financially because the "old" owners long ago agreed to split equally the television bonanza, this tilts the playing field. Now, Tagliabue must persuade these new owners to level off things again before any CBA can be signed.

Facing everyone is the nightmare of 2007, an uncapped year under the current CBA. That means there will be no restrictions on how much owners can spend on players. And it is the cap, along with

Parker opened the second half with a bang—and put his name in the Super Bowl record books—when he broke a 75-yard touchdown run to put the Steelers up 14-3.

the free-agent market, that has produced the wonderful competitive balance of today's NFL, where 11 teams have played in the seven Super Bowls of this century, where awful clubs have realistic playoff hopes for next season.

"When free agency started, fans were saying, 'I have guys I have rooted for my whole life and now they will be gone; I don't know who these players are that now are on my team,' " says Texans general manager Charley Casserly, a 29-year NFL veteran. "Now these same fans are saying, 'Every year, we have a chance.' It's become a 12-month league, a hot-stove league mentality that never existed before. You go from the Super Bowl to, *boom*, free agency, to *boom*, the Combine, to *boom*, the draft, to *boom*, training camp. It has increased the visibility of the league to new heights." To risk damaging this system, even for a year, is stupid. And to go into 2008 without a contract is the height of idiocy.

But with heightened visibility have come new pressures. Coaches feel it most. Here is a championship game featuring two of the longest-tenured coaches in the league, yet this new era of owners doesn't have the patience of a Rooney, who has employed two coaches in the past 37 years, or Allen, who has stayed with Mike Holmgren for seven. Ten coaching jobs alone have come open since the start of the 2005 season; there have been 19 coaching changes out of 32 teams the past two years.

"These new owners have spent a tremendous amount of money to buy a franchise, and they want quick results," FOX Sports analyst and former Cowboys and Dolphins coach Jimmy Johnson says. "Even though they are very intelligent people, they are not a lot different than the guys who paint their face and sit in the stadium. The only difference is they have a lot more money, and so sometimes they make decisions about coaches that don't involve patience."

This instability also trickles down to quarterback, a position at which the quality of play slipped badly this season. And this Super Bowl just added to the confusion. Do you continue to choose quarterbacks high in the draft, as exemplified by Ben Roethlisberger (11th player in the 2004 draft), even though so many of these top guys have fizzled? And because Roethlisberger excelled even as a rookie, do you start young quarterbacks in their first or second years even though so many of these youngsters struggle because of inexperience? Isn't it far better to develop quarterbacks methodically, much as it took Hasselbeck, a sixth-round pick, three years before he started and eight to play in a Super Bowl?

"But what are you going to do as a coach these days?" CBS Sports analyst Solomon Wilcots asks. "You see your peers being fired and owners without patience and you have this young, high-priced quarterback and the owner is wondering why he is not playing and you feel, 'Maybe I need to find out quickly if this guy can play because I might not have a lot of years to bring him along.' "

So what once made sense in the NFL no longer

is on the screen. These now are franchises worth up to $1 billion or more—there's that billion number again—and the league is as much about developing revenue as it is on-field competition. Consider the growth of the NFL Network. This fall, the network will show eight games live on Thursdays and Saturdays even though it still lacks overwhelming national cable penetration. The NFL says not to worry; free television will remain supreme. Yet, who would have thought that, after 36 years, *Monday Night Football*, the crown jewel of the league's television package, would leave free television for ESPN?

"I just worry about overexposure," says analyst John Madden, voted into the Hall of Fame last Saturday. "I don't want us to become like college basketball or football where you have games on every night. That's the direction that it's going in, and I really don't know it's a great direction."

For now, though, things are right, at least in Pittsburgh. But it certainly wasn't easy. After all, the Steelers triumph despite a fretful struggle by Roethlisberger, who played so well in the postseason but completes just nine of 21 attempts in this one for 123 yards, one interception and a woeful rating of 22.6, lowest of any winning quarterback in Super Bowl history. Still, he now is the youngest quarterback to win this game, in part because of a special first half play, a 37-yard strike to Ward off a scramble that sets up his own 1-yard touchdown run, good for a 7-3 halftime lead when Pittsburgh did nothing else in the first 30 minutes. And later, after the game, he too cries, sitting by his locker, head in his hands. Seattle accomplishes more in the first half, but an offensive interference call on receiver Darrell Jackson in the end zone nullifies his scoring grab.

Two other significant plays wrap up the game for the Steelers. The first comes on the second play of the third quarter, when Willie Parker rips off a record 75-yard touchdown scamper. Then in the final period, Pittsburgh resorts to one of its gadget calls, a pass by receiver Antwaan Randle El off a reverse that results in a 43-yard score to Ward. In between those plays, both quarterbacks throw awful interceptions and the Steelers accomplish what no one else in the playoffs had been able to do: control things against Seattle by running it. Pittsburgh finishes with 181 rushing yards, enough to support a defense that frustrates a more efficient opponent.

Seattle, trying to win its first Super Bowl, also is frustrated with its own inconsistencies. Here's how

Ward ended the game with 123 yards and a TD—plus the MVP trophy.

it unfolds for the Seahawks, normally one of the league's best red zone teams. Early in the fourth, trailing 14-10, a Hasselbeck completion to tight end Jerramy Stevens at the Steelers' 1-yard line is nullified by a holding penalty. Three plays later, Hasselbeck is intercepted, and Pittsburgh then scores moments later on the Randle El pass to go up by 11. "We did a lot of things right," says Seahawks center Robbie Tobeck. "We just couldn't finish them like we normally do."

But the Steelers finish what they set out to do: reward Rooney, get a ring for Cowher, send out Bettis with a flourish. And now it starts all over. "We've finished with rings for one hand," offensive tackle Max Starks says. "Now we'll start working on the second hand." **TSN**

STEELERS 21, SEAHAWKS 10
Sunday, February 5

Seattle	3	0	7	0—10
Pittsburgh	0	7	7	7—21

First Quarter
Sea.—FG, J. Brown 47, 14:38.
Second Quarter
Pit.—Roethlisberger 1 run (Reed kick), 13:05.
Third Quarter
Pit.—Parker 75 run (Reed kick), :22.
Sea.—Stevens 16 pass from Hasselbeck (J. Brown kick), 8:15.
Fourth Quarter
Pit.—Ward 43 pass from Randle El (Reed kick), 6:04.
Attendance—68,206.

	Seattle	Pittsburgh
First downs	20	14
Rushes-yards	25-137	33-181
Passing	259	158
Punt returns	4-27	2-32
Kickoff returns	4-71	2-43
Interception returns	2-76	1-24
Comp.-att.-int.	26-49-1	10-22-2
Sacked-yards lost	3-14	1-8
Punts	6-50	6-49
Fumbles-lost	0-0	0-0
Penalties-yards	7-70	3-20
Time of possession	33:02	26:58

INDIVIDUAL STATISTICS

RUSHING—Seattle, Alexander 20-95, Hasselbeck 3-35, Strong 2-7. Pittsburgh, Bettis 14-43, Parker 10-93, Roethlisberger 7-25, Ward 1-18, Haynes 1-2.

PASSING—Seattle, Hasselbeck 26-49-1-273. Pittsburgh, Roethlisberger 9-21-2-123, Randle El 1-1-0-43.

RECEIVING—Seattle, Engram 6-70, Jurevicius 5-93, Jackson 5-50, Stevens 2-15, Strong 2-15, Hannam 2-12, Alexander 2-2, Morris 1-6. Pittsburgh, Ward 5-123, Randle El 3-22, Wilson 1-20, Parker 1-1.

MISSED FIELD GOAL ATTEMPTS—Seattle, J. Brown 54, 50.

INTERCEPTIONS—Seattle, K. Herndon 1-76, Boulware 1-0. Pittsburgh, I. Taylor 1-24.

KICKOFF RETURNS—Seattle, Scobey 3-55, Morris 1-16. Pittsburgh, Colclough 2-43.

PUNT RETURNS—Seattle, Warrick 4-27. Pittsburgh, Randle El 2-32.

SACKS—Seattle, Wistrom 1. Pittsburgh, Townsend 1, Haggans 1, Hampton 1.

NFC SQUAD
OFFENSE
WR— Santana Moss, Washington*
Steve Smith, Carolina*
Larry Fitzgerald, Arizona
Torry Holt, St. Louis
T— Walter Jones, Seattle*
Orlando Pace, St. Louis*
Chris Samuels, Washington
G— Larry Allen, Dallas*
Steve Hutchinson, Seattle*
Mike Wahle, Carolina
C— Olin Kreutz, Chicago*
LeCharles Bentley, New Orleans
Robbie Tobeck, Seattle
TE— Alge Crumpler, Atlanta*
Jeremy Shockey, N.Y. Giants
Jason Witten, Dallas
QB— Matt Hasselbeck, Seattle*
Jake Delhomme, Carolina
Michael Vick, Atlanta
RB— Shaun Alexander, Seattle*
Tiki Barber, N.Y. Giants
Warrick Dunn, Atlanta
FB— Mack Strong, Seattle*
NOTE: C Kreutz was replaced due to injury by Tobeck; TE Shockey was replaced due to injury by Witten.

DEFENSE
DE— Julius Peppers, Carolina*
Michael Strahan, N.Y. Giants*
Osi Umenyiora, N.Y. Giants
IL— Shaun Rogers, Detroit*
Tommie Harris, Chicago*
Rod Coleman, Atlanta
La'Roi Glover, Dallas
OLB—Keith Brooking, Atlanta*
Derrick Brooks, Tampa Bay*
Lance Briggs, Chicago
ILB— Brian Urlacher, Chicago*
Jeremiah Trotter, Philadelphia
Lofa Tatupu, Seattle
CB— Ronde Barber, Tampa Bay*
DeAngelo Hall, Atlanta*
Nathan Vasher, Chicago
SS— Roy Williams, Dallas*

Brian Dawkins, Philadelphia
Mike Brown, Chicago
FS— Darren Sharper, Minnesota*
NOTE: IL Coleman was replaced due to injury by Glover; ILB Urlacher was replaced due to injury by Tatupu; SS Dawkins was replaced due to injury by Brown.

SPECIALISTS
P— Josh Bidwell, Tampa Bay
PK— Niel Rackers, Arizona
KR— Koren Robinson, Minnesota
ST— David Tyree, N.Y. Giants
LS— Mike Bartrum, Philadelphia

AFC SQUAD
OFFENSE
WR—Marvin Harrison, Indianapolis*
Chad Johnson, Cincinnati*
Chris Chambers, Miami
Rod Smith, Denver
T— Willie Anderson, Cincinnati*
Jonathan Ogden, Baltimore*
Willie Roaf, Kansas City
Tarik Glenn, Indianapolis
G— Alan Faneca, Pittsburgh*
Will Shields, Kansas City*
Brian Waters, Kansas City
C— Jeff Saturday, Indianapolis*
Jeff Hartings, Pittsburgh
TE— Antonio Gates, San Diego*
Tony Gonzalez, Kansas City
QB— Peyton Manning, Indianapolis*
Carson Palmer, Cincinnati
Trent Green, Kansas City
Tom Brady, New England
Jake Plummer, Denver
Steve McNair, Tennessee
RB— Edgerrin James, Indianapolis*
Larry Johnson, Kansas City
LaDainian Tomlinson, San Diego
FB— Lorenzo Neal, San Diego*
NOTE: T Roaf was replaced due to injury by Glenn; QB Palmer was replaced due to injury by Plummer; QB Brady was replaced due to injury by Green; QB

Plummer was replaced due to injury by McNair.

DEFENSE
DE— Dwight Freeney, Indianapolis*
Derrick Burgess, Oakland*
Jason Taylor, Miami
Kyle Vanden Bosch, Tennessee
IL— Marcus Stroud, Jacksonville*
Jamal Williams, San Diego*
Richard Seymour, New England
Casey Hampton, Pittsburgh
OLB—Cato June, Indianapolis*
Shawne Merriman, San Diego*
Joey Porter, Pittsburgh
ILB— Al Wilson, Denver*
Zach Thomas, Miami
Jonathan Vilma, N.Y. Jets
CB— Champ Bailey, Denver*
Deltha O'Neal, Cincinnati*
Ty Law, N.Y. Jets
SS— Troy Polamalu, Pittsburgh*
FS— Bob Sanders, Indianapolis*
John Lynch, Denver
NOTE: DE Taylor was replaced due to injury by Vanden Bosch; ILB Thomas was replaced due to injury by Vilma.

SPECIALISTS
P— Brian Moorman, Buffalo
PK— Shayne Graham, Cincinnati
KR— Jerome Mathis, Houston
ST— Hanik Milligan, San Diego
LS— Mike Schneck, Buffalo

*Elected starter.

AT ALOHA STADIUM, HONOLULU, FEBRUARY 12, 2006

Sunday, February 12

AFC	7	3	0	7—17
NFC	0	10	7	6—23

First Quarter
AFC—Chambers 16 pass from Manning (Graham kick), 5:09.
Second Quarter
NFC—FG Rackers 32, 7:45.
AFC—FG Graham 31, 3:22.
NFC—Crumpler 14 pass from Vick (Rackers kick), 0:02.
Third Quarter
NFC—Brooks 59 interception return (Rackers kick), 5:01.
Fourth Quarter
AFC—Green 1 run (Graham kick), 12:47.
NFC—FG Rackers 22, 6:29.
NFC—FG Rackers 20, 1:10.
Attendance—50,190.

Individual Statistics

RUSHING—AFC, L. Johnson 8-33; E. James 6-22; L. Tomlinson 5-13; T. Green 3-3; S. McNair 2-0. NFC, T. Barber 11-33; S. Moss 1-18; M. Vick 2-17; W. Dunn 7-12; L. Fitzgerald 1-12; S. Smith 1-6; M. Hasselbeck 1-0; M. Strong 1-0.

PASSING—AFC, P. Manning 13-26-1-139; T. Green 5-11-1-39; S. McNair 2-8-0-25. NFC, M. Hasselbeck 10-17-0-85; M. Vick 4-12-1-69; J. Delhomme 7-10-0-53.

RECEIVING—AFC, M. Harrison 4-74; T. Gonzalez 5-36; C. Chambers 2-34; L. Tomlinson 2-18; C. Johnson 2-15; R. Smith 2-13; A. Gates 2-7; L. Neal 1-6. NFC,

S. Smith 8-46; S. Moss 3-39; A. Crumpler 2-35; L. Fitzgerald 1-32; T. Holt 2-18; M. Strong 2-17; W. Dunn 1-14; T. Barber 1-6.

FIELD GOALS—AFC, S. Graham 1-1. NFC, N. Rackers 3-3.

INTERCEPTIONS—AFC, C. Bailey 1; J. Lynch 1. NFC D. Sharper 1; D. Brooks 1; R. Williams 1; N. Vasher 1.

KICKOFF RETURNS—AFC, J. Mathis 27.2; L. Neal 10.0. NFC, K. Robinson 23.5.

PUNT RETURNS—AFC, J. Mathis 12.0. NFC, S. Moss 12.0; S. Smith -6.0.

SACKS—AFC, K. Vanden Bosch 2.0; M. Stroud 1.5; C. Hampton 1.0; D. Burgess 0.5. NFC, S. Rogers 1.0; M. Strahan 1.0.

	AFC	NFC
First Downs	19	18
Rushes-yards	24-71	25-98
Passes completed-yards	20-189	21-181
Punt returns-yards	1-12	2-7
Kickoff returns-yards	5-119	4-94
Interception returns-yards	2-73	4-192
Comp.-Att.-Int.	20-45-4	21-39-2
Sacked-yds. lost	2-14	5-26
Punts-avg.	4-48.5	5-48.4
Penalties-Yards	8-59	8-55
Fumbles-Lost	3-2	6-2
Time Of Possession	27:59	32:01

PLAYER PARTICIPATION

COMPLETE LIST

Player, team	GP	GS
Abdullah, Hamza, Denver	1	0
Abraham, John, N.Y. Jets	16	15
Adams, Anthony, San Francisco	16	16
Adams, Blue, Tampa Bay	13	0
Adams, Charlie, Denver	16	2
Adams, Flozell, Dallas	6	6
Adams, Keith, Philadelphia	16	16
Adams, Mike, San Francisco	14	10
Adams, Sam, Buffalo	14	9
Aiken, Sam, Buffalo	16	2
Akers, David, Philadelphia	12	0
Albright, Ethan, Washington	16	0
Alexander, Brent, N.Y. Giants	16	16
Alexander, Eric, New England	1	0
Alexander, Roc, Denver	10	0
Alexander, Shaun, Seattle	16	16
Alexander, Stephen, Denver	16	15
Alexis, Rich, Jacksonville	2	0
Allen, David, St. Louis	4	0
Allen, Ian, Arizona	2	0
Allen, James, New Orleans	3	0
Allen, Jared, Kansas City	16	15
Allen, Kenderick, N.Y. Giants	14	0
Allen, Larry, Dallas	16	16
Allen, Will, N.Y. Giants	16	16
Allen, Will, Tampa Bay	13	8
Alstott, Mike, Tampa Bay	16	7
Amano, Eugene, Tennessee	16	0
Amato, Ken, Tennessee	7	0
Amey, Otis, San Francisco	11	0
Anderson, Bennie, Buffalo	16	14
Anderson, Charlie, Houston	16	0
Anderson, Courtney, Oakland	14	13
Anderson, Damien, Arizona	5	0
Anderson, Dwight, St. Louis	3	0
Anderson, Jason, Houston	1	0
Anderson, Marques, Den.-S.F.	10	0
Anderson, Mike, Denver	15	15
Anderson, Tim, Buffalo	16	12
Anderson, Willie, Cincinnati	16	16
Andrews, Shawn, Philadelphia	16	16
Andrews, Stacy, Cincinnati	14	0
Andruzzi, Joe, Cleveland	13	13
Angulo, Richard, Minnesota	2	0
Araguz, Leo, Seattle	4	0
Archibald, Ben, New Orleans	6	0
Archuleta, Adam, St. Louis	14	14
Armstrong, Derick, Houston	13	3
Arrington, J.J., Arizona	15	5
Arrington, LaVar, Washington	12	8
Ashworth, Tom, New England	14	11
Askew, B.J., N.Y. Jets	10	1
Askew, Matthias, Cincinnati	1	0
Asomugha, Nnamdi, Oakland	16	16
Atogwe, O.J., St. Louis	12	0
Awasom, Adrian, N.Y. Giants	5	0
Ayanbadejo, Brendon, Chicago	16	0
Ayanbadejo, Obafemi, Arizona	16	2
Ayodele, Akin, Jacksonville	16	11
Azumah, Jerry, Chicago	15	1
Baas, David, San Francisco	13	5
Babin, Jason, Houston	12	3
Babineaux, Jonathan, Atlanta	16	6
Babineaux, Jordan, Seattle	16	4
Backus, Jeff, Detroit	16	16
Badger, Brad, Oakland	16	8
Bailey, Boss, Detroit	11	11
Bailey, Champ, Denver	14	14
Bailey, Rodney, Seattle	8	0
Bajema, Billy, San Francisco	15	7
Baker, Chris, N.Y. Jets	8	8
Baker, Jason, Carolina	16	0
Baker, Rashad, Buffalo	14	0
Ball, Dave, San Diego-N.Y. Jets	5	0
Banks, Tony, Houston	3	0
Bannan, Justin, Buffalo	16	7
Bannister, Alex, Seattle	2	0
Banta-Cain, Tully, New England	13	0
Barber, Marion, Dallas	13	2
Barber, Ronde, Tampa Bay	16	16
Barber, Shawn, Kansas City	3	0
Barber, Tiki, N.Y. Giants	16	16
Barker, Bryan, St. Louis	11	0
Barlow, Kevan, San Francisco	12	12
Barnes, Darian, Miami	9	5
Barnes, Khalif, Jacksonville	13	12
Barnett, Nick, Green Bay	16	16
Barrett, David, N.Y. Jets	13	8
Barron, Alex, St. Louis	12	11
Barrow, Mike, Dallas	2	0
Barry, Kevin, Green Bay	16	1
Bartee, William, Kansas City	16	0
Bartell, Ronald, St. Louis	10	7
Barton, Eric, N.Y. Jets	4	3
Bartrum, Mike, Philadelphia	16	0
Bashir, Idrees, Carolina	11	0
Batch, Charlie, Pittsburgh	4	2
Battle, Arnaz, San Francisco	10	8
Bauman, Rashad, Cincinnati	11	1
Baxter, Gary, Cleveland	5	5
Baxter, Jarrod, Arizona	8	2
Beasley, Fred, San Francisco	9	7
Becht, Anthony, Tampa Bay	16	16
Beckham, Tony, Tennessee	15	2
Beisel, Monty, New England	15	6
Bell, Jacob, Tennessee	9	1
Bell, Jason, Houston	16	0
Bell, Kendrell, Kansas City	16	14
Bell, Marcus, Detroit	15	0
Bell, Tatum, Denver	15	1
Bell, Yeremiah, Miami	16	0
Bellamy, Jay, New Orleans	3	3
Bennett, Darren, Minnesota	1	0
Bennett, Drew, Tennessee	13	10
Bennett, Michael, Minnesota	16	6
Benson, Cedric, Chicago	9	1
Bentley, Kevin, Seattle	15	3
Bentley, LeCharles, New Orleans	14	14
Bergen, Adam, Arizona	16	9
Berger, Joe, Miami	3	0
Berger, Mitch, New Orleans	16	0
Berlin, Eddie, Chicago	5	0
Bernard, Rocky, Seattle	16	6
Berrian, Bernard, Chicago	11	2
Berry, Bertrand, Arizona	8	8
Berton, Sean, N.Y. Giants	14	0
Bettis, Jerome, Pittsburgh	12	0
Betts, Ladell, Washington	12	0
Beverly, Eric, Atlanta	16	2
Bidwell, Josh, Tampa Bay	16	0
Bigby, Atari, Green Bay	1	0
Bingham, Ryon, San Diego	1	0
Binn, David, San Diego	16	0
Bironas, Rob, Tennessee	16	0
Black, Jordan, Kansas City	16	10
Blackburn, Chase, N.Y. Giants	15	2
Blackstock, Darryl, Arizona	14	1
Blake, Jeff, Chicago	3	0
Blakley, Dwayne, Atlanta	16	1
Blaylock, Derrick, N.Y. Jets	7	1
Bledsoe, Drew, Dallas	16	16
Bly, Dre', Detroit	12	11
Bober, Chris, Kansas City	16	2
Bockwoldt, Colby, New Orleans	16	16
Bodden, Leigh, Cleveland	13	11
Body, Patrick, Cincinnati	6	0
Boerigter, Marc, Kansas City	10	0
Boiman, Rocky, Tennessee	15	2
Bolden, Juran, Tampa Bay	16	2
Boldin, Anquan, Arizona	14	14
Boley, Michael, Atlanta	16	11
Boller, Kyle, Baltimore	9	9
Bollinger, Brooks, N.Y. Jets	11	9
Booker, Fred, New Orleans	12	0
Booker, Marty, Miami	15	11
Boone, Alfonso, Chicago	16	1
Boschetti, Ryan, Washington	13	1
Boston, David, Miami	5	0
Boulware, Michael, Seattle	16	16
Boulware, Peter, Baltimore	15	0
Bouman, Todd, New Orleans	16	3
Bowen, Matt, Washington	13	1
Bowens, David, Miami	16	0
Brackett, Gary, Indianapolis	16	16
Bradford, Corey, Houston	16	6
Bradley, Jon, Tampa Bay	13	0
Bradley, Mark, Chicago	7	4
Brady, Kyle, Jacksonville	16	14
Brady, Tom, New England	16	16
Braham, Rich, Cincinnati	15	15
Branch, Calvin, Oakland	6	0
Branch, Deion, New England	16	15
Brandon, Sam, Denver	14	0
Brayton, Tyler, Oakland	16	3
Brees, Drew, San Diego	16	16
Brewer, Jack, Philadelphia	6	0
Bridges, Jeremy, Arizona	7	3
Brien, Doug, Chicago	3	0
Briggs, Lance, Chicago	16	16
Brock, Raheem, Indianapolis	16	16
Bronson, John, Arizona	1	0
Brooking, Keith, Atlanta	16	16
Brooks, Aaron, New Orleans	13	13
Brooks, Barrett, Pittsburgh	16	0
Brooks, Derrick, Tampa Bay	16	16
Brooks, Ethan, Dallas	2	0
Brooks, Greg, Cincinnati	11	0
Broughton, Nehemiah, Wash.	4	0
Brown, Alex, Chicago	16	16

Player, team	GP	GS	Player, team	GP	GS	Player, team	GP	GS
Brown, Antonio, Washington	7	0	Carr, David, Houston	16	16	Coleman, Rod, Atlanta	16	16
Brown, C.C., Houston	16	13	Carroll, Ahmad, Green Bay	16	16	Coles, Laveranues, N.Y. Jets	16	16
Brown, Chad, New England	15	5	Carstens, Jordan, Carolina	16	15	Collins, Jerome, St. Louis	3	0
Brown, Chris, Tennessee	15	14	Carswell, Dwayne, Denver	7	0	Collins, Kerry, Oakland	15	15
Brown, Courtney, Denver	14	13	Carter, Andre, San Francisco	16	14	Collins, Nick, Green Bay	16	16
Brown, Dee, Kansas City	8	0	Carter, Dale, Baltimore	15	2	Collins, Todd, Kansas City	2	0
Brown, Elton, Arizona	9	9	Carter, Drew, Carolina	3	0	Colombo, Marc, Chicago-Dallas	5	0
Brown, Fakhir, New Orleans	12	4	Carter, Dyshod, Arizona	3	0	Colquitt, Dustin, Kansas City	16	0
Brown, Jammal, New Orleans	13	13	Carter, Jerome, St. Louis	14	2	Colvin, Rosevelt, New England	16	11
Brown, Jason, Baltimore	6	1	Carter, Kevin, Miami	16	16	Condo, Jon, Dallas	3	0
Brown, Josh, Seattle	16	0	Carter, Tim, N.Y. Giants	15	1	Connolly, Daniel, Jacksonville	4	0
Brown, Kris, Houston	16	0	Carter, Tyrone, Pittsburgh	16	0	Considine, Sean, Philadelphia	6	0
Brown, Mark, N.Y. Jets	15	11	Carthon, Ran, Indianapolis	6	0	Conwell, Ernie, New Orleans	9	9
Brown, Mike, Chicago	12	12	Cartwright, Rock, Washington	16	0	Cook, Jameel, Tampa Bay	16	0
Brown, Milford, Houston	13	12	Cash, Antoine, Atlanta	3	0	Cooley, Chris, Washington	16	16
Brown, Orlando, Baltimore	9	9	Cash, Chris, Atlanta	3	0	Cooper, Deke, Jacksonville	16	12
Brown, Ralph, Minnesota	16	0	Cason, Aveion, St. Louis	2	0	Cooper, Jarrod, Oakland	16	10
Brown, Ray, Washington	14	2	Cassel, Matt, New England	2	0	Cooper, Marquis, Tampa Bay	12	0
Brown, Reggie, Philadelphia	16	11	Castillo, Luis, San Diego	16	15	Cooper, Stephen, San Diego	16	2
Brown, Ronnie, Miami	15	14	Caver, Quinton, Dallas	8	0	Copper, Terrance, Dallas	16	0
Brown, Ruben, Chicago	12	12	Celestin, Oliver, N.Y. Jets	12	0	Cortez, Jose, Dallas-Phila.-S.F.-Ind.	14	0
Brown, Sheldon, Philadelphia	16	16	Cesaire, Jacques, San Diego	16	5	Cotchery, Jerricho, N.Y. Jets	16	1
Brown, Troy, New England	13	3	Chamberlin, Frank, Houston	9	0	Cousin, Terry, Jacksonville	16	5
Browning, John, Kansas City	16	12	Chambers, Chris, Miami	16	16	Cowart, Sam, Minnesota	15	14
Bruce, Isaac, St. Louis	11	10	Chambers, Kirk, Cleveland	15	0	Cox, Curome, Denver	13	1
Bruener, Mark, Houston	16	15	Chapman, Kory, Indianapolis	3	0	Cox, Torrie, Tampa Bay	15	0
Brunell, Mark, Washington	16	15	Chase, Martin, Jacksonville	1	0	Craft, Jason, New Orleans	16	4
Bruschi, Tedy, New England	9	9	Chatham, Matt, New England	15	0	Cramer, Casey, Carolina	1	0
Bryant, Anthony, Tampa Bay	4	0	Chatman, Antonio, Green Bay	16	3	Crayton, Patrick, Dallas	11	0
Bryant, Antonio, Cleveland	16	15	Chavous, Corey, Minnesota	16	16	Cribbs, Joshua, Cleveland	14	0
Bryant, Fernando, Detroit	2	2	Childress, Brandon, New England	1	0	Crocker, Chris, Cleveland	16	16
Bryant, Matt, Tampa Bay	15	0	Chillar, Brandon, St. Louis	16	7	Crockett, Zack, Oakland	16	10
Bryant, Romby, Atlanta	3	0	Chrebet, Wayne, N.Y. Jets	8	0	Crowder, Channing, Miami	16	13
Bryant, Tony, New Orleans	16	1	Chukwurah, Patrick, Denver	14	0	Crowell, Angelo, Buffalo	15	13
Bryson, Shawn, Detroit	16	2	Cieslak, Brad, Buffalo	2	0	Crumpler, Alge, Atlanta	16	16
Buchanon, Phillip, Houston	10	6	Ciurciu, Vinny, Carolina	15	1	Cruz, Ronnie, Kansas City	14	0
Buckley, Terrell, N.Y. Giants	4	0	Claiborne, Chris, St. Louis	14	7	Culpepper, Daunte, Minnesota	7	7
Buckner, Brentson, Carolina	16	16	Clancy, Kendrick, N.Y. Giants	16	15	Cundiff, Billy, Dallas	6	0
Buenning, Dan, Tampa Bay	16	16	Clark, Dallas, Indianapolis	15	14	Curry, Donte', Detroit	13	2
Bulger, Marc, St. Louis	8	8	Clark, Danny, Oakland	16	15	Curry, Ronald, Oakland	2	0
Bullocks, Josh, New Orleans	16	13	Clark, Desmond, Chicago	16	16	Curtis, Kevin, St. Louis	16	9
Bulluck, Keith, Tennessee	16	16	Clark, Ryan, Washington	13	13	Dalton, Lional, Kansas City	16	14
Bulman, Tim, Arizona	8	1	Clarke, Adrien, Philadelphia	14	4	Daniels, Phillip, Washington	16	16
Burgess, Derrick, Oakland	16	12	Clauss, Jared, Tennessee	15	1	Daniels, Travis, Miami	16	14
Burleson, Nate, Minnesota	12	9	Claxton, Ben, Atlanta	2	0	Dansby, Karlos, Arizona	15	15
Burnett, Kevin, Dallas	13	0	Clayton, Mark, Baltimore	14	10	Darby, Chartric, Seattle	14	14
Burns, Joe, Buffalo	16	0	Clayton, Michael, Tampa Bay	14	10	Darche, Jean-Philippe, Seattle	16	0
Burns, Keith, Denver	15	1	Cleeland, Cam, St. Louis	9	3	Darilek, Trey, Philadelphia	15	0
Burress, Plaxico, N.Y. Giants	16	15	Clement, Anthony, San Francisco	14	6	Darius, Donovin, Jacksonville	2	2
Bush, Steve, San Francisco	15	2	Clements, Nate, Buffalo	16	16	Darling, Devard, Baltimore	10	0
Butler, James, N.Y. Giants	16	1	Clemons, Chris, Washington	14	1	Darling, James, Arizona	14	14
Butler, Kelly, Detroit	16	16	Clemons, Duane, Cincinnati	10	0	Davenport, Najeh, Green Bay	5	1
Butler, Terry, N.Y. Jets	1	0	Clemons, Nic, Washington	8	0	David, Jason, Indianapolis	16	16
Cain, Jeremy, Chicago	3	0	Clifton, Chad, Green Bay	16	16	Davis, Andra, Cleveland	16	16
Calahan, Jeremy, St. Louis	1	0	Cloud, Michael, N.E.-NYG	7	0	Davis, Andre', New England	9	4
Caldwell, Reche, San Diego	16	2	Coakley, Dexter, St. Louis	12	9	Davis, Anthony, Tampa Bay	16	16
Calico, Tyrone, Tennessee	12	6	Cobb, DeAndra, Atlanta	3	0	Davis, Chauncey, Atlanta	16	5
Campbell, Dan, Dallas	16	12	Cochran, Antonio, Arizona	3	0	Davis, Domanick, Houston	11	11
Campbell, Khary, Washington	15	0	Cody, Shaun, Detroit	16	2	Davis, Don, New England	16	0
Campbell, Mark, Buffalo	14	10	Colbert, Keary, Carolina	16	16	Davis, James, Detroit	16	14
Cantu, Rolando, Arizona	1	0	Colclough, Ricardo, Pittsburgh	14	0	Davis, Jim, Jacksonville	1	0
Canty, Chris, Dallas	16	2	Cole, Colin, Green Bay	16	4	Davis, Keith, Dallas	16	15
Carey, Vernon, Miami	16	14	Cole, Trent, Philadelphia	15	7	Davis, Leonard, Arizona	15	15
Carlisle, Cooper, Denver	16	16	Coleman, Cosey, Cleveland	14	14	Davis, Rashied, Chicago	12	0
Carney, John, New Orleans	16	0	Coleman, Erik, N.Y. Jets	16	16	Davis, Rob, Green Bay	16	0
Carpenter, Dwaine, S.F.-Stl.	3	0	Coleman, Kenyon, Dallas	12	5	Davis, Rod, Minnesota	16	1
Carpenter, Keion, Atlanta	15	15	Coleman, Marco, Denver	7	0	Davis, Russell, Arizona	3	3
Carr, Chris, Oakland	16	0	Coleman, Marcus, Houston	15	11	Davis, Sammy, San Diego	16	4

Player, team	GP	GS
Davis, Stephen, Carolina	13	11
Davis, Thomas, Carolina	16	1
Dawkins, Brian, Philadelphia	16	16
Dawson, Phil, Cleveland	16	0
Dayne, Ron, Denver	10	0
Dearth, James, N.Y. Jets	16	0
Delhomme, Jake, Carolina	16	16
DeLoach, Jerry, Houston	11	1
DeLoatch, Curtis, N.Y. Giants	16	13
Demps, Will, Baltimore	11	11
DeMulling, Rick, Detroit	13	5
Dendy, Patrick, Green Bay	4	0
Denney, John, Miami	16	0
Denney, Ryan, Buffalo	16	0
Detmer, Koy, Philadelphia	16	0
Devoe, Todd, Denver	14	0
DeVries, Jared, Detroit	16	0
Diamond, Lorenzo, Miami	16	8
Diehl, David, N.Y. Giants	16	16
Dielman, Kris, San Diego	16	14
Diem, Ryan, Indianapolis	14	14
Diggs, Na'il, Green Bay	9	6
Dilfer, Trent, Cleveland	11	11
Dillon, Corey, New England	12	10
Dinkins, Darnell, Baltimore	16	4
Dockery, Derrick, Washington	16	16
Dockett, Darnell, Arizona	16	16
Dorenbos, Jon, Tennessee	9	0
Dorsey, Ken, San Francisco	3	3
Dorsey, Nat, Cleveland	9	0
Doss, Mike, Indianapolis	15	14
Douglas, Marques, San Francisco	16	15
Draft, Chris, Carolina	16	3
Dreessen, Joel, N.Y. Jets	14	0
Driver, Donald, Green Bay	16	16
Droughns, Reuben, Cleveland	16	16
Drummond, Eddie, Detroit	12	0
Duckett, Damane, N.Y. Giants	8	0
Duckett, T.J., Atlanta	14	0
Dudley, Kevin, Atlanta	1	0
Dugan, Jeff, Minnesota	1	0
Duke, Wesley, Denver	3	0
Dunn, Jason, Kansas City	16	1
Dunn, Warrick, Atlanta	16	16
Dwight, Tim, New England	16	1
Dyson, Andre, Seattle	10	6
Earl, Glenn, Houston	10	7
Eason, Nick, Cleveland	16	0
Easy, Omar, Oakland	16	0
Echemandu, Adimchinobe, Minn.	2	0
Edinger, Paul, Minnesota	16	0
Edwards, Antuan, Atlanta	4	1
Edwards, Braylon, Cleveland	10	7
Edwards, Devonte, Minnesota	12	0
Edwards, Donnie, San Diego	16	16
Edwards, Dwan, Baltimore	12	1
Edwards, Eric, Arizona	16	9
Edwards, Kalimba, Detroit	16	2
Edwards, Marc, Chicago	8	5
Edwards, Ron, Buffalo	4	4
Edwards, Steve, Chicago	7	0
Edwards, Troy, Detroit	3	0
Ekejiuba, Isaiah, Oakland	10	0
Ekuban, Ebenezer, Denver	16	4
Elam, Jason, Denver	16	0
Elling, Aaron, Baltimore	9	0
Ellington, Dante, Arizona	2	0
Ellis, Greg, Dallas	16	13
Ellis, Shaun, N.Y. Jets	13	13
Emanuel, Ben, San Francisco	11	8
Emmons, Carlos, N.Y. Giants	9	8
Ena, Justin, Philadelphia	6	0
Engelberger, John, Denver	14	0
Engram, Bobby, Seattle	13	13
Enzor, Jamar, N.Y. Jets	1	0
Ephraim, Alonzo, Miami	13	3
Ernster, Paul, Denver	1	0
Essex, Trai, Pittsburgh	6	4
Estes, Patrick, San Francisco	7	0
Euhus, Tim, Buffalo	11	3
Evans, Demetric, Washington	16	3
Evans, Heath, Miami-N.E.	12	3
Evans, Lee, Buffalo	16	15
Evans, Troy, Houston	16	0
Ezekiel, Liam, Buffalo	2	0
Fabini, Jason, N.Y. Jets	9	9
Faggins, DeMarcus, Houston	13	10
Faine, Jeff, Cleveland	14	14
Fair, Terry, St. Louis	5	0
Faneca, Alan, Pittsburgh	16	16
Fanene, Jonathan, Cincinnati	3	1
Fargas, Justin, Oakland	14	0
Farrior, James, Pittsburgh	14	14
Farris, Jimmy, Washington	4	0
Farwell, Heath, Minnesota	7	0
Fason, Ciatrick, Minnesota	13	0
Faulk, Kevin, New England	8	2
Faulk, Marshall, St. Louis	16	1
Faulk, Trev, St. Louis	16	5
Fauria, Christian, New England	16	10
Favors, Greg, Jacksonville	1	0
Favre, Brett, Green Bay	16	16
Feagles, Jeff, N.Y. Giants	16	0
Feely, Jay, N.Y. Giants	16	0
Ferguson, Jason, Dallas	16	5
Ferguson, Nick, Denver	16	16
Ferguson, Robert, Green Bay	11	7
Fiedler, Jay, N.Y. Jets	2	0
Fields, Ronald, San Francisco	4	0
Fincher, Alfred, New Orleans	11	0
Finn, Jim, N.Y. Giants	16	13
Finneran, Brian, Atlanta	16	7
Fisher, Bryce, Seattle	16	15
Fisher, Tony, Green Bay	14	4
Fisher, Travis, St. Louis	8	8
Fisk, Jason, Cleveland	16	14
Fitzgerald, Larry, Arizona	16	16
Fitzpatrick, Ryan, St. Louis	4	3
FitzSimmons, Casey, Detroit	14	2
Flanagan, Mike, Green Bay	14	14
Fleming, Troy, Tennessee	13	2
Flemister, Zeron, Oakland	12	3
Fletcher, Bryan, Indianapolis	16	12
Fletcher, Derrick, Jacksonville	12	1
Fletcher, Jamar, San Diego	14	0
Fletcher, London, Buffalo	16	16
Flinn, Ryan, Green Bay	2	0
Florence, Drayton, San Diego	13	12
Flutie, Doug, New England	5	0
Flynn, Mike, Baltimore	16	16
Foley, Steve, San Diego	13	13
Fonoti, Toniu, San Diego-Minn.	3	3
Fontenot, Therrian, Green Bay	1	0
Foote, Larry, Pittsburgh	16	16
Ford, Carl, Chicago	10	0
Fordham, Todd, Carolina	16	0
Foreman, Jay, N.Y. Giants	1	0
Forney, Kynan, Atlanta	16	16
Foschi, John Paul, Oakland	10	5
Foster, DeShaun, Carolina	15	5
Foster, George, Denver	16	16
Fowler, Melvin, Minnesota	11	9
Fowler, Ryan, Dallas	14	3
Fox, Keyaron, Kansas City	2	0
Fox, Vernon, Detroit	14	0
Foxworth, Domonique, Denver	16	7
Fraley, Hank, Philadelphia	8	8
France, Todd, Phila.-Tampa Bay	4	0
Francisco, Aaron, Arizona	11	0
Franklin, Aubrayo, Baltimore	15	1
Franks, Bubba, Green Bay	10	8
Franz, Todd, Green Bay	5	0
Fraser, Simon, Cleveland	16	0
Frazier, Andre, Pittsburgh	11	0
Freeman, Arturo, New England	2	1
Freeney, Dwight, Indianapolis	16	16
Frerotte, Gus, Miami	16	15
Friedman, Lennie, Wash.-Chicago	11	0
Frost, Derrick, Washington	14	0
Frye, Charlie, Cleveland	7	5
Fujita, Scott, Dallas	16	8
Fuller, Vincent, Tennessee	2	0
Furrey, Mike, St. Louis	16	11
Gabriel, Doug, Oakland	14	2
Gado, Samkon, Green Bay	8	5
Gaffney, Jabar, Houston	16	13
Gage, Justin, Chicago	15	11
Gaines, Michael, Carolina	11	6
Gallery, Robert, Oakland	16	16
Gallishaw, Laroni, Minnesota	5	0
Galloway, Joey, Tampa Bay	16	16
Gamble, Chris, Carolina	15	15
Gammon, Kendall, Kansas City	10	0
Gandy, Dylan, Indianapolis	16	2
Gandy, Mike, Buffalo	16	16
Gandy, Wayne, New Orleans	16	16
Garcia, Jeff, Detroit	6	5
Gardner, Barry, N.Y. Jets	16	1
Gardner, Gilbert, Indianapolis	11	3
Gardner, Rich, Tennessee	13	0
Gardner, Rod, Carolina-Green Bay	12	1
Gardocki, Chris, Pittsburgh	16	0
Garrard, David, Jacksonville	7	5
Garza, Roberto, Chicago	16	7
Gates, Antonio, San Diego	15	15
Gay, Randall, New England	5	2
Gbaja-Biamila, Kabeer, Green Bay	16	16
Geathers, Robert, Cincinnati	16	16
Ghiaciuc, Eric, Cincinnati	5	1
Gibson, Derrick, Oakland	6	6
Gilbert, Tony, Jacksonville	16	0
Gilmore, Bryan, Miami	15	1
Gilmore, John, Chicago	16	0
Giordano, Matt, Indianapolis	15	0
Givens, David, New England	13	10
Gleason, Steve, New Orleans	13	1
Glenn, Aaron, Dallas	13	1
Glenn, Jason, Miami	16	0
Glenn, Tarik, Indianapolis	16	16
Glenn, Terry, Dallas	16	16
Glover, La'Roi, Dallas	16	13
Glymph, Junior, Atlanta	3	0
Goddard, Johnathan, Indianapolis	1	0
Godfrey, Randall, San Diego	14	14

Player, team	Att.	Cmp.	Pct.	Yds.	Avg. Gain	TD	Pct. TD	Long	Int.	Pct. Int.	Sack	Yds. Lost	Rat.
Hymes, Randy, Baltimore	2	0	0.0	0	0.00	0	0.0	0	0	0.0	0	0	39.6
Jackson, Frisman, Cleveland	0	0	...	0	...	0	...	...	0	...	1	2	...
Jones, Matt, Jacksonville	3	2	66.7	12	4.00	0	0.0	6	0	0.0	0	0	74.3
Jones, Pacman, Tennessee	0	0	...	0	...	0	...	...	0	...	1	13	...
Kingsbury, Kliff, N.Y. Jets	2	1	50.0	17	8.50	0	0.0	17	0	0.0	0	0	79.2
Kitna, Jon, Cincinnati	29	17	58.6	99	3.41	0	0.0	16	2	6.9	2	10	36.4
Leftwich, Byron, Jacksonville	302	175	57.9	2123	7.03	15	5.0	t45	5	1.7	23	110	89.3
Losman, J.P., Buffalo	228	113	49.6	1340	5.88	8	3.5	58	8	3.5	26	197	64.9
Maddox, Tommy, Pittsburgh	71	34	47.9	406	5.72	2	2.8	32	4	5.6	8	43	51.7
Manning, Peyton, Indianapolis	453	305	67.3	3747	8.27	28	6.2	t80	10	2.2	17	81	104.1
Mauck, Matt, Tennessee	27	15	55.6	136	5.04	0	0.0	17	1	3.7	1	8	53.9
McCardell, Keenan, San Diego	0	0	...	0	...	0	...	...	0	...	1	4	...
McNair, Steve, Tennessee	476	292	61.3	3161	6.64	16	3.4	57	11	2.3	20	134	82.4
Palmer, Carson, Cincinnati	509	345	67.8	3836	7.54	32	6.3	t70	12	2.4	19	105	101.1
Parrish, Roscoe, Buffalo	1	1	100.0	3	3.00	0	0.0	3	0	0.0	0	0	79.2
Pennington, Chad, N.Y. Jets	83	49	59.0	530	6.39	2	2.4	37	3	3.6	9	52	70.9
Plummer, Jake, Denver	456	277	60.7	3366	7.38	18	3.9	72	7	1.5	22	135	90.2
Randle El, Antwaan, Pittsburgh	3	3	100.0	67	22.33	1	33.3	t51	0	0.0	0	0	158.3
Rivers, Philip, San Diego	22	12	54.5	115	5.23	0	0.0	22	1	4.5	3	16	50.4
Roethlisberger, Ben, Pittsburgh	268	168	62.7	2385	8.90	17	6.3	t85	9	3.4	23	129	98.6
Rosenfels, Sage, Miami	61	34	55.7	462	7.57	4	6.6	t77	3	4.9	0	0	81.5
Smith, Hunter, Indianapolis	1	0	0.0	0	0.00	0	0.0	0	0	0.0	0	0	39.6
Smith, Rod, Denver	1	0	0.0	0	0.00	0	0.0	0	0	0.0	1	11	39.6
Sorgi, Jim, Indianapolis	61	42	68.9	444	7.28	3	4.9	45	1	1.6	3	14	99.4
Testaverde, Vinny, N.Y. Jets	106	60	56.6	777	7.33	1	0.9	47	6	5.7	12	102	59.4
Tomlinson, LaDainian, San Diego	4	3	75.0	47	11.75	3	75.0	t26	0	0.0	0	0	153.1
Tuiasosopo, Marques, Oakland	26	14	53.8	124	4.77	1	3.8	t20	2	7.7	6	40	47.6
Van Pelt, Bradlee, Denver	8	2	25.0	7	0.88	0	0.0	5	0	0.0	0	0	39.6
Volek, Billy, Tennessee	88	50	56.8	474	5.39	4	4.5	t55	2	2.3	9	45	77.6
Wright, Anthony, Baltimore	266	164	61.7	1582	5.95	6	2.3	48	9	3.4	19	147	71.7

t—touchdown.

NFC

Player, team	Att.	Cmp.	Pct.	Yds.	Avg. Gain	TD	Pct. TD	Long	Int.	Pct. Int.	Sack	Yds. Lost	Rat.
Barber, Marion, Dallas	0	0	...	0	...	0	...	...	0	...	1	3	...
Barber, Tiki, N.Y. Giants	1	0	0.0	0	0.00	0	0.0	0	0	0.0	0	0	39.6
Battle, Arnaz, San Francisco	2	2	100.0	27	13.50	0	0.0	24	0	0.0	0	0	118.8
Blake, Jeff, Chicago	9	8	88.9	55	6.11	1	11.1	17	0	0.0	0	0	129.2
Bledsoe, Drew, Dallas	499	300	60.1	3639	7.29	23	4.6	t71	17	3.4	49	295	83.7
Boldin, Anquan, Arizona	1	0	0.0	0	0.00	0	0.0	0	0	0.0	0	0	39.6
Bouman, Todd, New Orleans	122	68	55.7	722	5.92	2	1.6	43	7	5.7	8	59	54.7
Brooks, Aaron, New Orleans	431	240	55.7	2882	6.69	13	3.0	66	17	3.9	33	202	70.0
Brunell, Mark, Washington	454	262	57.7	3050	6.72	23	5.1	t78	10	2.2	27	213	85.9
Bulger, Marc, St. Louis	287	192	66.9	2297	8.00	14	4.9	t57	9	3.1	26	188	94.4
Culpepper, Daunte, Minnesota	216	139	64.4	1564	7.24	6	2.8	68	12	5.6	31	169	72.0
Delhomme, Jake, Carolina	435	262	60.2	3421	7.86	24	5.5	t80	16	3.7	28	214	88.1
Detmer, Koy, Philadelphia	56	32	57.1	238	4.25	0	0.0	24	3	5.4	3	15	45.1
Dorsey, Ken, San Francisco	90	48	53.3	481	5.34	2	2.2	44	2	2.2	6	28	66.9
Favre, Brett, Green Bay	607	372	61.3	3881	6.39	20	3.3	59	29	4.8	24	170	70.9
Fisher, Tony, Green Bay	1	1	100.0	14	14.00	0	0.0	14	0	0.0	0	0	118.8
Fitzpatrick, Ryan, St. Louis	135	76	56.3	777	5.76	4	3.0	t56	8	5.9	9	49	58.2
Foster, DeShaun, Carolina	1	0	0.0	0	0.00	0	0.0	0	0	0.0	0	0	39.6
Gado, Samkon, Green Bay	1	0	0.0	0	0.00	0	0.0	0	0	0.0	0	0	39.6
Garcia, Jeff, Detroit	173	102	59.0	937	5.42	3	1.7	49	6	3.5	6	34	65.1
Griese, Brian, Tampa Bay	174	112	64.4	1136	6.53	7	4.0	t80	7	4.0	12	76	79.6
Grossman, Rex, Chicago	39	20	51.3	259	6.64	1	2.6	54	2	5.1	1	9	59.7
Harrington, Joey, Detroit	330	188	57.0	2021	6.12	12	3.6	86	12	3.6	24	136	72.0
Hasselbeck, Matt, Seattle	449	294	65.5	3459	7.70	24	5.3	56	9	2.0	24	154	98.2
Johnson, Brad, Minnesota	294	184	62.6	1885	6.41	12	4.1	t80	4	1.4	23	134	88.9
Johnson, Keyshawn, Dallas	1	0	0.0	0	0.00	0	0.0	0	0	0.0	0	0	39.6
Manning, Eli, N.Y. Giants	557	294	52.8	3762	6.75	24	4.3	t78	17	3.1	28	184	75.9
Martin, Jamie, St. Louis	177	124	70.1	1277	7.21	5	2.8	t83	7	4.0	11	78	83.5
Maynard, Brad, Chicago	2	1	50.0	18	9.00	0	0.0	18	0	0.0	0	0	81.3
McCown, Josh, Arizona	270	163	60.4	1836	6.80	9	3.3	49	11	4.1	18	101	74.9
McMahon, Mike, Philadelphia	207	94	45.4	1158	5.59	5	2.4	48	8	3.9	19	96	55.2
McNabb, Donovan, Philadelphia	357	211	59.1	2507	7.02	16	4.5	t91	9	2.5	19	112	85.0
Navarre, John, Arizona	24	14	58.3	174	7.25	1	4.2	43	1	4.2	4	27	77.4
Orlovsky, Dan, Detroit	17	7	41.2	63	3.71	0	0.0	20	0	0.0	1	3	51.8
Orton, Kyle, Chicago	368	190	51.6	1869	5.08	9	2.4	54	13	3.5	30	190	59.7

Player, team	GP	GS	Player, team	GP	GS	Player, team	GP	GS
Goff, Mike, San Diego	16	16	Hall, Lamont, New Orleans	16	4	Hetherington, Chris, San Fran.	16	6
Goings, Nick, Carolina	16	1	Hall, Travis, San Francisco	16	1	Hicks, Artis, Philadelphia	14	14
Gold, Ian, Denver	16	16	Hallen, Bob, San Diego	9	3	Hicks, Eric, Kansas City	16	14
Goldberg, Adam, Minnesota	16	12	Hamilton, Ben, Denver	16	16	Hicks, Maurice, San Francisco	14	3
Gonzalez, Joaquin, Indianapolis	5	0	Hamilton, Bobby, Oakland	14	13	Hill, LeRoy, Seattle	15	9
Gonzalez, Tony, Kansas City	16	16	Hamilton, Remy, Detroit	1	0	Hill, Marquise, New England	8	0
Goodman, Andre', Detroit	15	8	Hamlin, Ken, Seattle	6	6	Hill, Renaldo, Oakland	16	13
Goodwin, Jonathan, N.Y. Jets	16	10	Hampton, Casey, Pittsburgh	16	15	Hill, Reynaldo, Tennessee	15	10
Goolsby, Mike, St. Louis	2	0	Hangartner, Geoff, Carolina	4	0	Hill, Shaun, Minnesota	1	0
Gordon, Lamar, Philadelphia	14	4	Hankton, Cortez, Jacksonville	5	0	Hillenmeyer, Hunter, Chicago	13	12
Gore, Frank, San Francisco	14	1	Hankton, Karl, Carolina	16	0	Hilliard, Ike, Tampa Bay	16	2
Gorin, Brandon, New England	12	8	Hannam, Ryan, Seattle	16	5	Hilton, Zachary, New Orleans	15	6
Gould, Robbie, Chicago	13	0	Hanson, Chris, Jacksonville	16	0	Hobbs, Ellis, New England	16	8
Gragg, Scott, N.Y. Jets	15	7	Hanson, Jason, Detroit	15	0	Hobson, Victor, N.Y. Jets	16	16
Graham, Ben, N.Y. Jets	16	0	Harden, Michael, Seattle	4	0	Hochstein, Russ, New England	16	7
Graham, Daniel, New England	11	9	Hardwick, Nick, San Diego	13	13	Hodel, Nathan, Arizona	16	0
Graham, Earnest, Tampa Bay	16	0	Hardy, Jermaine, Carolina	3	0	Hodgdon, Drew, Houston	4	3
Graham, Shayne, Cincinnati	16	0	Hargrove, Anthony, St. Louis	16	15	Hodge, Sedrick, New Orleans	13	12
Grant, Charles, New Orleans	16	14	Harper, Nick, Indianapolis	15	15	Hodges, Reggie, St. Louis-Phila.	8	0
Grant, DeLawrence, Oakland	9	0	Harrington, Joey, Detroit	12	11	Hodgins, James, Arizona	1	0
Grant, Deon, Jacksonville	16	16	Harris, Al, Green Bay	16	16	Hoke, Chris, Pittsburgh	15	0
Grasmanis, Paul, Philadelphia	2	0	Harris, Arlen, St. Louis	16	0	Holcomb, Kelly, Buffalo	10	8
Gray, Chris, Seattle	16	16	Harris, Chris, Chicago	14	13	Holdman, Warrick, Washington	14	7
Gray, Quinn, Jacksonville	1	0	Harris, Kwame, San Francisco	16	16	Holiday, Carlyle, Arizona	1	0
Green, Ahman, Green Bay	5	5	Harris, Marques, San Diego	11	0	Holland, Montrae, New Orleans	15	10
Green, Barrett, N.Y. Giants	1	0	Harris, Napoleon, Minnesota	15	3	Holliday, Vonnie, Miami	16	16
Green, Brandon, St. Louis	16	1	Harris, Nick, Detroit	16	0	Hollings, Tony, Houston	2	0
Green, Cornell, Denver	14	0	Harris, Quentin, Arizona	16	1	Hollowell, T.J., N.Y. Jets	2	0
Green, Eric, Arizona	12	5	Harris, Tommie, Chicago	16	16	Holly, Daven, Chicago	3	0
Green, Jarvis, New England	15	5	Harris, Walt, Washington	13	12	Holmes, Alex, Miami	8	0
Green, Justin, Baltimore	12	4	Harrison, James, Pittsburgh	16	3	Holmes, Earl, Detroit	11	10
Green, Louis, Denver	14	0	Harrison, Marvin, Indianapolis	15	15	Holmes, Priest, Kansas City	7	7
Green, Mike, Chicago	16	3	Harrison, Rodney, New England	3	3	Holt, Terrence, Detroit	10	10
Green, Roderick, Baltimore	16	0	Hart, Clinton, San Diego	16	5	Holt, Torry, St. Louis	14	14
Green, Trent, Kansas City	16	16	Hartings, Jeff, Pittsburgh	16	16	Hood, Roderick, Philadelphia	16	6
Green, William, Cleveland	8	0	Hartsock, Ben, Indianapolis	7	0	Hoover, Brad, Carolina	15	15
Greenwood, Morlon, Houston	16	16	Hartwell, Edgerton, Atlanta	5	5	Hope, Chris, Pittsburgh	16	16
Greer, Jabari, Buffalo	16	2	Hartwig, Justin, Tennessee	16	16	Hopkins, Brad, Tennessee	15	15
Gregg, Kelly, Baltimore	16	16	Hasselbeck, Matt, Seattle	16	16	Horn, Chris, Kansas City	14	3
Greisen, Nick, N.Y. Giants	16	12	Hasselbeck, Tim, N.Y. Giants	5	0	Horn, Joe, New Orleans	13	13
Griese, Brian, Tampa Bay	6	6	Hawkins, Artrell, New England	5	4	Horton, Jason, Green Bay	9	0
Griffin, Cornelius, Washington	13	12	Hawkins, Mike, Green Bay	11	1	Houser, Kevin, New Orleans	16	0
Griffin, Kris, Kansas City	8	0	Hawthorne, Anttaj, Oakland	2	0	Houshmandzadeh, T.J., Cincinnati	14	12
Griffith, Justin, Atlanta	16	15	Hawthorne, Michael, St. Louis	5	5	Houston, Cedric, N.Y. Jets	12	4
Griffith, Robert, Arizona	16	16	Hayden, Kelvin, Indianapolis	16	0	Hovan, Chris, Tampa Bay	16	16
Grigsby, Boomer, Kansas City	16	0	Haye, Jovan, Carolina	2	0	Howard, Brian, St. Louis	5	0
Groce, DeJuan, St. Louis	15	15	Haynes, Michael, Chicago	10	0	Howard, Darren, New Orleans	12	9
Groom, Andy, Washington	2	0	Haynes, Verron, Pittsburgh	14	0	Howard, Reggie, Miami	15	7
Grootegoed, Matt, Detroit	3	0	Haynesworth, Albert, Tennessee	14	14	Howell, John, Seattle	10	0
Gross, Jordan, Carolina	16	16	Hayward, Reggie, Jacksonville	15	15	Howry, Keenan, Minnesota	4	0
Grossman, Rex, Chicago	2	1	Heap, Todd, Baltimore	16	16	Huff, Orlando, Arizona	16	12
Grove, Jake, Oakland	10	8	Heard, Ronnie, Atlanta	16	5	Hulsey, Corey, Oakland	11	0
Guenther, Gregg, Tennessee	5	0	Hedgecock, Madison, St. Louis	16	7	Humphrey, Tory, Green Bay	1	0
Gurode, Andre, Dallas	16	2	Heiden, Steve, Cleveland	15	13	Hunter, Pete, Cleveland	4	0
Gutierrez, Brock, Detroit	14	0	Heitmann, Eric, San Francisco	16	16	Hunter, Wayne, Seattle	1	0
Haayer, Adam, Arizona	12	4	Heller, Will, Miami	7	0	Hunter, Will, Minnesota	13	0
Hackett, D.J., Seattle	13	3	Henderson, Devery, New Orleans	14	3	Hutchins, Von, Indianapolis	3	0
Hadnot, Rex, Miami	16	16	Henderson, E.J., Minnesota	15	14	Hutchinson, Steve, Seattle	16	16
Haggan, Mario, Buffalo	16	0	Henderson, John, Jacksonville	16	15	Hymes, Randy, Baltimore	16	3
Haggans, Clark, Pittsburgh	13	13	Henderson, William, Green Bay	16	8	Idonije, Israel, Chicago	11	1
Hakim, Az-Zahir, New Orleans	12	2	Henry, Anthony, Dallas	12	10	Ingram, Johnathan, Kansas City	2	0
Haley, Dennis, Baltimore	4	0	Henry, Chris, Cincinnati	14	5	Ioane, Junior, Houston	11	1
Hall, Andy, Philadelphia	1	0	Henry, Travis, Tennessee	9	1	Irons, Grant, Oakland	15	1
Hall, Carlos, Kansas City	14	2	Hentrich, Craig, Tennessee	16	0	Irons, Paul, Cleveland	2	1
Hall, Dante, Kansas City	16	2	Herndon, Kelly, Seattle	12	6	Irvin, Ken, Minnesota	7	1
Hall, DeAngelo, Atlanta	15	15	Herremans, Todd, Philadelphia	4	4	Ivy, Corey, St. Louis	16	5
Hall, James, Detroit	14	14	Herrera, Anthony, Minnesota	10	6	Iwuoma, Chidi, Pittsburgh	16	0
Hall, John, Washington	10	0	Herron, Noah, Pitts.-Green Bay	7	0	Izzo, Larry, New England	16	0

2005 REVIEW — Player participation

Player, team	GP	GS
Jackson, Alonzo, Phila.-N.Y. Giants	9	1
Jackson, Darrell, Seattle	6	6
Jackson, Dexter, Tampa Bay	11	10
Jackson, Eddie, Miami	15	1
Jackson, Frisman, Cleveland	12	0
Jackson, Grady, Green Bay	16	16
Jackson, Jamaal, Philadelphia	8	8
Jackson, James, Arizona	8	0
Jackson, Marlin, Indianapolis	15	1
Jackson, Nate, Denver	2	0
Jackson, Steven, St. Louis	15	15
Jackson, Terry, San Francisco	16	0
Jackson, Tyoka, St. Louis	16	2
Jackson, Vincent, San Diego	7	0
Jacobs, Brandon, N.Y. Giants	16	0
Jacobs, Taylor, Washington	15	3
Jacox, Kendyl, New Orleans	15	15
James, Bradie, Dallas	16	16
James, Edgerrin, Indianapolis	15	15
James, Erasmus, Minnesota	15	9
James, Jeno, Miami	16	16
James, Tory, Cincinnati	16	16
Jammer, Quentin, San Diego	16	16
Janikowski, Sebastian, Oakland	16	0
Jansen, Jon, Washington	16	16
Jasper, Ed, Oakland	15	1
Jefferson, Jason, Buffalo	5	0
Jefferson, Joseph, Indianapolis	4	2
Jenkins, Cullen, Green Bay	16	12
Jenkins, Kris, Carolina	1	1
Jenkins, Michael, Atlanta	14	12
Jennings, Brian, San Francisco	16	0
Jennings, Jonas, San Francisco	3	3
Jerman, Greg, Buffalo	10	3
Jimoh, Ade, Washington	16	0
Joe, Leon, Chicago	14	1
Johnson, Al, Dallas	16	16
Johnson, Andre, Houston	13	13
Johnson, Bethel, New England	11	1
Johnson, Brad, Minnesota	15	9
Johnson, Bryan, Chicago	7	6
Johnson, Bryant, Arizona	14	4
Johnson, Chad, Cincinnati	16	16
Johnson, Chris, St. Louis	14	1
Johnson, Darrien, N.Y. Jets	8	0
Johnson, Derrick, Kansas City	16	16
Johnson, Derrick, San Francisco	14	5
Johnson, Dirk, Philadelphia	7	0
Johnson, Eric, Arizona	3	0
Johnson, Jarret, Baltimore	16	12
Johnson, Jeremi, Cincinnati	16	11
Johnson, Kevin, Detroit	6	2
Johnson, Keyshawn, Dallas	16	14
Johnson, Kyle, Denver	16	14
Johnson, Landon, Cincinnati	16	10
Johnson, Larry, Kansas City	16	9
Johnson, Marcus, Minnesota	14	8
Johnson, Patrick, Baltimore	6	0
Johnson, Robert, Washington	2	0
Johnson, Rudi, Cincinnati	16	14
Johnson, Spencer, Minnesota	10	2
Johnson, Tank, Chicago	16	4
Johnson, Teyo, Arizona	7	3
Johnson, Thomas, Dallas	2	0
Johnson, Tim, Oakland	16	0
Johnson, Todd, Chicago	14	2
Johnson, Travis, Houston	15	3
Johnson, Trevor, N.Y. Jets	9	0
Johnstone, Lance, Minnesota	15	1
Jolley, Doug, N.Y. Jets	16	7
Jones, Adrian, N.Y. Jets	16	16
Jones, Aki, Washington	4	0
Jones, Brandon, Tennessee	10	8
Jones, Brian, Jacksonville	13	1
Jones, Dhani, Philadelphia	16	16
Jones, Donnie, Miami	16	0
Jones, Greg, Jacksonville	14	13
Jones, Jamal, Green Bay	2	0
Jones, Julius, Dallas	13	12
Jones, Kevin, Detroit	13	13
Jones, Levi, Cincinnati	15	15
Jones, Mark, Tampa Bay	16	0
Jones, Matt, Jacksonville	16	1
Jones, Nathan, Dallas	16	0
Jones, Pacman, Tennessee	15	13
Jones, Sean, Cleveland	16	0
Jones, Tebucky, Miami	6	6
Jones, Terry, Balt.-San Francisco	8	5
Jones, Thomas, Chicago	15	15
Jones, Walter, Seattle	15	15
Jordan, LaMont, Oakland	14	14
Jordan, Leander, San Diego	13	9
Joseph, William, N.Y. Giants	10	10
Jue, Bhawoh, San Diego	14	14
June, Cato, Indianapolis	13	13
Jurevicius, Joe, Seattle	16	11
Kacyvenski, Isaiah, Seattle	16	0
Kaczur, Nick, New England	14	11
Kaeding, Nate, San Diego	16	0
Kaesviharn, Kevin, Cincinnati	16	16
Kalu, N.D., Philadelphia	15	8
Kampman, Aaron, Green Bay	16	16
Karney, Mike, New Orleans	16	14
Kasay, John, Carolina	16	0
Kashama, Alain, Seattle	1	0
Kassell, Brad, Tennessee	16	14
Katula, Matt, Baltimore	16	0
Kearse, Jevon, Philadelphia	15	15
Keasey, Zak, Washington	1	0
Keisel, Brett, Pittsburgh	16	0
Kelley, Ethan, Cleveland	11	2
Kelly, Brian, Tampa Bay	16	16
Kelly, Lewis, N.Y. Giants	1	0
Kelly, Reggie, Cincinnati	15	14
Kelly, Tommy, Oakland	16	12
Kelsay, Chris, Buffalo	16	16
Kemoeatu, Maake, Baltimore	16	16
Kendall, Pete, N.Y. Jets	16	16
Kennedy, Jimmy, St. Louis	15	9
Kennedy, Kenoy, Detroit	16	16
Kennison, Eddie, Kansas City	16	16
Kerney, Patrick, Atlanta	16	16
Keys, Isaac, Arizona	6	0
Kiel, Terrence, San Diego	12	12
Killings, Cedric, Washington	10	1
King, Austin, Atlanta	16	1
King, Eric, Buffalo	16	1
Kingsbury, Kliff, N.Y. Jets	1	0
Kinney, Erron, Tennessee	14	14
Kirschke, Travis, Pittsburgh	16	0
Kitna, Jon, Cincinnati	3	0
Klecko, Dan, New England	10	0
Kleinsasser, Jim, Minnesota	16	16
Klemm, Adrian, Green Bay	16	8
Kluwe, Chris, Minnesota	15	0
Knight, Sammy, Kansas City	16	16
Koenen, Michael, Atlanta	16	0
Kolodziej, Ross, Arizona	16	14
Kooistra, Scott, Cincinnati	15	1
Koppen, Dan, New England	9	9
Kosier, Kyle, Detroit	16	11
Koutouvides, Niko, Seattle	12	0
Kozlowski, Brian, Washington	16	0
Kranchick, Matt, Pitts.-N.Y. Giants	6	1
Krause, Ryan, San Diego	3	0
Kreider, Dan, Pittsburgh	16	9
Kreutz, Olin, Chicago	16	16
Kriewaldt, Clint, Pittsburgh	16	2
Kuehl, Ryan, N.Y. Giants	16	0
Kyle, Jason, Carolina	16	0
Labinjo, Mike, Phila.-Indianapolis	7	1
LaBoy, Travis, Tennessee	15	7
Ladouceur, L.P., Dallas	13	0
Lake, Antwan, Atlanta	13	2
Landeta, Sean, Philadelphia	5	0
Lang, Kenard, Cleveland	16	5
Larson, Kyle, Cincinnati	16	0
Lavalais, Chad, Atlanta	14	14
Law, Ty, N.Y. Jets	16	16
Lawrie, Nate, Tampa Bay	5	0
Lawton, Luke, N.Y. Jets	4	0
Leach, Mike, Denver	16	0
Leach, Vonta, Green Bay	16	5
Leake, John, Atlanta-Green Bay	11	0
Leber, Ben, San Diego	9	6
Lechler, Shane, Oakland	16	0
Leckey, Nick, Arizona	14	9
Lee, Andy, San Francisco	16	0
Lee, Charles, Arizona	6	0
Lee, Donald, Green Bay	15	5
Lee, ReShard, Green Bay	7	1
Leftwich, Byron, Jacksonville	11	11
Legree, Lance, N.Y. Jets	16	4
Lehan, Michael, Cleveland	10	0
Lehman, Teddy, Detroit	5	0
Lehr, Matt, Atlanta	15	15
Leisle, Rodney, New Orleans	1	0
LeJeune, Norman, Miami	5	0
Lekkerkerker, Brad, Oakland	1	0
Lekkerkerker, Cory, San Diego	1	0
Lelie, Ashley, Denver	16	13
Lemon, Cleo, San Diego	1	0
Lenon, Paris, Green Bay	16	12
Leonhard, Jim, Buffalo	10	0
Lepsis, Matt, Denver	16	16
LeSueur, Jeremy, N.Y. Jets	3	0
Lewis, Alex, Detroit	1	1
Lewis, Chad, Philadelphia	8	0
Lewis, D.D., Seattle	12	12
Lewis, Damione, St. Louis	16	7
Lewis, Greg, Philadelphia	16	16
Lewis, Jamal, Baltimore	15	15
Lewis, Keith, San Francisco	16	4
Lewis, Kevin, N.Y. Giants	1	1
Lewis, Michael, New Orleans	2	0
Lewis, Michael, Philadelphia	16	16
Lewis, Ray, Baltimore	6	6
Light, Matt, New England	3	3
Lilja, Ryan, Indianapolis	16	16
Lindell, Rian, Buffalo	16	0
Little, Earl, Green Bay	4	0
Little, Leonard, St. Louis	14	14
Littleton, Jody, Cleveland	5	0
Liwienski, Chris, Minnesota	15	9

Player, team	GP	GS	Player, team	GP	GS	Player, team	GP	GS
Lloyd, Brandon, San Francisco	16	15	McCollum, Andy, St. Louis	16	16	Moore, Brandon, San Francisco	16	10
Locklear, Sean, Seattle	16	16	McCown, Josh, Arizona	9	6	Moore, Brandon, N.Y. Jets	16	16
Loeffler, Cullen, Minnesota	16	0	McCoy, LeRon, Arizona	10	4	Moore, Clarence, Baltimore	4	1
Logan, Mike, Pittsburgh	12	1	McCoy, Matt, Philadelphia	4	0	Moore, Dave, Tampa Bay	16	1
Long, Khari, Kansas City	1	0	McCrary, Fred, Atlanta	15	0	Moore, Eddie, Miami	5	0
Long, Rien, Tennessee	16	1	McCray, Bobby, Jacksonville	16	1	Moore, Eric, N.Y. Giants	8	0
Longwell, Ryan, Green Bay	16	0	McCree, Marlon, Carolina	16	15	Moore, Langston, Arizona	8	1
Looker, Dane, St. Louis	16	0	McCune, Robert, Washington	5	0	Moore, Larry, Cincinnati	4	0
Losman, J.P., Buffalo	9	8	McCutcheon, Daylon, Cleveland	16	16	Moore, Mewelde, Minnesota	16	8
Lowe, Omare, Atlanta	16	1	McDonald, Shaun, St. Louis	16	2	Moorehead, Aaron, Indianapolis	2	0
Loyd, Jeremy, St. Louis	4	0	McDougle, Stockar, Miami	8	2	Moorehead, Kindal, Carolina	15	0
Lucas, Chad, Green Bay	1	0	McFadden, Bryant, Pittsburgh	12	1	Moorman, Brian, Buffalo	16	0
Lucas, Ken, Carolina	15	15	McFarland, Anthony, Tampa Bay	15	15	Morant, Johnnie, Oakland	1	0
Luchey, Nick, Cincinnati	3	0	McFarland, Dylan, Buffalo	1	0	Morency, Vernand, Houston	13	1
Lynch, John, Denver	16	16	McGahee, Willis, Buffalo	16	15	Moreno, Zeke, Philadelphia	4	0
Lynch, Shawn, Arizona	2	1	McGarrahan, Scott, San Diego	2	0	Morey, Sean, Pittsburgh	15	0
Macklin, David, Arizona	16	15	McGee, Terrence, Buffalo	15	14	Morgan, Dan, Carolina	13	13
Maddox, Anthony, Jacksonville	5	0	McGinest, Willie, New England	16	16	Morgan, Donovan, Houston	3	0
Maddox, Tommy, Pittsburgh	5	2	McGowan, Brandon, Chicago	8	3	Morgan, Matt, St. Louis	1	0
Madison, Sam, Miami	15	15	McGraw, Jon, Detroit	8	2	Morgan, Quincy, Pittsburgh	16	0
Maese, Joe, Detroit	3	0	McHugh, Sean, Detroit	3	0	Morley, Steve, N.Y. Jets	7	0
Mahan, Sean, Tampa Bay	16	16	McIntosh, Damion, Miami	16	16	Morris, Maurice, Seattle	16	1
Mahe, Reno, Philadelphia	15	0	McIntyre, Corey, Cleveland	15	1	Morris, Rob, Indianapolis	14	0
Mallard, Wesly, N.E.-Tampa Bay	9	0	McKenzie, Chris, Houston	3	0	Morris, Sammy, Miami	16	2
Malone, Alfred, Houston	2	0	McKenzie, Kareem, N.Y. Giants	14	14	Morrison, Kirk, Oakland	16	15
Mangum, Kris, Carolina	14	9	McKenzie, Mike, New Orleans	15	15	Morrow, Harold, Arizona	14	0
Mankins, Logan, New England	16	16	McKie, Jason, Chicago	8	2	Morton, Chad, N.Y. Giants	16	0
Mannelly, Patrick, Chicago	16	0	McKinley, Alvin, Cleveland	16	16	Morton, Christian, Atlanta-Wash.	5	1
Manning, Eli, N.Y. Giants	16	16	McKinney, Seth, Miami	13	13	Morton, Johnnie, San Francisco	13	10
Manning, Peyton, Indianapolis	16	16	McKinney, Steve, Houston	16	16	Moses, J.J., Arizona	2	0
Manning, Roy, Green Bay	15	2	McKinnie, Bryant, Minnesota	16	16	Mosley, C.J., Minnesota	12	2
Manning Jr., Ricky, Carolina	16	3	McKinnon, Ronald, New Orleans	16	9	Moss, Randy, Oakland	16	15
Manuel, Marquand, Seattle	16	10	McMahon, Mike, Philadelphia	9	7	Moss, Santana, Washington	16	16
Manumaleuna, Brandon, St. Louis	14	14	McMichael, Randy, Miami	16	16	Moulds, Eric, Buffalo	15	15
Manuwai, Vince, Jacksonville	16	16	McMillan, David, Cleveland	4	0	Mruczkowski, Gene, New England	7	0
Mare, Olindo, Miami	16	0	McMullen, Billy, Philadelphia	16	0	Mruczkowski, Scott, San Diego	6	0
Marshall, Keyonta, Philadelphia	1	0	McNabb, Donovan, Philadelphia	9	9	Mughelli, Ovie, Baltimore	13	5
Marshall, Lemar, Washington	16	16	McNair, Steve, Tennessee	14	14	Muhammad, Muhsin, Chicago	15	15
Marshall, Rasheed, San Francisco	12	0	McQuarters, R.W., Detroit	16	11	Muhlbach, Don, Detroit	13	0
Martin, Curtis, N.Y. Jets	12	12	Meester, Brad, Jacksonville	12	12	Mulitalo, Edwin, Baltimore	16	15
Martin, David, Green Bay	12	8	Meier, Rob, Jacksonville	16	2	Mungro, James, Indianapolis	12	0
Martin, Jamie, St. Louis	8	5	Meier, Shad, New Orleans	1	0	Murphy, Matt, Houston	9	2
Martinez, Glenn, Detroit	5	0	Melton, Terrence, New Orleans	15	2	Murphy, Nick, Philadelphia	1	0
Mason, Derrick, Baltimore	16	16	Merriman, Shawne, San Diego	15	10	Murphy, Terrence, Green Bay	3	0
Massey, Chris, St. Louis	16	0	Metcalf, Terrence, Chicago	13	13	Myers, Chris, Denver	9	0
Mathis, Evan, Carolina	9	0	Mickens, Ray, Cleveland	16	0	Myers, Michael, Denver	16	15
Mathis, Jerome, Houston	12	0	Middlebrooks, Willie, S.F.	5	0	Myers, Ryan, N.Y. Jets	15	0
Mathis, Rashean, Jacksonville	16	16	Mikell, Quintin, Philadelphia	16	0	Myles, Reggie, Cincinnati	10	0
Mathis, Robert, Indianapolis	13	0	Mili, Itula, Seattle	2	0	Naeole, Chris, Jacksonville	15	15
Mauck, Matt, Tennessee	3	1	Miller, Billy, Cleveland	3	1	Nalen, Tom, Denver	16	16
Mawae, Kevin, N.Y. Jets	6	6	Miller, Caleb, Cincinnati	7	0	Nash, Damien, Tennessee	3	0
Maxwell, Jim, San Francisco	11	1	Miller, Fred, Chicago	15	15	Navarre, John, Arizona	1	0
Maxwell, Marcus, San Francisco	4	0	Miller, Heath, Pittsburgh	16	14	Navies, Hannibal, Cincinnati	15	1
Mayberry, Jermane, New Orleans	11	8	Miller, Josh, New England	16	0	Neal, Lorenzo, San Diego	16	15
Mayes, Adrian, Arizona	3	0	Miller, Justin, N.Y. Jets	16	8	Neal, Stephen, New England	16	16
Maynard, Brad, Chicago	16	0	Milligan, Hanik, San Diego	16	0	Nece, Ryan, Tampa Bay	16	14
McAddley, Jason, San Francisco	12	2	Milloy, Lawyer, Buffalo	16	16	Nedney, Joe, San Francisco	15	0
McAfee, Fred, New Orleans	16	0	Minor, Travis, Miami	16	0	Nelson, Jim, Baltimore	2	0
McAlister, Chris, Baltimore	14	13	Minter, Mike, Carolina	16	16	Nesbit, Jamar, New Orleans	16	4
McAllister, Deuce, New Orleans	5	5	Mitchell, Anthony, Cincinnati	16	0	Neufeld, Ryan, Buffalo	13	0
McBriar, Mat, Dallas	16	0	Mitchell, Jeff, Carolina	16	16	Newberry, Jeremy, San Francisco	10	10
McCadam, Kevin, Atlanta	16	0	Mitchell, Kawika, Kansas City	16	16	Newhouse, Reggie, Arizona	3	1
McCants, Darnerien, Philadelphia	12	0	Mitchell, Lance, Arizona	12	0	Newman, Keith, Minnesota	13	10
McCardell, Keenan, San Diego	16	16	Mitchell, Mel, New Orleans	13	0	Newman, Terence, Dallas	16	16
McCareins, Justin, N.Y. Jets	16	16	Mitchell, Qasim, Chicago	3	0	Newton, Cam, Atlanta	6	0
McChesney, Matt, N.Y. Jets	3	0	Moats, Ryan, Philadelphia	7	1	Nguyen, Dat, Dallas	8	4
McCleon, Dexter, Kansas City	11	5	Molinaro, Jim, Washington	3	0	Nicholson, Donte, Tampa Bay	9	0
McClure, Todd, Atlanta	16	16	Montgomery, Michael, Green Bay	12	0	Nickey, Donnie, Tennessee	16	0

Player, team	GP	GS
Nienhuis, Doug, N.Y. Jets	7	0
Noll, Ben, Dallas	4	0
Norman, Dennis, Jacksonville	16	4
Norris, Moran, Houston	16	5
Northcutt, Dennis, Cleveland	16	7
Norton, Zach, Baltimore	3	0
Novak, Nick, Washington-Arizona..	10	0
Nugent, Mike, N.Y. Jets	16	0
Nutten, Tom, St. Louis	8	6
Oben, Roman, San Diego	8	8
Odom, Antwan, Tennessee	16	9
Odom, Joe, Chicago	2	0
Offord, Willie, Minnesota	3	1
Ogbogu, Eric, Dallas	6	0
Ogden, Jonathan, Baltimore	16	16
Oglesby, Evan, Baltimore	3	0
Ogunleye, Adewale, Chicago	15	15
Ohalete, Ifeanyi, Cincinnati	15	12
O'Hara, Shaun, N.Y. Giants	16	16
Okeafor, Chike, Arizona	16	16
Okobi, Chukky, Pittsburgh	16	0
Olivea, Shane, San Diego	15	15
Olshansky, Igor, San Diego	14	12
Olson, Benji, Tennessee	16	16
O'Neal, Deltha, Cincinnati	15	14
O'Neil, Keith, Indianapolis	11	0
Orlovsky, Dan, Detroit	2	0
Orr, Shantee, Houston	16	12
Orton, Kyle, Chicago	15	15
Osgood, Kassim, San Diego	12	3
Owens, Chad, Jacksonville	1	0
Owens, Richard, Minnesota	16	2
Owens, Terrell, Philadelphia	7	7
Pace, Calvin, Arizona	5	1
Pace, Orlando, St. Louis	16	16
Palepoi, Anton, Arizona	3	0
Palmer, Carson, Cincinnati	16	16
Parker, Eric, San Diego	16	9
Parker, J'Vonne, Cleveland	4	0
Parker, Samie, Kansas City	12	9
Parker, Willie, Pittsburgh	15	15
Parrish, Roscoe, Buffalo	10	1
Parrish, Tony, San Francisco	9	9
Parry, Josh, Philadelphia	16	11
Parson, Rich, Washington	1	0
Pashos, Tony, Baltimore	16	7
Pass, Patrick, New England	12	4
Pathon, Jerome, Atlanta	8	0
Patten, David, Washington	9	7
Patterson, Dimitri, Washington	2	0
Patterson, Mike, Philadelphia	16	7
Paxton, Lonie, New England	16	0
Paymah, Karl, Denver	13	0
Payne, Seth, Houston	16	14
Payton, Jarrett, Tennessee	13	0
Pearman, Alvin, Jacksonville	16	0
Pearson, Kalvin, Tampa Bay	14	1
Pearson, Mike, Jacksonville	4	2
Peek, Antwan, Houston	16	16
Peelle, Justin, San Diego	16	4
Pennington, Chad, N.Y. Jets	3	3
Peppers, Julius, Carolina	16	16
Perkins, Antonio, Cleveland	1	0
Perry, Bruce, Philadelphia	2	1
Perry, Chris, Cincinnati	14	2
Perry, Ed, Kansas City	6	0
Perry, Tab, Cincinnati	16	0
Peterman, Stephen, Dallas	3	0
Peters, Jason, Buffalo	16	10
Peterson, Adrian, Chicago	16	0
Peterson, Julian, San Francisco	15	14
Peterson, Kenny, Green Bay	16	0
Peterson, Mike, Jacksonville	16	16
Peterson, Todd, Atlanta	16	0
Peterson, Will, N.Y. Giants	2	2
Petitgout, Luke, N.Y. Giants	16	15
Petitti, Rob, Dallas	16	16
Phifer, Roman, N.Y. Giants	2	0
Phillips, Jermaine, Tampa Bay	13	13
Phillips, Shaun, San Diego	15	3
Pickett, Cody, San Francisco	5	2
Pickett, Ryan, St. Louis	16	16
Pierce, Antonio, N.Y. Giants	13	13
Pierce, Brett, Dallas	10	1
Pile, Willie, Dallas	16	1
Piller, Zach, Tennessee	16	16
Pinner, Artose, Detroit	16	2
Pinnock, Andrew, San Diego	11	0
Pippens, Jerrell, San Diego	2	0
Pittman, Bryan, Houston	16	0
Pittman, Michael, Tampa Bay	16	4
Pitts, Chester, Houston	16	16
Player, Scott, Arizona	16	0
Plummer, Ahmed, San Francisco	3	3
Plummer, Jake, Denver	16	16
Polamalu, Troy, Pittsburgh	16	16
Polite, Lousaka, Dallas	14	3
Polk, DaShon, Houston	16	11
Pollack, David, Cincinnati	14	5
Pollard, Marcus, Detroit	16	16
Polley, Tommy, Baltimore	16	15
Ponder, Willie, N.Y. Giants	11	0
Pontbriand, Ryan, Cleveland	11	0
Pool, Brodney, Cleveland	13	0
Poole, Nate, New Orleans	7	0
Poole, Tyrone, New England	1	1
Pope, Derrick, Miami	12	2
Pope, Monsanto, Denver	2	0
Poppinga, Brady, Green Bay	12	1
Porter, Jerry, Oakland	16	14
Porter, Joey, Pittsburgh	16	16
Portis, Clinton, Washington	16	16
Posey, Jeff, Buffalo	16	15
Poteat, Hank, New England	10	1
Pouha, Sione, N.Y. Jets	14	0
Powell, Carl, Cincinnati	11	1
Preston, Duke, Buffalo	15	1
Price, Peerless, Dallas	7	1
Prioleau, Pierson, Washington	15	6
Proehl, Ricky, Carolina	16	0
Pruitt, Etric, Seattle	6	0
Pryce, Trevor, Denver	16	16
Pucillo, Mike, Cleveland	10	6
Putzier, Jeb, Denver	16	4
Quarles, Shelton, Tampa Bay	16	16
Rabach, Casey, Washington	16	16
Rackers, Neil, Arizona	15	0
Rackley, Derek, Atlanta	16	0
Rainer, Wali, Detroit	16	5
Raiola, Dominic, Detroit	16	16
Ramsey, Patrick, Washington	4	1
Randall, Marcus, Tennessee	3	0
Randle El, Antwaan, Pittsburgh	16	15
Rasheed, Saleem, San Francisco	9	1
Rasmussen, Kemp, Carolina	15	0
Ratliff, Jay, Dallas	4	1
Ratliff, Keiwan, Cincinnati	16	3
Rattay, Tim, San Francisco	4	4
Rayburn, Sam, Philadelphia	16	2
Raymer, Cory, Washington	2	0
Rayner, Dave, Indianapolis	14	0
Reagor, Montae, Indianapolis	13	12
Redding, Cory, Detroit	16	15
Reed, Ed, Baltimore	10	10
Reed, James, N.Y. Jets	16	15
Reed, Jeff, Pittsburgh	16	0
Reed, Josh, Buffalo	16	6
Reese, Ike, Atlanta	16	0
Reeves, Jacques, Dallas	16	0
Reid, Darrell, Indianapolis	8	1
Reid, Dexter, Indianapolis	16	0
Reid, Gabe, Chicago	16	3
Reid, Lamont, Arizona	10	1
Reyes, Tutan, Carolina	16	16
Reynolds, Robert, Tennessee	15	1
Rhodes, Dominic, Indianapolis	13	1
Rhodes, Kerry, N.Y. Jets	16	16
Ricard, Alan, Baltimore	2	2
Rice, Simeon, Tampa Bay	15	15
Richard, Kris, San Francisco	1	0
Richardson, David, Jacksonville	7	0
Richardson, Kyle, Cleveland	16	0
Richardson, Tony, Kansas City	16	16
Riddle, Ryan, Oakland	12	0
Ridgeway, Dante, N.Y. Jets	7	0
Riley, Victor, Houston	10	8
Rimpf, Brian, Baltimore	15	7
Ritzmann, Constantin, Atlanta	1	0
Rivera, Marco, Dallas	14	14
Rivers, Marcellus, Houston	16	5
Rivers, Philip, San Diego	2	0
Roaf, Willie, Kansas City	10	10
Robbins, Fred, N.Y. Giants	16	6
Roberson, Chris, Jacksonville	6	0
Robertson, Dewayne, N.Y. Jets	13	12
Robertson, Jamal, Carolina	6	0
Robinson, Bryan, Cincinnati	10	9
Robinson, Derreck, San Diego	3	0
Robinson, Dunta, Houston	16	16
Robinson, Jeff, St. Louis	5	1
Robinson, Koren, Minnesota	14	5
Robinson, Marcus, Minnesota	15	9
Roby, Courtney, Tennessee	13	6
Rodgers, Aaron, Green Bay	3	0
Roethlisberger, Ben, Pittsburgh	12	12
Rogers, Carlos, Washington	12	5
Rogers, Charles, Detroit	9	3
Rogers, Nick, Miami	3	0
Rogers, Shaun, Detroit	14	14
Rolle, Antrel, Arizona	5	4
Rolle, Samari, Baltimore	16	16
Roman, Mark, Green Bay	16	16
Romo, Tony, Dallas	16	0
Roos, Michael, Tennessee	16	16
Roper, Dedrick, Philadelphia	6	0
Rosenfels, Sage, Miami	4	1
Rosenthal, Mike, Minnesota	16	12
Ross, Oliver, Arizona	12	12
Rossum, Allen, Atlanta	10	0
Roth, Matt, Miami	16	0
Rouen, Tom, Seattle	12	0
Routt, Stanford, Oakland	14	2
Royal, Robert, Washington	15	14
Roye, Orpheus, Cleveland	16	16

Player, team	GP	GS	Player, team	GP	GS	Player, team	GP	GS
Rucker, Mike, Carolina	15	14	Shelton, Daimon, Buffalo	16	11	Spencer, Cody, Tennessee	16	0
Ruegamer, Grey, Green Bay	13	2	Shelton, L.J., Cleveland	16	16	Spencer, Shawntae, San Fran.	15	14
Ruff, Orlando, Cleveland	16	0	Shepherd, Edell, Tampa Bay	16	0	Spicer, Paul, Jacksonville	15	14
Rumph, Mike, San Francisco	3	3	Sheppard, Lito, Philadelphia	10	10	Spikes, Takeo, Buffalo	3	3
Runyan, Jon, Philadelphia	16	16	Shiancoe, Visanthe, N.Y. Giants	16	4	Spires, Greg, Tampa Bay	16	16
Russell, Brian, Cleveland	16	16	Shields, Will, Kansas City	16	16	Spragan, Donnie, Miami	16	9
Russell, Cliff, Miami	2	0	Shipp, Marcel, Arizona	15	11	Springs, Shawn, Washington	15	15
Ruud, Barrett, Tampa Bay	16	0	Shockey, Jeremy, N.Y. Giants	15	15	Sproles, Darren, San Diego	15	0
Ryan, Sean, Dallas	3	1	Short, Brandon, Carolina	16	15	St. Clair, John, Chicago	13	2
Saipaia, Blaine, St. Louis	9	3	Short, Jason, Philadelphia	6	0	St. Louis, Brad, Cincinnati	16	0
Salaam, Ephraim, Jacksonville	5	2	Shropshire, Darrell, Atlanta	10	0	Staley, Duce, Pittsburgh	5	1
Salave'a, Joe, Washington	14	13	Siavii, Junior, Kansas City	14	0	Stallworth, Donte', New Orleans	16	13
Sampson, Kevin, Kansas City	4	1	Simmons, Brian, Cincinnati	16	16	Stamer, Josh, Buffalo	16	0
Sams, B.J., Baltimore	14	0	Simmons, Jason, Houston	14	1	Stanley, Chad, Houston	16	0
Samuel, Asante, New England	15	15	Simmons, Kendall, Pittsburgh	16	16	Starks, Duane, New England	7	6
Samuels, Chris, Washington	16	16	Simms, Chris, Tampa Bay	11	10	Starks, Max, Pittsburgh	16	16
Sander, B.J., Green Bay	14	0	Simon, Corey, Indianapolis	13	13	Starks, Randy, Tennessee	16	16
Sanders, Bob, Indianapolis	14	14	Simoneau, Mark, Philadelphia	16	0	Starks, Scott, Jacksonville	16	0
Sanders, Deion, Baltimore	16	4	Sims, Barry, Oakland	16	16	Stecker, Aaron, New Orleans	15	4
Sanders, James, New England	10	2	Sims, Ryan, Kansas City	6	5	Steele, Ben, Green Bay	2	0
Sanders, Lewis, Houston	12	3	Sims, Wes, San Diego	2	0	Steinbach, Eric, Cincinnati	16	16
Sands, Terdell, Oakland	9	0	Singleton, Al, Dallas	8	7	Stepanovich, Alex, Arizona	9	9
Sandy, Justin, Tennessee	2	1	Sirmon, Peter, Tennessee	14	13	Steussie, Todd, Tampa Bay	15	0
Sape, Lauvale, Buffalo	9	0	Slaughter, Chad, Oakland	11	0	Stevens, Jerramy, Seattle	16	12
Sapp, Benny, Kansas City	16	3	Slaughter, T.J., New Orleans	10	1	Stevens, Larry, Cincinnati	7	0
Sapp, Cecil, Denver	16	0	Small, O.J., Tennessee	2	0	Stewart, Kordell, Baltimore	1	0
Sapp, Gerome, Indianapolis	16	2	Smart, Rod, Carolina	12	0	Stewart, Matt, Cleveland	14	12
Sapp, Warren, Oakland	10	10	Smiley, Justin, San Francisco	16	16	Stewart, Tony, Cincinnati	14	3
Saturday, Jeff, Indianapolis	16	16	Smith, Aaron, Pittsburgh	16	16	Stills, Gary, Kansas City	16	0
Sauerbrun, Todd, Denver	16	0	Smith, Alex, San Francisco	9	7	Stokes, Barry, Atlanta	16	1
Savage, Josh, Atlanta	1	0	Smith, Alex, Tampa Bay	16	10	Stokley, Brandon, Indianapolis	15	4
Scaife, Bo, Tennessee	16	5	Smith, Antonio, Arizona	11	8	Stone, Michael, New England	13	3
Scanlon, Rich, Kansas City	16	0	Smith, Antowain, New Orleans	16	7	Stone, Ron, Oakland	16	16
Schaub, Matt, Atlanta	16	1	Smith, Brady, Atlanta	5	5	Stoutmire, Omar, Washington	10	0
Schlesinger, Cory, Detroit	11	8	Smith, Corey, San Francisco	14	0	Stover, Matt, Baltimore	16	0
Schneck, Mike, Buffalo	16	0	Smith, Daryl, Jacksonville	16	16	Strahan, Michael, N.Y. Giants	16	16
Schobel, Aaron, Buffalo	16	16	Smith, Derek, San Francisco	16	16	Strait, Derrick, N.Y. Jets	16	2
Schobel, Bo, Tennessee	8	0	Smith, Dwight, New Orleans	15	15	Strickland, Donald, Ind.-Phi.	4	0
Schobel, Matt, Cincinnati	16	1	Smith, Hunter, Indianapolis	16	0	Strong, Mack, Seattle	16	7
Schulters, Lance, Miami	16	16	Smith, Jimmy, Jacksonville	16	16	Stroud, Marcus, Jacksonville	16	16
Schweigert, Stuart, Oakland	16	13	Smith, Jonathan, Buffalo	7	1	Stuvaints, Russell, Pittsburgh	4	0
Scifres, Mike, San Diego	16	0	Smith, Justin, Cincinnati	16	16	Suggs, Lee, Cleveland	8	0
Scobee, Josh, Jacksonville	16	0	Smith, Keith, Detroit	15	2	Suggs, Terrell, Baltimore	16	16
Scobey, Josh, Seattle	16	0	Smith, L.J., Philadelphia	16	16	Suisham, Shaun, Dallas	3	0
Scott, Bart, Baltimore	16	10	Smith, Marvel, Pittsburgh	13	12	Sullivan, Johnathan, New Orleans	15	0
Scott, Bryan, Atlanta	16	13	Smith, Mike, Baltimore	6	0	Surtain, Patrick, Kansas City	15	15
Scott, Chad, New England	3	0	Smith, Musa, Baltimore	1	0	Svitek, Will, Kansas City	1	0
Scott, Darrion, Minnesota	16	15	Smith, Paul, Detroit	12	5	Swancutt, Bill, Detroit	8	1
Scott, DeQuincy, San Diego	16	0	Smith, Raonall, Minnesota	16	6	Swinton, Reggie, Arizona	15	0
Scott, Guss, New England	5	2	Smith, Robaire, Houston	16	16	Szalay, Thatcher, Baltimore	3	0
Scott, Ian, Chicago	14	13	Smith, Rod, Denver	16	16	Tafoya, Joe, Seattle	15	1
Scott, Jake, Indianapolis	16	16	Smith, Shaun, Cincinnati	13	5	Tait, John, Chicago	15	15
Scott, Lynn, Dallas	6	0	Smith, Steve, Carolina	16	16	Tate, Robert, Arizona	13	5
Seau, Junior, Miami	7	5	Smith, Terrelle, Cleveland	16	15	Tatupu, Lofa, Seattle	16	16
Seidman, Mike, Carolina	12	1	Smith, Trent, San Francisco	5	2	Tauscher, Mark, Green Bay	16	16
Sellers, Mike, Washington	15	6	Smith, Will, New Orleans	16	9	Taylor, Ben, Cleveland	16	16
Sensabaugh, Gerald, Jacksonville	16	2	Smoot, Fred, Minnesota	11	8	Taylor, Chester, Baltimore	15	1
Seubert, Rich, N.Y. Giants	4	1	Snee, Chris, N.Y. Giants	16	16	Taylor, Eric, Minnesota	1	0
Seward, Adam, Carolina	4	0	Snow, Justin, Indianapolis	16	0	Taylor, Fred, Jacksonville	11	11
Seymour, Richard, New England	12	12	Snyder, Adam, San Francisco	16	8	Taylor, Ike, Pittsburgh	16	15
Shabazz, Siddeeq, New Orleans	2	0	Sopoaga, Isaac, San Francisco	16	1	Taylor, Jamaar, N.Y. Giants	5	0
Shaffer, Kevin, Atlanta	16	16	Sorensen, Nick, Jacksonville	10	0	Taylor, Jason, Miami	16	16
Shanle, Scott, Dallas	15	8	Sorgi, Jim, Indianapolis	5	0	Taylor, Sean, Washington	15	15
Sharper, Darren, Minnesota	14	14	Sowell, Jerald, N.Y. Jets	16	14	Taylor, Travis, Minnesota	16	13
Sharper, Jamie, Seattle	8	8	Spach, Stephen, Philadelphia	13	1	Teague, Trey, Buffalo	16	16
Shaw, Josh, Miami	1	0	Spears, Marcus, Dallas	16	10	Terrell, Claude, St. Louis	14	10
Shazor, Ernest, Arizona	2	0	Speegle, Nick, Cleveland	14	0	Terrell, David, Denver	1	0
Shea, Aaron, Cleveland	12	4	Spencer, Chris, Seattle	8	0			

2005 REVIEW Player participation

Player, team	GP	GS
Terrill, Craig, Seattle	16	0
Terry, Adam, Baltimore	7	0
Terry, Jeb, Tampa Bay	16	0
Testaverde, Vinny, N.Y. Jets	6	4
Thomas, Adalius, Baltimore	16	16
Thomas, Anthony, Dallas-N.O.	10	2
Thomas, Bryan, N.Y. Jets	16	4
Thomas, Dontarrious, Minnesota	14	2
Thomas, Fred, New Orleans	16	11
Thomas, Hollis, Philadelphia	16	12
Thomas, Joey, Green Bay-N.O.	11	1
Thomas, Josh, Indianapolis	12	2
Thomas, Juqua, Philadelphia	16	1
Thomas, Kiwaukee, Miami	10	0
Thomas, Pat, Jacksonville	9	0
Thomas, Randy, Washington	14	14
Thomas, Robert, Green Bay	10	9
Thomas, Sloan, Tennessee	1	0
Thomas, Tra, Philadelphia	10	10
Thomas, Zach, Miami	14	14
Thompson, Chaun, Cleveland	16	15
Thompson, Chris, Chicago	12	1
Thompson, Dominique, St. Louis	2	0
Thompson, Lamont, Tennessee	16	16
Thompson, Tyson, Dallas	15	0
Thornburg, Jeremy, San Fran.-G.B.	6	0
Thornton, Bruce, San Francisco	12	11
Thornton, David, Indianapolis	16	16
Thornton, John, Cincinnati	16	16
Thrash, James, Washington	12	2
Thurman, Andrae, Tenn.-G.B.	15	1
Thurman, Odell, Cincinnati	16	15
Tillman, Charles, Chicago	15	15
Tillman, Travares, Miami	16	10
Timmerman, Adam, St. Louis	16	16
Tinoisamoa, Pisa, St. Louis	16	16
Tobeck, Robbie, Seattle	16	16
Toefield, LaBrandon, Jacksonville	9	2
Tomlinson, LaDainian, San Diego	16	16
Tongue, Reggie, Oakland	4	1
Toomer, Amani, N.Y. Giants	16	16
Torbor, Reggie, N.Y. Giants	14	9
Torrence, Leigh, Atlanta	10	0
Towns, Lester, Arizona-Miami	6	1
Townsend, Deshea, Pittsburgh	16	15
Traylor, Keith, Miami	13	13
Treaudo, Ahmad, Atlanta	1	0
Treu, Adam, Oakland	16	10
Tripplett, Larry, Indianapolis	15	4
Trotter, Jeremiah, Philadelphia	15	15
Troupe, Ben, Tennessee	15	11
Trufant, Marcus, Seattle	15	15
Truluck, R-Kal, Arizona	7	0
Tubbs, Marcus, Seattle	13	12
Tuck, Justin, N.Y. Giants	14	1
Tucker, B.J., San Francisco	6	0
Tucker, Rex, St. Louis	8	3
Tucker, Ross, New England	1	0
Tucker, Ryan, Cleveland	16	16
Tucker, Torrin, Dallas	16	10
Tufts, Sean, Carolina	12	0
Tuiasosopo, Marques, Oakland	1	1
Tuman, Jerame, Pittsburgh	15	9
Turner, Larry, St. Louis	7	0
Turner, Michael, San Diego	16	0
Tynes, Lawrence, Kansas City	16	0
Tyree, David, N.Y. Giants	13	0
Udeze, Kenechi, Minnesota	3	2
Ulbrich, Jeff, San Francisco	5	5
Ulmer, Artie, Atlanta	9	0
Ulrich, Matt, Indianapolis	5	0
Umenyiora, Osi, N.Y. Giants	16	16
Unck, Mason, Cleveland	16	0
Underwood, Marviel, Green Bay	16	0
Urban, Jerheme, Seattle	4	1
Urlacher, Brian, Chicago	16	16
Utecht, Ben, Indianapolis	12	2
Van Pelt, Bradlee, Denver	3	0
Vanden Bosch, Kyle, Tennessee	16	16
Vanderjagt, Mike, Indianapolis	16	0
Vasher, Nathan, Chicago	16	15
Veal, Demetrin, Denver	15	0
Verdon, Jimmy, New Orleans	4	0
Vick, Michael, Atlanta	15	15
Villarrial, Chris, Buffalo	15	15
Vilma, Jonathan, N.Y. Jets	16	16
Vinatieri, Adam, New England	16	0
Vincent, Keydrick, Baltimore	9	9
Vincent, Troy, Buffalo	16	16
Vines, Scottie, Detroit	13	11
Volek, Billy, Tennessee	6	1
Vollers, Kurt, Indianapolis	2	0
von Oelhoffen, Kimo, Pittsburgh	16	16
Vrabel, Mike, New England	16	16
Waddell, Michael, Tennessee	16	1
Wade, Bobby, Chicago-Tennessee	14	1
Wade, John, Tampa Bay	16	16
Wade, Todd, Houston	9	9
Wahle, Mike, Carolina	16	16
Wahlroos, Drew, St. Louis	15	0
Wakefield, Fred, Arizona	15	9
Walker, Bracy, Detroit	16	4
Walker, Darwin, Philadelphia	13	12
Walker, Denard, Oakland	9	0
Walker, Frank, N.Y. Giants	7	0
Walker, Gary, Houston	11	11
Walker, Javon, Green Bay	1	1
Walker, Kenyatta, Tampa Bay	16	16
Walker, Langston, Oakland	6	6
Walker, Ramon, Houston	16	0
Wallace, Al, Carolina	16	2
Wallace, Rian, Pittsburgh	4	0
Wallace, Seneca, Seattle	7	0
Wallace, Taco, Green Bay	1	0
Walls, Lenny, Denver	7	3
Walls, Raymond, Arizona	7	2
Walter, Kevin, Cincinnati	16	2
Walter, Tyson, Houston	1	0
Walters, Troy, Indianapolis	16	1
Wand, Seth, Houston	13	0
Ward, B.J., Baltimore	15	0
Ward, Derrick, N.Y. Giants	14	0
Ward, Hines, Pittsburgh	15	15
Ware, DeMarcus, Dallas	16	16
Ware, Matt, Philadelphia	16	0
Warfield, Eric, Kansas City	11	10
Warner, Kurt, Arizona	10	10
Warren, Gerard, Denver	16	16
Warren, Greg, Pittsburgh	16	0
Warren, Ty, New England	16	16
Warrick, Peter, Seattle	13	5
Washington, Dewayne, K.C.	16	1
Washington, Fabian, Oakland	16	11
Washington, Kelley, Cincinnati	7	0
Washington, Marcus, Washington	16	16
Washington, Nate, Pittsburgh	1	0
Washington, Rashad, N.Y. Jets	16	0
Washington, Ted, Oakland	16	16
Washington, Todd, Houston	15	0
Waters, Brian, Kansas City	16	16
Watson, Ben, New England	15	9
Watson, Courtney, New Orleans	9	6
Watson, Kenny, Cincinnati	1	0
Watts, Darius, Denver	6	0
Wayne, Nate, Detroit	5	0
Wayne, Reggie, Indianapolis	16	16
Weary, Fred, Houston	4	4
Weaver, Anthony, Baltimore	10	8
Weaver, Leonard, Seattle	16	0
Webster, Corey, N.Y. Giants	15	2
Webster, Jason, Atlanta	15	13
Webster, Nate, Cincinnati	1	0
Weiner, Todd, Atlanta	15	15
Weinke, Chris, Carolina	3	0
Welbourn, John, Kansas City	12	9
Welker, Wes, Miami	16	1
Wells, Jonathan, Houston	15	0
Wells, Reggie, Arizona	9	9
Wells, Scott, Green Bay	16	10
Welsh, Jonathan, Indianapolis	6	0
Wesley, Dante, Carolina	16	0
Wesley, Greg, Kansas City	16	16
Westbrook, Brian, Philadelphia	12	12
Wharton, Travelle, Carolina	16	16
White, Chris, Green Bay	1	0
White, Dewayne, Tampa Bay	16	1
White, Dez, Atlanta	6	3
White, Jamel, Baltimore	5	0
White, Roddy, Atlanta	16	8
White, Tracy, Jacksonville	15	0
Whitehead, Willie, New Orleans	16	15
Whitfield, Bob, N.Y. Giants	16	2
Whitley, Taylor, Denver	2	0
Whitted, Alvis, Oakland	15	0
Whitticker, William, Green Bay	15	14
Whittle, Jason, N.Y. Giants	14	0
Wiegert, Zach, Houston	12	12
Wiegmann, Casey, Kansas City	16	16
Wiggins, Jermaine, Minnesota	16	8
Wilcox, Daniel, Baltimore	13	3
Wilds, Garnell, Carolina	3	0
Wiley, Marcellus, Jacksonville	11	1
Wilford, Ernest, Jacksonville	16	8
Wilfork, Vince, New England	16	16
Wilhelm, Matt, San Diego	16	0
Wilkerson, Jimmy, Kansas City	16	2
Wilkins, Jeff, St. Louis	16	0
Wilkins, Marcus, Cincinnati	15	0
Wilkinson, Dan, Detroit	16	16
Williams, Bobbie, Cincinnati	16	16
Williams, Brian, Minnesota	14	9
Williams, Carnell, Tampa Bay	14	14
Williams, Chad, Baltimore	16	3
Williams, Corey, Green Bay	12	0
Williams, D.J., Denver	16	14
Williams, Darrent, Denver	12	9
Williams, Demorrio, Atlanta	16	16
Williams, Jamal, San Diego	16	16
Williams, Jimmy, Seattle	14	1
Williams, Josh, Indianapolis	4	3
Williams, Kevin, Minnesota	14	14
Williams, Madieu, Cincinnati	4	3
Williams, Maurice, Jacksonville	16	16
Williams, Mike, Buffalo	9	6

Player, team	GP	GS	Player, team	GP	GS	Player, team	GP	GS
Williams, Mike, Detroit	14	4	Wilson, Al, Denver	15	15	Woodson, Charles, Oakland	6	6
Williams, Moe, Minnesota	6	1	Wilson, Cedrick, Pittsburgh	16	1	Woody, Damien, Detroit	16	16
Williams, Pat, Minnesota	16	16	Wilson, Eugene, New England	16	16	Woolfolk, Andre, Tennessee	13	7
Williams, Randal, Oakland	16	4	Wilson, George, Buffalo	3	0	Wortham, Cornelius, Seattle	8	0
Williams, Reggie, Jacksonville	16	7	Wilson, Gibril, N.Y. Giants	16	16	Wrighster, George, Jacksonville	16	6
Williams, Renauld, San Francisco	2	0	Wilson, Jerry, San Diego	9	1	Wright, Anthony, Baltimore	9	7
Williams, Ricky, Miami	12	4	Wilson, Kris, Kansas City	14	1	Wright, Jason, Cleveland	3	0
Williams, Roland, St. Louis	4	3	Wilson, Stanley, Detroit	9	0	Wright, Kenny, Jacksonville	16	16
Williams, Roy, Dallas	16	16	Wimbush, Derrick, Jacksonville	14	1	Wright, Kenyatta, N.Y. Jets	15	0
Williams, Roy, Detroit	13	12	Winborn, Jamie, S.F.-Jac.	8	2	Wright, Manuel, Miami	3	0
Williams, Roydell, Tennessee	10	2	Winfield, Antoine, Minnesota	16	16	Wright, Mike, New England	13	0
Williams, Shaud, Buffalo	16	0	Wire, Coy, Buffalo	13	0	Wyms, Ellis, Tampa Bay	16	1
Williams, Shaun, N.Y. Giants	8	0	Wishom, Jerron, Green Bay	5	0	Wynn, Dexter, Philadelphia	10	0
Williams, Tank, Tennessee	16	16	Wistrom, Grant, Seattle	16	16	Wynn, Renaldo, Washington	16	15
Williams, Todd, Tennessee	1	0	Witherspoon, Will, Carolina	15	15	Yates, Billy, New England	4	0
Williams, Walt, Green Bay	2	0	Withrow, Cory, Minnesota	16	7	Young, Brian, New Orleans	16	16
Williams, Willie, Pittsburgh	4	1	Witten, Jason, Dallas	16	16	Young, Bryant, San Francisco	13	13
Williams Jr., Harry, N.Y. Jets	1	0	Womack, Floyd, Seattle	11	1	Yovanovits, Dave, Cleveland	2	1
Williamson, Troy, Minnesota	14	3	Wong, Kailee, Houston	5	5	Zastudil, Dave, Baltimore	16	0
Willig, Matt, St. Louis	4	0	Woodfin, Zac, Baltimore	1	0	Zelenka, Joe, Jacksonville	16	0
Willis, Ray, Seattle	6	0	Woods, Jerome, Kansas City	7	0	Zereoue, Amos, New England	3	0
Wilson, Adrian, Arizona	16	16	Woods, LeVar, Detroit	6	3	Zgonina, Jeff, Miami	16	3

PLAYERS WITH TWO OR MORE CLUBS

Player, team	GP	GS	Player, team	GP	GS	Player, team	GP	GS
Anderson, Marques, Denver	6	0	Friedman, Lennie, Washington	10	0	Morton, Christian, Atlanta	4	1
Anderson, Marques, S.F.	4	0	Friedman, Lennie, Chicago	1	0	Morton, Christian, Washington	1	0
Ball, Dave, San Diego	2	0	Gardner, Rod, Carolina	10	0	Novak, Nick, Washington	5	0
Ball, Dave, N.Y. Jets	3	0	Gardner, Rod, Green Bay	2	1	Novak, Nick, Arizona	5	0
Carpenter, Dwaine, San Francisco	2	0	Herron, Noah, Pittsburgh	2	0	Strickland, Donald, Indianapolis	1	0
Carpenter, Dwaine, St. Louis	1	0	Herron, Noah, Green Bay	5	0	Strickland, Donald, Philadelphia	3	0
Cloud, Michael, New England	6	0	Hodges, Reggie, St. Louis	5	0	Thomas, Anthony, Dallas	6	2
Cloud, Michael, N.Y. Giants	1	0	Hodges, Reggie, Philadelphia	3	0	Thomas, Anthony, New Orleans	4	0
Colombo, Marc, Chicago	1	0	Jackson, Alonzo, Philadelphia	1	0	Thomas, Joey, Green Bay	6	1
Colombo, Marc, Dallas	4	0	Jackson, Alonzo, N.Y. Giants	8	1	Thomas, Joey, New Orleans	5	0
Cortez, Jose, Dallas	7	0	Jones, Terry, Baltimore	1	0	Thornburg, Jeremy, San Francisco	2	0
Cortez, Jose, Philadelphia	4	0	Jones, Terry, San Francisco	7	5	Thornburg, Jeremy, Green Bay	4	0
Cortez, Jose, San Francisco	1	0	Kranchick, Matt, Pittsburgh	4	1	Thurman, Andrae, Tennessee	5	0
Cortez, Jose, Indianapolis	2	0	Kranchick, Matt, N.Y. Giants	2	0	Thurman, Andrae, Green Bay	10	1
Evans, Heath, Miami	6	2	Labinjo, Mike, Philadelphia	5	1	Towns, Lester, Arizona	2	1
Evans, Heath, New England	6	1	Labinjo, Mike, Indianapolis	2	0	Towns, Lester, Miami	4	0
Fonoti, Toniu, San Diego	2	2	Leake, John, Atlanta	8	0	Wade, Bobby, Chicago	12	0
Fonoti, Toniu, Minnesota	1	1	Leake, John, Green Bay	3	0	Wade, Bobby, Tennessee	2	1
France, Todd, Philadelphia	3	0	Mallard, Wesly, New England	3	0	Winborn, Jamie, San Francisco	3	2
France, Todd, Tampa Bay	1	0	Mallard, Wesly, Tampa Bay	6	0	Winborn, Jamie, Jacksonville	5	0

2005 REVIEW Player participation

ATTENDANCE

REGULAR SEASON

Team	Home Attendance	Average	NFL Rank	Road Attendance	Average	NFL Rank
Arizona	401,035	50,129	32	519,813	64,977	25
Atlanta	565,106	70,638	10	539,514	67,439	16
Baltimore	563,076	70,385	11	533,939	66,742	19
Buffalo	575,248	71,906	9	514,960	64,370	27
Carolina	587,700	73,463	6	474,137	59,267	32
Chicago	496,965	62,121	27	518,191	64,774	26
Cincinnati	526,469	65,809	19	542,888	67,861	14
Cleveland	578,330	72,291	7	502,742	62,843	31
Dallas	505,258	63,157	26	575,780	71,973	5
Denver	608,790	76,099	5	558,598	69,825	8
Detroit	492,580	61,573	28	523,979	65,497	23
Green Bay	562,419	70,302	12	537,199	67,150	17
Houston	562,397	70,300	13	532,541	66,568	21
Indianapolis	457,373	57,172	29	548,125	68,516	12
Jacksonville	525,519	65,690	20	512,337	64,042	29
Kansas City	623,325	77,916	3	557,385	69,673	9
Miami	575,256	71,907	8	532,541	66,568	20
Minnesota	511,960	63,995	24	551,828	68,979	11
New England	550,048	68,756	15	586,855	73,357	3
New Orleans	*417,270	52,159	31	553,408	69,176	10
N.Y. Giants	628,519	78,565	2	**529,118	66,140	22
N.Y. Jets	619,958	77,495	4	582,723	72,840	4
Oakland	418,450	52,306	30	595,011	74,376	1
Philadelphia	541,393	67,674	16	568,306	71,038	6
Pittsburgh	507,434	63,429	25	541,305	67,663	15
St. Louis	523,685	65,461	21	513,176	64,147	28
San Diego	529,916	66,240	18	560,416	70,052	7
San Francisco	523,426	65,428	22	589,647	73,706	2
Seattle	532,954	66,619	17	534,972	66,872	18
Tampa Bay	521,741	65,218	23	523,095	65,387	24
Tennessee	553,192	69,149	14	505,986	63,248	30
Washington	716,999	89,625	1	543,276	67,910	13
NFL total	17,303,791	67,593		17,303,791	67593	

*Home attendance for New Orleans includes "home" game on Sept. 18 moved to Giants Stadium due to Hurricane Katrina.
**Road attendance for N.Y. Giants includes "road" game on Sept. 18 moved to Giants Stadium due to Hurricane Katrina.
Note: Attendance figures are unofficial and are based on box scores of games.

HISTORICAL

TOP REGULAR-SEASON HOME CROWDS

Team	Attendance	Date	Site	Opponent
Arizona	73,400	October 30, 1994	Sun Devil Stadium	Pittsburgh
Atlanta	71,253	November 21, 1993	Georgia Dome	Dallas
Baltimore	70,604	December 19, 2005	M&T Bank Stadium	Green Bay
Buffalo	80,368	October 4, 1992	Rich Stadium	Miami
Carolina	76,136	December 10, 1995	Clemson Memorial Stadium	San Francisco
Chicago	66,944	Occurred many times. Last time: January 6, 2002	Soldier Field	Jacksonville
Cincinnati	66,104	October 23, 2005	Paul Brown Stadium	Pittsburgh
Cleveland	85,703	September 21, 1970	Cleveland Stadium	N.Y. Jets
Dallas	80,259	November 24, 1966	Cotton Bowl	Cleveland
Denver	76,753	September 22, 2003	Invesco Field at Mile High	Oakland
Detroit	80,444	December 20, 1981	Pontiac Silverdome	Tampa Bay
Green Bay	70,688	September 19, 2004	Lambeau Field	Chicago
Houston	70,769	November 21, 2004	Reliant Stadium	Green Bay
Indianapolis	61,282	December 14, 1997	RCA Dome	Miami
Jacksonville	76,877	December 5, 2004	ALLTEL Stadium	Pittsburgh
Kansas City	82,893	October 2, 2000	Arrowhead Stadium	Seattle
Miami	78,914	November 19, 1972	Orange Bowl	N.Y. Jets
Minnesota	64,482	November 2, 2003	Metrodome	Green Bay
New England	68,756	Occurred many times. Last time: January 1, 2006	Gillette Stadium	Miami
New Orleans	83,437	November 12, 1967	Tulane Stadium	Dallas
		November 26, 1967	Tulane Stadium	Atlanta
New York Giants	78,907	September 15, 2003	Giants Stadium	Dallas

Team	Attendance	Date	Site	Opponent
New York Jets	79,469	September 20, 1998	Giants Stadium	Indianapolis
Oakland	74,121	September 23, 1973	Memorial Stadium; Berkeley, Cal.	Miami
Philadelphia	72,977	November 20, 2003	Lincoln Financial Field	Carolina
Pittsburgh	64,975	November 7, 2004	Heinz Field	Philadelphia
St. Louis	66,273	December 10, 2000	Trans World Dome	Minnesota
San Diego	68,537	October 10, 2005	Qualcomm Stadium	Pittsburgh
San Francisco	69,014	November 13, 1994	Candlestick Park	Dallas
Seattle	68,681	December 16, 2000	Husky Stadium	Oakland
Tampa Bay	73,523	December 7, 1997	Houlihan's Stadium	Green Bay
Tennessee	69,149	Occurred many times. Last time: December 18, 2005	The Coliseum	Seattle
Washington	90,588	December 18, 2005	FedEx Field	Dallas

YEAR BY YEAR

NATIONAL FOOTBALL LEAGUE

Year	Regular season*		Average	Postseason†		Year	Regular season*		Average	Postseason†	
1934	492,684	(60)	8,211	35,059	(1)	1985	13,345,047	(224)	59,567	660,667	(9)
1935	638,178	(53)	12,041	15,000	(1)	1986	13,588,551	(224)	60,663	683,901	(9)
1936	816,007	(54)	15,111	29,545	(1)	1987§	10,032,493	(168)	59,717	606,864	(9)
1937	963,039	(55)	17,510	15,878	(1)	1988	13,539,848	(224)	60,446	608,204	(9)
1938	937,197	(55)	17,040	48,120	(1)	1989	13,625,662	(224)	60,829	635,326	(9)
1939	1,071,200	(55)	19,476	32,279	(1)	1990	14,266,240	(224)	63,689	797,198	(11)
1940	1,063,025	(55)	19,328	36,034	(1)	1991	13,187,478	(224)	58,873	758,186	(11)
1941	1,108,615	(55)	20,157	55,870	(2)	1992	13,159,387	(224)	58,747	756,005	(11)
1942	887,920	(55)	16,144	36,006	(1)	1993	13,328,760	(224)	59,503	755,625	(11)
1943	969,128	(40)	24,228	71,315	(2)	1994	13,479,680	(224)	60,177	719,143	(11)
1944	1,019,649	(50)	20,393	46,016	(1)	1995	14,196,205	(240)	59,151	733,729	(11)
1945	1,270,401	(50)	25,408	32,178	(1)	1996	13,695,748	(240)	57,066	711,601	(11)
1946	1,732,135	(55)	31,493	58,346	(1)	1997	14,691,416	(240)	61,214	751,884	(11)
1947	1,837,437	(60)	30,624	66,268	(2)	1998	14,977,358	(240)	62,406	776,225	(11)
1948	1,525,243	(60)	25,421	36,309	(1)	1999	16,105,716	(248)	64,942	758,045	(11)
1949	1,391,735	(60)	23,196	27,980	(1)	2000	16,346,740	(248)	65,914	760,710	(11)
1950	1,977,753	(78)	25,356	136,647	(3)	2001	16,314,003	(248)	65,782	721,104	(11)
1951	1,913,019	(72)	26,570	57,522	(1)	2002	16,979,369	(256)	66,326	732,722	(11)
1952	2,052,126	(72)	28,502	97,507	(2)	2003	17,105,267	(256)	66,817	805,546	(11)
1953	2,164,585	(72)	30,064	54,577	(1)	2004	17,270,486	(256)	67,463	743,803	(11)
1954	2,190,571	(72)	30,425	43,827	(1)	2005	17,303,791	(256)	67,593	755,783	(11)
1955	2,521,836	(72)	35,026	85,693	(1)						
1956	2,551,263	(72)	35,434	56,836	(1)						
1957	2,836,318	(72)	39,393	119,579	(2)						
1958	3,006,124	(72)	41,752	123,659	(2)						
1959	3,140,000	(72)	43,617	57,545	(1)						
1960	3,128,296	(78)	40,106	67,325	(1)						
1961	3,986,159	(98)	40,675	39,029	(1)						
1962	4,003,421	(98)	40,851	64,892	(1)						
1963	4,163,643	(98)	42,486	45,801	(1)						
1964	4,563,049	(98)	46,562	79,544	(1)						
1965	4,634,021	(98)	47,286	100,304	(2)						
1966	5,337,044	(105)	50,829	135,098	(2)						
1967	5,938,924	(112)	53,026	241,754	(4)						
1968	5,882,313	(112)	52,521	291,279	(4)						
1969	6,096,127	(112)	54,430	242,841	(4)						
1970	9,533,333	(182)	52,381	410,371	(7)						
1971	10,076,035	(182)	55,363	430,244	(7)						
1972	10,445,827	(182)	57,395	435,466	(7)						
1973	10,730,933	(182)	58,961	458,515	(7)						
1974	10,236,322	(182)	56,244	412,180	(7)						
1975	10,213,193	(182)	56,116	443,811	(7)						
1976	11,070,543	(196)	56,482	428,733	(7)						
1977	11,018,632	(196)	56,218	483,588	(7)						
1978	12,771,800	(224)	57,017	578,107	(9)						
1979	13,182,039	(224)	58,848	582,266	(9)						
1980	13,392,230	(224)	59,787	577,186	(9)						
1981	13,606,990	(224)	60,745	587,361	(9)						
1982‡	7,367,438	(126)	58,472	985,952	(15)						
1983	13,277,222	(224)	59,273	625,068	(9)						
1984	13,398,112	(224)	59,813	614,809	(9)						

*Number of tickets sold, including no-shows; number of regular-season games in parentheses.

†Includes conference, league championship and Super Bowl games, but not Pro Bowl; number of postseason games in parentheses.

‡A 57-day players strike reduced 224-game schedule to 126 games.

§A 24-day players strike reduced 224-game schedule to 168 nonstrike games.

AMERICAN FOOTBALL LEAGUE

Year	Regular season*	Average	AFL Champ. Game
1960	926,156 (56)	16,538	32,183
1961	1,002,657 (56)	17,904	29,556
1962	1,147,302 (56)	20,487	37,981
1963	1,208,697 (56)	21,584	30,127
1964	1,447,875 (56)	25,855	40,242
1965	1,782,384 (56)	31,828	30,361
1966	2,160,369 (63)	34,291	42,080
1967	2,295,697 (63)	36,439	53,330
1968	2,635,004 (70)	37,643	62,627
1969	2,843,373 (70)	40,620	53,564

*Number of regular-season games in parentheses.

TRADES

(Covering May 2005 through April 2006)

MAY 19

Carolina traded P Todd Sauerbrun to **Denver** for P Jason Baker and a 2006 seventh-round draft pick. Panthers chose DE Stanley McClover.

JULY 14

Dallas traded CB Pete Hunter to the **New York Jets** for a conditional draft pick.

JULY 15

Denver traded CB Willie Middlebrooks to **San Francisco** for DE John Engelberger.

JULY 18

Buffalo traded RB Travis Henry to **Tennessee** for a 2006 third-round draft pick. Bills chose CB Ashton Youboty.

JULY 27

Washington traded WR Rod Gardner to **Carolina** for an undisclosed draft pick.

AUGUST 4

Seattle traded CB Kris Richard to **Miami** for DE Ronald Flemons.

AUGUST 11

New York Jets traded S Jon McGraw to **Detroit** for a conditional draft pick.

AUGUST 17

Dallas traded T Sam Wilder to **Tampa Bay** for an undisclosed draft pick.

AUGUST 22

Cleveland traded WR Andre Davis to **New England** for an undisclosed draft pick.

AUGUST 26

Jacksonville traded K Seth Marler to **Dallas** for an undisclosed draft pick.

AUGUST 28

Chicago traded DE Alain Kashama to **Seattle** for an undisclosed draft pick.

AUGUST 30

Miami traded LB Brendon Ayanbadejo to **Chicago** for TE John Owens and a conditional draft pick.

SEPTEMBER 4

Green Bay traded CB Chris Johnson to **St. Louis** for LB Robert Thomas.

Green Bay traded T/G Steve Morley to the **New York Jets** for an undisclosed draft pick.

Tennessee traded LB Rocky Calmus to **Indianapolis** for an undisclosed draft pick.

Minnesota traded OT Nat Dorsey to **Cleveland** for G/C Melvin Fowler.

Kansas City traded LB Scott Fujita to **Dallas** for a 2006 sixth-round draft pick and a conditional 2007 draft pick. Chiefs chose G Tre' Stallings.

OCTOBER 7

San Francisco traded LB Jamie Winborn to **Jacksonville** for an undisclosed draft pick.

OCTOBER 11

Miami traded RB Jesse Chatman to **New Orleans** for a conditional draft pick.

OCTOBER 18

San Diego traded OL Toniu Fonoti to **Minnesota** for an undisclosed draft pick.

Miami traded QB A.J. Feeley and an undisclosed draft pick to **San Diego** for QB Cleo Lemon.

San Francisco traded QB Tim Rattay to **Tampa Bay** for an undisclosed draft pick.

MARCH 12

San Francisco traded WR Brandon Lloyd to **Washington** for a 2006 third-round draft pick and a 2007 fourth-round draft pick. The 49ers chose WR Brandon Williams.

MARCH 15

Minnesota traded QB Daunte Culpepper to **Miami** for a 2006 second-round draft pick. Vikings chose C Ryan Cook.

MARCH 17

Washington traded QB Patrick Ramsey to the **New York Jets** for a 2006 sixth-round pick. Redskins chose SS Reed Doughty.

MARCH 20

Cleveland traded S Chris Crocker to **Atlanta** for a 2006 fourth-round draft pick. Browns chose G Isaac Sowells.

MARCH 22

Atlanta traded a 2006 first-round draft pick to **Denver** for 2006 first-round and third-round picks and a 2007 fourth-round pick. The Falcons traded the 2006 first-round pick to the **New York Jets** for DE John Abraham. Jets chose C Nick Mangold.

APRIL 6

Buffalo traded WR Eric Moulds to **Houston** for a 2006 fifth-round draft pick. Bills chose DT Kyle Williams.

New Orleans traded T Wayne Gandy to **Atlanta** for S Bryan Scott and a conditional draft choice.

APRIL 12

San Diego traded CB Sammy Davis to **San Francisco** for WR Rashaun Woods.

APRIL 19

Denver traded a 2006 first-round pick to **San Francisco** for 2006 second- and third-round picks. 49ers chose OLB Manny Lawson.

APRIL 25

Chicago traded S Mike Green to **Seattle** for a 2006 sixth-round draft pick. Chicago selected G Tyler Reed.

APRIL 29

St. Louis traded a 2006 first-round draft pick to **Denver** for 2006 first-round and third-round picks. Broncos chose QB Jay Cutler. Rams chose CB Tye Hill and DT Claude Wroten.

Cleveland traded a 2006 first-round draft pick to **Baltimore** for 2006 first-round and sixth-round draft picks. Ravens chose DT Haloti Ngata. Cleveland chose DE Kamerion Wimbley and DT Babatunde Oshinowo.

New York Giants traded a 2006 first-round draft pick to **Pittsburgh** for 2006 first-round, third-round and fourth-round draft picks. Steelers chose WR Santonio Holmes. Giants chose DE Mathias Kiwanuka, LB Gerris Wilkinson and OT Guy Whimper.

Chicago traded a 2006 first-round draft pick to **Buffalo** for 2006 second- and third-round draft picks. Bills chose DT John McCargo. Bears chose SS Danieal Manning and DT Dusty Dvoracek.

New Orleans traded a 2006 second-round draft pick to **Cleveland** for C Jeff Faine and a 2006 second-round draft pick. Saints chose FS Roman Harper. Browns chose LB D'Qwell Jackson.

New York Jets traded a 2006 second-round draft pick to **Washington** for 2006 second- and sixth-round draft picks and 2007 second-round pick. Redskins chose LB Rocky McIntosh.

Green Bay traded a 2006 second-round draft pick to **New England** for 2006 second- and third-round draft picks. Patriots chose WR Chad Jackson. Packers chose WR Greg Jennings and C Jason Spitz.

Green Bay traded WR Javon Walker to **Denver** for a 2006 second-round draft pick.

Green Bay traded 2006 second- and fifth-round picks to **Atlanta** for 2006 second-, third- and fifth-round picks. Falcons chose CB Jimmy Williams and OT Quinn Ojinnaka. Packers chose OT Daryn Colledge in the second round and QB/P Ingle Martin in the fifth.

Tennessee traded a 2006 second-round draft pick to **Philadelphia** for 2006 second- and fourth-round picks. Eagles chose OT Winston Justice. Titans chose RB LenDale White and LB Stephen Tulloch.

Baltimore traded a 2006 second-round draft pick to the **New York Giants** for two third-round draft choices. Giants chose WR Sinorice Moss. Ravens chose C Chris Chester and CB David Pittman.

Dallas traded a 2006 second-round draft pick to the **New York Jets** for second-, sixth- and seventh-round draft picks. Jets chose QB Kellen Clemons. Dallas chose TE Anthony Fasano in the second round and OT Pat McQuistan in the seventh.

Pittsburgh traded a 2006 second-round draft pick to **Minnesota** for two 2006 third-round draft picks. Vikings chose QB Tarvaris Jackson. Steelers chose FS Anthony Smith and WR Willie Reid.

New York Jets traded a 2006 third-round draft pick to **Philadelphia** for 2006 third- and seventh-round picks. Eagles chose DE Chris Gocong. Jets chose LB Anthony Schlegel and DT Titus Adams.

Dallas traded a 2006 third-round draft pick to **Jacksonville** for 2006 third- and fourth-round draft picks. Jaguars chose LB Clint Ingram. Cowboys chose DE Jason Hatcher and WR Skyler Green.

Green Bay traded a 2006 third-round draft pick to **St. Louis** for 2006 fourth- and sixth-round draft picks. Rams chose TE Dominique Byrd. Packers chose DT Johnny Jolly in the sixth round.

New Orleans traded a 2006 fourth-round draft pick to **Philadelphia** for DT Hollis Thomas and a 2006 fourth-round draft pick. Eagles chose G Max Jean-Gilles. Saints chose OT Jahri Evans.

Minnesota traded 2006 fourth- and sixth-round draft picks to **Philadelphia** for G Artis Hicks and a 2006 fourth-round draft pick. Vikings selected DE Ray Edwards.

San Diego traded a 2006 fourth-round draft pick to **St. Louis** for TE Brandon Manumaleuna. Rams chose DE Victor Adeyanju.

Green Bay traded a 2006 fourth-round draft choice to **Philadelphia** for 2006 fourth- and sixth-round draft picks. Eagles chose WR Jason Avant. Packers chose WR Will Blackmon and FS Tyrone Culver.

New York Jets traded a 2006 fifth-round draft pick to **Dallas** for 2006 fifth- and sixth-round draft picks. Dallas chose FS Pat Watkins. Jets chose TE Jason Pociask and CB Drew Coleman.

Jacksonville traded a 2006 sixth-round draft pick to **San Francisco** for two 2006 seventh-round draft picks. 49ers chose DE Melvin Oliver. Jaguars chose DE James Wyche and CB Dee Webb.

Tennessee traded a 2006 sixth-round draft pick to **Indianapolis** for a 2007 sixth-round draft pick. Colts chose CB T.J. Rushing.

2005 STATISTICS

Rushing

Passing

Receiving

Scoring

Interceptions

Sacks

Fumbles

Field goals

Punting

Punt returns

Kickoff returns

Tackles

Miscellaneous

RUSHING

AFC

Team	Att.	Yds.	Avg.	Long	TD
Denver	542	2539	4.7	68	25
Kansas City	520	2382	4.6	t49	26
Pittsburgh	549	2223	4.0	t80	21
San Diego	465	2072	4.5	t83	22
Jacksonville	502	1959	3.9	t71	18
Cincinnati	459	1910	4.2	33	15
Miami	444	1898	4.3	t65	11
Houston	437	1816	4.2	44	9
Indianapolis	465	1703	3.7	33	18
Buffalo	428	1607	3.8	39	6
Baltimore	452	1605	3.6	52	5
Tennessee	397	1525	3.8	t38	8
New England	439	1512	3.4	31	16
Cleveland	395	1503	3.8	t75	4
Oakland	361	1369	3.8	27	11
N.Y. Jets	384	1328	3.5	49	10
AFC total	7239	28951	...	t83	225
AFC average	452.4	1809.4	4.0	...	14.1

t—touchdown.

NFC

Team	Att.	Yds.	Avg.	Long	TD
Atlanta	531	2546	4.8	65	17
Seattle	519	2457	4.7	t88	29
N.Y. Giants	469	2209	4.7	t95	17
Washington	525	2183	4.2	52	15
Chicago	488	2099	4.3	42	11
Dallas	521	1861	3.6	51	13
Tampa Bay	457	1826	4.0	t71	13
San Francisco	428	1689	3.9	t73	9
New Orleans	423	1688	4.0	42	8
Carolina	487	1679	3.4	t70	17
St. Louis	380	1535	4.0	51	13
Detroit	404	1471	3.6	t77	10
Minnesota	381	1467	3.9	t61	10
Philadelphia	365	1432	3.9	t59	11
Green Bay	398	1352	3.4	t64	11
Arizona	360	1138	3.2	32	2
NFC total	7136	28632	...	t95	206
NFC average	446.0	1789.5	4.0	...	12.9
NFL total	14375	57583	...	t95	431
NFL average	449.2	1799.5	4.0	...	13.5

BESTS OF THE SEASON

Yards, season
NFC: 1880—Shaun Alexander, Seattle.
AFC: 1750—Larry Johnson, Kansas City.

Yards, game
NFC: 220—Tiki Barber, N.Y. Giants vs. Kansas City, Dec. 17 (29 attempts, 2 TDs)
AFC: 211—Larry Johnson, Kansas City at Houston, Nov. 20 (36 attempts, 2 TDs)

Longest gain
NFC: 95—Tiki Barber, N.Y. Giants at Oakland, Dec. 31 (TD).
AFC: 83—Michael Turner, San Diego at Indianapolis, Dec. 18 (TD)

Attempts, season
NFC: 370—Shaun Alexander, Seattle.
AFC: 360—Edgerrin James, Indianapolis.

Attempts, game
AFC: 37—Fred Taylor, Jacksonville at N.Y. Jets, Sep. 25 (98 yards, 1 TD)
NFC: 37—Carnell Williams, Tampa Bay at Green Bay, Sep. 25 (158 yards)

Yards per attempt, season
NFC: 5.9—Michael Vick, Atlanta.
AFC: 5.3—Tatum Bell, Denver.

Touchdowns, season
NFC: 27—Shaun Alexander, Seattle.
AFC: 20—Larry Johnson, Kansas City.

Team leaders, yards
AFC:

Baltimore	906	Jamal Lewis
Buffalo	1247	Willis McGahee
Cincinnati	1458	Rudi Johnson
Cleveland	1232	Reuben Droughns
Denver	1014	Mike Anderson
Houston	976	Domanick Davis
Indianapolis	1506	Edgerrin James
Jacksonville	787	Fred Taylor
Kansas City	1750	Larry Johnson
Miami	907	Ronnie Brown
N.Y. Jets	735	Curtis Martin
New England	733	Corey Dillon
Oakland	1025	LaMont Jordan
Pittsburgh	1202	Willie Parker
San Diego	1462	LaDainian Tomlinson
Tennessee	851	Chris Brown

NFC:

Arizona	451	Marcel Shipp
Atlanta	1416	Warrick Dunn
Carolina	879	DeShaun Foster
Chicago	1335	Thomas Jones
Dallas	993	Julius Jones
Detroit	664	Kevin Jones
Green Bay	582	Samkon Gado
Minnesota	662	Mewelde Moore
N.Y. Giants	1860	Tiki Barber
New Orleans	659	Antowain Smith
Philadelphia	617	Brian Westbrook
San Francisco	608	Frank Gore
Seattle	1880	Shaun Alexander
St. Louis	1046	Steven Jackson
Tampa Bay	1178	Carnell Williams
Washington	1516	Clinton Portis

NFL LEADERS

Player, team	Att.	Yds.	Avg.	Long	TD
Alexander, Shaun, Seattle	370	1880	5.1	t88	27
Barber, Tiki, N.Y. Giants	357	1860	5.2	t95	9
Johnson, Larry, Kansas City*	336	1750	5.2	t49	20
Portis, Clinton, Washington*	352	1516	4.3	t47	11
James, Edgerrin, Indianapolis*	360	1506	4.2	33	13
Tomlinson, LaDainian, San Diego*	339	1462	4.3	62	18
Johnson, Rudi, Cincinnati*	337	1458	4.3	33	12
Dunn, Warrick, Atlanta	280	1416	5.1	65	3
Jones, Thomas, Chicago	314	1335	4.3	42	9
McGahee, Willis, Buffalo*	325	1247	3.8	27	5
Droughns, Reuben, Cleveland*	309	1232	4.0	t75	2
Parker, Willie, Pittsburgh*	255	1202	4.7	t80	4
Williams, Carnell, Tampa Bay	290	1178	4.1	t71	6
Jackson, Steven, St. Louis*	254	1046	4.1	51	8
Jordan, LaMont, Oakland*	272	1025	3.8	26	9

Player, team	Att.	Yds.	Avg.	Long	TD
Anderson, Mike, Denver*	239	1014	4.2	t44	12
Jones, Julius, Dallas	257	993	3.9	51	5
Davis, Domanick, Houston*	230	976	4.2	44	2
Bell, Tatum, Denver*	173	921	5.3	68	8
Brown, Ronnie, Miami*	207	907	4.4	t65	4
Lewis, Jamal, Baltimore*	269	906	3.4	25	3
Foster, DeShaun, Carolina	205	879	4.3	t70	2
Brown, Chris, Tennessee*	224	851	3.8	t38	5
Taylor, Fred, Jacksonville*	194	787	4.1	t71	3
Williams, Ricky, Miami*	168	743	4.4	35	6
Martin, Curtis, N.Y. Jets*	220	735	3.3	49	5
Dillon, Corey, New England*	209	733	3.5	29	12
Jones, Kevin, Detroit	186	664	3.6	40	5
Moore, Mewelde, Minnesota	155	662	4.3	33	1
Smith, Antowain, New Orleans	166	659	4.0	42	3

*AFC.
t—touchdown.
Leader based on yards gained.

AFC

Player, team	Att.	Yds.	Avg.	Long	TD
Adams, Charlie, Denver	5	14	2.8	13	0
Anderson, Mike, Denver	239	1014	4.2	t44	12
Askew, B.J., N.Y. Jets	13	59	4.5	14	0
Banks, Tony, Houston	2	-2	-1.0	-1	0
Batch, Charlie, Pittsburgh	11	30	2.7	15	1
Bell, Tatum, Denver	173	921	5.3	68	8
Bennett, Drew, Tennessee	1	3	3.0	3	0
Bettis, Jerome, Pittsburgh	110	368	3.3	39	9
Blaylock, Derrick, N.Y. Jets	17	53	3.1	11	0
Boller, Kyle, Baltimore	23	66	2.9	9	1
Bollinger, Brooks, N.Y. Jets	35	135	3.9	15	0
Bradford, Corey, Houston	1	-2	-2.0	-2	0
Brady, Tom, New England	27	89	3.3	15	1
Brees, Drew, San Diego	21	49	2.3	9	1
Brown, Chris, Tennessee	224	851	3.8	t38	5
Brown, Dee, Kansas City	7	21	3.0	7	0
Brown, Kris, Houston	1	4	4.0	4	0
Brown, Ronnie, Miami	207	907	4.4	t65	4
Bryant, Antonio, Cleveland	1	3	3.0	3	0
Caldwell, Reche, San Diego	2	10	5.0	7	0
Carr, David, Houston	56	308	5.5	20	1
Carthon, Ran, Indianapolis	13	18	1.4	7	1
Cassel, Matt, New England	6	12	2.0	9	0
Chambers, Chris, Miami	12	92	7.7	61	0
Clayton, Mark, Baltimore	8	33	4.1	t11	1
Collins, Kerry, Oakland	17	39	2.3	t18	1
Collins, Todd, Kansas City	2	-2	-1.0	-1	0
Cotchery, Jerricho, N.Y. Jets	1	4	4.0	4	0
Crockett, Zack, Oakland	60	208	3.5	24	1
Davis, Domanick, Houston	230	976	4.2	44	2
Dayne, Ron, Denver	53	270	5.1	55	1
Dilfer, Trent, Cleveland	20	46	2.3	12	0
Dillon, Corey, New England	209	733	3.5	29	12
Droughns, Reuben, Cleveland	309	1232	4.0	t75	2
Dwight, Tim, New England	4	11	2.8	12	0
Evans, Heath, Mia.-N.E.*	52	192	3.7	21	0
Evans, Lee, Buffalo	4	38	9.5	39	0
Fargas, Justin, Oakland	5	28	5.6	15	0
Faulk, Kevin, New England	51	145	2.8	13	0
Fiedler, Jay, N.Y. Jets	1	0	0.0	0	0
Flutie, Doug, New England	5	-1	-.2	2	0
Frerotte, Gus, Miami	27	61	2.3	14	0
Frye, Charlie, Cleveland	18	60	3.3	16	1
Gabriel, Doug, Oakland	1	5	5.0	5	0
Gaffney, Jabar, Houston	4	13	3.3	10	0
Garrard, David, Jacksonville	31	172	5.5	28	3
Givens, David, New England	2	13	6.5	9	0
Graham, Ben, N.Y. Jets	1	0	0.0	0	0
Gray, Quinn, Jacksonville	3	1	0.3	3	0
Green, Justin, Baltimore	5	4	0.8	4	0
Green, Trent, Kansas City	35	82	2.3	13	0
Green, William, Cleveland	20	78	3.9	17	0
Hall, Dante, Kansas City	7	11	1.6	7	0
Haynes, Verron, Pittsburgh	74	274	3.7	20	3
Henry, Travis, Tennessee	88	335	3.8	29	0
Hentrich, Craig, Tennessee	1	0	0.0	0	0
Holcomb, Kelly, Buffalo	18	11	0.6	8	1
Holmes, Priest, Kansas City	119	451	3.8	t35	6
Houshmandzadeh, T.J., Cincinnati.	8	62	7.8	17	1
Houston, Cedric, N.Y. Jets	81	302	3.7	17	2
James, Edgerrin, Indianapolis	360	1506	4.2	33	13
Johnson, Andre, Houston	6	10	1.7	5	0
Johnson, Chad, Cincinnati	5	33	6.6	11	0
Johnson, Jeremi, Cincinnati	8	14	1.8	5	0
Johnson, Kyle, Denver	4	9	2.3	4	1
Johnson, Larry, Kansas City	336	1750	5.2	t49	20
Johnson, Rudi, Cincinnati	337	1458	4.3	33	12
Jones, Brandon, Tennessee	1	1	1.0	1	0
Jones, Donnie, Miami	1	0	0.0	0	0
Jones, Greg, Jacksonville	151	575	3.8	27	4
Jones, Matt, Jacksonville	12	51	4.3	25	0
Jordan, LaMont, Oakland	272	1025	3.8	26	9
Kennison, Eddie, Kansas City	7	43	6.1	23	0
Kitna, Jon, Cincinnati	2	14	7.0	11	0
Kreider, Dan, Pittsburgh	3	21	7.0	12	0
Lechler, Shane, Oakland	1	2	2.0	2	0
Leftwich, Byron, Jacksonville	31	67	2.2	9	2
Lelie, Ashley, Denver	5	84	16.8	39	0
Lewis, Jamal, Baltimore	269	906	3.4	25	3
Losman, J.P., Buffalo	31	154	5.0	30	0
Luchey, Nick, Cincinnati	1	0	0.0	0	0
Maddox, Tommy, Pittsburgh	8	26	3.3	16	0
Manning, Peyton, Indianapolis	33	45	1.4	12	0
Martin, Curtis, N.Y. Jets	220	735	3.3	49	5
Mauck, Matt, Tennessee	7	39	5.6	12	0
McCardell, Keenan, San Diego	2	6	3.0	3	0
McCareins, Justin, N.Y. Jets	1	8	8.0	8	0
McGahee, Willis, Buffalo	325	1247	3.8	27	5
McNair, Steve, Tennessee	32	139	4.3	19	1
Minor, Travis, Miami	5	17	3.4	9	0
Morency, Vernand, Houston	46	184	4.0	t25	2
Morris, Sammy, Miami	16	58	3.6	t9	1
Mungro, James, Indianapolis	7	15	2.1	7	0
Nash, Damien, Tennessee	6	32	5.3	8	0
Neal, Lorenzo, San Diego	29	98	3.4	9	0
Northcutt, Dennis, Cleveland	2	33	16.5	31	0
Osgood, Kassim, San Diego	1	4	4.0	4	0
Palmer, Carson, Cincinnati	34	41	1.2	14	1
Parker, Eric, San Diego	4	55	13.8	30	0
Parker, Willie, Pittsburgh	255	1202	4.7	t80	4
Parrish, Roscoe, Buffalo	2	-2	-1.0	4	0
Pass, Patrick, New England	54	245	4.5	31	3
Payton, Jarrett, Tennessee	33	105	3.2	15	2
Pearman, Alvin, Jacksonville	39	149	3.8	45	1
Pennington, Chad, N.Y. Jets	6	27	4.5	14	0
Perry, Chris, Cincinnati	61	279	4.6	30	0
Perry, Tab, Cincinnati	3	9	3.0	7	1
Pinnock, Andrew, San Diego	1	4	4.0	4	0
Plummer, Jake, Denver	46	151	3.3	22	2
Porter, Jerry, Oakland	1	-8	-8.0	-8	0
Randle El, Antwaan, Pittsburgh	12	73	6.1	43	0
Reed, Josh, Buffalo	1	-3	-3.0	-3	0
Rhodes, Dominic, Indianapolis	40	118	3.0	24	4
Richardson, Tony, Kansas City	6	20	3.3	8	0
Rivers, Philip, San Diego	1	-1	-1.0	-1	0
Roby, Courtney, Tennessee	2	16	8.0	11	0

2005 STATISTICS Rushing

Player, team	Att.	Yds.	Avg.	Long	TD
Roethlisberger, Ben, Pittsburgh.....	31	69	2.2	13	3
Rosenfels, Sage, Miami	6	15	2.5	12	0
Sanders, Deion, Baltimore	1	0	0.0	0	0
Sapp, Cecil, Denver	5	21	4.2	10	0
Shelton, Daimon, Buffalo	1	0	0.0	0	0
Smith, Jonathan, Buffalo	1	1	1.0	1	0
Smith, Rod, Denver	1	7	7.0	7	0
Smith, Terrelle, Cleveland	6	9	1.5	4	0
Sorgi, Jim, Indianapolis	12	1	0.1	6	0
Sowell, Jerald, N.Y. Jets	1	1	1.0	t1	1
Sproles, Darren, San Diego	8	50	6.3	21	0
Staley, Duce, Pittsburgh	38	148	3.9	17	1
Stanley, Chad, Houston	1	0	0.0	0	0
Stewart, Kordell, Baltimore	4	24	6.0	13	0
Suggs, Lee, Cleveland	8	15	1.9	7	0
Taylor, Chester, Baltimore	117	487	4.2	52	0
Taylor, Fred, Jacksonville	194	787	4.1	t71	3
Testaverde, Vinny, N.Y. Jets	7	4	0.6	2	2
Toefield, LaBrandon, Jacksonville..	36	142	3.9	t32	4
Tomlinson, LaDainian, San Diego..	339	1462	4.3	62	18
Tuiasosopo, Marques, Oakland......	2	19	9.5	10	0
Turner, Michael, San Diego	57	335	5.9	t83	3
Van Pelt, Bradlee, Denver	11	48	4.4	11	1
Volek, Billy, Tennessee	1	3	3.0	3	0
Wade, Bobby, Tennessee	1	1	1.0	1	0
Ward, Hines, Pittsburgh	3	10	3.3	7	0
Welker, Wes, Miami	1	5	5.0	5	0
Wells, Jonathan, Houston	90	325	3.6	t14	4
White, Jamel, Baltimore	6	17	2.8	5	0
Whitted, Alvis, Oakland	2	51	25.5	27	0
Williams, Reggie, Jacksonville	2	3	1.5	10	0
Williams, Ricky, Miami	168	743	4.4	35	6
Williams, Shaud, Buffalo	45	161	3.6	28	0
Wilson, Cedrick, Pittsburgh	1	0	0.0	0	0
Wilson, Kris, Kansas City	1	6	6.0	6	0
Wimbush, Derrick, Jacksonville	3	12	4.0	7	1
Wright, Anthony, Baltimore	18	68	3.8	22	0
Wright, Jason, Cleveland	11	27	2.5	t6	1
Zastudil, Dave, Baltimore	1	0	0.0	0	0
Zereoue, Amos, New England	7	14	2.0	12	0

*Includes both NFC and AFC statistics.
t—touchdown.

NFC

Player, team	Att.	Yds.	Avg.	Long	TD
Alexander, Shaun, Seattle	370	1880	5.1	t88	27
Alstott, Mike, Tampa Bay	34	80	2.4	9	6
Anderson, Damien, Arizona	2	7	3.5	6	0
Arrington, J.J., Arizona	112	370	3.3	32	2
Ayanbadejo, Obafemi, Arizona	22	46	2.1	11	0
Barber, Marion, Dallas	138	538	3.9	t28	5
Barber, Tiki, N.Y. Giants	357	1860	5.2	t95	9
Barlow, Kevan, San Francisco	176	581	3.3	29	3
Battle, Arnaz, San Francisco	8	11	1.4	9	0
Bennett, Michael, Minnesota	126	473	3.8	t61	3
Benson, Cedric, Chicago	67	272	4.1	36	0
Berrian, Bernard, Chicago	2	31	15.5	37	0
Betts, Ladell, Washington	89	338	3.8	22	1
Blake, Jeff, Chicago	1	-1	-1.0	-1	0
Bledsoe, Drew, Dallas	34	50	1.5	9	2
Boldin, Anquan, Arizona	12	45	3.8	11	0
Bouman, Todd, New Orleans	8	15	1.9	6	0
Brooks, Aaron, New Orleans	45	281	6.2	22	2
Broughton, Nehemiah, Was.	1	3	3.0	3	0
Brown, Antonio, Washington	2	7	3.5	4	0
Brown, Reggie, Philadelphia	1	5	5.0	5	0
Brunell, Mark, Washington	42	111	2.6	25	0
Bryson, Shawn, Detroit	64	306	4.8	t77	1
Bulger, Marc, St. Louis	9	29	3.2	9	0
Burleson, Nate, Minnesota	2	-6	-3.0	-2	0
Carter, Tim, N.Y. Giants	6	46	7.7	22	0
Cartwright, Rock, Washington	27	199	7.4	52	2
Cason, Aveion, St. Louis	10	65	6.5	14	1
Chatman, Antonio, Green Bay	8	34	4.3	11	0
Clayton, Michael, Tampa Bay	1	2	2.0	2	0
Cloud, Michael, N.E.-NYG*	24	59	2.5	15	0
Colbert, Keary, Carolina	1	6	6.0	6	0
Crayton, Patrick, Dallas	1	0	0.0	0	0
Culpepper, Daunte, Minnesota	24	147	6.1	18	1
Curtis, Kevin, St. Louis	1	5	5.0	t5	1
Davenport, Najeh, Green Bay	30	105	3.5	24	2
Davis, Stephen, Carolina	180	549	3.1	39	12
Delhomme, Jake, Carolina	24	31	1.3	12	1
Detmer, Koy, Philadelphia	1	1	1.0	1	0
Dorsey, Ken, San Francisco	4	11	2.8	6	0
Driver, Donald, Green Bay	2	13	6.5	9	0
Drummond, Eddie, Detroit	1	-3	-3.0	-3	0
Duckett, T.J., Atlanta	121	380	3.1	25	8
Dunn, Warrick, Atlanta	280	1416	5.1	65	3
Fason, Ciatrick, Minnesota	32	62	1.9	15	4
Faulk, Marshall, St. Louis	65	292	4.5	20	0
Favre, Brett, Green Bay	18	62	3.4	20	0
Fisher, Tony, Green Bay	60	173	2.9	17	1
Fitzgerald, Larry, Arizona	8	41	5.1	15	0
Fitzpatrick, Ryan, St. Louis	14	64	4.6	t14	2
Foster, DeShaun, Carolina	205	879	4.3	t70	2
Gado, Samkon, Green Bay	143	582	4.1	t64	6
Galloway, Joey, Tampa Bay	2	4	2.0	4	0
Garcia, Jeff, Detroit	17	51	3.0	14	1
Glenn, Terry, Dallas	2	-4	-2.0	t6	0
Goings, Nick, Carolina	37	133	3.6	17	0
Gordon, Lamar, Philadelphia	54	182	3.4	11	1
Gore, Frank, San Francisco	127	608	4.8	t72	3
Graham, Earnest, Tampa Bay	28	83	3.0	16	0
Green, Ahman, Green Bay	77	255	3.3	13	0
Griese, Brian, Tampa Bay	13	12	0.9	7	0
Griffith, Justin, Atlanta	15	65	4.3	19	0
Harrington, Joey, Detroit	24	80	3.3	15	0
Harris, Arlen, St. Louis	13	21	1.6	10	1
Hasselbeck, Matt, Seattle	36	124	3.4	23	1
Hasselbeck, Tim, N.Y. Giants	2	-3	-1.5	-1	0
Hedgecock, Madison, St. Louis	1	0	0.0	0	0
Henderson, Devery, New Orleans..	1	9	9.0	9	0
Henderson, William, Green Bay.....	1	-5	-5.0	-5	0
Herron, Noah, Pit.-G.B.*	48	123	2.6	17	2
Hetherington, Chris, San Francisco	1	3	3.0	3	0
Hicks, Maurice, San Francisco	59	308	5.2	t73	3
Hill, Shaun, Minnesota	2	-2	-1.0	-1	0
Holt, Torry, St. Louis	1	2	2.0	2	0
Hoover, Brad, Carolina	10	22	2.2	4	0
Jackson, Darrell, Seattle	1	7	7.0	7	0
Jackson, James, Arizona	4	11	2.8	3	0
Jackson, Steven, St. Louis	254	1046	4.1	51	8
Jackson, Terry, San Francisco	2	11	5.5	11	0
Jacobs, Brandon, N.Y. Giants	38	99	2.6	21	7
Johnson, Brad, Minnesota	18	53	2.9	16	0
Johnson, Bryan, Chicago	1	5	5.0	5	0
Johnson, Bryant, Arizona	1	0	0.0	0	0
Johnson, Keyshawn, Dallas	1	3	3.0	3	0
Jones, Julius, Dallas	257	993	3.9	51	5
Jones, Kevin, Detroit	186	664	3.6	40	5
Jones, Thomas, Chicago	314	1335	4.3	42	9
Karney, Mike, New Orleans	6	12	2.0	3	0
Lee, ReShard, Green Bay	11	16	1.5	4	0
Lewis, Greg, Philadelphia	2	13	6.5	8	0
Mahe, Reno, Philadelphia	20	87	4.4	13	0
Manning, Eli, N.Y. Giants	29	80	2.8	14	1
Manumaleuna, Brandon, St. Louis	1	2	2.0	2	0
Marshall, Rasheed, San Francisco.	1	-7	-7.0	-7	0

Player, team	Att.	Yds.	Avg.	Long	TD
Martin, Jamie, St. Louis	9	6	0.7	9	0
McAllister, Deuce, New Orleans	93	335	3.6	26	3
McCown, Josh, Arizona	29	139	4.8	12	0
McDonald, Shaun, St. Louis	1	7	7.0	7	0
McKie, Jason, Chicago	3	22	7.3	13	0
McMahon, Mike, Philadelphia	34	118	3.5	19	3
McNabb, Donovan, Philadelphia	25	55	2.2	11	1
Moats, Ryan, Philadelphia	55	278	5.1	t59	3
Moore, Mewelde, Minnesota	155	662	4.3	33	1
Morris, Maurice, Seattle	71	288	4.1	49	1
Moss, Santana, Washington	3	-3	-1.0	3	0
Newman, Terence, Dallas	1	4	4.0	4	0
Orton, Kyle, Chicago	24	44	1.8	15	0
Owens, Terrell, Philadelphia	1	2	2.0	2	0
Perry, Bruce, Philadelphia	16	74	4.6	11	0
Peterson, Adrian, Chicago	76	391	5.1	36	2
Pickett, Cody, San Francisco	13	42	3.2	12	0
Pinner, Artose, Detroit	106	349	3.3	19	3
Pittman, Michael, Tampa Bay	70	436	6.2	64	1
Polite, Lousaka, Dallas	2	8	4.0	6	0
Ponder, Willie, N.Y. Giants	1	4	4.0	4	0
Portis, Clinton, Washington	352	1516	4.3	t47	11
Price, Peerless, Dallas	1	9	9.0	9	0
Proehl, Ricky, Carolina	1	-8	-8.0	-8	0
Ramsey, Patrick, Washington	7	3	0.4	5	0
Rattay, Tim, San Francisco	7	18	2.6	13	0
Robertson, Jamal, Carolina	14	41	2.9	11	1
Robinson, Koren, Minnesota	4	27	6.8	t13	1
Rodgers, Aaron, Green Bay	2	7	3.5	8	0
Romo, Tony, Dallas	2	-2	-1.0	-1	0
Sander, B.J., Green Bay	1	-11	-11.0	-11	0
Schaub, Matt, Atlanta	9	76	8.4	23	0
Schlesinger, Cory, Detroit	1	1	1.0	1	0
Sellers, Mike, Washington	1	1	1.0	t1	1
Shipp, Marcel, Arizona	157	451	2.9	19	0
Simms, Chris, Tampa Bay	19	31	1.6	10	0
Smart, Rod, Carolina	3	6	2.0	6	0
Smith, Alex, San Francisco	30	103	3.4	19	0
Smith, Antowain, New Orleans	166	659	4.0	42	3
Smith, Paul, Detroit	4	16	4.0	6	0
Smith, Steve, Carolina	4	25	6.3	t20	1
Stallworth, Donte', New Orleans	2	2	1.0	3	0
Stecker, Aaron, New Orleans	95	363	3.8	32	0
Strong, Mack, Seattle	17	78	4.6	16	0
Taylor, Travis, Minnesota	2	3	1.5	5	0
Thomas, Anthony, Dal.-N.O.*	43	92	2.1	12	0
Thompson, Tyson, Dallas	46	182	4.0	16	0
Thrash, James, Washington	1	8	8.0	8	0
Vick, Michael, Atlanta	102	597	5.9	32	6
Vines, Scottie, Detroit	1	7	7.0	7	0
Wallace, Seneca, Seattle	6	-5	-.8	0	0
Ward, Derrick, N.Y. Giants	35	123	3.5	12	0
Warner, Kurt, Arizona	13	28	2.2	13	0
Warrick, Peter, Seattle	1	5	5.0	5	0
Weaver, Leonard, Seattle	17	80	4.7	24	0
Weinke, Chris, Carolina	8	-5	-.6	1	0
Westbrook, Brian, Philadelphia	156	617	4.0	31	3
White, Roddy, Atlanta	4	12	3.0	16	0
Wilkins, Jeff, St. Louis	1	-4	-4.0	-4	0
Williams, Carnell, Tampa Bay	290	1178	4.1	t71	6
Williams, Moe, Minnesota	13	20	1.5	9	0
Williamson, Troy, Minnesota	3	28	9.3	11	0

*Includes both NFC and AFC statistics.
t—touchdown.

PLAYERS WITH TWO CLUBS

Player, team	Att.	Yds.	Avg.	Long	TD
Cloud, Michael, New England	23	59	2.6	15	0
Cloud, Michael, N.Y. Giants	1	0	0.0	0	0
Evans, Heath, Miami	1	0	0.0	0	0
Evans, Heath, New England	51	192	3.8	21	0
Herron, Noah, Pittsburgh	3	2	0.7	1	0
Herron, Noah, Green Bay	45	121	2.7	17	2
Thomas, Anthony, Dallas	36	80	2.2	12	0
Thomas, Anthony, New Orleans	7	12	1.7	4	0

PASSING

TEAM

AFC

Team	Cmp.	Att.	Pct.	Gross Yds.	Sack	Yds. Lost	Net Yds.	Yds./Att.	Yds./Cmp.	TD	Pct. TD	Long	Int.	Pct. Int.
New England	352	564	62.4	4322	28	202	4120	7.66	12.28	28	4.96	71	15	2.7
Indianapolis	347	515	67.4	4191	20	95	4096	8.14	12.08	31	6.02	t80	11	2.1
Kansas City	317	507	62.5	4014	32	204	3810	7.92	12.66	17	3.35	t60	10	2.0
Cincinnati	362	538	67.3	3935	21	115	3820	7.31	10.87	32	5.95	t70	14	2.6
Oakland	316	591	53.5	3883	45	301	3582	6.57	12.29	21	3.55	79	14	2.4
Tennessee	358	594	60.3	3797	31	200	3597	6.39	10.61	20	3.37	57	14	2.4
San Diego	338	526	64.3	3738	31	243	3495	7.11	11.06	27	5.13	54	16	3.0
Miami	291	556	52.3	3458	26	158	3300	6.22	11.88	22	3.96	t77	16	2.9
Baltimore	335	562	59.6	3381	42	293	3088	6.02	10.09	17	3.02	48	21	3.7
Denver	279	465	60.0	3373	23	146	3227	7.25	12.09	18	3.87	72	7	1.5
Jacksonville	283	487	58.1	3352	32	162	3190	6.88	11.84	21	4.31	t45	6	1.2
Cleveland	297	497	59.8	3323	46	276	3047	6.69	11.19	15	3.02	t80	17	3.4
Pittsburgh	228	379	60.2	3104	32	178	2926	8.19	13.61	21	5.54	t85	14	3.7
N.Y. Jets	268	470	57.0	2989	53	347	2642	6.36	11.15	11	2.34	t60	15	3.2
Buffalo	269	459	58.6	2852	43	337	2515	6.21	10.60	18	3.92	65	16	3.5
Houston	270	449	60.1	2661	68	424	2237	5.93	9.86	15	3.34	t53	13	2.9
AFC total	8159	4910	...	56373	573	3681	52692	...	...	334	...	t85	219	...
AFC average	509.9	306.9	60.2	3523.3	35.8	230.1	3293.3	6.91	11.48	20.9	4.1	...	13.7	2.7

t—touchdown.

NFC

Team	Cmp.	Att.	Pct.	Gross Yds.	Sack	Yds. Lost	Net Yds.	Yds./Att.	Yds./Cmp.	TD	Pct. TD	Long	Int.	Pct. Int.
Arizona	419	670	62.5	4723	45	286	4437	7.05	11.27	21	3.13	63	21	3.1
St. Louis	392	599	65.4	4351	46	315	4036	7.26	11.10	23	3.84	t83	24	4.0
Green Bay	383	626	61.2	3964	27	198	3766	6.33	10.35	20	3.19	59	30	4.8
Philadelphia	337	620	54.4	3903	42	226	3677	6.30	11.58	21	3.39	t91	20	3.2
N.Y. Giants	294	558	52.7	3762	28	184	3578	6.74	12.80	24	4.30	t78	17	3.0
Dallas	300	500	60.0	3639	50	298	3341	7.28	12.13	23	4.60	t71	17	3.4
Seattle	307	474	64.8	3632	27	174	3458	7.66	11.83	25	5.27	56	10	2.1
New Orleans	308	553	55.7	3604	41	261	3343	6.52	11.70	15	2.71	66	24	4.3
Carolina	269	449	59.9	3485	28	214	3271	7.76	12.96	25	5.57	t80	16	3.6
Minnesota	323	510	63.3	3449	54	303	3146	6.76	10.68	18	3.53	t80	16	3.1
Washington	278	481	57.8	3346	31	240	3106	6.96	12.04	25	5.20	t78	11	2.3
Tampa Bay	303	487	62.2	3171	41	281	2890	6.51	10.47	17	3.49	t80	14	2.9
Detroit	297	520	57.1	3021	31	173	2848	5.81	10.17	15	2.88	86	18	3.5
Atlanta	247	451	54.8	2907	39	228	2679	6.45	11.77	19	4.21	58	13	2.9
Chicago	219	418	52.4	2201	31	199	2002	5.27	10.05	11	2.63	54	15	3.6
San Francisco	204	389	52.4	2190	48	292	1898	5.63	10.74	8	2.06	t89	21	5.4
NFC total	8305	4880	...	55348	609	3872	51476	...	...	310	...	t91	287	...
NFC average	519.1	305.0	58.8	3459.3	38.1	242.0	3217.3	6.66	11.34	19.4	3.7	...	17.9	3.5
NFL total	16464	9790	...	111721	1182	7553	104168	...	...	644	...	t91	506	...
NFL average	514.5	305.9	59.5	3491.3	36.9	236.0	3255.3	6.79	11.41	20.1	3.9	...	15.8	3.1

INDIVIDUAL

BESTS OF THE SEASON

Highest rating, season
AFC: 104.1—Peyton Manning, Indianapolis.
NFC: 98.2—Matt Hasselbeck, Seattle.
Completion percentage, season
AFC: 67.8—Carson Palmer, Cincinnati
NFC: 66.9—Marc Bulger, St. Louis
Attempts, season
NFC: 607—Brett Favre, Green Bay
AFC: 565—Kerry Collins, Oakland
Completions, season
NFC: 372—Brett Favre, Green Bay
AFC: 345—Carson Palmer, Cincinnati
Yards, season
AFC: 4110—Tom Brady, New England
NFC: 3881—Brett Favre, Green Bay

Yards, game
NFC: 442—Marc Bulger, St. Louis at N.Y. Giants, Oct. 2 (40-62, 2 TDs)
AFC: 386—Ben Roethlisberger, Pittsburgh vs. Cincinnati, Dec. 4 (29-41, 3 TDs)
Longest gain
NFC: 91—Donovan McNabb, (to Terrell Owens), Philadelphia at Denver, Oct. 30 (TD).
AFC: 85—Ben Roethlisberger, (to Hines Ward), Pittsburgh vs. New England, Sep. 25 (TD)
Yards per attempt, season
AFC: 8.90—Ben Roethlisberger, Pittsburgh.
NFC: 8.00—Marc Bulger, St. Louis
Touchdown passes, season
AFC: 32—Carson Palmer, Cincinnati.
NFC: 24—Jake Delhomme, Carolina; Matt Hasselbeck, Seattle; Eli Manning, N.Y. Giants.

Touchdown passes, game
AFC: 5—Donovan McNabb, Philadelphia vs. San Francisco, Sep. 18 (23-29, 342 yards)
NFC: 4—Peyton Manning, Indianapolis at Tennessee, Oct. 2 (20-27, 264 yards); Jake Plummer, Denver vs. Philadelphia, Oct. 30

(22-35, 309 yards); Drew Brees, San Diego vs. Buffalo, Nov. 20 (28-33, 339 yards)
Lowest interception percentage, season
AFC: 1.5—Jake Plummer, Denver
NFC: 1.4—Brad Johnson, Minnesota

NFL LEADERS

Player, team	Att.	Cmp.	Pct.	Yds.	Avg. Gain	TD	Pct. TD	Long	Int.	Pct. Int.	Sack	Yds. Lost	Rat.
Manning, Peyton, Indianapolis*	453	305	67.3	3747	8.27	28	6.2	t80	10	2.2	17	81	104.1
Palmer, Carson, Cincinnati*	509	345	67.8	3836	7.54	32	6.3	t70	12	2.4	19	105	101.1
Roethlisberger, Ben, Pittsburgh*	268	168	62.7	2385	8.90	17	6.3	t85	9	3.4	23	129	98.6
Hasselbeck, Matt, Seattle	449	294	65.5	3459	7.70	24	5.3	56	9	2.0	24	154	98.2
Bulger, Marc, St. Louis	287	192	66.9	2297	8.00	14	4.9	t57	9	3.1	26	188	94.4
Brady, Tom, New England*	530	334	63.0	4110	7.75	26	4.9	71	14	2.6	26	188	92.3
Plummer, Jake, Denver*	456	277	60.7	3366	7.38	18	3.9	72	7	1.5	22	135	90.2
Green, Trent, Kansas City*	507	317	62.5	4014	7.92	17	3.4	t60	10	2.0	32	204	90.1
Leftwich, Byron, Jacksonville*	302	175	57.9	2123	7.03	15	5.0	t45	5	1.7	23	110	89.3
Brees, Drew, San Diego*	500	323	64.6	3576	7.15	24	4.8	54	15	3.0	27	223	89.2
Johnson, Brad, Minnesota	294	184	62.6	1885	6.41	12	4.1	t80	4	1.4	23	134	88.9
Delhomme, Jake, Carolina	435	262	60.2	3421	7.86	24	5.5	t80	16	3.7	28	214	88.1
Brunell, Mark, Washington	454	262	57.7	3050	6.72	23	5.1	t78	10	2.2	27	213	85.9
Warner, Kurt, Arizona	375	242	64.5	2713	7.23	11	2.9	63	9	2.4	23	158	85.8
Holcomb, Kelly, Buffalo*	230	155	67.4	1509	6.56	10	4.3	65	8	3.5	17	140	85.6
McNabb, Donovan, Philadelphia	357	211	59.1	2507	7.02	16	4.5	t91	9	2.5	19	112	85.0
Bledsoe, Drew, Dallas	499	300	60.1	3639	7.29	23	4.6	t71	17	3.4	49	295	83.7
McNair, Steve, Tennessee*	476	292	61.3	3161	6.64	16	3.4	57	11	2.3	20	134	82.4
Simms, Chris, Tampa Bay	313	191	61.0	2035	6.50	10	3.2	t78	7	2.2	29	205	81.4
Collins, Kerry, Oakland*	565	302	53.5	3759	6.65	20	3.5	79	12	2.1	39	261	77.3
Carr, David, Houston*	423	256	60.5	2488	5.88	14	3.3	t53	11	2.6	68	424	77.2
Dilfer, Trent, Cleveland*	333	199	59.8	2321	6.97	11	3.3	t80	12	3.6	23	139	76.9
Manning, Eli, N.Y. Giants	557	294	52.8	3762	6.75	24	4.3	t78	17	3.1	28	184	75.9
McCown, Josh, Arizona	270	163	60.4	1836	6.80	9	3.3	49	11	4.1	18	101	74.9
Vick, Michael, Atlanta	387	214	55.3	2412	6.23	15	3.9	58	13	3.4	33	201	73.1
Bollinger, Brooks, N.Y. Jets*	266	150	56.4	1558	5.86	7	2.6	t60	6	2.3	32	193	72.9
Harrington, Joey, Detroit*	330	188	57.0	2021	6.12	12	3.6	86	12	3.6	24	136	72.0
Frerotte, Gus, Miami*	494	257	52.0	2996	6.06	18	3.6	t60	13	2.6	26	158	71.9
Boller, Kyle, Baltimore*	293	171	58.4	1799	6.14	11	3.8	t47	12	4.1	23	146	71.8
Wright, Anthony, Baltimore*	266	164	61.7	1582	5.95	6	2.3	48	9	3.4	19	147	71.7

*AFC.
t—touchdown.
Leader based on rating points, minimum 224 attempts.

AFC

Player, team	Att.	Cmp.	Pct.	Yds.	Avg. Gain	TD	Pct. TD	Long	Int.	Pct. Int.	Sack	Yds. Lost	Rat.
Banks, Tony, Houston	25	14	56.0	173	6.92	1	4.0	31	2	8.0	0	0	57.6
Batch, Charlie, Pittsburgh	36	23	63.9	246	6.83	1	2.8	43	1	2.8	1	6	81.5
Bennett, Drew, Tennessee	1	0	0.0	0	0.00	0	0.0	0	0	0.0	0	0	39.6
Boller, Kyle, Baltimore	293	171	58.4	1799	6.14	11	3.8	t47	12	4.1	23	146	71.8
Bollinger, Brooks, N.Y. Jets	266	150	56.4	1558	5.86	7	2.6	t60	6	2.3	32	193	72.9
Booker, Marty, Miami	1	0	0.0	0	0.00	0	0.0	0	0	0.0	0	0	39.6
Brady, Tom, New England	530	334	63.0	4110	7.75	26	4.9	71	14	2.6	26	188	92.3
Brees, Drew, San Diego	500	323	64.6	3576	7.15	24	4.8	54	15	3.0	27	223	89.2
Carr, David, Houston	423	256	60.5	2488	5.88	14	3.3	t53	11	2.6	68	424	77.2
Cassel, Matt, New England	24	13	54.2	183	7.63	2	8.3	36	1	4.2	1	1	89.4
Clayton, Mark, Baltimore	1	0	0.0	0	0.00	0	0.0	0	0	0.0	0	0	39.6
Collins, Kerry, Oakland	565	302	53.5	3759	6.65	20	3.5	79	12	2.1	39	261	77.3
Davis, Domanick, Houston	1	0	0.0	0	0.00	0	0.0	0	0	0.0	0	0	39.6
Dilfer, Trent, Cleveland	333	199	59.8	2321	6.97	11	3.3	t80	12	3.6	23	139	76.9
Fiedler, Jay, N.Y. Jets	13	8	61.5	107	8.23	1	7.7	t23	0	0.0	0	0	113.3
Flutie, Doug, New England	10	5	50.0	29	2.90	0	0.0	13	0	0.0	1	13	56.3
Frerotte, Gus, Miami	494	257	52.0	2996	6.06	18	3.6	t60	13	2.6	26	158	71.9
Frye, Charlie, Cleveland	164	98	59.8	1002	6.11	4	2.4	45	5	3.0	22	135	72.8
Gardocki, Chris, Pittsburgh	1	0	0.0	0	0.00	0	0.0	0	0	0.0	0	0	39.6
Garrard, David, Jacksonville	168	98	58.3	1117	6.65	4	2.4	37	1	0.6	8	45	83.9
Gray, Quinn, Jacksonville	14	8	57.1	100	7.14	2	14.3	26	0	0.0	1	7	119.0
Green, Trent, Kansas City	507	317	62.5	4014	7.92	17	3.4	t60	10	2.0	32	204	90.1
Hentrich, Craig, Tennessee	2	1	50.0	26	13.00	0	0.0	26	0	0.0	0	0	95.8
Holcomb, Kelly, Buffalo	230	155	67.4	1509	6.56	10	4.3	65	8	3.5	17	140	85.6

2005 STATISTICS *Passing*

Player, team	Att.	Cmp.	Pct.	Yds.	Avg. Gain	TD	Pct. TD	Long	Int.	Pct. Int.	Sack	Yds. Lost	Rat.
Pickett, Cody, San Francisco	35	14	40.0	140	4.00	0	0.0	28	2	5.7	3	16	28.3
Portis, Clinton, Washington	2	1	50.0	17	8.50	1	50.0	t17	0	0.0	0	0	118.8
Ramsey, Patrick, Washington	25	15	60.0	279	11.16	1	4.0	t72	1	4.0	4	27	95.3
Rattay, Tim, San Francisco	97	56	57.7	667	6.88	5	5.2	t89	6	6.2	10	63	70.3
Rodgers, Aaron, Green Bay	16	9	56.3	65	4.06	0	0.0	16	1	6.3	3	28	39.8
Sander, B.J., Green Bay	1	1	100.0	4	4.00	0	0.0	4	0	0.0	0	0	83.3
Schaub, Matt, Atlanta	64	33	51.6	495	7.73	4	6.3	53	0	0.0	6	27	98.1
Simms, Chris, Tampa Bay	313	191	61.0	2035	6.50	10	3.2	t78	7	2.2	29	205	81.4
Smith, Alex, San Francisco	165	84	50.9	875	5.30	1	0.6	47	11	6.7	29	185	40.8
Vick, Michael, Atlanta	387	214	55.3	2412	6.23	15	3.9	58	13	3.4	33	201	73.1
Wallace, Seneca, Seattle	25	13	52.0	173	6.92	1	4.0	42	1	4.0	3	20	70.9
Warner, Kurt, Arizona	375	242	64.5	2713	7.23	11	2.9	63	9	2.4	23	158	85.8
Weinke, Chris, Carolina	13	7	53.8	64	4.92	1	7.7	18	0	0.0	0	0	93.1
Westbrook, Brian, Philadelphia	0	0	...	0	...	0	...	...	0	...	1	3	...

t—touchdown.

RECEIVING

BESTS OF THE SEASON

Receptions, season
NFC: 103—Larry Fitzgerald, Arizona; Steve Smith, Carolina.
AFC: 97—Chad Johnson, Cincinnati.

Receptions, game
AFC: 15—Chris Chambers, Miami vs. Buffalo, Dec. 4 (238 yards, 1 TD).
NFC: 14—Steve Smith, Carolina at Chicago, Nov. 20 (169 yards).

Yards, season
NFC: 1563—Steve Smith, Carolina.
AFC: 1432—Chad Johnson, Cincinnati.

Yards, game
AFC: 238—Chris Chambers, Miami vs. Buffalo, Dec. 4 (15 receptions, 1 TD).
NFC: 204—Plaxico Burress, N.Y. Giants vs. St. Louis, Oct. 2 (10 receptions, 2 TDs).

Longest gain
NFC: 91—Terrell Owens, (from Donovan McNabb), Philadelphia at Denver, Oct. 30 (TD).
AFC: 85—Hines Ward, (from Ben Roethlisberger), Pittsburgh vs. New England, Sep. 25 (TD).

Yards per reception, season
AFC: 18.3—Ashley Lelie, Denver.
NFC: 18.3—Terry Glenn, Dallas.

Touchdowns, season
AFC: 12—Marvin Harrison, Indianapolis.
NFC: 12—Steve Smith, Carolina.

Team leaders, receptions

AFC:

Team	No.	Player
Baltimore	86	Derrick Mason
Buffalo	81	Eric Moulds
Cincinnati	97	Chad Johnson
Cleveland	69	Antonio Bryant
Denver	85	Rod Smith
Houston	63	Andre Johnson
Indianapolis	83	Reggie Wayne
Jacksonville	70	Jimmy Smith
Kansas City	78	Tony Gonzalez
Miami	82	Chris Chambers
N.Y. Jets	73	Laveranues Coles
New England	78	Deion Branch
Oakland	76	Jerry Porter
Pittsburgh	69	Hines Ward
San Diego	89	Antonio Gates
Tennessee	58	Drew Bennett

NFC:

Team	No.	Player
Arizona	103	Larry Fitzgerald
Atlanta	65	Alge Crumpler
Carolina	103	Steve Smith
Chicago	64	Muhsin Muhammad
Dallas	71	Keyshawn Johnson
Detroit	46	Marcus Pollard
Green Bay	86	Donald Driver
Minnesota	69	Jermaine Wiggins
N.Y. Giants	76	Plaxico Burress
New Orleans	70	Donte' Stallworth
Philadelphia	61	Brian Westbrook / L.J. Smith
San Francisco	48	Brandon Lloyd
Seattle	67	Bobby Engram
St. Louis	102	Torry Holt
Tampa Bay	83	Joey Galloway
Washington	84	Santana Moss

NFL LEADERS

Player, team	No.	Yds.	Avg.	Long	TD
Smith, Steve, Carolina	103	1563	15.2	t80	12
Fitzgerald, Larry, Arizona	103	1409	13.7	47	10
Boldin, Anquan, Arizona	102	1402	13.7	t54	7
Holt, Torry, St. Louis	102	1331	13.0	44	9
Johnson, Chad, Cincinnati*	97	1432	14.8	t70	9
Gates, Antonio, San Diego*	89	1101	12.4	38	10
Driver, Donald, Green Bay	86	1221	14.2	59	5
Mason, Derrick, Baltimore*	86	1073	12.5	t39	3
Smith, Rod, Denver*	85	1105	13.0	72	6
Moss, Santana, Washington	84	1483	17.7	t78	9
Galloway, Joey, Tampa Bay	83	1287	15.5	t80	10
Wayne, Reggie, Indianapolis*	83	1055	12.7	t66	5
Harrison, Marvin, Indianapolis*	82	1146	14.0	t80	12
Chambers, Chris, Miami*	82	1118	13.6	t77	11
Moulds, Eric, Buffalo*	81	816	10.1	t55	4
Branch, Deion, New England*	78	998	12.8	51	5
Houshmandzadeh, T.J., Cincinnati*	78	956	12.3	t43	7
Gonzalez, Tony, Kansas City*	78	905	11.6	39	2
Burress, Plaxico, N.Y. Giants	76	1214	16.0	t78	7
Porter, Jerry, Oakland*	76	942	12.4	t49	5
Heap, Todd, Baltimore*	75	855	11.4	48	7
Coles, Laveranues, N.Y. Jets*	73	845	11.6	43	5
Johnson, Keyshawn, Dallas	71	839	11.8	34	6
Cooley, Chris, Washington	71	774	10.9	32	7
Smith, Jimmy, Jacksonville*	70	1023	14.6	t45	6
Stallworth, Donte', New Orleans	70	945	13.5	43	7
McCardell, Keenan, San Diego*	70	917	13.1	54	9
Jordan, LaMont, Oakland*	70	563	8.0	28	2
Bryant, Antonio, Cleveland*	69	1009	14.6	54	4
Ward, Hines, Pittsburgh*	69	975	14.1	t85	11

*AFC.

t—touchdown.

Leader based on most passes caught.

AFC

Player, team	No.	Yds.	Avg.	Long	TD
Adams, Charlie, Denver	21	203	9.7	21	0
Aiken, Sam, Buffalo	4	57	14.3	22	0
Alexander, Stephen, Denver	21	170	8.1	15	1
Anderson, Courtney, Oakland	24	303	12.6	36	3
Anderson, Mike, Denver	18	212	11.8	t66	1
Armstrong, Derick, Houston	9	115	12.8	28	0
Ashworth, Tom, New England	1	1	1.0	t1	1
Askew, B.J., N.Y. Jets	1	11	11.0	11	0
Baker, Chris, N.Y. Jets	18	269	14.9	47	1
Bell, Tatum, Denver	18	104	5.8	14	0
Bennett, Drew, Tennessee	58	738	12.7	t55	4
Bettis, Jerome, Pittsburgh	4	40	10.0	16	0
Blaylock, Derrick, N.Y. Jets	3	17	5.7	10	0
Boerigter, Marc, Kansas City	8	119	14.9	38	0
Booker, Marty, Miami	39	686	17.6	t60	3
Boston, David, Miami	4	80	20.0	54	0
Bradford, Corey, Houston	34	436	12.8	t50	5
Brady, Kyle, Jacksonville	18	157	8.7	33	1
Branch, Deion, New England	78	998	12.8	51	5
Brown, Chris, Tennessee	25	327	13.1	57	2
Brown, Dee, Kansas City	3	23	7.7	9	1
Brown, Ronnie, Miami	32	232	7.3	38	1
Brown, Troy, New England	39	466	11.9	71	2
Bruener, Mark, Houston	2	22	11.0	19	0
Bryant, Antonio, Cleveland	69	1009	14.6	54	4
Burns, Joe, Buffalo	1	19	19.0	t19	1
Caldwell, Reche, San Diego	28	352	12.6	43	1

Player, team	No.	Yds.	Avg.	Long	TD	Player, team	No.	Yds.	Avg.	Long	TD
Calico, Tyrone, Tennessee	22	191	8.7	18	0	Johnson, Kyle, Denver	17	160	9.4	33	5
Campbell, Mark, Buffalo	19	139	7.3	27	0	Johnson, Larry, Kansas City	33	343	10.4	36	1
Carswell, Dwayne, Denver	2	3	1.5	t2	2	Johnson, Patrick, Baltimore	2	31	15.5	19	0
Carthon, Ran, Indianapolis	1	10	10.0	10	0	Johnson, Rudi, Cincinnati	23	90	3.9	15	0
Chambers, Chris, Miami	82	1118	13.6	t77	11	Jolley, Doug, N.Y. Jets	29	324	11.2	t60	1
Childress, Brandon, New England	3	32	10.7	21	0	Jones, Brandon, Tennessee	23	299	13.0	t38	2
Chrebet, Wayne, N.Y. Jets	15	153	10.2	20	0	Jones, Brian, Jacksonville	3	49	16.3	41	0
Clark, Dallas, Indianapolis	37	488	13.2	56	4	Jones, Greg, Jacksonville	10	65	6.5	10	0
Clayton, Mark, Baltimore	44	471	10.7	t47	2	Jones, Matt, Jacksonville	36	432	12.0	42	5
Coles, Laveranues, N.Y. Jets	73	845	11.6	43	5	Jordan, LaMont, Oakland	70	563	8.0	28	2
Cotchery, Jerricho, N.Y. Jets	19	251	13.2	45	0	Kelly, Reggie, Cincinnati	15	90	6.0	16	1
Cribbs, Joshua, Cleveland	1	7	7.0	7	0	Kennison, Eddie, Kansas City	68	1102	16.2	55	5
Crockett, Zack, Oakland	13	111	8.5	23	0	Kinney, Erron, Tennessee	55	543	9.9	27	2
Cruz, Ronnie, Kansas City	1	15	15.0	15	0	Kranchick, Matt, Pittsburgh	1	6	6.0	6	0
Curry, Ronald, Oakland	2	12	6.0	8	0	Kreider, Dan, Pittsburgh	7	43	6.1	9	0
Davis, Andre', New England	9	190	21.1	t60	1	Lelie, Ashley, Denver	42	770	18.3	56	1
Davis, Domanick, Houston	39	337	8.6	33	4	Lewis, Jamal, Baltimore	32	191	6.0	t15	1
Dayne, Ron, Denver	3	17	5.7	7	0	Manuwai, Vince, Jacksonville	1	-1	-1.0	-1	0
Devoe, Todd, Denver	9	87	9.7	t44	1	Martin, Curtis, N.Y. Jets	24	118	4.9	14	0
Diamond, Lorenzo, Miami	8	54	6.8	18	0	Mason, Derrick, Baltimore	86	1073	12.5	t39	3
Dillon, Corey, New England	22	181	8.2	25	1	Mathis, Jerome, Houston	5	65	13.0	t34	1
Dinkins, Darnell, Baltimore	6	55	9.2	15	0	McCardell, Keenan, San Diego	70	917	13.1	54	9
Dreessen, Joel, N.Y. Jets	5	41	8.2	17	0	McCareins, Justin, N.Y. Jets	43	713	16.6	45	2
Droughns, Reuben, Cleveland	39	369	9.5	51	0	McGahee, Willis, Buffalo	28	178	6.4	19	0
Duke, Wesley, Denver	2	22	11.0	21	1	McMichael, Randy, Miami	60	582	9.7	t30	5
Dunn, Jason, Kansas City	5	53	10.6	24	0	Miller, Heath, Pittsburgh	39	459	11.8	50	6
Dwight, Tim, New England	19	332	17.5	59	3	Minor, Travis, Miami	1	0	0.0	0	0
Edwards, Braylon, Cleveland	32	512	16.0	t80	3	Moore, Clarence, Baltimore	3	59	19.7	24	0
Euhus, Tim, Buffalo	3	17	5.7	9	0	Moorehead, Aaron, Indianapolis	7	75	10.7	24	0
Evans, Heath, Mia.-N.E.*	14	105	7.5	19	0	Morency, Vernand, Houston	10	87	8.7	16	0
Evans, Lee, Buffalo	48	743	15.5	65	7	Morgan, Donovan, Houston	4	42	10.5	14	0
Faine, Jeff, Cleveland	1	-1	-1.0	-1	0	Morgan, Quincy, Pittsburgh	9	150	16.7	t31	2
Fargas, Justin, Oakland	1	9	9.0	9	0	Morris, Sammy, Miami	8	54	6.8	18	0
Faulk, Kevin, New England	29	260	9.0	23	0	Moss, Randy, Oakland	60	1005	16.8	79	8
Fauria, Christian, New England	8	57	7.1	18	2	Moulds, Eric, Buffalo	81	816	10.1	t55	4
Fleming, Troy, Tennessee	10	69	6.9	18	1	Mughelli, Ovie, Baltimore	3	13	4.3	6	0
Fletcher, Bryan, Indianapolis	18	202	11.2	23	3	Mungro, James, Indianapolis	3	28	9.3	17	0
Foschi, John Paul, Oakland	6	37	6.2	11	0	Murphy, Matt, Houston	2	26	13.0	14	0
Gabriel, Doug, Oakland	37	554	15.0	38	3	Nash, Damien, Tennessee	3	14	4.7	7	0
Gaffney, Jabar, Houston	55	492	8.9	29	2	Neal, Lorenzo, San Diego	24	145	6.0	21	1
Gates, Antonio, San Diego	89	1101	12.4	38	10	Neufeld, Ryan, Buffalo	1	9	9.0	9	0
Gilmore, Bryan, Miami	5	105	21.0	t44	1	Nickey, Donnie, Tennessee	1	26	26.0	26	0
Givens, David, New England	59	738	12.5	40	2	Norris, Moran, Houston	1	4	4.0	t4	1
Gonzalez, Tony, Kansas City	78	905	11.6	39	2	Northcutt, Dennis, Cleveland	42	441	10.5	t58	2
Graham, Daniel, New England	16	235	14.7	t45	3	Osgood, Kassim, San Diego	2	21	10.5	15	0
Green, Justin, Baltimore	7	32	4.6	8	0	Parker, Eric, San Diego	57	725	12.7	49	3
Green, William, Cleveland	5	30	6.0	14	0	Parker, Samie, Kansas City	36	533	14.8	49	3
Guenther, Gregg, Tennessee	2	13	6.5	8	0	Parker, Willie, Pittsburgh	18	218	12.1	48	1
Hall, Dante, Kansas City	34	436	12.8	t52	3	Parrish, Roscoe, Buffalo	15	148	9.9	28	1
Hankton, Cortez, Jacksonville	3	15	5.0	8	0	Pass, Patrick, New England	22	227	10.3	39	0
Harrison, Marvin, Indianapolis	82	1146	14.0	t80	12	Payton, Jarrett, Tennessee	6	30	5.0	9	0
Hartsock, Ben, Indianapolis	2	8	4.0	7	0	Pearman, Alvin, Jacksonville	32	240	7.5	19	0
Haynes, Verron, Pittsburgh	11	113	10.3	18	0	Peelle, Justin, San Diego	11	38	3.5	11	1
Heap, Todd, Baltimore	75	855	11.4	48	7	Perry, Chris, Cincinnati	51	328	6.4	28	2
Heiden, Steve, Cleveland	43	401	9.3	t62	3	Perry, Tab, Cincinnati	4	21	5.3	13	1
Heller, Will, Miami	1	1	1.0	t1	1	Peters, Jason, Buffalo	2	5	2.5	4	1
Henry, Chris, Cincinnati	31	422	13.6	47	6	Porter, Jerry, Oakland	76	942	12.4	t49	5
Henry, Travis, Tennessee	13	117	9.0	42	0	Putzier, Jeb, Denver	37	481	13.0	32	0
Holmes, Alex, Miami	1	2	2.0	2	0	Randle El, Antwaan, Pittsburgh	35	558	15.9	t63	1
Holmes, Priest, Kansas City	21	197	9.4	t60	1	Reed, Josh, Buffalo	32	449	14.0	t51	2
Horn, Chris, Kansas City	18	187	10.4	50	0	Rhodes, Dominic, Indianapolis	12	88	7.3	15	0
Houshmandzadeh, T.J., Cincinnati	78	956	12.3	t43	7	Ricard, Alan, Baltimore	2	18	9.0	11	0
Houston, Cedric, N.Y. Jets	8	66	8.3	16	0	Richardson, Tony, Kansas City	9	68	7.6	22	1
Hymes, Randy, Baltimore	11	132	12.0	21	2	Ridgeway, Dante, N.Y. Jets	2	26	13.0	17	0
Irons, Paul, Cleveland	2	16	8.0	14	0	Rivers, Marcellus, Houston	24	168	7.0	20	0
Jackson, Frisman, Cleveland	24	287	12.0	t68	1	Roby, Courtney, Tennessee	21	289	13.8	32	1
Jackson, Vincent, San Diego	3	59	19.7	21	0	Roos, Michael, Tennessee	1	-7	-7.0	-7	0
James, Edgerrin, Indianapolis	44	337	7.7	20	1	Sapp, Cecil, Denver	2	17	8.5	12	0
Johnson, Andre, Houston	63	688	10.9	t53	2	Scaife, Bo, Tennessee	37	273	7.4	19	2
Johnson, Bethel, New England	4	67	16.8	t55	1	Schobel, Matt, Cincinnati	18	193	10.7	28	1
Johnson, Chad, Cincinnati	97	1432	14.8	t70	9	Shea, Aaron, Cleveland	18	153	8.5	27	1
Johnson, Jeremi, Cincinnati	12	65	5.4	t27	3	Shelton, Daimon, Buffalo	13	98	7.5	21	1

Player, team	No.	Yds.	Avg.	Long	TD
Small, O.J., Tennessee	1	6	6.0	6	0
Smith, Jimmy, Jacksonville	70	1023	14.6	t45	6
Smith, Jonathan, Buffalo	5	56	11.2	19	1
Smith, Musa, Baltimore	3	5	1.7	4	0
Smith, Rod, Denver	85	1105	13.0	72	6
Smith, Terrelle, Cleveland	12	58	4.8	9	1
Sowell, Jerald, N.Y. Jets	28	155	5.5	28	2
Sproles, Darren, San Diego	3	10	3.3	6	0
Staley, Duce, Pittsburgh	6	34	5.7	9	0
Stewart, Tony, Cincinnati	4	26	6.5	10	0
Stokley, Brandon, Indianapolis	41	543	13.2	45	1
Suggs, Lee, Cleveland	6	26	4.3	8	0
Taylor, Chester, Baltimore	41	292	7.1	20	1
Taylor, Fred, Jacksonville	13	83	6.4	13	0
Toefield, LaBrandon, Jacksonville..	3	17	5.7	11	0
Tomlinson, LaDainian, San Diego..	51	370	7.3	41	2
Troupe, Ben, Tennessee	55	530	9.6	35	4
Tuman, Jerame, Pittsburgh	3	57	19.0	27	0
Utecht, Ben, Indianapolis	3	59	19.7	t26	2
Vrabel, Mike, New England	3	4	1.3	t2	3
Wade, Bobby, Chi.-Ten.*	14	120	8.6	17	0
Walter, Kevin, Cincinnati	19	211	11.1	33	1
Walters, Troy, Indianapolis	14	152	10.9	39	3
Ward, Hines, Pittsburgh	69	975	14.1	t85	11
Washington, Kelley, Cincinnati	10	101	10.1	t18	1
Watson, Ben, New England	29	441	15.2	35	4
Watts, Darius, Denver	2	22	11.0	12	0
Wayne, Reggie, Indianapolis	83	1055	12.7	t66	5
Welker, Wes, Miami	29	434	15.0	47	0
Wells, Jonathan, Houston	22	179	8.1	20	0
Whitted, Alvis, Oakland	14	183	13.1	26	0
Wilcox, Daniel, Baltimore	20	154	7.7	t17	1
Wilford, Ernest, Jacksonville	41	681	16.6	39	7
Williams, Randal, Oakland	13	164	12.6	34	0
Williams, Reggie, Jacksonville	35	445	12.7	41	0
Williams, Ricky, Miami	17	93	5.5	19	0
Williams, Roydell, Tennessee	21	299	14.2	t50	2
Williams, Shaud, Buffalo	17	118	6.9	23	0
Wilson, Cedrick, Pittsburgh	26	451	17.3	46	0
Wilson, Kris, Kansas City	3	33	11.0	16	0
Wimbush, Derrick, Jacksonville	5	26	5.2	6	0
Wrighster, George, Jacksonville	13	120	9.2	27	2
Wright, Jason, Cleveland	3	15	5.0	15	0
Zereoue, Amos, New England	1	5	5.0	5	0

*Includes both NFC and AFC statistics.
t—touchdown.

NFC

Player, team	No.	Yds.	Avg.	Long	TD
Alexander, Shaun, Seattle	15	78	5.2	9	1
Alstott, Mike, Tampa Bay	25	222	8.9	24	1
Angulo, Richard, Minnesota	1	11	11.0	11	0
Arrington, J.J., Arizona	25	139	5.6	15	0
Ayanbadejo, Obafemi, Arizona	34	231	6.8	18	0
Bajema, Billy, San Francisco	5	54	10.8	24	0
Barber, Marion, Dallas	18	115	6.4	21	0
Barber, Tiki, N.Y. Giants	54	530	9.8	48	2
Barlow, Kevan, San Francisco	31	241	7.8	24	0
Bartrum, Mike, Philadelphia	2	6	3.0	t3	2
Battle, Arnaz, San Francisco	32	363	11.3	39	3
Baxter, Jarrod, Arizona	1	4	4.0	4	0
Beasley, Fred, San Francisco	2	12	6.0	6	0
Becht, Anthony, Tampa Bay	16	112	7.0	17	0
Bennett, Michael, Minnesota	27	124	4.6	20	2
Benson, Cedric, Chicago	1	3	3.0	3	0
Bergen, Adam, Arizona	28	270	9.6	32	1
Berlin, Eddie, Chicago	2	9	4.5	9	0
Berrian, Bernard, Chicago	13	246	18.9	54	0
Berton, Sean, N.Y. Giants	1	3	3.0	3	0
Betts, Ladell, Washington	10	78	7.8	26	1
Blakley, Dwayne, Atlanta	4	30	7.5	10	1

Player, team	No.	Yds.	Avg.	Long	TD
Boldin, Anquan, Arizona	102	1402	13.7	t54	7
Bradley, Mark, Chicago	18	230	12.8	54	0
Brown, Reggie, Philadelphia	43	571	13.3	t56	4
Bruce, Isaac, St. Louis	36	525	14.6	t46	3
Bryson, Shawn, Detroit	37	284	7.7	63	0
Bulger, Marc, St. Louis	1	1	1.0	1	0
Burleson, Nate, Minnesota	30	328	10.9	20	1
Burress, Plaxico, N.Y. Giants	76	1214	16.0	t78	7
Bush, Steve, San Francisco	3	21	7.0	10	0
Campbell, Dan, Dallas	3	24	8.0	18	1
Carter, Drew, Carolina	5	103	20.6	40	1
Carter, Tim, N.Y. Giants	10	186	18.6	44	0
Cartwright, Rock, Washington	2	23	11.5	17	0
Cason, Aveion, St. Louis	1	11	11.0	11	0
Chatman, Antonio, Green Bay	49	549	11.2	25	4
Clark, Desmond, Chicago	24	229	9.5	31	2
Clayton, Michael, Tampa Bay	32	372	11.6	41	0
Cleeland, Cam, St. Louis	5	17	3.4	t9	1
Colbert, Keary, Carolina	25	282	11.3	42	2
Conwell, Ernie, New Orleans	13	165	12.7	31	1
Cook, Jameel, Tampa Bay	7	43	6.1	11	1
Cooley, Chris, Washington	71	774	10.9	32	7
Copper, Terrance, Dallas	1	5	5.0	5	0
Crayton, Patrick, Dallas	22	341	15.5	t63	2
Crumpler, Alge, Atlanta	65	877	13.5	48	5
Curtis, Kevin, St. Louis	60	801	13.4	t83	6
Davenport, Najeh, Green Bay	2	3	1.5	2	0
Davis, Stephen, Carolina	5	45	9.0	21	0
Driver, Donald, Green Bay	86	1221	14.2	59	5
Duckett, T.J., Atlanta	6	63	10.5	19	0
Dunn, Warrick, Atlanta	29	220	7.6	24	1
Edwards, Eric, Arizona	12	133	11.1	63	1
Edwards, Marc, Chicago	10	66	6.6	13	2
Edwards, Troy, Detroit	2	15	7.5	8	0
Engram, Bobby, Seattle	67	778	11.6	56	3
Farris, Jimmy, Washington	1	18	18.0	18	0
Faulk, Marshall, St. Louis	44	291	6.6	18	1
Ferguson, Robert, Green Bay	27	366	13.6	51	3
Finn, Jim, N.Y. Giants	13	98	7.5	15	0
Finneran, Brian, Atlanta	50	611	12.2	53	2
Fisher, Tony, Green Bay	48	347	7.2	15	1
Fitzgerald, Larry, Arizona	103	1409	13.7	47	10
FitzSimmons, Casey, Detroit	10	45	4.5	11	1
Foster, DeShaun, Carolina	34	372	10.9	47	1
Franks, Bubba, Green Bay	25	207	8.3	24	1
Gado, Samkon, Green Bay	10	77	7.7	30	1
Gage, Justin, Chicago	31	346	11.2	25	2
Gaines, Michael, Carolina	12	155	12.9	38	2
Galloway, Joey, Tampa Bay	83	1287	15.5	t80	10
Gardner, Rod, Car.-G.B.*	13	151	11.6	33	1
Gilmore, John, Chicago	1	1	1.0	t1	1
Glenn, Terry, Dallas	62	1136	18.3	t71	7
Goings, Nick, Carolina	14	151	10.8	30	0
Gordon, Lamar, Philadelphia	11	79	7.2	18	0
Gore, Frank, San Francisco	15	131	8.7	47	0
Green, Ahman, Green Bay	19	147	7.7	20	0
Griffith, Justin, Atlanta	21	111	5.3	17	3
Hackett, D.J., Seattle	28	400	14.3	47	2
Hakim, Az-Zahir, New Orleans	34	489	14.4	42	2
Hall, Lamont, New Orleans	6	36	6.0	8	0
Hannam, Ryan, Seattle	13	89	6.8	20	1
Harrington, Joey, Detroit	1	-4	-4.0	-4	0
Harris, Arlen, St. Louis	4	34	8.5	17	0
Hedgecock, Madison, St. Louis	9	69	7.7	15	0
Henderson, Devery, New Orleans	22	343	15.6	66	3
Henderson, William, Green Bay	30	264	8.8	32	0
Hetherington, Chris, San Francisco	5	26	5.2	11	0
Hicks, Maurice, San Francisco	12	47	3.9	11	0
Hilliard, Ike, Tampa Bay	35	282	8.1	22	1
Hilton, Zachary, New Orleans	35	396	11.3	29	1
Holt, Torry, St. Louis	102	1331	13.0	44	9
Hoover, Brad, Carolina	14	87	6.2	12	0

Player, team	No.	Yds.	Avg.	Long	TD
orn, Joe, New Orleans	49	654	13.3	30	1
ackson, Darrell, Seattle	38	482	12.7	48	3
ackson, James, Arizona	2	31	15.5	19	0
ackson, Steven, St. Louis	43	320	7.4	27	2
ackson, Terry, San Francisco	10	67	6.7	12	0
acobs, Taylor, Washington	11	100	9.1	24	0
enkins, Michael, Atlanta	36	508	14.1	58	3
ohnson, Bryan, Chicago	5	15	3.0	7	0
ohnson, Bryant, Arizona	40	432	10.8	41	1
ohnson, Kevin, Detroit	17	133	7.8	25	0
ohnson, Keyshawn, Dallas	71	839	11.8	34	6
ohnson, Robert, Washington	1	14	14.0	14	0
ohnson, Teyo, Arizona	3	29	9.7	13	0
ones, Julius, Dallas	35	218	6.2	26	0
ones, Kevin, Detroit	20	109	5.5	28	0
ones, Terry, San Francisco	9	76	8.4	21	0
ones, Thomas, Chicago	26	143	5.5	41	0
urevicius, Joe, Seattle	55	694	12.6	52	10
arney, Mike, New Orleans	10	61	6.1	10	0
leinsasser, Jim, Minnesota	22	171	7.8	15	0
ozlowski, Brian, Washington	2	26	13.0	18	0
each, Vonta, Green Bay	5	19	3.8	9	0
ee, Charles, Arizona	11	152	13.8	49	0
ee, Donald, Green Bay	33	294	8.9	27	2
ee, ReShard, Green Bay	1	5	5.0	5	0
ewis, Chad, Philadelphia	5	64	12.8	17	0
ewis, Greg, Philadelphia	48	561	11.7	34	1
loyd, Brandon, San Francisco	48	733	15.3	t89	5
ooker, Dane, St. Louis	23	237	10.3	23	0
ahe, Reno, Philadelphia	12	68	5.7	12	0
angum, Kris, Carolina	23	202	8.8	24	2
anumaleuna, Brandon, St. Louis	13	129	9.9	33	1
arshall, Rasheed, San Francisco.	1	-1	-1.0	-1	0
artin, David, Green Bay	27	224	8.3	t21	3
artinez, Glenn, Detroit	1	11	11.0	11	0
cAddley, Jason, San Francisco	7	125	17.9	38	0
cAllister, Deuce, New Orleans	17	117	6.9	22	0
cCants, Darnerien, Philadelphia..	5	87	17.4	22	0
cCoy, LeRon, Arizona	18	191	10.6	24	1
cCrary, Fred, Atlanta	3	12	4.0	11	0
cDonald, Shaun, St. Louis	46	523	11.4	31	0
cKie, Jason, Chicago	4	15	3.8	11	0
cMullen, Billy, Philadelphia	18	268	14.9	38	1
oats, Ryan, Philadelphia	4	7	1.8	9	0
oore, Dave, Tampa Bay	1	5	5.0	5	0
oore, Mewelde, Minnesota	37	339	9.2	29	2
orris, Maurice, Seattle	5	48	9.6	20	0
orton, Johnnie, San Francisco	21	288	13.7	30	0
oss, Santana, Washington	84	1483	17.7	t78	9
uhammad, Muhsin, Chicago	64	750	11.7	33	4
urphy, Terrence, Green Bay	5	36	7.2	12	0
ewhouse, Reggie, Arizona	4	45	11.3	17	0
wens, Richard, Minnesota	2	18	9.0	12	0
wens, Terrell, Philadelphia	47	763	16.2	t91	6
arry, Josh, Philadelphia	13	89	6.8	13	0
athon, Jerome, Atlanta	1	18	18.0	18	0
atten, David, Washington	22	217	9.9	32	0
eterson, Adrian, Chicago	7	48	6.9	18	0
ierce, Brett, Dallas	2	15	7.5	10	0
inner, Artose, Detroit	21	181	8.6	24	0
ittman, Michael, Tampa Bay	36	300	8.3	t41	1
olite, Lousaka, Dallas	9	72	8.0	15	1
ollard, Marcus, Detroit	46	516	11.2	86	3
oole, Nate, New Orleans	3	63	21.0	42	0
ortis, Clinton, Washington	30	216	7.2	23	0
rice, Peerless, Dallas	6	96	16.0	58	0
roehl, Ricky, Carolina	25	441	17.6	69	4
eid, Gabe, Chicago	3	20	6.7	10	0
obinson, Jeff, St. Louis	1	28	28.0	28	0
obinson, Koren, Minnesota	22	347	15.8	t80	1
obinson, Marcus, Minnesota	31	515	16.6	68	5
ogers, Charles, Detroit	14	197	14.1	t35	1
Royal, Robert, Washington	18	131	7.3	29	1
Schlesinger, Cory, Detroit	8	31	3.9	8	1
Sellers, Mike, Washington	12	72	6.0	t19	7
Shepherd, Edell, Tampa Bay	6	103	17.2	46	1
Shiancoe, Visanthe, N.Y. Giants	8	91	11.4	17	0
Shipp, Marcel, Arizona	35	255	7.3	28	0
Shockey, Jeremy, N.Y. Giants	65	891	13.7	59	7
Simms, Chris, Tampa Bay	1	-3	-3.0	-3	0
Smith, Alex, Tampa Bay	41	367	9.0	24	2
Smith, Antowain, New Orleans	12	46	3.8	8	0
Smith, L.J., Philadelphia	61	682	11.2	48	3
Smith, Paul, Detroit	6	49	8.2	11	0
Smith, Steve, Carolina	103	1563	15.2	t80	12
Smith, Trent, San Francisco	3	7	2.3	6	0
Spach, Stephen, Philadelphia	7	42	6.0	8	0
Stallworth, Donte', New Orleans	70	945	13.5	43	7
Stecker, Aaron, New Orleans	35	281	8.0	41	0
Stevens, Jerramy, Seattle	45	554	12.3	t35	5
Strong, Mack, Seattle	22	166	7.5	27	0
Taylor, Travis, Minnesota	50	604	12.1	31	4
Thomas, Anthony, Dal.-N.O.*	4	13	3.3	6	0
Thompson, Dominique, St. Louis..	1	13	13.0	13	0
Thompson, Tyson, Dallas	3	16	5.3	8	0
Thrash, James, Washington	14	194	13.9	41	0
Thurman, Andrae, Green Bay	7	92	13.1	33	0
Toomer, Amani, N.Y. Giants	60	684	11.4	37	7
Tyree, David, N.Y. Giants	5	52	10.4	18	1
Urban, Jerheme, Seattle	7	151	21.6	46	0
Vick, Michael, Atlanta	1	-14	-14.0	-14	0
Vines, Scottie, Detroit	40	417	10.4	40	0
Walker, Javon, Green Bay	4	27	6.8	9	0
Ward, Derrick, N.Y. Giants	2	13	6.5	8	0
Warner, Kurt, Arizona	1	0	0.0	0	0
Warrick, Peter, Seattle	11	180	16.4	42	0
Weaver, Leonard, Seattle	1	12	12.0	12	0
Westbrook, Brian, Philadelphia	61	616	10.1	62	4
White, Dez, Atlanta	2	25	12.5	t14	1
White, Roddy, Atlanta	29	446	15.4	t54	3
Wiggins, Jermaine, Minnesota	69	568	8.2	24	1
Williams, Carnell, Tampa Bay	20	81	4.1	15	0
Williams, Mike, Detroit	29	350	12.1	49	1
Williams, Moe, Minnesota	8	52	6.5	25	0
Williams, Roland, St. Louis	3	21	7.0	12	0
Williams, Roy, Detroit	45	687	15.3	t51	8
Williams, Walt, Green Bay	1	19	19.0	19	0
Williamson, Troy, Minnesota	24	372	15.5	56	2
Witten, Jason, Dallas	66	757	11.5	34	6

t—touchdown.
*Includes both AFC and NFC statistics.

PLAYERS WITH TWO CLUBS

Player, team	No.	Yds.	Avg.	Long	TD
Evans, Heath, Miami	4	17	4.3	5	0
Evans, Heath, New England	10	88	8.8	19	0
Gardner, Rod, Carolina	9	84	9.3	15	1
Gardner, Rod, Green Bay	4	67	16.8	33	0
Thomas, Anthony, Dallas	2	5	2.5	5	0
Thomas, Anthony, New Orleans	2	8	4.0	6	0
Wade, Bobby, Chicago	10	80	8.0	17	0
Wade, Bobby, Tennessee	4	40	10.0	15	0

SCORING

TEAM
AFC

Team	Total TD	TD Rush	TD Pass	TD Misc.	XP	2Pt.	XPA	FG	FGA	Safeties	Total Pts.
Indianapolis	53	18	31	4	52	0	52	23	26	0	439
Cincinnati	48	15	32	1	47	1	47	28	32	0	421
San Diego	51	22	27	2	49	0	49	21	24	0	418
Kansas City	46	26	17	3	44	1	45	27	33	0	403
Denver	46	25	18	3	43	1	44	24	32	1	395
Pittsburgh	45	21	21	3	45	0	45	24	29	1	389
New England	46	16	28	2	41	1	42	20	25	0	379
Jacksonville	42	18	21	3	38	1	39	23	30	0	361
Miami	34	11	22	1	33	0	33	25	30	3	318
Tennessee	33	8	20	5	30	0	32	23	29	1	299
Oakland	33	11	21	1	30	1	30	20	30	0	290
Buffalo	26	6	18	2	26	0	26	29	35	1	271
Baltimore	25	5	17	3	23	1	23	30	35	0	265
Houston	26	9	15	2	24	1	24	26	34	0	260
N.Y. Jets	25	10	11	4	24	0	24	22	28	0	240
Cleveland	22	4	15	3	19	0	21	27	29	0	232
AFC total	601	225	334	42	568	8	576	392	481	7	5380
AFC average	37.6	14.1	20.9	2.6	35.5	0.5	36.0	24.5	30.1	0.4	336.3

NFC

Team	Total TD	TD Rush	TD Pass	TD Misc.	XP	2Pt.	XPA	FG	FGA	Safeties	Total Pts.
Seattle	57	29	25	3	56	0	57	18	25	0	452
N.Y. Giants	45	17	24	4	43	2	43	35	42	0	422
Carolina	45	17	25	3	43	0	44	26	34	0	391
St. Louis	40	13	23	4	36	2	36	27	31	1	363
Washington	44	15	25	4	42	1	42	17	21	0	359
Atlanta	39	17	19	3	35	4	35	24	27	1	351
Dallas	38	13	23	2	35	1	36	20	28	0	325
Arizona	26	2	21	3	20	3	21	43	45	0	311
Philadelphia	35	11	21	3	32	1	33	22	29	0	310
Minnesota	33	10	18	5	31	1	31	25	34	0	306
Tampa Bay	33	13	17	3	32	1	32	22	27	1	300
Green Bay	34	11	20	3	30	2	31	20	27	0	298
Chicago	28	11	11	6	26	0	27	22	31	0	260
Detroit	28	10	15	3	27	0	28	19	24	1	254
San Francisco	23	9	8	6	21	1	21	26	29	0	239
New Orleans	23	8	15	0	22	0	22	25	32	0	235
NFC total	571	206	310	55	531	19	539	391	486	4	5176
NFC average	35.7	12.9	19.4	3.4	33.2	1.2	33.7	24.4	30.4	0.3	323.5
NFL total	1172	431	644	97	1099	27	1115	783	967	11	10556
NFL average	36.6	13.5	20.1	3.0	34.3	0.8	34.8	24.5	30.2	0.3	329.9

INDIVIDUAL

BESTS OF THE SEASON

Points, season
NFC: 168—Shaun Alexander, Seattle.
AFC: 131—Shayne Graham, Cincinnati.
Touchdowns, season
NFC: 28—Shaun Alexander, Seattle.
AFC: 21—Larry Johnson, Kansas City.
Extra points, season
NFC: 56—Josh Brown, Seattle.
AFC: 52—Mike Vanderjagt, Indianapolis.
Field goals, season.
NFC: 40—Neil Rackers, Arizona.
AFC: 30—Matt Stover, Baltimore.
Field goal attempts, season
NFC: 42—Jay Feely, N.Y. Giants; Neil Rackers, Arizona.
AFC: 35—Rian Lindell, Buffalo.

Longest field goal
NFC: 58—Michael Koenen, Atlanta vs. New England, Oct. 9.
AFC: 53—Held by 5 players.
Most points, game ...
AFC: 24—LaDainian Tomlinson, San Diego at N.Y. Jets, Nov. 6.
NFC: 24—Shaun Alexander, Seattle vs. Arizona, Sep. 25; Shaun Alexander, Seattle vs. Houston, Oct. 16.
Team leaders, points
AFC:

Baltimore	113	Matt Stover
Buffalo	113	Rian Lindell
Cincinnati	131	Shayne Graham
Cleveland	100	Phil Dawson
Denver	115	Jason Elam
Houston	102	Kris Brown
Indianapolis	121	Mike Vanderjagt
Jacksonville	107	Josh Scobee

Kansas City	126	Larry Johnson
Miami	108	Olindo Mare
N.Y. Jets	90	Mike Nugent
New England	100	Adam Vinatieri
Oakland	90	SebastianJanikowski
Pittsburgh	117	Jeff Reed
San Diego	120	LaDainianTomlinson
Tennessee	99	Rob Bironas

NFC:

Arizona	140	Neil Rackers
Atlanta	104	Todd Peterson
Carolina	121	John Kasay
Chicago	82	Robbie Gould
Dallas	48	Terry Glenn
Detroit	84	Jason Hanson
Green Bay	90	Ryan Longwell
Minnesota	106	Paul Edinger
N.Y. Giants	148	Jay Feely
New Orleans	97	John Carney
Philadelphia	71	David Akers
San Francisco	97	Joe Nedney
Seattle	168	Shaun Alexander
St. Louis	117	Jeff Wilkins
Tampa Bay	94	Matt Bryant
Washington	68	Clinton Portis

NFL LEADERS

KICKERS

Player, team	XPM	XPA	FGM	FGA	Tot. Pts.
Feely, Jay, N.Y. Giants	43	43	35	42	148
Rackers, Neil, Arizona	20	20	40	42	140
Graham, Shayne, Cincinnati*	47	47	28	32	131
Tynes, Lawrence, Kansas City*	44	45	27	33	125
Kasay, John, Carolina	43	44	26	34	121
Vanderjagt, Mike, Indianapolis*	52	52	23	25	121
Wilkins, Jeff, St. Louis	36	36	27	31	117
Reed, Jeff, Pittsburgh*	45	45	24	29	117
Elam, Jason, Denver*	43	44	24	32	115
Stover, Matt, Baltimore*	23	23	30	34	113
Lindell, Rian, Buffalo*	26	26	29	35	113
Kaeding, Nate, San Diego*	49	49	21	24	112
Brown, Josh, Seattle	56	57	18	25	110
Mare, Olindo, Miami*	33	33	25	30	108
Scobee, Josh, Jacksonville*	38	39	23	30	107

Player, team	XPM	XPA	FGM	FGA	Tot. Pts.
Edinger, Paul, Minnesota	31	31	25	34	106
Peterson, Todd, Atlanta	35	35	23	25	104
Brown, Kris, Houston*	24	24	26	34	102
Vinatieri, Adam, New England*	40	41	20	25	100
Dawson, Phil, Cleveland*	19	21	27	29	100

*AFC.

NONKICKERS

Player, team	Tot. TD	RTD	PTD	MTD	2Pt.	Tot. Pts.
Alexander, Shaun, Seattle	28	27	1	0	0	168
Johnson, Larry, Kansas City*	21	20	1	0	0	126
Tomlinson, LaDainian, San Diego*	20	18	2	0	0	120
James, Edgerrin, Indianapolis*	14	13	1	0	0	84
Dillon, Corey, New England*	13	12	1	0	0	78
Anderson, Mike, Denver*	13	12	1	0	0	78
Smith, Steve, Carolina	13	1	12	0	0	78
Harrison, Marvin, Indianapolis*	12	0	12	0	0	72
Davis, Stephen, Carolina	12	12	0	0	0	72
Johnson, Rudi, Cincinnati*	12	12	0	0	0	72
Barber, Tiki, N.Y. Giants	11	9	2	0	1	68
Jordan, LaMont, Oakland*	11	9	2	0	1	68
Portis, Clinton, Washington	11	11	0	0	1	68
Ward, Hines, Pittsburgh*	11	0	11	0	0	66
Chambers, Chris, Miami*	11	0	11	0	0	66
Galloway, Joey, Tampa Bay	10	0	10	0	0	60
Jurevicius, Joe, Seattle	10	0	10	0	0	60
Gates, Antonio, San Diego*	10	0	10	0	0	60
Fitzgerald, Larry, Arizona	10	0	10	0	0	60
Jackson, Steven, St. Louis	10	8	2	0	0	60
McCardell, Keenan, San Diego*	9	0	9	0	0	54
Bettis, Jerome, Pittsburgh*	9	9	0	0	0	54
Holt, Torry, St. Louis	9	0	9	0	0	54
Jones, Thomas, Chicago	9	9	0	0	0	54
Moss, Santana, Washington	9	0	9	0	0	54
Johnson, Chad, Cincinnati*	9	0	9	0	0	54
Glenn, Terry, Dallas	8	1	7	0	0	48
Moss, Randy, Oakland*	8	0	8	0	0	48
Sellers, Mike, Washington	8	1	7	0	0	48
Houshmandzadeh, T.J., Cincinnati*	8	1	7	0	0	48

*AFC.

AFC

KICKERS

Player, team	XPM	XPA	FGM	FGA	Tot. Pts.
Bironas, Rob, Tennessee	30	32	23	29	99
Brown, Kris, Houston	24	24	26	34	102
Dawson, Phil, Cleveland	19	21	27	29	100
Elam, Jason, Denver	43	44	24	32	115
Flutie, Doug, New England	1	1	0	0	1
Graham, Shayne, Cincinnati	47	47	28	32	131
Janikowski, Sebastian, Oakland	30	30	20	30	90
Kaeding, Nate, San Diego	49	49	21	24	112
Lindell, Rian, Buffalo	26	26	29	35	113
Mare, Olindo, Miami	33	33	25	30	108
Nugent, Mike, N.Y. Jets	24	24	22	28	90
Reed, Jeff, Pittsburgh	45	45	24	29	117
Scobee, Josh, Jacksonville	38	39	23	30	107
Stover, Matt, Baltimore	23	23	30	34	113
Tynes, Lawrence, Kansas City	44	45	27	33	125
Vanderjagt, Mike, Indianapolis	52	52	23	25	121
Vinatieri, Adam, New England	40	41	20	25	100

NONKICKERS

Player, team	Tot. TD	RTD	PTD	MTD	2Pt.	Tot. Pts.
Alexander, Stephen, Denver	1	0	1	0	0	6
Anderson, Courtney, Oakland	3	0	3	0	0	18
Anderson, Mike, Denver	13	12	1	0	0	78
Ashworth, Tom, New England	1	0	1	0	0	6
Bailey, Champ, Denver	2	0	0	2	0	12
Baker, Chris, N.Y. Jets	1	0	1	0	0	6
Batch, Charlie, Pittsburgh	1	1	0	0	0	6
Bell, Tatum, Denver	8	8	0	0	0	48
Bennett, Drew, Tennessee	4	0	4	0	0	24
Bettis, Jerome, Pittsburgh	9	9	0	0	0	54
Bodden, Leigh, Cleveland	1	0	0	1	0	6
Boerigter, Marc, Kansas City	0	0	0	0	1	2
Boller, Kyle, Baltimore	1	1	0	0	0	6
Booker, Marty, Miami	3	0	3	0	0	18
Bradford, Corey, Houston	5	0	5	0	1	32
Brady, Kyle, Jacksonville	1	0	1	0	0	6
Brady, Tom, New England	1	1	0	0	0	6

Player, team	Tot. TD	RTD	PTD	MTD	2Pt.	Tot. Pts.
Branch, Deion, New England ..	5	0	5	0	0	30
Brees, Drew, San Diego	1	1	0	0	0	6
Brown, Chris, Tennessee	7	5	2	0	0	42
Brown, Dee, Kansas City	1	1	0	0	0	6
Brown, Mark, N.Y. Jets	1	0	0	1	0	6
Brown, Ronnie, Miami	5	4	1	0	0	30
Brown, Troy, New England	2	0	2	0	0	12
Bryant, Antonio, Cleveland.....	4	0	4	0	0	24
Burns, Joe, Buffalo	1	0	1	0	0	6
Caldwell, Reche, San Diego	1	0	1	0	0	6
Carr, David, Houston.............	1	1	0	0	0	6
Carswell, Dwayne, Denver	2	0	2	0	0	12
Carter, Kevin, Miami	0	0	0	0	0	*2
Carthon, Ran, Indianapolis	1	1	0	0	0	6
Chambers, Chris, Miami	11	0	11	0	0	66
Clark, Dallas, Indianapolis......	4	0	4	0	0	24
Clayton, Mark, Baltimore	3	1	2	0	0	18
Coles, Laveranues, N.Y. Jets...	5	0	5	0	0	30
Collins, Kerry, Oakland...........	1	1	0	0	0	6
Cooper, Jarrod, Oakland	1	0	0	1	0	6
Cribbs, Joshua, Cleveland.......	1	0	0	1	0	6
Crockett, Zack, Oakland	1	1	0	0	0	6
Davis, Andre', New England....	1	0	1	0	0	6
Davis, Domanick, Houston	6	2	4	0	0	36
Dayne, Ron, Denver................	1	1	0	0	0	6
Devoe, Todd, Denver.............	1	0	1	0	0	6
Dillon, Corey, New England.....	13	12	1	0	0	78
Droughns, Reuben, Cleveland.	2	2	0	0	0	12
Duke, Wesley, Denver.............	1	0	1	0	0	6
Dwight, Tim, New England	3	0	3	0	0	18
Edwards, Braylon, Cleveland...	3	0	3	0	0	18
Evans, Heath, New England	0	0	0	0	1	2
Evans, Lee, Buffalo	7	0	7	0	0	42
Fauria, Christian, New England	2	0	2	0	0	12
Fleming, Troy, Tennessee.......	1	0	1	0	0	6
Fletcher, Bryan, Indianapolis...	3	0	3	0	0	18
Fletcher, London, Buffalo........	0	0	0	0	0	*2
Flutie, Doug, New England......	0	0	0	0	0	1
Foote, Larry, Pittsburgh	0	0	0	0	0	*2
Frye, Charlie, Cleveland	1	1	0	0	0	6
Gabriel, Doug, Oakland	3	0	3	0	0	18
Gaffney, Jabar, Houston.........	2	0	2	0	0	12
Garrard, David, Jacksonville ...	3	3	0	0	1	20
Gates, Antonio, San Diego	10	0	10	0	0	60
Gilmore, Bryan, Miami...........	1	0	1	0	0	6
Givens, David, New England ...	2	0	2	0	0	12
Gonzalez, Tony, Kansas City ...	2	0	2	0	0	12
Graham, Daniel, New England	3	0	3	0	0	18
Green, Justin, Baltimore	0	0	0	0	1	2
Hall, Dante, Kansas City.........	4	0	3	1	0	24
Harrison, Marvin, Indianapolis	12	0	12	0	0	72
Hart, Clinton, San Diego	2	0	0	2	0	12
Haynes, Verron, Pittsburgh.....	3	3	0	0	0	18
Heap, Todd, Baltimore	7	0	7	0	0	42
Heiden, Steve, Cleveland........	3	0	3	0	0	18
Heller, Will, Miami	1	0	1	0	0	6
Henry, Chris, Cincinnati	6	0	6	0	0	36
Hill, Reynaldo, Tennessee	1	0	0	1	0	6
Holcomb, Kelly, Buffalo...........	1	1	0	0	0	6
Holmes, Priest, Kansas City....	7	6	1	0	0	42
Houshmandzadeh, T.J., Cincinnati	8	1	7	0	0	48
Houston, Cedric, N.Y. Jets......	2	2	0	0	0	12
Howard, Reggie, Miami	0	0	0	0	0	*2
Hymes, Randy, Baltimore	2	0	2	0	0	12
Jackson, Frisman, Cleveland...	1	0	1	0	0	6
James, Edgerrin, Indianapolis.	14	13	1	0	0	84
Johnson, Andre, Houston........	2	0	2	0	0	12
Johnson, Bethel, New England	1	0	1	0	0	6
Johnson, Chad, Cincinnati	9	0	9	0	0	54
Johnson, Jeremi, Cincinnati ...	3	0	3	0	0	18
Johnson, Kyle, Denver............	6	1	5	0	0	36
Johnson, Larry, Kansas City ...	21	20	1	0	0	126
Johnson, Rudi, Cincinnati.......	12	12	0	0	0	72
Jolley, Doug, N.Y. Jets	1	0	1	0	0	6
Jones, Brandon, Tennessee	2	0	2	0	0	12
Jones, Greg, Jacksonville	4	4	0	0	0	24
Jones, Matt, Jacksonville........	5	0	5	0	0	30
Jones, Pacman, Tennessee.....	1	0	0	1	0	6
Jordan, LaMont, Oakland........	11	9	2	0	1	68
June, Cato, Indianapolis.........	2	0	0	2	0	12
Kassell, Brad, Tennessee	1	0	0	1	0	6
Kelly, Reggie, Cincinnati	1	0	1	0	0	6
Kennison, Eddie, Kansas City .	5	0	5	0	0	30
Kinney, Erron, Tennessee........	2	0	2	0	0	12
Knight, Sammy, Kansas City...	1	0	0	1	0	6
Law, Ty, N.Y. Jets..................	1	0	0	1	0	6
Leftwich, Byron, Jacksonville .	2	2	0	0	0	12
Lelie, Ashley, Denver..............	1	0	1	0	0	6
Lewis, Jamal, Baltimore	4	3	1	0	0	24
Martin, Curtis, N.Y. Jets..........	5	5	0	0	0	30
Mason, Derrick, Baltimore	3	0	3	0	0	18
Mathis, Jerome, Houston	3	0	1	2	0	18
Mathis, Rashean, Jacksonville	1	0	0	1	0	6
McCardell, Keenan, San Diego	9	0	9	0	0	54
McCareins, Justin, N.Y. Jets ...	2	0	2	0	0	12
McGahee, Willis, Buffalo.........	5	5	0	0	0	30
McGee, Terrence, Buffalo........	2	0	0	2	0	12
McMichael, Randy, Miami	5	0	5	0	0	30
McNair, Steve, Tennessee.......	1	1	0	0	0	6
Miller, Heath, Pittsburgh	6	0	6	0	0	36
Miller, Justin, N.Y. Jets	1	0	0	1	0	6
Morency, Vernand, Houston ...	2	2	0	0	0	12
Morgan, Quincy, Pittsburgh....	2	0	2	0	0	12
Morris, Sammy, Miami...........	1	1	0	0	0	6
Moss, Randy, Oakland............	8	0	8	0	0	48
Moulds, Eric, Buffalo	4	0	4	0	0	24
Neal, Lorenzo, San Diego	1	0	1	0	0	6
Norris, Moran, Houston...........	1	0	1	0	0	6
Northcutt, Dennis, Cleveland ..	3	0	2	1	0	18
Odom, Antwan, Tennessee......	2	0	0	2	0	12
Palmer, Carson, Cincinnati......	1	1	0	0	0	6
Parker, Eric, San Diego	3	0	3	0	0	18
Parker, Samie, Kansas City	3	0	3	0	0	18
Parker, Willie, Pittsburgh	5	4	1	0	0	30
Parrish, Roscoe, Buffalo	1	0	1	0	0	6
Pass, Patrick, New England	3	0	3	0	0	18
Payton, Jarrett, Tennessee......	2	2	0	0	0	12
Pearman, Alvin, Jacksonville ..	1	1	0	0	0	6
Peelle, Justin, San Diego	1	0	1	0	0	6
Perry, Chris, Cincinnati	2	0	2	0	0	12
Perry, Tab, Cincinnati.............	2	1	1	0	0	12
Peters, Jason, Buffalo.............	1	0	1	0	0	6
Peterson, Mike, Jacksonville...	1	0	0	1	0	6
Plummer, Jake, Denver...........	2	2	0	0	0	12
Polamalu, Troy, Pittsburgh	1	0	0	1	0	6
Porter, Jerry, Oakland.............	5	0	5	0	0	30
Putzier, Jeb, Denver...............	0	0	0	0	1	2
Randle El, Antwaan, Pittsburgh	3	0	1	2	0	18
Reagor, Montae, Indianapolis .	1	0	0	1	0	6
Reed, James, N.Y. Jets	1	0	0	1	0	6
Reed, Josh, Buffalo	2	0	2	0	0	12
Reynolds, Robert, Tennessee .	0	0	0	0	0	*2
Rhodes, Dominic, Indianapolis	4	4	0	0	0	24
Richardson, Tony, Kansas City	1	0	1	0	0	6
Roby, Courtney, Tennessee.....	1	0	1	0	0	6
Roethlisberger, Ben, Pittsburgh	3	3	0	0	0	18
Sanders, James, New England	1	0	0	1	0	6
Scaife, Bo, Tennessee............	2	0	2	0	0	12
Schobel, Matt, Cincinnati........	1	0	1	0	1	8
Shea, Aaron, Cleveland...........	1	0	1	0	0	6
Shelton, Daimon, Buffalo........	1	0	1	0	0	6
Smith, Jimmy, Jacksonville	6	0	6	0	0	36
Smith, Jonathan, Buffalo	1	0	1	0	0	6

Player, team	Tot. TD	RTD	PTD	MTD	2Pt.	Tot. Pts.
Smith, Rod, Denver	6	0	6	0	0	36
Smith, Terrelle, Cleveland	1	0	1	0	0	6
Sowell, Jerald, N.Y. Jets	3	1	2	0	0	18
Staley, Duce, Pittsburgh	1	1	0	0	0	6
Stokley, Brandon, Indianapolis	1	0	1	0	0	6
Taylor, Chester, Baltimore	1	0	1	0	0	6
Taylor, Fred, Jacksonville	3	3	0	0	0	18
Taylor, Jason, Miami	1	0	0	1	0	*8
Testaverde, Vinny, N.Y. Jets	2	2	0	0	0	12
Thomas, Adalius, Baltimore	3	0	0	3	0	18
Thurman, Odell, Cincinnati	1	0	0	1	0	6
Toefield, LaBrandon, Jacksonville	4	4	0	0	0	24
Tomlinson, LaDainian, San Diego	20	18	2	0	0	120
Tripplett, Larry, Indianapolis	1	0	0	1	0	6
Troupe, Ben, Tennessee	4	0	4	0	0	24
Turner, Michael, San Diego	3	3	0	0	0	18
Utecht, Ben, Indianapolis	2	0	2	0	0	12
Van Pelt, Bradlee, Denver	1	1	0	0	0	6
Veal, Demetrin, Denver	0	0	0	0	0	*2
Vrabel, Mike, New England	4	0	3	1	0	24
Walter, Kevin, Cincinnati	1	0	1	0	0	6
Walters, Troy, Indianapolis	3	0	3	0	0	18
Ward, Hines, Pittsburgh	11	0	11	0	0	66
Warfield, Eric, Kansas City	1	0	0	1	0	6
Washington, Kelley, Cincinnati	1	0	1	0	0	6
Watson, Ben, New England	4	0	4	0	0	24
Wayne, Reggie, Indianapolis	5	0	5	0	0	30
Wells, Jonathan, Houston	4	4	0	0	0	24
Wilcox, Daniel, Baltimore	1	0	1	0	0	6
Wilford, Ernest, Jacksonville	7	0	7	0	0	42
Williams, Darrent, Denver	1	0	0	1	0	6
Williams, Ricky, Miami	6	6	0	0	0	36
Williams, Roydell, Tennessee	2	0	2	0	0	12
Wimbush, Derrick, Jacksonville	2	1	0	1	0	12
Wrighster, George, Jacksonville	2	0	2	0	0	12
Wright, Jason, Cleveland	1	1	0	0	0	6

*Includes safety.

NFC

KICKERS

Player, team	XPM	XPA	FGM	FGA	Tot. Pts
Akers, David, Philadelphia	23	23	16	22	71
Brien, Doug, Chicago	7	7	1	4	10
Brown, Josh, Seattle	56	57	18	25	110
Bryant, Matt, Tampa Bay	31	31	21	25	94
Carney, John, New Orleans	22	22	25	32	97
Cortez, Jose, Dal.-Phi.-S.F.	18	19	12	17	54
Cundiff, Billy, Dallas	14	14	5	8	29
Edinger, Paul, Minnesota	31	31	25	34	106
Feely, Jay, N.Y. Giants	43	43	35	42	148
France, Todd, Phi.-T.B.	6	6	7	9	27
Gould, Robbie, Chicago	19	20	21	27	82
Hall, John, Washington	27	27	12	14	63
Hamilton, Remy, Detroit	0	1	0	0	0
Hanson, Jason, Detroit	27	27	19	24	84
Kasay, John, Carolina	43	44	26	34	121
Koenen, Michael, Atlanta	0	0	1	2	3
Longwell, Ryan, Green Bay	30	31	20	27	90
Nedney, Joe, San Francisco	19	19	26	28	97
Novak, Nick, Was.-Ariz.	15	15	8	10	39
Peterson, Todd, Atlanta	35	35	23	25	104
Rackers, Neil, Arizona	20	20	40	42	140
Simoneau, Mark, Philadelphia	1	2	0	0	1
Suisham, Shaun, Dallas	8	8	3	4	17
Wilkins, Jeff, St. Louis	36	36	27	31	117

NONKICKERS

Player, team	Tot. TD	RTD	PTD	MTD	2Pt.	Tot. Pts.
Adams, Mike, San Francisco	1	0	0	1	0	6
Alexander, Shaun, Seattle	28	27	1	0	0	168
Allen, Will, Tampa Bay	1	0	0	1	0	6
Alstott, Mike, Tampa Bay	7	6	1	0	1	44
Amey, Otis, San Francisco	1	0	0	1	0	6
Archuleta, Adam, St. Louis	1	0	0	1	0	6
Arrington, J.J., Arizona	2	2	0	0	0	12
Ayanbadejo, Obafemi, Arizona	0	0	0	0	2	4
Bailey, Boss, Detroit	1	0	0	1	0	6
Barber, Marion, Dallas	5	5	0	0	0	30
Barber, Tiki, N.Y. Giants	11	9	2	0	1	68
Barlow, Kevan, San Francisco	3	3	0	0	0	18
Barnett, Nick, Green Bay	1	0	0	1	0	6
Bartrum, Mike, Philadelphia	2	0	2	0	0	12
Battle, Arnaz, San Francisco	3	0	3	0	0	18
Bennett, Michael, Minnesota	5	3	2	0	0	30
Bergen, Adam, Arizona	1	0	1	0	0	6
Betts, Ladell, Washington	3	1	1	1	0	18
Blackburn, Chase, N.Y. Giants	1	0	0	1	0	6
Blakley, Dwayne, Atlanta	1	0	1	0	0	6
Bledsoe, Drew, Dallas	2	2	0	0	0	12
Boldin, Anquan, Arizona	7	0	7	0	1	44
Briggs, Lance, Chicago	1	0	0	1	0	6
Brooks, Aaron, New Orleans	2	2	0	0	0	12
Brown, Antonio, Washington	1	0	0	1	0	6
Brown, Mike, Chicago	1	0	0	1	0	6
Brown, Reggie, Philadelphia	4	0	4	0	0	24
Brown, Sheldon, Philadelphia	2	0	0	2	0	12
Bruce, Isaac, St. Louis	3	0	3	0	0	18
Bryson, Shawn, Detroit	1	1	0	0	0	6
Burleson, Nate, Minnesota	1	0	1	0	0	6
Burress, Plaxico, N.Y. Giants	7	0	7	0	0	42
Campbell, Dan, Dallas	1	0	1	0	0	6
Carter, Drew, Carolina	1	0	1	0	0	6
Cartwright, Rock, Washington	2	2	0	0	0	12
Cason, Aveion, St. Louis	1	1	0	0	0	6
Chatman, Antonio, Green Bay	5	0	4	1	0	30
Chillar, Brandon, St. Louis	1	0	0	1	0	6
Clark, Desmond, Chicago	2	0	2	0	0	12
Cleeland, Cam, St. Louis	1	0	1	0	0	6
Colbert, Keary, Carolina	2	0	2	0	0	12
Conwell, Ernie, New Orleans	1	0	1	0	0	6
Cook, Jameel, Tampa Bay	1	0	1	0	0	6
Cooley, Chris, Washington	7	0	7	0	0	42
Crayton, Patrick, Dallas	2	0	2	0	0	12
Crumpler, Alge, Atlanta	5	0	5	0	1	32
Culpepper, Daunte, Minnesota	1	1	0	0	0	6
Curtis, Kevin, St. Louis	7	1	6	0	0	42
Dansby, Karlos, Arizona	2	0	0	2	0	12
Davenport, Najeh, Green Bay	2	2	0	0	0	12
Davis, Chauncey, Atlanta	1	0	0	1	0	6
Davis, Stephen, Carolina	12	12	0	0	0	72
Delhomme, Jake, Carolina	1	1	0	0	0	6
Driver, Donald, Green Bay	5	0	5	0	0	30
Duckett, T.J., Atlanta	8	8	0	0	0	48
Dunn, Warrick, Atlanta	4	3	1	0	0	24
Dyson, Andre, Seattle	2	0	0	2	0	12
Edwards, Devonte, Minnesota	1	0	0	1	0	6
Edwards, Eric, Arizona	1	0	1	0	0	6
Edwards, Marc, Chicago	2	0	2	0	0	12
Engram, Bobby, Seattle	3	0	3	0	0	18
Fason, Ciatrick, Minnesota	4	4	0	0	0	24
Faulk, Marshall, St. Louis	1	0	1	0	1	8
Ferguson, Robert, Green Bay	3	0	3	0	1	20
Finneran, Brian, Atlanta	2	0	2	0	3	18
Fisher, Tony, Green Bay	2	1	1	0	0	12
Fitzgerald, Larry, Arizona	10	0	10	0	0	60
Fitzpatrick, Ryan, St. Louis	2	2	0	0	0	12
FitzSimmons, Casey, Detroit	1	0	1	0	0	6

Player, team	Tot. TD	RTD	PTD	MTD	2Pt.	Tot. Pts.
Foster, DeShaun, Carolina	3	2	1	0	0	18
Franks, Bubba, Green Bay	1	0	1	0	0	6
Furrey, Mike, St. Louis	1	0	0	1	0	6
Gado, Samkon, Green Bay	7	6	1	0	0	42
Gage, Justin, Chicago	2	0	2	0	0	12
Gaines, Michael, Carolina	2	0	2	0	0	12
Galloway, Joey, Tampa Bay	10	0	10	0	0	60
Gamble, Chris, Carolina	1	0	0	1	0	6
Garcia, Jeff, Detroit	1	1	0	0	0	6
Gardner, Rod, Carolina	1	0	1	0	0	6
Gilmore, John, Chicago	1	0	1	0	0	6
Glenn, Terry, Dallas	8	1	7	0	0	48
Gordon, Lamar, Philadelphia	1	1	0	0	0	6
Gore, Frank, San Francisco	3	3	0	0	0	18
Griffith, Justin, Atlanta	3	0	3	0	0	18
Hackett, D.J., Seattle	2	0	2	0	0	12
Hakim, Az-Zahir, New Orleans	2	0	2	0	0	12
Hall, DeAngelo, Atlanta	1	0	0	1	0	6
Hannam, Ryan, Seattle	1	0	1	0	0	6
Harris, Al, Green Bay	1	0	0	1	0	6
Harris, Arlen, St. Louis	1	1	0	0	1	8
Hasselbeck, Matt, Seattle	1	1	0	0	0	6
Henderson, Devery, New Orleans	3	0	3	0	0	18
Henry, Anthony, Dallas	1	0	0	1	0	6
Herron, Noah, Green Bay	2	2	0	0	0	12
Hicks, Maurice, San Francisco	3	3	0	0	0	18
Hilliard, Ike, Tampa Bay	1	0	1	0	0	6
Hilton, Zachary, New Orleans	1	0	1	0	0	6
Holt, Torry, St. Louis	9	0	9	0	0	54
Horn, Joe, New Orleans	1	0	1	0	0	6
Jackson, Darrell, Seattle	3	0	3	0	0	18
Jackson, Steven, St. Louis	10	8	2	0	0	60
Jackson, Terry, San Francisco	0	0	0	0	1	2
Jacobs, Brandon, N.Y. Giants	7	7	0	0	0	42
Jenkins, Michael, Atlanta	3	0	3	0	0	18
Johnson, Bryant, Arizona	1	0	1	0	0	6
Johnson, Chris, St. Louis	1	0	0	1	0	6
Johnson, Derrick, San Francisco	1	0	0	1	0	6
Johnson, Keyshawn, Dallas	6	0	6	0	1	38
Jones, Julius, Dallas	5	5	0	0	0	30
Jones, Kevin, Detroit	5	5	0	0	0	30
Jones, Thomas, Chicago	9	9	0	0	0	54
Jurevicius, Joe, Seattle	10	0	10	0	0	60
Kennedy, Kenoy, Detroit	1	0	0	1	0	6
Lake, Antwan, Atlanta	0	0	0	0	0	*2
Lee, Donald, Green Bay	2	0	2	0	0	12
Lewis, Greg, Philadelphia	1	0	1	0	0	6
Lloyd, Brandon, San Francisco	5	0	5	0	0	30
Macklin, David, Arizona	1	0	0	1	0	6
Mangum, Kris, Carolina	2	0	2	0	0	12
Manning, Eli, N.Y. Giants	1	1	0	0	0	6
Manning, Ricky, Carolina	1	0	0	1	0	6
Manumaleuna, Brandon, St. Louis	1	0	1	0	0	6
Marshall, Lemar, Washington	1	0	0	1	0	6
Martin, David, Green Bay	3	0	3	0	1	20
McAllister, Deuce, New Orleans	3	3	0	0	0	18
McCoy, LeRon, Arizona	1	0	1	0	0	6
McFarland, Anthony, Tampa Bay	1	0	0	1	0	6
McMahon, Mike, Philadelphia	3	3	0	0	0	18
McMullen, Billy, Philadelphia	1	0	1	0	0	6
McNabb, Donovan, Philadelphia	1	1	0	0	0	6
Moats, Ryan, Philadelphia	3	3	0	0	0	18
Moore, Mewelde, Minnesota	4	1	2	1	0	24
Morris, Maurice, Seattle	1	1	0	0	0	6
Morton, Chad, N.Y. Giants	1	0	0	1	0	6
Moss, Santana, Washington	9	0	9	0	0	54
Muhammad, Muhsin, Chicago	4	0	4	0	0	24
Owens, Terrell, Philadelphia	6	0	6	0	0	36
Parrish, Tony, San Francisco	1	0	0	1	0	6
Peterson, Adrian, Chicago	2	2	0	0	0	12
Pierce, Antonio, N.Y. Giants	1	0	0	1	0	6
Pinner, Artose, Detroit	3	3	0	0	0	18
Pittman, Michael, Tampa Bay	2	1	1	0	0	12
Polite, Lousaka, Dallas	1	0	1	0	0	6
Pollard, Marcus, Detroit	3	0	3	0	0	18
Ponder, Willie, N.Y. Giants	1	0	0	1	0	6
Portis, Clinton, Washington	11	11	0	0	1	68
Proehl, Ricky, Carolina	4	0	4	0	0	24
Quarles, Shelton, Tampa Bay	0	0	0	0	0	*2
Robertson, Jamal, Carolina	1	1	0	0	0	6
Robinson, Koren, Minnesota	3	1	1	1	0	18
Robinson, Marcus, Minnesota	5	0	5	0	1	32
Rogers, Charles, Detroit	1	0	1	0	0	6
Rogers, Shaun, Detroit	1	0	0	1	0	6
Royal, Robert, Washington	1	0	1	0	0	6
Schlesinger, Cory, Detroit	1	0	1	0	0	6
Sellers, Mike, Washington	8	1	7	0	0	48
Sharper, Darren, Minnesota	2	0	0	2	0	12
Shepherd, Edell, Tampa Bay	1	0	1	0	0	6
Shockey, Jeremy, N.Y. Giants	7	0	7	0	1	44
Smith, Alex, Tampa Bay	2	0	2	0	0	12
Smith, Antowain, New Orleans	3	3	0	0	0	18
Smith, Derek, San Francisco	1	0	0	1	0	6
Smith, L.J., Philadelphia	3	0	3	0	0	18
Smith, Steve, Carolina	13	1	12	0	0	78
Spencer, Shawntae, San Francisco	1	0	0	0	0	6
Stallworth, Donte', New Orleans	7	0	7	0	0	42
Stevens, Jerramy, Seattle	5	0	5	0	0	30
Tatupu, Lofa, Seattle	1	0	0	1	0	6
Taylor, Sean, Washington	1	0	0	1	0	6
Taylor, Travis, Minnesota	4	0	4	0	0	24
Tillman, Charles, Chicago	1	0	0	1	0	6
Toomer, Amani, N.Y. Giants	7	0	7	0	0	42
Tyree, David, N.Y. Giants	1	0	1	0	0	6
Vasher, Nathan, Chicago	2	0	0	2	0	12
Vick, Michael, Atlanta	6	6	0	0	0	36
Wade, Bobby, Chicago	1	0	0	1	0	6
Ware, Matt, Philadelphia	1	0	0	1	0	6
Westbrook, Brian, Philadelphia	7	3	4	0	1	44
White, Dewayne, Tampa Bay	1	0	0	1	0	6
White, Dez, Atlanta	1	0	1	0	0	6
White, Roddy, Atlanta	3	0	3	0	0	18
Wiggins, Jermaine, Minnesota	1	0	1	0	0	6
Wilkinson, Dan, Detroit	0	0	0	0	0	*2
Williams, Carnell, Tampa Bay	6	6	0	0	0	36
Williams, Demorrio, Atlanta	1	0	0	1	0	6
Williams, Mike, Detroit	1	0	1	0	0	6
Williams, Roy, Dallas	1	0	0	1	0	6
Williams, Roy, Detroit	8	0	8	0	0	48
Williamson, Troy, Minnesota	2	0	2	0	0	12
Witherspoon, Will, Carolina	1	0	0	1	0	6
Witten, Jason, Dallas	6	0	6	0	0	36

*Includes safety.

NOTE: Team safety credited to St. Louis.

INTERCEPTIONS

AFC

Team	No.	Yds.	Avg.	Long	TD
Cincinnati	31	260	8.4	37	1
N.Y. Jets	21	279	13.3	t74	2
Denver	20	379	19.0	t80	3
Jacksonville	19	184	9.7	t41	2
Indianapolis	18	259	14.4	36	2
Buffalo	17	233	13.7	t46	1
Kansas City	16	232	14.5	t57	1
Pittsburgh	15	179	11.9	55	0
Cleveland	15	130	8.7	37	0
Miami	14	136	9.7	37	0
Baltimore	11	191	17.4	38	1
San Diego	10	205	20.5	t70	2
New England	10	85	8.5	t39	2
Tennessee	9	129	14.3	t52	2
Houston	7	46	6.6	29	0
Oakland	5	38	7.6	33	0
AFC total	238	2965	...	t80	19
AFC average	14.9	185.3	12.5	...	1.2

t—touchdown.

NFC

Team	No.	Yds.	Avg.	Long	TD
Chicago	24	524	21.8	95	4
Minnesota	24	392	16.3	t92	3
Carolina	23	440	19.1	t61	2
Detroit	19	308	16.2	t64	2
N.Y. Giants	17	354	20.8	71	1
Tampa Bay	17	223	13.1	42	0
Philadelphia	17	195	11.5	t40	1
Seattle	16	315	19.7	t72	2
Atlanta	16	268	16.8	65	0
San Francisco	16	220	13.8	t61	3
Washington	16	176	11.0	41	1
Arizona	15	285	19.0	t60	3
Dallas	15	187	12.5	t58	2
St. Louis	13	364	28.0	t85	2
Green Bay	10	205	20.5	t95	2
New Orleans	10	182	18.2	51	0
NFC total	268	4638	...	t95	28
NFC average	16.8	289.9	17.3	...	1.8
NFL total	506	7603	...	t95	47
NFL average	15.8	237.6	15.0	...	1.5

BESTS OF THE SEASON

Interceptions, season
AFC: 10—Ty Law, N.Y. Jets; Deltha O'Neal, Cincinnati.
NFC: 9—Darren Sharper, Minnesota.

Interceptions, game
AFC: 3—Ty Law, N.Y. Jets vs. Buffalo, Jan. 1; Deltha O'Neal, Cincinnati vs. Minnesota, Sep. 18; Greg Wesley, Kansas City vs. New England, Nov. 27.
NFC: 3—Darren Sharper, Minnesota at N.Y. Giants, Nov. 13; Ronde Barber, Tampa Bay at New Orleans, Dec. 4.

Yards, season
NFC: 276—Darren Sharper, Minnesota.
AFC: 195—Ty Law, N.Y. Jets.

Longest
NFC: 95—Nick Barnett, Green Bay vs. New Orleans, Oct. 9 (TD); Charles Tillman, Chicago vs. Green Bay, Dec. 4.
AFC: 80—Darrent Williams, Denver at Oakland, Nov. 13 (TD).

Touchdowns, season
AFC: 2—Champ Bailey, Denver; Clinton Hart, San Diego; Cato June, Indianapolis.
NFC: 2—Karlos Dansby, Arizona; Darren Sharper, Minnesota.

Team leaders, interceptions
AFC:

Baltimore	2	Deion Sanders, Adalius Thomas, Terrell Suggs
Buffalo	4	Terrence McGee, Troy Vincent
Cincinnati	10	Deltha O'Neal
Cleveland	3	Brian Russell, Leigh Bodden
Denver	8	Champ Bailey
Houston	2	Glenn Earl
Indianapolis	5	Cato June
Jacksonville	5	Rashean Mathis
Kansas City	6	Greg Wesley
Miami	4	Lance Schulters
N.Y. Jets	10	Ty Law
New England	3	Asante Samuel, Ellis Hobbs
Oakland	2	Stuart Schweigert
Pittsburgh	3	Chris Hope
San Diego	3	Bhawoh Jue
Tennessee	3	Reynaldo Hill

NFC:

Arizona	3	Karlos Dansby
Atlanta	6	DeAngelo Hall
Carolina	7	Chris Gamble
Chicago	8	Nathan Vasher
Dallas	4	Aaron Glenn
Detroit	6	Dre' Bly
Green Bay	3	Al Harris
Minnesota	9	Darren Sharper
N.Y. Giants	4	Brent Alexander
New Orleans	3	Jason Craft
Philadelphia	4	Sheldon Brown
San Francisco	4	Shawntae Spencer, Mike Adams
Seattle	4	Michael Boulware
St. Louis	4	Mike Furrey
Tampa Bay	5	Ronde Barber
Washington	4	Lemar Marshall

NFL LEADERS

Player, team	No.	Yds.	Avg.	Long	TD
Law, Ty, N.Y. Jets*	10	195	19.5	t74	1
O'Neal, Deltha, Cincinnati*	10	103	10.3	37	0
Sharper, Darren, Minnesota	9	276	30.7	t92	2
Vasher, Nathan, Chicago	8	145	18.1	46	1
Bailey, Champ, Denver*	8	139	17.4	t65	2
Gamble, Chris, Carolina	7	157	22.4	t61	1
Hall, DeAngelo, Atlanta	6	177	29.5	65	0
Wesley, Greg, Kansas City*	6	106	17.7	51	0
Lucas, Ken, Carolina	6	70	11.7	32	0
Bly, Dre', Detroit	6	54	9.0	28	0

*AFC.
t—touchdown.
Leader based on most interceptions.

2005 STATISTICS *Interceptions*

AFC

Player, team	No.	Yds.	Avg.	Long	TD
Bailey, Champ, Denver	8	139	17.4	t65	2
Baker, Rashad, Buffalo	1	18	18.0	18	0
Barrett, David, N.Y. Jets	5	28	5.6	13	0
Baxter, Gary, Cleveland	2	10	5.0	10	0
Bell, Yeremiah, Miami	1	0	0.0	0	0
Bodden, Leigh, Cleveland	3	6	2.0	6	0
Brackett, Gary, Indianapolis	3	50	16.7	31	0
Brown, C.C., Houston	1	5	5.0	5	0
Brown, Mark, N.Y. Jets	2	51	25.5	t33	1
Bulluck, Keith, Tennessee	2	16	8.0	16	0
Carter, Tyrone, Pittsburgh	1	3	3.0	3	0
Clements, Nate, Buffalo	2	0	0.0	0	0
Colclough, Ricardo, Pittsburgh	1	14	14.0	14	0
Coleman, Erik, N.Y. Jets	2	4	2.0	4	0
Coleman, Marcus, Houston	1	6	6.0	6	0
Cooper, Deke, Jacksonville	1	0	0.0	0	0
Cousin, Terry, Jacksonville	4	18	4.5	14	0
Cox, Curome, Denver	1	48	48.0	48	0
Crocker, Chris, Cleveland	2	35	17.5	24	0
Crowell, Angelo, Buffalo	2	3	1.5	2	0
Daniels, Travis, Miami	1	4	4.0	4	0
David, Jason, Indianapolis	2	13	6.5	13	0
Davis, Andra, Cleveland	1	14	14.0	14	0
Doss, Mike, Indianapolis	2	8	4.0	8	0
Earl, Glenn, Houston	2	2	1.0	2	0
Edwards, Donnie, San Diego	2	15	7.5	14	0
Evans, Troy, Houston	1	3	3.0	3	0
Ferguson, Nick, Denver	5	59	11.8	30	0
Fletcher, Jamar, San Diego	1	19	19.0	19	0
Fletcher, London, Buffalo	1	20	20.0	20	0
Florence, Drayton, San Diego	1	9	9.0	9	0
Foxworth, Domonique, Denver	2	23	11.5	23	0
Gardner, Gilbert, Indianapolis	1	16	16.0	16	0
Grant, Deon, Jacksonville	3	29	9.7	29	0
Harper, Nick, Indianapolis	3	41	13.7	21	0
Harrison, James, Pittsburgh	1	25	25.0	25	0
Hart, Clinton, San Diego	1	110	110.0	t70	2
Hill, Renaldo, Oakland	1	0	0.0	0	0
Hill, Reynaldo, Tennessee	3	88	29.3	t52	1
Hobbs, Ellis, New England	3	8	2.7	8	0
Hope, Chris, Pittsburgh	3	60	20.0	55	0
Howard, Reggie, Miami	1	5	5.0	5	0
Jackson, Marlin, Indianapolis	1	16	16.0	16	0
James, Tory, Cincinnati	5	5	1.0	5	0
Jammer, Quentin, San Diego	1	14	14.0	14	0
Jue, Bhawoh, San Diego	3	28	9.3	20	0
June, Cato, Indianapolis	5	115	23.0	36	2
Kaesviharn, Kevin, Cincinnati	3	9	3.0	6	0
Kassell, Brad, Tennessee	1	21	21.0	t21	1
Kelsay, Chris, Buffalo	1	17	17.0	17	0
Knight, Sammy, Kansas City	2	12	6.0	12	0
Law, Ty, N.Y. Jets	10	195	19.5	t74	1
Lewis, Ray, Baltimore	1	0	0.0	0	0
Lynch, John, Denver	2	2	1.0	1	0
Madison, Sam, Miami	2	11	5.5	11	0
Mathis, Rashean, Jacksonville	5	79	15.8	t41	1
McAlister, Chris, Baltimore	1	0	0.0	0	0
McCleon, Dexter, Kansas City	2	0	0.0	0	0
McCutcheon, Daylon, Cleveland	2	14	7.0	14	0
McFadden, Bryant, Pittsburgh	1	0	0.0	0	0
McGee, Terrence, Buffalo	4	97	24.3	t46	1
Milloy, Lawyer, Buffalo	1	0	0.0	0	0
Mitchell, Kawika, Kansas City	1	0	0.0	0	0
O'Neal, Deltha, Cincinnati	10	103	10.3	37	0
Ohalete, Ifeanyi, Cincinnati	1	15	15.0	15	0
Peterson, Mike, Jacksonville	3	54	18.0	t26	1
Polamalu, Troy, Pittsburgh	2	42	21.0	36	0
Pool, Brodney, Cleveland	1	1	1.0	1	0
Porter, Joey, Pittsburgh	2	9	4.5	9	0
Ratliff, Keiwan, Cincinnati	3	52	17.3	35	0
Reed, Ed, Baltimore	1	23	23.0	23	0
Rhodes, Kerry, N.Y. Jets	1	0	0.0	0	0
Robinson, Dunta, Houston	1	1	1.0	1	0
Rolle, Samari, Baltimore	1	11	11.0	11	0
Russell, Brian, Cleveland	3	50	16.7	37	0
Samuel, Asante, New England	3	15	5.0	15	0
Sanders, Bob, Indianapolis	1	0	0.0	0	0
Sanders, Deion, Baltimore	2	57	28.5	33	0
Sanders, James, New England	1	39	39.0	t39	1
Sanders, Lewis, Houston	1	29	29.0	29	0
Sapp, Warren, Oakland	1	3	3.0	3	0
Schobel, Aaron, Buffalo	1	0	0.0	0	0
Schulters, Lance, Miami	4	78	19.5	37	0
Schweigert, Stuart, Oakland	2	35	17.5	33	0
Simmons, Brian, Cincinnati	2	15	7.5	16	0
Smith, Aaron, Pittsburgh	1	0	0.0	0	0
Smith, Daryl, Jacksonville	1	0	0.0	0	0
Spragan, Donnie, Miami	1	0	0.0	0	0
Stewart, Matt, Cleveland	1	0	0.0	0	0
Suggs, Terrell, Baltimore	2	38	19.0	38	0
Surtain, Patrick, Kansas City	4	57	14.3	53	0
Taylor, Ike, Pittsburgh	1	0	0.0	0	0
Thomas, Adalius, Baltimore	2	48	24.0	28	1
Thomas, Zach, Miami	1	0	0.0	0	0
Thompson, Lamont, Tennessee	1	0	0.0	0	0
Thornton, John, Cincinnati	1	0	0.0	0	0
Thurman, Odell, Cincinnati	5	59	11.8	t30	1
Tillman, Travares, Miami	3	38	12.7	22	0
Townsend, Deshea, Pittsburgh	2	26	13.0	26	0
Vilma, Jonathan, N.Y. Jets	1	1	1.0	1	0
Vincent, Troy, Buffalo	4	78	19.5	42	0
Vrabel, Mike, New England	2	23	11.5	t24	1
Warfield, Eric, Kansas City	1	57	57.0	t57	1
Wesley, Greg, Kansas City	6	106	17.7	51	0
Wilhelm, Matt, San Diego	1	10	10.0	10	0
Williams, Chad, Baltimore	1	14	14.0	14	0
Williams, Darrent, Denver	2	108	54.0	t80	1
Williams, Madieu, Cincinnati	1	2	2.0	2	0
Williams, Tank, Tennessee	1	1	1.0	1	0
Wilson, Eugene, New England	1	0	0.0	0	0
Woodson, Charles, Oakland	1	0	0.0	0	0
Woolfolk, Andre, Tennessee	1	3	3.0	3	0
Wright, Kenny, Jacksonville	2	4	2.0	4	0

t—touchdown.

NFC

Player, team	No.	Yds.	Avg.	Long	TD
Adams, Mike, San Francisco	4	36	9.0	t40	1
Alexander, Brent, N.Y. Giants	4	45	11.3	24	0
Allen, Will, N.Y. Giants	0	17	...	17	0
Allen, Will, Tampa Bay	3	26	8.7	26	0
Archuleta, Adam, St. Louis	1	85	85.0	t85	1
Atogwe, O.J., St. Louis	1	42	42.0	42	0
Babineaux, Jordan, Seattle	3	56	18.7	25	0
Bailey, Boss, Detroit	1	34	34.0	t34	1
Barber, Ronde, Tampa Bay	5	105	21.0	42	0
Barnett, Nick, Green Bay	1	95	95.0	t95	1
Blackburn, Chase, N.Y. Giants	1	31	31.0	t31	1
Bly, Dre', Detroit	6	54	9.0	28	0
Bolden, Juran, Tampa Bay	2	46	23.0	28	0
Boulware, Michael, Seattle	4	107	26.8	40	0
Briggs, Lance, Chicago	2	30	15.0	20	1
Brooking, Keith, Atlanta	4	50	12.5	22	0
Brooks, Derrick, Tampa Bay	1	0	0.0	0	0
Brown, Mike, Chicago	3	116	38.7	72	1
Brown, Sheldon, Philadelphia	4	67	16.8	t40	1
Bullocks, Josh, New Orleans	1	51	51.0	51	0
Butler, James, N.Y. Giants	2	16	8.0	16	0
Carpenter, Keion, Atlanta	2	1	0.5	1	0
Carroll, Ahmad, Green Bay	2	38	19.0	38	0
Chavous, Corey, Minnesota	2	0	0.0	0	0
Clark, Ryan, Washington	3	10	3.3	6	0

Player, team	No.	Yds.	Avg.	Long	TD
Coakley, Dexter, St. Louis	1	16	16.0	16	0
Collins, Nick, Green Bay	1	0	0.0	0	0
Craft, Jason, New Orleans	3	63	21.0	39	0
Dansby, Karlos, Arizona	3	31	10.3	t18	2
Darling, James, Arizona	2	22	11.0	15	0
Dawkins, Brian, Philadelphia	3	24	8.0	24	0
DeLoatch, Curtis, N.Y. Giants	1	20	20.0	20	0
Dockett, Darnell, Arizona	1	14	14.0	14	0
Dyson, Andre, Seattle	1	72	72.0	t72	1
Edwards, Devonte, Minnesota	1	51	51.0	t51	1
Emanuel, Ben, San Francisco	1	38	38.0	35	0
Emmons, Carlos, N.Y. Giants	1	6	6.0	6	0
Furrey, Mike, St. Louis	4	143	35.8	t67	1
Gamble, Chris, Carolina	7	157	22.4	t61	1
Glenn, Aaron, Dallas	4	10	2.5	10	0
Goodman, Andre', Detroit	3	17	5.7	21	0
Green, Eric, Arizona	1	13	13.0	13	0
Green, Mike, Chicago	1	14	14.0	14	0
Griffin, Cornelius, Washington	1	0	0.0	0	0
Griffith, Robert, Arizona	1	11	11.0	11	0
Groce, DeJuan, St. Louis	2	0	0.0	0	0
Hall, DeAngelo, Atlanta	6	177	29.5	65	0
Harris, Al, Green Bay	3	30	10.0	t22	1
Harris, Chris, Chicago	3	44	14.7	44	0
Harris, Walt, Washington	1	0	0.0	0	0
Hawthorne, Michael, St. Louis	1	24	24.0	24	0
Henry, Anthony, Dallas	3	102	34.0	t58	1
Herndon, Kelly, Seattle	2	12	6.0	10	0
Hillenmeyer, Hunter, Chicago	1	0	0.0	0	0
Holt, Terrence, Detroit	2	51	25.5	51	0
Hood, Roderick, Philadelphia	3	17	5.7	17	0
Huff, Orlando, Arizona	1	3	3.0	3	0
Ivy, Corey, St. Louis	1	19	19.0	19	0
Jackson, Dexter, Tampa Bay	1	21	21.0	21	0
Jones, Dhani, Philadelphia	1	0	0.0	0	0
Kelly, Brian, Tampa Bay	4	19	4.8	14	0
Kennedy, Kenoy, Detroit	2	64	32.0	t64	1
Lehman, Teddy, Detroit	1	21	21.0	17	0
Lewis, Keith, San Francisco	1	2	2.0	2	0
Lewis, Michael, Philadelphia	2	13	6.5	13	0
Lucas, Ken, Carolina	6	70	11.7	32	0
Macklin, David, Arizona	2	79	39.5	t60	1
Manning Jr., Ricky, Carolina	2	20	10.0	10	0
Marshall, Lemar, Washington	4	55	13.8	27	1
McCree, Marlon, Carolina	3	73	24.3	46	0
McKenzie, Mike, New Orleans	1	11	11.0	11	0
McQuarters, R.W., Detroit	2	25	12.5	19	0
Minter, Mike, Carolina	1	47	47.0	47	0
Moore, Brandon, San Francisco	1	12	12.0	12	0
Newman, Keith, Minnesota	1	1	1.0	1	0
Newman, Terence, Dallas	3	16	5.3	12	0
Nguyen, Dat, Dallas	1	7	7.0	7	0
Offord, Willie, Minnesota	1	0	0.0	0	0
Parrish, Tony, San Francisco	2	34	17.0	t34	1
Patterson, Dimitri, Washington	1	20	20.0	20	0
Pierce, Antonio, N.Y. Giants	2	41	20.5	24	0
Rice, Simeon, Tampa Bay	1	6	6.0	6	0
Rogers, Carlos, Washington	2	14	7.0	14	0
Rolle, Antrel, Arizona	1	29	29.0	29	0
Roman, Mark, Green Bay	2	18	9.0	12	0
Scott, Bryan, Atlanta	1	15	15.0	15	0
Scott, Ian, Chicago	1	3	3.0	3	0
Sharper, Darren, Minnesota	9	276	30.7	t92	2
Sheppard, Lito, Philadelphia	3	72	24.0	34	0
Singleton, Al, Dallas	1	0	0.0	0	0
Slaughter, T.J., New Orleans	1	0	0.0	0	0
Smith, Derek, San Francisco	1	13	13.0	13	0
Smith, Dwight, New Orleans	2	53	26.5	28	0
Smoot, Fred, Minnesota	2	0	0.0	0	0
Spencer, Shawntae, San Francisco	4	85	21.3	t61	1
Springs, Shawn, Washington	1	2	2.0	2	0
Tate, Robert, Arizona	2	47	23.5	25	0
Tatupu, Lofa, Seattle	3	55	18.3	t38	1
Taylor, Sean, Washington	2	34	17.0	32	0
Thomas, Fred, New Orleans	2	4	2.0	4	0
Thomas, Robert, Green Bay	1	24	24.0	24	0
Thornton, Bruce, San Francisco	2	0	0.0	0	0
Tillman, Charles, Chicago	5	172	34.4	95	1
Tinoisamoa, Pisa, St. Louis	2	35	17.5	20	0
Torbor, Reggie, N.Y. Giants	1	37	37.0	37	0
Trotter, Jeremiah, Philadelphia	1	2	2.0	2	0
Trufant, Marcus, Seattle	1	7	7.0	7	0
Vasher, Nathan, Chicago	8	145	18.1	46	1
Walker, Bracy, Detroit	1	22	22.0	22	0
Walker, Frank, N.Y. Giants	1	71	71.0	71	0
Wallace, Al, Carolina	2	38	19.0	38	0
Washington, Marcus, Washington.	1	41	41.0	41	0
Wayne, Nate, Detroit	1	20	20.0	20	0
Webster, Jason, Atlanta	1	19	19.0	19	0
Williams, Brian, Minnesota	4	59	14.8	31	0
Williams, Demorrio, Atlanta	2	6	3.0	6	0
Williams, Jimmy, Seattle	2	6	3.0	6	0
Williams, Roy, Dallas	3	52	17.3	t46	1
Williams, Shaun, N.Y. Giants	2	34	17.0	34	0
Wilson, Adrian, Arizona	1	36	36.0	36	0
Wilson, Gibril, N.Y. Giants	2	36	18.0	19	0
Winfield, Antoine, Minnesota	4	5	1.3	4	0
Witherspoon, Will, Carolina	2	35	17.5	t35	1

t—touchdown.

SACKS

TEAM

AFC			NFC		
Team	**Sacks**	**Yards**	**Team**	**Sacks**	**Yards**
Miami	49	375	Seattle	50	302
Pittsburgh	47	312	Carolina	45	294
Jacksonville	47	277	Chicago	41	275
Indianapolis	46	318	N.Y. Giants	41	268
San Diego	46	289	St. Louis	41	195
Baltimore	42	270	Atlanta	37	257
Tennessee	41	246	Dallas	37	236
Buffalo	38	269	Arizona	37	217
Houston	37	206	Tampa Bay	36	229
Oakland	36	238	Washington	35	237
New England	33	223	Green Bay	35	196
N.Y. Jets	30	193	Minnesota	34	207
Kansas City	29	183	Detroit	31	187
Denver	28	190	Philadelphia	29	184
Cincinnati	28	180	San Francisco	28	193
Cleveland	23	142	New Orleans	25	165
AFC total	600	3911	**NFC total**	582	3642
AFC average	37.5	244.4	**NFC average**	36.4	227.6
			NFL total	1182	7553
			NFL average	36.9	236.0

INDIVIDUAL

BESTS OF THE SEASON

Sacks, season
AFC: 16.0—Derrick Burgess, Oakland.
NFC: 14.5—Osi Umenyiora, N.Y. Giants.

Sacks, game
NFC: 4.0—Phillip Daniels, Washington vs. Dallas, Dec. 18.
AFC: 3.0—Held by 13 players.

NFL LEADERS

Player, team	No.	Player, team	No.
Burgess, Derrick, Oakland*	16.0	Allen, Jared, Kansas City*	11.0
Umenyiora, Osi, N.Y. Giants	14.5	Abraham, John, N.Y. Jets*	10.5
Rice, Simeon, Tampa Bay	14.0	Porter, Joey, Pittsburgh*	10.5
Vanden Bosch, Kyle, Tennessee*	12.5	Coleman, Rod, Atlanta	10.5
Schobel, Aaron, Buffalo*	12.0	Peppers, Julius, Carolina	10.5
Taylor, Jason, Miami*	12.0	Merriman, Shawne, San Diego*	10.0
Mathis, Robert, Indianapolis*	11.5	Ogunleye, Adewale, Chicago	10.0
Strahan, Michael, N.Y. Giants	11.5	Little, Leonard, St. Louis	9.5
Freeney, Dwight, Indianapolis*	11.0	*AFC.	

AFC

Player, team	No.
Abraham, John, N.Y. Jets	10.5
Adams, Sam, Buffalo	3.0
Allen, Jared, Kansas City	11.0
Anderson, Charlie, Houston	1.0
Anderson, Tim, Buffalo	1.0
Ayodele, Akin, Jacksonville	2.5
Babin, Jason, Houston	4.0
Baker, Rashad, Buffalo	1.0
Bannan, Justin, Buffalo	1.5
Banta-Cain, Tully, New England	0.5
Beisel, Monty, New England	1.0
Bell, Kendrell, Kansas City	1.5
Bell, Yeremiah, Miami	3.0
Boulware, Peter, Baltimore	2.5
Bowens, David, Miami	6.0
Brackett, Gary, Indianapolis	1.0
Brayton, Tyler, Oakland	1.0
Brock, Raheem, Indianapolis	6.5

Player, team	No.
Brown, Courtney, Denver	2.0
Brown, Mark, N.Y. Jets	1.5
Browning, John, Kansas City	2.0
Bruschi, Tedy, New England	2.0
Bulluck, Keith, Tennessee	5.0
Burgess, Derrick, Oakland	16.0
Carter, Kevin, Miami	6.0
Carter, Tyrone, Pittsburgh	1.0
Castillo, Luis, San Diego	3.5
Cesaire, Jacques, San Diego	1.0
Chatham, Matt, New England	1.0
Clark, Danny, Oakland	1.0
Clauss, Jared, Tennessee	0.5
Clemons, Duane, Cincinnati	2.0
Colclough, Ricardo, Pittsburgh	1.0
Coleman, Marco, Denver	1.0
Colvin, Rosevelt, New England	7.0
Cooper, Jarrod, Oakland	0.5
Cooper, Stephen, San Diego	1.5
Cousin, Terry, Jacksonville	0.5

Player, team	No.
Crocker, Chris, Cleveland	2.0
Crowell, Angelo, Buffalo	3.0
Dalton, Lional, Kansas City	1.0
Davis, Andra, Cleveland	2.0
Davis, Sammy, San Diego	1.0
DeLoach, Jerry, Houston	1.0
Denney, Ryan, Buffalo	4.0
Eason, Nick, Cleveland	2.0
Edwards, Donnie, San Diego	3.0
Ekuban, Ebenezer, Denver	4.0
Ellis, Shaun, N.Y. Jets	2.5
Farrior, James, Pittsburgh	2.0
Fletcher, Jamar, San Diego	1.0
Fletcher, London, Buffalo	4.0
Foley, Steve, San Diego	4.5
Foote, Larry, Pittsburgh	3.0
Franklin, Aubrayo, Baltimore	1.0
Frazier, Andre, Pittsburgh	1.0
Freeney, Dwight, Indianapolis	11.0
Gardner, Gilbert, Indianapolis	1.0

Player, team	No.
Geathers, Robert, Cincinnati	3.0
Gibson, Derrick, Oakland	1.0
Godfrey, Randall, San Diego	1.0
Gold, Ian, Denver	3.0
Grant, DeLawrence, Oakland	1.0
Grant, Deon, Jacksonville	1.5
Green, Jarvis, New England	2.5
Green, Roderick, Baltimore	2.0
Greenwood, Morlon, Houston	2.0
Greer, Jabari, Buffalo	1.0
Gregg, Kelly, Baltimore	2.0
Haggans, Clark, Pittsburgh	9.0
Hall, Carlos, Kansas City	1.0
Hamilton, Bobby, Oakland	2.0
Harris, Marques, San Diego	1.0
Harrison, James, Pittsburgh	3.0
Hawkins, Artrell, New England	1.0
Haynesworth, Albert, Tennessee	3.0
Hayward, Reggie, Jacksonville	8.5
Henderson, John, Jacksonville	3.0
Hicks, Eric, Kansas City	4.0
Hobson, Victor, N.Y. Jets	1.0
Holliday, Vonnie, Miami	5.0
Howard, Reggie, Miami	2.0
Jasper, Ed, Oakland	2.0
Johnson, Derrick, Kansas City	2.0
Johnson, Jarret, Baltimore	1.5
Johnson, Travis, Houston	1.0
Jones, Tebucky, Miami	2.0
Kaesviharn, Kevin, Cincinnati	1.0
Keisel, Brett, Pittsburgh	3.0
Kelley, Ethan, Cleveland	1.0
Kelly, Tommy, Oakland	4.5
Kelsay, Chris, Buffalo	2.5
Kemoeatu, Maake, Baltimore	1.0
Kiel, Terrence, San Diego	1.0
Kirschke, Travis, Pittsburgh	1.0
Klecko, Dan, New England	0.5
Knight, Sammy, Kansas City	2.0
Labinjo, Mike, Indianapolis	0.5
LaBoy, Travis, Tennessee	6.5
Lang, Kenard, Cleveland	2.0
Leber, Ben, San Diego	2.0
Legree, Lance, N.Y. Jets	3.0
Lewis, Ray, Baltimore	1.0
Long, Rien, Tennessee	3.5
Lynch, John, Denver	4.0
Maddox, Anthony, Jacksonville	1.0
Malone, Alfred, Houston	1.0
Mathis, Robert, Indianapolis	11.5
McCray, Bobby, Jacksonville	5.5
McFadden, Bryant, Pittsburgh	1.0
McGinest, Willie, New England	6.0
McKenzie, Chris, Houston	1.0
McKinley, Alvin, Cleveland	5.0
Meier, Rob, Jacksonville	6.0
Merriman, Shawne, San Diego	10.0
Milloy, Lawyer, Buffalo	1.0
Mitchell, Anthony, Cincinnati	1.0
Mitchell, Kawika, Kansas City	2.0
Myers, Michael, Denver	1.0
Odom, Antwan, Tennessee	2.0
Olshansky, Igor, San Diego	3.0
Orr, Shantee, Houston	7.0
Payne, Seth, Houston	4.0
Peek, Antwan, Houston	6.0
Peterson, Mike, Jacksonville	6.0
Phillips, Shaun, San Diego	7.0
Polamalu, Troy, Pittsburgh	3.0
Polk, DaShon, Houston	3.5
Pollack, David, Cincinnati	4.5

Player, team	No.
Polley, Tommy, Baltimore	4.0
Pool, Brodney, Cleveland	1.0
Porter, Joey, Pittsburgh	10.5
Posey, Jeff, Buffalo	3.0
Poteat, Hank, New England	1.0
Powell, Carl, Cincinnati	1.0
Pryce, Trevor, Denver	4.0
Reagor, Montae, Indianapolis	5.5
Reed, James, N.Y. Jets	2.0
Rhodes, Kerry, N.Y. Jets	1.0
Robertson, Dewayne, N.Y. Jets	3.5
Robinson, Dunta, Houston	1.0
Roth, Matt, Miami	1.0
Routt, Stanford, Oakland	1.0
Roye, Orpheus, Cleveland	3.0
Sands, Terdell, Oakland	1.0
Sapp, Benny, Kansas City	2.5
Sapp, Warren, Oakland	5.0
Schobel, Aaron, Buffalo	12.0
Schobel, Bo, Tennessee	1.0
Schulters, Lance, Miami	2.0
Scott, Bart, Baltimore	4.0
Scott, DeQuincy, San Diego	4.5
Seau, Junior, Miami	1.0
Seymour, Richard, New England	4.0
Simmons, Brian, Cincinnati	4.0
Simmons, Jason, Houston	1.0
Sirmon, Peter, Tennessee	2.5
Smith, Aaron, Pittsburgh	2.0
Smith, Daryl, Jacksonville	4.0
Smith, Justin, Cincinnati	6.0
Smith, Robaire, Houston	1.5
Spicer, Paul, Jacksonville	7.5
Spikes, Takeo, Buffalo	1.0
Spragan, Donnie, Miami	1.0
Starks, Randy, Tennessee	3.0
Stroud, Marcus, Jacksonville	1.0
Suggs, Terrell, Baltimore	8.5
Taylor, Jason, Miami	12.0
Thomas, Adalius, Baltimore	9.0
Thomas, Bryan, N.Y. Jets	3.5
Thomas, Josh, Indianapolis	3.0
Thomas, Zach, Miami	2.0
Thompson, Chaun, Cleveland	5.0
Thompson, Lamont, Tennessee	1.0
Thornton, David, Indianapolis	2.0
Thornton, John, Cincinnati	2.0
Thurman, Odell, Cincinnati	1.5
Townsend, Deshea, Pittsburgh	3.0
Traylor, Keith, Miami	2.0
Tripplett, Larry, Indianapolis	4.0
Vanden Bosch, Kyle, Tennessee	12.5
Veal, Demetrin, Denver	1.0
Vilma, Jonathan, N.Y. Jets	0.5
von Oelhoffen, Kimo, Pittsburgh	3.5
Vrabel, Mike, New England	4.5
Waddell, Michael, Tennessee	0.5
Walker, Gary, Houston	1.0
Warren, Gerard, Denver	3.0
Warren, Ty, New England	1.5
Washington, Rashad, N.Y. Jets	1.0
Weaver, Anthony, Baltimore	2.0
Wilfork, Vince, New England	0.5
Wilhelm, Matt, San Diego	1.0
Williams, Chad, Baltimore	1.5
Williams, Darrent, Denver	1.0
Wilson, Al, Denver	3.0
Wong, Kailee, Houston	1.0
Wright, Manuel, Miami	1.0
Zgonina, Jeff, Miami	2.0

NFC

Player, team	No.
Adams, Anthony, San Francisco	2.5
Adams, Mike, San Francisco	1.0
Allen, Kenderick, N.Y. Giants	2.0
Archuleta, Adam, St. Louis	3.5
Atogwe, O.J., St. Louis	1.0
Azumah, Jerry, Chicago	1.0
Babineaux, Jonathan, Atlanta	0.5
Bailey, Boss, Detroit	1.0
Barber, Ronde, Tampa Bay	2.0
Barnett, Nick, Green Bay	1.0
Bernard, Rocky, Seattle	8.5
Berry, Bertrand, Arizona	6.0
Blackstock, Darryl, Arizona	1.0
Boone, Alfonso, Chicago	1.5
Boulware, Michael, Seattle	2.0
Briggs, Lance, Chicago	2.0
Brooking, Keith, Atlanta	3.5
Brooks, Derrick, Tampa Bay	3.0
Brown, Alex, Chicago	6.0
Brown, Mike, Chicago	1.0
Brown, Sheldon, Philadelphia	1.0
Bryant, Tony, New Orleans	4.0
Buckner, Brentson, Carolina	1.0
Burnett, Kevin, Dallas	1.0
Canty, Chris, Dallas	2.5
Carstens, Jordan, Carolina	4.0
Carter, Andre, San Francisco	4.5
Claiborne, Chris, St. Louis	0.5
Clancy, Kendrick, N.Y. Giants	2.0
Clark, Ryan, Washington	0.5
Clemons, Chris, Washington	2.0
Coakley, Dexter, St. Louis	2.0
Cody, Shaun, Detroit	1.5
Cole, Colin, Green Bay	2.0
Cole, Trent, Philadelphia	5.0
Coleman, Kenyon, Dallas	0.5
Coleman, Rod, Atlanta	10.5
Cowart, Sam, Minnesota	2.0
Craft, Jason, New Orleans	1.0
Daniels, Phillip, Washington	8.0
Dansby, Karlos, Arizona	4.0
Darby, Chartric, Seattle	2.5
Darling, James, Arizona	1.0
Davis, Chauncey, Atlanta	1.0
Davis, Thomas, Carolina	1.5
Dawkins, Brian, Philadelphia	3.5
DeVries, Jared, Detroit	3.0
Dockett, Darnell, Arizona	0.5
Douglas, Marques, San Francisco	1.0
Draft, Chris, Carolina	2.0
Edwards, Kalimba, Detroit	7.0
Ellis, Greg, Dallas	8.0
Emanuel, Ben, San Francisco	0.5
Evans, Demetric, Washington	3.0
Ferguson, Jason, Dallas	1.0
Fisher, Bryce, Seattle	9.0
Fujita, Scott, Dallas	2.0
Gbaja-Biamila, Kabeer, Green Bay	8.0
Glover, La'Roi, Dallas	3.0
Grant, Charles, New Orleans	2.5
Green, Brandon, St. Louis	3.0
Greisen, Nick, N.Y. Giants	1.0
Griffin, Cornelius, Washington	4.0
Hall, James, Detroit	5.0
Hall, Travis, San Francisco	0.5
Hargrove, Anthony, St. Louis	6.5
Harris, Al, Green Bay	3.0
Harris, Chris, Chicago	1.0
Harris, Napoleon, Minnesota	1.0
Harris, Tommie, Chicago	3.0

Player, team	No.
Haynes, Michael, Chicago	1.5
Henderson, E.J., Minnesota	1.0
Hill, LeRoy, Seattle	7.5
Hillenmeyer, Hunter, Chicago	1.0
Howard, Darren, New Orleans	3.5
Huff, Orlando, Arizona	1.0
Idonije, Israel, Chicago	1.0
Ivy, Corey, St. Louis	2.0
Jackson, Dexter, Tampa Bay	1.0
Jackson, Grady, Green Bay	1.0
Jackson, Tyoka, St. Louis	2.5
James, Bradie, Dallas	2.5
James, Erasmus, Minnesota	4.0
Jenkins, Cullen, Green Bay	3.0
Johnson, Derrick, San Francisco	1.0
Johnson, Tank, Chicago	5.0
Johnstone, Lance, Minnesota	7.5
Joseph, William, N.Y. Giants	2.0
Kalu, N.D., Philadelphia	2.0
Kampman, Aaron, Green Bay	6.5
Kearse, Jevon, Philadelphia	7.5
Kelly, Brian, Tampa Bay	1.0
Kennedy, Jimmy, St. Louis	3.0
Kerney, Patrick, Atlanta	6.5
Kolodziej, Ross, Arizona	3.0
Lake, Antwan, Atlanta	3.5
Lavalais, Chad, Atlanta	2.5
Lenon, Paris, Green Bay	1.5
Lewis, Damione, St. Louis	1.0
Lewis, Michael, Philadelphia	1.0
Little, Leonard, St. Louis	9.5
Marshall, Lemar, Washington	2.0
McFarland, Anthony, Tampa Bay	2.0
Minter, Mike, Carolina	1.5
Montgomery, Michael, Green Bay	1.0
Moore, Brandon, San Francisco	5.0
Moore, Langston, Arizona	1.0
Moorehead, Kindal, Carolina	5.0
Morgan, Dan, Carolina	3.0
Mosley, C.J., Minnesota	3.0
Nece, Ryan, Tampa Bay	2.0
Newman, Keith, Minnesota	3.0
Newman, Terence, Dallas	1.0
Nguyen, Dat, Dallas	1.0
Ogunleye, Adewale, Chicago	10.0
Okeafor, Chike, Arizona	7.5
Pace, Calvin, Arizona	1.0
Patterson, Mike, Philadelphia	3.5
Peppers, Julius, Carolina	10.5
Peterson, Julian, San Francisco	3.0
Peterson, Kenny, Green Bay	3.0
Pickett, Ryan, St. Louis	2.0
Pierce, Antonio, N.Y. Giants	2.5
Poppinga, Brady, Green Bay	2.0
Prioleau, Pierson, Washington	3.0
Quarles, Shelton, Tampa Bay	1.0
Ratliff, Jay, Dallas	1.0
Rayburn, Sam, Philadelphia	1.0
Redding, Cory, Detroit	1.0
Rice, Simeon, Tampa Bay	14.0
Robbins, Fred, N.Y. Giants	1.5
Rogers, Shaun, Detroit	5.5
Rucker, Mike, Carolina	7.5
Salave'a, Joe, Washington	0.5
Scott, Bryan, Atlanta	1.0
Scott, Darrion, Minnesota	4.0
Shanle, Scott, Dallas	1.5
Sheppard, Lito, Philadelphia	1.0
Short, Brandon, Carolina	0.5
Shropshire, Darrell, Atlanta	2.0
Smith, Antonio, Arizona	3.0
Smith, Brady, Atlanta	3.0
Smith, Dwight, New Orleans	1.0
Smith, Keith, Detroit	1.0
Smith, Raonall, Minnesota	1.0
Smith, Will, New Orleans	8.5
Spears, Marcus, Dallas	1.5
Spires, Greg, Tampa Bay	4.0
Strahan, Michael, N.Y. Giants	11.5
Tafoya, Joe, Seattle	1.0
Tatupu, Lofa, Seattle	4.0
Taylor, Sean, Washington	1.0
Terrill, Craig, Seattle	2.0
Thomas, Fred, New Orleans	3.0
Tillman, Charles, Chicago	1.0
Tinoisamoa, Pisa, St. Louis	1.5
Trotter, Jeremiah, Philadelphia	1.0
Trufant, Marcus, Seattle	1.0
Tubbs, Marcus, Seattle	5.5
Tuck, Justin, N.Y. Giants	1.0
Udeze, Kenechi, Minnesota	1.0
Umenyiora, Osi, N.Y. Giants	14.5
Urlacher, Brian, Chicago	6.0
Walker, Darwin, Philadelphia	2.5
Wallace, Al, Carolina	5.0
Ware, DeMarcus, Dallas	8.0
Washington, Marcus, Washington	7.5
Watson, Courtney, New Orleans	1.0
White, Dewayne, Tampa Bay	3.0
Whitehead, Willie, New Orleans	0.5
Wilkinson, Dan, Detroit	3.0
Williams, Brian, Minnesota	1.0
Williams, Corey, Green Bay	2.0
Williams, Demorrio, Atlanta	3.0
Williams, Kevin, Minnesota	4.0
Williams, Pat, Minnesota	1.5
Williams, Roy, Dallas	2.5
Wilson, Adrian, Arizona	8.0
Wilson, Gibril, N.Y. Giants	3.0
Wistrom, Grant, Seattle	4.0
Witherspoon, Will, Carolina	2.5
Woods, LeVar, Detroit	1.0
Wyms, Ellis, Tampa Bay	2.0
Wynn, Renaldo, Washington	0.5
Young, Bryant, San Francisco	8.0

FUMBLES

AFC

Team	Fum.	Own Fum. Rec.	Own Fum. *O.B.	Own Fum. Lost	TD	Opp Fum. Rec.	TD	†Yards	Total Rec.
Cincinnati	18	9	3	6	0	13	0	79	22
Indianapolis	14	5	1	8	0	13	2	123	18
Denver	19	8	2	9	0	16	0	-1	24
New England	19	9	1	9	0	8	0	21	17
Pittsburgh	22	13	0	9	0	15	1	111	28
Oakland	26	14	3	9	0	14	1	-6	28
Buffalo	26	12	4	10	0	13	0	15	25
Jacksonville	27	14	2	11	0	9	0	0	23
Houston	30	17	2	11	0	9	0	-14	26
Tennessee	27	12	3	12	0	11	2	102	23
Cleveland	27	14	0	13	0	8	0	5	22
Kansas City	23	10	0	13	0	15	1	72	25
San Diego	22	9	0	13	0	10	0	34	19
Miami	31	16	1	14	0	17	1	48	33
Baltimore	28	13	0	15	0	15	2	70	28
N.Y. Jets	36	16	1	19	0	7	1	60	23
AFC total	395	191	23	181	0	193	11	719	384
AFC average	24.7	11.9	1.4	11.3	0.0	12.1	0.7	44.9	24.0

*Fumbled out of bounds.
†Includes all fumble yardage (aborted plays and recoveries of own and opponents' fumbles).

NFC

Team	Fum.	Own Fum. Rec.	Own Fum. *O.B.	Own Fum. Lost	TD	Opp Fum. Rec.	TD	†Yards	Total Rec.
Seattle	18	9	2	7	0	11	1	43	20
N.Y. Giants	17	8	1	8	0	19	1	61	27
Tampa Bay	16	6	1	9	0	13	3	88	19
Carolina	23	11	2	10	0	19	1	78	30
Detroit	21	9	0	12	0	12	1	101	21
Chicago	32	18	1	13	0	10	0	38	28
St. Louis	24	9	2	13	0	14	0	-10	23
Dallas	36	20	2	14	0	11	0	93	31
Philadelphia	34	17	3	14	0	10	1	90	27
San Francisco	31	17	0	14	1	10	1	63	27
Green Bay	31	15	1	15	0	11	0	11	26
Minnesota	25	9	1	15	0	11	0	16	20
Atlanta	26	6	4	16	0	13	2	121	19
Arizona	26	10	0	16	0	11	0	-9	21
Washington	29	10	3	16	0	12	1	25	22
New Orleans	23	3	2	18	0	9	0	12	12
NFC total	412	177	25	210	1	196	12	821	373
NFC average	25.8	11.1	1.6	13.1	0.1	12.3	0.8	51.3	23.3
NFL total	807	368	48	391	1	389	23	1540	757
NFL average	25.2	11.5	1.5	12.2	0.0	12.2	0.7	48.1	23.7

*Fumbled out of bounds.
†Includes all fumble yardage (aborted plays and recoveries of own and opponents' fumbles).

INDIVIDUAL

BESTS OF THE SEASON

Fumbles, season
AFC: 17—David Carr, Houston.
NFC: 17—Drew Bledsoe, Dallas.

Fumbles, game
AFC: 6—Chad Pennington, N.Y. Jets at Kansas City, Sep. 11.
NFC: 3—Held by 9 players.

Own fumbles recovered, season
AFC: 6—David Carr, Houston.
NFC: 6—Alex Smith, San Francisco.

Own fumbles recovered, game
AFC: 3—Chad Pennington, N.Y. Jets at Kansas City, Sep. 11.
NFC: 3—Drew Bledsoe, Dallas vs. Washington, Sep. 19; Mike McMahon, Philadelphia at N.Y. Giants, Nov. 20.

Opponents' fumbles recovered, season
AFC: 4—Randall Godfrey, San Diego; Montae Reagor, Indianapolis.
NFC: 3—Held by 7 players.

Opponents' fumbles recovered, game
AFC: 2—Kawika Mitchell, Kansas City vs. N.Y. Jets, Sep. 11; Jared Allen, Kansas City vs. Washington, Oct. 16; Troy Polamalu, Pittsburgh at Green Bay, Nov. 6; Ellis Hobbs, New England at Miami, Nov. 13.
NFC: 2—Nick Barnett, Green Bay at Atlanta, Nov. 13; Ricky Manning, Carolina at Atlanta, Jan. 1.

Yards returning fumbles, season
NFC: 86—DeAngelo Hall, Atlanta.
AFC: 85—Jason Taylor, Miami.

Longest fumble return
AFC: 85—Jason Taylor, Miami vs. Denver, Sep. 11 (TD).
NFC: 80—Sheldon Brown, Philadelphia at Dallas, Oct. 9 (TD).

2005 STATISTICS Fumbles

AFC

Player, team	Fum.	Own Rec.	Opp. Rec.	Yds.	Tot. Rec.	TD
Abraham, John, N.Y. Jets	0	0	1	0	1	0
Adams, Charlie, Denver	4	0	0	0	0	0
Aiken, Sam, Buffalo	0	0	1	0	1	0
Alexander, Roc, Denver	0	0	1	0	1	0
Allen, Jared, Kansas City	0	0	2	0	2	0
Anderson, Bennie, Buffalo	0	1	0	0	1	0
Anderson, Charlie, Houston	0	0	1	0	1	0
Anderson, Courtney, Oakland	1	0	0	0	0	0
Anderson, Mike, Denver	2	0	0	0	0	0
Ashworth, Tom, New England.	0	1	0	0	1	0
Ayodele, Akin, Jacksonville	0	0	1	0	1	0
Badger, Brad, Oakland	0	2	0	0	2	0
Baker, Chris, N.Y. Jets	1	0	0	0	0	0
Barrett, David, N.Y. Jets	1	0	1	30	1	0
Batch, Charlie, Pittsburgh	1	2	0	0	2	0
Bell, Tatum, Denver	3	1	0	0	1	0
Bell, Yeremiah, Miami	0	0	2	12	2	0
Bironas, Rob, Tennessee	0	1	0	0	1	0
Bober, Chris, Kansas City	0	1	0	0	1	0
Boller, Kyle, Baltimore	8	4	0	0	4	0
Bollinger, Brooks, N.Y. Jets	3	2	0	-3	2	0
Brady, Kyle, Jacksonville	3	1	0	0	1	0
Brady, Tom, New England	4	0	0	0	0	0
Brandon, Sam, Denver	0	0	1	0	1	0
Brees, Drew, San Diego	8	0	0	0	0	0
Brock, Raheem, Indianapolis	0	0	1	15	1	0
Brown, Chris, Tennessee	4	0	0	0	0	0
Brown, Courtney, Denver	0	0	2	0	2	0
Brown, Mark, N.Y. Jets	0	1	0	0	1	0
Brown, Ronnie, Miami	4	2	0	0	2	0
Bruener, Mark, Houston	0	2	0	0	2	0
Bryant, Antonio, Cleveland	1	1	0	0	1	0
Buchanon, Phillip, Houston	2	2	0	0	2	0
Bulluck, Keith, Tennessee	0	0	1	0	1	0
Burgess, Derrick, Oakland	0	0	2	0	2	0
Burns, Keith, Denver	0	1	0	0	1	0
Caldwell, Reche, San Diego	2	0	0	0	0	0
Calico, Tyrone, Tennessee	1	0	0	0	0	0
Carey, Vernon, Miami	0	0	1	0	1	0
Carlisle, Cooper, Denver	0	2	0	0	2	0
Carr, Chris, Oakland	5	3	0	-1	3	0
Carr, David, Houston	17	6	0	-7	6	0
Carter, Kevin, Miami	0	0	1	0	1	0
Carter, Tyrone, Pittsburgh	0	0	1	0	1	0
Carthon, Ran, Indianapolis	1	0	0	0	0	0
Cassel, Matt, New England	2	1	0	-1	1	0
Chambers, Chris, Miami	5	2	0	-2	2	0
Clements, Nate, Buffalo	0	0	1	0	1	0
Clemons, Duane, Cincinnati	0	0	1	0	1	0
Colclough, Ricardo, Pittsburgh	1	0	0	0	0	0
Coleman, Marcus, Houston	1	0	0	0	0	0
Coles, Laveranues, N.Y. Jets	1	0	0	0	0	0
Collins, Kerry, Oakland	13	1	0	-16	1	0
Colvin, Rosevelt, New England	0	0	1	0	1	0
Cooper, Deke, Jacksonville	0	1	0	0	1	0
Cooper, Jarrod, Oakland	0	0	2	0	2	1
Cotchery, Jerricho, N.Y. Jets	2	1	0	0	1	0
Cousin, Terry, Jacksonville	0	1	0	0	1	0
Cribbs, Joshua, Cleveland	4	0	0	0	0	0
Crocker, Chris, Cleveland	0	0	1	0	1	0
Crockett, Zack, Oakland	1	1	0	0	1	0
Crowder, Channing, Miami	0	0	2	0	2	0
Daniels, Travis, Miami	0	0	1	0	1	0
David, Jason, Indianapolis	1	0	2	5	2	0
Davis, Domanick, Houston	2	1	0	0	1	0
Dayne, Ron, Denver	1	0	0	0	0	0
Demps, Will, Baltimore	0	0	2	22	2	0
Denney, John, Miami	1	0	0	-12	0	0
Denney, Ryan, Buffalo	0	0	1	0	1	0

Player, team	Fum.	Own Rec.	Opp. Rec.	Yds.	Tot. Rec.	TD
Devoe, Todd, Denver	0	0	2	0	2	0
Dilfer, Trent, Cleveland	9	0	0	-14	0	0
Dillon, Corey, New England	1	0	0	0	0	0
Dinkins, Darnell, Baltimore	0	1	0	0	1	0
Droughns, Reuben, Cleveland.	6	5	0	0	5	0
Dwight, Tim, New England	1	1	0	0	1	0
Ekuban, Ebenezer, Denver	0	0	1	0	1	0
Evans, Troy, Houston	0	1	0	0	1	0
Faneca, Alan, Pittsburgh	0	2	0	0	2	0
Farrior, James, Pittsburgh	0	0	1	0	1	0
Faulk, Kevin, New England	3	1	0	0	1	0
Ferguson, Nick, Denver	0	0	1	0	1	0
Fiedler, Jay, N.Y. Jets	1	1	0	-5	1	0
Fleming, Troy, Tennessee	0	1	0	0	1	0
Fletcher, London, Buffalo	0	0	2	0	2	0
Florence, Drayton, San Diego	1	0	0	0	0	0
Flutie, Doug, New England	2	1	0	-9	1	0
Foote, Larry, Pittsburgh	0	0	1	27	1	0
Foxworth, Domonique, Denver	0	1	1	9	2	0
Frerotte, Gus, Miami	13	4	0	-36	4	0
Frye, Charlie, Cleveland	7	2	0	-11	2	0
Garrard, David, Jacksonville	4	1	0	0	1	0
Gibson, Derrick, Oakland	0	0	1	0	1	0
Gilbert, Tony, Jacksonville	0	0	1	0	1	0
Godfrey, Randall, San Diego	0	0	4	35	4	0
Gold, Ian, Denver	0	0	2	0	2	0
Gonzalez, Tony, Kansas City	0	1	0	0	1	0
Graham, Ben, N.Y. Jets	1	0	0	-9	0	0
Graham, Daniel, New England	1	1	0	0	1	0
Gray, Quinn, Jacksonville	1	0	0	0	0	0
Green, Roderick, Baltimore	0	0	1	0	1	0
Green, Trent, Kansas City	8	1	0	-10	1	0
Greenwood, Morlon, Houston	0	0	2	0	2	0
Griffin, Kris, Kansas City	0	0	1	0	1	0
Hall, Carlos, Kansas City	0	0	1	0	1	0
Hall, Dante, Kansas City	5	2	0	0	2	0
Hamilton, Bobby, Oakland	0	0	2	8	2	0
Harper, Nick, Indianapolis	0	0	1	7	1	0
Harrison, James, Pittsburgh	0	1	0	0	1	0
Hart, Clinton, San Diego	0	0	2	-1	2	0
Hartings, Jeff, Pittsburgh	1	0	0	-9	0	0
Haynes, Verron, Pittsburgh	2	1	0	0	1	0
Hayward, Reggie, Jacksonville	0	0	1	0	1	0
Heap, Todd, Baltimore	1	1	0	0	1	0
Henry, Chris, Cincinnati	2	0	0	0	0	0
Henry, Travis, Tennessee	2	1	0	0	1	0
Hentrich, Craig, Tennessee	1	0	0	-3	0	0
Hobbs, Ellis, New England	1	1	1	7	2	0
Hobson, Victor, N.Y. Jets	0	0	1	43	1	0
Holcomb, Kelly, Buffalo	13	3	0	-31	3	0
Holliday, Vonnie, Miami	0	0	2	12	2	0
Holmes, Priest, Kansas City	1	0	0	0	0	0
Hope, Chris, Pittsburgh	0	0	1	6	1	0
Hopkins, Brad, Tennessee	0	1	0	0	1	0
Houshmandzadeh, T.J., Cincinnati	1	0	0	0	0	0
Houston, Cedric, N.Y. Jets	1	0	0	0	0	0
Howard, Reggie, Miami	0	1	0	0	1	0
Iwuoma, Chidi, Pittsburgh	0	0	1	0	1	0
Jackson, Eddie, Miami	0	0	1	0	1	0
Jackson, Marlin, Indianapolis	1	0	0	0	0	0
James, Edgerrin, Indianapolis	2	1	0	0	1	0
James, Tory, Cincinnati	0	0	1	26	1	0
Johnson, Andre, Houston	1	0	0	0	0	0
Johnson, Bethel, New England	1	1	0	0	1	0
Johnson, Chad, Cincinnati	1	0	0	0	0	0
Johnson, Derrick, Kansas City	0	0	1	0	1	0
Johnson, Jeremi, Cincinnati	2	1	0	0	1	0
Johnson, Larry, Kansas City	5	3	0	0	3	0
Johnson, Rudi, Cincinnati	1	2	0	0	2	0
Jolley, Doug, N.Y. Jets	1	0	0	0	0	0
Jones, Levi, Cincinnati	0	1	0	0	1	0

Player, team	Fum.	Own Rec.	Opp. Rec.	Yds.	Tot. Rec.	TD
Jones, Matt, Jacksonville........	2	2	0	0	2	0
Jones, Pacman, Tennessee.....	5	1	0	0	1	0
Jones, Sean, Cleveland...........	0	1	0	11	1	0
Jordan, LaMont, Oakland........	2	0	0	0	0	0
Jordan, Leander, San Diego.....	0	1	0	0	1	0
Kaesviharn, Kevin, Cincinnati..	0	0	3	0	3	0
Kassell, Brad, Tennessee........	0	0	3	0	3	0
Katula, Matt, Baltimore	1	0	0	-10	0	0
Keisel, Brett, Pittsburgh..........	0	0	1	0	1	0
Kelly, Reggie, Cincinnati	1	1	0	0	1	0
Kelsay, Chris, Buffalo	0	0	1	2	1	0
Kemoeatu, Maake, Baltimore..	0	0	1	0	1	0
Kennison, Eddie, Kansas City .	1	0	0	0	0	0
Kiel, Terrence, San Diego........	0	0	1	0	1	0
Kirschke, Travis, Pittsburgh....	0	0	1	0	1	0
Knight, Sammy, Kansas City...	0	0	2	80	2	1
LaBoy, Travis, Tennessee........	0	0	1	0	1	0
Law, Ty, N.Y. Jets....................	1	1	0	0	1	0
Leber, Ben, San Diego	0	0	1	0	1	0
Leftwich, Byron, Jacksonville .	8	1	0	0	1	0
Lewis, Jamal, Baltimore..........	5	0	0	0	0	0
Lewis, Ray, Baltimore	0	0	1	0	1	0
Lilja, Ryan, Indianapolis..........	0	1	0	0	1	0
Losman, J.P., Buffalo	7	3	0	-2	3	0
Maddox, Tommy, Pittsburgh...	2	0	0	-9	0	0
Mankins, Logan, New England	0	1	0	0	1	0
Manning, Peyton, Indianapolis	5	0	0	-1	0	0
Manuwai, Vince, Jacksonville .	0	2	0	0	2	0
Mare, Olindo, Miami	0	0	1	0	1	0
Martin, Curtis, N.Y. Jets..........	2	2	0	0	2	0
Mason, Derrick, Baltimore	1	0	0	0	0	0
Mathis, Jerome, Houston	3	1	0	0	1	0
Mathis, Rashean, Jacksonville	0	0	1	0	1	0
Mauck, Matt, Tennessee	1	0	0	0	0	0
Mawae, Kevin, N.Y. Jets.........	1	0	0	-6	0	0
McCray, Bobby, Jacksonville...	0	0	1	0	1	0
McDougle, Stockar, Miami......	0	1	0	0	1	0
McFadden, Bryant, Pittsburgh	0	0	1	9	1	0
McGahee, Willis, Buffalo.........	1	0	0	0	0	0
McGee, Terrence, Buffalo........	1	1	1	0	2	0
McGinest, Willie, New England	0	0	1	19	1	0
McKinney, Steve, Houston......	1	0	0	-1	0	0
McMichael, Randy, Miami.......	1	0	0	0	0	0
McNair, Steve, Tennessee.......	7	2	0	-1	2	0
Meier, Rob, Jacksonville	0	0	1	0	1	0
Mickens, Ray, Cleveland	0	0	1	13	1	0
Miller, Caleb, Cincinnati	0	0	1	0	1	0
Miller, Heath, Pittsburgh	0	1	0	0	1	0
Miller, Justin, N.Y. Jets	3	0	0	0	0	0
Milloy, Lawyer, Buffalo............	0	0	1	0	1	0
Mitchell, Kawika, Kansas City .	0	1	1	0	2	0
Morency, Vernand, Houston	1	0	1	0	1	0
Morey, Sean, Pittsburgh	0	1	0	0	1	0
Morgan, Quincy, Pittsburgh....	1	0	0	0	0	0
Morris, Rob, Indianapolis........	0	0	1	0	1	0
Morrison, Kirk, Oakland..........	0	0	2	0	2	0
Moss, Randy, Oakland............	0	1	0	0	1	0
Mughelli, Ovie, Baltimore	1	0	0	0	0	0
Myers, Michael, Denver..........	0	0	1	0	1	0
Naeole, Chris, Jacksonville	0	1	0	0	1	0
Navies, Hannibal, Cincinnati ...	0	0	1	0	1	0
Neal, Lorenzo, San Diego	0	1	0	0	1	0
Nickey, Donnie, Tennessee.....	0	1	0	0	1	0
O'Neal, Deltha, Cincinnati	0	0	1	26	1	0
Oben, Roman, San Diego	0	1	0	0	1	0
Odom, Antwan, Tennessee	0	0	2	52	2	2
Ogden, Jonathan, Baltimore ...	0	2	0	0	2	0
Olivea, Shane, San Diego	0	2	0	0	2	0
Olson, Benji, Tennessee..........	0	1	0	0	1	0
Owens, Chad, Jacksonville	2	1	0	0	1	0
Palmer, Carson, Cincinnati......	5	1	0	-2	1	0

Player, team	Fum.	Own Rec.	Opp. Rec.	Yds.	Tot. Rec.	TD
Parker, Eric, San Diego	2	1	0	0	1	0
Parker, J'Vonne, Cleveland......	0	0	1	0	1	0
Parker, Samie, Kansas City	2	0	0	0	0	0
Parker, Willie, Pittsburgh	4	2	0	0	2	0
Parrish, Roscoe, Buffalo.........	2	1	0	0	1	0
Pass, Patrick, New England	2	0	0	0	0	0
Payton, Jarrett, Tennessee......	0	1	0	0	1	0
Pearman, Alvin, Jacksonville ..	4	1	0	0	1	0
Peek, Antwan, Houston	0	0	2	0	2	0
Pennington, Chad, N.Y. Jets ...	8	4	0	-22	4	0
Perry, Chris, Cincinnati	2	1	0	0	1	0
Perry, Tab, Cincinnati.............	1	1	1	0	2	0
Peterson, Mike, Jacksonville...	0	0	1	0	1	0
Phillips, Shaun, San Diego	0	0	1	0	1	0
Plummer, Jake, Denver...........	4	1	0	-10	1	0
Polamalu, Troy, Pittsburgh	0	0	2	78	2	1
Pollack, David, Cincinnati	0	0	1	6	1	0
Polley, Tommy, Baltimore	0	0	1	2	1	0
Pool, Brodney, Cleveland	0	1	1	0	2	0
Porter, Jerry, Oakland	1	1	0	0	1	0
Porter, Joey, Pittsburgh	0	0	1	0	1	0
Posey, Jeff, Buffalo.................	0	0	1	46	1	0
Pucillo, Mike, Cleveland..........	0	1	0	0	1	0
Putzier, Jeb, Denver................	1	1	0	0	1	0
Randall, Marcus, Tennessee ...	0	1	0	0	1	0
Randle El, Antwaan, Pittsburgh	4	0	0	0	0	0
Ratliff, Keiwan, Cincinnati	0	0	1	0	1	0
Reagor, Montae, Indianapolis .	0	0	4	37	4	1
Reed, James, N.Y. Jets	0	0	2	33	2	1
Reid, Dexter, Indianapolis.......	0	1	0	0	1	0
Reynolds, Robert, Tennessee .	0	1	0	0	1	0
Rhodes, Dominic, Indianapolis	2	0	0	0	0	0
Rivers, Marcellus, Houston.....	0	0	1	0	1	0
Rivers, Philip, San Diego	2	0	0	0	0	0
Robinson, Dunta, Houston	0	1	0	0	1	0
Roby, Courtney, Tennessee.....	1	0	0	0	0	0
Roethlisberger, Ben, Pittsburgh	2	1	0	-1	1	0
Rosenfels, Sage, Miami	1	1	0	-11	1	0
Roth, Matt, Miami...................	0	0	1	0	1	0
Roye, Orpheus, Cleveland......	0	0	1	6	1	0
Ruff, Orlando, Cleveland	0	0	1	0	1	0
Sanders, Bob, Indianapolis.....	0	0	1	0	1	0
Sanders, Deion, Baltimore	1	0	0	0	0	0
Sanders, James, New England	0	0	1	0	1	0
Sands, Terdell, Oakland	0	0	1	0	1	0
Sape, Lauvale, Buffalo	0	0	1	0	1	0
Sapp, Cecil, Denver................	0	1	1	0	2	0
Saturday, Jeff, Indianapolis.....	0	1	1	0	2	0
Schobel, Aaron, Buffalo..........	0	0	1	0	1	0
Schobel, Matt, Cincinnati........	1	0	0	0	0	0
Schweigert, Stuart, Oakland	0	0	3	3	3	0
Scifres, Mike, San Diego.........	1	1	0	0	1	0
Scott, Bart, Baltimore	0	0	2	11	2	0
Sensabaugh, Gerald, Jacksonville	0	0	1	0	1	0
Seymour, Richard, New England	0	0	1	0	1	0
Shelton, Daimon, Buffalo........	1	0	0	0	0	0
Siavii, Junior, Kansas City.......	0	0	1	0	1	0
Simmons, Brian, Cincinnati	1	0	0	0	0	0
Simmons, Jason, Houston	0	0	1	0	1	0
Sims, Barry, Oakland	0	2	0	0	2	0
Sirmon, Peter, Tennessee.......	0	0	1	41	1	0
Slaughter, Chad, Oakland........	0	1	0	0	1	0
Smith, Aaron, Pittsburgh........	0	0	1	0	1	0
Smith, Jonathan, Buffalo.........	1	1	0	0	1	0
Smith, Justin, Cincinnati..........	0	0	1	0	1	0
Smith, Robaire, Houston	0	0	1	3	1	0
Smith, Rod, Denver	2	0	0	0	0	0
Smith, Terrelle, Cleveland	0	1	0	0	1	0
Sorgi, Jim, Indianapolis...........	1	0	0	0	0	0
Sowell, Jerald, N.Y. Jets	1	3	0	0	3	0
Speegle, Nick, Cleveland.........	0	0	1	0	1	0

Player, team	Fum.	Own Rec.	Opp. Rec.	Yds.	Tot. Rec.	TD
Spicer, Paul, Jacksonville	0	0	1	0	1	0
Sproles, Darren, San Diego	3	1	0	0	1	0
Staley, Duce, Pittsburgh	1	1	0	0	1	0
Stanley, Chad, Houston	1	0	0	-9	0	0
Stills, Gary, Kansas City..........	0	0	1	0	1	0
Stone, Ron, Oakland..............	0	2	0	0	2	0
Strait, Derrick, N.Y. Jets.........	0	0	1	0	1	0
Suggs, Terrell, Baltimore	0	0	1	0	1	0
Surtain, Patrick, Kansas City...	1	0	1	2	1	0
Taylor, Chester, Baltimore	3	0	0	0	0	0
Taylor, Fred, Jacksonville........	0	1	0	0	1	0
Taylor, Ike, Pittsburgh............	0	0	2	8	2	0
Taylor, Jason, Miami..............	0	0	2	85	2	1
Teague, Trey, Buffalo..............	0	1	0	0	1	0
Terry, Adam, Baltimore	0	1	0	0	1	0
Testaverde, Vinny, N.Y. Jets....	7	1	0	-5	1	0
Thomas, Adalius, Baltimore....	0	1	3	44	4	2
Thomas, Zach, Miami	0	0	1	0	1	0
Thompson, Chaun, Cleveland .	0	0	1	0	1	0
Thornton, John, Cincinnati	0	0	1	0	1	0
Thurman, Odell, Cincinnati	0	1	0	23	1	0
Tillman, Travares, Miami.........	0	0	1	0	1	0
Tomlinson, LaDainian, San Diego	3	1	0	0	1	0
Townsend, Deshea, Pittsburgh	0	0	1	2	1	0
Tripplett, Larry, Indianapolis ...	0	0	2	60	2	1
Troupe, Ben, Tennessee.........	2	0	0	0	0	0
Tuiasosopo, Marques, Oakland	2	0	0	0	0	0
Unck, Mason, Cleveland	0	2	0	0	2	0
Vanden Bosch, Kyle, Tennessee	0	0	1	0	1	0
Veal, Demetrin, Denver...........	0	0	1	0	1	0
Vilma, Jonathan, N.Y. Jets	1	0	1	4	1	0
Vincent, Troy, Buffalo.............	0	0	2	0	2	0
Volek, Billy, Tennessee...........	3	0	0	0	0	0
Wade, Todd, Houston	0	1	0	0	1	0
Walker, Ramon, Houston........	0	0	1	0	1	0
Ward, B.J., Baltimore.............	0	0	1	11	1	0
Ward, Hines, Pittsburgh	1	0	0	0	0	0
Warfield, Eric, Kansas City.....	0	0	2	0	2	0
Warren, Greg, Pittsburgh........	1	0	0	0	0	0
Warren, Ty, New England........	0	0	1	5	1	0
Washington, Dewayne, Kansas City	0	0	1	0	1	0
Washington, Fabian, Oakland .	0	0	1	0	1	0
Waters, Brian, Kansas City	0	1	0	0	1	0
Watson, Ben, New England.....	1	0	0	0	0	0
Wayne, Reggie, Indianapolis...	1	1	0	0	1	0
Weary, Fred, Houston	0	1	0	0	1	0
Weaver, Anthony, Baltimore....	0	0	1	0	1	0
Welker, Wes, Miami	5	4	0	0	4	0
Wells, Jonathan, Houston.......	1	0	0	0	0	0
Wilcox, Daniel, Baltimore........	0	0	1	0	1	0
Wilfork, Vince, New England...	0	0	1	0	1	0
Wilkerson, Jimmy, Kansas City	0	0	1	0	1	0
Williams, Darrent, Denver.......	2	0	1	0	1	0
Williams, Jamal, San Diego	0	0	1	0	1	0
Williams, Maurice, Jacksonville	0	1	0	0	1	0
Williams, Reggie, Jacksonville	2	0	0	0	0	0
Williams, Ricky, Miami	1	1	0	0	1	0
Williams, Shaud, Buffalo	0	0	1	0	1	0
Williams, Tank, Tennessee	0	0	1	5	1	0
Wilson, Al, Denver.................	0	0	1	0	1	0
Wilson, Cedrick, Pittsburgh	1	1	0	0	1	0
Wilson, Eugene, New England	0	0	1	0	1	0
Wimbush, Derrick, Jacksonville	1	0	0	0	0	0
Woodson, Charles, Oakland....	1	0	0	0	0	0
Woolfolk, Andre, Tennessee....	0	0	1	8	1	0
Wright, Anthony, Baltimore	5	2	0	-8	2	0
Zastudil, Dave, Baltimore........	1	1	0	-2	1	0
Zgonina, Jeff, Miami	0	0	1	0	1	0

NFC

Player, team	Fum.	Own Rec.	Opp. Rec.	Yds.	Tot. Rec.	TD
Adams, Mike, San Francisco...	0	0	1	0	1	0
Alexander, Brent, N.Y. Giants..	0	0	1	9	1	0
Alexander, Shaun, Seattle	5	0	0	0	0	0
Allen, David, St. Louis	1	0	0	0	0	0
Allen, Kenderick, N.Y. Giants...	0	0	2	2	2	0
Allen, Larry, Dallas................	0	1	0	0	1	0
Allen, Will, N.Y. Giants	0	0	1	0	1	0
Allen, Will, Tampa Bay	0	0	1	33	1	1
Amey, Otis, San Francisco	1	0	0	0	0	0
Archuleta, Adam, St. Louis	0	0	1	0	1	0
Arrington, J.J., Arizona	1	1	0	0	1	0
Atogwe, O.J., St. Louis	0	0	1	0	1	0
Ayanbadejo, Brendon, Chicago	0	1	0	0	1	0
Ayanbadejo, Obafemi, Arizona	1	0	0	0	0	0
Babineaux, Jonathan, Atlanta..	0	0	1	0	1	0
Babineaux, Jordan, Seattle	0	0	1	0	1	0
Bailey, Rodney, Seattle...........	0	0	1	0	1	0
Bajema, Billy, San Francisco...	0	1	0	0	1	0
Barber, Marion, Dallas	3	3	0	-5	3	0
Barber, Ronde, Tampa Bay......	0	0	1	4	1	0
Barber, Tiki, N.Y. Giants	1	1	0	0	1	0
Barlow, Kevan, San Francisco.	2	0	0	0	0	0
Barnett, Nick, Green Bay........	0	0	3	17	3	0
Barron, Alex, St. Louis............	0	1	0	0	1	0
Battle, Arnaz, San Francisco ...	1	0	0	0	0	0
Bennett, Michael, Minnesota...	5	1	0	0	1	0
Benson, Cedric, Chicago.........	1	1	0	0	1	0
Bergen, Adam, Arizona	0	1	0	0	1	0
Bernard, Rocky, Seattle...........	0	0	2	5	2	0
Berrian, Bernard, Chicago.......	1	0	0	0	0	0
Berry, Bertrand, Arizona..........	0	0	1	0	1	0
Betts, Ladell, Washington	3	0	0	0	0	0
Blackburn, Chase, N.Y. Giants.	0	0	1	0	1	0
Bledsoe, Drew, Dallas	17	3	0	-12	3	0
Bly, Dre', Detroit...................	1	0	1	0	1	0
Bockwoldt, Colby, New Orleans	0	0	1	0	1	0
Boldin, Anquan, Arizona	2	0	0	0	0	0
Bouman, Todd, New Orleans ..	4	0	0	0	0	0
Bradley, Mark, Chicago	1	0	0	0	0	0
Briggs, Lance, Chicago...........	0	0	2	0	2	0
Brooking, Keith, Atlanta	0	0	1	0	1	0
Brooks, Aaron, New Orleans...	4	2	0	-12	2	0
Brown, Antonio, Washington...	2	1	0	0	1	0
Brown, Reggie, Philadelphia ...	1	0	0	0	0	0
Brown, Sheldon, Philadelphia.	0	0	1	80	1	1
Brunell, Mark, Washington	11	1	0	-17	1	0
Bryant, Tony, New Orleans	0	0	1	5	1	0
Bryson, Shawn, Detroit..........	1	1	0	0	1	0
Buckner, Brentson, Carolina ...	0	0	1	0	1	0
Bulger, Marc, St. Louis...........	4	1	0	-8	1	0
Burleson, Nate, Minnesota......	0	2	0	0	2	0
Burress, Plaxico, N.Y. Giants ..	1	0	0	0	0	0
Butler, James, N.Y. Giants......	1	0	1	5	1	0
Butler, Kelly, Detroit	0	2	0	0	2	0
Carpenter, Keion, Atlanta	1	0	0	0	0	0
Carroll, Ahmad, Green Bay	1	0	0	0	0	0
Cartwright, Rock, Washington	1	0	0	0	0	0
Chavous, Corey, Minnesota	0	0	1	0	1	0
Chillar, Brandon, St. Louis	0	0	1	8	1	0
Clancy, Kendrick, N.Y. Giants..	0	0	1	0	1	0
Clarke, Adrien, Philadelphia	0	1	0	0	1	0
Clayton, Michael, Tampa Bay..	1	0	0	0	0	0
Clement, Anthony, San Francisco	0	1	0	0	1	0
Cody, Shaun, Detroit..............	0	0	1	0	1	0
Colbert, Keary, Carolina	1	0	0	0	0	0
Conwell, Ernie, New Orleans...	1	0	0	0	0	0
Cooley, Chris, Washington......	3	0	0	0	0	0
Crayton, Patrick, Dallas..........	3	2	0	0	2	0
Crumpler, Alge, Atlanta...........	1	0	0	0	0	0

Player, team	Fum.	Own Rec.	Opp. Rec.	Yds.	Tot. Rec.	TD
Culpepper, Daunte, Minnesota	5	0	0	-4	0	0
Curtis, Kevin, St. Louis	2	0	0	0	0	0
Daniels, Phillip, Washington	0	0	2	0	2	0
Dansby, Karlos, Arizona	0	0	2	0	2	0
Darche, Jean-Philippe, Seattle	0	0	1	0	1	0
Davenport, Najeh, Green Bay	1	1	0	0	1	0
Davis, Chauncey, Atlanta	0	0	2	24	2	1
Davis, James, Detroit	0	0	1	0	1	0
Davis, Keith, Dallas	0	0	1	5	1	0
Davis, Rashied, Chicago	2	1	0	0	1	0
Davis, Stephen, Carolina	2	0	0	0	0	0
Dawkins, Brian, Philadelphia	0	0	1	0	1	0
Delhomme, Jake, Carolina	12	3	0	-4	3	0
Detmer, Koy, Philadelphia	2	0	0	0	0	0
DeVries, Jared, Detroit	0	0	2	0	2	0
Diehl, David, N.Y. Giants	0	2	0	0	2	0
Diggs, Na'il, Green Bay	0	0	1	0	1	0
Dockery, Derrick, Washington	0	2	0	0	2	0
Dorsey, Ken, San Francisco	2	0	0	0	0	0
Douglas, Marques, San Francisco	0	0	2	0	2	0
Draft, Chris, Carolina	0	1	1	0	2	0
Drummond, Eddie, Detroit	1	0	0	0	0	0
Duckett, T.J., Atlanta	2	0	0	0	0	0
Dunn, Warrick, Atlanta	3	2	0	1	2	0
Dyson, Andre, Seattle	0	0	1	25	1	1
Edwards, Kalimba, Detroit	0	0	3	10	3	0
Ellis, Greg, Dallas	0	0	2	37	2	0
Emanuel, Ben, San Francisco	0	1	0	0	1	0
Engram, Bobby, Seattle	2	0	0	0	0	0
Evans, Demetric, Washington	0	0	1	0	1	0
Fason, Ciatrick, Minnesota	1	0	0	0	0	0
Faulk, Marshall, St. Louis	2	1	0	0	1	0
Favre, Brett, Green Bay	10	2	0	-1	2	0
Ferguson, Jason, Dallas	0	0	1	0	1	0
Finn, Jim, N.Y. Giants	1	0	0	0	0	0
Fisher, Tony, Green Bay	2	2	0	0	2	0
Fisher, Travis, St. Louis	0	0	1	0	1	0
Fitzpatrick, Ryan, St. Louis	3	1	0	-3	1	0
Flanagan, Mike, Green Bay	2	1	0	-15	1	0
Foster, DeShaun, Carolina	2	0	0	0	0	0
Fowler, Ryan, Dallas	0	0	1	9	1	0
Furrey, Mike, St. Louis	0	1	2	0	3	0
Gado, Samkon, Green Bay	4	0	0	0	0	0
Gage, Justin, Chicago	0	0	1	0	1	0
Gamble, Chris, Carolina	0	0	1	0	1	0
Garcia, Jeff, Detroit	1	0	0	-3	0	0
Gbaja-Biamila, Kabeer, Green Bay	0	0	3	0	3	0
Goings, Nick, Carolina	1	0	0	0	0	0
Goodman, Andre', Detroit	0	1	0	15	1	0
Gordon, Lamar, Philadelphia	3	1	0	1	1	0
Gore, Frank, San Francisco	2	1	0	0	1	0
Graham, Earnest, Tampa Bay	0	0	1	0	1	0
Grant, Charles, New Orleans	0	0	1	23	1	0
Green, Ahman, Green Bay	1	0	0	0	0	0
Green, Eric, Arizona	0	0	1	0	1	0
Green, Mike, Chicago	0	0	1	0	1	0
Greisen, Nick, N.Y. Giants	0	0	3	28	3	0
Griese, Brian, Tampa Bay	2	1	0	0	1	0
Griffin, Cornelius, Washington	0	0	1	0	1	0
Griffith, Justin, Atlanta	1	0	0	0	0	0
Gross, Jordan, Carolina	0	2	1	0	3	0
Hakim, Az-Zahir, New Orleans	1	0	0	0	0	0
Hall, DeAngelo, Atlanta	2	1	2	86	3	1
Hankton, Karl, Carolina	0	1	0	11	1	0
Hargrove, Anthony, St. Louis	0	0	2	0	2	0
Harrington, Joey, Detroit	7	1	0	-3	1	0
Harris, Arlen, St. Louis	0	1	0	0	1	0
Harris, Chris, Chicago	0	1	1	49	2	0
Harris, Quentin, Arizona	0	0	2	0	2	0
Harris, Tommie, Chicago	0	0	2	0	2	0
Hasselbeck, Matt, Seattle	4	0	0	0	0	0
Hawthorne, Michael, St. Louis	0	0	1	0	1	0
Heard, Ronnie, Atlanta	0	0	1	0	1	0
Heitmann, Eric, San Francisco	0	1	1	0	2	0
Henderson, E.J., Minnesota	0	0	1	0	1	0
Henderson, William, Green Bay	1	0	0	0	0	0
Holdman, Warrick, Washington	0	0	1	0	1	0
Holland, Montrae, New Orleans	0	1	0	0	1	0
Holt, Terrence, Detroit	0	1	1	38	2	0
Holt, Torry, St. Louis	2	1	0	0	1	0
Hood, Roderick, Philadelphia	1	0	0	0	0	0
Hoover, Brad, Carolina	0	1	0	0	1	0
Horn, Joe, New Orleans	2	0	0	0	0	0
Hovan, Chris, Tampa Bay	0	0	2	0	2	0
Howard, Darren, New Orleans	0	0	2	-2	2	0
Idonije, Israel, Chicago	1	1	0	0	1	0
Jackson, Steven, St. Louis	3	0	1	-7	1	0
Jacobs, Brandon, N.Y. Giants	1	0	0	0	0	0
Jansen, Jon, Washington	0	2	0	0	2	0
Jenkins, Cullen, Green Bay	0	0	1	-2	1	0
Jenkins, Michael, Atlanta	1	0	0	0	0	0
Jennings, Brian, San Francisco	0	0	1	0	1	0
Johnson, Al, Dallas	1	1	0	0	1	0
Johnson, Brad, Minnesota	5	1	0	-1	1	0
Johnson, Bryan, Chicago	0	1	0	0	1	0
Johnson, Chris, St. Louis	2	1	0	0	1	0
Johnson, Derrick, San Francisco	0	0	1	78	1	1
Johnson, Keyshawn, Dallas	3	0	0	0	0	0
Jones, Jamal, Green Bay	1	0	0	0	0	0
Jones, Julius, Dallas	4	1	0	0	1	0
Jones, Kevin, Detroit	2	2	0	23	2	0
Jones, Mark, Tampa Bay	1	1	0	0	1	0
Jones, Thomas, Chicago	2	0	0	0	0	0
Jones, Walter, Seattle	0	0	1	0	1	0
Joseph, William, N.Y. Giants	0	0	1	5	1	0
Jurevicius, Joe, Seattle	1	0	0	0	0	0
Kennedy, Kenoy, Detroit	1	0	0	0	0	0
Kerney, Patrick, Atlanta	0	0	3	2	3	0
Kleinsasser, Jim, Minnesota	1	0	0	0	0	0
Kolodziej, Ross, Arizona	0	0	2	0	2	0
Kreutz, Olin, Chicago	0	1	0	0	1	0
Leach, Vonta, Green Bay	0	2	0	0	2	0
Leckey, Nick, Arizona	0	1	0	0	1	0
Lee, ReShard, Green Bay	2	0	0	0	0	0
Lewis, Damione, St. Louis	0	0	1	0	1	0
Lewis, Michael, New Orleans	1	0	0	0	0	0
Lewis, Michael, Philadelphia	0	0	1	0	1	0
Little, Leonard, St. Louis	0	0	2	0	2	0
Lloyd, Brandon, San Francisco	1	0	0	0	0	0
Locklear, Sean, Seattle	0	2	0	0	2	0
Lucas, Ken, Carolina	0	0	1	24	1	0
Mahan, Sean, Tampa Bay	0	1	0	0	1	0
Mahe, Reno, Philadelphia	2	2	1	0	3	0
Manning, Eli, N.Y. Giants	9	0	0	0	0	0
Manning, Ricky, Carolina	0	0	3	11	3	1
Manuel, Marquand, Seattle	0	0	1	0	1	0
Manumaleuna, Brandon, St. Louis	2	0	0	0	0	0
Marshall, Rasheed, San Francisco	4	1	0	0	1	0
Martin, Jamie, St. Louis	2	0	0	0	0	0
Maxwell, Jim, San Francisco	0	0	1	0	1	0
Maynard, Brad, Chicago	1	1	0	0	1	0
McAddley, Jason, San Francisco	0	0	1	0	1	0
McAfee, Fred, New Orleans	2	0	0	0	0	0
McClure, Todd, Atlanta	0	1	0	0	1	0
McCown, Josh, Arizona	5	0	0	0	0	0
McCree, Marlon, Carolina	0	0	1	4	1	0
McDonald, Shaun, St. Louis	1	0	0	0	0	0
McFarland, Anthony, Tampa Bay	0	0	2	0	2	1
McGraw, Jon, Detroit	0	0	1	0	1	0
McKenzie, Kareem, N.Y. Giants	0	2	0	0	2	0
McKenzie, Mike, New Orleans	1	0	0	0	0	0
McKie, Jason, Chicago	0	1	0	0	1	0

2005 STATISTICS — Fumbles

Player, team	Fum.	Own Rec.	Opp. Rec.	Yds.	Tot. Rec.	TD
McKinnie, Bryant, Minnesota..	0	1	0	0	1	0
McMahon, Mike, Philadelphia.	8	3	0	-8	3	0
McMullen, Billy, Philadelphia..	1	0	0	0	0	0
McNabb, Donovan, Philadelphia	8	3	0	-18	3	0
McQuarters, R.W., Detroit.......	2	1	0	0	1	0
Moats, Ryan, Philadelphia	3	1	1	0	2	0
Moore, Brandon, San Francisco	1	0	1	9	1	0
Moore, Mewelde, Minnesota ..	2	2	0	0	2	0
Moorehead, Kindal, Carolina...	0	0	2	0	2	0
Morgan, Dan, Carolina.............	0	0	1	0	1	0
Morris, Maurice, Seattle	0	1	0	-1	1	0
Morton, Chad, N.Y. Giants	1	1	0	0	1	0
Morton, Christian, Atlanta.......	0	0	1	14	1	0
Moss, Santana, Washington ...	3	1	0	0	1	0
Navarre, John, Arizona	1	1	0	0	1	0
Newman, Keith, Minnesota.....	0	0	1	0	1	0
Newman, Terence, Dallas........	3	3	1	0	4	0
Nguyen, Dat, Dallas	0	0	2	0	2	0
Odom, Joe, Chicago	0	0	1	0	1	0
Ogunleye, Adewale, Chicago...	0	0	1	0	1	0
Orlovsky, Dan, Detroit.............	1	0	0	0	0	0
Orton, Kyle, Chicago	12	3	0	-11	3	0
Owens, Richard, Minnesota....	0	0	1	0	1	0
Pace, Calvin, Arizona	1	0	1	0	1	0
Pace, Orlando, St. Louis	0	1	1	0	2	0
Parry, Josh, Philadelphia	0	1	0	0	1	0
Pearson, Kalvin, Tampa Bay ...	0	0	1	0	1	0
Peppers, Julius, Carolina	0	0	1	10	1	0
Peterson, Adrian, Chicago	1	1	0	0	1	0
Peterson, Julian, San Francisco	0	0	1	0	1	0
Peterson, Kenny, Green Bay ...	0	1	1	18	2	0
Pickett, Cody, San Francisco...	3	1	0	-12	1	0
Pierce, Antonio, N.Y. Giants....	0	0	2	12	2	1
Pierce, Brett, Dallas	0	1	0	0	1	0
Pittman, Michael, Tampa Bay .	1	1	0	0	1	0
Polite, Lousaka, Dallas............	0	2	0	0	2	0
Pollard, Marcus, Detroit..........	1	0	0	0	0	0
Ponder, Willie, N.Y. Giants	1	0	1	0	1	0
Portis, Clinton, Washington	3	2	0	0	2	0
Prioleau, Pierson, Washington	0	1	1	4	2	0
Quarles, Shelton, Tampa Bay..	0	0	1	0	1	0
Ramsey, Patrick, Washington .	2	0	0	0	0	0
Rasmussen, Kemp, Carolina....	0	0	1	0	1	0
Rattay, Tim, San Francisco	3	1	0	-2	1	0
Rayburn, Sam, Philadelphia....	0	0	1	0	1	0
Redding, Cory, Detroit	0	0	1	0	1	0
Reeves, Jacques, Dallas	0	0	1	0	1	0
Robbins, Fred, N.Y. Giants	0	0	1	0	1	0
Robertson, Jamal, Carolina.....	1	0	0	0	0	0
Robinson, Koren, Minnesota ..	2	0	0	0	0	0
Rodgers, Aaron, Green Bay	2	0	0	0	0	0
Rogers, Shaun, Detroit	0	0	1	21	1	1
Roman, Mark, Green Bay........	0	0	2	0	2	0
Ross, Oliver, Arizona...............	0	1	0	0	1	0
Rossum, Allen, Atlanta	2	1	0	0	1	0
Rucker, Mike, Carolina............	0	0	2	11	2	0
Runyan, Jon, Philadelphia	0	2	0	1	2	0
Ruud, Barrett, Tampa Bay.......	0	0	1	0	1	0
Salave'a, Joe, Washington	0	0	1	0	1	0
Sander, B.J., Green Bay	1	1	0	0	1	0
Schaub, Matt, Atlanta	1	0	0	0	0	0
Scobey, Josh, Seattle..............	2	0	1	0	1	0
Scott, Bryan, Atlanta..............	0	0	1	0	1	0
Scott, Darrion, Minnesota.......	0	0	1	1	1	0
Seidman, Mike, Carolina.........	1	0	0	0	0	0
Sellers, Mike, Washington	0	0	1	0	1	0
Sharper, Darren, Minnesota....	1	0	1	14	1	0
Shepherd, Edell, Tampa Bay ...	1	0	0	0	0	0
Shipp, Marcel, Arizona............	4	1	0	0	1	0
Simms, Chris, Tampa Bay.......	6	1	0	-1	1	0
Smart, Rod, Carolina	1	0	0	0	0	0
Smith, Alex, San Francisco	11	6	0	-10	6	0
Smith, Antowain, New Orleans	2	0	0	0	0	0
Smith, Derek, San Francisco...	0	1	0	0	1	1
Smith, Dwight, New Orleans...	1	0	0	0	0	0
Smith, L.J., Philadelphia.........	1	0	0	0	0	0
Smith, Paul, Detroit	1	0	0	0	0	0
Smith, Raonall, Minnesota......	0	0	2	0	2	0
Smith, Steve, Carolina	2	2	0	5	2	0
Smith, Will, New Orleans	0	0	1	-2	1	0
Snee, Chris, N.Y. Giants..........	0	1	0	0	1	0
Snyder, Adam, San Francisco .	0	2	0	0	2	0
Spears, Marcus, Dallas	0	0	1	59	1	0
Stallworth, Donte', New Orleans	1	0	0	0	0	0
Stecker, Aaron, New Orleans ..	3	0	0	0	0	0
Stevens, Jerramy, Seattle	0	2	0	0	2	0
Stokes, Barry, Atlanta	0	1	0	0	1	0
Strahan, Michael, N.Y. Giants .	0	0	1	0	1	0
Swinton, Reggie, Arizona........	2	1	0	0	1	0
Tafoya, Joe, Seattle................	0	1	0	0	1	0
Tatupu, Lofa, Seattle..............	0	0	1	0	1	0
Tauscher, Mark, Green Bay	0	1	0	0	1	0
Taylor, Sean, Washington	0	0	1	39	1	1
Taylor, Travis, Minnesota	1	0	0	0	0	0
Terrill, Craig, Seattle	0	0	1	18	1	0
Thomas, Anthony, Dallas	0	1	0	0	1	0
Thomas, Fred, New Orleans....	0	0	2	0	2	0
Thomas, Juqua, Philadelphia..	0	0	1	16	1	0
Thompson, Chris, Chicago	0	0	1	0	1	0
Thompson, Tyson, Dallas	2	1	0	0	1	0
Thrash, James, Washington ...	1	0	0	0	0	0
Thurman, Andrae, Green Bay..	1	1	0	0	1	0
Tillman, Charles, Chicago	0	0	1	0	1	0
Torbor, Reggie, N.Y. Giants.....	0	0	1	0	1	0
Tubbs, Marcus, Seattle	0	0	1	0	1	0
Tucker, Torrin, Dallas	0	1	0	0	1	0
Tufts, Sean, Carolina..............	0	0	1	0	1	0
Tyree, David, N.Y. Giants.........	1	1	0	0	1	0
Umenyiora, Osi, N.Y. Giants	0	0	2	0	2	0
Vick, Michael, Atlanta	11	0	0	-6	0	0
Wade, Bobby, Chicago............	10	4	0	0	4	0
Wahle, Mike, Carolina.............	0	1	0	0	1	0
Walker, Darwin, Philadelphia ..	0	0	2	18	2	0
Wallace, Al, Carolina...............	0	0	1	6	1	0
Wallace, Seneca, Seattle.........	2	1	0	-4	1	0
Ware, Matt, Philadelphia.........	0	0	1	0	1	0
Warner, Kurt, Arizona..............	9	3	0	-9	3	0
Washington, Marcus, Washington	0	0	2	-1	2	0
Wells, Scott, Green Bay	2	2	0	-6	2	0
Wesley, Dante, Carolina	0	0	1	0	1	0
White, Dewayne, Tampa Bay...	0	0	3	52	3	1
White, Roddy, Atlanta	1	0	0	0	0	0
Whitehead, Willie, New Orleans	0	0	1	0	1	0
Whitticker, William, Green Bay	0	1	0	0	1	0
Williams, Brian, Minnesota......	1	0	0	0	0	0
Williams, Carnell, Tampa Bay .	3	1	0	0	1	0
Williams, Demorrio, Atlanta.....	0	0	1	0	1	0
Williams, Jimmy, Seattle.........	2	1	0	0	1	0
Williams, Kevin, Minnesota.....	0	0	1	6	1	0
Williams, Mike, Detroit	2	0	0	0	0	0
Williams, Moe, Minnesota	1	1	0	0	1	0
Williams, Pat, Minnesota........	0	1	0	0	1	0
Williams, Roy, Dallas	0	0	1	0	1	0
Wilson, Adrian, Arizona	0	0	2	0	2	0
Winfield, Antoine, Minnesota..	0	0	2	0	2	0
Wyms, Ellis, Tampa Bay	0	0	1	0	1	0
Wynn, Dexter, Philadelphia	4	3	0	0	3	0
Wynn, Renaldo, Washington ..	0	0	1	0	1	0

2005 STATISTICS *Fumbles*

FIELD GOALS

TEAM

AFC

Team	Made	Att.	Pct.	Long
Cleveland	27	29	.931	44
Indianapolis	23	26	.885	48
Cincinnati	28	32	.875	49
San Diego	21	24	.875	49
Baltimore	30	35	.857	49
Miami	25	30	.833	53
Buffalo	29	35	.829	53
Pittsburgh	24	29	.828	44
Kansas City	27	33	.818	52
New England	20	25	.800	49
Tennessee	23	29	.793	53
N.Y. Jets	22	28	.786	49
Jacksonville	23	30	.767	53
Houston	26	34	.765	53
Denver	24	32	.750	51
Oakland	20	30	.667	49
AFC total	392	481	...	53
AFC average	24.5	30.1	.815	...

NFC

Team	Made	Att.	Pct.	Long
Arizona	43	45	.956	54
San Francisco	26	29	.897	56
Atlanta	24	27	.889	58
St. Louis	27	31	.871	53
N.Y. Giants	35	42	.833	52
Tampa Bay	22	27	.815	50
Washington	17	21	.810	45
Detroit	19	24	.792	52
New Orleans	25	32	.781	49
Carolina	26	34	.765	52
Philadelphia	22	29	.759	50
Green Bay	20	27	.741	53
Minnesota	25	34	.735	56
Seattle	18	25	.720	55
Dallas	20	28	.714	56
Chicago	22	31	.710	48
NFC total	391	486	...	58
NFC average	24.4	30.4	.805	...
NFL total	783	967	...	58
NFL average	24.5	30.2	.810	...

INDIVIDUAL

BESTS OF THE SEASON

Field goal percentage, season
NFC: .952—Neil Rackers, Arizona.
AFC: .931—Phil Dawson, Cleveland.
Field goals, season
NFC: 40—Neil Rackers, Arizona.
AFC: 30—Matt Stover, Baltimore.
Field goal attempts, season
NFC: 42—Jay Feely, N.Y. Giants; Neil Rackers, Arizona.
AFC: 35—Rian Lindell, Buffalo.
Longest field goal
NFC: 58—Michael Koenen, Atlanta vs. New England, Oct. 9.
AFC: 53—By 5 players.
Average yards made, season
NFC: 39.1—Josh Brown, Seattle.
AFC: 35.5—Nate Kaeding, San Diego.

NFL LEADERS

Team	Made	Att.	Pct.	Long
Rackers, Neil, Arizona	40	42	.952	54
Dawson, Phil, Cleveland*	27	29	.931	44
Nedney, Joe, San Francisco	26	28	.929	56
Peterson, Todd, Atlanta	23	25	.920	43
Vanderjagt, Mike, Indianapolis*	23	25	.920	48
Stover, Matt, Baltimore*	30	34	.882	49
Graham, Shayne, Cincinnati*	28	32	.875	49
Kaeding, Nate, San Diego*	21	24	.875	49
Wilkins, Jeff, St. Louis	27	31	.871	53
Bryant, Matt, Tampa Bay	21	25	.840	50

*AFC.
Leader based on percentage, minimum 16 attempts.

AFC

Player, team	1-19	20-29	30-39	40-49	50 & Over	Totals	Avg. Yds. Att.	Avg. Yds. Made	Avg. Yds. Miss	Long
Bironas, Rob	0-0	10-10	6-7	5-7	2-5	23-29	37.4	34.6	48.3	53
Tennessee	...	1.000	.857	.714	.400	.793				
Brown, Kris	0-0	9-9	12-17	4-6	1-2	26-34	35.6	34.1	40.6	53
Houston	...	1.000	.706	.667	.500	.765				
Dawson, Phil	2-2	11-11	9-11	5-5	0-0	27-29	31.6	31.3	36.5	44
Cleveland	1.000	1.000	.818	1.000	...	.931				
Elam, Jason	0-0	9-10	5-5	9-13	1-4	24-32	38.0	35.3	46.0	51
Denver	...	.900	1.000	.692	.250	.750				
Elling, Aaron	0-0	0-0	0-0	0-0	0-1	0-1	54.0	-	54.0	0
Baltimore	...	...	...	...	.000	.000				
Graham, Shayne	0-0	11-11	10-11	7-9	0-1	28-32	34.0	32.8	43.0	49
Cincinnati	...	1.000	.909	.778	.000	.875				
Janikowski, Sebastian	1-1	7-8	5-6	7-12	0-3	20-30	37.6	33.6	45.6	49
Oakland	1.000	.875	.833	.583	.000	.667				
Kaeding, Nate	1-1	3-3	9-9	8-11	0-0	21-24	36.4	35.5	42.7	49
San Diego	1.000	1.000	1.000	.727	...	.875				
Lindell, Rian	0-0	8-9	11-13	7-10	3-3	29-35	35.3	34.7	38.3	53
Buffalo	...	.889	.846	.700	1.000	.829				
Mare, Olindo	0-0	9-10	9-12	6-6	1-2	25-30	34.8	34.6	35.8	53
Miami	...	.900	.750	1.000	.500	.833				
Nugent, Mike	0-0	8-9	7-7	7-10	0-2	22-28	35.7	33.5	43.8	49
N.Y. Jets	...	.889	1.000	.700	.000	.786				
Rayner, Dave	0-0	0-0	0-0	0-0	0-1	0-1	59.0	-	59.0	0
Indianapolis	...	...	...	...	.000	.000				

Player, team	1-19	20-29	30-39	40-49	50 & Over	Totals	Avg. Yds. Att.	Avg. Yds. Made	Avg. Yds. Miss	Long
Reed, Jeff	0-0	9-9	9-9	6-9	0-2	24-29	35.4	33.1	46.8	44
Pittsburgh		1.000	1.000	.667	.000	.828				
Scobee, Josh	0-0	9-9	7-8	5-10	2-3	23-30	36.4	34.0	44.0	53
Jacksonville	...	1.000	.875	.500	.667	.767				
Stover, Matt	1-1	8-8	10-11	11-14	0-0	30-34	35.9	34.9	43.3	49
Baltimore	1.000	1.000	.909	.786	...	.882				
Tynes, Lawrence	1-1	8-8	12-13	4-8	2-3	27-33	35.4	33.7	43.0	52
Kansas City	1.000	1.000	.923	.500	.667	.818				
Vanderjagt, Mike	1-1	9-9	6-7	7-8	0-0	23-25	32.8	32.2	39.5	48
Indianapolis	1.000	1.000	.857	.875	...	.920				
Vinatieri, Adam	0-0	7-7	9-10	4-6	0-2	20-25	36.4	33.9	46.4	49
New England	...	1.000	.900	.667	.000	.800				

NFC

Player, team	1-19	20-29	30-39	40-49	50 & Over	Totals	Avg. Yds. Att.	Avg. Yds. Made	Avg. Yds. Miss	Long
Akers, David	0-0	3-3	7-8	5-9	1-2	16-22	39.6	36.5	48.0	50
Philadelphia	...	1.000	.875	.556	.500	.727				
Brien, Doug	0-0	0-0	0-2	1-2	0-0	1-4	42.8	48.0	41.0	48
Chicago	...	...	.000	.500	...	.250				
Brown, Josh	0-0	5-5	4-5	4-7	5-8	18-25	41.3	39.1	46.9	55
Seattle	...	1.000	.800	.571	.625	.720				
Bryant, Matt	0-0	2-4	8-8	10-11	1-2	21-25	38.4	38.4	38.5	50
Tampa Bay	...	.500	1.000	.909	.500	.840				
Carney, John	1-1	12-13	4-6	8-12	0-0	25-32	33.6	32.2	38.4	49
New Orleans	1.000	.923	.667	.667	...	.781				
Cortez, Jose	0-0	5-6	4-5	3-6	0-0	12-17	35.3	33.3	40.2	45
Dal.-S.F.	...	.833	.800	.500	...	.706				
Cundiff, Billy	1-1	1-1	2-5	0-0	1-1	5-8	33.9	33.4	34.7	56
Dallas	1.000	1.000	.400	...	1.000	.625				
Edinger, Paul	0-0	11-11	3-8	8-10	3-5	25-34	36.5	35.5	39.4	56
Minnesota	...	1.000	.375	.800	.600	.735				
Feely, Jay	0-0	11-13	13-14	8-10	3-5	35-42	36.4	35.7	40.0	52
N.Y. Giants	...	.846	.929	.800	.600	.833				
France, Todd	0-0	4-4	1-1	2-4	0-0	7-9	33.8	31.6	41.5	44
Phi.-T.B.	...	1.000	1.000	.500	...	.778				
Gould, Robbie	0-0	9-9	9-10	3-8	0-0	21-27	35.0	32.3	44.7	45
Chicago	...	1.000	.900	.375	...	.778				
Hall, John	1-1	3-3	3-3	5-6	0-1	12-14	36.3	34.2	49.0	45
Washington	1.000	1.000	1.000	.833	.000	.857				
Hanson, Jason	1-1	9-9	3-3	4-7	2-4	19-24	35.7	32.4	48.2	52
Detroit	1.000	1.000	1.000	.571	.500	.792				
Kasay, John	1-1	8-8	8-8	6-9	3-8	26-34	38.9	35.2	50.8	52
Carolina	1.000	1.000	1.000	.667	.375	.765				
Koenen, Michael	0-0	0-0	0-0	0-0	1-2	1-2	56.5	58.0	55.0	58
Atlanta	...	...	...	...	.500	.500				
Longwell, Ryan	0-0	7-7	6-10	3-5	4-5	20-27	37.7	36.8	40.4	53
Green Bay	...	1.000	.600	.600	.800	.741				
Nedney, Joe	0-0	4-4	10-11	10-10	2-3	26-28	38.5	38.0	45.5	56
San Francisco	...	1.000	.909	1.000	.667	.929				
Novak, Nick	1-1	1-1	5-7	1-1	0-0	8-10	33.7	32.5	38.5	40
Was.-Ariz	1.000	1.000	.714	1.000	...	.800				
Peterson, Todd	0-0	9-10	11-11	3-4	0-0	23-25	31.6	31.0	38.5	43
Atlanta	...	.900	1.000	.750	...	.920				
Rackers, Neil	0-0	11-11	10-10	13-14	6-7	40-42	38.1	37.6	48.5	54
Arizona	...	1.000	1.000	.929	.857	.952				
Suisham, Shaun	0-0	3-3	0-0	0-1	0-0	3-4	27.8	21.3	47.0	22
Dallas	...	1.000	...	.000	...	.750				
Wilkins, Jeff	0-0	6-7	8-8	9-11	4-5	27-31	39.1	38.4	44.0	53
St. Louis	...	.857	1.000	.818	.800	.871				

PLAYERS WITH TWO CLUBS

Player, team	1-19	20-29	30-39	40-49	50 & Over	Totals	Avg. Yds. Att.	Avg. Yds. Made	Avg. Yds. Miss	Long
Cortez, Jose	0-0	5-6	4-4	3-6	0-0	12-16	32.3	33.3	29.5	45
Dallas	...	.833	1.000	.500	...	.750				
Cortez, Jose	0-0	0-0	0-1	0-0	0-0	0-1	34.0	-	34.0	...
San Francisco	...	...	.000	...	...	.000				
France, Todd	0-0	3-3	1-1	2-3	0-0	6-7	27.6	32.2	0.0	44
Philadelphia	...	1.000	1.000	.667	...	.857				
France, Todd	0-0	1-1	0-0	0-1	0-0	1-2	14.0	28.0	0.0	28
Tampa Bay	...	1.000	...	.000	...	.500				
Novak, Nick	0-0	1-1	3-5	1-1	0-0	5-7	25.1	35.2	0.0	40
Washington	...	1.000	.600	1.000	...	.714				
Novak, Nick	1-1	0-0	2-2	0-0	0-0	3-3	28.0	28.0	-	35
Arizona	1.000	...	1.000	...	...	1.000				

PUNTING

AFC

Team	Total Punts	Yards	Long	Avg.	TB	Blk.	Opp. Ret.	Ret. Yards	In. 20	Net Avg.
Buffalo	71	3242	68	45.7	9	0	42	285	22	39.1
Oakland	82	3744	64	45.7	9	0	39	460	26	37.9
New England	77	3431	59	44.6	4	1	42	405	22	38.3
Indianapolis	52	2301	58	44.3	5	0	25	272	23	37.1
San Diego	71	3104	71	43.7	8	0	26	244	25	38.0
N.Y. Jets	75	3251	59	43.3	6	0	36	305	19	37.7
Denver	73	3157	66	43.2	6	1	36	266	24	38.0
Tennessee	78	3371	59	43.2	14	0	32	144	21	37.8
Miami	89	3835	63	43.1	7	0	46	227	31	39.0
Baltimore	86	3685	60	42.8	7	1	55	481	12	35.6
Cincinnati	61	2591	75	42.5	8	1	32	260	13	35.6
Jacksonville	83	3517	74	42.4	11	1	29	236	33	36.9
Pittsburgh	69	2875	65	41.7	8	0	37	336	23	34.5
Cleveland	80	3234	61	40.4	9	0	36	347	24	33.8
Kansas City	65	2564	62	39.4	5	0	23	179	27	35.2
Houston	77	2990	61	38.8	1	0	33	219	29	35.7
AFC total	1189	50892	75	...	117	5	569	4666	374	...
AFC average	74.3	3180.8	...	42.8	7.3	0.3	35.6	291.6	23.4	36.9

Leader based on average.

NFC

Team	Total Punts	Yards	Long	Avg.	TB	Blk.	Opp. Ret.	Ret. Yards	In. 20	Net Avg.
Tampa Bay	90	4101	61	45.6	13	0	49	466	24	37.5
Detroit	84	3656	60	43.5	2	0	50	520	34	36.9
Arizona	74	3206	60	43.3	7	1	39	328	18	37.0
Minnesota	81	3505	62	43.3	6	0	45	495	19	35.7
Carolina	73	3154	59	43.2	5	0	36	235	23	38.6
New Orleans	71	3066	69	43.2	3	0	33	260	28	38.7
Dallas	82	3474	63	42.4	10	0	33	250	28	36.9
Atlanta	78	3300	67	42.3	9	0	35	238	23	36.9
N.Y. Giants	73	3070	56	42.1	3	0	36	309	26	37.0
St. Louis	73	3008	63	41.2	6	0	39	410	16	33.9
San Francisco	108	4447	58	41.2	3	1	62	471	15	36.3
Seattle	80	3282	62	41.0	8	0	41	343	25	34.7
Philadelphia	100	4073	59	40.7	3	1	57	312	25	37.0
Chicago	98	3965	63	40.5	11	1	39	312	24	35.0
Washington	87	3503	57	40.3	7	0	40	189	25	36.5
Green Bay	70	2726	53	38.9	2	0	49	339	11	33.5
NFC total	1322	55536	69	...	98	4	683	5477	364	...
NFC average	82.6	3471.0	...	42.0	6.1	0.3	42.7	342.3	22.8	36.4
NFL total	2511	106428	75	...	215	9	1252	10143	738	...
NFL average	78.5	3325.9	...	42.4	6.7	0.3	39.1	317.0	23.1	36.6

INDIVIDUAL

BESTS OF THE SEASON

Average yards per punt, season
AFC: 45.7—Brian Moorman, Buffalo.
NFC: 45.6—Josh Bidwell, Tampa Bay.
Net average yards per punt, season
AFC: 39.3—Donnie Jones, Miami.
NFC: 38.9—Jason Baker, Carolina.
Longest
AFC: 75—Kyle Larson, Cincinnati at Jacksonville, Oct. 9.

NFC: 69—Mitch Berger, New Orleans vs. Carolina, Dec. 18.
Punts, season
NFC: 107—Andy Lee, San Francisco.
AFC: 88—Donnie Jones, Miami.
Punts, game
NFC: 10—Scott Player, Arizona vs. Tennessee, Oct. 23; Derrick Frost, Washington at Philadelphia, Jan. 1; Sean Landeta, Philadelphia at Arizona, Dec. 24.
AFC: 9—Held by 9 players.

2005 STATISTICS   Punting

AFC

Player, team	Net Punts	Yards	Long	Avg.	Total Punts	TB	Blk.	Opp. Ret.	Ret. Yds.	In. 20	Net Avg.
Colquitt, Dustin, Kansas City	65	2564	62	39.4	65	5	0	23	179	27	35.2
Dawson, Phil, Cleveland	2	53	31	26.5	2	0	0	0	0	2	26.5
Elling, Aaron, Baltimore	1	32	32	32.0	1	0	0	0	0	1	32.0
Gardocki, Chris, Pittsburgh	67	2803	65	41.8	67	7	0	37	336	22	34.7
Graham, Ben, N.Y. Jets	74	3233	59	43.7	74	6	0	36	305	18	37.9
Hanson, Chris, Jacksonville	82	3517	74	42.9	83	11	1	29	236	33	36.9
Hentrich, Craig, Tennessee	78	3371	59	43.2	78	14	0	32	144	21	37.8
Jones, Donnie, Miami	88	3827	63	43.5	88	7	0	46	227	31	39.3
Larson, Kyle, Cincinnati	60	2591	75	43.2	61	8	1	32	260	13	35.6
Lechler, Shane, Oakland	82	3744	64	45.7	82	9	0	39	460	26	37.9
Mare, Olindo, Miami	1	8	8	8.0	1	0	0	0	0	0	8.0
Miller, Josh, New England	76	3431	59	45.1	77	4	1	42	405	22	38.3
Moorman, Brian, Buffalo	71	3242	68	45.7	71	9	0	42	285	22	39.1
Nugent, Mike, N.Y. Jets	1	18	18	18.0	1	0	0	0	0	1	18.0
Richardson, Kyle, Cleveland	78	3181	61	40.8	78	9	0	36	347	22	34.0
Roethlisberger, Ben, Pittsburgh	2	72	39	36.0	2	1	0	0	0	1	26.0
Sauerbrun, Todd, Denver	72	3157	66	43.8	73	6	1	36	266	24	38.0
Scifres, Mike, San Diego	71	3104	71	43.7	71	8	0	26	244	25	38.0
Smith, Hunter, Indianapolis	52	2301	58	44.3	52	5	0	25	272	23	37.1
Stanley, Chad, Houston	77	2990	61	38.8	77	1	0	33	219	29	35.7
Zastudil, Dave, Baltimore	84	3653	60	43.5	85	7	1	55	481	11	35.7

NFC

Player, team	Net Punts	Yards	Long	Avg.	Total Punts	TB	Blk.	Opp. Ret.	Ret. Yds.	In. 20	Net Avg.
Araguz, Leo, Seattle	18	723	53	40.2	18	1	0	8	78	4	34.7
Baker, Jason, Carolina	72	3118	59	43.3	72	4	0	36	235	23	38.9
Barker, Bryan, St. Louis	50	2137	63	42.7	50	4	0	31	277	13	35.6
Bennett, Darren, Minnesota	8	300	53	37.5	8	0	0	4	25	1	34.4
Berger, Mitch, New Orleans	71	3066	69	43.2	71	3	0	33	260	28	38.7
Bidwell, Josh, Tampa Bay	90	4101	61	45.6	90	13	0	49	466	24	37.5
Brown, Josh, Seattle	1	20	20	20.0	1	0	0	0	0	1	20.0
Cundiff, Billy, Dallas	1	35	35	35.0	1	1	0	0	0	0	15.0
Edinger, Paul, Minnesota	2	75	40	37.5	2	0	0	0	0	1	37.5
Feagles, Jeff, N.Y. Giants	73	3070	56	42.1	73	3	0	36	309	26	37.0
Flinn, Ryan, Green Bay	6	218	42	36.3	6	0	0	4	42	0	29.3
Frost, Derrick, Washington	76	3074	55	40.4	76	6	0	34	163	23	36.7
Gould, Robbie, Chicago	1	28	28	28.0	1	0	0	1	19	0	9.0
Groom, Andy, Washington	11	429	57	39.0	11	1	0	6	26	2	34.8
Harris, Nick, Detroit	84	3656	60	43.5	84	2	0	50	520	34	36.9
Hodges, Reggie, St.L.-Phi.*	41	1535	55	37.4	42	2	1	13	142	9	32.2
Johnson, Dirk, Philadelphia	39	1615	59	41.4	39	0	0	25	119	11	38.4
Kasay, John, Carolina	1	36	36	36.0	1	1	0	0	0	0	16.0
Kluwe, Chris, Minnesota	71	3130	62	44.1	71	6	0	41	470	17	35.8
Koenen, Michael, Atlanta	78	3300	67	42.3	78	9	0	35	238	23	36.9
Landeta, Sean, Philadelphia	34	1484	56	43.6	34	2	0	22	145	7	38.2
Lee, Andy, San Francisco	107	4447	58	41.6	108	3	1	62	471	15	36.3
Maynard, Brad, Chicago	96	3937	63	41.0	97	11	1	38	293	24	35.3
McBriar, Mat, Dallas	81	3439	63	42.5	81	9	0	33	250	28	37.1
Murphy, Nick, Philadelphia	7	275	44	39.3	7	0	0	5	39	1	33.7
Player, Scott, Arizona	73	3206	60	43.9	74	7	1	39	328	18	37.0
Rouen, Tom, Seattle	61	2539	62	41.6	61	7	0	33	265	20	35.0
Sander, B.J., Green Bay	64	2508	53	39.2	64	2	0	45	297	11	33.9
Wilkins, Jeff, St. Louis	1	35	35	35.0	1	1	0	0	0	0	15.0

*Includes both AFC and NFC statistics.

PLAYERS WITH TWO CLUBS

Player, team	Net Punts	Yards	Long	Avg.	Total Punts	TB	Blk.	Opp. Ret.	Ret. Yds.	In. 20	Net Avg.
Hodges, Reggie, St. Louis	22	836	55	38.0	22	1	0	8	133	3	31.0
Hodges, Reggie, Philadelphia	19	699	51	36.8	20	1	1	5	9	6	33.5

PUNT RETURNS

TEAM

AFC

Team	No.	FC	Yds.	Avg.	Long	TD
Baltimore	39	13	431	11.1	51	0
Pittsburgh	46	13	470	10.2	t81	2
Cleveland	37	13	373	10.1	t62	1
Buffalo	28	17	279	10.0	43	0
Tennessee	45	13	418	9.3	t52	1
Miami	43	23	390	9.1	47	0
Denver	33	17	281	8.5	52	0
New England	40	18	314	7.9	29	0
Jacksonville	53	15	415	7.8	24	0
Indianapolis	24	25	182	7.6	29	0
Houston	30	7	223	7.4	37	0
Kansas City	43	7	293	6.8	52	0
N.Y. Jets	34	12	219	6.4	18	0
San Diego	39	17	245	6.3	23	0
Cincinnati	28	14	157	5.6	13	0
Oakland	37	7	206	5.6	34	0
AFC total	599	231	4896	...	t81	4
AFC average	37.4	14.4	306.0	8.2	...	0.3

t—touchdown.

NFC

Team	No.	FC	Yds.	Avg.	Long	TD
Carolina	41	11	444	10.8	76	0
Tampa Bay	51	18	492	9.6	31	0
N.Y. Giants	49	16	453	9.2	58	1
Chicago	46	13	417	9.1	t73	0
Green Bay	45	18	381	8.5	t85	1
Philadelphia	53	24	448	8.5	44	0
Atlanta	31	23	261	8.4	29	0
Minnesota	41	14	344	8.4	t71	1
Arizona	50	16	385	7.7	32	0
Detroit	36	13	274	7.6	49	0
San Francisco	28	12	212	7.6	t75	1
New Orleans	46	5	320	7.0	42	0
Dallas	45	21	284	6.3	26	0
Washington	30	28	180	6.0	18	0
St. Louis	30	23	175	5.8	17	0
Seattle	31	23	177	5.7	24	0
NFC total	653	278	5247	...	t85	5
NFC average	40.8	17.4	327.9	8.0	...	0.3
NFL total	1252	509	10143	...	t85	9
NFL average	39.1	15.9	317.0	8.1	...	0.3

INDIVIDUAL

BESTS OF THE SEASON

Yards per attempt, season
NFC: 12.8—Reno Mahe, Philadelphia.
AFC: 12.2—B.J. Sams, Baltimore.
Yards, season
NFC: 492—Mark Jones, Tampa Bay.
AFC: 448—Antwaan Randle El, Pittsburgh.
Yards, game
NFC: 108—Reno Mahe, Philadelphia vs. Seattle, Dec. 5 (7 returns).
AFC: 94—Antwaan Randle El, Pittsburgh vs. Jacksonville, Oct. 16 (5 returns, 1 TD).
Longest
NFC: 85—Antonio Chatman, Green Bay vs. Chicago, Dec. 25 (TD).
AFC: 81—Antwaan Randle El, Pittsburgh vs. Detroit, Jan. 1 (TD).
Returns, season
NFC: 51—Mark Jones, Tampa Bay.
AFC: 49—Alvin Pearman, Jacksonville.
Returns, game
NFC: 9—Reggie Swinton, Arizona vs. Philadelphia, Dec. 24 (59 yards).
AFC: 8—Pacman Jones, Tennessee at Miami, Dec. 24 (25 yards).
Fair catches, season
AFC: 25—Troy Walters, Indianapolis.
NFC: 22—Jimmy Williams, Seattle.
Touchdowns, season
AFC: 2—Antwaan Randle El, Pittsburgh.
NFC: 1—Otis Amey, San Francisco; Antonio Chatman, Green Bay; Mewelde Moore, Minnesota; Chad Morton, N.Y. Giants.

NFL LEADERS

Player, team	No.	FC	Yds.	Avg.	Lg.	TD
Mahe, Reno, Philadelphia	21	9	269	12.8	44	0
Sams, B.J., Baltimore*	33	10	401	12.2	51	0
Moore, Mewelde, Minnesota	21	9	245	11.7	t71	1
Smith, Steve, Carolina	27	6	286	10.6	44	0
Northcutt, Dennis, Cleveland*	35	13	368	10.5	t62	1
Randle El, Antwaan, Pittsburgh*	44	12	448	10.2	t81	2

Player, team	No.	FC	Yds.	Avg.	Lg.	TD
Jones, Mark, Tampa Bay	51	18	492	9.6	31	0
Morton, Chad, N.Y. Giants	47	16	453	9.6	58	1
Wade, Bobby, Tennessee*	33	9	317	9.6	t73	1
Jones, Pacman, Tennessee*	29	8	272	9.4	t52	1
Welker, Wes, Miami*	43	23	390	9.1	47	0
Dwight, Tim, New England*	32	13	273	8.5	29	0
Chatman, Antonio, Green Bay	45	18	381	8.5	t85	1
Pearman, Alvin, Jacksonville*	49	15	410	8.4	24	0
Walters, Troy, Indianapolis*	21	25	172	8.2	29	0

*AFC.
t—touchdown.
Leader based on average return, minimum 20.

AFC

Player, team	No.	FC	Yds.	Avg.	Lg.	TD
Adams, Charlie, Denver	16	5	133	8.3	32	0
Brown, Troy, New England	7	5	30	4.3	7	0
Buchanon, Phillip, Houston	12	6	101	8.4	37	0
Carr, Chris, Oakland	34	7	186	5.5	34	0
Clayton, Mark, Baltimore	6	2	30	5.0	10	0
Clements, Nate, Buffalo	8	3	52	6.5	13	0
Cotchery, Jerricho, N.Y. Jets	23	7	182	7.9	18	0
Cribbs, Joshua, Cleveland	1	0	5	5.0	5	0
David, Jason, Indianapolis	1	0	0	0.0	0	0
Davis, Domanick, Houston	3	1	24	8.0	21	0
Dwight, Tim, New England	32	13	273	8.5	29	0
Hall, Dante, Kansas City	42	6	276	6.6	52	0
Harrison, James, Pittsburgh	0	1	0	...	...	0
Harrison, Marvin, Indianapolis	1	0	10	10.0	10	0
Iwuoma, Chidi, Pittsburgh	1	0	3	3.0	3	0
Jackson, Marlin, Indianapolis	1	0	0	0.0	0	0
Johnson, Bethel, New England	1	0	11	11.0	11	0
Jones, Brandon, Tennessee	5	0	75	15.0	32	0
Jones, Pacman, Tennessee	29	8	272	9.4	t52	1
Jones, Sean, Cleveland	1	0	0	0.0	0	0
Kennison, Eddie, Kansas City	1	1	17	17.0	17	0
Mathis, Jerome, Houston	12	0	68	5.7	19	0
Mathis, Rashean, Jacksonville	1	0	-1	-1.0	-1	0
McCardell, Keenan, San Diego	3	3	31	10.3	14	0
McCareins, Justin, N.Y. Jets	5	4	28	5.6	12	0
Miller, Justin, N.Y. Jets	6	1	9	1.5	12	0
Morgan, Donovan, Houston	3	0	30	10.0	23	0

2005 STATISTICS Punt returns

— 277 —

AFC

Player, team	No.	FC	Yds.	Avg.	Lg.	TD
Northcutt, Dennis, Cleveland ..	35	13	368	10.5	t62	1
Owens, Chad, Jacksonville	3	0	6	2.0	6	0
Parker, Eric, San Diego...........	18	9	106	5.9	15	0
Parrish, Roscoe, Buffalo.........	14	9	186	13.3	43	0
Pearman, Alvin, Jacksonville ..	49	15	410	8.4	24	0
Randle El, Antwaan, Pittsburgh	44	12	448	10.2	t81	2
Ratliff, Keiwan, Cincinnati.......	28	14	157	5.6	13	0
Sams, B.J., Baltimore..............	33	10	401	12.2	51	0
Sanders, Deion, Baltimore	0	1	0	...	...	0
Smith, Jonathan, Buffalo	6	5	41	6.8	17	0
Sproles, Darren, San Diego	18	5	108	6.0	23	0
Taylor, Ike, Pittsburgh.............	1	0	19	19.0	19	0
Thompson, Lamont, Tennessee	1	0	31	31.0	31	0
Thurman, Andrae, Tennessee ..	9	5	31	3.4	11	0
Walters, Troy, Indianapolis	21	25	172	8.2	29	0
Welker, Wes, Miami	43	23	390	9.1	47	0
Williams, Darrent, Denver.......	17	12	148	8.7	52	0
Williams, Tank, Tennessee	1	0	9	9.0	9	0
Woodson, Charles, Oakland	3	0	20	6.7	15	0

t—touchdown.

NFC

Player, team	No.	FC	Yds.	Avg.	Lg.	TD
Allen, David, St. Louis	7	6	38	5.4	12	0
Amey, Otis, San Francisco	11	2	125	11.4	t75	1
Atogwe, O.J., St. Louis............	0	1	0	...	...	0
Berrian, Bernard, Chicago.......	8	3	69	8.6	24	0
Blackburn, Chase, N.Y. Giants	1	0	0	0.0	0	0
Brown, Antonio, Washington ..	13	12	63	4.8	16	0
Burleson, Nate, Minnesota	5	0	21	4.2	10	0
Butler, James, N.Y. Giants........	1	0	0	0.0	0	0
Chatman, Antonio, Green Bay..	45	18	381	8.5	t85	1
Cobb, DeAndra, Atlanta	1	0	8	8.0	8	0
Crayton, Patrick, Dallas	23	9	166	7.2	25	0
Davis, Rashied, Chicago..........	5	1	31	6.2	21	0
Drummond, Eddie, Detroit	26	11	157	6.0	38	0
Engram, Bobby, Seattle	1	1	9	9.0	9	0
Fair, Terry, St. Louis	3	6	7	2.3	8	0
Finneran, Brian, Atlanta	2	8	7	3.5	5	0
Furrey, Mike, St. Louis	4	2	28	7.0	13	0
Gamble, Chris, Carolina	14	5	158	11.3	76	0
Hakim, Az-Zahir, New Orleans	34	4	260	7.6	42	0
Hall, DeAngelo, Atlanta	8	2	82	10.3	27	0
Howry, Keenan, Minnesota......	12	5	78	6.5	19	0
Jenkins, Michael, Atlanta	3	0	19	6.3	15	0
Johnson, Bryant, Arizona	1	2	9	9.0	9	0
Jones, Mark, Tampa Bay..........	51	18	492	9.6	31	0
Lewis, Michael, New Orleans ..	4	0	8	2.0	5	0
Looker, Dane, St. Louis	8	2	69	8.6	17	0
Mahe, Reno, Philadelphia........	21	9	269	12.8	44	0
Marshall, Rasheed, San Francisco	17	10	87	5.1	13	0
McDonald, Shaun, St. Louis....	8	6	33	4.1	14	0
McQuarters, R.W., Detroit........	10	2	117	11.7	49	0
Moore, Mewelde, Minnesota	21	9	245	11.7	t71	1
Morton, Chad, N.Y. Giants	47	16	453	9.6	58	1
Moses, J.J., Arizona	7	0	40	5.7	12	0
Moss, Santana, Washington....	7	1	40	5.7	14	0
Newman, Terence, Dallas	10	6	55	5.5	26	0
Price, Peerless, Dallas	12	6	63	5.3	11	0
Robinson, Koren, Minnesota ..	2	0	0	0.0	0	0
Rossum, Allen, Atlanta	17	12	145	8.5	29	0
Sheppard, Lito, Philadelphia ..	2	3	9	4.5	8	0
Smith, Steve, Carolina	27	6	286	10.6	44	0
Stallworth, Donte', New Orleans	7	1	52	7.4	27	0
Swinton, Reggie, Arizona	42	14	336	8.0	32	0
Taylor, Travis, Minnesota	1	0	0	0.0	0	0
Thomas, Fred, New Orleans	1	0	0	0.0	0	0
Thrash, James, Washington	10	15	77	7.7	18	0
Torrence, Leigh, Atlanta	0	1	0	...	...	0
Wade, Bobby, Chicago	33	9	317	9.6	t73	1
Warrick, Peter, Seattle	6	0	29	4.8	10	0
Westbrook, Brian, Philadelphia	8	2	60	7.5	23	0
Williams, Jimmy, Seattle	24	22	139	5.8	24	0
Wynn, Dexter, Philadelphia......	22	10	110	5.0	27	0

t—touchdown.

KICKOFF RETURNS

AFC

Team	No.	Yds.	Avg.	Long	TD
Buffalo	75	1992	26.6	t99	1
Houston	84	2173	25.9	t99	2
N.Y. Jets	71	1728	24.3	t95	1
Tennessee	70	1697	24.2	85	0
San Diego	69	1667	24.2	60	0
Jacksonville	50	1197	23.9	t91	1
Cincinnati	67	1580	23.6	94	0
Kansas City	68	1591	23.4	t96	1
Oakland	80	1832	22.9	62	0
New England	70	1555	22.2	65	0
Cleveland	68	1506	22.1	t90	1
Miami	68	1501	22.1	46	0
Pittsburgh	56	1208	21.6	74	0
Baltimore	60	1289	21.5	87	0
Denver	47	975	20.7	36	0
Indianapolis	51	1017	19.9	39	0
AFC total	1054	24508	...	t99	7
AFC average	65.9	1531.8	23.3	...	0.4

t—touchdown.

NFC

Team	No.	Yds.	Avg.	Long	TD
N.Y. Giants	63	1529	24.3	t95	1
Dallas	64	1523	23.8	49	0
Washington	62	1438	23.2	t94	2
Arizona	76	1719	22.6	90	0
Philadelphia	71	1578	22.2	53	0
Seattle	61	1347	22.1	53	0
Minnesota	71	1549	21.8	t86	1
Detroit	73	1576	21.6	73	0
St. Louis	74	1580	21.4	t99	1
Atlanta	70	1482	21.2	47	0
Carolina	53	1083	20.4	60	0
New Orleans	75	1516	20.2	46	0
Chicago	55	1092	19.9	40	0
Tampa Bay	59	1148	19.5	37	0
San Francisco	81	1540	19.0	40	0
Green Bay	75	1418	18.9	57	0
NFC total	1083	23118	...	t99	5
NFC average	67.7	1444.9	21.3	...	0.3
NFL total	2137	47626	...	t99	12
NFL average	66.8	1488.3	22.3	...	0.4

BESTS OF THE SEASON

Yards per attempt, season
AFC: 30.2—Terrence McGee, Buffalo.
NFC: 26.0—Koren Robinson, Minnesota.

Yards, season
AFC: 1752—Chris Carr, Oakland.
NFC: 1456—Reggie Swinton, Arizona.

Yards, game
AFC: 266—Jerome Mathis, Houston vs. Indianapolis, Oct. 23 (7 returns, 1 TD); Jerome Mathis, Houston vs. Kansas City, Nov. 20 (7 returns, 1 TD).
NFC: 202—Chris Johnson, St. Louis vs. Seattle, Oct. 9 (6 returns, 1 TD).

Longest
AFC: 99—Jerome Mathis, Houston vs. Kansas City, Nov. 20 (TD), Terrence McGee, Buffalo at Cincinnati, Dec. 24 (TD).
NFC: 99—Chris Johnson, St. Louis vs. Seattle, Oct. 9 (TD).

Returns, season
AFC: 73—Chris Carr, Oakland.
NFC: 63—Reggie Swinton, Arizona.

Returns, game
AFC: 8—Dante Hall, Kansas City vs. Philadelphia, Oct. 2 (234 yards, 1 TD); Tab Perry, Cincinnati vs. Indianapolis, Nov. 20 (181 yards); B.J. Sams, Baltimore at Cincinnati, Nov. 27 (145 yards).
NFC: 8—Maurice Hicks, San Francisco at Washington, Oct. 23 (133 yards); Chris Johnson, St. Louis at Indianapolis, Oct. 17 (151 yards); Allen Rossum, Atlanta vs. Green Bay, Nov. 13 (156 yards); DeAndra Cobb, Atlanta vs. Carolina, Jan. 1 (181 yards).

Touchdowns, season
AFC: 2—Jerome Mathis, Houston.
NFC: 1—Held by 5 players.

NFL LEADERS

Player, team	No.	Yds.	Avg.	Long	TD
McGee, Terrence, Buffalo*	46	1391	30.2	t99	1
Mathis, Jerome, Houston*	54	1542	28.6	t99	2
Miller, Justin, N.Y. Jets*	60	1577	26.3	t95	1
Jones, Pacman, Tennessee*	43	1127	26.2	85	0
Robinson, Koren, Minnesota	47	1221	26.0	t86	1
Betts, Ladell, Washington	24	621	25.9	t94	1

Player, team	No.	Yds.	Avg.	Long	TD
Ponder, Willie, N.Y. Giants	35	905	25.9	t95	1
Morgan, Quincy, Pittsburgh*	23	583	25.3	74	0
Thompson, Tyson, Dallas	57	1399	24.5	49	0
Wimbush, Derrick, Jacksonville*	39	955	24.5	t91	1
Perry, Tab, Cincinnati*	64	1562	24.4	94	0
Cribbs, Joshua, Cleveland*	45	1094	24.3	t90	1
Sproles, Darren, San Diego*	63	1528	24.3	58	0
Carr, Chris, Oakland*	73	1752	24.0	62	0
Hall, Dante, Kansas City*	65	1560	24.0	t96	1

*AFC.
t—touchdown.
Leader based on average return, minimum 20.

AFC

Player, team	No.	Yds.	Avg.	Long	TD
Adams, Charlie, Denver	10	218	21.8	32	0
Alexander, Roc, Denver	12	261	21.8	31	0
Alexis, Rich, Jacksonville	1	31	31.0	31	0
Anderson, Mike, Denver	1	18	18.0	18	0
Baker, Chris, N.Y. Jets	2	11	5.5	11	0
Banta-Cain, Tully, New England	1	14	14.0	14	0
Barrett, David, N.Y. Jets	1	0	0.0	0	0
Blaylock, Derrick, N.Y. Jets	1	17	17.0	17	0
Bowens, David, Miami	1	5	5.0	5	0
Brady, Kyle, Jacksonville	1	24	24.0	24	0
Bruener, Mark, Houston	1	11	11.0	11	0
Burns, Joe, Buffalo	3	46	15.3	19	0
Caldwell, Reche, San Diego	3	99	33.0	60	0
Carr, Chris, Oakland	73	1752	24.0	62	0
Carswell, Dwayne, Denver	1	0	0.0	0	0
Carthon, Ran, Indianapolis	5	92	18.4	25	0
Cloud, Michael, New England	1	15	15.0	15	0
Colclough, Ricardo, Pittsburgh	22	473	21.5	63	0
Cotchery, Jerricho, N.Y. Jets	4	105	26.3	30	0
Cribbs, Joshua, Cleveland	45	1094	24.3	t90	1
Davis, Andre', New England	3	108	36.0	65	0
Davis, Domanick, Houston	1	29	29.0	29	0
Dinkins, Darnell, Baltimore	f1	10	10.0	10	0
Droughns, Reuben, Cleveland	5	119	23.8	35	0

Player, team	No.	Yds.	Avg.	Long	TD
Dwight, Tim, New England	10	250	25.0	38	0
Engelberger, John, Denver	f1	5	5.0	5	0
Euhus, Tim, Buffalo	1	0	0.0	0	0
Faulk, Kevin, New England	4	81	20.3	26	0
Fleming, Troy, Tennessee	1	9	9.0	9	0
Flemister, Zeron, Oakland	2	16	8.0	8	0
Gabriel, Doug, Oakland	4	64	16.0	21	0
Gilmore, Bryan, Miami	3	84	28.0	29	0
Green, Justin, Baltimore	1	10	10.0	10	0
Green, William, Cleveland	5	79	15.8	22	0
Hall, Dante, Kansas City	65	1560	24.0	t96	1
Harrison, James, Pittsburgh	1	-2	-2.0	-2	0
Heller, Will, Miami	1	11	11.0	11	0
Hobbs, Ellis, New England	15	361	24.1	37	0
Hollings, Tony, Houston	2	46	23.0	28	0
Horn, Chris, Kansas City	3	31	10.3	11	0
Houston, Cedric, N.Y. Jets	2	18	9.0	18	0
Hulsey, Corey, Oakland	1	0	0.0	0	0
Izzo, Larry, New England	1	0	0.0	0	0
Jackson, Frisman, Cleveland	1	15	15.0	15	0
Jefferson, Joseph, Indianapolis	1	11	11.0	11	0
Johnson, Bethel, New England	31	694	22.4	54	0
Johnson, Kyle, Denver	1	8	8.0	8	0
Jones, Greg, Jacksonville	1	0	0.0	0	0
Jones, Pacman, Tennessee	43	1127	26.2	85	0
Keisel, Brett, Pittsburgh	2	23	11.5	12	0
Kreider, Dan, Pittsburgh	1	3	3.0	3	0
Lawton, Luke, N.Y. Jets	1	0	0.0	0	0
Leonhard, Jim, Buffalo	1	36	36.0	36	0
Mathis, Jerome, Houston	54	1542	28.6	t99	2
McCareins, Justin, N.Y. Jets	f0	0		...	0
McGee, Terrence, Buffalo	46	1391	30.2	t99	1
McIntyre, Corey, Cleveland	3	47	15.7	17	0
Miller, Justin, N.Y. Jets	60	1577	26.3	t95	1
Minor, Travis, Miami	2	22	11.0	19	0
Morency, Vernand, Houston	20	437	21.9	31	0
Morgan, Quincy, Pittsburgh	23	583	25.3	74	0
Mungro, James, Indianapolis	2	39	19.5	22	0
Neufeld, Ryan, Buffalo	3	39	13.0	23	0
Norris, Moran, Houston	1	2	2.0	2	0
O'Neal, Deltha, Cincinnati	1	14	14.0	14	0
Parker, Eric, San Diego	1	16	16.0	16	0
Parrish, Roscoe, Buffalo	10	261	26.1	45	0
Pass, Patrick, New England	2	31	15.5	21	0
Payton, Jarrett, Tennessee	2	24	12.0	24	0
Pearman, Alvin, Jacksonville	8	187	23.4	34	0
Perkins, Antonio, Cleveland	3	82	27.3	35	0
Perry, Tab, Cincinnati	64	1562	24.4	94	0
Pinnock, Andrew, San Diego	1	24	24.0	24	0
Randle El, Antwaan, Pittsburgh	1	16	16.0	16	0
Reed, Josh, Buffalo	4	69	17.3	24	0
Rhodes, Dominic, Indianapolis	41	855	20.9	39	0
Roby, Courtney, Tennessee	22	495	22.5	59	0
Sams, B.J., Baltimore	f44	998	22.7	87	0
Sapp, Cecil, Denver	2	28	14.0	20	0
Schobel, Matt, Cincinnati	2	4	2.0	4	0
Shea, Aaron, Cleveland	3	29	9.7	13	0
Shelton, Daimon, Buffalo	2	26	13.0	16	0
Smith, Jonathan, Buffalo	5	124	24.8	44	0
Smith, Terrelle, Cleveland	2	24	12.0	13	0
Sproles, Darren, San Diego	63	1528	24.3	58	0
Stone, Michael, New England	1	0	0.0	0	0
Taylor, Chester, Baltimore	12	253	21.1	45	0
Taylor, Ike, Pittsburgh	3	59	19.7	24	0
Turner, Michael, San Diego	1	0	0.0	0	0
Utecht, Ben, Indianapolis	1	7	7.0	7	0
Veal, Demetrin, Denver	1	6	6.0	6	0
Walters, Troy, Indianapolis	1	13	13.0	13	0
Watson, Ben, New England	1	1	1.0	1	0
Welker, Wes, Miami	61	1379	22.6	46	0
Wells, Jonathan, Houston	5	106	21.2	40	0
White, Jamel, Baltimore	2	18	9.0	9	0
Williams, Darrent, Denver	18	431	23.9	36	0
Wilson, Cedrick, Pittsburgh	3	53	17.7	29	0
Wimbush, Derrick, Jacksonville	39	955	24.5	t91	1
Wright, Jason, Cleveland	1	17	17.0	17	0

t—touchdown.
f—includes at least one fair catch.

NFC

Player, team	No.	Yds.	Avg.	Long	TD
Allen, David, St. Louis	23	472	20.5	32	0
Allen, Kenderick, N.Y. Giants	1	2	2.0	2	0
Alstott, Mike, Tampa Bay	1	2	2.0	2	0
Amey, Otis, San Francisco	14	241	17.2	25	0
Anderson, Damien, Arizona	1	7	7.0	7	0
Ayanbadejo, Obafemi, Arizona	1	16	16.0	16	0
Azumah, Jerry, Chicago	32	705	22.0	40	0
Barber, Marion, Dallas	3	58	19.3	21	0
Betts, Ladell, Washington	24	621	25.9	t94	1
Bradley, Jon, Tampa Bay	1	2	2.0	2	0
Bradley, Mark, Chicago	4	70	17.5	23	0
Broughton, Nehemiah, Washington	1	5	5.0	5	0
Brown, Antonio, Washington	19	439	23.1	t91	0
Bryant, Romby, Atlanta	8	137	17.1	23	0
Bryson, Shawn, Detroit	4	55	13.8	25	0
Campbell, Dan, Dallas	1	14	14.0	14	0
Carroll, Ahmad, Green Bay	19	390	20.5	57	0
Cartwright, Rock, Washington	4	82	20.5	25	0
Cason, Aveion, St. Louis	2	48	24.0	29	0
Chatman, Antonio, Green Bay	5	91	18.2	33	0
Cobb, DeAndra, Atlanta	16	359	22.4	39	0
Copper, Terrance, Dallas	2	32	16.0	21	0
Cox, Torrie, Tampa Bay	24	464	19.3	30	0
Davenport, Najeh, Green Bay	10	189	18.9	27	0
Davis, Rashied, Chicago	11	251	22.8	34	0
DeVries, Jared, Detroit	1	7	7.0	7	0
Drummond, Eddie, Detroit	49	1077	22.0	48	0
Duckett, T.J., Atlanta	2	36	18.0	18	0
Evans, Demetric, Washington	1	0	0.0	0	0
Fair, Terry, St. Louis	10	182	18.2	35	0
Fason, Ciatrick, Minnesota	2	4	2.0	4	0
Ferguson, Robert, Green Bay	2	44	22.0	22	0
Gaines, Michael, Carolina	2	24	12.0	13	0
Gilmore, John, Chicago	1	5	5.0	5	0
Glenn, Aaron, Dallas	1	20	20.0	20	0
Goings, Nick, Carolina	1	21	21.0	21	0
Gordon, Lamar, Philadelphia	3	64	21.3	25	0
Graham, Earnest, Tampa Bay	4	74	18.5	22	0
Green, Eric, Arizona	1	4	4.0	4	0
Griffith, Justin, Atlanta	8	149	18.6	23	0
Hakim, Az-Zahir, New Orleans	9	171	19.0	29	0
Hall, DeAngelo, Atlanta	2	45	22.5	23	0
Hall, Lamont, New Orleans	2	9	4.5	5	0
Hannam, Ryan, Seattle	f0	0	...	...	0
Harris, Arlen, St. Louis	1	21	21.0	21	0
Henderson, E.J., Minnesota	1	13	13.0	13	0
Henderson, William, Green Bay	2	20	10.0	10	0
Herrera, Anthony, Minnesota	1	6	6.0	6	0
Hicks, Maurice, San Francisco	34	689	20.3	40	0
Hood, Roderick, Philadelphia	38	900	23.7	53	0
Hoover, Brad, Carolina	1	10	10.0	10	0
Idonije, Israel, Chicago	1	0	0.0	0	0
Jackson, James, Arizona	1	14	14.0	14	0
Jacobs, Brandon, N.Y. Giants	2	58	29.0	33	0
Johnson, Bryant, Arizona	2	45	22.5	24	0
Johnson, Chris, St. Louis	38	857	22.6	t99	1
Johnson, Kevin, Detroit	1	14	14.0	14	0
Jones, Jamal, Green Bay	4	80	20.0	25	0
Jones, Mark, Tampa Bay	5	95	19.0	24	0
Leach, Vonta, Green Bay	3	39	13.0	20	0
Lee, ReShard, Green Bay	15	319	21.3	35	0
Lewis, Michael, New Orleans	8	137	17.1	20	0

Player, team	No.	Yds.	Avg.	Long	TD
Mahe, Reno, Philadelphia	1	19	19.0	19	0
Mangum, Kris, Carolina	1	9	9.0	9	0
Marshall, Rasheed, San Francisco.	26	488	18.8	29	0
Martinez, Glenn, Detroit	2	42	21.0	24	0
McAddley, Jason, San Francisco	7	122	17.4	22	0
McAfee, Fred, New Orleans	22	485	22.0	34	0
McKie, Jason, Chicago	3	29	9.7	17	0
McQuarters, R.W., Detroit	16	381	23.8	73	0
Moats, Ryan, Philadelphia	2	26	13.0	15	0
Moore, Mewelde, Minnesota	4	72	18.0	27	0
Morris, Maurice, Seattle	1	21	21.0	21	0
Morton, Chad, N.Y. Giants	24	559	23.3	41	0
Moses, J.J., Arizona	7	177	25.3	35	0
Murphy, Terrence, Green Bay	5	91	18.2	29	0
Owens, Richard, Minnesota	3	25	8.3	16	0
Parson, Rich, Washington	3	71	23.7	35	0
Pathon, Jerome, Atlanta	3	54	18.0	21	0
Patterson, Mike, Philadelphia	1	12	12.0	12	0
Perry, Bruce, Philadelphia	10	273	27.3	49	0
Peterson, Adrian, Chicago	2	32	16.0	19	0
Peterson, Kenny, Green Bay	1	5	5.0	5	0
Pittman, Michael, Tampa Bay	3	85	28.3	37	0
Ponder, Willie, N.Y. Giants	35	905	25.9	t95	1
Robertson, Jamal, Carolina	16	343	21.4	42	0
Robinson, Koren, Minnesota	47	1221	26.0	t86	1
Rossum, Allen, Atlanta	31	702	22.6	47	0
Scobey, Josh, Seattle	59	1326	22.5	53	0
Sellers, Mike, Washington	3	50	16.7	20	0
Shepherd, Edell, Tampa Bay	20	414	20.7	30	0
Shiancoe, Visanthe, N.Y. Giants	1	5	5.0	5	0
Smart, Rod, Carolina	29	615	21.2	60	0
Smith, Alex, Tampa Bay	1	12	12.0	12	0
Smith, Antowain, New Orleans	1	30	30.0	30	0
Smith, Steve, Carolina	3	61	20.3	33	0
Stecker, Aaron, New Orleans	31	672	21.7	46	0
Swinton, Reggie, Arizona	63	1456	23.1	90	0
Tafoya, Joe, Seattle	1	0	0.0	0	0
Thompson, Tyson, Dallas	57	1399	24.5	49	0
Thrash, James, Washington	7	170	24.3	31	0
Thurman, Andrae, Ten.-G.B.*	10	178	17.8	25	0
Vasher, Nathan, Chicago	1	0	0.0	0	0
Whitehead, Willie, New Orleans	2	12	6.0	12	0
Williams, Corey, Green Bay	1	14	14.0	14	0
Williams, Moe, Minnesota	1	16	16.0	16	0
Williamson, Troy, Minnesota	12	192	16.0	28	0
Wynn, Dexter, Philadelphia	16	284	17.8	27	0

*Includes both NFC and AFC statistics.
t—touchdown.
f—includes at least one fair catch.

PLAYERS WITH TWO CLUBS

Player, team	No.	Yds.	Avg.	Lg.	TD
Thurman, Andrae, Tennessee	2	42	21.0	25	0
Thurman, Andrae, Green Bay	8	136	17.0	23	0

TACKLES

BESTS OF THE SEASON

Tackles, season
AFC: 128—Jonathan Vilma, N.Y. Jets.
NFC: 103—Shelton Quarles, Tampa Bay.

Tackles, game
AFC: 17—Donnie Edwards, San Diego at Kansas City, Dec. 24.
NFC: 15—Eric Green, Arizona at St. Louis, Nov. 20.

NFL LEADERS

Player, team	Tk.	Ast.
Vilma, Jonathan, N.Y. Jets*	128	45
Edwards, Donnie, San Diego*	114	40
Thomas, Zach, Miami*	107	55
Fletcher, London, Buffalo* ..	104	54
Quarles, Shelton, Tampa Bay..	103	30
Bulluck, Keith, Tennessee*	102	36
Trotter, Jeremiah, Philadelphia	102	19
Urlacher, Brian, Chicago	98	24
Williams, Demorrio, Atlanta....	97	28
Peterson, Mike, Jacksonville*.	95	37
Brooks, Derrick, Tampa Bay ..	93	32
Brackett, Gary, Indianapolis* ..	92	35
Barnett, Nick, Green Bay........	92	47
Wilson, Adrian, Arizona	92	16
Lewis, Michael, Philadelphia..	91	14
Smith, Derek, San Francisco...	90	26
Davis, Andra, Cleveland*	89	60
Brooking, Keith, Atlanta	89	26
Wilson, Gibril, N.Y. Giants......	88	22
Morrison, Kirk, Oakland*........	87	25
*AFC		

AFC

Player, team	Tk.	Ast.
Abraham, John, N.Y. Jets	44	14
Adams, Sam, Buffalo	15	4
Allen, Jared, Kansas City	51	7
Anderson, Charlie, Houston....	6	1
Anderson, Tim, Buffalo	26	16
Askew, Matthias, Cincinnati ...	2	2
Asomugha, Nnamdi, Oakland .	55	5
Ayodele, Akin, Jacksonville	56	16
Babin, Jason, Houston............	26	11
Bailey, Champ, Denver............	60	6
Baker, Rashad, Buffalo............	5	1
Ball, Dave, San Diego-N.Y. Jets	4	2
Bannan, Justin, Buffalo...........	23	17
Banta-Cain, Tully, New England	3	2
Barrett, David, N.Y. Jets	40	8
Bartee, William, Kansas City ..	1	1
Barton, Eric, N.Y. Jets	13	8
Bauman, Rashad, Cincinnati ...	8	0
Baxter, Gary, Cleveland...........	19	4
Beckham, Tony, Tennessee	10	1
Beisel, Monty, New England ...	27	17
Bell, Jason, Houston................	7	0
Bell, Kendrell, Kansas City	32	9
Bell, Yeremiah, Miami.............	13	8
Bingham, Ryon, San Diego.....	1	0
Bodden, Leigh, Cleveland	47	10
Body, Patrick, Cincinnati.........	1	0
Boiman, Rocky, Tennessee	11	9
Boulware, Peter, Baltimore......	5	4
Bowens, David, Miami	16	3
Brackett, Gary, Indianapolis	92	35
Branch, Calvin, Oakland..........	2	0
Brandon, Sam, Denver............	12	7
Brayton, Tyler, Oakland...........	11	2
Brock, Raheem, Indianapolis..	36	9
Brown, C.C., Houston	52	26
Brown, Chad, New England	29	8

Player, team	Tk.	Ast.
Brown, Courtney, Denver........	20	4
Brown, Mark, N.Y. Jets	37	37
Browning, John, Kansas City..	31	4
Bruschi, Tedy, New England ...	36	25
Buchanon, Phillip, Houston	29	6
Bulluck, Keith, Tennessee	102	36
Burgess, Derrick, Oakland......	50	6
Burns, Keith, Denver...............	0	2
Carr, Chris, Oakland –	6	1
Carter, Dale, Baltimore	15	2
Carter, Kevin, Miami	34	19
Carter, Tyrone, Pittsburgh	9	2
Castillo, Luis, San Diego.........	37	12
Celestin, Oliver, N.Y. Jets	18	3
Cesaire, Jacques, San Diego...	17	8
Chase, Martin, Jacksonville.....	1	0
Chatham, Matt, New England .	8	1
Childress, Brandon, New England	4	0
Clark, Danny, Oakland............	82	31
Clauss, Jared, Tennessee........	13	5
Clements, Nate, Buffalo	81	21
Clemons, Duane, Cincinnati....	10	2
Colclough, Ricardo, Pittsburgh	12	3
Coleman, Erik, N.Y. Jets..........	80	36
Coleman, Marco, Denver	7	2
Coleman, Marcus, Houston	47	6
Colvin, Rosevelt, New England	41	20
Cooper, Deke, Jacksonville	42	10
Cooper, Jarrod, Oakland	35	14
Cooper, Stephen, San Diego ...	20	10
Cousin, Terry, Jacksonville.....	39	7
Cox, Curome, Denver..............	9	1
Cribbs, Joshua, Cleveland.......	1	0
Crocker, Chris, Cleveland	50	29
Crowder, Channing, Miami	53	32
Crowell, Angelo, Buffalo	77	38
Dalton, Lional, Kansas City.....	12	6
Daniels, Travis, Miami.............	46	14
Darius, Donovin, Jacksonville.	5	1
David, Jason, Indianapolis......	28	8
Davis, Andra, Cleveland	89	60
Davis, Don, New England	0	1
Davis, Jim, Jacksonville...........	1	1
Davis, Sammy, San Diego.......	23	3
DeLoach, Jerry, Houston	10	3
Demps, Will, Baltimore...........	46	4
Denney, Ryan, Buffalo.............	23	12
Doss, Mike, Indianapolis.........	56	19
Earl, Glenn, Houston..............	21	13
Eason, Nick, Cleveland............	11	8
Edwards, Donnie, San Diego ..	114	40
Edwards, Dwan, Baltimore......	17	7
Edwards, Ron, Buffalo.............	4	2
Ekuban, Ebenezer, Denver......	19	8
Ellis, Shaun, N.Y. Jets	31	7
Engelberger, John, Denver......	12	3
Evans, Troy, Houston	14	2
Faggins, DeMarcus, Houston..	40	7
Fanene, Jonathan, Cincinnati..	2	1
Farrior, James, Pittsburgh	76	45
Favors, Greg, Jacksonville	1	5
Ferguson, Nick, Denver...........	60	18
Fisk, Jason, Cleveland.............	23	16
Fletcher, Jamar, San Diego	20	8

Player, team	Tk.	Ast.
Fletcher, London, Buffalo........	104	54
Florence, Drayton, San Diego .	47	7
Foley, Steve, San Diego	28	10
Foote, Larry, Pittsburgh..........	76	25
Foster, George, Denver	0	1
Fox, Keyaron, Kansas City	1	0
Foxworth, Domonique, Denver	58	6
Franklin, Aubrayo, Baltimore...	18	2
Fraser, Simon, Cleveland	1	0
Frazier, Andre, Pittsburgh	2	0
Freeman, Arturo, New England	5	2
Freeney, Dwight, Indianapolis..	30	5
Gardner, Barry, N.Y. Jets.........	2	1
Gardner, Gilbert, Indianapolis..	14	5
Gardner, Rich, Tennessee	0	1
Gay, Randall, New England	10	1
Geathers, Robert, Cincinnati ...	25	9
Gibson, Derrick, Oakland	25	5
Gilbert, Tony, Jacksonville	3	0
Giordano, Matt, Indianapolis...	5	0
Goddard, Johnathan, Indianapolis	1	0
Godfrey, Randall, San Diego....	56	21
Gold, Ian, Denver....................	74	16
Grant, DeLawrence, Oakland...	2	1
Grant, Deon, Jacksonville........	55	11
Green, Jarvis, New England	24	11
Green, Roderick, Baltimore......	2	1
Greenwood, Morlon, Houston.	82	30
Greer, Jabari, Buffalo	19	6
Gregg, Kelly, Baltimore...........	36	25
Griffin, Kris, Kansas City	2	0
Haggan, Mario, Buffalo...........	3	2
Haggans, Clark, Pittsburgh.....	42	19
Hall, Carlos, Kansas City	11	3
Hamilton, Bobby, Oakland......	50	6
Hampton, Casey, Pittsburgh ...	25	17
Harper, Nick, Indianapolis.......	60	6
Harris, Marques, San Diego....	2	0
Harrison, James, Pittsburgh....	25	6
Harrison, Rodney, New England	9	4
Hart, Clinton, San Diego	26	8
Hawkins, Artrell, New England	11	5
Hawthorne, Anttaj, Oakland....	0	2
Hayden, Kelvin, Indianapolis...	14	4
Haynesworth, Albert, Tennessee	36	16
Hayward, Reggie, Jacksonville	27	6
Henderson, John, Jacksonville	53	19
Hicks, Eric, Kansas City	36	8
Hill, Marquise, New England...	2	1
Hill, Renaldo, Oakland............	72	14
Hill, Reynaldo, Tennessee	37	8
Hobbs, Ellis, New England	33	9
Hobson, Victor, N.Y. Jets	53	26
Hoke, Chris, Pittsburgh...........	3	3
Holliday, Vonnie, Miami	36	16
Hope, Chris, Pittsburgh...........	70	27
Howard, Reggie, Miami	36	10
Hutchins, Von, Indianapolis.....	3	1
Ioane, Junior, Houston	11	10
Irons, Grant, Oakland..............	3	1
Izzo, Larry, New England	3	0
Jackson, Eddie, Miami	1	1
Jackson, Marlin, Indianapolis .	38	12
James, Tory, Cincinnati...........	49	8

2005 STATISTICS *Tackles*

Player, team	Tk.	Ast.	Player, team	Tk.	Ast.	Player, team	Tk.	Ast.
Jammer, Quentin, San Diego..	60	12	Odom, Antwan, Tennessee	18	13	Smith, Daryl, Jacksonville	69	11
Jasper, Ed, Oakland	23	1	Ohalete, Ifeanyi, Cincinnati	36	15	Smith, Justin, Cincinnati.........	45	21
Jefferson, Joseph, Indianapolis	2	4	Olshansky, Igor, San Diego.....	18	11	Smith, Robaire, Houston	43	25
Johnson, Derrick, Kansas City	79	16	Orr, Shantee, Houston	34	11	Smith, Shaun, Cincinnati	18	8
Johnson, Jarret, Baltimore	26	12	Parker, J'Vonne, Cleveland......	1	0	Sorensen, Nick, Jacksonville ..	1	0
Johnson, Landon, Cincinnati..	58	24	Paymah, Karl, Denver	2	1	Speegle, Nick, Cleveland........	1	1
Johnson, Tim, Oakland	4	5	Payne, Seth, Houston	45	14	Spencer, Cody, Tennessee	1	0
Johnson, Travis, Houston	23	3	Peek, Antwan, Houston	30	17	Spicer, Paul, Jacksonville	30	7
Johnson, Trevor, N.Y. Jets	5	3	Peterson, Mike, Jacksonville...	95	37	Spikes, Takeo, Buffalo............	11	6
Jones, Pacman, Tennessee.....	43	9	Phillips, Shaun, San Diego	18	2	Spragan, Donnie, Miami	34	12
Jones, Sean, Cleveland	2	3	Polamalu, Troy, Pittsburgh	74	18	Sproles, Darren, San Diego	1	0
Jones, Tebucky, Miami	23	12	Polk, DaShon, Houston	62	30	Starks, Duane, New England ...	21	7
Jue, Bhawoh, San Diego	30	12	Pollack, David, Cincinnati	22	6	Starks, Randy, Tennessee	34	14
June, Cato, Indianapolis	67	35	Polley, Tommy, Baltimore	72	23	Starks, Scott, Jacksonville	2	2
Kaesviharn, Kevin, Cincinnati..	63	24	Pontbriand, Ryan, Cleveland...	0	1	Stewart, Matt, Cleveland..........	26	12
Kassell, Brad, Tennessee	50	24	Pool, Brodney, Cleveland	19	6	Stone, Michael, New England ..	27	5
Keisel, Brett, Pittsburgh...........	13	5	Poole, Tyrone, New England ...	1	0	Strait, Derrick, N.Y. Jets.........	29	9
Kelley, Ethan, Cleveland	15	6	Pope, Derrick, Miami	19	4	Stroud, Marcus, Jacksonville..	32	11
Kelly, Tommy, Oakland	37	10	Pope, Monsanto, Denver	2	0	Suggs, Terrell, Baltimore	46	23
Kelsay, Chris, Buffalo...............	26	19	Porter, Joey, Pittsburgh	39	18	Surtain, Patrick, Kansas City...	47	10
Kemoeatu, Maake, Baltimore..	30	10	Posey, Jeff, Buffalo	39	22	Taylor, Ben, Cleveland	75	35
Kiel, Terrence, San Diego........	49	15	Poteat, Hank, New England.....	17	4	Taylor, Ike, Pittsburgh	69	15
King, Eric, Buffalo	23	2	Pouha, Sione, N.Y. Jets..........	7	2	Taylor, Jason, Miami	52	21
Kirschke, Travis, Pittsburgh	6	6	Powell, Carl, Cincinnati	9	4	Thomas, Adalius, Baltimore....	69	15
Klecko, Dan, New England	5	4	Pryce, Trevor, Denver	31	2	Thomas, Bryan, N.Y. Jets.......	25	12
Knight, Sammy, Kansas City...	70	20	Ratliff, Keiwan, Cincinnati........	37	6	Thomas, Josh, Indianapolis.....	7	9
Kriewaldt, Clint, Pittsburgh	13	3	Reagor, Montae, Indianapolis .	27	9	Thomas, Kiwaukee, Miami	6	0
Labinjo, Mike, Phila.-Ind.*	4	1	Reed, Ed, Baltimore	33	4	Thomas, Pat, Jacksonville	5	0
LaBoy, Travis, Tennessee	28	13	Reed, James, N.Y. Jets	44	21	Thomas, Zach, Miami	107	55
Lang, Kenard, Cleveland	28	13	Reid, Darrell, Indianapolis	5	4	Thompson, Chaun, Cleveland..	61	21
Law, Ty, N.Y. Jets....................	45	17	Reid, Dexter, Indianapolis	3	0	Thompson, Lamont, Tennessee	62	19
Leber, Ben, San Diego	18	4	Reynolds, Robert, Tennessee .	7	4	Thornton, David, Indianapolis.	55	20
Legree, Lance, N.Y. Jets	21	8	Rhodes, Kerry, N.Y. Jets	80	20	Thornton, John, Cincinnati	24	18
Lehan, Michael, Cleveland	4	0	Richardson, David, Jacksonville	3	0	Thurman, Odell, Cincinnati	69	37
Leonhard, Jim, Buffalo	0	3	Roberson, Chris, Jacksonville.	1	0	Tillman, Travares, Miami.........	33	21
Lewis, Ray, Baltimore	38	8	Robertson, Dewayne, N.Y. Jets	28	15	Tongue, Reggie, Oakland	5	0
Logan, Mike, Pittsburgh	11	4	Robinson, Bryan, Cincinnati	9	9	Towns, Lester, Arizona-Miami*	6	1
Long, Rien, Tennessee.............	24	5	Robinson, Derreck, San Diego	1	1	Townsend, Deshea, Pittsburgh	41	14
Lynch, John, Denver	45	17	Robinson, Dunta, Houston	68	19	Traylor, Keith, Miami	22	10
Maddox, Anthony, Jacksonville	3	0	Rolle, Samari, Baltimore	39	2	Tripplett, Larry, Indianapolis....	25	5
Madison, Sam, Miami...............	46	10	Roth, Matt, Miami	15	5	Vanden Bosch, Kyle, Tennessee	40	26
Malone, Alfred, Houston	6	3	Routt, Stanford, Oakland	22	2	Veal, Demetrin, Denver	19	6
Martin, Curtis, N.Y. Jets	0	1	Roye, Orpheus, Cleveland	65	23	Vilma, Jonathan, N.Y. Jets	128	45
Mathis, Rashean, Jacksonville	55	9	Ruff, Orlando, Cleveland	17	10	Vincent, Troy, Buffalo..............	43	24
Mathis, Robert, Indianapolis..	29	7	Russell, Brian, Cleveland	44	22	von Oelhoffen, Kimo, Pittsburgh	23	13
McAlister, Chris, Baltimore	47	2	Samuel, Asante, New England	44	10	Vrabel, Mike, New England	69	35
McChesney, Matt, N.Y. Jets ...	3	0	Sanders, Bob, Indianapolis	72	20	Waddell, Michael, Tennessee..	13	5
McCleon, Dexter, Kansas City .	20	1	Sanders, Deion, Baltimore	27	2	Walker, Denard, Oakland.........	2	1
McCray, Bobby, Jacksonville..	14	3	Sanders, James, New England	9	3	Walker, Gary, Houston	20	10
McCutcheon, Daylon, Cleveland	71	7	Sanders, Lewis, Houston.........	22	1	Walls, Lenny, Denver	16	0
McFadden, Bryant, Pittsburgh	17	0	Sands, Terdell, Oakland	9	1	Ward, B.J., Baltimore...............	3	1
McGarrahan, Scott, San Diego	0	1	Sandy, Justin, Tennessee	2	0	Warfield, Eric, Kansas City	53	4
McGee, Terrence, Buffalo........	60	13	Sape, Lauvale, Buffalo	7	1	Warren, Gerard, Denver	14	5
McGinest, Willie, New England	45	12	Sapp, Benny, Kansas City	30	5	Warren, Ty, New England	40	28
McKenzie, Chris, Houston.......	4	0	Sapp, Gerome, Indianapolis....	10	1	Washington, Dewayne, Kansas City	9	1
McKinley, Alvin, Cleveland	45	23	Sapp, Warren, Oakland	28	4	Washington, Fabian, Oakland .	40	3
Meier, Rob, Jacksonville	29	6	Scanlon, Rich, Kansas City	3	0	Washington, Rashad, N.Y. Jets	4	7
Merriman, Shawne, San Diego	41	13	Schobel, Aaron, Buffalo	54	17	Washington, Ted, Oakland	38	10
Mickens, Ray, Cleveland	26	7	Schobel, Bo, Tennessee	8	1	Weaver, Anthony, Baltimore....	28	5
Miller, Caleb, Cincinnati	6	1	Schulters, Lance, Miami	57	20	Wesley, Greg, Kansas City	66	16
Miller, Justin, N.Y. Jets	31	9	Schweigert, Stuart, Oakland ...	61	14	Wiley, Marcellus, Jacksonville	6	0
Milloy, Lawyer, Buffalo.............	75	32	Scott, Bart, Baltimore	54	29	Wilfork, Vince, New England....	40	14
Mitchell, Anthony, Cincinnati .	17	2	Scott, Chad, New England	5	0	Wilhelm, Matt, San Diego	13	3
Mitchell, Kawika, Kansas City .	82	21	Scott, DeQuincy, San Diego....	11	2	Wilkerson, Jimmy, Kansas City	15	2
Morris, Rob, Indianapolis	10	3	Scott, Guss, New England	15	4	Williams, Chad, Baltimore	33	5
Morris, Sammy, Miami	1	0	Seau, Junior, Miami	18	18	Williams, D.J., Denver	39	16
Morrison, Kirk, Oakland	87	25	Sensabaugh, Gerald, Jacksonville	14	4	Williams, Darrent, Denver	48	4
Myers, Michael, Denver	25	6	Seymour, Richard, New England	36	11	Williams, Jamal, San Diego	40	13
Navies, Hannibal, Cincinnati ..	1	0	Shelton, Daimon, Buffalo.........	0	3	Williams, Josh, Indianapolis	3	3
Nickey, Donnie, Tennessee	2	0	Siavii, Junior, Kansas City	5	1	Williams, Madieu, Cincinnati ..	16	5
Northcutt, Dennis, Cleveland ..	1	0	Simmons, Brian, Cincinnati	52	32	Williams, Shaud, Buffalo.........	1	0
Norton, Zach, Baltimore	1	0	Simmons, Jason, Houston	17	6	Williams, Tank, Tennessee	58	20
O'Neal, Deltha, Cincinnati	56	9	Simon, Corey, Indianapolis	26	9	Williams, Willie, Pittsburgh	7	3
O'Neil, Keith, Indianapolis.......	14	4	Sims, Ryan, Kansas City	8	0	Wilson, Al, Denver	62	11
			Sirmon, Peter, Tennessee	46	22	Wilson, Eugene, New England	38	23
			Smith, Aaron, Pittsburgh	30	10	Wilson, Jerry, San Diego	12	2

Player, team	Tk.	Ast.
Winborn, Jamie, S.F.-Jack.*	10	5
Wire, Coy, Buffalo	4	2
Wong, Kailee, Houston	21	12
Woodson, Charles, Oakland	27	4
Woolfolk, Andre, Tennessee	40	12
Wright, Kenny, Jacksonville	55	9
Wright, Kenyatta, N.Y. Jets	1	1
Wright, Manuel, Miami	2	2
Wright, Mike, New England	9	4
Zgonina, Jeff, Miami	23	20

*Includes both AFC and NFC statistics.

NFC

Player, team	Tk.	Ast.
Adams, Anthony, San Francisco	24	16
Adams, Blue, Tampa Bay	0	1
Adams, Keith, Philadelphia	50	9
Adams, Mike, San Francisco	55	17
Alexander, Brent, N.Y. Giants	46	15
Allen, James, New Orleans	3	0
Allen, Kenderick, N.Y. Giants	14	6
Allen, Will, N.Y. Giants	62	8
Allen, Will, Tampa Bay	27	12
Anderson, Marques, Den.-S.F.*	0	1
Archuleta, Adam, St. Louis	53	16
Arrington, LaVar, Washington	39	8
Atogwe, O.J., St. Louis	3	1
Ayanbadejo, Brendon, Chicago	4	3
Azumah, Jerry, Chicago	33	4
Babineaux, Jonathan, Atlanta	24	7
Babineaux, Jordan, Seattle	47	11
Bailey, Boss, Detroit	38	20
Bailey, Rodney, Seattle	8	5
Barber, Ronde, Tampa Bay	82	16
Barnett, Nick, Green Bay	92	47
Bartell, Ronald, St. Louis	29	3
Bashir, Idrees, Carolina	1	1
Bell, Marcus, Detroit	15	6
Bellamy, Jay, New Orleans	8	2
Bentley, Kevin, Seattle	18	4
Bernard, Rocky, Seattle	43	9
Berry, Bertrand, Arizona	24	10
Blackburn, Chase, N.Y. Giants	6	9
Blackstock, Darryl, Arizona	7	2
Bly, Dre', Detroit	41	4
Bockwoldt, Colby, New Orleans	54	26
Bolden, Juran, Tampa Bay	33	5
Boley, Michael, Atlanta	36	19
Booker, Fred, New Orleans	1	1
Boone, Alfonso, Chicago	9	5
Boschetti, Ryan, Washington	4	2
Boulware, Michael, Seattle	58	15
Bowen, Matt, Washington	8	1
Bradley, Jon, Tampa Bay	1	0
Briggs, Lance, Chicago	83	24
Brooking, Keith, Atlanta	89	26
Brooks, Derrick, Tampa Bay	93	32
Brown, Alex, Chicago	39	7
Brown, Fakhir, New Orleans	28	1
Brown, Mike, Chicago	63	9
Brown, Ralph, Minnesota	23	2
Brown, Sheldon, Philadelphia	48	9
Bryant, Anthony, Tampa Bay	1	2
Bryant, Fernando, Detroit	8	1
Bryant, Tony, New Orleans	18	8
Buckner, Brentson, Carolina	28	8
Bullocks, Josh, New Orleans	52	14
Bulman, Tim, Arizona	7	0
Burnett, Kevin, Dallas	5	1
Butler, James, N.Y. Giants	14	4
Cain, Jeremy, Chicago	4	2
Calahan, Jeremy, St. Louis	1	0
Campbell, Khary, Washington	1	2

Player, team	Tk.	Ast.
Canty, Chris, Dallas	24	12
Carpenter, Keion, Atlanta	43	12
Carroll, Ahmad, Green Bay	40	3
Carstens, Jordan, Carolina	24	12
Carter, Andre, San Francisco	35	9
Carter, Dyshod, Arizona	1	0
Carter, Jerome, St. Louis	29	6
Cash, Chris, Atlanta	11	1
Chavous, Corey, Minnesota	54	17
Chillar, Brandon, St. Louis	35	7
Ciurciu, Vinny, Carolina	2	2
Claiborne, Chris, St. Louis	35	4
Clancy, Kendrick, N.Y. Giants	32	7
Clark, Ryan, Washington	42	15
Clemons, Chris, Washington	6	1
Clemons, Nic, Washington	2	0
Coakley, Dexter, St. Louis	29	9
Cody, Shaun, Detroit	17	11
Cole, Colin, Green Bay	24	15
Cole, Trent, Philadelphia	35	8
Coleman, Kenyon, Dallas	9	5
Coleman, Rod, Atlanta	35	5
Collins, Nick, Green Bay	60	17
Cooper, Marquis, Tampa Bay	3	3
Cowart, Sam, Minnesota	65	12
Cox, Torrie, Tampa Bay	1	1
Craft, Jason, New Orleans	29	3
Curry, Donte', Detroit	14	8
Daniels, Phillip, Washington	37	11
Dansby, Karlos, Arizona	68	18
Darby, Chartric, Seattle	19	11
Darling, James, Arizona	70	17
Davis, Chauncey, Atlanta	21	7
Davis, James, Detroit	35	24
Davis, Keith, Dallas	35	15
Davis, Rashied, Chicago	4	3
Davis, Rod, Minnesota	5	6
Davis, Russell, Arizona	5	0
Davis, Thomas, Carolina	22	6
Dawkins, Brian, Philadelphia	70	10
DeLoach, Curtis, N.Y. Giants	45	9
DeVries, Jared, Detroit	15	6
Diggs, Na'il, Green Bay	28	3
Dockett, Darnell, Arizona	20	12
Douglas, Marques, San Francisco	44	14
Draft, Chris, Carolina	40	9
Duckett, Damane, N.Y. Giants	1	0
Dyson, Andre, Seattle	20	1
Edwards, Antuan, Atlanta	11	0
Edwards, Devonte, Minnesota	6	0
Edwards, Kalimba, Detroit	25	7
Ellis, Greg, Dallas	25	10
Emanuel, Ben, San Francisco	32	4
Emmons, Carlos, N.Y. Giants	35	14
Ena, Justin, Philadelphia	1	1
Evans, Demetric, Washington	17	5
Fair, Terry, St. Louis	2	1
Faulk, Trev, St. Louis	26	6
Ferguson, Jason, Dallas	27	10
Fields, Ronald, San Francisco	4	3
Fincher, Alfred, New Orleans	1	0
Fisher, Bryce, Seattle	34	13
Fisher, Travis, St. Louis	37	0
Fowler, Ryan, Dallas	12	3
Fox, Vernon, Detroit	1	0
Francisco, Aaron, Arizona	0	1
Friedman, Lennie, Wash.-Chi.	0	1
Fujita, Scott, Dallas	42	9
Furrey, Mike, St. Louis	38	8
Gamble, Chris, Carolina	60	10
Gbaja-Biamila, Kabeer, Green Bay	37	16
Gleason, Steve, New Orleans	2	1
Glenn, Aaron, Dallas	29	3
Glover, La'Roi, Dallas	23	5
Glymph, Junior, Atlanta	4	1

Player, team	Tk.	Ast.
Goodman, Andre', Detroit	37	4
Grant, Charles, New Orleans	44	18
Grasmanis, Paul, Philadelphia	1	0
Green, Brandon, St. Louis	16	3
Green, Eric, Arizona	34	5
Green, Mike, Chicago	27	8
Greisen, Nick, N.Y. Giants	60	19
Griffin, Cornelius, Washington	34	1
Griffith, Robert, Arizona	52	14
Groce, DeJuan, St. Louis	45	4
Grootegoed, Matt, Detroit	1	2
Hall, DeAngelo, Atlanta	59	7
Hall, James, Detroit	52	8
Hall, Travis, San Francisco	14	6
Hamlin, Ken, Seattle	22	4
Harden, Michael, Seattle	4	1
Hargrove, Anthony, St. Louis	41	6
Harris, Al, Green Bay	46	7
Harris, Chris, Chicago	43	10
Harris, Napoleon, Minnesota	17	7
Harris, Quentin, Arizona	17	5
Harris, Tommie, Chicago	29	5
Harris, Walt, Washington	49	8
Hartwell, Edgerton, Atlanta	16	6
Hawkins, Mike, Green Bay	8	1
Hawthorne, Michael, St. Louis	17	5
Haynes, Michael, Chicago	6	3
Heard, Ronnie, Atlanta	22	2
Henderson, E.J., Minnesota	53	21
Henry, Anthony, Dallas	39	9
Herndon, Kelly, Seattle	51	4
Hill, LeRoy, Seattle	49	19
Hillenmeyer, Hunter, Chicago	38	18
Hodge, Sedrick, New Orleans	33	15
Holdman, Warrick, Washington	16	7
Holly, Daven, Chicago	0	2
Holmes, Earl, Detroit	51	24
Holt, Terrence, Detroit	32	10
Hood, Roderick, Philadelphia	34	1
Horton, Jason, Green Bay	6	1
Houser, Kevin, New Orleans	0	1
Hovan, Chris, Tampa Bay	35	10
Howard, Brian, St. Louis	2	0
Howard, Darren, New Orleans	24	9
Huff, Orlando, Arizona	49	20
Hunter, Will, Minnesota	3	2
Idonije, Israel, Chicago	10	4
Irvin, Ken, Minnesota	8	0
Ivy, Corey, St. Louis	51	7
Jackson, Alonzo, Phila.-N.Y.G.	8	2
Jackson, Dexter, Tampa Bay	32	13
Jackson, Grady, Green Bay	39	16
Jackson, Tyoka, St. Louis	13	3
James, Bradie, Dallas	72	20
James, Erasmus, Minnesota	23	5
Jenkins, Cullen, Green Bay	24	13
Jenkins, Kris, Carolina	0	2
Jimoh, Ade, Washington	9	0
Joe, Leon, Chicago	13	1
Johnson, Chris, St. Louis	23	1
Johnson, Derrick, San Francisco	30	7
Johnson, Eric, Arizona	1	0
Johnson, Spencer, Minnesota	20	9
Johnson, Tank, Chicago	19	6
Johnson, Thomas, Dallas	1	1
Johnson, Todd, Chicago	19	6
Johnstone, Lance, Minnesota	16	4
Jones, Aki, Washington	1	0
Jones, Dhani, Philadelphia	54	11
Jones, Nathan, Dallas	0	1
Joseph, William, N.Y. Giants	14	5
Kacyvenski, Isaiah, Seattle	2	0
Kalu, N.D., Philadelphia	26	4
Kampman, Aaron, Green Bay	60	22
Kashama, Alain, Seattle	1	1

Player, team	Tk.	Ast.
Kearse, Jevon, Philadelphia....	36	3
Kelly, Brian, Tampa Bay	42	9
Kennedy, Jimmy, St. Louis	23	10
Kennedy, Kenoy, Detroit..........	72	24
Kerney, Patrick, Atlanta	38	15
Killings, Cedric, Washington...	9	4
Kolodziej, Ross, Arizona	16	8
Koutouvides, Niko, Seattle......	1	1
Lake, Antwan, Atlanta	11	6
Lavalais, Chad, Atlanta............	17	8
Lehman, Teddy, Detroit.............	8	4
Lehr, Matt, Atlanta	0	1
Lenon, Paris, Green Bay	37	23
Lewis, D.D., Seattle.................	46	18
Lewis, Damione, St. Louis	27	7
Lewis, Keith, San Francisco	16	6
Lewis, Kevin, N.Y. Giants	4	0
Lewis, Michael, Philadelphia...	91	14
Little, Earl, Green Bay	1	1
Little, Leonard, St. Louis	45	11
Lowe, Omare, Atlanta	3	1
Lucas, Ken, Carolina	62	7
Macklin, David, Arizona	52	8
Manning, Roy, Green Bay	7	10
Manning Jr., Ricky, Carolina ...	27	6
Manuel, Marquand, Seattle	54	13
Marshall, Keyonta, Philadelphia	0	1
Marshall, Lemar, Washington .	77	19
Maxwell, Jim, San Francisco ..	4	1
McCree, Marlon, Carolina	73	14
McFarland, Anthony, Tampa Bay	18	9
McGowan, Brandon, Chicago .	22	5
McGraw, Jon, Detroit................	10	5
McKenzie, Mike, New Orleans.	40	5
McKinnon, Ronald, New Orleans	61	17
McQuarters, R.W., Detroit.......	46	11
Melton, Terrence, New Orleans	14	5
Middlebrooks, Willie, San Francisco	5	1
Mikell, Quintin, Philadelphia ...	8	1
Minter, Mike, Carolina..............	41	22
Mitchell, Jeff, Carolina	0	1
Montgomery, Michael, Green Bay	13	7
Moore, Brandon, San Francisco	49	21
Moore, Langston, Arizona........	8	1
Moore, Mewelde, Minnesota....	0	1
Moorehead, Kindal, Carolina...	19	5
Morgan, Dan, Carolina	59	18
Morton, Christian, Atl.-Wash. .	6	2
Mosley, C.J., Minnesota...........	15	4
Nece, Ryan, Tampa Bay	39	24
Newman, Keith, Minnesota	29	13
Newman, Terence, Dallas........	57	3
Nguyen, Dat, Dallas	25	4
Offord, Willie, Minnesota	3	1
Ogbogu, Eric, Dallas	1	0
Ogunleye, Adewale, Chicago...	36	4
Okeafor, Chike, Arizona...........	41	10
Pace, Calvin, Arizona	6	5
Parrish, Tony, San Francisco ...	34	10
Patterson, Mike, Philadelphia .	38	7
Pearson, Kalvin, Tampa Bay	12	1
Peppers, Julius, Carolina	38	12
Peterson, Julian, San Francisco	59	24
Peterson, Kenny, Green Bay ...	19	5
Peterson, Will, N.Y. Giants	6	2
Phillips, Jermaine, Tampa Bay	45	14
Pickett, Ryan, St. Louis	47	18
Pierce, Antonio, N.Y. Giants	78	20
Pile, Willie, Dallas	10	3
Plummer, Ahmed, San Francisco	17	7
Poppinga, Brady, Green Bay ...	7	4
Prioleau, Pierson, Washington	28	4
Pruitt, Etric, Seattle.................	1	0
Quarles, Shelton, Tampa Bay..	103	30
Rainer, Wali, Detroit................	28	7
Rasheed, Saleem, San Francisco	4	1
Rasmussen, Kemp, Carolina...	3	0
Ratliff, Jay, Dallas	3	1
Rayburn, Sam, Philadelphia....	14	2
Redding, Cory, Detroit	26	7
Reese, Ike, Atlanta	15	2
Reeves, Jacques, Dallas	7	3
Reid, Lamont, Arizona	14	1
Rice, Simeon, Tampa Bay	33	7
Robbins, Fred, N.Y. Giants......	17	9
Rogers, Carlos, Washington ...	39	4
Rogers, Shaun, Detroit............	30	11
Rolle, Antrel, Arizona	26	2
Roman, Mark, Green Bay........	70	20
Rosenthal, Mike, Minnesota....	0	1
Rossum, Allen, Atlanta	7	3
Rucker, Mike, Carolina	35	9
Rumph, Mike, San Francisco..	12	0
Ruud, Barrett, Tampa Bay	4	2
Salave'a, Joe, Washington	24	8
Savage, Josh, Atlanta	0	1
Scobey, Josh, Seattle..............	2	0
Scott, Bryan, Atlanta...............	51	11
Scott, Darrion, Minnesota........	40	18
Scott, Ian, Chicago	17	10
Seward, Adam, Carolina	2	1
Shanle, Scott, Dallas...............	30	11
Sharper, Darren, Minnesota.....	40	10
Sharper, Jamie, Seattle...........	29	8
Sheppard, Lito, Philadelphia...	28	4
Short, Brandon, Carolina	41	18
Shropshire, Darrell, Atlanta.....	8	5
Simoneau, Mark, Philadelphia	22	5
Singleton, Al, Dallas................	11	5
Slaughter, T.J., New Orleans...	9	2
Smith, Antonio, Arizona...........	16	0
Smith, Brady, Atlanta	8	0
Smith, Corey, San Francisco....	2	0
Smith, Derek, San Francisco...	90	26
Smith, Dwight, New Orleans....	63	10
Smith, Keith, Detroit................	14	4
Smith, Raonall, Minnesota......	18	4
Smith, Will, New Orleans.........	48	12
Smoot, Fred, Minnesota..........	37	4
Sopoaga, Isaac, San Francisco	16	6
Spears, Marcus, Dallas	19	12
Spencer, Shawntae, San Francisco	73	9
Spires, Greg, Tampa Bay	35	12
Springs, Shawn, Washington .	43	3
Stoutmire, Omar, Washington	8	1
Strahan, Michael, N.Y. Giants .	61	21
Strickland, Donald, Ind.-Phila.*	15	3
Sullivan, Johnathan, New Orleans	20	9
Tafoya, Joe, Seattle.................	7	7
Tate, Robert, Arizona	25	2
Tatupu, Lofa, Seattle................	86	19
Tauscher, Mark, Green Bay	1	0
Taylor, Sean, Washington	56	9
Terrill, Craig, Seattle	12	6
Thomas, Dontarrious, Minnesota	27	11
Thomas, Fred, New Orleans	56	19
Thomas, Hollis, Philadelphia...	27	8
Thomas, Joey, G.B.-N.O...........	10	3
Thomas, Juqua, Philadelphia..	11	2
Thomas, Robert, Green Bay....	27	11
Thompson, Chris, Chicago	4	3
Thornburg, Jeremy, S.F.-G.B...	1	0
Thornton, Bruce, San Francisco	36	4
Tillman, Charles, Chicago	85	11
Tinoisamoa, Pisa, St. Louis	68	23
Torbor, Reggie, N.Y. Giants.....	25	9
Torrence, Leigh, Atlanta...........	1	0

Player, team	Tk.	Ast.
Trotter, Jeremiah, Philadelphia	102	19
Trufant, Marcus, Seattle..........	55	9
Truluck, R-Kal, Arizona	0	2
Tubbs, Marcus, Seattle	27	13
Tuck, Justin, N.Y. Giants	15	4
Tucker, B.J., San Francisco.....	9	3
Tufts, Sean, Carolina	1	1
Udeze, Kenechi, Minnesota.....	5	0
Ulbrich, Jeff, San Francisco.....	31	10
Umenyiora, Osi, N.Y. Giants....	49	22
Underwood, Marviel, Green Bay	11	2
Urlacher, Brian, Chicago	98	24
Vasher, Nathan, Chicago.........	41	7
Walker, Bracy, Detroit	20	8
Walker, Darwin, Philadelphia ..	20	5
Wallace, Al, Carolina	20	5
Walls, Raymond, Arizona	7	2
Ware, DeMarcus, Dallas..........	47	11
Ware, Matt, Philadelphia..........	6	1
Washington, Marcus, Washington	73	20
Watson, Courtney, New Orleans	28	9
Wayne, Nate, Detroit...............	11	3
Webster, Corey, N.Y. Giants	37	1
Webster, Jason, Atlanta...........	75	6
Wesley, Dante, Carolina	9	0
White, Dewayne, Tampa Bay...	28	5
Whitehead, Willie, New Orleans	24	11
Wilds, Garnell, Carolina	2	0
Wilkinson, Dan, Detroit............	20	6
Williams, Brian, Minnesota......	32	10
Williams, Corey, Green Bay.....	17	9
Williams, Demorrio, Atlanta.....	97	28
Williams, Jimmy, Seattle..........	18	5
Williams, Kevin, Minnesota.....	31	11
Williams, Pat, Minnesota.........	42	25
Williams, Roy, Dallas...............	65	12
Williams, Shaun, N.Y. Giants ..	15	1
Wilson, Adrian, Arizona	92	16
Wilson, Gibril, N.Y. Giants.......	88	22
Wilson, Stanley, Detroit...........	2	0
Winfield, Antoine, Minnesota..	80	9
Wistrom, Grant, Seattle...........	41	11
Witherspoon, Will, Carolina.....	65	15
Woods, LeVar, Detroit..............	15	11
Wyms, Ellis, Tampa Bay	12	5
Wynn, Dexter, Philadelphia......	2	0
Wynn, Renaldo, Washington ..	25	6
Young, Brian, New Orleans.....	38	13
Young, Bryant, San Francisco.	32	4

*Includes both AFC and NFC statistics.

PLAYERS WITH TWO CLUBS

Player, team	Tk.	Ast.
Anderson, Marques, Denver ...	0	0
Anderson, Marques, San Francisco	0	1
Ball, Dave, San Diego	0	1
Ball, Dave, N.Y. Jets	4	1
Friedman, Lennie, Washington	0	0
Friedman, Lennie, Chicago	0	1
Labinjo, Mike, Philadelphia.....	4	0
Labinjo, Mike, Indianapolis.....	0	1
Jackson, Alonzo, Philadelphia.	2	0
Jackson, Alonzo, N.Y. Giants ..	6	2
Morton, Christian, Atlanta........	3	2
Morton, Christian, Washington	3	0
Strickland, Donald, Indianapolis	5	1
Strickland, Donald, Philadelphia	10	2
Thornburg, Jeremy, San Francisco	0	0
Thornburg, Jeremy, Green Bay	1	0
Towns, Lester, Arizona	6	1
Towns, Lester, Miami..............	0	0
Winborn, Jamie, San Francisco	8	5
Winborn, Jamie, Jacksonville .	2	0

CLUB RANKINGS BY YARDS

Team	OFFENSE			DEFENSE		
	Total	Rush	Pass	Total	Rush	Pass
Arizona	8	32	1*	8	10	12
Atlanta	12	1*	27	22	26	14
Baltimore	24	21	22	5	9	8
Buffalo	28	20	29	29	31	19
Carolina	22	19	17	3	4	9
Chicago	29	8	31	2	11	5
Cincinnati	6	11	5	28	20	26
Cleveland	26	25	23	T16	30	4
Dallas	13	13	15	10	15	11
Denver	5	2	18	15	2	29
Detroit	27	26	26	20	24	13
Green Bay	18	30	7	7	23	1*
Houston	30	15	30	31	32	24
Indianapolis	3	16	3	11	16	15
Jacksonville	T15	10	19	6	14	7
Kansas City	1*	4	6	25	7	30
Miami	14	12	16	18	17	20
Minnesota	25	27	20	21	19	22
New England	7	24	2	26	8	31
New Orleans	20	18	14	14	27	3
N.Y. Giants	4	6	11	24	12	27
N.Y. Jets	31	31	28	12	29	2
Oakland	21	29	10	27	25	18
Philadelphia	19	28	8	23	21	21
Pittsburgh	T15	5	24	4	3	16
San Diego	10	9	12	13	1*	28
San Francisco	32	17	32	32	18	32
Seattle	2	3	13	T16	5	25
St. Louis	9	22	4	30	28	23
Tampa Bay	23	14	25	1*	6	6
Tennessee	17	23	9	19	22	17
Washington	11	7	21	9	13	10

*NFL leader.
T-Tied for position.

TAKEAWAYS/GIVEAWAYS

AFC

	TAKEAWAYS			GIVEAWAYS			
	Int.	Fum.	Tot.	Int.	Fum.	Tot.	Net Diff.
Cincinnati	31	13	44	14	6	20	24
Denver	20	16	36	7	9	16	20
Indianapolis	18	13	31	11	8	19	12
Jacksonville	19	9	28	6	11	17	11
Kansas City	16	15	31	10	13	23	8
Pittsburgh	15	15	30	14	9	23	7
Buffalo	17	13	30	16	10	26	4
Miami	14	17	31	16	14	30	1
Oakland	5	14	19	14	9	23	-4
Tennessee	9	11	20	14	12	26	-6
New England	10	8	18	15	9	24	-6
N.Y. Jets	21	7	28	15	19	34	-6
Cleveland	15	8	23	17	13	30	-7
San Diego	10	10	20	16	12	28	-8
Houston	7	9	16	13	11	24	-8
Baltimore	11	15	26	21	15	36	-10

NFC

	TAKEAWAYS			GIVEAWAYS			
	Int.	Fum.	Tot.	Int.	Fum.	Tot.	Net Diff.
Carolina	23	19	42	16	10	26	16
N.Y. Giants	17	20	37	17	8	25	12
Seattle	16	11	27	10	7	17	10
Tampa Bay	17	13	30	14	9	23	7
Chicago	24	10	34	15	13	28	6
Minnesota	24	11	35	16	14	30	5
Detroit	19	12	31	18	12	30	1
Washington	16	12	28	11	16	27	1
Atlanta	16	13	29	13	16	29	0
Dallas	15	11	26	17	14	31	-5
Philadelphia	17	10	27	20	14	34	-7
San Francisco	16	10	26	21	14	35	-9
St. Louis	13	14	27	24	13	37	-10
Arizona	15	11	26	21	16	37	-11
Green Bay	10	11	21	30	15	45	-24
New Orleans	10	9	19	24	19	43	-24

CLUB LEADERS

	Offense	Defense
First downs	Ind. 363	T.B. 254
Rushing	Den. 145	Car. 72
Passing	Ariz. 224	G.B. 143
Penalty	Dal. 44	3 tied with 15
Rushes	Pit. 549	Den. 344
Net yards gained	Atl. 2546	S.D .1349
Average gain	Atl. 4.8	Pit. 3.4
Passes attempted	Ariz. 670	N.O. .418
Completed	Ariz. 419	N.O. 241
Percent completed	Ind. 67.4	Was. 54.4
Total yards gained	Ariz. 4723	G.B. 2876
Times sacked	Ind. 20	Sea. 50
Yards lost	Ind. 95	Mia. 375
Net yards gained	Ariz. 4437	G.B. 2680
Net yards per pass play	Ind. 7.66	Chi. 4.86
Yards gained per completion	Pit. 13.61	Chi. 10.05
Combined net yards gained	K.C. 6192	T.B. 4444
Percent total yards rushing	Chi. 51.2	Den. 27.2
Percent total yards passing	Ariz. 79.6	NYJ 55.8
Ball-control plays	Ariz. 075	Ariz. 936
Average yards per play	K.C. 5.85	Chi. 4.36
Avg. time of possession	Den. 32:37	—
Third-down efficiency	Ind. 48.7	Atl. 30.2
Interceptions	—	Cin. 31
Yards returned	—	Chi. 524
Returned for TD	—	Chi. 4
Punts	S.F. 108	—
Yards punted	S.F. 4447	—
Average yards per punt	Buf. 45.7	—
Punt returns	Phi., Jac. 53	K.C. 23
Yards returned	T.B. 492	Ten. 144
Average yds. per return	Bal. 11.1	Ten. 4.5
Returned for TD	Pit. 2	—
Kickoff returns	Hou. 84	S.F. .48
Yards returned	Hou. 2173	S.F. 960
Average yards per return	Buf. 26.6	Atl. 19.3
Returned for TD	Was., Hou. 2	—
Total Points Scored	Sea. 452	Chi. 202
Total TDs	Sea. 57	Chi. 20
TDs rushing	Sea. 26	Jac. 4
TDs passing	Cin. 32	Chi. 10
TDs on ret. and recov.	Chi., S.F. 6	Min. 0
Extra point kicks	Sea. 56	Chi. 19
2-Pt. conversions	Atl. 4	14 tied with 0
Safeties	Mia. 3	—
Field goals made	Ariz. 43	Den. 14
Field goals attempted	Ariz. 45	Den. 18
Percent successful	Ariz. 95.6	S.D. 69.0
Extra points	Sea. 56	Chi. 19

OFFENSE

	Bal.	Buf.	Cin.	Cle.	Den.	Hou.	Ind.	Jac.	K.C.	Mia.	N.E.	NYJ	Oak.	Pit.	S.D.	Ten.
First downs	286	259	342	241	330	243	363	301	347	274	334	251	294	297	337	279
Rushing	97	96	109	76	145	89	116	97	138	93	101	74	80	120	116	72
Passing	163	129	203	149	162	142	217	170	182	159	204	146	189	144	191	191
Penalty	26	34	30	16	23	12	30	34	27	22	29	31	25	33	30	16
Rushes	452	428	459	395	542	437	465	502	520	444	439	384	361	549	465	397
Net yards gained	1605	1607	1910	1503	2539	1816	1703	1959	2382	1898	1512	1328	1369	2223	2072	1525
Average gain	3.6	3.8	4.2	3.8	4.7	4.2	3.7	3.9	4.6	4.3	3.4	3.5	3.8	4.0	4.5	3.8
Average yards per game	100.3	100.4	119.4	93.9	158.7	113.5	106.4	122.4	148.9	118.6	94.5	83.0	85.6	138.9	129.5	95.3
Passes attempted	562	459	538	497	465	449	515	487	507	556	564	470	591	379	526	594
Completed	335	269	362	297	279	270	347	283	317	291	352	268	316	228	338	358
Percent completed	59.6	58.6	67.3	59.8	60.0	60.1	67.4	58.1	62.5	52.3	62.4	57.0	53.5	60.2	64.3	60.3
Total yards gained	3381	2852	3935	3323	3373	2661	4191	3352	4014	3458	4322	2989	3883	3104	3738	3797
Times sacked	42	43	21	46	23	68	20	32	32	26	28	53	45	32	31	31
Yards lost	293	337	115	276	146	424	95	162	204	158	202	347	301	178	243	200
Net yards gained	3088	2515	3820	3047	3227	2237	4096	3190	3810	3300	4120	2642	3582	2926	3495	3597
Average yards per game	193.0	157.2	238.8	190.4	201.7	139.8	256.0	199.4	238.1	206.3	257.5	165.1	223.9	182.9	218.4	224.8
Net yards per pass play	5.11	5.01	6.83	5.61	6.61	4.33	7.66	6.15	7.07	5.67	6.96	5.05	5.63	7.12	6.27	5.76
Yards gained per completion	10.09	10.60	10.87	11.19	12.09	9.86	12.08	11.84	12.66	11.88	12.28	11.15	12.29	13.61	11.06	10.61
Combined net yards gained	4693	4122	5730	4550	5766	4053	5799	5149	6192	5198	5632	3970	4951	5149	5567	5122
Percent total yards rushing	34.2	39.0	33.3	33.0	44.0	44.8	29.4	38.0	38.5	36.5	26.8	33.5	27.7	43.2	37.2	29.8
Percent total yards passing	65.8	61.0	66.7	67.0	56.0	55.2	70.6	62.0	61.5	63.5	73.2	66.5	72.3	56.8	62.8	70.2
Average yards per game	293.3	257.6	358.1	284.4	360.4	253.3	362.4	321.8	387.0	324.9	352.0	248.1	309.4	321.8	347.9	320.1
Ball-control plays	1056	930	1018	938	1030	954	1000	1021	1059	1026	1031	907	997	960	1022	1022
Average yards per play	4.4	4.4	5.6	4.9	5.6	4.2	5.8	5.0	5.8	5.1	5.5	4.4	5.0	5.4	5.4	5.0
Average time of possession	30:22	29:04	30:52	28:00	32:37	28:10	30:22	31:33	32:09	27:25	30:19	26:37	28:07	31:16	31:34	31:13
Third-down efficiency	39.1	36.8	42.9	33.0	36.2	34.2	48.7	41.3	42.7	35.1	42.1	35.3	39.7	35.4	42.3	34.4
Had intercepted	21	16	14	17	7	13	11	6	10	16	15	15	14	14	16	14
Yards opponents returned	256	209	247	215	43	225	136	90	196	127	188	147	336	194	230	293
Returned by oppponents for TD	3	2	1	0	0	3	0	0	1	0	2	1	4	1	1	4
Punts	86	71	61	80	73	77	52	83	65	89	77	75	82	69	71	78
Yards punted	3685	3242	2591	3234	3157	2990	2301	3517	2564	3835	3431	3251	3744	2875	3104	3371
Average yards per punt	42.8	45.7	42.5	40.4	43.2	38.8	44.3	42.4	39.4	43.1	44.6	43.3	45.7	41.7	43.7	43.2
Punt returns	39	28	28	37	33	30	24	53	43	43	40	34	37	46	39	45
Yards returned	431	279	157	373	281	223	182	415	293	390	314	219	206	470	245	418
Average yards per return	11.1	10.0	5.6	10.1	8.5	7.4	7.6	7.8	6.8	9.1	7.9	6.4	5.6	10.2	6.3	9.3
Returned for TD	0	0	0	1	0	0	0	0	0	0	0	0	0	2	0	1
Kickoff returns	60	75	67	68	47	84	51	50	68	68	70	71	80	56	69	70
Yards returned	1289	1992	1580	1506	975	2173	1017	1197	1591	1501	1555	1728	1832	1208	1667	1697
Average yards per return	21.5	26.6	23.6	22.1	20.7	25.9	19.9	23.9	23.4	22.1	22.2	24.3	22.9	21.6	24.2	24.2
Returned for TD	0	1	0	1	0	2	0	1	1	0	0	1	0	0	0	0
Fumbles	28	26	18	27	19	30	14	27	23	31	19	36	26	22	22	27
Lost	15	10	6	13	9	11	8	11	13	14	9	19	9	9	12	12
Out of bounds	0	4	3	0	2	2	1	2	0	1	1	1	3	0	1	3
Recovered for TD	0	0	0	0	0	0	0	0	0	0	0	0	0	0	0	0
Penalties	139	120	110	99	97	106	94	121	115	132	110	98	147	99	110	125
Yards penalized	1067	897	920	770	756	854	690	1006	890	1055	921	801	1132	876	890	1002
Total Points Scored	265	271	421	232	395	260	439	361	403	318	379	240	290	389	418	299
Total TDs	25	26	48	22	46	26	53	42	46	34	46	25	33	45	51	33
TDs rushing	5	6	15	4	25	9	18	18	26	11	16	10	11	21	22	8
TDs passing	17	18	32	15	18	15	31	21	17	22	28	11	21	21	27	20
TDs on returns and recoveries	3	2	1	3	3	2	4	3	3	1	2	4	1	3	2	5
Extra point kicks	23	26	47	19	43	24	52	38	44	33	41	24	30	45	49	30
Extra point kick att.	23	26	47	21	44	24	52	39	45	33	42	24	30	45	49	32
2-Pt. conversions	1	0	1	0	1	1	0	1	1	0	1	0	1	0	0	0
2-Pt. conversions att.	2	0	1	1	2	2	1	1	1	1	4	1	3	0	1	1
Safeties	0	1	0	0	1	0	0	0	0	3	0	0	0	1	0	1
Field goals made	30	29	28	27	24	26	23	23	27	25	20	22	20	24	21	23
Field goals attempted	35	35	32	29	32	34	26	30	33	30	25	28	30	29	24	29
Percent successful	85.7	82.9	87.5	93.1	75.0	76.5	88.5	76.7	81.8	83.3	80.0	78.6	66.7	82.8	87.5	79.3
Extra points	24	26	48	19	44	25	52	39	45	33	42	24	31	45	49	30
Field goals blocked	0	0	0	0	1	1	1	0	1	1	0	0	1	1	2	1	0

2005 STATISTICS Miscellaneous

DEFENSE

	Bal.	Buf.	Cin.	Cle.	Den.	Hou.	Ind.	Jac.	K.C.	Mia.	N.E.	NYJ	Oak.	Pit.	S.D.	Ten.
First downs	277	343	321	292	295	348	269	273	292	319	306	321	299	275	306	294
Rushing	79	146	109	116	82	123	91	79	84	94	94	136	100	75	90	89
Passing	161	169	185	161	183	188	163	158	189	183	179	151	165	179	189	180
Penalty	37	28	27	15	30	37	15	36	19	42	33	34	34	21	27	25
Rushes	431	489	429	527	344	506	398	434	383	480	437	554	507	402	386	449
Net yards gained	1591	2205	1850	2202	1363	2303	1762	1709	1570	1771	1580	2185	2049	1376	1349	1894
Average gain	3.7	4.5	4.3	4.2	4.0	4.6	4.4	3.9	4.1	3.7	3.6	3.9	4.0	3.4	3.5	4.2
Average yards per game	99.4	137.8	115.6	137.6	85.2	143.9	110.1	106.8	98.1	110.7	98.8	136.6	128.1	86.0	84.3	118.4
Passes attempted	525	503	519	471	613	469	509	482	559	549	527	463	486	549	567	470
Completed	296	314	324	279	344	304	343	285	325	323	296	284	296	315	338	296
Percent completed	56.4	62.4	62.4	59.2	56.1	64.8	67.4	59.1	58.1	58.8	56.2	61.3	60.9	57.4	59.6	63.0
Total yards gained	3228	3560	3749	3009	3833	3727	3469	3223	3862	3682	3926	2948	3481	3480	3888	3462
Times sacked	42	38	28	23	28	37	46	47	29	49	33	30	36	47	46	41
Yards lost	270	269	180	142	190	206	318	277	183	375	223	193	238	312	289	246
Net yards gained	2958	3291	3569	2867	3643	3521	3151	2946	3679	3307	3703	2755	3243	3168	3599	3216
Average yards per game	184.9	205.7	223.1	179.2	227.7	220.1	196.9	184.1	229.9	206.7	231.4	172.2	202.7	198.0	224.9	201.0
Net yards per pass play	5.22	6.08	6.52	5.80	5.68	6.96	5.68	5.57	6.26	5.53	6.61	5.59	6.21	5.32	5.87	6.29
Yards gained per completion	10.91	11.34	11.57	10.78	11.14	12.26	10.11	11.31	11.88	11.40	13.26	10.38	11.76	11.05	11.50	11.70
Combined net yards gained	4549	5496	5419	5069	5006	5824	4913	4655	5249	5078	5283	4940	5292	4544	4948	5110
Percent total yards rushing	35.0	40.1	34.1	43.4	27.2	39.5	35.9	36.7	29.9	34.9	29.9	44.2	38.7	30.3	27.3	37.1
Percent total yards passing	65.0	59.9	65.9	56.6	72.8	60.5	64.1	63.3	70.1	65.1	70.1	55.8	61.3	69.7	72.7	62.9
Average yards per game	284.3	343.5	338.7	316.8	312.9	364.0	307.1	290.9	328.1	317.4	330.2	308.8	330.8	284.0	309.3	319.4
Ball-control plays	998	1030	976	1021	985	1012	953	963	971	1078	997	1047	1029	998	999	960
Average yards per play	4.6	5.3	5.6	5.0	5.1	5.8	5.2	4.8	5.4	4.7	5.3	4.7	5.1	4.6	5.0	5.3
Average time of possession	29:38	30:56	29:09	32:00	27:23	31:50	29:38	28:27	27:51	32:35	29:41	33:23	31:53	28:44	28:26	28:47
Third-down efficiency	36.1	46.5	42.6	40.5	36.7	38.3	36.7	32.7	37.9	40.3	42.0	41.5	40.7	39.7	37.3	35.5
Intercepted by	11	17	31	15	20	7	18	19	16	14	10	21	5	15	10	9
Yards returned by	191	233	260	130	379	46	259	184	232	136	85	279	38	179	205	129
Returned for TD	1	1	1	0	3	0	2	2	1	0	2	2	0	0	2	2
Punts	89	62	50	72	81	63	67	88	69	92	81	62	76	80	78	85
Yards punted	3605	2492	2106	3058	3633	2528	2791	3763	3155	3957	3537	2787	3156	3463	3274	3746
Average yards per punt	40.5	40.2	42.1	42.5	44.9	40.1	41.7	42.8	45.7	43.0	43.7	45.0	41.5	43.3	42.0	44.1
Punt returns	55	42	32	36	36	33	25	29	23	46	42	36	39	37	26	32
Yards returned	481	285	260	347	266	219	272	236	179	227	405	305	460	336	244	144
Average yards per return	8.7	6.8	8.1	9.6	7.4	6.6	10.9	8.1	7.8	4.9	9.6	8.5	11.8	9.1	9.4	4.5
Returned for TD	1	0	0	0	0	1	0	1	0	0	0	0	0	0	0	0
Kickoff returns	62	64	85	56	67	55	89	56	83	56	68	60	56	77	83	57
Yards returned	1352	1308	1787	1182	1696	1194	1978	1327	2053	1425	1487	1250	1369	1685	1856	1290
Average yards per return	21.8	20.4	21.0	21.1	25.3	21.7	22.2	23.7	24.7	25.4	21.9	20.8	24.4	21.9	22.4	22.6
Returned for TD	0	1	1	0	0	0	1	0	1	0	0	0	0	0	0	0
Fumbles	28	24	31	21	29	24	32	21	33	35	13	24	22	30	23	20
Recovered by	15	13	13	8	16	9	13	9	15	17	8	7	14	15	10	11
Out of bounds	0	1	2	2	3	3	1	1	2	4	1	1	0	0	3	1
Recovered for TD	0	0	0	0	0	0	0	0	0	0	0	0	0	0	0	0
Penalties	110	124	110	97	139	105	119	130	90	105	132	115	101	120	110	95
Yards penalized	844	904	985	716	989	846	857	1055	805	827	1068	981	825	1031	831	718
Total points scored	299	367	350	301	258	431	247	269	325	317	338	355	383	258	312	421
Total TDs	30	44	39	31	31	50	27	30	38	35	38	38	40	27	36	51
TDs rushing	8	22	16	11	10	21	9	4	11	11	11	19	18	10	14	12
TDs passing	18	19	21	19	20	24	17	22	25	23	25	17	18	15	20	33
TDs on returns and recoveries	4	3	2	1	1	5	1	4	2	1	2	2	4	2	2	6
Extra point kicks	28	44	37	31	30	47	24	29	33	31	34	37	34	24	34	48
Extra point kick att.	29	44	37	31	30	47	24	30	33	32	34	37	37	25	35	49
2-Pt. conversions	1	0	2	0	0	0	2	0	2	1	1	0	1	0	0	1
2-Pt. conversions att.	1	0	2	0	1	2	3	0	5	3	4	0	3	1	1	2
Safeties	1	1	0	0	0	0	0	0	1	1	0	1	1	0	1	0
Field goals made	29	19	25	28	14	28	19	20	20	24	24	30	35	24	20	21
Field goals attempted	31	25	28	35	18	32	27	27	26	24	30	35	38	30	29	27
Percent successful	93.5	76.0	89.3	80.0	77.8	87.5	70.4	74.1	76.9	100.0	80.0	85.7	92.1	80.0	69.0	77.8
Extra points	29	44	39	31	30	47	26	29	35	32	35	37	35	24	34	50
Field goals blocked	0	0	0	2	1	0	0	1	2	0	0	0	1	1	0	2

OFFENSE

	Ariz.	Atl.	Car.	Chi.	Dal.	Det.	G.B.	Min.	N.O.	NYG	Phi.	St.L.	S.F.	Sea.	T.B.	Was.
First downs	304	313	278	233	318	258	318	285	312	312	282	314	191	361	268	301
Rushing	58	139	82	99	97	69	76	83	89	106	73	82	70	142	83	114
Passing	224	149	157	111	177	151	206	169	182	172	182	209	96	192	161	166
Penalty	22	25	39	23	44	38	36	33	41	34	27	23	25	27	24	21
Rushes	360	531	487	488	521	404	398	381	423	469	365	380	428	519	457	525
Net yards gained	1138	2546	1679	2099	1861	1471	1352	1467	1688	2209	1432	1535	1689	2457	1826	2183
Average gain	3.2	4.8	3.4	4.3	3.6	3.6	3.4	3.9	4.0	4.7	3.9	4.0	3.9	4.7	4.0	4.2
Average yards per game	71.1	159.1	104.9	131.2	116.3	91.9	84.5	91.7	105.5	138.1	89.5	95.9	105.6	153.6	114.1	136.4
Passes attempted	670	451	449	418	500	520	626	510	553	558	620	599	389	474	487	481
Completed	419	247	269	219	300	297	383	323	308	294	337	392	204	307	303	278
Percent completed	62.5	54.8	59.9	52.4	60.0	57.1	61.2	63.3	55.7	52.7	54.4	65.4	52.4	64.8	62.2	57.8
Total yards gained	4723	2907	3485	2201	3639	3021	3964	3449	3604	3762	3903	4351	2190	3632	3171	3346
Times sacked	45	39	28	31	50	31	27	54	41	28	42	46	48	27	41	31
Yards lost	286	228	214	199	298	173	198	303	261	184	226	315	292	174	281	240
Net yards gained	4437	2679	3271	2002	3341	2848	3766	3146	3343	3578	3677	4036	1898	3458	2890	3106
Average yards per game	277.3	167.4	204.4	125.1	208.8	178.0	235.4	196.6	208.9	223.6	229.8	252.3	118.6	216.1	180.6	194.1
Net yards per pass play	6.21	5.47	6.86	4.46	6.07	5.17	5.77	5.58	5.63	6.11	5.55	6.26	4.34	6.90	5.47	6.07
Yards gained per completion	11.27	11.77	12.96	10.05	12.13	10.17	10.35	10.68	11.70	12.80	11.58	11.10	10.74	11.83	10.47	12.04
Combined net yards gained	5575	5225	4950	4101	5202	4319	5118	4613	5031	5787	5109	5571	3587	5915	4716	5289
Percent total yards rushing	20.4	48.7	33.9	51.2	35.8	34.1	26.4	31.8	33.6	38.2	28.0	27.6	47.1	41.5	38.7	41.3
Percent total yards passing	79.6	51.3	66.1	48.8	64.2	65.9	73.6	68.2	66.4	61.8	72.0	72.4	52.9	58.5	61.3	58.7
Average yards per game	348.4	326.6	309.4	256.3	325.1	269.9	319.9	288.3	314.4	361.7	319.3	348.2	224.2	369.7	294.8	330.6
Ball-control plays	1075	1021	964	937	1071	955	1051	945	1017	1055	1027	1025	865	1020	985	1037
Average yards per play	5.2	5.1	5.1	4.4	4.9	4.5	4.9	4.9	4.9	5.5	5.0	5.4	4.1	5.8	4.8	5.1
Average time of possession	31:20	29:58	30:48	28:41	32:24	29:13	30:48	28:46	30:32	30:26	28:22	30:14	27:18	29:17	30:45	31:33
Third-down efficiency	38.1	42.9	42.2	28.8	40.5	38.8	41.2	32.7	38.9	39.6	32.7	36.5	24.0	39.6	39.4	42.2
Had intercepted	21	13	16	15	17	18	30	16	24	17	20	24	21	10	14	11
Yards opponents returned	334	163	335	66	326	271	370	220	456	302	339	268	265	93	480	183
Returned by opponents for TD	1	0	3	0	2	2	3	0	3	2	4	0	1	0	2	1
Punts	74	78	73	98	82	84	70	81	71	73	100	73	108	80	90	87
Yards punted	3206	3300	3154	3965	3474	3656	2726	3505	3066	3070	4073	3008	4447	3282	4101	3503
Average yards per punt	43.3	42.3	43.2	40.5	42.4	43.5	38.9	43.3	43.2	42.1	40.7	41.2	41.2	41.0	45.6	40.3
Punt returns	50	31	41	46	45	36	45	41	46	49	53	30	28	31	51	30
Yards returned	385	261	444	417	284	274	381	344	320	453	448	175	212	177	492	180
Average yards per return	7.7	8.4	10.8	9.1	6.3	7.6	8.5	8.4	7.0	9.2	8.5	5.8	7.6	5.7	9.6	6.0
Returned for TD	0	0	0	1	0	0	1	1	0	1	0	0	1	0	0	0
Kickoff returns	76	70	53	55	64	73	75	71	75	63	71	74	81	61	59	62
Yards returned	1719	1482	1083	1092	1523	1576	1418	1549	1516	1529	1578	1580	1540	1347	1148	1438
Average yards per return	22.6	21.2	20.4	19.9	23.8	21.6	18.9	21.8	20.2	24.3	22.2	21.4	19.0	22.1	19.5	23.2
Returned for TD	0	0	0	0	0	0	0	1	0	1	0	1	0	0	0	2
Fumbles	26	26	23	32	36	21	31	25	23	17	34	24	31	18	16	29
Lost	16	16	10	13	14	12	15	14	19	8	14	13	14	7	9	16
Out of bounds	0	4	2	1	2	0	1	2	2	1	3	2	0	2	1	3
Recovered for TD	0	0	0	0	0	0	0	0	0	0	0	0	1	0	0	0
Penalties	145	114	91	105	99	115	119	128	135	143	134	131	106	94	131	108
Yards penalized	1185	1043	732	850	739	838	918	1013	1130	1115	1130	941	780	846	1085	925
Total points scored	311	351	391	260	325	254	298	306	235	422	310	363	239	452	300	359
Total TDs	26	39	45	28	38	28	34	33	23	45	35	40	23	57	33	44
TDs rushing	2	17	17	11	13	10	11	10	8	17	11	13	9	29	13	15
TDs passing	21	19	25	11	23	15	20	18	15	24	21	23	8	25	17	25
TDs on returns and recoveries	3	3	3	6	2	3	3	5	0	4	3	4	6	3	3	4
Extra point kicks	20	35	43	26	35	27	30	31	22	43	32	36	21	56	32	42
Extra point kick att.	20	35	44	27	36	28	31	31	22	43	33	36	21	57	32	42
2-Pt. conversions	3	4	1	0	1	0	2	1	0	2	1	2	1	0	1	1
2-Pt. conversions att.	6	4	1	0	2	0	3	2	1	2	1	3	2	0	1	2
Safeties	0	1	0	0	0	1	0	0	0	0	0	1	0	0	1	0
Field goals made	43	24	26	22	20	19	20	25	25	35	22	27	26	18	22	17
Field goals attempted	45	27	34	31	28	24	27	34	32	42	29	31	29	25	27	21
Percent successful	95.6	88.9	76.5	71.0	71.4	79.2	74.1	73.5	78.1	83.3	75.9	87.1	89.7	72.0	81.5	81.0
2-Pt. conversions	3	4	0	0	1	0	2	1	0	2	1	2	1	0	1	1
Extra points	23	39	43	26	36	27	32	32	22	45	33	38	22	56	33	43
Field goals blocked	0	1	1	0	2	1	1	3	2	1	1	0	0	1	1	2

DEFENSE

	Ariz.	Atl.	Car.	Chi.	Dal.	Det.	G.B.	Min.	N.O.	NYG	Phi.	St.L.	S.F.	Sea.	T.B.	Was.
First downs	272	319	262	259	256	308	280	304	281	302	290	321	335	295	254	258
Rushing	83	122	72	83	87	109	107	96	103	83	91	116	115	78	75	74
Passing	158	167	160	153	150	166	143	177	145	189	171	178	205	194	148	158
Penalty	31	30	30	23	19	33	30	31	33	30	28	27	15	23	31	26
Rushes	411	438	408	443	414	488	504	462	503	428	506	459	486	420	438	411
Net yards gained	1632	2063	1465	1637	1731	2040	2010	1841	2145	1656	1883	2178	1832	1510	1515	1686
Average gain	4.0	4.7	3.6	3.7	4.2	4.2	4.0	4.0	4.3	3.9	3.7	4.7	3.8	3.6	3.5	4.1
Average yards per game	102.0	128.9	91.6	102.3	108.2	127.5	125.6	115.1	134.1	103.5	117.7	136.1	114.5	94.4	94.7	105.4
Passes attempted	488	526	528	550	495	487	430	533	418	580	503	507	576	571	476	535
Completed	301	320	305	313	271	295	252	319	241	329	297	314	374	331	275	291
Percent completed	61.7	60.8	57.8	56.9	54.7	60.6	58.6	59.8	57.7	56.7	59.0	61.9	64.9	58.0	57.8	54.4
Total yards gained	3314	3394	3351	3147	3319	3305	2876	3539	3014	3852	3507	3619	4620	3861	3158	3318
Times sacked	37	37	45	41	37	31	35	34	25	41	29	41	28	50	36	35
Yards lost	217	257	294	275	236	187	196	207	165	268	184	195	193	302	229	237
Net yards gained	3097	3137	3057	2872	3083	3118	2680	3332	2849	3584	3323	3424	4427	3559	2929	3081
Average yards per game	193.6	196.1	191.1	179.5	192.7	194.9	167.5	208.3	178.1	224.0	207.7	214.0	276.7	222.4	183.1	192.6
Net yards per pass play	5.90	5.57	5.34	4.86	5.80	6.02	5.76	5.88	6.43	5.77	6.25	6.25	7.33	5.73	5.72	5.41
Yards gained per completion	11.01	10.61	10.99	10.05	12.25	11.20	11.41	11.09	12.51	11.71	11.81	11.53	12.35	11.66	11.48	11.40
Combined net yards gained	4729	5200	4522	4509	4814	5158	4690	5173	4994	5240	5206	5602	6259	5069	4444	4767
Percent total yards rushing	34.5	39.7	32.4	36.3	36.0	39.6	42.9	35.6	43.0	31.6	36.2	38.9	29.3	29.8	34.1	35.4
Percent total yards passing	65.5	60.3	67.6	63.7	64.0	60.4	57.1	64.4	57.0	68.4	63.8	61.1	70.7	70.2	65.9	64.6
Average yards per game	295.6	325.0	282.6	281.8	300.9	322.4	293.1	323.3	312.1	327.5	325.4	350.1	391.2	316.8	277.8	297.9
Ball-control plays	936	1001	981	1034	946	1006	969	1029	946	1049	1038	1007	1090	1041	950	981
Average yards per play	5.1	5.2	4.6	4.4	5.1	5.1	4.8	5.0	5.3	5.0	5.0	5.6	5.7	4.9	4.7	4.9
Average time of possession	28:40	30:02	29:12	31:19	27:36	30:47	29:12	31:14	29:28	29:34	31:38	29:46	32:42	30:43	29:15	28:27
Third-down efficiency	34.2	30.2	40.7	31.9	34.6	39.4	35.9	43.0	40.5	39.8	34.3	40.2	38.5	38.0	35.0	36.5
Intercepted by	15	16	23	24	15	19	10	24	10	17	17	13	16	16	17	16
Yards returned by	285	268	440	524	187	308	205	392	182	354	195	364	220	315	223	176
Returned for TD	3	0	2	4	2	2	2	3	0	1	1	2	3	2	0	1
Punts	85	79	79	97	95	72	85	72	76	88	104	68	71	77	80	88
Yards punted	3753	3401	3562	3982	3892	2899	3597	3013	3462	3651	4361	2722	2846	3091	3509	3636
Average yards per punt	44.2	43.1	45.1	41.1	41.0	40.3	42.3	41.8	45.6	41.5	41.9	40.0	40.1	40.1	43.9	41.3
Punt returns	39	35	36	39	33	50	49	45	33	36	57	39	62	41	49	40
Yards returned	328	238	235	312	250	520	339	495	260	309	312	410	471	343	466	189
Average yards per return	8.4	6.8	6.5	8.0	7.6	10.4	6.9	11.0	7.9	8.6	5.5	10.5	7.6	8.4	9.5	4.7
Returned for TD	1	0	0	1	0	2	0	0	0	1	0	1	0	0	0	0
Kickoff returns	60	59	80	63	66	55	65	67	61	85	67	70	48	82	63	72
Yards returned	1700	1138	1702	1255	1432	1239	1404	1416	1404	1867	1416	1781	960	1802	1368	1503
Average yards per return	28.3	19.3	21.3	19.9	21.7	22.5	21.6	21.1	23.0	22.0	21.1	25.4	20.0	22.0	21.7	20.9
Returned for TD	3	0	0	0	0	1	0	0	0	1	1	0	0	1	1	0
Fumbles	24	22	25	26	21	24	33	22	19	29	25	27	18	25	25	32
Recovered	11	13	19	10	11	12	11	11	9	20	10	14	10	11	13	12
Out of bounds	0	2	1	1	1	2	1	3	1	1	3	3	0	2	1	3
Recovered for TD	1	0	0	0	0	0	0	0	0	0	0	0	0	0	0	0
Penalties	103	114	128	118	142	130	98	137	127	136	112	117	120	123	108	105
Yards penalized	819	981	1045	1016	1015	953	975	990	985	1180	911	1066	961	909	830	879
Total points scored	387	341	259	202	308	345	344	344	398	314	388	429	428	271	274	293
Total TDs	46	38	27	20	35	39	37	37	43	36	46	50	49	24	28	32
TDs rushing	22	18	9	9	13	15	10	14	16	12	15	22	19	5	10	15
TDs passing	17	18	15	10	18	19	22	23	20	20	24	26	28	18	15	15
TDs on returns and recoveries	7	2	3	1	4	5	5	0	7	4	7	2	2	1	3	2
Extra point kicks	44	38	22	19	35	37	33	34	43	35	46	49	43	21	26	29
Extra point kick att.	45	38	22	20	35	37	35	34	43	35	46	49	44	21	27	29
2-Pt. conversions	1	0	3	0	0	1	1	1	0	0	0	1	2	2	1	2
2-Pt. conversions att.	1	0	5	0	0	1	2	3	0	1	0	1	5	3	1	2
Safeties	1	0	0	0	0	0	0	1	2	0	0	0	0	0	0	1
Field goals made	21	25	23	21	21	24	29	28	31	21	22	26	29	34	26	22
Field goals attempted	24	30	27	29	27	30	34	33	39	30	27	33	36	42	33	31
Percent successful	87.5	83.3	85.2	72.4	77.8	80.0	85.3	84.8	79.5	70.0	81.5	78.8	80.6	81.0	78.8	71.0
Extra points	45	38	25	19	35	38	34	35	43	35	46	50	45	23	27	31
Field goals blocked	0	1	2	1	0	2	1	0	1	2	1	1	0	2	1	1

	AFC Offense Total	AFC Offense Average	AFC Defense Total	AFC Defense Average	NFC Offense Total	NFC Offense Average	NFC Defense Total	NFC Defense Average	NFL Total	NFL Average
First downs	4778	298.6	4830	301.9	4648	290.5	4596	287.3	9426	294.6
Rushing	1619	101.2	1587	99.2	1462	91.4	1494	93.4	3081	96.3
Passing	2741	171.3	2783	173.9	2704	169.0	2662	166.4	5445	170.2
Penalty	418	26.1	460	28.8	482	30.1	440	27.5	900	28.1
Rushes	7239	452.4	7156	447.3	7136	446.0	7219	451.2	14375	449.2
Net yards gained	28951	1809.4	28759	1797.4	28632	1789.5	28824	1801.5	57583	1799.5
Average gain	....	4.0	....	4.0	....	4.0	....	4.0	....	4.0
Average yards per game	....	113.1	....	112.3	....	111.8	....	112.6	....	112.5
Passes attempted	8159	509.9	8261	516.3	8305	519.1	8203	512.7	16464	514.5
Completed	4910	306.9	4962	310.1	4880	305.0	4828	301.8	9790	305.9
Percent completed	....	60.2	....	60.1	....	58.8	....	58.9	....	59.5
Total yards gained	56373	3523.3	56527	3532.9	55348	3459.3	55194	3449.6	111721	3491.3
Times sacked	573	35.8	600	37.5	609	38.1	582	36.4	1182	36.9
Yards lost	3681	230.1	3911	244.4	3872	242.0	3642	227.6	7553	236.0
Net yards gained	52692	3293.3	52616	3288.5	51476	3217.3	51552	3222.0	104168	3255.3
Average yards per game	....	205.8	....	205.5	....	201.1	....	201.4	....	203.5
Net yards per pass play	....	6.03	....	5.94	....	5.77	....	5.87	....	5.90
Yards gained per completion	....	11.48	....	11.39	....	11.34	....	11.43	....	11.41
Combined net yards gained	81643	5102.7	81375	5085.9	80108	5006.8	80376	5023.5	161751	5054.7
Percent total yards rushing	....	35.5	....	35.3	....	35.7	....	35.9	....	35.6
Percent total yards passing	....	64.5	....	64.7	....	64.3	....	64.1	....	64.4
Average yards per game	....	318.9	....	317.9	....	312.9	....	314.0	....	315.9
Ball-control plays	15971	998.2	16017	1001.1	16050	1003.1	16004	1000.3	32021	1000.7
Average yards per play	....	5.1	....	5.1	....	5.0	....	5.0	....	5.1
Third-down efficiency	....	38.7	....	39.1	....	37.5	....	37.1	....	38.1
Interceptions	219	13.7	238	14.9	287	17.9	268	16.8	506	15.8
Yards returned	3132	195.8	2965	185.3	4471	279.4	4638	289.9	7603	237.6
Returned for TD	23	1.4	19	1.2	24	1.5	28	1.8	47	1.5
Punts	1189	74.3	1195	74.7	1322	82.6	1316	82.3	2511	78.5
Yards punted	50892	3180.8	51051	3190.7	55536	3471.0	55377	3461.1	106428	3325.9
Average yards per punt	....	42.8	....	42.7	....	42.0	....	42.1	....	42.4
Punt returns	599	37.4	569	35.6	653	40.8	683	42.7	1252	39.1
Yards returned	4896	306.0	4666	291.6	5247	327.9	5477	342.3	10143	317.0
Average yards per return	....	8.2	....	8.2	....	8.0	....	8.0	....	8.1
Returned for TD	4	0.3	3	0.2	5	0.3	6	0.4	9	0.3
Kickoff returns	1054	65.9	1074	67.1	1083	67.7	1063	66.4	2137	66.8
Yards returned	24508	1531.8	24239	1514.9	23118	1444.9	23387	1461.7	47626	1488.3
Average yards per return	....	23.3	....	22.6	....	21.3	....	22.0	....	22.3
Returned for TD	7	0.4	4	0.3	5	0.3	8	0.5	12	0.4
Fumbles	395	24.7	410	25.6	412	25.8	397	24.8	807	25.2
Lost	180	11.3	193	12.1	210	13.1	197	12.3	390	12.2
Out of bounds	24	1.5	25	1.6	26	1.6	25	1.6	50	1.6
Own recovered for TD	0	0.0	0	0.0	1	0.1	1	0.1	1	0.0
Opponents recovered by	193	12.1	180	11.3	196	12.3	209	13.1	389	12.2
Opponents recovered for TD	11	0.7	9	0.6	12	0.8	14	0.9	23	0.7
Penalties	1822	113.9	1802	112.6	1898	118.6	1918	119.9	3720	116.3
Yards penalized	14527	907.9	14282	892.6	15270	954.4	15515	969.7	29797	931.2
Total points scored	5380	336.3	5231	326.9	5176	323.5	5325	332.8	10556	329.9
Total TDs	601	37.6	585	36.6	571	35.7	587	36.7	1172	36.6
TDs rushing	225	14.1	207	12.9	206	12.9	224	14.0	431	13.5
TDs passing	334	20.9	336	21.0	310	19.4	308	19.3	644	20.1
TDs on returns and recoveries	42	2.6	42	2.6	55	3.4	55	3.4	97	3.0
Extra point kicks	568	35.5	545	34.1	531	33.2	554	34.6	1099	34.3
Extra point kick att.	576	36.0	554	34.6	538	33.6	560	35.0	1114	34.8
2-Pt. conversions	8	0.5	12	0.8	19	1.2	15	0.9	27	0.8
2-Pt. conversion att.	22	1.4	28	1.8	30	1.9	25	1.6	52	1.6
Safeties	7	0.4	6	0.4	4	0.3	5	0.3	11	0.3
Field goals made	392	24.5	380	23.8	391	24.4	403	25.2	783	24.5
Field goals attempted	481	30.1	462	28.9	486	30.4	505	31.6	967	30.2
Percent successful	....	81.5	....	82.3	....	80.5	....	79.8	....	81.0
Extra points	576	36.0	557	68.1	550	34.4	569	35.6	1126	35.2
Field goals blocked	9	0.6	10	0.6	17	1.1	16	1.0	26	0.8

2005 STATISTICS *Miscellaneous*

RUSHING

Player, team	Opponent	Date	Att.	Yds.	TD
Tiki Barber, N.Y. Giants	vs. Kansas City	December 17	29	220	2
Larry Johnson, Kansas City	at Houston	November 20	36	211	2
Tiki Barber, N.Y. Giants	vs. Washington	October 30	24	206	1
Tiki Barber, N.Y. Giants	at Oakland	December 31	28	203	1
Larry Johnson, Kansas City	vs. Cincinnati	January 1	26	201	3
Julius Jones, Dallas	at Carolina	December 24	34	194	2
LaDainian Tomlinson, San Diego	vs. N.Y. Giants	September 25	21	192	3
LaDainian Tomlinson, San Diego	at Washington	November 27*	25	184	3
Steven Jackson, St. Louis	vs. Jacksonville	October 30	25	179	0
Shaun Alexander, Seattle	at Arizona	November 6	23	173	2
Shaun Alexander, Seattle	at Tennessee	December 18	26	172	1
Ricky Williams, Miami	vs. Tennessee	December 24	26	172	1
Samkon Gado, Green Bay	vs. Detroit	December 11*	29	171	1
Rudi Johnson, Cincinnati	vs. Cleveland	December 11	30	169	1
Larry Johnson, Kansas City	at N.Y. Giants	December 17	31	167	2
Reuben Droughns, Cleveland	vs. Miami	November 20	30	166	1
DeShaun Foster, Carolina	at Atlanta	January 1	18	165	1
Fred Taylor, Jacksonville	at St. Louis	October 30	22	165	1
Shaun Alexander, Seattle	vs. St. Louis	November 13	33	165	3
Willie Parker, Pittsburgh	vs. Tennessee	September 11	22	161	1
Carnell Williams, Tampa Bay	at Green Bay	September 25	37	158	0
Warrick Dunn, Atlanta	vs. N.Y. Jets	October 24	24	155	0
Domanick Davis, Houston	at Baltimore	December 4	29	155	0
Tiki Barber, N.Y. Giants	at Seattle	November 27*	26	151	0
Carnell Williams, Tampa Bay	vs. Atlanta	December 24*	31	150	1
Curtis Martin, N.Y. Jets	at Buffalo	October 16	18	148	1
Carnell Williams, Tampa Bay	at Minnesota	September 11	27	148	1
Clinton Portis, Washington	at Tampa Bay	November 13	23	144	1
Shaun Alexander, Seattle	vs. Atlanta	September 18	28	144	1
Edgerrin James, Indianapolis	vs. St. Louis	October 17	23	143	3
Larry Johnson, Kansas City	at Dallas	December 11	26	143	3
Willis McGahee, Buffalo	vs. N.Y. Jets	October 16	29	143	1
Shaun Alexander, Seattle	vs. Houston	October 16	22	141	4
Shaun Alexander, Seattle	vs. Arizona	September 25	22	140	4
Willis McGahee, Buffalo	vs. Atlanta	September 25	27	140	1
Larry Johnson, Kansas City	vs. Denver	December 4	30	140	2
LaDainian Tomlinson, San Diego	at Oakland	October 16	31	140	1
Thomas Jones, Chicago	vs. Detroit	September 18	20	139	2
Edgerrin James, Indianapolis	at Houston	October 23	21	139	2
Shaun Alexander, Seattle	vs. Indianapolis	December 24	21	139	2
Domanick Davis, Houston	at Tennessee	December 11	22	139	0
Thomas Jones, Chicago	vs. Baltimore	October 23	25	139	0
Thomas Jones, Chicago	at Cleveland	October 9	24	137	0
Clinton Portis, Washington	at St. Louis	December 4	27	136	2
Willis McGahee, Buffalo	at New England	October 30	31	136	0
Willie Parker, Pittsburgh	vs. Detroit	January 1	26	135	0
LaDainian Tomlinson, San Diego	at New England	October 2	25	134	2
Ronnie Brown, Miami	vs. Carolina	September 25	23	132	1
Fred Taylor, Jacksonville	vs. Cincinnati	October 9	24	132	0
LaMont Jordan, Oakland	vs. Cleveland	December 18	25	132	0
Larry Johnson, Kansas City	at Buffalo	November 13	27	132	0
Willie Parker, Pittsburgh	at Cincinnati	October 23	18	131	1
DeShaun Foster, Carolina	vs. Atlanta	December 4	24	131	1
Larry Johnson, Kansas City	vs. San Diego	December 24	32	131	1
Willie Parker, Pittsburgh	at Cleveland	December 24	17	130	1
Domanick Davis, Houston	vs. Tennessee	October 9	19	130	0
Deuce McAllister, New Orleans	vs. Buffalo	October 2	27	130	0
Carnell Williams, Tampa Bay	vs. Buffalo	September 18	24	128	1
Tiki Barber, N.Y. Giants	vs. St. Louis	October 2	24	128	1
Edgerrin James, Indianapolis	vs. Jacksonville	September 18	27	128	0
Tatum Bell, Denver	vs. Washington	October 9	12	127	2
Michael Pittman, Tampa Bay	vs. Miami	October 16	15	127	1
Marion Barber, Dallas	vs. Arizona	October 30	27	127	2
Warrick Dunn, Atlanta	vs. Minnesota	October 2	18	126	1
Mike Anderson, Denver	vs. Philadelphia	October 30	21	126	1
Rudi Johnson, Cincinnati	at Cleveland	September 11	26	126	1
LaMont Jordan, Oakland	vs. Dallas	October 2	26	126	1
Edgerrin James, Indianapolis	vs. Pittsburgh	November 28	29	124	0
Tiki Barber, N.Y. Giants	at Philadelphia	December 11*	32	124	0
Mewelde Moore, Minnesota	at Green Bay	November 21	22	122	0
Edgerrin James, Indianapolis	vs. Houston	November 13	26	122	1
LaMont Jordan, Oakland	vs. Buffalo	October 23	28	122	3

Player, team	Opponent	Date	Att.	Yds.	TD
Clinton Portis, Washington	vs. Chicago	September 11	21	121	0
Brian Westbrook, Philadelphia	vs. Green Bay	November 27	20	120	1
Mike Anderson, Denver	at N.Y. Giants	October 23	24	120	1
Adrian Peterson, Chicago	vs. San Francisco	November 13	24	120	1
Shaun Alexander, Seattle	at St. Louis	October 9	25	119	2
Larry Johnson, Kansas City	vs. New England	November 27	31	119	1
Rock Cartwright, Washington	at St. Louis	December 4	9	118	0
Warrick Dunn, Atlanta	vs. Philadelphia	September 12	21	117	0
Willis McGahee, Buffalo	vs. Houston	September 11	22	117	0
Rudi Johnson, Cincinnati	at Detroit	December 18	24	117	2
Warrick Dunn, Atlanta	at Detroit	November 24	17	116	0
Carnell Williams, Tampa Bay	at Atlanta	November 20	19	116	1
Reuben Droughns, Cleveland	vs. Tennessee	November 6	20	116	0
Mike Anderson, Denver	at Jacksonville	October 2	23	115	0
Shaun Alexander, Seattle	at San Francisco	November 20	24	115	2
Tiki Barber, N.Y. Giants	vs. Dallas	December 4	30	115	0
Ryan Moats, Philadelphia	vs. N.Y. Giants	December 11*	11	114	2
Tatum Bell, Denver	vs. New England	October 16	13	114	1
Rudi Johnson, Cincinnati	vs. Baltimore	November 27	27	114	2
Michael Turner, San Diego	at Indianapolis	December 18	8	113	1
Willis McGahee, Buffalo	at N.Y. Jets	January 1	22	113	0
Jamal Lewis, Baltimore	at Cincinnati	November 27	23	113	1
Mike Anderson, Denver	vs. N.Y. Jets	November 20	26	113	3
Tiki Barber, N.Y. Giants	vs. Philadelphia	November 20	21	112	0
Clinton Portis, Washington	vs. Dallas	December 18	23	112	0
Clinton Portis, Washington	at Philadelphia	January 1	27	112	2
Carnell Williams, Tampa Bay	at Carolina	December 11	29	112	2
Willie Parker, Pittsburgh	at Houston	September 18	25	111	1
Samkon Gado, Green Bay	at Philadelphia	November 27	26	111	1
Larry Johnson, Kansas City	vs. N.Y. Jets	September 11	9	110	2
Antowain Smith, New Orleans	vs. Chicago	November 6	17	110	0
Steven Jackson, St. Louis	at Houston	November 27*	25	110	1
Shaun Alexander, Seattle	vs. N.Y. Giants	November 27*	31	110	1
Maurice Hicks, San Francisco	at St. Louis	December 24	10	109	1
Shaun Alexander, Seattle	vs. San Francisco	December 11	21	108	1
Frank Gore, San Francisco	vs. Houston	January 1*	25	108	0
Edgerrin James, Indianapolis	vs. Cleveland	September 25	27	108	1
Clinton Portis, Washington	vs. N.Y. Giants	December 24	27	108	1
Ricky Williams, Miami	at New England	January 1	28	108	1
Tatum Bell, Denver	vs. Philadelphia	October 30	14	107	2
Larry Johnson, Kansas City	vs. Oakland	November 6	22	107	2
LaDainian Tomlinson, San Diego	at N.Y. Jets	November 6	25	107	3
Edgerrin James, Indianapolis	vs. Tennessee	December 4	28	107	1
Michael Bennett, Minnesota	vs. Detroit	November 6	18	106	0
Corey Dillon, New England	at Atlanta	October 9	23	106	0
Ronnie Brown, Miami	at New Orleans	October 30	23	106	0
Greg Jones, Jacksonville	vs. Baltimore	November 13	25	106	1
Thomas Jones, Chicago	vs. Cincinnati	September 25	27	106	1
Edgerrin James, Indianapolis	at San Francisco	October 9	21	105	1
Jamal Lewis, Baltimore	vs. Green Bay	December 19	22	105	1
Thomas Jones, Chicago	at Green Bay	December 25	25	105	1
Clinton Portis, Washington	at Arizona	December 11	26	105	1
Maurice Morris, Seattle	vs. Houston	October 16	8	104	1
Edgerrin James, Indianapolis	at New England	November 7	34	104	1
Clinton Portis, Washington	at Denver	October 9	20	103	0
Samkon Gado, Green Bay	at Atlanta	November 13	25	103	2
Greg Jones, Jacksonville	at Cleveland	December 4	27	103	0
Corey Dillon, New England	at Buffalo	December 11	22	102	1
LaBrandon Toefield, Jacksonville	vs. Tennessee	January 1	25	102	1
Jerome Bettis, Pittsburgh	vs. Chicago	December 11	17	101	2
Clinton Portis, Washington	vs. San Francisco	October 23	19	101	3
Fred Taylor, Jacksonville	at Houston	December 24	22	101	1
Mewelde Moore, Minnesota	vs. New Orleans	September 25	23	101	0
Kevan Barlow, San Francisco	vs. Tampa Bay	October 30	26	101	1
Reuben Droughns, Cleveland	vs. Detroit	October 23	19	100	0
Warrick Dunn, Atlanta	at New Orleans	October 16	22	100	1

*Overtime game.

PASSING

Player, team	Opponent	Date	Att.	Cmp.	Yds.	TD	Int.
Marc Bulger, St. Louis	at N.Y. Giants	October 2	62	40	442	2	3
Josh McCown, Arizona	vs. Carolina	October 9	46	29	398	2	3
Ben Roethlisberger, Pittsburgh	vs. Cincinnati	December 4	41	29	386	3	3
Josh McCown, Arizona	vs. San Francisco	October 2	46	32	385	2	0
Aaron Brooks, New Orleans	vs. N.Y. Giants	September 19	45	27	375	1	3
Tom Brady, New England	at Pittsburgh	September 25	41	31	372	0	1
Donovan McNabb, Philadelphia	at Kansas City	October 2	48	33	369	3	1

Player, team	Opponent	Date	Att.	Cmp.	Yds.	TD	Int.
Donovan McNabb, Philadelphia	vs. Oakland	September 25	52	30	365	2	1
Peyton Manning, Indianapolis	at Cincinnati	November 20	40	24	365	3	1
Drew Bledsoe, Dallas	at San Francisco	September 25	38	24	363	2	2
Marc Bulger, St. Louis	at San Francisco	September 11	56	34	362	2	1
Gus Frerotte, Miami	vs. New England	November 13	47	25	360	2	1
Kurt Warner, Arizona	at Detroit	November 13	45	29	359	1	0
Jamie Martin, St. Louis	vs. San Francisco	December 24	41	33	354	1	1
Kurt Warner, Arizona	at San Francisco	December 4	45	29	354	1	2
Eli Manning, N.Y. Giants	at San Diego	September 25	41	24	352	2	0
Tom Brady, New England	at Atlanta	October 9	27	22	350	3	1
Trent Green, Kansas City	at San Diego	October 30	43	31	347	2	0
Kerry Collins, Oakland	at Philadelphia	September 25	42	24	345	2	0
Eli Manning, N.Y. Giants	at Seattle	November 27*	53	29	344	2	1
Trent Green, Kansas City	vs. Cincinnati	January 1	29	23	344	1	0
Aaron Brooks, New Orleans	at New England	November 20	50	27	343	2	1
Steve McNair, Tennessee	vs. San Francisco	November 27	41	23	343	3	1
Brett Favre, Green Bay	vs. Cleveland	September 18	44	32	342	3	2
Donovan McNabb, Philadelphia	vs. San Francisco	September 18	29	23	342	5	0
Jake Delhomme, Carolina	vs. Minnesota	October 30	30	21	341	3	0
Trent Green, Kansas City	at Dallas	December 11	32	20	340	1	0
Drew Brees, San Diego	vs. Buffalo	November 20	33	28	339	4	0
Carson Palmer, Cincinnati	vs. Minnesota	September 18	40	27	337	3	1
Marc Bulger, St. Louis	vs. Seattle	October 9	40	26	336	2	1
Peyton Manning, Indianapolis	vs. San Diego	December 18	45	26	336	1	2
Trent Dilfer, Cleveland	at Green Bay	September 18	32	21	336	3	0
Carson Palmer, Cincinnati	vs. Indianapolis	November 20	38	25	335	2	1
Kurt Warner, Arizona	vs. Seattle	November 6	48	29	334	1	3
Drew Bledsoe, Dallas	vs. Kansas City	December 11	34	22	332	3	0
Kerry Collins, Oakland	vs. N.Y. Giants	December 31	48	26	331	3	0
Mark Brunell, Washington	at Kansas City	October 16	41	25	331	3	0
Tom Brady, New England	at Buffalo	December 11	38	29	329	2	2
Kurt Warner, Arizona	vs. St. Louis	September 18	42	29	327	0	1
Brooks Bollinger, N.Y. Jets	at Miami	December 18	42	28	327	2	0
Drew Brees, San Diego	vs. Kansas City	October 30	43	25	324	3	1
Peyton Manning, Indianapolis	at Jacksonville	December 11	36	24	324	2	0
Trent Green, Kansas City	vs. New England	November 27	26	19	323	1	0
Mark Brunell, Washington	at Denver	October 9	53	30	322	2	0
Peyton Manning, Indianapolis	at New England	November 7	37	28	321	3	1
Brett Favre, Green Bay	vs. Chicago	December 25	51	30	317	0	4
Matt Hasselbeck, Seattle	at St. Louis	October 9	38	27	316	2	0
Kurt Warner, Arizona	vs. Jacksonville	November 27	46	29	315	2	1
Brett Favre, Green Bay	at Minnesota	October 23	36	28	315	2	0
Eli Manning, N.Y. Giants	at Philadelphia	December 11*	44	28	312	1	3
Drew Bledsoe, Dallas	vs. N.Y. Giants	October 16*	37	26	312	1	1
Kerry Collins, Oakland	vs. Denver	November 13	50	26	310	2	3
Steve McNair, Tennessee	vs. Seattle	December 18	38	23	310	2	0
Ryan Fitzpatrick, St. Louis	at Houston	November 27*	30	19	310	3	1
Jake Plummer, Denver	vs. Philadelphia	October 30	35	22	309	4	0
Kelly Holcomb, Buffalo	at Cincinnati	December 24	31	24	308	1	1
Tom Brady, New England	vs. Oakland	September 8	38	24	306	2	0
Michael Vick, Atlanta	vs. Tampa Bay	November 20	38	21	306	2	0
Marc Bulger, St. Louis	at Seattle	November 13	40	28	304	1	1
Donovan McNabb, Philadelphia	at Washington	November 6	35	22	304	1	1
Brett Favre, Green Bay	at Carolina	October 3	47	28	303	4	1
Brian Griese, Tampa Bay	vs. Detroit	October 2	39	22	302	2	3
Carson Palmer, Cincinnati	vs. Baltimore	November 27	30	22	302	3	1
Daunte Culpepper, Minnesota	vs. New Orleans	September 25	29	21	300	3	0

*Overtime game.

RECEIVING

Player, team	Opponent	Date	No.	Yds.	TD
Chris Chambers, Miami	vs. Buffalo	December 4	15	238	1
Plaxico Burress, N.Y. Giants	vs. St. Louis	October 2	10	204	2
Steve Smith, Carolina	vs. Minnesota	October 30	11	201	1
Chad Johnson, Cincinnati	vs. Indianapolis	November 20	8	189	1
Santana Moss, Washington	at Kansas City	October 16	10	173	1
Terrell Owens, Philadelphia	at Kansas City	October 2	11	171	1
Steve Smith, Carolina	at Miami	September 25	11	170	3
Steve Smith, Carolina	at Chicago	November 20	14	169	0
Joey Galloway, Tampa Bay	vs. Detroit	October 2	7	166	1
Torry Holt, St. Louis	vs. San Francisco	December 24	10	163	1
Torry Holt, St. Louis	vs. Tennessee	September 25	9	163	1
Anquan Boldin, Arizona	vs. Carolina	October 9	10	162	1
Santana Moss, Washington	vs. N.Y. Giants	December 24	5	160	3

Player, team	Opponent	Date	No.	Yds.	TD
Andre Johnson, Houston	vs. St. Louis	November 27*	12	159	1
Santana Moss, Washington	at Dallas	September 19	5	159	2
Terry Glenn, Dallas	vs. Washington	September 19	6	157	1
Anquan Boldin, Arizona	at San Francisco	December 4	11	156	1
Larry Fitzgerald, Arizona	at N.Y. Giants	September 11	13	155	1
Terrell Owens, Philadelphia	at Denver	October 30	3	154	1
Eddie Kennison, Kansas City	vs. Cincinnati	January 1	7	151	0
Joey Galloway, Tampa Bay	at San Francisco	October 30	8	149	1
Koren Robinson, Minnesota	at Detroit	December 4	4	148	1
T.J. Houshmandzadeh, Cincinnati	vs. Baltimore	November 27	9	147	1
Antonio Gates, San Diego	vs. Kansas City	October 30	10	145	3
Ernest Wilford, Jacksonville	at St. Louis	October 30	6	145	1
Joe Horn, New Orleans	vs. N.Y. Giants	September 19	9	143	1
Terrell Owens, Philadelphia	vs. San Francisco	September 18	5	143	2
Jerry Porter, Oakland	at Washington	November 20	6	142	1
Brandon Lloyd, San Francisco	vs. Dallas	September 25	4	142	2
Larry Fitzgerald, Arizona	at Detroit	November 13	9	141	1
Donte' Stallworth, New Orleans	vs. N.Y. Giants	September 19	8	141	0
Brian Westbrook, Philadelphia	vs. Oakland	September 25	6	140	1
Chad Johnson, Cincinnati	vs. Minnesota	September 18	7	139	1
Steve Smith, Carolina	vs. New Orleans	September 11	8	138	1
Joey Galloway, Tampa Bay	vs. Chicago	November 27	7	138	0
Terry Glenn, Dallas	vs. Kansas City	December 11	6	138	1
Rod Smith, Denver	at Buffalo	December 17	11	137	1
Joe Jurevicius, Seattle	at St. Louis	October 9	9	137	1
Joe Jurevicius, Seattle	vs. N.Y. Giants	November 27*	8	137	2
Marvin Harrison, Indianapolis	at Jacksonville	December 11	6	137	2
David Givens, New England	vs. Tampa Bay	December 17	6	137	1
Terry Glenn, Dallas	at San Francisco	September 25	5	137	0
Larry Fitzgerald, Arizona	vs. Carolina	October 9	9	136	1
Hines Ward, Pittsburgh	vs. Cincinnati	December 4	9	135	2
Chad Johnson, Cincinnati	at Tennessee	October 16	8	135	1
Marvin Harrison, Indianapolis	vs. San Diego	December 18	8	135	0
Anquan Boldin, Arizona	at Houston	December 18	8	134	1
Antonio Gates, San Diego	at N.Y. Jets	November 6	8	132	1
Steve Smith, Carolina	at Atlanta	January 1	9	131	1
Darrell Jackson, Seattle	vs. Atlanta	September 18	8	131	0
Joey Galloway, Tampa Bay	vs. Washington	November 13	7	131	1
Torry Holt, St. Louis	at Houston	November 27*	10	130	1
David Givens, New England	at Pittsburgh	September 25	9	130	0
Jimmy Smith, Jacksonville	vs. Seattle	September 11	7	130	2
Randy Moss, Oakland	at New England	September 8	5	130	1
Torry Holt, St. Louis	vs. Arizona	November 20	11	129	1
Donte' Stallworth, New Orleans	vs. Buffalo	October 2	8	129	0
Larry Fitzgerald, Arizona	at San Francisco	December 4	8	129	0
Jeremy Shockey, N.Y. Giants	at Dallas	October 16*	5	129	1
Marvin Harrison, Indianapolis	at New England	November 7	9	128	2
Frisman Jackson, Cleveland	vs. Cincinnati	September 11	8	128	1
Plaxico Burress, N.Y. Giants	at Oakland	December 31	5	128	1
Marvin Harrison, Indianapolis	vs. Pittsburgh	November 28	4	128	1
Jeremy Shockey, N.Y. Giants	at Seattle	November 27*	10	127	1
Randy Moss, Oakland	vs. Kansas City	September 18	5	127	1
Torry Holt, St. Louis	vs. Seattle	October 9	8	126	1
Torry Holt, St. Louis	at San Francisco	September 11	10	125	0
Eric Moulds, Buffalo	at New England	October 30	9	125	1
Darrell Jackson, Seattle	vs. Arizona	September 25	8	125	1
Dallas Clark, Indianapolis	at Cincinnati	November 20	6	125	1
Reggie Wayne, Indianapolis	at New England	November 7	9	124	1
Hines Ward, Pittsburgh	vs. Cleveland	November 13	8	124	1
Chris Baker, N.Y. Jets	at Kansas City	September 11	7	124	1
Antonio Gates, San Diego	vs. Miami	December 11	13	123	1
Keenan McCardell, San Diego	vs. Dallas	September 11	9	123	2
Antonio Bryant, Cleveland	vs. Baltimore	January 1	9	123	1
Rod Smith, Denver	vs. New England	October 16	6	123	1
Steve Smith, Carolina	at Detroit	October 16	6	123	1
Jerry Porter, Oakland	at Tennessee	October 30	6	123	2
Randy Moss, Oakland	vs. Dallas	October 2	4	123	0
Brandon Stokley, Indianapolis	at Seattle	December 24	5	122	0
Shaun McDonald, St. Louis	at N.Y. Giants	October 2	9	121	0
Chris Chambers, Miami	at San Diego	December 11	8	121	2
Keyshawn Johnson, Dallas	vs. N.Y. Giants	October 16*	8	120	0
L.J. Smith, Philadelphia	vs. San Francisco	September 18	9	119	1
Anquan Boldin, Arizona	vs. St. Louis	September 18	8	119	0
Steve Smith, Carolina	at Arizona	October 9	8	119	2
Brandon Lloyd, San Francisco	vs. Seattle	November 20	7	119	1
Andre Johnson, Houston	vs. Jacksonville	December 24	7	119	1
Daniel Graham, New England	at Atlanta	October 9	5	119	1

Player, team	Opponent	Date	No.	Yds.	TD
Terry Glenn, Dallas	vs. Philadelphia	October 9	7	118	2
Donald Driver, Green Bay	vs. Seattle	January 1	6	118	0
Ernest Wilford, Jacksonville	at Houston	December 24	4	118	1
Chad Johnson, Cincinnati	vs. Buffalo	December 24	9	117	1
Roy Williams, Detroit	vs. Arizona	November 13	7	117	3
Matt Jones, Jacksonville	vs. Baltimore	November 13	5	117	1
Reggie Wayne, Indianapolis	at Cincinnati	November 20	5	117	1
Lee Evans, Buffalo	at Miami	December 4	5	117	3
Anquan Boldin, Arizona	vs. San Francisco	October 2	8	116	1
Santana Moss, Washington	at Denver	October 9	8	116	0
Randy Moss, Oakland	vs. N.Y. Giants	December 31	7	116	2
Ben Troupe, Tennessee	vs. Seattle	December 18	6	116	0
Justin McCareins, N.Y. Jets	at Buffalo	October 16	5	116	0
Anquan Boldin, Arizona	vs. Jacksonville	November 27	10	115	0
Eddie Kennison, Kansas City	at San Diego	October 30	7	115	1
Donald Driver, Green Bay	at Atlanta	November 13	10	114	0
Anquan Boldin, Arizona	vs. Washington	December 11	9	114	0
Donald Driver, Green Bay	at Minnesota	October 23	8	114	1
Plaxico Burress, N.Y. Giants	vs. Philadelphia	November 20	6	113	1
Eddie Kennison, Kansas City	at Denver	September 26	8	112	0
Terrell Owens, Philadelphia	at Atlanta	September 12	7	112	0
Santana Moss, Washington	vs. San Francisco	October 23	5	112	1
Tiki Barber, N.Y. Giants	vs. Minnesota	November 13	8	111	0
Roy Williams, Detroit	at New Orleans	December 24	4	111	0
Eric Moulds, Buffalo	vs. Denver	December 17	9	110	0
Todd Heap, Baltimore	vs. Green Bay	December 19	9	110	2
Ashley Lelie, Denver	vs. Oakland	December 24	6	110	0
Hines Ward, Pittsburgh	vs. New England	September 25	4	110	2
Marvin Harrison, Indianapolis	at Tennessee	October 2	9	109	2
Scottie Vines, Detroit	at Minnesota	November 6	9	109	0
Eddie Kennison, Kansas City	vs. Philadelphia	October 2	7	109	1
Plaxico Burress, N.Y. Giants	at Seattle	November 27*	6	109	0
Jimmy Smith, Jacksonville	vs. Denver	October 2	5	109	1
Marvin Harrison, Indianapolis	vs. Houston	November 13	7	108	1
Antonio Gates, San Diego	at New England	October 2	6	108	0
Az-Zahir Hakim, New Orleans	at Green Bay	October 9	5	108	0
Roddy White, Atlanta	vs. Tampa Bay	November 20	4	108	0
Eddie Kennison, Kansas City	vs. Denver	December 4	4	108	0
Jeremy Shockey, N.Y. Giants	at Philadelphia	December 11*	10	107	0
Deion Branch, New England	at Atlanta	October 9	8	107	0
Donald Driver, Green Bay	vs. Chicago	December 25	6	107	0
Lee Evans, Buffalo	at Cincinnati	December 24	5	107	1
Braylon Edwards, Cleveland	at Green Bay	September 18	3	107	1
Bobby Engram, Seattle	at Washington	October 2*	9	106	0
Steve Smith, Carolina	at Tampa Bay	November 6	5	106	1
T.J. Houshmandzadeh, Cincinnati	vs. Houston	October 2	8	105	0
Anquan Boldin, Arizona	at St. Louis	November 20	8	105	1
Mark Clayton, Baltimore	at Denver	December 11	7	105	1
Hines Ward, Pittsburgh	at Cleveland	December 24	7	105	1
Donald Driver, Green Bay	vs. Cleveland	September 18	6	105	1
Marcus Pollard, Detroit	vs. Carolina	October 16	3	105	1
Kevin Curtis, St. Louis	vs. Jacksonville	October 30	3	105	1
Chris Brown, Tennessee	vs. San Francisco	November 27	3	105	1
Larry Fitzgerald, Arizona	at St. Louis	November 20	9	104	1
Alge Crumpler, Atlanta	at Detroit	November 24	7	104	2
Steve Heiden, Cleveland	at Green Bay	September 18	6	104	2
Marty Booker, Miami	vs. Denver	September 11	5	104	1
Ricky Proehl, Carolina	vs. Dallas	December 24	2	104	1
Derrick Mason, Baltimore	vs. Minnesota	December 25	9	103	1
Brian Finneran, Atlanta	vs. New England	October 9	5	103	0
Steve Smith, Carolina	vs. Tampa Bay	December 11	5	103	1
Doug Jolley, N.Y. Jets	at Miami	December 18	9	102	1
Larry Fitzgerald, Arizona	vs. Seattle	November 6	8	102	0
Jimmy Smith, Jacksonville	vs. Indianapolis	December 11	8	102	1
Larry Fitzgerald, Arizona	vs. San Francisco	October 2	7	102	1
Brandon Lloyd, San Francisco	at Arizona	October 2	7	102	0
Marty Booker, Miami	vs. New England	November 13	5	102	0
Donte' Stallworth, New Orleans	vs. Carolina	December 18	5	102	1
Jeremy Shockey, N.Y. Giants	at San Diego	September 25	6	101	0
Chris Chambers, Miami	at Oakland	November 27	6	101	0
Doug Gabriel, Oakland	vs. Buffalo	October 23	5	101	1
Corey Bradford, Houston	vs. Jacksonville	December 24	4	101	1
Doug Gabriel, Oakland	vs. N.Y. Giants	December 31	8	100	0
Az-Zahir Hakim, New Orleans	at St. Louis	October 23	6	100	1
Courtney Anderson, Oakland	at Philadelphia	September 25	5	100	0
Priest Holmes, Kansas City	vs. Washington	October 16	5	100	1

*Overtime game.

OFFENSE

TOTAL SCORES

Team	Series	TD Rush	TD Pass	Total TDs	TD Efficiency Pct.	FGM	Total Scores	Scoring Efficiency Pct.
Cincinnati Bengals	62	15	20	35	56.45	20	55	88.71
Pittsburgh Steelers	56	19	15	34	60.71	21	55	98.21
Seattle Seahawks	60	27	16	43	71.67	11	54	90.00
Indianapolis Colts	61	18	19	37	60.66	16	53	86.89
New England Patriots	58	16	21	37	63.79	15	52	89.66
Atlanta Falcons	54	16	15	31	57.41	19	50	92.59
Denver Broncos	58	21	14	35	60.34	15	50	86.21
New York Giants	59	13	14	27	45.76	22	49	83.05
Kansas City Chiefs	54	20	8	28	51.85	20	48	88.89
Carolina Panthers	53	15	16	31	58.49	17	48	90.57
San Diego Chargers	50	19	16	35	70.00	12	47	94.00
Dallas Cowboys	53	11	17	28	52.83	17	45	84.91
Jacksonville Jaguars	49	15	14	29	59.18	15	44	89.80
St. Louis Rams	51	12	12	24	47.06	19	43	84.31
Minnesota Vikings	51	9	14	23	45.10	17	40	78.43
Washington Redskins	47	13	17	30	63.83	10	40	85.11
Miami Dolphins	52	7	14	21	40.38	18	39	75.00
Buffalo Bills	49	6	11	17	34.69	21	38	77.55
Arizona Cardinals	46	2	11	13	28.26	25	38	82.61
Oakland Raiders	45	11	10	21	46.67	16	37	82.22
Chicago Bears	43	10	10	20	46.51	16	36	83.72
Tennessee Titans	46	7	15	22	47.83	14	36	78.26
Green Bay Packers	46	9	13	22	47.83	13	35	76.09
New York Jets	43	10	9	19	44.19	15	34	79.07
Philadelphia Eagles	41	8	14	22	53.66	12	34	82.93
Tampa Bay Buccaneers	39	11	9	20	51.28	14	34	87.18
New Orleans Saints	42	7	9	16	38.10	17	33	78.57
Houston Texans	37	8	8	16	43.24	17	33	89.19
Baltimore Ravens	42	5	11	16	38.10	16	32	76.19
Cleveland Browns	39	3	8	11	28.21	20	31	79.49
Detroit Lions	36	9	9	18	50.00	12	30	83.33
San Francisco 49ers	28	6	5	11	39.29	16	27	96.43
Tot.	1550	378	414	792	51.10	528	1320	85.16
Avg.	48.4	11.8	12.9	24.8	51.10	16.5	41.3	85.16

SCORING EFFICIENCY

Team	Series	TD Rush	TD Pass	Total TDs	TD Efficiency Pct.	FGM	Total Scores	Scoring Efficiency Pct.
Pittsburgh Steelers	56	19	15	34	60.71	21	55	98.21
San Francisco 49ers	28	6	5	11	39.29	16	27	96.43
San Diego Chargers	50	19	16	35	70.00	12	47	94.00
Atlanta Falcons	54	16	15	31	57.41	19	50	92.59
Carolina Panthers	53	15	16	31	58.49	17	48	90.57
Seattle Seahawks	60	27	16	43	71.67	11	54	90.00
Jacksonville Jaguars	49	15	14	29	59.18	15	44	89.80
New England Patriots	58	16	21	37	63.79	15	52	89.66
Houston Texans	37	8	8	16	43.24	17	33	89.19
Kansas City Chiefs	54	20	8	28	51.85	20	48	88.89
Cincinnati Bengals	62	15	20	35	56.45	20	55	88.71
Tampa Bay Buccaneers	39	11	9	20	51.28	14	34	87.18
Indianapolis Colts	61	18	19	37	60.66	16	53	86.89
Denver Broncos	58	21	14	35	60.34	15	50	86.21
Washington Redskins	47	13	17	30	63.83	10	40	85.11
Dallas Cowboys	53	11	17	28	52.83	17	45	84.91
St. Louis Rams	51	12	12	24	47.06	19	43	84.31
Chicago Bears	43	10	10	20	46.51	16	36	83.72
Detroit Lions	36	9	9	18	50.00	12	30	83.33
New York Giants	59	13	14	27	45.76	22	49	83.05
Philadelphia Eagles	41	8	14	22	53.66	12	34	82.93
Arizona Cardinals	46	2	11	13	28.26	25	38	82.61
Oakland Raiders	45	11	10	21	46.67	16	37	82.22
Cleveland Browns	39	3	8	11	28.21	20	31	79.49
New York Jets	43	10	9	19	44.19	15	34	79.07
New Orleans Saints	42	7	9	16	38.10	17	33	78.57
Minnesota Vikings	51	9	14	23	45.10	17	40	78.43
Tennessee Titans	46	7	15	22	47.83	14	36	78.26
Buffalo Bills	49	6	11	17	34.69	21	38	77.55
Baltimore Ravens	42	5	11	16	38.10	16	32	76.19
Green Bay Packers	46	9	13	22	47.83	13	35	76.09
Miami Dolphins	52	7	14	21	40.38	18	39	75.00
Tot.	1550	378	414	792	51.10	528	1320	85.16
Avg.	48.4	11.8	12.9	24.8	51.10	16.5	41.3	85.16

2005 STATISTICS *Miscellaneous*

TOTAL SCORES

Team	Series	TD Rush	TD Pass	Total TDs	TD Efficiency Pct.	FGM	Total Scores	Scoring Efficiency Pct.
Chicago Bears	40	8	5	13	32.50	16	29	72.50
Dallas Cowboys	38	12	7	19	50.00	11	30	78.95
Carolina Panthers	39	8	8	16	41.03	14	30	76.92
Indianapolis Colts	39	7	12	19	48.72	12	31	79.49
Washington Redskins	37	10	7	17	45.95	14	31	83.78
Jacksonville Jaguars	36	4	15	19	52.78	12	31	86.11
Denver Broncos	39	10	12	22	56.41	11	33	84.62
Kansas City Chiefs	45	7	14	21	46.67	14	35	77.78
New York Giants	43	11	13	24	55.81	11	35	81.40
Pittsburgh Steelers	48	10	13	23	47.92	12	35	72.92
Arizona Cardinals	44	16	8	24	54.55	14	38	86.36
Tampa Bay Buccaneers	45	10	12	22	48.89	16	38	84.44
Baltimore Ravens	42	7	12	19	45.24	20	39	92.86
Seattle Seahawks	47	5	14	19	40.43	21	40	85.11
Atlanta Falcons	49	15	11	26	53.06	15	41	83.67
Cleveland Browns	50	10	12	22	44.00	20	42	84.00
Miami Dolphins	51	8	18	26	50.98	16	42	82.35
Minnesota Vikings	53	11	14	25	47.17	17	42	79.25
New England Patriots	48	11	16	27	56.25	15	42	87.50
San Diego Chargers	55	14	15	29	52.73	13	42	76.36
Green Bay Packers	47	9	16	25	53.19	18	43	91.49
Detroit Lions	53	14	13	27	50.94	17	44	83.02
Cincinnati Bengals	48	13	13	26	54.17	19	45	93.75
New York Jets	52	17	9	26	50.00	20	46	88.46
Buffalo Bills	52	22	11	33	63.46	14	47	90.38
New Orleans Saints	57	15	13	28	49.12	21	49	85.96
Philadelphia Eagles	52	12	17	29	55.77	20	49	94.23
Tennessee Titans	56	11	23	34	60.71	16	50	89.29
Oakland Raiders	59	15	12	27	45.76	27	54	91.53
San Francisco 49ers	64	19	14	33	51.56	22	55	85.94
St. Louis Rams	62	17	19	36	58.06	20	56	90.32
Houston Texans	60	20	16	36	60.00	20	56	93.33
Tot.	1550	378	414	792	51.10	528	1320	85.16
Avg.	48.4	11.8	12.9	24.8	51.10	16.5	41.3	85.16

SCORING EFFICIENCY

Team	Series	TD Rush	TD Pass	Total TDs	TD Efficiency Pct.	FGM	Total Scores	Scoring Efficiency Pct.
Chicago Bears	40	8	5	13	32.50	16	29	72.50
Pittsburgh Steelers	48	10	13	23	47.92	12	35	72.92
San Diego Chargers	55	14	15	29	52.73	13	42	76.36
Carolina Panthers	39	8	8	16	41.03	14	30	76.92
Kansas City Chiefs	45	7	14	21	46.67	14	35	77.78
Dallas Cowboys	38	12	7	19	50.00	11	30	78.95
Minnesota Vikings	53	11	14	25	47.17	17	42	79.25
Indianapolis Colts	39	7	12	19	48.72	12	31	79.49
New York Giants	43	11	13	24	55.81	11	35	81.40
Miami Dolphins	51	8	18	26	50.98	16	42	82.35
Detroit Lions	53	14	13	27	50.94	17	44	83.02
Atlanta Falcons	49	15	11	26	53.06	15	41	83.67
Washington Redskins	37	10	7	17	45.95	14	31	83.78
Cleveland Browns	50	10	12	22	44.00	20	42	84.00
Tampa Bay Buccaneers	45	10	12	22	48.89	16	38	84.44
Denver Broncos	39	10	12	22	56.41	11	33	84.62
Seattle Seahawks	47	5	14	19	40.43	21	40	85.11
San Francisco 49ers	64	19	14	33	51.56	22	55	85.94
New Orleans Saints	57	15	13	28	49.12	21	49	85.96
Jacksonville Jaguars	36	4	15	19	52.78	12	31	86.11
Arizona Cardinals	44	16	8	24	54.55	14	38	86.36
New England Patriots	48	11	16	27	56.25	15	42	87.50
New York Jets	52	17	9	26	50.00	20	46	88.46
Tennessee Titans	56	11	23	34	60.71	16	50	89.29
St. Louis Rams	62	17	19	36	58.06	20	56	90.32
Buffalo Bills	52	22	11	33	63.46	14	47	90.38
Green Bay Packers	47	9	16	25	53.19	18	43	91.49
Oakland Raiders	59	15	12	27	45.76	27	54	91.53
Baltimore Ravens	42	7	12	19	45.24	20	39	92.86
Houston Texans	60	20	16	36	60.00	20	56	93.33
Cincinnati Bengals	48	13	13	26	54.17	19	45	93.75
Philadelphia Eagles	52	12	17	29	55.77	20	49	94.23
Tot.	1550	378	414	792	51.10	528	1320	85.16
Avg.	48.4	11.8	12.9	24.8	51.10	16.5	41.3	85.16

2005 STATISTICAL LEADERS

2005 National Football League leaders
2005 NFL active career leaders

2005 NFL LEADERS

PRIMARY STATISTICS

Points

Player, team	TD	FG	PAT	Pts.
S. Alexander, Sea.	28	0	0	168
J. Feely, NYG	0	35	43	148
N. Rackers, Ariz.	0	40	20	140
S. Graham, Cin.	0	28	47	131
L. Johnson, K.C.	21	0	0	126
L. Tynes, K.C.	0	27	44	125
J. Kasay, Car.	0	26	43	121
M. Vanderjagt, Ind.	0	23	52	121
L. Tomlinson, S.D.	20	0	0	120
2 tied with				117

Touchdowns

Player, team	Rush.	Rec.	Misc.	Tot.
S. Alexander, Sea.	27	1	0	28
L. Johnson, K.C.	20	1	0	21
L. Tomlinson, S.D.	18	2	0	20
E. James, Ind.	13	1	0	14
M. Anderson, Den.	12	1	0	13
C. Dillon, N.E.	12	1	0	13
S. Smith, Car.	1	12	0	13
S. Davis, Car.	12	0	0	12
M. Harrison, Ind.	0	12	0	12
R. Johnson, Cin.	12	0	0	12

Rushing Yards

Player, team	Att.	Avg.	Yds.
S. Alexander, Sea.	370	5.1	1880
T. Barber, NYG	357	5.2	1860
L. Johnson, K.C.	336	5.2	1750
C. Portis, Was.	352	4.3	1516
E. James, Ind.	360	4.2	1506
L. Tomlinson, S.D.	339	4.3	1462
R. Johnson, Cin.	337	4.3	1458
W. Dunn, Atl.	280	5.1	1416
T. Jones, Chi.	314	4.3	1335
W. McGahee, Buf.	325	3.8	1247

Passer Rating†

(minimum 224 attempts)

Player, team	Att.	Rating
P. Manning, Ind.	453	104.1
C. Palmer, Cin.	509	101.1
B. Roethlisberger, Pit.	268	98.6
M. Hasselbeck, Sea.	449	98.2
M. Bulger, St.L.	287	94.4
T. Brady, N.E.	530	92.3
J. Plummer, Den.	456	90.2
T. Green, K.C.	507	90.1
B. Leftwich, Jac.	302	89.3
D. Brees, S.D.	500	89.2

Passing Yards

Player, team	Att.	Y/A	Yds.
T. Brady, N.E.	530	7.75	4110
T. Green, K.C.	507	7.92	4014
B. Favre, G.B.	607	6.39	3881
C. Palmer, Cin.	509	7.54	3836
E. Manning, NYG	557	6.75	3762
K. Collins, Oak.	565	6.65	3759
P. Manning, Ind.	453	8.27	3747
D. Bledsoe, Dal.	499	7.29	3639
D. Brees, S.D.	500	7.15	3576
M. Hasselbeck, Sea.	449	7.70	3459

Receptions

Player, team	No.
L. Fitzgerald, Ariz.	103
S. Smith, Car.	103
A. Boldin, Ariz.	102
T. Holt, St.L.	102
C. Johnson, Cin.	97
A. Gates, S.D.	89
D. Driver, G.B.	86
D. Mason, Bal.	86
R. Smith, Den.	85
S. Moss, Was.	84

Receiving Yards

Player, team	No.	Avg.	Yds.
S. Smith, Car.	103	15.2	1563
S. Moss, Was.	84	17.7	1483
C. Johnson, Cin.	97	14.8	1432
L. Fitzgerald, Ariz.	103	13.7	1409
A. Boldin, Ariz.	102	13.7	1402
T. Holt, St.L.	102	13.0	1331
J. Galloway, T.B.	83	15.5	1287
D. Driver, G.B.	86	14.2	1221
P. Burress, NYG	76	16.0	1214
M. Harrison, Ind.	82	14.0	1146

Fumbles

Player, team	Lost	Fum.
D. Bledsoe, Dal.	8	17
D. Carr, Hou.	6	17
K. Collins, Oak.	4	13
G. Frerotte, Mia.	4	13
K. Holcomb, Buf.	5	13
J. Delhomme, Car.	6	12
K. Orton, Chi.	5	12
M. Brunell, Was.	6	11
A. Smith, S.F.	3	11
M. Vick, Atl.	5	11

Interceptions

Player, team	Ret. Yds.	Int.
T. Law, NYJ	195	10
D. O'Neal, Cin.	103	10
D. Sharper, Min.	276	9
C. Bailey, Den.	139	8
N. Vasher, Chi.	145	8
C. Gamble, Car.	157	7
D. Bly, Det.	54	6
D. Hall, Atl.	177	6
K. Lucas, Car.	70	6
G. Wesley, K.C.	106	6

Sacks

Player, team	No.
D. Burgess, Oak.	16.0
O. Umenyiora, NYG	14.5
S. Rice, T.B.	14.0
K. Vanden Bosch, Ten.	12.5
A. Schobel, Buf.	12.0
J. Taylor, Mia.	12.0
R. Mathis, Ind.	11.5
M. Strahan, NYG	11.5
J. Allen, K.C.	11.0
D. Freeney, Ind.	11.0

Kickoff Return Average

(minimum 20 returns)

Player, team	No.	Yds.	Avg.
T. McGee, Buf.	46	1391	30.2
J. Mathis, Hou.	54	1542	28.6
J. Miller, NYJ	60	1577	26.3
P. Jones, Ten.	43	1127	26.2
K. Robinson, Min.	47	1221	26.0
L. Betts, Was.	24	621	25.9
W. Ponder, NYG	35	905	25.9
Q. Morgan, Pit.	23	583	25.3
T. Thompson, Dal.	57	1399	24.5
D. Wimbush, Jac.	39	955	24.5

Punt Return Average

(minimum 20 returns)

Player, team	No.	Yds.	Avg.
R. Mahe, Phi.	21	269	12.8
B. Sams, Bal.	33	401	12.2
M. Moore, Min.	21	245	11.7
S. Smith, Car.	27	286	10.6
D. Northcutt, Cle.	35	368	10.5
A. Randle El, Pit.	44	448	10.2
M. Jones, T.B.	51	492	9.6
C. Morton, NYG	47	453	9.6
B. Wade, Chi., Ten.	33	317	9.6
P. Jones, Ten.	29	272	9.4

†**Passer Rating** denotes the NFL formula used to rate quarterbacks. *Step 1:* Complete passes divided by pass attempts. Subtract 0.3, then divide by 0.2. *Step 2:* Passing yards divided by pass attempts. Subtract 3, then divide by 4. *Step 3:* Touchdown passes divided by pass attempts, then divide by .05. *Step 4:* Start with .095, and subtract interceptions divided by attempts. Divide the difference by .04. *Step 5:* The sum of each step cannot be greater than 2.375 or less than zero. Add the sums of Steps 1 through 4, multiply by 100 and divide by 6.

2005 STATISTICAL LEADERS *NFL*

Touchdowns

Player, team	No.
C. Palmer, Cin.	32
P. Manning, Ind.	28
T. Brady, N.E.	26
D. Brees, S.D.	24
J. Delhomme, Car.	24
M. Hasselbeck, Sea.	24
E. Manning, NYG	24
D. Bledsoe, Dal.	23
M. Brunell, Was.	23
2 tied with	20

Completions

Player, team	Att.	Cmp.
B. Favre, G.B.	607	372
C. Palmer, Cin.	509	345
T. Brady, N.E.	530	334
D. Brees, S.D.	500	323
T. Green, K.C.	507	317
P. Manning, Ind.	453	305
K. Collins, Oak.	565	302
D. Bledsoe, Dal.	499	300
M. Hasselbeck, Sea.	449	294
E. Manning, NYG	557	294

Interception Pct.
(minimum 224 attempts)

Player, team	Att.	Int.	Pct.
B. Johnson, Min.	294	4	1.4
J. Plummer, Den.	456	7	1.5
B. Leftwich, Jac.	302	5	1.7
T. Green, K.C.	507	10	2.0
M. Hasselbeck, Sea.	449	9	2.0
K. Collins, Oak.	565	12	2.1
M. Brunell, Was.	454	10	2.2
P. Manning, Ind.	453	10	2.2
C. Simms, T.B.	313	7	2.2
B. Bollinger, NYJ	266	6	2.3

Longest Completion

Player, team	Yds.
D. McNabb, Phi.	91
T. Rattay, S.F.	89
J. Harrington, Det.	86
B. Roethlisberger, Pit.	85
J. Martin, St.L.	83
5 tied with	80

Yards per Attempt
(minimum 224 attempts)

Player, team	Att.	Yds.	Y/A
B. Roethlisberger, Pit.	268	2385	8.90
P. Manning, Ind.	453	3747	8.27
M. Bulger, St.L.	287	2297	8.00
T. Green, K.C.	507	4014	7.92
J. Delhomme, Car.	435	3421	7.86
T. Brady, N.E.	530	4110	7.75
M. Hasselbeck, Sea.	449	3459	7.70
C. Palmer, Cin.	509	3836	7.54
J. Plummer, Den.	456	3366	7.38
D. Bledsoe, Dal.	499	3639	7.29

Completion Pct.
(minimum 224 attempts)

Player, team	Att.	Cmp.	Pct.
C. Palmer, Cin.	509	345	67.8
K. Holcomb, Buf.	230	155	67.4
P. Manning, Ind.	453	305	67.3
M. Bulger, St.L.	287	192	66.9
M. Hasselbeck, Sea.	449	294	65.5
D. Brees, S.D.	500	323	64.6
K. Warner, Ariz.	375	242	64.5
T. Brady, N.E.	530	334	63.0
B. Roethlisberger, Pit.	268	168	62.7
B. Johnson, Min.	294	184	62.6

Passing Yards per Game
(minimum 7 games)

Player, team	Yds.	G	Y/G
M. Bulger, St.L.	2297	8	287.1
D. McNabb, Phi.	2507	9	278.6
K. Warner, Ariz.	2713	10	271.3
T. Brady, N.E.	4110	16	256.9
T. Green, K.C.	4014	16	250.9
K. Collins, Oak.	3759	15	250.6
B. Favre, G.B.	3881	16	242.6
C. Palmer, Cin.	3836	16	239.8
E. Manning, NYG	3762	16	235.1
P. Manning, Ind.	3747	16	234.2

Times Sacked

Player, team	No.
D. Carr, Hou.	68
D. Bledsoe, Dal.	49
K. Collins, Oak.	39
A. Brooks, N.O.	33
M. Vick, Atl.	33
B. Bollinger, NYJ	32
T. Green, K.C.	32
D. Culpepper, Min.	31
K. Orton, Chi.	30
2 tied with	29

Attempts

Player, team	No.
B. Favre, G.B.	607
K. Collins, Oak.	565
E. Manning, NYG	557
T. Brady, N.E.	530
C. Palmer, Cin.	509
T. Green, K.C.	507
D. Brees, S.D.	500
D. Bledsoe, Dal.	499
G. Frerotte, Mia.	494
S. McNair, Ten.	476

Interceptions

Player, team	Att.	Int.
B. Favre, G.B.	607	29
D. Bledsoe, Dal.	499	17
A. Brooks, N.O.	431	17
E. Manning, NYG	557	17
J. Delhomme, Car.	435	16
D. Brees, S.D.	500	15
T. Brady, N.E.	530	14
G. Frerotte, Mia.	494	13
K. Orton, Chi.	368	13
M. Vick, Atl.	387	13

Big Play Passes†

Player, team	No.
T. Brady, N.E.	32
J. Delhomme, Car.	32
T. Green, K.C.	30
E. Manning, NYG	30
C. Palmer, Cin.	27
D. Bledsoe, Dal.	26
K. Collins, Oak.	25
M. Hasselbeck, Sea.	25
J. Plummer, Den.	24
2 tied with	23

Sack Percentage
(minimum 224 attempts; pass plays*)

Player, team	PP*	Skd.	Pct.
C. Palmer, Cin.	528	19	3.6
P. Manning, Ind.	470	17	3.6
B. Favre, G.B.	631	24	3.8
S. McNair, Ten.	496	20	4.0
J. Plummer, Den.	478	22	4.6
T. Brady, N.E.	556	26	4.7
E. Manning, NYG	585	28	4.8
G. Frerotte, Mia.	520	26	5.0
D. McNabb, Phi.	376	19	5.1
M. Hasselbeck, Sea.	473	24	5.1

†**Big Play Passes** denote pass completions of 25 or more yards. ***Pass Plays** denote passing attempts plus times sacked.

RUSHING STATISTICS

Attempts

Player, team	No.
S. Alexander, Sea.	370
E. James, Ind.	360
T. Barber, NYG	357
C. Portis, Was.	352
L. Tomlinson, S.D.	339
R. Johnson, Cin.	337
L. Johnson, K.C.	336
W. McGahee, Buf.	325
T. Jones, Chi.	314
R. Droughns, Cle.	309

Yards per Attempt
(minimum 100 attempts)

Player, team	Att.	Yds.	Avg.
M. Vick, Atl.	102	597	5.9
T. Bell, Den.	173	921	5.3
T. Barber, NYG	357	1860	5.2
L. Johnson, K.C.	336	1750	5.2
S. Alexander, Sea.	370	1880	5.1
W. Dunn, Atl.	280	1416	5.1
F. Gore, S.F.	127	608	4.8
W. Parker, Pit.	255	1202	4.7
R. Williams, Mia.	168	743	4.4
R. Brown, Mia.	207	907	4.4

Touchdowns

Player, team	No.
S. Alexander, Sea.	27
L. Johnson, K.C.	20
L. Tomlinson, S.D.	18
E. James, Ind.	13
M. Anderson, Den.	12
S. Davis, Car.	12
C. Dillon, N.E.	12
R. Johnson, Cin.	12
C. Portis, Was.	11
4 tied with	9

Big Running Plays†

Player, team	No.
S. Alexander, Sea.	54
L. Johnson, K.C.	47
T. Barber, NYG	43
R. Johnson, Cin.	39
L. Tomlinson, S.D.	38
C. Portis, Was.	34
W. Dunn, Atl.	33
T. Jones, Chi.	33
3 tied with	31

Longest Run

Player, team	Yds.
T. Barber, NYG	95
S. Alexander, Sea.	88
M. Turner, S.D.	83
W. Parker, Pit.	80
S. Bryson, Det.	77
R. Droughns, Cle.	75
M. Hicks, S.F.	73
F. Gore, S.F.	72
2 tied with	71

Yards per Attempt, Grass
(minimum 40 attempts)

Player, team	Att.	Yds.	Avg.
M. Pittman, T.B.	56	384	6.9
A. Peterson, Chi.	64	348	5.4
T. Bell, Den.	153	812	5.3
L. Johnson, K.C.	252	1308	5.2
S. Alexander, Sea.	146	762	5.2
T. Barber, NYG	112	538	4.8
F. Gore, S.F.	115	535	4.7
R. Moats, Phi.	43	200	4.7
M. Moore, Min.	45	209	4.6
W. Parker, Pit.	193	888	4.6

Yards per Attempt, Turf
(minimum 40 attempts)

Player, team	Att.	Yds.	Avg.
D. Foster, Car.	40	239	6.0
M. Vick, Atl.	73	434	5.9
C. Williams, T.B.	46	264	5.7
S. Bryson, Det.	44	241	5.5
T. Barber, NYG	245	1322	5.4
W. Dunn, Atl.	208	1108	5.3
L. Johnson, K.C.	84	442	5.3
W. Parker, Pit.	62	314	5.1
S. Alexander, Sea.	224	1127	5.0
C. Taylor, Bal.	76	357	4.7

Yards per Attempt, Att 21+§
(minimum 20 attempts)

Player, team	Att.	Yds.	Avg.
C. Williams, T.B.	52	357	6.9
L. Tomlinson, S.D.	37	240	6.5
T. Barber, NYG	60	313	5.2
L. Jordan, Oak.	29	137	4.7
R. Johnson, Cin.	46	216	4.7
J. Jones, Dal.	34	154	4.5
D. Davis, Hou.	32	144	4.5
E. James, Ind.	74	301	4.1
C. Portis, Was.	52	209	4.0
L. Johnson, K.C.	84	327	3.9

Pct. TD, Inside 3-Yard Line
(minimum 5 attempts)

Player, team	Att.	TD	TD%
C. Dillon, N.E.	8	7	87.5
T. Duckett, Atl.	8	7	87.5
M. Alstott, T.B.	7	6	85.7
T. Jones, Chi.	7	6	85.7
S. Alexander, Sea.	16	12	75.0
R. Johnson, Cin.	8	6	75.0
M. Anderson, Den.	12	8	66.7
L. Tomlinson, S.D.	12	8	66.7
J. Bettis, Pit.	10	6	60.0
S. Jackson, St.L.	5	3	60.0

Times Stuffed*

Player, team	No.
S. Jackson, St.L.	47
S. Alexander, Sea.	41
T. Barber, NYG	34
J. Lewis, Bal.	32
L. Tomlinson, S.D.	31
R. Droughns, Cle.	30
W. Parker, Pit.	30
J. Jones, Dal.	29
T. Jones, Chi.	29
C. Williams, T.B.	28

Times Stuffed per Attempt*
(minimum 100 attempts)

Player, team	Att.	Stuffed	Avg.
M. Anderson, Den.	239	9	.038
T. Duckett, Atl.	121	6	.050
A. Smith, N.O.	166	9	.054
L. Johnson, K.C.	336	19	.057
W. Dunn, Atl.	280	16	.057
A. Pinner, Det.	106	7	.066
R. Johnson, Cin.	337	23	.068
D. Foster, Car.	205	14	.068
D. Davis, Hou.	230	16	.070
S. Davis, Car.	180	13	.072

4th Qtr. Rushing Yards

Player, team	Att.	Yds.
T. Barber, NYG	92	462
C. Williams, T.B.	72	404
S. Alexander, Sea.	84	359
L. Johnson, K.C.	93	354
L. Tomlinson, S.D.	72	352
R. Johnson, Cin.	70	345
E. James, Ind.	80	310
T. Jones, Chi.	72	296
W. McGahee, Buf.	77	290
M. Anderson, Den.	58	268

†**Big Running Plays** denote running plays gaining 10 or more yards. §**Yards per Attempt, Att. 21+** denotes the average yards gained on all rushing attempts a player makes beyond his first 20 attempts in a game. Example: A player with 25 rushing attempts in a game is credited with only the yardage gained on his last five attempts. ***Times Stuffed** denotes the number of times a ballcarrier is tackled behind the line of scrimmage on a rushing attempt. Any rush for zero yards is *not* counted as a stuff.

Yards per Reception
(minimum 30 receptions)

Player, team	No.	Yds.	Avg.
A. Lelie, Den.	42	770	18.3
T. Glenn, Dal.	62	1136	18.3
S. Moss, Was.	84	1483	17.7
M. Booker, Mia.	39	686	17.6
R. Moss, Oak.	60	1005	16.8
M. Robinson, Min.	31	515	16.6
E. Wilford, Jac.	41	681	16.6
J. McCareins, NYJ	43	713	16.6
T. Owens, Phi.	47	763	16.2
E. Kennison, K.C.	68	1102	16.2

Yards After Catch (YAC)*

Player, team	No.	Yds.
S. Smith, Car.	103	810
S. Moss, Was.	84	616
L. Jordan, Oak.	70	548
A. Boldin, Ariz.	102	542
T. Barber, NYG	54	525
C. Cooley, Was.	71	487
B. Westbrook, Phi.	61	484
L. Tomlinson, S.D.	51	463
A. Gates, S.D.	89	431
R. Smith, Den.	85	423

1st Down Receptions△

Player, team	No.
C. Johnson, Cin.	74
S. Smith, Car.	70
A. Boldin, Ariz.	68
L. Fitzgerald, Ariz.	67
D. Driver, G.B.	63
T. Holt, St.L.	63
A. Gates, S.D.	62
S. Moss, Was.	60
C. Chambers, Mia.	59
M. Harrison, Ind.	59

4th Qtr TD Receptions

Player, team	No.
L. Fitzgerald, Ariz.	5
C. Chambers, Mia.	4
M. Harrison, Ind.	4
10 tied with	3

Touchdowns

Player, team	No.
M. Harrison, Ind.	12
S. Smith, Car.	12
C. Chambers, Mia.	11
H. Ward, Pit.	11
L. Fitzgerald, Ariz.	10
J. Galloway, T.B.	10
A. Gates, S.D.	10
J. Jurevicius, Sea.	10
4 tied with	9

Average Throw§
(minimum 32 targets)

Player, team	Tgt.	Yds.	Avg.
A. Lelie, Den.	88	1600	18.2
R. White, Atl.	68	1228	18.1
T. Glenn, Dal.	118	2074	17.6
T. Williamson, Min.	52	872	16.8
R. Moss, Oak.	124	2014	16.2
M. Jenkins, Atl.	71	1135	16.0
G. Lewis, Phi.	105	1651	15.7
R. Ferguson, G.B.	57	895	15.7
R. Proehl, Car.	50	780	15.6
C. Wilson, Pit.	53	824	15.5

Longest Reception

Player, team	Yds.
T. Owens, Phi.	91
B. Lloyd, S.F.	89
M. Pollard, Det.	86
H. Ward, Pit.	85
K. Curtis, St.L.	83
5 tied with	80

Receptions Lost on Penalty Ω

Player, team	No.
E. Kennison, K.C.	8
A. Boldin, Ariz.	6
C. Johnson, Cin.	6
S. Smith, Car.	6
P. Burress, NYG	5
E. Moulds, Buf.	5
J. Wiggins, Min.	5
11 tied with	4

Target†

Player, team	No.
A. Boldin, Ariz.	171
P. Burress, NYG	166
C. Chambers, Mia.	166
L. Fitzgerald, Ariz.	165
T. Holt, St.L.	163
C. Johnson, Cin.	155
J. Galloway, T.B.	152
S. Smith, Car.	150
D. Driver, G.B.	146
J. Porter, Oak.	142

Pct. Receptions per Target¥
(minimum 50 targets)

Player, team	No.	Tgt.	Pct.
E. James, Ind.	44	50	88.0
C. Perry, Cin.	51	62	82.3
C. Taylor, Bal.	41	52	78.8
S. Jackson, St.L.	43	55	78.2
T. Barber, NYG	54	70	77.1
E. Kinney, Ten.	55	72	76.4
M. Faulk, St.L.	44	58	75.9
H. Miller, Pit.	39	52	75.0
J. Wiggins, Min.	69	92	75.0
J. Witten, Dal.	66	89	74.2

Big Catches∑

Player, team	No.
S. Moss, Was.	18
S. Smith, Car.	16
L. Fitzgerald, Ariz.	14
J. Galloway, T.B.	13
C. Johnson, Cin.	12
A. Boldin, Ariz.	11
A. Bryant, Cle.	11
T. Glenn, Dal.	11
E. Kennison, K.C.	11
5 tied with	10

Passes Dropped∞

Player, team	No.
L. Jordan, Oak.	12
P. Burress, NYG	11
M. Muhammad, Chi.	11
D. Stallworth, N.O.	11
E. Kennison, K.C.	10
A. Gates, S.D.	9
C. Johnson, Cin.	9
5 tied with	8

†**Target** denotes the intended receiver of a pass. ***Yards After Catch (YAC)** denotes the number of yards a receiver gains from the spot on the field at which he establishes possession of a thrown football to the play's end. A receiver catching a pass in the end zone receives credit for no yards after the catch, regardless of the length of the entire pass play. Example: With the line of scrimmage on the offensive team's own 15-yard line, a receiver catches a pass on his own 25-yard line and is tackled (or runs out of bounds) at his team's 39-yard line. While he gets credit for a 24-yard reception, the receiver is credited with 14 yards after catch (YAC). §**Average Throw** denotes the average distance that all passes intended for a given receiver travel in the air before hitting the ground, being touched by a player, going out of bounds or crossing the goal line. ¥**Pct. Receptions per Target** denotes the percentage of time a pass intended for a receiver was caught by that receiver. △**1st Down Receptions** denote the number of receptions resulting in a first down. ∑**Big Catches** denote receptions of 25 or more yards. Ω**Receptions Lost on Penalty** denote the number of receptions nullified by a penalty. ∞**Passes Dropped** denote any incomplete pass which was catchable with normal effort. To determine if a pass was dropped, STATS, Inc. compares and reviews the judgment of multiple reporters.

DEFENSIVE STATISTICS

Tackles

Player, team	No.
J. Vilma, NYJ	128
D. Edwards, S.D.	114
Z. Thomas, Mia.	107
L. Fletcher, Buf.	104
S. Quarles, T.B.	103
K. Bulluck, Ten.	102
J. Trotter, Phi.	102
B. Urlacher, Chi.	98
D. Williams, Atl.	97
M. Peterson, Jac.	95

Interception Return Yards

Player, team	Int.	Yds.
D. Sharper, Min.	9	276
T. Law, NYJ	10	195
D. Hall, Atl.	6	177
C. Tillman, Chi.	5	172
C. Gamble, Car.	7	157
N. Vasher, Chi.	8	145
M. Furrey, St.L.	4	143
C. Bailey, Den.	8	139
M. Brown, Chi.	3	116
C. June, Ind.	5	115

Touchdowns

Player, team	No.
A. Thomas, Bal.	3
C. Bailey, Den.	2
S. Brown, Phi.	2
K. Dansby, Ariz.	2
A. Dyson, Sea.	2
C. Hart, S.D.	2
C. June, Ind.	2
A. Odom, Ten.	2
D. Sharper, Min.	2
51 tied with	1

Forced Fumbles

Player, team	No.
J. Allen, K.C.	7
R. Mathis, Ind.	7
J. Abraham, NYJ	6
D. Freeney, Ind.	6
S. Rice, T.B.	6
O. Thurman, Cin.	5
19 tied with	4

Assists

Player, team	No.
A. Davis, Cle.	60
Z. Thomas, Mia.	55
L. Fletcher, Buf.	54
N. Barnett, G.B.	47
J. Farrior, Pit.	45
J. Vilma, NYJ	45
D. Edwards, S.D.	40
A. Crowell, Buf.	38
3 tied with	37

Yards per Int. Return

(minimum 4 interceptions)

Player, team	Int.	Yds.	Avg.
M. Furrey, St.L.	4	143	35.8
C. Tillman, Chi.	5	172	34.4
D. Sharper, Min.	9	276	30.7
D. Hall, Atl.	6	177	29.5
M. Boulware, Sea.	4	107	26.8
T. McGee, Buf.	4	97	24.3
C. June, Ind.	5	115	23.0
C. Gamble, Car.	7	157	22.4
S. Spencer, S.F.	4	85	21.3
R. Barber, T.B.	5	105	21.0

Stuffs*

Player, team	No.
Z. Thomas, Mia.	12.0
R. Pickett, St.L.	11.0
J. Trotter, Phi.	11.0
D. Smith, S.F.	10.5
D. Ware, Dal.	10.0
I. Gold, Den.	9.0
O. Huff, Ariz.	9.0
P. Williams, Min.	9.0
A. Crowell, Buf.	8.5
C. Okeafor, Ariz.	8.5

Fumbles Recovered

Player, team	No.
R. Godfrey, S.D.	4
M. Reagor, Ind.	4
11 tied with	3

Sack Yards

Player, team	Sacks	Yds.
R. Mathis, Ind.	11.5	110.0
D. Burgess, Oak.	16.0	104.0
O. Umenyiora, NYG	14.5	95.5
S. Rice, T.B.	14.0	89.0
A. Schobel, Buf.	12.0	81.0
J. Taylor, Mia.	12.0	80.0
K. Vanden Bosch, Ten.	12.5	79.5
J. Abraham, NYJ	10.5	75.0
A. Thomas, Bal.	9.0	75.0
D. Freeney, Ind.	11.0	71.5

Passes Defensed†

Player, team	No.
S. Brown, Phi.	27
B. Dawkins, Phi.	24
C. Bailey, Den.	23
R. Barber, T.B.	20
D. O'Neal, Cin.	20
I. Taylor, Pit.	20
Q. Jammer, S.D.	19
S. Spencer, S.F.	19
T. Law, NYJ	18
4 tied with	17

Stuff Yards¥

Player, team	Stuffs	Yds.
Z. Thomas, Mia.	12.0	32.5
C. Okeafor, Ariz.	8.5	26.0
O. Roye, Cle.	7.0	26.0
M. Strahan, NYG	7.5	24.5
A. Carter, S.F.	4.0	24.0
D. Smith, S.F.	10.5	23.5
M. Lewis, Phi.	6.0	22.0
G. Walker, Hou.	5.5	22.0
P. Williams, Min.	9.0	22.0
2 tied with		21.0

Blocked FGs/Punts/PATs

Player, team	No.
C. Jenkins, G.B.	3
A. Boone, Chi.	2
L. Walker, Oak.	2
24 tied with	1

†**Passes Defensed** denote any passes which a defender, through contact with the football, causes to be incomplete. Interceptions are included in passes defensed. *****Stuffs** denote the number of times a ball carrier, including a quarterback on a rushing play, is tackled behind the line of scrimmage on a rushing attempt. Any rush for zero yards is *not* counted as a stuff. ¥**Stuff Yards** denote the number of yards lost as the result of being stuffed (see "Stuffs" explanation).

Return Touchdowns

Player, team	No.
J. Mathis, Hou.	2
A. Randle El, Pit.	2
17 tied with	1

Field Goals

Player, team	No.
N. Rackers, Ariz.	40
J. Feely, NYG	35
M. Stover, Bal.	30
R. Lindell, Buf.	29
S. Graham, Cin.	28
P. Dawson, Cle.	27
L. Tynes, K.C.	27
J. Wilkins, St.L.	27
3 tied with	26

40+ Yd FG Pct.
(minimum 10 attempts)

Player, team	Made	Att.	Pct.
J. Nedney, S.F.	12	13	92.3
N. Rackers, Ariz.	19	21	90.5
M. Bryant, T.B.	11	13	84.6
J. Wilkins, St.L.	13	16	81.3
M. Stover, Bal.	11	14	78.6
R. Lindell, Buf.	10	13	76.9
P. Edinger, Min.	11	15	73.3
J. Feely, NYG	11	15	73.3
N. Kaeding, S.D.	8	11	72.7
2 tied with			70.0

Net Punting Average¥
(minimum 40 punts)

Player, team	Punts	Yds.	Avg.
D. Jones, Mia.	88	3460	39.3
B. Moorman, Buf.	71	2777	39.1
J. Baker, Car.	72	2803	38.9
M. Berger, N.O.	71	2746	38.7
J. Miller, N.E.	77	2946	38.3
M. Scifres, S.D.	71	2700	38.0
T. Sauerbrun, Den.	73	2771	38.0
B. Graham, NYJ	74	2808	37.9
S. Lechler, Oak.	82	3104	37.9
C. Hentrich, Ten.	78	2947	37.8

Tackles

Player, team	No.
R. Scanlon, K.C.	19
M. Underwood, G.B.	19
B. Ayanbadejo, Chi.	18
G. Sapp, Ind.	18
J. Scobey, Sea.	17
7 tied with	16

Field Goal Pct.
(minimum 16 attempts)

Player, team	Made	Att.	Pct.
N. Rackers, Ariz.	40	42	95.2
P. Dawson, Cle.	27	29	93.1
J. Nedney, S.F.	26	28	92.9
T. Peterson, Atl.	23	25	92.0
M. Vanderjagt, Ind.	23	25	92.0
M. Stover, Bal.	30	34	88.2
S. Graham, Cin.	28	32	87.5
N. Kaeding, S.D.	21	24	87.5
J. Wilkins, St.L.	27	31	87.1
M. Bryant, T.B.	21	25	84.0

Net Kickoff Average*

Player, team	Avg.
J. Wilkins, St.L.	64.2
J. Kasay, Car.	63.8
A. Elling, Bal.	63.4
J. Brown, Sea.	63.4
N. Rackers, Ariz.	63.3
O. Mare, Mia.	63.2
M. Berger, N.O.	63.1
P. Edinger, Min.	63.1
J. Cortez, Dal.-Phi.-S.F., Ind.	62.6
R. Lindell, Buf.	62.5

Inside-20 Pct.∞
(minimum 40 punts)

Player, team	Punts	In-20	Pct.
H. Smith, Ind.	52	23	44.2
D. Colquitt, K.C.	65	27	41.5
N. Harris, Det.	84	34	40.5
C. Hanson, Jac.	82	33	40.2
M. Berger, N.O.	71	28	39.4
C. Stanley, Hou.	77	29	37.7
J. Feagles, NYG	73	26	35.6
D. Jones, Mia.	88	31	35.2
M. Scifres, S.D.	71	25	35.2
M. McBriar, Dal.	81	28	34.6

Hang Time†
(minimum 40 punts)

Player, team	Punts	Seconds
C. Kluwe, Min.	71	4.52
M. Scifres, S.D.	71	4.47
C. Hanson, Jac.	82	4.39
D. Colquitt, K.C.	65	4.37
J. Miller, N.E.	76	4.37
S. Player, Ariz.	73	4.37
C. Hentrich, Ten.	78	4.31
H. Smith, Ind.	52	4.31
J. Feagles, NYG	73	4.31
S. Lechler, Oak.	82	4.29

Inside-40 Yard FG Pct.
(minimum 10 attempts)

Player, team	Made	Att.	Pct.
J. Hanson, Det.	13	13	100.0
N. Kaeding, S.D.	13	13	100.0
J. Kasay, Car.	17	17	100.0
N. Rackers, Ariz.	21	21	100.0
J. Reed, Pit.	18	18	100.0
S. Graham, Cin.	21	22	95.5
L. Tynes, K.C.	21	22	95.5
T. Peterson, Atl.	20	21	95.2
M. Stover, Bal.	19	20	95.0
R. Gould, Chi.	18	19	94.7

Gross Punting Average
(minimum 40 punts)

Player, team	Punts	Yds.	Avg.
B. Moorman, Buf.	71	3242	45.7
S. Lechler, Oak.	82	3744	45.7
J. Bidwell, T.B.	90	4101	45.6
J. Miller, N.E.	76	3431	45.1
H. Smith, Ind.	52	2301	44.3
C. Kluwe, Min.	71	3130	44.1
S. Player, Ariz.	73	3206	43.9
T. Sauerbrun, Den.	72	3157	43.8
M. Scifres, S.D.	71	3104	43.7
B. Graham, NYJ	74	3233	43.7

Touchback Pct.
(minimum 40 punts)

Player, team	Punts	TB	Pct.
C. Stanley, Hou.	77	1	1.3
N. Harris, Det.	84	2	2.4
A. Lee, S.F.	107	3	2.8
B. Sander, G.B.	64	2	3.1
J. Feagles, NYG	73	3	4.1
M. Berger, N.O.	71	3	4.2
R. Hodges, St.L., Phi.	41	2	4.9
J. Miller, N.E.	76	4	5.3
J. Baker, Car.	72	4	5.6
D. Colquitt, K.C.	65	5	7.7

†**Hang Time** denotes the average time in seconds from when the ball strikes the punter's foot until it is touched by another player or hits the ground. If a punt is deflected at the line of scrimmage, that deflection is ignored. ***Net Kickoff Average** denotes kickoff yards, minus return yards, minus 20 yards for every touchback, divided by the number of kickoffs. ¥**Net Punting Average** denotes gross punting average, minus return yards, minus 20 yards for every touchback, divided by the total number of punts. ∞**Inside-20 Percentage** denotes the percentage of punts which are considered inside-20. According to the NFL, "Credit a player with an inside-20 when his punt is not returned to the receivers' 20-yard line or beyond. Also credit an inside-20 when a punt does not penetrate the 20, but the returner carries the ball back inside the 20 and his return ends there. A touchback is *not* an inside-20."

NFL ACTIVE CAREER LEADERS

PRIMARY STATISTICS

Points

Player	No.
John Carney	1634
Matt Stover	1594
Jason Elam	1557
Jason Hanson	1420
John Kasay	1305
Jeff Wilkins	1188
Adam Vinatieri	1158
Ryan Longwell	1054
Todd Peterson	1043
Mike Vanderjagt	995

Total Touchdowns

Player	No.
Marshall Faulk	136
Marvin Harrison	110
Terrell Owens	103
Shaun Alexander	100
Curtis Martin	100
Randy Moss	99
Jerome Bettis	94
Priest Holmes	94
LaDainian Tomlinson	80
Isaac Bruce	77

Rushing Yards

Player	Yds.
Curtis Martin	14101
Jerome Bettis	13662
Marshall Faulk	12279
Corey Dillon	10429
Edgerrin James	9226
Tiki Barber	8787
Fred Taylor	8367
Warrick Dunn	8321
Priest Holmes	8035
Stephen Davis	7875

Rushing Yards per Attempt

(minimum 750 attempts)

Player	Att.	Yds.	Avg.
Clinton Portis	1258	5930	4.7
Tiki Barber	1890	8787	4.6
Priest Holmes	1734	8035	4.6
Ahman Green	1605	7432	4.6
Charlie Garner	1537	7097	4.6
Fred Taylor	1831	8367	4.6
Shaun Alexander	1717	7817	4.6
Jamal Lewis	1508	6669	4.4
Mike Anderson	865	3822	4.4
Marshall Faulk	2836	12279	4.3

Rushing Touchdowns

Player	No.
Marshall Faulk	100
Jerome Bettis	91
Curtis Martin	90
Shaun Alexander	89
Priest Holmes	86
LaDainian Tomlinson	72
Corey Dillon	69
Stephen Davis	65
Edgerrin James	64
Mike Alstott	55

Rushing Attempts

Player	No.
Curtis Martin	3518
Jerome Bettis	3479
Marshall Faulk	2836
Corey Dillon	2419
Edgerrin James	2188
Warrick Dunn	1970
Stephen Davis	1905
Tiki Barber	1890
Fred Taylor	1831
Antowain Smith	1784

Receptions

Player	No.
Marvin Harrison	927
Jimmy Smith	862
Keenan McCardell	825
Isaac Bruce	813
Rod Smith	797
Marshall Faulk	767
Keyshawn Johnson	744
Terrell Owens	716
Eric Moulds	675
Ricky Proehl	666

Receiving Yards

Player	Yds.
Marvin Harrison	12331
Jimmy Smith	12287
Isaac Bruce	12278
Rod Smith	10877
Keenan McCardell	10680
Terrell Owens	10535
Randy Moss	10147
Keyshawn Johnson	9756
Torry Holt	9487
Eric Moulds	9096

Receiving Touchdowns

Player	No.
Marvin Harrison	110
Terrell Owens	101
Randy Moss	98
Isaac Bruce	77
Jimmy Smith	67
Rod Smith	65
Joey Galloway	64
Keenan McCardell	62
Keyshawn Johnson	60
Tony Gonzalez	56

Yards per Reception

(minimum 200 receptions)

Player	No.	Yds.	Avg.
Derrick Alexander	417	6971	16.7
Santana Moss	235	3899	16.6
Randy Moss	634	10147	16.0
Plaxico Burress	337	5378	16.0
Corey Bradford	201	3182	15.8
Joey Galloway	550	8501	15.5
Torry Holt	619	9487	15.3
Eddie Kennison	482	7384	15.3
Isaac Bruce	813	12278	15.1
Koren Robinson	235	3514	15.0

Fumbles

Player	No.
Brett Favre	130
Kerry Collins	121
Drew Bledsoe	120
Vinny Testaverde	113
Steve McNair	84
Daunte Culpepper	81
Trent Dilfer	74
Tony Banks	73
Jon Kitna	72
Mark Brunell	71

Games Played

Player	No.
Marvin Harrison	110
Terrell Owens	101
Randy Moss	98
Isaac Bruce	77
Jimmy Smith	67
Rod Smith	65
Joey Galloway	64
Keenan McCardell	62
Keyshawn Johnson	60
Tony Gonzalez	56

Passing Yards

Player	Yds.
Brett Favre	53615
Vinny Testaverde	45252
Drew Bledsoe	43447
Kerry Collins	33637
Peyton Manning	33189
Mark Brunell	30037
Jeff George	27602
Jake Plummer	27259
Steve McNair	27141
Brad Johnson	25798

Touchdowns

Player	No.
Brett Favre	396
Vinny Testaverde	269
Drew Bledsoe	244
Peyton Manning	244
Mark Brunell	174
Kerry Collins	173
Steve McNair	156
Brad Johnson	155
Jeff George	154
2 tied with	150

Yards per Attempt
(minimum 1500 attempts)

Player	Att.	Yds.	Y/A
Kurt Warner	2340	19214	8.21
Marc Bulger	1518	11932	7.86
Daunte Culpepper	2607	20162	7.73
Trent Green	3329	25621	7.70
Peyton Manning	4333	33189	7.66
Jake Delhomme	1503	11160	7.43
Matt Hasselbeck	2205	15925	7.22
Tom Brady	2548	18035	7.08
Brian Griese	2318	16344	7.05
Brett Favre	7611	53615	7.04

Attempts

Player	No.
Brett Favre	7611
Drew Bledsoe	6548
Vinny Testaverde	6526
Kerry Collins	5082
Mark Brunell	4334
Peyton Manning	4333
Jake Plummer	4033
Jeff George	3967
Steve McNair	3871
Brad Johnson	3798

Completions

Player	No.
Brett Favre	4678
Drew Bledsoe	3749
Vinny Testaverde	3691
Kerry Collins	2826
Peyton Manning	2769
Mark Brunell	2576
Brad Johnson	2350
Jake Plummer	2309
Steve McNair	2305
Jeff George	2298

Completion Pct.
(minimum 1500 attempts)

Player	Att.	Cmp.	Pct.
Kurt Warner	2340	1537	65.7
Marc Bulger	1518	987	65.0
Daunte Culpepper	2607	1678	64.4
Peyton Manning	4333	2769	63.9
Brian Griese	2318	1463	63.1
Drew Brees	1809	1125	62.2
Tom Brady	2548	1577	61.9
Brad Johnson	3798	2350	61.9
Brett Favre	7611	4678	61.5
Jeff Garcia	2785	1695	60.9

Passer Rating†
(minimum 1500 attempts)

Player	Att.	Rating
Kurt Warner	2340	94.1
Peyton Manning	4333	93.5
Daunte Culpepper	2607	91.5
Marc Bulger	1518	90.6
Tom Brady	2548	88.5
Trent Green	3329	88.3
Matt Hasselbeck	2205	86.6
Brett Favre	7611	86.0
Jeff Garcia	2785	85.8
Drew Brees	1809	84.9

Interceptions

Player	No.
Vinny Testaverde	261
Brett Favre	255
Drew Bledsoe	198
Kerry Collins	166
Jake Plummer	148
Peyton Manning	130
Trent Dilfer	117
Jeff George	113
Jon Kitna	104
Steve McNair	103

Interception Pct.
(minimum 1500 attempts)

Player	Att.	Int.	Pct.
Donovan McNabb	2943	66	2.2
Mark Brunell	4334	102	2.4
Jeff Garcia	2785	71	2.5
Matt Hasselbeck	2205	57	2.6
Tom Brady	2548	66	2.6
Steve McNair	3871	103	2.7
Brad Johnson	3798	102	2.7
Trent Green	3329	92	2.8
Jeff George	3967	113	2.8
Drew Brees	1809	53	2.9

Passing Yards per Game
(minimum 1500 attempts)

Player	Yds.	G	Y/G
Marc Bulger	11932	44	271.2
Kurt Warner	19214	73	263.2
Peyton Manning	33189	128	259.3
Daunte Culpepper	20162	81	248.9
Trent Green	25621	104	246.4
Brett Favre	53615	225	238.3
Drew Bledsoe	43447	188	231.1
Tom Brady	18035	80	225.4
Aaron Brooks	19156	85	225.4
Kerry Collins	33637	152	221.3

Times Sacked

Player	No.
Drew Bledsoe	451
Vinny Testaverde	408
Brett Favre	403
Mark Brunell	377
Jeff George	358
Kerry Collins	296
Jake Plummer	266
Jeff Blake	248
Trent Dilfer	236
Donovan McNabb	234

Sack Percentage
(minimum 1500 attempts; pass plays*)

Player	PP*	Skd.	Pct.
Peyton Manning	4489	156	3.5
Joey Harrington	1879	77	4.1
Jeff Garcia	2918	133	4.6
Doug Flutie	2258	107	4.7
Drew Brees	1901	92	4.8
Brett Favre	8014	403	5.0
Brad Johnson	4011	213	5.3
Kerry Collins	5378	296	5.5
Steve McNair	4100	229	5.6
Jake Delhomme	1593	90	5.6

†Passer Rating denotes the NFL formula used to rate quarterbacks. *Step 1:* Complete passes divided by pass attempts. Subtract 0.3, then divide by 0.2. *Step 2:* Passing yards divided by pass attempts. Subtract 3, then divide by 4. *Step 3:* Touchdown passes divided by pass attempts, then divide by .05. *Step 4:* Start with .095, and subtract interceptions divided by attempts. Divide the difference by .04. *Step 5:* The sum of each step cannot be greater than 2.375 or less than zero. Add the sums of Steps 1 through 4, multiply by 100 and divide by 6. ***Pass Plays** denote passing attempts plus times sacked.

SPECIAL TEAMS

Field Goals

Player	No.
John Carney	390
Matt Stover	380
Jason Elam	341
Jason Hanson	327
John Kasay	310
Adam Vinatieri	263
Jeff Wilkins	251
Todd Peterson	235
Ryan Longwell	226
Olindo Mare	219

Field Goal Pct.
(minimum 100 FG Made)

Player	Made	Att.	Pct.
Mike Vanderjagt	217	248	87.5
Phil Dawson	135	161	83.9
Matt Stover	380	457	83.2
Jeff Wilkins	251	306	82.0
Olindo Mare	219	267	82.0
David Akers	155	189	82.0
Adam Vinatieri	263	321	81.9
Ryan Longwell	226	277	81.6
John Carney	390	480	81.3
Jason Hanson	327	404	80.9

Inside-40 Yard FG Pct.
(minimum 50 FG Made)

Player	Made	Att.	Pct.
Jason Hanson	217	226	96.0
Mike Vanderjagt	138	146	94.5
David Akers	97	103	94.2
Matt Stover	261	278	93.9
Jason Elam	223	239	93.3
Joe Nedney	102	110	92.7
Sebastian Janikowski	86	93	92.5
Jeff Wilkins	169	183	92.3
John Kasay	207	225	92.0
Jeff Reed	64	70	91.4

40-49 Yard FG Pct.
(minimum 25 FG Made)

Player	Made	Att.	Pct.
Mike Vanderjagt	65	81	80.2
Shayne Graham	29	37	78.4
Doug Brien	68	92	73.9
Todd Peterson	65	89	73.0
Olindo Mare	53	73	72.6
Ryan Longwell	61	85	71.8
Paul Edinger	48	67	71.6
John Kasay	74	104	71.2
Matt Stover	107	151	70.9
Adam Vinatieri	70	99	70.7

50+ Yard FG Pct.
(minimum 10 FG Made)

Player	Made	Att.	Pct.
Jeff Wilkins	20	29	69.0
Paul Edinger	16	24	66.7
Neil Rackers	14	21	66.7
Mike Vanderjagt	14	21	66.7
Jason Elam	35	58	60.3
Ryan Longwell	13	22	59.1
David Akers	10	17	58.8
Rian Lindell	10	17	58.8
John Carney	19	34	55.9
Olindo Mare	13	24	54.2

Gross Punting Average
(minimum 250 punts)

Player	Punts	Yds.	Avg.
Shane Lechler	442	20266	45.9
Todd Sauerbrun	832	36600	44.0
Tom Rouen	810	35189	43.4
Darren Bennett	836	36316	43.4
Brian Moorman	379	16461	43.4
Tom Tupa	873	37862	43.4
Hunter Smith	425	18429	43.4
Chris Hanson	356	15427	43.3
Sean Landeta	1401	60707	43.3
Mitch Berger	710	30680	43.2

Net Punting Average†
(minimum 250 punts)

Player	Punts	Yds.	Avg.
Matt Turk	792	29501	37.2
Craig Hentrich	899	33047	36.8
Shane Lechler	444	16267	36.6
Darren Bennett	839	30721	36.6
Brian Moorman	380	13872	36.5
Chris Hanson	358	13030	36.4
Tom Rouen	819	29670	36.2
Josh Bidwell	481	17361	36.1
Brad Maynard	842	30390	36.1
Todd Sauerbrun	839	30233	36.0

Inside-20 Pct. *
(minimum 250 punts)

Player	Punts	In-20	Pct.
Craig Hentrich	896	313	34.9
Josh Miller	704	235	33.4
Chris Hanson	356	116	32.6
Hunter Smith	425	138	32.5
Mitch Berger	710	227	32.0
Matt Turk	790	252	31.9
Kyle Richardson	572	182	31.8
Brad Maynard	837	266	31.8
Jeff Feagles	1437	456	31.7
Shane Lechler	442	140	31.7

Touchback Pct.
(minimum 250 punts)

Player	Punts	TB	Pct.
Nick Harris	416	27	6.5
Chad Stanley	518	34	6.6
Jason Baker	300	20	6.7
Darren Bennett	836	62	7.4
Chris Mohr	1152	87	7.6
Jeff Feagles	1437	112	7.8
Leo Araguz	322	27	8.4
Brad Maynard	837	71	8.5
Chris Gardocki	1112	99	8.9
Scott Player	648	59	9.1

Kickoff Return Average
(minimum 75 returns)

Player	No.	Yds.	Avg.
Terrence McGee	106	2921	27.6
Bethel Johnson	102	2557	25.1
Steve Smith	96	2372	24.7
Eddie Drummond	151	3677	24.4
Ladell Betts	78	1898	24.3
Terry Fair	111	2698	24.3
Kevin Kasper	77	1869	24.3
Jerry Azumah	119	2885	24.2
Dante Hall	307	7437	24.2
Michael Lewis	206	4989	24.2

Punt Return Average
(minimum 75 returns)

Player	No.	Yds.	Avg.
Santana Moss	95	1092	11.5
B.J. Sams	88	976	11.1
Michael Lewis	126	1371	10.9
Allen Rossum	207	2229	10.8
Az-Zahir Hakim	165	1773	10.7
Phillip Buchanon	84	891	10.6
Dennis Northcutt	174	1837	10.6
Troy Brown	244	2554	10.5
Bobby Engram	101	1053	10.4
Deion Sanders	212	2199	10.4

Return Touchdowns

Player	No.
Dante Hall	10
Deion Sanders	9
Eddie Drummond	6
Allen Rossum	6
Steve Smith	6
Tim Dwight	5
Joey Galloway	5
Antwaan Randle El	5
Karl Williams	5
4 tied with	4

†**Net Punting Average** denotes gross punting yards, minus return yards, minus 20 yards for every touchback, divided by the total number of punts. ***Inside-20 Percentage** denotes the percentage of punts which are considered inside-20. According to the NFL, "Credit a player with an inside-20 when his punt is not returned to the receivers' 20-yard line or beyond. Also credit an inside-20 when a punt does not penetrate the 20, but the returner carries the ball back inside the 20 and his return ends there. A touchback is *not* an inside-20."

DEFENSE

Interceptions

Player	No.
Deion Sanders	53
Terrell Buckley	50
Troy Vincent	47
Ty Law	46
Darren Sharper	45
Ashley Ambrose	42
Aaron Glenn	39
Donnie Abraham	38
Sammy Knight	37
Tory James	35

Yards per Interception Return
(minimum 20 interceptions)

Player	Int.	Yds.	Avg.
Ed Reed	22	680	30.9
Deion Sanders	53	1331	25.1
Derrick Brooks	21	481	22.9
Tony Parrish	30	670	22.3
Otis Smith	29	645	22.2
Darren Sharper	45	953	21.2
Greg Wesley	26	503	19.3
Anthony Henry	20	385	19.3
Marcus Coleman	25	476	19.0
Dewayne Washington	31	569	18.4

Sacks

Player	No.
Michael Strahan	129.5
Simeon Rice	119.0
Jason Taylor	92.5
Kevin Carter	92.0
Warren Sapp	84.5
Hugh Douglas	80.0
Chad Brown	78.0
Willie McGinest	78.0
Bryant Young	77.5
La'Roi Glover	71.5

Fumbles Recovered

Player	No.
Jason Taylor	21
Junior Seau	17
Chad Brown	15
Willie McGinest	15
Takeo Spikes	14
Michael Strahan	14
Sammy Knight	13
Brian Dawkins	12
3 tied with	11

Interception Return Yards

Player	Yds.
Deion Sanders	1331
Darren Sharper	953
Terrell Buckley	793
Ty Law	778
Troy Vincent	711
Ed Reed	680
Tony Parrish	670
Otis Smith	645
Sammy Knight	606
Dewayne Washington	569

Int. Return TDs

Player	No.
Deion Sanders	9
Ty Law	7
Darren Sharper	7
Otis Smith	7
Terrell Buckley	6
Dre' Bly	5
Derrick Brooks	5
Aaron Glenn	5
Dewayne Washington	5
12 tied with	4

Forced Fumbles

Player	No.
Simeon Rice	30
Jason Taylor	27
Jevon Kearse	24
Dwight Freeney	23
Leonard Little	23
Michael Strahan	23
Mike Barrow	22
Derrick Brooks	21
Brian Dawkins	21
3 tied with	19

Defensive Touchdowns

Player	No.
Deion Sanders	10
Darren Sharper	9
Dre' Bly	7
Terrell Buckley	7
Ty Law	7
Otis Smith	7
Dewayne Washington	7
4 tied with	6

100-Yard Rushing Games

Player	No.
Jerome Bettis	61
Curtis Martin	57
Edgerrin James	49
Marshall Faulk	41
Corey Dillon	39
Fred Taylor	38
Shaun Alexander	33
Clinton Portis	32
Priest Holmes	31
Ricky Williams	31

400-Yard Passing Games

Player	No.
Drew Bledsoe	6
Peyton Manning	6
Marc Bulger	4
Vinny Testaverde	4
Matt Hasselbeck	3
7 tied with	2

1,000-Yd. Rushing Seasons

Player	No.
Curtis Martin	10
Jerome Bettis	8
Corey Dillon	7
Marshall Faulk	7
Shaun Alexander	5
Tiki Barber	5
Ahman Green	5
Edgerrin James	5
Fred Taylor	5
LaDainian Tomlinson	5

4,000-Yd. Passing Seasons

Player	No.
Peyton Manning	6
Brett Favre	4
Drew Bledsoe	3
Trent Green	3
Kurt Warner	2
9 tied with	1

200-Yard Rushing Games

Player	No.
Tiki Barber	4
LaDainian Tomlinson	4
Corey Dillon	3
Marshall Faulk	3
Edgerrin James	2
Larry Johnson	2
Jamal Lewis	2
Clinton Portis	2
Ricky Williams	2
11 tied with	1

100-Yard Receiving Games

Player	No.
Marvin Harrison	53
Jimmy Smith	46
Randy Moss	45
Isaac Bruce	39
Torry Holt	39
Terrell Owens	36
Rod Smith	30
Keenan McCardell	27
Eric Moulds	26
Muhsin Muhammad	26

1,500-Yd. Rushing Seasons

Player	No.
Edgerrin James	4
Clinton Portis	3
Shaun Alexander	2
Tiki Barber	2
Priest Holmes	2
Curtis Martin	2
LaDainian Tomlinson	2
8 tied with	1

1,000-Yd. Rec. Seasons

Player	No.
Jimmy Smith	9
Rod Smith	8
Isaac Bruce	7
Marvin Harrison	7
Randy Moss	7
Torry Holt	6
Terrell Owens	6
Derrick Mason	5
Keenan McCardell	5
Amani Toomer	5

300-Yard Passing Games

Player	No.
Brett Favre	45
Drew Bledsoe	37
Kurt Warner	35
Peyton Manning	34
Kerry Collins	30
Vinny Testaverde	30
Trent Green	29
Mark Brunell	25
Daunte Culpepper	19
Jeff George	18

200-Yard Receiving Games

Player	No.
Isaac Bruce	3
Plaxico Burress	2
Torry Holt	2
Jimmy Smith	2
14 tied with	1

3,000-Yd. Passing Seasons

Player	No.
Brett Favre	14
Drew Bledsoe	9
Peyton Manning	8
Mark Brunell	6
Kerry Collins	6
Trent Green	6
Vinny Testaverde	6
Brad Johnson	5
Steve McNair	5
7 tied with	4

1,500-Yd. Rec. Seasons

Player	No.
Marvin Harrison	3
Torry Holt	2
David Boston	1
Isaac Bruce	1
Randy Moss	1
Jimmy Smith	1
Rod Smith	1
Steve Smith	1

HISTORY

Championship games

Year-by-year standings

Super Bowls

Pro Bowls

Records

Statistical leaders

Coaching records

Hall of Fame

The Sporting News awards

First-round draft choices

Team by team

CHAMPIONSHIP GAMES

NFL (1933-1969); NFC (1970-2004)

RESULTS

Season	Date	Winner	Loser	Score	Site	Attendance
1933	Dec. 17	Chicago Bears	N.Y. Giants	23-21	Chicago	26,000
1934	Dec. 9	N.Y. Giants	Chicago Bears	30-13	N.Y. Giants	35,059
1935	Dec. 15	Detroit	N.Y. Giants	26-7	Detroit	15,000
1936	Dec. 13	Green Bay	Boston Redskins	21-6	N.Y. Giants	29,545
1937	Dec. 12	Washington	Chicago Bears	28-21	Chicago	15,870
1938	Dec. 11	N.Y. Giants	Green Bay	23-17	N.Y. Giants	48,120
1939	Dec. 10	Green Bay	N.Y. Giants	27-0	Milwaukee	32,279
1940	Dec. 8	Chicago Bears	Washington	73-0	Washington	36,034
1941	Dec. 21	Chicago Bears	N.Y. Giants	37-9	Chicago	13,341
1942	Dec. 13	Washington	Chicago Bears	14-6	Washington	36,006
1943	Dec. 26	Chicago Bears	Washington	41-21	Chicago	34,320
1944	Dec. 17	Green Bay	N.Y. Giants	14-7	N.Y. Giants	46,016
1945	Dec. 16	Cleveland Rams	Washington	15-14	Cleveland	32,178
1946	Dec. 15	Chicago Bears	N.Y. Giants	24-14	N.Y. Giants	58,346
1947	Dec. 28	Chicago Cardinals	Philadelphia	28-21	Chicago	30,759
1948	Dec. 19	Philadelphia	Chicago Cardinals	7-0	Philadelphia	36,309
1949	Dec. 18	Philadelphia	L.A. Rams	14-0	L.A. Rams	27,980
1950	Dec. 24	Cleveland Browns	L.A. Rams	30-28	Cleveland	29,751
1951	Dec. 23	L.A. Rams	Cleveland Browns	24-17	L.A. Rams	57,522
1952	Dec. 28	Detroit	Cleveland Browns	17-7	Cleveland	50,934
1953	Dec. 27	Detroit	Cleveland Browns	17-16	Detroit	54,577
1954	Dec. 26	Cleveland Browns	Detroit	56-10	Cleveland	43,827
1955	Dec. 26	Cleveland Browns	L.A. Rams	38-14	L.A. Rams	85,693
1956	Dec. 30	N.Y. Giants	Chicago Bears	47-7	N.Y. Giants	56,836
1957	Dec. 29	Detroit	Cleveland Browns	59-14	Detroit	55,263
1958	Dec. 28	Baltimore	N.Y. Giants	23-17*	N.Y. Giants	64,185
1959	Dec. 27	Baltimore	N.Y. Giants	31-16	Baltimore	57,545
1960	Dec. 26	Philadelphia	Green Bay	17-13	Philadelphia	67,325
1961	Dec. 31	Green Bay	N.Y. Giants	37-0	Green Bay	39,029
1962	Dec. 30	Green Bay	N.Y. Giants	16-7	N.Y. Giants	64,892
1963	Dec. 29	Chicago Bears	N.Y. Giants	14-10	Chicago	45,801
1964	Dec. 27	Cleveland Browns	Baltimore	27-0	Cleveland	79,544
1965	Jan. 2	Green Bay	Cleveland Browns	23-12	Green Bay	50,777
1966	Jan. 1	Green Bay	Dallas	34-27	Dallas	74,152
1967	Dec. 31	Green Bay	Dallas	21-17	Green Bay	50,861
1968	Dec. 29	Baltimore	Cleveland Browns	34-0	Cleveland	78,410
1969	Jan. 4	Minnesota	Cleveland Browns	27-7	Minnesota	46,503
1970	Jan. 3	Dallas	San Francisco	17-10	San Francisco	59,364
1971	Jan. 2	Dallas	San Francisco	14-3	Dallas	63,409
1972	Dec. 31	Washington	Dallas	26-3	Washington	53,129
1973	Dec. 30	Minnesota	Dallas	27-10	Dallas	64,422
1974	Dec. 29	Minnesota	L.A. Rams	14-10	Minnesota	48,444
1975	Jan. 4	Dallas	L.A. Rams	37-7	L.A. Rams	88,919
1976	Dec. 26	Minnesota	L.A. Rams	24-13	Minnesota	48,379
1977	Jan. 1	Dallas	Minnesota	23-6	Dallas	64,293
1978	Jan. 7	Dallas	L.A. Rams	28-0	L.A. Rams	71,086
1979	Jan. 6	L.A. Rams	Tampa Bay	9-0	Tampa Bay	72,033
1980	Jan. 11	Philadelphia	Dallas	20-7	Philadelphia	70,696
1981	Jan. 10	San Francisco	Dallas	28-27	San Francisco	60,525
1982	Jan. 22	Washington	Dallas	31-17	Washington	55,045
1983	Jan. 8	Washington	San Francisco	24-21	Washington	55,363
1984	Jan. 6	San Francisco	Chicago Bears	23-0	San Francisco	61,040
1985	Jan. 12	Chicago Bears	L.A. Rams	24-0	Chicago	63,522
1986	Jan. 11	N.Y. Giants	Washington	17-0	N.Y. Giants	76,633
1987	Jan. 17	Washington	Minnesota	17-10	Washington	55,212
1988	Jan. 8	San Francisco	Chicago Bears	28-3	Chicago	64,830
1989	Jan. 14	San Francisco	L.A. Rams	30-3	San Francisco	64,769
1990	Jan. 20	N.Y. Giants	San Francisco	15-13	San Francisco	65,750
1991	Jan. 12	Washington	Detroit	41-10	Washington	55,585
1992	Jan. 17	Dallas	San Francisco	30-20	San Francisco	64,920
1993	Jan. 23	Dallas	San Francisco	38-21	Dallas	64,902
1994	Jan. 15	San Francisco	Dallas	38-28	San Francisco	69,125
1995	Jan. 14	Dallas	Green Bay	38-27	Dallas	65,135
1996	Jan. 12	Green Bay	Carolina	30-13	Green Bay	60,216
1997	Jan. 11	Green Bay	San Francisco	23-10	San Francisco	68,987
1998	Jan. 17	Atlanta	Minnesota	30-27*	Minnesota	64,060

Season	Date	Winner	Loser	Score	Site	Attendance
1999	Jan. 23	St. Louis	Tampa Bay	11-6	St. Louis	66,496
2000	Jan. 14	N.Y. Giants	Minnesota	41-0	New York	79,310
2001	Jan. 27	St. Louis	Philadelphia	29-24	St. Louis	66,502
2002	Jan. 19	Tampa Bay	Philadelphia	27-10	Philadelphia	66,713
2003	Jan. 18	Carolina	Philadelphia	14-3	Philadelphia	65,158
2004	Jan. 23	Philadelphia	Atlanta	27-10	Philadelphia	67,717
2005	Jan. 22	Seattle	Carolina	34-14	Seattle	67,837

*Overtime.

COMPOSITE STANDINGS

	W	L	Pct.	PF	PA		W	L	Pct.	PF	PA
Seattle Seahawks	1	0	1.000	34	14	Arizona Cardinals*	1	1	.500	28	28
Green Bay Packers	10	3	.769	303	177	Atlanta Falcons	1	1	.500	40	54
Baltimore Colts	3	1	.750	88	60	San Francisco 49ers	5	7	.417	245	222
Detroit Lions	4	2	.667	139	141	Cleveland Browns	4	7	.364	224	253
Washington Redskins†	7	5	.583	222	255	St. Louis Rams‡	5	9	.357	163	300
Philadelphia Eagles	5	4	.556	143	128	New York Giants	6	11	.353	281	322
Chicago Bears	7	6	.538	286	245	Carolina Panthers	1	2	.333	41	67
Dallas Cowboys	8	8	.500	361	319	Tampa Bay Buccaneers	1	2	.333	33	30
Minnesota Vikings	4	4	.500	135	151						

*Both games played when franchise was in Chicago; won 28-21, lost 7-0.
†One game played when franchise was in Boston; lost 21-6.
‡One game played when franchise was in Cleveland; won 15-14. 11 games played when franchise was in Los Angeles, record of 2-9.

AFL (1960-1969); AFC (1970-2004)
RESULTS

Season	Date	Winner	Loser	Score	Site	Attendance
1960	Jan. 1	Houston	L.A. Chargers	24-16	Houston	32,183
1961	Dec. 24	Houston	San Diego	10-3	San Diego	29,556
1962	Dec. 23	Dallas Texans	Houston	20-17*	Houston	37,981
1963	Jan. 5	San Diego	Boston Patriots	51-10	San Diego	30,127
1964	Dec. 26	Buffalo	San Diego	20-7	Buffalo	40,242
1965	Dec. 26	Buffalo	San Diego	23-0	San Diego	30,361
1966	Jan. 1	Kansas City	Buffalo	31-7	Buffalo	42,080
1967	Dec. 31	Oakland	Houston	40-7	Oakland	53,330
1968	Dec. 29	N.Y. Jets	Oakland	27-23	New York	62,627
1969	Jan. 4	Kansas City	Oakland	17-7	Oakland	53,564
1970	Jan. 3	Baltimore	Oakland	27-17	Baltimore	54,799
1971	Jan. 2	Miami	Baltimore	21-0	Miami	76,622
1972	Dec. 31	Miami	Pittsburgh	21-17	Pittsburgh	50,845
1973	Dec. 30	Miami	Oakland	27-10	Miami	79,325
1974	Dec. 29	Pittsburgh	Oakland	24-13	Oakland	53,800
1975	Jan. 4	Pittsburgh	Oakland	16-10	Pittsburgh	50,609
1976	Dec. 26	Oakland	Pittsburgh	24-7	Oakland	53,821
1977	Jan. 1	Denver	Oakland	20-17	Denver	75,044
1978	Jan. 7	Pittsburgh	Houston	34-5	Pittsburgh	50,725
1979	Jan. 6	Pittsburgh	Houston	27-13	Pittsburgh	50,475
1980	Jan. 11	Oakland	San Diego	34-27	San Diego	52,428
1981	Jan. 10	Cincinnati	San Diego	27-7	Cincinnati	46,302
1982	Jan. 23	Miami	N.Y. Jets	14-0	Miami	67,396
1983	Jan. 8	L.A. Raiders	Seattle	30-14	Los Angeles	88,734
1984	Jan. 6	Miami	Pittsburgh	45-28	Miami	76,029
1985	Jan. 12	New England	Miami	31-14	Miami	74,978
1986	Jan. 11	Denver	Cleveland	23-20*	Cleveland	79,915
1987	Jan. 17	Denver	Cleveland	38-33	Denver	75,993
1988	Jan. 8	Cincinnati	Buffalo	21-10	Cincinnati	59,747
1989	Jan. 14	Denver	Cleveland	37-21	Denver	76,046
1990	Jan. 20	Buffalo	L.A. Raiders	51-3	Buffalo	80,234
1991	Jan. 12	Buffalo	Denver	10-7	Buffalo	80,272
1992	Jan. 17	Buffalo	Miami	29-10	Miami	72,703
1993	Jan. 23	Buffalo	Kansas City	30-13	Buffalo	76,642
1994	Jan. 15	San Diego	Pittsburgh	17-13	Pittsburgh	61,545
1995	Jan. 14	Pittsburgh	Indianapolis	20-16	Pittsburgh	61,062
1996	Jan. 12	New England	Jacksonville	20-6	New England	60,190
1997	Jan. 11	Denver	Pittsburgh	24-21	Pittsburgh	61,382
1998	Jan. 17	Denver	N.Y. Jets	23-10	Denver	75,482
1999	Jan. 23	Tennessee	Jacksonville	33-14	Jacksonville	75,206
2000	Jan. 14	Baltimore	Oakland	16-3	Oakland	62,784
2001	Jan. 27	New England	Pittsburgh	24-17	Pittsburgh	64,704
2002	Jan. 19	Oakland	Tennessee	41-24	Oakland	62,544
2003	Jan. 18	New England	Indianapolis	24-14	New England	68,436
2004	Jan. 23	New England	Pittsburgh	41-27	New England	65,242
2005	Jan. 22	Pittsburgh	Denver	34-17	Denver	76,775

*Overtime.

COMPOSITE STANDINGS

Team	W	L	Pct.	PF	PA	Team	W	L	Pct.	PF	PA
Cincinnati Bengals	2	0	1.000	48	17	Tennessee Titans▲	3	5	.375	133	195
Baltimore Ravens	1	0	1.000	16	3	Oakland Raiders§	5	9	.357	272	304
New England Patriots‡	5	1	.833	150	129	New York Jets	1	2	.333	37	60
Buffalo Bills	6	2	.750	180	92	San Diego Chargers*	2	6	.250	128	161
Denver Broncos	6	2	.750	189	166	Indianapolis Colts∞	1	3	.250	57	82
Kansas City Chiefs†	3	1	.750	81	61	Seattle Seahawks	0	1	.000	14	30
Miami Dolphins	5	2	.714	152	115	Jacksonville Jaguars	0	2	.000	20	53
Pittsburgh Steelers	6	7	.462	285	270	Cleveland Browns	0	3	.000	74	98

*One game played when franchise was in Los Angeles; lost 24-16.
†One game played when franchise was in Dallas (Texans); won 20-17.
‡One game played when franchise was in Boston; lost 51-10.
§Two games played when franchise was in Los Angeles; record of 1-1.
∞Two games played when franchise was in Baltimore; record of 1-1.
▲Six games played when franchise was in Houston (Oilers); record of 2-4.

POSTSEASON GAME COMPOSITE STANDINGS

Team	W	L	Pct.	PF	PA	Team	W	L	Pct.	PF	PA
Baltimore Ravens	5	2	.714	142	73	Indianapolis Colts■	13	16	.448	556	602
Carolina Panthers	6	3	.667	206	170	New York Jets	8	10	.444	372	352
Green Bay Packers	24	14	.632	888	723	Jacksonville Jaguars	4	5	.444	211	228
Pittsburgh Steelers	28	18	.609	1066	928	St. Louis Rams†	19	24	.442	770	944
New England Patriots§	17	11	.607	569	542	New York Giants	16	22	.421	647	722
San Francisco 49ers	25	17	.595	1044	853	Minnesota Vikings	18	24	.429	824	957
Dallas Cowboys	32	22	.593	1281	1008	Atlanta Falcons	6	8	.429	298	331
Washington Redskins‡	23	16	.590	805	672	Tampa Bay Buccaneers	6	8	.429	216	255
Oakland Raiders◆	25	18	.581	1028	797	Detroit Lions	7	10	.412	365	404
Denver Broncos	17	15	.531	694	794	Kansas City Chiefs*	8	12	.400	332	422
Miami Dolphins	20	19	.513	780	848	Cincinnati Bengals	5	8	.385	263	288
Philadelphia Eagles	16	16	.500	606	561	Seattle Seahawks	5	8	.385	256	264
Buffalo Bills	14	15	.483	681	658	San Diego Chargers▲	7	12	.368	349	448
Chicago Bears	14	16	.467	619	614	Cleveland Browns	11	20	.355	629	738
Tennessee Titans▼	14	17	.452	563	732	Arizona Cardinals∞	2	5	.286	122	182
						New Orleans Saints	1	5	.167	103	185

*One game played when franchise was in Dallas (Texans); won 20-17.
†One game played when franchise was in Cleveland; won 15-14. 32 games played when franchise was in Los Angeles; record of 12-20.
‡One game played when franchise was in Boston; lost 21-6.
§Two games played when franchise was in Boston; won 26-8, lost 51-10.
∞Two games played when franchise was in Chicago; won 28-21, lost 7-0. Three games played when franchise was in St. Louis; lost 35-23, lost 30-14, lost 41-16.
▲One game played when franchise was in Los Angeles; lost 24-16.
◆12 games played when franchise was in Los Angeles; record of 6-6.
■15 games played when franchise was in Baltimore; record of 8-7.
▼22 games played when franchise was in Houston; record of 9-13.

CHAMPIONS OF DEFUNCT PRO FOOTBALL LEAGUES
ALL-AMERICAN FOOTBALL CONFERENCE

Year	Winner	Coach	Loser	Coach	Score, Site
1946	Cleveland Browns	Paul Brown	N.Y. Yankees	Ray Flaherty	14-9, Cleveland
1947	Cleveland Browns	Paul Brown	N.Y. Yankees	Ray Flaherty	14-3, New York
1948	Cleveland Browns	Paul Brown	Buffalo Bills	Red Dawson	49-7, Cleveland
1949	Cleveland Browns	Paul Brown	S.F. 49ers	Buck Shaw	21-7, Cleveland

NOTE: Cleveland Browns and San Francisco 49ers joined the NFL after the AAFC folded in 1949.

WORLD FOOTBALL LEAGUE

Year	Winner	Coach	Loser	Coach	Score, Site
1974	Birmingham Americans	Jack Gotta	Florida Blazers	Jack Pardee	22-21, Birmingham
1975	League folded October 22				

UNITED STATES FOOTBALL LEAGUE

Year	Winner	Coach	Loser	Coach	Score, Site
1983	Michigan Panthers	Jim Stanley	Philadelphia Stars	Jim Mora	24-22, Denver
1984	Philadelphia Stars	Jim Mora	Arizona Wranglers	George Allen	23-3, Tampa
1985	Baltimore Stars	Jim Mora	Oakland Invaders	Charlie Sumner	28-24, E. Rutherford, N.J.
1986	League folded				

HISTORY Championship games

YEAR-BY-YEAR STANDINGS

1920

Team	W	L	T	Pct.
Akron Pros*	8	0	3	1.000
Decatur Staleys	10	1	2	.909
Buffalo All-Americans	9	1	1	.900
Chicago Cardinals	6	2	2	.750
Rock Island Independents	6	2	2	.750
Dayton Triangles	5	2	2	.714
Rochester Jeffersons	6	3	2	.667
Canton Bulldogs	7	4	2	.636
Detroit Heralds	2	3	3	.400
Cleveland Tigers	2	4	2	.333
Chicago Tigers	2	5	1	.286
Hammond Pros	2	5	0	.286
Columbus Panhandles	2	6	2	.250
Muncie Flyers	0	1	0	.000

*No official standings were maintained for the 1920 season, and the championship was awarded to the Akron Pros in a League meeting on April 30, 1921. Clubs played schedules which included games against non-league opponents. Records of clubs against all opponents are listed above.

1921

Team	W	L	T	Pct.
Chicago Staleys	9	1	1	.900
Buffalo All-Americans	9	1	2	.900
Akron Pros	8	3	1	.727
Canton Bulldogs	5	2	3	.714
Rock Island Independents	4	2	1	.667
Evansville Crimson Giants	3	2	0	.600
Green Bay Packers	3	2	1	.600
Dayton Triangles	4	4	1	.500
Chicago Cardinals	3	3	2	.500
Rochester Jeffersons	2	3	0	.400
Cleveland Indians	3	5	0	.375
Washington Senators	1	2	0	.333
Cincinnati Celts	1	3	0	.250
Hammond Pros	1	3	1	.250
Minneapolis Marines	1	3	0	.250
Detroit Heralds	1	5	1	.167
Columbus Panhandles	1	8	0	.111
Tonawanda Kardex	0	1	0	.000
Muncie Flyers	0	2	0	.000
Louisville Brecks	0	2	0	.000
New York Giants	0	2	0	.000

1922

Team	W	L	T	Pct.
Canton Bulldogs	10	0	2	1.000
Chicago Bears	9	3	0	.750
Chicago Cardinals	8	3	0	.727
Toledo Maroons	5	2	2	.714
Rock Island Independents	4	2	1	.667
Racine Legion	6	4	1	.600
Dayton Triangles	4	3	1	.571
Green Bay Packers	4	3	3	.571
Buffalo All-Americans	5	4	1	.556
Akron Pros	3	5	2	.375
Milwaukee Badgers	2	4	3	.333
Oorang Indians	3	6	0	.333
Minneapolis Marines	1	3	0	.250
Louisville Brecks	1	3	0	.250
Evansville Crimson Giants	0	3	0	.000
Rochester Jeffersons	0	4	1	.000
Hammond Pros	0	5	1	.000
Columbus Panhandles	0	8	0	.000

1923

Team	W	L	T	Pct.
Canton Bulldogs	11	0	1	1.000
Chicago Bears	9	2	1	.818
Green Bay Packers	7	2	1	.778
Milwaukee Badgers	7	2	3	.778
Cleveland Indians	3	1	3	.750
Chicago Cardinals	8	4	0	.667
Duluth Kelleys	4	3	0	.571
Buffalo All-Americans	5	4	3	.556
Columbus Tigers	5	4	1	.556
Racine Legion	4	4	2	.500
Toledo Maroons	3	3	2	.500
Rock Island Independents	2	3	3	.400
Minneapolis Marines	2	5	2	.286
St. Louis All-Stars	1	4	2	.200
Hammond Pros	1	5	1	.167
Dayton Triangles	1	6	1	.143
Akron Indians	1	6	0	.143
Oorang Indians	1	10	0	.091
Louisville Brecks	0	3	0	.000
Rochester Jeffersons	0	4	0	.000

1924

Team	W	L	T	Pct.
Cleveland Bulldogs	7	1	1	.875
Chicago Bears	6	1	4	.857
Frankford Yellow Jackets	11	2	1	.846
Duluth Kelleys	5	1	0	.833
Rock Island Independents	5	2	2	.714
Green Bay Packers	7	4	0	.636
Racine Legion	4	3	3	.571
Chicago Cardinals	5	4	1	.556
Buffalo Bisons	6	5	0	.545
Columbus Tigers	4	4	0	.500
Hammond Pros	2	2	1	.500
Milwaukee Badgers	5	8	0	.385
Akron Indians	2	6	0	.250
Dayton Triangles	2	6	0	.250
Kansas City Blues	2	7	0	.222
Kenosha Maroons	0	4	1	.000
Minneapolis Marines	0	6	0	.000
Rochester Jeffersons	0	7	0	.000

1925

Team	W	L	T	Pct.
Chicago Cardinals	11	2	1	.846
Pottsville Maroons	10	2	0	.833
Detroit Panthers	8	2	2	.800
New York Giants	8	4	0	.667
Akron Indians	4	2	2	.667
Frankford Yellow Jackets	13	7	0	.650
Chicago Bears	9	5	3	.643
Rock Island Independents	5	3	3	.625
Green Bay Packers	8	5	0	.615
Providence Steam Roller	6	5	1	.545
Canton Bulldogs	4	4	0	.500
Cleveland Bulldogs	5	8	1	.385
Kansas City Cowboys	2	5	1	.286
Hammond Pros	1	4	0	.200
Buffalo Bisons	1	6	2	.143
Duluth Kelleys	0	3	0	.000
Rochester Jeffersons	0	6	1	.000
Milwaukee Badgers	0	6	0	.000
Dayton Triangles	0	7	1	.000
Columbus Tigers	0	9	0	.000

1926

Team	W	L	T	Pct.
Frankford Yellow Jackets	14	1	2	.933
Chicago Bears	12	1	3	.923
Pottsville Maroons	10	2	2	.833
Kansas City Cowboys	8	3	0	.727
Green Bay Packers	7	3	3	.700
Los Angeles Buccaneers	6	3	1	.667
New York Giants	8	4	1	.667
Duluth Eskimos	6	5	3	.545
Buffalo Rangers	4	4	2	.500
Chicago Cardinals	5	6	1	.455
Providence Steam Roller	5	7	1	.417
Detroit Panthers	4	6	2	.400
Hartford Blues	3	7	0	.300
Brooklyn Lions	3	8	0	.273
Milwaukee Badgers	2	7	0	.222
Akron Pros	1	4	3	.200
Dayton Triangles	1	4	1	.200
Racine Tornadoes	1	4	0	.200
Columbus Tigers	1	6	0	.143
Canton Bulldogs	1	9	3	.100
Hammond Pros	0	4	0	.000
Louisville Colonels	0	4	0	.000

1927

Team	W	L	T	Pct.
New York Giants	11	1	1	.917
Green Bay Packers	7	2	1	.778
Chicago Bears	9	3	2	.750
Cleveland Bulldogs	8	4	1	.667
Providence Steam Roller	8	5	1	.615
New York Yankees	7	8	1	.467
Frankford Yellow Jackets	6	9	3	.400
Pottsville Maroons	5	8	0	.385
Chicago Cardinals	3	7	1	.300
Dayton Triangles	1	6	1	.143
Duluth Eskimos	1	8	0	.111
Buffalo Bisons	0	5	0	.000

1928

Team	W	L	T	Pct.
Providence Steam Roller	8	1	2	.889
Frankford Yellow Jackets	11	3	2	.786
Detroit Wolverines	7	2	1	.778
Green Bay Packers	6	4	3	.600
Chicago Bears	7	5	1	.583
New York Giants	4	7	2	.364
New York Yankees	4	8	1	.333
Pottsville Maroons	2	8	0	.200
Chicago Cardinals	1	5	0	.167
Dayton Triangles	0	7	0	.000

1929

Team	W	L	T	Pct.
Green Bay Packers	12	0	1	1.000
New York Giants	13	1	1	.929
Frankford Yellow Jackets	10	4	5	.714
Chicago Cardinals	6	6	1	.500
Boston Bulldogs	4	4	0	.500
Staten Island Stapletons	3	4	3	.429
Providence Steam Roller	4	6	2	.400
Orange Tornadoes	3	5	4	.375
Chicago Bears	4	9	2	.308
Buffalo Bisons	1	7	1	.125
Minneapolis Red Jackets	1	9	0	.100
Dayton Triangles	0	6	0	.000

1930

Team	W	L	T	Pct.
Green Bay Packers	10	3	1	.769
New York Giants	13	4	0	.765
Chicago Bears	9	4	1	.692
Brooklyn Dodgers	7	4	1	.636
Providence Steam Roller	6	4	1	.600
Staten Island Stapletons	5	5	2	.500
Chicago Cardinals	5	6	2	.455
Portsmouth Spartans	5	6	3	.455
Frankford Yellow Jackets	4	13	1	.222
Minneapolis Red Jackets	1	7	1	.125
Newark Tornadoes	1	10	1	.091

1931

Team	W	L	T	Pct.
Green Bay Packers	12	2	0	.857
Portsmouth Spartans	11	3	0	.786
Chicago Bears	8	5	0	.615
Chicago Cardinals	5	4	0	.556
New York Giants	7	6	1	.538
Providence Steam Roller	4	4	3	.500
Staten Island Stapletons	4	6	1	.400
Cleveland Indians	2	8	0	.200
Brooklyn Dodgers	2	12	0	.143
Frankford Yellow Jackets	1	6	1	.143

1932

Team	W	L	T	Pct.
Chicago Bears	7	1	6	.875
Green Bay Packers	10	3	1	.769
Portsmouth Spartans	6	2	4	.750
Boston Braves	4	4	2	.500
New York Giants	4	6	2	.400
Brooklyn Dodgers	3	9	0	.250
Chicago Cardinals	2	6	2	.250
Staten Island Stapletons	2	7	3	.222

NOTE: Chicago Bears and Portsmouth finished regularly scheduled games tied for first place. Bears won playoff game, which counted in standings, 9-0.

1933

EASTERN DIVISION

Team	W	L	T	Pct.	PF	PA
N.Y. Giants	11	3	0	.786	244	101
Brooklyn	5	4	1	.556	93	54
Boston	5	5	2	.500	103	97
Philadelphia	3	5	1	.375	77	158
Pittsburgh	3	6	2	.333	67	208

WESTERN DIVISION

Team	W	L	T	Pct.	PF	PA
Chicago Bears	10	2	1	.833	133	82
Portsmouth	6	5	0	.545	128	87
Green Bay	5	7	1	.417	170	107
Cincinnati	3	6	1	.333	38	110
Chi. Cardinals	1	9	1	.100	52	101

PLAYOFFS

NFL championship
Chicago Bears 23 vs. N.Y. Giants 21

1934

EASTERN DIVISION						
Team	W	L	T	Pct.	PF	PA
N.Y. Giants	8	5	0	.615	147	107
Boston	6	6	0	.500	107	94
Brooklyn	4	7	0	.364	61	153
Philadelphia	4	7	0	.364	127	85
Pittsburgh	2	10	0	.167	51	206

WESTERN DIVISION						
Team	W	L	T	Pct.	PF	PA
Chicago Bears	13	0	0	1.000	286	86
Detroit	10	3	0	.769	238	59
Green Bay	7	6	0	.538	156	112
Chi. Cardinals	5	6	0	.455	80	84
St. Louis	1	2	0	.333	27	61
Cincinnati	0	8	0	.000	10	243

PLAYOFFS

NFL championship
N.Y. Giants 30 vs. Chicago Bears 13

1935

EASTERN DIVISION						
Team	W	L	T	Pct.	PF	PA
N.Y. Giants	9	3	0	.750	180	96
Brooklyn	5	6	1	.455	90	141
Pittsburgh	4	8	0	.333	100	209
Boston	2	8	1	.200	65	123
Philadelphia	2	9	0	.182	60	179

WESTERN DIVISION						
Team	W	L	T	Pct.	PF	PA
Detroit	7	3	2	.700	191	111
Green Bay	8	4	0	.667	181	96
Chicago Bears	6	4	2	.600	192	106
Chi. Cardinals	6	4	2	.600	99	97

PLAYOFFS

NFL championship
Detroit 26 vs. N.Y. Giants 7

NOTE: One game between Boston and Philadelphia was cancelled.

1936

EASTERN DIVISION						
Team	W	L	T	Pct.	PF	PA
Boston	7	5	0	.583	149	110
Pittsburgh	6	6	0	.500	98	187
N.Y. Giants	5	6	1	.455	115	163
Brooklyn	3	8	1	.273	92	161
Philadelphia	1	11	0	.083	51	206

WESTERN DIVISION						
Team	W	L	T	Pct.	PF	PA
Green Bay	10	1	1	.909	248	118
Chicago Bears	9	3	0	.750	222	94
Detroit	8	4	0	.667	235	102
Chi. Cardinals	3	8	1	.273	74	143

PLAYOFFS

NFL championship
Green Bay 21, Boston 6, at New York.

1937

EASTERN DIVISION						
Team	W	L	T	Pct.	PF	PA
Washington	8	3	0	.727	195	120
N.Y. Giants	6	3	2	.667	128	109
Pittsburgh	4	7	0	.364	122	145
Brooklyn	3	7	1	.300	82	174
Philadelphia	2	8	1	.200	86	177

WESTERN DIVISION						
Team	W	L	T	Pct.	PF	PA
Chicago Bears	9	1	1	.900	201	100
Green Bay	7	4	0	.636	220	122
Detroit	7	4	0	.636	180	105
Chi. Cardinals	5	5	1	.500	135	165
Cleveland	1	10	0	.091	75	207

PLAYOFFS

NFL championship
Washington 28 at Chicago Bears 21

1938

EASTERN DIVISION						
Team	W	L	T	Pct.	PF	PA
N.Y. Giants	8	2	1	.800	194	79
Washington	6	3	2	.667	148	154
Brooklyn	4	4	3	.500	131	161
Philadelphia	5	6	0	.455	154	164
Pittsburgh	2	9	0	.182	79	169

WESTERN DIVISION						
Team	W	L	T	Pct.	PF	PA
Green Bay	8	3	0	.727	223	118
Detroit	7	4	0	.636	119	108
Chicago Bears	6	5	0	.545	194	148
Cleveland	4	7	0	.364	131	215
Chi. Cardinals	2	9	0	.182	111	168

PLAYOFFS

NFL championship
N.Y. Giants 23 vs. Green Bay 17

1939

EASTERN DIVISION						
Team	W	L	T	Pct.	PF	PA
N.Y. Giants	9	1	1	.900	168	85
Washington	8	2	1	.800	242	94
Brooklyn	4	6	1	.400	108	219
Philadelphia	1	9	1	.100	105	200
Pittsburgh	1	9	1	.100	114	216

WESTERN DIVISION						
Team	W	L	T	Pct.	PF	PA
Green Bay	9	2	0	.818	233	153
Chicago Bears	8	3	0	.727	298	157
Detroit	6	5	0	.545	145	150
Cleveland	5	5	1	.500	195	164
Chi. Cardinals	1	10	0	.091	84	254

PLAYOFFS

NFL championship
Green Bay 27 vs. N.Y. Giants 0

1940

EASTERN DIVISION						
Team	W	L	T	Pct.	PF	PA
Washington	9	2	0	.818	245	142
Brooklyn	8	3	0	.727	186	120
N.Y. Giants	6	4	1	.600	131	133
Pittsburgh	2	7	2	.222	60	178
Philadelphia	1	10	0	.091	111	211

WESTERN DIVISION						
Team	W	L	T	Pct.	PF	PA
Chicago Bears	8	3	0	.727	238	152
Green Bay	6	4	1	.600	238	155
Detroit	5	5	1	.500	138	153
Cleveland	4	6	1	.400	171	191
Chi. Cardinals	2	7	2	.222	139	222

PLAYOFFS

NFL championship
Chicago Bears 73 at Washington 0

1941

EASTERN DIVISION

Team	W	L	T	Pct.	PF	PA
N.Y. Giants	8	3	0	.727	238	114
Brooklyn	7	4	0	.636	158	127
Washington	6	5	0	.545	176	174
Philadelphia	2	8	1	.200	119	218
Pittsburgh	1	9	1	.100	103	276

WESTERN DIVISION

Team	W	L	T	Pct.	PF	PA
Chicago Bears	10	1	0	.909	396	147
Green Bay	10	1	0	.909	258	120
Detroit	4	6	1	.400	121	195
Chi. Cardinals	3	7	1	.300	127	197
Cleveland	2	9	0	.182	116	244

PLAYOFFS

Western Division playoff
Chicago Bears 33 vs. Green Bay 14

NFL championship
Chicago Bears 37 vs. N.Y. Giants 9

1942

EASTERN DIVISION

Team	W	L	T	Pct.	PF	PA
Washington	10	1	0	.909	227	102
Pittsburgh	7	4	0	.636	167	119
N.Y. Giants	5	5	1	.500	155	139
Brooklyn	3	8	0	.273	100	168
Philadelphia	2	9	0	.182	134	239

WESTERN DIVISION

Team	W	L	T	Pct.	PF	PA
Chicago Bears	11	0	0	1.000	376	84
Green Bay	8	2	1	.800	300	215
Cleveland	5	6	0	.455	150	207
Chi. Cardinals	3	8	0	.273	98	209
Detroit	0	11	0	.000	38	263

PLAYOFFS

NFL championship
Washington 14 vs. Chicago Bears 6

1943

EASTERN DIVISION

Team	W	L	T	Pct.	PF	PA
Washington	6	3	1	.667	229	137
N.Y. Giants	6	3	1	.667	197	170
Phil.-Pitt.	5	4	1	.556	225	230
Brooklyn	2	8	0	.200	65	234

NOTE: Cleveland Rams did not play in 1943.

WESTERN DIVISION

Team	W	L	T	Pct.	PF	PA
Chicago Bears	8	1	1	.889	303	157
Green Bay	7	2	1	.778	264	172
Detroit	3	6	1	.333	178	218
Chi. Cardinals	0	10	0	.000	95	238

PLAYOFFS

Eastern Division playoff
Washington 28 at N.Y. Giants 0

NFL championship
Chicago Bears 41 vs. Washington 21

1944

EASTERN DIVISION

Team	W	L	T	Pct.	PF	PA
N.Y. Giants	8	1	1	.889	206	75
Philadelphia	7	1	2	.875	267	131
Washington	6	3	1	.667	169	180
Boston	2	8	0	.200	82	233
Brooklyn	0	10	0	.000	69	166

WESTERN DIVISION

Team	W	L	T	Pct.	PF	PA
Green Bay	8	2	0	.800	238	141
Chicago Bears	6	3	1	.667	258	172
Detroit	6	3	1	.667	216	151
Cleveland	4	6	0	.400	188	224
Card-Pitt	0	10	0	.000	108	328

PLAYOFFS

NFL championship
Green Bay 14 at N.Y. Giants 7

1945

EASTERN DIVISION

Team	W	L	T	Pct.	PF	PA
Washington	8	2	0	.800	209	121
Philadelphia	7	3	0	.700	272	133
N.Y. Giants	3	6	1	.333	179	198
Boston	3	6	1	.333	123	211
Pittsburgh	2	8	0	.200	79	220

WESTERN DIVISION

Team	W	L	T	Pct.	PF	PA
Cleveland	9	1	0	.900	244	136
Detroit	7	3	0	.700	195	194
Green Bay	6	4	0	.600	258	173
Chicago Bears	3	7	0	.300	192	235
Chi. Cardinals	1	9	0	.100	98	228

PLAYOFFS

NFL championship
Cleveland 15 vs. Washington 14

1946

AAFC

EASTERN DIVISION

Team	W	L	T	Pct.	PF	PA
New York	10	3	1	.769	270	192
Brooklyn	3	10	1	.231	226	339
Buffalo	3	10	1	.231	249	370
Miami	3	11	0	.214	167	378

WESTERN DIVISION

Team	W	L	T	Pct.	PF	PA
Cleveland	12	2	0	.857	423	137
San Francisco	9	5	0	.643	307	189
Los Angeles	7	5	2	.583	305	290
Chicago	5	6	3	.455	263	315

PLAYOFFS

AAFC championship
Cleveland 14 vs. New York 9

NFL

EASTERN DIVISION

Team	W	L	T	Pct.	PF	PA
N.Y. Giants	7	3	1	.700	236	162
Philadelphia	6	5	0	.545	231	220
Washington	5	5	1	.500	171	191
Pittsburgh	5	5	1	.500	136	117
Boston	2	8	1	.200	189	273

WESTERN DIVISION

Team	W	L	T	Pct.	PF	PA
Chicago Bears	8	2	1	.800	289	193
Los Angeles	6	4	1	.600	277	257
Green Bay	6	5	0	.545	148	158
Chi. Cardinals	6	5	0	.545	260	198
Detroit	1	10	0	.091	142	310

PLAYOFFS

NFL championship
Chicago Bears 24 at N.Y. Giants 14

1947

AAFC

EASTERN DIVISION

Team	W	L	T	Pct.	PF	PA
New York	11	2	1	.846	378	239
Buffalo	8	4	2	.667	320	288
Brooklyn	3	10	1	.231	181	340
Baltimore	2	11	1	.154	167	377

WESTERN DIVISION

Team	W	L	T	Pct.	PF	PA
Cleveland	12	1	1	.923	410	185
San Francisco	8	4	2	.667	327	264
Los Angeles	7	7	0	.500	328	256
Chicago	1	13	0	.071	263	425

PLAYOFFS

AAFC championship
Cleveland 14 at New York 3

NFL

EASTERN DIVISION

Team	W	L	T	Pct.	PF	PA
Philadelphia	8	4	0	.667	308	242
Pittsburgh	8	4	0	.667	240	259
Boston	4	7	1	.364	168	256
Washington	4	8	0	.333	295	367
N.Y. Giants	2	8	2	.200	190	309

WESTERN DIVISION

Team	W	L	T	Pct.	PF	PA
Chi. Cardinals	9	3	0	.750	306	231
Chicago Bears	8	4	0	.667	363	241
Green Bay	6	5	1	.545	274	210
Los Angeles	6	6	0	.500	259	214
Detroit	3	9	0	.250	231	305

PLAYOFFS

Eastern Division playoff
Philadelphia 21 at Pittsburgh 0

NFL championship
Chicago Cardinals 28 vs. Philadelphia 21

1948

AAFC

EASTERN DIVISION

Team	W	L	T	Pct.	PF	PA
Buffalo	7	7	0	.500	360	358
Baltimore	7	7	0	.500	333	327
New York	6	8	0	.429	265	301
Brooklyn	2	12	0	.143	253	387

WESTERN DIVISION

Team	W	L	T	Pct.	PF	PA
Cleveland	14	0	0	1.000	389	190
San Francisco	12	2	0	.857	495	248
Los Angeles	7	7	0	.500	258	305
Chicago	1	13	0	.071	202	439

PLAYOFFS

Eastern Division playoff
Buffalo 28 vs. Baltimore 17

AAFC championship
Cleveland 49 vs. Buffalo 7

NFL

EASTERN DIVISION

Team	W	L	T	Pct.	PF	PA
Philadelphia	9	2	1	.818	376	156
Washington	7	5	0	.583	291	287
N.Y. Giants	4	8	0	.333	297	388
Pittsburgh	4	8	0	.333	200	243
Boston	3	9	0	.250	174	372

WESTERN DIVISION

Team	W	L	T	Pct.	PF	PA
Chi. Cardinals	11	1	0	.917	395	226
Chicago Bears	10	2	0	.833	375	151
Los Angeles	6	5	1	.545	327	269
Green Bay	3	9	0	.250	154	290
Detroit	2	10	0	.167	200	407

PLAYOFFS

NFL championship
Philadelphia 7 vs. Chicago Cardinals 0

1949

AAFC

Team	W	L	T	Pct.	PF	PA
Cleveland	9	1	2	.900	339	171
San Francisco	9	3	0	.750	416	227
Brooklyn-N.Y.	8	4	0	.667	196	206
Buffalo	5	5	2	.500	236	256
Chicago	4	8	0	.333	179	268
Los Angeles	4	8	0	.333	253	322
Baltimore	1	11	0	.083	172	341

PLAYOFFS

AAFC Semifinals
Cleveland 31 vs. Buffalo 21
San Francisco 17 vs. Brooklyn-N.Y. 7

AAFC championship
Cleveland 21 vs. San Francisco 7

NFL

EASTERN DIVISION

Team	W	L	T	Pct.	PF	PA
Philadelphia	11	1	0	.917	364	134
Pittsburgh	6	5	1	.545	224	214
N.Y. Giants	6	6	0	.500	287	298
Washington	4	7	1	.364	268	339
N.Y. Bulldogs	1	10	1	.091	153	368

WESTERN DIVISION

Team	W	L	T	Pct.	PF	PA
Los Angeles	8	2	2	.800	360	239
Chicago Bears	9	3	0	.750	332	218
Chi. Cardinals	6	5	1	.545	360	301
Detroit	4	8	0	.333	237	259
Green Bay	2	10	0	.167	114	329

PLAYOFFS

NFL championship
Philadelphia 14 at Los Angeles 0

1950

AMERICAN CONFERENCE

Team	W	L	T	Pct.	PF	PA
Cleveland	10	2	0	.833	310	144
N.Y. Giants	10	2	0	.833	268	150
Philadelphia	6	6	0	.500	254	141
Pittsburgh	6	6	0	.500	180	195
Chi. Cardinals	5	7	0	.417	233	287
Washington	3	9	0	.250	232	326

NATIONAL CONFERENCE

Team	W	L	T	Pct.	PF	PA
Los Angeles	9	3	0	.750	466	309
Chicago Bears	9	3	0	.750	279	207
N.Y. Yanks	7	5	0	.583	366	367
Detroit	6	6	0	.500	321	285
Green Bay	3	9	0	.250	244	406
San Francisco	3	9	0	.250	213	300
Baltimore	1	11	0	.083	213	462

PLAYOFFS

American Conference playoff
Cleveland 8 vs. N.Y. Giants 3

National Conference playoff
Los Angeles 24 vs. Chicago Bears 14

NFL championship
Cleveland 30 vs. Los Angeles 28

AMERICAN CONFERENCE

Team	W	L	T	Pct.	PF	PA
Cleveland	11	1	0	.917	331	152
N.Y. Giants	9	2	1	.818	254	161
Washington	5	7	0	.417	183	296
Pittsburgh	4	7	1	.364	183	235
Philadelphia	4	8	0	.333	234	264
Chi. Cardinals	3	9	0	.250	210	287

NATIONAL CONFERENCE

Team	W	L	T	Pct.	PF	PA
Los Angeles	8	4	0	.667	392	261
Detroit	7	4	1	.636	336	259
San Francisco	7	4	1	.636	255	205
Chicago Bears	7	5	0	.583	286	282
Green Bay	3	9	0	.250	254	375
N.Y. Yanks	1	9	2	.100	241	382

PLAYOFFS

NFL championship
Los Angeles 24 vs. Cleveland 17

AMERICAN CONFERENCE

Team	W	L	T	Pct.	PF	PA
Cleveland	8	4	0	.667	310	213
N.Y. Giants	7	5	0	.583	234	231
Philadelphia	7	5	0	.583	252	271
Pittsburgh	5	7	0	.417	300	273
Chi. Cardinals	4	8	0	.333	172	221
Washington	4	8	0	.333	240	287

NATIONAL CONFERENCE

Team	W	L	T	Pct.	PF	PA
Detroit	9	3	0	.750	344	192
Los Angeles	9	3	0	.750	349	234
San Francisco	7	5	0	.583	285	221
Green Bay	6	6	0	.500	295	312
Chicago Bears	5	7	0	.417	245	326
Dallas Texans	1	11	0	.083	182	427

PLAYOFFS

National Conference playoff
Detroit 31 vs. Los Angeles 21

NFL championship
Detroit 17 at Cleveland 7

EASTERN CONFERENCE

Team	W	L	T	Pct.	PF	PA
Cleveland	11	1	0	.917	348	162
Philadelphia	7	4	1	.636	352	215
Washington	6	5	1	.545	208	215
Pittsburgh	6	6	0	.500	211	263
N.Y. Giants	3	9	0	.250	179	277
Chi. Cardinals	1	10	1	.091	190	337

WESTERN CONFERENCE

Team	W	L	T	Pct.	PF	PA
Detroit	10	2	0	.833	271	205
San Francisco	9	3	0	.750	372	237
Los Angeles	8	3	1	.727	366	236
Chicago Bears	3	8	1	.273	218	262
Baltimore	3	9	0	.250	182	350
Green Bay	2	9	1	.182	200	338

PLAYOFFS

NFL championship
Detroit 17 vs. Cleveland 16

EASTERN CONFERENCE

Team	W	L	T	Pct.	PF	PA
Cleveland	9	3	0	.750	336	162
Philadelphia	7	4	1	.636	284	230
N.Y. Giants	7	5	0	.583	293	184
Pittsburgh	5	7	0	.417	219	263
Washington	3	9	0	.250	207	432
Chi. Cardinals	2	10	0	.167	183	347

WESTERN CONFERENCE

Team	W	L	T	Pct.	PF	PA
Detroit	9	2	1	.818	337	189
Chicago Bears	8	4	0	.667	301	279
San Francisco	7	4	1	.636	313	251
Los Angeles	6	5	1	.545	314	285
Green Bay	4	8	0	.333	234	251
Baltimore	3	9	0	.250	131	279

PLAYOFFS

NFL championship
Cleveland 56 vs. Detroit 10

EASTERN CONFERENCE

Team	W	L	T	Pct.	PF	PA
Cleveland	9	2	1	.818	349	218
Washington	8	4	0	.667	246	222
N.Y. Giants	6	5	1	.545	267	223
Chi. Cardinals	4	7	1	.364	224	252
Philadelphia	4	7	1	.364	248	231
Pittsburgh	4	8	0	.333	195	285

WESTERN CONFERENCE

Team	W	L	T	Pct.	PF	PA
Los Angeles	8	3	1	.727	260	231
Chicago Bears	8	4	0	.667	294	251
Green Bay	6	6	0	.500	258	276
Baltimore	5	6	1	.455	214	239
San Francisco	4	8	0	.333	216	298
Detroit	3	9	0	.250	230	275

PLAYOFFS

NFL championship
Cleveland 38 at Los Angeles 14

EASTERN CONFERENCE

Team	W	L	T	Pct.	PF	PA
N.Y. Giants	8	3	1	.727	264	197
Chi. Cardinals	7	5	0	.583	240	182
Washington	6	6	0	.500	183	225
Cleveland	5	7	0	.417	167	177
Pittsburgh	5	7	0	.417	217	250
Philadelphia	3	8	1	.273	143	215

WESTERN CONFERENCE

Team	W	L	T	Pct.	PF	PA
Chicago Bears	9	2	1	.818	363	246
Detroit	9	3	0	.750	300	188
San Francisco	5	6	1	.455	233	284
Baltimore	5	7	0	.417	270	322
Green Bay	4	8	0	.333	264	342
Los Angeles	4	8	0	.333	291	307

PLAYOFFS

NFL championship
N.Y. Giants 47 vs. Chicago Bears 7

HISTORY Year-by-year standings

EASTERN CONFERENCE

Team	W	L	T	Pct.	PF	PA
Cleveland	9	2	1	.818	269	172
N.Y. Giants	7	5	0	.583	254	211
Pittsburgh	6	6	0	.500	161	178
Washington	5	6	1	.455	251	230
Philadelphia	4	8	0	.333	173	230
Chi. Cardinals	3	9	0	.250	200	299

WESTERN CONFERENCE

Team	W	L	T	Pct.	PF	PA
Detroit	8	4	0	.667	251	231
San Francisco	8	4	0	.667	260	264
Baltimore	7	5	0	.583	303	235
Los Angeles	6	6	0	.500	307	278
Chicago Bears	5	7	0	.417	203	211
Green Bay	3	9	0	.250	218	311

PLAYOFFS

Western Conference playoff
Detroit 31 at San Francisco 27

NFL championship
Detroit 59 vs. Cleveland 14

EASTERN CONFERENCE

Team	W	L	T	Pct.	PF	PA
N.Y. Giants	9	3	0	.750	246	183
Cleveland	9	3	0	.750	302	217
Pittsburgh	7	4	1	.636	261	230
Washington	4	7	1	.364	214	268
Chi. Cardinals	2	9	1	.182	261	356
Philadelphia	2	9	1	.182	235	306

WESTERN CONFERENCE

Team	W	L	T	Pct.	PF	PA
Baltimore	9	3	0	.750	381	203
Chicago Bears	8	4	0	.667	298	230
Los Angeles	8	4	0	.667	344	278
San Francisco	6	6	0	.500	257	324
Detroit	4	7	1	.364	261	276
Green Bay	1	10	1	.091	193	382

PLAYOFFS

Eastern Conference playoff
N.Y. Giants 10 vs. Cleveland 0

NFL championship
Baltimore 23 at N.Y. Giants 17 (OT)

EASTERN CONFERENCE

Team	W	L	T	Pct.	PF	PA
N.Y. Giants	10	2	0	.833	284	170
Cleveland	7	5	0	.583	270	214
Philadelphia	7	5	0	.583	268	278
Pittsburgh	6	5	1	.545	257	216
Washington	3	9	0	.250	185	350
Chi. Cardinals	2	10	0	.167	234	324

WESTERN CONFERENCE

Team	W	L	T	Pct.	PF	PA
Baltimore	9	3	0	.750	374	251
Chicago Bears	8	4	0	.667	252	196
Green Bay	7	5	0	.583	248	246
San Francisco	7	5	0	.583	255	237
Detroit	3	8	1	.273	203	275
Los Angeles	2	10	0	.167	242	315

PLAYOFFS

NFL championship
Baltimore 31 vs. N.Y. Giants 16

EASTERN DIVISION

Team	W	L	T	Pct.	PF	PA
Houston	10	4	0	.714	379	285
N.Y. Titans	7	7	0	.500	382	399
Buffalo	5	8	1	.385	296	303
Boston Patriots	5	9	0	.357	286	349

WESTERN DIVISION

Team	W	L	T	Pct.	PF	PA
L.A. Chargers	10	4	0	.714	373	336
Dallas Texans	8	6	0	.571	362	253
Oakland	6	8	0	.429	319	388
Denver	4	9	1	.308	309	393

PLAYOFFS

AFL championship
Houston 24 vs. L.A. Chargers 16

NFL

EASTERN CONFERENCE

Team	W	L	T	Pct.	PF	PA
Philadelphia	10	2	0	.833	321	246
Cleveland	8	3	1	.727	362	217
N.Y. Giants	6	4	2	.600	271	261
St. Louis	6	5	1	.545	288	230
Pittsburgh	5	6	1	.455	240	275
Washington	1	9	2	.100	178	309

WESTERN CONFERENCE

Team	W	L	T	Pct.	PF	PA
Green Bay	8	4	0	.667	332	209
Detroit	7	5	0	.583	239	212
San Francisco	7	5	0	.583	208	205
Baltimore	6	6	0	.500	288	234
Chicago	5	6	1	.455	194	299
L.A. Rams	4	7	1	.364	265	297
Dallas Cowboys	0	11	1	.000	177	369

PLAYOFFS

NFL championship
Philadelphia 17 vs. Green Bay 13

EASTERN DIVISION

Team	W	L	T	Pct.	PF	PA
Houston	10	3	1	.769	513	242
Boston Patriots	9	4	1	.692	413	313
N.Y. Titans	7	7	0	.500	301	390
Buffalo	6	8	0	.429	294	342

WESTERN DIVISION

Team	W	L	T	Pct.	PF	PA
San Diego	12	2	0	.857	396	219
Dallas Texans	6	8	0	.429	334	343
Denver	3	11	0	.214	251	432
Oakland	2	12	0	.143	237	458

PLAYOFFS

AFL championship
Houston 10 at San Diego 3

HISTORY *Year-by-year standings*

NFL

EASTERN CONFERENCE

Team	W	L	T	Pct.	PF	PA
N.Y. Giants	10	3	1	.769	368	220
Philadelphia	10	4	0	.714	361	297
Cleveland	8	5	1	.615	319	270
St. Louis	7	7	0	.500	279	267
Pittsburgh	6	8	0	.429	295	287
Dallas Cowboys	4	9	1	.308	236	380
Washington	1	12	1	.077	174	392

WESTERN CONFERENCE

Team	W	L	T	Pct.	PF	PA
Green Bay	11	3	0	.786	391	223
Detroit	8	5	1	.615	270	258
Baltimore	8	6	0	.571	302	307
Chicago	8	6	0	.571	326	302
San Francisco	7	6	1	.538	346	272
Los Angeles	4	10	0	.286	263	333
Minnesota	3	11	0	.214	285	407

PLAYOFFS

NFL championship
Green Bay 37 vs. N.Y. Giants 0

1962

AFL

EASTERN DIVISION

Team	W	L	T	Pct.	PF	PA
Houston	11	3	0	.786	387	270
Boston Patriots	9	4	1	.692	346	295
Buffalo	7	6	1	.538	309	272
N.Y. Titans	5	9	0	.357	278	423

WESTERN DIVISION

Team	W	L	T	Pct.	PF	PA
Dallas Texans	11	3	0	.786	389	233
Denver	7	7	0	.500	353	334
San Diego	4	10	0	.286	314	392
Oakland	1	13	0	.071	213	370

PLAYOFFS

AFL championship
Dallas Texans 20 at Houston 17 (OT)

NFL

EASTERN CONFERENCE

Team	W	L	T	Pct.	PF	PA
N.Y. Giants	12	2	0	.857	398	283
Pittsburgh	9	5	0	.643	312	363
Cleveland	7	6	1	.538	291	257
Washington	5	7	2	.417	305	376
Dallas Cowboys	5	8	1	.385	398	402
St. Louis	4	9	1	.308	287	361
Philadelphia	3	10	1	.231	282	356

WESTERN CONFERENCE

Team	W	L	T	Pct.	PF	PA
Green Bay	13	1	0	.929	415	148
Detroit	11	3	0	.786	315	177
Chicago	9	5	0	.643	321	287
Baltimore	7	7	0	.500	293	288
San Francisco	6	8	0	.429	282	331
Minnesota	2	11	1	.154	254	410
Los Angeles	1	12	1	.077	220	334

PLAYOFFS

NFL championship
Green Bay 16 at N.Y. Giants 7

1963

AFL

EASTERN DIVISION

Team	W	L	T	Pct.	PF	PA
Boston Patriots	7	6	1	.538	327	257
Buffalo	7	6	1	.538	304	291
Houston	6	8	0	.429	302	372
N.Y. Jets	5	8	1	.385	249	399

WESTERN DIVISION

Team	W	L	T	Pct.	PF	PA
San Diego	11	3	0	.786	399	256
Oakland	10	4	0	.714	363	288
Kansas City	5	7	2	.417	347	263
Denver	2	11	1	.154	301	473

PLAYOFFS

Eastern Division playoff
Boston 26 at Buffalo 8

AFL championship
San Diego 51 vs. Boston 10

NFL

EASTERN CONFERENCE

Team	W	L	T	Pct.	PF	PA
N.Y. Giants	11	3	0	.786	448	280
Cleveland	10	4	0	.714	343	262
St. Louis	9	5	0	.643	341	283
Pittsburgh	7	4	3	.636	321	295
Dallas	4	10	0	.286	305	378
Washington	3	11	0	.214	279	398
Philadelphia	2	10	2	.167	242	381

WESTERN CONFERENCE

Team	W	L	T	Pct.	PF	PA
Chicago	11	1	2	.917	301	144
Green Bay	11	2	1	.846	369	206
Baltimore	8	6	0	.571	316	285
Detroit	5	8	1	.385	326	265
Minnesota	5	8	1	.385	309	390
Los Angeles	5	9	0	.357	210	350
San Francisco	2	12	0	.143	198	391

PLAYOFFS

NFL championship
Chicago 14 vs. N.Y. Giants 10

1964

AFL

EASTERN DIVISION

Team	W	L	T	Pct.	PF	PA
Buffalo	12	2	0	.857	400	242
Boston Patriots	10	3	1	.769	365	297
N.Y. Jets	5	8	1	.385	278	315
Houston	4	10	0	.286	310	355

WESTERN DIVISION

Team	W	L	T	Pct.	PF	PA
San Diego	8	5	1	.615	341	300
Kansas City	7	7	0	.500	366	306
Oakland	5	7	2	.417	303	350
Denver	2	11	1	.154	240	438

PLAYOFFS

AFL championship
Buffalo 20 vs. San Diego 7

NFL

EASTERN CONFERENCE

Team	W	L	T	Pct.	PF	PA
Cleveland	10	3	1	.769	415	293
St. Louis	9	3	2	.750	357	331
Philadelphia	6	8	0	.429	312	313
Washington	6	8	0	.429	307	305
Dallas	5	8	1	.385	250	289
Pittsburgh	5	9	0	.357	253	315
N.Y. Giants	2	10	2	.167	241	399

WESTERN CONFERENCE

Team	W	L	T	Pct.	PF	PA
Baltimore	12	2	0	.857	428	225
Green Bay	8	5	1	.615	342	245
Minnesota	8	5	1	.615	355	296
Detroit	7	5	2	.583	280	260
Los Angeles	5	7	2	.417	283	339
Chicago	5	9	0	.357	260	379
San Francisco	4	10	0	.286	236	330

PLAYOFFS

NFL championship
Cleveland 27 vs. Baltimore 0

1965

AFL

EASTERN DIVISION

Team	W	L	T	Pct.	PF	PA
Buffalo	10	3	1	.769	313	226
N.Y. Jets	5	8	1	.385	285	303
Boston Patriots	4	8	2	.333	244	302
Houston	4	10	0	.286	298	429

WESTERN DIVISION

Team	W	L	T	Pct.	PF	PA
San Diego	9	2	3	.818	340	227
Oakland	8	5	1	.615	298	239
Kansas City	7	5	2	.583	322	285
Denver	4	10	0	.286	303	392

PLAYOFFS

AFL championship
Buffalo 23 at San Diego 0

NFL

EASTERN CONFERENCE

Team	W	L	T	Pct.	PF	PA
Cleveland	11	3	0	.786	363	325
Dallas	7	7	0	.500	325	280
N.Y. Giants	7	7	0	.500	270	338
Washington	6	8	0	.429	257	301
Philadelphia	5	9	0	.357	363	359
St. Louis	5	9	0	.357	296	309
Pittsburgh	2	12	0	.143	202	397

WESTERN CONFERENCE

Team	W	L	T	Pct.	PF	PA
Green Bay	10	3	1	.769	316	224
Baltimore	10	3	1	.769	389	284
Chicago	9	5	0	.643	409	275
San Francisco	7	6	1	.538	421	402
Minnesota	7	7	0	.500	383	403
Detroit	6	7	1	.462	257	295
Los Angeles	4	10	0	.286	269	328

PLAYOFFS

Western Conference playoff
Green Bay 13 vs. Baltimore 10 (OT)

NFL championship
Green Bay 23 vs. Cleveland 12

1966

AFL

EASTERN DIVISION

Team	W	L	T	Pct.	PF	PA
Buffalo	9	4	1	.692	358	255
Boston Patriots	8	4	2	.667	315	283
N.Y. Jets	6	6	2	.500	322	312
Houston	3	11	0	.214	335	396
Miami	3	11	0	.214	213	362

WESTERN DIVISION

Team	W	L	T	Pct.	PF	PA
Kansas City	11	2	1	.846	448	276
Oakland	8	5	1	.615	315	288
San Diego	7	6	1	.538	335	284
Denver	4	10	0	.286	196	381

PLAYOFFS

AFL championship
Kansas City 31 at Buffalo 7

NFL

EASTERN CONFERENCE

Team	W	L	T	Pct.	PF	PA
Dallas	10	3	1	.769	445	239
Cleveland	9	5	0	.643	403	259
Philadelphia	9	5	0	.643	326	340
St. Louis	8	5	1	.615	264	265
Washington	7	7	0	.500	351	355
Pittsburgh	5	8	1	.385	316	347
Atlanta	3	11	0	.214	204	437
N.Y. Giants	1	12	1	.077	263	501

WESTERN CONFERENCE

Team	W	L	T	Pct.	PF	PA
Green Bay	12	2	0	.857	335	163
Baltimore	9	5	0	.643	314	226
Los Angeles	8	6	0	.571	289	212
San Francisco	6	6	2	.500	320	325
Chicago	5	7	2	.417	234	272
Detroit	4	9	1	.308	206	317
Minnesota	4	9	1	.308	292	304

PLAYOFFS

NFL championship
Green Bay 34 at Dallas 27

Super Bowl 1
Green Bay 35, Kansas City 10, at Los Angeles.

1967

AFL

EASTERN DIVISION

Team	W	L	T	Pct.	PF	PA
Houston	9	4	1	.692	258	199
N.Y. Jets	8	5	1	.615	371	329
Buffalo	4	10	0	.286	237	285
Miami	4	10	0	.286	219	407
Boston Patriots	3	10	1	.231	280	389

WESTERN DIVISION

Team	W	L	T	Pct.	PF	PA
Oakland	13	1	0	.929	468	233
Kansas City	9	5	0	.643	408	254
San Diego	8	5	1	.615	360	352
Denver	3	11	0	.214	256	409

PLAYOFFS

AFL championship
Oakland 40 vs. Houston 7

NFL

EASTERN CONFERENCE

CAPITOL DIVISION

Team	W	L	T	Pct.	PF	PA
Dallas	9	5	0	.643	342	268
Philadelphia	6	7	1	.462	351	409
Washington	5	6	3	.455	347	353
New Orleans	3	11	0	.214	233	379

CENTURY DIVISION

Team	W	L	T	Pct.	PF	PA
Cleveland	9	5	0	.643	334	297
N.Y. Giants	7	7	0	.500	369	379
St. Louis	6	7	1	.462	333	356
Pittsburgh	4	9	1	.308	281	320

WESTERN CONFERENCE

COASTAL DIVISION

Team	W	L	T	Pct.	PF	PA
Los Angeles	11	1	2	.917	398	196
Baltimore	11	1	2	.917	394	198
San Francisco	7	7	0	.500	273	337
Atlanta	1	12	1	.077	175	422

CENTRAL DIVISION

Team	W	L	T	Pct.	PF	PA
Green Bay	9	4	1	.692	332	209
Chicago	7	6	1	.538	239	218
Detroit	5	7	2	.417	260	259
Minnesota	3	8	3	.273	233	294

PLAYOFFS

Conference championships
Dallas 52 vs. Cleveland 14
Green Bay 28 vs. Los Angeles 7

NFL championship
Green Bay 21 vs. Dallas 17

Super Bowl 2
Green Bay 33, Oakland 14, at Miami.

1968

AFL

EASTERN DIVISION

Team	W	L	T	Pct.	PF	PA
N.Y. Jets	11	3	0	.786	419	280
Houston	7	7	0	.500	303	248
Miami	5	8	1	.385	276	355
Boston Patriots	4	10	0	.286	229	406
Buffalo	1	12	1	.077	199	367

WESTERN DIVISION

Team	W	L	T	Pct.	PF	PA
Oakland	12	2	0	.857	453	233
Kansas City	12	2	0	.857	371	170
San Diego	9	5	0	.643	382	310
Denver	5	9	0	.357	255	404
Cincinnati	3	11	0	.214	215	329

PLAYOFFS

Western Division playoff
Oakland 41 vs. Kansas City 6

AFL championship
N.Y. Jets 27 vs. Oakland 23

NFL

EASTERN CONFERENCE

CAPITOL DIVISION

Team	W	L	T	Pct.	PF	PA
Dallas	12	2	0	.857	431	186
N.Y. Giants	7	7	0	.500	294	325
Washington	5	9	0	.357	249	358
Philadelphia	2	12	0	.143	202	351

CENTURY DIVISION

Team	W	L	T	Pct.	PF	PA
Cleveland	10	4	0	.714	394	273
St. Louis	9	4	1	.692	325	289
New Orleans	4	9	1	.308	246	327
Pittsburgh	2	11	1	.154	244	397

WESTERN CONFERENCE

COASTAL DIVISION

Team	W	L	T	Pct.	PF	PA
Baltimore	13	1	0	.929	402	144
Los Angeles	10	3	1	.769	312	200
San Francisco	7	6	1	.538	303	310
Atlanta	2	12	0	.143	170	389

CENTRAL DIVISION

Team	W	L	T	Pct.	PF	PA
Minnesota	8	6	0	.571	282	242
Chicago	7	7	0	.500	250	333
Green Bay	6	7	1	.462	281	227
Detroit	4	8	2	.333	207	241

PLAYOFFS

Conference championships
Cleveland 31 vs. Dallas 20
Baltimore 24 vs. Minnesota 14

NFL championship
Baltimore 34 at Cleveland 0

Super Bowl 3
N.Y. Jets 16, Baltimore 7, at Miami.

1969

AFL

EASTERN DIVISION

Team	W	L	T	Pct.	PF	PA
N.Y. Jets	10	4	0	.714	353	269
Houston	6	6	2	.500	278	279
Boston Patriots	4	10	0	.286	266	316
Buffalo	4	10	0	.286	230	359
Miami	3	10	1	.231	233	332

WESTERN DIVISION

Team	W	L	T	Pct.	PF	PA
Oakland	12	1	1	.923	377	242
Kansas City	11	3	0	.786	359	177
San Diego	8	6	0	.571	288	276
Denver	5	8	1	.385	297	344
Cincinnati	4	9	1	.308	280	367

PLAYOFFS

Divisional games
Kansas City 13 at N.Y. Jets 6
Oakland 56 vs. Houston 7

AFL championship
Kansas City 17 at Oakland 7

NFL

EASTERN CONFERENCE

CAPITOL DIVISION

Team	W	L	T	Pct.	PF	PA
Dallas	11	2	1	.846	369	223
Washington	7	5	2	.583	307	319
New Orleans	5	9	0	.357	311	393
Philadelphia	4	9	1	.308	279	377

CENTURY DIVISION

Team	W	L	T	Pct.	PF	PA
Cleveland	10	3	1	.769	351	300
N.Y. Giants	6	8	0	.429	264	298
St. Louis	4	9	1	.308	314	389
Pittsburgh	1	13	0	.071	218	404

WESTERN CONFERENCE

COASTAL DIVISION

Team	W	L	T	Pct.	PF	PA
Los Angeles	11	3	0	.786	320	243
Baltimore	8	5	1	.615	279	268
Atlanta	6	8	0	.429	276	268
San Francisco	4	8	2	.333	277	319

CENTRAL DIVISION

Team	W	L	T	Pct.	PF	PA
Minnesota	12	2	0	.857	379	133
Detroit	9	4	1	.692	259	188
Green Bay	8	6	0	.571	269	221
Chicago	1	13	0	.071	210	339

PLAYOFFS

Conference championships
Cleveland 38 at Dallas 14
Minnesota 23 vs. Los Angeles 20

NFL championship
Minnesota 27 vs. Cleveland 7

Super Bowl 4
Kansas City 23, Minnesota 7, at New Orleans.

AMERICAN CONFERENCE

EASTERN DIVISION

Team	W	L	T	Pct.	PF	PA
Baltimore*	11	2	1	.846	321	234
Miami†	10	4	0	.714	297	228
N.Y. Jets	4	10	0	.286	255	286
Buffalo	3	10	1	.231	204	337
Boston Patriots	2	12	0	.143	149	361

CENTRAL DIVISION

Team	W	L	T	Pct.	PF	PA
Cincinnati*	8	6	0	.571	312	255
Cleveland	7	7	0	.500	286	265
Pittsburgh	5	9	0	.357	210	272
Houston	3	10	1	.231	217	352

WESTERN DIVISION

Team	W	L	T	Pct.	PF	PA
Oakland*	8	4	2	.667	300	293
Kansas City	7	5	2	.583	272	244
San Diego	5	6	3	.455	282	278
Denver	5	8	1	.385	253	264

*Division champion.
†Wild-card team.

NATIONAL CONFERENCE

EASTERN DIVISION

Team	W	L	T	Pct.	PF	PA
Dallas*	10	4	0	.714	299	221
N.Y. Giants	9	5	0	.643	301	270
St. Louis	8	5	1	.615	325	228
Washington	6	8	0	.429	297	314
Philadelphia	3	10	1	.231	241	332

CENTRAL DIVISION

Team	W	L	T	Pct.	PF	PA
Minnesota*	12	2	0	.857	335	143
Detroit†	10	4	0	.714	347	202
Green Bay	6	8	0	.429	196	293
Chicago	6	8	0	.429	256	261

WESTERN DIVISION

Team	W	L	T	Pct.	PF	PA
San Francisco*	10	3	1	.769	352	267
Los Angeles	9	4	1	.692	325	202
Atlanta	4	8	2	.333	206	261
New Orleans	2	11	1	.154	172	347

PLAYOFFS

AFC divisional games
Baltimore 17 vs. Cincinnati 0
Oakland 21 vs. Miami 14

AFC championship
Baltimore 27 vs. Oakland 17

NFC divisional games
Dallas 5 vs. Detroit 0
San Francisco 17 at Minnesota 14

NFC championship
Dallas 17 at San Francisco 10

Super Bowl 5
Baltimore 16, Dallas 13, at Miami.

AMERICAN CONFERENCE

EASTERN DIVISION

Team	W	L	T	Pct.	PF	PA
Miami*	10	3	1	.769	315	174
Baltimore†	10	4	0	.714	313	140
New England	6	8	0	.429	238	325
N.Y. Jets	6	8	0	.429	212	299
Buffalo	1	13	0	.071	184	394

CENTRAL DIVISION

Team	W	L	T	Pct.	PF	PA
Cleveland*	9	5	0	.643	285	273
Pittsburgh	6	8	0	.429	246	292
Houston	4	9	1	.308	251	330
Cincinnati	4	10	0	.286	284	265

WESTERN DIVISION

Team	W	L	T	Pct.	PF	PA
Kansas City*	10	3	1	.769	302	208
Oakland	8	4	2	.667	344	278
San Diego	6	8	0	.429	311	341
Denver	4	9	1	.308	203	275

*Division champion.
†Wild-card team.

NATIONAL CONFERENCE

EASTERN DIVISION

Team	W	L	T	Pct.	PF	PA
Dallas*	11	3	0	.786	406	222
Washington†	9	4	1	.679	276	190
Philadelphia	6	7	1	.462	221	302
St. Louis	4	9	1	.308	231	279
N.Y. Giants	4	10	0	.286	228	362

CENTRAL DIVISION

Team	W	L	T	Pct.	PF	PA
Minnesota*	11	3	0	.786	245	139
Detroit	7	6	1	.538	341	286
Chicago	6	8	0	.429	185	276
Green Bay	4	8	2	.333	274	298

WESTERN DIVISION

Team	W	L	T	Pct.	PF	PA
San Francisco*	9	5	0	.643	300	216
Los Angeles	8	5	1	.615	313	260
Atlanta	7	6	1	.538	274	277
New Orleans	4	8	2	.333	266	347

PLAYOFFS

AFC divisional games
Miami 27 at Kansas City 24 (OT)
Baltimore 20 at Cleveland 3

AFC championship
Miami 21 vs. Baltimore 0

NFC divisional games
Dallas 20 at Minnesota 12
San Francisco 24 vs. Washington 20

NFC championship
Dallas 14 vs. San Francisco 3

Super Bowl 6
Dallas 24, Miami 3, at New Orleans.

AMERICAN CONFERENCE

EASTERN DIVISION

Team	W	L	T	Pct.	PF	PA
Miami*	14	0	0	1.000	385	171
N.Y. Jets	7	7	0	.500	367	324
Baltimore	5	9	0	.357	235	252
Buffalo	4	9	1	.321	257	377
New England	3	11	0	.214	192	446

CENTRAL DIVISION

Team	W	L	T	Pct.	PF	PA
Pittsburgh*	11	3	0	.786	343	175
Cleveland†	10	4	0	.714	268	249
Cincinnati	8	6	0	.571	299	229
Houston	1	13	0	.071	164	380

WESTERN DIVISION

Team	W	L	T	Pct.	PF	PA
Oakland*	10	3	1	.750	365	248
Kansas City	8	6	0	.571	287	254
Denver	5	9	0	.357	325	350
San Diego	4	9	1	.321	264	344

*Division champion.
†Wild-card team.

NATIONAL CONFERENCE

EASTERN DIVISION

Team	W	L	T	Pct.	PF	PA
Washington*	11	3	0	.786	336	218
Dallas†	10	4	0	.714	319	240
N.Y. Giants	8	6	0	.571	331	247
St. Louis	4	9	1	.321	193	303
Philadelphia	2	11	1	.179	145	352

CENTRAL DIVISION

Team	W	L	T	Pct.	PF	PA
Green Bay*	10	4	0	.714	304	226
Detroit	8	5	1	.607	339	290
Minnesota	7	7	0	.500	301	252
Chicago	4	9	1	.321	225	275

WESTERN DIVISION

Team	W	L	T	Pct.	PF	PA
San Francisco*	8	5	1	.607	353	249
Atlanta	7	7	0	.500	269	274
Los Angeles	6	7	1	.464	291	286
New Orleans	2	11	1	.179	215	361

PLAYOFFS

AFC divisional games
Pittsburgh 13 vs. Oakland 7
Miami 20 vs. Cleveland 14

AFC championship
Miami 21 at Pittsburgh 17

NFC divisional games
Dallas 30 at San Francisco 28
Washington 16 vs. Green Bay 3

NFC championship
Washington 26 vs. Dallas 3

Super Bowl 7
Miami 14, Washington 7, at Los Angeles.

HISTORY Year-by-year standings

1973

AMERICAN CONFERENCE

EASTERN DIVISION

Team	W	L	T	Pct.	PF	PA
Miami*	12	2	0	.857	343	150
Buffalo	9	5	0	.643	259	230
New England	5	9	0	.357	258	300
N.Y. Jets	4	10	0	.286	240	306
Baltimore	4	10	0	.286	226	341

CENTRAL DIVISION

Team	W	L	T	Pct.	PF	PA
Cincinnati*	10	4	0	.714	286	231
Pittsburgh†	10	4	0	.714	347	210
Cleveland	7	5	2	.571	234	255
Houston	1	13	0	.071	199	447

WESTERN DIVISION

Team	W	L	T	Pct.	PF	PA
Oakland*	9	4	1	.679	292	175
Kansas City	7	5	2	.571	231	192
Denver	7	5	2	.571	354	296
San Diego	2	11	1	.179	188	386

*Division champion.
†Wild-card team.

NATIONAL CONFERENCE

EASTERN DIVISION

Team	W	L	T	Pct.	PF	PA
Dallas*	10	4	0	.714	382	203
Washington†	10	4	0	.714	325	198
Philadelphia	5	8	1	.393	310	393
St. Louis	4	9	1	.321	286	365
N.Y. Giants	2	11	1	.179	226	362

CENTRAL DIVISION

Team	W	L	T	Pct.	PF	PA
Minnesota*	12	2	0	.857	296	168
Detroit	6	7	1	.464	271	247
Green Bay	5	7	2	.429	202	259
Chicago	3	11	0	.214	195	334

WESTERN DIVISION

Team	W	L	T	Pct.	PF	PA
Los Angeles*	12	2	0	.857	388	178
Atlanta	9	5	0	.643	318	224
San Francisco	5	9	0	.357	262	319
New Orleans	5	9	0	.357	163	312

PLAYOFFS

AFC divisional games
Oakland 33 vs. Pittsburgh 14
Miami 34 vs. Cincinnati 16

AFC championship
Miami 27 vs. Oakland 10

NFC divisional games
Minnesota 27 vs. Washington 20
Dallas 27 vs. Los Angeles 16

NFC championship
Minnesota 27 at Dallas 10

Super Bowl 8
Miami 24, Minnesota 7, at Houston.

1974

AMERICAN CONFERENCE

EASTERN DIVISION

Team	W	L	T	Pct.	PF	PA
Miami*	11	3	0	.786	327	216
Buffalo†	9	5	0	.643	264	244
New England	7	7	0	.500	348	289
N.Y. Jets	7	7	0	.500	279	300
Baltimore	2	12	0	.143	190	329

CENTRAL DIVISION

Team	W	L	T	Pct.	PF	PA
Pittsburgh*	10	3	1	.750	305	189
Houston	7	7	0	.500	236	282
Cincinnati	7	7	0	.500	283	259
Cleveland	4	10	0	.286	251	344

WESTERN DIVISION

Team	W	L	T	Pct.	PF	PA
Oakland*	12	2	0	.857	355	228
Denver	7	6	1	.536	302	294
Kansas City	5	9	0	.357	233	293
San Diego	5	9	0	.357	212	285

*Division champion.
†Wild-card team.

NATIONAL CONFERENCE

EASTERN DIVISION

Team	W	L	T	Pct.	PF	PA
St. Louis*	10	4	0	.714	285	218
Washington†	10	4	0	.714	320	196
Dallas	8	6	0	.571	297	235
Philadelphia	7	7	0	.500	242	217
N.Y. Giants	2	12	0	.143	195	299

CENTRAL DIVISION

Team	W	L	T	Pct.	PF	PA
Minnesota*	10	4	0	.714	310	195
Detroit	7	7	0	.500	256	270
Green Bay	6	8	0	.429	210	206
Chicago	4	10	0	.286	152	279

WESTERN DIVISION

Team	W	L	T	Pct.	PF	PA
Los Angeles*	10	4	0	.714	263	181
San Francisco	6	8	0	.429	226	236
New Orleans	5	9	0	.357	166	263
Atlanta	3	11	0	.214	111	271

PLAYOFFS

AFC divisional games
Oakland 28 vs. Miami 26
Pittsburgh 32 vs. Buffalo 14

AFC championship
Pittsburgh 24 at Oakland 13

NFC divisional games
Minnesota 30 vs. St. Louis 14
Los Angeles 19 vs. Washington 10

NFC championship
Minnesota 14 vs. Los Angeles 10

Super Bowl 9
Pittsburgh 16, Minnesota 6, at New Orleans.

1975

AMERICAN CONFERENCE

EASTERN DIVISION

Team	W	L	T	Pct.	PF	PA
Baltimore*	10	4	0	.714	395	269
Miami	10	4	0	.714	357	222
Buffalo	8	6	0	.571	420	355
N.Y. Jets	3	11	0	.214	258	433
New England	3	11	0	.214	258	358

CENTRAL DIVISION

Team	W	L	T	Pct.	PF	PA
Pittsburgh*	12	2	0	.857	373	162
Cincinnati†	11	3	0	.786	340	246
Houston	10	4	0	.714	293	226
Cleveland	3	11	0	.214	218	372

WESTERN DIVISION

Team	W	L	T	Pct.	PF	PA
Oakland*	11	3	0	.786	375	255
Denver	6	8	0	.429	254	307
Kansas City	5	9	0	.357	282	341
San Diego	2	12	0	.143	189	345

*Division champion.
†Wild-card team.

NATIONAL CONFERENCE

EASTERN DIVISION

Team	W	L	T	Pct.	PF	PA
St. Louis*	11	3	0	.786	356	276
Dallas†	10	4	0	.714	350	268
Washington	8	6	0	.571	325	276
N.Y. Giants	5	9	0	.357	216	306
Philadelphia	4	10	0	.286	225	302

CENTRAL DIVISION

Team	W	L	T	Pct.	PF	PA
Minnesota*	12	2	0	.857	377	180
Detroit	7	7	0	.500	245	262
Chicago	4	10	0	.286	191	379
Green Bay	4	10	0	.286	226	285

WESTERN DIVISION

Team	W	L	T	Pct.	PF	PA
Los Angeles*	12	2	0	.857	312	135
San Francisco	5	9	0	.357	255	286
Atlanta	4	10	0	.286	240	289
New Orleans	2	12	0	.143	165	360

PLAYOFFS

AFC divisional games
Pittsburgh 28 vs. Baltimore 10
Oakland 31 vs. Cincinnati 28

AFC championship
Pittsburgh 16 vs. Oakland 10

NFC divisional games
Los Angeles 35 vs. St. Louis 23
Dallas 17 at Minnesota 14

NFC championship
Dallas 37 at Los Angeles 7

Super Bowl 10
Pittsburgh 21, Dallas 17, at Miami.

AMERICAN CONFERENCE

EASTERN DIVISION

Team	W	L	T	Pct.	PF	PA
Baltimore*	11	3	0	.786	417	246
New England†	11	3	0	.786	376	236
Miami	6	8	0	.429	263	264
N.Y. Jets	3	11	0	.214	169	383
Buffalo	2	12	0	.143	245	363

CENTRAL DIVISION

Team	W	L	T	Pct.	PF	PA
Pittsburgh*	10	4	0	.714	342	138
Cincinnati	10	4	0	.714	335	210
Cleveland	9	5	0	.643	267	287
Houston	5	9	0	.357	222	273

WESTERN DIVISION

Team	W	L	T	Pct.	PF	PA
Oakland*	13	1	0	.929	350	237
Denver	9	5	0	.643	315	206
San Diego	6	8	0	.429	248	285
Kansas City	5	9	0	.357	290	376
Tampa Bay	0	14	0	.000	125	412

*Division champion.
†Wild-card team.

NATIONAL CONFERENCE

EASTERN DIVISION

Team	W	L	T	Pct.	PF	PA
Dallas*	11	3	0	.786	296	194
Washington†	10	4	0	.714	291	217
St. Louis	10	4	0	.714	309	267
Philadelphia	4	10	0	.286	165	286
N.Y. Giants	3	11	0	.214	170	250

CENTRAL DIVISION

Team	W	L	T	Pct.	PF	PA
Minnesota*	11	2	1	.821	305	176
Chicago	7	7	0	.500	253	216
Detroit	6	8	0	.429	262	220
Green Bay	5	9	0	.357	218	299

WESTERN DIVISION

Team	W	L	T	Pct.	PF	PA
Los Angeles*	10	3	1	.750	351	190
San Francisco	8	6	0	.571	270	190
Atlanta	4	10	0	.286	172	312
New Orleans	4	10	0	.286	253	346
Seattle	2	12	0	.143	229	429

PLAYOFFS

AFC divisional games
Oakland 24 vs. New England 21
Pittsburgh 40 at Baltimore 14

AFC championship
Oakland 24 vs. Pittsburgh 7

NFC divisional games
Minnesota 35 vs. Washington 20
Los Angeles 14 at Dallas 12

NFC championship
Minnesota 24 vs. Los Angeles 13

Super Bowl 11
Oakland 32, Minnesota 14, at Pasadena, Calif.

AMERICAN CONFERENCE

EASTERN DIVISION

Team	W	L	T	Pct.	PF	PA
Baltimore*	10	4	0	.714	295	221
Miami	10	4	0	.714	313	197
New England	9	5	0	.643	278	217
Buffalo	3	11	0	.214	160	313
N.Y. Jets	3	11	0	.214	191	300

CENTRAL DIVISION

Team	W	L	T	Pct.	PF	PA
Pittsburgh*	9	5	0	.643	283	243
Cincinnati	8	6	0	.571	238	235
Houston	8	6	0	.571	299	230
Cleveland	6	8	0	.429	269	267

WESTERN DIVISION

Team	W	L	T	Pct.	PF	PA
Denver*	12	2	0	.857	274	148
Oakland†	11	3	0	.786	351	230
San Diego	7	7	0	.500	222	205
Seattle	5	9	0	.357	282	373
Kansas City	2	12	0	.143	225	349

*Division champion.
†Wild-card team.

NATIONAL CONFERENCE

EASTERN DIVISION

Team	W	L	T	Pct.	PF	PA
Dallas*	12	2	0	.857	345	212
Washington	9	5	0	.643	196	189
St. Louis	7	7	0	.500	272	287
Philadelphia	5	9	0	.357	220	207
N.Y. Giants	5	9	0	.357	181	265

CENTRAL DIVISION

Team	W	L	T	Pct.	PF	PA
Minnesota*	9	5	0	.643	231	227
Chicago†	9	5	0	.643	255	253
Detroit	6	8	0	.429	183	252
Green Bay	4	10	0	.286	134	219
Tampa Bay	2	12	0	.143	103	223

WESTERN DIVISION

Team	W	L	T	Pct.	PF	PA
Los Angeles*	10	4	0	.714	302	146
Atlanta	7	7	0	.500	179	129
San Francisco	5	9	0	.357	220	260
New Orleans	3	11	0	.214	232	336

PLAYOFFS

AFC divisional games
Denver 34 vs. Pittsburgh 21
Oakland 37 at Baltimore 31 (OT)

AFC championship
Denver 20 vs. Oakland 17

NFC divisional games
Dallas 37 vs. Chicago 7
Minnesota 14 at Los Angeles 7

NFC championship
Dallas 23 vs. Minnesota 6

Super Bowl 12
Dallas 27, Denver 10, at New Orleans.

HISTORY *Year-by-year standings*

THE '76 BUCS: THE WRONG KIND OF FAME

Four seasons after the Miami Dolphins went through an entire season without losing a game, another Florida team also made NFL history, but not the kind it would have preferred. In their inaugural season the Tampa Bay Buccaneers failed to win a game, going 0-14 as a member of the AFC's Western Division. Coach John McKay's Bucs scored a league-low 125 points and allowed 412, a total surpassed only by the league's other 1976 expansion team, the Seattle Seahawks. Tampa Bay failed to score more than 20 points in any game and did not come within three points of winning a game. One of those three-point defeats came in Week 6, when the Seahawks beat the Bucs, 13-10, a victory preserved when veteran linebacker Mike Curtis blocked a 35-yard field goal attempt by Bucs kicker Dave Green with 42 seconds left.

1978

AMERICAN CONFERENCE

EASTERN DIVISION

Team	W	L	T	Pct.	PF	PA
New England*	11	5	0	.688	358	286
Miami†	11	5	0	.688	372	254
N.Y. Jets	8	8	0	.500	359	364
Buffalo	5	11	0	.313	302	354
Baltimore	5	11	0	.313	239	421

CENTRAL DIVISION

Team	W	L	T	Pct.	PF	PA
Pittsburgh*	14	2	0	.875	356	195
Houston†	10	6	0	.625	283	298
Cleveland	8	8	0	.500	334	356
Cincinnati	4	12	0	.250	252	284

WESTERN DIVISION

Team	W	L	T	Pct.	PF	PA
Denver*	10	6	0	.625	282	198
Oakland	9	7	0	.563	311	283
Seattle	9	7	0	.563	345	358
San Diego	9	7	0	.563	355	309
Kansas City	4	12	0	.250	243	327

*Division champion.
†Wild-card team.

NATIONAL CONFERENCE

EASTERN DIVISION

Team	W	L	T	Pct.	PF	PA
Dallas*	12	4	0	.750	384	208
Philadelphia†	9	7	0	.563	270	250
Washington	8	8	0	.500	273	283
St. Louis	6	10	0	.375	248	296
N.Y. Giants	6	10	0	.375	264	298

CENTRAL DIVISION

Team	W	L	T	Pct.	PF	PA
Minnesota*	8	7	1	.531	294	306
Green Bay	8	7	1	.531	249	269
Detroit	7	9	0	.438	290	300
Chicago	7	9	0	.438	253	274
Tampa Bay	5	11	0	.313	241	259

WESTERN DIVISION

Team	W	L	T	Pct.	PF	PA
Los Angeles*	12	4	0	.750	316	245
Atlanta†	9	7	0	.563	240	290
New Orleans	7	9	0	.438	281	298
San Francisco	2	14	0	.125	219	350

PLAYOFFS

AFC wild-card game
Houston 17 at Miami 9

AFC divisional games
Houston 31 at New England 14
Pittsburgh 33 vs. Denver 10

AFC championship
Pittsburgh 34 vs. Houston 5

NFC wild-card game
Atlanta 14 vs. Philadelphia 13

NFC divisional games
Dallas 27 vs. Atlanta 20
Los Angeles 34 vs. Minnesota 10

NFC championship
Dallas 28 at Los Angeles 0

Super Bowl 13
Pittsburgh 35, Dallas 31, at Miami.

1979

AMERICAN CONFERENCE

EASTERN DIVISION

Team	W	L	T	Pct.	PF	PA
Miami*	10	6	0	.625	341	257
New England	9	7	0	.563	411	326
N.Y. Jets	8	8	0	.500	337	383
Buffalo	7	9	0	.438	268	279
Baltimore	5	11	0	.313	271	351

CENTRAL DIVISION

Team	W	L	T	Pct.	PF	PA
Pittsburgh*	12	4	0	.750	416	262
Houston†	11	5	0	.688	362	331
Cleveland	9	7	0	.563	359	352
Cincinnati	4	12	0	.250	337	421

WESTERN DIVISION

Team	W	L	T	Pct.	PF	PA
San Diego*	12	4	0	.750	411	246
Denver†	10	6	0	.625	289	262
Seattle	9	7	0	.563	378	372
Oakland	9	7	0	.563	365	337
Kansas City	7	9	0	.438	238	262

*Division champion.
†Wild-card team.

NATIONAL CONFERENCE

EASTERN DIVISION

Team	W	L	T	Pct.	PF	PA
Dallas*	11	5	0	.688	371	313
Philadelphia†	11	5	0	.688	339	282
Washington	10	6	0	.625	348	295
N.Y. Giants	6	10	0	.375	237	323
St. Louis	5	11	0	.313	307	358

CENTRAL DIVISION

Team	W	L	T	Pct.	PF	PA
Tampa Bay*	10	6	0	.625	273	237
Chicago†	10	6	0	.625	306	249
Minnesota	7	9	0	.438	259	337
Green Bay	5	11	0	.313	246	316
Detroit	2	14	0	.125	219	365

WESTERN DIVISION

Team	W	L	T	Pct.	PF	PA
Los Angeles*	9	7	0	.563	323	309
New Orleans	8	8	0	.500	370	360
Atlanta	6	10	0	.375	300	388
San Francisco	2	14	0	.125	308	416

PLAYOFFS

AFC wild-card game
Houston 13 vs. Denver 7

AFC divisional games
Houston 17 at San Diego 14
Pittsburgh 34 vs. Miami 14

AFC championship
Pittsburgh 27 vs. Houston 13

NFC wild-card game
Philadelphia 27 vs. Chicago 17

NFC divisional games
Tampa Bay 24 vs. Philadelphia 17
Los Angeles 21 at Dallas 19

NFC championship
Los Angeles 9 at Tampa Bay 0

Super Bowl 14
Pittsburgh 31, Los Angeles 19, at Pasadena, Calif.

SMASHING '78 DEBUT FOR BIG EARL

Houston running back Earl Campbell, winner of the Heisman Trophy at Texas the year before and the league's top draft pick, gave NFL fans a preview of things to come by rushing for a league-high 1,450 yards and scoring 13 touchdowns in one of the most electrifying rookie seasons in NFL history. Campbell dethroned defending league rushing champ Walter Payton by 55 yards despite carrying the ball 31 fewer times. More important, he took a team that had not been to the playoffs in the eight previous seasons to the AFC championship game. Campbell's best game of 1978 came under the brightest of lights: a 199-yard, four-touchdown performance in a 35-30 victory over Miami on Monday, November 20. He capped his big evening by scoring the Oilers' final touchdown on an 81-yard run in the fourth quarter.

AMERICAN CONFERENCE

EASTERN DIVISION

Team	W	L	T	Pct.	PF	PA
Buffalo*	11	5	0	.688	320	260
New England	10	6	0	.625	441	325
Miami	8	8	0	.500	266	305
Baltimore	7	9	0	.438	355	387
N.Y. Jets	4	12	0	.250	302	395

CENTRAL DIVISION

Team	W	L	T	Pct.	PF	PA
Cleveland*	11	5	0	.688	357	310
Houston†	11	5	0	.688	295	251
Pittsburgh	9	7	0	.563	352	313
Cincinnati	6	10	0	.375	244	312

WESTERN DIVISION

Team	W	L	T	Pct.	PF	PA
San Diego*	11	5	0	.688	418	327
Oakland†	11	5	0	.688	364	306
Kansas City	8	8	0	.500	319	336
Denver	8	8	0	.500	310	323
Seattle	4	12	0	.250	291	408

*Division champion.
†Wild-card team.

NATIONAL CONFERENCE

EASTERN DIVISION

Team	W	L	T	Pct.	PF	PA
Philadelphia*	12	4	0	.750	384	222
Dallas†	12	4	0	.750	454	311
Washington	6	10	0	.375	261	293
St. Louis	5	11	0	.313	299	350
N.Y. Giants	4	12	0	.250	249	425

CENTRAL DIVISION

Team	W	L	T	Pct.	PF	PA
Minnesota*	9	7	0	.563	317	308
Detroit	9	7	0	.563	334	272
Chicago	7	9	0	.438	304	264
Tampa Bay	5	10	1	.344	271	341
Green Bay	5	10	1	.344	231	371

WESTERN DIVISION

Team	W	L	T	Pct.	PF	PA
Atlanta*	12	4	0	.750	405	272
Los Angeles†	11	5	0	.688	424	289
San Francisco	6	10	0	.375	320	415
New Orleans	1	15	0	.063	291	487

PLAYOFFS

AFC wild-card game
Oakland 27 vs. Houston 7

AFC divisional games
San Diego 20 vs. Buffalo 14
Oakland 14 at Cleveland 12

AFC championship
Oakland 34 at San Diego 27

NFC wild-card game
Dallas 34 vs. Los Angeles 13

NFC divisional games
Philadelphia 31 vs. Minnesota 16
Dallas 30 at Atlanta 27

NFC championship
Philadelphia 20 vs. Dallas 7

Super Bowl 15
Oakland 27, Philadelphia 10, at New Orleans.

AMERICAN CONFERENCE

EASTERN DIVISION

Team	W	L	T	Pct.	PF	PA
Miami*	11	4	1	.719	345	275
N.Y. Jets†	10	5	1	.656	355	287
Buffalo†	10	6	0	.625	311	276
Baltimore	2	14	0	.125	259	533
New England	2	14	0	.125	322	370

CENTRAL DIVISION

Team	W	L	T	Pct.	PF	PA
Cincinnati*	12	4	0	.750	421	304
Pittsburgh	8	8	0	.500	356	297
Houston	7	9	0	.438	281	355
Cleveland	5	11	0	.313	276	375

WESTERN DIVISION

Team	W	L	T	Pct.	PF	PA
San Diego*	10	6	0	.625	478	390
Denver	10	6	0	.625	321	289
Kansas City	9	7	0	.563	343	290
Oakland	7	9	0	.438	273	343
Seattle	6	10	0	.375	322	388

*Division champion.
†Wild-card team.

NATIONAL CONFERENCE

EASTERN DIVISION

Team	W	L	T	Pct.	PF	PA
Dallas*	12	4	0	.750	367	277
Philadelphia†	10	6	0	.625	368	221
N.Y. Giants†	9	7	0	.563	295	257
Washington	8	8	0	.500	347	349
St. Louis	7	9	0	.438	315	408

CENTRAL DIVISION

Team	W	L	T	Pct.	PF	PA
Tampa Bay*	9	7	0	.563	315	268
Detroit	8	8	0	.500	397	322
Green Bay	8	8	0	.500	324	361
Minnesota	7	9	0	.438	325	369
Chicago	6	10	0	.375	253	324

WESTERN DIVISION

Team	W	L	T	Pct.	PF	PA
San Francisco*	13	3	0	.813	357	250
Atlanta	7	9	0	.438	426	355
Los Angeles	6	10	0	.375	303	351
New Orleans	4	12	0	.250	207	378

PLAYOFFS

AFC wild-card game
Buffalo 31 at New York Jets 27

AFC divisional games
San Diego 41 at Miami 38 (OT)
Cincinnati 28 vs. Buffalo 21

AFC championship
Cincinnati 27 vs. San Diego 7

NFC wild-card game
N.Y. Giants 27 at Philadelphia 21

NFC divisional games
Dallas 38 vs. Tampa Bay 0
San Francisco 38 vs. N.Y. Giants 24

NFC championship
San Francisco 28 vs. Dallas 27

Super Bowl 16
San Francisco 26, Cincinnati 21, at Pontiac, Mich.

HISTORY *Year-by-year standings*

LT: A ROOKIE TO REMEMBER

The 1981 season was a big one for rookies (six made the Pro Bowl), but none had more impact than Giants linebacker Lawrence Taylor, who had no problem adjusting to the pro game after an All-American career at North Carolina. The second player drafted in 1981, Taylor was simply marvelous, helping to make a good New York defense with veterans like linebacker Harry Carson and cornerback Mark Haynes great. In 16 games (all starts) Taylor had 133 tackles, 10.5 sacks, recovered a fumble and intercepted a pass. He followed that up with 14 tackles and two sacks in two playoff games, the Giants' first postseason action since 1963. For his efforts Taylor was a unanimous All-NFL first-team selection, a Pro Bowl starter and the Associated Press Defensive Player of the Year.

1982

AMERICAN CONFERENCE

Team	W	L	T	Pct.	PF	PA
L.A. Raiders	8	1	0	.889	260	200
Miami	7	2	0	.778	198	131
Cincinnati	7	2	0	.778	232	177
Pittsburgh	6	3	0	.667	204	146
San Diego	6	3	0	.667	288	221
N.Y. Jets	6	3	0	.667	245	166
New England	5	4	0	.556	143	157
Cleveland	4	5	0	.444	140	182
Buffalo	4	5	0	.444	150	154
Seattle	4	5	0	.444	127	147
Kansas City	3	6	0	.333	176	184
Denver	2	7	0	.222	148	226
Houston	1	8	0	.111	136	245
Baltimore	0	8	1	.056	113	236

NATIONAL CONFERENCE

Team	W	L	T	Pct.	PF	PA
Washington	8	1	0	.889	190	128
Dallas	6	3	0	.667	226	145
Green Bay	5	3	1	.611	226	169
Minnesota	5	4	0	.556	187	198
Atlanta	5	4	0	.556	183	199
St. Louis	5	4	0	.556	135	170
Tampa Bay	5	4	0	.556	158	178
Detroit	4	5	0	.444	181	176
New Orleans	4	5	0	.444	129	160
N.Y. Giants	4	5	0	.444	164	160
San Francisco	3	6	0	.333	209	206
Chicago	3	6	0	.333	141	174
Philadelphia	3	6	0	.333	191	195
L.A. Rams	2	7	0	.222	200	250

PLAYOFFS

AFC first round
Miami 28 vs. New England 13
L.A. Raiders 27 vs. Cleveland 10
New York Jets 44 at Cincinnati 17
San Diego 31 at Pittsburgh 28

AFC second round
N.Y. Jets 17 at L.A. Raiders 14
Miami 34 vs. San Diego 13

AFC championship
Miami 14 vs. New York Jets 0

NFC first round
Washington 31 vs. Detroit 7
Green Bay 41 vs. St. Louis 16
Minnesota 30 vs. Atlanta 24
Dallas 30 vs. Tampa Bay 17

NFC second round
Washington 21 vs. Minnesota 7
Dallas 37 vs. Green Bay 26

NFC championship
Washington 31 vs. Dallas 17

Super Bowl 17
Washington 27, Miami 17, at Pasadena, Calif.

As a result of a 57-day players' strike, the 1982 NFL regular season schedule was reduced from 16 weeks to 9. At the conclusion of the regular season, a 16-team Super Bowl Tournament was held. Eight teams from each conference were seeded 1 through 8 based on their records during regular season play.

Miami finished ahead of Cincinnati based on a better conference record. Pittsburgh won common games tiebreaker with San Diego after New York Jets were eliminated from a three-way tie based on conference record. Cleveland finished ahead of Buffalo and Seattle based on a better conference record. Minnesota, Atlanta, St. Louis and Tampa Bay seeds were determined by best won-lost record in conference games. Detroit finished ahead of New Orleans and the New York Giants based on a better conference record.

1983

AMERICAN CONFERENCE

EASTERN DIVISION

Team	W	L	T	Pct.	PF	PA
Miami*	12	4	0	.750	389	250
New England	8	8	0	.500	274	289
Buffalo	8	8	0	.500	283	351
Baltimore	7	9	0	.438	264	354
N.Y. Jets	7	9	0	.438	313	331

CENTRAL DIVISION

Team	W	L	T	Pct.	PF	PA
Pittsburgh*	10	6	0	.625	355	303
Cleveland	9	7	0	.563	356	342
Cincinnati	7	9	0	.438	346	302
Houston	2	14	0	.125	288	460

WESTERN DIVISION

Team	W	L	T	Pct.	PF	PA
L.A. Raiders*	12	4	0	.750	442	338
Seattle†	9	7	0	.563	403	397
Denver†	9	7	0	.563	302	327
San Diego	6	10	0	.375	358	462
Kansas City	6	10	0	.375	386	367

*Division champion.
†Wild-card team.

NATIONAL CONFERENCE

EASTERN DIVISION

Team	W	L	T	Pct.	PF	PA
Washington*	14	2	0	.875	541	332
Dallas†	12	4	0	.750	479	360
St. Louis	8	7	1	.531	374	428
Philadelphia	5	11	0	.313	233	322
N.Y. Giants	3	12	1	.219	267	347

CENTRAL DIVISION

Team	W	L	T	Pct.	PF	PA
Detroit*	9	7	0	.563	347	286
Green Bay	8	8	0	.500	429	439
Chicago	8	8	0	.500	311	301
Minnesota	8	8	0	.500	316	348
Tampa Bay	2	14	0	.125	241	380

WESTERN DIVISION

Team	W	L	T	Pct.	PF	PA
San Francisco*	10	6	0	.625	432	293
L.A. Rams†	9	7	0	.563	361	344
New Orleans	8	8	0	.500	319	337
Atlanta	7	9	0	.438	370	389

PLAYOFFS

AFC wild-card game
Seattle 31 vs. Denver 7

AFC divisional games
Seattle 27 at Miami 20
L.A. Raiders 38 vs. Pittsburgh 10

AFC championship game
L.A. Raiders 30 vs. Seattle 14

NFC wild-card game
Los Angeles Rams 24 at Dallas 17

NFC divisional games
San Francisco 24 vs. Detroit 23
Washington 51 vs. L.A. Rams 7

NFC championship
Washington 24 vs. San Francisco 21

Super Bowl 18
L.A. Raiders 38, Washington 9, at Tampa, Fla.

CAPITAL GAINS FOR THE REDSKINS

Although they failed to successfully defend their Super Bowl championship, the Washington Redskins did just about everything else right in 1983, especially on offense. Washington scored 541 points, the most in NFL history and 62 more than the next highest scoring team that year. Running back John Riggins scored a record 24 touchdowns, rushed for a club-record 1,347 yards and set a league mark over two seasons by rushing for a TD in 13 consecutive games. Mark Moseley's 161 points set a new league standard for kickers. But as good as Riggins and Moseley were, the league's Most Valuable Player, in voting conducted by the Associated Press, was quarterback Joe Theismann, who threw 29 TD passes, compiled a 97.0 passer rating and had streaks of 161 and 104 consecutive passes without an interception.

AMERICAN CONFERENCE

EASTERN DIVISION

Team	W	L	T	Pct.	PF	PA
Miami*	14	2	0	.875	513	298
New England	9	7	0	.563	362	352
N.Y. Jets	7	9	0	.438	332	364
Indianapolis	4	12	0	.250	239	414
Buffalo	2	14	0	.125	250	454

CENTRAL DIVISION

Team	W	L	T	Pct.	PF	PA
Pittsburgh*	9	7	0	.563	387	310
Cincinnati	8	8	0	.500	339	339
Cleveland	5	11	0	.313	250	297
Houston	3	13	0	.188	240	437

WESTERN DIVISION

Team	W	L	T	Pct.	PF	PA
Denver*	13	3	0	.813	353	241
Seattle†	12	4	0	.750	418	282
L.A. Raiders†	11	5	0	.688	368	278
Kansas City	8	8	0	.500	314	324
San Diego	7	9	0	.438	394	413

*Division champion.
†Wild-card team.

NATIONAL CONFERENCE

EASTERN DIVISION

Team	W	L	T	Pct.	PF	PA
Washington*	11	5	0	.688	426	310
N.Y. Giants†	9	7	0	.563	299	301
St. Louis	9	7	0	.563	423	345
Dallas	9	7	0	.563	308	308
Philadelphia	6	9	1	.406	278	320

CENTRAL DIVISION

Team	W	L	T	Pct.	PF	PA
Chicago*	10	6	0	.625	325	248
Green Bay	8	8	0	.500	390	309
Tampa Bay	6	10	0	.375	335	380
Detroit	4	11	1	.281	283	408
Minnesota	3	13	0	.188	276	484

WESTERN DIVISION

Team	W	L	T	Pct.	PF	PA
San Francisco*	15	1	0	.938	475	227
L.A. Rams†	10	6	0	.625	346	316
New Orleans	7	9	0	.438	298	361
Atlanta	4	12	0	.250	281	382

PLAYOFFS

AFC wild-card game
Seattle 13 vs. Los Angeles Raiders 7

AFC divisional games
Miami 31 vs. Seattle 10
Pittsburgh 24 at Denver 17

AFC championship
Miami 45 vs. Pittsburgh 28

NFC wild-card game
N.Y. Giants 16 at L.A. Rams 13

NFC divisional games
San Francisco 21 vs. N.Y. Giants 10
Chicago 23 at Washington 19

NFC championship
San Francisco 23 vs. Chicago 0

Super Bowl 19
San Francisco 38, Miami 16, at Stanford, Calif.

AMERICAN CONFERENCE

EASTERN DIVISION

Team	W	L	T	Pct.	PF	PA
Miami*	12	4	0	.750	428	320
N.Y. Jets†	11	5	0	.688	393	264
New England†	11	5	0	.688	362	290
Indianapolis	5	11	0	.313	320	386
Buffalo	2	14	0	.125	200	381

CENTRAL DIVISION

Team	W	L	T	Pct.	PF	PA
Cleveland*	8	8	0	.500	287	294
Cincinnati	7	9	0	.438	441	437
Pittsburgh	7	9	0	.438	379	355
Houston	5	11	0	.313	284	412

WESTERN DIVISION

Team	W	L	T	Pct.	PF	PA
L.A. Raiders*	12	4	0	.750	354	308
Denver	11	5	0	.688	380	329
Seattle	8	8	0	.500	349	303
San Diego	8	8	0	.500	467	435
Kansas City	6	10	0	.375	317	360

*Division champion.
†Wild-card team.

NATIONAL CONFERENCE

EASTERN DIVISION

Team	W	L	T	Pct.	PF	PA
Dallas*	10	6	0	.625	357	333
N.Y. Giants†	10	6	0	.625	399	283
Washington	10	6	0	.625	297	312
Philadelphia	7	9	0	.438	286	310
St. Louis	5	11	0	.313	278	414

CENTRAL DIVISION

Team	W	L	T	Pct.	PF	PA
Chicago*	15	1	0	.938	456	198
Green Bay	8	8	0	.500	337	355
Minnesota	7	9	0	.438	346	359
Detroit	7	9	0	.438	307	366
Tampa Bay	2	14	0	.125	294	448

WESTERN DIVISION

Team	W	L	T	Pct.	PF	PA
L.A. Rams*	11	5	0	.688	340	277
San Francisco†	10	6	0	.625	411	263
New Orleans	5	11	0	.313	294	401
Atlanta	4	12	0	.250	282	452

PLAYOFFS

AFC wild-card game
New England 26 at N.Y. Jets 14

AFC divisional games
Miami 24 vs. Cleveland 21
New England 27 at L.A. Raiders 20

AFC championship
New England 31 at Miami 14

NFC wild-card game
N.Y. Giants 17 vs. San Francisco 3

NFC divisional games
Los Angeles Rams 20 vs. Dallas 0
Chicago 21 vs. New York Giants 0

NFC championship
Chicago 24 vs. Los Angeles Rams 0

Super Bowl 20
Chicago 46, New England 10, at New Orleans.

HISTORY *Year-by-year standings*

DA BEARS

The 1985 Chicago Bears may not have been the best team ever, but they were certainly among the most colorful. Running back Walter Payton suggested his teammates could have stepped right from the pages of *One Flew Over the Cuckoo's Nest*. Rookie defensive tackle William Perry, whose girth earned him the nickname "The Refrigerator," said "I was big when I was little" when queried about his weight. The players cut a popular music video "The Super Bowl Shuffle"—while the regular season was still in progress. But there were good reasons for the cockiness: The Bears were good. They scored 456 points and allowed 198, one of the lowest totals ever for a 16-game season. Their final record, including the playoffs, was 18-1, and they outscored their three postseason opponents by a combined 91-10. Chicago's 46-10 rout of New England in the Super Bowl was the most lopsided in the game's first 20 years.

1986

AMERICAN CONFERENCE

EASTERN DIVISION

Team	W	L	T	Pct.	PF	PA
New England*	11	5	0	.688	412	307
N.Y. Jets†	10	6	0	.625	364	386
Miami	8	8	0	.500	430	405
Buffalo	4	12	0	.250	287	348
Indianapolis	3	13	0	.188	229	400

CENTRAL DIVISION

Team	W	L	T	Pct.	PF	PA
Cleveland*	12	4	0	.750	391	310
Cincinnati	10	6	0	.625	409	394
Pittsburgh	6	10	0	.375	307	336
Houston	5	11	0	.313	274	329

WESTERN DIVISION

Team	W	L	T	Pct.	PF	PA
Denver*	11	5	0	.688	378	327
Kansas City†	10	6	0	.625	358	326
Seattle	10	6	0	.625	366	293
L.A. Raiders	8	8	0	.500	323	346
San Diego	4	12	0	.250	335	396

*Division champion.
†Wild-card team.

NATIONAL CONFERENCE

EASTERN DIVISION

Team	W	L	T	Pct.	PF	PA
N.Y. Giants*	14	2	0	.875	371	236
Washington†	12	4	0	.750	368	296
Dallas	7	9	0	.438	346	337
Philadelphia	5	10	1	.344	256	312
St. Louis	4	11	1	.281	218	351

CENTRAL DIVISION

Team	W	L	T	Pct.	PF	PA
Chicago*	14	2	0	.875	352	187
Minnesota	9	7	0	.563	398	273
Detroit	5	11	0	.313	277	326
Green Bay	4	12	0	.250	254	418
Tampa Bay	2	14	0	.125	239	473

WESTERN DIVISION

Team	W	L	T	Pct.	PF	PA
San Francisco*	10	5	1	.656	374	247
L.A. Rams†	10	6	0	.625	309	267
Atlanta	7	8	1	.469	280	280
New Orleans	7	9	0	.438	288	287

PLAYOFFS

AFC wild-card game
N.Y. Jets 35 vs. Kansas City 15

AFC divisional games
Cleveland 23 vs. N.Y. Jets 20 (OT)
Denver 22 vs. New England 17

AFC championship
Denver 23 at Cleveland 20 (OT)

NFC wild-card game
Washington 19 vs. L.A. Rams 7

NFC divisional games
Washington 27 at Chicago 13
N.Y. Giants 49 vs. San Francisco 3

NFC championship
N.Y. Giants 17 vs. Washington 0

Super Bowl 21
New York Giants 39, Denver 20, at Pasadena, Calif.

1987

AMERICAN CONFERENCE

EASTERN DIVISION

Team	W	L	T	Pct.	PF	PA
Indianapolis*	9	6	0	.600	300	238
New England	8	7	0	.533	320	293
Miami	8	7	0	.533	362	335
Buffalo	7	8	0	.467	270	305
N.Y. Jets	6	9	0	.400	334	360

CENTRAL DIVISION

Team	W	L	T	Pct.	PF	PA
Cleveland*	10	5	0	.667	390	239
Houston†	9	6	0	.600	345	349
Pittsburgh	8	7	0	.533	285	299
Cincinnati	4	11	0	.267	285	370

WESTERN DIVISION

Team	W	L	T	Pct.	PF	PA
Denver*	10	4	1	.700	379	288
Seattle†	9	6	0	.600	371	314
San Diego	8	7	0	.533	253	317
L.A. Raiders	5	10	0	.333	301	289
Kansas City	4	11	0	.267	273	388

*Division champion.
†Wild-card team.

NATIONAL CONFERENCE

EASTERN DIVISION

Team	W	L	T	Pct.	PF	PA
Washington*	11	4	0	.733	379	285
Dallas	7	8	0	.467	340	348
St. Louis	7	8	0	.467	362	368
Philadelphia	7	8	0	.467	337	380
N.Y. Giants	6	9	0	.400	280	312

CENTRAL DIVISION

Team	W	L	T	Pct.	PF	PA
Chicago*	11	4	0	.733	356	282
Minnesota†	8	7	0	.533	336	335
Green Bay	5	9	1	.367	255	300
Tampa Bay	4	11	0	.267	286	360
Detroit	4	11	0	.267	269	384

WESTERN DIVISION

Team	W	L	T	Pct.	PF	PA
San Francisco*	13	2	0	.867	459	253
New Orleans†	12	3	0	.800	422	283
L.A. Rams	6	9	0	.400	317	361
Atlanta	3	12	0	.200	205	436

PLAYOFFS

AFC wild-card game
Houston 23 vs. Seattle 20 (OT)

AFC divisional games
Cleveland 38 vs. Indianapolis 21
Denver 34 vs. Houston 10

AFC championship
Denver 38 vs. Cleveland 33

NFC wild-card game
Minnesota 44 at New Orleans 10

NFC divisional games
Minnesota 36 at San Francisco 24
Washington 21 at Chicago 17

NFC championship
Washington 17 vs. Minnesota 10

Super Bowl 22
Washington 42, Denver 10, at San Diego.

NOTE: The 1987 NFL regular season was reduced from 224 games to 210 (16 to 15 for each team) due to players' strike.

REPLACEMENT BALL

Frustrated in their attempts to gain a fairer form of unrestricted free agency, NFL players went on strike for the second time in league history on September 22, 1987. The work stoppage forced the cancellation of all Week 3 games and brought about three subsequent weeks of what came to be called "replacement football." With their regular players on strike, team owners quickly assembled new squads consisting of former NFL and United States Football League players, castoffs and amateur dreamers willing to cross a picket line. The result? There was a wide discrepancy in the quality of the teams, depending largely on how much effort management invested in assembling new rosters. The defending Super Bowl champion Giants, for example, lost all three of their replacement games (which counted in the standings) and never recovered once their regular players returned, finishing the season 6-9 and out of the playoffs. The Redskins, meanwhile, went 3-0 in replacement ball, helping to propel them to an 11-4 regular-season finish en route to the club's second Super Bowl title in six years.

AMERICAN CONFERENCE

EASTERN DIVISION

Team	W	L	T	Pct.	PF	PA
Buffalo*	12	4	0	.750	329	237
Indianapolis	9	7	0	.563	354	315
New England	9	7	0	.563	250	284
N.Y. Jets	8	7	1	.531	372	354
Miami	6	10	0	.375	319	380

CENTRAL DIVISION

Team	W	L	T	Pct.	PF	PA
Cincinnati*	12	4	0	.750	448	329
Cleveland†	10	6	0	.625	304	288
Houston†	10	6	0	.625	424	365
Pittsburgh	5	11	0	.313	336	421

WESTERN DIVISION

Team	W	L	T	Pct.	PF	PA
Seattle*	9	7	0	.563	339	329
Denver	8	8	0	.500	327	352
L.A. Raiders	7	9	0	.438	325	369
San Diego	6	10	0	.375	231	332
Kansas City	4	11	1	.281	254	320

*Division champion.
†Wild-card team.

NATIONAL CONFERENCE

EASTERN DIVISION

Team	W	L	T	Pct.	PF	PA
Philadelphia*	10	6	0	.625	379	319
N.Y. Giants	10	6	0	.625	359	304
Washington	7	9	0	.438	345	387
Phoenix	7	9	0	.438	344	398
Dallas	3	13	0	.188	265	381

CENTRAL DIVISION

Team	W	L	T	Pct.	PF	PA
Chicago*	12	4	0	.750	312	215
Minnesota†	11	5	0	.688	406	233
Tampa Bay	5	11	0	.313	261	350
Detroit	4	12	0	.250	220	313
Green Bay	4	12	0	.250	240	315

WESTERN DIVISION

Team	W	L	T	Pct.	PF	PA
San Francisco*	10	6	0	.625	369	294
L.A. Rams†	10	6	0	.625	407	293
New Orleans	10	6	0	.625	312	283
Atlanta	5	11	0	.313	244	315

PLAYOFFS

AFC wild-card game
Houston 24 at Cleveland 23

AFC divisional games
Cincinnati 21 vs. Seattle 13
Buffalo 17 vs. Houston 10

AFC championship
Cincinnati 21 vs. Buffalo 10

NFC wild-card game
Minnesota 28 vs. L.A. Rams 17

NFC divisional games
Chicago 20 vs. Philadelphia 12
San Francisco 34 vs. Minnesota 9

NFC championship
San Francisco 28 at Chicago 3

Super Bowl 23
San Francisco 20, Cincinnati 16, at Miami.

AMERICAN CONFERENCE

EASTERN DIVISION

Team	W	L	T	Pct.	PF	PA
Buffalo*	9	7	0	.563	409	317
Indianapolis	8	8	0	.500	298	301
Miami	8	8	0	.500	331	379
New England	5	11	0	.313	297	391
N.Y. Jets	4	12	0	.250	253	411

CENTRAL DIVISION

Team	W	L	T	Pct.	PF	PA
Cleveland*	9	6	1	.594	334	254
Houston†	9	7	0	.563	365	412
Pittsburgh†	9	7	0	.563	265	326
Cincinnati	8	8	0	.500	404	285

WESTERN DIVISION

Team	W	L	T	Pct.	PF	PA
Denver*	11	5	0	.688	362	226
Kansas City	8	7	1	.531	318	286
L.A. Raiders	8	8	0	.500	315	297
Seattle	7	9	0	.438	241	327
San Diego	6	10	0	.375	266	290

*Division champion.
†Wild-card team.

NATIONAL CONFERENCE

EASTERN DIVISION

Team	W	L	T	Pct.	PF	PA
N.Y. Giants*	12	4	0	.750	348	252
Philadelphia†	11	5	0	.688	342	274
Washington	10	6	0	.625	386	308
Phoenix	5	11	0	.313	258	377
Dallas	1	15	0	.063	204	393

CENTRAL DIVISION

Team	W	L	T	Pct.	PF	PA
Minnesota*	10	6	0	.625	351	275
Green Bay	10	6	0	.625	362	356
Detroit	7	9	0	.438	312	364
Chicago	6	10	0	.375	358	377
Tampa Bay	5	11	0	.313	320	419

WESTERN DIVISION

Team	W	L	T	Pct.	PF	PA
San Francisco*	14	2	0	.875	442	253
L.A. Rams†	11	5	0	.688	426	344
New Orleans	9	7	0	.563	386	301
Atlanta	3	13	0	.188	279	437

PLAYOFFS

AFC wild-card game
Pittsburgh 26 at Houston 23 (OT)

AFC divisional games
Cleveland 34 vs. Buffalo 30
Denver 24 vs. Pittsburgh 23

AFC championship
Denver 37 vs. Cleveland 21

NFC wild-card game
L.A. Rams 21 at Philadelphia 7

NFC divisional games
L.A. Rams 19 at N.Y. Giants 13 (OT)
San Francisco 41 vs. Minnesota 13

NFC championship
San Francisco 30 vs. L.A. Rams 3

Super Bowl 24
San Francisco 55, Denver 10, at New Orleans.

HISTORY *Year-by-year standings*

END OF AN ERA

Longtime NFL commissioner Pete Rozelle announced his retirement on March 22, 1989, after nearly thirty years running the league. The choice by default when commissioner Bert Bell died in 1960, Rozelle compiled an impressive list of accomplishments: creating the Super Bowl, masterminding the merge of the AFL and NFL, inventing *Monday Night Football,* persuading owners to accept a revenue-sharing agreement, negotiating the first leaguewide TV contract and bringing football into the television era. A search committee chose Paul Tagliabue to replace Rozelle.

1990

AMERICAN CONFERENCE

EASTERN DIVISION

Team	W	L	T	Pct.	PF	PA
Buffalo*	13	3	0	.813	428	263
Miami†	12	4	0	.750	336	242
Indianapolis	7	9	0	.438	281	353
N.Y. Jets	6	10	0	.375	295	345
New England	1	15	0	.063	181	446

CENTRAL DIVISION

Team	W	L	T	Pct.	PF	PA
Cincinnati*	9	7	0	.563	360	352
Houston†	9	7	0	.563	405	307
Pittsburgh	9	7	0	.563	292	240
Cleveland	3	13	0	.188	228	462

WESTERN DIVISION

Team	W	L	T	Pct.	PF	PA
L.A. Raiders*	12	4	0	.750	337	268
Kansas City†	11	5	0	.688	369	257
Seattle	9	7	0	.563	306	286
San Diego	6	10	0	.375	315	281
Denver	5	11	0	.313	331	374

*Division champion.
†Wild-card team.

NATIONAL CONFERENCE

EASTERN DIVISION

Team	W	L	T	Pct.	PF	PA
N.Y. Giants*	13	3	0	.813	335	211
Philadelphia†	10	6	0	.625	396	299
Washington†	10	6	0	.625	381	301
Dallas	7	9	0	.438	244	308
Phoenix	5	11	0	.313	268	396

CENTRAL DIVISION

Team	W	L	T	Pct.	PF	PA
Chicago*	11	5	0	.688	348	280
Tampa Bay	6	10	0	.375	264	367
Detroit	6	10	0	.375	373	413
Green Bay	6	10	0	.375	271	347
Minnesota	6	10	0	.375	351	326

WESTERN DIVISION

Team	W	L	T	Pct.	PF	PA
San Francisco*	14	2	0	.875	353	239
New Orleans†	8	8	0	.500	274	275
L.A. Rams	5	11	0	.313	345	412
Atlanta	5	11	0	.313	348	365

PLAYOFFS

AFC wild-card playoffs
Miami 17 vs. Kansas City 16
Cincinnati 41 vs. Houston 14

AFC divisional playoffs
Buffalo 44 vs. Miami 34
L.A. Raiders 20 vs. Cincinnati 10

AFC championship
Buffalo 51 vs. L.A. Raiders 3

NFC wild-card playoffs
Washington 20 at Philadelphia 6
Chicago 16 vs. New Orleans 6

NFC divisional playoffs
San Francisco 28 vs. Washington 10
N.Y. Giants 31 vs. Chicago 3

NFC championship
N.Y. Giants 15 at San Francisco 13

Super Bowl 25
N.Y. Giants 20 vs. Buffalo 19, at Tampa, Fla.

1991

AMERICAN CONFERENCE

EASTERN DIVISION

Team	W	L	T	Pct.	PF	PA
Buffalo*	13	3	0	.813	458	318
N.Y. Jets†	8	8	0	.500	314	293
Miami	8	8	0	.500	343	349
New England	6	10	0	.375	211	305
Indianapolis	1	15	0	.063	143	381

CENTRAL DIVISION

Team	W	L	T	Pct.	PF	PA
Houston*	11	5	0	.688	386	251
Pittsburgh	7	9	0	.438	292	344
Cleveland	6	10	0	.375	293	298
Cincinnati	3	13	0	.188	263	435

WESTERN DIVISION

Team	W	L	T	Pct.	PF	PA
Denver*	12	4	0	.750	304	235
Kansas City†	10	6	0	.625	322	252
L.A. Raiders†	9	7	0	.563	298	297
Seattle	7	9	0	.438	276	261
San Diego	4	12	0	.250	274	342

*Division champion.
†Wild-card team.

NATIONAL CONFERENCE

EASTERN DIVISION

Team	W	L	T	Pct.	PF	PA
Washington*	14	2	0	.875	485	224
Dallas†	11	5	0	.688	342	310
Philadelphia	10	6	0	.625	285	244
N.Y. Giants	8	8	0	.500	281	297
Phoenix	4	12	0	.250	196	344

CENTRAL DIVISION

Team	W	L	T	Pct.	PF	PA
Detroit*	12	4	0	.750	339	295
Chicago†	11	5	0	.688	299	269
Minnesota	8	8	0	.500	301	306
Green Bay	4	12	0	.250	273	313
Tampa Bay	3	13	0	.188	199	365

WESTERN DIVISION

Team	W	L	T	Pct.	PF	PA
New Orleans*	11	5	0	.688	341	211
Atlanta†	10	6	0	.625	361	338
San Francisco	10	6	0	.625	393	239
L.A. Rams	3	13	0	.188	234	390

PLAYOFFS

AFC wild-card playoffs
Kansas City 10 vs. L.A. Raiders 6
Houston 17 vs. N.Y. Jets 10

AFC divisional playoffs
Denver 26 vs. Houston 24
Buffalo 37 vs. Kansas City 14

AFC championship
Buffalo 10 vs. Denver 7

NFC wild-card playoffs
Atlanta 27 at New Orleans 20
Dallas 17 at Chicago 13

NFC divisional playoffs
Washington 24 vs. Atlanta 7
Detroit 38 vs. Dallas 6

NFC championship
Washington 41 vs. Detroit 10

Super Bowl 26
Washington 37 vs. Buffalo 24, at Minneapolis.

HISTORY *Year-by-year standings*

GIANTS AND BILLS GO DOWN TO THE WIRE

One year after the most lopsided Super Bowl ever, the Giants and Bills staged the closest, with New York edging Buffalo, 20-19, at Tampa Stadium in Super Bowl 25 when Bills kicker Scott Norwood missed a 47-yard field goal attempt with eight seconds left. Although Norwood wore the goat horns afterward, his teammates did little early in the contest to prevent the game from coming down to a last-minute kick. A Buffalo offense that had scored a league-high 428 points during the regular season and 95 in the first two playoff games did little in its biggest test of the season. Only running back Thurman Thomas (135 yards rushing) had what could be considered a superior game. The Giants' offense, meanwhile, put together scoring drives of 87, 75 and 74 yards. A 14-play, 75-yard drive that took 9 minutes, 29 seconds off the clock went into the books as the most time-consuming drive in Super Bowl history.

AMERICAN CONFERENCE

EASTERN DIVISION

Team	W	L	T	Pct.	PF	PA
Miami*	11	5	0	.688	340	281
Buffalo†	11	5	0	.688	381	283
Indianapolis	9	7	0	.563	216	302
N.Y. Jets	4	12	0	.250	220	315
New England	2	14	0	.125	205	363

CENTRAL DIVISION

Team	W	L	T	Pct.	PF	PA
Pittsburgh*	11	5	0	.688	299	225
Houston†	10	6	0	.625	352	258
Cleveland	7	9	0	.438	272	275
Cincinnati	5	11	0	.313	274	364

WESTERN DIVISION

Team	W	L	T	Pct.	PF	PA
San Diego*	11	5	0	.688	335	241
Kansas City†	10	6	0	.625	348	282
Denver	8	8	0	.500	262	329
L.A. Raiders	7	9	0	.438	249	281
Seattle	2	14	0	.125	140	312

*Division champion.
†Wild-card team.

NATIONAL CONFERENCE

EASTERN DIVISION

Team	W	L	T	Pct.	PF	PA
Dallas*	13	3	0	.813	409	243
Philadelphia†	11	5	0	.688	354	245
Washington†	9	7	0	.563	300	255
N.Y. Giants	6	10	0	.375	306	367
Phoenix	4	12	0	.250	243	332

CENTRAL DIVISION

Team	W	L	T	Pct.	PF	PA
Minnesota*	11	5	0	.688	374	249
Green Bay	9	7	0	.563	276	296
Tampa Bay	5	11	0	.313	267	365
Chicago	5	11	0	.313	295	361
Detroit	5	11	0	.313	273	332

WESTERN DIVISION

Team	W	L	T	Pct.	PF	PA
San Francisco*	14	2	0	.875	431	236
New Orleans†	12	4	0	.750	330	202
Atlanta	6	10	0	.375	327	414
L.A. Rams	6	10	0	.375	313	383

PLAYOFFS

AFC wild-card playoffs
San Diego 17 vs. Kansas City 0
Buffalo 41 vs. Houston 38 (OT)

AFC divisional playoffs
Buffalo 24 at Pittsburgh 3
Miami 31 vs. San Diego 0

AFC championship
Buffalo 29 at Miami 10

NFC wild-card playoffs
Washington 24 at Minnesota 7
Philadelphia 36 at New Orleans 20

NFC divisional playoffs
San Francisco 20 vs. Washington 13
Dallas 34 vs. Philadelphia 10

NFC championship
Dallas 30 at San Francisco 20

Super Bowl 27
Dallas 52 vs. Buffalo 17, at Pasadena, Calif.

AMERICAN CONFERENCE

EASTERN DIVISION

Team	W	L	T	Pct.	PF	PA
Buffalo*	12	4	0	.750	329	242
Miami	9	7	0	.563	349	351
N.Y. Jets	8	8	0	.500	270	247
New England	5	11	0	.313	238	286
Indianapolis	4	12	0	.250	189	378

CENTRAL DIVISION

Team	W	L	T	Pct.	PF	PA
Houston*	12	4	0	.750	368	238
Pittsburgh†	9	7	0	.563	308	281
Cleveland	7	9	0	.438	304	307
Cincinnati	3	13	0	.188	187	319

WESTERN DIVISION

Team	W	L	T	Pct.	PF	PA
Kansas City*	11	5	0	.688	328	291
L.A. Raiders†	10	6	0	.625	306	326
Denver†	9	7	0	.563	373	284
San Diego	8	8	0	.500	322	290
Seattle	6	10	0	.375	280	314

*Division champion.
†Wild-card team.

NATIONAL CONFERENCE

EASTERN DIVISION

Team	W	L	T	Pct.	PF	PA
Dallas*	12	4	0	.750	376	229
N.Y. Giants†	11	5	0	.688	288	205
Philadelphia	8	8	0	.500	293	315
Phoenix	7	9	0	.438	326	269
Washington	4	12	0	.250	230	345

CENTRAL DIVISION

Team	W	L	T	Pct.	PF	PA
Detroit*	10	6	0	.625	298	292
Minnesota†	9	7	0	.563	277	290
Green Bay†	9	7	0	.563	340	282
Chicago	7	9	0	.438	234	230
Tampa Bay	5	11	0	.313	237	376

WESTERN DIVISION

Team	W	L	T	Pct.	PF	PA
San Francisco*	10	6	0	.625	473	295
New Orleans	8	8	0	.500	317	343
Atlanta	6	10	0	.375	316	385
L.A. Rams	5	11	0	.313	221	367

PLAYOFFS

AFC wild-card playoffs
Kansas City 27 vs. Pittsburgh 24 (OT)
L.A. Raiders 42 vs. Denver 24

AFC divisional playoffs
Buffalo 29 vs. L.A. Raiders 23
Kansas City 28 at Houston 20

AFC championship
Buffalo 30 vs. Kansas City 13

NFC wild-card playoffs
Green Bay 28 at Detroit 24
N.Y. Giants 17 vs. Minnesota 10

NFC divisional playoffs
San Francisco 44 vs. N.Y. Giants 3
Dallas 27 vs. Green Bay 17

NFC championship
Dallas 38 vs. San Francisco 21

Super Bowl 28
Dallas 30 vs. Buffalo 13, at Atlanta.

HISTORY *Year-by-year standings*

MONTANA IN THE MIDWEST

Although he was unable to take the Chiefs to the same heights he did the San Francisco 49ers a decade earlier, Joe Montana closed out his illustrious career with two relatively productive, if injury-plagued, seasons in Kansas City. Montana, who never completely recovered from injuries suffered in the 1990 NFC title game against the Giants (broken right hand, bruised sternum) that forced him to miss the entire 1991 season and all but one game in '92, played only 38 of 64 quarters for the Chiefs in 1993. Nevertheless, he was the AFC's No. 2-rated quarterback and guided Kansas City to within one game of the Super Bowl. Using the old Montana magic, he spearheaded come-from-behind playoff victories over the Steelers and Oilers before the Chiefs finally succumbed, 30-13, at Buffalo in the AFC championship game.

AMERICAN CONFERENCE

EASTERN DIVISION

Team	W	L	T	Pct.	PF	PA
Miami*	10	6	0	.625	389	327
New England†	10	6	0	.625	351	312
Indianapolis	8	8	0	.500	307	320
Buffalo	7	9	0	.438	340	356
N.Y. Jets	6	10	0	.375	264	320

CENTRAL DIVISION

Team	W	L	T	Pct.	PF	PA
Pittsburgh*	12	4	0	.750	316	234
Cleveland†	11	5	0	.688	340	204
Cincinnati	3	13	0	.188	276	406
Houston	2	14	0	.125	226	352

WESTERN DIVISION

Team	W	L	T	Pct.	PF	PA
San Diego*	11	5	0	.688	381	306
Kansas City†	9	7	0	.563	319	298
L.A. Raiders	9	7	0	.563	303	327
Denver	7	9	0	.438	347	396
Seattle	6	10	0	.375	287	323

*Division champion.
†Wild-card team.

NATIONAL CONFERENCE

EASTERN DIVISION

Team	W	L	T	Pct.	PF	PA
Dallas*	12	4	0	.750	414	248
N.Y. Giants	9	7	0	.563	279	305
Arizona	8	8	0	.500	235	267
Philadelphia	7	9	0	.438	308	308
Washington	3	13	0	.188	320	412

CENTRAL DIVISION

Team	W	L	T	Pct.	PF	PA
Minnesota*	10	6	0	.625	356	314
Green Bay†	9	7	0	.563	382	287
Detroit†	9	7	0	.563	357	342
Chicago†	9	7	0	.563	271	307
Tampa Bay	6	10	0	.375	251	351

WESTERN DIVISION

Team	W	L	T	Pct.	PF	PA
San Francisco*	13	3	0	.813	505	296
New Orleans	7	9	0	.438	348	407
Atlanta	7	9	0	.438	317	385
L.A. Rams	4	12	0	.250	286	365

PLAYOFFS

AFC wild-card playoffs
Miami 27 vs. Kansas City 17
Cleveland 20 vs. New England 13

AFC divisional playoffs
Pittsburgh 29 vs. Cleveland 9
San Diego 22 vs. Miami 21

AFC championship
San Diego 17 at Pittsburgh 13

NFC wild-card playoffs
Green Bay 16 vs. Detroit 12
Chicago 35 at Minnesota 18

NFC divisional playoffs
San Francisco 44 vs. Chicago 15
Dallas 35 vs. Green Bay 9

NFC championship
San Francisco 38 vs. Dallas 28

Super Bowl 29
San Francisco 49 vs. San Diego 26 at Miami.

AMERICAN CONFERENCE

EASTERN DIVISION

Team	W	L	T	Pct.	PF	PA
Buffalo*	10	6	0	.625	350	335
Indianapolis†	9	7	0	.563	331	316
Miami†	9	7	0	.563	398	332
New England	6	10	0	.375	294	377
N.Y. Jets	3	13	0	.188	233	384

CENTRAL DIVISION

Team	W	L	T	Pct.	PF	PA
Pittsburgh*	11	5	0	.689	407	327
Cincinnati	7	9	0	.438	349	374
Houston	7	9	0	.438	348	324
Cleveland	5	11	0	.313	289	356
Jacksonville	4	12	0	.250	275	404

WESTERN DIVISION

Team	W	L	T	Pct.	PF	PA
Kansas City*	13	3	0	.813	358	241
San Diego†	9	7	0	.563	321	323
Seattle	8	8	0	.500	363	366
Denver	8	8	0	.500	388	345
Oakland	8	8	0	.500	348	332

*Division champion.
†Wild-card team.

NATIONAL CONFERENCE

EASTERN DIVISION

Team	W	L	T	Pct.	PF	PA
Dallas*	12	4	0	.750	435	291
Philadelphia†	10	6	0	.625	318	338
Washington	6	10	0	.375	326	359
N.Y. Giants	5	11	0	.313	290	340
Arizona	4	12	0	.250	275	422

CENTRAL DIVISION

Team	W	L	T	Pct.	PF	PA
Green Bay*	11	5	0	.689	404	314
Detroit†	10	6	0	.625	436	336
Chicago	9	7	0	.563	392	360
Minnesota	8	8	0	.500	412	385
Tampa Bay	7	9	0	.438	238	335

WESTERN DIVISION

Team	W	L	T	Pct.	PF	PA
San Francisco*	11	5	0	.688	457	258
Atlanta†	9	7	0	.563	362	349
St. Louis	7	9	0	.438	309	418
Carolina	7	9	0	.438	289	325
New Orleans	7	9	0	.438	319	348

PLAYOFFS

AFC wild-card playoffs
Buffalo 37 vs. Miami 22
Indianapolis 35 at San Diego 20

AFC divisional playoffs
Pittsburgh 40 vs. Buffalo 21
Indianapolis 10 at Kansas City 7

AFC championship
Pittsburgh 20 vs. Indianapolis 16

NFC wild-card playoffs
Philadelphia 58 vs. Detroit 37
Green Bay 37 vs. Atlanta 20

NFC divisional playoffs
Green Bay 27 at San Francisco 17
Dallas 30 vs. Philadelphia 11

NFC championship
Dallas 38 vs. Green Bay 27

Super Bowl 30
Dallas 27 vs. Pittsburgh 17, at Tempe, Ariz.

A RECORD-SETTING YEAR

In 1995, NFL players broke several long-standing records. Miami quarterback Dan Marino, in Dolphins coach Don Shula's last season, put himself atop the career passing charts by breaking Fran Tarkenton's records for attempts (6,467), completions (3,686), yards (47,003) and touchdown passes (342). Dallas running back Emmitt Smith set the career mark for touchdowns in a season when he broke John Riggins' record of 24. San Francisco receiver Jerry Rice broke Art Monk's record for career receptions and Charlie Hennigan's mark for receiving yards in a season. Rice ended the 1995 regular season with 942 receptions for his career and 1,848 yards for the season.

AMERICAN CONFERENCE

EASTERN DIVISION

Team	W	L	T	Pct.	PF	PA
New England*	11	5	0	.687	418	313
Buffalo†	10	6	0	.625	319	266
Indianapolis†	9	7	0	.563	317	334
Miami	8	8	0	.500	339	325
N.Y. Jets	1	15	0	.063	279	454

CENTRAL DIVISION

Team	W	L	T	Pct.	PF	PA
Pittsburgh*	10	6	0	.625	344	257
Jacksonville†	9	7	0	.563	325	335
Cincinnati	8	8	0	.500	372	369
Houston	8	8	0	.500	345	319
Baltimore	4	12	0	.250	371	441

WESTERN DIVISION

Team	W	L	T	Pct.	PF	PA
Denver*	13	3	0	.813	391	275
Kansas City	9	7	0	.563	297	300
San Diego	8	8	0	.500	310	376
Oakland	7	9	0	.438	340	293
Seattle	7	9	0	.438	317	376

*Division champion.
†Wild-card team.

NATIONAL CONFERENCE

EASTERN DIVISION

Team	W	L	T	Pct.	PF	PA
Dallas*	10	6	0	.625	286	250
Philadelphia†	10	6	0	.625	363	341
Washington	9	7	0	.563	364	312
Arizona	7	9	0	.438	300	397
N.Y. Giants	6	10	0	.375	242	297

CENTRAL DIVISION

Team	W	L	T	Pct.	PF	PA
Green Bay*	13	3	0	.813	456	210
Minnesota†	9	7	0	.563	298	315
Chicago	7	9	0	.438	283	305
Tampa Bay	6	10	0	.375	221	293
Detroit	5	11	0	.313	302	368

WESTERN DIVISION

Team	W	L	T	Pct.	PF	PA
Carolina*	12	4	0	.750	367	218
San Francisco†	12	4	0	.750	398	257
St. Louis	6	10	0	.375	303	409
Atlanta	3	13	0	.188	309	461
New Orleans	3	13	0	.188	229	339

PLAYOFFS

AFC wild-card playoffs
Jacksonville 30 at Buffalo 27
Pittsburgh 42 vs. Indianapolis 14
AFC divisional playoffs
Jacksonville 30 at Denver 27
New England 28 vs. Pittsburgh 3
AFC championship
New England 20 vs. Jacksonville 6
NFC wild-card playoffs
Dallas 40 vs. Minnesota 15
San Francisco 14 vs. Philadelphia 0
NFC divisional playoffs
Green Bay 35 vs. San Francisco 14
Carolina 26 vs. Dallas 17
NFC championship
Green Bay 30 vs. Carolina 13
Super Bowl 31
Green Bay 35, New England 21, at New Orleans.

AMERICAN CONFERENCE

EASTERN DIVISION

Team	W	L	T	Pct.	PF	PA
New England*	10	6	0	.625	369	289
Miami†	9	7	0	.563	339	327
N.Y. Jets	9	7	0	.563	348	287
Buffalo	6	10	0	.375	255	367
Indianapolis	3	13	0	.188	313	401

CENTRAL DIVISION

Team	W	L	T	Pct.	PF	PA
Pittsburgh*	11	5	0	.688	372	307
Jacksonville†	11	5	0	.688	394	318
Tennessee	8	8	0	.500	333	310
Cincinnati	7	9	0	.438	355	405
Baltimore	6	9	1	.406	326	345

WESTERN DIVISION

Team	W	L	T	Pct.	PF	PA
Kansas City*	13	3	0	.813	375	232
Denver†	12	4	0	.750	472	287
Seattle	8	8	0	.500	365	362
Oakland	4	12	0	.250	324	419
San Diego	4	12	0	.250	266	425

*Division champion.
†Wild-card team.

NATIONAL CONFERENCE

EASTERN DIVISION

Team	W	L	T	Pct.	PF	PA
N.Y. Giants*	10	5	1	.656	307	265
Washington	8	7	1	.531	327	289
Philadelphia	6	9	1	.406	317	372
Dallas	6	10	0	.375	304	314
Arizona	4	12	0	.250	283	379

CENTRAL DIVISION

Team	W	L	T	Pct.	PF	PA
Green Bay*	13	3	0	.813	422	282
Tampa Bay†	10	6	0	.625	299	263
Detroit†	9	7	0	.563	379	306
Minnesota†	9	7	0	.563	354	359
Chicago	4	12	0	.250	263	421

WESTERN DIVISION

Team	W	L	T	Pct.	PF	PA
San Francisco*	13	3	0	.813	375	265
Carolina	7	9	0	.438	265	314
Atlanta	7	9	0	.438	320	361
New Orleans	6	10	0	.375	237	327
St. Louis	5	11	0	.313	299	359

PLAYOFFS

AFC wild-card playoffs
Denver 42 vs. Jacksonville 17
New England 17 vs. Miami 3
AFC divisional playoffs
Pittsburgh 7 vs. New England 6
Denver 14 at Kansas City 10
AFC championship
Denver 24 at Pittsburgh 21
NFC wild-card playoffs
Minnesota 23 at N.Y. Giants 22
Tampa Bay 20 vs. Detroit 10
NFC divisional playoffs
San Francisco 38 vs. Minnesota 22
Green Bay 21 vs. Tampa Bay 7
NFC championship
Green Bay 23 at San Francisco 10
Super Bowl 32
Denver 31 vs. Green Bay 24, at San Diego.

HISTORY *Year-by-year standings*

ELWAY, BRONCOS REACH THE TOP

One year after a humbling first-round loss at home to Jacksonville in the 1996 playoffs, the Denver Broncos made sure history did not repeat, whipping the Jaguars, 42-17, in a first-round rematch at Mile High Stadium. That was impressive, but what happened next was more impressive: two straight road playoff victories and the franchise's first-ever Super Bowl title. Prior to the three-game winning streak, the Broncos had won just one other road playoff game in their 37-year history. Although running back Terrell Davis was the Broncos' star and won Super Bowl 32 MVP honors, their leader was veteran quarterback John Elway, who finally scaled the NFL mountaintop after three crushing Super Bowl defeats earlier in his career. Denver thus became the first AFC team in 14 years and only the second wild-card team to win the Super Bowl.

1998

AMERICAN CONFERENCE

EASTERN DIVISION

Team	W	L	T	Pct.	PF	PA
N.Y. Jets*	12	4	0	.750	416	266
Miami†	10	6	0	.625	321	265
Buffalo†	10	6	0	.625	400	333
New England†	9	7	0	.563	337	329
Indianapolis	3	13	0	.188	310	444

CENTRAL DIVISION

Team	W	L	T	Pct.	PF	PA
Jacksonville*	11	5	0	.688	392	338
Tennessee	8	8	0	.500	330	320
Pittsburgh	7	9	0	.438	263	303
Baltimore	6	10	0	.375	269	335
Cincinnati	3	13	0	.188	268	452

WESTERN DIVISION

Team	W	L	T	Pct.	PF	PA
Denver*	14	2	0	.875	501	309
Oakland	8	8	0	.500	288	356
Seattle	8	8	0	.500	372	310
Kansas City	7	9	0	.438	327	363
San Diego	5	11	0	.313	241	342

*Division champion.
†Wild-card team.

NATIONAL CONFERENCE

EASTERN DIVISION

Team	W	L	T	Pct.	PF	PA
Dallas*	10	6	0	.625	381	275
Arizona†	9	7	0	.563	325	378
N.Y. Giants	8	8	0	.500	287	309
Washington	6	10	0	.375	319	421
Philadelphia	3	13	0	.188	161	344

CENTRAL DIVISION

Team	W	L	T	Pct.	PF	PA
Minnesota*	15	1	0	.938	556	296
Green Bay†	11	5	0	.688	408	319
Tampa Bay	8	8	0	.500	314	295
Detroit	5	11	0	.313	306	378
Chicago	4	12	0	.250	276	368

WESTERN DIVISION

Team	W	L	T	Pct.	PF	PA
Atlanta*	14	2	0	.875	442	289
San Francisco†	12	4	0	.750	479	328
New Orleans	6	10	0	.375	305	359
Carolina	4	12	0	.250	336	413
St. Louis	4	12	0	.250	285	378

PLAYOFFS

AFC wild-card playoffs
Miami 24 vs. Buffalo 17
Jacksonville 25 vs. New England 10
AFC divisional playoffs
Denver 38 vs. Miami 3
New York Jets 34 vs. Jacksonville 24
AFC championship
Denver 23 vs. New York Jets 10
NFC wild-card playoffs
Arizona 20 at Dallas 7
San Francisco 30 vs. Green Bay 27
NFC divisional playoffs
Atlanta 20 vs. San Francisco 18
Minnesota 41 vs. Arizona 21
NFC championship
Atlanta 30 at Minnesota 27 (OT)
Super Bowl 33
Denver 34 vs. Atlanta 19, at Miami.

1999

AMERICAN CONFERENCE

EASTERN DIVISION

Team	W	L	T	Pct.	PF	PA
Indianapolis*	13	3	0	.813	423	333
Buffalo†	11	5	0	.688	320	229
Miami†	9	7	0	.563	326	336
N.Y. Jets	8	8	0	.500	308	309
New England	8	8	0	.500	299	284

CENTRAL DIVISION

Team	W	L	T	Pct.	PF	PA
Jacksonville*	14	2	0	.875	396	217
Tennessee†	13	3	0	.813	392	324
Baltimore	8	8	0	.500	324	277
Pittsburgh	6	10	0	.375	317	320
Cincinnati	4	12	0	.250	283	460
Cleveland	2	14	0	.125	217	437

WESTERN DIVISION

Team	W	L	T	Pct.	PF	PA
Seattle*	9	7	0	.563	338	298
Kansas City	9	7	0	.563	390	322
San Diego	8	8	0	.500	269	316
Oakland	8	8	0	.500	390	329
Denver	6	10	0	.375	314	318

*Division champion.
†Wild-card team.

NATIONAL CONFERENCE

EASTERN DIVISION

Team	W	L	T	Pct.	PF	PA
Washington*	10	6	0	.625	443	377
Dallas†	8	8	0	.500	352	276
N.Y. Giants	7	9	0	.438	299	358
Arizona	6	10	0	.375	245	382
Philadelphia	5	11	0	.313	272	357

CENTRAL DIVISION

Team	W	L	T	Pct.	PF	PA
Tampa Bay*	11	5	0	.688	270	235
Minnesota†	10	6	0	.625	399	335
Detroit†	8	8	0	.500	322	323
Green Bay	8	8	0	.500	357	341
Chicago	6	10	0	.375	272	341

WESTERN DIVISION

Team	W	L	T	Pct.	PF	PA
St. Louis*	13	3	0	.813	526	242
Carolina	8	8	0	.500	421	381
Atlanta	5	11	0	.313	285	380
San Francisco	4	12	0	.250	295	453
New Orleans	3	13	0	.188	260	434

PLAYOFFS

AFC wild-card playoffs
Miami 20 at Seattle 17
Tennessee 22 vs. Buffalo 16
AFC divisional playoffs
Tennessee 19 at Indianapolis 16
Jacksonville 62 vs. Miami 7
AFC championship
Tennessee 33 at Jacksonville 14
NFC wild-card playoffs
Minnesota 27 vs. Dallas 10
Washington 27 vs. Detroit 13
NFC divisional playoffs
St. Louis 49 vs. Minnesota 37
Tampa Bay 14 vs. Washington 13
NFC championship
St. Louis 11 vs. Tampa Bay 6
Super Bowl 34
St. Louis 23 vs. Tennessee 16, at Atlanta.

RAMS, RAVENS MAKE DRAMATIC TURNAROUNDS

The ability of teams to turn around their fortunes seemingly overnight was never more evident than during the 1999 and 2000 seasons. The St. Louis Rams, 4-12 in 1998, and the Baltimore Ravens, 8-8 in 1999, rebounded to win Super Bowls the following seasons. The turnaround of the Rams was truly astonishing. In danger of finishing with the NFL's worst record of the 1990s, the Rams—45-99 from 1990 through '98—scored a league-high 526 points (third most in NFL history and 241 more than they had the year before) and won 16 games (including playoffs) by an average score of 33-13. The Ravens, meanwhile, used defense to win their first league championship. Baltimore allowed just 165 points—fewest ever in a 16-game season—en route to becoming the third wild-card team to win the Super Bowl.

AMERICAN CONFERENCE

EASTERN DIVISION

Team	W	L	T	Pct.	PF	PA
Miami*	11	5	0	.688	323	226
Indianapolis†	10	6	0	.625	429	326
N.Y. Jets	9	7	0	.563	321	321
Buffalo	8	8	0	.500	315	350
New England	5	11	0	.313	276	338

CENTRAL DIVISION

Team	W	L	T	Pct.	PF	PA
Tennessee*	13	3	0	.813	346	191
Baltimore†	12	4	0	.750	333	165
Pittsburgh	9	7	0	.563	321	255
Jacksonville	7	9	0	.438	367	327
Cincinnati	4	12	0	.250	185	359
Cleveland	3	13	0	.188	161	419

WESTERN DIVISION

Team	W	L	T	Pct.	PF	PA
Oakland*	12	4	0	.750	479	299
Denver†	11	5	0	.688	485	369
Kansas City	7	9	0	.438	355	354
Seattle	6	10	0	.375	320	405
San Diego	1	15	0	.063	269	440

*Division champion.
†Wild-card team.

NATIONAL CONFERENCE

EASTERN DIVISION

Team	W	L	T	Pct.	PF	PA
N.Y. Giants*	12	4	0	.750	328	246
Philadelphia†	11	5	0	.688	351	245
Washington	8	8	0	.500	281	269
Dallas	5	11	0	.313	294	361
Arizona	3	13	0	.188	210	443

CENTRAL DIVISION

Team	W	L	T	Pct.	PF	PA
Minnesota*	11	5	0	.688	397	371
Tampa Bay†	10	6	0	.625	388	269
Green Bay	9	7	0	.563	353	323
Detroit	9	7	0	.563	307	307
Chicago	5	11	0	.313	216	355

WESTERN DIVISION

Team	W	L	T	Pct.	PF	PA
New Orleans*	10	6	0	.625	354	305
St. Louis†	10	6	0	.625	540	471
Carolina	7	9	0	.438	310	310
San Francisco	6	10	0	.375	388	422
Atlanta	4	12	0	.250	252	413

PLAYOFFS

AFC wild-card playoffs
Miami 23 vs. Indianapolis 17 (OT)
Baltimore 21 vs. Denver 3
AFC divisional playoffs
Oakland 27 vs. Miami 0
Baltimore 24 at Tennessee 10
AFC championship
Baltimore 16 at Oakland 3
NFC wild-card playoffs
New Orleans 31 vs. St. Louis 28
Philadelphia 21 vs. Tampa Bay 3
NFC divisional playoffs
Minnesota 34 vs. New Orleans 16
N.Y. Giants 20 vs. Philadelphia 10
NFC championship
N.Y. Giants 41 vs. Minnesota 0
Super Bowl 35
Baltimore 34 vs. N.Y. Giants 7, at Tampa.

AMERICAN CONFERENCE

EASTERN DIVISION

Team	W	L	T	Pct.	PF	PA
New England*	11	5	0	.688	371	272
Miami†	11	5	0	.688	344	290
N.Y. Jets†	10	6	0	.625	308	295
Indianapolis	6	10	0	.375	413	486
Buffalo	3	13	0	.188	265	420

CENTRAL DIVISION

Team	W	L	T	Pct.	PF	PA
Pittsburgh*	13	3	0	.812	352	212
Baltimore†	10	6	0	.625	303	265
Cleveland	7	9	0	.438	285	319
Tennessee	7	9	0	.438	336	388
Jacksonville	6	10	0	.375	294	286
Cincinnati	6	10	0	.375	226	309

WESTERN DIVISION

Team	W	L	T	Pct.	PF	PA
Oakland*	10	6	0	.625	399	327
Seattle	9	7	0	.562	301	324
Denver	8	8	0	.500	340	339
Kansas City	6	10	0	.375	320	344
San Diego	5	11	0	.312	332	321

*Division champion.
†Wild-card team.

NATIONAL CONFERENCE

EASTERN DIVISION

Team	W	L	T	Pct.	PF	PA
Philadelphia*	11	5	0	.688	343	208
Washington	8	8	0	.500	256	303
N.Y. Giants	7	9	0	.438	294	321
Arizona	7	9	0	.438	295	343
Dallas	5	11	0	.312	246	338

CENTRAL DIVISION

Team	W	L	T	Pct.	PF	PA
Chicago*	13	3	0	.812	338	203
Green Bay†	12	4	0	.750	390	266
Tampa Bay†	9	7	0	.562	324	280
Minnesota	5	11	0	.312	290	390
Detroit	2	14	0	.125	270	424

WESTERN DIVISION

Team	W	L	T	Pct.	PF	PA
St. Louis*	14	2	0	.875	503	273
San Francisco†	12	4	0	.750	409	282
New Orleans	7	9	0	.438	333	409
Atlanta	7	9	0	.438	291	377
Carolina	1	15	0	.062	253	410

PLAYOFFS

AFC wild-card playoffs
Oakland 38 vs. N.Y. Jets 24
Baltimore 20 at Miami 3
AFC divisional playoffs
New England 16 vs. Oakland 13 (OT)
Pittsburgh 27 vs. Baltimore 10
AFC championship
New England 24 at Pittsburgh 17
NFC wild-card playoffs
Philadelphia 31 vs. Tampa Bay 9
Green Bay 25 vs. San Francisco 15
NFC divisional playoffs
Philadelphia 33 at Chicago 19
St. Louis 45 vs. Green Bay 17
NFC championship
St. Louis 29 vs. Philadelphia 24
Super Bowl 36
New England 20 vs. St. Louis 17, at New Orleans.

HISTORY *Year-by-year standings*

THIS ONE WAS TRULY SUPER

The terrorist attacks of September 11, 2001, forced the NFL to move its Week 2 games scheduled for September 16-17 to the end of the regular season, resulting in the first February Super Bowl in league history. And what a Super Bowl it was, as the New England Patriots beat the heavily favored St. Louis Rams, 20-17, on a 48-yard field goal by Adam Vinatieri as time expired. Vinatieri's kick capped a nine-play, 53-yard drive engineered by quarterback Tom Brady (who completed five passes on the march) without the benefit of a timeout after the Rams had scored two touchdowns in final 10 minutes to tie the game at 17-17. At 24 years and 184 days old, Brady became the youngest quarterback to win a Super Bowl and the third-youngest player (after Marcus Allen and Lynn Swann) to be named the game's MVP.

2002

AMERICAN CONFERENCE

EAST DIVISION

Team	W	L	T	Pct.	PF	PA
N.Y. Jets*	9	7	0	.563	359	336
New England	9	7	0	.563	381	346
Miami	9	7	0	.563	378	301
Buffalo	8	8	0	.500	379	397

NORTH DIVISION

Team	W	L	T	Pct.	PF	PA
Pittsburgh*	10	5	1	.656	390	345
Cleveland†	9	7	0	.563	344	320
Baltimore	7	9	0	.438	316	354
Cincinnati	2	14	0	.125	279	456

SOUTH DIVISION

Team	W	L	T	Pct.	PF	PA
Tennessee*	11	5	0	.688	367	324
Indianapolis†	10	6	0	.625	349	313
Jacksonville	6	10	0	.375	328	315
Houston	4	12	0	.250	213	356

WEST DIVISION

Team	W	L	T	Pct.	PF	PA
Oakland*	11	5	0	.688	450	304
Denver	9	7	0	.563	392	344
San Diego	8	8	0	.500	333	367
Kansas City	8	8	0	.500	467	399

*Division champion.
†Wild-card team.

NATIONAL CONFERENCE

EAST DIVISION

Team	W	L	T	Pct.	PF	PA
Philadelphia*	12	4	0	.750	415	241
N.Y. Giants†	10	6	0	.625	320	279
Washington	7	9	0	.438	307	365
Dallas	5	11	0	.313	217	329

NORTH DIVISION

Team	W	L	T	Pct.	PF	PA
Green Bay*	12	4	0	.750	398	328
Minnesota	6	10	0	.375	390	442
Chicago	4	12	0	.250	281	379
Detroit	3	13	0	.188	306	451

SOUTH DIVISION

Team	W	L	T	Pct.	PF	PA
Tampa Bay*	12	4	0	.750	346	196
Atlanta†	9	6	1	.594	402	314
New Orleans	9	7	0	.563	432	388
Carolina	7	9	0	.438	258	302

WEST DIVISION

Team	W	L	T	Pct.	PF	PA
San Francisco*	10	6	0	.625	367	351
St. Louis	7	9	0	.438	316	369
Seattle	7	9	0	.438	355	369
Arizona	5	11	0	.313	262	417

PLAYOFFS

AFC wild-card playoffs
N.Y. Jets 41 vs. Indianapolis 0
Pittsburgh 36 vs. Cleveland 33
AFC divisional playoffs
Tennessee 34 vs. Pittsburgh 31 (OT)
Oakland 30 vs. N.Y. Jets 10
AFC championship
Oakland 41 vs. Tennessee 24
NFC wild-card playoffs
Atlanta 27 at Green Bay 7
San Francisco 39 vs. N.Y. Giants 38
NFC divisional playoffs
Philadelphia 20 vs. Atlanta 6
Tampa Bay 31 vs. San Francisco 6
NFC championship
Tampa Bay 27 at Philadelphia 10
Super Bowl 37
Tampa Bay 48 vs. Oakland 21, at San Diego.

2003

AMERICAN CONFERENCE

EAST DIVISION

Team	W	L	T	Pct.	PF	PA
New England*	14	2	0	.875	348	238
Miami	10	6	0	.625	311	261
Buffalo	6	10	0	.375	243	279
N.Y. Jets	6	10	0	.375	283	299

NORTH DIVISION

Team	W	L	T	Pct.	PF	PA
Baltimore*	10	6	0	.625	391	281
Cincinnati	8	8	0	.500	346	384
Pittsburgh	6	10	0	.375	300	327
Cleveland	5	11	0	.313	254	322

SOUTH DIVISION

Team	W	L	T	Pct.	PF	PA
Indianapolis*	12	4	0	.750	447	336
Tennessee†	12	4	0	.750	435	324
Jacksonville	5	11	0	.313	276	331
Houston	5	11	0	.313	255	380

WEST DIVISION

Team	W	L	T	Pct.	PF	PA
Kansas City*	13	3	0	.813	484	332
Denver†	10	6	0	.625	381	301
Oakland	4	12	0	.250	270	379
San Diego		4	12	0	.250	313

*Division champion.
†Wild-card team.

NATIONAL CONFERENCE

EAST DIVISION

Team	W	L	T	Pct.	PF	PA
Philadelphia*	12	4	0	.750	374	287
Dallas†	10	6	0	.625	289	260
Washington	5	11	0	.313	287	372
N.Y. Giants	4	12	0	.250	243	387

NORTH DIVISION

Team	W	L	T	Pct.	PF	PA
Green Bay*	10	6	0	.625	442	307
Minnesota	9	7	0	.563	416	353
Chicago	7	9	0	.438	283	346
Detroit	5	11	0	.313	270	379

SOUTH DIVISION

Team	W	L	T	Pct.	PF	PA
Carolina*	11	5	0	.688	325	304
New Orleans	8	8	0	.500	340	326
Tampa Bay	7	9	0	.438	301	264
Atlanta	5	11	0	.313	299	422

WEST DIVISION

Team	W	L	T	Pct.	PF	PA
St. Louis*	12	4	0	.750	447	328
Seattle†	10	6	0	.625	404	327
San Francisco	7	9	0	.438	384	337
Arizona	4	12	0	.250	225	452

PLAYOFFS

AFC wild-card playoffs
Tennessee 20 at Baltimore 17
Indianapolis 41 vs. Denver 10
AFC divisional playoffs
New England 17 vs. Tennessee 14
Indianapolis 38 at Kansas City 31
AFC championship
New England 24 vs. Indianapolis 14
NFC wild-card playoffs
Carolina 29 vs. Dallas 10
Green Bay 33 vs. Seattle 27 (OT)
NFC divisional playoffs
Carolina 29 at St. Louis 23 (OT)
Philadelphia 20 vs. Green Bay 17 (OT)
NFC championship
Carolina 14 at Philadelphia 3
Super Bowl 38
New England 32, Carolina 29, at Houston.

BUILDING A DYNASTY

In one of the closest Super Bowls in NFL history, the Patriots defeated the Panthers, 32-29 on a last-minute field goal. New England, which had won 15 straight and was making its case as the first NFL dynasty since the Cowboys of the 1990s, received a scare from the Panthers, who had been 1-15 just two seasons earlier.

AMERICAN CONFERENCE

EAST DIVISION

Team	W	L	T	Pct.	PF	PA
New England*	14	2	0	.875	437	260
N.Y. Jets†	10	6	0	.625	333	261
Buffalo	9	7	0	.562	395	284
Miami	4	12	0	.250	275	354

NORTH DIVISION

Team	W	L	T	Pct.	PF	PA
Pittsburgh*	15	1	0	.938	372	251
Baltimore	9	7	0	.562	317	268
Cincinnati	8	8	0	.500	374	372
Cleveland	4	12	0	.250	276	390

SOUTH DIVISION

Team	W	L	T	Pct.	PF	PA
Indianapolis*	12	4	0	.750	522	351
Jacksonville	9	7	0	.562	261	280
Houston	7	9	0	.438	309	339
Tennessee	5	11	0	.312	344	439

WEST DIVISION

Team	W	L	T	Pct.	PF	PA
San Diego*	12	4	0	.750	446	313
Denver†	10	6	0	.625	381	304
Kansas City	7	9	0	.438	483	435
Oakland	5	11	0	.312	320	442

*Division champion.
†Wild-card team.

NATIONAL CONFERENCE

EAST DIVISION

Team	W	L	T	Pct.	PF	PA
Philadelphia*	13	3	0	.812	386	260
N.Y. Giants	6	10	0	.375	303	347
Dallas	6	10	0	.375	293	405
Washington	6	10	0	.375	240	265

NORTH DIVISION

Team	W	L	T	Pct.	PF	PA
Green Bay*	10	6	0	.625	424	380
Minnesota†	8	8	0	.500	405	395
Detroit	6	10	0	.375	296	350
Chicago	5	11	0	.312	231	331

SOUTH DIVISION

Team	W	L	T	Pct.	PF	PA
Atlanta*	11	5	0	.688	340	337
New Orleans	8	8	0	.500	348	405
Carolina	7	9	0	.438	355	339
Tampa Bay	5	11	0	.312	301	304

WEST DIVISION

Team	W	L	T	Pct.	PF	PA
Seattle*	9	7	0	.562	371	373
St. Louis†	8	8	0	.500	319	392
Arizona	6	10	0	.375	284	322
San Francisco	2	14	0	.125	259	452

PLAYOFFS

AFC wild-card playoffs
N.Y. Jets 20 at San Diego 17
Indianapolis 49 vs. Denver 24

AFC divisional playoffs
Pittsburgh 20 vs. N.Y. Jets 17 (OT)
New England 20 vs. Indianapolis 3

AFC championship
New England 41 at Pittsburgh 27

NFC wild-card playoffs
St. Louis 27 at Seattle 20
Minnesota 31 at Green Bay 17

NFC divisional playoffs
Atlanta 47 vs. St. Louis 17
Philadelphia 27 vs. Minnesota 14

NFC championship
Philadelphia 27 vs. Atlanta 10

Super Bowl 39
New England 24, Philadelphia 21, at Jacksonville.

SUPER BOWLS

SUMMARIES

SUPER BOWL 1

JANUARY 15, 1967, AT LOS ANGELES

Kansas City (AFL)	0	10	0	0 — 10
Green Bay (NFL)	7	7	14	7 — 35

Winning coach—Vince Lombardi.
Most Valuable Player—Bart Starr.
Attendance—61,946.

SUPER BOWL 2

JANUARY 14, 1968, AT MIAMI

Green Bay (NFL)	3	13	10	7 — 33
Oakland (AFL)	0	7	0	7 — 14

Winning coach—Vince Lombardi.
Most Valuable Player—Bart Starr.
Attendance—75,546.

SUPER BOWL 3

JANUARY 12, 1969, AT MIAMI

New York (AFL)	0	7	6	3 — 16
Baltimore (NFL)	0	0	0	7 — 7

Winning coach—Weeb Ewbank.
Most Valuable Player—Joe Namath.
Attendance—75,389.

SUPER BOWL 4

JANUARY 11, 1970, AT NEW ORLEANS

Minnesota (NFL)	0	0	7	0 — 7
Kansas City (AFL)	3	13	7	0 — 23

Winning coach—Hank Stram.
Most Valuable Player—Len Dawson.
Attendance—80,562.

SUPER BOWL 5

JANUARY 17, 1971, AT MIAMI

Baltimore (AFC)	0	6	0	10 — 16
Dallas (NFC)	3	10	0	0 — 13

Winning coach—Don McCafferty.
Most Valuable Player—Chuck Howley.
Attendance—79,204.

SUPER BOWL 6

JANUARY 16, 1972, AT NEW ORLEANS

Dallas (NFC)	3	7	7	7 — 24
Miami (AFC)	0	3	0	0 — 3

Winning coach—Tom Landry.
Most Valuable Player—Roger Staubach.
Attendance—81,023.

SUPER BOWL 7

JANUARY 14, 1973, AT LOS ANGELES

Miami (AFC)	7	7	0	0 — 14
Washington (NFC)	0	0	0	7 — 7

Winning coach—Don Shula.
Most Valuable Player—Jake Scott.
Attendance—90,182.

SUPER BOWL 8

JANUARY 13, 1974, AT HOUSTON

Minnesota (NFC)	0	0	0	7 — 7
Miami (AFC)	14	3	7	0 — 24

Winning coach—Don Shula.
Most Valuable Player—Larry Csonka.
Attendance—71,882.

SUPER BOWL 9

JANUARY 12, 1975, AT NEW ORLEANS

Pittsburgh (AFC)	0	2	7	7 — 16
Minnesota (NFC)	0	0	0	6 — 6

Winning coach—Chuck Noll.
Most Valuable Player—Franco Harris.
Attendance—80,997.

SUPER BOWL 10

JANUARY 18, 1976, AT MIAMI

Dallas (NFC)	7	3	0	7 — 17
Pittsburgh (AFC)	7	0	0	14 — 21

Winning coach—Chuck Noll.
Most Valuable Player—Lynn Swann.
Attendance—80,187.

SUPER BOWL 11

JANUARY 9, 1977, AT PASADENA, CALIF.

Oakland (AFC)	0	16	3	13 — 32
Minnesota (NFC)	0	0	7	7 — 14

Winning coach—John Madden.
Most Valuable Player—Fred Biletnikoff.
Attendance—103,438.

SUPER BOWL 12

JANUARY 15, 1978, AT NEW ORLEANS

Dallas (NFC)	10	3	7	7 — 27
Denver (AFC)	0	0	10	0 — 10

Winning coach—Tom Landry.
Most Valuable Players—Harvey Martin and Randy White.
Attendance—75,583.

SUPER BOWL 13

JANUARY 21, 1979, AT MIAMI

Pittsburgh (AFC)	7	14	0	14 — 35
Dallas (NFC)	7	7	3	14 — 31

Winning coach—Chuck Noll.
Most Valuable Player—Terry Bradshaw.
Attendance—79,484.

SUPER BOWL 14

JANUARY 20, 1980, PASADENA, CALIF.

Los Angeles (NFC)	7	6	6	0 — 19
Pittsburgh (AFC)	3	7	7	14 — 31

Winning coach—Chuck Noll.
Most Valuable Player—Terry Bradshaw.
Attendance—103,985.

SUPER BOWL 15

JANUARY 25, 1981, AT NEW ORLEANS

Oakland (AFC)	14	0	10	3 — 27
Philadelphia (NFC)	0	3	0	7 — 10

Winning coach—Tom Flores.
Most Valuable Player—Jim Plunkett.
Attendance—76,135.

SUPER BOWL 16

JANUARY 24, 1982, AT PONTIAC, MICH.

San Francisco (NFC)	7	13	0	6 — 26
Cincinnati (AFC)	0	0	7	14 — 21

Winning coach—Bill Walsh.
Most Valuable Player—Joe Montana.
Attendance—81,270.

SUPER BOWL 17

JANUARY 30, 1983, AT PASADENA, CALIF.

Miami (AFC)	7	10	0	0 — 17
Washington (NFC)	0	10	3	14 — 27

Winning coach—Joe Gibbs.
Most Valuable Player—John Riggins.
Attendance—103,667.

SUPER BOWL 18

JANUARY 22, 1984, AT TAMPA

Washington (NFC)	0	3	6	0 — 9
Los Angeles (AFC)	7	14	14	3 — 38

Winning coach—Tom Flores.
Most Valuable Player—Marcus Allen.
Attendance—72,920.

SUPER BOWL 19

JANUARY 20, 1985, AT STANFORD, CALIF.

Miami (AFC)	10	6	0	0 — 16
San Francisco (NFC)	7	21	10	0 — 38

Winning coach—Bill Walsh.
Most Valuable Player—Joe Montana.
Attendance—84,059.

SUPER BOWL 20

JANUARY 26, 1986, AT NEW ORLEANS

Chicago (NFC)	13	10	21	2 — 46
New England (AFC)	3	0	0	7 — 10

Winning coach—Mike Ditka.
Most Valuable Player—Richard Dent.
Attendance—73,818.

SUPER BOWL 21

JANUARY 25, 1987, AT PASADENA, CALIF.

Denver (AFC)	10	0	0	10 — 20
N.Y. Giants (NFC)	7	2	17	13 — 39

Winning coach—Bill Parcells.
Most Valuable Player—Phil Simms.
Attendance—101,063.

SUPER BOWL 22

JANUARY 31, 1988, AT SAN DIEGO

Washington (NFC)	0	35	0	7 — 42
Denver (AFC)	10	0	0	0 — 10

Winning coach—Joe Gibbs.
Most Valuable Player—Doug Williams.
Attendance—73,302.

SUPER BOWL 23

JANUARY 22, 1989, AT MIAMI

Cincinnati (AFC)	0	3	10	3 — 16
San Francisco (NFC)	3	0	3	14 — 20

Winning coach—Bill Walsh.
Most Valuable Player—Jerry Rice.
Attendance—75,179.

SUPER BOWL 24

JANUARY 28, 1990, AT NEW ORLEANS

San Francisco (NFC)	13	14	14	14 — 55
Denver (AFC)	3	0	7	0 — 10

Winning coach—George Seifert.
Most Valuable Player—Joe Montana.
Attendance—72,919.

SUPER BOWL 25

JANUARY 27, 1991, AT TAMPA

Buffalo (AFC)	3	9	0	7 — 19
New York (NFC)	3	7	7	3 — 20

Winning coach—Bill Parcells.
Most Valuable Player—Ottis Anderson.
Attendance—73,813.

SUPER BOWL 26

JANUARY 26, 1992, AT MINNEAPOLIS

Washington (NFC)	0	17	14	6 — 37
Buffalo (AFC)	0	0	10	14 — 24

Winning coach—Joe Gibbs.
Most Valuable Player—Mark Rypien.
Attendance—63,130.

SUPER BOWL 27

JANUARY 31, 1993, AT PASADENA, CALIF.

Buffalo (AFC)	7	3	7	0 — 17
Dallas (NFC)	14	14	3	21 — 52

Winning coach—Jimmy Johnson.
Most Valuable Player—Troy Aikman.
Attendance—98,374.

SUPER BOWL 28

JANUARY 30, 1994, AT ATLANTA

Dallas (NFC)	6	0	14	10 — 30
Buffalo (AFC)	3	10	0	0 — 13

Winning coach—Jimmy Johnson.
Most Valuable Player—Emmitt Smith.
Attendance—72,817.

SUPER BOWL 29

JANUARY 29, 1995, AT MIAMI

San Diego (AFC)	7	3	8	8 — 26
San Francisco (NFC)	14	14	14	7 — 49

Winning coach—George Seifert.
Most Valuable Player—Steve Young.
Attendance—74,107.

SUPER BOWL 30

JANUARY 28, 1996, AT TEMPE, ARIZ.

Dallas (NFC)	10	3	7	7 — 27
Pittsburgh (AFC)	0	7	0	10 — 17

Winning coach—Barry Switzer.
Most Valuable Player—Larry Brown.
Attendance—76,347.

SUPER BOWL 31

JANUARY 26, 1997, AT NEW ORLEANS

New England (AFC)	14	0	7	0 — 21
Green Bay (NFC)	10	17	8	0 — 35

Winning coach—Mike Holmgren.
Most Valuable Player—Desmond Howard.
Attendance—72,301.

SUPER BOWL 32

JANUARY 25, 1998, AT SAN DIEGO

Green Bay (NFC)	7	7	3	7 — 24
Denver (AFC)	7	10	7	7 — 31

Winning coach—Mike Shanahan.
Most Valuable Player—Terrell Davis.
Attendance—68,912.

SUPER BOWL 33

JANUARY 31, 1999, AT MIAMI

Denver (AFC)	7	10	0	17 — 34
Atlanta (NFC)	3	3	0	13 — 19

Winning coach—Mike Shanahan.
Most Valuable Player—John Elway.
Attendance—74,803.

SUPER BOWL 34

JANUARY 30, 2000, AT ATLANTA

St. Louis (NFC)	3	6	7	7 — 23
Tennessee (AFC)	0	0	6	10 — 16

Winning coach—Dick Vermeil.
Most Valuable Player—Kurt Warner.
Attendance—72,625.

SUPER BOWL 35

JANUARY 28, 2001, AT TAMPA

Baltimore (AFC)	7	3	14	10 — 34
N.Y. Giants (NFC)	0	0	7	0 — 7

Winning coach—Brian Billick.
Most Valuable Player—Ray Lewis.
Attendance—71,921.

SUPER BOWL 36

FEBRUARY 3, 2002, AT NEW ORLEANS

St. Louis (NFC)	3	0	0	14 — 17
New England (AFC)	0	14	3	3 — 20

Winning coach—Bill Belichick.
Most Valuable Player—Tom Brady.
Attendance—72,922.

SUPER BOWL 37

JANUARY 26, 2003, AT SAN DIEGO

Oakland (AFC)	3	0	6	12 — 21
Tampa Bay (NFC)	3	17	14	14 — 48

Winning coach—Jon Gruden.
Most Valuable Player—Dexter Jackson.
Attendance—67,603.

SUPER BOWL 38

FEBRUARY 1, 2004, AT HOUSTON

Carolina (NFC)	0	10	0	19 — 29
New England (AFC)	0	14	0	18 — 32

Winning coach—Bill Belichick.
Most Valuable Player—Tom Brady.
Attendance—71,525.

SUPER BOWL 39

FEBRUARY 6, 2005, AT JACKSONVILLE

New England (AFC)	0	7	7	10 — 24
Philadelphia Eagles (NFC)	0	7	7	7 — 21

Winning coach—Bill Belichick.
Most Valuable Player—Deion Branch.
Attendance—78,125.

SUPER BOWL 40

FEBRUARY 5, 2006, AT DETROIT

Seattle Seahawks (NFC)	3	0	7	0 — 10
Pittsburgh Steelers (AFC)	0	7	7	7 — 21

Winning coach—Bill Cowher.
Most Valuable Player—Hines Ward.
Attendance—68,206.

PRO BOWLS

RESULTS

Date	Site	Winning team, score	Losing team, score	Att.
1-15-39	Wrigley Field, Los Angeles	New York Giants, 13	Pro All-Stars, 10	†20,000
1-14-40	Gilmore Stadium, Los Angeles	Green Bay Packers, 16	NFL All-Stars, 7	†18,000
12-29-40	Gilmore Stadium, Los Angeles	Chicago Bears, 28	NFL All-Stars, 14	21,624
1-4-42	Polo Grounds, New York	Chicago Bears, 35	NFL All-Stars, 24	17,725
12-27-42	Shibe Park, Philadelphia	NFL All-Stars, 17	Washington Redskins, 14	18,671
1943-50	No game was played.			
1-14-51	Los Angeles Memorial Coliseum	American Conference, 28	National Conference, 27	53,676
1-12-52	Los Angeles Memorial Coliseum	National Conference, 30	American Conference, 13	19,400
1-10-53	Los Angeles Memorial Coliseum	National Conference, 27	American Conference, 7	34,208
1-17-54	Los Angeles Memorial Coliseum	East, 20	West, 9	44,214
1-16-55	Los Angeles Memorial Coliseum	West, 26	East, 19	43,972
1-15-56	Los Angeles Memorial Coliseum	East, 31	West, 30	37,867
1-13-57	Los Angeles Memorial Coliseum	West, 19	East, 10	44,177
1-12-58	Los Angeles Memorial Coliseum	West, 26	East, 7	66,634
1-11-59	Los Angeles Memorial Coliseum	East, 28	West, 21	72,250
1-17-60	Los Angeles Memorial Coliseum	West, 38	East, 21	56,876
1-15-61	Los Angeles Memorial Coliseum	West, 35	East, 31	62,971
1-7-62*	Balboa Stadium, San Diego	West, 47	East, 27	20,973
1-14-62	Los Angeles Memorial Coliseum	West, 31	East, 30	57,409
1-13-63*	Balboa Stadium, San Diego	West, 21	East, 14	27,641
1-13-63	Los Angeles Memorial Coliseum	East, 30	West, 20	61,374
1-12-64	Los Angeles Memorial Coliseum	West, 31	East, 17	67,242
1-19-64*	Balboa Stadium, San Diego	West, 27	East, 24	20,016
1-10-65	Los Angeles Memorial Coliseum	West, 34	East, 14	60,598
1-16-65*	Jeppesen Stadium, Houston	West, 38	East, 14	15,446
1-15-66*	Rice Stadium, Houston	AFL All-Stars, 30	Buffalo Bills, 19	35,572
1-15-66	Los Angeles Memorial Coliseum	East, 36	West, 7	60,124
1-21-67*	Oakland-Alameda County Coliseum	East, 30	West, 23	18,876
1-22-67	Los Angeles Memorial Coliseum	East, 20	West, 10	15,062
1-21-68*	Gator Bowl, Jacksonville, Fla.	East, 25	West, 24	40,103
1-21-68	Los Angeles Memorial Coliseum	West, 38	East, 20	53,289
1-19-69*	Gator Bowl, Jacksonville, Fla.	West, 38	East, 25	41,058
1-19-69	Los Angeles Memorial Coliseum	West, 10	East, 7	32,050
1-17-70*	Astrodome, Houston	West, 26	East, 3	30,170
1-18-70	Los Angeles Memorial Coliseum	West, 16	East, 13	57,786
1-24-71	Los Angeles Memorial Coliseum	NFC, 27	AFC, 6	48,222
1-23-72	Los Angeles Memorial Coliseum	AFC, 26	NFC, 13	53,647
1-21-73	Texas Stadium, Irving	AFC, 33	NFC, 28	37,091
1-20-74	Arrowhead Stadium, Kansas City	AFC, 15	NFC, 13	66,918

Date	Site	Winning team, score	Losing team, score	Att.
1-20-75	Orange Bowl, Miami	NFC, 17	AFC, 10	26,484
1-26-76	Louisiana Superdome, New Orleans	NFC, 23	AFC, 20	30,546
1-17-77	Kingdome, Seattle	AFC, 24	NFC, 14	64,752
1-23-78	Tampa Stadium	NFC, 14	AFC, 13	51,337
1-29-79	Los Angeles Memorial Coliseum	NFC, 13	AFC, 7	46,281
1-27-80	Aloha Stadium, Honolulu	NFC, 37	AFC, 27	49,800
2-1-81	Aloha Stadium, Honolulu	NFC, 21	AFC, 7	50,360
1-31-82	Aloha Stadium, Honolulu	AFC, 16	NFC, 13	50,402
2-6-83	Aloha Stadium, Honolulu	NFC, 20	AFC, 19	49,883
1-29-84	Aloha Stadium, Honolulu	NFC, 45	AFC, 3	50,445
1-27-85	Aloha Stadium, Honolulu	AFC, 22	NFC, 14	50,385
2-2-86	Aloha Stadium, Honolulu	NFC, 28	AFC, 24	50,101
2-1-87	Aloha Stadium, Honolulu	AFC, 10	NFC, 6	50,101
2-7-88	Aloha Stadium, Honolulu	AFC, 15	NFC, 6	50,113
1-29-89	Aloha Stadium, Honolulu	NFC, 34	AFC, 3	50,113
2-4-90	Aloha Stadium, Honolulu	NFC, 27	AFC, 21	50,445
2-3-91	Aloha Stadium, Honolulu	AFC, 23	NFC, 21	50,345
2-2-92	Aloha Stadium, Honolulu	NFC, 21	AFC, 15	50,209
2-7-93	Aloha Stadium, Honolulu	AFC, 23 (OT)	NFC, 20	50,007
2-6-94	Aloha Stadium, Honolulu	NFC, 17	AFC, 3	50,026
2-5-95	Aloha Stadium, Honolulu	AFC, 41	NFC, 13	49,121
2-4-96	Aloha Stadium, Honolulu	NFC, 20	AFC, 13	50,034
2-2-97	Aloha Stadium, Honolulu	AFC, 26 (OT)	NFC, 23	50,031
2-1-98	Aloha Stadium, Honolulu	AFC, 29	NFC, 24	49,995
2-7-99	Aloha Stadium, Honolulu	AFC, 23	NFC, 10	50,075
2-6-00	Aloha Stadium, Honolulu	NFC, 51	AFC, 31	50,112
2-4-01	Aloha Stadium, Honolulu	AFC, 38	NFC, 17	50,128
2-9-02	Aloha Stadium, Honolulu	AFC, 38	NFC, 30	50,301
2-2-03	Aloha Stadium, Honolulu	AFC, 45	NFC, 20	50,125
2-8-04	Aloha Stadium, Honolulu	NFC, 55	AFC, 52	50,127
2-13-05	Aloha Stadium, Honolulu	AFC, 38	NFC, 27	50,225
2-12-06	Aloha Stadium, Honolulu	NFC, 23	AFC, 17	50,190

*AFL game.   †Estimated figure.

OUTSTANDING PLAYER AWARDS

Year—Player, team
1951— Otto Graham, Cleveland Browns
1952— Dan Towler, Los Angeles Rams
1953— Dan Doll, Detroit Lions
1954— Chuck Bednarik, Philadelphia Eagles
1955— Billy Wilson, San Francisco 49ers
1956— Ollie Matson, Chicago Cardinals
1957— Bert Rechichar, Baltimore Colts (back)
　　　 Ernie Stautner, Pittsburgh Steelers (lineman)
1958— Hugh McElhenny, San Francisco 49ers (back)
　　　 Gene Brito, Washington Redskins (lineman)
1959— Frank Gifford, New York Giants (back)
　　　 Doug Atkins, Chicago Bears (lineman)
1960— Johnny Unitas, Baltimore Colts (back)
　　　 Gene Lipscomb, Baltimore Colts (lineman)
1961— Johnny Unitas, Baltimore Colts (back)
　　　 Sam Huff, New York Giants (lineman)
1962— Cotton Davidson, Dallas Texans*
　　　 Jim Brown, Cleveland Browns (back)
　　　 Henry Jordan, Green Bay Packers (lineman)
1963— Curtis McClinton, Dallas Texans* (offense)
　　　 Earl Faison, San Diego Chargers* (defense)
　　　 Jim Brown, Cleveland Browns (back)
　　　 Gene Lipscomb, Pittsburgh Steelers (lineman)
1964— Keith Lincoln, San Diego Chargers* (offense)
　　　 Archie Matsos, Oakland Raiders* (defense)
　　　 Johnny Unitas, Baltimore Colts (back)
　　　 Gino Marchetti, Baltimore Colts (lineman)
1965— Keith Lincoln, San Diego Chargers* (offense)
　　　 Willie Brown, Denver Broncos* (defense)
　　　 Fran Tarkenton, Minnesota Vikings (back)
　　　 Terry Barr, Detroit Lions (lineman)
1966— Joe Namath, New York Jets* (offense)
　　　 Frank Buncom, San Diego Chargers* (defense)
　　　 Jim Brown, Cleveland Browns (back)
　　　 Dale Meinert, St. Louis Cardinals (lineman)
1967— Babe Parilli, Boston Patriots* (offense)
　　　 Verlon Biggs, New York Jets* (defense)
　　　 Gale Sayers, Chicago Bears (back)
　　　 Floyd Peters, Philadelphia Eagles (lineman)
1968— Joe Namath, New York Jets* (offense)
　　　 Don Maynard, New York Jets* (offense)
　　　 Speedy Duncan, San Diego Chargers (defense)
　　　 Gale Sayers, Chicago Bears (back)
　　　 Dave Robinson, Green Bay Packers (lineman)
1969— Len Dawson, Kansas City Chiefs* (offense)
　　　 George Webster, Houston* (defense)

Year—Player, team
　　　 Roman Gabriel, Los Angeles Rams (back)
　　　 Merlin Olsen, Los Angeles Rams (lineman)
1970— John Hadl, San Diego Chargers*
　　　 Gale Sayers, Chicago Bears (back)
　　　 George Andrie, Dallas Cowboys (lineman)
1971— Mel Renfro, Dallas Cowboys (back)
　　　 Fred Carr, Green Bay Packers (lineman)
1972— Jan Stenerud, Kansas City Chiefs (offense)
　　　 Willie Lanier, Kansas City Chiefs (defense)
1973— O.J. Simpson, Buffalo Bills
1974— Garo Yepremian, Miami Dolphins
1975— James Harris, Los Angeles Rams
1976— Billy Johnson, Houston Oilers
1977— Mel Blount, Pittsburgh Steelers
1978— Walter Payton, Chicago Bears
1979— Ahmad Rashad, Minnesota Vikings
1980— Chuck Muncie, New Orleans Saints
1981— Eddie Murray, Detroit Lions
1982— Kellen Winslow, San Diego Chargers
　　　 Lee Roy Selmon, Tampa Bay Buccaneers
1983— Dan Fouts, San Diego Chargers
　　　 John Jefferson, Green Bay Packers
1984— Joe Theismann, Washington Redskins
1985— Mark Gastineau, New York Jets
1986— Phil Simms, New York Giants
1987— Reggie White, Philadelphia Eagles
1988— Bruce Smith, Buffalo Bills
1989— Randall Cunningham, Philadelphia Eagles
1990— Jerry Gray, Los Angeles Rams
1991— Jim Kelly, Buffalo Bills
1992— Michael Irvin, Dallas Cowboys
1993— Steve Tasker, Buffalo Bills
1994— Andre Rison, Atlanta Falcons
1995— Marshall Faulk, Indianapolis Colts
1996— Jerry Rice, San Francisco 49ers
1997— Mark Brunell, Jacksonville Jaguars
1998— Warren Moon, Seattle Seahawks
1999— Ty Law, New England Patriots
　　　 Keyshawn Johnson, New York Jets
2000— Randy Moss, Minnesota Vikings
2001— Rich Gannon, Oakland Raiders
2002— Rich Gannon, Oakland Raiders
2003— Ricky Williams, Miami Dolphins
2004— Marc Bulger, St. Louis Rams
2005— Peyton Manning, Indianapolis Colts
2006— Derrick Brooks, Tampa Bay Buccaneers
　　　 *AFL game.

RECORDS

INDIVIDUAL SERVICE
PLAYERS

Most years played
26—George Blanda, Chicago Bears, Baltimore, Houston, Oakland, 1949 through 1975, except 1959.

Most years with one club
20—Jackie Slater, L.A. Rams, St. Louis Rams, 1976 through 1995.
Darrell Green, Washington, 1983 through 2002.

Most games played, career
354—Morten Andersen, New Orleans, Atlanta, N.Y. Giants, Kansas City, Minnesota, 1985 through 1989, 1991 through 1995, 1997-98, 2002-04.

Most consecutive games played, career
288—Jeff Feagles, New England, Philadelphia, Arizona, Seattle, N.Y. Giants, 1988 through 2005 (current).

COACHES

Most years as head coach
40—George Halas, Chicago Bears, 1920 through 1929, 1933 through 1942, 1946 through 1955 and 1958 through 1967.

Most games won as head coach
328—Don Shula, Baltimore, 1963 through 1969; Miami, 1970 through 1995.

Most games lost as head coach
165—Dan Reeves, Denver, 1981 through 1992; N.Y. Giants, 1993 through 1996; Atlanta, 1997 through 2003.

INDIVIDUAL OFFENSE
RUSHING

YARDS

Most yards, career
18,355—Emmitt Smith, Dallas, Arizona, 1990 through 2004.

Most yards, season
2,105—Eric Dickerson, Los Angeles Rams, 1984.

Most yards, season, by a quarterback
968—Bobby Douglass, Chicago, 1972.

Most years leading league in yards
8—Jim Brown, Cleveland, 1957 through 1965, except 1962.

Most consecutive years leading league in yards
5—Jim Brown, Cleveland, 1957 through 1961.

Most years with 1,000 or more yards
11—Emmitt Smith, Dallas, 1991 through 2001.

Most consecutive years with 1,000 or more yards
11—Emmitt Smith, Dallas, 1991 through 2001.

Most yards, game
295—Jamal Lewis, Baltimore vs. Cleveland, Sept. 14, 2003.

Most games with 200 or more yards, career
6—O.J. Simpson, Buffalo, San Francisco, 1969 through 1979.

Most games with 200 or more yards, season
4—Earl Campbell, Houston, 1980.

Most consecutive games with 200 or more yards, season
2—O.J. Simpson, Buffalo, Dec. 9 through 16, 1973.
O.J. Simpson, Buffalo, Nov. 25 through Dec. 5, 1976.
Earl Campbell, Houston, Oct. 19 through 26, 1980.
Ricky Williams, Miami, Dec. 1 through 9, 2002.

Most games with 100 or more yards, career
78—Emmitt Smith, Dallas, Arizona, 1990 through 2004.

Most games with 100 or more yards, season
14—Barry Sanders, Detroit, 1997.

Most consecutive games with 100 or more yards, career
14—Barry Sanders, Detroit, Sept. 14 through Dec. 21, 1997.

Most consecutive games with 100 or more yards, season
14—Barry Sanders, Detroit, Sept. 14 through Dec. 21, 1997.

Longest run from scrimmage
99 yards—Tony Dorsett, Dallas at Minnesota, Jan. 3, 1983 (TD).

ATTEMPTS

Most attempts, career
4,409—Emmitt Smith, Dallas, Arizona, 1990 through 2004.

Most attempts, season
410—Jamal Anderson, Atlanta, 1998.

Most attempts, game
45—Jamie Morris, Washington at Cincinnati, Dec. 17, 1988 (OT).
43—Butch Woolfolk, New York Giants at Philadelphia, Nov. 20, 1983.
James Wilder, Tampa Bay vs. Green Bay, Sept. 30, 1984 (OT).
Rudi Johnson, Cincinnati vs. Houston, Nov. 9, 2003.

Most years leading league in attempts
6—Jim Brown, Cleveland, 1958 through 1965, except 1960 and 1962.

Most consecutive years leading league in attempts
4—Steve Van Buren, Philadelphia, 1947 through 1950.
Walter Payton, Chicago, 1976 through 1979.

TOUCHDOWNS

Most touchdowns, career
164—Emmitt Smith, Dallas, Arizona, 1990 through 2004.

Most touchdowns, season
27—Priest Holmes, Kansas City, 2003.
Shaun Alexander, Seattle, 2005.

Most years leading league in touchdowns
5—Jim Brown, Cleveland, 1957 through 1959, 1963, 1965.

Most consecutive years leading league in touchdowns
3—Steve Van Buren, Philadelphia, 1947 through 1949.
Jim Brown, Cleveland, 1957 through 1959.
Abner Haynes, Dallas Texans, 1960 through 1962.
Cookie Gilchrist, Buffalo, 1962 through 1964.
Leroy Kelly, Cleveland, 1966 through 1968.

Most touchdowns, game
6—Ernie Nevers, Chicago Cardinals vs. Chicago Bears, Nov. 28, 1929.

Most consecutive games with one or more touchdowns, career
18—LaDainian Tomlinson, San Diego, Oct. 3, 2004 through Oct. 16, 2005.

Most consecutive games with one or more touchdowns, season
12—John Riggins, Washington, Sept. 5 through Nov. 27, 1983.
LaDainian Tomlinson, San Diego, Oct. 3, 2004 through Dec. 26, 2004.

PASSING

PASSER RATING

Highest rating, career (1,500 or more attempts)
96.8—Steve Young, Tampa Bay, San Francisco, 1985 through 1999.

Highest rating, season (qualifiers)
121.1—Peyton Manning, Indianapolis, 2004.

ATTEMPTS

Most attempts, career
8,358—Dan Marino, Miami, 1983 through 1999.

Most attempts, season
691—Drew Bledsoe, New England, 1994.

Most years leading league in attempts
5—Dan Marino, Miami, 1984, 1986, 1988, 1992, 1997.

Most consecutive years leading league in attempts
3—Johnny Unitas, Baltimore, 1959 through 1961.
  George Blanda, Houston, 1963 through 1965.
  Drew Bledsoe, New England, 1994 through 1996.

Most attempts, game
70—Drew Bledsoe, New England vs. Minnesota, Nov. 13, 1994 (OT).
69—Vinny Testaverde, N.Y. Jets at Baltimore, Dec. 24, 2000.

COMPLETIONS

Most completions, career
4,967—Dan Marino, Miami, 1983 through 1999.

Most completions, season
418—Rich Gannon, Oakland, 2002.

Most years leading league in completions
6—Dan Marino, Miami, 1984, 1985, 1986, 1988, 1992, 1997.

Most consecutive years leading league in completions
3—George Blanda, Houston, 1963 through 1965.
  Dan Marino, Miami, 1984 through 1986.

Most completions, game
45—Drew Bledsoe, New England vs. Minnesota, Nov. 13, 1994 (OT).
43—Rich Gannon, Oakland at Pittsburgh, Sept. 15, 2002.

Most consecutive completions, game
21—Rich Gannon, Oakland at Denver, Nov. 11, 2002.

YARDS

Most yards, career
61,361—Dan Marino, Miami, 1983 through 1999.

Most yards, season
5,084—Dan Marino, Miami, 1984.

Most years leading league in yards
5—Sonny Jurgensen, Philadelphia, Washington, 1961, 1962, 1966, 1967, 1969.
  Dan Marino, Miami, 1984 through 1986, 1988, 1992.

Most consecutive years leading league in yards
4—Dan Fouts, San Diego, 1979 through 1982.

Most years with 3,000 or more yards
14—Brett Favre, Green Bay, 1992 through 2005.

Most yards, game
554—Norm Van Brocklin, Los Angeles vs. New York Yanks, Sept. 28, 1951.

Most games with 400 or more yards, career
13—Dan Marino, Miami, 1983 through 1999.

Most games with 400 or more yards, season
4—Dan Marino, Miami, 1984.

Most consecutive games with 400 or more yards, season
2—Dan Fouts, San Diego, Dec. 11 through 20, 1982.
  Dan Marino, Miami, Dec. 2 through 9, 1984.
  Phil Simms, New York Giants, Oct. 6 through 13, 1985.

Most games with 300 or more yards, career
63—Dan Marino, Miami, 1983 through 1999.

Most games with 300 or more yards, season
10—Rich Gannon, Oakland, 2002.

Most consecutive games with 300 or more yards, season
6—Steve Young, San Francisco, Sept. 6 through Oct. 18, 1998.
  Kurt Warner, St. Louis, Sept. 4 through Oct. 15, 2000.
  Rich Gannon, Oakland, Sept. 15 through Oct. 27, 2002.

Longest pass completion
99 yards—Frank Filchock, Washington vs. Pittsburgh, Oct. 15, 1939 (TD).
  George Izo, Washington at Cleveland, Sept. 15, 1963 (TD).
  Karl Sweetan, Detroit at Baltimore, Oct. 16, 1966 (TD).
  Sonny Jurgensen, Washington at Chicago, Sept. 15, 1968 (TD).
  Jim Plunkett, Los Angeles Raiders vs. Washington, Oct. 2, 1983 (TD).
  Ron Jaworski, Philadelphia vs. Atlanta, Nov. 10, 1985 (TD).
  Stan Humphries, San Diego at Seattle, Sept. 18, 1994 (TD).
  Brett Favre, Green Bay at Chicago, Sept. 11, 1995 (TD).
  Trent Green, Kansas City vs. San Diego, Dec. 22, 2002 (TD).
  Jeff Garcia, Cleveland vs. Cincinnati, Oct. 17, 2004 (TD).

YARDS PER ATTEMPT

Most yards per attempt, career (1,500 or more attempts)
8.63—Otto Graham, Cleveland, 1950 through 1955 (13,499 yards, 1,565 attempts).

Most yards per attempt, season (qualifiers)
11.17—Tommy O'Connell, Cleveland, 1957 (1,229 yards, 110 attempts).

Most years leading league in yards per attempt
7—Sid Luckman, Chicago Bears, 1939 through 1943, 1946, 1947.

Most consecutive years leading league in yards per attempt
5—Sid Luckman, Chicago Bears, 1939 through 1943.

Most yards per attempt, game (20 or more attempts)
18.58—Sammy Baugh, Washington vs. Boston, Oct. 31, 1948 (446 yards, 24 attempts).

TOUCHDOWNS

Most touchdowns, career
420—Dan Marino, Miami, 1983 through 1999.

Most touchdowns, season
49—Peyton Manning, Indianapolis, 2004.

Most years leading league in touchdowns
4—Johnny Unitas, Baltimore, 1957 through 1960.
  Len Dawson, Dallas Texans, Kansas City, 1962 through 1966, except 1964.
  Steve Young, San Francisco, 1992 through 1994, 1998.
  Brett Favre, Green Bay, 1995 through 1997, 2003.

Most consecutive years leading league in touchdowns
4—Johnny Unitas, Baltimore, 1957 through 1960.

Most touchdowns, game
7—Sid Luckman, Chicago Bears at New York Giants, Nov. 14, 1943.
  Adrian Burk, Philadelphia at Washington, Oct. 17, 1954.
  George Blanda, Houston vs. New York Titans, Nov. 19, 1961.
  Y.A. Tittle, New York Giants vs. Washington, Oct. 28, 1962.
  Joe Kapp, Minnesota vs. Baltimore, Sept. 28, 1969.

INTERCEPTIONS

Most interceptions, career
277—George Blanda, Chicago Bears, Baltimore, Houston, Oakland, 1949 through 1975, except 1959.

Most interceptions, season
42—George Blanda, Houston, 1962.

Most interceptions, game
8—Jim Hardy, Chicago Cardinals vs. Philadelphia, Sept. 24, 1950.

Most attempts with no interceptions, game
70—Drew Bledsoe, New England vs. Minnesota, Nov. 13, 1994 (OT).
63—Rich Gannon, Minnesota at New England, Oct. 20, 1991 (OT).
60—Davey O'Brien, Philadelphia at Washington, Dec. 1, 1940.

INTERCEPTION PERCENTAGE

Lowest interception percentage, career (1,500 or more attempts)
2.11—Neil O'Donnell, Pittsburgh, N.Y. Jets, Cincinnati, Tennessee, 1991 through 2003 (3,229 attempts, 68 interceptions).

Lowest interception percentage, season (qualifiers)
0.66—Joe Ferguson, Buffalo, 1976 (151 attempts, one interception).

Most years leading league in lowest interception percentage
5—Sammy Baugh, Washington, 1940, 1942, 1944, 1945, 1947.

SACKS (SINCE 1963)

Most times sacked, career
516—John Elway, Denver, 1983 through 1998.

Most times sacked, season
76—David Carr, Houston, 2002.

Most times sacked, game
12—Bert Jones, Baltimore vs. St. Louis, Oct. 26, 1980.
    Warren Moon, Houston vs. Dallas, Sept. 29, 1985.

RECEIVING

RECEPTIONS

Most receptions, career
1,549—Jerry Rice, San Francisco, Oakland, 1985 through 2004.

Most receptions, season
143—Marvin Harrison, Indianapolis, 2002.

Most years leading league in receptions
8—Don Hutson, Green Bay, 1936 through 1945, except 1938 and 1940.

Most consecutive years leading league in receptions
5—Don Hutson, Green Bay, 1941 through 1945.

Most receptions, game
20—Terrell Owens, San Francisco vs. Chicago, Dec. 17, 2000.

Most consecutive games with one or more receptions
274—Jerry Rice, San Francisco, Oakland, Dec. 9, 1985 through Sept. 12, 2004.

YARDS

Most yards, career
22,895—Jerry Rice, San Francisco, Oakland, 1985 through 2004.

Most yards, season
1,848—Jerry Rice, San Francisco, 1995.

Most years leading league in yards
7—Don Hutson, Green Bay, 1936 through 1944, except 1937 and 1940.

Most consecutive years leading league in yards
4—Don Hutson, Green Bay, 1941 through 1944.

Most years with 1,000 or more yards
14—Jerry Rice, San Francisco, Oakland, 1986 through 1996, 1998, 2001 through 2002.

Most yards, game
336—Willie Anderson, Los Angeles Rams at New Orleans, Nov. 26, 1989 (OT).
309—Stephone Paige, Kansas City vs. San Diego, Dec. 22, 1985.

Most games with 200 or more yards, career
5—Lance Alworth, San Diego, Dallas, 1962 through 1972.

Most games with 200 or more yards, season
3—Charley Hennigan, Houston, 1961.

Most games with 100 or more yards, career
76—Jerry Rice, San Francisco, Oakland, 1985 through 2004.

Most games with 100 or more yards, season
11—Michael Irvin, Dallas, 1995.

Most consecutive games with 100 or more yards, season
9—Larry Johnson, Kansas City, 2005.

Longest reception
99 yards—Andy Farkas, Washington vs. Pittsburgh, Oct. 15, 1939 (TD).
    Bobby Mitchell, Washington at Cleveland, Sept. 15, 1963 (TD).
    Pat Studstill, Detroit at Baltimore, Oct. 16, 1966 (TD).

Gerry Allen, Washington at Chicago, Sept. 15, 1968 (TD).
Cliff Branch, Los Angeles Raiders vs. Washington, Oct. 2, 1983 (TD).
Mike Quick, Philadelphia vs. Atlanta, Nov. 10, 1985 (TD).
Tony Martin, San Diego at Seattle, Sept. 18, 1994 (TD).
Robert Brooks, Green Bay at Chicago, Sept. 11, 1995 (TD).
Marc Boerigter, Kansas City vs. San Diego, Dec. 22, 2002 (TD).
Andre Davis, Cleveland vs. Cincinnati, Oct. 17, 2004 (TD).

TOUCHDOWNS

Most touchdowns, career
197—Jerry Rice, San Francisco, Oakland, 1985 through 2004.

Most touchdowns, season
22—Jerry Rice, San Francisco, 1987.

Most years leading league in touchdowns
9—Don Hutson, Green Bay, 1935 through 1944, except 1939.

Most consecutive years leading league in touchdowns
5—Don Hutson, Green Bay, 1940 through 1944.

Most touchdowns, game
5—Bob Shaw, Chicago Cardinals vs. Baltimore, Oct. 2, 1950.
    Kellen Winslow, San Diego at Oakland, Nov. 22, 1981.
    Jerry Rice, San Francisco at Atlanta, Oct. 14, 1990.

Most consecutive games with one or more touchdowns
13—Jerry Rice, San Francisco, Dec. 19, 1986 through Dec. 27, 1987.

COMBINED NET YARDS

(Rushing, receiving, interception returns, punt returns, kickoff returns and fumble returns)

ATTEMPTS

Most attempts, career
4,924—Emmitt Smith, Dallas, Arizona, 1990 through 2004.

Most attempts, season
496—James Wilder, Tampa Bay, 1984.

Most attempts, game
48—James Wilder, Tampa Bay at Pittsburgh, Oct. 30, 1983.

YARDS

Most yards, career
23,546—Jerry Rice, San Francisco, Oakland, Seattle, 1985 through 2004.

Most yards, season
2,690—Derrick Mason, Tennessee, 2000.

Most years leading league in yards
5—Jim Brown, Cleveland, 1958 through 1961, 1964.

Most consecutive years leading league in yards
4—Jim Brown, Cleveland, 1958 through 1961.

Most yards, game
404—Glyn Milburn, Denver vs. Seattle, Dec. 10, 1995.

SCORING

POINTS

Most points, career
2,434—Gary Anderson, Pittsburgh, Philadelphia, San Francisco, Minnesota, Tennessee, 1982 through 2004.

Most points, season
176—Paul Hornung, Green Bay, 1960.

Most years leading league in points
5—Don Hutson, Green Bay, 1940 through 1944.
    Gino Cappelletti, Boston, 1961 through 1966, except 1962.

Most consecutive years leading league in points
5—Don Hutson, Green Bay, 1940 through 1944.

Most years with 100 or more points
14—Gary Anderson, Pittsburgh, Philadelphia, San Francisco, Minnesota, Tennessee, 1983 through 1985, 1988, 1991 through 1994, 1996 through 2000, 2003.
Morten Andersen, New Orleans, Atlanta, N.Y. Giants, Kansas City, 1985 through 1989, 1991 through 1995, 1997-98, 2002-03.

Most points, game
40—Ernie Nevers, Chicago Cardinals vs. Chicago Bears, Nov. 28, 1929.

Most consecutive games with one or more points
332—Morten Andersen, New Orleans, Atlanta, N.Y. Giants, Kansas City, Minnesota, Dec. 11, 1983 through Jan. 5, 2005.

TOUCHDOWNS

Most touchdowns, career
208—Jerry Rice, San Francisco, Oakland, 1985 through 2004.

Most touchdowns, season
28—Shaun Alexander, Seattle, 2005.

Most years leading league in touchdowns
8—Don Hutson, Green Bay, 1935 through 1938 and 1941 through 1944.

Most consecutive years leading league in touchdowns
4—Don Hutson, Green Bay, 1935 through 1938 and 1941 through 1944.

Most touchdowns, game
6—Ernie Nevers, Chicago Cardinals vs. Chicago Bears, Nov. 28, 1929.
Dub Jones, Cleveland vs. Chicago Bears, Nov. 25, 1951.
Gale Sayers, Chicago vs. San Francisco, Dec. 12, 1965.

Most consecutive games with one or more touchdowns
18—Lenny Moore, Baltimore, Oct. 27, 1963 through Sept. 19, 1965.
LaDainian Tomlinson, San Diego, Oct. 3, 2005 through October 16, 2006.

EXTRA POINTS

Most extra points attempted, career
959—George Blanda, Chicago Bears, Baltimore, Houston, Oakland, 1949 through 1975, except 1959.

Most extra points made, career
943—George Blanda, Chicago Bears, Baltimore, Houston, Oakland, 1949 through 1975, except 1959.

Most extra points attempted, season
70—Uwe von Schamann, Miami, 1984.

Most extra points made, season
66—Uwe von Schamann, Miami, 1984.

Most extra points attempted, game
10—Charlie Gogolak, Washington vs. New York Giants, Nov. 27, 1966.

Most extra points made, game
9—Pat Harder, Chicago Cardinals at New York Giants, Oct. 17, 1948.
Bob Waterfield, Los Angeles vs. Baltimore, Oct. 22, 1950.
Charlie Gogolak, Washington vs. New York Giants, Nov. 27, 1966.

FIELD GOALS AND FIELD GOAL PERCENTAGE

Most field goals attempted, career
672—Gary Anderson, Pittsburgh, Philadelphia, San Francisco, Minnesota, Tennessee, 1982 through 2004.

Most field goals made, career
538—Gary Anderson, Pittsburgh, Philadelphia, San Francisco, Minnesota, 1982 through 2004.

Most field goals attempted, season
49—Bruce Gossett, Los Angeles, 1966.
Curt Knight, Washington, 1971.

Most field goals made, season
40—Neil Rackers, Arizona, 40, 2005.

Most field goals attempted, game
9—Jim Bakken, St. Louis at Pittsburgh, Sept. 24, 1967.

Most field goals made, game
7—Jim Bakken, St. Louis at Pittsburgh, Sept. 24, 1967.
Rich Karlis, Minnesota vs. Los Angeles Rams, Nov. 5, 1989 (OT).
Chris Boniol, Dallas vs. Green Bay, Nov. 18, 1996.
Billy Cundiff, Dallas at N.Y. Giants, Sept. 15, 2003 (OT).

Most field goals made, one quarter
4—Garo Yepremian, Detroit vs. Minnesota, Nov. 13, 1966, second quarter.
Curt Knight, Washington at New York Giants, Nov. 15, 1970, second quarter.
Roger Ruzek, Dallas vs. New York Giants, Nov. 2, 1987, fourth quarter.
Cary Blanchard, Indianapolis at Buffalo, Sept. 21, 1997, second quarter.
Sebastian Janikowski, Oakland at Chicago, Oct. 5, 2003, second quarter.
Jeff Wilkins, St. Louis vs. Baltimore, Nov. 9, 2003, fourth quarter.
Lawrence Tynes, Kansas City vs. New England, Nov. 27, 2005, second quarter.

Most consecutive games with one or more field goals made, career
38—Matt Stover, Baltimore, Oct. 31, 1999 through Dec. 2, 2001.

Most consecutive field goals made, career
42—Mike Vanderjagt, Indianapolis, Dec. 22, 2002 through Sept. 4, 2004.

Most field goals of 50 or more yards, career
40—Morten Andersen, New Orleans, Atlanta, N.Y. Giants, Kansas City, Minnesota, 1982 through 2004.

Most field goals of 50 or more yards, season
8—Morten Andersen, Atlanta, 1995.

Most field goals of 50 or more yards, game
3—Morten Andersen, Atlanta vs. New Orleans, Dec. 10, 1995.
Neil Rackers, Arizona vs. Seattle, Oct. 24, 2004.

Longest field goal made
63 yards—Tom Dempsey, New Orleans vs. Detroit, Nov. 8, 1970.
Jason Elam, Denver vs. Jacksonville, Oct. 25, 1998.

Highest field goal percentage, career (100 or more made)
87.5—Mike Vanderjagt, Indianapolis, 1998 through 2005 (248 attempted, 217 made).

Highest field goal percentage, season (qualifiers)
100.00—Tony Zendejas, Los Angeles Rams, 1991 (17 made).
Gary Anderson, Minnesota, 1998 (35 made).
Jeff Wilkins, St. Louis, 2000 (17 made).
Mike Vanderjagt, Indianapolis, 2003 (37 made).

SAFETIES

Most safeties, career
4—Ted Hendricks, Baltimore, Green Bay, Oakland, Los Angeles Raiders, 1969 through 1983.
Doug English, Detroit, 1975 through 1985, except 1980.
Derrick Thomas, Kansas City, 1989 through 1999.

Most safeties, season
2—Held by many players.

Most safeties, game
2—Fred Dryer, Los Angeles vs. Green Bay, Oct. 21, 1973.

PUNTING

Most punts, career
1,437—Jeff Feagles, New England, Philadelphia, Arizona, Seattle, N.Y. Giants, 1988 through 2005.

Most punts, season
114—Bob Parsons, Chicago, 1981.
  Chad Stanley, Houston, 2002.

Most seasons leading league in punting
4—Sammy Baugh, Washington, 1940 through 1943.
  Jerrel Wilson, Kansas City, 1965, 1968, 1972, 1973.

Most consecutive seasons leading league in punting
4—Sammy Baugh, Washington, 1940 through 1943.

Most punts, game
16— Leo Araguz, Oakland vs. San Diego, Oct. 11, 1998.

Longest punt
98 yards—Steve O'Neal, New York Jets at Denver, Sept. 21,
  1969.

FUMBLES

Most fumbles, career
161—Warren Moon, Houston, Minnesota, Seattle, Kansas City,
  1984 through 2000.

Most fumbles, season
23—Kerry Collins, N.Y. Giants, 2001.
  Daunte Culpepper, Minnesota, 2002.

Most fumbles, game
7—Len Dawson, Kansas City vs. San Diego, Nov. 15, 1964.

PUNT RETURNS

Most punt returns, career
463—Brian Mitchell, Washington, Philadelphia, N.Y. Giants,
  1990 through 2003.

Most punt returns, season
70—Danny Reece, Tampa Bay, 1979.

Most years leading league in punt returns
3—Les "Speedy" Duncan, San Diego, Washington, 1965, 1966,
  1971.
  Rick Upchurch, Denver, 1976, 1978, 1982.

Most punt returns, game
11—Eddie Brown, Washington at Tampa Bay, Oct. 9, 1977.

YARDS

Most yards, career
4,999—Brian Mitchell, Washington, Philadelphia, N.Y. Giants, 1990
  through 2003.

Most yards, season
875—Desmond Howard, Green Bay, 1996.

Most yards, game
207—LeRoy Irvin, Los Angeles at Atlanta, Oct. 11, 1981.

Longest punt return
103 yards—Robert Bailey, Los Angeles Rams at New Orleans,
  Oct. 23, 1994 (TD).

FAIR CATCHES

Most fair catches, career
231—Brian Mitchell, Washington, Philadelphia, N.Y. Giants,
  1990 through 2003.

Most fair catches, season
33—Brian Mitchell, Philadelphia, 2000.

Most fair catches, game
7—Lem Barney, Detroit vs. Chicago, Nov. 21, 1976.
  Bobby Morse, Philadelphia vs. Buffalo, Dec. 27, 1987.

TOUCHDOWNS

Most touchdowns, career
10—Eric Metcalf, Cleveland, Atlanta, San Diego, Arizona,
  Carolina, Washington, Green Bay, 1989 through 2002,
  except 2000.

Most touchdowns, season
4—Jack Christiansen, Detroit, 1951.
  Rick Upchurch, Denver, 1976.

Most touchdowns, game
2—Jack Christiansen, Detroit vs. Los Angeles, Oct. 14, 1951.
  Jack Christiansen, Detroit vs. Green Bay, Nov. 22, 1951.
  Dick Christy, New York Titans vs. Denver, Sept. 24, 1961.
  Rick Upchurch, Denver vs. Cleveland, Sept. 26, 1976.
  LeRoy Irvin, Los Angeles at Atlanta, Oct. 11, 1981.
  Vai Sikahema, St. Louis vs. Tampa Bay, Dec. 21, 1986.
  Todd Kinchen, Los Angeles Rams vs. Atlanta, Dec. 27,
  1992.
  Eric Metcalf, Cleveland vs. Pittsburgh, Oct. 24, 1993.
  Eric Metcalf, San Diego at Cincinnati, Nov. 2, 1997.
  Darrien Gordon, Denver vs. Carolina, Nov. 9, 1997.
  Jermaine Lewis, Baltimore vs. Seattle, Dec. 7, 1997.
  Jermaine Lewis, Baltimore vs. N.Y. Jets, Dec. 24, 2000.
  Steve Smith, Carolina vs. Cincinnati, Dec. 8, 2002.

KICKOFF RETURNS

Most kickoff returns, career
607—Brian Mitchell, Washington, Philadelphia, N.Y. Giants, 1990
  through 2003.

Most kickoff returns, season
82—MarTay Jenkins, Arizona, 2000.

Most years leading league in kickoff returns
3—Abe Woodson, San Francisco, 1959, 1962, 1963.

Most kickoff returns, game
10—Desmond Howard, Oakland at Seattle, Oct. 26, 1997.

YARDS

Most yards, career
14,014—Brian Mitchell, Washington, Philadelphia, N.Y. Giants, 1990
  through 2003.

Most yards, season
2,186—MarTay Jenkins, Arizona, 2000.

Most years leading league in yards
3—Bruce Harper, New York Jets, 1977 through 1979.
  Tyrone Hughes, New Orleans, 1994 through 1996.

Most yards, game
304—Tyrone Hughes, New Orleans vs. Los Angeles Rams, Oct.
  23, 1994.

Longest kickoff return
106 yards—Al Carmichael, Green Bay vs. Chicago Bears, Oct. 7,
  1956 (TD).
  Noland Smith, K.C. at Denver, Dec. 17, 1967 (TD).
  Roy Green, St. Louis at Dallas, Oct. 21, 1979 (TD).

TOUCHDOWNS

Most touchdowns, career
6—Ollie Matson, Chicago Cardinals, Los Angeles Rams, Detroit,
  Philadelphia, 1952 through 1964, except 1953.
  Gale Sayers, Chicago, 1965 through 1971.
  Travis Williams, Green Bay, Los Angeles, 1967 through 1971.
  Mel Gray, New Orleans, Detroit, Houston, Tennessee, Phila-
  delphia, 1986 through 1997.
  Dante Hall, Kansas City, 2000 through 2005.

Most touchdowns, season
4—Travis Williams, Green Bay, 1967.
  Cecil Turner, Chicago, 1970.

Most touchdowns, game
2—Timmy Brown, Philadelphia vs. Dallas, Nov. 6, 1966.
  Travis Williams, Green Bay vs. Cleveland, Nov. 12, 1967.
  Ron Brown, Los Angeles Rams vs. Green Bay, Nov. 24, 1985.
  Tyrone Hughes, New Orleans vs. Los Angeles Rams, Oct.
  23, 1994.
  Chad Morton, N.Y. Jets at Buffalo, Sept. 8, 2002 (OT).

COMBINED KICK RETURNS

(KICKOFFS AND PUNTS)

Most kick returns, career
1,070—Brian Mitchell, Washington, Philadelphia, N.Y. Giants, 1990 through 2003.

Most kick returns, season
114—Michael Lewis, New Orleans, 2002.

Most kick returns, game
13—Stump Mitchell, St. Louis at Atlanta, Oct. 18, 1981.
Ronnie Harris, New England at Pittsburgh, Dec. 5, 1993.

YARDS

Most yards, career
19,013—Brian Mitchell, Washington, Philadelphia, N.Y. Giants, 1990 through 2003.

Most yards, season
2,432—Michael Lewis, New Orleans, 2002.

Most yards, game
347—Tyrone Hughes, New Orleans vs. Los Angeles Rams, Oct. 23, 1994.

TOUCHDOWNS

Most touchdowns, career
13—Brian Mitchell, Washington, Philadelphia, N.Y. Giants, 1990 through 2003.

Most touchdowns, season
4—Jack Christiansen, Detroit, 1951.
Emlen Tunnell, New York Giants, 1951.
Gale Sayers, Chicago, 1967.
Travis Williams, Green Bay, 1967.
Cecil Turner, Chicago, 1970.
Billy "White Shoes" Johnson, Houston, 1975.
Rick Upchurch, Denver, 1976.
Dante Hall, Kansas City, 2003.
Eddie Drummond, Detroit, 2004.

Most touchdowns, game
2—Held by many players.

INDIVIDUAL DEFENSE

INTERCEPTIONS

Most interceptions, career
81—Paul Krause, Washington, Minnesota, 1964 through 1979.

Most interceptions, season
14—Dick "Night Train" Lane, Los Angeles, 1952.

Most interceptions, game
4—Held by many players.

Most consecutive games with one or more interceptions
8—Tom Morrow, Oakland, 1962 through 1963.

Most yards on interceptions, career
1,483—Rod Woodson, Pittsburgh, San Francisco, Baltimore, Oakland, 1987 through 2003.

Most yards on interceptions, season
358—Ed Reed, Baltimore, 2004.

Most yards on interceptions, game
177—Charlie McNeil, San Diego vs. Houston, Sept. 24, 1961.

Longest interception return
106—Ed Reed, Baltimore vs. Cleveland, Nov. 7, 2004.

TOUCHDOWNS

Most touchdowns, career
12—Rod Woodson, Pittsburgh, San Francisco, Baltimore, Oakland, 1987 through 2003.

Most touchdowns, season
4—Ken Houston, Houston, 1971.
Jim Kearney, Kansas City, 1972.
Eric Allen, Philadelphia, 1993.

Most touchdowns, game
2—Held by many players.

FUMBLES RECOVERED

Most fumbles recovered (own and opponents'), career
56—Warren Moon, Houston, Minnesota, Seattle, Kansas City, 1984 through 2000.

Most fumbles recovered (own), career
56—Warren Moon, Houston, Minnesota, Seattle, Kansas City, 1984 through 2000.

Most opponents' fumbles recovered, career
29—Jim Marshall, Cleveland, Minnesota, 1960 through 1979.

Most fumbles recovered (own and opponents'), season
12—David Carr, Houston, 2002.

Most fumbles recovered (own), season
12—David Carr, Houston, 2002.

Most opponents' fumbles recovered, season
9—Don Hultz, Minnesota, 1963.

Most fumbles recovered (own and opponents'), game
4—Otto Graham, Cleveland at New York Giants, Oct. 25, 1953.
Sam Etcheverry, St. Louis at New York Giants, Sept. 17, 1961.
Roman Gabriel, Los Angeles at San Francisco, Oct. 12, 1969.
Joe Ferguson, Buffalo vs. Miami, Sept. 18, 1977.
Randall Cunningham, Philadelphia at Los Angeles Raiders, Nov. 30, 1986 (OT).

Most fumbles recovered (own), game
4—Otto Graham, Cleveland at New York Giants, Oct. 25, 1953.
Sam Etcheverry, St. Louis at New York Giants, Sept. 17, 1961.
Roman Gabriel, Los Angeles at San Francisco, Oct. 12, 1969.
Joe Ferguson, Buffalo vs. Miami, Sept. 18, 1977.
Randall Cunningham, Philadelphia at Los Angeles Raiders, Nov. 30, 1986 (OT).

Most opponents' fumbles recovered, game
3—Held by many players.

Longest fumble return
104 yards—Jack Tatum, Oakland at Green Bay, Sept. 24, 1972 (TD).
Aeneas Williams, Arizona vs. Washington, Nov. 5, 2000 (TD).

TOUCHDOWNS

Most touchdowns (own and opponents' recovered), career
5—Jessie Tuggle, Atlanta, 1987 through 2000.
Jason Taylor, Miami, 1997 through 2005.

Most touchdowns (own recovered), career
2—Held by many players.

Most touchdowns (opponents' recovered), career
5—Jessie Tuggle, Atlanta, 1987 through 2000.
Jason Taylor, Miami, 1997 through 2005.

Most touchdowns (opponents' recovered), season
2—Held by many players.

Most touchdowns (opponents' recovered), game
2—Fred "Dippy" Evans, Chicago Bears vs. Washington, Nov. 28, 1948.

SACKS (SINCE 1982)

Most sacks, career
200—Bruce Smith, Buffalo, Washington, 1985 through 2003.

Most sacks, season
22.5—Michael Strahan, N.Y. Giants, 2001.

Most sacks, game
7—Derrick Thomas, Kansas City vs. Seattle, Nov. 11, 1990.

CHAMPIONSHIPS

Most league championships won
12—Green Bay, 1929, 1930, 1931, 1936, 1939, 1944, 1961, 1962, 1965, 1966, 1967, 1996.

Most consecutive league championships won
3—Green Bay, 1929 through 1931.
    Green Bay, 1965 through 1967.

Most first-place finishes during regular season (since 1933)
20—N.Y. Giants, 1933-35, 1938-39, 1941, 1944, 1946, 1956, 1958-59, 1961-63, 1986, 1989-90, 1997, 2000, 2005.

Most consecutive first-place finishes during regular season (since 1933)
7—Los Angeles, 1973 through 1979.

GAMES WON

Most games won, season
15—San Francisco, 1984.
    Chicago, 1985.
    Minnesota, 1998.
    Pittsburgh, 2004.

Most consecutive games won, season
14—Miami, Sept. 17 through Dec. 16, 1972.
    Pittsburgh, Sept. 26, 2004 through Jan. 2, 2005.

Most consecutive games won from start of season
14—Miami, Sept. 17 through Dec. 16, 1972 (entire season).

Most consecutive games won at end of season
14—Miami, Sept. 17 through Dec. 16, 1972 (entire season).
    Pittsburgh, Sept. 26, 2004 through Jan. 2, 2005.

Most consecutive undefeated games, season
14—Miami, Sept. 17 through Dec. 16, 1972 (entire season).
    Pittsburgh, Sept. 26, 2004 through Jan. 2, 2005.

Most consecutive games won
18—New England Patriots, Oct. 5, 2003 through Oct. 24, 2004.

Most consecutive undefeated games
25—Canton, 1921 through 1923 (won 22, tied three).

Most consecutive home games won
27—Miami, Oct. 17, 1971 through Dec. 15, 1974.

Most consecutive undefeated home games
30—Green Bay, 1928 through 1933 (won 27, tied three).

Most consecutive road games won
18—San Francisco, Nov. 27, 1988 through Dec. 30, 1990.

Most consecutive undefeated road games
18—San Francisco, Nov. 27, 1988 through Dec. 30, 1990 (won 18).

GAMES LOST

Most games lost, season
15—New Orleans, 1980.
    Dallas, 1989.
    New England, 1990.
    Indianapolis, 1991.
    New York Jets, 1996.
    San Diego, 2000.
    Carolina, 2001.

Most consecutive games lost
26—Tampa Bay, Sept. 12, 1976 through Dec. 4, 1977.

Most consecutive winless games
26—Tampa Bay, Sept. 12, 1976 through Dec. 4, 1977 (lost 26).

Most consecutive games lost, season
15—Carolina, Sept. 23, 2001 through Jan. 6, 2002.

Most consecutive games lost from start of season
14—Tampa Bay, Sept. 12 through Dec. 12, 1976 (entire season).

New Orleans, Sept. 7 through Dec. 7, 1980.

Most consecutive games lost at end of season
15—Carolina, Sept. 23, 2001 through Jan. 6, 2002.

Most consecutive winless games, season
15—Carolina, Sept. 23, 2001 through Jan. 6, 2002 (lost 15).

Most consecutive home games lost
14—Dallas, Oct. 9, 1988 through Dec. 24, 1989.

Most consecutive winless home games
14—Dallas, Oct. 9, 1988 through Dec. 24, 1989 (lost 14).

Most consecutive road games lost
24—Detroit, Sept. 9, 2001 through Dec. 21, 2003.

Most consecutive winless road games
24—Detroit, Sept. 9, 2001 through Dec. 21, 2003.

TIE GAMES

Most tie games, season
6—Chicago Bears, 1932.

Most consecutive tie games
3—Chicago Bears, Sept. 25 through Oct. 9, 1932.

TEAM OFFENSE

RUSHING

Most years leading league in rushing
16—Chicago Bears, 1932, 1934, 1935, 1939, 1940, 1941, 1942, 1951, 1955, 1956, 1968, 1977, 1983, 1984, 1985, 1986.

Most consecutive years leading league in rushing
4—Chicago Bears, 1939 through 1942.
    Chicago Bears, 1983 through 1986.

ATTEMPTS

Most attempts, season
681—Oakland, 1977.

Most attempts, game
72—Chicago Bears vs. Brooklyn, Oct. 20, 1935.

Most attempts by both teams, game
108—Chicago Cardinals 70, Green Bay 38, Dec. 5, 1948.

Fewest attempts, game
6—Chicago Cardinals at Brooklyn, Oct. 29, 1933.

Fewest attempts by both teams, game
34—Houston 22, Atlanta 12, Dec. 5, 1993.
    San Francisco 19, Atlanta 15, Dec. 24, 1995.
    Philadelphia 14, San Diego 20, Oct. 23, 2005.

YARDS

Most yards, season
3,165—New England, 1978.

Fewest yards, season
298—Philadelphia, 1940.

Most yards, game
426—Detroit vs. Pittsburgh, Nov. 4, 1934.

Most yards by both teams, game
595—Los Angeles 371, New York Yanks 224, Nov. 18, 1951.

Fewest yards, game
-53—Detroit at Chicago Cardinals, Oct. 17, 1943.

Fewest yards by both teams, game
-15—Detroit -53, Chicago Cardinals 38, Oct. 17, 1943.

TOUCHDOWNS

Most touchdowns, season
36—Green Bay, 1962.

Fewest touchdowns, season
1—Brooklyn, 1934.

Most touchdowns, game
8—Kansas City vs. Atlanta, Oct. 24, 2004.

Most touchdowns by both teams, game
8—Los Angeles 6, New York Yanks 2, Nov. 18, 1951.
   Chicago Bears 5, Green Bay 3, Nov. 6, 1955.
   Cleveland 6, Los Angeles 2, Nov. 24, 1957.
   Denver 5, Kansas City 3, Dec. 7, 2003.
   Kansas City 8, Atlanta 0, Oct. 24, 2004.

PASSING

ATTEMPTS

Most attempts, season
709—Minnesota, 1981.

Fewest attempts, season
102—Cincinnati, 1933.

Most attempts, game
70—New England vs. Minnesota, Nov. 13, 1994 (OT).
69—N.Y. Jets at Baltimore, Dec. 24, 2000.

Most attempts by both teams, game
112—New England 70, Minnesota 42, Nov. 13, 1994 (OT).
104—Miami 55, New York Jets 49, Oct. 18, 1987 (OT).
   N.Y. Jets 58, San Francisco 46, Sept. 6, 1998 (OT).
103—Cincinnati 68, Pittsburgh 35, Dec. 30, 2001 (OT).
102—San Francisco 57, Atlanta 45, Oct. 6, 1985.

Fewest attempts, game
0—Green Bay vs. Portsmouth, Oct. 8, 1933.
   Detroit at Cleveland, Sept. 10, 1937.
   Pittsburgh vs. Brooklyn, Nov. 16, 1941.
   Pittsburgh vs. Los Angeles, Nov. 13, 1949.
   Cleveland vs. Philadelphia, Dec. 3, 1950.

Fewest attempts by both teams, game
4—Detroit 3, Chicago Cardinals 1, Nov. 3, 1935.
   Cleveland 4, Detroit 0, Sept. 10, 1937.

COMPLETIONS

Most completions, season
432—San Francisco, 1995.

Fewest completions, season
25—Cincinnati, 1933.

Most completions, game
45—New England vs. Minnesota, Nov. 13, 1994 (OT).
43—Washington at Detroit, Nov. 4, 1990 (OT).
   Oakland at Pittsburgh, Sept. 15, 2002.

Most completions by both teams, game
71—New England 45, Minnesota 26, Nov. 13, 1994 (OT).
68—San Francisco 37, Atlanta 31, Oct. 6, 1985.
   Oakland 34, Denver 34, Nov. 11, 2002.

Fewest completions, game
0—Held by many teams. Last team: Buffalo vs. New York Jets,
   Sept. 29, 1974.

Fewest completions by both teams, game
1—Philadelphia 1, Chicago Cardinals 0, Nov. 8, 1936.
   Cleveland 1, Detroit 0, Sept. 10, 1937.
   Detroit 1, Chicago Cardinals 0, Sept. 15, 1940.
   Pittsburgh 1, Brooklyn 0, Nov. 29, 1942.

YARDS

Most yards, season
5,232—St. Louis, 2000.

Most years leading league in yards
10—San Diego, 1965, 1968, 1971, 1978 through 1983, 1985.

Most consecutive years leading league in yards
6—San Diego, 1978 through 1983.

Fewest yards, season
302—Chicago Cardinals, 1934.

Most yards, game
554—Los Angeles vs. New York Yanks, Sept. 28, 1951.

Most yards by both teams, game
884—New York Jets 449, Miami 435, Sept. 21, 1986
   (OT).
883—San Diego 486, Cincinnati 397, Dec. 20, 1982.

Fewest yards, game
-53—Denver at Oakland, Sept. 10, 1967.

Fewest yards by both teams, game
-11—Green Bay -10, Dallas -1, Oct. 24, 1965.

TOUCHDOWNS

Most touchdowns, season
51—Indianapolis, 2004.

Fewest touchdowns, season
0—Cincinnati, 1933.
   Pittsburgh, 1945.

Most touchdowns, game
7—Chicago Bears at New York Giants, Nov. 14, 1943.
   Philadelphia at Washington, Oct. 17, 1954.
   Houston vs. New York Titans, Nov. 19, 1961.
   Houston vs. New York Titans, Oct. 14, 1962.
   New York Giants vs. Washington, Oct. 28, 1962.
   Minnesota vs. Baltimore, Sept. 28, 1969.
   San Diego at Oakland, Nov. 22, 1981.

Most touchdowns by both teams, game
12—New Orleans 6, St. Louis 6, Nov. 2, 1969.

INTERCEPTIONS

Most interceptions, season
48—Houston, 1962.

Fewest interceptions, season
5—Cleveland, 1960.
   Green Bay, 1966.
   Kansas City, 1990.
   New York Giants, 1990.

Most interceptions, game
9—Detroit vs. Green Bay, Oct. 24, 1943.
   Pittsburgh vs. Philadelphia, Dec. 12, 1965.

Most interceptions by both teams, game
13—Denver 8, Houston 5, Dec. 2, 1962.

SACKS

Most sacks allowed, season
104—Philadelphia, 1986.

Most years leading league in fewest sacks allowed
10—Miami, 1973 and 1982 through 1990.

Most consecutive years leading league in fewest sacks allowed
9—Miami, 1982 through 1990.

Fewest sacks allowed, season
7—Miami, 1988.

Most sacks allowed, game
12—Pittsburgh vs. Dallas, Nov. 20, 1966.
   Baltimore vs. St. Louis, Oct. 26, 1980.
   Detroit vs. Chicago, Dec. 16, 1984.
   Houston vs. Dallas, Sept. 29, 1985.

Most sacks allowed by both teams, game
18—Green Bay 10, San Diego 8, Sept. 24, 1978.

SCORING

POINTS

Most points, season
556—Minnesota, 1998.

Most points, game
72—Washington vs. New York Giants, Nov. 27, 1966.

Most points by both teams, game
113—Washington 72, New York Giants 41, Nov. 27, 1966.

Fewest points by both teams, game
0—Occurred many times. Last time: New York Giants 0, Detroit 0, Nov. 7, 1943.

Most points in a shutout victory
64—Philadelphia vs. Cincinnati, Nov. 6, 1934.

Fewest points in a shutout victory
2—Green Bay at Chicago Bears, Oct. 16, 1932.
   Chicago Bears at Green Bay, Sept. 18, 1938.

Most points in first half of game
49—Green Bay vs. Tampa Bay, Oct. 2, 1983.

Most points in first half of game by both teams
70—Houston 35, Oakland 35, Dec. 22, 1963.

Most points in second half of game
49—Chicago Bears at Philadelphia, Nov. 30, 1941.

Most points in second half of game by both teams
65—Washington 38, New York Giants 27, Nov. 27, 1966.

Most points in one quarter
41—Green Bay vs. Detroit, Oct. 7, 1945, second quarter.
   Los Angeles vs. Detroit, Oct. 29, 1950, third quarter.

Most points in one quarter by both teams
49—Oakland 28, Houston 21, Dec. 22, 1963, second quarter.

Most points in first quarter
35—Green Bay vs. Cleveland, Nov. 12, 1967.

Most points in first quarter by both teams
42—Green Bay 35, Cleveland 7, Nov. 12, 1967.

Most points in second quarter
41—Green Bay vs. Detroit, Oct. 7, 1945.

Most points in second quarter by both teams
49—Oakland 28, Houston 21, Dec. 22, 1963.

Most points in third quarter
41—Los Angeles vs. Detroit, Oct. 29, 1950.

Most points in third quarter by both teams
48—Los Angeles 41, Detroit 7, Oct. 29, 1950.

Most points in fourth quarter
31—Oakland vs. Denver, Dec. 17, 1960.
   Oakland vs. San Diego, Dec. 8, 1963.
   Atlanta at Green Bay, Sept. 13, 1981.

Most points in fourth quarter by both teams
42—Chicago Cardinals 28, Philadelphia 14, Dec. 7, 1947.
   Green Bay 28, Chicago Bears 14, Nov. 6, 1955.
   New York Jets 28, Boston 14, Oct. 27, 1968.
   Pittsburgh 21, Cleveland 21, Oct. 18, 1969.
   Kansas City 21, New England 21, Sept. 22, 2002.

Most consecutive games without being shut out
420—San Francisco, Oct. 16, 1977 through Sept. 26, 2004.

TIMES SHUT OUT

Most times shut out, season
8—Frankford, 1927 (lost six, tied two).
   Brooklyn, 1931 (lost eight).

Most consecutive times shut out
8—Rochester, 1922 through 1924 (lost eight).

TOUCHDOWNS

Most touchdowns, season
70—Miami, 1984.

Most years leading league in touchdowns
13—Chicago Bears, 1932, 1934, 1935, 1939, 1941, 1942, 1943, 1944, 1946, 1947, 1948, 1956, 1965.

Most consecutive years leading league in touchdowns
4—Chicago Bears, 1941 through 1944.
   Los Angeles, 1949 through 1952.
   San Francisco, 1992 through 1995.

Most touchdowns, game
10—Philadelphia vs. Cincinnati, Nov. 6, 1934.

Los Angeles vs. Baltimore, Oct. 22, 1950.
Washington vs. New York Giants, Nov. 27, 1966.

Most touchdowns by both teams, game
16—Washington 10, New York Giants 6, Nov. 27, 1966.

Most consecutive games with one or more touchdowns
166—Cleveland, 1957 through 1969.

EXTRA POINTS

Most extra points, season
66—Miami, 1984.

Fewest extra points, season
2—Chicago Cardinals, 1933.

Most extra points, game
10—Los Angeles vs. Baltimore, Oct. 22, 1950.

Most extra points by both teams, game
14—Chicago Cardinals 9, New York Giants 5, Oct. 17, 1948.
   Houston 7, Oakland 7, Dec. 22, 1963.
   Washington 9, New York Giants 5, Nov. 27, 1966.

FIELD GOALS

Most field goals attempted, season
49—Los Angeles, 1966.
   Washington, 1971.

Most field goals made, season
43—Arizona, 2005.

Most field goals attempted, game
9—St. Louis at Pittsburgh, Sept. 24, 1967.

Most field goals made, game
7—St. Louis at Pittsburgh, Sept. 24, 1967.
   Minnesota vs. Los Angeles Rams, Nov. 5, 1989 (OT).
   Dallas vs. Green Bay, Nov. 18, 1996.
   Dallas at N.Y. Giants, Sept. 15, 2003 (OT).

Most field goals attempted by both teams, game
12—New York Giants

Most field goals made by both teams, game
9—San Diego 5, Kansas City 4, Sept. 29, 1996.
   Miami 6, New England 3, Oct. 17, 1999.

Most consecutive games with one or more field goals made
38—Baltimore, Oct. 31, 1999 through Dec. 2, 2001.

SAFETIES

Most safeties, season
4—Cleveland, 1927.
   Detroit, 1962.
   Seattle, 1993.
   San Francisco, 1996.
   Tennessee, 1999.

Most safeties, game
3—Los Angeles Rams vs. New York Giants, Sept. 30, 1984.

Most safeties by both teams, game
3—Los Angeles Rams 3, New York Giants 0, Sept. 30, 1984.

FIRST DOWNS

Most first downs, season
398—Kansas City, 2004.

Most first downs, game
39—New York Jets vs. Miami, Nov. 27, 1988.
   Washington at Detroit, Nov. 4, 1990 (OT).

Most first downs by both teams, game
64—Kansas City 32, Seattle 32, Nov. 24, 2002.

PUNTING

Most punts, season
116—Houston, 2002.

Fewest punts, season
23—San Diego, 1982.

Most punts, game
17—Chicago Bears vs. Green Bay, Oct. 22, 1933.
  Cincinnati vs. Pittsburgh, Oct. 22, 1933.

Most punts by both teams, game
31—Chicago Bears 17, Green Bay 14, Oct. 22, 1933.
  Cincinnati 17, Pittsburgh 14, Oct. 22, 1933.

Fewest punts, game
0—Held by many teams.

Fewest punts by both teams, game
0—Buffalo 0, San Francisco 0, Sept. 13, 1992.

FUMBLES

Most fumbles, season
56—Chicago Bears, 1938.
  San Francisco, 1978.

Fewest fumbles, season
7—Kansas City, 2002.

Most fumbles, game
10—Phil-Pitt vs. New York, Oct. 9, 1943.
  Detroit at Minnesota, Nov. 12, 1967.
  Kansas City vs. Houston, Oct. 12, 1969.
  San Francisco at Detroit, Dec. 17, 1978.

Most fumbles by both teams, game
14—Washington 8, Pittsburgh 6, Nov. 14, 1937.
  Chicago Bears 7, Cleveland 7, Nov. 24, 1940.
  St. Louis 8, New York Giants 6, Sept. 17, 1961.
  Kansas City 10, Houston 4, Oct. 12, 1969.

LOST

Most fumbles lost, season
36—Chicago Cardinals, 1959.

Fewest fumbles lost, season
2—Kansas City, 2002.

Most fumbles lost, game
8—St. Louis at Washington, Oct. 25, 1976.
  Cleveland at Pittsburgh, Dec. 23, 1990.

RECOVERED

Most fumbles recovered (own and opponents'), season
58—Minnesota, 1963.

Fewest fumbles recovered (own and opponents'), season
9—San Francisco, 1982.

Most fumbles recovered (own and opponents'), game
10—Denver vs. Buffalo, Dec. 13, 1964.
  Pittsburgh vs. Houston, Dec. 9, 1973.
  Washington vs. St. Louis, Oct. 25, 1976.

Most fumbles recovered (own), season
37—Chicago Bears, 1938.

Fewest fumbles recovered (own), season
2—Washington, 1958.
  Miami, 2000.

TOUCHDOWNS

Most touchdowns on fumbles recovered (own and opponents'), season
5—Chicago Bears, 1942.
  Los Angeles, 1952.
  San Francisco, 1965.
  Oakland, 1978.

Most touchdowns on own fumbles recovered, season
2—Held by many teams. Last team: Buffalo, 2000.

Most touchdowns on fumbles recovered (own and opponents'), game
2—Held by many teams.

Most touchdowns on fumbles recovered (own and opponents'), both teams, game
3—Detroit 2, Minnesota 1, Dec. 9, 1962.
  Green Bay 2, Dallas 1, Nov. 29, 1964.
  Oakland 2, Buffalo 1, Dec. 24, 1967.

Oakland 2, Philadelphia 1, Sept. 24, 1995.
  Tennessee 2, Pittsburgh 1, Jan. 2, 2000.

Most touchdowns on own fumbles recovered, game
2—Miami vs. New England, Sept. 1, 1996.

Most touchdowns on opponents' fumbles recovered by both teams, game
3—Green Bay 2, Dallas 1, Nov. 29, 1964.
  Oakland 2, Buffalo 1, Dec. 24, 1967.
  Oakland 2, Philadelphia 1, Sept. 24, 1995.
  Tennessee 2, Pittsburgh 1, Jan. 2, 2000.

TURNOVERS

Most turnovers, season
63—San Francisco, 1978.

Fewest turnovers, season
12—Kansas City, 1982.

Most turnovers, game
12—Detroit vs. Chicago Bears, Nov. 22, 1942.
  Chicago Cardinals vs. Philadelphia, Sept. 24, 1950.
  Pittsburgh vs. Philadelphia, Dec. 12, 1965.

Most turnovers by both teams, game
17—Detroit 12, Chicago Bears 5, Nov. 22, 1942.
  Boston 9, Philadelphia 8, Dec. 8, 1946.

PUNT RETURNS

Most punt returns, season
71—Pittsburgh, 1976.
  Tampa Bay, 1979.
  Los Angeles Raiders, 1985.

Fewest punt returns, season
12—Baltimore, 1981.
  San Diego, 1982.

Most punt returns, game
12—Philadelphia at Cleveland, Dec. 3, 1950.

Most punt returns by both teams, game
17—Philadelphia 12, Cleveland 5, Dec. 3, 1950.

YARDS

Most yards, season
875—Green Bay, 1996.

Fewest yards, season
27—St. Louis, 1965.

Most yards, game
231—Detroit vs. San Francisco, Oct. 6, 1963.

Most yards by both teams, game
282—Los Angeles 219, Atlanta 63, Oct. 11, 1981.

TOUCHDOWNS

Most touchdowns, season
5—Chicago Cardinals, 1959.

Most touchdowns, game
2—Held by many teams.

Most touchdowns by both teams, game
2—Occurred many times.

KICKOFF RETURNS

Most kickoff returns, season
89—Cleveland, 1999.

Fewest kickoff returns, season
17—N.Y. Giants, 1944.

Most kickoff returns, game
12—N.Y. Giants at Washington, Nov. 27, 1966.

Most kickoff returns by both teams, game
19—N.Y. Giants 12, Washington 7, Nov. 27, 1966.

YARDS

Most yards, season
2,296—Arizona, 2000.

Fewest yards, season
282—N.Y. Giants, 1940.

Most yards, game
367—Baltimore vs. Minnesota, Dec. 13, 1998.

Most yards by both teams, game
560—Detroit 362, Los Angeles 198, Oct. 29, 1950.

TOUCHDOWNS

Most touchdowns, season
4—Green Bay, 1967.
   Chicago, 1970.
   Detroit, 1994.

Most touchdowns, game
2—Chicago Bears at Green Bay, Sept. 22, 1940.
   Chicago Bears vs. Green Bay, Nov. 9, 1952.
   Philadelphia vs. Dallas, Nov. 6, 1966.
   Green Bay vs. Cleveland, Nov. 12, 1967.
   Los Angeles Rams vs. Green Bay, Nov. 24, 1985.
   New Orleans vs. Los Angeles Rams, Oct. 23, 1994.
   Baltimore vs. Minnesota, Dec. 13, 1998.
   N.Y. Jets at Buffalo, Sept. 8, 2002 (OT).

Most touchdowns by both teams, game (each team scoring)
3—Baltimore (2) vs. Minnesota (1), Dec. 13, 1998.

PENALTIES

Most penalties, season
158—Kansas City, 1998.

Fewest penalties, season
19—Detroit, 1937.

Most penalties, game
22—Brooklyn at Green Bay, Sept. 17, 1944.
   Chicago Bears at Philadelphia, Nov. 26, 1944.
   San Francisco at Buffalo, Oct. 4, 1998.

Most penalties by both teams, game
37—Cleveland 21, Chicago Bears 16, Nov. 25, 1951.

Fewest penalties, game
0—Held by many teams. Last team: Oakland at San Diego, Dec. 4, 2005.

Fewest penalties by both teams, game
0—Brooklyn 0, Pittsburgh 0, Oct. 28, 1934.
   Brooklyn 0, Boston 0, Sept. 28, 1936.
   Cleveland 0, Chicago Bears 0, Oct. 9, 1938.
   Pittsburgh 0, Philadelphia 0, Nov. 10, 1940.

YARDS PENALIZED

Most yards penalized, season
1,304—Kansas City, 1998.

Fewest yards penalized, season
139—Detroit, 1937.

Most yards penalized, game
212—Tennessee vs. Baltimore, Oct. 10, 1999.

Most yards penalized by both teams, game
374—Cleveland 209, Chicago Bears 165, Nov. 25, 1951.

Fewest yards penalized, game
0—Held by many teams. Last team: Oakland at San Diego, Dec. 4, 2005.

Fewest yards penalized by both teams, game
0—Brooklyn 0, Pittsburgh 0, Oct. 28, 1934.
   Brooklyn 0, Boston 0, Sept. 28, 1936.
   Cleveland 0, Chicago Bears 0, Oct. 9, 1938.
   Pittsburgh 0, Philadelphia 0, Nov. 10, 1940.

TEAM DEFENSE
RUSHING

YARDS ALLOWED

Most yards allowed, season
3,228—Buffalo, 1978.

Fewest yards allowed, season
519—Chicago Bears, 1942.

TOUCHDOWNS ALLOWED

Most touchdowns allowed, season
36—Oakland, 1961.

Fewest touchdowns allowed, season
2—Detroit, 1934.
   Dallas, 1968.
   Minnesota, 1971.

PASSING

YARDS ALLOWED

Most yards allowed, season
4,541—Atlanta, 1995.

Fewest yards allowed, season
545—Philadelphia, 1934.

TOUCHDOWNS ALLOWED

Most touchdowns allowed, season
40—Denver, 1963.

Fewest touchdowns allowed, season
1—Portsmouth, 1932.
   Philadelphia, 1934.

YARDS ALLOWED

(RUSHING AND PASSING)

Most yards allowed rushing and passing, season
6,793—Baltimore, 1981.

Fewest yards allowed rushing and passing, season
1,539—Chicago Cardinals, 1934.

SCORING

POINTS ALLOWED

Most points allowed, season
533—Baltimore, 1981.

Fewest points allowed, season (since 1932)
44—Chicago Bears, 1932.

SHUTOUTS

Most shutouts, season
10—Pottsville, 1926 (won nine, tied one).
   N.Y. Giants, 1927 (won nine, tied one).

Most consecutive shutouts
13—Akron, 1920 through 1921 (won 10, tied three).

TOUCHDOWNS ALLOWED

Most touchdowns allowed, season
68—Baltimore, 1981.

Fewest touchdowns allowed, season (since 1932)
6—Chicago Bears, 1932.
   Brooklyn, 1933.

FIRST DOWNS ALLOWED

Most first downs allowed, season
406—Baltimore, 1981.

Fewest first downs allowed, season
77—Detroit, 1935.

Most first downs allowed by rushing, season
179—Detroit, 1985.

Fewest first downs allowed by rushing, season
35—Chicago Bears, 1942.

Most first downs allowed by passing, season
230—Atlanta, 1995.

Fewest first downs allowed by passing, season
33—Chicago Bears, 1943.

Most first downs allowed by penalties, season
56—Kansas City, 1998.

Fewest first downs allowed by penalties, season
1—Boston, 1944.

INTERCEPTIONS

Most interceptions, season
49—San Diego, 1961.

Fewest interceptions, season
3—Houston, 1982.

Most interceptions, game
9—Green Bay at Detroit, Oct. 24, 1943.
    Philadelphia at Pittsburgh, Dec. 12, 1965.

Most yards returning interceptions, season
929—San Diego, 1961.

Fewest yards returning interceptions, season
5—Los Angeles, 1959.

Most yards returning interceptions, game
325—Seattle vs. Kansas City, Nov. 4, 1984.

Most touchdowns returning interceptions, season
9—San Diego, 1961.

Most touchdowns returning interceptions, game
4—Seattle vs. Kansas City, Nov. 4, 1984.

Most touchdowns returning interceptions by both teams, game
4—Philadelphia 3, Pittsburgh 1, Dec. 12, 1965.
    Seattle 4, Kansas City 0, Nov. 4, 1984.

FUMBLES

Most opponents' fumbles forced, season
50—Minnesota, 1963.
    San Francisco, 1978.

Fewest opponents' fumbles forced, season
11—Cleveland, 1956.
    Baltimore, 1982.
    Tennessee, 1998.

RECOVERED

Most opponents' fumbles recovered, season
31—Minnesota, 1963.

Fewest opponents' fumbles recovered, season
3—Los Angeles, 1974.
    Green Bay, 1995.

Most opponents' fumbles recovered, game
8—Washington vs. St. Louis, Oct. 25, 1976.
    Pittsburgh vs. Cleveland, Dec. 23, 1990.

TOUCHDOWNS

Most touchdowns on opponents' fumbles recovered, season
4—Held by many teams. Last team: Kansas City, 1999.

Most touchdowns on opponents' fumbles recovered, game
2—Held by many teams. Last team: San Francisco at Arizona, Oct. 2, 2005.

TURNOVERS

Most opponents' turnovers, season
66—San Diego, 1961.

Fewest opponents' turnovers, season
11—Baltimore, 1982.

Most opponents' turnovers, game
12—Chicago Bears at Detroit, Nov. 22, 1942.
    Philadelphia at Chicago Cardinals, Sept. 24, 1950.
    Philadelphia at Pittsburgh, Dec. 12, 1965.

SACKS

Most sacks, season
72—Chicago, 1984.

Fewest sacks, season
11—Baltimore, 1982.

Most sacks, game
12—Dallas at Pittsburgh, Nov. 20, 1966.
    St. Louis at Baltimore, Oct. 26, 1980.
    Chicago at Detroit, Dec. 16, 1984.
    Dallas at Houston, Sept. 29, 1985.

PUNTS RETURNED

Most punts returned by opponents, season
71—Tampa Bay, 1976.
    Tampa Bay, 1977.

Fewest punts returned by opponents, season
7—Washington, 1962.
    San Diego, 1982.

Most yards allowed on punts returned by opponents, season
932—Green Bay, 1949.

Fewest yards allowed on punts returned by opponents, season
22—Green Bay, 1967.

Most touchdowns allowed on punts returned by opponents, season
4—New York, 1959.
    Atlanta, 1992.

KICKOFFS RETURNED

Most kickoffs returned by opponents, season
91—Washington, 1983.

Fewest kickoffs returned by opponents, season
10—Brooklyn, 1943.

Most yards allowed on kickoffs returned by opponents, season
2,194—St. Louis, 2001.

Fewest yards allowed on kickoffs returned by opponents, season
225—Brooklyn, 1943.

Most touchdowns allowed on kickoffs returned by opponents, season
4—Minnesota, 1998.

STATISTICAL LEADERS

CAREER MILESTONES

TOP 20 RUSHERS

Player	League	Years	Att.	Yds.	Avg.	Long	TD
Emmitt Smith	NFL	15	4,409	18,355	4.2	t75	164
Walter Payton	NFL	13	3,838	16,726	4.4	76	110
Barry Sanders	NFL	10	3,062	15,269	5.0	85	99
Curtis Martin*	NFL	11	3,518	14,101	4.0	t70	90
Jerome Bettis*	NFL	13	3,479	13,662	3.9	t71	91
Eric Dickerson	NFL	11	2,996	13,259	4.4	t85	90
Tony Dorsett	NFL	12	2,936	12,739	4.3	t99	77
Jim Brown	NFL	9	2,359	12,312	5.2	t80	106
Marshall Faulk*	NFL	12	2,836	12,279	4.3	t71	100
Marcus Allen	NFL	16	3,022	12,243	4.1	t61	123
Franco Harris	NFL	13	2,949	12,120	4.1	t75	91
Thurman Thomas	NFL	13	2,877	12,074	4.2	t80	65
John Riggins	NFL	14	2,916	11,352	3.9	t66	104
O.J. Simpson	AFL-NFL	11	2,404	11,236	4.7	t94	61
Ricky Watters	NFL	10	2,622	10,643	4.1	57	78
Eddie George	NFL	9	2,865	10,441	3.6	76	68
Corey Dillon*	NFL	9	2,419	10,429	4.3	96	69
Ottis Anderson	NFL	14	2,562	10,273	4.0	t76	81
Joe Perry	AAFC-NFL	16	1,929	9,723	5.0	t78	71
Earl Campbell	NFL	8	2,187	9,407	4.3	t81	74

*Active through 2005 season.

TOP 20 PASSERS

Player	League	Years	Att.	Cmp.	Yds.	TD	Int.	Rat.
Steve Young	NFL	15	4,149	2,667	33,124	232	107	96.8
Kurt Warner*	NFL	8	2,340	1,537	19,214	119	78	94.1
Peyton Manning*	NFL	8	4,333	2,769	33,189	244	130	93.5
Joe Montana	NFL	15	5,391	3,409	40,551	273	139	92.3
Daunte Culpepper*	NFL	7	2,607	1,678	20,162	135	86	91.5
Marc Bulger*	NFL	5	1,518	987	11,932	71	51	90.6
Tom Brady*	NFL	6	2,548	1,577	18,035	123	66	88.5
Trent Green*	NFL	8	3,329	2,022	25,621	150	92	88.3
Matt Hasselbeck*	NFL	7	2,205	1,342	15,925	96	57	86.64
Otto Graham	AAFC-NFL	10	2,626	1,464	23,584	174	135	86.63
Dan Marino	NFL	17	8,358	4,967	61,361	420	252	86.4
Brett Favre*	NFL	15	7,610	4,678	53,615	396	255	86.0
Jeff Garcia*	NFL	7	2,785	1,695	19,076	126	71	85.8
Drew Brees*	NFL	5	1,809	1,125	12,348	80	53	84.9
Brian Griese*	NFL	8	2,318	1,463	16,344	103	78	84.8
Rich Gannon	NFL	16	4,206	2,533	28,743	180	104	84.7
Jake Delhomme*	NFL	5	1,503	888	11,160	75	52	84.5
Jim Kelly	NFL	11	4,779	2,874	35,467	237	175	84.39
Brad Johnson*	NFL	14	3,798	2,350	25,798	155	102	84.36
Donovan McNabb*	NFL	7	2,943	1,718	19,433	134	66	84.1

*Active through 2005 season; minimum 1,500 attempts.

TOP 20 RECEIVERS

Player	League	Years	No.	Yds.	Avg.	Long	TD
Jerry Rice	NFL	20	1,549	22,895	14.8	t96	197
Cris Carter	NFL	16	1,101	13,899	12.6	t80	130
Tim Brown	NFL	17	1,094	14,934	13.7	t80	100
Andre Reed	NFL	16	951	13,198	13.9	t83	87
Art Monk	NFL	16	940	12,721	13.5	t79	68
Marvin Harrison*	NFL	10	927	12,331	13.3	80	110
Jimmy Smith*	NFL	13	862	12,287	14.3	75	67
Irving Fryar	NFL	17	851	12,785	15.0	t80	84
Larry Centers	NFL	14	827	6,797	8.2	54	28
Keenan McCardell*	NFL	14	825	10,680	12.9	t76	62
Steve Largent	NFL	14	819	13,089	16.0	t74	100
Shannon Sharpe	NFL	14	815	10,060	12.3	t82	62
Henry Ellard	NFL	16	814	13,777	16.9	t81	65
Isaac Bruce*	NFL	12	813	12,278	15.1	t80	77
Rod Smith*	NFL	11	797	10,877	13.6	85	65

Player	League	Years	No.	Yds.	Avg.	Long	TD
Marshall Faulk*	NFL	12	767	6,875	9.0	85	36
James Lofton	NFL	16	764	14,004	18.3	t80	75
Charlie Joiner	AFL-NFL	18	750	12,146	16.2	t87	65
Michael Irvin	NFL	12	750	11,904	15.9	t87	65
Keyshawn Johnson*	NFL	10	744	9,756	13.1	76	60

*Active through 2005 season.

TOP 20 SCORERS

Player	League	Years	TD	XP Made	FG Made	Total
Gary Anderson	NFL	23	0	820	538	2,434
Morten Andersen	NFL	23	0	798	520	2,358
George Blanda	NFL-AFL	26	9	942	335	2,002
Norm Johnson	NFL	18	0	638	366	1,736
Nick Lowery	NFL	18	0	562	383	1,711
Jan Stenerud	AFL-NFL	19	0	580	373	1,699
John Carney*	NFL	18	0	464	390	1,634
Lou Groza	AAFC-NFL	21	1	810	264	1,608
Eddie Murray	NFL	19	0	538	352	1,594
Matt Stover*	NFL	15	0	454	380	1,594
Al Del Greco	NFL	17	0	543	347	1,584
Jason Elam*	NFL	13	0	534	341	1,557
Steve Christie	NFL	15	0	468	336	1,476
Pat Leahy	NFL	18	0	558	304	1,470
Jim Turner	AFL-NFL	16	1	521	304	1,439
Matt Bahr	NFL	17	0	522	300	1,422
Jason Hanson*	NFL	14	0	439	327	1,420
Mark Moseley	NFL	16	0	482	300	1,382
Jim Bakken	NFL	17	0	534	282	1,380
Fred Cox	NFL	15	0	519	282	1,365

*Active through 2005 season.

YEAR BY YEAR

AFC

RUSHING
(Based on most net yards)

	Net Yds.	Att.	TD
1960—Abner Haynes, Dallas	875	156	9
1961—Billy Cannon, Houston	948	200	6
1962—Cookie Gilchrist, Buffalo	1096	214	13
1963—Clem Daniels, Oakland	1099	215	3
1964—Cookie Gilchrist, Buffalo	981	230	6
1965—Paul Lowe, San Diego	1121	222	7
1966—Jim Nance, Boston	1458	299	11
1967—Jim Nance, Boston	1216	269	7
1968—Paul Robinson, Cincinnati	1023	238	8
1969—Dick Post, San Diego	873	182	6
1970—Floyd Little, Denver	901	209	3
1971—Floyd Little, Denver	1133	284	6
1972—O.J. Simpson, Buffalo	1251	292	6
1973—O.J. Simpson, Buffalo	2003	332	12
1974—Otis Armstrong, Denver	1407	263	9
1975—O.J. Simpson, Buffalo	1817	329	16
1976—O.J. Simpson, Buffalo	1503	290	8
1977—Mark van Eeghen, Oakland	1273	324	7
1978—Earl Campbell, Houston	1450	302	13
1979—Earl Campbell, Houston	1697	368	19
1980—Earl Campbell, Houston	1934	373	13
1981—Earl Campbell, Houston	1376	361	10
1982—Freeman McNeil, N.Y. Jets	786	151	6
1983—Curt Warner, Seattle	1449	335	13
1984—Earnest Jackson, San Diego	1179	296	8
1985—Marcus Allen, L.A. Raiders	1759	380	11
1986—Curt Warner, Seattle	1481	319	13
1987—Eric Dickerson, Indianapolis	1011	223	5
1988—Eric Dickerson, Indianapolis	1659	388	14
1989—Christian Okoye, Kansas City	1480	370	12
1990—Thurman Thomas, Buffalo	1297	271	11
1991—Thurman Thomas, Buffalo	1407	288	7
1992—Barry Foster, Pittsburgh	1690	390	11
1993—Thurman Thomas, Buffalo	1315	355	6
1994—Chris Warren, Seattle	1545	333	9

	Net Yds.	Att.	TD
1995—Curtis Martin, New England	1487	368	14
1996—Terrell Davis, Denver	1538	345	13
1997—Terrell Davis, Denver	1750	369	15
1998—Terrell Davis, Denver	2008	392	21
1999—Edgerrin James, Indianapolis	1553	369	13
2000—Edgerrin James, Indianapolis	1709	387	13
2001—Priest Holmes, Kansas City	1555	327	8
2002—Ricky Williams, Miami	1853	383	16
2003—Jamal Lewis, Baltimore	2066	387	14
2004—Curtis Martin, N.Y. Jets	1697	371	12
2005—Larry Johnson, Kansas City	1750	336	20

PASSING
(Based on highest passer rating among qualifiers*)

	Att.	Com.	Yds.	TD	Int.	Rat.
1960— Jack Kemp, S.D.	406	211	3018	20	25	67.1
1961— George Blanda, Hou.	362	187	3330	36	22	91.3
1962— Len Dawson, Dal.	310	189	2759	29	17	98.3
1963— Tobin Rote, S.D.	286	170	2510	20	17	86.7
1964— Len Dawson, K.C.	354	199	2879	30	18	89.9
1965— John Hadl, S.D.	348	174	2798	20	21	71.3
1966— Len Dawson, K.C.	284	159	2527	26	10	101.7
1967— Daryle Lamonica, Oak.	425	220	3228	30	20	80.8
1968— Len Dawson, K.C.	224	131	2109	17	9	98.6
1969— Greg Cook, Cin.	197	106	1854	15	11	88.3
1970— Daryle Lamonica, Oak.	356	179	2516	22	15	76.5
1971— Bob Griese, Mia.	263	145	2089	19	9	90.9
1972— Earl Morrall, Mia.	150	83	1360	11	7	91.0
1973— Ken Stabler, Oak.	260	163	1997	14	10	88.3
1974— Ken Anderson, Cin.	328	213	2667	18	10	95.7
1975— Ken Anderson, Cin.	377	228	3169	21	11	93.9
1976— Ken Stabler, Oak.	291	194	2737	27	17	103.4
1977— Bob Griese, Mia.	307	180	2252	22	13	87.8
1978— Terry Bradshaw, Pit.	368	207	2915	28	20	84.7
1979— Dan Fouts, S.D.	530	332	4082	24	24	82.6
1980— Brian Sipe, Cle.	554	337	4132	30	14	91.4
1981— Ken Anderson, Cin.	479	300	3754	29	10	98.4

HISTORY *Statistical leaders*

	Att.	Com.	Yds.	TD	Int.	Rat.
1982— Ken Anderson, Cin.	309	218	2495	12	9	95.3
1983— Dan Marino, Mia.	296	173	2210	20	6	96.0
1984— Dan Marino, Mia.	564	362	5084	48	17	108.9
1985— Ken O'Brien, NYJ	488	297	3888	25	8	96.2
1986— Dan Marino, Mia.	623	378	4746	44	23	92.5
1987— Bernie Kosar, Cle.	389	241	3033	22	9	95.4
1988— Boomer Esiason, Cin.	388	223	3572	28	14	97.4
1989— Boomer Esiason, Cin.	455	258	3525	28	11	92.1
1990— Jim Kelly, Buf.	346	219	2829	24	9	101.2
1991— Jim Kelly, Buf.	474	304	3844	33	17	97.6
1992— Warren Moon, Hou.	346	224	2521	18	12	89.3
1993— John Elway, Den.	551	348	4030	25	10	92.8
1994— Dan Marino, Mia.	615	385	4453	30	17	89.2
1995— Jim Harbaugh, Ind.	314	200	2575	17	5	100.7
1996— John Elway, Den.	466	287	3328	26	14	89.2
1997— Mark Brunell, Jac.†	435	264	3281	18	7	91.17
1998— Vinny Testaverde, NYJ	421	259	3256	29	7	101.6
1999— Peyton Manning, Ind.	533	331	4135	26	15	90.7
2000— Brian Griese, Den.	336	216	2688	19	4	102.9
2001— Rich Gannon, Oak.	549	361	3828	27	9	95.5
2002— Chad Pennington, NYJ	399	275	3120	22	6	104.2
2003— Steve McNair, Ten.	400	250	3215	24	7	100.4
2004— Peyton Manning, Ind.	497	336	4557	49	10	121.1
2005— Peyton Manning, Ind.	453	305	3747	28	10	104.1

*This chart includes passer rating points for all leaders, although the same rating system was not used for determining leading quarterbacks prior to 1973. The old system was less equitable, yet similar to the new one in that the rating was based on percentage of completions, touchdown passes, percentage of interceptions and average gain in yards.

†Brunell and Jeff George of Oakland (521, 290, 3917, 29, 9), tied with 91.2 rating points, but rounded to another decimal place, Brunell's rating is higher, 91.17 to 91.15.

RECEIVING

(Based on most receptions)

	No.	Yds.	TD
1960—Lionel Taylor, Denver	92	1235	12
1961—Lionel Taylor, Denver	100	1176	4
1962—Lionel Taylor, Denver	77	908	4
1963—Lionel Taylor, Denver	78	1101	10
1964—Charley Hennigan, Houston	101	1546	8
1965—Lionel Taylor, Denver	85	1131	6
1966—Lance Alworth, San Diego	73	1383	13
1967—George Sauer, N.Y. Jets	75	1189	6
1968—Lance Alworth, San Diego	68	1312	10
1969—Lance Alworth, San Diego	64	1003	4
1970—Marlin Briscoe, Buffalo	57	1036	8
1971—Fred Biletnikoff, Oakland	61	929	9
1972—Fred Biletnikoff, Oakland	58	802	7
1973—Fred Willis, Houston	57	371	1
1974—Lydell Mitchell, Baltimore	72	544	2
1975—Reggie Rucker, Cleveland	60	770	3
Lydell Mitchell, Baltimore	60	544	4
1976—MacArthur Lane, Kansas City	66	686	1
1977—Lydell Mitchell, Baltimore	71	620	4
1978—Steve Largent, Seattle	71	1168	8
1979—Joe Washington, Baltimore	82	750	3
1980—Kellen Winslow, San Diego	89	1290	9
1981—Kellen Winslow, San Diego	88	1075	10
1982—Kellen Winslow, San Diego	54	721	6
1983—Todd Christensen, L.A. Raiders	92	1247	12
1984—Ozzie Newsome, Cleveland	89	1001	5
1985—Lionel James, San Diego	86	1027	6
1986—Todd Christensen, L.A. Raiders	95	1153	8
1987—Al Toon, N.Y. Jets	68	976	5
1988—Al Toon, N.Y. Jets	93	1067	5
1989—Andre Reed, Buffalo	88	1312	9
1990—Haywood Jeffires, Houston	74	1048	8
Drew Hill, Houston	74	1019	5
1991—Haywood Jeffires, Houston	100	1181	7
1992—Haywood Jeffires, Houston	90	913	9
1993—Reggie Langhorne, Indianapolis	85	1038	3
1994—Ben Coates, New England	96	1174	7
1995—Carl Pickens, Cincinnati	99	1234	17

	No.	Yds.	TD
1996—Carl Pickens, Cincinnati	100	1180	12
1997—Tim Brown, Oakland	104	1408	5
1998—O.J. McDuffie, Miami	90	1050	7
1999—Jimmy Smith, Jacksonville	116	1636	6
2000—Marvin Harrison, Indianapolis	102	1413	14
2001—Rod Smith, Denver	113	1343	11
2002—Marvin Harrison, Indianapolis	143	1722	11
2003—LaDainian Tomlinson, San Diego	100	725	4
2004—Tony Gonzalez, Kansas City	102	1258	7
2005—Chad Johnson, Cincinnati	97	1432	9

SCORING

(Based on most total points)

	TD	PAT	FG	Tot.
1960— Gene Mingo, Denver	6	33	18	123
1961— Gino Cappelletti, Boston	8	48	17	147
1962— Gene Mingo, Denver	4	32	27	137
1963— Gino Cappelletti, Boston	2	35	22	113
1964— Gino Cappelletti, Boston	7	36	25	155
1965— Gino Cappelletti, Boston	9	27	17	132
1966— Gino Cappelletti, Boston	6	35	16	119
1967— George Blanda, Oakland	0	56	20	116
1968— Jim Turner, N.Y. Jets	0	43	34	145
1969— Jim Turner, N.Y. Jets	0	33	32	129
1970— Jan Stenerud, Kansas City	0	26	30	116
1971— Garo Yepremian, Miami	0	33	28	117
1972— Bobby Howfield, N.Y. Jets	0	40	27	121
1973— Roy Gerela, Pittsburgh	0	36	29	123
1974— Roy Gerela, Pittsburgh	0	33	20	93
1975— O.J. Simpson, Buffalo	23	0	0	138
1976— Toni Linhart, Baltimore	0	49	20	109
1977— Errol Mann, Oakland	0	39	20	99
1978— Pat Leahy, N.Y. Jets	0	41	22	107
1979— John Smith, New England	0	46	23	115
1980— John Smith, New England	0	51	26	129
1981— Jim Breech, Cincinnati	0	49	22	115
Nick Lowery, Kansas City	0	37	26	115
1982— Marcus Allen, L.A. Raiders	14	0	0	84
1983— Gary Anderson, Pittsburgh	0	38	27	119
1984— Gary Anderson, Pittsburgh	0	45	24	117
1985— Gary Anderson, Pittsburgh	0	40	33	139
1986— Tony Franklin, New England	0	44	32	140
1987— Jim Breech, Cincinnati	0	25	24	97
1988— Scott Norwood, Buffalo	0	33	32	129
1989— David Treadwell, Denver	0	39	27	120
1990— Nick Lowery, Kansas City	0	37	34	139
1991— Pete Stoyanovich, Miami	0	28	31	121
1992— Pete Stoyanovich, Miami	0	34	30	124
1993— Jeff Jaeger, L.A. Raiders	0	27	35	132
1994— John Carney, San Diego	0	33	34	135
1995— Norm Johnson, Pittsburgh	0	39	34	141
1996— Cary Blanchard, Indianapolis	0	27	36	135
1997— Mike Hollis, Jacksonville	0	41	31	134
1998— Steve Christie, Buffalo	0	41	33	140
1999— Mike Vanderjagt, Indianapolis	0	43	34	145
2000— Matt Stover, Baltimore	0	30	35	135
2001— Mike Vanderjagt, Indianapolis	0	41	28	125
2002— Priest Holmes, Kansas City	24	0	0	144
2003— Priest Holmes, Kansas City	27	0	0	162
2004— Adam Vinatieri, New England	0	48	31	141
2005— Shayne Graham, Cincinnati	0	47	28	131

FIELD GOALS

	No.
1960— Gene Mingo, Denver	18
1961— Gino Cappelletti, Boston	17
1962— Gene Mingo, Denver	27
1963— Gino Cappelletti, Boston	22
1964— Gino Cappelletti, Boston	25
1965— Pete Gogolak, Buffalo	28
1966— Mike Mercer, Oakland-Kansas City	21
1967— Jan Stenerud, Kansas City	21
1968— Jim Turner, N.Y. Jets	34
1969— Jim Turner, N.Y. Jets	32

HISTORY Statistical leaders

	No.
1970— Jan Stenerud, Kansas City	30
1971— Garo Yepremian, Miami	28
1972— Roy Gerela, Pittsburgh	28
1973— Roy Gerela, Pittsburgh	29
1974— Roy Gerela, Pittsburgh	20
1975— Jan Stenerud, Kansas City	22
1976— Jan Stenerud, Kansas City	21
1977— Errol Mann, Oakland	20
1978— Pat Leahy, N.Y. Jets	22
1979— John Smith, New England	23
1980— John Smith, New England	26
Fred Steinfort, Denver	26
1981— Nick Lowery, Kansas City	26
1982— Nick Lowery, Kansas City	19
1983— Raul Allegre, Baltimore	30
1984— Gary Anderson, Pittsburgh	24
Matt Bahr, Cleveland	24
1985— Gary Anderson, Pittsburgh	33
1986— Tony Franklin, New England	32
1987— Dean Biasucci, Indianapolis	24
Jim Breech, Cincinnati	24
1988— Scott Norwood, Buffalo	32
1989— David Treadwell, Denver	27
1990— Nick Lowery, Kansas City	34
1991— Pete Stoyanovich, Miami	31
1992— Pete Stoyanovich, Miami	30
1993— Jeff Jaeger, L.A. Raiders	35
1994— John Carney, San Diego	34
1995— Norm Johnson, Pittsburgh	34
1996— Cary Blanchard, Indianapolis	36
1997— Cary Blanchard, Indianapolis	32
1998— Al Del Greco, Tennessee	36
1999— Olindo Mare, Miami	39
2000— Matt Stover, Baltimore	35
2001— Jason Elam, Denver	31
2002— Adam Vinatieri, New England	27
2003— Mike Vanderjagt, Indianapolis	37
2004— Adam Vinatieri, New England	31
2005— Matt Stover, Baltimore	30

INTERCEPTIONS

	No.	Yds.
1960— Austin Gonsoulin, Denver	11	98
1961— Bill Atkins, Buffalo	10	158
1962— Lee Riley, N.Y. Titans	11	122
1963— Fred Glick, Houston	12	180
1964— Dainard Paulson, N.Y. Jets	12	157
1965— W.K. Hicks, Houston	9	156
1966— Johnny Robinson, Kansas City	10	136
Bobby Hunt, Kansas City	10	113
1967— Miller Farr, Houston	10	264
Tom Janik, Buffalo	10	222
Dick Westmoreland, Miami	10	127
1968— Dave Grayson, Oakland	10	195
1969— Emmitt Thomas, Kansas City	9	146
1970— Johnny Robinson, Kansas City	10	155
1971— Ken Houston, Houston	9	220
1972— Mike Sensibaugh, Kansas City	8	65
1973— Dick Anderson, Miami	8	136
Mike Wagner, Pittsburgh	8	134
1974— Emmitt Thomas, Kansas City	12	214
1975— Mel Blount, Pittsburgh	11	121
1976— Ken Riley, Cincinnati	9	141
1977— Lyle Blackwood, Baltimore	10	163
1978— Thom Darden, Cleveland	10	200
1979— Mike Reinfeldt, Houston	12	205
1980— Lester Hayes, Oakland	13	273
1981— John Harris, Seattle	10	155
1982— Ken Riley, Cincinnati	5	88
Bobby Jackson, N.Y. Jets	5	84
Dwayne Woodruff, Pittsburgh	5	53
Donnie Shell, Pittsburgh	5	27
1983— Ken Riley, Cincinnati	8	89
Vann McElroy, Los Angeles	8	68
1984— Kenny Easley, Seattle	10	126
1985— Albert Lewis, Kansas City	8	59
Eugene Daniel, Indianapolis	8	53
1986— Deron Cherry, Kansas City	9	150

	No.	Yds.
1987— Mike Prior, Indianapolis	6	57
Mark Kelso, Buffalo	6	25
Keith Bostic, Houston	6	-14
1988— Erik McMillan, N.Y. Jets	8	168
1989— Felix Wright, Cleveland	9	91
1990— Richard Johnson, Houston	8	100
1991— Ronnie Lott, L.A. Raiders	8	52
1992— Henry Jones, Buffalo	8	263
1993— Eugene Robinson, Seattle	9	80
Nate Odomes, Buffalo	9	65
1994— Eric Turner, Cleveland	9	199
1995— Willie Williams, Pittsburgh	7	122
1996— Tyrone Braxton, Denver	9	128
1997— Mark McMillian, Kansas City	8	274
Darryl Williams, Seattle	8	172
1998— Ty Law, New England	9	133
1999— Rod Woodson, Baltimore	7	195
Sam Madison, Miami	7	164
James Hasty, Kansas City	7	98
2000— Samari Rolle, Tennessee	7	140
Brian Walker, Miami	7	80
2001— Anthony Henry, Cleveland	10	177
2002— Rod Woodson, Oakland	8	225
2003— Ed Reed, Baltimore	7	132
Marcus Coleman, Houston	7	95
Patrick Surtain, Miami	7	59
2004— Ed Reed, Baltimore	9	358
2005— Ty Law, N.Y. Jets	10	195
Deltha O'Neal, Cincinnati	10	103

PUNTING

(Based on highest average yardage per punt by qualifiers)

	No.	Avg.
1960— Paul Maguire, L.A. Chargers	43	40.5
1961— Bill Atkins, Buffalo	85	44.5
1962— Jim Fraser, Denver	55	43.6
1963— Jim Fraser, Denver	81	44.4
1964— Jim Fraser, Denver	73	44.2
1965— Jerrel Wilson, Kansas City	69	45.4
1966— Bob Scarpitto, Denver	76	45.8
1967— Bob Scarpitto, Denver	105	44.9
1968— Jerrel Wilson, Kansas City	63	45.1
1969— Dennis Partee, San Diego	71	44.6
1970— Dave Lewis, Cincinnati	79	46.2
1971— Dave Lewis, Cincinnati	72	44.8
1972— Jerrel Wilson, Kansas City	66	44.8
1973— Jerrel Wilson, Kansas City	80	45.5
1974— Ray Guy, Oakland	74	42.2
1975— Ray Guy, Oakland	68	43.8
1976— Marv Bateman, Buffalo	86	42.8
1977— Ray Guy, Oakland	59	43.3
1978— Pat McInally, Cincinnati	91	43.1
1979— Bob Grupp, Kansas City	89	43.6
1980— Luke Prestridge, Denver	70	43.9
1981— Pat McInally, Cincinnati	72	45.4
1982— Luke Prestridge, Denver	45	45.0
1983— Rohn Stark, Baltimore	91	45.3
1984— Jim Arnold, Kansas City	98	44.9
1985— Rohn Stark, Indianapolis	78	45.9
1986— Rohn Stark, Indianapolis	76	45.2
1987— Ralf Mojsiejenko, San Diego	67	42.9
1988— Harry Newsome, Pittsburgh	65	45.4
1989— Greg Montgomery, Houston	56	43.3
1990— Mike Horan, Denver	58	44.4
1991— Reggie Roby, Miami	54	45.7
1992— Greg Montgomery, Houston	53	46.9
1993— Greg Montgomery, Houston	54	45.6
1994— Jeff Gossett, L.A. Raiders	77	43.9
1995— Rick Tuten, Seattle	83	45.0
1996— John Kidd, Miami	78	46.3
1997— Tom Tupa, New England	78	45.8
1998— Craig Hentrich, Tennessee	69	47.2
1999— Tom Rouen, Denver	84	46.5
2000— Darren Bennett, San Diego	92	46.2
2001— Shane Lechler, Oakland	73	46.2
2002— Chris Hanson, Jacksonville	81	44.2
2003— Shane Lechler, Oakland	96	46.9
2004— Shane Lechler, Oakland	73	46.7
2005— Brian Moorman, Buffalo	71	45.7

PUNT RETURNS
(Based on most total yards)

	No.	Yds.	Avg.
1960— Abner Haynes, Dallas	14	215	15.4
1961— Dick Christy, N.Y. Titans	18	383	21.3
1962— Dick Christy, N.Y. Titans	15	250	16.7
1963— Claude Gibson, Oakland	26	307	11.8
1964— Bobby Jancik, Houston	12	220	18.3
1965— Leslie Duncan, San Diego	30	464	15.5
1966— Leslie Duncan, San Diego	18	238	13.2
1967— Floyd Little, Denver	16	270	16.9
1968— Noland Smith, Kansas City	18	270	15.0
1969— Bill Thompson, Denver	25	288	11.5
1970— Ed Podolak, Kansas City	23	311	13.5
1971— Leroy Kelly, Cleveland	30	292	9.7
1972— Chris Farasopoulos, N.Y. Jets	17	179	10.5
1973— Ron Smith, San Diego	27	352	13.0
1974— Lemar Parrish, Cincinnati	18	338	18.8
1975— Billy Johnson, Houston	40	612	15.3
1976— Rick Upchurch, Denver	39	536	13.7
1977— Billy Johnson, Houston	35	539	15.4
1978— Rick Upchurch, Denver	36	493	13.7
1979— Tony Nathan, Miami	28	306	10.9
1980— J.T. Smith, Kansas City	40	581	14.5
1981— James Brooks, San Diego	22	290	13.2
1982— Rick Upchurch, Denver	15	242	16.1
1983— Kirk Springs, N.Y. Jets	23	287	12.5
1984— Mike Martin, Cincinnati	24	376	15.7
1985— Irving Fryar, New England	37	520	14.1
1986— Bobby Joe Edmonds, Seattle	34	419	12.3
1987— Bobby Joe Edmonds, Seattle	20	251	12.6
1988— Jojo Townsell, N.Y. Jets	35	409	11.7
1989— Clarence Verdin, Indianapolis	23	296	12.9
1990— Clarence Verdin, Indianapolis	31	396	12.8
1991— Rod Woodson, Pittsburgh	28	320	11.4
1992— Rod Woodson, Pittsburgh	32	364	11.4
1993— Tim Brown, L.A. Raiders	40	465	11.6
1994— Tim Brown, L.A. Raiders	40	487	12.2
1995— Tamarick Vanover, Kansas City	51	540	10.6
1996— David Meggett, New England	52	588	11.3
1997— Leon Johnson, N.Y. Jets	51	619	12.1
1998— Reggie Barlow, Jacksonville	43	555	12.9
1999— Charlie Rogers, Seattle	22	318	14.5
2000— Derrick Mason, Tennessee	51	662	13.0
2001— Jermaine Lewis, Baltimore	42	519	12.4
2002— Santana Moss, N.Y. Jets	25	413	16.5
2003— Antwaan Randle El, Pittsburgh	45	542	12.0
2004— B.J. Sams, Baltimore	55	575	10.5
2005— Antwaan Randle El, Pittsburgh	44	448	10.2

KICKOFF RETURNS
(Based on most total yards)

	No.	Yds.	Avg.
1960— Ken Hall, Houston	19	594	31.3
1961— Dave Grayson, Dallas	16	453	28.3
1962— Bobby Jancik, Houston	24	726	30.3
1963— Bobby Jancik, Houston	45	1317	29.3
1964— Bo Roberson, Oakland	36	975	27.1
1965— Abner Haynes, Denver	34	901	26.5
1966— Goldie Sellers, Denver	19	541	28.5
1967— Zeke Moore, Houston	14	405	28.9
1968— George Atkinson, Oakland	32	802	25.1
1969— Bill Thompson, Denver	18	513	28.5
1970— Jim Duncan, Baltimore	20	707	35.4
1971— Mercury Morris, Miami	15	423	28.2
1972— Bruce Laird, Baltimore	29	843	29.1
1973— Wallace Francis, Buffalo	23	687	29.9
1974— Greg Pruitt, Cleveland	22	606	27.5
1975— Harold Hart, Oakland	17	518	30.5
1976— Duriel Harris, Miami	17	559	32.9
1977— Raymond Clayborn, New England	28	869	31.0
1978— Keith Wright, Cleveland	30	789	26.3
1979— Larry Brunson, Oakland	17	441	25.9
1980— Horace Ivory, New England	36	992	27.6
1981— Carl Roaches, Houston	28	769	27.5
1982— Mike Mosley, Buffalo	18	487	27.1
1983— Fulton Walker, Miami	36	962	26.7
1984— Bobby Humphery, N.Y. Jets	22	675	30.7
1985— Glen Young, Cleveland	35	898	25.7

(Continuation of PUNT RETURNS)

	No.	Yds.	Avg.
1986— Lupe Sanchez, Pittsburgh	25	591	23.6
1987— Paul Palmer, Kansas City	38	923	24.3
1988— Tim Brown, L.A. Raiders	41	1098	26.8
1989— Rod Woodson, Pittsburgh	36	982	27.3
1990— Kevin Clark, Denver	20	505	25.3
1991— Nate Lewis, San Diego	23	578	25.1
1992— Jon Vaughn, New England	20	564	28.2
1993— Clarence Verdin, Indianapolis	50	1050	21.0
1994— Andre Coleman, San Diego	49	1293	26.4
1995— Andre Coleman, San Diego	62	1411	22.8
1996— Mel Gray, Houston	50	1224	24.5
1997— Kevin Williams, Arizona	59	1458	24.7
1998— Vaughn Hebron, Denver	46	1216	26.4
1999— Tremain Mack, Cincinnati	51	1382	27.1
2000— Charlie Rogers, Seattle	66	1629	24.7
2001— Ronney Jenkins, San Diego	58	1541	26.6
2002— Chad Morton, N.Y. Jets	58	1509	26.0
2003— Dante Hall, Kansas City	57	1478	25.9
2004— Dante Hall, Kansas City	68	1718	25.3
2005— Chris Carr, Oakland	73	1752	24.0

SACKS

	No.
1982— Jesse Baker, Houston	7.5
1983— Mark Gastineau, N.Y. Jets	19.0
1984— Mark Gastineau, N.Y. Jets	22.0
1985— Andre Tippett, New England	16.5
1986— Sean Jones, L.A. Raiders	15.5
1987— Andre Tippett, New England	12.5
1988— Greg Townsend, L.A. Raiders	11.5
1989— Lee Williams, San Diego	14.0
1990— Derrick Thomas, Kansas City	20.0
1991— William Fuller, Houston	15.0
1992— Leslie O'Neal, San Diego	17.0
1993— Neil Smith, Kansas City	15.0
1994— Kevin Greene, Pittsburgh	14.0
1995— Bryce Paup, Buffalo	17.5
1996— Michael McCrary, Seattle	13.5
Bruce Smith, Buffalo	13.5
1997— Bruce Smith, Buffalo	14.0
1998— Michael Sinclair, Seattle	16.5
1999— Jevon Kearse, Tennessee	14.5
2000— Trace Armstrong, Miami	16.5
2001— Peter Boulware, Baltimore	15.0
2002— Jason Taylor, Miami	18.5
2003— Adewale Ogunleye, Miami	15.0
2004— Dwight Freeney, Indianapolis	16.0
2005— Derrick Burgess, Oakland	16.0

NFC

RUSHING
(Based on most net yards)

	Net Yds.	Att.	TD
1960—Jim Brown, Cleveland	1257	215	9
1961—Jim Brown, Cleveland	1408	305	8
1962—Jim Taylor, Green Bay	1474	272	19
1963—Jim Brown, Cleveland	1863	291	12
1964—Jim Brown, Cleveland	1446	280	7
1965—Jim Brown, Cleveland	1544	289	17
1966—Gale Sayers, Chicago	1231	229	8
1967—Leroy Kelly, Cleveland	1205	235	11
1968—Leroy Kelly, Cleveland	1239	248	16
1969—Gale Sayers, Chicago	1032	236	8
1970—Larry Brown, Washington	1125	237	5
1971—John Brockington, Green Bay	1105	216	4
1972—Larry Brown, Washington	1216	285	8
1973—John Brockington, Green Bay	1144	265	3
1974—Lawrence McCutcheon, L.A. Rams	1109	236	3
1975—Jim Otis, St. Louis	1076	269	5
1976—Walter Payton, Chicago	1390	311	13
1977—Walter Payton, Chicago	1852	339	14
1978—Walter Payton, Chicago	1395	333	11
1979—Walter Payton, Chicago	1610	369	14
1980—Walter Payton, Chicago	1460	317	6
1981—George Rogers, New Orleans	1674	378	13

HISTORY Statistical leaders

	Net Yds.	Att.	TD
1982—Tony Dorsett, Dallas	745	177	5
1983—Eric Dickerson, L.A. Rams	1808	390	18
1984—Eric Dickerson, L.A. Rams	2105	379	14
1985—Gerald Riggs, Atlanta	1719	397	10
1986—Eric Dickerson, L.A. Rams	1821	404	11
1987—Charles White, L.A. Rams	1374	324	11
1988—Herschel Walker, Dallas	1514	361	5
1989—Barry Sanders, Detroit	1470	280	14
1990—Barry Sanders, Detroit	1304	255	13
1991—Emmitt Smith, Dallas	1563	365	12
1992—Emmitt Smith, Dallas	1713	373	18
1993—Emmitt Smith, Dallas	1486	283	9
1994—Barry Sanders, Detroit	1883	331	7
1995—Emmitt Smith, Dallas	1773	377	25
1996—Barry Sanders, Detroit	1553	307	11
1997—Barry Sanders, Detroit	2053	335	11
1998—Jamal Anderson, Atlanta	1846	410	14
1999—Stephen Davis, Washington	1405	290	17
2000—Robert Smith, Minnesota	1521	295	7
2001—Stephen Davis, Washington	1432	356	5
2002—Deuce McAllister, New Orleans	1388	325	13
2003—Ahman Green, Green Bay	1883	355	15
2004—Shaun Alexander, Seattle	1696	353	16
2005—Shaun Alexander, Seattle	1880	370	27

PASSING

(Based on highest passer rating among qualifiers*)

	Att.	Com.	Yds.	TD	Int.	Rat.
1960— Milt Plum, Cle.	250	151	2297	21	5	110.4
1961— Milt Plum, Cle.	302	177	2416	18	10	90.3
1962— Bart Starr, G.B.	285	178	2438	12	9	90.7
1963— Y.A. Tittle, NYG	367	221	3145	36	14	104.8
1964— Bart Starr, G.B.	272	163	2144	15	4	97.1
1965— Rudy Bukich, Chi.	312	176	2641	20	9	93.7
1966— Bart Starr, G.B.	251	156	2257	14	3	105.0
1967— Sonny Jurgensen, Was.	508	288	3747	31	16	87.3
1968— Earl Morrall, Bal.	317	182	2909	26	17	93.2
1969— Sonny Jurgensen, Was.	442	274	3102	22	15	85.4
1970— John Brodie, S.F.	378	223	2941	24	10	93.8
1971— Roger Staubach, Dal.	211	126	1882	15	4	104.8
1972— Norm Snead, NYG	325	196	2307	17	12	84.0
1973— Roger Staubach, Dal.	286	179	2428	23	15	94.6
1974— Sonny Jurgensen, Was.	167	107	1185	11	5	94.5
1975— Fran Tarkenton, Min.	425	273	2994	25	13	91.8
1976— James Harris, L.A.	158	91	1460	8	6	89.6
1977— Roger Staubach, Dal.	361	210	2620	18	9	87.0
1978— Roger Staubach, Dal.	413	231	3190	25	16	84.9
1979— Roger Staubach, Dal.	461	267	3586	27	11	92.3
1980— Ron Jaworski, Phi.	451	257	3529	27	12	91.0
1981— Joe Montana, S.F.	488	311	3565	19	12	88.4
1982— Joe Theismann, Was.	252	161	2033	13	9	91.3
1983— Steve Bartkowski, Atl.	432	274	3167	22	5	97.6
1984— Joe Montana, S.F.	432	279	3630	28	10	102.9
1985— Joe Montana, S.F.	494	303	3653	27	13	91.3
1986— Tommy Kramer, Min.	372	208	3000	24	10	92.6
1987— Joe Montana, S.F.	398	266	3054	31	13	102.1
1988— Wade Wilson, Min.	332	204	2746	15	9	91.5
1989— Joe Montana, S.F.	386	271	3521	26	8	112.4
1990— Phil Simms, NYG	311	184	2284	15	4	92.7
1991— Steve Young, S.F.	279	180	2517	17	8	101.8
1992— Steve Young, S.F.	402	268	3465	25	7	107.0
1993— Steve Young, S.F.	462	314	4023	29	16	101.5
1994— Steve Young, S.F.	461	324	3969	35	10	112.8
1995— Brett Favre, G.B.	570	359	4413	38	13	99.5
1996— Steve Young, S.F.	316	214	2410	14	6	97.2
1997— Steve Young, S.F.	356	241	3029	19	6	104.7
1998— Ran. Cunningham, Min.	425	259	3704	34	10	106.0
1999— Kurt Warner, St.L.	499	325	4353	41	13	109.2
2000— Trent Green, St.L.	240	145	2063	16	5	101.8
2001— Kurt Warner, St.L.	546	375	4830	36	22	101.4
2002— Brad Johnson, T.B.	451	281	3049	22	6	92.9
2003— Daunte Culpepper, Min.	454	295	3479	25	11	96.4
2004— Daunte Culpepper, Min.	548	379	4717	39	11	110.9
2005— Matt Hasselbeck, Sea.	449	294	3459	24	9	98.2

*This chart includes passer rating points for all leaders, although the same rating system was not used for determining leading quarterbacks prior to 1973. The old system was less equitable, yet similar to the new one in that the rating was based on percentage of completions, touchdown passes, percentage of interceptions and average gain in yards.

RECEIVING

(Based on most receptions)

	No.	Yds.	TD
1960—Raymond Berry, Baltimore	74	1298	10
1961—Jim Phillips, L.A. Rams	78	1092	5
1962—Bobby Mitchell, Washington	72	1384	11
1963—Bobby Joe Conrad, St. Louis	73	967	10
1964—Johnny Morris, Chicago	93	1200	10
1965—Dave Parks, San Francisco	80	1344	12
1966—Charley Taylor, Washington	72	1119	12
1967—Charley Taylor, Washington	70	990	9
1968—Clifton McNeil, San Francisco	71	994	7
1969—Dan Abramowicz, New Orleans	73	1015	7
1970—Dick Gordon, Chicago	71	1026	13
1971—Bob Tucker, N.Y. Giants	59	791	4
1972—Harold Jackson, Philadelphia	62	1048	4
1973—Harold Carmichael, Philadelphia	67	1116	9
1974—Charles Young, Philadelphia	63	696	3
1975—Chuck Foreman, Minnesota	73	691	9
1976—Drew Pearson, Dallas	58	806	6
1977—Ahmad Rashad, Minnesota	51	681	2
1978—Rickey Young, Minnesota	88	704	5
1979—Ahmad Rashad, Minnesota	80	1156	9
1980—Earl Cooper, San Francisco	83	567	4
1981—Dwight Clark, San Francisco	85	1105	4
1982—Dwight Clark, San Francisco	60	913	5
1983—Roy Green, St. Louis	78	1227	14
Charlie Brown, Washington	78	1225	8
Earnest Gray, N.Y. Giants	78	1139	5
1984—Art Monk, Washington	106	1372	7
1985—Roger Craig, San Francisco	92	1016	6
1986—Jerry Rice, San Francisco	86	1570	15
1987—J.T. Smith, St. Louis	91	1117	8
1988—Henry Ellard, L.A. Rams	86	1414	10
1989—Sterling Sharpe, Green Bay	90	1423	12
1990—Jerry Rice, San Francisco	100	1502	13
1991—Michael Irvin, Dallas	93	1523	8
1992—Sterling Sharpe, Green Bay	108	1461	13
1993—Sterling Sharpe, Green Bay	112	1274	11
1994—Cris Carter, Minnesota	122	1256	7
1995—Herman Moore, Detroit	123	1686	14
1996—Jerry Rice, San Francisco	108	1254	8
1997—Herman Moore, Detroit	104	1293	8
1998—Frank Sanders, Arizona	89	1145	3
1999—Muhsin Muhammad, Carolina	96	1253	8
2000—Muhsin Muhammad, Carolina	102	1183	6
2001—Keyshawn Johnson, Tampa Bay	106	1266	1
2002—Randy Moss, Minnesota	106	1347	7
2003—Torry Holt, St. Louis	117	1696	12
2004—Joe Horn, New Orleans	94	1399	11
2005—Steve Smith, Carolina	103	1563	12
Larry Fitzgerald, Arizona	103	1409	10

SCORING

(Based on most total points)

	TD	PAT	FG	Tot.
1960—Paul Hornung, Green Bay	15	41	15	176
1961—Paul Hornung, Green Bay	10	41	15	146
1962—Jim Taylor, Green Bay	19	0	0	114
1963—Don Chandler, N.Y. Giants	0	52	18	106
1964—Lenny Moore, Baltimore	20	0	0	120
1965—Gale Sayers, Chicago	22	0	0	132
1966—Bruce Gossett, L.A. Rams	0	29	28	113
1967—Jim Bakken, St. Louis	0	36	27	117
1968—Leroy Kelly, Cleveland	20	0	0	120
1969—Fred Cox, Minnesota	0	43	26	121
1970—Fred Cox, Minnesota	0	35	30	125
1971—Curt Knight, Washington	0	27	29	114
1972—Chester Marcol, Green Bay	0	29	33	128
1973—David Ray, L.A. Rams	0	40	30	130
1974—Chester Marcol, Green Bay	0	19	25	94
1975—Chuck Foreman, Minnesota	22	0	0	132
1976—Mark Moseley, Washington	0	31	22	97
1977—Walter Payton, Chicago	16	0	0	96
1978—Frank Corral, L.A. Rams	0	31	29	118
1979—Mark Moseley, Washington	0	39	25	114
1980—Eddie Murray, Detroit	0	35	27	116
1981—Eddie Murray, Detroit	0	46	25	121
Rafael Septien, Dallas	0	40	27	121

	TD	PAT	FG	Tot.
1982— Wendell Tyler, L.A. Rams	13	0	0	78
1983— Mark Moseley, Washington	0	62	33	161
1984— Ray Wersching, S.F.	0	56	25	131
1985— Kevin Butler, Chicago	0	51	31	144
1986— Kevin Butler, Chicago	0	36	28	120
1987— Jerry Rice, San Francisco	23	0	0	138
1988— Mike Cofer, San Francisco	0	40	27	121
1989— Mike Cofer, San Francisco	0	49	29	136
1990— Chip Lohmiller, Washington	0	41	30	131
1991— Chip Lohmiller, Washington	0	56	31	149
1992— Morten Andersen, New Orleans	0	33	29	120
Chip Lohmiller, Washington	0	30	30	120
1993— Jason Hanson, Detroit	0	28	34	130
1994— Fuad Reveiz, Minnesota	0	30	34	132
1995— Emmitt Smith, Dallas	25	0	0	150
1996— John Kasay, Carolina	0	34	37	145
1997— Richie Cunningham, Dallas	0	24	34	126
1998— Gary Anderson, Minnesota	0	59	35	164
1999— Jeff Wilkins, St. Louis	0	64	20	124
2000— Marshall Faulk, St. Louis	26	0	0	*160
2001— Marshall Faulk, St. Louis	21	0	0	†128
2002— Jay Feely, Atlanta	0	42	32	138
2003— Jeff Wilkins, St. Louis	0	46	39	163
2004— David Akers, Philadelphia	0	41	27	122
2005— Shaun Alexander, Seattle	28	0	0	168

*Includes two 2-Pt. conversions.
†Includes one 2-Pt. conversion.

FIELD GOALS

	No.
1960— Tommy Davis, San Francisco	19
1961— Steve Myhra, Baltimore	21
1962— Lou Michaels, Pittsburgh	26
1963— Jim Martin, Baltimore	24
1964— Jim Bakken, St. Louis	25
1965— Fred Cox, Minnesota	23
1966— Bruce Gossett, L.A. Rams	28
1967— Jim Bakken, St. Louis	27
1968— Mac Percival, Chicago	25
1969— Fred Cox, Minnesota	26
1970— Fred Cox, Minnesota	30
1971— Curt Knight, Washington	29
1972— Chester Marcol, Green Bay	33
1973— David Ray, L.A. Rams	30
1974— Chester Marcol, Green Bay	25
1975— Toni Fritsch, Dallas	22
1976— Mark Moseley, Washington	22
1977— Mark Moseley, Washington	21
1978— Frank Corral, L.A. Rams	29
1979— Mark Moseley, Washington	25
1980— Eddie Murray, Detroit	27
1981— Rafael Septien, Dallas	27
1982— Mark Moseley, Washington	20
1983— Ali Haji-Sheikh, N.Y. Giants	35
1984— Paul McFadden, Philadelphia	30
1985— Morten Andersen, New Orleans	31
Kevin Butler, Chicago	31
1986— Kevin Butler, Chicago	28
1987— Morten Andersen, New Orleans	28
1988— Mike Cofer, San Francisco	27
1989— Rich Karlis, Minnesota	31
1990— Chip Lohmiller, Washington	30
1991— Chip Lohmiller, Washington	31
1992— Chip Lohmiller, Washington	30
1993— Jason Hanson, Detroit	34
1994— Fuad Reveiz, Minnesota	34
1995— Morten Andersen, Atlanta	31
1996— John Kasay, Carolina	37
1997— Richie Cunningham, Dallas	34
1998— Gary Anderson, Minnesota	35
1999— Martin Gramatica, Tampa Bay	27
2000— Ryan Longwell, Green Bay	33
2001— Jay Feely, Atlanta	29
2002— Jay Feely, Atlanta	32
Martin Gramatica, Tampa Bay	32
2003— Jeff Wilkins, St. Louis	39
2004— David Akers, Philadelphia	27
2005— Neil Rackers, Arizona	40

INTERCEPTIONS

	No.	Yds.
1960— Dave Baker, San Francisco	10	96
Jerry Norton, St. Louis	10	96
1961— Dick Lynch, N.Y. Giants	9	60
1962— Willie Wood, Green Bay	9	132
1963— Dick Lynch, N.Y. Giants	9	251
Rosie Taylor, Chicago	9	172
1964— Paul Krause, Washington	12	140
1965— Bobby Boyd, Baltimore	9	78
1966— Larry Wilson, St. Louis	10	180
1967— Lem Barney, Detroit	10	232
Dave Whitsell, New Orleans	10	178
1968— Willie Williams, N.Y. Giants	10	103
1969— Mel Renfro, Dallas	10	118
1970— Dick LeBeau, Detroit	9	96
1971— Bill Bradley, Philadelphia	11	248
1972— Bill Bradley, Philadelphia	9	73
1973— Bobby Bryant, Minnesota	7	105
1974— Ray Brown, Atlanta	8	164
1975— Paul Krause, Minnesota	10	201
1976— Monte Jackson, L.A. Rams	10	173
1977— Rolland Lawrence, Atlanta	7	138
1978— Ken Stone, St. Louis	9	139
Willie Buchanon, Green Bay	9	93
1979— Lemar Parrish, Washington	9	65
1980— Nolan Cromwell, L.A. Rams	8	140
1981— Everson Walls, Dallas	11	133
1982— Everson Walls, Dallas	7	61
1983— Mark Murphy, Washington	9	127
1984— Tom Flynn, Green Bay	9	106
1985— Everson Walls, Dallas	9	31
1986— Ronnie Lott, San Francisco	10	134
1987— Barry Wilburn, Washington	9	135
1988— Scott Case, Atlanta	10	47
1989— Eric Allen, Philadelphia	8	38
1990— Mark Carrier, Chicago	10	39
1991— Ray Crockett, Detroit	6	141
Deion Sanders, Atlanta	6	119
Aeneas Williams, Phoenix	6	60
Tim McKyer, Atlanta	6	24
1992— Audray McMillian, Minnesota	8	157
1993— Deion Sanders, Atlanta	7	91
1994— Aeneas Williams, Arizona	9	89
1995— Orlando Thomas, Minnesota	9	108
1996— Keith Lyle, St. Louis	9	152
1997— Ryan McNeil, St. Louis	9	127
1998— Kwamie Lassiter, Arizona	8	80
1999— Donnie Abraham, Tampa Bay	7	115
Troy Vincent, Philadelphia	7	91
2000— Darren Sharper, Green Bay	9	109
2001— Ronde Barber, Tampa Bay	10	86
2002— Brian Kelly, Tampa Bay	8	68
2003— Tony Parrish, San Francisco	9	202
Brian Russell, Minnesota	9	185
2004— Ken Lucas, Seattle	6	46
Chris Gamble, Carolina	6	15
2005— Darren Sharper, Minnesota	9	276

PUNTING

(Based on highest average yardage per punt by qualifiers)

	No.	Avg.
1960— Jerry Norton, St. Louis	39	45.6
1961— Yale Lary, Detroit	52	48.4
1962— Tommy Davis, San Francisco	48	45.6
1963— Yale Lary, Detroit	35	48.9
1964— Bobby Walden, Minnesota	72	46.4
1965— Gary Collins, Cleveland	65	46.7
1966— David Lee, Baltimore	49	45.6
1967— Billy Lothridge, Atlanta	87	43.7
1968— Billy Lothridge, Atlanta	75	44.3
1969— David Lee, Baltimore	57	45.3
1970— Julian Fagan, New Orleans	77	42.5
1971— Tom McNeill, Philadelphia	73	42.0
1972— Dave Chapple, L.A. Rams	53	44.2
1973— Tom Wittum, San Francisco	79	43.7
1974— Tom Blanchard, New Orleans	88	42.1
1975— Herman Weaver, Detroit	80	42.0
1976— John James, Atlanta	101	42.1
1977— Tom Blanchard, New Orleans	82	42.4
1978— Tom Skladany, Detroit	86	42.5

	No.	Avg.
1979— Dave Jennings, N.Y. Giants	104	42.7
1980— Dave Jennings, N.Y. Giants	94	44.8
1981— Tom Skladany, Detroit	64	43.5
1982— Carl Birdsong, St. Louis	54	43.8
1983— Frank Garcia, Tampa Bay	95	42.2
1984— Brian Hansen, New Orleans	69	43.8
1985— Rick Donnelly, Atlanta	59	43.6
1986— Sean Landeta, N.Y. Giants	79	44.8
1987— Rick Donnelly, Atlanta	61	44.0
1988— Jim Arnold, Detroit	97	42.4
1989— Rich Camarillo, Phoenix	76	43.4
1990— Sean Landeta, N.Y. Giants	75	44.1
1991— Harry Newsome, Minnesota	68	45.5
1992— Harry Newsome, Minnesota	72	45.0
1993— Jim Arnold, Detroit	72	44.5
1994— Sean Landeta, L.A. Rams	78	44.8
1995— Sean Landeta, St. Louis	83	44.3
1996— Matt Turk, Washington	75	45.1
1997— Mark Royals, New Orleans	88	45.9
1998— Mark Royals, New Orleans	88	45.6
1999— Mitch Berger, Minnesota	61	45.4
2000— Mitch Berger, Minnesota	62	44.7
2001— Todd Sauerbrun, Carolina	93	47.5
2002— Todd Sauerbrun, Carolina	104	45.5
2003— Todd Sauerbrun, Carolina	77	44.6
2004— Tom Tupa, Washington	103	44.1
2005— Josh Bidwell, Tampa Bay	90	45.6

PUNT RETURNS

(Based on most total yards)

	No.	Yds.	Avg.
1960— Abe Woodson, San Francisco	13	174	13.4
1961— Willie Wood, Green Bay	14	225	16.1
1962— Pat Studstill, Detroit	29	457	15.8
1963— Dick James, Washington	16	214	13.4
1964— Tommy Watkins, Detroit	16	238	14.9
1965— Leroy Kelly, Cleveland	17	265	15.6
1966— Johnny Roland, St. Louis	20	221	11.1
1967— Ben Davis, Cleveland	18	229	12.7
1968— Bob Hayes, Dallas	15	312	20.8
1969— Alvin Haymond, L.A. Rams	33	435	13.2
1970— Bruce Taylor, San Francisco	43	516	12.0
1971— Les Duncan, Washington	22	233	10.6
1972— Ken Ellis, Green Bay	14	215	15.4
1973— Bruce Taylor, San Francisco	15	207	13.8
1974— Dick Jauron, Detroit	17	286	16.8
1975— Terry Metcalf, St. Louis	23	285	12.4
1976— Eddie Brown, Washington	48	646	13.5
1977— Larry Marshall, Philadelphia	46	489	10.6
1978— Jackie Wallace, L.A. Rams	52	618	11.9
1979— John Sciarra, Philadelphia	16	182	11.4
1980— Kenny Johnson, Atlanta	23	281	12.2
1981— LeRoy Irvin, L.A. Rams	46	615	13.4
1982— Billy Johnson, Atlanta	24	273	11.4
1983— Henry Ellard, L.A. Rams	16	217	13.6
1984— Henry Ellard, L.A. Rams	30	403	13.4
1985— Henry Ellard, L.A. Rams	37	501	13.5
1986— Vai Sikahema, St. Louis	43	522	12.1
1987— Mel Gray, New Orleans	24	352	14.7
1988— John Taylor, San Francisco	44	556	12.6
1989— Walter Stanley, Detroit	36	496	13.8
1990— Johnny Bailey, Chicago	36	399	11.1
1991— Mel Gray, Detroit	25	385	15.4
1992— Johnny Bailey, Phoenix	20	263	13.2
1993— Tyrone Hughes, New Orleans	37	503	13.6
1994— Brian Mitchell, Washington	32	452	14.1
1995— Eric Guliford, Carolina	43	475	11.0
1996— Desmond Howard, Green Bay	58	875	15.1
1997— Karl Williams, Tampa Bay	46	597	13.0
1998— Brian Mitchell, Washington	44	506	11.5
1999— Glyn Milburn, Chicago	30	346	11.5
2000— Az-Zahir Hakim, St. Louis	32	489	15.3
2001— Brian Mitchell, Philadelphia	39	467	12.0
2002— Michael Lewis, New Orleans	44	625	14.2
2003— Allen Rossum, Atlanta	39	545	14.0
2004— Allen Rossum, Atlanta	37	457	12.4
2005— Mark Jones, Tampa Bay	51	492	9.6

KICKOFF RETURNS

(Based on most total yards)

	No.	Yds.	Avg.
1960— Tom Moore, Green Bay	12	397	33.1
1961— Dick Bass, L.A. Rams	23	698	30.3
1962— Abe Woodson, San Francisco	37	1157	31.3
1963— Abe Woodson, San Francisco	29	935	32.2
1964— Clarence Childs, N.Y. Giants	34	987	29.0
1965— Tommy Watkins, Detroit	17	584	34.4
1966— Gale Sayers, Chicago	23	718	31.2
1967— Travis Williams, Green Bay	18	739	41.1
1968— Preston Pearson, Baltimore	15	527	35.1
1969— Bobby Williams, Detroit	17	563	33.1
1970— Cecil Turner, Chicago	23	752	32.7
1971— Travis Williams, L.A. Rams	25	743	29.7
1972— Ron Smith, Chicago	30	924	30.8
1973— Carl Garrett, Chicago	16	486	30.4
1974— Terry Metcalf, St. Louis	20	623	31.2
1975— Walter Payton, Chicago	14	444	31.7
1976— Cullen Bryant, L.A. Rams	16	459	28.7
1977— Wilbert Montgomery, Phila.	23	619	26.9
1978— Steve Odom, Green Bay	25	677	27.1
1979— Jimmy Edwards, Minnesota	44	1103	25.1
1980— Rich Mauti, New Orleans	31	798	25.7
1981— Mike Nelms, Washington	37	1099	29.7
1982— Alvin Hall, Detroit	16	426	26.6
1983— Darrin Nelson, Minnesota	18	445	24.7
1984— Barry Redden, L.A. Rams	23	530	23.0
1985— Ron Brown, L.A. Rams	28	918	32.8
1986— Dennis Gentry, Chicago	20	576	28.8
1987— Sylvester Stamps, Atlanta	24	660	27.5
1988— Donnie Elder, Tampa Bay	34	772	22.7
1989— Mel Gray, Detroit	24	640	26.7
1990— Dave Meggett, N.Y. Giants	21	492	23.4
1991— Mel Gray, Detroit	36	929	25.8
1992— Deion Sanders, Atlanta	40	1067	26.7
1993— Tony Smith, Atlanta	38	948	24.9
1994— Tyrone Hughes, New Orleans	63	1556	24.7
1995— Tyrone Hughes, New Orleans	66	1617	24.5
1996— Tyrone Hughes, New Orleans	70	1791	25.6
1997— Glyn Milburn, Detroit	55	1315	23.9
1998— Glyn Milburn, Chicago	62	1550	25.0
1999— Tony Horne, St. Louis	30	892	29.7
2000— MarTay Jenkins, Arizona	82	2186	26.7
2001— Darrick Vaughn, Atlanta	61	1491	24.4
2002— Michael Lewis, New Orleans	70	1807	25.8
2003— Josh Scobey, Arizona	73	1684	23.1
2004— Allen Rossum, Atlanta	58	1250	21.6
2005— Reggie Swinton, Arizona	63	1456	23.1

SACKS

	No.
1982— Doug Martin, Minnesota	11.5
1983— Fred Dean, San Francisco	17.5
1984— Richard Dent, Chicago	17.5
1985— Richard Dent, Chicago	17.0
1986— Lawrence Taylor, N.Y. Giants	20.5
1987— Reggie White, Philadelphia	21.0
1988— Reggie White, Philadelphia	18.0
1989— Chris Doleman, Minnesota	21.0
1990— Charles Haley, San Francisco	16.0
1991— Pat Swilling, New Orleans	17.0
1992— Clyde Simmons, Philadelphia	19.0
1993— Renaldo Turnbull, New Orleans	13.0
	Reggie White, Green Bay	13.0
1994— Ken Harvey, Washington	13.5
	John Randle, Minnesota	13.5
1995— William Fuller, Philadelphia	13.0
	Wayne Martin, New Orleans	13.0
1996— Kevin Greene, Carolina	14.5
1997— John Randle, Minnesota	15.5
1998— Reggie White, Green Bay	16.0
1999— Kevin Carter, St. Louis	17.0
2000— La'Roi Glover, New Orleans	17.0
2001— Michael Strahan, N.Y. Giants	22.5
2002— Simeon Rice, Tampa Bay	15.5
2003— Michael Strahan, N.Y. Giants	18.5
2004— Bertrand Berry, Arizona	14.5
2005— Osi Umenyiora, N.Y. Giants	14.5

COACHING RECORDS

COACHES WITH 100 OR MORE CAREER VICTORIES

(Ranked according to career wins)

		REGULAR SEASON				POSTSEASON			CAREER			
	Yrs.	Won	Lost	Tied	Pct.	Won	Lost	Pct.	Won	Lost	Tied	Pct.
Don Shula	33	328	156	6	.676	19	17	.528	347	173	6	.665
George Halas	40	318	148	31	.671	6	3	.667	324	151	31	.671
Tom Landry	29	250	162	6	.605	20	16	.556	270	178	6	.601
Curly Lambeau	33	226	132	22	.624	3	2	.600	229	134	22	.623
Chuck Noll	23	193	148	1	.566	16	8	.667	209	156	1	.572
Dan Reeves	23	190	165	2	.535	11	9	.550	201	174	2	.536
Chuck Knox	22	186	147	1	.558	7	11	.389	193	158	1	.550
Marty Schottenheimer*	20	186	124	1	.602	5	12	.294	191	136	1	.584
Bill Parcells*	18	163	123	1	.570	11	7	.611	174	130	1	.572
Paul Brown	21	166	100	6	.621	4	8	.333	170	108	6	.609
Bud Grant	18	158	96	5	.620	10	12	.455	168	108	5	.607
Joe Gibbs*	14	140	76	0	.648	17	6	.739	157	82	0	.657
Steve Owen	23	153	100	17	.598	2	8	.200	155	108	17	.584
Marv Levy	17	143	112	0	.561	11	8	.579	154	120	0	.562
Bill Cowher*	14	141	82	1	.632	12	9	.571	153	91	1	.627
Mike Holmgren*	14	138	86	0	.616	11	9	.550	149	94	0	.613
Hank Stram	17	131	97	10	.571	5	3	.625	136	100	10	.573
Weeb Ewbank	20	130	129	7	.502	4	1	.800	134	130	7	.507
Mike Shanahan*	13	122	74	0	.622	8	5	.615	130	79	0	.622
Mike Ditka	14	121	95	0	.560	6	6	.500	127	101	0	.557
Dick Vermeil*	15	120	109	0	.524	6	5	.545	126	114	0	.525
Jim Mora	15	125	106	0	.541	0	6	.000	125	112	0	.527
George Seifert	11	114	62	0	.648	10	5	.667	124	67	0	.649
Sid Gillman	18	122	99	7	.550	1	5	.167	123	104	7	.541
George Allen	12	116	47	5	.705	2	7	.222	118	54	5	.681
Don Coryell	14	111	83	1	.572	3	6	.333	114	89	1	.561
John Madden	10	103	32	7	.750	9	7	.563	112	39	7	.731
Dennis Green*	12	108	83	0	.565	4	8	.333	112	91	0	.552
Bill Belichick*	11	99	77	0	.563	11	2	.846	110	79	0	.582
Tony Dungy*	10	102	58	0	.638	5	8	.385	107	66	0	.618
Buddy Parker	15	104	75	9	.577	3	1	.750	107	76	9	.581
Vince Lombardi	10	96	34	6	.728	9	1	.900	105	35	6	.740
Tom Flores	12	97	87	0	.527	8	3	.727	105	90	0	.538
Bill Walsh	10	92	59	1	.609	10	4	.714	102	63	1	.617
Jeff Fisher*	12	97	85	0	.533	5	4	.556	102	89	0	.534

*Active NFL coaches in 2005.

2006 COACHES' CAREER RECORDS

(Ranked according to career NFL percentages*)

	WITH CURRENT CLUB							CAREER							CAREER TOTALS			
	Regular season				Postseason			Regular season				Postseason			Reg. + Postseason			
Coach, current team	Yrs.	W	L	T	Pct.	App.	W-L	Pct.	Yrs.	W	L	T	Pct.	App.	W-L	Pct.	W	L	T	Pct.
Joe Gibbs, Washington	14	140	76	0	.648	9	17-6	.739	14	140	76	0	.648	9	17-6	.739	157	82	0	.657
Bill Cowher, Pittsburgh	14	141	82	1	.632	10	12-9	.571	14	141	82	1	.632	10	12-9	.571	153	91	1	.627
Mike Shanahan, Denver	11	114	62	0	.648	7	8-5	.615	13	122	74	0	.622	7	8-5	.615	130	79	0	.622
Andy Reid, Philadelphia	7	70	42	0	.625	5	7-5	.583	7	70	42	0	.625	5	7-5	.583	77	47	0	.621
Tony Dungy, Indianapolis	4	48	16	0	.750	4	3-4	.429	10	102	58	0	.638	8	5-8	.385	107	66	0	.618
Mike Holmgren, Seattle	7	63	49	0	.563	4	2-4	.333	14	138	86	0	.616	10	11-9	.550	149	95	0	.611
Jim Mora Jr., Atlanta	2	19	13	0	.594	1	1-1	.500	2	19	13	0	.594	1	1-1	.500	20	14	0	.588
Marty Schottenheimer, S.D.	4	33	31	0	.516	1	0-1	.000	20	186	124	1	.600	12	5-12	.294	191	136	1	.584
Bill Belichick, New England	6	63	33	0	.656	4	10-1	.909	11	99	77	0	.563	5	11-2	.846	110	79	0	.582
Art Shell, Oakland	6	54	38	0	.587	3	2-3	.400	6	54	38	0	.587	3	2-3	.400	56	41	0	.577
John Fox, Carolina	4	36	28	0	.563	2	5-2	.714	4	36	28	0	.563	2	5-2	.714	41	30	0	.577
Jon Gruden, Tampa Bay	4	35	29	0	.547	2	3-1	.750	8	73	55	0	.570	4	5-3	.625	78	58	0	.574
Bill Parcells, Dallas	3	25	23	0	.521	1	0-1	.000	18	163	123	1	.570	9	11-7	.611	174	130	1	.572
Brian Billick, Baltimore	7	62	50	0	.554	3	5-2	.714	7	62	50	0	.554	3	5-2	.714	67	52	0	.563
Nick Saban, Miami	1	9	7	0	.563				1	9	7	0	.563				9	7	0	.563
Dennis Green, Arizona	2	11	21	0	.344				12	108	83	0	.565	8	4-8	.333	112	91	0	.552
Marvin Lewis, Cincinnati	3	27	21	0	.563	1	0-1	.000	3	27	21	0	.563	1	0-1	.000	27	22	0	.551
Jeff Fisher, Tennessee	12	97	85	0	.533	4	5-4	.556	12	97	85	0	.533	4	5-4	.556	102	89	0	.534
Jack Del Rio, Jacksonville	3	26	22	0	.542	1	0-1	.000	3	26	22	0	.542	1	0-1	.000	26	23	0	.531
Tom Coughlin, N.Y. Giants	2	17	15	0	.531	1	0-1	.000	10	85	75	0	.531	5	4-5	.444	89	80	0	.527
Lovie Smith, Chicago	2	16	16	0	.500	1	0-1	.000	2	16	16	0	.500	1	0-1	.000	16	17	0	.485
Herman Edwards, K.C.	5	39	41	0	.488	3	2-3	.400	5	39	41	0	.488	3	2-3	.400	41	44	0	.482
Dick Jauron, Buffalo									6	36	49	0	.424	1	0-1	.000	36	50	0	.419
Romeo Crennel, Cleveland	1	6	10	0	.375				1	6	10	0	.375				6	10	0	.375
Mike Nolan, San Francisco	1	4	12	0	.250				1	4	12	0	.250				4	12	0	.250

*First year as NFL head coach: Brad Childress, Minnesota; Gary Kubiak, Houston; Scott Linehan, St. Louis; Eric Mangini, N.Y. Jets; Rod Marinelli, Detroit; Mike McCarthy, Green Bay; Sean Payton, New Orleans.

HALL OF FAME

ROSTER OF MEMBERS
SIX NEW INDUCTEES IN 2006

Troy Aikman, Harry Carson, John Madden, Warren Moon, Reggie White and Rayfield Wright were inducted into Pro Football's Hall of Fame in 2006, expanding the list of former stars honored at Canton, Ohio, to 235.

HISTORY Hall of Fame

Name	Elec. year	College	Pos.	NFL teams
Adderley, Herb	1980	Michigan State	CB	Green Bay Packers, 1961-69; Dallas Cowboys, 1970-72
Aikman, Troy†	2006	Oklahoma, UCLA	QB	Dallas Cowboys, 1989-2000
Allen, George	2002	Michigan	*	Coach, Los Angeles Rams, 1966-70; Washington Redskins, 1971-77
Allen, Marcus†	2003	USC	RB	Los Angeles Raiders, 1982-92; Kansas City Chiefs, 1993-97
Alworth, Lance†	1978	Arkansas	WR	San Diego Chargers, 1962-70; Dallas Cowboys, 1971-72
Atkins, Doug	1982	Tennessee	DE	Cleveland Browns, 1953-54; Chicago Bears, 1955-66; New Orleans Saints, 1967-69
Badgro, Morris (Red)	1981	Southern California	E	New York Yankees, 1927; New York Giants, 1930-35; Brooklyn Dodgers, 1936
Barney, Lem	1992	Jackson State	CB	Detroit Lions, 1967-77
Battles, Cliff	1968	W. Virginia Wesleyan	HB/QB	Boston Braves, 1932; Boston Redskins, 1933-36; Washington Redskins, 1937; coach, Brooklyn Dodgers, 1946-47
Baugh, Sammy	1963	Texas Christian	QB	Washington Redskins, 1937-52; coach, New York Titans, 1960-61; Houston Oilers, 1964
Bednarik, Chuck	1967	Pennsylvania	C/LB	Philadelphia Eagles, 1949-62
Bell, Bert	1963	Pennsylvania	*	NFL Commissioner, 1946-59
Bell, Bobby	1983	Minnesota	LB	Kansas City Chiefs, 1963-74
Berry, Raymond†	1973	Southern Methodist	E	Baltimore Colts, 1955-67; coach, New England Patriots, 1984-89
Bethea, Elvin	2003	North Carolina A&T	DE	Houston Oilers, 1968-83
Bidwill, Charles W.	1967	Loyola	*	Owner, Chicago Cardinals, 1933-47
Biletnikoff, Fred	1988	Florida State	WR	Oakland Raiders, 1965-78
Blanda, George†	1981	Kentucky	QB/PK	Chicago Bears, 1949-58; Baltimore Colts, 1950; Houston Oilers, 1960-66; Oakland Raiders, 1967-75
Blount, Mel†	1989	Southern	CB	Pittsburgh Steelers, 1970-83
Bradshaw, Terry†	1989	Louisiana Tech	QB	Pittsburgh Steelers, 1970-83
Brown, Bob	2004	Nebraska	T	Philadelphia Eagles, 1964-68; Los Angeles Rams, 1969-70; Oakland Raiders, 1971-73
Brown, Jim†	1971	Syracuse	FB	Cleveland Browns, 1957-65
Brown, Paul	1967	Miami of Ohio	*	Coach, Cleveland Browns, 1946-62; Cincinnati Bengals, 1968-75
Brown, Roosevelt	1975	Morgan State	T	New York Giants, 1953-65
Brown, Willie†	1984	Grambling	DB	Denver Broncos, 1963-66; Oakland Raiders, 1967-78
Buchanan, Buck	1990	Grambling	DT	Kansas City Chiefs, 1963-75
Buoniconti, Nick	2001	Notre Dame	LB	Boston Patriots, 1962-68; Miami Dolphins, 1969-76
Butkus, Dick†	1979	Illinois	LB	Chicago Bears, 1965-73
Campbell, Earl†	1991	Texas	RB	Houston Oilers, 1978-84; New Orleans Saints, 1984-85
Canadeo, Tony	1974	Gonzaga	HB	Green Bay Packers, 1941-44, 46-52
Carr, Joe	1963		*	NFL President, 1921-39
Carson, Harry	2006	South Carolina St.	LB	New York Giants, 1976-88
Casper, Dave	2002	Notre Dame	TE	Oakland Raiders, 1974-80; Houston Oilers, 1980-83; Minnesota Vikings, 1983; Los Angeles Raiders, 1984
Chamberlin, Guy	1965	Nebraska	E*	Player/coach, Canton Bulldogs, 1919, 22-23; Decatur Staleys, 1920; Cleveland Bulldogs, 1924; Frankford Yellow Jackets, 1925-26; Chicago Staleys, 1921; Chicago Cardinals, 1927-28
Christiansen, Jack	1970	Colorado A&M	DB	Detroit Lions, 1951-58; coach, San Francisco 49ers, 1963-67
Clark, Dutch	1963	Colorado College	QB	Portsmouth Spartans, Detroit Lions, 1931-38
Connor, George	1975	Notre Dame	T/LB	Chicago Bears, 1948-55
Conzelman, Jimmy	1964	Washington (Mo.)	HB*	Player/coach/executive, Decatur Staleys, 1920; Rock Island Independents, 1921-22; Milwaukee Badgers, 1922-24; Detroit Panthers, 1925-26; Providence Steam Roller, 1927-30; Chicago Cardinals, 1940-42, 46-48
Creekmur, Lou	1996	William & Mary	T/G	Detroit Lions, 1950-59
Csonka, Larry	1987	Syracuse	RB	Miami Dolphins, 1968-74, 79; New York Giants, 1976-78
Davis, Al	1992	Syracuse	*	Coach/general manager/president, Oakland-Los Angeles Raiders, 1963-present
Davis, Willie	1981	Grambling	DE	Cleveland Browns, 1958-59; Green Bay Packers, 1960-69
Dawson, Len	1987	Purdue	QB	Pittsburgh Steelers, 1957-59; Cleveland Browns, 1960-61; Dallas Texans, 1962; Kansas City Chiefs, 1963-75
DeLamielleure, Joe	2003	Michigan State	G	Buffalo Bills, 1973-79, 1985; Cleveland Browns, 1980-84
Dickerson, Eric†	1999	Southern Methodist	RB	Los Angeles Rams, 1983-87; Indianapolis Colts, 1987-91; Los Angeles Raiders, 1992; Atlanta Falcons, 1993
Dierdorf, Dan	1996	Michigan	T/C	St. Louis Cardinals, 1971-83
Ditka, Mike	1988	Pittsburgh	TE	Chicago Bears, 1961-66; Philadelphia Eagles, 1967-68; Dallas Cowboys, 1969-72; coach, Chicago Bears, 1982-92; New Orleans Saints, 1997-99
Donovan, Art	1968	Boston College	DT	Baltimore Colts, 1950, 53-61; New York Yanks, 1951; Dallas Texans, 1952
Dorsett, Tony	1994	Pittsburgh	RB	Dallas Cowboys, 1977-87; Denver Broncos, 1988
Driscoll, Paddy	1965	Northwestern	TB/HB/QB	Player, Hammond Pros, 1919; Decatur Staleys, 1920; Chicago Cardinals, 1920-25; Chicago Bears, 1926-29; coach, Chicago Cardinals, 1920-22; Chicago Bears, 1956-57

Name	Elec. year	College	Pos.	NFL teams
Dudley, Bill	1966	Virginia	HB	Pittsburgh Steelers, 1942, 45-46; Detroit Lions, 1947-49; Washington Redskins, 1950-51, 53
Edwards, Turk	1969	Washington State	T	Boston Braves, 1932; Boston Redskins, 1933-36; Washington Redskins, 1937-40
Eller, Carl	2004	Minnesota	DE	Minnesota Vikings, 1964-78; Seattle Seahawks, 1979
Elway, John†	2004	Stanford	QB	Denver Broncos, 1983-1998
Ewbank, Weeb	1978	Miami of Ohio	*	Coach, Baltimore Colts, 1954-62; New York Jets, 1963-73
Fears, Tom	1970	UCLA	E	Los Angeles Rams, 1948-56; coach, New Orleans Saints, 1967-70
Finks, Jim	1995	Tulsa	QB*	Pittsburgh Steelers, 1949-55; administrator, Minnesota Vikings, 1964-73; Chicago Bears, 1974-82; New Orleans Saints, 1986-93
Flaherty, Ray	1976	Gonzaga	E*	Los Angeles Wildcats, 1926; New York Yankees, 1927-28, AFL; New York Giants, 1928-35; coach, Boston Redskins, 1936; Washington Redskins, 1937-42; New York Yankees, 1946-48 AAFC; Chicago Hornets, 1949
Ford, Len	1976	Michigan	E	Los Angeles Dons, 1948-49 AAFC; Cleveland Browns, 1950-57; Green Bay Packers, 1958
Fortmann, Danny	1965	Colgate	G	Chicago Bears, 1936-43
Fouts, Dan†	1993	Oregon	QB	San Diego Chargers, 1973-87
Friedman, Benny	2005	Michigan	QB	Cleveland Bulldogs, 1927; Detroit Wolverines, 1928; New York Giants, 1929-31; Brooklyn Dodgers, 1932-34
Gatski, Frank	1985	Marshall	C	Cleveland Browns, 1946-56; Detroit Lions, 1957
George, Bill	1974	Wake Forest	LB	Chicago Bears, 1952-65; Los Angeles Rams, 1966
Gibbs, Joe	1996	San Diego State	*	Washington Redskins, 1981-92
Gifford, Frank	1977	USC	HB/E	New York Giants, 1952-60, 62-64
Gillman, Sid	1983	Ohio State	*	Coach, Los Angeles Rams, 1955-59; Los Angeles Chargers, 1960; San Diego Chargers, 1961-69, 71; Houston Oilers, 1973-74
Graham, Otto	1965	Northwestern	QB	Cleveland Browns, 1946-55; coach, Washington Redskins, 1966-68
Grange, Red	1963	Illinois	HB	Chicago Bears, 1925, 29-34; New York Yankees, 1926-27
Grant, Bud	1994	Minnesota	WR*	Philadelphia Eagles, 1951-52; coach, Minnesota Vikings, 1967-83, 1985
Greene, Joe†	1987	North Texas State	DT	Pittsburgh Steelers, 1969-81
Gregg, Forrest†	1977	Southern Methodist	T	Green Bay Packers, Dallas Cowboys, 1956, 58-71; coach, Cleveland Browns, 1975-77; Cincinnati Bengals, 1980-83; Green Bay Packers, 1984-87
Griese, Bob	1990	Purdue	QB	Miami Dolphins, 1967-80
Groza, Lou	1974	Ohio State	T/PK	Cleveland Browns, 1946-59, 61-67
Guyon, Joe	1966	Carlisle, Georgia Tech	HB	Canton Bulldogs, 1919-20; Cleveland Indians, 1921; Oorang Indians, 1922-23; Rock Island Independents, 1924; Kansas City Cowboys, 1924-25; New York Giants, 1927
Halas, George	1963	Illinois	E*	Player/coach/founder, Chicago Bears, 1920-83
Ham, Jack†	1988	Penn State	LB	Pittsburgh Steelers, 1971-82
Hampton, Dan	2002	Arkansas	DT-DE	Chicago Bears, 1979-90
Hannah, John†	1991	Alabama	G	New England Patriots, 1973-85
Harris, Franco†	1990	Penn State	RB	Pittsburgh Steelers, 1972-83; Seattle Seahawks, 1984
Haynes, Mike	1997	Arizona State	CB	New England Patriots, 1976-82; Los Angeles Raiders, 1983-89
Healey, Ed	1964	Dartmouth	T	Rock Island Independents, 1920-22; Chicago Bears, 1922-27
Hein, Mel	1963	Washington State	C	New York Giants, 1931-45
Hendricks, Ted	1990	Miami	LB	Baltimore Colts, 1969-73; Green Bay Packers, 1974; Oakland/Los Angeles Raiders, 1975-83
Henry, Wilbur (Pete)	1963	Wash. & Jefferson	T	Canton Bulldogs, 1920-23, 25-26; New York Giants, 1927; Pottsville Maroons, 1927-28
Herber, Arnie	1966	Regis	HB/QB	Green Bay Packers, 1930-40; New York Giants, 1944-45
Hewitt, Bill	1971	Michigan	E	Chicago Bears, 1932-36; Philadelphia Eagles, 1937-39; Philadelphia/Pittsburgh, 1943
Hinkle, Clarke	1964	Bucknell	FB	Green Bay Packers, 1932-41
Hirsch, Elroy (Crazylegs)	1968	Wisconsin	E/HB	Chicago Rockets, 1946-48 AAFC; Los Angeles Rams, 1949-57
Hornung, Paul	1986	Notre Dame	RB	Green Bay Packers, 1957-62, 64-66
Houston, Ken†	1986	Prairie View	DB	Houston Oilers, 1967-72; Washington Redskins, 1973-80
Hubbard, Cal	1963	Centenary, Geneva	T/E	New York Giants, 1927-28, 36; Green Bay Packers, 1929-33, 35; Pittsburgh Pirates, 1936
Huff, Sam	1982	West Virginia	LB	New York Giants, 1956-63; Washington Redskins, 1964-67, 69
Hunt, Lamar	1972	Southern Methodist	*	Founder, American Football League, 1959; president, Dallas Texans, 1960-62; Kansas City Chiefs, 1963-present
Hutson, Don	1963	Alabama	E	Green Bay Packers, 1935-45
Johnson, Jimmy	1994	UCLA	DB	San Francisco 49ers, 1961-76
Johnson, John Henry	1987	Arizona State	FB	San Francisco 49ers, 1954-56; Detroit Lions, 1957-59; Pittsburgh Steelers, 1960-65; Houston Oilers, 1966
Joiner, Charlie	1996	Grambling	WR	Houston Oilers, 1969-72; Cincinnati Bengals, 1972-75; San Diego Chargers, 1976-86
Jones, Deacon†	1980	South Carolina State	DE	Los Angeles Rams, 1961-71; San Diego Chargers, 1972-73; Washington Redskins, 1974
Jones, Stan	1991	Maryland	G/DT	Chicago Bears, 1954-65; Washington Redskins, 1966
Jordan, Henry	1995	Virginia	DT	Cleveland Browns, 1957-58; Green Bay Packers, 1959-69
Jurgensen, Sonny	1983	Duke	QB	Philadelphia Eagles, 1957-63; Washington Redskins, 1964-74
Kelly, Jim†	2002	Miami	QB	Buffalo Bills, 1986-96
Kelly, Leroy	1994	Morgan State	RB	Cleveland Browns, 1964-73
Kiesling, Walter	1966	St. Thomas (Minn.)	G/T*	Player, Duluth Eskimos, 1926-27; Pottsville Maroons, 1928; Chicago Cardinals, 1929-33; Chicago Bears, 1934; Green Bay Packers, 1935-36; Pittsburgh Pirates, 1937-38. Coach, Pittsburgh Pirates, 1939-40; Pittsburgh Steelers, 1941-42; Philadelphia-Pittsburgh, 1943; Chicago-Pittsburgh, 1944; Pittsburgh Steelers, 1954-56

Name	Elec. year	College	Pos.	NFL teams
Kinard, Frank (Bruiser)	1971	Mississippi	T	Bro. Dodgers, 1938-43; Bro. Tigers, 1944; N.Y. Yankess, 1946-47
Krause, Paul	1998	Iowa	S	Washington Redskins, 1964-67; Minnesota Vikings, 1968-79
Lambeau, Curly	1963	Notre Dame	TB/FB/E*	Player/coach/founder, Green Bay Packers, 1919-49; Chicago Cardinals, 1950-51; Washington Redskins, 1952-53
Lambert, Jack†	1990	Kent State	LB	Pittsburgh Steelers, 1974-84
Landry, Tom†	1990	Texas	*	Coach, Dallas Cowboys, 1960-88
Lane, Dick (Night Train)	1974	Scottsbluff J.C.	DB	Los Angeles Rams, 1952-53; Chicago Cardinals, 1954-59; Detroit Lions, 1960-65
Langer, Jim†	1987	South Dakota State	C	Miami Dolphins, 1970-79; Minnesota Vikings, 1980-81
Lanier, Willie	1986	Morgan State	LB	Kansas City Chiefs, 1967-77
Largent, Steve†	1995	Tulsa	WR	Seattle Seahawks, 1976-89
Lary, Yale	1979	Texas A&M	DB	Detroit Lions, 1952-53, 56-64
Lavelli, Dante	1975	Ohio State	E	Cleveland Browns, 1946-56
Layne, Bobby	1967	Texas	QB	Chicago Bears, 1948; New York Bulldogs, 1949; Detroit Lions, 1950-58; Pittsburgh Steelers, 1958-62
Leemans, Tuffy	1978	George Washington	FB	New York Giants, 1936-43
Levy, Marv†	2001	Coe College	*	Kansas City Chiefs, 1978-82; Buffalo Bills, 1986-97
Lilly, Bob†	1980	Texas Christian	DT	Dallas Cowboys, 1961-74
Little, Larry	1993	Bethune Cookman	G	San Diego Chargers, 1967-68; Miami Dolphins, 1969-80
Lofton, James	2003	Stanford	WR	Green Bay Packers, 1978-86; Los Angeles Raiders, 1987-88; Buffalo Bills, 1989-92; Los Angeles Rams, 1993; Philadelphia Eagles, 1993
Lombardi, Vince	1971	Fordham	*	Coach, Green Bay Packers, 1959-67; Washington Redskins, 1969
Long, Howie	2000	Villanova	DE	Oakland/Los Angeles Raiders, 1981-93
Lott, Ronnie†	2000	USC	DB	San Francisco 49ers, 1981-90; Los Angeles Raiders, 1991-92; New York Jets, 1993-94
Luckman, Sid	1965	Columbia	QB	Chicago Bears, 1939-50
Lyman, Roy (Link)	1964	Nebraska	T	Canton Bulldogs, 1922-23; Cleveland Bulldogs, 1924; Frankford Yellow Jackets, 1925; Chicago Bears, 1926-28, 30-31, 33-34
Mack, Tom	1999	Michigan	G	Los Angeles Rams, 1966-78
Mackey, John	1992	Syracuse	TE	Baltimore Colts, 1963-71; San Diego Chargers, 1972
Madden, John	2006	San Mateo J.C., Cal Poly	*	Coach, Oakland Raiders 1969-78
Mara, Tim	1963		*	Founder, New York Giants, 1925-59
Mara, Wellington	1997	Fordham	*	President, New York Giants, 1965-2005
Marchetti, Gino†	1972	San Francisco	DE	Dallas Texans, 1952; Baltimore Colts, 1953-66
Marino, Dan†	2005	Pittsburgh	QB	Miami Dolphins, 1983-99
Marshall, George Preston	1963	Randolph-Macon	*	Founder, Washington Redskins, 1932-65
Matson, Ollie†	1972	San Francisco	HB	Chicago Cardinals, 1952, 54-58; Los Angeles Rams, 1959-62; Detroit Lions, 1963; Philadelphia Eagles, 1964-66
Maynard, Don	1987	Texas Western College	WR	New York Giants, 1958; New York Jets, 1960-72; St. Louis Cardinals, 1973
McAfee, George	1966	Duke	HB	Chicago Bears, 1940-41, 45-50
McCormack, Mike	1984	Kansas	T	New York Yanks, 1951; Cleveland Browns, 1954-62
McDonald, Tommy	1998	Oklahoma	WR	Philadelphia Eagles, 1957-63; Dallas Cowboys, 1964; Los Angeles Rams, 1965-66; Atlanta Falcons, 1967; Cleveland Browns,1968
McElhenny, Hugh†	1970	Washington	HB	San Francisco 49ers, 1952-60; Minnesota Vikings, 1961-62; New York Giants, 1963; Detroit Lions, 1964
McNally, Johnny Blood	1963	St. John's (Minn.)	HB	Milwaukee Badgers, 1925-26; Duluth Eskimos, 1926-27; Pottsville Maroons, 1928; Green Bay Packers, 1929-33, 35-36; Pittsburgh Pirates, 1934, 37-38
Michalske, August (Mike)	1964	Penn State	G	New York Yankees, 1926 AFL; New York Yankees, 1927-28; Green Bay Packers, 1929-35, 37
Millner, Wayne	1968	Notre Dame	E	Boston Redskins, 1936; Washington Redskins, 1937-41, 45
Mitchell, Bobby	1983	Illinois	RB/FL/WR	Cleveland Browns, 1958-61; Washington Redskins, 1962-68
Mix, Ron	1979	USC	T	Los Angeles Chargers, 1960; San Diego Chargers, 1961-69; Oakland Raiders, 1971
Montana, Joe†	2000	Notre Dame	QB	San Francisco 49ers, 1979-92; Kansas City Chiefs, 1993-94
Moon, Warren†	2006	West L.A. J.C., Washington	QB	Houston Oilers, 1984-93; Minnesota Vikings, 1994-96; Seattle Seahawks 1997-98; Kansas City Chiefs 1999-2000
Moore, Lenny	1975	Penn State	HB	Baltimore Colts, 1956-67
Motley, Marion	1968	Nevada	FB/LB	Cleveland Browns, 1946-53; Pittsburgh Steelers, 1955
Munchak, Mike	2001	Penn State	G	Houston Oilers, 1982-93
Munoz, Anthony†	1998	USC	OT	Cincinnati Bengals, 1980-92
Musso, George	1982	Milliken	G/DT	Chicago Bears, 1933-44
Nagurski, Bronko	1963	Minnesota	FB/T	Chicago Bears, 1930-37, 43
Namath, Joe	1985	Alabama	QB	New York Jets, 1965-76; Los Angeles Rams, 1977
Neale, Earle (Greasy)	1969	W. Virginia Wesleyan	*	Coach, Philadelphia Eagles, 1941-50
Nevers, Ernie	1963	Stanford	FB	Duluth Eskimos, 1926-27; Chicago Cardinals, 1929-31
Newsome, Ozzie	1999	Alabama	TE	Cleveland Browns, 1978-90
Nitschke, Ray†	1978	Illinois	LB	Green Bay Packers, 1958-72
Noll, Chuck†	1993	Dayton	*	Coach, Pittsburgh Steelers, 1969-91
Nomellini, Leo†	1969	Minnesota	DT	San Francisco 49ers, 1950-63
Olsen, Merlin†	1982	Utah State	DT	Los Angeles Rams, 1962-76
Otto, Jim†	1980	Miami	C	Oakland Raiders, 1960-74
Owen, Steve	1966	Phillips	T/G	Player/coach, Kansas City Cowboys, 1924-25; Cleveland Bulldogs, 1925; New York Giants, 1926-53
Page, Alan	1988	Notre Dame	DT	Minnesota Vikings, 1967-78; Chicago Bears, 1978-81
Parker, Clarence (Ace)	1972	Duke	HB/QB	Brooklyn Dodgers, 1937-41; Boston Yanks, 1945; New York Yankees, 1946
Parker, Jim†	1973	Ohio State	G	Baltimore Colts, 1957-67
Payton, Walter†	1993	Jackson State	RB	Chicago Bears, 1975-87
Perry, Joe†	1969	Compton J.C.	FB	San Francisco 49ers, 1940-60, 63; Baltimore Colts, 1961-62
Pihos, Pete	1970	Indiana	E	Philadelphia Eagles, 1947-55

Name	Elec. year	College	Pos.	NFL teams
Pollard, Fritz	2005	Brown	HB	Akron Pros/Indians, 1919-21, 1925-26; Milwaukee Badgers, 1922-23; Hammond Pros, 1925; Gilberton Cadamounts 1923-24; Providence Steam Roller, 1925
Ray, Hugh (Shorty)	1966	Illinois	*	NFL technical adviser and supervisor of officials, 1938-52
Reeves, Daniel F.	1967	Georgetown	*	Founder, Cleveland/Los Angeles Rams, 1941-71
Renfro, Mel	1996	Oregon	DB	Dallas Cowboys, 1964-77
Riggins, John	1992	Kansas	HB	New York Jets, 1971-75; Washington Redskins, 1976-85
Ringo, Jim	1981	Syracuse	C	Green Bay Packers, 1953-63; Philadelphia Eagles, 1964-67
Robustelli, Andy	1971	Arnold	DE	Los Angeles Rams, 1951-55; New York Giants, 1956-64
Rooney, Arthur J.	1964	Georgetown	*	Founder, Pittsburgh Steelers, 1933-88
Rooney, Dan	2000	Duquesne	*	Pittsburgh Steelers, 1955-present
Rozelle, Pete	1985	San Francisco	*	NFL Commissioner, 1960-89
St. Clair, Bob	1990	San Francisco	T	San Francisco 49ers, 1953-63
Sanders, Barry†	2004	Oklahoma State	RB	Detroit Lions, 1989-98
Sayers, Gale†	1977	Kansas	RB	Chicago Bears, 1965-71
Schmidt, Joe	1973	Pittsburgh	LB	Detroit Lions, 1953-65; coach, Detroit Lions, 1967-72
Schramm, Tex	1991	Texas	*	President/general manager, Dallas Cowboys, 1960-89
Selmon, Lee Roy	1995	Oklahoma	DE	Tampa Bay Buccaneers, 1976-84
Shaw, Billy	1999	Georgia Tech	G	Buffalo Bills, 1961-69
Shell, Art	1989	Md.-Eastern Shore	T	Oakland/Los Angeles Raiders, 1968-82; coach, Los Angeles Raiders, 1989-94, 2006-present
Shula, Don†	1997	John Carroll	DB*	Cleveland Browns, 1951-52; Baltimore Colts, 1953-56; Washington Redskins, 1957; coach, Baltimore Colts, 1963-69, Miami Dolphins, 1970-95
Simpson, O.J.†	1985	USC	RB	Buffalo Bills, 1969-77; San Francisco 49ers, 1978-79
Singletary, Mike†	1998	Baylor	LB	Chicago Bears, 1981-92
Slater, Jackie†	2001	Jackson State	T	Los Angeles Rams, 1976-94; St. Louis Rams, 1995
Smith, Jackie	1994	N'western Louisiana	TE	St. Louis Cardinals, 1963-77; Dallas Cowboys, 1978
Stallworth, John	2002	Alabama A&M	WR	Pittsburgh Steelers, 1974-87
Starr, Bart†	1977	Alabama	QB	Green Bay Packers, 1956-71; coach, Green Bay Packers, 1975-83
Staubach, Roger†	1985	Navy	QB	Dallas Cowboys, 1969-79
Stautner, Ernie†	1969	Boston College	DT	Pittsburgh Steelers, 1950-63
Stenerud, Jan†	1991	Montana State	PK	Kansas City Chiefs, 1967-79; Green Bay Packers, 1980-83; Minnesota Vikings, 1984-85
Stephenson, Dwight	1998	Alabama	C	Miami Dolphins, 1980-87
Stram, Hank	2003	Purdue	*	Dallas Texans, 1960-62; Kansas City Chiefs, 1963-74; New Orleans Saints, 1976-77
Strong, Ken	1967	New York U.	HB/PK	Staten Island Stapletons, 1929-32; New York Giants, 1933-35, 39, 44-47; New York Yankees, 1936-37 AFL
Stydahar, Joe	1967	West Virginia	T	Chicago Bears, 1936-42, 45-46
Swann, Lynn	2001	USC	WR	Pittsburgh Steelers, 1974-82
Tarkenton, Fran	1986	Georgia	QB	Minnesota Vikings, 1961-66, 72-78; New York Giants, 1967-71
Taylor, Charley	1984	Arizona State	WR	Washington Redskins, 1964-75, 77
Taylor, Jim	1976	Louisiana State	FB	Green Bay Packers, 1958-66; New Orleans Saints, 1967
Taylor, Lawrence†	1999	North Carolina	LB	New York Giants, 1981-93
Thorpe, Jim	1963	Carlisle	HB	Canton Bulldogs, 1915-17, 19-20, 26; Cleveland Indians, 1921; Oorang Indians, 1922-23; Rock Island Independents, 1924; New York Giants, 1925; Chicago Cardinals, 1928
Tittle, Y.A.	1971	Louisiana State	QB	Baltimore Colts, 1948-50; San Francisco 49ers, 1951-60; New York Giants, 1961-64
Trafton, George	1964	Notre Dame	C	Decatur Staleys, 1920; Chicago Staleys, 1921; Chicago Bears, 1923-32
Trippi, Charley	1968	Georgia	HB	Chicago Cardinals, 1947-55
Tunnell, Emlen	1967	Iowa	DB	New York Giants, 1948-58; Green Bay Packers, 1959-61
Turner, Clyde (Bulldog)	1966	Hardin-Simmons	C/LB	Chicago Bears, 1940-52; coach, New York Titans, 1962
Unitas, John†	1979	Louisville	QB	Baltimore Colts, 1956-72; San Diego Chargers, 1973
Upshaw, Gene†	1987	Texas A&I	G	Oakland Raiders, 1967-81
Van Brocklin, Norm	1971	Oregon	QB	Los Angeles Rams, 1949-57; Philadelphia Eagles, 1958-60; coach, Minnesota Vikings, 1961-66; Atlanta Falcons, 1968-74
Van Buren, Steve	1965	Louisiana State	HB	Philadelphia Eagles, 1944-51
Walker, Doak	1986	Southern Methodist	RB	Detroit Lions, 1950-55
Walsh, Bill	1993	San Jose State	*	Coach, San Francisco 49ers, 1979-88
Warfield, Paul†	1983	Ohio State	WR	Cleveland Browns, 1964-69, 76-77; Miami Dolphins, 1970-74
Waterfield, Bob	1965	UCLA	QB	Cleveland Rams, Los Angeles Rams, 1945-52; coach, Los Angeles Rams, 1960-62
Webster, Mike	1997	Wisconsin	C-G	Pittsburgh Steelers, 1974-88; Kansas City Chiefs, 1989-90
Weinmeister, Arnie	1984	Washington	T	New York Yankees, 1948-49; New York Giants, 1950-53
White, Randy	1994	Maryland	DT	Dallas Cowboys, 1975-88
White, Reggie†	2006	Tennessee	DE/DT	Philadelphia Eagles, 1985-92; Green Bay Packers, 1993-98; Carolina Panthers, 2000
Wilcox, Dave	2000	Oregon	LB	San Francisco 49ers, 1964-74
Willis, Bill	1977	Ohio State	G	Cleveland Browns, 1946-53
Wilson, Larry†	1978	Utah	DB	St. Louis Cardinals, 1960-72
Winslow, Kellen	1995	Missouri	TE	San Diego Chargers, 1979-87
Wojciechowicz, Alex	1968	Fordham	C/LB	Detroit Lions, 1938-46; Philadelphia Eagles, 1946-50
Wood, Willie	1989	USC	S	Green Bay Packers, 1960-71
Wright, Rayfield	2006	Fort Valley State	T	Dallas Cowboys, 1967-79
Yary, Ron	2001	USC	OT	Minnesota Vikings, 1968-81; Los Angeles Rams, 1982
Young, Steve†	2005	Brigham Young	QB	Tampa Bay Buccaneers, 1985-86; San Francisco 49ers, 1987-99
Youngblood, Jack	2001	Florida	DE	Los Angeles Rams, 1971-84

†Elected in his first year of eligibility.
*Hall of Fame member was selected for contributions other than as a player.
Abbreviations of positions: C—Center, CB—Cornerback, DB—Defensive back, DE—Defensive end, DT—Defensive tackle, E—End, FB—Fullback, FL—Flanker, G—Guard, HB—Halfback, LB—Linebacker, PK—Placekicker, QB—Quarterback, RB—Running back, S—Safety, T—Tackle, TB—Tailback, TE—Tight end.

SPORTING NEWS AWARDS

PLAYER OF THE YEAR

1954—Lou Groza, OT/K, Cleveland
1955—Otto Graham, QB, Cleveland
1956—Frank Gifford, HB, N.Y. Giants
1957—Jim Brown, RB, Cleveland
1958—Jim Brown, RB, Cleveland
1959—Johnny Unitas, QB, Baltimore
1960—Norm Van Brocklin, QB, Philadelphia
1961—Paul Hornung, HB, Green Bay
1962—Y.A. Tittle, QB, N.Y. Giants
1963—Y.A. Tittle, QB, N.Y. Giants
1964—Johnny Unitas, QB, Baltimore
1965—Jim Brown, RB, Cleveland
1966—Bart Starr, QB, Green Bay
1967—Johnny Unitas, QB, Baltimore
1968—Earl Morrall, QB, Baltimore
1969—Roman Gabriel, QB, L.A. Rams
1970—NFC: John Brodie, QB, San Francisco
       AFC: George Blanda, QB/PK, Oakland
1971—NFC: Roger Staubach, QB, Dallas
       AFC: Bob Griese, QB, Miami
1972—NFC: Larry Brown, RB, Washington
       AFC: Earl Morrall, QB, Miami
1973—NFC: John Hadl, QB, L.A. Rams
       AFC: O.J. Simpson, RB, Buffalo
1974—NFC: Chuck Foreman, RB, Minnesota
       AFC: Ken Stabler, QB, Oakland
1975—NFC: Fran Tarkenton, QB, Minnesota
       AFC: O.J. Simpson, RB, Buffalo
1976—NFC: Walter Payton, RB, Chicago
       AFC: Ken Stabler, QB, Oakland
1977—NFC: Walter Payton, RB, Chicago
       AFC: Craig Morton, QB, Denver
1978—NFC: Archie Manning, QB, New Orleans

AFC: Earl Campbell, RB, Houston
1979—NFC: Ottis Anderson, RB, St. Louis
       AFC: Dan Fouts, QB, San Diego
1980—Brian Sipe, QB, Cleveland
1981—Ken Anderson, QB, Cincinnati
1982—Mark Moseley, PK, Washington
1983—Eric Dickerson, RB, L.A. Rams
1984—Dan Marino, QB, Miami
1985—Marcus Allen, RB, L.A. Raiders
1986—Lawrence Taylor, LB, N.Y. Giants
1987—Jerry Rice, WR, San Francisco
1988—Boomer Esiason, QB, Cincinnati
1989—Joe Montana, QB, San Francisco
1990—Jerry Rice, WR, San Francisco
1991—Thurman Thomas, RB, Buffalo
1992—Steve Young, QB, San Francisco
1993—Emmitt Smith, RB, Dallas
1994—Steve Young, QB, San Francisco
1995—Brett Favre, QB, Green Bay
1996—Brett Favre, QB, Green Bay
1997—Barry Sanders, RB, Detroit
1998—Terrell Davis, RB, Denver
1999—Kurt Warner, QB, St. Louis
2000—Marshall Faulk, RB, St. Louis
2001—Marshall Faulk, RB, St. Louis
2002—Rich Gannon, QB, Oakland
2003—Peyton Manning, QB, Indianapolis
2004—Peyton Manning, QB, Indianapolis
2005—Shaun Alexander, RB, Seattle
   NOTE: From 1970-79, a player was selected as Player of the Year for both the NFC and AFC. In 1980 The Sporting News reinstated the selection of one player as Player of the Year for the entire NFL.

ROOKIE OF THE YEAR

1955—Alan Ameche, FB, Baltimore
1956—J.C. Caroline, HB, Chicago
1957—Jim Brown, FB, Cleveland
1958—Bobby Mitchell, HB, Cleveland
1959—Nick Pietrosante, FB, Detroit
1960—Gail Cogdill, E, Detroit
1961—Mike Ditka, E, Chicago
1962—Ronnie Bull, HB, Chicago
1963—Paul Flatley, WR, Minnesota
1964—Charley Taylor, HB, Washington
1965—Gale Sayers, RB, Chicago
1966—Tommy Nobis, LB, Atlanta
1967—Mel Farr, RB, Detroit
1968—Earl McCullouch, WR, Detroit
1969—Calvin Hill, RB, Dallas
1970—NFC: Bruce Taylor, CB, San Francisco
       AFC: Dennis Shaw, QB, Buffalo
1971—NFC: John Brockington, RB, Green Bay
       AFC: Jim Plunkett, QB, New England
1972—NFC: Chester Marcol, PK, Green Bay
       AFC: Franco Harris, RB, Pittsburgh
1973—NFC: Chuck Foreman, RB, Minnesota
       AFC: Boobie Clark, RB, Cincinnati
1974—NFC: Wilbur Jackson, RB, San Francisco
       AFC: Don Woods, RB, San Diego
1975—NFC: Steve Bartkowski, QB, Atlanta
       AFC: Robert Brazile, LB, Houston
1976—NFC: Sammy White, WR, Minnesota
       AFC: Mike Haynes, CB, New England
1977—NFC: Tony Dorsett, RB, Dallas
       AFC: A.J. Duhe, DT, Miami
1978—NFC: Al Baker, DE, Detroit
       AFC: Earl Campbell, RB, Houston

1979—NFC: Ottis Anderson, RB, St. Louis
       AFC: Jerry Butler, WR, Buffalo
1980—Billy Sims, RB, Detroit
1981—George Rogers, RB, New Orleans
1982—Marcus Allen, RB, L.A. Raiders
1983—Dan Marino, QB, Miami
1984—Louis Lipps, WR, Pittsburgh
1985—Eddie Brown, WR, Cincinnati
1986—Rueben Mayes, RB, New Orleans
1987—Robert Awalt, TE, St. Louis
1988—Keith Jackson, TE, Philadelphia
1989—Barry Sanders, RB, Detroit
1990—Richmond Webb, T, Miami
1991—Mike Croel, LB, Denver
1992—Santana Dotson, DL, Tampa Bay
1993—Jerome Bettis, RB, L.A. Rams
1994—Marshall Faulk, RB, Indianapolis
1995—Curtis Martin, RB, New England
1996—Eddie George, RB, Houston
1997—Warrick Dunn, RB, Tampa Bay
1998—Randy Moss, WR, Minnesota
1999—Edgerrin James, RB, Indianapolis
2000—Brian Urlacher, LB, Chicago
2001—Kendrell Bell, LB, Pittsburgh
2002—Clinton Portis, RB, Denver
2003—Anquan Boldin, WR, Arizona
2004—Ben Roethlisberger, Pittsburgh
2005—Shawne Merriman, San Diego
   NOTE: From 1970-79, a player was selected as Rookie of the Year for both the NFC and AFC. In 1980 The Sporting News reinstated the selection of one player as Rookie of the year for the entire NFL.

NFL EXECUTIVE OF THE YEAR

1947—Jimmy Conzelman, Chi. Cardinals
1948—Earle (Greasy) Neale, Philadelphia
1949—Paul Brown, Cleveland (AAFC)
1950—Steve Owen, N.Y. Giants
1951—Paul Brown, Cleveland
1952—J. Hampton Pool, L.A. Rams
1953—Paul Brown, Cleveland
1954—None
1955—Joe Kuharich, Washington
1956—Jim Lee Howell, N.Y. Giants
1961—Vince Lombardi, Green Bay
1962—None
1963—George Halas, Chicago
1964—Don Shula, Baltimore
1965—George Halas, Chicago
1966—Tom Landry, Dallas
1967—George Allen, L.A. Rams
1968—Don Shula, Baltimore
1969—Bud Grant, Minnesota
1970—Don Shula, Miami
1971—George Allen, Washington
1972—Don Shula, Miami
1973—Chuck Knox, L.A. Rams
1974—Don Coryell, St. Louis
1975—Ted Marchibroda, Baltimore
1976—Chuck Fairbanks, New England
1977—Red Miller, Denver
1978—Jack Patera, Seattle
1979—Dick Vermeil, Philadelphia

1980—Chuck Knox, Buffalo
1981—Bill Walsh, San Francisco
1982—Joe Gibbs, Washington
1983—Joe Gibbs, Washington
1984—Chuck Knox, Seattle
1985—Mike Ditka, Chicago
1986—Bill Parcells, N.Y. Giants
1987—Jim Mora, New Orleans
1988—Marv Levy, Buffalo
1989—Lindy Infante, Green Bay
1990—George Seifert, San Francisco
1991—Joe Gibbs, Washington
1992—Bill Cowher, Pittsburgh
1993—Dan Reeves, N.Y. Giants
1994—George Seifert, San Francisco
1995—Ray Rhodes, Philadelphia
1996—Dom Capers, Carolina
1997—Jim Fassel, N.Y. Giants
1998—Dan Reeves, Atlanta
1999—Dick Vermeil, St. Louis
2000—Andy Reid, Philadelphia
2001—Dick Jauron, Chicago
2002—Andy Reid, Philadelphia
2003—Bill Belichick, New England
2004—Bill Cowher, Pittsburgh
2005—Tony Dungy, Indianapolis
NOTE: The Coach of the Year Award was not given from 1957-60.

NFL EXECUTIVE OF THE YEAR

1955—Dan Reeves, L.A. Rams
1956—George Halas, Chicago
1972—Dan Rooney, Pittsburgh
1973—Jim Finks, Minnesota
1974—Art Rooney, Pittsburgh
1975—Joe Thomas, Baltimore
1976—Al Davis, Oakland
1977—Tex Schramm, Dallas
1978—John Thompson, Seattle
1979—John Sanders, San Diego
1980—Eddie LeBaron, Atlanta
1981—Paul Brown, Cincinnati
1982—Bobby Beathard, Washington
1983—Bobby Beathard, Washington
1984—George Young, N.Y. Giants
1985—Mike McCaskey, Chicago
1986—George Young, N.Y. Giants
1987—Jim Finks, New Orleans
1988—Bill Polian, Buffalo

1989—John McVay, San Francisco
1990—George Young, N.Y. Giants
1991—Bill Polian, Buffalo
1992—Ron Wolf, Green Bay
1993—George Young, N.Y. Giants
1994—Carmen Policy, San Francisco
1995—Bill Polian, Carolina
1996—Bill Polian, Carolina
1997—George Young, N.Y. Giants
1998—Jeff Diamond, Minnesota
1999—Bill Polian, Indianapolis
2000—Randy Mueller, New Orleans
2001—Dan Rooney, Pittsburgh
2002—Bruce Allen, Oakland
2003—Scott Pioli, New England
2004—Scott Pioli, New England
2005—Art Rooney II, Pittsburgh
NOTE: The Executive of the Year Award was not given from 1957-71.

2005 NFL ALL-PRO TEAM

OFFENSE

WR—Chad Johnson, Cincinnati
WR—Steve Smith, Carolina
TE—Antonio Gates, San Diego
T—Walter Jones, Seattle
T—Willie Roaf, Kansas City
G—Alan Faneca, Pittsburgh
G—Steve Hutchinson, Seattle
C—Olin Kreutz, Chicago
QB—Peyton Manning, Indianapolis
RB—Shaun Alexander, Seattle
RB—LaDainian Tomlinson, San Diego

DEFENSE

E—Dwight Freeney, Indianapolis
E—Michael Strahan, N.Y. Giants
T—Marcus Stroud, Jacksonville
T—Jamal Williams, San Diego
LB—Shawne Merriman, San Diego
LB—Brian Urlacher, Chicago
LB—Al Wilson, Denver
CB—Champ Bailey, Denver
CB—Deltha O'Neal, Cincinnati
S—Troy Polamalu, Pittsburgh
S—Darren Sharper, Minnesota

SPECIALISTS

K—Neil Rackers, Arizona
P—Brian Moorman, Buffalo
KR—Jerome Mathis, Houston
PR—B.J. Sams, Baltimore

FIRST-ROUND DRAFT CHOICES

(Note: Players in boldface are in Pro Football's Hall of Fame and those in italics are former Heisman Trophy winners. In years in which draft order was not announced, players are arranged alphabetically by team.)

1936
FIRST ROUND—NFL

No. Team	Player selected	Pos.	College
1. Philadelphia	*Jay Berwanger*	B	Chicago
2. Boston	Riley Smith	B	Alabama
3. Pittsburgh	Bill Shakespeare	B	Notre Dame
4. Brooklyn	Dick Crayne	B	Iowa
5. Chi. Cardinals	Jim Lawrence	B	Texas Christian
6. Chi. Bears	**Joe Stydahar**	T	West Virginia
7. Green Bay	Russ Letlow	G	San Francisco
8. Detroit	Sid Wagner	G	Michigan State
9. New York	Art Lewis	T	Ohio

Total number of picks in draft: 81.

OTHER NOTEWORTHY PICKS

Round/Overall—Team, Player selected, Pos., College
2/18—New York, **Tuffy Leemans**, B, George Washington; 3/23—Chi. Cardinals, Eddie Erdelatz, E, St. Mary's (Calif.); 4/31—Brooklyn, Bear Bryant, E, Alabama; 8/65—Boston, **Wayne Millner**, E, Notre Dame; 9/78—Chi. Bears, **Dan Fortmann**, G, Colgate.

1937
FIRST ROUND—NFL

No. Team	Player selected	Pos.	College
1. Philadelphia	Sam Francis	B	Nebraska
2. Brooklyn	Ed Goddard	B	Washington State
3. Chi. Cardinals	Buzz Buivid	B	Marquette
4. New York	Ed Widseth	T	Minnesota
5. Pittsburgh	Mike Basrak	C	Duquesne
6. Boston	**Sammy Baugh**	QB	Texas Christian
7. Detroit	Lloyd Cardwell	B	Nebraska
8. Chi. Bears	Les McDonald	E	Nebraska
9. Green Bay	Eddie Jankowski	B	Wisconsin
10. League*	Johnny Drake	B	Purdue

*The league selected for an extra franchise under the likelihood that one would be awarded. The Cleveland Rams received Drake when they were admitted to the league prior to the 1937 season.
Total number of picks in draft: 100.

OTHER NOTEWORTHY PICKS

Round/Overall—Team, Player selected, Pos., College
2/13—Brooklyn, **Ace Parker**, B, Duke; 3/29—Green Bay, Bud Wilkinson, T, Minnesota; 9/87—Detroit, *Larry Kelley*, E, Yale.

1938
FIRST ROUND—NFL

No. Team	Player selected	Pos.	College
1. Cleveland	Corbett Davis	B	Indiana
2. Philadelphia	Jim McDonald	B	Ohio State
3. Brooklyn	Boyd Brumbaugh	B	Duquesne
4. Pittsburgh	Whizzer White	B	Colorado
5. Chi. Cardinals	Jack Robbins	B	Arkansas
6. Detroit	**Alex Wojciechowicz**	C	Fordham
7. Green Bay	Cecil Isbell	B	Purdue
8. New York	George Karamatic	B	Gonzaga
9. Washington	Andy Farkas	B	Detroit
10. Chi. Bears	Joe Gray	B	Oregon State

Total number of picks in draft: 110.

OTHER NOTEWORTHY PICKS

Round/Overall—Team, Player selected, Pos., College
3/18—Brooklyn, **Frank (Bruiser) Kinard**, T, Mississippi; 12/106—Detroit, *Clint Frank*, B, Yale.

1939
FIRST ROUND—NFL

No. Team	Player selected	Pos.	College
1. Chi. Cardinals	Ki Aldrich	C	Texas Christian
2. Chi. Bears	**Sid Luckman**	QB	Columbia
3. Cleveland	Parker Hall	B	Mississippi
4. Philadelphia	*Davey O'Brien*	B	Texas Christian
5. Brooklyn	Bob MacLeod	B	Dartmouth
6. Chi. Bears	Bill Osmanski	B	Holy Cross
7. Detroit	John Pingel	B	Michigan State
8. Washington	I.B. Hale	T	Texas Christian
9. Green Bay	Larry Buhler	B	Minnesota
10. New York	Walt Nielsen	B	Arizona

Team not selecting in first round: Pittsburgh.
Total number of picks in draft: 200.

OTHER NOTEWORTHY PICKS

Round/Overall—Team, Player selected, Pos., College
11/91—Chi. Cardinals, Bowden Wyatt, E, Tennessee.

1940
FIRST ROUND—NFL

No. Team	Player selected	Pos.	College
1. Chi. Cardinals	George Cafego	B	Tennessee
2. Philadelphia	**George McAfee**	B	Duke
3. Pittsburgh	Kay Eakin	B	Arkansas
4. Brooklyn	Banks McFadden	B	Clemson
5. Cleveland	Olie Cordill	B	Rice
6. Detroit	Doyle Nave	B	USC
7. Chi. Bears	**Bulldog Turner**	C	Hardin-Simmons
8. Washington	Ed Boell	B	New York U.
9. Green Bay	Hal Van Every	B	Minnesota
10. New York	Grenny Lansdell	B	USC

Total number of picks in draft: 200.

OTHER NOTEWORTHY PICKS

Round/Overall—Team, Player selected, Pos., College
2/11—Chi. Cardinals, George (Snuffy) Stirnweiss, B, North Carolina; 2/14—Brooklyn, *Nile Kinnick*, B, Iowa; 4/27—Pittsburgh, Frank (Pop) Ivy, E, Oklahoma; 9/77—Chi. Bears, Hampton Pool, E, Stanford.

1941
FIRST ROUND—NFL

No. Team	Player selected	Pos.	College
1. Chi. Bears	*Tom Harmon*	B	Michigan
2. Chi. Cardinals	John Kimbrough	B	Texas A&M
3. Chi. Bears	Norm Standlee	B	Stanford
4. Cleveland	Rudy Mucha	C	Washington
5. Detroit	Jim Thomason	B	Texas A&M
6. New York	George Franck	B	Minnesota
7. Green Bay	George Paskvan	B	Wisconsin
8. Brooklyn	Dean McAdams	B	Washington
9. Chi. Bears	Don Scott	B	Ohio State
10. Washington	Forest Evashevski	B	Michigan

Teams not selecting in first round: Philadelphia, Pittsburgh.
Total number of picks in draft: 200.

OTHER NOTEWORTHY PICKS

Round/Overall—Team, Player selected, Pos., College
2/13—Chi. Cardinals, Paul Christman, QB, Missouri; 9/77—Green Bay, **Tony Canadeo**, B, Gonzaga.

HISTORY *First-round draft choices*

1942

FIRST ROUND—NFL

No. Team	Player selected	Pos.	College
1. Pittsburgh	**Bill Dudley**	B	Virginia
2. Cleveland	Jack Wilson	B	Baylor
3. Philadelphia	Pete Kmetovic	B	Stanford
4. Chi. Cardinals	Steve Lach	B	Duke
5. Detroit	Bob Westfall	B	Michigan
6. Washington	Spec Sanders	B	Texas
7. Brooklyn	Bob Robertson	B	USC
8. New York	Merle Hapes	B	Mississippi
9. Green Bay	Urban Odson	T	Minnesota
10. Chi. Bears	Frankie Albert	B	Stanford

Total number of picks in draft: 200.

OTHER NOTEWORTHY PICKS

Round/Overall—Team, Player selected, Pos., College

7/58—New York, Tommy Prothro, B, Duke; 13/119—Green Bay, *Bruce Smith*, B, Minnesota; 15/134—Chi. Cardinals, Marv Harshman, B, Pacific Lutheran; 15/135—Detroit, Mac Speedie, E, Utah; 18/167—Brooklyn, Ralph Miller, B, Kansas.

1943

FIRST ROUND—NFL

No. Team	Player selected	Pos.	College
1. Detroit	*Frank Sinkwich*	B	Georgia
2. Philadelphia	Joe Muha	B	Virginia Military
3. Chi. Cardinals	Glenn Dobbs	B	Tulsa
4. Brooklyn	Paul Governali	B	Columbia
5. Cleveland	Mike Holovak	B	Boston College
6. New York	Steve Filipowicz	B	Fordham
7. Pittsburgh	Bill Daley	B	Minnesota
8. Green Bay	Dick Wildung	T	Minnesota
9. Chi. Bears	Bob Steuber	B	Missouri
10. Washington	Jack Jenkins	B	Vanderbilt

Note: Philadelphia and Pittsburgh franchises merged for 1943 season (but after draft); Cleveland franchise suspended operations for one year (but after draft).

Total number of picks in draft: 300.

OTHER NOTEWORTHY PICKS

Round/Overall—Team, Player selected, Pos., College

6/45—Cleveland, *Les Horvath*, B, Ohio State, 13/116—New York, Don McCafferty, T, Ohio State; 17/157—Pittsburgh, Nick Skorich, G, Cincinnati.

1944

FIRST ROUND—NFL

No. Team	Player selected	Pos.	College
1. Boston	*Angelo Bertelli*	QB	Notre Dame
2. Chi. Cardinals	Pat Harder	B	Wisconsin
3. Brooklyn	Creighton Miller	B	Notre Dame
4. Detroit	**Otto Graham**	QB	Northwestern
5. Philadelphia	**Steve Van Buren**	B	Louisiana State
6. New York	Billy Hillenbrand	B	Indiana
7. Green Bay	Merv Pregulman	G	Michigan
8. Washington	Mike Micka	B	Colgate
9. Chi. Bears	Ray Evans	B	Kansas
10. Pittsburgh	Johnny Podesto	B	St. Mary's (Cal.)
11. Cleveland	Tony Butkovich	B	Illinois

Note: Chi. Cardinals and Pittsburgh franchises merged for 1944 season (but after draft).

Total number of picks in draft: 330.

OTHER NOTEWORTHY PICKS

Round/Overall—Team, Player selected, Pos., College

5/42—Cleveland, **Bob Waterfield**, B, UCLA; 8/71—Green Bay, Alex Agase, G, Illinois; 10/88—Chi. Cardinals, Lou Saban, B, Indiana; 12/112—Detroit, Jack Lescoulie, G, UCLA.

1945

FIRST ROUND—NFL

No. Team	Player selected	Pos.	College
1. Chi. Cardinals	**Charley Trippi**	B	Georgia
2. Pittsburgh	Paul Duhart	B	Florida
3. Brooklyn	Joe Renfroe	B	Tulane
4. Boston	Eddie Prokop	B	Georgia Tech
5. Cleveland	**Crazylegs Hirsch**	B	Wisconsin
6. Detroit	Frank Szymanski	C	Notre Dame
7. Chi. Bears	Don Lund	B	Michigan
8. Washington	Jim Hardy	QB	USC
9. Philadelphia	John Yonaker	E	Notre Dame
10. New York	Elmer Barbour	B	Wake Forest
11. Green Bay	Walt Schlinkman	B	Texas Tech

Note: Boston and Brooklyn franchises merged for 1945 season (but after draft).

Total number of picks in draft: 330.

OTHER NOTEWORTHY PICKS

Round/Overall—Team, Player selected, Pos., College

3/25—Philadelphia, Alvin Dark, B, Louisiana State; 5/41—Philadelphia, **Pete Pihos**, E, Indiana; 11/103—Cleveland, **Tom Fears**, E, UCLA; 13/127—Washington, Charlie Conerly, QB, Mississippi; 15/145—Pittsburgh, **George Connor**, T, Notre Dame; 17/166—Brooklyn, **Arnie Weinmeister**, E, Washington.

1946

FIRST ROUND—NFL

No. Team	Player selected	Pos.	College
1. Boston	Frank Dancewicz	QB	Notre Dame
2. Chi. Cardinals	Dub Jones	B	Tulane
3. Pittsburgh	*Doc Blanchard*	B	Army
4. Chi. Bears	*Johnny Lujack*	QB	Notre Dame
5. New York	**George Connor**	T	Notre Dame
6. Green Bay	Johnny Strzykalski	B	Marquette
7. Philadelphia	Leo Riggs	B	USC
8. Detroit	Bill Dellastatious	B	Missouri
9. Washington	Cal Rossi	B	UCLA
10. Los Angeles	Emil Sitko	B	Notre Dame

Total number of picks in draft: 300.

OTHER NOTEWORTHY PICKS

Round/Overall—Team, Player selected, Pos., College

3/19—Chi. Bears, Frank Broyles, QB, Georgia Tech; 9/74—Chi. Bears, Walt Dropo, E, Connecticut.

1947

SPECIAL SELECTIONS—AAFC

These special selections were made prior to the regular AAFC draft and the draft order was not announced.

Team	Player selected	Pos.	College
Brooklyn	*Doc Blanchard*	B	Army
Brooklyn	Choo-Choo Roberts	B	UT-Chattanooga
Buffalo	Bob Fenimore	B	Oklahoma State
Buffalo	Frank Aschenbrenner	B	Northwestern
Buffalo	Cal Richardson	E	Tulsa
Buffalo	Red Cochran	B	Wake Forest
Chicago	*Johnny Lujack*	QB	Notre Dame
Chicago	Bernie Gallagher	T	Pennsylvania
Cleveland	Dick Hoerner	B	Iowa
Cleveland	Robert Lawrence Rice	C	Tulane
Los Angeles	Herman Wedemeyer	B	St. Mary's (Cal.)
Miami	Arnold Tucker	QB	Army
Miami	Ernie Case	B	UCLA
New York	Buddy Young	B	Illinois
New York	**Charley Trippi**	B	Georgia
San Francisco	*Glenn Davis*	B	Army

Note: Miami dropped out of league after draft, but Miami's selections went to new Baltimore franchise formed after draft.

Total number of special selection picks: 16.

FIRST ROUND—AAFC

No.	Team	Player selected	Pos.	College
1.	Miami	Elmer Madar	E	Michigan
2.	Buffalo	Alton Baldwin	E	Arkansas
3.	Brooklyn	Neill Armstrong	E	Oklahoma State
4.	Chicago	George Sullivan	T	Notre Dame
5.	Los Angeles	Burr Baldwin	E	UCLA
6.	San Francisco	Clyde LeForce	B	Tulsa
7.	New York	Ben Raimondi	B	Indiana
8.	Cleveland	Bob Chappuis	B	Michigan

Note: Miami dropped out of league after draft, but Miami's selections went to new Baltimore franchise formed after draft.

Total number of picks in regular rounds of draft (excluding special selections): 170.

OTHER NOTEWORTHY PICKS

Round/Overall—Team, Player selected, Pos., College
2/11—Brooklyn, Charlie Conerly, QB, Mississippi; 6/47—New York, Walt Dropo, E, Connecticut; 10/78—San Francisco, Frank Broyles, QB, Georgia Tech.

FIRST ROUND—NFL

No.	Team	Player selected	Pos.	College
1.	Chi. Bears	Bob Fenimore	B	Oklahoma State
2.	Detroit	*Glenn Davis*	B	Army
3.	Boston	Fritz Barzilauskas	G	Yale
4.	Washington	Cal Rossi	B	UCLA
5.	Pittsburgh	Hub Bechtol	E	Texas
6.	Green Bay	Ernie Case	B	UCLA
7.	Chi. Cardinals	Tex Coulter	T	Army
8.	Philadelphia	Neill Armstrong	E	Oklahoma State
9.	Los Angeles	Herman Wedemeyer	B	St. Mary's (Cal.)
10.	New York	Vic Schwall	B	Northwestern
11.	Chi. Bears	Don Kindt	B	Wisconsin

Note: From 1947-58 one team was granted a "bonus selection," which became the first overall pick in the draft. Each team was allowed only one bonus selection during this period.

Total number of picks in draft: 300.

OTHER NOTEWORTHY PICKS

Round/Overall—Team, Player selected, Pos., College
12/103—Los Angeles, **Dante Lavelli**, E, Ohio State; 13/109—Pittsburgh, Ara Parseghian, B, Miami (Ohio); 20/184—New York, **Tom Landry**, B, Texas; 22/204—New York, **Art Donovan**, T, Boston College; 31/293—Chi. Bears, Ed Ehlers, B, Purdue.

1948

FIRST ROUND—AAFC

No.	Team	Player selected	Pos.	College
1.	Chicago	Tony (Skippy) Minisi	B	Pennsylvania
2.	Baltimore	**Bobby Layne**	QB	Texas
3.	Brooklyn	Harry Gilmer	QB	Alabama
4.	Los Angeles	Vaughn Mancha	C	Alabama
5.	San Francisco	Joe Scott	B	San Francisco
6.	Buffalo	Clyde Scott	B	Arkansas
7.	New York	Lowell Tew	B	Alabama
8.	Cleveland	Jeff Durkota	B	Penn State

Total number of picks in draft: 217.

OTHER NOTEWORTHY PICKS

Round/Overall—Team, Player selected, Pos., College
3/14—Los Angeles, **Len Ford**, E, Michigan; 19/128—New York, **Tom Landry**, B, Texas; 25/177—Cleveland, Ara Parseghian, B, Miami of Ohio; 28/198—Los Angeles, **Lou Creekmur**, T, William & Mary.

FIRST ROUND—NFL

No.	Team	Player selected	Pos.	College
1.	Washington	Harry Gilmer	QB	Alabama
2.	New York	Tony (Skippy) Minisi	B	Pennsylvania

No.	Team	Player selected	Pos.	College
3.	Chi. Bears	**Bobby Layne**	QB	Texas
4.	Washington	Lowell Tew	B	Alabama
5.	Boston	Vaughn Mancha	C	Alabama
6.	Detroit	**Y.A. Tittle**	QB	Louisiana State
7.	Green Bay	Earl (Jug) Girard	B	Wisconsin
8.	Philadelphia	Clyde Scott	B	Arkansas
9.	Pittsburgh	Dan Edwards	E	Georgia
10.	Chi. Bears	Max Bumgardner	E	Texas
11.	Chi. Cardinals	Jim Spavital	B	Oklahoma State

Note: From 1947-58 one team was granted a "bonus selection," which became the first pick in the draft. Each team was allowed only one bonus selection during this period; team not selecting in first round: Los Angeles.

Total number of picks in draft: 300.

OTHER NOTEWORTHY PICKS

Round/Overall—Team, Player selected, Pos., College
26/243—Philadelphia, **Lou Creekmur**, T, William & Mary; 29/274—Pittsburgh, Abe Gibron, G, Purdue.

1949

SECRET DRAFT—AAFC

These players were selected in the first round of a secret two-round draft in July 1948 in order for the AAFC to have a chance of luring star college players before the NFL could negotiate with them.

Team	Player selected	Pos.	College
Baltimore	Dick Harris	C	Texas
Brooklyn	**Chuck Bednarik**	C	Pennsylvania
Buffalo	Abe Gibron	G	Purdue
Chicago	Terry Brennan	B	Notre Dame
Chicago	Pete Elliott	B	Michigan
Cleveland	Gene Derricotte	B	Michigan
Los Angeles	Dan Dworsky	C	Michigan
San Francisco	**Ernie Stautner**	T	Boston College

Team not selecting in first round: New York.

Total number of picks in secret draft: 16.

FIRST ROUND—AAFC

No.	Team	Player selected	Pos.	College
1.	Chicago	Stan Heath	QB	Nevada
2.	Brooklyn	Joe Sullivan	B	Dartmouth
3.	New York	Bobby Thomason	QB	Virginia Military
4.	Baltimore	George Sims	B	Baylor
5.	Los Angeles	George Taliaferro	B	Indiana
6.	Buffalo	Bill Kay	T	Iowa
7.	San Francisco	Chester Fritz	B	Missouri
8.	Cleveland	Jack Mitchell	QB	Oklahoma

Note: Brooklyn and New York franchises merged for 1949 season (but after draft).

Total number of picks in regular rounds of draft (excluding secret draft selections): 192.

OTHER NOTEWORTHY PICKS

Round/Overall—Team, Player selected, Pos., College
2/9—Chicago, **George Blanda**, QB, Kentucky; 4/22—Chicago, **Jim Finks**, QB, Tulsa; 9/69—Cleveland, *Doak Walker*, B, SMU; 11/78—Chicago, **Norm Van Brocklin**, QB, Oregon.

FIRST ROUND—NFL

No.	Team	Player selected	Pos.	College
1.	Philadelphia	**Chuck Bednarik**	C	Pennsylvania
2.	Detroit	Johnny Rauch	QB	Georgia
3.	Boston	*Doak Walker*	B	SMU
4.	New York	Paul Page	B	SMU
5.	Green Bay	Stan Heath	QB	Nevada
6.	Pittsburgh	Bobby Gage	B	Clemson
7.	Los Angeles	Bobby Thomason	QB	Virginia Military
8.	Washington	Rob Goode	B	Texas A&M
9.	Philadelphia	Frank Tripucka	QB	Notre Dame
10.	Chi. Cardinals	Bill Fischer	G	Notre Dame
11.	Chi. Bears	Dick Harris	C	Texas

Note: From 1947-58 one team was granted a "bonus selection," which became the first overall pick in the draft. Each team was allowed only one bonus selection during this period.
Total number of picks in draft: 251.

OTHER NOTEWORTHY PICKS

Round/Overall—Team, Player selected, Pos., College
2/14—New York, Al DeRogatis, T, Duke; 4/37—Los Angeles, **Norm Van Brocklin**, QB, Oregon; 6/55—New York, Abe Gibron, G, Purdue; 12/116—Pittsburgh, **Jim Finks**, B, Tulsa; 12/119—Chi. Bears, **George Blanda**, QB, Kentucky; 25/247—Los Angeles, Clay Matthews Sr., T, Georgia Tech.

1950
FIRST ROUND—NFL

No.	Team	Player selected	Pos.	College
1.	Detroit	Leon Hart	E	Notre Dame
2.	Baltimore	Adrian Burk	QB	Baylor
3.	Chi. Bears	Chuck Hunsinger	B	Florida
4.	Green Bay	Clayton Tonnemaker	C	Minnesota
5.	Detroit	Joe Watson	C	Rice
6.	Washington	George Thomas	B	Oklahoma
7.	N.Y. Giants	Travis Tidwell	B	Auburn
8.	Pittsburgh	Lynn Chandnois	B	Michigan State
9.	Los Angeles	Ralph Pasquariello	B	Villanova
10.	Chi. Bears	Fred (Curly) Morrison	B	Ohio State
11.	San Francisco	**Leo Nomellini**	T	Minnesota
12.	Los Angeles	Stan West	G	Oklahoma
13.	Cleveland	Ken Carpenter	B	Oregon State
14.	Philadelphia	**Bud Grant**	E	Minnesota

Note: From 1947-58 one team was granted a "bonus selection," which became the first overall pick in the draft. Each team was allowed only one bonus selection during this period; teams not selecting in first round: Chi. Cardinals, N.Y. Bulldogs.
Total number of picks in draft: 391.

OTHER NOTEWORTHY PICKS

Round/Overall—Team, Player selected, Pos., College
2/22—Pittsburgh, **Ernie Stautner**, T, Boston College; 10/123—Washington, Eddie LeBaron, QB, Pacific; 16/201—Washington, Charlie (Choo-Choo) Justice, B, North Carolina; 20/250—N.Y. Bulldogs, Darrell Royal, B, Oklahoma.

1951
FIRST ROUND—NFL

No.	Team	Player selected	Pos.	College
1.	N.Y. Giants	Kyle Rote	B	SMU
2.	Chi. Bears	Bob Williams	QB	Notre Dame*
3.	San Francisco	Y.A. Tittle	QB	Louisiana State*
4.	Washington	Leon Heath	B	Oklahoma
5.	Green Bay	Bob Gain	T	Kentucky
6.	Chi. Cardinals	Jerry Groom	C	Notre Dame
7.	Philadelphia	Ebert Van Buren	B	Louisiana State
8.	Philadelphia	Chet Mutryn	B	Xavier*
9.	Pittsburgh	Butch Avinger	B	Alabama
10.	Chi. Bears	Billy Stone	B	Bradley*
11.	Los Angeles	Bud McFadin	G	Texas
12.	Chi. Bears	Gene Schroeder	E	Virginia
13.	N.Y. Giants	Jim Spavital	B	Oklahoma State*
14.	Cleveland	Kenny Konz	B	Louisiana State

*Players drafted from Baltimore franchise, which disbanded following 1950 season.
Note: From 1947-58 one team was granted a "bonus selection," which became the first overall pick in the draft. Each team was allowed only one bonus selection during this period; teams not selecting in first round: Detroit, N.Y. Yanks.
Total number of picks in draft: 362.

OTHER NOTEWORTHY PICKS

Round/Overall—Team, Player selected, Pos., College
2/23—Chi. Bears, **Bill George**, T, Wake Forest; 3/34—N.Y. Yanks, **Mike McCormack**, T, Kansas; 4/50—Cleveland, **Art Donovan**, T,

Boston College; 6/69—Detroit, **Jack Christiansen**, B, Colorado State; 9/110—Cleveland, **Don Shula**, B, John Carroll; 19/228—Los Angeles, **Andy Robustelli**, E, Arnold.

1952
FIRST ROUND—NFL

No.	Team	Player selected	Pos.	College
1.	Los Angeles	Bill Wade	QB	Vanderbilt
2.	N.Y. Yanks	Les Richter	G	California
3.	Chi. Cardinals	**Ollie Matson**	B	San Francisco
4.	Green Bay	Babe Parilli	QB	Kentucky
5.	Philadelphia	Johnny Bright	B	Drake
6.	Pittsburgh	Ed Modzelewski	B	Maryland
7.	Washington	Larry Isbell	B	Baylor
8.	Chi. Bears	Jim Dooley	B	Miami
9.	San Francisco	**Hugh McElhenny**	B	Washington
10.	Cleveland	Bert Rechichar	B	Tennessee
11.	N.Y. Giants	**Frank Gifford**	B	USC
12.	Cleveland	Harry Agganis	QB	Boston University
13.	Los Angeles	Bob Carey	E	Michigan State

Note: Shortly after draft, N.Y. Yanks franchise was sold back to league and the club played in 1952 as Dallas Texans; from 1947-58 one team was granted a "bonus selection," which became the first overall pick in the draft. Each team was allowed only one bonus selection during this period; team not selecting in first round: Detroit.
Total number of picks in draft: 360.

OTHER NOTEWORTHY PICKS

Round/Overall—Team, Player selected, Pos., College
2/14—N.Y. Yanks, **Gino Marchetti**, T, San Francisco; 3/26—Cleveland, Don Klosterman, QB, Loyola, Calif.; 3/34—Detroit, **Yale Lary**, B, Texas A&M; 4/45—Detroit, Pat Summerall, E, Arkansas; 7/79—Washington, Vic Janowicz, B, Ohio State; 15/176—Chi. Bears, Dick Kazmaier, B, Princeton.

1953
FIRST ROUND—NFL

No.	Team	Player selected	Pos.	College
1.	San Francisco	Harry Babcock	E	Georgia
2.	Baltimore	Billy Vessels	B	Oklahoma
3.	Washington	Jack Scarbath	B	Maryland
4.	Chi. Cardinals	Johnny Olszewski	B	California
5.	Pittsburgh	Ted Marchibroda	QB	Detroit
6.	Chi. Bears	Billy Anderson	B	Compton J.C.
7.	Green Bay	Al Carmichael	B	USC
8.	New York	Bobby Marlow	B	Alabama
9.	Los Angeles	Donn Moomaw	C	UCLA
10.	San Francisco	Tom Stolhanske	E	Texas
11.	Cleveland	**Doug Atkins**	T	Tennessee
12.	Los Angeles	Ed Barker	E	Washington State
13.	Detroit	Harley Sewell	G	Texas

Note: From 1947-58 one team was granted a "bonus selection," which became the first overall pick in the draft. Each team was allowed only one bonus selection during this period; team not selecting in first round: Philadelphia.
Total number of picks in draft: 360.

OTHER NOTEWORTHY PICKS

Round/Overall—Team, Player selected, Pos., College
2/17—Chi. Bears, Zeke Bratkowski, QB, Georgia; 2/18—Pittsburgh, **John Henry Johnson**, B, Arizona State; 3/32—San Francisco, **Bob St. Clair**, T, Tulsa; 5/54—Chi. Bears, **Stan Jones**, T, Maryland; 7/79—Green Bay, **Jim Ringo**, C, Syracuse; 7/81—Philadelphia, Ray Malavasi, G, Mississippi State; 7/85—Detroit, **Joe Schmidt**, C, Pittsburgh; 10/117—Philadelphia, Tom Brookshier, B, Colorado; 20/239—Cleveland, **Chuck Noll**, T, Dayton; 25/292—Chi. Cardinals, Haywood Sullivan, B, Florida; 27/321—New York, **Roosevelt Brown**, T, Morgan State; 30/352—Washington, Bob Mathias, B, Stanford.

1954
FIRST ROUND—NFL

No. Team	Player selected	Pos.	College
1. Cleveland	Bobby Garrett	QB	Stanford
2. Chi. Cardinals	Lamar McHan	QB	Arkansas
3. Green Bay	Art Hunter	T	Notre Dame
4. Green Bay	Veryl Switzer	B	Kansas State
5. Baltimore	Cotton Davidson	QB	Baylor
6. Chi. Bears	Stan Wallace	B	Illinois
7. Pittsburgh	*Johnny Lattner*	B	Notre Dame
8. Washington	Steve Meilinger	E	Kentucky
9. Philadelphia	Neil Worden	B	Notre Dame
10. Los Angeles	Ed Beatty	C	Mississippi
11. San Francisco	Bernie Faloney	B	Maryland
12. Cleveland	John Bauer	G	Illinois
13. Detroit	Dick Chapman	T	Rice

Note: From 1947-58 one team was granted a "bonus selection," which became the first overall pick in the draft. Each team was allowed only one bonus selection during this period; team not selecting in first round: New York.
Total number of picks in draft: 360.

OTHER NOTEWORTHY PICKS

Round/Overall—Team, Player selected, Pos., College
4/41—New York, Dick Nolan, B, Maryland; 5/51—Green Bay, Max McGee, B, Tulane; 15/174—Chi. Bears, Harlon Hill, E, North Alabama; 20/232—Baltimore, **Raymond Berry**, E, Southern Methodist; 25/293—Baltimore, Pepper Rodgers, B, Georgia Tech.

1955
FIRST ROUND—NFL

No. Team	Player selected	Pos.	College
1. Baltimore	George Shaw	B	Oregon
2. Chi. Cardinals	Max Boydston	E	Oklahoma
3. Baltimore	*Alan Ameche*	B	Wisconsin
4. Washington	Ralph Guglielmi	QB	Notre Dame
5. Green Bay	Tom Bettis	G	Purdue
6. Pittsburgh	Frank Varrichione	T	Notre Dame
7. Los Angeles	Larry Morris	C	Georgia Tech
8. New York	Joe Heap	B	Notre Dame
9. Philadelphia	Dick Bielski	B	Maryland
10. San Francisco	Dickie Moegle	B	Rice
11. Chi. Bears	Ron Drzewiecki	B	Marquette
12. Detroit	Dave Middleton	B	Auburn
13. Cleveland	Kurt Burris	C	Oklahoma

Total number of picks in draft: 360.

OTHER NOTEWORTHY PICKS

Round/Overall—Team, Player selected, Pos., College
3/31—New York, Rosey Grier, T, Penn State; 3/34—San Francisco, Carroll Hardy, B, Colorado; 9/102—Pittsburgh, **Johnny Unitas**, QB, Louisville; 12/139—Los Angeles, Jim Hanifan, E, California; 13/155—Chi. Bears, Norm Cash, B, Sul Ross; 30/354—Los Angeles, K.C. Jones, E, San Francisco.

1956
FIRST ROUND—NFL

No. Team	Player selected	Pos.	College
1. Pittsburgh	Gary Glick	QB	Colorado State
2. San Francisco	Earl Morrall	QB	Michigan State
3. Detroit	*Hopalong Cassady*	B	Ohio State
4. Philadelphia	Bob Pellegrini	C	Maryland
5. Pittsburgh	Art Davis	B	Mississippi State
6. Los Angeles	Joe Marconi	B	West Virginia
7. Chi. Cardinals	Joe Childress	B	Auburn
8. Green Bay	Jack Losch	B	Miami
9. Baltimore	**Lenny Moore**	B	Penn State
10. Chi. Bears	Menan (Tex) Schriewer	E	Texas

No. Team	Player selected	Pos.	College
11. Los Angeles	Charlie Horton	B	Vanderbilt
12. Washington	Ed Vereb	B	Maryland
13. Cleveland	Preston Carpenter	B	Arkansas

Note: From 1947-58 one team was granted a "bonus selection," which became the first overall pick in the draft. Each team was allowed only one bonus selection during this period; team not selecting in first round: New York.
Total number of picks in draft: 360.

OTHER NOTEWORTHY PICKS

Round/Overall—Team, Player selected, Pos., College
2/20—Green Bay, **Forrest Gregg**, T, SMU; 3/30—New York, **Sam Huff**, T, West Virginia; 5/54—Philadelphia, Fuzzy Thurston, G, Valparaiso; 15/181—Cleveland, **Willie Davis**, E, Grambling; 16/186—Chi. Cardinals, George Welsh, QB, Navy; 17/200—Green Bay, **Bart Starr**, QB, Alabama; 21/251—Washington, Howard Schnellenberger, E, Kentucky.

1957
FIRST ROUND—NFL

No. Team	Player selected	Pos.	College
1. Green Bay	**Paul Hornung**	QB	Notre Dame
2. Los Angeles	Jon Arnett	B	USC
3. San Francisco	John Brodie	QB	Stanford
4. Green Bay	Ron Kramer	E	Michigan
5. Pittsburgh	**Len Dawson**	QB	Purdue
6. Cleveland	**Jim Brown**	B	Syracuse
7. Philadelphia	Clarence Peaks	B	Michigan State
8. Baltimore	**Jim Parker**	G	Ohio State
9. Washington	Don Bosseler	B	Miami
10. Chi. Cardinals	Jerry Tubbs	C	Oklahoma
11. Los Angeles	Del Shofner	B	Baylor
12. Detroit	Bill Glass	G	Baylor
13. Chi. Bears	Earl Leggett	T	Louisiana State

Note: From 1947-58 one team was granted a "bonus selection," which became the first overall pick in the draft. Each team was allowed only one bonus selection during this period; team not selecting in first round: New York.
Total number of picks in draft: 360.

OTHER NOTEWORTHY PICKS

Round/Overall—Team, Player selected, Pos., College
2/14—Los Angeles, Jack Pardee, B, Texas A&M; 3/31—Philadelphia, **Tommy McDonald**, B, Oklahoma; 4/43—Philadelphia, **Sonny Jurgensen**, QB, Duke; 5/52—Cleveland, **Henry Jordan**, T, Virginia; 5/53—Cleveland, Milt Campbell, B, Indiana; 9/109—New York, **Don Maynard**, B, Texas Western College; 17/203—Detroit, Jack Kemp, QB, Occidental; 29/346—Chi. Cardinals, Lee Corso, B, Florida State.

1958
FIRST ROUND—NFL

No. Team	Player selected	Pos.	College
1. Chi. Cardinals	King Hill	QB	Rice
2. Chi. Cardinals	*John David Crow*	B	Texas A&M
3. Green Bay	Dan Currie	C	Michigan State
4. Los Angeles	Lou Michaels	T	Kentucky
5. Los Angeles	Jim Phillips	E	Auburn
6. Philadelphia	Walt Kowalczyk	B	Michigan State
7. Chi. Bears	Chuck Howley	G	West Virginia
8. San Francisco	Jim Pace	B	Michigan
9. San Francisco	Charlie Krueger	T	Texas A&M
10. Detroit	Alex Karras	T	Iowa
11. Baltimore	Lenny Lyles	B	Louisville
12. New York	Phil King	B	Vanderbilt
13. Cleveland	Jim Shofner	B	Texas Christian

Note: From 1947-58 one team was granted a "bonus selection," which became the first overall pick in the draft. Each team was allowed only one bonus selection during this period; teams not selecting in first round: Pittsburgh, Washington.
Total number of picks in draft: 360.

OTHER NOTEWORTHY PICKS

Round/Overall—Team, Player selected, Pos., College
2/15—Green Bay, **Jim Taylor**, B, Louisiana State; 3/36—Green Bay, **Ray Nitschke**, B, Illinois; 4/39—Green Bay, Jerry Kramer, G, Idaho; 7/84—Cleveland, **Bobby Mitchell**, B, Illinois; 13/154—Baltimore, Jerry Richardson, E, Wofford; 19/223—Pittsburgh, Gene Keady, B, Kansas State; 21/244—Philadelphia, **John Madden**, T, Cal Poly-SLO.

1959

FIRST ROUND—NFL

No.	Team	Player selected	Pos.	College
1.	Green Bay	Randy Duncan	QB	Iowa
2.	Los Angeles	Dick Bass	B	Pacific
3.	Chi. Cardinals	Billy Stacy	B	Mississippi State
4.	Washington	Don Allard	QB	Boston College
5.	San Francisco	Dave Baker	QB	Oklahoma
6.	Detroit	Nick Pietrosante	B	Notre Dame
7.	Chi. Bears	Don Clark	B	Ohio State
8.	San Francisco	Dan James	C	Ohio State
9.	Los Angeles	Paul Dickson	T	Baylor
10.	New York	Lee Grosscup	QB	Utah
11.	Cleveland	Rich Kreitling	E	Illinois
12.	Baltimore	Jackie Burkett	C	Auburn

Teams not selecting in first round: Philadelphia, Pittsburgh.
Total number of picks in draft: 360.

OTHER NOTEWORTHY PICKS

Round/Overall—Team, Player selected, Pos., College
5/58—Cleveland, Dick LeBeau, B, Ohio State; 18/209—Washington, Joe Kapp, QB, California; 19/222—San Francisco, Tom Osborne, B, Hastings.

1960

AFL

Eight players were selected as territorial picks by the AFL prior to its first draft. The actual draft was held in two stages consisting of a total of 53 rounds. The draft order was not announced. Shortly after the draft, Minneapolis withdrew from the league when it was offered an NFL franchise (to begin play in 1961). Oakland was then allowed to join as the eighth AFL team, and it received the Minneapolis draft list. Before Oakland was admitted to the league, however, other AFL teams had signed a number of players drafted by Minneapolis. The AFL then held an allocation draft for Oakland. Each AFL team protected 11 players and Oakland was allowed to choose 24 unprotected players. Below is the list of AFL territorial picks.

Team	Player selected	Pos.	College
Boston	Gerhard Schwedes	HB	Syracuse
Buffalo	Richie Lucas	QB	Penn State
Dallas	Don Meredith	QB	SMU
Denver	Roger LeClerc	C	Trinity (Ct.)
Houston	*Billy Cannon*	B	Louisiana State
Los Angeles	Monty Stickles	E	Notre Dame
Minneapolis	Dale Hackbart	QB	Wisconsin
New York	George Izo	QB	Notre Dame

Total number of territorial picks: 8.
Total number of regular draft picks (including territorial): 424.
Total number of allocation picks for Oakland franchise: 24

OTHER NOTEWORTHY PICKS

Team, Player selected, Pos., College
Boston, Foge Fazio, C, Pittsburgh; Boston, **Ron Mix**, T, USC; Buffalo, **Larry Wilson**, DB, Utah; Houston, Jim Marshall, T/G, Ohio State; Los Angeles, Paul Maguire, E, The Citadel; Minneapolis, **Jim Otto**, C, Miami.

FIRST ROUND—NFL

No.	Team	Player selected	Pos.	College
1.	Los Angeles	*Billy Cannon*	B	Louisiana State
2.	Chi. Cardinals	George Izo	QB	Notre Dame
3.	Detroit	Johnny Robinson	HB	Louisiana State

No.	Team	Player selected	Pos.	College
4.	Washington	Richie Lucas	QB	Penn State
5.	Green Bay	Tom Moore	B	Vanderbilt
6.	Pittsburgh	Jack Spikes	FB	Texas Christian
7.	Chi. Bears	Roger Davis	G	Syracuse
8.	Cleveland	Jim Houston	E	Ohio State
9.	Philadelphia	Ron Burton	HB	Northwestern
10.	Baltimore	**Ron Mix**	T	USC
11.	San Francisco	Monty Stickles	E	Notre Dame
12.	New York	Lou Cordileone	T	Clemson

Note: Chi. Cardinals moved to St. Louis prior to 1960 season (but after draft); expansion Dallas team joined league after draft.
Total number of picks in draft: 240.

OTHER NOTEWORTHY PICKS

Round/Overall—Team, Player selected, Pos., College
3/32—Chi. Bears, Don Meredith, QB, SMU; 4/44—Cleveland, Jim Marshall, T, Ohio State; 7/74—Chi. Cardinals, **Larry Wilson**, DB, Utah.

1961

FIRST ROUND—AFL

Team	Player selected	Pos.	College
Boston	Tommy Mason	HB	Tulane
Buffalo	Ken Rice	T	Auburn
Dallas	E.J. Holub	C	Texas Tech
Denver	Bob Gaiters	HB	New Mexico St.
Houston	**Mike Ditka**	E	Pittsburgh
Los Angeles	Earl Faison	E	Indiana
New York	Tom Brown	G	Minnesota
Oakland	Joe Rutgens	T	Illinois

Note: Los Angeles team moved to San Diego prior to 1961 season (but after draft).
Total number of picks in draft: 240.

OTHER NOTEWORTHY PICKS

Round—Team, Player selected, Pos., College
2—Buffalo, **Billy Shaw**, T, Georgia Tech; 2—Dallas, **Bob Lilly**, T, Texas Christian; 2—New York, **Herb Adderley**, HB, Michigan State; 4—Los Angeles, **Jimmy Johnson**, HB, UCLA; 5—Boston, **Fran Tarkenton**, QB, Georgia; 5—Buffalo, Norm Snead, QB, Wake Forest; 5—Los Angeles, Billy Kilmer, QB, UCLA; 6—Houston, Jake Gibbs, QB, Mississippi; 19—Boston, *Joe Bellino*, B, Navy.

FIRST ROUND—NFL

No.	Team	Player selected	Pos.	College
1.	Minnesota	Tommy Mason	HB	Tulane
2.	Washington	Norm Snead	QB	Wake Forest
3.	Washington	Joe Rutgens	T	Illinois
4.	Los Angeles	Marlin McKeever	LB	USC
5.	Chicago	**Mike Ditka**	E	Pittsburgh
6.	San Francisco	**Jimmy Johnson**	B	UCLA
7.	Baltimore	Tom Matte	HB	Ohio State
8.	St. Louis	Ken Rice	T	Auburn
9.	San Francisco	Bernie Casey	B	Bowling Green
10.	Cleveland	Bobby Crespino	E	Mississippi
11.	San Francisco	Billy Kilmer	QB	UCLA
12.	Green Bay	**Herb Adderley**	B	Michigan State
13.	Dallas	**Bob Lilly**	T	Texas Christian
14.	Philadelphia	Art Baker	FB	Syracuse

Teams not selecting in first round: Dallas, Detroit, New York, Pittsburgh.
Total number of picks in draft: 280.

OTHER NOTEWORTHY PICKS

Round/Overall—Team, Player selected, Pos., College
3/29—Minnesota, **Fran Tarkenton**, QB, Georgia; 9/125—Cleveland, Jake Gibbs, QB, Mississippi; 14/184—Dallas, **Billy Shaw**, T, Georgia Tech; 14/186—Los Angeles, **Deacon Jones**, T, South Carolina State; 17/227—Washington, *Joe Bellino*, B, Navy.

HISTORY — First-round draft choices

1962

FIRST ROUND—AFL

No. Team	Player selected	Pos.	College
1. Oakland	Roman Gabriel	QB	N.C. State
2. Denver	**Merlin Olsen**	T	Utah State
3. Dallas	Ronnie Bull	B	Baylor
4. Buffalo	*Ernie Davis*	B	Syracuse
5. New York	Sandy Stephens	QB	Minnesota
6. Boston	Gary Collins	E	Maryland
7. Houston	Ray Jacobs	T	Howard Payne
8. San Diego	Bob Ferguson	B	Ohio State

Total number of picks in draft: 272.

OTHER NOTEWORTHY PICKS

Round/Overall—Team, Player selected, Pos., College
2/9—Oakland, **Lance Alworth**, HB, Arkansas; 3/24—San Diego, John Hadl, QB, Kansas; 13/102—Boston, **Nick Buoniconti**, G, Notre Dame.

FIRST ROUND—NFL

No. Team	Player selected	Pos.	College
1. Washington	*Ernie Davis*	B	Syracuse
2. Los Angeles	Roman Gabriel	QB	N.C. State
3. Los Angeles	**Merlin Olsen**	T	Utah State
4. Cleveland	Gary Collins	E	Maryland
5. Pittsburgh	Bob Ferguson	B	Ohio State
6. St. Louis	Fate Echols	T	Northwestern
7. Chicago	Ronnie Bull	B	Baylor
8. San Francisco	**Lance Alworth**	B	Arkansas
9. Baltimore	Wendell Harris	B	Louisiana State
10. Detroit	John Hadl	QB	Kansas
11. Cleveland	Leroy Jackson	B	Western Illinois
12. St. Louis	Irv Goode	C	Kentucky
13. New York	Jerry Hillebrand	E	Colorado
14. Green Bay	Earl Gros	B	Louisiana State

Teams not selecting in first round: Dallas, Minnesota, Philadelphia.
Total number of picks in draft: 280.

OTHER NOTEWORTHY PICKS

Round/Overall—Team, Player selected, Pos., College
7/95—Cleveland, John Havlicek, E, Ohio State; 17/238—Green Bay, **Buck Buchanan**, T, Grambling.

1963

FIRST ROUND—AFL

No. Team	Player selected	Pos.	College
1. Dallas	**Buck Buchanan**	T	Grambling
2. San Diego	Walt Sweeney	E	Syracuse
3. New York	Jerry Stovall	B	Louisiana State
4. Buffalo	Dave Behrman	C	Michigan State
5. Denver	Kermit Alexander	B	UCLA
6. Houston	Danny Brabham	FB	Arkansas
7. Boston	Art Graham	E	Boston College
8. Dallas	Ed Budde	T	Michigan State

Team not selecting in first round: Oakland.
Total number of picks in draft: 232.

OTHER NOTEWORTHY PICKS

Round/Overall—Team, Player selected, Pos., College
5/35—New York, **John Mackey**, E, Syracuse; 7/56—Dallas, **Bobby Bell**, T, Minnesota; 12/90—San Diego, *Terry Baker*, QB, Oregon State; 24/188—Buffalo, Daryle Lamonica, QB, Notre Dame.

FIRST ROUND—NFL

No. Team	Player selected	Pos.	College
1. Los Angeles	*Terry Baker*	B	Oregon State
2. St. Louis	Jerry Stovall	B	Louisiana State
3. Minnesota	Jim Dunaway	T	Mississippi
4. Philadelphia	Ed Budde	T	Michigan State
5. Baltimore	Bob Vogel	T	Ohio State
6. Dallas	Lee Roy Jordan	LB	Alabama
7. Washington	Pat Richter	E	Wisconsin
8. San Francisco	Kermit Alexander	B	UCLA
9. Cleveland	Tom Hutchinson	E	Kentucky
10. Los Angeles	Rufus Guthrie	G	Georgia Tech
11. Chicago	Dave Behrman	C	Michigan State
12. Detroit	Daryl Sanders	T	Ohio State
13. St. Louis	Don Brumm	DE	Purdue
14. Green Bay	Dave Robinson	E	Penn State

Teams not selecting in first round: New York, Pittsburgh.
Total number of picks in draft: 280.

OTHER NOTEWORTHY PICKS

Round/Overall—Team, Player selected, Pos., College
2/16—Minnesota, **Bobby Bell**, T, Minnesota; 2/19—Baltimore, **John Mackey**, E, Syracuse; 10/129—St. Louis, **Jackie Smith**, E, Northwestern (La.) State; 12/168—Green Bay, Daryle Lamonica, QB, Notre Dame; 19/265—New York, **Buck Buchanan**, T, Grambling.

1964

FIRST ROUND—AFL

No. Team	Player selected	Pos.	College
1. Boston	Jack Concannon	QB	Boston College
2. Kansas City	Pete Beathard	QB	USC
3. New York	Matt Snell	FB	Ohio State
4. Denver	Bob Brown	T	Nebraska
5. Buffalo	**Carl Eller**	T	Minnesota
6. Houston	Scott Appleton	T	Texas
7. Oakland	Tony Lorick	HB	Arizona State
8. San Diego	Ted Davis	E	Georgia Tech

Total number of picks in draft: 208.

OTHER NOTEWORTHY PICKS

Round/Overall—Team, Player selected, Pos., College
2/9—Houston, **Charley Taylor**, HB, Arizona State; 4/28—Buffalo, **Paul Warfield**, HB, Ohio State; 6/46—Houston, **Dave Wilcox**, DE, Oregon; 9/67—New York, Sherman Lewis, HB, Michigan State; 10/79—Oakland, **Mel Renfro**, HB, Oregon; 12/89—Denver, **Paul Krause**, DB, Iowa; 14/105—Denver, Bob Hayes, HB, Florida A&M; 16/122—Kansas City, *Roger Staubach*, QB, Navy; 18/140—Boston, Joe Tiller, T, Montana State; 23/183—Oakland, Bill Curry, C, Georgia Tech.

FIRST ROUND—NFL

No. Team	Player selected	Pos.	College
1. San Francisco	Dave Parks	E	Texas Tech
2. Philadelphia	**Bob Brown**	T	Nebraska
3. Washington	**Charley Taylor**	HB	Arizona State
4. Dallas	Scott Appleton	T	Texas
5. Detroit	Pete Beathard	QB	USC
6. Minnesota	**Carl Eller**	T	Minnesota
7. Los Angeles	Bill Munson	QB	Utah State
8. Baltimore	Marv Woodson	HB	Indiana
9. St. Louis	Ken Kortas	T	Louisville
10. Pittsburgh	Paul Martha	HB	Pittsburgh
11. Cleveland	**Paul Warfield**	HB	Ohio State
12. New York	Joe Don Looney	B	Oklahoma
13. Green Bay	Lloyd Voss	T	Nebraska
14. Chicago	Dick Evey	T	Tennessee

Total number of picks in draft: 280.

OTHER NOTEWORTHY PICKS

Round/Overall—Team, Player selected, Pos., College
2/17—Dallas, **Mel Renfro**, B, Oregon; 2/18—Washington, **Paul Krause**, B, Iowa; 3/29—San Francisco, **Dave Wilcox**, DE, Oregon; 7/88—Dallas, Bob Hayes, HB, Florida A&M; 7/89—Detroit, Bill Parcells, T, Wichita State; 8/110—Cleveland, **Leroy Kelly**, HB, Morgan State; 10/129—Dallas, *Roger Staubach*, QB, Navy; 18/250—Cleveland, Sherman Lewis, HB, Michigan State.

FIRST ROUND—AFL

Team	Player selected	Pos.	College
Boston	Jerry Rush	T	Michigan State
Buffalo	Jim Davidson	T	Ohio State
Houston	Lawrence Elkins	E	Baylor
Kansas City	**Gale Sayers**	HB	Kansas
New York	**Joe Namath**	QB	Alabama
New York	Tom Nowatzke	FB	Indiana
Oakland	Harry Schuh	T	Memphis State
San Diego	Steve DeLong	DE	Tennessee

Team not selecting in first round: Denver.
Total number of picks in draft: 160.

OTHER NOTEWORTHY PICKS

Round—Team, Player selected, Pos., College
2—Denver, **Dick Butkus**, LB, Illinois; 2—New York, *John Huarte*, QB, Notre Dame; 2—Oakland, **Fred Biletnikoff**, E, Florida State; 7—Buffalo, Marty Schottenheimer, LB, Pittsburgh; 7—San Diego, Jack Snow, E, Notre Dame; 10—Oakland, Craig Morton, QB, California.

REDSHIRT—AFL

The AFL held a separate draft for future picks in 1965 and 1966.

Team	Player selected	Pos.	College
Boston	Dave McCormick	T	Louisiana State
Buffalo	Ken Ambrusko	HB	Maryland
Denver	Miller Farr	HB	Wichita State
Houston	Donny Anderson	HB	Texas Tech
Kansas City	Alphonse Dotson	T	Grambling
New York	Johnny Roland	HB	Missouri
Oakland	Larry Todd	HB	Arizona State
San Diego	Gary Garrison	E	San Diego State

Total number of picks in draft: 96.

OTHER NOTEWORTHY PICKS

Round—Team, Player selected, Pos., College
9—New York, Rich Kotite, E, Wagner.

FIRST ROUND—NFL

No.	Team	Player selected	Pos.	College
1.	New York	Tucker Frederickson	B	Auburn
2.	San Francisco	Ken Willard	FB	North Carolina
3.	Chicago	**Dick Butkus**	LB	Illinois
4.	Chicago	**Gale Sayers**	HB	Kansas
5.	Dallas	Craig Morton	QB	California
6.	Chicago	Steve DeLong	DE	Tennessee
7.	Green Bay	Donny Anderson	HB	Texas Tech
8.	Minnesota	Jack Snow	E	Notre Dame
9.	Los Angeles	Clancy Williams	HB	Washington State
10.	Green Bay	Lawrence Elkins	E	Baylor
11.	Detroit	Tom Nowatzke	FB	Indiana
12.	St. Louis	**Joe Namath**	QB	Alabama
13.	San Francisco	George Donnelly	B	Illinois
14.	Baltimore	Mike Curtis	LB	Duke

Teams not selecting in first round: Cleveland, Philadelphia, Pittsburgh, Washington.
Total number of picks in draft: 280.

OTHER NOTEWORTHY PICKS

Round/Overall—Team, Player selected, Pos., College
3/39—Detroit, **Fred Biletnikoff**, E, Florida State; 4/49—Baltimore, Marty Schottenheimer, LB, Pittsburgh; 6/76—Philadelphia, *John Huarte*, QB, Notre Dame; 17/238—Baltimore, Rick Reichardt, HB, Wisconsin; 19/257—Dallas, Merv Rettenmund, HB, Ball State.

FIRST ROUND—AFL

Team	Player selected	Pos.	College
Boston	Karl Singer	T	Purdue
Buffalo	Mike Dennis	HB	Mississippi
Denver	Jerry Shay	T	Purdue
Houston	Tommy Nobis	LB	Texas
Kansas City	Aaron Brown	E	Minnesota
Miami	Jim Grabowski	FB	Illinois
Miami	Rick Norton	QB	Kentucky
New York	Bill Yearby	T	Michigan
Oakland	Rodger Bird	HB	Kentucky
San Diego	Don Davis	T	Cal State-L.A.

Total number of picks in draft: 181.

OTHER NOTEWORTHY PICKS

Round—Team, Player selected, Pos., College
15—Oakland, Steve Renko, FB, Kansas; 17—Kansas City, Walt Garrison, FB, Oklahoma State; 20—Kansas City, *Mike Garrett*, HB, USC.

REDSHIRT—AFL

The AFL held a separate draft for future picks in 1965 and 1966.

Team	Player selected	Pos.	College
Boston	Willie Townes	T	Tulsa
Buffalo	Jack Gregory	E	UT-Chattanooga
Denver	Nick Eddy	HB	Notre Dame
Houston	Tom Fisher	LB	Tennessee
Kansas City	George Youngblood	E/DB	Cal State-L.A.
Miami	John Roderick	E	SMU
New York	Don Parker	E	Virginia
Oakland	Rod Sherman	HB	USC
San Diego	Bob Windsor	E	Kentucky

Total number of picks in draft: 99.

OTHER NOTEWORTHY PICKS

Round—Team, Player selected, Pos., College
3—Kansas City, **Jan Stenerud**, K, Montana State; Boston, Ray Perkins, E, Alabama.

FIRST ROUND—NFL

No.	Team	Player selected	Pos.	College
1.	Atlanta	Tommy Nobis	LB	Texas
2.	Los Angeles	**Tom Mack**	T	Michigan
3.	Pittsburgh	Dick Leftridge	FB	West Virginia
4.	Philadelphia	Randy Beisler	DE	Indiana
5.	Dallas	John Niland	G	Iowa
6.	Washington	Charlie Gogolak	K	Princeton
7.	Minnesota	Jerry Shay	T	Purdue
8.	St. Louis	Carl McAdams	LB	Oklahoma
9.	Green Bay	Jim Grabowski	FB	Illinois
10.	New York	Francis Peay	T	Missouri
11.	San Francisco	Stan Hindman	T	Mississippi
12.	Chicago	George Rice	T	Louisiana State
13.	Green Bay	Gale Gillingham	T	Minnesota
14.	Cleveland	Milt Morin	E	Massachusetts
15.	Baltimore	Sam Ball	T	Kentucky
16.	Atlanta	Randy Johnson	QB	Texas A&I

Team not selecting in first round: Detroit.
Total number of picks in draft: 305.

OTHER NOTEWORTHY PICKS

Round/Overall—Team, Player selected, Pos., College
2/18—Los Angeles, *Mike Garrett*, HB, USC; 5/79—Dallas, Walt Garrison, HB, Oklahoma State; 7/110—Baltimore, Ray Perkins, E, Alabama; 20/296—Dallas, Lou Hudson, FL, Minnesota.

1967
FIRST ROUND—AFL-NFL

From 1967 through 1969 the AFL and NFL held a combined draft. The league is noted in parentheses after each team's name.

No. Team	Player selected	Pos.	College
1. Baltimore (N)	Bubba Smith	DT	Michigan State
2. Minnesota (N)	Clint Jones	HB	Michigan State
3. San Fran. (N)	*Steve Spurrier*	QB	Florida
4. Miami (A)	**Bob Griese**	QB	Purdue
5. Houston (A)	George Webster	LB	Michigan State
6. Denver (A)	Floyd Little	HB	Syracuse
7. Detroit (N)	Mel Farr	HB	UCLA
8. Minnesota (N)	Gene Washington	FL	Michigan State
9. Green Bay (N)	Bob Hyland	G	Boston College
10. Chicago (N)	Loyd Phillips	DE	Arkansas
11. San Fran. (N)	Cas Banaszek	TE/LB	Northwestern
12. N.Y. Jets (A)	Paul Seiler	G	Notre Dame
13. Wash. (N)	Ray McDonald	FB	Idaho
14. San Diego (A)	Ron Billingsley	DT	Wyoming
15. Minnesota (N)	**Alan Page**	DE	Notre Dame
16. St. Louis (N)	Dave Williams	FL	Washington
17. Oakland (A)	**Gene Upshaw**	G/T	Texas A&I
18. Cleveland (N)	Bob Matheson	LB	Duke
19. Phil. (N)	Harry Jones	HB	Arkansas
20. Baltimore (N)	Jim Detwiler	HB	Michigan
21. Boston (A)	John Charles	DB	Purdue
22. Buffalo (A)	John Pitts	FL/DB	Arizona State
23. Houston (A)	Tom Regner	G	Notre Dame
24. Kan. City (A)	Gene Trosch	DT	Miami
25. Green Bay (N)	Don Horn	QB	San Diego State
26. New Orl. (N)	Les Kelley	HB	Alabama

Teams not selecting in first round: Atlanta (N), Dallas (N), Los Angeles (N), N.Y. Giants (N), Pittsburgh (N).
Total number of picks in draft: 445.

OTHER NOTEWORTHY PICKS

Round/Overall—Team, Player selected, Pos., College
2/34—Detroit (N), **Lem Barney**, DB, Jackson State; 2/50—Kansas City (A), **Willie Lanier**, LB, Morgan State; 9/214—Houston (A), **Ken Houston**, DB, Prairie View A&M; 9/226—Los Angeles, Tommie Smith, HB, San Jose State; 11/285—Dallas (N), Pat Riley, FL, Kentucky; 17/443—Kansas City, Dave Lattin, FL, Texas-El Paso; 17/445—New Orleans, Jimmy Walker, E, Providence.

1968
FIRST ROUND—AFL-NFL

From 1967 through 1969 the AFL and NFL held a combined draft. The league is noted in parentheses after each team's name.

No. Team	Player selected	Pos.	College
1. Minnesota (N)	**Ron Yary**	T	USC
2. Cincinnati (A)	Bob Johnson	C	Tennessee
3. Atlanta (N)	Claude Humphrey	DE	Tennessee State
4. San Diego (A)	Russ Washington	T	Missouri
5. Green Bay (N)	Fred Carr	LB	Texas-El Paso
6. Boston (A)	Dennis Byrd	DT	N.C. State
7. New Orl. (N)	Kevin Hardy	DE	Notre Dame
8. Miami (A)	**Larry Csonka**	RB	Syracuse
9. Buffalo (A)	Haven Moses	E	San Diego State
10. Pittsburgh (N)	Mike Taylor	T	USC
11. Detroit (N)	Greg Landry	QB	Massachusetts
12. Wash. (N)	Jim Smith	DB	Oregon
13. St. Louis (N)	MacArthur Lane	RB	Utah State
14. Phil. (N)	Tim Rossovich	DE	USC
15. San Fran. (N)	Forrest Blue	C	Auburn
16. Chicago (N)	Mike Hull	RB	USC
17. N.Y. Jets (A)	Lee White	RB	Weber State
18. San Diego (A)	Jim Hill	DB	Texas A&I
19. Kan. City (A)	Mo Moorman	G	Texas A&M
20. Dallas (N)	Dennis Homan	E	Alabama
21. Cleveland (N)	Marvin Upshaw	DE	Trinity (Tex.)
22. Kan. City (A)	George Daney	G	Texas-El Paso

No. Team	Player selected	Pos.	College
23. Baltimore (N)	John Williams	T	Minnesota
24. Detroit (N)	Earl McCullouch	E	USC
25. Oakland (A)	Eldridge Dickey	QB	Tennessee State
26. Green Bay (N)	Bill Lueck	G	Arizona
27. Miami (A)	Doug Crusan	T	Indiana

Teams not selecting in first round: Denver (A), Houston (A), Los Angeles (N), N.Y. Giants (N).
Total number of picks in draft: 462.

OTHER NOTEWORTHY PICKS

Round/Overall—Team, Player selected, Pos., College
2/30—Los Angeles (N), *Gary Beban*, QB, UCLA; 2/31—Denver (A), Curley Culp, DE, Arizona State; 2/52—Oakland (A), Ken Stabler, QB, Alabama; 3/77—Houston (A), **Elvin Bethea**, DE, North Carolina A&T; 3/80—Oakland (A), **Art Shell**, T, Maryland-Eastern Shore; 5/118—Miami (A), Jim Kiick, RB, Wyoming; 9/240—Miami (A), Tom Paciorek, DB, Houston; 16/417—Pittsburgh (N), Rocky Bleier, RB, Notre Dame.

1969
FIRST ROUND—AFL-NFL

From 1967 through 1969 the AFL and NFL held a combined draft. The league is noted in parentheses after each team's name.

No. Team	Player selected	Pos.	College
1. Buffalo (A)	**O.J. Simpson**	RB	USC
2. Atlanta (N)	George Kunz	T	Notre Dame
3. Phil. (N)	Leroy Keyes	RB	Purdue
4. Pittsburgh (N)	**Joe Greene**	DT	North Texas State
5. Cincinnati (A)	Greg Cook	QB	Cincinnati
6. Boston (A)	Ron Sellers	SE	Florida State
7. San Fran. (N)	Ted Kwalick	TE	Penn State
8. Los Ang. (A)	Larry Smith	RB	Florida
9. San Diego (A)	Marty Domres	QB	Columbia
10. Los Ang. (N)	Jim Seymour	SE	Notre Dame
11. Miami (A)	Bill Stanfill	DE	Georgia
12. Green Bay (N)	Rich Moore	DT	Villanova
13. N.Y. Giants (N)	Fred Dryer	DE	San Diego State
14. Chicago (N)	Rufus Mayes	T	Ohio State
15. Houston (A)	Ron Pritchard	LB	Arizona State
16. San Fran. (N)	Gene Washington	FL	Stanford
17. New Orl. (N)	John Shinners	G	Xavier
18. San Diego (A)	Bob Babich	LB	Miami (Ohio)
19. St. Louis (N)	Roger Wehrli	DB	Missouri
20. Cleveland (N)	Ron Johnson	RB	Michigan
21. Los Ang. (N)	Bob Klein	TE	USC
22. Oakland (A)	Art Thoms	DT	Syracuse
23. Kan. City (A)	Jim Marsalis	DB	Tennessee State
24. Dallas (N)	Calvin Hill	RB	Yale
25. Baltimore (N)	Eddie Hinton	FL	Oklahoma
26. N.Y. Jets (A)	Dave Foley	T	Ohio State

Teams not selecting in first round: Denver (A), Detroit (N), Minnesota (N), Washington (N).
Total number of picks in draft: 442.

OTHER NOTEWORTHY PICKS

Round/Overall—Team, Player selected, Pos., College
2/33—Baltimore (N), **Ted Hendricks**, LB, Miami; 2/39—Minnesota (N), Ed White, G, California; 3/63—Miami (A), Mercury Morris, RB, West Texas State; 4/80—Philadelphia (N), Bob Kuechenberg, G, Notre Dame; 4/93—Houston (A), **Charlie Joiner**, DB, Grambling; 8/192—Buffalo (A), James Harris, QB, Grambling; 10/238—Pittsburgh (A), L.C. Greenwood, LB, Arkansas-Pine Bluff; 17/429—N.Y. Giants (N), Ken Riley, LB, Texas-Arlington.

1970
FIRST ROUND—NFL

No. Team	Player selected	Pos.	College
1. Pittsburgh	**Terry Bradshaw**	QB	Louisiana Tech
2. Green Bay	Mike McCoy	DT	Notre Dame

No. Team	Player selected	Pos.	College
3. Cleveland	Mike Phipps	QB	Purdue
4. Boston	Phil Olsen	DT	Utah State
5. Buffalo	Al Cowlings	DE	USC
6. Philadelphia	Steve Zabel	TE	Oklahoma
7. Cincinnati	Mike Reid	DT	Penn State
8. St. Louis	Larry Stegent	RB	Texas A&M
9. San Francisco	Cedrick Hardman	DE	North Texas State
10. New Orleans	Ken Burrough	WR	Texas Southern
11. Denver	Bobby Anderson	RB	Colorado
12. Atlanta	John Small	LB	The Citadel
13. N.Y. Giants	Jim Files	LB	Oklahoma
14. Houston	Doug Wilkerson	G	N.C. Central
15. San Diego	Walker Gillette	WR	Richmond
16. Green Bay	Rich McGeorge	TE	Elon
17. San Francisco	Bruce Taylor	DB	Boston University
18. Baltimore	Norm Bulaich	RB	Texas Christian
19. Detroit	*Steve Owens*	RB	Oklahoma
20. N.Y. Jets	Steve Tannen	DB	Florida
21. Cleveland	Bob McKay	T	Texas
22. Los Angeles	Jack Reynolds	LB	Tennessee
23. Dallas	Duane Thomas	RB	West Texas State
24. Oakland	Raymond Chester	TE	Morgan State
25. Minnesota	John Ward	T	Oklahoma State
26. Kansas City	Sid Smith	T	USC

Teams not selecting in first round: Chicago, Miami, Washington.
Total number of picks in draft: 442.

OTHER NOTEWORTHY PICKS

Round/Overall—Team, Player selected, Pos., College
3/53—Pittsburgh, **Mel Blount**, DB, Southern (La.); 3/66—Dallas, Charlie Waters, DB, Clemson; 7/159—Miami, Jake Scott, DB, Georgia; 8/201—St. Louis, Mike Holmgren, QB, USC; 14/346—Philadelphia, Mark Moseley, K, Stephen F. Austin.

1971

FIRST ROUND—NFL

No. Team	Player selected	Pos.	College
1. Boston	*Jim Plunkett*	QB	Stanford
2. New Orleans	Archie Manning	QB	Mississippi
3. Houston	Dan Pastorini	QB	Santa Clara
4. Buffalo	J.D. Hill	WR	Arizona State
5. Philadelphia	Richard Harris	DE	Grambling
6. N.Y. Jets	**John Riggins**	RB	Kansas
7. Atlanta	Joe Profit	RB	N.E. Louisiana
8. Pittsburgh	Frank Lewis	WR	Grambling
9. Green Bay	John Brockington	RB	Ohio State
10. Los Angeles	Isiah Robertson	LB	Southern (La.)
11. Chicago	Joe Moore	RB	Missouri
12. Denver	Marv Montgomery	T	USC
13. San Diego	Leon Burns	RB	Long Beach State
14. Cleveland	Clarence Scott	DB	Kansas State
15. Cincinnati	Vernon Holland	T	Tennessee State
16. Kansas City	Elmo Wright	WR	Houston
17. St. Louis	Norm Thompson	DB	Utah
18. N.Y. Giants	Rocky Thompson	WR	West Texas State
19. Oakland	Jack Tatum	DB	Ohio State
20. Los Angeles	**Jack Youngblood**	DE	Florida
21. Detroit	Bob Bell	DT	Cincinnati
22. Baltimore	Don McCauley	RB	North Carolina
23. San Francisco	Tim Anderson	DB	Ohio State
24. Minnesota	Leo Hayden	RB	Ohio State
25. Dallas	Tody Smith	DE	USC
26. Baltimore	Leonard Dunlap	DB	North Texas State

Note: Boston franchise changed its name to New England (but after draft); teams not selecting in first round: Miami, Washington.
Total number of picks in draft: 442.

OTHER NOTEWORTHY PICKS

Round/Overall—Team, Player selected, Pos., College
2/27—Boston, Julius Adams, DT, Texas Southern; 2/34—Pittsburgh, **Jack Ham**, LB, Penn State; 2/43—St. Louis, **Dan**

Dierdorf, T, Michigan; 3/67—Cincinnati, Ken Anderson, QB, Augustana (Ill.); 4/79—Denver, Lyle Alzado, DE, Yankton; 4/99—Miami, Joe Theismann, QB, Notre Dame; 6/147—St. Louis, Mel Gray, WR, Missouri; 7/161—Philadelphia, Harold Carmichael, WR, Southern (La.).

1972

FIRST ROUND—NFL

No. Team	Player selected	Pos.	College
1. Buffalo	Walt Patulski	DE	Notre Dame
2. Cincinnati	Sherman White	DE	California
3. Chicago	Lionel Antoine	T	Southern Illinois
4. St. Louis	Bobby Moore	WR	Oregon
5. Denver	Riley Odoms	TE	Houston
6. Houston	Gregory Sampson	DE	Stanford
7. Green Bay	Willie Buchanon	DB	San Diego State
8. New Orleans	Royce Smith	G	Georgia
9. N.Y. Jets	Jerome Barkum	WR	Jackson State
10. Minnesota	Jeff Siemon	LB	Stanford
11. Green Bay	Jerry Tagge	QB	Nebraska
12. Chicago	Craig Clemons	DB	Iowa
13. Pittsburgh	**Franco Harris**	RB	Penn State
14. Philadelphia	John Reaves	QB	Florida
15. Atlanta	Clarence Ellis	DB	Notre Dame
16. Detroit	Herb Orvis	DE	Colorado
17. N.Y. Giants	Eldridge Small	DB	Texas A&I
18. Cleveland	Thom Darden	DB	Michigan
19. San Francisco	Terry Beasley	WR	Auburn
20. N.Y. Jets	Mike Taylor	LB	Michigan
21. Oakland	Mike Siani	WR	Villanova
22. Baltimore	Tom Drougas	T	Oregon
23. Kansas City	Jeff Kinney	RB	Nebraska
24. N.Y. Giants	Larry Jacobson	DE	Nebraska
25. Miami	Mike Kadish	DT	Notre Dame
26. Dallas	Bill Thomas	RB	Boston College

Teams not selecting in first round: Los Angeles, New England, San Diego, Washington.
Total number of picks in draft: 442.

OTHER NOTEWORTHY PICKS

Round/Overall—Team, Player selected, Pos., College
2/27—Buffalo, Reggie McKenzie, G, Michigan; 2/40—Atlanta, *Pat Sullivan*, QB, Auburn; 2/50—Minnesota, Ed Marinaro, RB, Cornell; 4/98—Oakland, Cliff Branch, WR, Colorado; 5/110—St. Louis, Conrad Dobler, G, Wyoming; 7/167—Chicago, Jim Fassel, QB, Long Beach State; 13/330—Cleveland, Brian Sipe, QB, San Diego State.

1973

FIRST ROUND—NFL

No. Team	Player selected	Pos.	College
1. Houston	John Matuszak	DE	Tampa
2. Baltimore	Bert Jones	QB	Louisiana State
3. Philadelphia	Jerry Sisemore	T	Texas
4. New England	**John Hannah**	G	Alabama
5. St. Louis	Dave Butz	DT	Purdue
6. Philadelphia	Charle Young	TE	USC
7. Buffalo	Paul Seymour	T	Michigan
8. Chicago	Wally Chambers	DE	Eastern Kentucky
9. Denver	Otis Armstrong	RB	Purdue
10. Baltimore	Joe Ehrmann	DT	Syracuse
11. New England	Sam Cunningham	RB	USC
12. Minnesota	Chuck Foreman	RB	Miami
13. N.Y. Jets	Burgess Owens	DB	Miami
14. Houston	George Amundson	RB	Iowa State
15. Cincinnati	Isaac Curtis	WR	San Diego State
16. Cleveland	Steve Holden	WR	Arizona State
17. Detroit	Ernest Price	DE	Texas A&I
18. San Francisco	Mike Holmes	DB	Texas Southern
19. New England	Darryl Stingley	WR	Purdue
20. Dallas	Billy Joe DuPree	TE	Michigan State
21. Green Bay	Barry Smith	WR	Florida State

No. Team	Player selected	Pos.	College
22. Cleveland	Pete Adams	T	USC
23. Oakland	Ray Guy	P	Southern Miss
24. Pittsburgh	J.T. Thomas	DB	Florida State
25. San Diego	*Johnny Rodgers*	WR	Nebraska
26. Buffalo	**Joe DeLamielleure**	G	Michigan State

Teams not selecting in first round: Atlanta, Kansas City, Los Angeles, Miami, New Orleans, N.Y. Giants, Washington.
Total number of picks in draft: 442.

OTHER NOTEWORTHY PICKS

Round/Overall—Team, Player selected, Pos., College
2/30—Cleveland, Greg Pruitt, RB, Oklahoma; 2/37—Los Angeles, Ron Jaworski, QB, Youngstown State; 3/53—Dallas, Harvey Martin, DE, East Texas State; 3/57—Buffalo, Joe Ferguson, QB, Arkansas; 3/84—San Diego, **Dan Fouts**, QB, Oregon; 4/88—Denver, Tom Jackson, LB, Louisville; 4/91—Detroit, Dick Jauron, RB, Yale; 17/423—Buffalo, John Stearns, DB, Colorado; 17/429—Minnesota, Dave Winfield, TE, Minnesota.

1974

FIRST ROUND—NFL

No. Team	Player selected	Pos.	College
1. Dallas	Ed Jones	DE	Tennessee State
2. San Diego	Bo Matthews	RB	Colorado
3. N.Y. Giants	John Hicks	G	Ohio State
4. Chicago	Waymond Bryant	LB	Tennessee State
5. Baltimore	John Dutton	DE	Nebraska
6. N.Y. Jets	Carl Barzilauskas	DT	Indiana
7. St. Louis	J.V. Cain	TE	Colorado
8. Detroit	Ed O'Neil	LB	Penn State
9. San Francisco	Wilbur Jackson	RB	Alabama
10. San Francisco	Bill Sandifer	DT	UCLA
11. Los Angeles	*John Cappelletti*	RB	Penn State
12. Green Bay	Barty Smith	RB	Richmond
13. New Orleans	Rick Middleton	LB	Ohio State
14. Denver	Randy Gradishar	LB	Ohio State
15. San Diego	Don Goode	LB	Kansas
16. Kansas City	Woody Green	RB	Arizona State
17. Minnesota	Fred McNeill	LB	UCLA
18. Buffalo	Reuben Gant	TE	Oklahoma State
19. Oakland	Henry Lawrence	T	Florida A&M
20. Chicago	Dave Gallagher	DL	Michigan
21. Pittsburgh	**Lynn Swann**	WR	USC
22. Dallas	Charley Young	RB	N.C. State
23. Cincinnati	Bill Kollar	DT	Montana State
24. Baltimore	Roger Carr	WR	Louisiana Tech
25. Minnesota	Steve Riley	T	USC
26. Miami	Donald Reese	DE	Jackson State

Teams not selecting in first round: Atlanta, Cleveland, Houston, New England, Philadelphia, Washington.
Total number of picks in draft: 442.

OTHER NOTEWORTHY PICKS

Round/Overall—Team, Player selected, Pos., College
2/45—Oakland, **Dave Casper**, TE, Notre Dame; 2/46—Pittsburgh, **Jack Lambert**, LB, Kent State; 3/53—Dallas, Danny White, QB, Arizona State; 3/78—Miami, Nat Moore, WR, Florida; 4/82—Pittsburgh, **John Stallworth**, WR, Alabama A&M; 5/125—Pittsburgh, **Mike Webster**, C, Wisconsin; 10/236—N.Y. Giants, Ray Rhodes, WR, Tulsa; 15/365—Houston, Billy (White Shoes) Johnson, WR, Widener; 15/376—Green Bay, Dave Wannstedt, T, Pittsburgh.

1975

FIRST ROUND—NFL

No. Team	Player selected	Pos.	College
1. Atlanta	Steve Bartkowski	QB	California
2. Dallas	**Randy White**	DE/LB	Maryland
3. Baltimore	Ken Huff	G	North Carolina
4. Chicago	**Walter Payton**	RB	Jackson State
5. Cleveland	Mack Mitchell	DE	Houston
6. Houston	Robert Brazile	LB	Jackson State

No. Team	Player selected	Pos.	College
7. New Orleans	Larry Burton	WR	Purdue
8. San Diego	Gary Johnson	DT	Grambling
9. Los Angeles	Mike Fanning	DT	Notre Dame
10. San Francisco	Jimmy Webb	DT	Mississippi State
11. Los Angeles	Dennis Harrah	T	Miami
12. New Orleans	Kurt Schumacher	T	Ohio State
13. Detroit	Lynn Boden	G	South Dakota St.
14. Cincinnati	Glenn Cameron	LB	Florida
15. Houston	Don Hardeman	RB	Texas A&I
16. New England	Russ Francis	TE	Oregon
17. Denver	Louis Wright	DB	San Jose State
18. Dallas	Thomas Henderson	LB	Langston
19. Buffalo	Tom Ruud	LB	Nebraska
20. Los Angeles	Doug France	T	Ohio State
21. St. Louis	Tim Gray	DB	Texas A&M
22. San Diego	Mike Williams	DB	Louisiana State
23. Miami	Darryl Carlton	T	Tampa
24. Oakland	Neal Colzie	DB	Ohio State
25. Minnesota	Mark Mullaney	DE	Colorado State
26. Pittsburgh	Dave Brown	DB	Michigan

Teams not selecting in first round: Green Bay, Kansas City, N.Y. Giants, N.Y. Jets, Philadelphia, Washington.
Total number of picks in draft: 442.

OTHER NOTEWORTHY PICKS

Round/Overall—Team, Player selected, Pos., College
4/95—Denver, Rick Upchurch, WR, Minnesota; 5/116—New England, Steve Grogan, QB, Kansas State; 7/176—Los Angeles, Pat Haden, QB, USC.

1976

FIRST ROUND—NFL

No. Team	Player selected	Pos.	College
1. Tampa Bay	**Lee Roy Selmon**	DE	Oklahoma
2. Seattle	Steve Niehaus	DT	Notre Dame
3. New Orleans	Chuck Muncie	RB	California
4. San Diego	Joe Washington	RB	Oklahoma
5. New England	**Mike Haynes**	DB	Arizona State
6. N.Y. Jets	Richard Todd	QB	Alabama
7. Cleveland	Mike Pruitt	RB	Purdue
8. Chicago	Dennis Lick	T	Wisconsin
9. Atlanta	Bubba Bean	RB	Texas A&M
10. Detroit	James Hunter	DB	Grambling
11. Cincinnati	Billy Brooks	WR	Oklahoma
12. New England	Pete Brock	C	Colorado
13. N.Y. Giants	Troy Archer	DE	Colorado
14. Kansas City	Rod Walters	G	Iowa
15. Denver	Tom Glassic	G	Virginia
16. Detroit	Lawrence Gaines	RB	Wyoming
17. Miami	Larry Gordon	LB	Arizona State
18. Buffalo	Mario Clark	DB	Oregon
19. Miami	Kim Bokamper	LB	San Jose State
20. Baltimore	Ken Novak	DT	Purdue
21. New England	Tim Fox	DB	Ohio State
22. St. Louis	Mike Dawson	DT	Arizona
23. Green Bay	Mark Koncar	T	Colorado
24. Cincinnati	*Archie Griffin*	RB	Ohio State
25. Minnesota	James White	DT	Oklahoma State
26. Los Angeles	Kevin McLain	LB	Colorado State
27. Dallas	Aaron Kyle	DB	Wyoming
28. Pittsburgh	Bennie Cunningham	TE	Clemson

Teams not selecting in first round: Houston, Oakland, Philadelphia, San Francisco, Washington.
Total number of picks in draft: 487.

OTHER NOTEWORTHY PICKS

Round/Overall—Team, Player selected, Pos., College
2/42—San Francisco, Randy Cross, C, UCLA; 3/86—Los Angeles, **Jackie Slater**, G, Jackson State; 4/105—N.Y. Giants, **Harry Carson**, LB, South Carolina State; 4/117—Houston, **Steve Largent**, WR, Tulsa; 14/393—Washington, Quinn Buckner, DB, Indiana.

1977

FIRST ROUND—NFL

No.	Team	Player selected	Pos.	College
1.	Tampa Bay	Ricky Bell	RB	USC
2.	Dallas	*Tony Dorsett*	RB	Pittsburgh
3.	Cincinnati	Eddie Edwards	DT	Miami,
4.	N.Y. Jets	Marvin Powell	T	USC
5.	N.Y. Giants	Gary Jeter	DT	USC
6.	Atlanta	Wilson Faumuina	T	Kentucky
7.	New Orleans	Joe Campbell	DE	Maryland
8.	Cincinnati	Wilson Whitley	DT	Houston
9.	Green Bay	Mike Butler	DE	Kansas
10.	Kansas City	Gary Green	DB	Baylor
11.	Houston	Morris Towns	T	Missouri
12.	Buffalo	Phil Dokes	DT	Oklahoma State
13.	Miami	A.J. Duhe	DT	Louisiana State
14.	Seattle	Steve August	G	Tulsa
15.	Chicago	Ted Albrecht	T	California
16.	New England	Raymond Clayborn	DB	Texas
17.	Cleveland	Robert Jackson	LB	Texas A&M
18.	Denver	Steve Schindler	G	Boston College
19.	St. Louis	Steve Pisarkiewicz	QB	Missouri
20.	Atlanta	Wilson Faumina	DT	San Jose State
21.	Pittsburgh	Robin Cole	LB	New Mexico
22.	Cincinnati	Mike Cobb	TE	Michigan State
23.	Los Angeles	Bob Brudzinski	LB	Ohio State
24.	San Diego	Bob Rush	C	Memphis State
25.	New England	Stanley Morgan	WR	Tennessee
26.	Baltimore	Randy Burke	WR	Kentucky
27.	Minnesota	Tommy Kramer	QB	Rice
28.	Green Bay	Ezra Johnson	DE	Morris Brown

Teams not selecting in first round: Detroit, Oakland, Philadelphia, San Francisco, Washington.
Total number of picks in draft: 335.

OTHER NOTEWORTHY PICKS

Round/Overall—Team, Player selected, Pos., College
2/31—Los Angeles, Nolan Cromwell, DB, Kansas; 4/91—Los Angeles, Vince Ferragamo, QB, Nebraska; 6/140—Chicago, Vince Evans, QB, USC; 6/144—N.Y. Jets, Joe Klecko, DT, Temple; 6/154—Philadelphia, Wilbert Montgomery, RB, Abilene Christian; 10/275—Dallas, Steve DeBerg, QB, San Jose State; 11/295—San Francisco, Brian Billick, TE, Brigham Young.

1978

FIRST ROUND—NFL

No.	Team	Player selected	Pos.	College
1.	Houston	*Earl Campbell*	RB	Texas
2.	Kansas City	Art Still	DE	Kentucky
3.	New Orleans	Wes Chandler	WR	Florida
4.	N.Y. Jets	Chris Ward	T	Ohio State
5.	Buffalo	Terry Miller	RB	Oklahoma State
6.	Green Bay	James Lofton	WR	Stanford
7.	San Francisco	Ken MacAfee	TE	Notre Dame
8.	Cincinnati	Ross Browner	DE	Notre Dame
9.	Seattle	Keith Simpson	DB	Memphis State
10.	N.Y. Giants	Gordon King	T	Stanford
11.	Detroit	Luther Bradley	DB	Notre Dame
12.	Cleveland	Clay Matthews	LB	USC
13.	Atlanta	Mike Kenn	T	Michigan
14.	San Diego	John Jefferson	WR	Arizona State
15.	St. Louis	Steve Little	K	Arkansas
16.	Cincinnati	Blair Bush	C	Washington
17.	Tampa Bay	Doug Williams	QB	Grambling
18.	New England	Bob Cryder	G	Alabama
19.	St. Louis	Ken Greene	DB	Washington State
20.	Los Angeles	Elvis Peacock	RB	Oklahoma
21.	Minnesota	Randy Holloway	DE	Pittsburgh
22.	Pittsburgh	Ron Johnson	DB	Eastern Michigan

No.	Team	Player selected	Pos.	College
23.	Cleveland	**Ozzie Newsome**	WR	Alabama
24.	San Francisco	Dan Bunz	LB	Long Beach State
25.	Baltimore	Reese McCall	TE	Auburn
26.	Green Bay	John Anderson	LB	Michigan
27.	Denver	Don Latimer	DT	Miami
28.	Dallas	Larry Bethea	DE	Michigan State

Teams not selecting in first round: Chicago, Miami, Oakland, Philadelphia, Washington.
Total number of picks in draft: 334.

OTHER NOTEWORTHY PICKS

Round/Overall—Team, Player selected, Pos., College
2/56—Dallas, Todd Christensen, RB, Brigham Young; 8/206—Detroit, Jim Breech, K, California; 8/215—New England, Mosi Tatupu, RB, USC.

1979

FIRST ROUND—NFL

No.	Team	Player selected	Pos.	College
1.	Buffalo	Tom Cousineau	LB	Ohio State
2.	Kansas City	Mike Bell	DE	Colorado State
3.	Cincinnati	Jack Thompson	QB	Washington State
4.	Chicago	**Dan Hampton**	DT	Arkansas
5.	Buffalo	Jerry Butler	WR	Clemson
6.	Baltimore	Barry Krauss	LB	Alabama
7.	N.Y. Giants	Phil Simms	QB	Morehead State
8.	St. Louis	Ottis Anderson	RB	Miami
9.	Chicago	Al Harris	DE	Arizona State
10.	Detroit	Keith Dorney	T	Penn State
11.	New Orleans	Russell Erxleben	K/P	Texas
12.	Cincinnati	Charles Alexander	RB	Louisiana State
13.	San Diego	**Kellen Winslow**	TE	Missouri
14.	N.Y. Jets	Marty Lyons	DE	Alabama
15.	Green Bay	Eddie Lee Ivery	RB	Georgia Tech
16.	Minnesota	Ted Brown	RB	N.C. State
17.	Atlanta	Don Smith	DE	Miami
18.	Seattle	Manu Tuiasosopo	DT	UCLA
19.	Los Angeles	George Andrews	LB	Nebraska
20.	Cleveland	Willis Adams	WR	Houston
21.	Philadelphia	Jerry Robinson	LB	UCLA
22.	Denver	Kelvin Clark	T	Nebraska
23.	Kansas City	Steve Fuller	QB	Clemson
24.	Miami	Jon Giesler	T	Michigan
25.	New England	Rick Sanford	DB	South Carolina
26.	Los Angeles	Kent Hill	T	Georgia Tech
27.	Dallas	Robert Shaw	C	Tennessee
28.	Pittsburgh	Greg Hawthorne	RB	Baylor

Teams not selecting in first round: Houston, Oakland, San Francisco, Tampa Bay, Washington.
Total number of picks in draft: 330.

OTHER NOTEWORTHY PICKS

Round/Overall—Team, Player selected, Pos., College
2/41—N.Y. Jets, Mark Gastineau, DE, East Central Oklahoma; 2/51—Buffalo, Jim Haslett, LB, Indiana, Pa.; 2/52—New England, Bob Golic, LB, Notre Dame; 3/82—San Francisco, **Joe Montana**, QB, Notre Dame; 6/165—Pittsburgh, Matt Bahr, K, Penn State; 7/173—St. Louis, Kirk Gibson, WR, Michigan State; 10/249—San Francisco, Dwight Clark, WR, Clemson, 12/328—Los Angeles, Drew Hill, WR, Georgia Tech.

1980

FIRST ROUND—NFL

No.	Team	Player selected	Pos.	College
1.	Detroit	*Billy Sims*	RB	Oklahoma
2.	N.Y. Jets	Johnny (Lam) Jones	WR	Texas
3.	Cincinnati	**Anthony Munoz**	T	USC
4.	Green Bay	Bruce Clark	DE	Penn State
5.	Baltimore	Curtis Dickey	RB	Texas A&M

No. Team	Player selected	Pos.	College
6. St. Louis	Curtis Greer	DE	Michigan
7. Atlanta	Junior Miller	TE	Nebraska
8. N.Y. Giants	Mark Haynes	DB	Colorado
9. Minnesota	Doug Martin	DT	Washington
10. Seattle	Jacob Green	DE	Texas A&M
11. Kansas City	Brad Budde	G	USC
12. New Orleans	Stan Brock	T	Colorado
13. San Francisco	Earl Cooper	RB	Rice
14. New England	Roland James	DB	Tennessee
15. Oakland	Marc Wilson	QB	Brigham Young
16. Buffalo	Jim Ritcher	C	N.C. State
17. Los Angeles	Johnnie Johnson	DB	Texas
18. Washington	Art Monk	WR	Syracuse
19. Chicago	Otis Wilson	LB	Louisville
20. San Francisco	Jim Stuckey	DT	Clemson
21. Miami	Don McNeal	DB	Alabama
22. Tampa Bay	Ray Snell	G	Wisconsin
23. Philadelphia	Roynell Young	DB	Alcorn State
24. Baltimore	Derrick Hatchett	DB	Texas
25. New England	Vagas Ferguson	RB	Notre Dame
26. Green Bay	George Cumby	LB	Oklahoma
27. Cleveland	*Charles White*	RB	USC
28. Pittsburgh	Mark Malone	QB	Arizona State

Teams not selecting in first round: Dallas, Denver, Houston, San Diego.

Total number of picks in draft: 333.

OTHER NOTEWORTHY PICKS

Round/Overall—Team, Player selected, Pos., College
2/29—Buffalo, Joe Cribbs, RB, Auburn; 2/43—Oakland, Matt Millen, LB, Penn State; 2/48—Miami, **Dwight Stephenson**, C, Alabama; 3/73—New England, Steve McMichael, DT, Texas; 7/166—Detroit, Eddie Murray, K, Tulane.

1981

FIRST ROUND—NFL

No. Team	Player selected	Pos.	College
1. New Orleans	*George Rogers*	RB	South Carolina
2. N.Y. Giants	**Lawrence Taylor**	LB	North Carolina
3. N.Y. Jets	Freeman McNeil	RB	UCLA
4. Seattle	Kenny Easley	DB	UCLA
5. St. Louis	E.J. Junior	LB	Alabama
6. Green Bay	Rich Campbell	QB	California
7. Tampa Bay	Hugh Green	LB	Pittsburgh
8. San Francisco	**Ronnie Lott**	DB	USC
9. Los Angeles	Mel Owens	LB	Michigan
10. Cincinnati	David Verser	WR	Kansas
11. Chicago	Keith Van Horne	T	USC
12. Baltimore	Randy McMillan	RB	Pittsburgh
13. Miami	David Overstreet	RB	Oklahoma
14. Kansas City	Willie Scott	TE	South Carolina
15. Denver	Dennis Smith	DB	USC
16. Detroit	Mark Nichols	WR	San Jose State
17. Pittsburgh	Keith Gary	DE	Oklahoma
18. Baltimore	Donnell Thompson	DT	North Carolina
19. New England	Brian Holloway	T	Stanford
20. Washington	Mark May	T	Pittsburgh
21. Oakland	Ted Watts	DB	Texas Tech
22. Cleveland	Hanford Dixon	DB	Southern Miss
23. Oakland	Curt Marsh	T	Washington
24. San Diego	James Brooks	RB	Auburn
25. Atlanta	Bobby Butler	DB	Florida State
26. Dallas	Howard Richards	T	Missouri
27. Philadelphia	Leonard Mitchell	DE	Houston
28. Buffalo	Booker Moore	RB	Penn State

Teams not selecting in first round: Houston, Minnesota.
Total number of picks in draft: 332.

OTHER NOTEWORTHY PICKS

Round/Overall—Team, Player selected, Pos., College
2/34—Tampa Bay, James Wilder, RB, Missouri; 2/37—Cincinnati, Cris Collinsworth, WR, Florida; 2/38—Chicago, **Mike Singletary**,

LB, Baylor; 2/48—Oakland, **Howie Long**, DT, Villanova; 3/69—Washington, Russ Grimm, C, Pittsburgh; 5/119—Washington, Dexter Manley, DE, Oklahoma State; 7/177—Chicago, Jeff Fisher, DB, USC; 8/210—Minnesota, Wade Wilson, QB, East Texas State; 8/213—N.Y. Jets, J.C. Watts, DB, Oklahoma; Supplemental—New Orleans, Dave Wilson, QB, Illinois.

1982

FIRST ROUND—NFL

No. Team	Player selected	Pos.	College
1. New England	Ken Sims	DT	Texas
2. Baltimore	Johnie Cooks	LB	Mississippi State
3. Cleveland	Chip Banks	LB	USC
4. Baltimore	Art Schlichter	QB	Ohio State
5. Chicago	Jim McMahon	QB	Brigham Young
6. Seattle	Jeff Bryant	DE	Clemson
7. Minnesota	Darrin Nelson	RB	Stanford
8. Houston	**Mike Munchak**	G	Penn State
9. Atlanta	Gerald Riggs	RB	Arizona State
10. Oakland	*Marcus Allen*	RB	USC
11. Kansas City	Anthony Hancock	WR	Tennessee
12. Pittsburgh	Walter Abercrombie	RB	Baylor
13. New Orleans	Lindsay Scott	WR	Georgia
14. Los Angeles	Barry Redden	RB	Richmond
15. Detroit	Jimmy Williams	LB	Nebraska
16. St. Louis	Luis Sharpe	T	UCLA
17. Tampa Bay	Sean Farrell	G	Penn State
18. N.Y. Giants	Butch Woolfolk	RB	Michigan
19. Buffalo	Perry Tuttle	WR	Clemson
20. Philadelphia	Mike Quick	WR	N.C. State
21. Denver	Gerald Willhite	RB	San Jose State
22. Green Bay	Ron Hallstrom	G	Iowa
23. N.Y. Jets	Bob Crable	LB	Notre Dame
24. Miami	Roy Foster	G	USC
25. Dallas	Rod Hill	DB	Kentucky State
26. Cincinnati	Glen Collins	DE	Mississippi State
27. New England	Lester Williams	DT	Miami

Note: Oakland franchise moved to Los Angeles (but after draft); teams not selecting in first round: San Diego, San Francisco, Washington.

Total number of picks in draft: 334.

OTHER NOTEWORTHY PICKS

Round/Overall—Team, Player selected, Pos., College
2/41—New England, Andre Tippett, LB, Iowa; 2/45—N.Y. Giants, Joe Morris, RB, Syracuse; 2/52—Miami, Mark Duper, WR, Northwestern (La.) State; 4/86—New Orleans, Morten Andersen, K, Michigan State; 5/131—Denver, Sammy Winder, RB, Southern Mississippi; 7/171—Buffalo, Gary Anderson, K, Syracuse.

1983

FIRST ROUND—NFL

No. Team	Player selected	Pos.	College
1. Baltimore	**John Elway**	QB	Stanford
2. L.A. Rams	**Eric Dickerson**	RB	SMU
3. Seattle	Curt Warner	RB	Penn State
4. Denver	Chris Hinton	G	Northwestern
5. San Diego	Billy Ray Smith	LB	Arkansas
6. Chicago	Jimbo Covert	T	Pittsburgh
7. Kansas City	Todd Blackledge	QB	Penn State
8. Philadelphia	Michael Haddix	RB	Mississippi State
9. Houston	Bruce Matthews	G	USC
10. N.Y. Giants	Terry Kinard	DB	Clemson
11. Green Bay	Tim Lewis	DB	Pittsburgh
12. Buffalo	Tony Hunter	TE	Notre Dame
13. Detroit	James Jones	RB	Florida
14. Buffalo	**Jim Kelly**	QB	Miami
15. New England	Tony Eason	QB	Illinois
16. Atlanta	Mike Pitts	DE	Alabama

No.	Team	Player selected	Pos.	College
17.	St. Louis	Leonard Smith	DB	McNeese State
18.	Chicago	Willie Gault	WR	Tennessee
19.	Minnesota	Joey Browner	DB	USC
20.	San Diego	Gary Anderson	WR	Arkansas
21.	Pittsburgh	Gabriel Rivera	DT	Texas Tech
22.	San Diego	Gill Byrd	DB	San Jose State
23.	Dallas	Jim Jeffcoat	DE	Arizona State
24.	N.Y. Jets	Ken O'Brien	QB	UC Davis
25.	Cincinnati	Dave Rimington	C	Nebraska
26.	L.A. Raiders	Don Mosebar	T	USC
27.	Miami	**Dan Marino**	QB	Pittsburgh
28.	Washington	Darrell Green	DB	Texas A&I

Teams not selecting in first round: Cleveland, New Orleans, San Francisco, Tampa Bay.
Total number of picks in draft: 335.

OTHER NOTEWORTHY PICKS

Round/Overall—Team, Player selected, Pos., College
2/32—L.A. Rams, Henry Ellard, WR, Fresno State; 2/37—N.Y. Giants, Leonard Marshall, DT, Louisiana State; 2/49—San Francisco, Roger Craig, RB, Nebraska; 3/84—Washington, Charles Mann, DE, Nevada; 6/167—Miami, Reggie Roby, P, Iowa; 8/203—Chicago, Richard Dent, DE, Tennessee State; 8/223—Miami, Mark Clayton, WR, Louisville; 12/334—Miami, Anthony Carter, WR, Michigan.

1984

FIRST ROUND—NFL

No.	Team	Player selected	Pos.	College
1.	New England	Irving Fryar	WR	Nebraska
2.	Houston	Dean Steinkuhler	T	Nebraska
3.	N.Y. Giants	Carl Banks	LB	Michigan State
4.	Philadelphia	Kenny Jackson	WR	Penn State
5.	Kansas City	Bill Maas	DT	Pittsburgh
6.	San Diego	Mossy Cade	DB	Texas
7.	Cincinnati	Ricky Hunley	LB	Arizona
8.	Indianapolis	Leonard Coleman	DB	Vanderbilt
9.	Atlanta	Rick Bryan	DT	Oklahoma
10.	N.Y. Jets	Russell Carter	DB	SMU
11.	Chicago	Wilber Marshall	LB	Florida
12.	Green Bay	Alphonso Carreker	DE	Florida State
13.	Minnesota	Keith Millard	DE	Washington State
14.	Miami	Jackie Shipp	LB	Oklahoma
15.	N.Y. Jets	Ron Faurot	DE	Arkansas
16.	Cincinnati	Pete Koch	DE	Maryland
17.	St. Louis	Clyde Duncan	WR	Tennessee
18.	Cleveland	Don Rogers	DB	UCLA
19.	Indianapolis	Ron Solt	G	Maryland
20.	Detroit	David Lewis	TE	California
21.	Kansas City	John Alt	T	Iowa
22.	Seattle	Terry Taylor	DB	Southern Illinois
23.	Pittsburgh	Louis Lipps	WR	Southern Miss
24.	San Francisco	Todd Shell	LB	Brigham Young
25.	Dallas	Billy Cannon Jr.	LB	Texas A&M
26.	Buffalo	Greg Bell	RB	Notre Dame
27.	N.Y. Giants	Bill Roberts	T	Ohio State
28.	Cincinnati	Brian Blados	T	North Carolina

Teams not selecting in first round: Denver, L.A. Raiders, L.A. Rams, New Orleans, Tampa Bay, Washington.
Total number of picks in draft: 336.

OTHER NOTEWORTHY PICKS

Round/Overall—Team, Player selected, Pos., College
2/38—Cincinnati, Boomer Esiason, QB, Maryland; 3/59—N.Y. Giants, Jeff Hostetler, QB, West Virginia; 10/280—Cleveland, Earnest Byner, RB, East Carolina.

FIRST ROUND—NFL SUPPLEMENTAL

In 1984, the NFL held a three-round supplemental draft for the contract rights to USFL and CFL players.

No.	Team	Player selected	Pos.	College
1.	Tampa Bay	**Steve Young**	QB	Brigham Young
2.	Houston	*Mike Rozier*	RB	Nebraska

No.	Team	Player selected	Pos.	College
3.	N.Y. Giants	Gary Zimmerman	G	Oregon
4.	Philadelphia	**Reggie White**	DE	Tennessee
5.	Kansas City	Mark Adickes	T	Baylor
6.	San Diego	Lee Williams	DE	Bethune-Cookman
7.	Cincinnati	Wayne Peace	QB	Florida
8.	Indianapolis	Paul Bergmann	TE	UCLA
9.	Atlanta	Joey Jones	WR	Alabama
10.	N.Y. Jets	Ken Hobart	QB	Idaho
11.	Cleveland	Kevin Mack	RB	Clemson
12.	Green Bay	Buford Jordan	RB	McNeese State
13.	Minnesota	Allanda Smith	DB	Texas Christian
14.	Buffalo	Dwight Drane	DB	Oklahoma
15.	New Orleans	Vaughan Johnson	LB	N.C. State
16.	New England	Ricky Sanders	WR/PR	SW Texas State
17.	St. Louis	Mike Ruether	C	Texas
18.	Cleveland	Mike Johnson	LB	Virginia Tech
19.	Denver	Freddie Gilbert	DE	Georgia
20.	Detroit	Alphonso Williams	WR	Nevada
21.	L.A. Rams	William Fuller	DE	North Carolina
22.	Seattle	Gordon Hudson	TE	Brigham Young
23.	Pittsburgh	Duane Gunn	WR	Indiana
24.	San Francisco	Derrick Crawford	WR	Memphis State
25.	Dallas	Todd Fowler	TE	Stephen F. Austin
26.	Miami	Danny Knight	WR	Mississippi State
27.	Washington	Tony Zendejas	K	Nevada
28.	L.A. Raiders	Chris Woods	WR	Auburn

Team not selecting in first round: Chicago.
Total number of picks in supplemental draft: 84.

1985

FIRST ROUND—NFL

No.	Team	Player selected	Pos.	College
1.	Buffalo	Bruce Smith	DE	Virginia Tech
2.	Atlanta	Bill Fralic	T	Pittsburgh
3.	Houston	Ray Childress	DE	Texas A&M
4.	Minnesota	Chris Doleman	LB	Pittsburgh
5.	Indianapolis	Duane Bickett	LB	USC
6.	Detroit	Lomas Brown	T	Florida
7.	Green Bay	Ken Ruettgers	T	USC
8.	Tampa Bay	Ron Holmes	DE	Washington
9.	Philadelphia	Kevin Allen	T	Indiana
10.	N.Y. Jets	Al Toon	WR	Wisconsin
11.	Houston	Richard Johnson	DB	Wisconsin
12.	San Diego	Jim Lachey	G	Ohio State
13.	Cincinnati	Eddie Brown	WR	Miami
14.	Buffalo	Derrick Burroughs	DB	Memphis State
15.	Kansas City	Ethan Horton	RB	North Carolina
16.	San Francisco	Jerry Rice	WR	Miss Valley
17.	Dallas	Kevin Brooks	DE	Michigan
18.	St. Louis	Freddie Joe Nunn	LB	Mississippi
19.	N.Y. Giants	George Adams	RB	Kentucky
20.	Pittsburgh	Darryl Sims	DE	Wisconsin
21.	L.A. Rams	Jerry Gray	DB	Texas
22.	Chicago	William Perry	DT	Clemson
23.	L.A. Raiders	Jessie Hester	WR	Florida State
24.	New Orleans	Alvin Toles	LB	Tennessee
25.	Cincinnati	Emanuel King	LB	Alabama
26.	Denver	Steve Sewell	RB	Oklahoma
27.	Miami	Lorenzo Hampton	RB	Florida
28.	New England	Trevor Matich	C	Brigham Young

Teams not selecting in first round: Cleveland, Seattle, Washington.
Total number of picks in draft: 336.

OTHER NOTEWORTHY PICKS

Round/Overall—Team, Player selected, Pos., College
2/37—Philadelphia, Randall Cunningham, QB/P, UNLV; 3/68—New Orleans, Jack Del Rio, LB, USC; 4/86—Buffalo, Andre Reed, WR, Kutztown; 4/100—N.Y. Giants, Mark Bavaro, TE, Notre Dame; 5/114—Dallas, *Herschel Walker*, RB, Georgia; 6/158—St. Louis, Jay Novacek, TE, Wyoming; 11/285—L.A. Rams, *Doug Flutie*, QB, Boston College; Supplemental—Cleveland, Bernie Kosar, QB, Miami.

1986
FIRST ROUND—NFL

No.	Team	Player selected	Pos.	College
1.	Tampa Bay	*Bo Jackson*	RB	Auburn
2.	Atlanta	Tony Casillas	NT	Oklahoma
3.	Houston	Jim Everett	QB	Purdue
4.	Indianapolis	Jon Hand	DE	Alabama
5.	St. Louis	Anthony Bell	LB	Michigan State
6.	New Orleans	Jim Dombrowski	T	Virginia
7.	Kansas City	Brian Jozwiak	T	West Virginia
8.	San Diego	Leslie O'Neal	DE	Oklahoma State
9.	Pittsburgh	John Rienstra	G	Temple
10.	Philadelphia	Keith Byars	RB	Ohio State
11.	Cincinnati	Joe Kelly	LB	Washington
12.	Detroit	Chuck Long	QB	Iowa
13.	San Diego	James Fitzpatrick	T	USC
14.	Minnesota	Gerald Robinson	DE	Auburn
15.	Seattle	John L. Williams	RB	Florida
16.	Buffalo	Ronnie Harmon	RB	Iowa
17.	Atlanta	Tim Green	LB	Syracuse
18.	Dallas	Mike Sherrard	WR	UCLA
19.	N.Y. Giants	Eric Dorsey	DE	Notre Dame
20.	Buffalo	Will Wolford	T	Vanderbilt
21.	Cincinnati	Tim McGee	WR	Tennessee
22.	N.Y. Jets	Mike Haight	T	Iowa
23.	L.A. Rams	Mike Schad	T	Queens (Canada)
24.	L.A. Raiders	Bob Buczkowski	DE	Pittsburgh
25.	Tampa Bay	Roderick Jones	DB	SMU
26.	New England	Reggie Dupard	RB	SMU
27.	Chicago	Neal Anderson	RB	Florida

Teams not selecting in first round: Cleveland, Denver, Green Bay, Miami, San Francisco, Washington.
Total number of picks in draft: 333.

OTHER NOTEWORTHY PICKS

Round/Overall—Team, Player selected, Pos., College
2/51—N.Y. Giants, Pepper Johnson, LB, Ohio State; 3/56—San Francisco, Tom Rathman, RB, Nebraska; 3/60—New Orleans, Pat Swilling, LB, Georgia Tech; 3/76—San Francisco, John Taylor, WR, Delaware State; 4/96—San Francisco, Charles Haley, LB, James Madison; 6/146—Washington, Mark Rypien, QB, Washington State; 9/233—Philadelphia, Clyde Simmons, DE, Western Carolina; 12/327—L.A. Rams, Marcus Dupree, RB, Oklahoma.

1987
FIRST ROUND—NFL

No.	Team	Player selected	Pos.	College
1.	Tampa Bay	*Vinny Testaverde*	QB	Miami
2.	Indianapolis	Cornelius Bennett	LB	Alabama
3.	Houston	Alonzo Highsmith	RB	Miami
4.	Green Bay	Brent Fullwood	RB	Auburn
5.	Cleveland	Mike Junkin	LB	Duke
6.	St. Louis	Kelly Stouffer	QB	Colorado State
7.	Detroit	Reggie Rogers	DE	Washington
8.	Buffalo	Shane Conlan	LB	Penn State
9.	Philadelphia	Jerome Brown	DT	Miami
10.	Pittsburgh	Rod Woodson	DB	Purdue
11.	New Orleans	Shawn Knight	DT	Brigham Young
12.	Dallas	Danny Noonan	DT	Nebraska
13.	Atlanta	Chris Miller	QB	Oregon
14.	Minnesota	D.J. Dozier	RB	Penn State
15.	L.A. Raiders	John Clay	T	Missouri
16.	Miami	John Bosa	DE	Boston College
17.	Cincinnati	Jason Buck	DE	Brigham Young
18.	Seattle	Tony Woods	LB	Pittsburgh
19.	Kansas City	Paul Palmer	RB	Temple
20.	Houston	Haywood Jeffires	WR	N.C. State
21.	N.Y. Jets	Roger Vick	RB	Texas A&M
22.	San Francisco	Harris Barton	T	North Carolina
23.	New England	Bruce Armstrong	T	Louisville
24.	San Diego	Rod Bernstine	TE	Texas A&M
25.	San Francisco	Terrence Flagler	RB	Clemson

No.	Team	Player selected	Pos.	College
26.	Chicago	Jim Harbaugh	QB	Michigan
27.	Denver	Ricky Nattiel	WR	Florida
28.	N.Y. Giants	Mark Ingram	WR	Michigan State

Teams not selecting in first round: L.A. Rams, Washington.
Total number of picks in draft: 335.

OTHER NOTEWORTHY PICKS

Round/Overall—Team, Player selected, Pos., College
2/53—San Diego, Louis Brock, DB, USC; 4/98—New England, Rich Gannon, QB, Delaware; 4/110—L.A. Raiders, Steve Beuerlein, QB, Notre Dame; 5/117—Washington, Timmy Smith, RB, Texas Tech; 5/122—Pittsburgh, Hardy Nickerson, LB, California; 7/183—L.A. Raiders, Bo Jackson, RB, Auburn; 10/255—Green Bay, Don Majkowski, QB, Virginia; 10/261—Pittsburgh, Merril Hoge, RB, Idaho State; 12/313—Tampa Bay, Mike Shula, QB, Alabama; Supplemental—Seattle, Brian Bosworth, LB, Oklahoma; Philadelphia, Cris Carter, WR, Ohio State.

1988
FIRST ROUND—NFL

No.	Team	Player selected	Pos.	College
1.	Atlanta	Aundray Bruce	LB	Auburn
2.	Kansas City	Neil Smith	DE	Nebraska
3.	Detroit	Bennie Blades	DB	Miami
4.	Tampa Bay	Paul Gruber	T	Wisconsin
5.	Cincinnati	Rickey Dixon	DB	Oklahoma
6.	L.A. Raiders	*Tim Brown*	WR	Notre Dame
7.	Green Bay	Sterling Sharpe	WR	South Carolina
8.	N.Y. Jets	Dave Cadigan	T	USC
9.	L.A. Raiders	Terry McDaniel	DB	Tennessee
10.	N.Y. Giants	Eric Moore	T	Indiana
11.	Dallas	Michael Irvin	WR	Miami
12.	Phoenix	Ken Harvey	LB	California
13.	Philadelphia	Keith Jackson	TE	Oklahoma
14.	L.A. Rams	Gaston Green	RB	UCLA
15.	San Diego	Anthony Miller	WR	Tennessee
16.	Miami	Eric Kumerow	DE	Ohio State
17.	New England	John Stephens	RB	NW (La.) State
18.	Pittsburgh	Aaron Jones	DE	Eastern Kentucky
19.	Minnesota	Randall McDaniel	G	Arizona State
20.	L.A. Rams	Aaron Cox	WR	Arizona State
21.	Cleveland	Clifford Charlton	LB	Florida
22.	Houston	Lorenzo White	RB	Michigan State
23.	Chicago	Brad Muster	RB	Stanford
24.	New Orleans	Craig Heyward	RB	Pittsburgh
25.	L.A. Raiders	Scott Davis	DE	Illinois
26.	Denver	Ted Gregory	NT	Syracuse
27.	Chicago	Wendell Davis	WR	Louisiana State

Teams not selecting in first round: Buffalo, Indianapolis, San Francisco, Seattle, Washington.
Total number of picks in draft: 333.

OTHER NOTEWORTHY PICKS

Round/Overall—Team, Player selected, Pos., College
2/29—Detroit, Chris Spielman, LB, Ohio State; 2/30—Philadelphia, Eric Allen, DB, Arizona State; 2/36—N.Y. Giants, John (Jumbo) Elliott, T, Michigan; 2/40—Buffalo, Thurman Thomas, RB, Oklahoma State; 2/41—Dallas, Ken Norton Jr., LB, UCLA; 2/44—Pittsburgh, Dermontti Dawson, G, Kentucky; 2/46—L.A. Rams, Willie (Flipper) Anderson, WR, UCLA; 3/76—Indianapolis, Chris Chandler, QB, Washington; 3/80—San Francisco, Bill Romanowski, LB, Boston College.

1989
FIRST ROUND—NFL

No.	Team	Player selected	Pos.	College
1.	Dallas	**Troy Aikman**	QB	UCLA
2.	Green Bay	Tony Mandarich	T	Michigan State
3.	Detroit	*Barry Sanders*	RB	Oklahoma State

No.	Team	Player selected	Pos.	College
4.	Kansas City	Derrick Thomas	LB	Alabama
5.	Atlanta	Deion Sanders	CB	Florida State
6.	Tampa Bay	Broderick Thomas	LB	Nebraska
7.	Pittsburgh	Tim Worley	RB	Georgia
8.	San Diego	Burt Grossman	DE	Pittsburgh
9.	Miami	Sammie Smith	RB	Florida State
10.	Phoenix	Eric Hill	LB	Louisiana State
11.	Chicago	Donnell Woolford	CB	Clemson
12.	Chicago	Trace Armstrong	DE	Florida
13.	Cleveland	Eric Metcalf	RB	Texas
14.	N.Y. Jets	Jeff Lageman	LB	Virginia
15.	Seattle	Andy Heck	T	Notre Dame
16.	New England	Hart Lee Dykes	WR	Oklahoma State
17.	Phoenix	Joe Wolf	G	Boston College
18.	N.Y. Giants	Brian Williams	G	Minnesota
19.	New Orleans	Wayne Martin	DE	Arkansas
20.	Denver	Steve Atwater	S	Arkansas
21.	L.A. Rams	Bill Hawkins	DE	Miami
22.	Indianapolis	Andre Rison	WR	Michigan State
23.	Houston	David Williams	T	Florida
24.	Pittsburgh	Tom Ricketts	T	Pittsburgh
25.	Miami	Louis Oliver	S	Florida
26.	L.A. Rams	Cleveland Gary	RB	Miami
27.	Atlanta	Shawn Collins	WR	Northern Arizona
28.	San Francisco	Keith DeLong	LB	Tennessee

Teams not selecting in first round: Buffalo, Cincinnati, L.A. Raiders, Minnesota, Philadelphia, Washington.
Total number of picks in draft: 335.

OTHER NOTEWORTHY PICKS

Round/Overall—Team, Player selected, Pos., College
2/34—Pittsburgh, Carnell Lake, DB, UCLA; 2/39—Dallas, Daryl Johnston, RB, Syracuse; 2/56—San Francisco, Wesley Walls, TE, Mississippi; 7/173—Buffalo, Brian Jordan, DB, Richmond; Supplemental—Dallas, Steve Walsh, QB, Miami; Supplemental—Denver, Bobby Humphrey, RB, Alabama; Phoenix, Timm Rosenbach, QB, Washington State.

1990

FIRST ROUND—NFL

No.	Team	Player selected	Pos.	College
1.	Indianapolis	Jeff George	QB	Illinois
2.	N.Y. Jets	Blair Thomas	RB	Penn State
3.	Seattle	Cortez Kennedy	DT	Miami
4.	Tampa Bay	Keith McCants	LB	Alabama
5.	San Diego	Junior Seau	LB	USC
6.	Chicago	Mark Carrier	DB	USC
7.	Detroit	Andre Ware	QB	Houston
8.	New England	Chris Singleton	LB	Arizona
9.	Miami	Richmond Webb	T	Texas A&M
10.	New England	Ray Agnew	DE	N.C. State
11.	L.A. Raiders	Anthony Smith	DE	Arizona
12.	Cincinnati	James Francis	LB	Baylor
13.	Kansas City	Percy Snow	LB	Michigan State
14.	New Orleans	Renaldo Turnbull	DE	West Virginia
15.	Houston	Lamar Lathon	LB	Houston
16.	Buffalo	James Williams	DB	Fresno State
17.	Dallas	Emmitt Smith	RB	Florida
18.	Green Bay	Tony Bennett	LB	Mississippi
19.	Green Bay	Darrell Thompson	RB	Minnesota
20.	Atlanta	Steve Broussard	RB	Washington State
21.	Pittsburgh	Eric Green	TE	Liberty (Va.)
22.	Philadelphia	Ben Smith	DB	Georgia
23.	L.A. Rams	Bern Brostek	C	Washington
24.	N.Y. Giants	Rodney Hampton	RB	Georgia
25.	San Francisco	Dexter Carter	RB	Florida State

Teams not selecting in first round: Cleveland, Denver, Minnesota, Phoenix, Washington.
Total number of picks in draft: 331.

OTHER NOTEWORTHY PICKS

Round/Overall—Team, Player selected, Pos., College
2/48—Green Bay, LeRoy Butler, DB, Florida State; 3/70—Pittsburgh, Neil O'Donnell, QB, Maryland; 5/115—Phoenix, Larry Centers, RB, Stephen F. Austin; 5/130—Washington, Brian Mitchell, RB, Southwestern Louisiana; 7/180—Kansas City, Dave Szott, G, Penn State; 7/192—Denver, Shannon Sharpe, WR, Savannah State; 9/241—Minnesota, Terry Allen, RB, Clemson; 10/265—Buffalo, Mike Lodish, DT, UCLA; 12/329—N.Y. Giants, Matt Stover, K, Louisiana Tech.

1991

FIRST ROUND—NFL

No.	Team	Player selected	Pos.	College
1.	Dallas	Russell Maryland	DL	Miami
2.	Cleveland	Eric Turner	S	UCLA
3.	Atlanta	Bruce Pickens	CB	Nebraska
4.	Denver	Mike Croel	LB	Nebraska
5.	L.A. Rams	Todd Lyght	CB	Notre Dame
6.	Phoenix	Eric Swann	DL	No college
7.	Tampa Bay	Charles McRae	T	Tennessee
8.	Philadelphia	Antone Davis	T	Tennessee
9.	San Diego	Stanley Richard	CB	Texas
10.	Detroit	Herman Moore	WR	Virginia
11.	New England	Pat Harlow	T	USC
12.	Dallas	Alvin Harper	WR	Tennessee
13.	Atlanta	Mike Pritchard	WR	Colorado
14.	New England	Leonard Russell	RB	Arizona State
15.	Pittsburgh	Huey Richardson	DE	Florida
16.	Seattle	Dan McGwire	QB	San Diego State
17.	Washington	Bobby Wilson	DT	Michigan State
18.	Cincinnati	Alfred Williams	LB	Colorado
19.	Green Bay	Vincent Clark	DB	Ohio State
20.	Dallas	Kelvin Pritchett	DT	Mississippi
21.	Kansas City	Harvey Williams	RB	Louisiana State
22.	Chicago	Stan Thomas	T	Texas
23.	Miami	Randal Hill	WR	Miami
24.	L.A. Raiders	Todd Marinovich	QB	USC
25.	San Francisco	Ted Washington	DL	Louisville
26.	Buffalo	Henry Jones	S	Illinois
27.	N.Y. Giants	Jarrod Bunch	FB	Michigan

Teams not selecting in first round: Houston, Indianapolis, Minnesota, New Orleans, N.Y. Jets.
Total number of picks in draft: 334.

OTHER NOTEWORTHY PICKS

Round/Overall—Team, Player selected, Pos., College
2/33—Atlanta, Brett Favre, QB, Southern Mississippi; 2/45—San Francisco, Ricky Watters, RB, Notre Dame; 3/59—Phoenix, Aeneas Williams, DB, Southern; 3/70—Dallas, Erik Williams, T, Central State (Ohio); 3/83—N.Y. Giants, Ed McCaffrey, WR, Stanford; 4/100—L.A. Raiders, Rocket Ismail, WR, Notre Dame; 5/113—Miami, Bryan Cox, LB, Western Illinois; 5/124—New England, Ben Coates, TE, Livingstone; 7/173—Dallas, Leon Lett, DT, Emporia State; 12/326—Washington, Keenan McCardell, WR, UNLV.

1992

FIRST ROUND—NFL

No.	Team	Player selected	Pos.	College
1.	Indianapolis	Steve Emtman	DL	Washington
2.	Indianapolis	Quentin Coryatt	LB	Texas A&M
3.	L.A. Rams	Sean Gilbert	DL	Pittsburgh
4.	Washington	Desmond Howard	WR	Michigan
5.	Green Bay	Terrell Buckley	DB	Florida State
6.	Cincinnati	David Klingler	QB	Houston
7.	Miami	Troy Vincent	DB	Wisconsin
8.	Atlanta	Bob Whitfield	OL	Stanford

No.	Team	Player selected	Pos.	College
9.	Cleveland	Tommy Vardell	FB	Stanford
10.	Seattle	Ray Roberts	OL	Virginia
11.	Pittsburgh	Leon Searcy	T	Miami
12.	Miami	Marco Coleman	LB	Georgia Tech
13.	New England	Eugene Chung	OL	Virginia Tech
14.	N.Y. Giants	Derek Brown	TE	Notre Dame
15.	N.Y. Jets	Johnny Mitchell	TE	Nebraska
16.	L.A. Raiders	Chester McGlockton	DT	Clemson
17.	Dallas	Kevin Smith	DB	Texas A&M
18.	San Francisco	Dana Hall	DB	Washington
19.	Atlanta	Tony Smith	RB	Southern Miss
20.	Kansas City	Dale Carter	DB	Tennessee
21.	New Orleans	Vaughn Dunbar	RB	Indiana
22.	Chicago	Alonzo Spellman	DL	Ohio State
23.	San Diego	Chris Mims	DL	Tennessee
24.	Dallas	Robert Jones	LB	East Carolina
25.	Denver	Tommy Maddox	QB	UCLA
26.	Detroit	Robert Porcher	DL	S. Carolina State
27.	Buffalo	John Fina	OL	Arizona
28.	Cincinnati	Darryl Williams	DB	Miami

Teams not selecting in first round: Houston, Minnesota, Philadelphia, Phoenix, Tampa Bay.
Total number of picks in draft: 336.

OTHER NOTEWORTHY PICKS

Round/Overall—Team, Player selected, Pos., College
2/31—Cincinnati, Carl Pickens, WR, Tennessee; 2/36—Dallas, Jimmy Smith, WR, Jackson State; 2/37—Dallas, Darren Woodson, DB, Arizona State; 2/56—Detroit, Jason Hanson, K, Washington; 3/62—Green Bay, Robert Brooks, WR, South Carolina; 5/132—Tampa Bay, Santana Dotson, DE, Baylor; 6/166—N.Y. Jets, Jeff Blake, QB, East Carolina; 9/227—Minnesota, Brad Johnson, QB, Florida State; 9/230—Green Bay, *Ty Detmer*, QB, Brigham Young; Supplemental—N.Y. Giants, Dave Brown, QB, Duke.

1993
FIRST ROUND—NFL

No.	Team	Player selected	Pos.	College
1.	New England	Drew Bledsoe	QB	Washington State
2.	Seattle	Rick Mirer	QB	Notre Dame
3.	Phoenix	Garrison Hearst	RB	Georgia
4.	N.Y. Jets	Marvin Jones	LB	Florida State
5.	Cincinnati	John Copeland	DE	Alabama
6.	Tampa Bay	Eric Curry	DE	Alabama
7.	Chicago	Curtis Conway	WR	USC
8.	New Orleans	Willie Roaf	T	Louisiana Tech
9.	Atlanta	Lincoln Kennedy	T	Washington
10.	L.A. Rams	Jerome Bettis	RB	Notre Dame
11.	Denver	Dan Williams	DE	Toledo
12.	L.A. Raiders	Patrick Bates	DB	Texas A&M
13.	Houston	Brad Hopkins	T	Illinois
14.	Cleveland	Steve Everitt	C	Michigan
15.	Green Bay	Wayne Simmons	LB	Clemson
16.	Indianapolis	Sean Dawkins	WR	California
17.	Washington	Tom Carter	DB	Notre Dame
18.	Phoenix	Ernest Dye	T	South Carolina
19.	Philadelphia	Lester Holmes	T	Jackson State
20.	New Orleans	Irv Smith	TE	Notre Dame
21.	Minnesota	Robert Smith	RB	Ohio State
22.	San Diego	Darrien Gordon	DB	Stanford
23.	Pittsburgh	Deon Figures	DB	Colorado
24.	Philadelphia	Leonard Renfro	DT	Colorado
25.	Miami	O.J. McDuffie	WR	Penn State
26.	San Francisco	Dana Stubblefield	DT	Kansas
27.	San Francisco	Todd Kelly	DE	Tennessee
28.	Buffalo	Thomas Smith	DB	North Carolina
29.	Green Bay	George Teague	DB	Alabama

Teams not selecting in first round: Dallas, Detroit, Kansas City, N.Y. Giants.
Total number of picks in draft: 224.

OTHER NOTEWORTHY PICKS

Round/Overall—Team, Player selected, Pos., College
2/40—N.Y. Giants, Michael Strahan, DE, Texas Southern; 2/44—Pittsburgh, Chad Brown, LB, Colorado; 3/65—Indianapolis, Ray Buchanan, DB, Louisville; 3/70—Denver, Jason Elam, K, Hawaii; 3/82—Tampa Bay, John Lynch, DB, Stanford; 5/118—Green Bay, Mark Brunell, QB, Washington; 6/160—Washington, Frank Wycheck, TE, Maryland; 7/192—Minnesota, *Gino Torretta*, QB, Miami; 8/207—N.Y. Giants, Jessie Armstead, LB, Miami; 8/219—San Francisco, Elvis Grbac, QB, Michigan; 8/222—San Diego, Trent Green, QB, Indiana.

1994
FIRST ROUND—NFL

No.	Team	Player selected	Pos.	College
1.	Cincinnati	Dan Wilkinson	DT	Ohio State
2.	Indianapolis	Marshall Faulk	RB	San Diego State
3.	Washington	Heath Shuler	QB	Tennessee
4.	New England	Willie McGinest	DE	USC
5.	Indianapolis	Trev Alberts	LB	Nebraska
6.	Tampa Bay	Trent Dilfer	QB	Fresno State
7.	San Francisco	Bryant Young	DT	Notre Dame
8.	Seattle	Sam Adams	DE	Texas A&M
9.	Cleveland	Antonio Langham	DB	Alabama
10.	Arizona	Jamir Miller	LB	UCLA
11.	Chicago	John Thierry	LB	Alcorn State
12.	N.Y. Jets	Aaron Glenn	DB	Texas A&M
13.	New Orleans	Joe Johnson	DE	Louisville
14.	Philadelphia	Bernard Williams	T	Georgia
15.	L.A. Rams	Wayne Gandy	T	Auburn
16.	Green Bay	Aaron Taylor	T	Notre Dame
17.	Pittsburgh	Charles Johnson	WR	Colorado
18.	Minnesota	Dewayne Washington	CB	N.C. State
19.	Minnesota	Todd Steussie	T	California
20.	Miami	Tim Bowens	DT	Mississippi
21.	Detroit	Johnnie Morton	WR	USC
22.	L.A. Raiders	Rob Fredrickson	LB	Michigan State
23.	Dallas	Shante Carver	DE	Arizona State
24.	N.Y. Giants	Thomas Lewis	WR	Indiana
25.	Kansas City	Greg Hill	RB	Texas A&M
26.	Houston	Henry Ford	DE	Arkansas
27.	Buffalo	Jeff Burris	DB	Notre Dame
28.	San Francisco	William Floyd	RB	Florida State
29.	Cleveland	Derrick Alexander	WR	Michigan

Teams not selecting in first round: Atlanta, Denver, San Diego.
Total number of picks in draft: 222.

OTHER NOTEWORTHY PICKS

Round/Overall—Team, Player selected, Pos., College
2/33—L.A. Rams, Isaac Bruce, WR, Memphis State; 2/36—Seattle, Kevin Mawae, C, Louisiana State; 2/42—Philadelphia, Charlie Garner, RB, Tennessee; 2/46—Dallas, Larry Allen, G, Sonoma State; 2/59—N.Y. Giants, Jason Sehorn, DB, USC; 5/145—San Diego, Rodney Harrison, DB, Western Illinois; 5/149—Green Bay, Dorsey Levens, RB, Georgia Tech; 7/197—Washington, Gus Frerotte, QB, Tulsa; 7/201—Atlanta, Jamal Anderson, RB, Utah; 7/218—Denver, Tom Nalen, C, Boston College.

1995
FIRST ROUND—NFL

No.	Team	Player selected	Pos.	College
1.	Cincinnati	Ki-Jana Carter	RB	Penn State
2.	Jacksonville	Tony Boselli	T	USC
3.	Houston	Steve McNair	QB	Alcorn State
4.	Washington	Michael Westbrook	WR	Colorado
5.	Carolina	Kerry Collins	QB	Penn State
6.	St. Louis	Kevin Carter	DE	Florida
7.	Philadelphia	Mike Mamula	DE	Boston College
8.	Seattle	Joey Galloway	WR	Ohio State

No. Team	Player selected	Pos.	College
9. N.Y. Jets	Kyle Brady	TE	Penn State
10. San Francisco	J.J. Stokes	WR	UCLA
11. Minnesota	Derrick Alexander	DE	Florida State
12. Tampa Bay	Warren Sapp	DT	Miami
13. New Orleans	Mark Fields	LB	Washington State
14. Buffalo	Ruben Brown	G	Pittsburgh
15. Indianapolis	Ellis Johnson	DT	Florida
16. N.Y. Jets	Hugh Douglas	DE	Central State (Ohio)
17. N.Y. Giants	Tyrone Wheatley	RB	Michigan
18. Los Angeles	Napoleon Kaufman	RB	Washington
19. Jacksonville	James Stewart	RB	Tennessee
20. Detroit	Luther Elliss	DT	Utah
21. Chicago	*Rashaan Salaam*	RB	Colorado
22. Carolina	Tyrone Poole	DB	Ft. Valley (Ga.) St.
23. New England	Ty Law	DB	Michigan
24. Minnesota	Korey Stringer	T	Ohio State
25. Miami	Billy Milner	T	Houston
26. Atlanta	Devin Bush	DB	Florida State
27. Pittsburgh	Mark Bruener	TE	Washington
28. Tampa Bay	Derrick Brooks	LB	Florida State
29. Carolina	Blake Brockermeyer	T	Texas
30. Cleveland	Craig Powell	LB	Ohio State
31. Kansas City	Trezelle Jenkins	T	Michigan
32. Green Bay	Craig Newsome	DB	Arizona State

Note: Los Angeles franchise moved to Oakland (but after draft); teams not selecting in first round: Arizona, Dallas, Denver, San Diego.

Total number of picks in draft: 249.

OTHER NOTEWORTHY PICKS

Round/Overall—Team, Player selected, Pos., College
2/50—Philadelphia, Bobby Taylor, DB, Notre Dame; 2/60—Pittsburgh, Kordell Stewart, QB, Colorado; 3/74—New England, Curtis Martin, RB, Pittsburgh; 3/90—Green Bay, Antonio Freeman, WR, Virginia Tech; 6/196—Denver, Terrell Davis, RB, Georgia; 7/230—Green Bay, Adam Timmerman, G, South Dakota State.

1996
FIRST ROUND—NFL

No. Team	Player selected	Pos.	College
1. N.Y. Jets	Keyshawn Johnson	WR	USC
2. Jacksonville	Kevin Hardy	LB	Illinois
3. Arizona	Simeon Rice	DE	Illinois
4. Baltimore	Jonathan Ogden	T	UCLA
5. N.Y. Giants	Cedric Jones	DE	Oklahoma
6. St. Louis	Lawrence Phillips	RB	Nebraska
7. New England	Terry Glenn	WR	Ohio State
8. Carolina	Tim Biakabutuka	RB	Michigan
9. Oakland	Rickey Dudley	TE	Ohio State
10. Cincinnati	Willie Anderson	T	Auburn
11. New Orleans	Alex Molden	DB	Oregon
12. Tampa Bay	Regan Upshaw	DE	California
13. Chicago	Walt Harris	DB	Miss. State
14. Houston	*Eddie George*	RB	Ohio State
15. Denver	John Mobley	LB	Kutztown (Pa.)
16. Minnesota	Duane Clemons	DE	California
17. Detroit	Reggie Brown	LB	Texas A&M
18. St. Louis	Eddie Kennison	WR	Louisiana State
19. Indianapolis	Marvin Harrison	WR	Syracuse
20. Miami	Daryl Gardener	DT	Baylor
21. Seattle	Pete Kendall	T	Boston College
22. Tampa Bay	Marcus Jones	DT	North Carolina
23. Detroit	Jeff Hartings	G	Penn State
24. Buffalo	Eric Moulds	WR	Miss. State
25. Philadelphia	Jermane Mayberry	T	Tex. A&M-K'ville
26. Baltimore	Ray Lewis	LB	Miami
27. Green Bay	John Michels	T	USC
28. Kansas City	Jerome Woods	DB	Memphis
29. Pittsburgh	Jamain Stephens	T	N. Carolina A&T
30. Washington	Andre Johnson	T	Penn State

Teams not selecting in first round: Atlanta, Dallas, San Diego, San Francisco.

Total number of picks in draft: 254.

OTHER NOTEWORTHY PICKS

Round/Overall—Team, Player selected, Pos., College
2/33—Jacksonville, Tony Brackens, DE, Texas; 2/34—N.Y. Giants, Amani Toomer, WR, Michigan; 2/35—Tampa Bay, Mike Alstott, RB, Purdue; 2/36—New England, Lawyer Milloy, DB, Washington; 2/61—Philadelphia, Brian Dawkins, DB, Clemson; 3/89—San Francisco, Terrell Owens, WR, UT-Chattanooga; 4/102—Washington, Stephen Davis, RB, Auburn; 5/135—Kansas City, Joe Horn, WR, Itawamba JC; 5/154—Miami, Zach Thomas, LB, Texas Tech.

1997
FIRST ROUND—NFL

No. Team	Player selected	Pos.	College
1. St. Louis	Orlando Pace	T	Ohio State
2. Oakland	Darrell Russell	DT	USC
3. Seattle	Shawn Springs	CB	Ohio State
4. Baltimore	Peter Boulware	DE	Florida State
5. Detroit	Bryant Westbrook	DB	Texas
6. Seattle	Walter Jones	T	Florida State
7. N.Y. Giants	Ike Hilliard	WR	Florida
8. N.Y. Jets	James Farrior	LB	Virginia
9. Arizona	Tom Knight	DB	Iowa
10. New Orleans	Chris Naeole	G	Colorado
11. Atlanta	Michael Booker	DB	Nebraska
12. Tampa Bay	Warrick Dunn	RB	Florida State
13. Kansas City	Tony Gonzalez	TE	California
14. Cincinnati	Reinard Wilson	LB	Florida State
15. Miami	Yatil Green	WR	Miami
16. Tampa Bay	Reidel Anthony	WR	Florida
17. Washington	Kenard Lang	DE	Miami
18. Houston	Kenny Holmes	DE	Miami
19. Indianapolis	Tarik Glenn	T	California
20. Minnesota	Dwayne Rudd	LB	Alabama
21. Jacksonville	Renaldo Wynn	DT	Notre Dame
22. Dallas	David LaFleur	TE	Louisiana State
23. Buffalo	Antowain Smith	RB	Houston
24. Pittsburgh	Chad Scott	DB	Maryland
25. Philadelphia	Jon Harris	DE	Virginia
26. San Francisco	Jim Druckenmiller	QB	Virginia Tech
27. Carolina	Rae Carruth	WR	Colorado
28. Denver	Trevor Pryce	DT	Clemson
29. New England	Chris Canty	DB	Kansas State
30. Green Bay	Ross Verba	T	Iowa

Teams not selecting in first round: Chicago, San Diego.
Total number of picks in draft: 240.

OTHER NOTEWORTHY PICKS

Round/Overall—Team, Player selected, Pos., College
2/34—Baltimore, Jamie Sharper, LB, Virginia; 2/36—N.Y. Giants, Tiki Barber, RB, Virginia; 2/42—Arizona, Jake Plummer, QB, Arizona State; 2/43—Cincinnati, Corey Dillon, RB, Washington; 2/44—Miami, Sam Madison, DB, Louisville; 2/60—Green Bay, Darren Sharper, DB, William & Mary; 3/71—Philadelphia, Duce Staley, RB, South Carolina; 3/73—Miami, Jason Taylor, DE, Akron; 4/99—New Orleans, *Danny Wuerffel*, QB, Florida.

1998
FIRST ROUND—NFL

No. Team	Player selected	Pos.	College
1. Indianapolis	Peyton Manning	QB	Tennessee
2. San Diego	Ryan Leaf	QB	Washington State
3. Arizona	Andre Wadsworth	DE	Florida State
4. Oakland	*Charles Woodson*	DB	Michigan
5. Chicago	Curtis Enis	RB	Penn State
6. St. Louis	Grant Wistrom	DE	Nebraska
7. New Orleans	Kyle Turley	T	San Diego State
8. Dallas	Greg Ellis	DE	North Carolina
9. Jacksonville	Fred Taylor	RB	Florida
10. Baltimore	Duane Starks	DB	Miami
11. Philadelphia	Tra Thomas	T	Florida State

No.	Team	Player selected	Pos.	College
12.	Atlanta	Keith Brooking	LB	Georgia Tech
13.	Cincinnati	Takeo Spikes	LB	Auburn
14.	Carolina	Jason Peter	DT	Nebraska
15.	Seattle	Anthony Simmons	LB	Clemson
16.	Tennessee	Kevin Dyson	WR	Utah
17.	Cincinnati	Brian Simmons	LB	North Carolina
18.	New England	Robert Edwards	RB	Georgia
19.	Green Bay	Vonnie Holliday	DT	North Carolina
20.	Detroit	Terry Fair	DB	Tennessee
21.	Minnesota	Randy Moss	WR	Marshall
22.	New England	Tebucky Jones	DB	Syracuse
23.	Oakland	Mo Collins	T	Florida
24.	N.Y. Giants	Shaun Williams	DB	UCLA
25.	Jacksonville	Donovin Darius	DB	Syracuse
26.	Pittsburgh	Alan Faneca	G	Louisiana State
27.	Kansas City	Victor Riley	T	Auburn
28.	San Francisco	R.W. McQuarters	DB	Oklahoma State
29.	Miami	John Avery	RB	Mississippi
30.	Denver	Marcus Nash	WR	Tennessee

Teams not selecting in first round: Buffalo, N.Y. Jets, Tampa Bay, Washington.
Total number of picks in draft: 241.

OTHER NOTEWORTHY PICKS

Round/Overall—Team, Player selected, Pos., College
2/38—Dallas, Flozell Adams, T, Michigan State; 2/39—Buffalo, Sam Cowart, LB, Florida State; 2/60—Detroit, Charlie Batch, QB, Eastern Michigan; 3/76—Seattle, Ahman Green, RB, Nebraska; 3/91—Denver, Brian Griese, QB, Michigan; 3/92—Pittsburgh, Hines Ward, WR, Georgia; 5/150—Green Bay, Corey Bradford, WR, Jackson State; 6/173—Minnesota, Matt Birk, C, Harvard; 6/187—Green Bay, Matt Hasselbeck, QB, Boston College; 7/226—Arizona, Pat Tillman, DB, Arizona State.

1999
FIRST ROUND—NFL

No.	Team	Player selected	Pos.	College
1.	Cleveland	Tim Couch	QB	Kentucky
2.	Philadelphia	Donovan McNabb	QB	Syracuse
3.	Cincinnati	Akili Smith	QB	Oregon
4.	Indianapolis	Edgerrin James	RB	Miami
5.	New Orleans	*Ricky Williams*	RB	Texas
6.	St. Louis	Torry Holt	WR	N.C. State
7.	Washington	Champ Bailey	DB	Georgia
8.	Arizona	David Boston	WR	Ohio State
9.	Detroit	Chris Claiborne	LB	USC
10.	Baltimore	Chris McAlister	DB	Arizona
11.	Minnesota	Daunte Culpepper	QB	Central Florida
12.	Chicago	Cade McNown	QB	UCLA
13.	Pittsburgh	Troy Edwards	WR	Louisiana Tech
14.	Kansas City	John Tait	T	Brigham Young
15.	Tampa Bay	Anthony McFarland	DT	Louisiana State
16.	Tennessee	Jevon Kearse	DE	Florida
17.	New England	Damien Woody	C	Boston College
18.	Oakland	Matt Stinchcomb	T	Georgia
19.	N.Y. Giants	Luke Petitgout	T	Notre Dame
20.	Dallas	Ebenezer Ekuban	DE	North Carolina
21.	Arizona	L.J. Shelton	T	Eastern Michigan
22.	Seattle	Lamar King	DE	Saginaw Valley St.
23.	Buffalo	Antoine Winfield	DB	Ohio State
24.	San Francisco	Reggie McGrew	DT	Florida
25.	Green Bay	Antuan Edwards	DB	Clemson
26.	Jacksonville	Fernando Bryant	DB	Alabama
27.	Detroit	Aaron Gibson	T	Wisconsin
28.	New England	Andy Katzenmoyer	LB	Ohio State
29.	Minnesota	Dimitrius Underwood	DE	Michigan State
30.	Atlanta	Patrick Kerney	DE	Virginia
31.	Denver	Al Wilson	LB	Tennessee

Teams not selecting in first round: Carolina, Miami, N.Y. Jets, San Diego.
Total number of picks in draft: 253.

OTHER NOTEWORTHY PICKS

Round/Overall—Team, Player selected, Pos., College
2/36—Indianapolis, Mike Peterson, LB, Florida; 2/41—St. Louis, Dre' Bly, DB, North Carolina; 2/53—Buffalo, Peerless Price, WR, Tennessee; 3/73—Pittsburgh, Joey Porter, LB, Colorado State; 3/78—Chicago, Marty Booker, WR, Northeast Louisiana; 3/80—Tampa Bay, Martin Gramatica, K, Kansas State; 4/131—Green Bay, Aaron Brooks, QB, Virginia; 7/213—Green Bay, Donald Driver, WR, Alcorn State.

2000
FIRST ROUND—NFL

No.	Team	Player selected	Pos.	College
1.	Cleveland	Courtney Brown	DE	Penn State
2.	Washington	LaVar Arrington	LB	Penn State
3.	Washington	Chris Samuels	T	Alabama
4.	Cincinnati	Peter Warrick	WR	Florida State
5.	Baltimore	Jamal Lewis	RB	Tennessee
6.	Philadelphia	Corey Simon	DT	Florida State
7.	Arizona	Thomas Jones	RB	Virginia
8.	Pittsburgh	Plaxico Burress	WR	Michigan State
9.	Chicago	Brian Urlacher	LB	New Mexico
10.	Baltimore	Travis Taylor	WR	Florida
11.	N.Y. Giants	*Ron Dayne*	RB	Wisconsin
12.	N.Y. Jets	Shaun Ellis	DE	Tennessee
13.	N.Y. Jets	John Abraham	LB	South Carolina
14.	Green Bay	Bubba Franks	TE	Miami
15.	Denver	Deltha O'Neal	DB	California
16.	San Francisco	Julian Peterson	LB	Michigan State
17.	Oakland	Sebastian Janikowski	K	Florida State
18.	N.Y. Jets	Chad Pennington	QB	Marshall
19.	Seattle	Shaun Alexander	RB	Alabama
20.	Detroit	Stockar McDougle	T	Oklahoma
21.	Kansas City	Sylvester Morris	WR	Jackson State
22.	Seattle	Chris McIntosh	T	Wisconsin
23.	Carolina	Rashard Anderson	DB	Jackson State
24.	San Francisco	Ahmed Plummer	DB	Ohio State
25.	Minnesota	Chris Hovan	DT	Boston College
26.	Buffalo	Erik Flowers	DE	Arizona State
27.	N.Y. Jets	Anthony Becht	TE	West Virginia
28.	Indianapolis	Rob Morris	LB	Brigham Young
29.	Jacksonville	R. Jay Soward	WR	USC
30.	Tennessee	Keith Bulluck	LB	Syracuse
31.	St. Louis	Trung Canidate	RB	Arizona

Teams not selecting in first round: Atlanta, Dallas, Miami, New England, New Orleans, San Diego, Tampa Bay.
Total number of picks in draft: 254.

OTHER NOTEWORTHY PICKS

Round/Overall—Team, Player selected, Pos., College
2/33—New Orleans, Darren Howard, DE, Kansas State; 3/78—N.Y. Jets, Laveranues Coles, WR, Florida State; 3/80—Seattle, Darrell Jackson, WR, Florida; 5/142—Oakland, Shane Lechler, P, Texas A&M; 5/149—Green Bay, Kabeer Gbaja-Biamila, DE, San Diego State; 5/153—Kansas City, Dante Hall, RB, Texas A&M; 6/168—New Orleans, Marc Bulger, QB, West Virginia; 6/174—Chicago, Paul Edinger, K, Michigan State; 6/199—New England, Tom Brady, QB, Michigan.

2001
FIRST ROUND—NFL

No.	Team	Player selected	Pos.	College
1.	Atlanta	Michael Vick	QB	Virginia Tech
2.	Arizona	Leonard Davis	T	Texas
3.	Cleveland	Gerard Warren	DT	Florida
4.	Cincinnati	Justin Smith	DE	Missouri
5.	San Diego	LaDainian Tomlinson	RB	Texas Christian
6.	New England	Richard Seymour	DT	Georgia
7.	San Francisco	Andre Carter	DE	California
8.	Chicago	David Terrell	WR	Michigan
9.	Seattle	Koren Robinson	WR	North Carolina St.
10.	Green Bay	Jamal Reynolds	DE	Florida State
11.	Carolina	Dan Morgan	LB	Miami
12.	St. Louis	Damione Lewis	DT	Miami
13.	Jacksonville	Marcus Stroud	DT	Georgia
14.	Tampa Bay	Kenyatta Walker	T	Florida
15.	Washington	Rod Gardner	WR	Clemson
16.	N.Y. Jets	Santana Moss	WR	Miami
17.	Seattle	Steve Hutchinson	G	Michigan
18.	Detroit	Jeff Backus	T	Michigan
19.	Pittsburgh	Casey Hampton	DT	Texas
20.	St. Louis	Adam Archuleta	DB	Arizona State
21.	Buffalo	Nate Clements	DB	Ohio State
22.	N.Y. Giants	Will Allen	DB	Syracuse
23.	New Orleans	Deuce McAllister	RB	Mississippi
24.	Denver	Willie Middlebrooks	DB	Minnesota
25.	Philadelphia	Freddie Mitchell	WR	UCLA
26.	Miami	Jamar Fletcher	DB	Wisconsin
27.	Minnesota	Michael Bennett	RB	Wisconsin
28.	Oakland	Derrick Gibson	DB	Florida State
29.	St. Louis	Ryan Pickett	DT	Ohio State

No.	Team	Player selected	Pos.	College
30.	Indianapolis	Reggie Wayne	WR	Miami
31.	Baltimore	Todd Heap	TE	Arizona State

Teams not selecting in first round: Dallas, Kansas City, Tennessee.
Total number of picks in draft: 246.

OTHER NOTEWORTHY PICKS

Round/Overall—Team, Player selected, Pos., College
2/32—San Diego, Drew Brees, QB, Purdue; 2/36—Cincinnati, Chad Johnson, WR, Oregon State; 2/39—Pittsburgh, Kendrell Bell, LB, Georgia; 2/52—Miami, Chris Chambers, WR, Wisconsin; 2/53—Dallas, Quincy Carter, QB, Georgia; 2/58—Buffalo, Travis Henry, RB, Tennessee; 3/74—Carolina, Steve Smith, WR, Utah; 3/80—San Francisco, Kevan Barlow, RB, Pittsburgh; 4/100—Cincinnati, Rudi Johnson, RB, Auburn; 4/106—Carolina, Chris Weinke, QB, Florida State.

2002
FIRST ROUND—NFL

No.	Team	Player selected	Pos.	College
1.	Houston	David Carr	QB	Fresno State
2.	Carolina	Julius Peppers	DE	North Carolina
3.	Detroit	Joey Harrington	QB	Oregon
4.	Buffalo	Mike Williams	T	Texas
5.	San Diego	Quentin Jammer	DB	Texas
6.	Kansas City	Ryan Sims	DT	North Carolina
7.	Minnesota	Bryant McKinnie	T	Miami
8.	Dallas	Roy Williams	DB	Oklahoma
9.	Jacksonville	John Henderson	DT	Tennessee
10.	Cincinnati	Levi Jones	T	Arizona State
11.	Indianapolis	Dwight Freeney	DE	Syracuse
12.	Arizona	Wendell Bryant	DT	Wisconsin
13.	New Orleans	Donte' Stallworth	WR	Tennessee
14.	N.Y. Giants	Jeremy Shockey	TE	Miami
15.	Tennessee	Albert Haynesworth	DT	Tennessee
16.	Cleveland	William Green	RB	Boston College
17.	Oakland	Phillip Buchanon	DB	Miami
18.	Atlanta	T.J. Duckett	RB	Michigan State
19.	Denver	Ashley Lelie	WR	Hawaii
20.	Green Bay	Javon Walker	WR	Florida State
21.	New England	Daniel Graham	TE	Colorado
22.	N.Y. Jets	Bryan Thomas	DE	Ala.-Birmingham
23.	Oakland	Napoleon Harris	LB	Northwestern
24.	Baltimore	Ed Reed	S	Miami
25.	New Orleans	Charles Grant	DE	Georgia
26.	Philadelphia	Lito Sheppard	DB	Florida
27.	San Francisco	Mike Rumph	DB	Miami
28.	Seattle	Jerramy Stevens	TE	Washington
29.	Chicago	Marc Colombo	T	Boston College
30.	Pittsburgh	Kendall Simmons	G	Auburn
31.	St. Louis	Robert Thomas	LB	UCLA
32.	Washington	Patrick Ramsey	QB	Tulane

Teams not selecting in first round: Miami, Tampa Bay.
Total number of picks in draft: 261.

OTHER NOTEWORTHY PICKS

Round/Overall—Team, Player selected, Pos., College
2/36—Buffalo, Josh Reed, WR, Louisiana State; 2/51—Denver, Clinton Portis, RB, Miami; 2/62—Pittsburgh, Antwaan Randle El, WR, Indiana; 3/81—Arizona, Josh McCown, QB, Sam Houston State; 3/91—Philadelphia, Brian Westbrook, RB, Villanova; 3/92—Green Bay, Marques Anderson, DB, UCLA; 3/95—St. Louis, Eric Crouch, WR, Nebraska; 4/114—Miami, Randy McMichael, TE, Georgia.

2003
FIRST ROUND—NFL

No.	Team	Player selected	Pos.	College
1.	Cincinnati	Carson Palmer	QB	USC
2.	Detroit	Charles Rogers	WR	Michigan State
3.	Houston	Andre Johnson	WR	Miami
4.	N.Y. Jets	Dwayne Robertson	DT	Kentucky
5.	Dallas	Terence Newman	DB	Kansas State
6.	New Orleans	Johnathan Sullivan	DT	Georgia
7.	Jacksonville	Byron Leftwich	QB	Marshall
8.	Carolina	Jordan Gross	T	Utah
9.	Minnesota	Kevin Williams	DT	Oklahoma State
10.	Baltimore	Terrell Suggs	DE	Arizona State
11.	Seattle	Marcus Trufant	DB	Washington State

No.	Team	Player selected	Pos.	College
12.	St. Louis	Jimmy Kennedy	DT	Penn State
13.	New England	Ty Warren	DT	Texas A&M
14.	Chicago	Michael Haynes	DE	Penn State
15.	Philadelphia	Jerome McDougle	DE	Miami
16.	Pittsburgh	Troy Polamalu	DB	USC
17.	Arizona	Bryant Johnson	WR	Penn State
18.	Arizona	Calvin Pace	DE	Wake Forest
19.	Baltimore	Kyle Boller	QB	California
20.	Denver	George Foster	T	Georgia
21.	Cleveland	Jeff Faine	C	Notre Dame
22.	Chicago	Rex Grossman	QB	Florida
23.	Buffalo	Willis McGahee	RB	Miami
24.	Indianapolis	Dallas Clark	TE	Iowa
25.	N.Y. Giants	William Joseph	DT	Miami
26.	San Francisco	Kwame Harris	T	Stanford
27.	Kansas City	Larry Johnson	RB	Penn State
28.	Tennessee	Andre Woolfolk	DB	Oklahoma
29.	Green Bay	Nick Barnett	LB	Oregon State
30.	San Diego	Sammy Davis	DB	Texas A&M
31.	Oakland	Nnamadi Asomugha	DB	California
32.	Oakland	Tyler Brayton	DE	Colorado

Teams not selecting in first round: Atlanta, Miami, Tampa Bay, Washington.
Total number of picks in draft: 262.

OTHER NOTEWORTHY PICKS

Round/Overall—Team, Player selected, Pos., College
2/54—Arizona, Anquan Boldin, WR, Florida State; 3/82—Carolina, Ricky Manning, CB, UCLA; 3/97—Tampa Bay, Chris Simms, QB, Texas; 4/101—Houston, Domanick Davis, RB, LSU; 4/105—Minnesota, Onterrio Smith, RB, Oregon; 6/192—Houston, Drew Henson, QB, Michigan; 7/241—San Francisco, Ken Dorsey, QB, Miami

2004
FIRST ROUND—NFL

No.	Team	Player selected	Pos.	College
1.	San Diego*	Eli Manning	QB	Mississippi
2.	Oakland	Robert Gallery	T	Iowa
3.	Arizona	Larry Fitzgerald	WR	Pittsburgh
4.	N.Y. Giants*	Philip Rivers	QB	N.C. State
5.	Washington	Sean Taylor	S	Miami
6.	Cleveland	Kellen Winslow	TE	Miami
7.	Detroit	Roy Williams	WR	Texas
8.	Atlanta	DeAngelo Hall	DB	Virginia Tech
9.	Jacksonville	Reggie Williams	WR	Washington
10.	Houston	Dunta Robinson	DB	South Carolina
11.	Pittsburgh	Ben Roethlisberger	QB	Miami (Ohio)
12.	N.Y. Jets	Jonathan Vilma	LB	Miami
13.	Buffalo	Lee Evans	WR	Wisconsin
14.	Chicago	Tommie Harris	DT	Oklahoma
15.	Tampa Bay	Michael Clayton	WR	LSU
16.	Philadelphia	Shawn Andrews	T	Arkansas
17.	Denver	D.J. Williams	LB	Miami
18.	New Orleans	Will Smith	DE	Ohio State
19.	Miami	Vernon Carey	T	Miami
20.	Minnesota	Kenechi Udeze	DE	USC
21.	New England	Vince Wilfork	DT	Miami
22.	Buffalo	J.P. Losman	QB	Tulane
23.	Seattle	Marcus Tubbs	DT	Texas
24.	St. Louis	Steven Jackson	RB	Oregon State
25.	Green Bay	Ahmad Carroll	DB	Arkansas
26.	Cincinnati	Chris Perry	RB	Michigan
27.	Houston	Jason Babin	LB	Western Michigan
28.	Carolina	Chris Gamble	DB	Ohio State
29.	Atlanta	Michael Jenkins	WR	Ohio State
30.	Detroit	Kevin Jones	RB	Virginia Tech
31.	San Francisco	Rashaun Woods	WR	Oklahoma State
32.	New England	Ben Watson	TE	Georgia

Teams not selecting in first round: Baltimore, Dallas, Indianapolis, Kansas City, Tennessee.
Total number of picks in draft: 255.

OTHER NOTEWORTHY PICKS

Round/Overall—Team, Player selected, Pos., College
2/33—Arizona, Karlos Dansby, LB, Auburn; 2/43—Dallas, Julius Jones, RB, Notre Dame; 2/43—Seattle, Michael Boulware, LB, Florida State; 2/62—Carolina, Keary Colbert, WR, USC; 4/110—Nathan Vasher, DB, Texas; 5/148—Chicago, Craig Krenzel, QB, Ohio State; 7/202—Arizona, John Navarre, QB, Michigan.

2005

FIRST ROUND—NFL

No.	Team	Player selected	Pos.	College
1.	San Francisco	Alex Smith	QB	Utah
2.	Miami	Ronnie Brown	RB	Auburn
3.	Cleveland	Braylon Edwards	WR	Michigan
4.	Chicago	Cedric Benson	RB	Texas
5.	Tampa Bay	Cadillac Williams	RB	Auburn
6.	Tennessee	Pacman Jones	CB	West Virginia
7.	Minnesota	Troy Williamson	WR	South Carolina
8.	Arizona	Antrel Rolle	CB	Miami
9.	Washington	Carlos Rogers	CB	Auburn
10.	Detroit	Mike Williams	WR	USC
11.	Dallas	Demarcus Ware	DE	Troy State
12.	San Diego	Shawne Merriman	LB	Maryland
13.	New Orleans	Jammal Brown	OT	Oklahoma
14.	Carolina	Thomas Davis	FS	Georgia
15.	Kansas City	Derrick Johnson	LB	Texas
16.	Houston	Travis Johnson	DT	Florida State
17.	Cincinnati	David Pollack	DE	Georgia
18.	Minnesota	Erasmus James	DE	Wisconsin
19.	St. Louis	Alex Barron	OT	Florida State
20.	Dallas	Marcus Spears	DE	Louisiana State
21.	Jacksonville	Matt Jones	WR	Arkansas
22.	Baltimore	Mark Clayton	WR	Oklahoma
23.	Oakland	Fabian Washington	CB	Nebraska
24.	Green Bay	Aaron Rodgers	QB	California
25.	Washington	Jason Campbell	QB	Auburn
26.	Seattle	Chris Spencer	C	Mississippi
27.	Atlanta	Roddy White	WR	UAB
28.	San Diego	Luis Castillo	DT	Northwestern
29.	Indianapolis	Marlin Jackson	CB	Michigan
30.	Pittsburgh	Heath Miller	TE	Virginia
31.	Philadelphia	Mike Patterson	DT	Southern Cal
32.	New England	Logan Mankins	G	Fresno State

Teams not selecting in first round: Buffalo, Denver, N.Y. Giants, N.Y. Jets.

Total number of picks in draft: 255.

OTHER NOTEWORTHY PICKS

Round/Overall—Team, Player selected, Pos., College
2/45—Seattle, Lofa Tatupu, LB, USC; 2/48—Cincinnati, Odell Thurman, LB, Georgia; 2/51—Green Bay, Nick Collins, S, Bethune-Cookman; 2/52—Jacksonville, Khalif Barnes, OT, Washington; 3/67—Cleveland, Charlie Frye, QB, Akron; 3/70—Miami, Channing Crowder, LB, Florida; 3/98—Seattle, Leroy Hill, LB, Clemson; 3/100—New England, Nick Kaczur, OT, Toledo; 4/106—Chicago, Kyle Orton, QB, Purdue.

TEAM BY TEAM

YEAR-BY-YEAR RECORDS

		REGULAR SEASON						PLAYOFFS			
Year	W	L	T	Pct.	PF	PA	Finish	W	L	Highest round	Coach
1920*	6	2	2	.750	...	...	T4th				Paddy Driscoll
1921*	3	3	2	.500	...	...	T8th				Paddy Driscoll
1922*	8	3	0	.727	...	...	3rd				Paddy Driscoll
1923*	8	4	0	.667	...	...	6th				Arnold Horween
1924*	5	4	1	.556	...	...	8th				Arnold Horween
1925*	11	2	1	.846	...	...	1st				Norman Barry
1926*	5	6	1	.455	...	...	10th				Norman Barry
1927*	3	7	1	.300	...	...	9th				Guy Chamberlin
1928*	1	5	0	.167	...	...	9th				Fred Gillies
1929*	6	6	1	.500	...	...	T4th				Dewey Scanlon
1930*	5	6	2	.455	...	...	T7th				Ernie Nevers
1931*	5	4	0	.556	...	...	4th				LeRoy Andrews, E. Nevers
1932*	2	6	2	.250	...	...	7th				Jack Chevigny
1933*	1	9	1	.100	52	101	5th/Western Div.	—	—		Paul Schissler
1934*	5	6	0	.455	80	84	4th/Western Div.	—	—		Paul Schissler
1935*	6	4	2	.600	99	97	T3rd/Western Div.	—	—		Milan Creighton
1936*	3	8	1	.273	74	143	4th/Western Div.	—	—		Milan Creighton
1937*	5	5	1	.500	135	165	4th/Western Div.	—	—		Milan Creighton
1938*	2	9	0	.182	111	168	5th/Western Div.	—	—		Milan Creighton
1939*	1	10	0	.091	84	254	5th/Western Div.	—	—		Ernie Nevers
1940*	2	7	2	.222	139	222	5th/Western Div.	—	—		Jimmy Conzelman
1941*	3	7	1	.300	127	197	4th/Western Div.	—	—		Jimmy Conzelman
1942*	3	8	0	.273	98	209	4th/Western Div.	—	—		Jimmy Conzelman
1943*	0	10	0	.000	95	238	4th/Western Div.	—	—		Phil Handler
1944†	0	10	0	.000	108	328	5th/Western Div.	—	—		P. Handler-Walt Kiesling
1945*	1	9	0	.100	98	228	5th/Western Div.	—	—		Phil Handler
1946*	6	5	0	.545	260	198	T3rd/Western Div.	—	—		Jimmy Conzelman
1947*	9	3	0	.750	306	231	1st/Western Div.	1	0	NFL champ	Jimmy Conzelman
1948*	11	1	0	.917	395	226	1st/Western Div.	0	1	NFL championship game	Jimmy Conzelman
1949*	6	5	1	.545	360	301	3rd/Western Div.	—	—		P. Handler-Buddy Parker
1950*	5	7	0	.417	233	287	5th/American Conf.	—	—		Curly Lambeau
1951*	3	9	0	.250	210	287	6th/American Conf.	—	—		Curly Lambeau, P. Handler-Cecil Isbell
1952*	4	8	0	.333	172	221	T5th/American Conf.	—	—		Joe Kuharich
1953*	1	10	1	.091	190	337	6th/Eastern Conf.	—	—		Joe Stydahar
1954*	2	10	0	.167	183	347	6th/Eastern Conf.	—	—		Joe Stydahar
1955*	4	7	1	.364	224	252	T4th/Eastern Conf.	—	—		Ray Richards
1956*	7	5	0	.583	240	182	2nd/Eastern Conf.	—	—		Ray Richards
1957*	3	9	0	.250	200	299	6th/Eastern Conf.	—	—		Ray Richards
1958*	2	9	1	.182	261	356	T5th/Eastern Conf.	—	—		Pop Ivy
1959*	2	10	0	.167	234	324	6th/Eastern Conf.	—	—		Pop Ivy
1960‡	6	5	1	.545	288	230	4th/Eastern Conf.	—	—		Pop Ivy
1961‡	7	7	0	.500	279	267	4th/Eastern Conf.	—	—		Pop Ivy
1962‡	4	9	1	.308	287	361	6th/Eastern Conf.	—	—		Wally Lemm
1963‡	9	5	0	.643	341	283	3rd/Eastern Conf.	—	—		Wally Lemm
1964‡	9	3	2	.750	357	331	2nd/Eastern Conf.	—	—		Wally Lemm
1965‡	5	9	0	.357	296	309	T5th/Eastern Conf.	—	—		Wally Lemm
1966‡	8	5	1	.615	264	265	4th/Eastern Conf.	—	—		Charley Winner
1967‡	6	7	1	.462	333	356	3rd/Century Div.	—	—		Charley Winner
1968‡	9	4	1	.692	325	289	2nd/Century Div.	—	—		Charley Winner
1969‡	4	9	1	.308	314	389	3rd/Century Div.	—	—		Charley Winner
1970‡	8	5	1	.615	325	228	3rd/NFC Eastern Div.	—	—		Charley Winner
1971‡	4	9	1	.308	231	279	4th/NFC Eastern Div.	—	—		Bob Hollway
1972‡	4	9	1	.308	193	303	4th/NFC Eastern Div.	—	—		Bob Hollway
1973‡	4	9	1	.308	286	365	4th/NFC Eastern Div.	—	—		Don Coryell
1974‡	10	4	0	.714	285	218	1st/NFC Eastern Div.	0	1	NFC div. playoff game	Don Coryell
1975‡	11	3	0	.786	356	276	1st/NFC Eastern Div.	0	1	NFC div. playoff game	Don Coryell
1976‡	10	4	0	.714	309	267	3rd/NFC Eastern Div.	—	—		Don Coryell
1977‡	7	7	0	.500	272	287	3rd/NFC Eastern Div.	—	—		Don Coryell
1978‡	6	10	0	.375	248	296	4th/NFC Eastern Div.	—	—		Bud Wilkinson
1979‡	5	11	0	.313	307	358	5th/NFC Eastern Div.	—	—		B. Wilkinson, Larry Wilson
1980‡	5	11	0	.313	299	350	4th/NFC Eastern Div.	—	—		Jim Hanifan
1981‡	7	9	0	.438	315	408	5th/NFC Eastern Div.	—	—		Jim Hanifan
1982‡	5	4	0	.556	135	170	6th/NFC	0	1	NFC first-round pl. game	Jim Hanifan
1983‡	8	7	1	.531	374	428	3rd/NFC Eastern Div.	—	—		Jim Hanifan
1984‡	9	7	0	.563	423	345	3rd/NFC Eastern Div.	—	—		Jim Hanifan
1985‡	5	11	0	.313	278	414	5th/NFC Eastern Div.	—	—		Jim Hanifan
1986‡	4	11	1	.281	218	351	5th/NFC Eastern Div.	—	—		Gene Stallings
1987‡	7	8	0	.467	362	368	3rd/NFC Eastern Div.	—	—		Gene Stallings
1988§	7	9	0	.438	344	398	4th/NFC Eastern Div.	—	—		Gene Stallings

HISTORY *Team by team*

	REGULAR SEASON						PLAYOFFS			
Year	W	L	T	Pct.	PF	PA	Finish	W	L	Highest round	Coach
1989§	5	11	0	.313	258	377	4th/NFC Eastern Div.	—	—		G. Stallings, Hank Kuhlmann
1990§	5	11	0	.313	268	396	5th/NFC Eastern Div.	—	—		Joe Bugel
1991§	4	12	0	.250	196	344	5th/NFC Eastern Div.	—	—		Joe Bugel
1992§	4	12	0	.250	243	332	5th/NFC Eastern Div.	—	—		Joe Bugel
1993§	7	9	0	.438	326	269	4th/NFC Eastern Div.	—	—		Joe Bugel
1994	8	8	0	.500	235	267	3rd/NFC Eastern Div.	—	—		Buddy Ryan
1995	4	12	0	.250	275	422	5th/NFC Eastern Div.	—	—		Buddy Ryan
1996	7	9	0	.438	300	397	4th/NFC Eastern Div.	—	—		Vince Tobin
1997	4	12	0	.250	283	379	5th/NFC Eastern Div.	—	—		Vince Tobin
1998	9	7	0	.563	325	378	2nd/NFC Eastern Div.	1	1	NFC div. playoff game	Vince Tobin
1999	6	10	0	.375	245	382	4th/NFC Eastern Div.	—	—		Vince Tobin
2000	3	13	0	.188	210	443	5th/NFC Eastern Div.	—	—		V. Tobin, Dave McGinnis
2001	7	9	0	.438	295	343	4th/NFC Eastern Div.	—	—		Dave McGinnis
2002	5	11	0	.313	262	417	4th/NFC West Div.	—	—		Dave McGinnis
2003	4	12	0	.250	225	452	4th/NFC West Div.	—	—		Dave McGinnis
2004	6	10	0	.375	284	322	3rd/NFC West Div.	—	—		Dennis Green
2005	5	11	0	.312	311	387	3rd/NFC West Div.	—	—		Dennis Green

*Chicago Cardinals.
†Card-Pitt, a combined squad of Chicago Cardinals and Pittsburgh Steelers.
‡St. Louis Cardinals.
§Phoenix Cardinals.

FIRST-ROUND DRAFT PICKS

1936—Jim Lawrence, B, Texas Christian
1937—Ray Buivid, B, Marquette
1938—Jack Robbins, B, Arkansas
1939—Charles Aldrich, C, Texas Christian*
1940—George Cafego, B, Tennessee*
1941—John Kimbrough, B, Texas A&M
1942—Steve Lach, B, Duke
1943—Glenn Dobbs, B, Tulsa
1944—Pat Harder, B, Wisconsin
1945—Charley Trippi, B, Georgia*
1946—Dub Jones, B, Tulane
1947—DeWitt (Tex) Coulter, T, Army
1948—Jim Spavital, B, Oklahoma State
1949—Bill Fischer, G, Notre Dame
1950—None
1951—Jerry Groom, C, Notre Dame
1952—Ollie Matson, B, San Francisco
1953—Johnny Olszewski, QB, California
1954—Lamar McHan, B, Arkansas
1955—Max Boydston, E, Oklahoma
1956—Joe Childress, B, Auburn
1957—Jerry Tubbs, C, Oklahoma
1958—King Hill, B, Rice*
       John David Crow, B, Texas A&M
1959—Billy Stacy, B, Mississippi State
1960—George Izo, QB, Notre Dame
1961—Ken Rice, T, Auburn
1962—Fate Echols, DT, Northwestern
       Irv Goode, C, Kentucky
1963—Jerry Stovall, DB, LSU
       Don Brumm, E, Purdue
1964—Ken Kortas, DT, Louisville
1965—Joe Namath, QB, Alabama
1966—Carl McAdams, LB, Oklahoma
1967—Dave Williams, WR, Washington
1968—MacArthur Lane, RB, Utah State
1969—Roger Wehrli, DB, Missouri
1970—Larry Stegent, RB, Texas A&M
1971—Norm Thompson, DB, Utah
1972—Bobby Moore, RB, Oregon

1973—Dave Butz, DT, Purdue
1974—J.V. Cain, TE, Colorado
1975—Tim Gray, DB, Texas A&M
1976—Mike Dawson, DT, Arizona
1977—Steve Pisarkiewicz, QB, Missouri
1978—Steve Little, K, Arkansas
       Ken Greene, DB, Washington State
1979—Ottis Anderson, RB, Miami (Fla.)
1980—Curtis Greer, DE, Michigan
1981—E.J. Junior, LB, Alabama
1982—Luis Sharpe, T, UCLA
1983—Leonard Smith, DB, McNeese State
1984—Clyde Duncan, WR, Tennessee
1985—Freddie Joe Nunn, LB, Mississippi
1986—Anthony Bell, LB, Michigan State
1987—Kelly Stouffer, QB, Colorado State
1988—Ken Harvey, LB, California
1989—Eric Hill, LB, LSU
       Joe Wolf, G, Boston College
1990—None
1991—Eric Swann, DL, None
1992—None
1993—Garrison Hearst, RB, Georgia
       Ernest Dye, T, South Carolina
1994—Jamir Miller, LB, UCLA
1995—None
1996—Simeon Rice, DE, Illinois
1997—Tom Knight, DB, Iowa
1998—Andre Wadsworth, DE, Florida State
1999—David Boston, WR, Ohio State
       L.J. Shelton, T, Eastern Michigan
2000—Thomas Jones, RB, Virginia
2001—Leonard Davis, T, Texas
2002—Wendell Bryant, DT, Wisconsin
2003—Bryant Johnson, WR, Penn State
       Calvin Pace, DE, Wake Forest
2004—Larry Fitzgerald, WR, Pittsburgh
2005—Antrel Rolle, CB, Miami
2006—Matt Leinart, QB, USC
       *First player chosen in draft.

FRANCHISE RECORDS

Most rushing yards, career
7,999—Ottis Anderson
Most rushing yards, season
1,605—Ottis Anderson, 1979
Most rushing yards, game
214—LeShon Johnson at N.O., Sept. 22,1996

Most rushing touchdowns, season
14—John David Crow, 1962
Most passing attempts, season
560—Neil Lomax, 1984
Most passing attempts, game
61—Neil Lomax at S.D., Sept. 20, 1987

Most passes completed, season
345—Neil Lomax, 1984
Most passes completed, game
37—Neil Lomax at Was., Dec. 16, 1984
       Kent Graham vs. St.L., Sept. 29, 1996 (OT)
Most passing yards, career
34,639—Jim Hart

HISTORY *Team by team*

Most passing yards, season
4,614—Neil Lomax, 1984
Most passing yards, game
522—Boomer Esiason at Was., Nov. 10, 1996 (OT)
468—Neil Lomax at Was., Dec. 16, 1984
Most touchdown passes, season
28—Charley Johnson, 1963
Neil Lomax, 1984
Most pass receptions, career
535—Larry Centers
Most pass receptions, season
103—Larry Fitzgerald, 2005

Most pass receptions, game
16—Sonny Randle at NYG, Nov. 4, 1962
Most receiving yards, career
8,497—Roy Green
Most receiving yards, season
1,598—David Boston, 2001
Most receiving yards, game
256—Sonny Randle vs. NYG, Nov. 4, 1962
Most receiving touchdowns, season
16—Sonny Randle, 1960
Most touchdowns, career
69—Roy Green
Most field goals, season
40—Neil Rackers, 2005

Longest field goal
55 yards—Greg Davis at Sea., Dec. 19, 1993
Greg Davis at Det., Sept. 17, 1995
Most interceptions, career
52—Larry Wilson
Most interceptions, season
12—Bob Nussbaumer, 1949
Most sacks, career
66—Freddie Joe Nunn
Most sacks, season
16.5—Simeon Rice, 1999

SERIES RECORDS

Arizona vs.: Atlanta 13-9; Baltimore 1-2; Buffalo 3-5; Carolina 2-4; Chicago 26-54-6; Cincinnati 3-5; Cleveland 11-33-3; Dallas 28-54-1; Denver 0-6-1; Detroit 21-31-5; Green Bay 22-41-4; Houston 0-1; Indianapolis 6-7; Jacksonville 0-2; Kansas City 2-6-1; Miami 1-8; Minnesota 9-8; New England 6-5; New Orleans 13-11; N.Y. Giants 41-78-2; N.Y. Jets 2-4; Oakland 2-4; Philadelphia 53-52-5; Pittsburgh 22-31-3; St. Louis 23-27-2; San Diego 3-7; San Francisco 12-17; Seattle 7-7; Tampa Bay 8-7; Tennessee 5-3; Washington 44-71-2. NOTE: Includes records for entire franchise, from 1920 to present; does not include records when team combined with Pittsburgh squad and was known as Card-Pitt in 1944.

COACHING RECORDS

LeRoy Andrews, 0-1-0; Norman Barry, 16-8-2; Joe Bugel, 20-44-0; Guy Chamberlain, 3-7-1; Jack Chevigny, 2-6-2; Jimmy Conzelman, 34-31-3 (1-1); Don Coryell, 42-27-1 (0-2); Milan Creighton, 16-26-4; Paddy Driscoll, 17-8-4; Chuck Drulis-Ray Prochaska-Ray Willsey*, 2-0-0; Fred Gillies, 1-5-0; Dennis Green, 11-21; Phil Handler, 1-29-0; Phil Handler-Cecil Isbell*, 1-1-0; Phil Handler-Buddy Parker*, 2-4-0; Jim Hanifan, 39-49-1 (0-1); Bob Hollway, 8-18-2; Arnold Horween, 13-8-1; Frank Ivy, 17-29-2; Joe Kuharich, 4-8-0; Hank Kuhlmann, 0-5-0; Curly Lambeau, 7-15-0; Wally Lemm, 27-26-3; Dave McGinnis, 17-40-0; Ernie Nevers, 11-19-2; Buddy Parker, 4-1-1; Ray Richards, 14-21-1; Buddy Ryan, 12-20-0; Dewey Scanlon, 6-6-1; Paul Schissler, 6-15-1; Gene Stallings, 23-34-1; Joe Stydahar, 3-20-1; Vince Tobin, 28-43-0 (1-1); Bud Wilkinson, 9-20-0; Larry Wilson, 2-1-0; Charley Winner, 35-30-5.
NOTE: Playoff games in parentheses.
*Co-coaches.

RETIRED UNIFORM NUMBERS

No.	Player
8	Larry Wilson
40	Pat Tillman
77	Stan Mauldin
88	J.V. Cain
99	Marshall Goldberg

ATLANTA FALCONS
YEAR-BY-YEAR RECORDS

	REGULAR SEASON						PLAYOFFS			
Year	W	L	T	Pct.	PF	PA	Finish	W	L	Highest round	Coach
1966	3	11	0	.214	204	437	7th/Eastern Conf.	—	—		Norb Hecker
1967	1	12	1	.077	175	422	4th/Coastal Div.	—	—		Norb Hecker
1968	2	12	0	.143	170	389	4th/Coastal Div.	—	—		N. Hecker, N. Van Brocklin
1969	6	8	0	.429	276	268	3rd/Coastal Div.	—	—		Norm Van Brocklin
1970	4	8	2	.333	206	261	3rd/NFC Western Div.	—	—		Norm Van Brocklin
1971	7	6	1	.538	274	277	3rd/NFC Western Div.	—	—		Norm Van Brocklin
1972	7	7	0	.500	269	274	2nd/NFC Western Div.	—	—		Norm Van Brocklin
1973	9	5	0	.643	318	224	2nd/NFC Western Div.	—	—		Norm Van Brocklin
1974	3	11	0	.214	111	271	4th/NFC Western Div.	—	—		N. Van Brocklin, M. Campbell
1975	4	10	0	.286	240	289	3rd/NFC Western Div.	—	—		Marion Campbell
1976	4	10	0	.286	172	312	3rd/NFC Western Div.	—	—		M. Campbell, Pat Peppler
1977	7	7	0	.500	179	129	2nd/NFC Western Div.	—	—		Leeman Bennett
1978	9	7	0	.563	240	290	2nd/NFC Western Div.	1	1	NFC div. playoff game	Leeman Bennett
1979	6	10	0	.375	300	388	3rd/NFC Western Div.	—	—		Leeman Bennett
1980	12	4	0	.750	405	272	1st/NFC Western Div.	0	1	NFC div. playoff game	Leeman Bennett
1981	7	9	0	.438	426	355	2nd/NFC Western Div.	—	—		Leeman Bennett
1982	5	4	0	.556	183	199	5th/NFC	0	1	NFC first-round pl. game	Leeman Bennett
1983	7	9	0	.438	370	389	4th/NFC Western Div.	—	—		Dan Henning
1984	4	12	0	.250	281	382	4th/NFC Western Div.	—	—		Dan Henning
1985	4	12	0	.250	282	452	4th/NFC Western Div.	—	—		Dan Henning
1986	7	8	1	.469	280	280	3rd/NFC Western Div.	—	—		Dan Henning
1987	3	12	0	.200	205	436	4th/NFC Western Div.	—	—		Marion Campbell
1988	5	11	0	.313	244	315	4th/NFC Western Div.	—	—		Marion Campbell
1989	3	13	0	.188	279	437	4th/NFC Western Div.	—	—		M. Campbell, Jim Hanifan
1990	5	11	0	.313	348	365	4th/NFC Western Div.	—	—		Jerry Glanville
1991	10	6	0	.625	361	338	2nd/NFC Western Div.	1	1	NFC div. playoff game	Jerry Glanville
1992	6	10	0	.375	327	414	3rd/NFC Western Div.	—	—		Jerry Glanville
1993	6	10	0	.375	316	385	3rd/NFC Western Div.	—	—		Jerry Glanville

			REGULAR SEASON					PLAYOFFS			
Year	W	L	T	Pct.	PF	PA	Finish	W	L	Highest round	Coach
1994	7	9	0	.438	317	385	3rd/NFC Western Div.	—	—		June Jones
1995	9	7	0	.563	362	349	2nd/NFC Western Div.	0	1	NFC wild-card game	June Jones
1996	3	13	0	.188	309	461	4th/NFC Western Div.	—	—		June Jones
1997	7	9	0	.438	320	361	3rd/NFC Western Div.	—	—		Dan Reeves
1998	14	2	0	.875	442	289	1st/NFC Western Div.	2	1	Super Bowl	Dan Reeves
1999	5	11	0	.313	285	380	3rd/NFC Western Div.	—	—		Dan Reeves
2000	4	12	0	.250	252	413	5th/NFC Western Div.	—	—		Dan Reeves
2001	7	9	0	.438	291	377	4th/NFC Western Div.	—	—		Dan Reeves
2002	9	6	1	.594	402	314	2nd/NFC South Div.	1	1	NFC div. playoff game	Dan Reeves
2003	5	11	0	.313	299	422	4th/NFC South Div.	—	—		Dan Reeves, Wade Phillips
2004	11	5	0	.688	340	337	1st/NFC South Div.	1	1	NFC championship game	Jim Mora Jr.
2005	8	8	0	.500	351	341	3rd/NFC South Div.	—	—		Jim Mora Jr.

FIRST-ROUND DRAFT PICKS

1966—Tommy Nobis, LB, Texas*
    Randy Johnson, QB, Texas A&I
1967—None
1968—Claude Humphrey, DE, Tennessee State
1969—George Kunz, T, Notre Dame
1970—John Small, LB, Citadel
1971—Joe Profit, RB, Northeast Louisiana State
1972—Clarence Ellis, DB, Notre Dame
1973—None
1974—None
1975—Steve Bartkowski, QB, California*
1976—Bubba Bean, RB, Texas A&M
1977—Warren Bryant, T, Kentucky
    Wilson Faumuina, DT, San Jose State
1978—Mike Kenn, T, Michigan
1979—Don Smith, DE, Miami (Fla.)
1980—Junior Miller, TE, Nebraska
1981—Bobby Butler, DB, Florida State
1982—Gerald Riggs, RB, Arizona State
1983—Mike Pitts, DE, Alabama
1984—Rick Bryan, DT, Oklahoma
1985—Bill Fralic, T, Pittsburgh
1986—Tony Casillas, DT, Oklahoma
    Tim Green, LB, Syracuse

1987—Chris Miller, QB, Oregon
1988—Aundray Bruce, LB, Auburn*
1989—Deion Sanders, DB, Florida State
    Shawn Collins, WR, Northern Arizona
1990—Steve Broussard, RB, Washington State
1991—Bruce Pickens, CB, Nebraska
    Mike Pritchard, WR, Colorado
1992—Bob Whitfield, T, Stanford
    Tony Smith, RB, Southern Mississippi
1993—Lincoln Kennedy, T, Washington
1994—None
1995—Devin Bush, DB, Florida State
1996—None
1997—Michael Booker, DB, Nebraska
1998—Keith Brooking, LB, Georgia Tech
1999—Patrick Kerney, DE, Virginia
2000—None
2001—Michael Vick, QB, Virginia Tech*
2002—T.J. Duckett, FB, Michigan State
2003—None
2004—DeAngelo Hall, CB, Virginia Tech
    Michael Jenkins, WR, Ohio State
2005—Sharod "Roddy" White, WR, Alabama-Birmingham
2006—None
    *First player chosen in draft.

FRANCHISE RECORDS

Most rushing yards, career
6,631—Gerald Riggs
Most rushing yards, season
1,846—Jamal Anderson, 1998
Most rushing yards, game
202—Gerald Riggs at N.O., Sept. 2, 1984
Most rushing touchdowns, season
14—Jamal Anderson, 1998
Most passing attempts, season
557—Jeff George, 1995
Most passing attempts, game
66—Chris Miller vs. Det., Dec. 24, 1989
Most passes completed, season
336—Jeff George, 1995
Most passes completed, game
37—Chris Miller vs. Det., Dec. 24, 1989
Most passing yards, career
23,470—Steve Bartkowski
Most passing yards, season
4,143—Jeff George, 1995

Most passing yards, game
431—Chris Chandler vs. Buf., Dec. 23, 2001
Most touchdown passes, season
31—Steve Bartkowski, 1980
Most pass receptions, career
573—Terance Mathis
Most pass receptions, season
111—Terance Mathis, 1994
Most pass receptions, game
15—William Andrews vs. Pit., Nov. 15, 1981
Most receiving yards, career
7,349—Terance Mathis
Most receiving yards, season
1,358—Alfred Jenkins, 1981
Most receiving yards, game
198—Terance Mathis at N.O., Dec. 13, 1998

Most receiving touchdowns, season
15—Andre Rison, 1993
Most touchdowns, career
57—Terance Mathis
Most field goals, season
32—Jay Feely, 2002
Longest field goal
59 yards—Morten Andersen vs. S.F., Dec. 24, 1995
Most interceptions, career
39—Rolland Lawrence
Most interceptions, season
10—Scott Case, 1988
Most sacks, career
94.5—Claude Humphrey
Most sacks, season
16—Joel Williams, 1980

SERIES RECORDS

Atlanta vs.: Arizona 9-13; Baltimore 1-1; Buffalo 5-4; Carolina 14-8; Chicago 10-12; Cincinnati 3-7; Cleveland 2-9; Dallas 7-12; Denver 4-7; Detroit 9-22; Green Bay 10-12; Houston 0-1; Indianapolis 1-12; Jacksonville 1-2; Kansas City 1-5; Miami 3-7; Minnesota 8-14; New England 6-5; New Orleans 43-30; N.Y. Giants 10-7; N.Y. Jets 5-4; Oakland 4-7; Philadelphia 10-11-1; Pittsburgh 1-11-1; St. Louis 24-46-2; San Diego 6-1; San Francisco 26-44-1; Seattle 2-8; Tampa Bay 10-15; Tennessee 5-6; Washington 4-14-1.

HISTORY *Team by team*

COACHING RECORDS

Leeman Bennett, 46-41-0 (1-3); Marion Campbell, 17-51-0; Jerry Glanville, 27-37-0 (1-1); Jim Hanifan, 0-4-0; Norb Hecker, 4-26-1; Dan Henning, 22-41-1; June Jones, 19-29-0 (0-1); Jim Mora Jr., 19-13-0 (1-1); Pat Peppler, 3-6-0; Wade Phillips, 2-1-0; Dan Reeves, 49-59-1 (3-2); Norm Van Brocklin, 37-49-3.
NOTE: Playoff games in parentheses.

BALTIMORE RAVENS
YEAR-BY-YEAR RECORDS

	REGULAR SEASON							PLAYOFFS			
Year	W	L	T	Pct.	PF	PA	Finish	W	L	Highest round	Coach
1996	4	12	0	.250	371	441	5th/AFC Central Div.	—	—		Ted Marchibroda
1997	6	9	1	.406	326	345	5th/AFC Central Div.	—	—		Ted Marchibroda
1998	6	10	0	.375	269	335	4th/AFC Central Div.	—	—		Ted Marchibroda
1999	8	8	0	.500	324	277	3rd/AFC Central Div.	—	—		Brian Billick
2000	12	4	0	.750	333	165	2nd/AFC Central Div.	4	0	Super Bowl champ	Brian Billick
2001	10	6	0	.625	303	265	2nd/AFC Central Div.	1	1	AFC div. playoff game	Brian Billick
2002	7	9	0	.438	316	354	3rd/AFC North Div.	—	—		Brian Billick
2003	10	6	0	.625	391	281	1st/AFC North Div.	0	1	AFC wild-card game	Brian Billick
2004	9	7	0	.562	317	268	2nd/AFC North Div.	—	—		Brian Billick
2005	6	10	0	.375	265	299	3rd/AFC North Div.	—	—		Brian Billick

FIRST-ROUND DRAFT PICKS

1996—Jonathan Ogden, T, UCLA
    Ray Lewis, LB, Miami (Fla.)
1997—Peter Boulware, DE, Florida State
1998—Duane Starks, DB, Miami (Fla.)
1999—Chris McAlister, DB, Arizona
2000—Jamal Lewis, RB, Tennessee
    Travis Taylor, WR, Florida

2001—Todd Heap, TE, Arizona State
2002—Ed Reed, S, Miami (Fla.)
2003—Terrell Suggs, DE, Arizona State
    Kyle Boller, QB, California
2004—None
2005—Mark Clayton, WR, Oklahoma
2006—Haloti Ngata, DT, Oregon

FRANCHISE RECORDS

Most rushing yards, career
6,669—Jamal Lewis
Most rushing yards, season
2,066—Jamal Lewis, 2003
Most rushing yards, game
295—Jamal Lewis vs. Cle., Sept. 14, 2003
Most rushing touchdowns, season
14—Jamal Lewis, 2003
Most passing attempts, season
549—Vinny Testaverde, 1996
Most passing attempts, game
63—Elvis Grbac at Cin., Sept. 23, 2001
Most passes completed, season
325—Vinny Testaverde, 1996
Most passes completed, game
33—Elvis Grbac at Cin., Sept. 23, 2001
Most passing yards, career
7,148—Vinny Testaverde

Most passing yards, season
4,177—Vinny Testaverde, 1996
Most passing yards, game
429—Vinny Testaverde vs. St.L., Oct. 27, 1996 (OT)
366—Vinny Testaverde vs. Jac., Nov. 24, 1996 (OT)
353—Vinny Testaverde vs. N.E., Oct. 6, 1996
Most touchdown passes, season
33—Vinny Testaverde, 1996
Most pass receptions, career
243—Todd Heap
Most pass receptions, season
76—Michael Jackson, 1996
Most pass receptions, game
13—Priest Holmes vs. Ten., Oct. 11, 1998
Most receiving yards, career
2,893—Todd Heap
Most receiving yards, season
1,201—Michael Jackson, 1996

Most receiving yards, game
258—Qadry Ismail at Pit., Dec. 12, 1999
Most receiving touchdowns, season
14—Michael Jackson, 1996
Most touchdowns, career
38—Jamal Lewis
Most field goals, season
35—Matt Stover, 2000
Longest field goal
56 yards—Wade Richey vs. Cle., Sept. 14, 2003
Most interceptions, career
22—Ed Reed
Most interceptions, season
9—Ed Reed, 2004
Most sacks, career
67.5—Peter Boulware
Most sacks, season
15—Peter Boulware, 2001

SERIES RECORDS

Baltimore vs.: Arizona 2-1; Atlanta 1-1; Buffalo 1-1; Carolina 0-2; Chicago 1-2; Cincinnati 12-8; Cleveland 9-5; Dallas 2-0; Denver 3-2; Detroit 1-1; Green Bay 1-2; Houston 2-0; Indianapolis 2-4; Jacksonville 6-9; Kansas City 0-3; Miami 1-4; Minnesota 2-1; New England 0-3; New Orleans 2-1; N.Y. Giants 2-0; N.Y. Jets 4-1; Oakland 2-1; Philadelphia, 0-1-1; Pittsburgh 7-13; St. Louis 1-2; San Diego 2-2; San Francisco 1-1; Seattle 2-0; Tampa Bay 0-2; Tennessee 7-7; Washington 2-1.

COACHING RECORDS

Brian Billick, 62-50-0 (5-2); Ted Marchibroda, 16-31-1.
NOTE: Playoff games in parentheses.

HISTORY *Team by team*

BUFFALO BILLS
YEAR-BY-YEAR RECORDS

	REGULAR SEASON							PLAYOFFS			
Year	W	L	T	Pct.	PF	PA	Finish	W	L	Highest round	Coach
1960*	5	8	1	.385	296	303	3rd/Eastern Div.	—	—		Buster Ramsey
1961*	6	8	0	.429	294	342	4th/Eastern Div.	—	—		Buster Ramsey
1962*	7	6	1	.538	309	272	3rd/Eastern Div.	—	—		Lou Saban
1963*	7	6	1	.538	304	291	2nd/Eastern Div.	0	1	E. Div. championship game	Lou Saban
1964*	12	2	0	.857	400	242	1st/Eastern Div.	1	0	AFL champ	Lou Saban
1965*	10	3	1	.769	313	226	1st/Eastern Div.	1	0	AFL champ	Lou Saban
1966*	9	4	1	.692	358	255	1st/Eastern Div.	0	1	AFL championship game	Joe Collier
1967*	4	10	0	.286	237	285	T3rd/Eastern Div.	—	—		Joe Collier
1968*	1	12	1	.077	199	367	5th/Eastern Div.	—	—		J. Collier, H. Johnson
1969*	4	10	0	.286	230	359	T3rd/Eastern Div.	—	—		John Rauch
1970	3	10	1	.231	204	337	4th/AFC Eastern Div.	—	—		John Rauch
1971	1	13	0	.071	184	394	5th/AFC Eastern Div.	—	—		Harvey Johnson
1972	4	9	1	.321	257	377	4th/AFC Eastern Div.	—	—		Lou Saban
1973	9	5	0	.643	259	230	2nd/AFC Eastern Div.	—	—		Lou Saban
1974	9	5	0	.643	264	244	2nd/AFC Eastern Div.	0	1	AFC div. playoff game	Lou Saban
1975	8	6	0	.571	420	355	3rd/AFC Eastern Div.	—	—		Lou Saban
1976	2	12	0	.143	245	363	5th/AFC Eastern Div.	—	—		Lou Saban, Jim Ringo
1977	3	11	0	.214	160	313	5th/AFC Eastern Div.	—	—		Jim Ringo
1978	5	11	0	.313	302	354	4th/AFC Eastern Div.	—	—		Chuck Knox
1979	7	9	0	.438	268	279	4th/AFC Eastern Div.	—	—		Chuck Knox
1980	11	5	0	.688	320	260	1st/AFC Eastern Div.	0	1	AFC div. playoff game	Chuck Knox
1981	10	6	0	.625	311	276	3rd/AFC Eastern Div.	1	1	AFC div. playoff game	Chuck Knox
1982	4	5	0	.444	150	154	9th/AFC	—	—		Chuck Knox
1983	8	8	0	.500	283	351	3rd/AFC Eastern Div.	—	—		Kay Stephenson
1984	2	14	0	.125	250	454	5th/AFC Eastern Div.	—	—		Kay Stephenson
1985	2	14	0	.125	200	381	5th/AFC Eastern Div.	—	—		Kay Stephenson, Hank Bullough
1986	4	12	0	.250	287	348	4th/AFC Eastern Div.	—	—		H. Bullough, M. Levy
1987	7	8	0	.467	270	305	4th/AFC Eastern Div.	—	—		Marv Levy
1988	12	4	0	.750	329	237	1st/AFC Eastern Div.	1	1	AFC championship game	Marv Levy
1989	9	7	0	.563	409	317	1st/AFC Eastern Div.	0	1	AFC div. playoff game	Marv Levy
1990	13	3	0	.813	428	263	1st/AFC Eastern Div.	2	1	Super Bowl	Marv Levy
1991	13	3	0	.813	458	318	1st/AFC Eastern Div.	2	1	Super Bowl	Marv Levy
1992	11	5	0	.688	381	283	2nd/AFC Eastern Div.	3	1	Super Bowl	Marv Levy
1993	12	4	0	.750	329	242	1st/AFC Eastern Div.	2	1	Super Bowl	Marv Levy
1994	7	9	0	.438	340	356	4th/AFC Eastern Div.	—	—		Marv Levy
1995	10	6	0	.625	350	335	1st/AFC Eastern Div.	1	1	AFC div. playoff game	Marv Levy
1996	10	6	0	.625	319	266	2nd/AFC Eastern Div.	0	1	AFC wild-card game	Marv Levy
1997	6	10	0	.375	255	367	4th/AFC Eastern Div.	—	—		Marv Levy
1998	10	6	0	.625	400	333	3rd/AFC Eastern Div.	0	1	AFC wild-card game	Wade Phillips
1999	11	5	0	.688	320	229	2nd/AFC Eastern Div.	0	1	AFC wild-card game	Wade Phillips
2000	8	8	0	.500	315	350	4th/AFC Eastern Div.	—	—		Wade Phillips
2001	3	13	0	.188	265	420	5th/AFC Eastern Div.	—	—		Gregg Williams
2002	8	8	0	.500	379	397	4th/AFC East Div.	—	—		Gregg Williams
2003	6	10	0	.375	243	279	3rd/AFC East Div.	—	—		Gregg Williams
2004	9	7	0	.562	395	284	3rd/AFC East Div.	—	—		Mike Mularkey
2005	5	11	0	.312	271	367	3rd/AFC East Div.	—	—		Mike Mularkey

*American Football League.

FIRST-ROUND DRAFT PICKS

1960—Richie Lucas, QB, Penn State
1961—Ken Rice, T, Auburn* (AFL)
1962—Ernie Davis, RB, Syracuse
1963—Dave Behrman, C, Michigan State
1964—Carl Eller, DE, Minnesota
1965—Jim Davidson, T, Ohio State
1966—Mike Dennis, RB, Mississippi
1967—John Pitts, DB, Arizona State
1968—Haven Moses, WR, San Diego State
1969—O.J. Simpson, RB, USC*
1970—Al Cowlings, DE, USC
1971—J.D. Hill, WR, Arizona State
1972—Walt Patulski, DE, Notre Dame*
1973—Paul Seymour, T, Michigan
    Joe DeLamielleure, G, Michigan State
1974—Reuben Gant, TE, Oklahoma State
1975—Tom Ruud, LB, Nebraska
1976—Mario Clark, DB, Oregon
1977—Phil Dokes, DT, Oklahoma State
1978—Terry Miller, RB, Oklahoma State
1979—Tom Cousineau, LB, Ohio State*

    Jerry Butler, WR, Clemson
1980—Jim Ritcher, C, N.C. State
1981—Booker Moore, RB, Penn State
1982—Perry Tuttle, WR, Clemson
1983—Tony Hunter, TE, Notre Dame
    Jim Kelly, QB, Miami (Fla.)
1984—Greg Bell, RB, Notre Dame
1985—Bruce Smith, DE, Virginia Tech*
    Derrick Burroughs, DB, Memphis State
1986—Ronnie Harmon, RB, Iowa
    Will Wolford, T, Vanderbilt
1987—Shane Conlan, LB, Penn State
1988—None
1989—None
1990—James Williams, DB, Fresno State
1991—Henry Jones, S, Illinois
1992—John Fina, T, Arizona
1993—Thomas Smith, DB, North Carolina
1994—Jeff Burris, DB, Notre Dame
1995—Ruben Brown, G, Pittsburgh
1996—Eric Moulds, WR, Mississippi State

1997—Antowain Smith, RB, Houston
1998—None
1999—Antoine Winfield, DB, Ohio State
2000—Erik Flowers, DE, Arizona State
2001—Nate Clements, DB, Ohio State
2002—Mike Williams, T, Texas
2003—Willis McGahee, RB, Miami (Fla.)

2004—Lee Evans, WR, Wisconsin
      J.P. Losman, QB, Tulane
2005—None
2006—Donte Whitner, DB, Ohio State
      John McCargo, DT, N.C. State
*First player chosen in draft.

FRANCHISE RECORDS

Most rushing yards, career
11,938—Thurman Thomas
Most rushing yards, season
2,003—O.J. Simpson, 1973
Most rushing yards, game
273—O.J. Simpson at Det., Nov. 25,1976
Most rushing touchdowns, season
16—O.J. Simpson, 1975
Most passing attempts, season
610—Drew Bledsoe, 2002
Most passing attempts, game
55—Joe Ferguson at Mia., Oct. 9, 1983
Most passes completed, season
375—Drew Bledsoe, 2002
Most passes completed, game
38—Joe Ferguson at Mia., Oct. 9, 1983
Most passing yards, career
35,467—Jim Kelly
Most passing yards, season
4,359—Drew Bledsoe, 2002

Most passing yards, game
463—Drew Bledsoe at Min., Sept. 15,
      2002 (OT)
419—Joe Ferguson at Mia., Oct. 9, 1983(OT)
403—Jim Kelly at S.F., Sept. 13, 1992
Most touchdown passes, season
33—Jim Kelly, 1991
Most pass receptions, career
941—Andre Reed
Most pass receptions, season
100—Eric Moulds, 2002
Most pass receptions, game
15—Andre Reed vs. G.B., Nov. 20, 1994
Most receiving yards, career
13,095—Andre Reed
Most receiving yards, season
1,368—Eric Moulds, 1998
Most receiving yards, game
255—Jerry Butler vs. NYJ, Sept. 23, 1979

Most receiving touchdowns, season
11—Bill Brooks, 1995
Most touchdowns, career
87—Andre Reed
      Thurman Thomas
Most field goals, season
33—Steve Christie, 1998
Longest field goal
59 yards—Steve Christie vs. Mia., Sept.
      26, 1993
Most interceptions, career
40—George Byrd
Most interceptions, season
10—Billy Atkins, 1961
      Tom Janik, 1967
Most sacks, career
171—Bruce Smith
Most sacks, season
19—Bruce Smith, 1990

SERIES RECORDS

Buffalo vs.: Arizona 5-3; Atlanta 4-5; Baltimore 1-1; Carolina 3-1; Chicago 4-5; Cincinnati 13-9; Cleveland 5-7; Dallas 3-4; Denver 17-14-1; Detroit 3-3-1; Green Bay 6-3; Houston 2-1; Indianapolis 34-29-1; Jacksonville 3-2; Kansas City 19-16-1; Miami 30-49-1; Minnesota 3-7; New England 40-50-1; New Orleans 4-4; N.Y. Giants 6-3; N.Y. Jets 49-41; Oakland 15-19; Philadelphia 5-5; Pittsburgh 8-10; St. Louis 5-4; San Diego 9-19-2; San Francisco 5-4; Seattle 4-6; Tampa Bay 2-6; Tennessee 14-23; Washington 6-4.

COACHING RECORDS

Hank Bullough, 4-17-0; Joe Collier, 13-16-1 (0-1); Harvey Johnson, 2-23-1; Chuck Knox, 37-36-0 (1-2); Marv Levy, 112-70-0 (11-8); Mike Mularkey, 14-18-0; Wade Phillips, 29-19-0 (0-2); Buster Ramsey, 11-16-1; John Rauch, 7-20-1; Jim Ringo, 3-20-0; Lou Saban, 68-45-4 (2-2); Kay Stephenson, 10-26-0; Gregg Williams, 17-31-0.
NOTE: Playoff games in parentheses.

RETIRED UNIFORM NUMBERS

No.	Player
12	Jim Kelly

CAROLINA PANTHERS
YEAR-BY-YEAR RECORDS

		REGULAR SEASON							PLAYOFFS		
Year	W	L	T	Pct.	PF	PA	Finish	W	L	Highest round	Coach
1995	7	9	0	.438	289	325	4th/NFC Western Div.	—	—		Dom Capers
1996	12	4	0	.750	367	218	1st/NFC Western Div.	1	1	NFC championship game	Dom Capers
1997	7	9	0	.438	265	314	2nd/NFC Western Div.	—	—		Dom Capers
1998	4	12	0	.250	336	413	4th/NFC Western Div.	—	—		Dom Capers
1999	8	8	0	.500	421	381	3rd/NFC Western Div.	—	—		George Seifert
2000	7	9	0	.438	310	310	3rd/NFC Western Div.	—	—		George Seifert
2001	1	15	0	.063	253	410	5th/NFC Western Div.	—	—		George Seifert
2002	7	9	0	.438	258	302	4th/NFC South Div.	—	—		John Fox
2003	11	5	0	.688	325	304	1st/NFC South Div.	3	1	Super Bowl	John Fox
2004	7	9	0	.438	355	339	3rd/NFC South Div.	—	—		John Fox
2005	11	5	0	.688	391	259	2nd/NFC South Div.	2	1	NFC championship game	John Fox

FIRST-ROUND DRAFT PICKS

1995—Kerry Collins, QB, Penn State
      Tyrone Poole, DB, Fort Valley (Ga.) St.
      Blake Brockermeyer, T, Texas
1996—Tim Biakabutuka, RB, Michigan
1997—Rae Carruth, WR, Colorado
1998—Jason Peter, DT, Nebraska
1999—None

2000—Rashard Anderson, DB, Jackson State
2001—Dan Morgan, LB, Miami
2002—Julius Peppers, DE, North Carolina
2003—Jordan Gross, T, Utah
2004—Chris Gamble, CB, Ohio State
2005—Thomas Davis, FS, Georgia
2006—DeAngelo Williams, RB, Memphis

Most rushing yards, career
2,530—Tim Biakabatuka
Most rushing yards, season
1,444—Stephen Davis, 2003
Most rushing yards, game
178—Stephen Davis at. N.O., Oct. 26, 2003
Most rushing touchdowns, season
12—Stephen Davis, 2005
Most passing attempts, season
571—Steve Beuerlein, 1999
Most passing attempts, game
63—Chris Weinke vs. Ari., Dec. 30, 2001
Most passes completed, season
343—Steve Beuerlein, 1999
Most passes completed, game
36—Chris Weinke vs. Ari., Dec. 30, 2001
Most passing yards, career
12,690—Steve Beuerlein

Most passing yards, season
4,436—Steve Beuerlein, 1999
Most passing yards, game
373—Steve Beuerlein at Green Bay, Dec. 12, 1999
Most touchdown passes, season
36—Steve Beuerlein, 1999
Most pass receptions, career
578—Muhsin Muhammad
Most pass receptions, season
103—Steve Smith, 2005
Most pass receptions, game
14—Steve Smith at Chi., Nov. 20, 2005
Most receiving yards, career
7,751—Muhsin Muhammad
Most receiving yards, season
1,563—Steve Smith, 2005
Most receiving yards, game
201—Steve Smith vs. Min., Oct. 30, 200

Most receiving touchdowns, season
16—Muhsin Muhammad, 2004
Most touchdowns, career
44—Muhsin Muhammad
  Wesley Walls
Most field goals, season
37—John Kasay, 1996
Longest field goal
56 yards—John Kasay vs. G.B., Sept. 27, 1998
Most interceptions, career
25—Eric Davis
Most interceptions, season
8—Doug Evans, 2001
Most sacks, career
47.5—Mike Rucker
Most sacks, season
15—Kevin Greene, 1998

SERIES RECORDS

Carolina vs.: Arizona 4-2; Atlanta 8-14; Baltimore 2-0; Buffalo 1-3; Chicago 2-2; Cincinnati 2-0; Cleveland 2-0; Dallas 1-5; Denver 0-2; Detroit 3-1; Green Bay 3-5; Houston 0-1; Indianapolis 3-0; Jacksonville 1-2; Kansas City 1-2; Miami 0-3; Minnesota 3-3; New England 3-0; New Orleans 11-11; N.Y. Giants 3-0; N.Y. Jets 2-2; Oakland 1-2; Philadelphia 1-3; Pittsburgh 1-2; St. Louis 8-7; San Diego 2-1; San Francisco 8-7; Seattle 1-2.

COACHING RECORDS

Dom Capers, 30-34-0 (1-1); John Fox, 36-28-0 (5-2); George Seifert, 16-32-0.
NOTE: Playoff games in parentheses.

RETIRED UNIFORM NUMBERS

No.	Player
51	Sam Mills

CHICAGO BEARS
YEAR-BY-YEAR RECORDS

			REGULAR SEASON						PLAYOFFS		
Year	W	L	T	Pct.	PF	PA	Finish	W	L	Highest round	Coach
1920*	10	1	2	.909	...	...	2nd				George Halas
1921†	9	1	1	.900	...	...	1st				George Halas
1922	9	3	0	.750	...	...	2nd				George Halas
1923	9	2	1	.818	...	...	2nd				George Halas
1924	6	1	4	.857	...	...	2nd				George Halas
1925	9	5	3	.643	...	...	7th				George Halas
1926	12	1	3	.923	...	...	2nd				George Halas
1927	9	3	2	.750	...	...	3rd				George Halas
1928	7	5	1	.583	...	...	5th				George Halas
1929	4	9	2	.308	...	...	9th				George Halas
1930	9	4	1	.692	...	...	3rd				Ralph Jones
1931	8	5	0	.615	...	...	3rd				Ralph Jones
1932	7	1	6	.875	...	...	1st				Ralph Jones
1933	10	2	1	.833	133	82	1st/Western Div.	1	0	NFL champ	George Halas
1934	13	0	0	1.000	286	86	1st/Western Div.	0	1	NFL championship game	George Halas
1935	6	4	2	.600	192	106	T3rd/Western Div.	—	—		George Halas
1936	9	3	0	.750	222	94	2nd/Western Div.	—	—		George Halas
1937	9	1	1	.900	201	100	1st/Western Div.	0	1	NFL championship game	George Halas
1938	6	5	0	.545	194	148	3rd/Western Div.	—	—		George Halas
1939	8	3	0	.727	298	157	2nd/Western Div.	—	—		George Halas
1940	8	3	0	.727	238	152	1st/Western Div.	1	0	NFL champ	George Halas
1941	10	1	0	.909	396	147	1st/Western Div.	2	0	NFL champ	George Halas
1942	11	0	0	1.000	376	84	1st/Western Div.	0	1	NFL championship game	George Halas, Hunk Anderson-Luke Johnsos
1943	8	1	1	.889	303	157	1st/Western Div.	1	0	NFL champ	H. Anderson-L. Johnsos
1944	6	3	1	.667	258	172	T2nd/Western Div.	—	—		H. Anderson-L. Johnsos
1945	3	7	0	.300	192	235	4th/Western Div.	—	—		H. Anderson-L. Johnsos
1946	8	2	1	.800	289	193	1st/Western Div.	1	0	NFL champ	George Halas

	REGULAR SEASON							PLAYOFFS			
Year	W	L	T	Pct.	PF	PA	Finish	W	L	Highest round	Coach
1947	8	4	0	.667	363	241	2nd/Western Div.	—	—		George Halas
1948	10	2	0	.833	375	151	2nd/Western Div.	—	—		George Halas
1949	9	3	0	.750	332	218	2nd/Western Div.	—	—		George Halas
1950	9	3	0	.750	279	207	2nd/National Conf.	0	1	Nat. Conf. champ. game	George Halas
1951	7	5	0	.583	286	282	4th/National Conf.	—	—		George Halas
1952	5	7	0	.417	245	326	5th/National Conf.	—	—		George Halas
1953	3	8	1	.273	218	262	T4th/Western Conf.	—	—		George Halas
1954	8	4	0	.667	301	279	2nd/Western Conf.	—	—		George Halas
1955	8	4	0	.667	294	251	2nd/Western Conf.	—	—		George Halas
1956	9	2	1	.818	363	246	1st/Western Conf.	0	1	NFL championship game	Paddy Driscoll
1957	5	7	0	.417	203	211	5th/Western Conf.	—	—		Paddy Driscoll
1958	8	4	0	.667	298	230	T2nd/Western Conf.	—	—		George Halas
1959	8	4	0	.667	252	196	2nd/Western Conf.	—	—		George Halas
1960	5	6	1	.455	194	299	5th/Western Conf.	—	—		George Halas
1961	8	6	0	.571	326	302	T3rd/Western Conf.	—	—		George Halas
1962	9	5	0	.643	321	287	3rd/Western Conf.	—	—		George Halas
1963	11	1	2	.917	301	144	1st/Western Conf.	1	0	NFL champ	George Halas
1964	5	9	0	.357	260	379	6th/Western Conf.	—	—		George Halas
1965	9	5	0	.643	409	275	3rd/Western Conf.	—	—		George Halas
1966	5	7	2	.417	234	272	5th/Western Conf.	—	—		George Halas
1967	7	6	1	.538	239	218	2nd/Central Div.	—	—		Jim Dooley
1968	7	7	0	.500	250	333	2nd/Central Div.	—	—		Jim Dooley
1969	1	13	0	.071	210	339	4th/Central Div.	—	—		Jim Dooley
1970	6	8	0	.429	256	261	3rd/NFC Central Div.	—	—		Jim Dooley
1971	6	8	0	.429	185	276	3rd/NFC Central Div.	—	—		Abe Gibron
1972	4	9	1	.321	225	275	4th/NFC Central Div.	—	—		Abe Gibron
1973	3	11	0	.214	195	334	4th/NFC Central Div.	—	—		Abe Gibron
1974	4	10	0	.286	152	279	4th/NFC Central Div.	—	—		Jack Pardee
1975	4	10	0	.286	191	379	3rd/NFC Central Div.	—	—		Jack Pardee
1976	7	7	0	.500	253	216	2nd/NFC Central Div.	—	—		Jack Pardee
1977	9	5	0	.643	255	253	2nd/NFC Central Div.	0	1	NFC div. playoff game	Jack Pardee
1978	7	9	0	.438	253	274	4th/NFC Central Div.	—	—		Neill Armstrong
1979	10	6	0	.625	306	249	2nd/NFC Central Div.	0	1	NFC wild-card game	Neill Armstrong
1980	7	9	0	.438	304	264	3rd/NFC Central Div.	—	—		Neill Armstrong
1981	6	10	0	.375	253	324	5th/NFC Central Div.	—	—		Neill Armstrong
1982	3	6	0	.333	141	174	12th/NFC	—	—		Mike Ditka
1983	8	8	0	.500	311	301	3rd/NFC Central Div.	—	—		Mike Ditka
1984	10	6	0	.625	325	248	1st/NFC Central Div.	1	1	NFC championship game	Mike Ditka
1985	15	1	0	.938	456	198	1st/NFC Central Div.	3	0	Super Bowl champ	Mike Ditka
1986	14	2	0	.875	352	187	1st/NFC Central Div.	0	1	NFC div. playoff game	Mike Ditka
1987	11	4	0	.733	356	282	1st/NFC Central Div.	0	1	NFC div. playoff game	Mike Ditka
1988	12	4	0	.750	312	215	1st/NFC Central Div.	1	1	NFC championship game	Mike Ditka
1989	6	10	0	.375	358	377	4th/NFC Central Div.	—	—		Mike Ditka
1990	11	5	0	.688	348	280	1st/NFC Central Div.	1	1	NFC div. playoff game	Mike Ditka
1991	11	5	0	.688	299	269	2nd/NFC Central Div.	0	1	NFC wild-card game	Mike Ditka
1992	5	11	0	.313	295	361	4th/NFC Central Div.	—	—		Dave Wannstedt
1993	7	9	0	.438	234	230	4th/NFC Central Div.	—	—		Dave Wannstedt
1994	9	7	0	.563	271	307	4th/NFC Central Div.	1	1	NFC div. playoff game	Dave Wannstedt
1995	9	7	0	.563	392	360	3rd/NFC Central Div.	—	—		Dave Wannstedt
1996	7	9	0	.438	283	305	3rd/NFC Central Div.	—	—		Dave Wannstedt
1997	4	12	0	.250	263	421	5th/NFC Central Div.	—	—		Dave Wannstedt
1998	4	12	0	.250	276	368	5th/NFC Central Div.	—	—		Dave Wannstedt
1999	6	10	0	.375	272	341	5th NFC Central Div.	—	—		Dick Jauron
2000	5	11	0	.313	216	355	5th/NFC Central Div.	—	—		Dick Jauron
2001	13	3	0	.813	338	203	1st/NFC Central Div.	0	1	NFC div. playoff game	Dick Jauron
2002	4	12	0	.250	281	379	3rd/NFC North Div.	—	—		Dick Jauron
2003	7	9	0	.438	283	346	3rd/NFC North Div.	—	—		Dick Jauron
2004	5	11	0	.312	231	331	4th/NFC North Div.	—	—		Lovie Smith
2005	11	5	0	.688	260	202	1st/NFC North Div.	0	1	NFC div. playoff game	Lovie Smith

*Decatur Staleys.
†Chicago Staleys.

FIRST-ROUND DRAFT PICKS

1936—Joe Stydahar, T, West Virginia
1937—Les McDonald, E, Nebraska
1938—Joe Gray, B, Oregon State
1939—Sid Luckman, QB, Columbia
      Bill Osmanski, B, Holy Cross
1940—C. Turner, C, Hardin-Simmons
1941—Tom Harmon, B, Michigan*
      Norm Standlee, B, Stanford
      Don Scott, B, Ohio State

1942—Frankie Albert, B, Stanford
1943—Bob Steuber, B, Missouri
1944—Ray Evans, B, Kansas
1945—Don Lund, B, Michigan
1946—Johnny Lujack, QB, Notre Dame
1947—Bob Fenimore, B, Oklahoma State*
      Don Kindt, B, Wisconsin
1948—Bobby Layne, QB, Texas
      Max Bumgardner, E, Texas

1949—Dick Harris, C, Texas
1950—Chuck Hunsinger, B, Florida
1951—Bob Williams, B, Notre Dame
    Billy Stone, B, Bradley
    Gene Schroeder, E, Virginia
1952—Jim Dooley, B, Miami
1953—Billy Anderson, B, Compton (Ca.) J.C.
1954—Stan Wallace, B, Illinois
1955—Ron Drzewiecki, B, Marquette
1956—Menan (Tex) Schriewer, E, Texas
1957—Earl Leggett, DT, LSU
1958—Chuck Howley, G, West Virginia
1959—Don Clark, B, Ohio State
1960—Roger Davis, G, Syracuse
1961—Mike Ditka, E, Pittsburgh
1962—Ron Bull, RB, Baylor
1963—Dave Behrman, C, Michigan State
1964—Dick Evey, DT, Tennessee
1965—Dick Butkus, LB, Illinois
    Gale Sayers, RB, Kansas
    Steve DeLong, DE, Tennessee
1966—George Rice, DT, LSU
1967—Loyd Phillips, DE, Arkansas
1968—Mike Hull, RB, USC
1969—Rufus Mayes, T, Ohio State
1970—None
1971—Joe Moore, RB, Missouri
1972—Lionel Antoine, T, Southern Illinois
    Craig Clemons, DB, Iowa
1973—Wally Chambers, DE, Eastern Kentucky
1974—Waymond Bryant, LB, Tennessee State
    Dave Gallagher, DE, Michigan
1975—Walter Payton, RB, Jackson State
1976—Dennis Lick, T, Wisconsin
1977—Ted Albrecht, T, California

1978—None
1979—Dan Hampton, DT, Arkansas
    Al Harris, DE, Arizona State
1980—Otis Wilson, LB, Louisville
1981—Keith Van Horne, T, USC
1982—Jim McMahon, QB, Brigham Young
1983—Jimbo Covert, T, Pittsburgh
    Willie Gault, WR, Tennessee
1984—Wilber Marshall, LB, Florida
1985—William Perry, DT, Clemson
1986—Neal Anderson, RB, Florida
1987—Jim Harbaugh, QB, Michigan
1988—Brad Muster, RB, Stanford
    Wendell Davis, WR, LSU
1989—Donnell Woolford, DB, Clemson
    Trace Armstrong, DE, Florida
1990—Mark Carrier, DB, USC
1991—Stan Thomas, T, Texas
1992—Alonzo Spellman, DE, Ohio State
1993—Curtis Conway, WR, USC
1994—John Thierry, LB, Alcorn State
1995—Rashaan Salaam, RB, Colorado
1996—Walt Harris, DB, Mississippi State
1997—None
1998—Curtis Enis, RB, Penn State
1999—Cade McNown, QB, UCLA
2000—Brian Urlacher, LB, New Mexico
2001—David Terrell, WR, Michigan
2002—Marc Colombo, T, Boston College
2003—Michael Haynes, DE, Penn State
    Rex Grossman, QB, Florida
2004—Tommie Harris, DT, Oklahoma
2005—Cedric Benson, RB, Texas
2006—None
*First player chosen in draft.

FRANCHISE RECORDS

Most rushing yards, career
16,726—Walter Payton
Most rushing yards, season
1,852—Walter Payton, 1977
Most rushing yards, game
275—Walter Payton vs. Min., Nov. 20, 1977
Most rushing touchdowns, season
14—Gale Sayers, 1965
    Walter Payton, 1977
    Walter Payton, 1979
Most passing attempts, season
522—Erik Kramer, 1995
Most passing attempts, game
60—Erik Kramer vs. NYJ, Nov. 16, 1997
Most passes completed, season
315—Erik Kramer, 1995
Most passes completed, game
34—Jim Miller vs. Min., Nov. 14, 1999 (OT)
33—Bill Wade at Was., Oct. 25, 1964

Most passing yards, career
14,686—Sid Luckman
Most passing yards, season
3,838—Erik Kramer, 1995
Most passing yards, game
468—Johnny Lujack vs. Chi. Cards, Dec. 11, 1949
Most touchdown passes, season
29—Erik Kramer, 1995
Most pass receptions, career
492—Walter Payton
Most pass receptions, season
100—Marty Booker, 2001
Most pass receptions, game
14—Jim Keane at NYG, Oct. 23, 1949
Most receiving yards, career
5,059—Johnny Morris
Most receiving yards, season
1,400—Marcus Robinson, 1999
Most receiving yards, game
214—Harlon Hill at S.F., Oct. 31, 1954

Most receiving touchdowns, season
13—Ken Kavanaugh, 1947
    Dick Gordon, 1970
Most touchdowns, career
125—Walter Payton
Most field goals, season
31—Kevin Butler, 1985
Longest field goal
55 yards—Bob Thomas at L.A. Rams, Nov. 23, 1975
    Kevin Butler vs. Min., Oct. 25, 1993
    Kevin Butler at T.B., Dec. 12, 1993
Most interceptions, career
38—Gary Fencik
Most interceptions, season
10—Mark Carrier, 1990
Most sacks, career
124.5—Richard Dent
Most sacks, season
17.5—Richard Dent, 1984

SERIES RECORDS

Chicago vs.: Arizona 54-26-6; Atlanta 12-10; Baltimore 2-1; Buffalo 5-4; Carolina 2-2; Cincinnati 3-5; Cleveland 4-9; Dallas 8-10; Denver 6-6; Detroit 85-62-5; Green Bay 86-78-6; Houston 0-1; Indianapolis 17-22; Jacksonville 2-2; Kansas City 5-4; Miami 3-6; Minnesota 39-48-2; New England 3-6; New Orleans 11-11; N.Y. Giants 26-17-2; N.Y. Jets 5-3; Oakland 5-6; Philadelphia 24-8-1; Pittsburgh 16-7-1; St. Louis 47-34-3; San Diego 5-4; San Francisco 28-27-1; Seattle 2-6; Tampa Bay 34-17; Tennessee 5-4; Washington 20-17-1. NOTE: Includes records as Decatur Staleys in 1920 and Chicago Staleys in 1921.

COACHING RECORDS

Hunk Anderson-Luke Johnsos*, 23-11-2 (1-1); Neill Armstrong, 30-34-0 (0-1); Mike Ditka, 106-62-0 (6-6); Jim Dooley, 20-36-0; Paddy Driscoll, 14-9-1 (0-1); Abe Gibron, 11-30-1; George Halas, 318-148-32 (6-4); Dick Jauron, 35-45-0 (0-1); Ralph Jones, 24-10-7; Jack Pardee, 20-22-0 (0-1); Lovie Smith, 16-16-0 (0-1); Dave Wannstedt, 40-56-0 (1-1).
NOTE: Playoff games in parentheses.
*Co-coaches.

RETIRED UNIFORM NUMBERS

No.	Player	No.	Player
3	Bronko Nagurski	42	Sid Luckman
5	George McAfee	51	Dick Butkus
7	George Halas	56	Bill Hewitt
28	Willie Galimore	61	Bill George
34	Walter Payton	66	Bulldog Turner
40	Gale Sayers	77	Red Grange
41	Brian Piccolo		

CINCINNATI BENGALS
YEAR-BY-YEAR RECORDS

	REGULAR SEASON						PLAYOFFS			
Year	W	L	T	Pct.	PF	PA	Finish	W	L	Highest round	Coach
1968*	3	11	0	.214	215	329	5th/Western Div.	—	—		Paul Brown
1969*	4	9	1	.308	280	367	5th/Western Div.	—	—		Paul Brown
1970	8	6	0	.571	312	255	1st/AFC Central Div.	0	1	AFC div. playoff game	Paul Brown
1971	4	10	0	.286	284	265	4th/AFC Central Div.	—	—		Paul Brown
1972	8	6	0	.571	299	229	3rd/AFC Central Div.	—	—		Paul Brown
1973	10	4	0	.714	286	231	1st/AFC Central Div.	0	1	AFC div. playoff game	Paul Brown
1974	7	7	0	.500	283	259	2nd/AFC Central Div.	—	—		Paul Brown
1975	11	3	0	.786	340	246	2nd/AFC Central Div.	0	1	AFC div. playoff game	Paul Brown
1976	10	4	0	.714	335	210	2nd/AFC Central Div.	—	—		Bill Johnson
1977	8	6	0	.571	238	235	3rd/AFC Central Div.	—	—		Bill Johnson
1978	4	12	0	.250	252	284	4th/AFC Central Div.	—	—		B. Johnson, H. Rice
1979	4	12	0	.250	337	421	4th/AFC Central Div.	—	—		Homer Rice
1980	6	10	0	.375	244	312	4th/AFC Central Div.	—	—		Forrest Gregg
1981	12	4	0	.750	421	304	1st/AFC Central Div.	2	1	Super Bowl	Forrest Gregg
1982	7	2	0	.778	232	177	3rd/AFC	0	1	AFC first-round pl. game	Forrest Gregg
1983	7	9	0	.438	346	302	3rd/AFC Central Div.	—	—		Forrest Gregg
1984	8	8	0	.500	339	339	2nd/AFC Central Div.	—	—		Sam Wyche
1985	7	9	0	.438	441	437	2nd/AFC Central Div.	—	—		Sam Wyche
1986	10	6	0	.625	409	394	4th/AFC Central Div.	—	—		Sam Wyche
1987	4	11	0	.267	285	370	4th/AFC Central Div.	—	—		Sam Wyche
1988	12	4	0	.750	448	329	1st/AFC Central Div.	2	1	Super Bowl	Sam Wyche
1989	8	8	0	.500	404	285	4th/AFC Central Div.	—	—		Sam Wyche
1990	9	7	0	.563	360	352	1st/AFC Central Div.	1	1	AFC div. playoff game	Sam Wyche
1991	3	13	0	.188	263	435	4th/AFC Central Div.	—	—		Sam Wyche
1992	5	11	0	.313	274	364	4th/AFC Central Div.	—	—		David Shula
1993	3	13	0	.188	187	319	4th/AFC Central Div.	—	—		David Shula
1994	3	13	0	.188	276	406	3rd/AFC Central Div.	—	—		David Shula
1995	7	9	0	.438	349	374	2nd/AFC Central Div.	—	—		David Shula
1996	8	8	0	.500	372	369	3rd/AFC Central Div.	—	—		D. Shula, B. Coslet
1997	7	9	0	.438	355	405	4th/AFC Central Div.	—	—		Bruce Coslet
1998	3	13	0	.188	268	452	5th/AFC Central Div.	—	—		Bruce Coslet
1999	4	12	0	.250	283	460	5th/AFC Central Div.	—	—		Bruce Coslet
2000	4	12	0	.250	185	359	5th/AFC Central Div.	—	—		B. Coslet, Dick LeBeau
2001	6	10	0	.375	226	309	6th/AFC Central Div.	—	—		Dick LeBeau
2002	2	14	0	.125	279	456	4th/AFC North Div.	—	—		Dick LeBeau
2003	8	8	0	.500	346	384	2nd/AFC North Div.	—	—		Marvin Lewis
2004	8	8	0	.500	374	372	3rd/AFC North Div.	—	—		Marvin Lewis
2005	11	5	0	.688	421	350	1st/AFC North Div.	0	1	AFC wild-card game	Marvin Lewis

*American Football League.

FIRST-ROUND DRAFT PICKS

1968—Bob Johnson, C, Tennessee
1969—Greg Cook, QB, Cincinnati
1970—Mike Reid, DT, Penn State
1971—Vernon Holland, T, Tennessee State
1972—Sherman White, DE, California
1973—Issac Curtis, WR, San Diego State
1974—Bill Kollar, DT, Montana State
1975—Glenn Cameron, LB, Florida
1976—Billy Brooks, WR, Oklahoma
    Archie Griffin, RB, Ohio State
1977—Eddie Edwards, DT, Miami (Fla.)
    Wilson Whitley, DT, Houston
    Mike Cobb, TE, Michigan State
1978—Ross Browner, DE, Notre Dame
    Blair Bush, C, Washington
1979—Jack Thompson, QB, Washington State
    Charles Alexander, RB, LSU

1980—Anthony Munoz, T, USC
1981—David Verser, WR, Kansas
1982—Glen Collins, DE, Mississippi State
1983—Dave Rimington, C, Nebraska
1984—Ricky Hunley, LB, Arizona
    Pete Koch, DE, Maryland
    Brian Blados, T, North Carolina
1985—Eddie Brown, WR, Miami (Fla.)
    Emanuel King, LB, Alabama
1986—Joe Kelly, LB, Washington
    Tim McGee, WR, Tennessee
1987—Jason Buck, DE, Brigham Young
1988—Rickey Dixon, S, Oklahoma
1989—None
1990—James Francis, LB, Baylor
1991—Alfred Williams, LB, Colorado

HISTORY *Team by team*

1992—David Klingler, QB, Houston
Darryl Williams, DB, Miami
1993—John Copeland, DE, Alabama
1994—Dan Wilkinson, DT, Ohio State*
1995—Ki-Jana Carter, RB, Penn State*
1996—Willie Anderson, T, Auburn
1997—Reinard Wilson, LB, Florida State
1998—Takeo Spikes, LB, Auburn
Brian Simmons, LB, North Carolina

1999—Akili Smith, QB, Oregon
2000—Peter Warrick, WR, Florida State
2001—Justin Smith, DE, Missouri
2002—Levi Jones, T, Arizona State
2003—Carson Palmer, QB, USC*
2004—Chris Perry, RB, Michigan
2005—David Pollack, DE, Georgia
2006—Johnathan Joseph, CB, South Carolina
*First player chosen in draft.

FRANCHISE RECORDS

Most rushing yards, career
8,061—Corey Dillon
Most rushing yards, season
1,458—Rudi Johnson, 2005
Most rushing yards, game
278—Corey Dillon vs. Den., Oct. 22, 2000
Most rushing touchdowns, season
15—Ickey Woods, 1988
Most passing attempts, season
581—Jon Kitna, 2001
Most passing attempts, game
68—Jon Kitna vs. Pit., Dec. 30, 2001 (OT)
56—Ken Anderson at S.D., Dec. 20, 1982
Most passes completed, season
345—Carson Palmer, 2005
Most passes completed, game
40—Ken Anderson at S.D., Dec. 20, 1982

Most passing yards, career
32,838—Ken Anderson
Most passing yards, season
3,959—Boomer Esiason, 1986
Most passing yards, game
490—Boomer Esiason at L.A. Rams, Oct. 7, 1990
Most touchdown passes, season
32—Carson Palmer, 2005
Most pass receptions, career
530—Carl Pickens
Most pass receptions, season
100—Carl Pickens, 1996
Most pass receptions, game
13—Carl Pickens vs. Pit., Oct. 11, 1998
Most receiving yards, career
7,101—Isaac Curtis
Most receiving yards, season
1,432—Chad Johnson, 2005

Most receiving yards, game
216—Eddie Brown vs. Pit., Nov. 16, 1988
Most receiving touchdowns, season
17—Carl Pickens, 1995
Most touchdowns, career
70—Pete Johnson
Most field goals, season
29—Doug Pelfrey, 1995
Longest field goal
55 yards—Chris Bahr vs. Hou., Sept. 23, 1979
Most interceptions, career
65—Ken Riley
Most interceptions, season
10—Deltha O'Neal, 2005
Most sacks, career
83.5—Eddie Edwards
Most sacks, season
22—Coy Bacon, 1976

SERIES RECORDS

Cincinnati vs.: Arizona 5-3; Atlanta 7-3; Baltimore 8-12; Buffalo 9-13; Carolina 0-2; Chicago 5-3; Cleveland 32-33; Dallas 4-5; Denver 8-15; Detroit 6-3; Green Bay 5-5; Houston 3-0; Indianapolis 8-13; Jacksonville 5-11; Kansas City 10-12; Miami 4-12; Minnesota 5-5; New England 8-11; New Orleans 5-5; N.Y. Giants 5-2; N.Y. Jets 6-12; Oakland 7-17; Philadelphia 7-3; Pittsburgh 29-43; St. Louis 5-5; San Diego 10-17; San Francisco 3-7; Seattle 8-8; Tampa Bay 3-5; Tennessee 30-38-1; Washington 3-4.

COACHING RECORDS

Paul Brown, 55-56-1 (0-3); Bruce Coslet, 21-39-0; Forrest Gregg, 32-25-0 (2-2); Bill Johnson, 18-15-0; Dick LeBeau, 12-33-0; Marvin Lewis, 27-21-0 (0-1); Homer Rice, 8-19-0; Dave Shula, 19-52-0; Sam Wyche, 61-66-0 (3-2).
NOTE: Playoff games in parentheses.

RETIRED UNIFORM NUMBERS

No.	Player
54	Bob Johnson

CLEVELAND BROWNS
YEAR-BY-YEAR RECORDS

			REGULAR SEASON					PLAYOFFS		
Year	W	L	T	Pct.	PF	PA	Finish	W	L	Highest round	Coach
1946*	12	2	0	.857	423	137	1st/Western Div.	1	0	AAFC champ	Paul Brown
1947*	12	1	1	.923	410	185	1st/Western Div.	1	0	AAFC champ	Paul Brown
1948*	14	0	0	1.000	389	190	1st/Western Div.	1	0	AAFC champ	Paul Brown
1949*	9	1	2	.900	339	171	1st	2	0	AAFC champ	Paul Brown
1950	10	2	0	.833	310	144	1st/American Conf.	2	0	NFL champ	Paul Brown
1951	11	1	0	.917	331	152	1st/American Conf.	0	1	NFL championship game	Paul Brown
1952	8	4	0	.667	310	213	1st/American Conf.	0	1	NFL championship game	Paul Brown
1953	11	1	0	.917	348	162	1st/Eastern Conf.	0	1	NFL championship game	Paul Brown
1954	9	3	0	.750	336	162	1st/Eastern Conf.	1	0	NFL champ	Paul Brown
1955	9	2	1	.818	349	218	1st/Eastern Conf.	1	0	NFL champ	Paul Brown
1956	5	7	0	.417	167	177	4th/Eastern Conf.	—	—		Paul Brown
1957	9	2	1	.818	269	172	1st/Eastern Conf.	0	1	NFL championship game	Paul Brown
1958	9	3	0	.750	302	217	2nd/Eastern Conf.	0	1	E. Conf. championship game	Paul Brown
1959	7	5	0	.583	270	214	T2nd/Eastern Conf.	—	—		Paul Brown
1960	8	3	1	.727	362	217	2nd/Eastern Conf.	—	—		Paul Brown
1961	8	5	1	.615	319	270	3rd/Eastern Conf.	—	—		Paul Brown
1962	7	6	1	.538	291	257	3rd/Eastern Conf.	—	—		Paul Brown
1963	10	4	0	.714	343	262	2nd/Eastern Conf.	—	—		Blanton Collier
1964	10	3	1	.769	415	293	1st/Eastern Conf.	1	0	NFL champ	Blanton Collier
1965	11	3	0	.786	363	325	1st/Eastern Conf.	0	1	NFL championship game	Blanton Collier
1966	9	5	0	.643	403	259	T2nd/Eastern Conf.	—	—		Blanton Collier

		REGULAR SEASON							PLAYOFFS			
Year	W	L	T	Pct.	PF	PA	Finish	W	L	Highest round	Coach
1967	9	5	0	.643	334	297	1st/Century Div.	0	1	E. Conf. championship game	Blanton Collier
1968	10	4	0	.714	394	273	1st/Century Div.	1	1	NFL championship game	Blanton Collier
1969	10	3	1	.769	351	300	1st/Century Div.	1	1	NFL championship game	Blanton Collier
1970	7	7	0	.500	286	265	2nd/AFC Central Div.	—	—		Blanton Collier
1971	9	5	0	.643	285	273	1st/AFC Central Div.	0	1	AFC div. playoff game	Nick Skorich
1972	10	4	0	.714	268	249	2nd/AFC Central Div.	0	1	AFC div. playoff game	Nick Skorich
1973	7	5	2	.571	234	255	3rd/AFC Central Div.	—	—		Nick Skorich
1974	4	10	0	.286	251	344	4th/AFC Central Div.	—	—		Nick Skorich
1975	3	11	0	.214	218	372	4th/AFC Central Div.	—	—		Forrest Gregg
1976	9	5	0	.643	267	287	3rd/AFC Central Div.	—	—		Forrest Gregg
1977	6	8	0	.429	269	267	4th/AFC Central Div.	—	—		F. Gregg, Dick Modzelewski
1978	8	8	0	.500	334	356	3rd/AFC Central Div.	—	—		Sam Rutigliano
1979	9	7	0	.563	359	352	3rd/AFC Central Div.	—	—		Sam Rutigliano
1980	11	5	0	.688	357	310	1st/AFC Central Div.	0	1	AFC div. playoff game	Sam Rutigliano
1981	5	11	0	.313	276	375	4th/AFC Central Div.	—	—		Sam Rutigliano
1982	4	5	0	.444	140	182	8th/AFC	0	1	AFC first-round pl. game	Sam Rutigliano
1983	9	7	0	.563	356	342	2nd/AFC Central Div.	—	—		Sam Rutigliano
1984	5	11	0	.313	250	297	3rd/AFC Central Div.	—	—		Rutigliano, Schottenheimer
1985	8	8	0	.500	287	294	1st/AFC Central Div.	0	1	AFC div. playoff game	Marty Schottenheimer
1986	12	4	0	.750	391	310	1st/AFC Central Div.	1	1	AFC championship game	Marty Schottenheimer
1987	10	5	0	.667	390	239	1st/AFC Central Div.	1	1	AFC championship game	Marty Schottenheimer
1988	10	6	0	.625	304	288	2nd/AFC Central Div.	0	1	AFC wild-card game	Marty Schottenheimer
1989	9	6	1	.594	334	254	1st/AFC Central Div.	1	1	AFC championship game	Bud Carson
1990	3	13	0	.188	228	462	4th/AFC Central Div.	—	—		Bud Carson, Jim Shofner
1991	6	10	0	.375	293	298	3rd/AFC Central Div.	—	—		Bill Belichick
1992	7	9	0	.438	272	275	3rd/AFC Central Div.	—	—		Bill Belichick
1993	7	9	0	.438	304	307	3rd/AFC Central Div.	—	—		Bill Belichick
1994	11	5	0	.688	340	204	2nd/AFC Central Div.	1	1	AFC div. playoff game	Bill Belichick
1995	5	11	0	.313	289	356	4th/AFC Central Div.	—	—		Bill Belichick
1999	2	14	0	.125	217	437	6th/AFC Central Div.	—	—		Chris Palmer
2000	3	13	0	.188	161	419	6th/AFC Central Div.	—	—		Chris Palmer
2001	7	9	0	.438	285	319	3rd/AFC Central Div.	—	—		Butch Davis
2002	9	7	0	.563	344	320	2nd/AFC North Div.	0	1	AFC wild-card game	Butch Davis
2003	5	11	0	.313	254	322	4th/AFC North Div.	—	—		Butch Davis
2004	4	12	0	.250	276	390	4th/AFC North Div.	—	—		B. Davis, Terry Robiskie
2005	6	10	0	.375	232	301	4th/AFC North Div.	—	—		Romeo Crennel

*All-America Football Conference.

FIRST-ROUND DRAFT PICKS

1950—Ken Carpenter, B, Oregon State
1951—Ken Konz, B, LSU
1952—Bert Rechichar, DB, Tennessee
    Harry Agganis, QB, Boston University
1953—Doug Atkins, DT, Tennessee
1954—Bobby Garrett, QB, Stanford*
    John Bauer, G, Illinois
1955—Kent Burris, C, Oklahoma
1956—Preston Carpenter, B, Arkansas
1957—Jim Brown, B, Syracuse
1958—Jim Shofner, DB, Texas Christian
1959—Rich Kreitling, DE, Illinois
1960—Jim Houston, DE, Ohio State
1961—Bobby Crespino, E, Mississippi
1962—Gary Collins, WR, Maryland
    Leroy Jackson, B, Western Illinois
1963—Tom Hutchinson, TE, Kentucky
1964—Paul Warfield, WR, Ohio State
1965—None
1966—Milt Morin, TE, Massachusetts
1967—Bob Matheson, LB, Duke
1968—M. Upshaw, DE, Trinity (Tex.)
1969—Ron Johnson, RB, Michigan
1970—Mike Phipps, QB, Purdue
    Bob McKay, T, Texas
1971—Clarence Scott, DB, Kansas State
1972—Thom Darden, DB, Michigan
1973—Steve Holden, WR, Arizona State
    Pete Adams, G, USC
1974—None
1975—Mack Mitchell, DE, Houston

1976—Mike Pruitt, RB, Purdue
1977—Robert Jackson, LB, Texas A&M
1978—Clay Matthews, LB, USC
    Ozzie Newsome, WR, Alabama
1979—Willis Adams, WR, Houston
1980—Charles White, RB, USC
1981—Hanford Dixon, CB, Southern Mississippi
1982—Chip Banks, LB, USC
1983—None
1984—Don Rogers, DB, UCLA
1985—None
1986—None
1987—Mike Junkin, LB, Duke
1988—Clifford Charlton, LB, Florida
1989—Eric Metcalf, RB, Texas
1990—None
1991—Eric Turner, S, UCLA
1992—Tommy Vardell, FB, Stanford
1993—Steve Everitt, C, Michigan
1994—Antonio Langham, DB, Alabama
    Derrick Alexander, WR, Michigan
1995—Craig Powell, LB, Ohio State
1999—Tim Couch, QB, Kentucky*
2000—Courtney Brown, DE, Penn State*
2001—Gerard Warren, DT, Florida
2002—William Green, RB, Boston College
2003—Jeff Faine, C, Notre Dame
2004—Kellen Winslow, TE, Miami (Fla.)
2005—Braylon Edwards, WR, Michigan
2006—Kamerion Wimbley, DE, Florida State
   *First player chosen in draft.

FRANCHISE RECORDS

Most rushing yards, career
12,312—Jim Brown
Most rushing yards, season
1,863—Jim Brown, 1963
Most rushing yards, game
237—Jim Brown vs. L.A., Nov. 24, 1957
Jim Brown vs. Phi., Nov. 19, 1961
Most rushing touchdowns, season
17—Jim Brown, 1958
Jim Brown, 1965
Most passing attempts, season
567—Brian Sipe, 1981
Most passing attempts, game
57—Brian Sipe vs. S.D., Sept. 7, 1981
Most passes completed, season
337—Brian Sipe, 1980
Most passes completed, game
36—Tim Couch at Ten., Sept. 22, 2002 (OT)
33—Brian Sipe vs. S.D., Dec. 5, 1982

Most passing yards, career
23,713—Brian Sipe
Most passing yards, season
4,132—Brian Sipe, 1980
Most passing yards, game
444—Brian Sipe vs. Bal., Oct. 25, 1981
Most touchdown passes, season
30—Brian Sipe, 1980
Most pass receptions, career
662—Ozzie Newsome
Most pass receptions, season
89—Ozzie Newsome, 1983
Ozzie Newsome, 1984
Most pass receptions, game
14—Ozzie Newsome vs. NYJ, Oct. 14, 1984
Most receiving yards, career
7,980—Ozzie Newsome
Most receiving yards, season
1,236—Webster Slaughter, 1989

Most receiving yards, game
191—Ozzie Newsome vs. NYJ, Oct. 14, 1984
Most receiving touchdowns, season
13—Gary Collins, 1963
Most touchdowns, career
126—Jim Brown
Most field goals, season
29—Matt Stover, 1995
Longest field goal
60 yards—Steve Cox at Cin., Oct. 21, 1984
Most interceptions, career
45—Thom Darden
Most interceptions, season
10—Thom Darden, 1978
Anthony Henry, 2001
Most sacks, career
76.5—Clay Matthews
Most sacks, season
14.5—Bill Glass, 1965

SERIES RECORDS

Cleveland vs.: Arizona 33-11-3; Atlanta 9-2; Baltimore 5-9; Buffalo 7-5; Carolina 0-2; Chicago 9-4; Cincinnati 33-32; Dallas 15-10; Denver 5-15; Detroit 4-13; Green Bay 7-9; Houston 2-1; Indianapolis 13-11; Jacksonville 2-8; Kansas City 8-9-2; Miami 5-7; Minnesota 3-9; New England 11-8; New Orleans 11-3; N.Y. Giants 25-19-2; N.Y. Jets 10-7; Oakland 6-9; Philadelphia 31-14-1; Pittsburgh 55-51; St. Louis 8-9; San Diego 7-12-1; San Francisco 10-6; Seattle 4-11; Tampa Bay 5-1; Tennessee 33-26; Washington 33-9-1.

COACHING RECORDS

Bill Belichick, 36-44-0 (1-1); Paul Brown, 158-48-8 (9-5); Bud Carson, 11-13-1 (1-1); Blanton Collier, 76-34-2 (3-4); Romeo Crennel, 6-10-0; Butch Davis, 24-35-0 (0-1); Forrest Gregg 18-23-0; Dick Modzelewski, 0-1-0; Chris Palmer, 5-27-0; Terry Robiskie, 1-4-0; Sam Rutigliano, 47-50-0 (0-2); Marty Schottenheimer, 44-27-0 (2-4); Jim Shofner, 1-6-0; Nick Skorich, 30-24-2 (0-2).
NOTE: Playoff games in parentheses.

RETIRED UNIFORM NUMBERS

No.	Player
14	Otto Graham
32	Jim Brown
45	Ernie Davis
46	Don Fleming
76	Lou Groza

DALLAS COWBOYS
YEAR-BY-YEAR RECORDS

		REGULAR SEASON						PLAYOFFS			
Year	W	L	T	Pct.	PF	PA	Finish	W	L	Highest round	Coach
1960	0	11	1	.000	177	369	7th/Western Conf.	—	—		Tom Landry
1961	4	9	1	.308	236	380	6th/Eastern Conf.	—	—		Tom Landry
1962	5	8	1	.385	398	402	5th/Eastern Conf.	—	—		Tom Landry
1963	4	10	0	.286	305	378	5th/Eastern Conf.	—	—		Tom Landry
1964	5	8	1	.385	250	289	5th/Eastern Conf.	—	—		Tom Landry
1965	7	7	0	.500	325	280	T2nd/Eastern Conf.	—	—		Tom Landry
1966	10	3	1	.769	445	239	1st/Eastern Conf.	0	1	NFL championship game	Tom Landry
1967	9	5	0	.643	342	268	1st/Capitol Div.	1	1	NFL championship game	Tom Landry
1968	12	2	0	.857	431	186	1st/Capitol Div.	0	1	E. Conf. championship game	Tom Landry
1969	11	2	1	.846	369	223	1st/Capitol Div.	0	1	E. Conf. championship game	Tom Landry
1970	10	4	0	.714	299	221	1st/NFC Eastern Div.	2	1	Super Bowl	Tom Landry
1971	11	3	0	.786	406	222	1st/NFC Eastern Div.	3	0	Super Bowl champ	Tom Landry
1972	10	4	0	.714	319	240	2nd/NFC Eastern Div.	1	1	NFC championship game	Tom Landry
1973	10	4	0	.714	382	203	1st/NFC Eastern Div.	1	1	NFC championship game	Tom Landry
1974	8	6	0	.571	297	235	3rd/NFC Eastern Div.	—	—		Tom Landry
1975	10	4	0	.714	350	268	2nd/NFC Eastern Div.	2	1	Super Bowl	Tom Landry
1976	11	3	0	.786	296	194	1st/NFC Eastern Div.	0	1	NFC div. playoff game	Tom Landry
1977	12	2	0	.857	345	212	1st/NFC Eastern Div.	3	0	Super Bowl champ	Tom Landry
1978	12	4	0	.750	384	208	1st/NFC Eastern Div.	2	1	Super Bowl	Tom Landry
1979	11	5	0	.688	371	313	1st/NFC Eastern Div.	0	1	NFC div. playoff game	Tom Landry
1980	12	4	0	.750	454	311	2nd/NFC Eastern Div.	2	1	NFC championship game	Tom Landry
1981	12	4	0	.750	367	277	1st/NFC Eastern Div.	1	1	NFC championship game	Tom Landry
1982	6	3	0	.667	226	145	2nd/NFC	2	1	NFC championship game	Tom Landry
1983	12	4	0	.750	479	360	2nd/NFC Eastern Div.	0	1	NFC wild-card game	Tom Landry
1984	9	7	0	.563	308	308	4th/NFC Eastern Div.	—	—		Tom Landry

	REGULAR SEASON						PLAYOFFS			
Year	W	L	T	Pct.	PF	PA	Finish	W	L	Highest round	Coach
1985	10	6	0	.625	357	333	1st/NFC Eastern Div.	0	1	NFC div. playoff game	Tom Landry
1986	7	9	0	.438	346	337	3rd/NFC Eastern Div.	—	—		Tom Landry
1987	7	8	0	.467	340	348	2nd/NFC Eastern Div.	—	—		Tom Landry
1988	3	13	0	.188	265	381	5th/NFC Eastern Div.	—	—		Tom Landry
1989	1	15	0	.063	204	393	5th/NFC Eastern Div.	—	—		Jimmy Johnson
1990	7	9	0	.438	244	308	4th/NFC Eastern Div.	—	—		Jimmy Johnson
1991	11	5	0	.688	342	310	2nd/NFC Eastern Div.	1	1	NFC div. playoff game	Jimmy Johnson
1992	13	3	0	.813	409	243	1st/NFC Eastern Div.	3	0	Super Bowl champ	Jimmy Johnson
1993	12	4	0	.750	376	229	1st/NFC Eastern Div.	3	0	Super Bowl champ	Jimmy Johnson
1994	12	4	0	.750	414	248	1st/NFC Eastern Div.	1	1	NFC championship game	Barry Switzer
1995	12	4	0	.750	435	291	1st/NFC Eastern Div.	3	0	Super Bowl champ	Barry Switzer
1996	10	6	0	.625	286	250	1st/NFC Eastern Div.	1	1	NFC div. playoff game	Barry Switzer
1997	6	10	0	.375	304	314	4th/NFC Eastern Div.	—	—		Barry Switzer
1998	10	6	0	.625	381	275	1st/NFC Eastern Div.	0	1	NFC wild-card game	Chan Gailey
1999	8	8	0	.500	352	276	2nd/NFC Eastern Div.	0	1	NFC wild-card game	Chan Gailey
2000	5	11	0	.313	294	361	4th/NFC Eastern Div.	—	—		Dave Campo
2001	5	11	0	.313	246	338	5th/NFC Eastern Div.	—	—		Dave Campo
2002	5	11	0	.313	217	329	4th/NFC East Div.	—	—		Dave Campo
2003	10	6	0	.625	289	260	2nd/NFC East Div.	0	1	NFC wild-card game	Bill Parcells
2004	6	10	0	.375	293	405	3rd/NFC East Div.	—	—		Bill Parcells
2005	9	7	0	.562	325	308	3rd/NFC East Div.	—	—		Bill Parcells

FIRST-ROUND DRAFT PICKS

1961—Bob Lilly, DT, Texas Christian
1962—None
1963—Lee Roy Jordan, LB, Alabama
1964—Scott Appleton, DT, Texas
1965—Craig Morton, QB, California
1966—John Niland, G, Iowa
1967—None
1968—Dennis Homan, WR, Alabama
1969—Calvin Hill, RB, Yale
1970—Duane Thomas, RB, West Texas State
1971—Tody Smith, DE, USC
1972—Bill Thomas, RB, Boston College
1973—Billy Joe DuPree, TE, Michigan State
1974—Ed Jones, DE, Tennessee State*
    Charles Young, RB, N.C. State
1975—Randy White, LB, Maryland
    Thomas Henderson, LB, Langston
1976—Aaron Kyle, DB, Wyoming
1977—Tony Dorsett, RB, Pittsburgh
1978—Larry Bethea, DE, Michigan State
1979—Robert Shaw, C, Tennessee
1980—None
1981—Howard Richards, T, Missouri
1982—Rod Hill, DB, Kentucky State
1983—Jim Jeffcoat, DE, Arizona State
1984—Billy Cannon Jr., LB, Texas A&M

1985—Kevin Brooks, DE, Michigan
1986—Mike Sherrard, WR, UCLA
1987—Danny Noonan, DT, Nebraska
1988—Michael Irvin, WR, Miami (Fla.)
1989—Troy Aikman, QB, UCLA*
1990—Emmitt Smith, RB, Florida
1991—Russell Maryland, DL, Miami (Fla.)*
    Alvin Harper, WR, Tennessee
    Kelvin Pritchett, DT, Mississippi
1992—Kevin Smith, DB, Texas A&M
    Robert Jones, LB, East Carolina
1993—None
1994—Shante Carver, DE, Arizona State
1995—None
1996—None
1997—David LaFleur, TE, LSU
1998—Greg Ellis, DE, North Carolina
1999—Ebenezer Ekuban, DE, North Carolina
2000—None
2001—None
2002—Roy Williams, DB, Oklahoma
2003—Terence Newman, DB, Kansas State
2004—None
2005—Demarcus Ware, DE, Troy State
    Marcus Spears, DE, LSU
2006—Bobby Carpenter, LB, Ohio State
*First player chosen in draft.

FRANCHISE RECORDS

Most rushing yards, career
17,162—Emmitt Smith

Most rushing yards, season
1,773—Emmitt Smith, 1995

Most rushing yards, game
237—Emmitt Smith at Phi., Oct. 31, 1993

Most rushing touchdowns, season
25—Emmitt Smith, 1995

Most passing attempts, season
533—Danny White, 1983

Most passing attempts, game
57—Troy Aikman vs. Min., Nov. 26, 1998

Most passes completed, season
334—Danny White, 1983

Most passes completed, game
34—Troy Aikman at NYG, Oct. 5, 1997
    Troy Aikman vs. Min., Nov. 26, 1998

Most passing yards, career
32,942—Troy Aikman

Most passing yards, season
3,980—Danny White, 1983

Most passing yards, game
460—Don Meredith at S.F., Nov. 10, 1963

Most touchdown passes, season
29—Danny White, 1983

Most pass receptions, career
750—Michael Irvin

Most pass receptions, season
111—Michael Irvin, 1995

Most pass receptions, game
13—Lance Rentzel vs. Was., Nov. 19, 1967

Most receiving yards, career
11,904—Michael Irvin

Most receiving yards, season
1,603—Michael Irvin, 1995

Most receiving yards, game
246—Bob Hayes at Was., Nov. 13, 1966

Most receiving touchdowns, season
14—Frank Clarke, 1962

Most touchdowns, career
164—Emmitt Smith

Most field goals, season
34—Richie Cunningham, 1997

Longest field goal
56 yards—Billy Cundiff vs. Detroit,
    Nov. 20, 2005

Most interceptions, career
52—Mel Renfro

Most interceptions, season
11—Everson Walls, 1981

Most sacks, career
113—Harvey Martin

Most sacks, season
23—Harvey Martin, 1977

SERIES RECORDS

Dallas vs.: Arizona 54-28-1; Atlanta 12-7; Baltimore 0-2; Buffalo 4-3; Carolina 5-1; Chicago 10-8; Cincinnati 5-4; Cleveland 10-15; Denver 4-5; Detroit 10-8; Green Bay 10-10; Houston 0-1; Indianapolis 7-5; Jacksonville 2-1; Kansas City 5-3; Miami 3-7; Minnesota 9-10; New England 7-2; New Orleans 14-7; N.Y. Giants 51-34-2; N.Y. Jets 6-2; Oakland 3-6; Philadelphia 51-39; Pittsburgh 14-12; St. Louis 9-10; San Diego 6-2; San Francisco 9-14-1; Seattle 6-4; Tampa Bay 6-3; Tennessee 6-5; Washington 54-34-2.

COACHING RECORDS

Dave Campo, 15-33-0; Chan Gailey, 18-14-0 (0-2); Jimmy Johnson, 44-36-0 (7-1); Tom Landry, 250-162-6 (20-16); Bill Parcells, 25-23-0 (0-1); Barry Switzer, 40-24-0 (5-2). NOTE: Playoff games in parentheses.

RETIRED UNIFORM NUMBERS

No.	Player
	None

DENVER BRONCOS
YEAR-BY-YEAR RECORDS

	REGULAR SEASON							PLAYOFFS			
Year	W	L	T	Pct.	PF	PA	Finish	W	L	Highest round	Coach
1960*	4	9	1	.308	309	393	4th/Western Div.	—	—		Frank Filchock
1961*	3	11	0	.214	251	432	3rd/Western Div.	—	—		Frank Filchock
1962*	7	7	0	.500	353	334	2nd/Western Div.	—	—		Jack Faulkner
1963*	2	11	1	.154	301	473	4th/Western Div.	—	—		Jack Faulkner
1964*	2	11	1	.154	240	438	4th/Western Div.	—	—		J. Faulkner, M. Speedie
1965*	4	10	0	.286	303	392	4th/Western Div.	—	—		Mac Speedie
1966*	4	10	0	.286	196	381	4th/Western Div.	—	—		M. Speedie, Ray Malavasi
1967*	3	11	0	.214	256	409	4th/Western Div.	—	—		Lou Saban
1968*	5	9	0	.357	255	404	4th/Western Div.	—	—		Lou Saban
1969*	5	8	1	.385	297	344	4th/Western Div.	—	—		Lou Saban
1970	5	8	1	.385	253	264	4th/AFC Western Div.	—	—		Lou Saban
1971	4	9	1	.308	203	275	4th/AFC Western Div.	—	—		Lou Saban, Jerry Smith
1972	5	9	0	.357	325	350	3rd/AFC Western Div.	—	—		John Ralston
1973	7	5	2	.571	354	296	2nd/AFC Western Div.	—	—		John Ralston
1974	7	6	1	.536	302	294	2nd/AFC Western Div.	—	—		John Ralston
1975	6	8	0	.429	254	307	2nd/AFC Western Div.	—	—		John Ralston
1976	9	5	0	.643	315	206	2nd/AFC Western Div.	—	—		John Ralston
1977	12	2	0	.857	274	148	1st/AFC Western Div.	2	1	Super Bowl	Red Miller
1978	10	6	0	.625	282	198	1st/AFC Western Div.	0	1	AFC div. playoff game	Red Miller
1979	10	6	0	.625	289	262	2nd/AFC Western Div.	0	1	AFC wild-card game	Red Miller
1980	8	8	0	.500	310	323	4th/AFC Western Div.	—	—		Red Miller
1981	10	6	0	.625	321	289	2nd/AFC Western Div.	—	—		Dan Reeves
1982	2	7	0	.222	148	226	12th/AFC	—	—		Dan Reeves
1983	9	7	0	.563	302	327	3rd/AFC Western Div.	0	1	AFC wild-card game	Dan Reeves
1984	13	3	0	.813	353	241	1st/AFC Western Div.	0	1	AFC div. playoff game	Dan Reeves
1985	11	5	0	.688	380	329	2nd/AFC Western Div.	—	—		Dan Reeves
1986	11	5	0	.688	378	327	1st/AFC Western Div.	2	1	Super Bowl	Dan Reeves
1987	10	4	1	.700	379	288	1st/AFC Western Div.	2	1	Super Bowl	Dan Reeves
1988	8	8	0	.500	327	352	2nd/AFC Western Div.	—	—		Dan Reeves
1989	11	5	0	.688	362	226	1st/AFC Western Div.	2	1	Super Bowl	Dan Reeves
1990	5	11	0	.313	331	374	5th/AFC Western Div.	—	—		Dan Reeves
1991	12	4	0	.750	304	235	1st/AFC Western Div.	1	1	AFC championship game	Dan Reeves
1992	8	8	0	.500	262	329	3rd/AFC Western Div.	—	—		Dan Reeves
1993	9	7	0	.563	373	284	3rd/AFC Western Div.	0	1	AFC wild-card game	Wade Phillips
1994	7	9	0	.438	347	396	4th/AFC Western Div.	—	—		Wade Phillips
1995	8	8	0	.500	388	345	4th/AFC Western Div.	—	—		Mike Shanahan
1996	13	3	0	.813	391	275	1st/AFC Western Div.	0	1	AFC div. playoff game	Mike Shanahan
1997	12	4	0	.750	472	287	2nd/AFC Western Div.	4	0	Super Bowl champ	Mike Shanahan
1998	14	2	0	.875	501	309	1st/AFC Western Div.	3	0	Super Bowl champ	Mike Shanahan
1999	6	10	0	.375	314	318	5th/AFC Western Div.	—	—		Mike Shanahan
2000	11	5	0	.688	485	369	2nd/AFC Western Div.	0	1	AFC wild-card game	Mike Shanahan
2001	8	8	0	.500	340	339	3rd/AFC Western Div.	—	—		Mike Shanahan
2002	9	7	0	.563	392	344	2nd/AFC West Div.	—	—		Mike Shanahan
2003	10	6	0	.625	381	301	2nd/AFC West Div.	0	1	AFC wild-card game	Mike Shanahan
2004	10	6	0	.625	381	304	2nd/AFC West Div.	0	1	AFC wild-card game	Mike Shanahan
2005	13	3	0	.812	395	258	1st/AFC West Div.	1	1	AFC div. playoff game	Mike Shanahan

*American Football League.

FIRST-ROUND DRAFT PICKS

1960—Roger Leclerc, C, Trinity (Conn.)
1961—Bob Gaiters, RB, New Mexico State
1962—Merlin Olsen, DT, Utah State
1963—Kermit Alexander, DB, UCLA
1964—Bob Brown, T, Nebraska
1965—None
1966—Jerry Shay, DT, Purdue

1967—Floyd Little, RB, Syracuse
1968—None
1969—None
1970—Bob Anderson, RB, Colorado
1971—Marv Montgomery, T, USC
1972—Riley Odoms, TE, Houston
1973—Otis Armstrong, RB, Purdue

1974—Randy Gradishar, LB, Ohio State	1991—Mike Croel, LB, Nebraska
1975—Louis Wright, DB, San Jose State	1992—Tommy Maddox, QB, UCLA
1976—Tom Glassic, G, Virginia	1993—Dan Williams, DE, Toledo
1977—Steve Schindler, G, Boston College	1994—None
1978—Don Latimer, DT, Miami (Fla.)	1995—None
1979—Kelvin Clark, T, Nebraska	1996—John Mobley, LB, Kutztown (Pa.)
1980—None	1997—Trevor Pryce, DT, Clemson
1981—Dennis Smith, DB, USC	1998—Marcus Nash, WR, Tennessee
1982—Gerald Willhite, RB, San Jose State	1999—Al Wilson, LB, Tennessee
1983—Chris Hinton, G, Northwestern	2000—Deltha O'Neal, DB, California
1984—None	2001—Willie Middlebrooks, DB, Minnesota
1985—Steve Sewell, RB, Oklahoma	2002—Ashley Lelie, WR, Hawaii
1986—None	2003—George Foster, T, Georgia
1987—Ricky Nattiel, WR, Florida	2004—D.J. Williams, LB, Miami (Fla.)
1988—Ted Gregory, DT, Syracuse	2005—None
1989—Steve Atwater, DB, Arkansas	2006—Jay Cutler, QB, Vanderbilt
1990—None	

FRANCHISE RECORDS

Most rushing yards, career
7,607—Terrell Davis
Most rushing yards, season
2,008—Terrell Davis, 1998
Most rushing yards, game
251—Mike Anderson at N.O., Dec. 3, 2000
Most rushing touchdowns, season
21—Terrell Davis, 1998
Most passing attempts, season
605—John Elway, 1985
Most passing attempts, game
59—John Elway at G.B., Oct. 10, 1993
Most passes completed, season
348—John Elway, 1993
Most passes completed, game
36—John Elway vs. S.D., Sept. 4, 1994
Gus Frerotte vs. S.D., Nov. 19, 2000
Most passing yards, career
51,475—John Elway
Most passing yards, season
4,089—Jake Plummer, 2004

Most passing yards, game
462—Gus Frerotte vs. S.D., Nov. 19, 2000
Most touchdown passes, season
27—John Elway, 1997
Jake Plummer, 2004
Most pass receptions, career
797—Rod Smith
Most pass receptions, season
113—Rod Smith, 2001
Most pass receptions, game
14—Rod Smith at Ari., Sept. 23, 2001
Most receiving yards, career
10,877—Rod Smith
Most receiving yards, season
1,602—Rod Smith, 2000
Most receiving yards, game
214—Shannon Sharpe at K.C., Oct. 20,
2002 (OT)
199—Lionel Taylor vs. Buf., Nov. 27, 1960

Most receiving touchdowns, season
14—Anthony Miller, 1995
Most touchdowns, career
68—Rod Smith
Most field goals, season
31—Jason Elam, 1995, 2001
Longest field goal
63 yards—Jason Elam vs. Jac., Oct. 25,
1998
Most interceptions, career
44—Steve Foley
Most interceptions, season
11—Goose Gonsoulin, 1960
Most sacks, career
97.5—Simon Fletcher
Most sacks, season
16—Simon Fletcher, 1992

SERIES RECORDS

Denver vs.: Arizona 6-0-1; Atlanta 7-4; Baltimore 2-3; Buffalo 14-17-1; Carolina 2-0; Chicago 6-6; Cincinnati 15-8; Cleveland 15-5; Dallas 5-4; Detroit 6-3; Green Bay 5-4-1; Houston 1-0; Indianapolis 11-4; Jacksonville 3-2; Kansas City 40-51; Miami 3-10-1; Minnesota 4-7; New England 24-15; New Orleans 6-2; N.Y. Giants 4-5; N.Y. Jets 15-14-1; Oakland 36-53-2; Philadelphia 4-6; Pittsburgh 11-7-1; St. Louis 5-5; San Diego 52-39-1; San Francisco 6-4; Seattle 33-17; Tampa Bay 4-2; Tennessee 12-20-1; Washington 6-4.

COACHING RECORDS

Jack Faulkner, 9-22-1; Frank Filchock, 7-20-1; Ray Malavasi, 4-8-0; Red Miller, 40-22-0 (2-3); Wade Phillips, 16-16-0 (0-1); John Ralston, 34-33-3; Dan Reeves, 110-73-1 (7-6); Lou Saban, 20-42-3; Mike Shanahan, 114-62-0 (8-5); Jerry Smith, 2-3-0; Mac Speedie, 6-19-1. NOTE: Playoff games in parentheses.

RETIRED UNIFORM NUMBERS

No.	Player
7	John Elway
18	Frank Tripucka
44	Floyd Little

DETROIT LIONS
YEAR-BY-YEAR RECORDS

			REGULAR SEASON						PLAYOFFS		
Year	W	L	T	Pct.	PF	PA	Finish	W	L	Highest round	Coach
1930*	5	6	3	.455	...	...	T7th				Tubby Griffen
1931*	11	3	0	.786	...	...	2nd				Potsy Clark
1932*	6	2	4	.750	...	...	3rd				Potsy Clark
1933*	6	5	0	.545	128	87	2nd/Western Div.	—	—		Potsy Clark
1934	10	3	0	.769	238	59	2nd/Western Div.	—	—		Potsy Clark
1935	7	3	2	.700	191	111	1st/Western Div.	1	0	NFL champ	Potsy Clark
1936	8	4	0	.667	235	102	3rd/Western Div.	—	—		Potsy Clark
1937	7	4	0	.636	180	105	T2nd/Western Div.	—	—		Dutch Clark
1938	7	4	0	.636	119	108	2nd/Western Div.	—	—		Dutch Clark
1939	6	5	0	.545	145	150	3rd/Western Div.	—	—		Gus Henderson

Year	W	L	T	Pct.	PF	PA	Finish	W	L	Highest round	Coach
					REGULAR SEASON				**PLAYOFFS**			
1940	5	5	1	.500	138	153	3rd/Western Div.	—	—		Potsy Clark
1941	4	6	1	.400	121	195	3rd/Western Div.	—	—		Bill Edwards
1942	0	11	0	.000	38	263	5th/Western Div.	—	—		B. Edwards, John Karcis
1943	3	6	1	.333	178	218	3rd/Western Div.	—	—		Gus Dorais
1944	6	3	1	.667	216	151	T2nd/Western Div.	—	—		Gus Dorais
1945	7	3	0	.700	195	194	2nd/Western Div.	—	—		Gus Dorais
1946	1	10	0	.091	142	310	5th/Western Div.	—	—		Gus Dorais
1947	3	9	0	.250	231	305	5th/Western Div.	—	—		Gus Dorais
1948	2	10	0	.167	200	407	5th/Western Div.	—	—		Bo McMillin
1949	4	8	0	.333	237	259	4th/Western Div.	—	—		Bo McMillin
1950	6	6	0	.500	321	285	4th/National Conf.	—	—		Bo McMillin
1951	7	4	1	.636	336	259	T2nd/National Conf.	—	—		Buddy Parker
1952	9	3	0	.750	344	192	1st/National Conf.	2	0	NFL champ	Buddy Parker
1953	10	2	0	.833	271	205	1st/Western Conf.	1	0	NFL champ	Buddy Parker
1954	9	2	1	.818	337	189	1st/Western Conf.	0	1	NFL championship game	Buddy Parker
1955	3	9	0	.250	230	275	6th/Western Conf.	—	—		Buddy Parker
1956	9	3	0	.750	300	188	2nd/Western Conf.	—	—		Buddy Parker
1957	8	4	0	.667	251	231	1st/Western Conf.	2	0	NFL champ	George Wilson
1958	4	7	1	.364	261	276	5th/Western Conf.	—	—		George Wilson
1959	3	8	1	.273	203	275	5th/Western Conf.	—	—		George Wilson
1960	7	5	0	.583	239	212	T2nd/Western Conf.	—	—		George Wilson
1961	8	5	1	.615	270	258	2nd/Western Conf.	—	—		George Wilson
1962	11	3	0	.786	315	177	2nd/Western Conf.	—	—		George Wilson
1963	5	8	1	.385	326	265	T4th/Western Conf.	—	—		George Wilson
1964	7	5	2	.583	280	260	4th/Western Conf.	—	—		George Wilson
1965	6	7	1	.462	257	295	6th/Western Conf.	—	—		Harry Gilmer
1966	4	9	1	.308	206	317	T6th/Western Conf.	—	—		Harry Gilmer
1967	5	7	2	.417	260	259	3rd/Central Div.	—	—		Joe Schmidt
1968	4	8	2	.333	207	241	4th/Central Div.	—	—		Joe Schmidt
1969	9	4	1	.692	259	188	2nd/Central Div.	—	—		Joe Schmidt
1970	10	4	0	.714	347	202	2nd/NFC Central Div.	0	1	NFC div. playoff game	Joe Schmidt
1971	7	6	1	.538	341	286	2nd/NFC Central Div.	—	—		Joe Schmidt
1972	8	5	1	.607	339	290	2nd/NFC Central Div.	—	—		Joe Schmidt
1973	6	7	1	.464	271	247	2nd/NFC Central Div.	—	—		Don McCafferty
1974	7	7	0	.500	256	270	2nd/NFC Central Div.	—	—		Rick Forzano
1975	7	7	0	.500	245	262	2nd/NFC Central Div.	—	—		Rick Forzano
1976	6	8	0	.429	262	220	3rd/NFC Central Div.	—	—		R. Forzano, T. Hudspeth
1977	6	8	0	.429	183	252	3rd/NFC Central Div.	—	—		Tommy Hudspeth
1978	7	9	0	.438	290	300	3rd/NFC Central Div.	—	—		Monte Clark
1979	2	14	0	.125	219	365	5th/NFC Central Div.	—	—		Monte Clark
1980	9	7	0	.563	334	272	2nd/NFC Central Div.	—	—		Monte Clark
1981	8	8	0	.500	397	322	2nd/NFC Central Div.	—	—		Monte Clark
1982	4	5	0	.444	181	176	8th/NFC	0	1	NFC first-round pl. game	Monte Clark
1983	9	7	0	.563	347	286	1st/NFC Central Div.	0	1	NFC div. playoff game	Monte Clark
1984	4	11	1	.281	283	408	4th/NFC Central Div.	—	—		Monte Clark
1985	7	9	0	.438	307	366	4th/NFC Central Div.	—	—		Darryl Rogers
1986	5	11	0	.313	277	326	3rd/NFC Central Div.	—	—		Darryl Rogers
1987	4	11	0	.267	269	384	5th/NFC Central Div.	—	—		Darryl Rogers
1988	4	12	0	.250	220	313	4th/NFC Central Div.	—	—		Darryl Rogers
1989	7	9	0	.438	312	364	3rd/NFC Central Div.	—	—		Wayne Fontes
1990	6	10	0	.375	373	413	3rd/NFC Central Div.	—	—		Wayne Fontes
1991	12	4	0	.750	339	295	1st/NFC Central Div.	1	1	NFC championship game	Wayne Fontes
1992	5	11	0	.313	273	332	3rd/NFC Central Div.	—	—		Wayne Fontes
1993	10	6	0	.625	298	292	1st/NFC Central Div.	0	1	NFC wild-card game	Wayne Fontes
1994	9	7	0	.563	357	342	3rd/NFC Central Div.	0	1	NFC wild-card game	Wayne Fontes
1995	10	6	0	.625	436	336	2nd/NFC Central Div.	0	1	NFC wild-card game	Wayne Fontes
1996	5	11	0	.313	302	368	5th/NFC Central Div.	—	—		Wayne Fontes
1997	9	7	0	.563	379	306	3rd/NFC Central Div.	0	1	NFC wild-card game	Bobby Ross
1998	5	11	0	.313	306	378	4th/NFC Central Div.	—	—		Bobby Ross
1999	8	8	0	.500	322	323	3rd/NFC Central Div.	0	1	NFC wild-card game	Bobby Ross
2000	9	7	0	.563	307	307	4th/NFC Central Div.	—	—		B. Ross, Gary Moeller
2001	2	14	0	.125	270	424	5th/NFC Central Div.	—	—		Marty Mornhinweg
2002	3	13	0	.188	306	451	4th/NFC North Div.	—	—		Marty Mornhinweg
2003	5	11	0	.313	270	379	4th/NFC North Div.	—	—		Steve Mariucci
2004	6	10	0	.375	296	350	3rd/NFC North Div.	—	—		Steve Mariucci
2005	5	11	0	.312	254	345	3rd/NFC North Div.	—	—		S. Mariucci, Dick Jauron

*Portsmouth Spartans.

FIRST-ROUND DRAFT PICKS

1936—Sid Wagner, G, Michigan State
1937—Lloyd Cardwell, B, Nebraska
1938—Alex Wojciechowicz, C, Fordham
1939—John Pingel, B, Michigan State

1940—Doyle Nave, B, USC
1941—Jim Thomason, B, Texas A&M
1942—Bob Westfall, B, Michigan
1943—Frank Sinkwich, B, Georgia*

1944—Otto Graham, B, Northwestern
1945—Frank Szymanski, C, Notre Dame
1946—Bill Dellastatious, B, Missouri
1947—Glenn Davis, B, Army
1948—Y.A. Tittle, B, LSU
1949—John Rauch, B, Georgia
1950—Leon Hart, E, Notre Dame*
    Joe Watson, C, Rice
1951—None
1952—None
1953—Harley Sewell, G, Texas
1954—Dick Chapman, T, Rice
1955—Dave Middleton, B, Auburn
1956—Hopalong Cassady, B, Ohio State
1957—Bill Glass, G, Baylor
1958—Alex Karras, T, Iowa
1959—Nick Pietrosante, B, Notre Dame
1960—John Robinson, DB, LSU
1961—None
1962—John Hadl, QB, Kansas
1963—Daryl Sanders, T, Ohio State
1964—Pete Beathard, QB, USC
1965—Tom Nowatzke, RB, Indiana
1966—None
1967—Mel Farr, RB, UCLA
1968—Greg Landry, QB, Massachusetts
    Earl McCullouch, E, USC
1969—None
1970—Steve Owens, RB, Oklahoma
1971—Bob Bell, DT, Cincinnati
1972—Herb Orvis, DE, Colorado
1973—Ernie Price, DE, Texas A&I
1974—Ed O'Neil, LB, Penn State
1975—Lynn Boden, G, South Dakota State
1976—James Hunter, DB, Grambling State

    Lawrence Gaines, FB, Wyoming
1977—None
1978—Luther Bradley, DB, Notre Dame
1979—Keith Dorney, T, Penn State
1980—Billy Sims, RB, Oklahoma*
1981—Mark Nichols, WR, San Jose State
1982—Jimmy Williams, LB, Nebraska
1983—James Jones, RB, Florida
1984—David Lewis, TE, California
1985—Lomas Brown, T, Florida
1986—Chuck Long, QB, Iowa
1987—Reggie Rogers, DE, Washington
1988—Bennie Blades, S, Miami (Fla.)
1989—Barry Sanders, RB, Oklahoma State
1990—Andre Ware, QB, Houston
1991—Herman Moore, WR, Virginia
1992—Robert Porcher, DE, South Carolina State
1993—None
1994—Johnnie Morton, WR, USC
1995—Luther Elliss, DT, Utah
1996—Reggie Brown, LB, Texas A&M
    Jeff Hartings, G, Penn State
1997—Bryant Westbrook, DB, Texas
1998—Terry Fair, DB, Tennessee
1999—Chris Claiborne, LB, USC
    Aaron Gibson, T, Wisconsin
2000—Stockar McDougle, T, Oklahoma
2001—Jeff Backus, T, Michigan
2002—Joey Harrington, QB, Oregon
2003—Charles Rogers, WR, Michigan State
2004—Roy Williams, WR, Texas
    Kevin Jones, RB, Virginia Tech
2005—Mike Williams, WR, USC
2006—Ernie Sims, LB, Florida State
*First player chosen in draft.

FRANCHISE RECORDS

Most rushing yards, career
15,269—Barry Sanders

Most rushing yards, season
2,053—Barry Sanders, 1997

Most rushing yards, game
237—Barry Sanders vs. T.B., Nov. 13, 1994

Most rushing touchdowns, season
16—Barry Sanders, 1991

Most passing attempts, season
583—Scott Mitchell, 1995

Most passing attempts, game
62—Charlie Batch at Ari., Nov. 18, 2001

Most passes completed, season
346—Scott Mitchell, 1995

Most passes completed, game
36—Charlie Batch at Ari., Nov. 18, 2001

Most passing yards, career
15,710—Bobby Layne

Most passing yards, season
4,338—Scott Mitchell, 1995

Most passing yards, game
436—Charlie Batch at Ari., Nov. 18, 2001

Most touchdown passes, season
32—Scott Mitchell, 1995

Most pass receptions, career
670—Herman Moore

Most pass receptions, season
123—Herman Moore, 1995

Most pass receptions, game
14—Herman Moore vs. Chi., Dec. 4, 1995

Most receiving yards, career
9,174—Herman Moore

Most receiving yards, season
1,686—Herman Moore, 1995

Most receiving yards, game
302—Cloyce Box vs. Bal., Dec. 3, 1950

Most receiving touchdowns, season
15—Cloyce Box, 1952

Most touchdowns, career
109—Barry Sanders

Most field goals, season
34—Jason Hanson, 1993

Longest field goal
56 yards—Jason Hanson vs. Cle., Oct. 8, 1995

Most interceptions, career
62—Dick LeBeau

Most interceptions, season
12—Don Doll, 1950
    Jack Christiansen, 1953

Most sacks, career
95.5—Robert Porcher

Most sacks, season
23—Al Baker, 1978

SERIES RECORDS

Detroit vs.: Arizona 31-21-5; Atlanta 22-9; Baltimore 1-1; Buffalo 3-3-1; Carolina 1-3; Chicago 62-85-5; Cincinnati 3-6; Cleveland 13-4; Dallas 8-10; Denver 3-6; Green Bay 64-80-7; Houston 1-0; Indianapolis 18-19-2; Jacksonville 1-2; Kansas City 3-7; Miami 2-6; Minnesota 29-58-2; New England 4-4; New Orleans 9-8-1; N.Y. Giants 20-17-1; N.Y. Jets 6-4; Oakland 3-6; Philadelphia 12-12-2; Pittsburgh 14-14-1; St. Louis 37-40-1; San Diego 3-5; San Francisco 26-31-1; Seattle 4-5; Tampa Bay 26-24; Tennessee 3-6; Washington 10-25. NOTE: Includes records as Portsmouth Spartans from 1930 through 1933.

COACHING RECORDS

Dutch Clark, 14-8-0; Monte Clark, 43-61-1 (0-2); Potsy Clark, 53-25-7 (1-0); Gus Dorais, 20-31-2; Bill Edwards, 4-9-1; Wayne Fontes, 66-67-0 (1-4); Rick Forzano, 15-17-0; Harry Gilmer, 10-16-2; Hal Griffen, 5-6-3; Elmer Henderson, 6-5-0; Tommy Hudspeth, 11-13-0; Dick Jauron, 1-4-0; John Karcis, 0-8-0; Steve Mariucci, 15-28-0; Don McCafferty, 6-7-1; Alvin McMillin, 12-24-0; Gary Moeller, 4-3-0; Marty Mornhinweg, 5-27-0; Buddy Parker, 47-23-2 (3-1); Darryl Rogers, 18-40-0; Bobby Ross, 27-30-0 (0-2); Joe Schmidt, 43-34-7 (0-1); George Wilson, 53-45-6 (2-0). NOTE: Playoff games in parentheses.

RETIRED UNIFORM NUMBERS

No.	Player
7	Dutch Clark
22	Bobby Layne
37	Doak Walker
56	Joe Schmidt

HISTORY *Team by team*

	REGULAR SEASON							PLAYOFFS			
Year	W	L	T	Pct.	PF	PA	Finish	W	L	Highest round	Coach
1921	3	2	1	.600	...	...	T6th				Curly Lambeau
1922	4	3	3	.571	...	...	T7th				Curly Lambeau
1923	7	2	1	.778	...	...	3rd				Curly Lambeau
1924	7	4	0	.636	...	...	6th				Curly Lambeau
1925	8	5	0	.615	...	...	9th				Curly Lambeau
1926	7	3	3	.700	...	...	5th				Curly Lambeau
1927	7	2	1	.778	...	...	2nd				Curly Lambeau
1928	6	4	3	.600	...	...	4th				Curly Lambeau
1929	12	0	1	1.000	...	...	1st				Curly Lambeau
1930	10	3	1	.769	...	...	1st				Curly Lambeau
1931	12	2	0	.857	...	...	1st				Curly Lambeau
1932	10	3	1	.769	...	...	2nd				Curly Lambeau
1933	5	7	1	.417	170	107	3rd/Western Div.	—	—		Curly Lambeau
1934	7	6	0	.538	156	112	3rd/Western Div.	—	—		Curly Lambeau
1935	8	4	0	.667	181	96	2nd/Western Div.	—	—		Curly Lambeau
1936	10	1	1	.909	248	118	1st/Western Div.	1	0	NFL champ	Curly Lambeau
1937	7	4	0	.636	220	122	T2nd/Western Div.	—	—		Curly Lambeau
1938	8	3	0	.727	223	118	1st/Western Div.	0	1	NFL championship game	Curly Lambeau
1939	9	2	0	.818	233	153	1st/Western Div.	1	0	NFL champ	Curly Lambeau
1940	6	4	1	.600	238	155	2nd/Western Div.	—	—		Curly Lambeau
1941	10	1	0	.909	258	120	2nd/Western Div.	0	1	W. Div. championship game	Curly Lambeau
1942	8	2	1	.800	300	215	2nd/Western Div.	—	—		Curly Lambeau
1943	7	2	1	.778	264	172	2nd/Western Div.	—	—		Curly Lambeau
1944	8	2	0	.800	238	141	1st/Western Div.	1	0	NFL champ	Curly Lambeau
1945	6	4	0	.600	258	173	3rd/Western Div.	—	—		Curly Lambeau
1946	6	5	0	.545	148	158	T3rd/Western Div.	—	—		Curly Lambeau
1947	6	5	1	.545	274	210	3rd/Western Div.	—	—		Curly Lambeau
1948	3	9	0	.250	154	290	4th/Western Div.	—	—		Curly Lambeau
1949	2	10	0	.167	114	329	5th/Western Div.	—	—		Curly Lambeau
1950	3	9	0	.250	244	406	T5th/National Conf.	—	—		Gene Ronzani
1951	3	9	0	.250	254	375	5th/National Conf.	—	—		Gene Ronzani
1952	6	6	0	.500	295	312	4th/National Conf.	—	—		Gene Ronzani
1953	2	9	1	.182	200	338	6th/Western Conf.	—	—		Gene Ronzani, Hugh Devore-S. McLean
1954	4	8	0	.333	234	251	5th/Western Conf.	—	—		Lisle Blackbourn
1955	6	6	0	.500	258	276	3rd/Western Conf.	—	—		Lisle Blackbourn
1956	4	8	0	.333	264	342	5th/Western Conf.	—	—		Lisle Blackbourn
1957	3	9	0	.250	218	311	6th/Western Conf.	—	—		Lisle Blackbourn
1958	1	10	1	.091	193	382	6th/Western Conf.	—	—		Scooter McLean
1959	7	5	0	.583	248	246	T3rd/Western Conf.	—	—		Vince Lombardi
1960	8	4	0	.667	332	209	1st/Western Conf.	0	1	NFL championship game	Vince Lombardi
1961	11	3	0	.786	391	223	1st/Western Conf.	1	0	NFL champ	Vince Lombardi
1962	13	1	0	.929	415	148	1st/Western Conf.	1	0	NFL champ	Vince Lombardi
1963	11	2	1	.846	369	206	2nd/Western Conf.	—	—		Vince Lombardi
1964	8	5	1	.615	342	245	T2nd/Western Conf.	—	—		Vince Lombardi
1965	10	3	1	.769	316	224	1st/Western Conf.	2	0	NFL champ	Vince Lombardi
1966	12	2	0	.857	335	163	1st/Western Conf.	2	0	Super Bowl champ	Vince Lombardi
1967	9	4	1	.692	332	209	1st/Central Div.	3	0	Super Bowl champ	Vince Lombardi
1968	6	7	1	.462	281	227	3rd/Central Div.	—	—		Phil Bengtson
1969	8	6	0	.571	269	221	3rd/Central Div.	—	—		Phil Bengtson
1970	6	8	0	.429	196	293	4th/NFC Central Div.	—	—		Phil Bengtson
1971	4	8	2	.333	274	298	4th/NFC Central Div.	—	—		Dan Devine
1972	10	4	0	.714	304	226	1st/NFC Central Div.	0	1	NFC div. playoff game	Dan Devine
1973	5	7	2	.429	202	259	3rd/NFC Central Div.	—	—		Dan Devine
1974	6	8	0	.429	210	206	3rd/NFC Central Div.	—	—		Dan Devine
1975	4	10	0	.286	226	285	4th/NFC Central Div.	—	—		Bart Starr
1976	5	9	0	.357	218	299	4th/NFC Central Div.	—	—		Bart Starr
1977	4	10	0	.286	134	219	4th/NFC Central Div.	—	—		Bart Starr
1978	8	7	1	.531	249	269	2nd/NFC Central Div.	—	—		Bart Starr
1979	5	11	0	.313	246	316	4th/NFC Central Div.	—	—		Bart Starr
1980	5	10	1	.344	231	371	5th/NFC Central Div.	—	—		Bart Starr
1981	8	8	0	.500	324	361	3rd/NFC Central Div.	—	—		Bart Starr
1982	5	3	1	.611	226	169	3rd/NFC	1	1	NFC second-round pl. game	Bart Starr
1983	8	8	0	.500	429	439	2nd/NFC Central Div.	—	—		Bart Starr
1984	8	8	0	.500	390	309	2nd/NFC Central Div.	—	—		Forrest Gregg
1985	8	8	0	.500	337	355	2nd/NFC Central Div.	—	—		Forrest Gregg
1986	4	12	0	.250	254	418	4th/NFC Central Div.	—	—		Forrest Gregg
1987	5	9	1	.367	255	300	3rd/NFC Central Div.	—	—		Forrest Gregg
1988	4	12	0	.250	240	315	5th/NFC Central Div.	—	—		Lindy Infante
1989	10	6	0	.625	362	356	2nd/NFC Central Div.	—	—		Lindy Infante

Year	W	L	T	Pct.	PF	PA	Finish	W	L	Highest round	Coach
1990	6	10	0	.375	271	347	4th/NFC Central Div.	—	—		Lindy Infante
1991	4	12	0	.250	273	313	4th/NFC Central Div.	—	—		Lindy Infante
1992	9	7	0	.563	276	296	2nd/NFC Central Div.	—	—		Mike Holmgren
1993	9	7	0	.563	340	282	3rd/NFC Central Div.	1	1	NFC div. playoff game	Mike Holmgren
1994	9	7	0	.563	382	287	2nd/NFC Central Div.	1	1	NFC div. playoff game	Mike Holmgren
1995	11	5	0	.689	404	314	1st/NFC Central Div.	2	1	NFC championship game	Mike Holmgren
1996	13	3	0	.813	456	210	1st/NFC Central Div.	3	0	Super Bowl champ	Mike Holmgren
1997	13	3	0	.813	422	282	1st/NFC Central Div.	2	1	Super Bowl	Mike Holmgren
1998	11	5	0	.688	408	319	2nd/NFC Central Div.	0	1	NFC wild-card game	Mike Holmgren
1999	8	8	0	.500	357	341	4th/NFC Central Div.	—	—		Ray Rhodes
2000	9	7	0	.563	353	323	3rd/NFC Central Div.	—	—		Mike Sherman
2001	12	4	0	.750	390	266	2nd/NFC Central Div.	1	1	NFC div. playoff game	Mike Sherman
2002	12	4	0	.750	398	328	1st/NFC North Div.	0	1	NFC wild-card game	Mike Sherman
2003	10	6	0	.625	442	307	1st/NFC North Div.	1	1	NFC div. playoff game	Mike Sherman
2004	10	6	0	.625	424	380	1st/NFC North Div.	0	1	NFC wild-card game	Mike Sherman
2005	4	12	0	.250	298	344	4th/NFC North Div.	—	—		Mike Sherman

(Column headers: Year, W, L, T, Pct., PF, PA, Finish under **REGULAR SEASON**; W, L, Highest round under **PLAYOFFS**; Coach)

FIRST-ROUND DRAFT PICKS

1936—Russ Letlow, G, San Francisco
1937—Ed Jankowski, B, Wisconsin
1938—Cecil Isbell, B, Purdue
1939—Larry Buhler, B, Minnesota
1940—Hal Van Every, B, Minnesota
1941—George Paskvan, B, Wisconsin
1942—Urban Odson, T, Minnesota
1943—Dick Wildung, T, Minnesota
1944—Merv Pregulman, G, Michigan
1945—Walt Schlinkman, G, Texas Tech
1946—Johnny Strzykalski, B, Marquette
1947—Ernie Case, B, UCLA
1948—Earl Girard, B, Wisconsin
1949—Stan Heath, B, Nevada
1950—Clayton Tonnemaker, C, Minnesota
1951—Bob Gain, T, Kentucky
1952—Babe Parilli, QB, Kentucky
1953—Al Carmichael, B, USC
1954—Art Hunter, T, Notre Dame
     Veryl Switzer, B, Kansas State
1955—Tom Bettis, G, Purdue
1956—Jack Losch, B, Miami
1957—Paul Hornung, B, Notre Dame*
     Ron Kramer, E, Michigan
1958—Dan Currie, C, Michigan State
1959—Randy Duncan, B, Iowa*
1960—Tom Moore, RB, Vanderbilt
1961—Herb Adderley, DB, Michigan State
1962—Earl Gros, RB, LSU
1963—Dave Robinson, LB, Penn State
1964—Lloyd Voss, DT, Nebraska
1965—Donny Anderson, RB, Texas Tech
     Larry Elkins, E, Baylor
1966— Jim Grabowski, RB, Illinois
     Gale Gillingham, T, Minnesota
1967—Bob Hyland, C, Boston College
     Don Horn, QB, San Diego State
1968—Fred Carr, LB, Texas-El Paso
     Bill Lueck, G, Arizona
1969—Rich Moore, DT, Villanova
1970—Mike McCoy, DT, Notre Dame
     Rich McGeorge, TE, Elon
1971—John Brockington, RB, Ohio State

1972—Willie Buchanon, DB, San Diego State
     Jerry Tagge, QB, Nebraska
1973—Barry Smith, WR, Florida State
1974—Barty Smith, RB, Richmond
1975—None
1976—Mark Koncar, T, Colorado
1977—Mike Butler, DE, Kansas
     Ezra Johnson, DE, Morris Brown
1978—James Lofton, WR, Stanford
     John Anderson, LB, Michigan
1979—Eddie Lee Ivery, RB, Georgia Tech
1980—Bruce Clark, DE, Penn State
     George Cumby, LB, Oklahoma
1981—Rich Campbell, QB, California
1982—Ron Hallstrom, G, Iowa
1983—Tim Lewis, DB, Pittsburgh
1984—Alphonso Carreker, DE, Florida State
1985—Ken Ruettgers, T, USC
1986—None
1987—Brent Fullwood, RB, Auburn
1988—Sterling Sharpe, WR, South Carolina
1989—Tony Mandarich, T, Michigan State
1990—Tony Bennett, LB, Mississippi
     Darrell Thompson, RB, Minnesota
1991—Vincent Clark, DB, Ohio State
1992—Terrell Buckley, DB, Florida State
1993—Wayne Simmons, LB, Clemson
     George Teague, DB, Alabama
1994—Aaron Taylor, T, Notre Dame
1995—Craig Newsome, DB, Arizona State
1996—John Michels, T, USC
1997—Ross Verba, T, Iowa
1998—Vonnie Holliday, DT, North Carolina
1999—Antuan Edwards, DB, Clemson
2000—Bubba Franks, TE, Miami (Fla.)
2001—Jamal Reynolds, DE, Florida State
2002—Javon Walker, WR, Florida State
2003—Nick Barnett, LB, Oregon State
2004—Ahmad Carroll, CB, Arkansas
2005—Aaron Rodgers, QB, California
2006—A.J. Hawk, LB, Ohio State
     *First player chosen in draft.

FRANCHISE RECORDS

Most rushing yards, career
8,207—Jim Taylor

Most rushing yards, season
1,883—Ahman Green, 2003

Most rushing yards, game
218—Ahman Green vs. Den., Dec. 28, 2003

Most rushing touchdowns, season
19—Jim Taylor, 1962

Most passing attempts, season
607—Brett Favre, 2005

Most passing attempts, game
61—Brett Favre vs. S.F., Oct. 14, 1996 (OT)
59—Don Majkowski at Det., Nov. 12, 1989

Most passes completed, season
372—Brett Favre, 2005

Most passes completed, game
36—Brett Favre at Chi., Dec. 5, 1993

Most passing yards, career
53,615—Brett Favre

Most passing yards, season
4,458—Lynn Dickey, 1983

Most passing yards, game
418—Lynn Dickey at T.B., Oct. 12, 1980

Most touchdown passes, season
39—Brett Favre, 1996

Most pass receptions, career
595—Sterling Sharpe
Most pass receptions, season
112—Sterling Sharpe, 1993
Most pass receptions, game
14—Don Hutson at NYG, Nov. 22, 1942
Most receiving yards, career
9,656—James Lofton
Most receiving yards, season
1,497—Robert Brooks, 1995

Most receiving yards, game
257—Bill Howton vs. L.A. Rams, Oct. 21, 1956
Most receiving touchdowns, season
18—Sterling Sharpe, 1994
Most touchdowns, career
105—Don Hutson
Most field goals, season
33—Chester Marcol, 1972
Ryan Longwell, 2000

Longest field goal
54 yards—Chris Jacke at Det., Jan. 2, 1994
Ryan Longwell at Ten., Dec. 16, 2001
Most interceptions, career
52—Bobby Dillon
Most interceptions, season
10—Irv Comp, 1943
Most sacks, career
84—Ezra Johnson
Most sacks, season
20.5—Ezra Johnson, 1978

SERIES RECORDS

Green Bay vs.: Arizona 41-22-4; Atlanta 12-10; Baltimore 2-1; Buffalo 3-6; Carolina 5-3; Chicago 78-86-6; Cincinnati 5-5; Cleveland 9-7; Dallas 11-9; Denver 4-5-1; Detroit 80-64-7; Houston 1-0; Indianapolis 19-20-1; Jacksonville 2-1; Kansas City 1-6-1; Miami 2-9; Minnesota 44-44-1; New England 4-3; New Orleans 14-5; N.Y. Giants 24-21-2; N.Y. Jets 2-7; Oakland 4-5; Philadelphia 22-12; Pittsburgh 18-13; St. Louis 40-44-2; San Diego 7-1; San Francisco 27-25-1; Seattle 6-4; Tampa Bay 29-19-1; Tennessee 4-5; Washington 16-12-1.

COACHING RECORDS

Phil Bengtson, 20-21-1; Lisle Blackbourn, 17-31-0; Dan Devine, 25-27-4 (0-1); Hugh Devore-Ray (Scooter) McLean, 0-2-0*; Forrest Gregg, 25-37-1; Mike Holmgren, 75-37-0 (9-5); Lindy Infante, 24-40-0; Curly Lambeau, 209-104-21 (3-2); Vince Lombardi, 89-29-4 (9-1); Ray (Scooter) McLean, 1-10-1; Ray Rhodes, 8-8-0; Gene Ronzani, 14-31-1; Mike Sherman, 57-39-0 (2-4); Bart Starr, 52-76-3 (1-1). NOTE: Playoff games in parentheses. *Co-coaches.

RETIRED UNIFORM NUMBERS

No.	Player
3	Tony Canadeo
14	Don Hutson
15	Bart Starr
66	Ray Nitschke
92	Reggie White

HOUSTON TEXANS
YEAR-BY-YEAR RECORDS

			REGULAR SEASON				PLAYOFFS			
Year	W	L	T	Pct.	PF	PA	Finish	W	L	Highest round	Coach
2002	4	12	0	.250	213	356	4th/AFC South Div.	—	—		Dom Capers
2003	5	11	0	.313	255	380	4th/AFC South Div.	—	—		Dom Capers
2004	7	9	0	.438	309	339	3rd/AFC South Div.	—	—		Dom Capers
2005	2	14	0	.125	260	431	4th/AFC South Div.	—	—		Dom Capers

FIRST-ROUND DRAFT PICKS

2002—David Carr, QB, Fresno State*
2003—Andre Johnson, WR, Miami
2004—Dunta Robinson, CB, South Carolina
Jason Babin, LB, Western Michigan

2005—Travis Johnson, DT, Florida State
2006—Mario Williams, DE, N.C. State*
*First player chosen in draft.

FRANCHISE RECORDS

Most rushing yards, career
3,195—Domanick Davis
Most rushing yards, season
1,188—Domanick Davis, 2004
Most rushing yards, game
155—Domanick Davis at Bal., Dec. 4, 2005.
Most rushing touchdowns, season
13—Domanick Davis, 2004
Most passing attempts, season
444—David Carr, 2002
Most passing attempts, game
42—David Carr at Ten., Oct. 12, 2003
Most passes completed, season
256—David Carr, 2005
Most passes completed, game
25—David Carr at Ten., Oct. 12, 2003
David Carr vs. StL., Nov. 27, 2005
Most passing yards, career
10,624—David Carr

Most passing yards, season
3,531—David Carr, 2004
Most passing yards, game
371—David Carr at Ten., Oct. 12, 2003
Most touchdown passes, season
16—David Carr, 2004
Most pass receptions, career
208—Andre Johnson
Most pass receptions, season
79—Andre Johnson, 2004
Most pass receptions, game
12—Andre Johnson vs. StL., Nov. 27, 2005
Most receiving yards, career
2,806—Andre Johnson
Most receiving yards, season
1,136—Andre Johnson, 2004
Most receiving yards, game
159—Andre Johnson vs. StL., Nov. 27, 2005

Most receiving touchdowns, season
6—Corey Bradford, 2002
Most touchdowns, career
28—Domanick Davis
Most field goals, season
26—Kris Brown, 2005
Longest field goal
53 yards—Kris Brown vs. Jac., Dec. 24, 2005
Most interceptions, career
11—Aaron Glenn
Marcus Coleman
Most interceptions, season
7—Marcus Coleman, 2003
Most sacks, career
15—Kailee Wong
Most sacks, season
8—Jeff Posey, 2002

SERIES RECORDS

Houston vs.: Arizona 1-0; Atlanta 1-0; Baltimore 0-2; Buffalo 1-2; Carolina 1-0; Chicago 1-0; Cincinnati 0-3; Cleveland 1-2; Dallas 1-0; Denver 0-1; Detroit 0-1; Green Bay 0-1; Indianapolis 0-8; Jacksonville 4-4; Kansas City 1-2; Miami 1-0; Minnesota 0-1; New England 0-1; New Orleans 0-1; N.Y. Giants 1-0; N.Y. Jets 0-2; Oakland 1-0; Philadelphia 0-1; Pittsburgh 1-1; St. Louis 0-1; San Diego 0-2; San Francisco 0-1; Seattle 0-1; Tampa Bay 0-1; Tennessee 2-6; Washington 0-1.

Dom Capers, 18-46-0.

No.	Player
	None

INDIANAPOLIS COLTS
YEAR-BY-YEAR RECORDS

		REGULAR SEASON					PLAYOFFS			
Year	W	L	T	Pct.	PF	PA	Finish	W	L	Highest round	Coach
1953*	3	9	0	.250	182	350	5th/Western Conf.	—	—		Keith Molesworth
1954*	3	9	0	.250	131	279	6th/Western Conf.	—	—		Weeb Ewbank
1955*	5	6	1	.455	214	239	4th/Western Conf.	—	—		Weeb Ewbank
1956*	5	7	0	.417	270	322	4th/Western Conf.	—	—		Weeb Ewbank
1957*	7	5	0	.583	303	235	3rd/Western Conf.	—	—		Weeb Ewbank
1958*	9	3	0	.750	381	203	1st/Western Conf.	1	0	NFL champ	Weeb Ewbank
1959*	9	3	0	.750	374	251	1st/Western Conf.	1	0	NFL champ	Weeb Ewbank
1960*	6	6	0	.500	288	234	4th/Western Conf.	—	—		Weeb Ewbank
1961*	8	6	0	.571	302	307	T3rd/Western Conf.	—	—		Weeb Ewbank
1962*	7	7	0	.500	293	288	4th/Western Conf.	—	—		Weeb Ewbank
1963*	8	6	0	.571	316	285	3rd/Western Conf.	—	—		Don Shula
1964*	12	2	0	.857	428	225	1st/Western Conf.	0	1	NFL championship game	Don Shula
1965*	10	3	1	.769	389	284	2nd/Western Conf.	0	1	W. Conf. champ. game	Don Shula
1966*	9	5	0	.643	314	226	2nd/Western Conf.	—	—		Don Shula
1967*	11	1	2	.917	394	198	2nd/Coastal Div.	—	—		Don Shula
1968*	13	1	0	.929	402	144	1st/Coastal Div.	2	1	Super Bowl	Don Shula
1969*	8	5	1	.615	279	268	2nd/Coastal Div.	—	—		Don Shula
1970*	11	2	1	.846	321	234	1st/AFC Eastern Div.	3	0	Super Bowl champ	Don McCafferty
1971*	10	4	0	.714	313	140	2nd/AFC Eastern Div.	1	1	AFC championship game	Don McCafferty
1972*	5	9	0	.357	235	252	3rd/AFC Eastern Div.	—	—		McCafferty, John Sandusky
1973*	4	10	0	.286	226	341	4th/AFC Eastern Div.	—	—		Howard Schnellenberger
1974*	2	12	0	.143	190	329	5th/AFC Eastern Div.	—	—		H. Schnellenberger, Joe Thomas
1975*	10	4	0	.714	395	269	1st/AFC Eastern Div.	0	1	AFC div. playoff game	Ted Marchibroda
1976*	11	3	0	.786	417	246	1st/AFC Eastern Div.	0	1	AFC div. playoff game	Ted Marchibroda
1977*	10	4	0	.714	295	221	1st/AFC Eastern Div.	0	1	AFC div. playoff game	Ted Marchibroda
1978*	5	11	0	.313	239	421	5th/AFC Eastern Div.	—	—		Ted Marchibroda
1979*	5	11	0	.313	271	351	5th/AFC Eastern Div.	—	—		Ted Marchibroda
1980*	7	9	0	.438	355	387	4th/AFC Eastern Div.	—	—		Mike McCormack
1981*	2	14	0	.125	259	533	4th/AFC Eastern Div.	—	—		Mike McCormack
1982*	0	8	1	.056	113	236	14th/AFC	—	—		Frank Kush
1983*	7	9	0	.438	264	354	4th/AFC Eastern Div.	—	—		Frank Kush
1984	4	12	0	.250	239	414	4th/AFC Eastern Div.	—	—		Frank Kush, Hal Hunter
1985	5	11	0	.313	320	386	4th/AFC Eastern Div.	—	—		Rod Dowhower
1986	3	13	0	.188	229	400	5th/AFC Eastern Div.	—	—		Rod Dowhower, Ron Meyer
1987	9	6	0	.600	300	238	1st/AFC Eastern Div.	0	1	AFC div. playoff game	Ron Meyer
1988	9	7	0	.563	354	315	2nd/AFC Eastern Div.	—	—		Ron Meyer
1989	8	8	0	.500	298	301	2nd/AFC Eastern Div.	—	—		Ron Meyer
1990	7	9	0	.438	281	353	3rd/AFC Eastern Div.	—	—		Ron Meyer
1991	1	15	0	.063	143	381	5th/AFC Eastern Div.	—	—		Ron Meyer, Rick Venturi
1992	9	7	0	.563	216	302	3rd/AFC Eastern Div.	—	—		Ted Marchibroda
1993	4	12	0	.250	189	378	5th/AFC Eastern Div.	—	—		Ted Marchibroda
1994	8	8	0	.500	307	320	4th/AFC Eastern Div.	—	—		Ted Marchibroda
1995	9	7	0	.563	331	316	2nd/AFC Eastern Div.	2	1	AFC championship game	Ted Marchibroda
1996	9	7	0	.563	317	334	3rd/AFC Eastern Div.	0	1	AFC wild-card game	Lindy Infante
1997	3	13	0	.188	313	401	5th/AFC Eastern Div.	—	—		Lindy Infante
1998	3	13	0	.188	310	444	5th/AFC Eastern Div.	—	—		Jim Mora
1999	13	3	0	.813	423	333	1st/AFC Eastern Div.	0	1	AFC div. playoff game	Jim Mora
2000	10	6	0	.625	429	326	2nd/AFC Eastern Div.	0	1	AFC wild-card game	Jim Mora
2001	6	10	0	.375	413	486	4th/AFC Eastern Div.	—	—		Jim Mora
2002	10	6	0	.625	349	313	2nd/AFC South Div.	0	1	AFC wild-card game	Tony Dungy
2003	12	4	0	.750	447	336	1st/AFC South Div.	2	1	AFC championship game	Tony Dungy
2004	12	4	0	.750	522	351	1st/AFC South Div.	1	1	AFC div. playoff game	Tony Dungy
2005	14	2	0	.875	439	247	1st/AFC South Div.	0	1	AFC div. playoff game	Tony Dungy

*Baltimore Colts.

FIRST-ROUND DRAFT PICKS

1953—Billy Vessels, B, Oklahoma
1954—Cotton Davidson, B, Baylor
1955—George Shaw, B, Oregon*
    Alan Ameche, B, Wisconsin
1956—Lenny Moore, B, Penn State
1957—Jim Parker, G, Ohio State

1958—Lenny Lyles, B, Louisville
1959—Jackie Burkett, C, Auburn
1960—Ron Mix, T, USC
1961—Tom Matte, RB, Ohio State
1962—Wendell Harris, DB, LSU
1963—Bob Vogel, T, Ohio State

HISTORY *Team by team*

1964—Marv Woodson, DB, Indiana
1965—Mike Curtis, LB, Duke
1966—Sam Ball, T, Kentucky
1967—Bubba Smith, DT, Michigan State*
    Jim Detwiler, RB, Michigan
1968—John Williams, G, Minnesota
1969—Eddie Hinton, WR, Oklahoma
1970—Norm Bulaich, RB, Texas Christian
1971—Don McCauley, RB, North Carolina
    Leonard Dunlap, DB, North Texas State
1972—Tom Drougas, T, Oregon
1973—Bert Jones, QB, LSU
    Joe Ehrmann, DT, Syracuse
1974—John Dutton, DE, Nebraska
    Roger Carr, WR, Louisiana Tech
1975—Ken Huff, G, North Carolina
1976—Ken Novak, DT, Purdue
1977—Randy Burke, WR, Kentucky
1978—Reese McCall, TE, Auburn
1979—Barry Krauss, LB, Alabama
1980—Curtis Dickey, RB, Texas A&M
    Derrick Hatchett, DB, Texas
1981—Randy McMillan, RB, Pittsburgh
    Donnell Thompson, DT, North Carolina
1982—Johnie Cooks, LB, Mississippi State
    Art Schlichter, QB, Ohio State
1983—John Elway, QB, Stanford*

1984—L. Coleman, DB, Vanderbilt
    Ron Solt, G, Maryland
1985—Duane Bickett, LB, USC
1986—Jon Hand, DE, Alabama
1987—Cornelius Bennett, LB, Alabama
1988—None
1989—Andre Rison, WR, Michigan State
1990—Jeff George, QB, Illinois*
1991—None
1992—Steve Emtman, DE, Washington*
    Quentin Coryatt, LB, Texas A&M
1993—Sean Dawkins, WR, California
1994—Marshall Faulk, RB, San Diego State
    Trev Alberts, LB, Nebraska
1995—Ellis Johnson, DT, Florida
1996—Marvin Harrison, WR, Syracuse
1997—Tarik Glenn, T, California
1998—Peyton Manning, QB, Tennessee*
1999—Edgerrin James, RB, Miami (Fla.)
2000—Rob Morris, LB, Brigham Young
2001—Reggie Wayne, WR, Miami (Fla.)
2002—Dwight Freeney, DE, Syracuse
2003—Dallas Clark, TE, Iowa
2004—None
2005—Marlin Jackson, CB, Michigan
2006—Joseph Addai, RB, Indianapolis
*First player chosen in draft.

FRANCHISE RECORDS

Most rushing yards, career
9,226—Edgerrin James
Most rushing yards, season
1,709—Edgerrin James, 2000
Most rushing yards, game
219—Edgerrin James at Sea., Oct. 15, 2000
Most rushing touchdowns, season
16—Lenny Moore, 1964
Most passing attempts, season
591—Peyton Manning, 2002
Most passing attempts, game
59—Jeff George at Was., Nov. 7, 1993
Most passes completed, season
392—Peyton Manning, 2002
Most passes completed, game
37—Jeff George at Was., Nov. 7, 1993
    Peyton Manning vs. Ten., Nov. 3, 2002
Most passing yards, career
39,768—Johnny Unitas
Most passing yards, season
4,557—Peyton Manning, 2004

Most passing yards, game
440—Peyton Manning vs. Jac., Sept. 25, 2000
Most touchdown passes, season
49—Peyton Manning, 2004
Most pass receptions, career
927—Marvin Harrison
Most pass receptions, season
143—Marvin Harrison, 2002
Most pass receptions, game
14—Marvin Harrison at Cle., Dec. 26, 1999
    Marvin Harrison vs. Dal., Nov. 17, 2002
Most receiving yards, career
12,331—Marvin Harrison
Most receiving yards, season
1,722—Marvin Harrison, 2002
Most receiving yards, game
224—Raymond Berry at Was., Nov. 10, 1957
Most receiving touchdowns, season
15—Marvin Harrison, 2001
    Marvin Harrison, 2004

Most touchdowns, career
113—Lenny Moore
Most field goals, season
37—Mike Vanderjagt, 2003
Longest field goal
58 yards—Dan Miller at S.D., Dec. 26, 1982
Most interceptions, career
57—Bob Boyd
Most interceptions, season
11—Tom Keane, 1953
Most sacks, career
56.5—Fred Cook
Most sacks, season
17—John Dutton, 1975

SERIES RECORDS

Indianapolis vs.: Arizona 7-6; Atlanta 12-1; Baltimore 4-2; Buffalo 29-34-1; Carolina 0-3; Chicago 22-17; Cincinnati 13-8; Cleveland 11-13; Dallas 5-7; Denver 4-11; Detroit 20-18-2; Green Bay 20-19-1; Houston 8-0; Jacksonville 8-2; Kansas City 8-7; Miami 22-44; Minnesota 13-7-1; New England 25-41; New Orleans 4-5; N.Y. Giants 6-6; N.Y. Jets 39-25; Oakland 3-7; Philadelphia 9-6; Pittsburgh 5-14; St. Louis 22-17-2; San Diego 8-13; San Francisco 23-18; Seattle 5-4; Tampa Bay 6-4; Tennessee 13-9; Washington 17-10. NOTE: Includes records as Baltimore Colts from 1953 through 1983.

COACHING RECORDS

Rod Dowhower, 5-24-0; Tony Dungy, 48-16-0 (3-4); Weeb Ewbank, 59-52-1 (2-0); Hal Hunter, 0-1-0; Lindy Infante, 12-20-0 (0-1); Frank Kush, 11-28-1; Ted Marchibroda, 71-67-0 (2-4); Don McCafferty, 22-10-1 (4-1); Mike McCormack, 9-23-0; Ron Meyer, 36-35-0 (0-1); Keith Molesworth, 3-9-0; Jim Mora, 32-32-0 (0-2); John Sandusky, 4-5-0; Howard Schnellenberger, 4-13-0; Don Shula, 71-23-4 (2-3); Joe Thomas, 2-9-0; Rick Venturi, 1-10.
NOTE: Playoff games in parentheses.

RETIRED UNIFORM NUMBERS

No.	Player
19	Johnny Unitas
22	Buddy Young
24	Lenny Moore
70	Art Donovan
77	Jim Parker
82	Raymond Berry
89	Gino Marchetti

JACKSONVILLE JAGUARS

YEAR-BY-YEAR RECORDS

		REGULAR SEASON							PLAYOFFS		
Year	W	L	T	Pct.	PF	PA	Finish	W	L	Highest round	Coach
1995	4	12	0	.250	275	404	5th/AFC Central Div.	—	—		Tom Coughlin
1996	9	7	0	.563	325	335	2nd/AFC Central Div.	2	1	AFC championship game	Tom Coughlin
1997	11	5	0	.688	394	318	2nd/AFC Central Div.	0	1	AFC wild-card game	Tom Coughlin
1998	11	5	0	.688	392	338	1st/AFC Central Div.	1	1	AFC div. playoff game	Tom Coughlin
1999	14	2	0	.875	396	217	1st/AFC Central Div.	1	1	AFC championship game	Tom Coughlin
2000	7	9	0	.438	367	327	4th/AFC Central Div.	—	—		Tom Coughlin
2001	6	10	0	.375	294	286	5th/AFC Central Div.	—	—		Tom Coughlin
2002	6	10	0	.375	328	315	3rd/AFC South Div.	—	—		Tom Coughlin
2003	5	11	0	.313	276	331	3rd/AFC South Div.	—	—		Jack Del Rio
2004	9	7	0	.562	261	280	2nd/AFC South Div.	—	—		Jack Del Rio
2005	12	4	0	.750	361	269	2nd/AFC South Div.	0	1	AFC wild-card game	Jack Del Rio

FIRST-ROUND DRAFT PICKS

1995—Tony Boselli, T, USC
James Stewart, RB, Tennessee
1996—Kevin Hardy, LB, Illinois
1997—Renaldo Wynn, DT, Notre Dame
1998—Fred Taylor, RB, Florida
Donovin Darius, DB, Syracuse
1999—Fernando Bryant, DB, Alabama

2000—R. Jay Soward, WR, USC
2001—Marcus Stroud, DT, Georgia
2002—John Henderson, DT, Tennessee
2003—Byron Leftwich, QB, Marshall
2004—Reggie Williams, WR, Washington
2005—Matt Jones, WR, Arkansas
2006—Marcedes Lewis, TE, UCLA

FRANCHISE RECORDS

Most rushing yards, career
8,367—Fred Taylor
Most rushing yards, season
1,572—Fred Taylor, 2003
Most rushing yards, game
234—Fred Taylor at Pit., Nov. 19, 2000
Most rushing touchdowns, season
14—Fred Taylor, 1998
Most passing attempts, season
557—Mark Brunell, 1996
Most passing attempts, game
52—Mark Brunell at St.L., Oct. 20, 1996
Most passes completed, season
353—Mark Brunell, 1996
Most passes completed, game
37—Mark Brunell at St.L., Oct. 20, 1996
Most passing yards, career
25,698—Mark Brunell
Most passing yards, season
4,367—Mark Brunell, 1996

Most passing yards, game
432—Mark Brunell at N.E., Sept. 22, 1996
Most touchdown passes, season
20—Mark Brunell, 1998, 2000
Most pass receptions, career
862—Jimmy Smith
Most pass receptions, season
116—Jimmy Smith, 1999
Most pass receptions, game
16—Keenan McCardell at St.L., Oct. 20, 1996
Most receiving yards, career
12,287—Jimmy Smith
Most receiving yards, season
1,636—Jimmy Smith, 1999
Most receiving yards, game
291—Jimmy Smith at Bal., Sept. 10, 2000
Most receiving touchdowns, season
8—Jimmy Smith, 1998, 2000, 2001

Most touchdowns, career
69—Jimmy Smith
Most field goals, season
31—Mike Hollis, 1997
Mike Hollis, 1999
Longest field goal
53 yards—Mike Hollis vs. Pit., Oct. 8, 1995
Mike Hollis vs. Car., Sept. 29, 1996
Seth Marler vs. S.D., Oct. 5, 2003
Josh Scobee vs. Cin., Oct. 9, 2005
Most interceptions, career
15—Aaron Beasley
Most interceptions, season
6—Aaron Beasley, 1999
Marlon McCree, 2002
Most sacks, career
55—Tony Brackens
Most sacks, season
12—Tony Brackens, 1999

HISTORY   Team by team

SERIES RECORDS

Jacksonville vs.: Arizona 2-0; Atlanta 2-1; Baltimore 9-6; Buffalo 2-3; Carolina 2-1; Chicago 2-2; Cincinnati 11-5; Cleveland 8-2; Dallas 1-2; Denver 2-3; Detroit 2-1; Green Bay 1-2; Houston 4-4; Indianapolis 2-8; Kansas City 4-1; Miami 1-1; Minnesota 1-2; New England 0-4; New Orleans 2-1; N.Y. Giants 1-2; N.Y. Jets 4-2; Oakland 2-1; Philadelphia 2-0; Pittsburgh 9-8; St. Louis 0-2; San Diego 1-1; San Francisco 2-0; Seattle 2-3; Tampa Bay 2-1; Tennessee 10-12; Washington 1-2.

COACHING RECORDS

Tom Coughlin, 68-60-0 (4-4); Jack Del Rio, 26-22-0 (0-1).
NOTE: Playoff games in parentheses.

RETIRED UNIFORM NUMBERS

No.	Player
	None

KANSAS CITY CHIEFS

YEAR-BY-YEAR RECORDS

		REGULAR SEASON							PLAYOFFS		
Year	W	L	T	Pct.	PF	PA	Finish	W	L	Highest round	Coach
1960*†	8	6	0	.571	362	253	2nd/Western Div.	—	—		Hank Stram
1961*†	6	8	0	.429	334	343	2nd/Western Div.	—	—		Hank Stram
1962*†	11	3	0	.786	389	233	1st/Western Div.	1	0	AFL champ	Hank Stram
1963*	5	7	2	.417	347	263	3rd/Western Div.	—	—		Hank Stram
1964*	7	7	0	.500	366	306	2nd/Western Div.	—	—		Hank Stram

Year	W	L	T	Pct.	PF	PA	Finish	W	L	Highest round	Coach
					REGULAR SEASON					**PLAYOFFS**	
1965*	7	5	2	.583	322	285	3rd/Western Div.	—	—		Hank Stram
1966*	11	2	1	.846	448	276	1st/Western Div.	1	1	Super Bowl	Hank Stram
1967*	9	5	0	.643	408	254	2nd/Western Div.	—	—		Hank Stram
1968*	12	2	0	.857	371	170	2nd/Western Div.	0	1	W. Div. champ. game	Hank Stram
1969*	11	3	0	.786	359	177	2nd/Western Div.	3	0	Super Bowl champ	Hank Stram
1970	7	5	2	.583	272	244	2nd/AFC Western Div.	—	—		Hank Stram
1971	10	3	1	.769	302	208	1st/AFC Western Div.	0	1	AFC div. playoff game	Hank Stram
1972	8	6	0	.571	287	254	2nd/AFC Western Div.	—	—		Hank Stram
1973	7	5	2	.571	231	192	3rd/AFC Western Div.	—	—		Hank Stram
1974	5	9	0	.357	233	293	3rd/AFC Western Div.	—	—		Hank Stram
1975	5	9	0	.357	282	341	3rd/AFC Western Div.	—	—		Paul Wiggin
1976	5	9	0	.357	290	376	4th/AFC Western Div.	—	—		Paul Wiggin
1977	2	12	0	.143	225	349	5th/AFC Western Div.	—	—		Paul Wiggin, Tom Bettis
1978	4	12	0	.250	243	327	5th/AFC Western Div.	—	—		Marv Levy
1979	7	9	0	.438	238	262	5th/AFC Western Div.	—	—		Marv Levy
1980	8	8	0	.500	319	336	3rd/AFC Western Div.	—	—		Marv Levy
1981	9	7	0	.563	343	290	3rd/AFC Western Div.	—	—		Marv Levy
1982	3	6	0	.333	176	184	11th/AFC	—	—		Marv Levy
1983	6	10	0	.375	386	367	5th/AFC Western Div.	—	—		John Mackovic
1984	8	8	0	.500	314	324	4th/AFC Western Div.	—	—		John Mackovic
1985	6	10	0	.375	317	360	5th/AFC Western Div.	—	—		John Mackovic
1986	10	6	0	.625	358	326	2nd/AFC Western Div.	0	1	AFC wild-card game	John Mackovic
1987	4	11	0	.267	273	388	5th/AFC Western Div.	—	—		Frank Gansz
1988	4	11	1	.281	254	320	5th/AFC Western Div.	—	—		Frank Gansz
1989	8	7	1	.531	318	286	2nd/AFC Western Div.	—	—		Marty Schottenheimer
1990	11	5	0	.688	369	257	2nd/AFC Western Div.	0	1	AFC wild-card game	Marty Schottenheimer
1991	10	6	0	.625	322	252	2nd/AFC Western Div.	1	1	AFC div. playoff game	Marty Schottenheimer
1992	10	6	0	.625	348	282	2nd/AFC Western Div.	0	1	AFC wild-card game	Marty Schottenheimer
1993	11	5	0	.688	328	291	1st/AFC Western Div.	2	1	AFC championship game	Marty Schottenheimer
1994	9	7	0	.563	319	298	2nd/AFC Western Div.	0	1	AFC wild-card game	Marty Schottenheimer
1995	13	3	0	.813	358	241	1st/AFC Western Div.	0	1	AFC div. playoff game	Marty Schottenheimer
1996	9	7	0	.563	297	300	2nd/AFC Western Div.	—	—		Marty Schottenheimer
1997	13	3	0	.813	375	232	1st/AFC Western Div.	0	1	AFC div. playoff game	Marty Schottenheimer
1998	7	9	0	.438	327	363	4th/AFC Western Div.	—	—		Marty Schottenheimer
1999	9	7	0	.563	390	322	2nd/AFC Western Div.	—	—		Gunther Cunningham
2000	7	9	0	.438	355	354	3rd/AFC Western Div.	—	—		Gunther Cunningham
2001	6	10	0	.375	320	344	4th/AFC Western Div.	—	—		Dick Vermeil
2002	8	8	0	.500	467	399	4th/AFC West Div.	—	—		Dick Vermeil
2003	13	3	0	.813	484	332	1st/AFC West Div.	0	1	AFC div. playoff game	Dick Vermeil
2004	7	9	0	.438	483	435	3rd/AFC West Div.	—	—		Dick Vermeil
2005	10	6	0	.625	403	325	2nd/AFC West Div.	—	—		Dick Vermeil

*American Football League.
†Dallas Texans.

FIRST-ROUND DRAFT PICKS

1960—Don Meredith, QB, Southern Methodist
1961—E.J. Holub, C, Texas Tech
1962—Ronnie Bull, RB, Baylor
1963—Buck Buchanan, DT, Grambling* (AFL)
  Ed Budde, G, Michigan State
1964—Pete Beathard, QB, USC
1965—Gale Sayers, RB, Kansas
1966—Aaron Brown, DE, Minnesota
1967—Gene Trosch, DE, Miami
1968—Mo Moorman, G, Texas A&M
  George Daney, G, Texas-El Paso
1969—Jim Marsalis, DB, Tennessee State
1970—Sid Smith, T, USC
1971—Elmo Wright, WR, Houston
1972—Jeff Kinney, RB, Nebraska
1973—None
1974—Woody Green, RB, Arizona State
1975—None
1976—Rod Walters, G, Iowa
1977—Gary Green, DB, Baylor
1978—Art Still, DE, Kentucky
1979—Mike Bell, DE, Colorado State
  Steve Fuller, QB, Clemson
1980—Brad Budde, G, USC
1981—Willie Scott, TE, South Carolina
1982—Anthony Hancock, WR, Tennessee
1983—Todd Blackledge, QB, Penn State

1984—Bill Maas, DT, Pittsburgh
  John Alt, T, Iowa
1985—Ethan Horton, RB, North Carolina
1986—Brian Jozwiak, T, West Virginia
1987—Paul Palmer, RB, Temple
1988—Neil Smith, DE, Nebraska
1989—Derrick Thomas, LB, Alabama
1990—Percy Snow, LB, Michigan State
1991—Harvey Williams, RB, LSU
1992—Dale Carter, DB, Tennessee
1993—None
1994—Greg Hill, RB, Texas A&M
1995—Trezelle Jenkins, T, Michigan
1996—Jerome Woods, DB, Memphis
1997—Tony Gonzalez, TE, California
1998—Victor Riley, T, Auburn
1999—John Tait, T, Brigham Young
2000—Sylvester Morris, WR, Jackson State
2001—None
2002—Ryan Sims, DT, North Carolina
2003—Larry Johnson, RB, Penn State
2004—None
2005—Derrick Johnson, LB, Texas
2006—Tamba Hali, DE, Penn State
  *First player chosen in draft.

FRANCHISE RECORDS

Most rushing yards, career
5,933—Priest Holmes

Most rushing yards, season
1,750—Larry Johnson, 2005

Most rushing yards, game
211—Larry Johnson at Hou., Nov. 20,2005

Most rushing touchdowns, season
27—Priest Holmes, 2003

Most passing attempts, season
603—Bill Kenney, 1983

Most passing attempts, game
55—Joe Montana at S.D., Oct. 9, 1994
Steve Bono at Mia., Dec. 12, 1994

Most passes completed, season
346—Bill Kenney, 1983

Most passes completed, game
39—Elvis Grbac at Oak., Nov. 5, 2000

Most passing yards, career
28,507—Len Dawson

Most passing yards, season
4,591—Trent Green, 2004

Most passing yards, game
504—Elvis Grbac at Oak., Nov. 5, 2000

Most touchdown passes, season
30—Len Dawson, 1964

Most pass receptions, career
648—Tony Gonzalez

Most pass receptions, season
102—Tony Gonzalez, 2004

Most pass receptions, game
12—Ed Podolak vs. Den., Oct. 7, 1973

Most receiving yards, career
7,810—Tony Gonzalez

Most receiving yards, season
1,391—Derrick Alexander, 2000

Most receiving yards, game
309—Stephone Paige vs. S.D., Dec. 22, 1985

Most receiving touchdowns, season
12—Chris Burford, 1962

Most touchdowns, career
83—Priest Holmes

Most field goals, season
34—Nick Lowery, 1990

Longest field goals
58 yards—Nick Lowery at Was., Sept. 18, 1983
Nick Lowery vs. L.A. Raiders, Sept. 12, 1985

Most interceptions, career
58—Emmitt Thomas

Most interceptions, season
12—Emmitt Thomas, 1974

Most sacks, career
126.5—Derrick Thomas

Most sacks, season
20—Derrick Thomas, 1990

SERIES RECORDS

Kansas City vs.: Arizona 6-2-1; Atlanta 5-1; Baltimore 3-0; Buffalo 16-19-1; Carolina 2-1; Chicago 4-5; Cincinnati 12-10; Cleveland 9-8-2; Dallas 3-5; Denver 51-40; Detroit 7-3; Green Bay 6-1-1; Houston 2-1; Indianapolis 7-8; Jacksonville 1-4; Miami 12-10; Minnesota 4-4; New England 16-11-3; New Orleans 4-4; N.Y. Giants 2-9; N.Y. Jets 16-14-1; Oakland 47-42-2; Philadelphia 2-3; Pittsburgh 8-16; St. Louis 4-4; San Diego 48-42-1; San Francisco 3-6; Seattle 30-18; Tampa Bay 5-4; Tennessee 25-18; Washington 6-1.
NOTE: Includes records as Dallas Texans from 1960 through 1962.

COACHING RECORDS

Tom Bettis, 1-6-0; Gunther Cunningham, 16-16-0; Frank Gansz, 8-22-1; Marv Levy, 31-42-0; John Mackovic, 30-34-0 (0-1); Marty Schottenheimer, 101-58-1 (3-7); Hank Stram, 124-76-10 (5-3); Dick Vermeil, 44-36-0 (0-1); Paul Wiggin, 11-24-0.
NOTE: Playoff games in parentheses.

RETIRED UNIFORM NUMBERS

No.	Player	No.	Player
3	Jan Stenerud	36	Mack Lee Hill
16	Len Dawson	63	Willie Lanier
28	Abner Haynes	78	Bobby Bell
33	Stone Johnson	86	Buck Buchanan

MIAMI DOLPHINS
YEAR-BY-YEAR RECORDS

Year	W	L	T	Pct.	PF	PA	Finish	W	L	Highest round	Coach
1966*	3	11	0	.214	213	362	T4th/Eastern Div.	—	—		George Wilson
1967*	4	10	0	.286	219	407	T3rd/Eastern Div.	—	—		George Wilson
1968*	5	8	1	.385	276	355	3rd/Eastern Div.	—	—		George Wilson
1969*	3	10	1	.231	233	332	5th/Eastern Div.	—	—		George Wilson
1970	10	4	0	.714	297	228	2nd/AFC Eastern Div.	0	1	AFC div. playoff game	Don Shula
1971	10	3	1	.769	315	174	1st/AFC Eastern Div.	2	1	Super Bowl	Don Shula
1972	14	0	0	1.000	385	171	1st/AFC Eastern Div.	3	0	Super Bowl champ	Don Shula
1973	12	2	0	.857	343	150	1st/AFC Eastern Div.	3	0	Super Bowl champ	Don Shula
1974	11	3	0	.786	327	216	1st/AFC Eastern Div.	0	1	AFC div. playoff game	Don Shula
1975	10	4	0	.714	357	222	2nd/AFC Eastern Div.	—	—		Don Shula
1976	6	8	0	.429	263	264	3rd/AFC Eastern Div.	—	—		Don Shula
1977	10	4	0	.714	313	197	2nd/AFC Eastern Div.	—	—		Don Shula
1978	11	5	0	.688	372	254	2nd/AFC Eastern Div.	0	1	AFC wild-card game	Don Shula
1979	10	6	0	.625	341	257	1st/AFC Eastern Div.	0	1	AFC div. playoff game	Don Shula
1980	8	8	0	.500	266	305	3rd/AFC Eastern Div.	—	—		Don Shula
1981	11	4	1	.719	345	275	1st/AFC Eastern Div.	0	1	AFC div. playoff game	Don Shula
1982	7	2	0	.778	198	131	2nd/AFC	3	1	Super Bowl	Don Shula
1983	12	4	0	.750	389	250	1st/AFC Eastern Div.	0	1	AFC div. playoff game	Don Shula
1984	14	2	0	.875	513	298	1st/AFC Eastern Div.	2	1	Super Bowl	Don Shula
1985	12	4	0	.750	428	320	1st/AFC Eastern Div.	1	1	AFC championship game	Don Shula
1986	8	8	0	.500	430	405	3rd/AFC Eastern Div.	—	—		Don Shula
1987	8	7	0	.533	362	335	3rd/AFC Eastern Div.	—	—		Don Shula
1988	6	10	0	.375	319	380	5th/AFC Eastern Div.	—	—		Don Shula
1989	8	8	0	.500	331	379	3rd/AFC Eastern Div.	—	—		Don Shula
1990	12	4	0	.750	336	242	2nd/AFC Eastern Div.	1	1	AFC div. playoff game	Don Shula
1991	8	8	0	.500	343	349	3rd/AFC Eastern Div.	—	—		Don Shula
1992	11	5	0	.688	340	281	1st/AFC Eastern Div.	1	1	AFC championship game	Don Shula
1993	9	7	0	.563	349	351	2nd/AFC Eastern Div.	—	—		Don Shula

	REGULAR SEASON							PLAYOFFS			
Year	W	L	T	Pct.	PF	PA	Finish	W	L	Highest round	Coach
1994	10	6	0	.625	389	327	1st/AFC Eastern Div.	1	1	AFC div. playoff game	Don Shula
1995	9	7	0	.563	398	332	3rd/AFC Eastern Div.	0	1	AFC wild-card game	Don Shula
1996	8	8	0	.500	339	325	4th/AFC Eastern Div.	—	—		Jimmy Johnson
1997	9	7	0	.563	339	327	2nd/AFC Eastern Div.	0	1	AFC wild-card game	Jimmy Johnson
1998	10	6	0	.625	321	265	2nd/AFC Eastern Div.	1	1	AFC div. playoff game	Jimmy Johnson
1999	9	7	0	.563	326	336	3rd/AFC Eastern Div.	1	1	AFC div. playoff game	Jimmy Johnson
2000	11	5	0	.688	323	226	1st/AFC Eastern Div.	1	1	AFC div. playoff game	Dave Wannstedt
2001	11	5	0	.688	344	290	2nd/AFC Eastern Div.	0	1	AFC wild-card game	Dave Wannstedt
2002	9	7	0	.563	378	301	3rd/AFC East Div.	—	—		Dave Wannstedt
2003	10	6	0	.625	311	261	2nd/AFC East Div.	—	—		Dave Wannstedt
2004	4	12	0	.250	275	354	4th/AFC East Div.	—	—		D. Wannstedt, Jim Bates
2005	9	7	0	.562	318	317	2nd/AFC East Div.	—	—		Nick Saban

*American Football League.

FIRST-ROUND DRAFT PICKS

1966—Jim Grabowski, RB, Illinois*
    Rick Norton, QB, Kentucky
1967—Bob Griese, QB, Purdue
1968—Larry Csonka, RB, Syracuse
    Doug Crusan, T, Indiana
1969—Bill Stanfill, DE, Georgia
1970—None
1971—None
1972—Mike Kadish, DT, Notre Dame
1973—None
1974—Don Reese, DE, Jackson State
1975—Darryl Carlton, T, Tampa
1976—Larry Gordon, LB, Arizona State
    Kim Bokamper, LB, San Jose State
1977—A.J. Duhe, DT, LSU
1978—None
1979—Jon Giesler, T, Michigan
1980—Don McNeal, DB, Alabama
1981—David Overstreet, RB, Oklahoma
1982—Roy Foster, G, USC
1983—Dan Marino, QB, Pittsburgh
1984—Jackie Shipp, LB, Oklahoma
1985—Lorenzo Hampton, RB, Florida
1986—None

1987—John Bosa, DE, Boston College
1988—Eric Kumerow, DE, Ohio State
1989—Sammie Smith, RB, Florida State
    Louis Oliver, DB, Florida
1990—Richmond Webb, T, Texas A&M
1991—Randal Hill, WR, Miami
1992—Troy Vincent, DB, Wisconsin
    Marco Coleman, LB, Georgia Tech
1993—O.J. McDuffie, WR, Penn State
1994—Tim Bowens, DT, Mississippi
1995—Billy Milner, T, Houston
1996—Daryl Gardener, DT, Baylor
1997—Yatil Green, WR, Miami (Fla.)
1998—John Avery, RB, Mississippi
1999—None
2000—None
2001—Jamar Fletcher, DB, Wisconsin
2002—None
2003—None
2004—Vernon Carey, OT, Miami (Fla.)
2005—Ronnie Brown, RB, Auburn
2006—Jason Allen, S, Tennessee
*First player chosen in draft.

FRANCHISE RECORDS

Most rushing yards, career
6,737—Larry Csonka
Most rushing yards, season
1,853—Ricky Williams, 2002
Most rushing yards, game
228—Ricky Williams at Buf., Dec. 1, 2002
Most rushing touchdowns, season
16—Ricky Williams, 2002
Most passing attempts, season
623—Dan Marino, 1986
Most passing attempts, game
60—Dan Marino vs. NYJ, Oct. 23, 1988
    Dan Marino at N.E., Nov. 23, 1997
Most passes completed, season
385—Dan Marino, 1994
Most passes completed, game
39—Dan Marino at Buf., Nov. 16, 1986
Most passing yards, career
61,361—Dan Marino

Most passing yards, season
5,084—Dan Marino, 1984
Most passing yards, game
521—Dan Marino vs. NYJ, Oct. 23, 1988
Most touchdown passes, season
48—Dan Marino, 1984
Most pass receptions, career
550—Mark Clayton
Most pass receptions, season
90—O.J. McDuffie, 1998
Most pass receptions, game
15—Chris Chambers vs. Buf., Dec. 4, 2005
Most receiving yards, career
8,869—Mark Duper
Most receiving yards, season
1,389—Mark Clayton, 1984
Most receiving yards, game
238—Chris Chambers vs. Buf., Dec. 4, 2005

Most receiving touchdowns, season
18—Mark Clayton, 1984
Most touchdowns, career
82—Mark Clayton
Most field goals, season
39—Olindo Mare, 1999
Longest field goal
59 yards—Pete Stoyanovich at NYJ, Nov. 12, 1989
Most interceptions, career
35—Jake Scott
Most interceptions, season
10—Dick Westmoreland, 1967
Most sacks, career
92.5—Jason Taylor
Most sacks, season
18.5—Bill Stanfill, 1973
    Jason Taylor, 2002

SERIES RECORDS

Miami vs.: Arizona 8-1; Atlanta 7-3; Baltimore 4-1; Buffalo 49-30-1; Carolina 3-0; Chicago 6-3; Cincinnati 12-4; Cleveland 7-5; Dallas 7-3; Denver 10-3-1; Detroit 6-2; Green Bay 9-2; Houston 0-1; Indianapolis 44-22; Jacksonville 1-1; Kansas City 10-12; Minnesota 4-4; New England 46-32; New Orleans 6-3; N.Y. Giants 2-3; N.Y. Jets 38-41-1; Oakland 11-15-1; Philadelphia 7-4; Pittsburgh 9-8; St. Louis 8-2; San Diego 11-10; San Francisco 5-4; Seattle 6-3; Tampa Bay 4-4; Tennessee 16-13; Washington 6-3.

COACHING RECORDS

Jim Bates, 3-4-0; Jimmy Johnson, 36-28-0 (2-3); Nick Saban, 9-7-0; Don Shula, 257-133-2 (17-14); Dave Wannstedt, 42-31-0 (1-2); George Wilson, 15-39-2.
NOTE: Playoff games in parentheses.

RETIRED UNIFORM NUMBERS

No.	Player
12	Bob Griese
13	Dan Marino
39	Larry Csonka

MINNESOTA VIKINGS
YEAR-BY-YEAR RECORDS

	REGULAR SEASON							PLAYOFFS		
Year	W	L	T	Pct.	PF	PA	Finish	W	L	Highest round	Coach
1961	3	11	0	.214	285	407	7th/Western Conf.	—	—		Norm Van Brocklin
1962	2	11	1	.154	254	410	6th/Western Conf.	—	—		Norm Van Brocklin
1963	5	8	1	.385	309	390	T4th/Western Conf.	—	—		Norm Van Brocklin
1964	8	5	1	.615	355	296	T2nd/Western Conf.	—	—		Norm Van Brocklin
1965	7	7	0	.500	383	403	5th/Western Conf.	—	—		Norm Van Brocklin
1966	4	9	1	.308	292	304	T6th/Western Conf.	—	—		Norm Van Brocklin
1967	3	8	3	.273	233	294	4th/Central Div.	—	—		Bud Grant
1968	8	6	0	.571	282	242	1st/Central Div.	0	1	W. Conf. champ. game	Bud Grant
1969	12	2	0	.857	379	133	1st/Central Div.	2	1	Super Bowl	Bud Grant
1970	12	2	0	.857	335	143	1st/NFC Central Div.	0	1	NFC div. playoff game	Bud Grant
1971	11	3	0	.786	245	139	1st/NFC Central Div.	0	1	NFC div. playoff game	Bud Grant
1972	7	7	0	.500	301	252	3rd/NFC Central Div.	—	—		Bud Grant
1973	12	2	0	.857	296	168	1st/NFC Central Div.	2	1	Super Bowl	Bud Grant
1974	10	4	0	.714	310	195	1st/NFC Central Div.	2	1	Super Bowl	Bud Grant
1975	12	2	0	.857	377	180	1st/NFC Central Div.	0	1	NFC div. playoff game	Bud Grant
1976	11	2	1	.821	305	176	1st/NFC Central Div.	2	1	Super Bowl	Bud Grant
1977	9	5	0	.643	231	227	1st/NFC Central Div.	1	1	NFC championship game	Bud Grant
1978	8	7	1	.531	294	306	1st/NFC Central Div.	0	1	NFC div. playoff game	Bud Grant
1979	7	9	0	.438	259	337	3rd/NFC Central Div.	—	—		Bud Grant
1980	9	7	0	.563	317	308	1st/NFC Central Div.	0	1	NFC div. playoff game	Bud Grant
1981	7	9	0	.438	325	369	4th/NFC Central Div.	—	—		Bud Grant
1982	5	4	0	.556	187	198	4th/NFC	1	1	NFC second-round pl. game	Bud Grant
1983	8	8	0	.500	316	348	4th/NFC Central Div.	—	—		Les Steckel
1984	3	13	0	.188	276	484	5th/NFC Central Div.	—	—		Les Steckel
1985	7	9	0	.438	346	359	3rd/NFC Central Div.	—	—		Bud Grant
1986	9	7	0	.563	398	273	2nd/NFC Central Div.	—	—		Jerry Burns
1987	8	7	0	.533	336	335	2nd/NFC Central Div.	2	1	NFC championship game	Jerry Burns
1988	11	5	0	.688	406	233	2nd/NFC Central Div.	1	1	NFC div. playoff game	Jerry Burns
1989	10	6	0	.625	351	275	1st/NFC Central Div.	0	1	NFC div. playoff game	Jerry Burns
1990	6	10	0	.375	351	326	5th/NFC Central Div.	—	—		Jerry Burns
1991	8	8	0	.500	301	306	3rd/NFC Central Div.	—	—		Jerry Burns
1992	11	5	0	.688	374	249	1st/NFC Central Div.	0	1	NFC wild-card game	Dennis Green
1993	9	7	0	.563	277	290	2nd/NFC Central Div.	0	1	NFC wild-card game	Dennis Green
1994	10	6	0	.625	356	314	1st/NFC Central Div.	0	1	NFC wild-card game	Dennis Green
1995	8	8	0	.500	412	385	4th/NFC Central Div.	—	—		Dennis Green
1996	9	7	0	.563	298	315	2nd/NFC Central Div.	0	1	NFC wild-card game	Dennis Green
1997	9	7	0	.563	354	359	4th/NFC Central Div.	1	1	NFC div. playoff game	Dennis Green
1998	15	1	0	.938	556	296	1st/NFC Central Div.	1	1	NFC championship game	Dennis Green
1999	10	6	0	.625	399	335	2nd/NFC Central Div.	1	1	NFC div. playoff game	Dennis Green
2000	11	5	0	.688	397	371	1st/NFC Central Div.	1	1	NFC championship game	Dennis Green
2001	5	11	0	.313	290	390	4th/NFC Central Div.	—	—		Dennis Green, Mike Tice
2002	6	10	0	.375	390	442	2nd/NFC North Div.	—	—		Mike Tice
2003	9	7	0	.563	416	353	2nd/NFC North Div.	—	—		Mike Tice
2004	8	8	0	.500	405	395	2nd/NFC North Div.	1	1	NFC div. playoff game	Mike Tice
2005	9	7	0	.562	306	344	2nd/NFC North Div.	—	—		Mike Tice

HISTORY *Team by team*

FIRST-ROUND DRAFT PICKS

1961—Tommy Mason, RB, Tulane*
1962—None
1963—Jim Dunaway, T, Mississippi
1964—Carl Eller, DE, Minnesota
1965—Jack Snow, WR, Notre Dame
1966—Jerry Shay, DT, Purdue
1967—Clint Jones, RB, Michigan State
    Gene Washington, WR, Michigan State
    Alan Page, DT, Notre Dame
1968—Ron Yary, T, USC*
1969—None
1970—John Ward, DT, Oklahoma State
1971—Leo Hayden, RB, Ohio State
1972—Jeff Siemon, LB, Stanford
1973—Chuck Foreman, RB, Miami (Fla.)

1974—Fred McNeill, LB, UCLA
    Steve Riley, T, USC
1975—Mark Mullaney, DE, Colorado State
1976—James White, DT, Oklahoma State
1977—Tommy Kramer, QB, Rice
1978—Randy Holloway, DE, Pittsburgh
1979—Ted Brown, RB, N.C. State
1980—Doug Martin, DT, Washington
1981—None
1982—Darrin Nelson, RB, Stanford
1983—Joey Browner, DB, USC
1984—Keith Millard, DE, Washington State
1985—Chris Doleman, LB, Pittsburgh
1986—Gerald Robinson, DE, Auburn
1987—D.J. Dozier, RB, Penn State

1988—Randall McDaniel, G, Arizona State
1989—None
1990—None
1991—None
1992—None
1993—Robert Smith, RB, Ohio State
1994—DeWayne Washington, CB, N.C. State
　　　Todd Steussie, T, California
1995—Derrick Alexander, DE, Florida State
　　　Korey Stringer, T, Ohio State
1996—Duane Clemons, DE, California
1997—Dwayne Rudd, LB, Alabama

1998—Randy Moss, WR, Marshall
1999—Daunte Culpepper, QB, Central Florida
　　　Dimitrius Underwood, DE, Michigan State
2000—Chris Hovan, DT, Boston College
2001—Michael Bennett, RB, Wisconsin
2002—Bryant McKinnie, T, Miami (Fla.)
2003—Kevin Williams, DT, Oklahoma State
2004—Kenechi Udeze, DE, USC
2005—Troy Williamson, WR, South Carolina
　　　Erasmus James, DE, Wisconsin
2006—Chad Greenway, LB, Iowa
　　*First player chosen in draft.

FRANCHISE RECORDS

Most rushing yards, career
6,818—Robert Smith
Most rushing yards, season
1,521—Robert Smith, 2000
Most rushing yards, game
200—Chuck Foreman at Phi., Oct. 24, 1976
Most rushing touchdowns, season
13—Chuck Foreman, 1975
　　Chuck Foreman, 1976
　　Terry Allen, 1992
Most passing attempts, season
606—Warren Moon, 1995
Most passing attempts, game
63—Rich Gannon at N.E., Oct. 20, 1991
Most passes completed, season
377—Warren Moon, 1995
Most passes completed, game
38—Tommy Kramer vs. Cle., Dec. 14, 1980
　　Tommy Kramer vs. G.B., Nov. 29, 1981
Most passing yards, career
33,098—Fran Tarkenton

Most passing yards, season
4,717—Daunte Culpepper, 2004
Most passing yards, game
490—Tommy Kramer at Was., Nov. 2, 1986
　　(OT)
456—Tommy Kramer vs. Cle., Dec. 14,
　　1980
Most touchdown passes, season
39—Daunte Culpepper, 2004
Most pass receptions, career
1,004—Cris Carter
Most pass receptions, season
122—Cris Carter, 1994, 1995
Most pass receptions, game
15—Rickey Young at N.E., Dec. 16, 1979
Most receiving yards, career
12,383—Cris Carter
Most receiving yards, season
1,632—Randy Moss, 2003
Most receiving yards, game
210—Sammy White vs. Det., Nov. 7, 1976

Most receiving touchdowns, season
17—Cris Carter, 1995
　　Randy Moss, 1998
　　Randy Moss, 2003
Most touchdowns, career
110—Cris Carter
Most field goals, season
35—Gary Anderson, 1998
Longest field goal
56 yards—Paul Edinger vs. Green Bay,
　　Oct. 23, 2005
Most interceptions, career
53—Paul Krause
Most interceptions, season
10—Paul Krause, 1975
Most sacks, career
130—Carl Eller
Most sacks, season
21—Chris Doleman, 1989

SERIES RECORDS

Minnesota vs.: Arizona 8-9; Atlanta 14-8; Baltimore 1-2; Buffalo 7-3; Carolina 3-3; Chicago 48-39-2; Cincinnati 5-5; Cleveland 9-3; Dallas 10-9; Denver 7-4; Detroit 58-29-2; Green Bay 44-44-1; Houston 1-0; Indianapolis 7-13-1; Jacksonville 2-1; Kansas City 4-4; Miami 4-4; New England 4-5; New Orleans 17-7; N.Y. Giants 10-8; N.Y. Jets 1-6; Oakland 3-8; Philadelphia 11-8; Pittsburgh 8-6; St. Louis 17-13-2; San Diego 4-5; San Francisco 18-17-1; Seattle 3-6; Tampa Bay 31-19; Tennessee 7-3; Washington 5-7.

COACHING RECORDS

Jerry Burns, 52-43-0 (3-3); Bud Grant, 158-96-5 (10-12); Dennis Green, 97-62-0 (4-8); Les Steckel, 3-13-0; Mike Tice, 32-33-0 (1-1); Norm Van Brocklin, 29-51-4.
NOTE: Playoff games in parentheses.

RETIRED UNIFORM NUMBERS

No.	Player
10	Fran Tarkenton
53	Mick Tingelhoff
70	Jim Marshall
77	Korey Stringer
80	Cris Carter
88	Alan Page

NEW ENGLAND PATRIOTS
YEAR-BY-YEAR RECORDS

| | | | REGULAR SEASON | | | | | PLAYOFFS | | |
Year	W	L	T	Pct.	PF	PA	Finish	W	L	Highest round	Coach
1960*†	5	9	0	.357	286	349	4th/Eastern Div.	—	—		Lou Saban
1961*†	9	4	1	.692	413	313	2nd/Eastern Div.	—	—		Lou Saban, Mike Holovak
1962*†	9	4	1	.692	346	295	2nd/Eastern Div.	—	—		Mike Holovak
1963*†	7	6	1	.538	327	257	1st/Eastern Div.	1	1	AFL championship game	Mike Holovak
1964*†	10	3	1	.769	365	297	2nd/Eastern Div.	—	—		Mike Holovak
1965*†	4	8	2	.333	244	302	3rd/Eastern Div.	—	—		Mike Holovak
1966*†	8	4	2	.667	315	283	2nd/Eastern Div.	—	—		Mike Holovak
1967*†	3	10	1	.231	280	389	5th/Eastern Div.	—	—		Mike Holovak
1968*†	4	10	0	.286	229	406	4th/Eastern Div.	—	—		Mike Holovak
1969*†	4	10	0	.286	266	316	T3rd/Eastern Div.	—	—		Clive Rush
1970†	2	12	0	.143	149	361	5th/AFC Eastern Div.	—	—		Clive Rush, John Mazur
1971	6	8	0	.429	238	325	3rd/AFC Eastern Div.	—	—		John Mazur
1972	3	11	0	.214	192	446	5th/AFC Eastern Div.	—	—		J. Mazur, Phil Bengtson
1973	5	9	0	.357	258	300	3rd/AFC Eastern Div.	—	—		Chuck Fairbanks

		REGULAR SEASON						PLAYOFFS			
Year	W	L	T	Pct.	PF	PA	Finish	W	L	Highest round	Coach
1974	7	7	0	.500	348	289	3rd/AFC Eastern Div.	—	—		Chuck Fairbanks
1975	3	11	0	.214	258	358	4th/AFC Eastern Div.	—	—		Chuck Fairbanks
1976	11	3	0	.786	376	236	2nd/Eastern Div.	0	1	AFC div. playoff game	Chuck Fairbanks
1977	9	5	0	.643	278	217	3rd/AFC Eastern Div.	—	—		Chuck Fairbanks
1978	11	5	0	.688	358	286	1st/AFC Eastern Div.	0	1	AFC div. playoff game	Chuck Fairbanks, Hank Bullough-R. Erhardt
1979	9	7	0	.563	411	326	2nd/AFC Eastern Div.	—	—		Ron Erhardt
1980	10	6	0	.625	441	325	2nd/AFC Eastern Div.	—	—		Ron Erhardt
1981	2	14	0	.125	322	370	5th/AFC Eastern Div.	—	—		Ron Erhardt
1982	5	4	0	.556	143	157	7th/AFC	0	1	AFC first-round pl. game	Ron Meyer
1983	8	8	0	.500	274	289	2nd/AFC Eastern Div.	—	—		Ron Meyer
1984	9	7	0	.563	362	352	2nd/AFC Eastern Div.	—	—		R. Meyer, R. Berry
1985	11	5	0	.688	362	290	3rd/AFC Eastern Div.	3	1	Super Bowl	Raymond Berry
1986	11	5	0	.688	412	307	1st/AFC Eastern Div.	0	1	AFC div. playoff game	Raymond Berry
1987	8	7	0	.533	320	293	2nd/AFC Eastern Div.	—	—		Raymond Berry
1988	9	7	0	.563	250	284	3rd/AFC Eastern Div.	—	—		Raymond Berry
1989	5	11	0	.313	297	391	4th/AFC Eastern Div.	—	—		Raymond Berry
1990	1	15	0	.063	181	446	5th/AFC Eastern Div.	—	—		Rod Rust
1991	6	10	0	.375	211	305	4th/AFC Eastern Div.	—	—		Dick MacPherson
1992	2	14	0	.125	205	363	5th/AFC Eastern Div.	—	—		Dick MacPherson
1993	5	11	0	.313	238	286	4th/AFC Eastern Div.	—	—		Bill Parcells
1994	10	6	0	.625	351	312	2nd/AFC Eastern Div.	0	1	AFC wild-card game	Bill Parcells
1995	6	10	0	.375	294	377	4th/AFC Eastern Div.	—	—		Bill Parcells
1996	11	5	0	.687	418	313	1st/AFC Eastern Div.	2	1	Super Bowl	Bill Parcells
1997	10	6	0	.625	369	289	1st/AFC Eastern Div.	1	1	AFC div. playoff game	Pete Carroll
1998	9	7	0	.563	337	329	4th/AFC Eastern Div.	0	1	AFC wild-card game	Pete Carroll
1999	8	8	0	.500	299	284	5th/AFC Eastern Div.	—	—		Pete Carroll
2000	5	11	0	.313	276	338	5th/AFC Eastern Div.	—	—		Bill Belichick
2001	11	5	0	.688	371	272	1st/AFC Eastern Div.	3	0	Super Bowl champ	Bill Belichick
2002	9	7	0	.563	381	346	2nd/AFC East Div.	—	—		Bill Belichick
2003	14	2	0	.875	348	238	1st/AFC East Div.	3	0	Super Bowl champ	Bill Belichick
2004	14	2	0	.875	437	260	1st/AFC East Div.	3	0	Super Bowl champ	Bill Belichick
2005	10	6	0	.625	379	338	1st/AFC East Div.	1	1	AFC div. playoff game	Bill Belichick

*American Football League.
†Boston Patriots.

FIRST-ROUND DRAFT PICKS

1960—Ron Burton, RB, Northwestern
1961—Tommy Mason, RB, Tulane
1962—Gary Collins, WR, Maryland
1963—Art Graham, E, Boston College
1964—Jack Concannon, QB, Boston College* (AFL)
1965—Jerry Rush, DE, Michigan State
1966—Karl Singer, T, Purdue
1967—John Charles, DB, Purdue
1968—Dennis Byrd, DE, N.C. State
1969—Ron Sellers, WR, Florida State
1970—Phil Olsen, DT, Utah State
1971—Jim Plunkett, QB, Stanford*
1972—None
1973—John Hannah, G, Alabama
    Sam Cunningham, RB, USC
    Darryl Stingley, WR, Purdue
1974—None
1975—Russ Francis, TE, Oregon
1976—Mike Haynes, DB, Arizona State
    Pete Brock, C, Colorado
    Tim Fox, DB, Ohio State
1977—Raymond Clayborn, DB, Texas
    Stanley Morgan, WR, Tennessee
1978—Bob Cryder, G, Alabama
1979—Rick Sanford, DB, South Carolina
1980—Roland James, DB, Tennessee
    Vagas Ferguson, RB, Notre Dame
1981—Brian Holloway, T, Stanford
1982—Kenneth Sims, DT, Texas*
    Lester Williams, DT, Miami

1983—Tony Eason, QB, Illinois
1984—Irving Fryar, WR, Nebraska*
1985—Trevor Matich, C, Brigham Young
1986—Reggie Dupard, RB, Southern Methodist
1987—Bruce Armstrong, T, Louisville
1988—J. Stephens, RB, Northwestern Louisiana State
1989—Hart Lee Dykes, WR, Oklahoma State
1990—Chris Singleton, LB, Arizona
    Ray Agnew, DE, N.C. State
1991—Pat Harlow, T, USC
    Leonard Russell, RB, Arizona State
1992—Eugene Chung, T, Virginia Tech
1993—Drew Bledsoe, QB, Washington State*
1994—Willie McGinest, DE, USC
1995—Ty Law, DB, Michigan
1996—Terry Glenn, WR, Ohio State
1997—Chris Canty, DB, Kansas State
1998—Robert Edwards, RB, Georgia
    Tebucky Jones, DB, Syracuse
1999—Damien Woody, C, Boston College
    Andy Katzenmoyer, LB, Ohio State
2000—None
2001—Richard Seymour, DT, Georgia
2002—Daniel Graham, TE, Colorado
2003—Ty Warren, NT, Texas A&M
2004—Vince Wilfork, DT, Miami
    Ben Watson, TE, Georgia
2005—Logan Mankins, G, Fresno State
2006—Laurence Maroney, RB, Minnesota
    *First player chosen in draft.

FRANCHISE RECORDS

Most rushing yards, career
5,453—Sam Cunningham
Most rushing yards, season
1,635—Corey Dillon, 2004

Most rushing yards, game
212—Tony Collins vs. NYJ, Sept. 18, 1983
Most rushing touchdowns, season
14—Curtis Martin, 1995

Curtis Martin, 1996
Most passing attempts, season
691—Drew Bledsoe, 1994

Most passing attempts, game
70—Drew Bledsoe vs. Min., Nov. 13, 1994 (OT)
60—Drew Bledsoe at Pit., Dec. 16, 1995
Most passes completed, season
400—Drew Bledsoe, 1994
Most passes completed, game
45—Drew Bledsoe vs. Min., Nov. 13, 1994 (OT)
39—Drew Bledsoe at Pit., Dec. 16, 1995
Tom Brady vs. K.C., Sept. 22, 2002 (OT)
Most passing yards, career
29,657—Drew Bledsoe
Most passing yards, season
4,555—Drew Bledsoe, 1994
Most passing yards, game
426—Drew Bledsoe vs. Min., Nov. 13, 1994 (OT)

423—Drew Bledsoe vs. Mia., Nov. 23, 1998
Most touchdown passes, season
31—Babe Parilli, 1964
Most pass receptions, career
534—Stanley Morgan
Most pass receptions, season
101—Troy Brown, 2001
Most pass receptions, game
16—Troy Brown vs. K.C., Sept. 22, 2002 (OT)
13—Terry Glenn at Cle., Oct. 3, 1999
Most receiving yards, career
10,352—Stanley Morgan
Most receiving yards, season
1,491—Stanley Morgan, 1986
Most receiving yards, game
214—Terry Glenn at Cle., Oct. 3, 1999

Most receiving touchdowns, season
12—Stanley Morgan, 1979
Most touchdowns, career
68—Stanley Morgan
Most field goals, season
32—Tony Franklin, 1986
Longest field goal
57 yards—Adam Vinatieri at Chi., Nov. 10, 2002
Most interceptions, career
36—Raymond Clayborn
Ty Law
Most interceptions, season
11—Ron Hall, 1964
Most sacks, career
100—Andre Tippett
Most sacks, season
18.5—Andre Tippett, 1984

SERIES RECORDS

New England vs.: Arizona 5-6; Atlanta 5-6; Baltimore 3-0; Buffalo 50-40-1; Carolina 0-3; Chicago 6-3; Cincinnati 11-8; Cleveland 8-11; Dallas 2-7; Denver 15-24; Detroit 4-4; Green Bay 3-4; Houston 1-0; Indianapolis 41-25; Jacksonville 4-0; Kansas City 11-16-3; Miami 32-46; Minnesota 5-4; New Orleans 8-3; N.Y. Giants 4-3; N.Y. Jets 43-47-1; Oakland 13-14-1; Philadelphia 3-6; Pittsburgh 6-12; St. Louis 4-5; San Diego 17-13-2; San Francisco 3-7; Seattle 7-7; Tampa Bay 4-2; Tennessee 19-15-1; Washington 1-6.
NOTE: Includes records as Boston Patriots from 1960 through 1970.

COACHING RECORDS

Bill Belichick, 63-33-0 (10-1); Phil Bengtson, 1-4-0; Raymond Berry, 48-39-0 (3-2); Hank Bullough, 0-1-0; Pete Carroll, 27-21-0 (1-2); Ron Erhardt, 21-27-0; Chuck Fairbanks, 46-39-0 (0-2); Mike Holovak, 52-46-9 (1-1); Dick MacPherson, 8-24-0; John Mazur, 9-21-0; Ron Meyer, 18-15-0 (0-1); Bill Parcells, 32-32-0 (2-2); Clive Rush, 5-16-0; Rod Rust, 1-15-0; Lou Saban, 7-12-0.
NOTE: Playoff games in parentheses.

RETIRED UNIFORM NUMBERS

No.	Player
20	Gino Cappelletti
40	Mike Haynes
57	Steve Nelson
73	John Hannah
78	Bruce Armstrong
79	Jim Hunt
89	Bob Dee

NEW ORLEANS SAINTS
YEAR-BY-YEAR RECORDS

	REGULAR SEASON						**PLAYOFFS**			
Year	W	L	T	Pct.	PF	PA	Finish	W	L	Highest round	Coach
1967	3	11	0	.214	233	379	4th/Capitol Div.	—	—		Tom Fears
1968	4	9	1	.308	246	327	3rd/Century Div.	—	—		Tom Fears
1969	5	9	0	.357	311	393	3rd/Capitol Div.	—	—		Tom Fears
1970	2	11	1	.154	172	347	4th/NFC Western Div.	—	—		Tom Fears, J.D. Roberts
1971	4	8	2	.333	266	347	4th/NFC Western Div.	—	—		J.D. Roberts
1972	2	11	1	.179	215	361	4th/NFC Western Div.	—	—		J.D. Roberts
1973	5	9	0	.357	163	312	3rd/NFC Western Div.	—	—		John North
1974	5	9	0	.357	166	263	3rd/NFC Western Div.	—	—		John North
1975	2	12	0	.143	165	360	4th/NFC Western Div.	—	—		J. North, Ernie Hefferle
1976	4	10	0	.286	253	346	4th/NFC Western Div.	—	—		Hank Stram
1977	3	11	0	.214	232	336	4th/NFC Western Div.	—	—		Hank Stram
1978	7	9	0	.438	281	298	3rd/NFC Western Div.	—	—		Dick Nolan
1979	8	8	0	.500	370	360	2nd/NFC Western Div.	—	—		Dick Nolan
1980	1	15	0	.063	291	487	4th/NFC Western Div.	—	—		Dick Nolan, Dick Stanfel
1981	4	12	0	.250	207	378	4th/NFC Western Div.	—	—		Bum Phillips
1982	4	5	0	.444	129	160	9th/NFC	—	—		Bum Phillips
1983	8	8	0	.500	319	337	3rd/NFC Western Div.	—	—		Bum Phillips
1984	7	9	0	.438	298	361	3rd/NFC Western Div.	—	—		Bum Phillips
1985	5	11	0	.313	294	401	3rd/NFC Western Div.	—	—		B. Phillips, Wade Phillips
1986	7	9	0	.438	288	287	4th/NFC Western Div.	—	—		Jim Mora
1987	12	3	0	.800	422	283	2nd/NFC Western Div.	0	1	NFC wild-card game	Jim Mora
1988	10	6	0	.625	312	283	3rd/NFC Western Div.	—	—		Jim Mora
1989	9	7	0	.563	386	301	3rd/NFC Western Div.	—	—		Jim Mora
1990	8	8	0	.500	274	275	2nd/NFC Western Div.	0	1	NFC wild-card game	Jim Mora
1991	11	5	0	.688	341	211	1st/NFC Western Div.	0	1	NFC wild-card game	Jim Mora
1992	12	4	0	.750	330	202	2nd/NFC Western Div.	0	1	NFC wild-card game	Jim Mora
1993	8	8	0	.500	317	343	2nd/NFC Western Div.	—	—		Jim Mora
1994	7	9	0	.438	348	407	2nd/NFC Western Div.	—	—		Jim Mora
1995	7	9	0	.438	319	348	5th/NFC Western Div.	—	—		Jim Mora
1996	3	13	0	.188	229	339	5th/NFC Western Div.	—	—		Jim Mora, Rick Venturi

	REGULAR SEASON							PLAYOFFS			
Year	W	L	T	Pct.	PF	PA	Finish	W	L	Highest round	Coach
1997	6	10	0	.375	237	327	4th/NFC Western Div.	—	—		Mike Ditka
1998	6	10	0	.375	305	359	3rd/NFC Western Div.	—	—		Mike Ditka
1999	3	13	0	.188	260	434	5th/NFC Western Div.	—	—		Mike Ditka
2000	10	6	0	.625	354	305	1st/NFC Western Div.	1	1	NFC div. playoff game	Jim Haslett
2001	7	9	0	.438	333	409	3rd/NFC Western Div.	—	—		Jim Haslett
2002	9	7	0	.563	432	388	3rd/NFC South Div.	—	—		Jim Haslett
2003	8	8	0	.500	340	326	2nd/NFC South Div.	—	—		Jim Haslett
2004	8	8	0	.500	348	405	2nd/NFC South Div.	—	—		Jim Haslett
2005	3	13	0	.188	235	398	4th/NFC South Div.	—	—		Jim Haslett

FIRST-ROUND DRAFT PICKS

1967—Les Kelley, RB, Alabama
1968—Kevin Hardy, DE, Notre Dame
1969—John Shinners, G, Xavier (Ohio)
1970—Ken Burrough, WR, Texas Southern
1971—Archie Manning, QB, Mississippi
1972—Royce Smith, G, Georgia
1973—None
1974—Rick Middleton, LB, Ohio State
1975—Larry Burton, WR, Purdue
　　　Kurt Schumacher, T, Ohio State
1976—Chuck Muncie, RB, California
1977—Joe Campbell, DE, Maryland
1978—Wes Chandler, WR, Florida
1979—Russell Erxleben, P, Texas
1980—Stan Brock, T, Colorado
1981—George Rogers, RB, South Carolina*
1982—Lindsay Scott, WR, Georgia
1983—None
1984—None
1985—Alvin Toles, LB, Tennessee
1986—Jim Dombrowski, T, Virginia
1987—Shawn Knight, DT, Brigham Young

1988—Craig Heyward, RB, Pittsburgh
1989—Wayne Martin, DE, Arkansas
1990—Renaldo Turnbull, DE, West Virginia
1991—None
1992—Vaughn Dunbar, RB, Indiana
1993—Willie Roaf, T, Louisiana Tech
　　　Irv Smith, TE, Notre Dame
1994—Joe Johnson, DE, Louisville
1995—Mark Fields, LB, Washington State
1996—Alex Molden, DB, Oregon
1997—Chris Naeole, G, Colorado
1998—Kyle Turley, T, San Diego State
1999—Ricky Williams, RB, Texas
2000—None
2001—Deuce McAllister, RB, Mississippi
2002—Donte' Stallworth, WR, Tennessee
　　　Charles Grant, DE, Georgia
2003—Johnathan Sullivan, DT, Georgia
2004—Will Smith, DE, Ohio State
2005—Jammal Brown, OT, Oklahoma
2006—Reggie Bush, RB, USC
*First player chosen in draft.

FRANCHISE RECORDS

Most rushing yards, career
4,529—Deuce McAllister
Most rushing yards, season
1,674—George Rogers, 1981
Most rushing yards, game
206—George Rogers vs. St.L., Sept. 4, 1983
Most rushing touchdowns, season
13—George Rogers, 1981
　　　Dalton Hilliard, 1989
　　　Deuce McAllister, 2002
Most passing attempts, season
567—Jim Everett, 1995
Most passing attempts, game
55—Jim Everett at S.F., Sept. 25, 1994
Most passes completed, season
346—Jim Everett, 1994
Most passes completed, game
33—Archie Manning at G.B., Sept. 10, 1978
　　　Jeff Blake at S.D., Sept. 10, 2000

Most passing yards, career
21,734—Archie Manning
Most passing yards, season
3,970—Jim Everett, 1995
Most passing yards, game
441—Aaron Brooks vs. Den., Dec. 3, 2000
Most touchdown passes, season
27—Aaron Brooks, 2002
Most pass receptions, career
532—Eric Martin
Most pass receptions, season
94—Joe Horn, 2000
　　　Joe Horn, 2004
Most pass receptions, game
14—Tony Galbreath at G.B., Sept. 10, 1978
Most receiving yards, career
7,854—Eric Martin
Most receiving yards, season
1,399—Joe Horn, 2004

Most receiving yards, game
205—Wes Chandler vs. Atl., Sept. 2, 1979
Most receiving touchdowns, season
10—Joe Horn, 2003
Most touchdowns, career
53—Dalton Hilliard
Most field goals, season
31—Morten Andersen, 1985
　　　John Carney, 2002
Longest field goal
63 yards—Tom Dempsey vs. Det., Nov. 8, 1970
Most interceptions, career
37—Dave Waymer
Most interceptions, season
10—Dave Whitsell, 1967
Most sacks, career
123—Rickey Jackson
Most sacks, season
17—Pat Swilling, 1991
　　　La'Roi Glover, 2000

SERIES RECORDS

New Orleans vs.: Arizona 11-13; Atlanta 30-43; Baltimore 1-2; Buffalo 4-4; Carolina 11-11; Chicago 11-11; Cincinnati 5-5; Cleveland 3-11; Dallas 7-14; Denver 2-6; Detroit 8-9-1; Green Bay 5-14; Houston 1-0; Indianapolis 5-4; Jacksonville 1-2; Kansas City 4-4; Miami 3-6; Minnesota 7-17; New England 3-8; N.Y. Giants 9-14; N.Y. Jets 5-5; Oakland 4-5-1; Philadelphia 8-14; Pittsburgh 6-6; St. Louis 29-37; San Diego 2-7; San Francisco 20-45-2; Seattle 4-5; Tampa Bay 17-11; Tennessee 4-6-1; Washington 7-13.

COACHING RECORDS

Mike Ditka, 15-33-0; Tom Fears, 13-34-2; Jim Haslett, 45-51-0 (1-1); Ernie Hefferle, 1-7-0; Jim Mora, 93-74-0 (0-4); Dick Nolan, 15-29-0; John North, 11-23-0; Bum Phillips, 27-42-0; Wade Phillips, 1-3-0; J.D. Roberts, 7-25-3; Dick Stanfel, 1-3-0; Hank Stram, 7-21-0; Rick Venturi, 1-7-0.
NOTE: Playoff games in parentheses.

RETIRED UNIFORM NUMBERS

No.	Player
31	Jim Taylor
81	Doug Atkins

YEAR-BY-YEAR RECORDS

	REGULAR SEASON						PLAYOFFS			
Year	W	L	T	Pct.	PF	PA	Finish	W	L	Highest round	Coach
1925	8	4	0	.667	122	67	T4th				Bob Folwell
1926	8	4	1	.667	147	51	T6th				Joe Alexander
1927	11	1	1	.917	197	20	1st				Earl Potteiger
1928	4	7	2	.364	79	136	6th				Earl Potteiger
1929	13	1	1	.929	312	86	2nd				LeRoy Andrews
1930	13	4	0	.765	308	98	2nd				L. Andrews, Benny Friedman-Steve Owen
1931	7	6	1	.538	154	100	5th				Steve Owen
1932	4	6	2	.400	93	113	5th				Steve Owen
1933	11	3	0	.786	244	101	1st/Eastern Div.	0	1	NFL championship game	Steve Owen
1934	8	5	0	.615	147	107	1st/Eastern Div.	1	0	NFL champ	Steve Owen
1935	9	3	0	.750	180	96	1st/Eastern Div.	0	1	NFL championship game	Steve Owen
1936	5	6	1	.455	115	163	3rd/Eastern Div.	—	—		Steve Owen
1937	6	3	2	.667	128	109	2nd/Eastern Div.	—	—		Steve Owen
1938	8	2	1	.800	194	79	1st/Eastern Div.	1	0	NFL champ	Steve Owen
1939	9	1	1	.900	168	85	1st/Eastern Div.	0	1	NFL championship game	Steve Owen
1940	6	4	1	.600	131	133	3rd/Eastern Div.	—	—		Steve Owen
1941	8	3	0	.727	238	114	1st/Eastern Div.	0	1	NFL championship game	Steve Owen
1942	5	5	1	.500	155	139	3rd/Eastern Div.	—	—		Steve Owen
1943	6	3	1	.667	197	170	2nd/Eastern Div.	0	1	E. Div. champ. game	Steve Owen
1944	8	1	1	.889	206	75	1st/Eastern Div.	0	1	NFL championship game	Steve Owen
1945	3	6	1	.333	179	198	T3rd/Eastern Div.	—	—		Steve Owen
1946	7	3	1	.700	236	162	1st/Eastern Div.	0	1	NFL championship game	Steve Owen
1947	2	8	2	.200	190	309	5th/Eastern Div.	—	—		Steve Owen
1948	4	8	0	.333	297	388	T3rd/Eastern Div.	—	—		Steve Owen
1949	6	6	0	.500	287	298	3rd/Eastern Div.	—	—		Steve Owen
1950	10	2	0	.833	268	150	2nd/American Conf.	0	1	Am. Conf. champ. game	Steve Owen
1951	9	2	1	.818	254	161	2nd/American Conf.	—	—		Steve Owen
1952	7	5	0	.583	234	231	T2nd/American Conf.	—	—		Steve Owen
1953	3	9	0	.250	179	277	5th/Eastern Conf.	—	—		Steve Owen
1954	7	5	0	.583	293	184	3rd/Eastern Conf.	—	—		Jim Lee Howell
1955	6	5	1	.545	267	223	3rd/Eastern Conf.	—	—		Jim Lee Howell
1956	8	3	1	.727	264	197	1st/Eastern Conf.	1	0	NFL champ	Jim Lee Howell
1957	7	5	0	.583	254	211	2nd/Eastern Conf.	—	—		Jim Lee Howell
1958	9	3	0	.750	246	183	1st/Eastern Conf.	1	1	NFL championship game	Jim Lee Howell
1959	10	2	0	.833	284	170	1st/Eastern Conf.	0	1	NFL championship game	Jim Lee Howell
1960	6	4	2	.600	271	261	3rd/Eastern Conf.	—	—		Jim Lee Howell
1961	10	3	1	.769	368	220	1st/Eastern Conf.	0	1	NFL championship game	Allie Sherman
1962	12	2	0	.857	398	283	1st/Eastern Conf.	0	1	NFL championship game	Allie Sherman
1963	11	3	0	.786	448	280	1st/Eastern Conf.	0	1	NFL championship game	Allie Sherman
1964	2	10	2	.167	241	399	7th/Eastern Conf.	—	—		Allie Sherman
1965	7	7	0	.500	270	338	T2nd/Eastern Conf.	—	—		Allie Sherman
1966	1	12	1	.077	263	501	8th/Eastern Conf.	—	—		Allie Sherman
1967	7	7	0	.500	369	379	2nd/Century Div.	—	—		Allie Sherman
1968	7	7	0	.500	294	325	2nd/Capitol Div.	—	—		Allie Sherman
1969	6	8	0	.429	264	298	2nd/Century Div.	—	—		Alex Webster
1970	9	5	0	.643	301	270	2nd/NFC Eastern Div.	—	—		Alex Webster
1971	4	10	0	.286	228	362	5th/NFC Eastern Div.	—	—		Alex Webster
1972	8	6	0	.571	331	247	3rd/NFC Eastern Div.	—	—		Alex Webster
1973	2	11	1	.179	226	362	5th/NFC Eastern Div.	—	—		Alex Webster
1974	2	12	0	.143	195	299	5th/NFC Eastern Div.	—	—		Bill Arnsparger
1975	5	9	0	.357	216	306	4th/NFC Eastern Div.	—	—		Bill Arnsparger
1976	3	11	0	.214	170	250	5th/NFC Eastern Div.	—	—		B. Arnsparger, J. McVay
1977	5	9	0	.357	181	265	5th/NFC Eastern Div.	—	—		John McVay
1978	6	10	0	.375	264	298	5th/NFC Eastern Div.	—	—		John McVay
1979	6	10	0	.375	237	323	4th/NFC Eastern Div.	—	—		Ray Perkins
1980	4	12	0	.250	249	425	5th/NFC Eastern Div.	—	—		Ray Perkins
1981	9	7	0	.563	295	257	3rd/NFC Eastern Div.	1	1	NFC div. playoff game	Ray Perkins
1982	4	5	0	.444	164	160	10th/NFC	—	—		Ray Perkins
1983	3	12	1	.219	267	347	5th/NFC Eastern Div.	—	—		Bill Parcells
1984	9	7	0	.563	299	301	2nd/NFC Eastern Div.	1	1	NFC div. playoff game	Bill Parcells
1985	10	6	0	.625	399	283	2nd/NFC Eastern Div.	1	1	NFC div. playoff game	Bill Parcells
1986	14	2	0	.875	371	236	1st/NFC Eastern Div.	3	0	Super Bowl champ	Bill Parcells

			REGULAR SEASON							PLAYOFFS		
Year	W	L	T	Pct.	PF	PA	Finish	W	L	Highest round	Coach
1987	6	9	0	.400	280	312	5th/NFC Eastern Div.	—	—		Bill Parcells
1988	10	6	0	.625	359	304	2nd/NFC Eastern Div.	—	—		Bill Parcells
1989	12	4	0	.750	348	252	1st/NFC Eastern Div.	0	1	NFC div. playoff game	Bill Parcells
1990	13	3	0	.813	335	211	1st/NFC Eastern Div.	3	0	Super Bowl champ	Bill Parcells
1991	8	8	0	.500	281	297	4th/NFC Eastern Div.	—	—		Ray Handley
1992	6	10	0	.375	306	367	4th/NFC Eastern Div.	—	—		Ray Handley
1993	11	5	0	.688	288	205	2nd/NFC Eastern Div.	1	1	NFC div. playoff game	Dan Reeves
1994	9	7	0	.563	279	305	2nd/NFC Eastern Div.	—	—		Dan Reeves
1995	5	11	0	.313	290	340	4th/NFC Eastern Div.	—	—		Dan Reeves
1996	6	10	0	.375	242	297	5th/NFC Eastern Div.	—	—		Dan Reeves
1997	10	5	1	.656	307	265	1st/NFC Eastern Div.	0	1	NFC wild-card game	Jim Fassel
1998	8	8	0	.500	287	309	3rd/NFC Eastern Div.	—	—		Jim Fassel
1999	7	9	0	.438	299	358	3rd/NFC Eastern Div.	—	—		Jim Fassel
2000	12	4	0	.750	328	246	1st/NFC Eastern Div.	2	1	Super Bowl	Jim Fassel
2001	7	9	0	.438	294	321	3rd/NFC Eastern Div.	—	—		Jim Fassel
2002	10	6	0	.625	320	279	2nd/NFC East Div.	0	1	NFC wild-card game	Jim Fassel
2003	4	12	0	.250	243	387	4th/NFC East Div.	—	—		Jim Fassel
2004	6	10	0	.375	303	347	2nd/NFC East Div.	—	—		Tom Coughlin
2005	11	5	0	.688	422	314	1st/NFC East Div.	0	1	NFC wild-card game	Tom Coughlin

FIRST-ROUND DRAFT PICKS

1936—Art Lewis, T, Ohio
1937—Ed Widseth, T, Minnesota
1938—George Karamatic, B, Gonzaga
1939—Walt Nielsen, B, Arizona
1940—Grenville Lansdell, B, USC
1941—George Franck, B, Minnesota
1942—Merle Hapes, B, Mississippi
1943—Steve Filipowicz, B, Fordham
1944—Billy Hillenbrand, B, Indiana
1945—Elmer Barbour, B, Wake Forest
1946—George Connor, T, Notre Dame
1947—Vic Schwall, B, Northwestern
1948—Tony Minisi, B, Pennsylvania
1949—Paul Page, B, Southern Methodist
1950—Travis Tidwell, B, Auburn
1951—Kyle Rote, B, Southern Methodist*
　　　Jim Spavital, B, Oklahoma State
1952—Frank Gifford, B, USC
1953—Bobby Marlow, B, Alabama
1954—None
1955—Joe Heap, B, Notre Dame
1956—None
1957—None
1958—Phil King, B, Vanderbilt
1959—Lee Grosscup, B, Utah
1960—Lou Cordileone, G, Clemson
1961—None
1962—Jerry Hillebrand, LB, Colorado
1963—None
1964—Joe Don Looney, RB, Oklahoma
1965—Tucker Frederickson, RB, Auburn*
1966—Francis Peay, T, Missouri
1967—None
1968—None
1969—Fred Dryer, DE, San Diego State
1970—Jim Files, LB, Oklahoma
1971—Rocky Thompson, RB, West Texas State
1972—Eldridge Small, DB, Texas A&I
　　　Larry Jacobson, DE, Nebraska
1973—None
1974—John Hicks, G, Ohio State
1975—None
1976—Troy Archer, DE, Colorado
1977—Gary Jeter, DT, Southern Cal
1978—Gordon King, T, Stanford
1979—Phil Simms, QB, Morehead State
1980—Mark Haynes, DB, Colorado
1981—Lawrence Taylor, LB, North Carolina
1982—Butch Woolfolk, RB, Michigan
1983—Terry Kinard, DB, Clemson
1984—Carl Banks, LB, Michigan State
　　　Bill Roberts, T, Ohio State
1985—George Adams, RB, Kentucky
1986—Eric Dorsey, DE, Notre Dame
1987—Mark Ingram, WR, Michigan State
1988—Eric Moore, T, Indiana
1989—Brian Williams, G, Minnesota
1990—Rodney Hampton, RB, Georgia
1991—Jarrod Bunch, FB, Michigan
1992—Derek Brown, TE, Notre Dame
1993—None
1994—Thomas Lewis, WR, Indiana
1995—Tyrone Wheatley, RB, Michigan
1996—Cedric Jones, DE, Oklahoma
1997—Ike Hilliard, WR, Florida
1998—Shaun Williams, DB, UCLA
1999—Luke Petitgout, T, Notre Dame
2000—Ron Dayne, RB, Wisconsin
2001—Will Allen, DB, Syracuse
2002—Jeremy Shockey, TE, Miami (Fla.)
2003—William Joseph, DT, Miami (Fla.)
2004—Philip Rivers, QB, N.C. State
2005—None
2006—Mathias Kiwanuka, DE, Boston College
　*First player chosen in draft.

FRANCHISE RECORDS

Most rushing yards, career
8,787—Tiki Barber

Most rushing yards, season
1,860—Tiki Barber, 2005

Most rushing yards, game
220—Tiki Barber vs. K.C., Dec. 17, 2005

Most rushing touchdowns, season
21—Joe Morris, 1985

Most passing attempts, season
568—Kerry Collins, 2001

Most passing attempts, game
62—Phil Simms at Cin., Oct. 13, 1985

Most passes completed, season
335—Kerry Collins, 2002

Most passes completed, game
40—Phil Simms at Cin., Oct. 13, 1985

Most passing yards, career
33,462—Phil Simms

Most passing yards, season
4,073—Kerry Collins, 2002
Most passing yards, game
513—Phil Simms at Cin., Oct. 13, 1985
Most touchdown passes, season
36—Y.A. Tittle, 1963
Most pass receptions, career
529—Amani Toomer
Most pass receptions, season
82—Amani Toomer, 2002
Most pass receptions, game
13—Tiki Barber at Dal., Jan. 2, 2000

Most receiving yards, career
7,797—Amani Toomer
Most receiving yards, season
1,343—Amani Toomer, 2002
Most receiving yards, game
269—Del Shofner vs. Was., Oct. 28, 1962
Most receiving touchdowns, season
13—Homer Jones, 1967
Most touchdowns, career
78—Frank Gifford
Most field goals, season
35—Ali Haji-Sheikh, 1983
        Jay Feely, 2005

Longest field goal
56 yards—Ali Haji-Sheikh vs. G.B., Sept. 26, 1983
        Ali Haji-Sheikh at Det., Nov. 7, 1983
Most interceptions, career
74—Emlen Tunnell
Most interceptions, season
11—Otto Schellbacher, 1951
        Jimmy Patton, 1958
Most sacks, career
132.5—Lawrence Taylor
Most sacks, season
22.5—Michael Strahan, 2001

SERIES RECORDS

N.Y. Giants vs.: Arizona 78-41-2; Atlanta 7-10; Baltimore, 0-2; Buffalo 3-6; Carolina 0-3; Chicago 17-26-2; Cincinnati 2-5; Cleveland 19-25-2; Dallas 34-51-2; Denver 5-4; Detroit 17-20-1; Green Bay 21-24-2; Houston 0-1; Indianapolis 6-6; Jacksonville 2-1; Kansas City 9-2; Miami 3-2; Minnesota 8-10; New England 3-4; New Orleans 14-9; N.Y. Jets 6-4; Oakland 3-7; Philadelphia 75-65-2; Pittsburgh 43-28-3; St. Louis 12-25; San Diego 5-4; San Francisco 12-13; Seattle 7-4; Tampa Bay 9-6; Tennessee 5-3; Washington 82-60-4.

COACHING RECORDS

Joe Alexander, 8-4-1; LeRoy Andrews, 24-5-1; Bill Arnsparger, 7-28-0; Tom Coughlin, 17-15-0 (0-1); Jim Fassel, 69-58-1 (2-4); Bob Folwell, 8-4-0; Benny Friedman, 2-0-0; Ray Handley, 14-18-0; Jim Lee Howell, 53-27-4 (2-2); John McVay, 14-23-0; Steve Owen, 153-100-17 (2-8); Bill Parcells, 77-49-1 (8-3); Ray Perkins, 23-34-0 (1-1); Earl Potteiger, 15-8-3; Dan Reeves, 31-33-0 (1-1); Allie Sherman, 57-51-4 (0-3); Alex Webster, 29-40-1. NOTE: Playoff games in parentheses.

RETIRED UNIFORM NUMBERS

No.	Player	No.	Player
1	Ray Flaherty	32	Al Blozis
4	Tuffy Leemans	40	Joe Morrison
7	Mel Hein	42	Charlie Conerly
11	Phil Simms	50	Ken Strong
14	Y.A. Tittle	56	Lawrence Taylor
16	Frank Gifford		

NEW YORK JETS
YEAR-BY-YEAR RECORDS

			REGULAR SEASON						PLAYOFFS		
Year	W	L	T	Pct.	PF	PA	Finish	W	L	Highest round	Coach
1960*†	7	7	0	.500	382	399	2nd/Eastern Div.	—	—		Sammy Baugh
1961*†	7	7	0	.500	301	390	3rd/Eastern Div.	—	—		Sammy Baugh
1962*†	5	9	0	.357	278	423	4th/Eastern Div.	—	—		Bulldog Turner
1963*	5	8	1	.385	249	399	4th/Eastern Div.	—	—		Weeb Ewbank
1964*	5	8	1	.385	278	315	3rd/Eastern Div.	—	—		Weeb Ewbank
1965*	5	8	1	.385	285	303	2nd/Eastern Div.	—	—		Weeb Ewbank
1966*	6	6	2	.500	322	312	3rd/Eastern Div.	—	—		Weeb Ewbank
1967*	8	5	1	.615	371	329	2nd/Eastern Div.	—	—		Weeb Ewbank
1968*	11	3	0	.786	419	280	1st/Eastern Div.	2	0	Super Bowl champ	Weeb Ewbank
1969*	10	4	0	.714	353	269	1st/Eastern Div.	0	1	Div. playoff game	Weeb Ewbank
1970	4	10	0	.286	255	286	3rd/AFC Eastern Div.	—	—		Weeb Ewbank
1971	6	8	0	.429	212	299	4th/AFC Eastern Div.	—	—		Weeb Ewbank
1972	7	7	0	.500	367	324	2nd/AFC Eastern Div.	—	—		Weeb Ewbank
1973	4	10	0	.286	240	306	5th/AFC Eastern Div.	—	—		Weeb Ewbank
1974	7	7	0	.500	279	300	4th/AFC Eastern Div.	—	—		Charley Winner
1975	3	11	0	.214	258	433	5th/AFC Eastern Div.	—	—		C. Winner, Ken Shipp
1976	3	11	0	.214	169	383	4th/AFC Eastern Div.	—	—		Lou Holtz, Mike Holovak
1977	3	11	0	.214	191	300	4th/AFC Eastern Div.	—	—		Walt Michaels
1978	8	8	0	.500	359	364	3rd/AFC Eastern Div.	—	—		Walt Michaels
1979	8	8	0	.500	337	383	3rd/AFC Eastern Div.	—	—		Walt Michaels
1980	4	12	0	.250	302	395	5th/AFC Eastern Div.	—	—		Walt Michaels
1981	10	5	1	.656	355	287	2nd/AFC Eastern Div.	0	1	AFC wild-card game	Walt Michaels
1982	6	3	0	.667	245	166	6th/AFC	2	1	AFC championship game	Walt Michaels
1983	7	9	0	.438	313	331	5th/AFC Eastern Div.	—	—		Joe Walton
1984	7	9	0	.438	332	364	3rd/AFC Eastern Div.	—	—		Joe Walton
1985	11	5	0	.688	393	264	2nd/AFC Eastern Div.	0	1	AFC wild-card game	Joe Walton
1986	10	6	0	.625	364	386	2nd/AFC Eastern Div.	1	1	AFC div. playoff game	Joe Walton
1987	6	9	0	.400	334	360	5th/AFC Eastern Div.	—	—		Joe Walton
1988	8	7	1	.531	372	354	4th/AFC Eastern Div.	—	—		Joe Walton
1989	4	12	0	.250	253	411	5th/AFC Eastern Div.	—	—		Joe Walton
1990	6	10	0	.375	295	345	4th/AFC Eastern Div.	—	—		Bruce Coslet
1991	8	8	0	.500	314	293	2nd/AFC Eastern Div.	0	1	AFC wild-card game	Bruce Coslet
1992	4	12	0	.250	220	315	4th/AFC Eastern Div.	—	—		Bruce Coslet
1993	8	8	0	.500	270	247	3rd/AFC Eastern Div.	—	—		Bruce Coslet
1994	6	10	0	.375	264	320	5th/AFC Eastern Div.	—	—		Pete Carroll
1995	3	13	0	.188	233	384	5th/AFC Eastern Div.	—	—		Rich Kotite
1996	1	15	0	.063	279	454	5th/AFC Eastern Div.	—	—		Rich Kotite
1997	9	7	0	.563	348	287	3rd/AFC Eastern Div.	—	—		Bill Parcells

			REGULAR SEASON					**PLAYOFFS**			
Year	W	L	T	Pct.	PF	PA	Finish	W	L	Highest round	Coach
1998	12	4	0	.750	416	266	1st/AFC Eastern Div.	1	1	AFC championship game	Bill Parcells
1999	8	8	0	.500	308	309	4th/AFC Eastern Div.	—	—		Bill Parcells
2000	9	7	0	.563	321	321	3rd/AFC Eastern Div.	—	—		Al Groh
2001	10	6	0	.625	308	295	3rd/AFC Eastern Div.	0	1	AFC wild-card game	Herman Edwards
2002	9	7	0	.563	359	336	1st/AFC East Div.	1	1	AFC div. playoff game	Herman Edwards
2003	6	10	0	.375	283	299	4th/AFC East Div.				Herman Edwards
2004	10	6	0	.625	333	261	2nd/AFC East Div.	1	1	AFC div. playoff game	Herman Edwards
2005	4	12	0	.250	240	355	4th/AFC East Div.	—	—		Herman Edwards

*American Football League.
†New York Titans.

FIRST-ROUND DRAFT PICKS

1960—George Izo, QB, Notre Dame
1961—Tom Brown, G, Minnesota
1962—Sandy Stephens, QB, Minnesota
1963—Jerry Stovall, HB, LSU
1964—Matt Snell, RB, Ohio State
1965—Joe Namath, QB, Alabama
     Tom Nowatzke, RB, Indiana
1966—Bill Yearby, DT, Michigan
1967—Paul Seiler, G, Notre Dame
1968—Lee White, RB, Weber State
1969—Dave Foley, T, Ohio State
1970—Steve Tannen, DB, Florida
1971—John Riggins, RB, Kansas
1972—Jerome Barkum, WR, Jackson State
1972—Mike Taylor, LB, Michigan
1973—Burgess Owens, DB, Miami
1974—Carl Barzilauskas, DT, Indiana
1975—None
1976—Richard Todd, QB, Alabama
1977—Marvin Powell, T, USC
1978—Chris Ward, T, Ohio State
1979—Marty Lyons, DE, Alabama
1980—Lam Jones, WR, Texas
1981—Freeman McNeil, RB, UCLA
1982—Bob Crable, LB, Notre Dame
1983—Ken O'Brien, QB, California-Davis
1984—Russell Carter, DB, Southern Methodist
     Ron Faurot, DE, Arkansas

1985—Al Toon, WR, Wisconsin
1986—Mike Haight, T, Iowa
1987—Roger Vick, RB, Texas A&M
1988—Dave Cadigan, T, USC
1989—Jeff Lageman, LB, Virginia
1990—Blair Thomas, RB, Penn State
1991—None
1992—Johnny Mitchell, TE, Nebraska
1993—Marvin Jones, LB, Florida State
1994—Aaron Glenn, DB, Texas A&M
1995—Kyle Brady, TE, Penn State
     Hugh Douglas, DE, Central State (Ohio)
1996—Keyshawn Johnson, WR, USC*
1997—James Farrior, LB, Virginia
1998—None
1999—None
2000—Shaun Ellis, DE, Tennessee
     John Abraham, LB, South Carolina
     Chad Pennington, QB, Marshall
     Anthony Becht, TE, West Virginia
2001—Santana Moss, WR, Miami (Fla.)
2002—Bryan Thomas, DE, Alabama-Birmingham
2003—Dewayne Robertson, DT, Kentucky
2004—Jonathan Vilma, LB, Miami (Fla.)
2005—None
2006—D'Brickashaw Ferguson, OT, Virginia
     Nick Mangold, C, Ohio State
*First player chosen in draft.

FRANCHISE RECORDS

Most rushing yards, career
10,302—Curtis Martin
Most rushing yards, season
1,697—Curtis Martin, 2004
Most rushing yards, game
203—Curtis Martin vs. Ind., Dec. 3, 2000
Most rushing touchdowns, season
12—Curtis Martin, 2004
Most passing attempts, season
590—Vinny Testaverde, 2000
Most passing attempts, game
69—Vinny Testaverde at Bal., Dec. 24, 2000
Most passes completed, season
328—Vinny Testaverde, 2000
Most passes completed, game
42—Richard Todd vs. S.F., Sept. 21, 1980
     Vinny Testaverde vs. Sea., Dec. 6, 1998
Most passing yards, career
27,057—Joe Namath

Most passing yards, season
4,007—Joe Namath, 1967
Most passing yards, game
496—Joe Namath at Bal., Sept. 24, 1972
Most touchdown passes, season
29—Vinny Testaverde, 1998
Most pass receptions, career
627—Don Maynard
Most pass receptions, season
93—Al Toon, 1988
Most pass receptions, game
17—Clark Gaines vs. S.F., Sept. 21, 1980
Most receiving yards, career
11,732—Don Maynard
Most receiving yards, season
1,434—Don Maynard, 1967
Most receiving yards, game
228—Don Maynard at Oak., Nov. 17, 1968

Most receiving touchdowns, season
14—Art Powell, 1960
     Don Maynard, 1965
Most touchdowns, career
88—Don Maynard
Most field goals, season
34—Jim Turner, 1968
Longest field goal
55 yards—Pat Leahy vs. Chi., Dec. 14, 1985
     John Hall at Sea., Aug. 31, 1997
Most interceptions, career
34—Bill Baird
Most interceptions, season
12—Dainard Paulson, 1964
Most sacks, career
107.5—Mark Gastineau
Most sacks, season
22—Mark Gastineau, 1984

SERIES RECORDS

N.Y. Jets vs.: Arizona 4-2; Atlanta 4-5; Baltimore 1-4; Buffalo 41-49; Carolina 2-2; Chicago 3-5; Cincinnati 12-6; Cleveland 7-10; Dallas 2-6; Denver 14-15-1; Detroit 4-6; Green Bay 7-2; Houston 2-0; Indianapolis 25-39; Jacksonville 2-4; Kansas City 14-16-1; Miami 41-38-1; Minnesota 6-1; New England 47-43-1; New Orleans 5-5; N.Y. Giants 4-6; Oakland 13-19-2; Philadelphia 0-7; Pittsburgh 2-15; St. Louis 2-9; San Diego 11-18-1; San Francisco 2-8; Seattle 8-8; Tampa Bay 8-1; Tennessee 14-20-1; Washington 1-7.

NOTE: Includes records as New York Titans from 1960 through 1962.

COACHING RECORDS

Sammy Baugh, 14-14-0; Pete Carroll, 6-10-0; Bruce Coslet, 26-38-0 (0-1); Herman Edwards, 39-41-0 (2-3); Weeb Ewbank, 71-77-6 (2-1); Al Groh, 9-7-0; Mike Holovak, 0-1-0; Lou Holtz, 3-10-0; Rich Kotite, 4-28-0; Walt Michaels, 39-47-1 (2-2); Bill Parcells, 29-19-0 (1-1); Ken Shipp, 1-4-0; Clyde Turner, 5-9-0; Joe Walton, 53-57-1 (1-2); Charley Winner, 9-14-0.
NOTE: Playoff games in parentheses.

OAKLAND RAIDERS
YEAR-BY-YEAR RECORDS

Year	W	L	T	Pct.	PF	PA	Finish	W	L	Highest round	Coach
				REGULAR SEASON						PLAYOFFS	
1960*	6	8	0	.429	319	388	3rd/Western Div.	—	—		Eddie Erdelatz
1961*	2	12	0	.143	237	458	4th/Western Div.	—	—		E. Erdelatz, Marty Feldman
1962*	1	13	0	.071	213	370	4th/Western Div.	—	—		M. Feldman, Red Conkright
1963*	10	4	0	.714	363	288	2nd/Western Div.	—	—		Al Davis
1964*	5	7	2	.417	303	350	3rd/Western Div.	—	—		Al Davis
1965*	8	5	1	.615	298	239	2nd/Western Div.	—	—		Al Davis
1966*	8	5	1	.615	315	288	2nd/Western Div.	—	—		John Rauch
1967*	13	1	0	.929	468	233	1st/Western Div.	1	1	Super Bowl	John Rauch
1968*	12	2	0	.857	453	233	1st/Western Div.	1	1	AFL championship game	John Rauch
1969*	12	1	1	.923	377	242	1st/Western Div.	1	1	AFL championship game	John Madden
1970	8	4	2	.667	300	293	1st/AFC Western Div.	1	1	AFC championship game	John Madden
1971	8	4	2	.667	344	278	2nd/AFC Western Div.	—	—		John Madden
1972	10	3	1	.750	365	248	1st/AFC Western Div.	0	1	AFC div. playoff game	John Madden
1973	9	4	1	.679	292	175	1st/AFC Western Div.	1	1	AFC championship game	John Madden
1974	12	2	0	.857	355	228	1st/AFC Western Div.	1	1	AFC championship game	John Madden
1975	11	3	0	.786	375	255	1st/AFC Western Div.	1	1	AFC championship game	John Madden
1976	13	1	0	.929	350	237	1st/AFC Western Div.	3	0	Super Bowl champ	John Madden
1977	11	3	0	.786	351	230	2nd/AFC Western Div.	1	1	AFC championship game	John Madden
1978	9	7	0	.563	311	283	2nd/AFC Western Div.	—	—		John Madden
1979	9	7	0	.563	365	337	4th/AFC Western Div.	—	—		Tom Flores
1980	11	5	0	.688	364	306	2nd/AFC Western Div.	4	0	Super Bowl champ	Tom Flores
1981	7	9	0	.438	273	343	4th/AFC Western Div.	—	—		Tom Flores
1982†	8	1	0	.889	260	200	1st/AFC	1	1	AFC second-round pl. game	Tom Flores
1983†	12	4	0	.750	442	338	1st/AFC Western Div.	3	0	Super Bowl champ	Tom Flores
1984†	11	5	0	.688	368	278	3rd/AFC Western Div.	0	1	AFC wild-card game	Tom Flores
1985†	12	4	0	.750	354	308	1st/AFC Western Div.	0	1	AFC div. playoff game	Tom Flores
1986†	8	8	0	.500	323	346	4th/AFC Western Div.	—	—		Tom Flores
1987†	5	10	0	.333	301	289	4th/AFC Western Div.	—	—		Tom Flores
1988†	7	9	0	.438	325	369	3rd/AFC Western Div.	—	—		Mike Shanahan
1989†	8	8	0	.500	315	297	3rd/AFC Western Div.	—	—		Mike Shanahan, Art Shell
1990†	12	4	0	.750	337	268	1st/AFC Western Div.	1	1	AFC championship game	Art Shell
1991†	9	7	0	.563	298	297	3rd/AFC Western Div.	0	1	AFC wild-card game	Art Shell
1992†	7	9	0	.438	249	281	4th/AFC Western Div.	—	—		Art Shell
1993†	10	6	0	.625	306	326	2nd/AFC Western Div.	1	1	AFC div. playoff game	Art Shell
1994†	9	7	0	.563	303	327	3rd/AFC Western Div.	—	—		Art Shell
1995	8	8	0	.500	348	332	5th/AFC Western Div.	—	—		Mike White
1996	7	9	0	.438	340	293	4th/AFC Western Div.	—	—		Mike White
1997	4	12	0	.250	324	419	4th/AFC Western Div.	—	—		Joe Bugel
1998	8	8	0	.500	288	356	2nd/AFC Western Div.	—	—		Jon Gruden
1999	8	8	0	.500	390	329	4th/AFC Western Div.	—	—		Jon Gruden
2000	12	4	0	.750	479	299	1st/AFC Western Div.	1	1	AFC championship game	Jon Gruden
2001	10	6	0	.625	399	327	1st/AFC Western Div.	1	1	AFC div. playoff game	Jon Gruden
2002	11	5	0	.688	450	304	1st/AFC West Div.	2	1	Super Bowl	Bill Callahan
2003	4	12	0	.250	270	379	3rd/AFC West Div.	—	—		Bill Callahan
2004	5	11	0	.312	320	442	4th/AFC West Div.	—	—		Norv Turner
2005	4	12	0	.250	290	383	4th/AFC West Div.	—	—		Norv Turner

*American Football League.
†Los Angeles Raiders.

FIRST-ROUND DRAFT PICKS

1960—Dale Hackbart, DB, Wisconsin
1961—Joe Rutgens, DT, Illinois
1962—Roman Gabriel, QB, N.C. State* (AFL)
1963—None
1964—Tony Lorick, RB, Arizona State
1965—Harry Schuh, T, Memphis State
1966—Rodger Bird, DB, Kentucky
1967—Gene Upshaw, G, Texas A&I
1968—Eldridge Dickey, QB, Tennessee State

1969—Art Thoms, DT, Syracuse
1970—Raymond Chester, TE, Morgan State
1971—Jack Tatum, DB, Ohio State
1972—Mike Siani, WR, Villanova
1973—Ray Guy, P, So. Mississippi
1974—Henry Lawrence, T, Florida A&M
1975—Neal Colzie, DB, Ohio State
1976—None
1977—None

HISTORY Team by team

1978—None
1979—None
1980—Marc Wilson, QB, Brigham Young
1981—Ted Watts, DB, Texas Tech
      Curt Marsh, T, Washington
1982—Marcus Allen, RB, USC
1983—Don Mosebar, T, USC
1984—None
1985—Jessie Hester, WR, Florida State
1986—Bob Buczkowski, DE, Pittsburgh
1987—John Clay, T, Missouri
1988—Tim Brown, WR, Notre Dame
      Terry McDaniel, CB, Tennessee
      Scott Davis, DE, Illinois
1989—None
1990—Anthony Smith, DE, Arizona
1991—Todd Marinovich, QB, USC
1992—Chester McGlockton, DT, Clemson

1993—Patrick Bates, DB, Texas A&M
1994—Rob Fredrickson, LB, Michigan State
1995—Napoleon Kaufman, RB, Washington
1996—Rickey Dudley, TE, Ohio State
1997—Darrell Russell, DT, USC
1998—Charles Woodson, DB, Michigan
      Mo Collins, T, Florida
1999—Matt Stinchcomb, T, Georgia
2000—Sebastian Janikowski, PK, Florida State
2001—Derrick Gibson, DB, Florida State
2002—Phillip Buchanon, DB, Miami (Fla.)
      Napoleon Harris, LB, Northwestern
2003—Nnamdi Asomugha, DB, California
      Tyler Brayton, DE, Colorado
2004—Robert Gallery, T, Iowa
2005—Fabian Washington, CB, Nebraska
2006—Michael Huff, DB, Texas
*First player chosen in draft.

FRANCHISE RECORDS

Most rushing yards, career
8,545—Marcus Allen
Most rushing yards, season
1,759—Marcus Allen, 1985
Most rushing yards, game
227—Napoleon Kaufman vs. Den., Oct.
    19, 1997
Most rushing touchdowns, season
16—Pete Banaszak, 1975
Most passing attempts, season
618—Rich Gannon, 2002
Most passing attempts, game
64—Rich Gannon at Pit., Sept. 15,
    2002
Most passes completed, season
418—Rich Gannon, 2002
Most passes completed, game
43—Rich Gannon at Pit., Sept. 15, 2002
Most passing yards, career
19,078—Ken Stabler

Most passing yards, season
4,689—Rich Gannon, 2002
Most passing yards, game
424—Jeff Hostetler vs. S.D., Oct. 18, 1993
Most touchdown passes, season
34—Daryle Lamonica, 1969
Most pass receptions, career
1,070—Tim Brown
Most pass receptions, season
104—Tim Brown, 1997
Most pass receptions, game
14—Tim Brown vs. Jac., Dec. 21, 1997
Most receiving yards, career
14,734—Tim Brown
Most receiving yards, season
1,408—Tim Brown, 1997
Most receiving yards, game
247—Art Powell vs. Hou., Dec. 22, 1963
Most receiving touchdowns, season
16—Art Powell, 1964

Most touchdowns, career
104—Tim Brown
Most field goals, season
35—Jeff Jaeger, 1993
Longest field goal
55 yards—Sebastian Janikowski at Det.,
    Nov. 2, 2003
Most interceptions, career
39—Willie Brown
    Lester Hayes
Most interceptions, season
13—Lester Hayes, 1980
Most sacks, career
107.5—Greg Townsend
Most sacks, season
17.5—Tony Cline, 1970

SERIES RECORDS

Oakland vs.: Arizona 4-2; Atlanta 7-4; Baltimore 1-2; Buffalo 19-15; Carolina 2-1; Chicago 6-5; Cincinnati 17-7; Cleveland 9-6; Dallas 6-3; Denver 53-36-2; Detroit 6-3; Green Bay 5-4; Houston 0-1; Indianapolis 7-3; Jacksonville 1-2; Kansas City 42-47-2; Miami 15-11-1; Minnesota 8-3; New England 14-13-1; New Orleans 5-4-1; N.Y. Giants 7-3; N.Y. Jets 19-13-2; Philadelphia 4-5; Pittsburgh 8-8; St. Louis 7-3; San Diego 54-36-2; San Francisco 6-4; Seattle 27-22; Tampa Bay 5-1; Tennessee 23-17; Washington 7-3.
NOTE: Includes records as Los Angeles Raiders from 1982 through 1994.

COACHING RECORDS

Joe Bugel, 4-12-0; Bill Callahan, 15-17-0 (2-1); Red Conkright, 1-8-0; Al Davis, 23-16-3; Eddie Erdelatz, 6-10-0; Marty Feldman, 2-15-0; Tom Flores, 83-53-0 (8-3); Jon Gruden, 38-26-0 (2-2); John Madden, 103-32-7 (9-7); John Rauch, 33-8-1 (2-2); Mike Shanahan, 8-12-0; Art Shell, 54-38-0 (2-3); Norv Turner, 9-23-0; Mike White, 15-17-0.
NOTE: Playoff games in parentheses.

RETIRED UNIFORM NUMBERS

No.   **Player**
None

PHILADELPHIA EAGLES
YEAR-BY-YEAR RECORDS

	REGULAR SEASON							PLAYOFFS			
Year	W	L	T	Pct.	PF	PA	Finish	W	L	Highest round	Coach
1933	3	5	1	.375	77	158	4th/Eastern Div.	—	—		Lud Wray
1934	4	7	0	.364	127	85	T3rd/Eastern Div.	—	—		Lud Wray
1935	2	9	0	.182	60	179	5th/Eastern Div.	—	—		Lud Wray
1936	1	11	0	.083	51	206	5th/Eastern Div.	—	—		Bert Bell
1937	2	8	1	.200	86	177	5th/Eastern Div.	—	—		Bert Bell
1938	5	6	0	.455	154	164	4th/Eastern Div.	—	—		Bert Bell
1939	1	9	1	.100	105	200	T4th/Eastern Div.	—	—		Bert Bell
1940	1	10	0	.091	111	211	5th/Eastern Div.	—	—		Bert Bell

	REGULAR SEASON							PLAYOFFS			
Year	W	L	T	Pct.	PF	PA	Finish	W	L	Highest round	Coach
1941	2	8	1	.200	119	218	4th/Eastern Div.	—	—		Greasy Neale
1942	2	9	0	.182	134	239	5th/Eastern Div.	—	—		Greasy Neale
1943*	5	4	1	.556	225	230	3rd/Eastern Div.	—	—		G. Neale-Walt Kiesling
1944	7	1	2	.875	267	131	2nd/Eastern Div.	—	—		Greasy Neale
1945	7	3	0	.700	272	133	2nd/Eastern Div.	—	—		Greasy Neale
1946	6	5	0	.545	231	220	2nd/Eastern Div.	—	—		Greasy Neale
1947	8	4	0	.667	308	242	1st/Eastern Div.	1	1	NFL championship game	Greasy Neale
1948	9	2	1	.818	376	156	1st/Eastern Div.	1	0	NFL champ	Greasy Neale
1949	11	1	0	.917	364	134	1st/Eastern Div.	1	0	NFL champ	Greasy Neale
1950	6	6	0	.500	254	141	T3rd/American Conf.	—	—		Greasy Neale
1951	4	8	0	.333	234	264	5th/American Conf.	—	—		Bo McMillin, Wayne Millner
1952	7	5	0	.583	252	271	T2nd/American Conf.	—	—		Jim Trimble
1953	7	4	1	.636	352	215	2nd/Eastern Conf.	—	—		Jim Trimble
1954	7	4	1	.636	284	230	2nd/Eastern Conf.	—	—		Jim Trimble
1955	4	7	1	.364	248	231	T4th/Eastern Conf.	—	—		Jim Trimble
1956	3	8	1	.273	143	215	6th/Eastern Conf.	—	—		Hugh Devore
1957	4	8	0	.333	173	230	5th/Eastern Conf.	—	—		Hugh Devore
1958	2	9	1	.182	235	306	T5th/Eastern Conf.	—	—		Buck Shaw
1959	7	5	0	.583	268	278	T2nd/Eastern Conf.	—	—		Buck Shaw
1960	10	2	0	.833	321	246	1st/Eastern Conf.	1	0	NFL champ	Buck Shaw
1961	10	4	0	.714	361	297	2nd/Eastern Conf.	—	—		Nick Skorich
1962	3	10	1	.231	282	356	7th/Eastern Conf.	—	—		Nick Skorich
1963	2	10	2	.167	242	381	7th/Western Conf.	—	—		Nick Skorich
1964	6	8	0	.429	312	313	T3rd/Eastern Conf.	—	—		Joe Kuharich
1965	5	9	0	.357	363	359	T5th/Eastern Conf.	—	—		Joe Kuharich
1966	9	5	0	.643	326	340	T2nd/Eastern Conf.	—	—		Joe Kuharich
1967	6	7	1	.462	351	409	2nd/Capitol Div.	—	—		Joe Kuharich
1968	2	12	0	.143	202	351	4th/Capitol Div.	—	—		Joe Kuharich
1969	4	9	1	.308	279	377	4th/Capitol Div.	—	—		Jerry Williams
1970	3	10	1	.231	241	332	5th/NFC Eastern Div.	—	—		Jerry Williams
1971	6	7	1	.462	221	302	3rd/NFC Eastern Div.	—	—		J. Williams, Ed Khayat
1972	2	11	1	.179	145	352	5th/NFC Eastern Div.	—	—		Ed Khayat
1973	5	8	1	.393	310	393	3rd/NFC Eastern Div.	—	—		Mike McCormack
1974	7	7	0	.500	242	217	4th/NFC Eastern Div.	—	—		Mike McCormack
1975	4	10	0	.286	225	302	5th/NFC Eastern Div.	—	—		Mike McCormack
1976	4	10	0	.286	165	286	4th/NFC Eastern Div.	—	—		Dick Vermeil
1977	5	9	0	.357	220	207	4th/NFC Eastern Div.	—	—		Dick Vermeil
1978	9	7	0	.563	270	250	2nd/NFC Eastern Div.	0	1	NFC wild-card game	Dick Vermeil
1979	11	5	0	.688	339	282	2nd/NFC Eastern Div.	1	1	NFC div. playoff game	Dick Vermeil
1980	12	4	0	.750	384	222	1st/NFC Eastern Div.	2	1	Super Bowl	Dick Vermeil
1981	10	6	0	.625	368	221	2nd/NFC Eastern Div.	0	1	NFC wild-card game	Dick Vermeil
1982	3	6	0	.333	191	195	13th/NFC	—	—		Dick Vermeil
1983	5	11	0	.313	233	322	4th/NFC Eastern Div.	—	—		Marion Campbell
1984	6	9	1	.406	278	320	5th/NFC Eastern Div.	—	—		Marion Campbell
1985	7	9	0	.438	286	310	4th/NFC Eastern Div.	—	—		M. Campbell, Fred Bruney
1986	5	10	1	.344	256	312	4th/NFC Eastern Div.	—	—		Buddy Ryan
1987	7	8	0	.467	337	380	4th/NFC Eastern Div.	—	—		Buddy Ryan
1988	10	6	0	.625	379	319	1st/NFC Eastern Div.	0	1	NFC div. playoff game	Buddy Ryan
1989	11	5	0	.688	342	274	2nd/NFC Eastern Div.	0	1	NFC wild-card game	Buddy Ryan
1990	10	6	0	.625	396	299	2nd/NFC Eastern Div.	0	1	NFC wild-card game	Buddy Ryan
1991	10	6	0	.625	285	244	3rd/NFC Eastern Div.	—	—		Rich Kotite
1992	11	5	0	.688	354	245	2nd/NFC Eastern Div.	1	1	NFC div. playoff game	Rich Kotite
1993	8	8	0	.500	293	315	3rd/NFC Eastern Div.	—	—		Rich Kotite
1994	7	9	0	.438	308	308	4th/NFC Eastern Div.	—	—		Rich Kotite
1995	10	6	0	.625	318	338	2nd/NFC Eastern Div.	1	1	NFC div. playoff game	Ray Rhodes
1996	10	6	0	.625	363	341	2nd/NFC Eastern Div.	0	1	NFC wild-card game	Ray Rhodes
1997	6	9	1	.406	317	372	3rd/NFC Eastern Div.	—	—		Ray Rhodes
1998	3	13	0	.188	161	344	5th/NFC Eastern Div.	—	—		Ray Rhodes
1999	5	11	0	.313	272	357	5th/NFC Eastern Div.	—	—		Andy Reid
2000	11	5	0	.688	351	245	2nd/NFC Eastern Div.	1	1	NFC div. playoff game	Andy Reid
2001	11	5	0	.688	343	208	1st/NFC Eastern Div.	2	1	NFC championship game	Andy Reid
2002	12	4	0	.750	415	241	1st/NFC East Div.	1	1	NFC championship game	Andy Reid
2003	12	4	0	.750	374	260	1st/NFC East Div.	1	1	NFC championship game	Andy Reid
2004	13	3	0	.812	386	260	1st/NFC East Div.	2	1	Super Bowl	Andy Reid
2005	6	10	0	.375	310	388	4th/NFC East Div.	—	—		Andy Reid

*Phil-Pitt "Steagles," a combined squad of Philadelphia Eagles and Pittsburgh Steelers.

FIRST-ROUND DRAFT PICKS

1936—Jay Berwanger, B, Chicago*
1937—Sam Francis, B, Nebraska*
1938—Jim McDonald, B, Ohio State

1939—Davey O'Brien, B, Texas Christian
1940—George McAfee, B, Duke
1941—None

1942—Pete Kmetovic, B, Stanford
1943—Joe Muha, B, Virginia Military
1944—Steve Van Buren, B, LSU
1945—John Yonaker, E, Notre Dame
1946—Leo Riggs, B, USC
1947—Neill Armstrong, E, Oklahoma State
1948—Clyde Scott, B, Arkansas
1949—Chuck Bednarik, C, Pennsylvania*
     Frank Tripucka, QB, Notre Dame
1950—Bud Grant, E, Minnesota
1951—Ebert Van Buren, B, LSU
     Chet Mutryn, B, Xavier
1952—John Bright, B, Drake
1953—None
1954—Neil Worden, B, Notre Dame
1955—Dick Bielski, B, Maryland
1956—Bob Pellegrini, C, Maryland
1957—Clarence Peaks, B, Michigan State
1958—Walter Kowalczyk, B, Michigan State
1959—None
1960—Ron Burton, B, Northwestern
1961—Art Baker, B, Syracuse
1962—None
1963—Ed Budde, T, Michigan State
1964—Bob Brown, T, Nebraska
1965—None
1966—Randy Beisler, DE, Indiana
1967—Harry Jones, RB, Arkansas
1968—Tim Rossovich, DE, USC
1969—Leroy Keyes, RB, Purdue
1970—Steve Zabel, E, Oklahoma
1971—Richard Harris, DE, Grambling State
1972—John Reaves, QB, Florida
1973—Jerry Sisemore, T, Texas
     Charle Young, TE, USC

1974—None
1975—None
1976—None
1977—None
1978—None
1979—Jerry Robinson, LB, UCLA
1980—Roynell Young, DB, Alcorn State
1981—Leonard Mitchell, DE, Houston
1982—Mike Quick, WR, N.C. State
1983—Michael Haddix, RB, Mississippi State
1984—Kenny Jackson, WR, Penn State
1985—Kevin Allen, T, Indiana
1986—Keith Byars, RB, Ohio State
1987—Jerome Brown, DT, Miami (Fla.)
1988—Keith Jackson, TE, Oklahoma
1989—None
1990—Ben Smith, DB, Georgia
1991—Antone Davis, T, Tennessee
1992—None
1993—Lester Holmes, T, Jackson State
     Leonard Renfro, DT, Colorado
1994—Bernard Williams, T, Georgia
1995—Mike Mamula, DE, Boston College
1996—Jermane Mayberry, T, Texas A&M-Kingsville
1997—Jon Harris, DE, Virginia
1998—Tra Thomas, T, Florida State
1999—Donovan McNabb, QB, Syracuse
2000—Corey Simon, DT, Florida State
2001—Freddie Mitchell, WR, UCLA
2002—Lito Sheppard, DB, Florida
2003—Jerome McDougle, DE, Miami (Fla.)
2004—Shawn Andrews, T, Arkansas
2005—Mike Patterson, DT, USC
2006—Brodrick Bunkley, DT, Florida State
*First player chosen in draft.

FRANCHISE RECORDS

Most rushing yards, career
6,538—Wilbert Montgomery
Most rushing yards, season
1,512—Wilbert Montgomery, 1979
Most rushing yards, game
205—Steve Van Buren vs. Pit., Nov. 27, 1949
Most rushing touchdowns, season
15—Steve Van Buren, 1945
Most passing attempts, season
569—Donovan McNabb, 2000
Most passing attempts, game
62—Randall Cunningham at Chi., Oct. 2, 1989
Most passes completed, season
330—Donovan McNabb, 2000
Most passes completed, game
35—Donovan McNabb vs. S.D., Oct. 23, 2005
Most passing yards, career
26,963—Ron Jaworski

Most passing yards, season
3,875—Donovan McNabb, 2004
Most passing yards, game
447—Randall Cunningham at Was., Sept. 17, 1989
Most touchdown passes, season
32—Sonny Jurgensen, 1961
Most pass receptions, career
589—Harold Carmichael
Most pass receptions, season
88—Irving Fryar, 1996
Most pass receptions, game
14—Don Looney at Was., Dec. 1, 1940
Most receiving yards, career
8,978—Harold Carmichael
Most receiving yards, season
1,409—Mike Quick, 1983
Most receiving yards, game
237—Tommy McDonald vs. NYG, Dec. 10, 1961

Most receiving touchdowns, season
14—Terrell Owens, 2004
Most touchdowns, career
79—Harold Carmichael
Most field goals, season
30—Paul McFadden, 1984
     David Akers, 2002
Longest field goal
59 yards—Tony Franklin at Dal., Nov. 12, 1979
Most interceptions, career
34—Eric Allen
     Bill Bradley
Most interceptions, season
11—Bill Bradley, 1971
Most sacks, career
124—Reggie White
Most sacks, season
21—Reggie White, 1987

SERIES RECORDS

Philadelphia vs.: Arizona 52-53-5; Atlanta 11-10-1; Baltimore, 1-0-1; Buffalo 5-5; Carolina 3-1; Chicago 8-24-1; Cincinnati 3-7; Cleveland 14-31-1; Dallas 39-51; Denver 6-4; Detroit 12-12-2; Green Bay 12-22; Houston 1-0; Indianapolis 6-9; Jacksonville 0-2; Kansas City 3-2; Miami 4-7; Minnesota 8-11; New England 6-3; New Orleans 14-8; N.Y. Giants 65-75-2; N.Y. Jets 7-0; Oakland 5-4; Pittsburgh 45-27-3; St. Louis 16-17-1; San Diego 4-5; San Francisco 8-16-1; Seattle 6-4; Tampa Bay 5-4; Tennessee 6-2; Washington 62-74-5.
NOTE: Does not include records when team combined with Pittsburgh squad and was known as Phil-Pitt in 1943.

COACHING RECORDS

Bert Bell, 10-44-2; Fred Bruney, 1-0-0; Marion Campbell, 17-29-1; Hugh Devore, 7-16-1; Ed Khayat, 8-15-2; Rich Kotite, 36-28-0 (1-1); Joe Kuharich, 28-41-1; Mike McCormack, 16-25-1; Alvin McMillin, 2-0-0; Wayne Millner, 2-8-0; Earle (Greasy) Neale, 63-43-5 (3-1); Andy Reid, 70-42-0 (7-5); Ray Rhodes, 29-34-1 (1-2); Buddy Ryan, 43-35-1 (0-3); Buck Shaw, 19-16-1 (1-0); Nick Skorich, 15-24-3; Jim Trimble, 25-20-3; Dick Vermeil, 54-47-0 (3-4); Jerry Williams, 7-22-2; Lud Wray, 9-21-1.
NOTE: Playoff games in parentheses.

PITTSBURGH STEELERS
YEAR-BY-YEAR RECORDS

	REGULAR SEASON							PLAYOFFS			
Year	W	L	T	Pct.	PF	PA	Finish	W	L	Highest round	Coach
1933*	3	6	2	.333	67	208	5th/Eastern Div.	—	—		Jap Douds
1934*	2	10	0	.167	51	206	5th/Eastern Div.	—	—		Luby DiMello
1935*	4	8	0	.333	100	209	3rd/Eastern Div.	—	—		Joe Bach
1936*	6	6	0	.500	98	187	2nd/Eastern Div.	—	—		Joe Bach
1937*	4	7	0	.364	122	145	3rd/Eastern Div.	—	—		Johnny Blood
1938*	2	9	0	.182	79	169	5th/Eastern Div.	—	—		Johnny Blood
1939*	1	9	1	.100	114	216	T4th/Eastern Div.	—	—		J. Blood-W. Kiesling
1940*	2	7	2	.222	60	178	4th/Eastern Div.	—	—		Walt Kiesling
1941	1	9	1	.100	103	276	5th/Eastern Div.	—	—		Bert Bell-Buff Donelli-Walt Kiesling
1942	7	4	0	.636	167	119	2nd/Eastern Div.	—	—		Walt Kiesling
1943†	5	4	1	.556	225	230	3rd/Eastern Div.	—	—		W. Kiesling-Greasy Neale
1944‡	0	10	0	.000	108	328	5th/Western Div.	—	—		W. Kiesling-Phil Handler
1945	2	8	0	.200	79	220	5th/Eastern Div.	—	—		Jim Leonard
1946	5	5	1	.500	136	117	T3rd/Eastern Div.	—	—		Jock Sutherland
1947	8	4	0	.667	240	259	2nd/Eastern Div.	0	1	E. Div. champ. game	Jock Sutherland
1948	4	8	0	.333	200	243	T3rd/Eastern Div.	—	—		John Michelosen
1949	6	5	1	.545	224	214	2nd/Eastern Div.	—	—		John Michelosen
1950	6	6	0	.500	180	195	T3rd/American Conf.	—	—		John Michelosen
1951	4	7	1	.364	183	235	4th/American Conf.	—	—		John Michelosen
1952	5	7	0	.417	300	273	4th/American Conf.	—	—		Joe Bach
1953	6	6	0	.500	211	263	4th/Eastern Conf.	—	—		Joe Bach
1954	5	7	0	.417	219	263	4th/Eastern Conf.	—	—		Walt Kiesling
1955	4	8	0	.333	195	285	6th/Eastern Conf.	—	—		Walt Kiesling
1956	5	7	0	.417	217	250	5th/Eastern Conf.	—	—		Walt Kiesling
1957	6	6	0	.500	161	178	3rd/Eastern Conf.	—	—		Buddy Parker
1958	7	4	1	.636	261	230	3rd/Eastern Conf.	—	—		Buddy Parker
1959	6	5	1	.545	257	216	4th/Eastern Conf.	—	—		Buddy Parker
1960	5	6	1	.455	240	275	5th/Eastern Conf.	—	—		Buddy Parker
1961	6	8	0	.429	295	287	5th/Eastern Conf.	—	—		Buddy Parker
1962	9	5	0	.643	312	363	2nd/Eastern Conf.	—	—		Buddy Parker
1963	7	4	3	.636	321	295	4th/Eastern Conf.	—	—		Buddy Parker
1964	5	9	0	.357	253	315	6th/Eastern Conf.	—	—		Buddy Parker
1965	2	12	0	.143	202	397	7th/Eastern Conf.	—	—		Mike Nixon
1966	5	8	1	.385	316	347	6th/Eastern Conf.	—	—		Bill Austin
1967	4	9	1	.308	281	320	4th/Century Div.	—	—		Bill Austin
1968	2	11	1	.154	244	397	4th/Century Div.	—	—		Bill Austin
1969	1	13	0	.071	218	404	4th/Century Div.	—	—		Chuck Noll
1970	5	9	0	.357	210	272	3rd/AFC Central Div.	—	—		Chuck Noll
1971	6	8	0	.429	246	292	2nd/AFC Central Div.	—	—		Chuck Noll
1972	11	3	0	.786	343	175	1st/AFC Central Div.	1	1	AFC championship game	Chuck Noll
1973	10	4	0	.714	347	210	2nd/AFC Central Div.	0	1	AFC div. playoff game	Chuck Noll
1974	10	3	1	.750	305	189	1st/AFC Central Div.	3	0	Super Bowl champ	Chuck Noll
1975	12	2	0	.857	373	162	1st/AFC Central Div.	3	0	Super Bowl champ	Chuck Noll
1976	10	4	0	.714	342	138	1st/AFC Central Div.	1	1	AFC championship game	Chuck Noll
1977	9	5	0	.643	283	243	1st/AFC Central Div.	0	1	AFC div. playoff game	Chuck Noll
1978	14	2	0	.875	356	195	1st/AFC Central Div.	3	0	Super Bowl champ	Chuck Noll
1979	12	4	0	.750	416	262	1st/AFC Central Div.	3	0	Super Bowl champ	Chuck Noll
1980	9	7	0	.563	352	313	3rd/AFC Central Div.	—	—		Chuck Noll
1981	8	8	0	.500	356	297	2nd/AFC Central Div.	—	—		Chuck Noll
1982	6	3	0	.667	204	146	4th/AFC	0	1	AFC first-round pl. game	Chuck Noll
1983	10	6	0	.625	355	303	1st/AFC Central Div.	0	1	AFC div. playoff game	Chuck Noll
1984	9	7	0	.563	387	310	1st/AFC Central Div.	1	1	AFC championship game	Chuck Noll
1985	7	9	0	.438	379	355	3rd/AFC Central Div.	—	—		Chuck Noll
1986	6	10	0	.375	307	336	3rd/AFC Central Div.	—	—		Chuck Noll
1987	8	7	0	.533	285	299	3rd/AFC Central Div.	—	—		Chuck Noll
1988	5	11	0	.313	336	421	4th/AFC Central Div.	—	—		Chuck Noll
1989	9	7	0	.563	265	326	3rd/AFC Central Div.	1	1	AFC div. playoff game	Chuck Noll
1990	9	7	0	.563	292	240	3rd/AFC Central Div.	—	—		Chuck Noll
1991	7	9	0	.438	292	344	2nd/AFC Central Div.	—	—		Chuck Noll

HISTORY Team by team

			REGULAR SEASON						PLAYOFFS			
Year	W	L	T	Pct.	PF	PA	Finish	W	L	Highest round	Coach
1992	11	5	0	.688	299	225	1st/AFC Central Div.	0	1	AFC div. playoff game	Bill Cowher
1993	9	7	0	.563	308	281	2nd/AFC Central Div.	0	1	AFC wild-card game	Bill Cowher
1994	12	4	0	.750	316	234	1st/AFC Central Div.	1	1	AFC championship game	Bill Cowher
1995	11	5	0	.688	407	327	1st/AFC Central Div.	2	1	Super Bowl	Bill Cowher
1996	10	6	0	.625	344	257	1st/AFC Central Div.	1	1	AFC div. playoff game	Bill Cowher
1997	11	5	0	.688	372	307	1st/AFC Central Div.	1	1	AFC championship game	Bill Cowher
1998	7	9	0	.438	263	303	3rd/AFC Central Div.	—	—		Bill Cowher
1999	6	10	0	.375	317	320	4th/AFC Central Div.	—	—		Bill Cowher
2000	9	7	0	.563	321	255	3rd/AFC Central Div.	—	—		Bill Cowher
2001	13	3	0	.813	352	212	1st/AFC Central Div.	1	1	AFC championship game	Bill Cowher
2002	10	5	1	.656	390	345	1st/AFC North Div.	1	1	AFC div. playoff game	Bill Cowher
2003	6	10	0	.375	300	327	3rd/AFC North Div.	—	—		Bill Cowher
2004	15	1	0	.938	372	251	1st/AFC North Div.	1	1	AFC championship game	Bill Cowher
2005	11	5	0	.688	389	258	2nd/AFC North Div.	4	0	Super Bowl champ	Bill Cowher

*Pittsburgh Pirates.
†Phil-Pitt "Steagles," a combined squad of Philadelphia Eagles and Pittsburgh Steelers.
‡Card-Pitt, a combined squad of Chicago Cardinals and Pittsburgh Steelers.

FIRST-ROUND DRAFT PICKS

1936—Bill Shakespeare, B, Notre Dame
1937—Mike Basrak, C, Duquesne
1938—Byron White, B, Colorado
      Frank Filchock, B, Indiana
1939—None
1940—Kay Eakin, B, Arkansas
1941—Chet Gladchuk, C, Boston College
1942—Bill Dudley, B, Virginia*
1943—Bill Daley, B, Minnesota
1944—Johnny Podesto, B, St. Mary's (Calif.)
1945—Paul Duhart, B, Florida
1946—Doc Blanchard, B, Army
1947—Hub Bechtol, E, Texas
1948—Dan Edwards, E, Georgia
1949—Bobby Gage, B, Clemson
1950—Lynn Chandnois, B, Michigan State
1951—Clarence Avinger, B, Alabama
1952—Ed Modzelewski, B, Maryland
1953—Ted Marchibroda, QB, St. Bonaventure
1954—John Lattner, B, Notre Dame
1955—Frank Varrichione, T, Notre Dame
1956—Gary Glick, B, Colorado State*
      Art Davis, B, Mississippi State
1957—Len Dawson, QB, Purdue
1958—None
1959—None
1960—Jack Spikes, B, Texas Christian
1961—None
1962—Bob Ferguson, RB, Ohio State
1963—None
1964—Paul Martha, RB, Pittsburgh
1965—None
1966—Dick Leftridge, RB, West Virginia
1967—None
1968—Mike Taylor, T, USC
1969—Joe Greene, DT, North Texas State
1970—Terry Bradshaw, QB, Louisiana Tech*

1971—Frank Lewis, WR, Grambling State
1972—Franco Harris, RB, Penn State
1973—James Thomas, DB, Florida State
1974—Lynn Swann, WR, USC
1975—Dave Brown, DB, Michigan
1976—Bennie Cunningham, TE, Clemson
1977—Robin Cole, LB, New Mexico
1978—Ron Johnson, DB, Eastern Michigan
1979—Greg Hawthorne, RB, Baylor
1980—Mark Malone, QB, Arizona State
1981—Keith Gary, DE, Oklahoma
1982—Walter Abercrombie, RB, Baylor
1983—Gabriel Rivera, DT, Texas Tech
1984—Louis Lipps, WR, Southern Mississippi
1985—Darryl Sims, DT, Wisconsin
1986—John Rienstra, G, Temple
1987—Rod Woodson, DB, Purdue
1988—Aaron Jones, DE, Eastern Kentucky
1989—Tim Worley, RB, Georgia
      Tom Ricketts, T, Pittsburgh
1990—Eric Green, TE, Liberty (Va.)
1991—Huey Richardson, DE, Florida
1992—Leon Searcy, T, Miami (Fla.)
1993—Deon Figures, DB, Colorado
1994—Charles Johnson, WR, Colorado
1995—Mark Bruener, TE, Washington
1996—Jermain Stephens, T, North Carolina A&T
1997—Chad Scott, DB, Maryland
1998—Alan Faneca, G, LSU
1999—Troy Edwards, WR, Louisiana Tech
2000—Plaxico Burress, WR, Michigan State
2001—Casey Hampton, DT, Texas
2002—Kendall Simmons, G, Auburn
2003—Troy Polamalu, DB, USC
2004—Ben Roethlisberger, QB, Miami (Ohio)
2005—Heath Miller, TE, Virginia
2006—Santonio Holmes, WR, Ohio State
    *First player chosen in draft.

FRANCHISE RECORDS

Most rushing yards, career
11,950—Franco Harris

Most rushing yards, season
1,690—Barry Foster, 1992

Most rushing yards, game
218—John Fuqua at Phi., Dec. 20, 1970

Most rushing touchdowns, season
14—Franco Harris, 1976

Most passing attempts, season
519—Tommy Maddox, 2003

Most passing attempts, game
57—Tommy Maddox vs. Hou., Dec. 8, 2002

Most passes completed, season
298—Tommy Maddox, 2003

Most passes completed, game
34—Neil O'Donnell at Chi., Nov. 5, 1995(OT)
33—Neil O'Donnell at G.B., Dec. 24, 1995

Most passing yards, career
27,989—Terry Bradshaw

Most passing yards, season
3,724—Terry Bradshaw, 1979

Most passing yards, game
473—Tommy Maddox vs. Atl., Nov. 10, 2002 (OT)
409—Bobby Layne vs. Chi. Cardinals, Dec. 13, 1958

Most touchdown passes, season
28—Terry Bradshaw, 1978

Most pass receptions, career
574—Hines Ward, 2005

Most pass receptions, season
112—Hines Ward, 2002

Most pass receptions, game
14—Courtney Hawkins vs. Ten., Nov. 1, 1998
Most receiving yards, career
8,723—John Stallworth
Most receiving yards, season
1,398—Yancey Thigpen, 1997
Most receiving yards, game
253—Plaxico Burress vs. Atl., Nov. 10, 2002 (OT)
235—Buddy Dial vs. Cle., Oct. 22, 1961

Most receiving touchdowns, season
12—Buddy Dial, 1961
    Louis Lipps, 1985
    Hines Ward, 2002
Most touchdowns, career
100—Franco Harris
Most field goals, season
34—Norm Johnson, 1995
Longest field goal
55 yards—Gary Anderson vs. S.D., Nov. 25, 1984

Kris Brown at K.C., Oct. 14, 2001
Most interceptions, career
57—Mel Blount
Most interceptions, season
11—Mel Blount, 1975
Most sacks, career
77—Jason Gildon
Most sacks, season
15—Mike Merriweather, 1984

SERIES RECORDS

Pittsburgh vs.: Arizona 31-22-3; Atlanta 11-1-1; Baltimore 13-7; Buffalo 10-8; Carolina 2-1; Chicago 7-16-1; Cincinnati 43-29; Cleveland 51-55; Dallas 12-14; Denver 7-11-1; Detroit 14-14-1; Green Bay 13-18; Houston 1-1; Indianapolis 14-5; Jacksonville 8-9; Kansas City 16-8; Miami 8-9; Minnesota 6-8; New England 12-6; New Orleans 6-6; N.Y. Giants 28-43-3; N.Y. Jets 15-2; Oakland 8-8; Philadelphia 27-45-3; St. Louis 5-15-2; San Diego 19-5; San Francisco 8-10; Seattle 7-8; Tampa Bay 6-1; Tennessee 38-28; Washington 30-42-3.
NOTE: Includes records as Pittsburgh Pirates from 1933 through 1940; does not include records when team combined with Philadelphia squad and was known as Phil-Pitt in 1943 and when team combined with Chicago Cardinals squad and was known as Card-Pitt in 1944.

COACHING RECORDS

Bill Austin, 11-28-3; Joe Bach, 21-27-0; Bert Bell, 0-2-0; Bill Cowher, 141-82-1 (12-9); Luby DiMelio, 2-10-0; Aldo Donelli, 0-5-0; Forrest Douds, 3-6-2; Walt Kiesling, 30-55-5; Jim Leonard, 2-8-0; Johnny (Blood) McNally, 6-19-0; Johnny Michelosen, 20-26-2; Mike Nixon, 2-12-0; Chuck Noll, 193-148-1 (16-8); Buddy Parker, 51-47-6 (0-1); Jock Sutherland, 13-9-1 (0-1).
NOTE: Playoff games in parentheses.

RETIRED UNIFORM NUMBERS

No.	Player
70	Ernie Stautner

HISTORY Team by team

ST. LOUIS RAMS

YEAR-BY-YEAR RECORDS

		REGULAR SEASON						PLAYOFFS			
Year	W	L	T	Pct.	PF	PA	Finish	W	L	Highest round	Coach
1937*	1	10	0	.091	75	207	5th/Western Div.	—	—		Hugo Bezdek
1938*	4	7	0	.364	131	215	4th/Western Div.	—	—		Hugo Bezdek, Art Lewis
1939*	5	5	1	.500	195	164	4th/Western Div.	—	—		Dutch Clark
1940*	4	6	1	.400	171	191	4th/Western Div.	—	—		Dutch Clark
1941*	2	9	0	.182	116	244	5th/Western Div.	—	—		Dutch Clark
1942*	5	6	0	.455	150	207	3rd/Western Div.	—	—		Dutch Clark
1943*	Rams did not play in 1943.										
1944*	4	6	0	.400	188	224	4th/Western Div.	—	—		Buff Donelli
1945*	9	1	0	.900	244	136	1st/Western Div.	1	0	NFL champ	Adam Walsh
1946†	6	4	1	.600	277	257	2nd/Western Div.	—	—		Adam Walsh
1947†	6	6	0	.500	259	214	4th/Western Div.	—	—		Bob Snyder
1948†	6	5	1	.545	327	269	3rd/Western Div.	—	—		Clark Shaughnessy
1949†	8	2	2	.800	360	239	1st/Western Div.	0	1	NFL championship game	Clark Shaughnessy
1950†	9	3	0	.750	466	309	1st/National Conf.	1	1	NFL championship game	Joe Stydahar
1951†	8	4	0	.667	392	261	1st/National Conf.	1	0	NFL champ	Joe Stydahar
1952†	9	3	0	.750	349	234	2nd/National Conf.	0	1	Nat. Conf. champ. game	J. Stydahar, Hamp Pool
1953†	8	3	1	.727	366	236	3rd/Western Conf.	—	—		Hamp Pool
1954†	6	5	1	.545	314	285	4th/Western Conf.	—	—		Hamp Pool
1955†	8	3	1	.727	260	231	1st/Western Conf.	0	1	NFL championship game	Sid Gillman
1956†	4	8	0	.333	291	307	6th/Western Conf.	—	—		Sid Gillman
1957†	6	6	0	.500	307	278	4th/Western Conf.	—	—		Sid Gillman
1958†	8	4	0	.667	344	278	T2nd/Western Conf.	—	—		Sid Gillman
1959†	2	10	0	.167	242	315	6th/Western Conf.	—	—		Sid Gillman
1960†	4	7	1	.364	265	297	6th/Western Conf.	—	—		Bob Waterfield
1961†	4	10	0	.286	263	333	6th/Western Conf.	—	—		Bob Waterfield
1962†	1	12	1	.077	220	334	7th/Western Conf.	—	—		B. Waterfield, H. Svare
1963†	5	9	0	.357	210	350	6th/Western Conf.	—	—		Harland Svare
1964†	5	7	2	.417	283	339	5th/Western Conf.	—	—		Harland Svare
1965†	4	10	0	.286	269	328	7th/Western Conf.	—	—		Harland Svare
1966†	8	6	0	.571	289	212	3rd/Western Conf.	—	—		George Allen
1967†	11	1	2	.917	398	196	1st/Coastal Div.	0	1	W. Conf. champ. game	George Allen
1968†	10	3	1	.769	312	200	2nd/Coastal Div.	—	—		George Allen
1969†	11	3	0	.786	320	243	1st/Coastal Div.	0	1	W. Conf. champ. game	George Allen
1970†	9	4	1	.692	325	202	2nd/NFC Western Div.	—	—		George Allen
1971†	8	5	1	.615	313	260	2nd/NFC Western Div.	—	—		Tommy Prothro
1972†	6	7	1	.464	291	286	3rd/NFC Western Div.	—	—		Tommy Prothro
1973†	12	2	0	.857	388	178	1st/NFC Western Div.	0	1	NFC div. playoff game	Chuck Knox
1974†	10	4	0	.714	263	181	1st/NFC Western Div.	1	1	NFC championship game	Chuck Knox

	REGULAR SEASON							PLAYOFFS			
Year	W	L	T	Pct.	PF	PA	Finish	W	L	Highest round	Coach
1975†	12	2	0	.857	312	135	1st/NFC Western Div.	1	1	NFC championship game	Chuck Knox
1976†	10	3	1	.750	351	190	1st/NFC Western Div.	1	1	NFC championship game	Chuck Knox
1977†	10	4	0	.714	302	146	1st/NFC Western Div.	0	1	NFC div. playoff game	Chuck Knox
1978†	12	4	0	.750	316	245	1st/NFC Western Div.	1	1	NFC championship game	Ray Malavasi
1979†	9	7	0	.563	323	309	1st/NFC Western Div.	2	1	Super Bowl	Ray Malavasi
1980†	11	5	0	.688	424	289	2nd/NFC Western Div.	0	1	NFC wild-card game	Ray Malavasi
1981†	6	10	0	.375	303	351	3rd/NFC Western Div.	—	—		Ray Malavasi
1982†	2	7	0	.222	200	250	14th/NFC	—	—		Ray Malavasi
1983†	9	7	0	.563	361	344	2nd/NFC Western Div.	1	1	NFC div. playoff game	John Robinson
1984†	10	6	0	.625	346	316	2nd/NFC Western Div.	0	1	NFC wild-card game	John Robinson
1985†	11	5	0	.688	340	277	1st/NFC Western Div.	1	1	NFC championship game	John Robinson
1986†	10	6	0	.625	309	267	2nd/NFC Western Div.	0	1	NFC wild-card game	John Robinson
1987†	6	9	0	.400	317	361	3rd/NFC Western Div.	—	—		John Robinson
1988†	10	6	0	.625	407	293	2nd/NFC Western Div.	0	1	NFC wild-card game	John Robinson
1989†	11	5	0	.688	426	344	2nd/NFC Western Div.	2	1	NFC championship game	John Robinson
1990†	5	11	0	.313	345	412	3rd/NFC Western Div.	—	—		John Robinson
1991†	3	13	0	.188	234	390	4th/NFC Western Div.	—	—		John Robinson
1992†	6	10	0	.375	313	383	4th/NFC Western Div.	—	—		Chuck Knox
1993†	5	11	0	.313	221	367	4th/NFC Western Div.	—	—		Chuck Knox
1994†	4	12	0	.250	286	365	4th/NFC Western Div.	—	—		Chuck Knox
1995	7	9	0	.438	309	418	3rd/NFC Western Div.	—	—		Rich Brooks
1996	6	10	0	.375	303	409	3rd/NFC Western Div.	—	—		Rich Brooks
1997	5	11	0	.313	299	359	5th/NFC Western Div.	—	—		Dick Vermeil
1998	4	12	0	.250	285	378	5th/NFC Western Div.	—	—		Dick Vermeil
1999	13	3	0	.813	526	242	1st/NFC Western Div.	3	0	Super Bowl champ	Dick Vermeil
2000	10	6	0	.625	540	471	2nd/NFC Western Div.	0	1	NFC wild-card game	Mike Martz
2001	14	2	0	.875	503	273	1st/NFC Western Div.	2	1	Super Bowl	Mike Martz
2002	7	9	0	.438	316	369	2nd/NFC West Div.	—	—		Mike Martz
2003	12	4	0	.750	447	328	1st/NFC West Div.	0	1	NFC div. playoff game	Mike Martz
2004	8	8	0	.500	319	392	2nd/NFC West Div.	1	1	NFC div. playoff game	Mike Martz
2005	6	10	0	.375	363	429	2nd/NFC West Div.	—	—		Mike Martz, Joe Vitt

*Cleveland Rams.
†Los Angeles Rams.

FIRST-ROUND DRAFT PICKS

1937—Johnny Drake, B, Purdue
1938—Corbett Davis, B, Indiana*
1939—Parker Hall, B, Mississippi
1940—Ollie Cordill, B, Rice
1941—Rudy Mucha, C, Washington
1942—Jack Wilson, B, Baylor
1943—Mike Holovak, B, Boston College
1944—Tony Butkovich, B, Illinois
1945—Elroy Hirsch, B, Wisconsin
1946—Emil Sitko, B, Notre Dame
1947—Herman Wedemeyer, B, St. Mary's (Cal.)
1948—None
1949—Bobby Thomason, B, Virginia Military
1950—Ralph Pasquariello, B, Villanova
    Stan West, G, Oklahoma
1951—Bud McFadin, G, Texas
1952—Bill Wade, QB, Vanderbilt*
    Bob Carey, E, Michigan State
1953—Donn Moomaw, C, UCLA
    Ed Barker, E, Washington State
1954—Ed Beatty, C, Mississippi
1955—Larry Morris, C, Georgia Tech
1956—Joe Marconi, B, West Virginia
    Charlie Horton, B, Vanderbilt
1957—Jon Arnett, B, USC
    Del Shofner, B, Baylor
1958—Lou Michaels, T, Kentucky
    Jim Phillips, E, Auburn
1959—Dick Bass, B, Pacific
    Paul Dickson, G, Baylor
1960—Billy Cannon, RB, LSU*
1961—Marlin McKeever, LB, USC
1962—Roman Gabriel, QB, N.C. State
    Merlin Olsen, DT, Utah State
1963—Terry Baker, QB, Oregon State*
    Rufus Guthrie, G, Georgia Tech
1964—Bill Munson, QB, Utah State

1965—Clancy Williams, DB, Washington State
1966—Tom Mack, G, Michigan
1967—None
1968—None
1969—Larry Smith, RB, Florida
    Jim Seymour, E, Notre Dame
    Bob Klein, TE, USC
1970—Jack Reynolds, LB, Tennessee
1971—Isiah Robertson, LB, Southern
    Jack Youngblood, DE, Florida
1972—None
1973—None
1974—John Cappelletti, RB, Penn State
1975—Mike Fanning, DT, Notre Dame
    Dennis Harrah, G, Miami (Fla.)
    Doug France, T, Ohio State
1976—Kevin McLain, LB, Colorado State
1977—Bob Brudzinski, LB, Ohio State
1978—Elvis Peacock, RB, Oklahoma
1979—George Andrews, LB, Nebraska
    Kent Hill, G, Georgia Tech
1980—Johnnie Johnson, DB, Texas
1981—Mel Owens, LB, Michigan
1982—Barry Redden, RB, Richmond
1983—Eric Dickerson, RB, Southern Methodist
1984—None
1985—Jerry Gray, DB, Texas
1986—Mike Schad, T, Queens College (Ont.)
1987—None
1988—Gaston Green, RB, UCLA
    Aaron Cox, WR, Arizona State
1989—Bill Hawkins, DE, Miami (Fla.)
    Cleveland Gary, RB, Miami (Fla.)
1990—Bern Brostek, C, Washington
1991—Todd Lyght, CB, Notre Dame
1992—Sean Gilbert, DE, Pittsburgh
1993—Jerome Bettis, RB, Notre Dame

HISTORY Team by team

1994—Wayne Gandy, T, Auburn
1995—Kevin Carter, DE, Florida
1996—Lawrence Phillips, RB, Nebraska
    Eddie Kennison, WR, LSU
1997—Orlando Pace, T, Ohio State*
1998—Grant Wistrom, DE, Nebraska
1999—Torry Holt, WR, N.C. State
2000—Trung Canidate, RB, Arizona
2001—Damione Lewis, DT, Miami (Fla.)

Adam Archuleta, DB, Arizona State
Ryan Pickett, DT, Ohio State
2002—Robert Thomas, LB, UCLA
2003—Jimmy Kennedy, DT, Penn State
2004—Steven Jackson, RB, Oregon State
2005—Alex Barron, OT, Florida State
2006—Tye Hill, CB, Clemson
  *First player chosen in draft.

FRANCHISE RECORDS

Most rushing yards, career
7,245—Eric Dickerson

Most rushing yards, season
2,105—Eric Dickerson, 1984

Most rushing yards, game
247—Willie Ellison vs. N.O., Dec. 5, 1971

Most rushing touchdowns, season
18—Eric Dickerson, 1983
    Marshall Faulk, 2000

Most passing attempts, season
554—Jim Everett, 1990

Most passing attempts, game
62—Marc Bulger at NYG, Oct. 2, 2005

Most passes completed, season
375—Kurt Warner, 2001

Most passes completed, game
40—Marc Bulger at NYG, Oct. 2, 2005

Most passing yards, career
23,758—Jim Everett

Most passing yards, season
4,830—Kurt Warner, 2001

Most passing yards, game
554—Norm Van Brocklin at N.Y. Yanks,
    Sept. 28, 1951

Most touchdown passes, season
41—Kurt Warner, 1999

Most pass receptions, career
813—Isaac Bruce

Most pass receptions, season
119—Isaac Bruce, 1995

Most pass receptions, game
18—Tom Fears vs. G.B., Dec. 3, 1950

Most receiving yards, career
12,278—Isaac Bruce

Most receiving yards, season
1,781—Isaac Bruce, 1995

Most receiving yards, game
336—Willie Anderson at N.O., Nov. 26,
    1989

Most receiving touchdowns, season
17—Elroy Hirsch, 1951

Most touchdowns, career
85—Marshall Faulk

Most field goals, season
39—Jeff Wilkins, 2003

Longest field goal
57 yards—Jeff Wilkins vs. Ari., Sept. 27,
    1998

Most interceptions, career
46—Ed Meador

Most interceptions, season
14—Night Train Lane, 1952

Most sacks, career
159.5—Deacon Jones

Most sacks, season
22—Deacon Jones, 1964
    Deacon Jones, 1968

SERIES RECORDS

St. Louis vs.: Arizona 27-23-2; Atlanta 46-24-2; Baltimore 2-1; Buffalo 4-5; Carolina 7-8; Chicago 34-47-3; Cincinnati 5-5; Cleveland 9-8; Dallas 10-9; Denver 5-5; Detroit 40-37-1; Green Bay 44-40-2; Houston 1-0; Indianapolis 17-22-2; Jacksonville 2-0; Kansas City 4-4; Miami 2-8; Minnesota 13-17-2; New England 5-4; New Orleans 37-29; N.Y. Giants 25-12; N.Y. Jets 9-2; Oakland 3-7; Philadelphia 17-16-1; Pittsburgh 15-5-2; San Diego 5-3; San Francisco 58-52-2; Seattle 9-6; Tampa Bay 9-6; Tennessee 6-3; Washington 6-20-1. NOTE: Includes records as Cleveland Rams from 1937 through 1945 and Los Angeles Rams from 1946 through 1994.

COACHING RECORDS

George Allen, 47-17-4 (2-2); Hugo Bezdek, 1-13-0; Rich Brooks, 13-19-0; Dutch Clark, 16-26-2; Aldo Donelli, 4-6-0; Sid Gillman, 28-31-1 (0-1); Chuck Knox, 69-48-1 (3-5); Art Lewis, 4-4-0; Ray Malavasi, 40-33-0 (3-3); Mike Martz, 53-32-0 (3-4); Hamp Pool, 23-10-2 (0-1); Tommy Prothro, 14-12-2; John Robinson, 75-68-0 (4-6); Clark Shaughnessy, 14-7-3 (0-1); Bob Snyder, 6-6-0; Joe Stydahar, 17-8-0 (2-1); Harland Svare, 14-31-3; Dick Vermeil, 22-26-0 (3-0); Joe Vitt, 4-7; Adam Walsh, 15-5-1 (1-0); Bob Waterfield, 9-24-1. NOTE: Playoff games in parentheses.

RETIRED UNIFORM NUMBERS

No.	Player
7	Bob Waterfield
29	Eric Dickerson
74	Merlin Olsen
78	Jackie Slater
85	Jack Youngblood

SAN DIEGO CHARGERS
YEAR-BY-YEAR RECORDS

	REGULAR SEASON							PLAYOFFS			
Year	W	L	T	Pct.	PF	PA	Finish	W	L	Highest round	Coach
1960*†	10	4	0	.714	373	336	1st/Western Div.	0	1	AFL championship game	Sid Gillman
1961*	12	2	0	.857	396	219	1st/Western Div.	0	1	AFL championship game	Sid Gillman
1962*	4	10	0	.286	314	392	3rd/Western Div.	—	—		Sid Gillman
1963*	11	3	0	.786	399	256	1st/Western Div.	1	0	AFL champ	Sid Gillman
1964*	8	5	1	.615	341	300	1st/Western Div.	0	1	AFL championship game	Sid Gillman
1965*	9	2	3	.818	340	227	1st/Western Div.	0	1	AFL championship game	Sid Gillman
1966*	7	6	1	.538	335	284	3rd/Western Div.	—	—		Sid Gillman
1967*	8	5	1	.615	360	352	3rd/Western Div.	—	—		Sid Gillman
1968*	9	5	0	.643	382	310	3rd/Western Div.	—	—		Sid Gillman
1969*	8	6	0	.571	288	276	3rd/Western Div.	—	—		S. Gillman, C. Waller
1970	5	6	3	.455	282	278	3rd/AFC Western Div.	—	—		Charlie Waller
1971	6	8	0	.429	311	341	3rd/AFC Western Div.	—	—		S. Gillman, H. Svare
1972	4	9	1	.308	264	344	4th/AFC Western Div.	—	—		Harland Svare
1973	2	11	1	.179	188	386	4th/AFC Western Div.	—	—		H. Svare, Ron Waller
1974	5	9	0	.357	212	285	4th/AFC Western Div.	—	—		Tommy Prothro

					REGULAR SEASON				PLAYOFFS		
Year	W	L	T	Pct.	PF	PA	Finish	W	L	Highest round	Coach
1975	2	12	0	.143	189	345	4th/AFC Western Div.	—	—		Tommy Prothro
1976	6	8	0	.429	248	285	3rd/AFC Western Div.	—	—		Tommy Prothro
1977	7	7	0	.500	222	205	3rd/AFC Western Div.	—	—		Tommy Prothro
1978	9	7	0	.563	355	309	4th/AFC Western Div.	—	—		T. Prothro, Don Coryell
1979	12	4	0	.750	411	246	1st/AFC Western Div.	0	1	AFC div. playoff game	Don Coryell
1980	11	5	0	.688	418	327	1st/AFC Western Div.	1	1	AFC championship game	Don Coryell
1981	10	6	0	.625	478	390	1st/AFC Western Div.	1	1	AFC championship game	Don Coryell
1982	6	3	0	.667	288	221	5th/AFC	1	1	AFC second-round pl. game	Don Coryell
1983	6	10	0	.375	358	462	4th/AFC Western Div.	—	—		Don Coryell
1984	7	9	0	.438	394	413	5th/AFC Western Div.	—	—		Don Coryell
1985	8	8	0	.500	467	435	4th/AFC Western Div.	—	—		Don Coryell
1986	4	12	0	.250	335	396	5th/AFC Western Div.	—	—		D. Coryell, Al Saunders
1987	8	7	0	.533	253	317	3rd/AFC Western Div.	—	—		Al Saunders
1988	6	10	0	.375	231	332	4th/AFC Western Div.	—	—		Al Saunders
1989	6	10	0	.375	266	290	5th/AFC Western Div.	—	—		Dan Henning
1990	6	10	0	.375	315	281	4th/AFC Western Div.	—	—		Dan Henning
1991	4	12	0	.250	274	342	5th/AFC Western Div.	—	—		Dan Henning
1992	11	5	0	.688	335	241	1st/AFC Western Div.	1	1	AFC div. playoff game	Bobby Ross
1993	8	8	0	.500	322	290	4th/AFC Western Div.	—	—		Bobby Ross
1994	11	5	0	.688	381	306	1st/AFC Western Div.	2	1	Super Bowl	Bobby Ross
1995	9	7	0	.563	321	323	2nd/AFC Western Div.	0	1	AFC wild-card game	Bobby Ross
1996	8	8	0	.500	310	376	3rd/AFC Western Div.	—	—		Bobby Ross
1997	4	12	0	.250	266	425	5th/AFC Western Div.	—	—		Kevin Gilbride
1998	5	11	0	.313	241	342	5th/AFC Western Div.	—	—		K. Gilbride, June Jones
1999	8	8	0	.500	269	316	3rd/AFC Western Div.	—	—		Mike Riley
2000	1	15	0	.063	269	440	5th/AFC Western Div.	—	—		Mike Riley
2001	5	11	0	.313	332	321	5th/AFC Western Div.	—	—		Mike Riley
2002	8	8	0	.500	333	367	3rd/AFC West Div.	—	—		Marty Schottenheimer
2003	4	12	0	.250	313	441	4th/AFC West Div.	—	—		Marty Schottenheimer
2004	12	4	0	.750	446	313	1st/AFC West Div	0	1	AFC wild-card game	Marty Schottenheimer
2005	9	7	0	.562	418	312	3rd/AFC West Div.	—	—		Marty Schottenheimer

*American Football League.
†Los Angeles Chargers.

FIRST-ROUND DRAFT PICKS

1960—Monty Stickles, E, Notre Dame
1961—Earl Faison, E, Indiana
1962—Bob Ferguson, RB, Ohio State
1963—Walt Sweeney, E, Syracuse
1964—Ted Davis, E, Georgia Tech
1965—Steve DeLong, DE, Tennessee
1966—Don Davis, T, Los Angeles State
1967—Ron Billingsley, DT, Wyoming
1968—Russ Washington, T, Missouri
    Jim Hill, DB, Texas A&I
1969—Marty Domres, QB, Columbia
    Bob Babich, LB, Miami (Ohio)
1970—Walker Gillette, WR, Richmond
1971—Leon Burns, RB, Long Beach State
1972—None
1973—Johnny Rodgers, WR, Nebraska
1974—Bo Matthews, RB, Colorado
    Don Goode, LB, Kansas
1975—Gary Johnson, DT, Grambling State
    Mike Williams, DB, Louisiana State
1976—Joe Washington, RB, Oklahoma
1977—Bob Rush, C, Memphis State
1978—John Jefferson, WR, Arizona State
1979—Kellen Winslow, TE, Missouri
1980—None
1981—James Brooks, RB, Auburn
1982—None
1983—Billy Ray Smith, LB, Arkansas

    Gary Anderson, WR, Arkansas
    Gill Byrd, DB, San Jose State
1984—Mossy Cade, DB, Texas
1985—Jim Lachey, G, Ohio State
1986—Leslie O'Neal, DE, Oklahoma State
    Jim FitzPatrick, T, USC
1987—Rod Bernstine, TE, Texas A&M
1988—Anthony Miller, WR, Tennessee
1989—Burt Grossman, DE, Pittsburgh
1990—Junior Seau, LB, USC
1991—Stanley Richard, CB, Texas
1992—Chris Mims, DT, Tennessee
1993—Darrien Gordon, DB, Stanford
1994—None
1995—None
1996—None
1997—None
1998—Ryan Leaf, QB, Washington State
1999—None
2000—None
2001—LaDainian Tomlinson, RB, Texas Christian
2002—Quentin Jammer, DB, Texas
2003—Sammy Davis, DB, Texas A&M
2004—Eli Manning, QB, Mississippi*
2005—Shawne Merriman, OLB, Maryland
    Luis Castillo, DT, Northwestern
2006—Antonio Cromartie, CB, Florida State
    *First player chosen in draft.

FRANCHISE RECORDS

Most rushing yards, career
7,361—LaDainian Tomlinson

Most rushing yards, season
1,683—LaDainian Tomlinson, 2002

Most rushing yards, game
243—LaDainian Tomlinson vs. Oak., Dec. 28, 2003

Most rushing touchdowns, season
19—Chuck Muncie, 1981

Most passing attempts, season
609—Dan Fouts, 1981

Most passing attempts, game
58—Mark Herrmann at K.C., Dec. 22, 1985

Most passes completed, season
360—Dan Fouts, 1981

Most passes completed, game
37—Dan Fouts vs. Mia., Nov. 18, 1984
(OT)
Mark Herrmann at K.C., Dec. 22, 1985

Most passing yards, career
43,040—Dan Fouts
Most passing yards, season
4,802—Dan Fouts, 1981
Most passing yards, game
444—Dan Fouts vs. NYG, Oct. 19, 1980
　　　　Dan Fouts at S.F., Dec. 11, 1982
Most touchdown passes, season
33—Dan Fouts, 1981
Most pass receptions, career
586—Charlie Joiner
Most pass receptions, season
100—LaDainian Tomlinson, 2003
Most pass receptions, game
15—Kellen Winslow at G.B., Oct. 7, 1984

Most receiving yards, career
9,584—Lance Alworth
Most receiving yards, season
1,602—Lance Alworth, 1965
Most receiving yards, game
260—Wes Chandler vs. Cin., Dec. 20, 1982
Most receiving touchdowns, season
14—Lance Alworth, 1965
　　　Tony Martin, 1996
Most touchdowns, career
83—Lance Alworth
Most field goals, season
34—John Carney, 1994

Longest field goal
54 yards—John Carney vs. Sea., Nov. 10, 1991
　　　　John Carney vs. Buf., Sept. 6, 1998
　　　　John Carney at K.C., Sept. 17, 2000
Most interceptions, career
42—Gill Byrd
Most interceptions, season
9—Charlie McNeil, 1961
Most sacks, career
105.5—Leslie O'Neal
Most sacks, season
17.5—Gary Johnson, 1980

SERIES RECORDS

San Diego vs.: Arizona 7-3; Atlanta 1-6; Baltimore 2-2; Buffalo 19-9-2; Carolina 1-2; Chicago 4-5; Cincinnati 17-10; Cleveland 12-7-1; Dallas 2-6; Denver 39-52-1; Detroit 5-3; Green Bay 1-7; Houston 2-0; Indianapolis 13-8; Jacksonville 1-1; Kansas City 42-48-1; Miami 10-11; Minnesota 5-4; New England 13-17-2; New Orleans 7-2; N.Y. Giants 4-5; N.Y. Jets 18-11-1; Oakland 36-54-2; Philadelphia 5-4; Pittsburgh 5-19; St. Louis 3-5; San Francisco 4-6; Seattle 22-25; Tampa Bay 7-1; Tennessee 20-13-1; Washington 2-6.
NOTE: Includes records as Los Angeles Chargers in 1960.

COACHING RECORDS

Don Coryell, 69-56-0 (3-4); Kevin Gilbride, 6-16-0; Sid Gillman, 86-53-6 (1-4); Dan Henning, 16-32-0; June Jones, 3-7-0; Tommy Prothro, 21-39-0; Mike Riley, 14-34-0; Bobby Ross, 47-33-0 (3-3); Al Saunders, 17-22-0; Marty Schottenheimer, 33-31-0 (0-1); Harland Svare, 7-17-2; Charlie Waller, 9-7-3; Ron Waller, 1-5-0.
NOTE: Playoff games in parentheses.

RETIRED UNIFORM NUMBERS

No.	Player
14	Dan Fouts
19	Lance Alworth

SAN FRANCISCO 49ERS
YEAR-BY-YEAR RECORDS

	REGULAR SEASON							PLAYOFFS			
Year	W	L	T	Pct.	PF	PA	Finish	W	L	Highest round	Coach
1946*	9	5	0	.643	307	189	2nd/Western Div.	—	—		Buck Shaw
1947*	8	4	2	.667	327	264	2nd/Western Div.	—	—		Buck Shaw
1948*	12	2	0	.857	495	248	2nd/Western Div.	—	—		Buck Shaw
1949*	9	3	0	.750	416	227	2nd	—	—		Buck Shaw
1950	3	9	0	.250	213	300	T5th/National Conf.	—	—		Buck Shaw
1951	7	4	1	.636	255	205	T2nd/National Conf.	—	—		Buck Shaw
1952	7	5	0	.583	285	221	3rd/National Conf.	—	—		Buck Shaw
1953	9	3	0	.750	372	237	2nd/Western Conf.	—	—		Buck Shaw
1954	7	4	1	.636	313	251	3rd/Western Conf.	—	—		Buck Shaw
1955	4	8	0	.333	216	298	5th/Western Conf.	—	—		Red Strader
1956	5	6	1	.455	233	284	3rd/Western Conf.	—	—		Frankie Albert
1957	8	4	0	.667	260	264	2nd/Western Conf.	0	1	W. Conf. champ. game	Frankie Albert
1958	6	6	0	.500	257	324	4th/Western Conf.	—	—		Frankie Albert
1959	7	5	0	.583	255	237	T3rd/Western Conf.	—	—		Red Hickey
1960	7	5	0	.583	208	205	T2nd/Western Conf.	—	—		Red Hickey
1961	7	6	1	.538	346	272	5th/Western Conf.	—	—		Red Hickey
1962	6	8	0	.429	282	331	5th/Western Conf.	—	—		Red Hickey
1963	2	12	0	.143	198	391	7th/Western Conf.	—	—		R. Hickey, J. Christiansen
1964	4	10	0	.286	236	330	7th/Western Conf.	—	—		Jack Christiansen
1965	7	6	1	.538	421	402	4th/Western Conf.	—	—		Jack Christiansen
1966	6	6	2	.500	320	325	4th/Western Conf.	—	—		Jack Christiansen
1967	7	7	0	.500	273	337	3rd/Coastal Div.	—	—		Jack Christiansen
1968	7	6	1	.538	303	310	3rd/Coastal Div.	—	—		Dick Nolan
1969	4	8	2	.333	277	319	4th/Coastal Div.	—	—		Dick Nolan
1970	10	3	1	.769	352	267	1st/NFC Western Div.	1	1	NFC championship game	Dick Nolan
1971	9	5	0	.643	300	216	1st/NFC Western Div.	1	1	NFC championship game	Dick Nolan
1972	8	5	1	.607	353	249	1st/NFC Western Div.	0	1	NFC div. playoff game	Dick Nolan
1973	5	9	0	.357	262	319	4th/NFC Western Div.	—	—		Dick Nolan
1974	6	8	0	.429	226	236	2nd/NFC Western Div.	—	—		Dick Nolan
1975	5	9	0	.357	255	286	2nd/NFC Western Div.	—	—		Dick Nolan
1976	8	6	0	.571	270	190	2nd/NFC Western Div.	—	—		Monte Clark
1977	5	9	0	.357	220	260	3rd/NFC Western Div.	—	—		Ken Meyer
1978	2	14	0	.125	219	350	4th/NFC Western Div.	—	—		P. McCulley, F. O'Connor
1979	2	14	0	.125	308	416	4th/NFC Western Div.	—	—		Bill Walsh

			REGULAR SEASON						PLAYOFFS		
Year	W	L	T	Pct.	PF	PA	Finish	W	L	Highest round	Coach
1980	6	10	0	.375	320	415	3rd/NFC Western Div.	—	—		Bill Walsh
1981	13	3	0	.813	357	250	1st/NFC Western Div.	3	0	Super Bowl champ	Bill Walsh
1982	3	6	0	.333	209	206	11th/NFC	—	—		Bill Walsh
1983	10	6	0	.625	432	293	1st/NFC Western Div.	1	1	NFC championship game	Bill Walsh
1984	15	1	0	.938	475	227	1st/NFC Western Div.	3	0	Super Bowl champ	Bill Walsh
1985	10	6	0	.625	411	263	2nd/NFC Western Div.	0	1	NFC wild-card game	Bill Walsh
1986	10	5	1	.656	374	247	1st/NFC Western Div.	0	1	NFC div. playoff game	Bill Walsh
1987	13	2	0	.867	459	253	1st/NFC Western Div.	0	1	NFC div. playoff game	Bill Walsh
1988	10	6	0	.625	369	294	1st/NFC Western Div.	3	0	Super Bowl champ	Bill Walsh
1989	14	2	0	.875	442	253	1st/NFC Western Div.	3	0	Super Bowl champ	George Seifert
1990	14	2	0	.875	353	239	1st/NFC Western Div.	1	1	NFC championship game	George Seifert
1991	10	6	0	.625	393	239	3rd/NFC Western Div.	—	—		George Seifert
1992	14	2	0	.875	431	236	1st/NFC Western Div.	1	1	NFC championship game	George Seifert
1993	10	6	0	.625	473	295	1st/NFC Western Div.	1	1	NFC championship game	George Seifert
1994	13	3	0	.813	505	296	1st/NFC Western Div.	3	0	Super Bowl champ	George Seifert
1995	11	5	0	.688	457	258	1st/NFC Western Div.	0	1	NFC div. playoff game	George Seifert
1996	12	4	0	.750	398	257	2nd/NFC Western Div.	1	1	NFC div. playoff game	George Seifert
1997	13	3	0	.813	375	265	1st/NFC Western Div.	1	1	NFC championship game	Steve Mariucci
1998	12	4	0	.750	479	328	2nd/NFC Western Div.	1	1	NFC div. playoff game	Steve Mariucci
1999	4	12	0	.250	295	453	4th/NFC Western Div.	—	—		Steve Mariucci
2000	6	10	0	.375	388	422	4th/NFC Western Div.	—	—		Steve Mariucci
2001	12	4	0	.750	409	282	2nd/NFC Western Div.	0	1	NFC wild-card game	Steve Mariucci
2002	10	6	0	.625	367	351	1st/NFC West Div.	1	1	NFC div. playoff game	Steve Mariucci
2003	7	9	0	.438	384	337	3rd/NFC West Div.	—	—		Dennis Erickson
2004	2	14	0	.125	259	452	4th/NFC West Div.	—	—		Dennis Erickson
2005	4	12	0	.250	239	428	4th/NFC West Div.	—	—		Mike Nolan

*All-America Football Conference.

FIRST-ROUND DRAFT PICKS

1950—Leo Nomellini, T, Minnesota
1951—Y.A. Tittle, QB, LSU
1952—Hugh McElhenny, RB, Washington
1953—Harry Babcock, E, Georgia*
      Tom Stolhandske, E, Texas
1954—Bernie Faloney, QB, Maryland
1955—Dick Moegel, HB, Rice
1956—Earl Morrall QB, Michigan State
1957—John Brodie, QB, Stanford
1958—Jim Pace, RB, Michigan
      Charles Krueger, T, Texas A&M
1959—Dave Baker, RB, Oklahoma
      Dan James, C, Ohio State
1960—Monty Stickles, E, Notre Dame
1961—Jim Johnson, RB, UCLA
      Bernie Casey, RB, Bowling Green State
      Billy Kilmer, QB, UCLA
1962—Lance Alworth, RB, Arkansas
1963—Kermit Alexander, RB, UCLA
1964—Dave Parks, E, Texas Tech*
1965—Ken Willard, RB, North Carolina
      George Donnelly, DB, Illinois
1966—Stan Hindman, DE, Mississippi
1967—Steve Spurrier, QB, Florida
      Cas Banaszek, LB, Northwestern
1968—Forrest Blue, C, Auburn
1969—Ted Kwalick, TE, Penn State
      Gene Washington, WR, Stanford
1970—Cedrick Hardman, DE, North Texas State
      Bruce Taylor, DB, Boston University
1971—Tim Anderson, DB, Ohio State
1972—Terry Beasley, WR, Auburn
1973—Mike Holmes, DB, Tex. Southern
1974—Wilbur Jackson, RB, Alabama
      Bill Sandifer, DT, UCLA
1975—Jimmy Webb, DT, Mississippi State
1976—None
1977—None

1978—Ken McAfee, TE, Notre Dame
      Dan Bunz, LB, Long Beach State
1979—None
1980—Earl Cooper, RB, Rice
      Jim Stuckey, DT, Clemson
1981—Ronnie Lott, DB, USC
1982—None
1983—None
1984—Todd Shell, LB, Brigham Young
1985—Jerry Rice, WR, Missssippi Valley State
1986—None
1987—Harris Barton, T, North Carolina
      Terrence Flager, RB, Clemson
1988—None
1989—Keith DeLong, LB, Tennessee
1990—Dexter Carter, RB, Florida State
1991—Ted Washington, DL, Louisville
1992—Dana Hall, DB, Washington
1993—Dana Stubblefield, DT, Kansas
      Todd Kelly, DE, Tennessee
1994—Bryant Young, DT, Notre Dame
      William Floyd, RB, Florida State
1995—J.J. Stokes, WR, UCLA
1996—None
1997—Jim Druckenmiller, QB, Virginia Tech
1998—R.W. McQuarters, DB, Oklahoma State
1999—Reggie McGrew, DT, Florida
2000—Julian Peterson, LB, Michigan State
      Ahmed Plummer, DB, Ohio State
2001—Andre Carter, DE, California
2002—Mike Rumph, CB, Miami (Fla.)
2003—Kwame Harris, T, Stanford
2004—Rashaun Woods, WR, Oklahoma State
2005—Alex Smith, QB, Utah*
2006—Vernon Davis, TE, Maryland
      Manny Lawson, OLB, N.C. State
    *First player chosen in draft.

FRANCHISE RECORDS

Most rushing yards, career
7,344—Joe Perry

Most rushing yards, season
1,570—Garrison Hearst, 1998

Most rushing yards, game
201—Charlie Garner at Dal., Sept. 24, 2000

Most rushing touchdowns, season
10—Joe Perry, 1953
   J.D. Smith, 1959
   Billy Kilmer, 1961
   Ricky Watters, 1993
   Derek Loville, 1995
Most passing attempts, season
578—Steve DeBerg, 1979
Most passing attempts, game
60—Joe Montana at Was., Nov. 17, 1986
Most passes completed, season
355—Jeff Garcia, 2000
Most passes completed, game
37—Joe Montana at Atl., Nov. 6, 1985
Most passing yards, career
35,124—Joe Montana
Most passing yards, season
4,278—Jeff Garcia, 2000

Most passing yards, game
476—Joe Montana at Atl., Oct. 14, 1990
Most touchdown passes, season
36—Steve Young, 1998
Most pass receptions, career
1,281—Jerry Rice
Most pass receptions, season
122—Jerry Rice, 1995
Most pass receptions, game
20—Terrell Owens vs. Chi., Dec. 17, 2000
Most receiving yards, career
19,247—Jerry Rice
Most receiving yards, season
1,848—Jerry Rice, 1995
Most receiving yards, game
289—Jerry Rice vs. Min., Dec. 18, 1995

Most receiving touchdowns, season
22—Jerry Rice, 1987
Most touchdowns, career
187—Jerry Rice
Most field goals, season
30—Jeff Wilkins, 1996
Longest field goal
56 yards—Mike Cofer at Atl., Oct. 14, 1990
   Joe Nedney at StL., Dec. 24, 2005
Most interceptions, career
51—Ronnie Lott
Most interceptions, season
10—Dave Baker, 1960
   Ronnie Lott, 1986
Most sacks, career
112.5—Cedrick Hardman
Most sacks, season
18—Cedrick Hardman, 1971

SERIES RECORDS

San Francisco vs.: Arizona 17-12; Atlanta 44-26-1; Baltimore 1-1; Buffalo 4-5; Carolina 7-8; Chicago 27-28-1; Cincinnati 7-3; Cleveland 6-10; Dallas 14-9-1; Denver 4-6; Detroit 31-26-1; Green Bay 25-27-1; Houston 1-0; Indianapolis 18-23; Jacksonville 0-2; Kansas City 6-3; Miami 4-5; Minnesota 17-18-1; New England 7-3; New Orleans 45-20-2; N.Y. Giants 13-12; N.Y. Jets 8-2; Oakland 4-6; Philadelphia 16-8-1; Pittsburgh 10-8; St. Louis 52-58-2; San Diego 6-4; Seattle 6-8; Tampa Bay 14-3; Tennessee 7-3; Washington 13-9-1. NOTE: Includes records only from 1950 to present.

COACHING RECORDS

Frankie Albert, 19-16-1 (0-1); Jack Christiansen, 26-38-3; Monte Clark, 8-6-0; Dennis Erickson, 9-23-0; Red Hickey, 27-27-1; Steve Mariucci, 57-39-0 (3-4); Pete McCulley, 1-8-0; Ken Meyer, 5-9-0; Dick Nolan, 54-53-5 (2-3); Mike Nolan, 4-12; Fred O'Connor, 1-6-0; George Seifert, 98-30-0 (10-5); Buck Shaw, 33-25-2; Red Strader, 4-8-0; Bill Walsh, 92-59-1 (10-4). NOTE: Playoff games in parentheses.

RETIRED UNIFORM NUMBERS

No.	Player	No.	Player
12	John Brodie	42	Ronnie Lott
16	Joe Montana	70	Charlie Krueger
34	Joe Perry	73	Leo Nomellini
37	Jimmy Johnson	79	Bob St. Clair
39	Hugh McElhenny	87	Dwight Clark

SEATTLE SEAHAWKS

YEAR-BY-YEAR RECORDS

	REGULAR SEASON							PLAYOFFS			
Year	W	L	T	Pct.	PF	PA	Finish	W	L	Highest round	Coach
1976	2	12	0	.143	229	429	5th/NFC Western Div.	—	—		Jack Patera
1977	5	9	0	.357	282	373	4th/AFC Western Div.	—	—		Jack Patera
1978	9	7	0	.563	345	358	3rd/AFC Western Div.	—	—		Jack Patera
1979	9	7	0	.563	378	372	3rd/AFC Western Div.	—	—		Jack Patera
1980	4	12	0	.250	291	408	5th/AFC Western Div.	—	—		Jack Patera
1981	6	10	0	.375	322	388	5th/AFC Western Div.	—	—		Jack Patera
1982	4	5	0	.444	127	147	10th/AFC	—	—		J. Patera, Mike McCormack
1983	9	7	0	.562	403	397	2nd/AFC Western Div.	2	1	AFC championship game	Chuck Knox
1984	12	4	0	.750	418	282	2nd/AFC Western Div.	1	1	AFC div. playoff game	Chuck Knox
1985	8	8	0	.500	349	303	3rd/AFC Western Div.	—	—		Chuck Knox
1986	10	6	0	.625	366	293	3rd/AFC Western Div.	—	—		Chuck Knox
1987	9	6	0	.600	371	314	2nd/AFC Western Div.	0	1	AFC wild-card game	Chuck Knox
1988	9	7	0	.563	339	329	1st/AFC Western Div.	0	1	AFC div. playoff game	Chuck Knox
1989	7	9	0	.438	241	327	4th/AFC Western Div.	—	—		Chuck Knox
1990	9	7	0	.563	306	286	3rd/AFC Western Div.	—	—		Chuck Knox
1991	7	9	0	.438	276	261	4th/AFC Western Div.	—	—		Chuck Knox
1992	2	14	0	.125	140	312	5th/AFC Western Div.	—	—		Tom Flores
1993	6	10	0	.375	280	314	5th/AFC Western Div.	—	—		Tom Flores
1994	6	10	0	.375	287	323	5th/AFC Western Div.	—	—		Tom Flores
1995	8	8	0	.500	363	366	3rd/AFC Western Div.	—	—		Dennis Erickson
1996	7	9	0	.438	317	376	5th/AFC Western Div.	—	—		Dennis Erickson
1997	8	8	0	.500	365	362	3rd/AFC Western Div.	—	—		Dennis Erickson
1998	8	8	0	.500	372	310	3rd/AFC Western Div.	—	—		Dennis Erickson
1999	9	7	0	.563	338	298	1st/AFC Western Div.	0	1	AFC wild-card game	Mike Holmgren
2000	6	10	0	.375	320	405	4th/AFC Western Div.	—	—		Mike Holmgren
2001	9	7	0	.563	301	324	2nd/AFC Western Div.	—	—		Mike Holmgren
2002	7	9	0	.438	355	369	3rd/NFC West Div.	—	—		Mike Holmgren
2003	10	6	0	.625	404	327	2nd/NFC West Div.	0	1	NFC wild-card game	Mike Holmgren
2004	9	7	0	.562	371	373	1st/NFC West Div.	0	1	NFC wild-card game	Mike Holmgren
2005	13	3	0	.812	452	271	1st/NFC West Div.	2	1	Super Bowl	Mike Holmgren

FIRST-ROUND DRAFT PICKS

1976—Steve Niehaus, DT, Notre Dame
1977—Steve August, G, Tulsa
1978—Keith Simpson, DB, Memphis State
1979—Manu Tuiasosopo, DT, UCLA
1980—Jacob Green, DE, Texas A&M
1981—Kenny Easley, DB, UCLA
1982—Jeff Bryant, DE, Clemson
1983—Curt Warner, RB, Penn State
1984—Terry Taylor, DB, Southern Illinois
1985—None
1986—John L. Williams, RB, Florida
1987—Tony Woods, LB, Pittsburgh
1988—None
1989—Andy Heck, T, Notre Dame
1990—Cortez Kennedy, DT, Miami
1991—Dan McGwire, QB, San Diego State
1992—Ray Roberts, T, Virginia

1993—Rick Mirer, QB, Notre Dame
1994—Sam Adams, DE, Texas A&M
1995—Joey Galloway, WR, Ohio State
1996—Pete Kendall, T, Boston College
1997—Shawn Springs, CB, Ohio State
    Walter Jones, T, Florida State
1998—Anthony Simmons, LB, Clemson
1999—Lamar King, DE, Saginaw Valley State
2000—Shaun Alexander, RB, Alabama
    Chris McIntosh, T, Wisconsin
2001—Koren Robinson, WR, N.C. State
    Steve Hutchinson, G, Michigan
2002—Jerramy Stevens, TE, Washington
2003—Marcus Trufant, DB, Washington State
2004—Marcus Tubbs, DT, Texas
2005—Chris Spencer, C, Mississippi
2006—Kelly Jennings, CB, Miami (Fla.)

FRANCHISE RECORDS

Most rushing yards, career
7,817—Shaun Alexander

Most rushing yards, season
1,880—Shaun Alexander, 2005

Most rushing yards, game
266—Shaun Alexander vs. Oak., Nov. 11, 2001

Most rushing touchdowns, season
27—Shaun Alexander, 2005

Most passing attempts, season
532—Dave Krieg, 1985

Most passing attempts, game
55—Matt Hasselbeck at S.F., Dec. 1, 2002

Most passes completed, season
313—Warren Moon, 1997
    Matt Hasselbeck, 2003

Most passes completed, game
36—Matt Hasselbeck at S.D., Dec. 29, 2002 (OT)
33—Dave Krieg vs. Atl., Oct. 13, 1985

Most passing yards, career
26,132—Dave Krieg

Most passing yards, season
3,841—Matt Hasselbeck, 2003

Most passing yards, game
449—Matt Hasselbeck at S.D., Dec. 29, 2002 (OT)
427—Matt Hasselbeck at S.F., Dec. 1, 2002

Most touchdown passes, season
32—Dave Krieg, 1984

Most pass receptions, career
819—Steve Largent

Most pass receptions, season
87—Darrell Jackson, 2004

Most pass receptions, game
15—Steve Largent vs. Det., Oct. 18, 1987

Most receiving yards, career
13,089—Steve Largent

Most receiving yards, season
1,287—Steve Largent, 1985

Most receiving yards, game
261—Steve Largent vs. Det., Oct. 18, 1987

Most receiving touchdowns, season
13—Daryl Turner, 1985

Most touchdowns, career
101—Steve Largent

Most field goals, season
34—Todd Peterson, 1999

Longest field goal
58 yards—Josh Brown at G.B., Oct. 5, 2003

Most interceptions, career
50—Dave Brown

Most interceptions, season
10—John Harris, 1981
    Kenny Easley, 1984

Most sacks, career
116—Jacob Green

Most sacks, season
16.5—Michael Sinclair, 1998

SERIES RECORDS

Seattle vs.: Arizona 7-7; Atlanta 8-2; Baltimore 0-2; Buffalo 6-4; Carolina 2-1; Chicago 6-2; Cincinnati 8-8; Cleveland 11-4; Dallas 4-6; Denver 17-33; Detroit 5-4; Green Bay 4-6; Houston 1-0; Indianapolis 4-5; Jacksonville 3-2; Kansas City 18-30; Miami 3-6; Minnesota 6-3; New England 7-7; New Orleans 5-4; N.Y. Giants 4-7; N.Y. Jets 8-8; Oakland 22-27; Philadelphia 4-5; Pittsburgh 8-7; St. Louis 6-9; San Diego 25-22; San Francisco 8-6; Tampa Bay 5-1; Tennessee 9-4; Washington 5-9.

COACHING RECORDS

Dennis Erickson, 31-33-0; Tom Flores, 14-34-0; Mike Holmgren, 63-49-0 (2-4); Chuck Knox, 80-63-0 (3-4); Mike McCormack, 4-3-0; Jack Patera, 35-59-0.
NOTE: Playoff games in parentheses.

RETIRED UNIFORM NUMBERS

No.	Player
12	Fans/the twelfth man
80	Steve Largent

TAMPA BAY BUCCANEERS
YEAR-BY-YEAR RECORDS

	REGULAR SEASON							PLAYOFFS			
Year	W	L	T	Pct.	PF	PA	Finish	W	L	Highest round	Coach
1976	0	14	0	.000	125	412	5th/AFC Western Div.	—	—		John McKay
1977	2	12	0	.143	103	223	5th/NFC Central Div.	—	—		John McKay
1978	5	11	0	.313	241	259	5th/NFC Central Div.	—	—		John McKay
1979	10	6	0	.625	273	237	1st/NFC Central Div.	1	1	NFC championship game	John McKay
1980	5	10	1	.344	271	341	4th/NFC Central Div.	—	—		John McKay
1981	9	7	0	.563	315	268	1st/NFC Central Div.	0	1	NFC div. playoff game	John McKay
1982	5	4	0	.556	158	178	7th/NFC	0	1	NFC first-round pl. game	John McKay
1983	2	14	0	.125	241	380	5th/NFC Central Div.	—	—		John McKay

HISTORY Team by team

Year	W	L	T	Pct.	PF	PA	Finish	W	L	Highest round	Coach
							REGULAR SEASON			**PLAYOFFS**	
1984	6	10	0	.375	335	380	3rd/NFC Central Div.	—	—		John McKay
1985	2	14	0	.125	294	448	5th/NFC Central Div.	—	—		Leeman Bennett
1986	2	14	0	.125	239	473	5th/NFC Central Div.	—	—		Leeman Bennett
1987	4	11	0	.267	286	360	4th/NFC Central Div.	—	—		Ray Perkins
1988	5	11	0	.313	261	350	3rd/NFC Central Div.	—	—		Ray Perkins
1989	5	11	0	.313	320	419	5th/NFC Central Div.	—	—		Ray Perkins
1990	6	10	0	.375	264	367	2nd/NFC Central Div.	—	—		R. Perkins, R. Williamson
1991	3	13	0	.188	199	365	5th/NFC Central Div.	—	—		Richard Williamson
1992	5	11	0	.313	267	365	3rd/NFC Central Div.	—	—		Sam Wyche
1993	5	11	0	.313	237	376	3rd/NFC Central Div.	—	—		Sam Wyche
1994	6	10	0	.375	251	351	5th/NFC Central Div.	—	—		Sam Wyche
1995	7	9	0	.438	238	335	5th/NFC Central Div.	—	—		Sam Wyche
1996	6	10	0	.375	221	293	5th/NFC Central Div.	—	—		Tony Dungy
1997	10	6	0	.625	299	263	2nd/NFC Central Div.	1	1	NFC div. playoff game	Tony Dungy
1998	8	8	0	.500	314	295	3rd/NFC Central Div.	—	—		Tony Dungy
1999	11	5	0	.688	270	235	1st/NFC Central Div.	1	1	NFC championship game	Tony Dungy
2000	10	6	0	.625	388	269	2nd/NFC Central Div.	0	1	NFC wild-card game	Tony Dungy
2001	9	7	0	.563	324	280	3rd/NFC Central Div.	0	1	NFC wild-card game	Tony Dungy
2002	12	4	0	.750	346	196	1st/NFC South Div.	3	0	Super Bowl champ	Jon Gruden
2003	7	9	0	.438	301	264	3rd/NFC South Div.	—	—		Jon Gruden
2004	5	11	0	.312	301	304	4th/NFC South Div.	—	—		Jon Gruden
2005	11	5	0	.688	300	274	1st/NFC South Div.	0	1	NFC wild-card game	Jon Gruden

FIRST-ROUND DRAFT PICKS

1976—Lee Roy Selmon, DE, Oklahoma*
1977—Ricky Bell, RB, USC*
1978—Doug Williams, QB, Grambling State
1979—None
1980—Ray Snell, G, Wisconsin
1981—Hugh Green, LB, Pittsburgh
1982—Sean Farrell, G, Penn State
1983—None
1984—None
1985—Ron Holmes, DE, Washington
1986—Bo Jackson, RB, Auburn*
     Rod Jones, DB, Southern Methodist
1987—Vinny Testaverde, QB, Miami (Fla.)*
1988—Paul Gruber, T, Wisconsin
1989—Broderick Thomas, LB, Nebraska
1990—Keith McCants, LB, Alabama
1991—Charles McRae, T, Tennessee
1992—None

1993—Eric Curry, DE, Alabama
1994—Trent Dilfer, QB, Fresno State
1995—Warren Sapp, DT, Miami (Fla.)
     Derrick Brooks, LB, Florida State
1996—Regan Upshaw, DE, California
     Marcus Jones, DT, North Carolina
1997—Warrick Dunn, RB, Florida State
     Reidel Anthony, WR, Florida
1998—None
1999—Anthony McFarland, DT, LSU
2000—None
2001—Kenyatta Walker, T, Florida
2002—None
2003—None
2004—Michael Clayton, WR, LSU
2005—Carnell "Cadillac" Williams, RB, Auburn
2006—Davin Joseph, G, Oklahoma
     *First player chosen in draft.

FRANCHISE RECORDS

Most rushing yards, career
5,957—James Wilder

Most rushing yards, season
1,544—James Wilder, 1984

Most rushing yards, game
219—James Wilder at Min., Nov. 6, 1983

Most rushing touchdowns, season
13—James Wilder, 1984

Most passing attempts, season
570—Brad Johnson, 2003

Most passing attempts, game
61—Brad Johnson vs. Car., Sept. 14, 2003

Most passes completed, season
354—Brad Johnson, 2003

Most passes completed, game
40—Brad Johnson vs. Chi., Nov. 18, 2001

Most passing yards, career
14,820—Vinny Testaverde

Most passing yards, season
3,811—Brad Johnson, 2003

Most passing yards, game
486—Doug Williams at Min., Nov. 16, 1980

Most touchdown passes, season
26—Brad Johnson, 2003

Most pass receptions, career
430—James Wilder

Most pass receptions, season
106—Keyshawn Johnson, 2001

Most pass receptions, game
13—James Wilder vs. Min., Sept. 15, 1985

Most receiving yards, career
5,018—Mark Carrier

Most receiving yards, season
1,422—Mark Carrier, 1989

Most receiving yards, game
212—Mark Carrier at N.O., Dec. 6, 1987

Most receiving touchdowns, season
10—Joey Galloway, 2005

Most touchdowns, career
68—Mike Alstott

Most field goals, season
32—Martin Gramatica, 2002

Longest field goal
57 yards—Michael Husted at L.A. Raiders, Dec. 19, 1993

Most interceptions, career
31—Donnie Abraham

Most interceptions, season
10—Ronde Barber, 2001

Most sacks, career
78.5—Lee Roy Selmon

Most sacks, season
16.5—Warren Sapp, 2000

SERIES RECORDS

Tampa Bay vs.: Arizona 7-8; Atlanta 15-10; Baltimore 2-0; Buffalo 6-2; Carolina 5-6; Chicago 17-34; Cincinnati 5-3; Cleveland 1-5; Dallas 3-6; Denver 2-4; Detroit 24-26; Green Bay 19-29-1; Houston 1-0; Indianapolis 4-6; Jacksonville 1-2; Kansas City 4-5; Miami 4-4; Minnesota 19-31; New England 2-4; New Orleans 11-17; N.Y. Giants 6-9; N.Y. Jets 1-8; Oakland 1-5; Philadelphia 4-5; Pittsburgh 1-6; St. Louis 6-9; San Diego 1-7; San Francisco 3-14; Seattle 1-5; Tennessee 1-7; Washington 6-8.

COACHING RECORDS

Leeman Bennett, 4-28-0; Tony Dungy, 54-42-0 (2-4); Jon Gruden, 35-29-0 (3-1); John McKay, 44-88-1 (1-3); Ray Perkins, 19-41-0; Richard Williamson, 4-15-0; Sam Wyche, 23-41-0.
NOTE: Playoff games in parentheses.

RETIRED UNIFORM NUMBERS

No.	Player
63	Lee Roy Selmon

TENNESSEE TITANS
YEAR-BY-YEAR RECORDS

Year	W	L	T	Pct.	PF	PA	Finish	W	L	Highest round	Coach
1960*†	10	4	0	.714	379	285	1st/Eastern Div.	1	0	AFL champ	Lou Rymkus
1961*†	10	3	1	.769	513	242	1st/Eastern Div.	1	0	AFL champ	L. Rymkus, Wally Lemm
1962*†	11	3	0	.786	387	270	1st/Eastern Div.	0	1	AFL championship game	Pop Ivy
1963*†	6	8	0	.429	302	372	3rd/Eastern Div.	—	—		Pop Ivy
1964*†	4	10	0	.286	310	355	4th/Eastern Div.	—	—		Sammy Baugh
1965*†	4	10	0	.286	298	429	4th/Eastern Div.	—	—		Hugh Taylor
1966*†	3	11	0	.214	335	396	T4th/Eastern Div.	—	—		Wally Lemm
1967*†	9	4	1	.692	258	199	1st/Eastern Div.	0	1	AFL championship game	Wally Lemm
1968*†	7	7	0	.500	303	248	2nd/Eastern Div.	—	—		Wally Lemm
1969*†	6	6	2	.500	278	279	2nd/Eastern Div.	0	1	Div. playoff game	Wally Lemm
1970†	3	10	1	.231	217	352	4th/AFC Central Div.	—	—		Wally Lemm
1971†	4	9	1	.308	251	330	3rd/AFC Central Div.	—	—		Ed Hughes
1972†	1	13	0	.071	164	380	4th/AFC Central Div.	—	—		Bill Peterson
1973†	1	13	0	.071	199	447	4th/AFC Central Div.	—	—		B. Peterson, S. Gillman
1974†	7	7	0	.500	236	282	3rd/AFC Central Div.	—	—		Sid Gillman
1975†	10	4	0	.714	293	226	3rd/AFC Central Div.	—	—		Bum Phillips
1976†	5	9	0	.357	222	273	4th/AFC Central Div.	—	—		Bum Phillips
1977†	8	6	0	.571	299	230	2nd/AFC Central Div.	—	—		Bum Phillips
1978†	10	6	0	.625	283	298	2nd/AFC Central Div.	2	1	AFC championship game	Bum Phillips
1979†	11	5	0	.688	362	331	2nd/AFC Central Div.	2	1	AFC championship game	Bum Phillips
1980†	11	5	0	.688	295	251	2nd/AFC Central Div.	0	1	AFC wild-card game	Bum Phillips
1981†	7	9	0	.438	281	355	3rd/AFC Central Div.	—	—		Ed Biles
1982†	1	8	0	.111	136	245	13th/AFC	—	—		Ed Biles
1983†	2	14	0	.125	288	460	4th/AFC Central Div.	—	—		Ed Biles, Chuck Studley
1984†	3	13	0	.188	240	437	4th/AFC Central Div.	—	—		Hugh Campbell
1985†	5	11	0	.313	284	412	4th/AFC Central Div.	—	—		H. Campbell, J. Glanville
1986†	5	11	0	.313	274	329	4th/AFC Central Div.	—	—		Jerry Glanville
1987†	9	6	0	.600	345	349	2nd/AFC Central Div.	1	1	AFC div. playoff game	Jerry Glanville
1988†	10	6	0	.625	424	365	3rd/AFC Central Div.	1	1	AFC div. playoff game	Jerry Glanville
1989†	9	7	0	.563	365	412	2nd/AFC Central Div.	0	1	AFC wild-card game	Jerry Glanville
1990†	9	7	0	.563	405	307	2nd/AFC Central Div.	0	1	AFC wild-card game	Jack Pardee
1991†	11	5	0	.688	386	251	1st/AFC Central Div.	1	1	AFC div. playoff game	Jack Pardee
1992†	10	6	0	.625	352	258	2nd/AFC Central Div.	0	1	AFC wild-card game	Jack Pardee
1993†	12	4	0	.750	368	238	1st/AFC Central Div.	0	1	AFC div. playoff game	Jack Pardee
1994†	2	14	0	.125	226	352	4th/AFC Central Div.	—	—		Jack Pardee, Jeff Fisher
1995†	7	9	0	.438	348	324	3rd/AFC Central Div.	—	—		Jeff Fisher
1996†	8	8	0	.500	345	319	4th/AFC Central Div.	—	—		Jeff Fisher
1997†	8	8	0	.500	333	310	3rd/AFC Central Div.	—	—		Jeff Fisher
1998‡	8	8	0	.500	330	320	2nd/AFC Central Div.	—	—		Jeff Fisher
1999	13	3	0	.813	392	324	2nd/AFC Central Div.	3	1	Super Bowl	Jeff Fisher
2000	13	3	0	.813	346	191	1st/AFC Central Div.	0	1	AFC div. playoff game	Jeff Fisher
2001	7	9	0	.438	336	388	4th/AFC Central Div.	—	—		Jeff Fisher
2002	11	5	0	.688	367	324	1st/AFC South Div.	1	1	AFC championship game	Jeff Fisher
2003	12	4	0	.750	435	324	2nd/AFC South Div.	1	1	AFC div. playoff game	Jeff Fisher
2004	5	11	0	.312	344	439	4th/AFC South Div.	—	—		Jeff Fisher
2005	4	12	0	.250	299	421	3rd/AFC South Div.	—	—		Jeff Fisher

*American Football League.
†Houston Oilers.
‡Tennessee Oilers.

FIRST-ROUND DRAFT PICKS

1960—Billy Cannon, RB, Louisiana State
1961—Mike Ditka, E, Pittsburgh
1962—Ray Jacobs, DT, Howard Payne
1963—Danny Brabham, LB, Arkansas
1964—Scott Appleton, DT, Texas
1965—Lawrence Elkins, WR, Baylor* (AFL)
1966—Tommy Nobis, LB, Texas
1967—George Webster, LB, Michigan State
    Tom Regner, G, Notre Dame
1968—None
1969—Ron Pritchard, LB, Arizona State

1970—Doug Wilkerson, G, North Carolina Central
1971—Dan Pastorini, QB, Santa Clara
1972—Greg Sampson, DE, Stanford
1973—John Matuszak, DE, Tampa*
    George Amundson, RB, Iowa State
1974—None
1975—Robert Brazile, LB, Jackson State
    Don Hardeman, RB, Texas A&I
1976—None
1977—Morris Towns, T, Missouri
1978—Earl Campbell, RB, Texas*

HISTORY Team by team

1979—None
1980—None
1981—None
1982—Mike Munchak, G, Penn State
1983—Bruce Matthews, G, USC
1984—Dean Steinkuhler, T, Nebraska
1985—Ray Childress, DE, Texas A&M
    Richard Johnson, DB, Wisconsin
1986—Jim Everett, QB, Purdue
1987—Alonzo Highsmith, RB, Miami (Fla.)
    Haywood Jeffries, WR, N.C. State
1988—Lorenzo White, RB, Michigan State
1989—David Williams, T, Florida
1990—Lamar Lathon, LB, Houston
1991—None
1992—None

1993—Brad Hopkins, T, Illinois
1994—Henry Ford, DE, Arkansas
1995—Steve McNair, QB, Alcorn State
1996—Eddie George, RB, Ohio State
1997—Kenny Holmes, DE, Miami (Fla.)
1998—Kevin Dyson, WR, Utah
1999—Jevon Kearse, DE, Florida
2000—Keith Bulluck, LB, Syracuse
2001—None
2002—Albert Haynesworth, DT, Tennessee
2003—Andre Woolfolk, DB, Oklahoma
2004—None
2005—Adam "Pacman" Jones, CB, West Virginia
2006—Vince Young, QB, Texas
    *First player chosen in draft.

FRANCHISE RECORDS

Most rushing yards, career
10,009—Eddie George
Most rushing yards, season
1,934—Earl Campbell, 1980
Most rushing yards, game
216—Billy Cannon at N.Y. Titans, Dec. 10, 1961
    Eddie George vs. Oak., Aug. 31, 1997 (OT)
Most rushing touchdowns, season
19—Earl Campbell, 1979
Most passing attempts, season
655—Warren Moon, 1991
Most passing attempts, game
68—George Blanda at Buf., Nov. 1, 1964
Most passes completed, season
404—Warren Moon, 1991
Most passes completed, game
41—Warren Moon vs. Dal., Nov. 10, 1991
Most passing yards, career
33,685—Warren Moon

Most passing yards, season
4,690—Warren Moon, 1991
Most passing yards, game
527—Warren Moon at K.C., Dec. 16, 1990
Most touchdown passes, season
36—George Blanda, 1961
Most pass receptions, career
542—Ernest Givins
Most pass receptions, season
101—Charlie Hennigan, 1964
Most pass receptions, game
13—Charlie Hennigan at Boston, Oct. 13, 1961
    Haywood Jeffires at NYJ, Oct. 13, 1991
Most receiving yards, career
7,935—Ernest Givins
Most receiving yards, season
1,746—Charlie Hennigan, 1961
Most receiving yards, game
272—Charlie Hennigan at Boston, Oct. 13, 1961

Most receiving touchdowns, season
17—Bill Groman, 1961
Most touchdowns, career
74—Eddie George
Most field goals, season
36—Al Del Greco, 1998
Longest field goal
56 yards—Al Del Greco vs. S.F., Oct. 27, 1996
Most interceptions, career
45—Jim Norton
Most interceptions, season
12—Freddy Glick, 1963
    Mike Reinfeldt, 1979
Most sacks, career
105—Elvin Bethea
Most sacks, season
16—Elvin Bethea, 1973

SERIES RECORDS

Tennessee vs.: Arizona 3-5; Atlanta 6-5; Baltimore 7-7; Buffalo 23-14; Carolina 1-1; Chicago 4-5; Cincinnati 38-30-1; Cleveland 26-33; Dallas 5-6; Denver 20-12-1; Detroit 6-3; Green Bay 5-4; Houston 6-2; Indianapolis 9-13; Jacksonville 12-10; Kansas City 18-25; Miami 13-16; Minnesota 3-7; New England 15-19-1; New Orleans 6-4-1; N.Y. Giants 3-5; N.Y. Jets 20-14-1; Oakland 17-23; Philadelphia 2-6; Pittsburgh 28-38; St. Louis 13-20-1; San Diego 13-20-1; San Francisco 4-7; Seattle 4-9; Tampa Bay 7-1; Washington 5-3. NOTE: Includes records as Houston Oilers from 1960 through 1996.

COACHING RECORDS

Sammy Baugh, 4-10-0; Ed Biles, 8-23-0; Hugh Campbell, 8-22-0; Jeff Fisher, 97-85-0 (5-4); Sid Gillman, 8-15-0; Jerry Glanville, 33-32-0 (2-3); Ed Hughes, 4-9-1; Frank Ivy, 17-11-0 (0-1); Wally Lemm, 37-38-4 (1-2); Jack Pardee, 43-31-0 (1-4); Bill Peterson, 1-18-0; Bum Phillips, 55-35-0 (4-3); Lou Rymkus, 11-7-1 (1-0); Chuck Studley, 2-8-0; Hugh Taylor, 4-10-0.
NOTE: Playoff games in parentheses.

RETIRED UNIFORM NUMBERS

No.	Player
34	Earl Campbell
43	Jim Norton
63	Mike Munchak
65	Elvin Bethea
74	Bruce Matthews

WASHINGTON REDSKINS
YEAR-BY-YEAR RECORDS

| | | | REGULAR SEASON | | | | | | PLAYOFFS | | |
Year	W	L	T	Pct.	PF	PA	Finish	W	L	Highest round	Coach
1932*	4	4	2	.500	55	79	4th				Lud Wray
1933†	5	5	2	.500	103	97	3rd/Eastern Div.	—	—		Lone Star Dietz
1934†	6	6	0	.500	107	94	2nd/Eastern Div.	—	—		Lone Star Dietz
1935†	2	8	1	.200	65	123	4th/Eastern Div.	—	—		Eddie Casey
1936†	7	5	0	.583	149	110	1st/Eastern Div.	0	1	NFL championship game	Ray Flaherty
1937	8	3	0	.727	195	120	1st/Eastern Div.	1	0	NFL champ	Ray Flaherty
1938	6	3	2	.667	148	154	2nd/Eastern Div.				Ray Flaherty
1939	8	2	1	.800	242	94	2nd/Eastern Div.	—	—		Ray Flaherty
1940	9	2	0	.818	245	142	1st/Eastern Div.	0	1	NFL championship game	Ray Flaherty

		REGULAR SEASON							PLAYOFFS		
Year	W	L	T	Pct.	PF	PA	Finish	W	L	Highest round	Coach
1941	6	5	0	.545	176	174	3rd/Eastern Div.	—	—		Ray Flaherty
1942	10	1	0	.909	227	102	1st/Eastern Div.	1	0	NFL champ	Ray Flaherty
1943	6	3	1	.667	229	137	1st/Eastern Div.	1	1	NFL championship game	Dutch Bergman
1944	6	3	1	.667	169	180	3rd/Eastern Div.	—	—		Dudley DeGroot
1945	8	2	0	.800	209	121	1st/Eastern Div.	0	1	NFL championship game	Dudley DeGroot
1946	5	5	1	.500	171	191	T3rd/Eastern Div.	—	—		Turk Edwards
1947	4	8	0	.333	295	367	4th/Eastern Div.	—	—		Turk Edwards
1948	7	5	0	.583	291	287	2nd/Eastern Div.	—	—		Turk Edwards
1949	4	7	1	.364	268	339	4th/Eastern Div.	—	—		John Whelchel, H. Ball
1950	3	9	0	.250	232	326	6th/American Conf.	—	—		Herman Ball
1951	5	7	0	.417	183	296	3rd/American Conf.	—	—		Herman Ball, Dick Todd
1952	4	8	0	.333	240	287	T5th/American Conf.	—	—		Curly Lambeau
1953	6	5	1	.545	208	215	3rd/Eastern Conf.	—	—		Curly Lambeau
1954	3	9	0	.250	207	432	5th/Eastern Conf.	—	—		Joe Kuharich
1955	8	4	0	.667	246	222	2nd/Eastern Conf.	—	—		Joe Kuharich
1956	6	6	0	.500	183	225	3rd/Eastern Conf.	—	—		Joe Kuharich
1957	5	6	1	.455	251	230	4th/Eastern Conf.	—	—		Joe Kuharich
1958	4	7	1	.364	214	268	4th/Eastern Conf.	—	—		Joe Kuharich
1959	3	9	0	.250	185	350	5th/Eastern Conf.	—	—		Mike Nixon
1960	1	9	2	.100	178	309	6th/Eastern Conf.	—	—		Mike Nixon
1961	1	12	1	.077	174	392	7th/Eastern Conf.	—	—		Bill McPeak
1962	5	7	2	.417	305	376	4th/Eastern Conf.	—	—		Bill McPeak
1963	3	11	0	.214	279	398	6th/Eastern Conf.	—	—		Bill McPeak
1964	6	8	0	.429	307	305	T3rd/Eastern Conf.	—	—		Bill McPeak
1965	6	8	0	.429	257	301	4th/Eastern Conf.	—	—		Bill McPeak
1966	7	7	0	.500	351	355	5th/Eastern Conf.	—	—		Otto Graham
1967	5	6	3	.455	347	353	3rd/Capitol Div.	—	—		Otto Graham
1968	5	9	0	.357	249	358	3rd/Capitol Div.	—	—		Otto Graham
1969	7	5	2	.583	307	319	2nd/Capitol Div.	—	—		Vince Lombardi
1970	6	8	0	.429	297	314	4th/NFC Eastern Div.	—	—		Bill Austin
1971	9	4	1	.692	276	190	2nd/NFC Eastern Div.	0	1	NFC div. playoff game	George Allen
1972	11	3	0	.786	336	218	1st/NFC Eastern Div.	2	1	Super Bowl	George Allen
1973	10	4	0	.714	325	198	2nd/NFC Eastern Div.	0	1	NFC div. playoff game	George Allen
1974	10	4	0	.714	320	196	2nd/NFC Eastern Div.	0	1	NFC div. playoff game	George Allen
1975	8	6	0	.571	325	276	3rd/NFC Eastern Div.	—	—		George Allen
1976	10	4	0	.714	291	217	2nd/NFC Eastern Div.	0	1	NFC div. playoff game	George Allen
1977	9	5	0	.643	196	189	2nd/NFC Eastern Div.	—	—		George Allen
1978	8	8	0	.500	273	283	3rd/NFC Eastern Div.	—	—		Jack Pardee
1979	10	6	0	.625	348	295	3rd/NFC Eastern Div.	—	—		Jack Pardee
1980	6	10	0	.375	261	293	3rd/NFC Eastern Div.	—	—		Jack Pardee
1981	8	8	0	.500	347	349	4th/NFC Eastern Div.	—	—		Joe Gibbs
1982	8	1	0	.889	190	128	1st/NFC	4	0	Super Bowl champ	Joe Gibbs
1983	14	2	0	.875	541	332	1st/NFC Eastern Div.	2	1	Super Bowl	Joe Gibbs
1984	11	5	0	.688	426	310	1st/NFC Eastern Div.	0	1	NFC div. playoff game	Joe Gibbs
1985	10	6	0	.625	297	312	3rd/NFC Eastern Div.	—	—		Joe Gibbs
1986	12	4	0	.750	368	296	2nd/NFC Eastern Div.	2	1	NFC championship game	Joe Gibbs
1987	11	4	0	.733	379	285	1st/NFC Eastern Div.	3	0	Super Bowl champ	Joe Gibbs
1988	7	9	0	.438	345	387	3rd/NFC Eastern Div.	—	—		Joe Gibbs
1989	10	6	0	.625	386	308	3rd/NFC Eastern Div.	—	—		Joe Gibbs
1990	10	6	0	.625	381	301	3rd/NFC Eastern Div.	1	1	NFC div. playoff game	Joe Gibbs
1991	14	2	0	.875	485	224	1st/NFC Eastern Div.	3	0	Super Bowl champ	Joe Gibbs
1992	9	7	0	.563	300	255	2nd/NFC Eastern Div.	1	1	NFC div. playoff game	Joe Gibbs
1993	4	12	0	.250	230	345	5th/NFC Eastern Div.	—	—		Richie Petitbon
1994	3	13	0	.188	320	412	5th/NFC Eastern Div.	—	—		Norv Turner
1995	6	10	0	.375	326	359	3rd/NFC Eastern Div.	—	—		Norv Turner
1996	9	7	0	.563	364	312	3rd/NFC Eastern Div.	—	—		Norv Turner
1997	8	7	1	.533	327	289	2nd/NFC Eastern Div.	—	—		Norv Turner
1998	6	10	0	.375	319	421	4th/NFC Eastern Div.	—	—		Norv Turner
1999	10	6	0	.625	443	377	1st/NFC Eastern Div.	1	1	NFC div. playoff game	Norv Turner
2000	8	8	0	.500	281	269	3rd/NFC Eastern Div.	—	—		N. Turner, Terry Robiskie
2001	8	8	0	.500	256	303	2nd/NFC Eastern Div.	—	—		Marty Schottenheimer
2002	7	9	0	.438	307	365	3rd/NFC East Div.	—	—		Steve Spurrier
2003	5	11	0	.313	287	372	4th/NFC East Div.	—	—		Steve Spurrier
2004	6	10	0	.375	240	265	4th/NFC East Div.	—	—		Joe Gibbs
2005	10	6	0	.625	359	293	2nd/NFC East Div.	1	1	NFC div. playoff game	Joe Gibbs

*Boston Braves.
†Boston Redskins.

FIRST-ROUND DRAFT PICKS

1936—Riley Smith, QB, Alabama
1937—Sammy Baugh, QB, Texas Christian
1938—Andy Farkas, B, Detroit
1939—I.B. Hale, T, Texas Christian

1940—Ed Boell, B, New York University
1941—Forrest Evashevski, B, Michigan
1942—Orban Sanders, B, Texas
1943—Jack Jenkins, B, Missouri

1944—Mike Micka, B, Colgate
1945—Jim Hardy, B, USC
1946—Cal Rossi, B, UCLA
1947—Cal Rossi, B, UCLA
1948—Harry Gilmer, QB, Alabama*
1949—Rob Goode, RB, Texas A&M
1950—George Thomas, RB, Oklahoma
1951—Leon Heath, RB, Oklahoma
1952—Larry Isbell, QB, Baylor
1953—Jack Scarbath, QB, Maryland
1954—Steve Meilinger, TE, Kentucky
1955—Ralph Guglielmi, QB, Notre Dame
1956—Ed Vereb, RB, Maryland
1957—Don Bosseler, RB, Miami (Fla.)
1958—None
1959—Don Allard, QB, Boston College
1960—Richie Lucas, QB, Penn State
1961—Norm Snead, QB, Wake Forest
       Joe Rutgens, T, Illinois
1962—Ernie Davis, RB, Syracuse*
1963—Pat Richter, TE, Wisconsin
1964—Charley Taylor, RB, Arizona State
1965—None
1966—Charlie Gogolak, K, Princeton
1967—Ray McDonald, RB, Idaho
1968—Jim Smith, DB, Oregon
1969—None
1970—None
1971—None
1972—None
1973—None
1974—None
1975—None
1976—None

1977—None
1978—None
1979—None
1980—Art Monk, WR, Syracuse
1981—Mark May, T, Pittsburgh
1982—None
1983—Darrell Green, DB, Texas A&I
1984—None
1985—None
1986—None
1987—None
1988—None
1989—None
1990—None
1991—Bobby Wilson, DT, Michigan State
1992—Desmond Howard, WR, Michigan
1993—Tom Carter, DB, Notre Dame
1994—Heath Shuler, QB, Tennessee
1995—Michael Westbrook, WR, Colorado
1996—Andre Johnson, T, Penn State
1997—Kenard Lang, DE, Miami (Fla.)
1998—None
1999—Champ Bailey, DB, Georgia
2000—LaVar Arrington, LB, Penn State
       Chris Samuels, T, Alabama
2001—Rod Gardner, WR, Clemson
2002—Patrick Ramsey, QB, Tulane
2003—None
2004—Sean Taylor, S, Miami (Fla.)
2005—Carlos Rogers, CB, Auburn
      Jason Campbell, QB, Auburn
2006—None
*First player chosen in draft.

FRANCHISE RECORDS

Most rushing yards, career
7,472—John Riggins
Most rushing yards, season
1,516—Clinton Portis, 2005
Most rushing yards, game
221—Gerald Riggs vs. Phi., Sept. 17, 1989
Most rushing touchdowns, season
24—John Riggins, 1983
Most passing attempts, season
541—Jay Schroeder, 1986
Most passing attempts, game
58—Jay Schroeder vs. S.F., Dec. 1, 1985
Most passes completed, season
316—Brad Johnson, 1999
Most passes completed, game
32—Sonny Jurgensen at Cle., Nov. 26, 1967
    John Friesz at NYG, Sept. 18, 1994
    Brad Johnson at S.F., Dec. 26, 1999 (OT)
Most passing yards, career
25,206—Joe Theismann

Most passing yards, season
4,109—Jay Schroeder, 1986
Most passing yards, game
471—Brad Johnson at S.F. Dec. 26, 1999 (OT)
446—Sammy Baugh vs. N.Y. Yanks, Oct. 31, 1948
Most touchdown passes, season
31—Sonny Jurgensen, 1967
Most pass receptions, career
888—Art Monk
Most pass receptions, season
106—Art Monk, 1984
Most pass receptions, game
13—Art Monk vs. Cin., Dec. 15, 1985
    Kelvin Bryant vs. NYG, Dec. 7, 1986
    Art Monk at Det., Nov. 4, 1990
Most receiving yards, career
12,026—Art Monk
Most receiving yards, season
1,483—Santana Moss, 2005

Most receiving yards, game
255—Anthony Allen vs. St.L., Oct. 4, 1987
Most receiving touchdowns, season
12—Hugh Taylor, 1952
    Charley Taylor, 1966
    Jerry Smith, 1967
    Ricky Sanders, 1988
Most touchdowns, career
90—Charley Taylor
Most field goals, season
33—Mark Moseley, 1983
Longest field goal
57 yards—Steve Cox vs. Sea., Sept. 28, 1986
Most interceptions, career
54—Darrell Green
Most interceptions, season
13—Dan Sandifer, 1948
Most sacks, career
97.5—Dexter Manley
Most sacks, season
18.0—Dexter Manley, 1986

SERIES RECORDS

Washington vs.: Arizona 71-44-2; Atlanta 14-4-1; Baltimore 1-2; Buffalo 4-6; Carolina 6-1; Chicago 17-20-1; Cincinnati 4-3; Cleveland 9-33-1; Dallas 34-54-2; Denver 4-6; Detroit 25-10; Green Bay 12-16-1; Houston 1-0; Indianapolis 10-17; Jacksonville 2-1; Kansas City 1-6; Miami 3-6; Minnesota 7-5; New England 6-1; New Orleans 13-7; N.Y. Giants 60-82-4; N.Y. Jets 7-1; Oakland 3-7; Philadelphia 74-62-5; Pittsburgh 42-30-4; St. Louis 20-6-1; San Diego 6-2; San Francisco 9-13-1; Seattle 9-5; Tampa Bay 8-6; Tennessee 3-5. NOTE: Includes records as Boston Braves in 1932 and Boston Redskins from 1933 through 1936.

COACHING RECORDS

George Allen, 67-30-1 (2-5); Bill Austin, 6-8-0; Herman Ball, 4-16-0; Dutch Bergman, 6-3-1 (1-1); Eddie Casey, 2-8-1; Dudley DeGroot, 14-5-1 (0-1); William Dietz, 11-11-2; Turk Edwards, 16-18-1; Ray Flaherty, 54-21-3 (2-2); Joe Gibbs, 140-76-0 (17-6); Otto Graham, 17-22-3; Joe Kuharich, 26-32-2; Curly Lambeau, 10-13-1; Vince Lombardi, 7-5-2; Bill McPeak, 21-46-3; Mike Nixon, 4-18-2; Jack Pardee, 24-24-0; Richie Petitbon, 4-12-0; Terry Robiskie, -1-2-0; Marty Schottenheimer, 8-8-0; Steve Spurrier, 12-20-0; Dick Todd, 5-4-0; Norv Turner, 49-59-1 (1-1); John Whelchel, 3-3-1; Lud Wray, 4-4-2. NOTE: Playoff games in parentheses.

RETIRED UNIFORM NUMBERS

No.	Player
33	Sammy Baugh